Lecture Notes in Computer Science 16551

The series Lecture Notes in Computer Science (LNCS), including its subseries Lecture Notes in Artificial Intelligence (LNAI) and Lecture Notes in Bioinformatics (LNBI), has established itself as a medium for the publication of new developments in computer science and information technology research, teaching, and education.

LNCS enjoys close cooperation with the computer science R & D community, the series counts many renowned academics among its volume editors and paper authors, and collaborates with prestigious societies. Its mission is to serve this international community by providing an invaluable service, mainly focused on the publication of conference and workshop proceedings and postproceedings. LNCS commenced publication in 1973.

Shi Bai · Edoardo Persichetti
Editors

Public-Key Cryptography – PKC 2026

29th IACR International Conference
on Practice and Theory of Public-Key Cryptography
West Palm Beach, FL, USA, May 25–28, 2026
Proceedings, Part I

Springer

Editors
Shi Bai
Shanghai Jiao Tong University
Shanghai, China

Edoardo Persichetti
Florida Atlantic University
Boca Raton, FL, USA

ISSN 0302-9743 ISSN 1611-3349 (electronic)
Lecture Notes in Computer Science
ISBN 978-3-032-26730-6 ISBN 978-3-032-26731-3 (eBook)
https://doi.org/10.1007/978-3-032-26731-3

This Springer imprint is published by the registered company Springer Nature Switzerland AG
The registered company address is: Gewerbestrasse 11, 6330 Cham, Switzerland

Preface

The 29th International Conference on Practice and Theory of Public-Key Cryptography (PKC 2026) was held in West Palm Beach, Florida, USA, from May 25 to 28, 2026. The conference was sponsored by the International Association for Cryptologic Research (IACR) and serves as the IACR's flagship conference dedicated specifically to public-key cryptography.

PKC 2026 brought together a vibrant international community of cryptography researchers, with authors representing a wide range of countries. The conference solicited original research papers on all aspects of public-key cryptography. This year, we particularly welcomed submissions on the theme "Mathematics of Public-Key Cryptography".

The conference received 259 submissions, which were reviewed by a program committee of 78 experts, including four area chairs, together with 253 external reviewers. The selection process took about two months for independent reviewing and another two months for discussion. During the discussion phase, the program chairs facilitated interactions between authors and reviewers by contacting authors to address critical questions that arose, ensuring informed decision-making. In the end, the program committee selected 65 papers for inclusion in PKC 2026. Papers were reviewed in the usual double-blind manner, with an average of about three reviews per paper. Program committee members were limited to three submissions (or four if all were coauthored with students), and their submissions were subject to additional scrutiny. The two program chairs were not permitted to submit papers.

The Best Paper Award was presented to "SQIsign with Fixed-Precision Integer Arithmetic" by Won Kim, Jeonghwan Lee, Hyeonhak Kim, and Changmin Lee.

The Test of Time Award Committee, consisting of Shi Bai, Tung Chou, Jiaxin Pan, Edoardo Persichetti, and Moti Yung, selected the recipient of the PKC 2026 Test of Time Award.

PKC is a remarkable undertaking, and it is made possible only through the hard work and significant contributions of many individuals:

- We would like to thank Veronika Kuchta and Francesco Sica (Florida Atlantic University, USA) for making the general arrangements such a success.
- We would like to express our sincere gratitude to all the authors for their trust in us, for choosing PKC 2026 as a forum for presenting their research, and for giving us the opportunity to consider their work. The quality, diversity, and creativity of their submissions were essential to shaping the program and to making PKC 2026 a vibrant and stimulating conference.
- We also thank the Program Committee, external reviewers, session chairs, invited speaker, and presenters for their tremendous work and contributions to the success of PKC 2026.

– Special thanks to the area chairs: Paulo Barreto, Mark Manulis, Pratyay Mukherjee, and Jean-Pierre Tillich. Their expertise and sound judgment were critical in helping us reach good decisions.

We hope you enjoyed the conference and the warm welcome at PKC 2026.

May 2026

Shi Bai
Edoardo Persichetti

Organization

General Chairs

Veronika Kuchta	Florida Atlantic University, USA
Francesco Sica	Florida Atlantic University, USA

Program Committee Chairs

Shi Bai	Shanghai Jiao Tong University, China
Edoardo Persichetti	Florida Atlantic University, USA

Steering Committee

Masayuki Abe	NTT, Japan
Shi Bai	Shanghai Jiao Tong University, China
Jung Hee Cheon	Seoul National University, South Korea
Tung Chou	Academia Sinica, Taiwan
Yvo Desmedt	University of Texas at Dallas, USA
Goichiro Hanaoka (Chair)	National Institute of Advanced Industrial Science and Technology, Japan
Tibor Jager	University of Wuppertal, Germany
Aggelos Kiayias	University of Edinburgh and IOG, UK
Tanja Lange	Eindhoven University of Technology, the Netherlands
Jiaxin Pan	University of Kassel, Germany
Edoardo Persichetti	Florida Atlantic University, USA
Duong Hieu Phan	Télécom Paris, Institut Polytechnique de Paris, France
Yu Yu	Shanghai Jiao Tong University, China
Moti Yung (Secretary)	Google LLC and Columbia University, USA
Yuliang Zheng	University of Alabama at Birmingham, USA

Program Committee

Sarah Arpin	Virginia Tech, USA
Gennaro Avitabile	IMDEA Software Institute, Spain
Gustavo Banegas	Inria, France
Razvan Barbulescu	University of Bordeaux, France
Paulo Barreto	University of Washington Tacoma, USA
Andrea Basso	IBM Research Europe, Switzerland
Lubjana Beshaj	West Point Military Academy, USA
Jean-François Biasse	University of South Florida, USA
Pierre Briaud	Simula Research Lab, Norway
Daniel Cabarcas	Universidad Nacional de Colombia, Colombia
Sofía Celi	Brave, Portugal
Yanbo Chen	University of Ottawa, Canada
Jie Chen	Wuhan University, China
Mingjie Chen	KU Leuven, Belgium
Giulio Codogni	University of Rome Tor Vergata, Italy
Bernardo David	IT University of Copenhagen, Denmark
Jintai Ding	Xi'an Jiaotong-Liverpool University, China
Dung Hoang Duong	University of Wollongong, Australia
Muhammed Esgin	Monash University, Australia
Simona Etinski	Centrum Wiskunde & Informatica, the Netherlands
Luca De Feo	IBM Research Europe, Switzerland
Tako Boris Fouotsa	University of Manchester, UK
Daniele Friolo	Sapienza University of Rome, Italy
Satrajit Ghosh	Indian Institute of Technology Kharagpur, India
Valerie Gilchrist	Université Libre de Bruxelles, Belgium
Calvin Abou Haidar	NTT Social Informatics Laboratories, Japan
Lucjan Hanzlik	CISPA, Germany
Kristina Hostáková	ETH Zurich, Switzerland
Kathrin Hövelmanns	Eindhoven University of Technology, the Netherlands
Andreas Hülsing	Eindhoven University of Technology & SandboxAQ, the Netherlands
Tibor Jager	University of Wuppertal, Germany
Octavio Pérez Kempner	NTT Social Informatics Laboratories, Japan
Miran Kim	Hanyang University, South Korea
Elena Kirshanova	Technology Innovation Institute, United Arab Emirates
Chelsea Komlo	University of Waterloo, Canada

Péter Kutas	Eötvös Loránd University, Hungary & University of Birmingham, UK
Jason LeGrow	Virginia Tech, USA
Changmin Lee	Korea University, South Korea
Damien Ligier	DESILO, South Korea
Feng-Hao Liu	Washington State University, USA
Zeyu Liu	Yale University, USA
Patrick Longa	Microsoft Research, USA
Julian Loss	Ruhr University Bochum, Germany
Johanna Loyer	Inria, France
Julio López	University of Campinas, Brazil
Mark Manulis	University of the Bundeswehr, Germany
Alexander May	Ruhr University Bochum, Germany
Kirill Morozov	University of North Texas, USA
Pratyay Mukherjee	Hashgraph, India
Jiaxin Pan	University of Kassel, Germany
Yanbin Pan	Academy of Mathematics and Systems Science, China
Robi Pedersen	Technical University of Denmark, Denmark
Geovandro Pereira	LG Electronics, USA
Federico Pintore	University of Trento, Italy
Longjiang Qu	National University of Defense Technology, China
Matthieu Rivain	CryptoExperts, France
Simona Samardjiska	Radboud University, the Netherlands
Paolo Santini	Marche Polytechnic University, Italy
Santanu Sarkar	Indian Institute of Technology Madras, India
Palash Sarkar	Indian Statistical Institute, Kolkata, India
Luisa Siniscalchi	Technical University of Denmark, Denmark
Yongsoo Song	Seoul National University, South Korea
Fang Song	Portland State University, USA
Akira Takahashi	JPMorgan, USA
Jean-Pierre Tillich	Inria, France
Fernando Virdia	King's College London, UK
Zhedong Wang	Shanghai Jiao Tong University, China
Violetta Weger	Technical University of Munich, Germany
Wessel van Woerden	PQShield, UK
David Wu	University of Texas at Austin, USA
Keita Xagawa	Technology Innovation Institute, United Arab Emirates
Yu Yu	Shanghai Jiao Tong University, China
Yang Yu	Tsinghua University, China

Runzhi Zeng	University of Kassel, Germany
Fangguo Zhang	Sun Yat-sen University, China
Zhenfeng Zhang	Chinese Academy of Sciences, China
Hong-Sheng Zhou	Virginia Commonwealth University, USA
Paul Zimmermann	Inria, France

Additional Reviewers

Ittai Abraham
Hamza Abusalah
Anasuya Acharya
Saed Alsayigh
Zhiyuan An
Luong Duc Anh
Daniel Augot
Liljana Babinkostova
Renas Bacho
John Baena
Karim Baghery
David Balbás
Jiawei Bao
Mohammed Barhoush
James Bartusek
Michele Battagliola
Marvin Beckmann
Nidhish Bhimrajka
Nina Bindel
Jan Bormet
Vincenzo Botta
Pedro Branco
Dung Bui
Benedikt Bünz
Roberto Cabral
André Chailloux
Suvradip Chakraborty
Jeff Champion
Huanhuan Chen
Qian Chen
Clemence Chevignard
Jesus Chi-Domínguez
Ilaria Chillotti
Michele Ciampi
Simone Colombo
Craig Costello
Geoffroy Couteau
Dipayan Das
Pratish Datta
Nicolas David
Angelo De Caro
Thomas Debris-Alazard
Hugo Delavenne
Giovanni Deligios
Pierpaolo Della Monica
David Dervishi
Julien Devevey
Ben Dowling
Qiuyan Du
Samed Düzlü
Friedrich Eisenbrand
Youssef El Housni
Gökberk Erdogan
Jonathan Eriksen
Daniel Escudero
Thomas Espitau
Sebastian Faller
Yansong Feng
Andrea Flamini
Scott Fluhrer
Mariana Gama
Andrea Gangemi
Albert Garreta
Decio Gazzoni
Robin Geelen
Matthias Geihs
Tyler Genao
Ashrujit Ghoshal
Sara Giammusso
Emanuele Giunta
Lewis Glabush
Boru Gong
Junqing Gong
Scott Griffy

Xiaojie Guo
Guillaume Hanrot
Keitaro Hashimoto
Raphael Heitjohann
Hans Heum
Minki Hhan
Felicitas Hoermann
Clement Hoffmann
Ga Hee Hong
Annamaria Iezzi
Hansraj Jangir
Chanho Jeon
Sohyun Jeon
Mahavir Jhawar
Haoxiang Jin
Antoine Joux
Abul Kalam
Chethan Kamath
Simon Holmgaard Kamp
Jiayi Kang
Taehun Kang
Alexander Karenin
Marcel Keller
Xuan Thanh Khuc
Hyeonhak Kim
Jongmin Kim
Won Kim
Lisa Kohl
Markulf Kohlweiss
Mikhail Kudinov
Hyunji Kwag
Qiqi Lai
Yongkang Lang
Mario Larangeira
Jun Bo Lau
Abel Laval
Dania Lazzarini
Hyeonbum Lee
Mira Lee
Yesol Lee
Chen Li
Minzhang Li
Yu Li
Bei Liang
Chuanwei Lin
Kaizhan Lin
Yini Lin
Yunhao Ling
Charles Liu
Jiahui Liu
Xiangyu Liu
Zhen Liu
George Lu
Yuan Lu
Hengyi Luo
Joseph Macula
William Mahaney
Mary Maller
Lola Mallordy
Mriganka Mandal
Siva Maradana
Varun Maram
Laurane Marco
Takahiro Matsuda
Krystal Maughan
Matthias Meijers
Nikolas Melissaris
Fei Meng
Pierre Meyer
Francesco Migliaro
Omid Mir
Sara Montanari
Eduardo Morais
Tomoki Moriya
Travis Morrison
Marzio Mula
Jade Nardi
Tom Neuschulten
Tran Ngo
Ky Nguyen
Guilhem Niot
Charles Olivier-Anclin
Eli Orvis
Hussien Othman
Nikhil Pappu
Jeongeun Park
Hilder Pereira
Lam Pham
Rafael del Pino
Erik Pohle

Anmoal Porwal
Thomas Prest
Yue Qin
Tian Qiu
Rahul Rachuri
Arka Rai Choudhuri
Lars Ran
Simon Rastikian
Andrea Reale
Krijn Reijnders
Omar Renawi
Filip Richter
Doreen Riepel
Guilherme Rito
Stefan Ritterhoff
Maxime Roméas
Michael Rosenberg
Luis Ruiz-Lopez
Matteo Salvino
Swagata Sasmal
Rahul Satish
Hugo Sauerbier Couvee
Sina Schaeffler
Michael Schaller
Sven Schäge
Gabrielle Sculllard
Melvin Seitner
István András Seres
Yannick Seurin
Kecheng Shi
Shumin Si
Daniel Slamanig
Freeman Slaughter
Enrico Sorbera
Sebastian Spindler
Katherine Stange
Damien Stehlé
Shifeng Sun
Hyewon Sung
Erkan Tairi
Gang Tang
Haibo Tian
Marcel Tiepelt
Monika Trimoska
Joost van der Laan
Daan van Gent
Barry Van Leeuwen
Hernán Vanegas
Marloes Venema
Javier Verbel
Damien Vergnaud
Viktoria Villanyi
Mikhail Volkov
Benedikt Wagner
Alexandre Wallet
Xicheng Wan
Hongxiao Wang
Wei Wang
Weijie Wang
Xiao Wang
Yi Wang
Yunhao Wang
Yuntao Wang
Yuyu Wang
Weiqiang Wen
Stella Wohnig
Ivy K. Y. Woo
Han Xia
Binwu Xiang
Jun Xu
Jiahao Xuan
Anshu Yadav
Saikumar Yadugiri
Jiayun Yan
Kang Yang
Xinrui Yang
Guangbei Yi
Eylon Yogev
Yuanzhuo Yu
Aaram Yun
Oliver Zajonc
Fahong Zhang
Wenbin Zhang
Yijian Zhang
Tianyu Zhao
Ziyu Zhao
Biming Zhou
Lukas Zobernig
Chiara-Marie Zok

Contents

Lattice Foundations and KEM

Hardness of M-LWE with General Distributions and Applications to Leaky Variants

Katharina Boudgoust[1(✉)], Corentin Jeudy[2], Erkan Tairi[3], and Weiqiang Wen[4]

[1] CNRS, Univ Montpellier, LIRMM, Montpellier, France
katharina.boudgoust@lirmm.fr

[2] Orange Labs, Applied Crypto Group, Rennes, France
corentin.jeudy@orange.com

[3] University of California, Berkeley, USA
erkan.tairi@berkeley.edu

[4] Télécom Paris, Institut Polytechnique de Paris, Paris, France
weiqiang.wen@telecom-paris.fr

Abstract. The Module Learning With Errors (M-LWE) problem has become a fundamental hardness assumption for lattice-based cryptography. It offers an attractive trade-off between strong robustness guarantees, sometimes directly based on worst-case lattice problems, and efficiency of the subsequent cryptographic primitives. Different flavors of M-LWE have then been introduced towards improving performance. Such variants look at different secret-error distributions and might allow for additional hints on the secret-error vector. Existing hardness results however only cover restricted classes of said distributions, or are tailored to specific leakage models. This lack of generality hinders the design of efficient and versatile cryptographic schemes, as each new distribution or leakage model requires a separate and nontrivial hardness evaluation.

In this work, we address this limitation by establishing the hardness of search M-LWE under *general distributions*. As a first step, we show that M-LWE remains hard when the *error vector* follows an arbitrary bounded distribution with sufficient entropy, with some restriction on the number of samples. Building on this, we then reduce to the Hermite Normal Form (HNF) where the *secret-error vector* follows said arbitrary distribution. Overall, our result shows that the actual shape of the distribution does not matter, as long as it keeps sufficient entropy.

To demonstrate the versatility of our framework, we further analyze a range of leakage scenarios. By examining the residual entropy given the leakage, we show that our results of M-LWE with general distributions encompass various types of leakage. More precisely, we cover exact and approximate linear hints which are widely used in recent cryptographic designs, as well as quadratic, and even non-algebraic forms, some of which were not yet covered by any theoretical hardness guarantees. The generality of our results aims at facilitating future cryptographic designs and security analyses.

E. Tairi—Work done while the author was at ENS Paris.

S. Bai and E. Persichetti (Eds.): PKC 2026, LNCS 16551, pp. 3–37, 2026.
https://doi.org/10.1007/978-3-032-26731-3_1

Keywords: Module Learning With Errors · General Distributions · Entropy · Leakage

1 Introduction

After being introduced in the pioneering work by Regev [52], the Learning With Errors (LWE) problem has induced a number of cryptographic applications through its versatility and robustness. Its connection to worst-case lattice problems is a source of confidence in the security of the cryptosystems that rely on it. While said systems were lacking efficiency, the introduction of structured variants [18,34,38,49,53] like Module Learning With Errors (M-LWE) [34] allowed for new optimizations and trade-off avenues, while preserving some trustworthy guarantees of robustness. Since then, many primitives have become practical thanks to these theoretical advances. The most undeniable examples are the recently standardized key encapsulation and signature schemes ML-KEM [9] and ML-DSA [26], whose security is directly based on the hardness of M-LWE. Similarly, a plethora of other primitives benefited from the versatility of M-LWE like advanced encryption schemes including fully homomorphic encryption [47], zero-knowledge arguments [33], threshold schemes [21], etc. The caveat, however, is that the genericity of M-LWE opens up to very different parameter selections, all of which must be carefully assessed to ensure the best balance between efficiency and security.

Concretely, for a ring R, the M-LWE problem consists in recovering a secret vector $\mathbf{s}$ in an R-module given some noisy linear system $(\mathbf{A}, \mathbf{t} = \mathbf{A}\mathbf{s} + \mathbf{e} \bmod q)$ with uniformly random $\mathbf{A}$, where $\mathbf{e}$ is a somewhat short error, or distinguishing such a pair $(\mathbf{A}, \mathbf{t})$ from random. Several parameters can then be tweaked and yield very different regimes both in terms of efficiency and exposure to efficient attacks: the degree n of R, the rank d of the module (i.e., the dimension of $\mathbf{s}$), the modulus q, the number of samples m (i.e., the dimension of $\mathbf{e}$), but also the distributions of $\mathbf{s}$ and $\mathbf{e}$. Far from being mere theoretical constraints, hasty parameter selection can lead to security issues rendering the M-LWE problem easy to solve (e.g., large modulus, noise-to-sample ratio too small, small lattice dimension nd, etc.). In particular, the distributions of $\mathbf{s}$ and $\mathbf{e}$ vary from one construction to the next so that they are tailored to make said constructions as efficient as possible. This multiplicity of distributions contrasts with the very few theoretical results that support them with proven mathematical evidence. Although not too concerning for practical constructions (as the hardness is estimated using the well-known lattice estimator [3]), it still questions the theoretical foundation of said systems and somewhat weakens our confidence in the robustness of M-LWE in such new parameter settings.

To make up for this lack of theoretical arguments, many papers have proven results for specific choices of distributions, trying to cover the most widely used ones. Although they do not cover the range of parameters used in practical schemes, they still act as a confidence booster that nothing is fundamentally wrong with these distributions and, if attacks arise, one could always increase the parameters to fall in the scope of the reduction. The first such results focused on the secret distribution [19,30,42]. They proved that it could be taken to be uniform binary (or with a small bound) while being as hard as the standard formulation of LWE (i.e., with $\mathbf{s}$ uniform over $\mathbb{Z}_q^d$ and $\mathbf{e}$ from a discrete Gaussian distribution). They were later generalized to M-LWE in [10,11,13], however, only the uniform distribution with small coefficients were covered. A study initiated by Brakerski and Döttling [16] aimed at abstracting the actual shape of the secret distribution while still being able to prove the hardness of LWE based on well-known assumptions. More precisely, the hardness was proven making the least amount of assumptions on the secret distribution beyond the entropy it carried. They were able to show that, as long as the secret distribution had sufficient min-entropy, LWE in that setting is no easier than the standard formulation. This result was later extended in [17] to the ring setting proving that R-LWE [38] with arbitrary (albeit with sufficient entropy) distributions is at least as hard as (a generalized version of) NTRU [32]. Both these approaches were later extended to the case of M-LWE in [35] (reduction from standard M-LWE) and [12] (reduction from Module-NTRU). Although these provide evidence that the actual shape of the secret distribution is not so important in the hardness of (R/M-)LWE, they all rely on Gaussian error distributions, and thus do not cover variants with different error distributions.

Changing the error distribution has shown to be a little more delicate, as it is the cornerstone of LWE. Indeed, even if no error leads to a trivial problem, having an error distribution that is too short or too sparse is also insecure as shown for example through algebraic attacks [7,54]. More precisely, there is an intricate constraint between the error distribution (and its sparsity) and the number of samples m. This constraint actually comes up in the first reduction provided by [44], where they showed LWE with uniform small errors stays as hard as LWE with Gaussian errors, if $m = d + O(d/\log d)$ where d is the secret dimension. The specific case of binary errors was then further investigated in [54], where they did not require a uniform distribution. They obtained different requirements on m depending on the sparsity of the distribution. The former was later extended to the module setting in [13] showing similar constraints for uniform bounded errors. But again, only variants of (M-)LWE with uniform bounded errors or sparse binary errors were provided with this evidence of robustness, which falls short of generally covering the distributions used across the cryptographic literature. Taking the opposite view, wandering off the distributions covered by reductions or estimated using [3] is often frowned upon, thus limiting the range of available distributions to parameterize LWE with.

Meanwhile, several works have introduced so-called *hint* or *extended* variants of LWE (and structured counterparts) so as to give more flexibility and improve or unlock certain applications. This has been done not only in the context of reductions [11,13,15,19], but also in many different cryptographic constructions [1,4,5,24,27,31,33,36,37,40,46,48,55]. These variants not only give $(\mathbf{A}, \mathbf{t})$ to the adversary, but also give out *hints* or *leakages* $f(\mathbf{s}, \mathbf{e})$ for a leakage function f that vary depending on the application. Although these variants generally lead to more efficient primitives, one has to ensure that the hint or leakage does not provide the adversary sufficient information to solve LWE. Indeed, the leakage changes the distribution of $(\mathbf{s}, \mathbf{e})$ from the adversary's perspective because this side information reduces the original secret-error space. In some cases, reductions from known flavours of LWE are proven, but always adopt a tailored approach to cover their specific variant. For that, one of the popular solutions is to characterize the distribution of $(\mathbf{s}, \mathbf{e})$ conditioned on some specific leaked value $f(\mathbf{s}, \mathbf{e}) = c$ (see e.g., [33, Lem. 7] or [27, Lem. 1]). This is a non-trivial task in general, which is why most results, to our knowledge, impose Gaussian distributions in order to rely on their nice convolution properties. On the other hand, certain variants are not supported by any theoretical insights, which makes it unclear whether the hints hinder security. Overall, because the distribution of $(\mathbf{s}, \mathbf{e})$ changes due to the leakage, there is no general hardness result covering these cases.

1.1 Our Contributions

In this paper, we provide a general study of the hardness of M-LWE with arbitrary error and secret distributions. Such a global study is especially motivated by the recent introduction of various leaky M-LWE variants, and was, prior to our work, was lacking. In particular, we provide the first hardness results for non-linear leakage. We provide a detailed description of our contributions below, with a high-level pictorial description of our results given in Fig. 1.

We start by focusing on general error distributions in Sect. 4. We generalize the approach of [13,44,54] from bounded uniform to general bounded error distributions, placing only minimal amount of requirements on it. Analogous to the series of works initiated by [16] for the secret distribution, we show that one can prove the hardness of M-LWE with bounded error distribution $\mathcal{X}$ from standard M-LWE, solely based on the entropy of $\mathcal{X}$. The restriction of $\mathcal{X}$ being bounded comes naturally in the M-LWE problem as one usually uses small errors to obtain more efficient schemes. In addition to this bound, we obtain a limitation on the number of samples. Abstracting the distribution unfortunately makes this limitation on the number of samples harder to pin down than with the uniform over hypercube case covered in [13]. Nevertheless, the combination of both these small restrictions helps ruling out trivial attacks for extreme distributions (for example when all the entropy would lie in a single coefficient). We discuss further these restrictions in Sect. 4. Overall, the main constraint on the error distribution comes from its entropy. It then yields interesting insights on the hardness of M-LWE: the concrete shape of the error distribution does not matter too much, provided it has sufficient entropy. Our proof also suggests that as long as the entropy stays the same, the hardness of M-LWE for two different error distributions does not drastically change, even if the two distributions are not cryptographically close (in terms of statistical distance, Rényi divergence or other metrics). It then opens for attractive perspectives for cryptographic designs where one could opt for a more suitable error distribution and arguing the underlying hardness based on the entropy alone. Our main result is summarized with the following informal theorem, and the full statement is provided in Theorem 4.1. Following [13,44], the high-level proof strategy is to show uninvertibility (Sect. 4.1) and second-preimage-resistance (Sect. 4.2), which

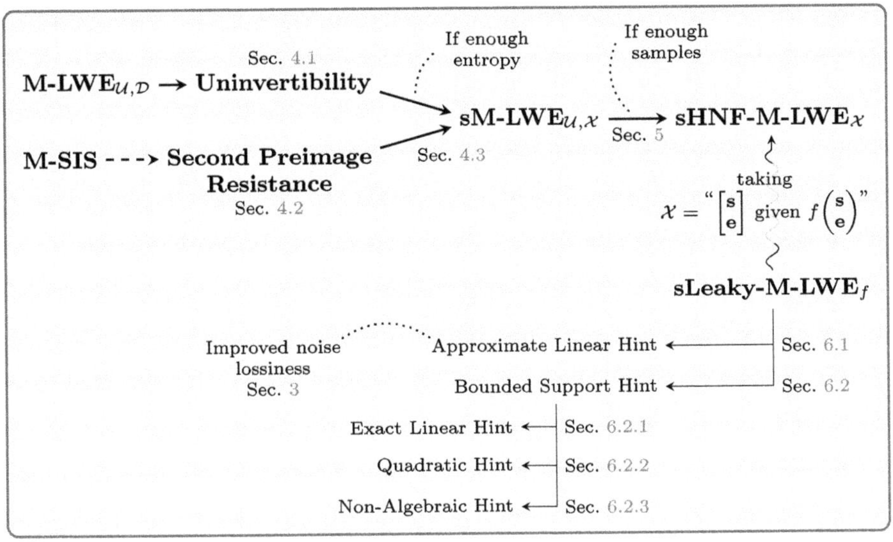

Fig. 1. High-level overview of our results and proof structure. The prefix "**s**" refers to the search variant. The subscript $\mathcal{U}$ designates a uniform distribution of secrets modulo q, while $\mathcal{D}$, $\mathcal{X}$ are error distributions representing the starting distribution (for which hardness of M-LWE is assumed) and target distribution (for which we want to prove hardness of M-LWE), respectively. In the case of HNF-M-LWE, $\mathcal{X}$ is the joint distribution of $(\mathbf{s}, \mathbf{e})$. The dashed arrow signifies it is optional and can be removed by relying on the statistical version of Lemma 4.3. The squiggly arrow means Leaky-M-LWE$_f$ is interpreted as HNF-M-LWE$_{\mathcal{X}}$ for $\mathcal{X}$ being the conditional distribution of $(\mathbf{s}, \mathbf{e})$ given the leakage $f(\mathbf{s}, \mathbf{e})$. The angled arrows specify which families of leakage functions f are tackled in this paper and where.

imply the hardness of the search variant of M-LWE with general error distribution $\mathcal{X}$. Second-preimage resistance can either be obtained statistically, or computationally assuming the hardness of M-SIS. Uninvertibility can be guaranteed assuming M-LWE with an error distribution $\mathcal{D}$ for which hardness has already been established.

Theorem 1.1 (Informal). *Let $m > d > k \geq 1$, modulus q and ring R be of degree n, and assume decision M-LWE with secret distribution $U(R_q^k)$ and error distribution $\mathcal{D}$ over R^{m-d+k} and M-SIS in dimension $m-d$ are hard. Then, for a distribution $\mathcal{X}$ over R^m, the search M-LWE with secret distribution $U(R_q^d)$ and error distribution $\mathcal{X}$ is hard provided that*

$$H_\infty(\mathcal{X}) \gtrsim \lambda + \log_2\left(\mathrm{Vol}(\mathcal{B}_{n(m-d+k)}(r_{\mathcal{D},\mathcal{X}}))\right),$$

where the $n(m-d+k)$-hyperball radius $r_{\mathcal{D},\mathcal{X}}$ depends on a norm bound on $\mathcal{X}$ and spectral norm bound on $\mathcal{D}$. Here, λ denotes the security parameter and $\gtrsim$ refers to an asymptotic behavior.

By setting $\mathcal{D}$ to the discrete Gaussian and $\mathcal{X}$ to the bounded uniform distributions, we recover the results of [13]. We then extend this result to the Hermite Normal Form (HNF) of M-LWE in Sect. 5. The HNF is often the preferred regime for M-LWE as it allows for replacing a large uniform secret by a secret of small norm, hence improving the efficiency of the subsequent cryptographic primitive. This regime is usually described by the fact that the secret distribution is the same as the error distribution, i.e., $\mathbf{t} = \mathbf{A}\mathbf{s} + \mathbf{e}$ for $\mathbf{s}$ drawn from $\mathscr{D}^d$ and $\mathbf{e}$ from $\mathscr{D}^m$. However, this suggests that all the entries of $\mathbf{s}$ and $\mathbf{e}$ are independent and identically distributed according to $\mathscr{D}$. A more natural and general formulation is to define $\mathbf{t} = [\mathbf{A} \mid \mathbf{I}_m]\mathbf{x}$ for $\mathbf{x}$ drawn from a distribution $\mathcal{X}$ over R^{m+d}. Here, $\mathbf{I}_m$ denotes the m-dimensional identity matrix over R. In that case, the vector $\mathbf{x}$ can be seen as the concatenation $[\mathbf{s} \mid \mathbf{e}]$, but no independence condition or specific shape is required for $\mathcal{X}$. Reducing M-LWE with $\mathbf{s}$ uniform in R_q^d and $\mathbf{e}$ sampled from $\mathcal{X}$ to this formulation with $\mathbf{x}$ drawn from $\mathcal{X}$ is fairly common [6,13,34]. A small subtlety however arises in the reduction when $\mathcal{X}$ is not invariant under permutation, e.g., not of the form $\mathcal{X} = \mathscr{D}^{m+d}$. Indeed, the reduction interprets $\mathbf{e}$ in the former problem as $\mathbf{x}$ in the latter. But for that, it requires to identify an invertible submatrix of $\mathbf{A}$ and to permute $\mathbf{e}$ so that the new "secret part" (the first d entries of $\mathbf{x}$) matches with the rows of this submatrix. As a result, the distribution of the resulting $\mathbf{x}$ is $\mathbf{P}\mathcal{X}$ for a random permutation matrix $\mathbf{P}$. Albeit equivalent to the standard HNF formulation for permutation-invariant distributions, it shows that the HNF transform needs to account for this permutation at the risk of yielding an insecure problem. We thus introduce the *permuted* HNF-M-LWE (pHNF-M-LWE) problem with distribution $\mathcal{X}$ as the problem of finding $\mathbf{x}$ given $\mathbf{A}$ and $\mathbf{t} = [\mathbf{A} \mid \mathbf{I}_m]\mathbf{P}\mathbf{x}$ for $\mathbf{x}$ drawn from $\mathcal{X}$, and random permutation matrix $\mathbf{P}$. Our proof then shows that pHNF-M-LWE with rank d, m samples and secret-error distribution $\mathcal{X}$ is at least as hard as M-LWE with rank d, $m + d$ samples, and error distribution $\mathcal{X}$. We also provide an alternative (looser) reduction to avoid this permutation intricacy and reduce to the regular formulation of HNF-M-LWE.

At this stage, we proved in Sects. 4+5 that HNF-M-LWE with secret-error distribution $\mathcal{X}$ and M-LWE with error distribution $\mathcal{X}$ are at least as hard as the standard formulation of M-LWE if $\mathcal{X}$ has sufficient entropy. Even though not considered surprising results by themselves, they required substantial technical rigorousness to be proven for M-LWE. Besides giving more freedom in the choice of distributions to instantiate M-LWE with, our findings also provide a systematic study of *leaky* and *hint* variants of M-LWE by simply relying on entropy considerations. Concretely, if one is given $f(\mathbf{x})$ in addition to $[\mathbf{A} \mid \mathbf{I}_m]\mathbf{x}$, we can consider the conditional distribution of $\mathbf{x}$ given $f(\mathbf{x})$. Having abstracted the distribution in our proof then allows to encompass these oddly-shaped distributions as long as they are bounded (which follows from the bound on $\mathbf{x}$) and that they have sufficient entropy. Proving hardness then comes down to estimating the conditional entropy of $\mathbf{x}$ given $f(\mathbf{x})$, i.e., how much information $f(\mathbf{x})$ provides on $\mathbf{x}$. For that we use the average conditional min-entropy, denoted $\widetilde{H}_\infty(\mathbf{x} \mid f(\mathbf{x}))$, which is well suited for security arguments, as detailed in Sect. 6.

Computing this quantity is non-trivial in general, but one can still derive meaningful lower bounds that are sufficient in some cases. We start in Sect. 6.1 with studying the setting covered in [5,27,33] of approximate linear hints $f(\mathbf{x}) = \mathbf{M}\mathbf{x} + \mathbf{f}$, with $\mathbf{M}$ arbitrary (possibly adversarial) and $\mathbf{f}$ Gaussian. Our result provides the hardness of this variant even when $\mathbf{x}$ does not follow a Gaussian distribution. As we explained, previous works required $\mathbf{x}$ to be Gaussian in order to characterize the conditional distribution of $\mathbf{x}$ given $f(\mathbf{x})$ using convolution techniques. In our case, we can lower bound $\widetilde{H}_\infty(\mathbf{x} \mid \mathbf{M}\mathbf{x} + \mathbf{f})$ by $H_\infty(\mathbf{x}) - O(\sqrt{nk} \left\|\mathbf{M}\mathbf{x}\right\|_2 / \sigma)$, where n is the ring degree, k is the number of hints and σ is the Gaussian parameter of $\mathbf{f}$, and without requiring $\mathbf{x}$ to be Gaussian. The latter point was identified as a limitation in the Raccoon signature scheme [51], where the hardness of *Hint*-M-LWE [33] required Gaussian distributions which were incompatible with the sums of uniforms of [51]. As a side contribution of potentially independent interest, detailed in Sect. 3, we generalize the notion of noise lossiness from [16] and results thereof to what we call *linear noise lossiness*. We indeed show that their "*flooding at the source*" technique is not always optimal. At a high level, they decompose the Gaussian $\mathbf{f}$ into $\mathbf{M}\mathbf{f}_1 + \mathbf{f}_2$, argue that $\widetilde{H}_\infty(\mathbf{x} \mid \mathbf{M}\mathbf{x} + \mathbf{f}) \geq \widetilde{H}_\infty(\mathbf{x} \mid \mathbf{x} + \mathbf{f}_1)$, and then choose the Gaussian parameter of $\mathbf{f}_1$ sufficiently large to flood $\mathbf{x}$. This Gaussian decomposition and inequality are a bit loose, and we show that one can directly use $\mathbf{f}$ to hide the leaked information $\mathbf{M}\mathbf{x}$. Getting rid of these first two steps removes unnecessary restrictions, giving more flexibility for the trade-off between the size of the mask $\mathbf{f}$ and the remaining guaranteed min-entropy of $\mathbf{x}$.

We then show in Sect. 6.2 that our approach also covers more general leakage variants, some of which were not proven hard prior to our work. We mentioned that the key methodology is to lower bound $\widetilde{H}_\infty(\mathbf{x} \mid f(\mathbf{x}))$. This can be done for arbitrary leakage functions, as long as the range of $f(\mathbf{x})$ is bounded. Indeed, we have $\widetilde{H}_\infty(\mathbf{x} \mid f(\mathbf{x})) \geq H_\infty(\mathbf{x}) - \log_2|f(\operatorname{Supp}\mathcal{X})|$. It means that for sufficiently small leakage space, one can derive a meaningful hardness result solely based on the entropy of $\mathcal{X}$. We note that if the entropy $H_\infty(\mathbf{x})$ of $\mathbf{x}$ is large enough to begin with, one can cover leakage that has an exponential leakage space, i.e., $\log_2|f(\operatorname{Supp}\mathcal{X})| = \Omega(\lambda)$, where λ is the security parameter. Conversely, such large leakage spaces are precluded in proofs based on guessing arguments which are used when no better alternative is known (e.g., [46]). Additionally, this bound on $\widetilde{H}_\infty(\mathbf{x} \mid f(\mathbf{x}))$ is agnostic to the specific shape of f which then allows us to cover many different types of leakage. We describe in the paper how to cover existing variants with exact linear hints [1,4,11,36,55], i.e., f linear (possibly adversarial), quadratic hints [46], but also non-algebraic hints [37]. In particular, until now, each of these either required a tailored reduction or was not covered by any theoretical hardness evidence (e.g., Known-Covariance variant in [46]). We explain in details in the full version [14, App. A] how to instantiate it to provide the first theoretical hardness evidence for the (module version of the) Known-Covariance variant proposed in [46]. To summarize, our results encompass most leakage variants, to our knowledge, by providing a unified methodology for studying their hardness.

1.2 Limitations and Open Problems

Similar to many other theoretical reductions, our results do not cover parameter ranges considered in practice. This is partly due to the generality of our results, which may lead to looser arguments than the ones focusing on specific settings. We thus interpret our findings as confidence booster in the studied variants of M-LWE. In particular, we think the impact of our work is most important when looking at variants of M-LWE where no prior reduction was known, such as non-linear yet algebraic leakage, e.g., [46], or non-algebraic leakage, e.g., from side-channel measurements. Tightening our results would reduce the gap between theory and practice, which we leave as an interesting research direction.

Our results hold for general number fields, including the case of degree $n = 1$, thus covering the unstructured case of LWE. Nonetheless, our analysis necessitates the evaluation of norms on the multiplication matrices of ring elements, which is better understood in (power-of-two) cyclotomic fields. On the opposite extreme, we highlight that our results, as stated in Theorem 1.1, require $d > 1$ and hence do not cover the ring setting. This was already left open for the general small secret distribution case. Indeed, previous papers rely on a low-rank factorization which is naturally not rank-preserving. We note that even [17], which focuses on R-LWE with entropic secret, inherently cannot reach small secrets.

Perhaps the most relevant limitation of our work is that our main result (Theorem 4.1) only guarantees the hardness of the *search* variant of M-LWE with general error (and secret) distributions. This restriction is also present in prior works that study M-LWE with small error distributions [13,44,54]. Moreover, we note that the existing search-to-decision reductions for M-LWE are not error preserving for ring degree $n > 1$ [34,43]. We believe it is an important and challenging open problem to extend our results to the *decision* variant.

2 Preliminaries

We use $\mathbb{N}, \mathbb{Z}, \mathbb{R}, \mathbb{C}$ to denote the set of natural numbers, the ring of integers, the field of reals and the field of complex numbers respectively. For two integers $a \leq b$, we define $[a, b] = \{a, \ldots, b\}$ and $[b] = [1, b]$. For a positive integer q and a ring R, we define the quotient ring $R_q = R/qR$. For a ring R, we denote by $R^\times$ its unit group, and we abuse notation by defining $\mathbb{N}^\times = \mathbb{N} \setminus \{0\}$ to be the set of positive integers. Vectors and matrices over a ring R are written in bold lowercase and bold uppercase respectively. We use $\|\mathbf{x}\|_p$ to denote the usual ℓ_p norm over $\mathbb{C}^n$. Recall that for $p > r \geq 1$, we have $\|\cdot\|_p \leq \|\cdot\|_r \leq n^{1/r-1/p} \|\cdot\|_p$. We use $\mathcal{B}_{p,n}(r)$ to denote the closed n-dimensional ℓ_p-norm ball of radius r, i.e., $\mathcal{B}_{p,n}(r) = \{\mathbf{x} \in \mathbb{R}^n : \|\mathbf{x}\|_p \leq r\}$. For $\alpha, \beta \geq 1$, we define the (α, β)-induced matrix norm of a matrix $\mathbf{A} \in \mathbb{C}^{n \times m}$ by $\|\mathbf{A}\|_{\alpha,\beta} = \sup_{\mathbf{x} \neq \mathbf{0}} \|\mathbf{A}\mathbf{x}\|_\beta / \|\mathbf{x}\|_\alpha$. This norm has simpler expressions for some known pairs (α, β). For example, we have $\|\mathbf{A}\|_{1,1} = \max_{j \in [m]} \|\mathbf{A}\mathbf{e}_j\|_1$, $\|\mathbf{A}\|_{1,2} = \max_{j \in [m]} \|\mathbf{A}\mathbf{e}_j\|_2$, and $\|\mathbf{A}\|_{\infty,\infty} = \|\mathbf{A}^T\|_{1,1}$, $\|\mathbf{A}\|_{2,\infty} = \|\mathbf{A}^T\|_{1,2}$, and $\|\mathbf{A}\|_{2,2} = \lambda_{\max}(\mathbf{A}^T\mathbf{A})^{1/2}$, where $\lambda_{\max}(\mathbf{A}^T\mathbf{A})$ denotes the largest eigenvalue, and $\mathbf{e}_j$ is the j-th canonical basis vector of $\mathbb{C}^m$.

When $\alpha = \beta$, we abbreviate the matrix norm by $\|\cdot\|_{\alpha,\beta} =: \|\cdot\|_\alpha$. In particular, $\|\cdot\|_{2,2}$ is generally noted $\|\cdot\|_2$ in the literature and called the spectral norm.

2.1 Algebraic Number Theory

A number field $K = \mathbb{Q}(\zeta)$ is a field extension of $\mathbb{Q}$ of finite degree n obtained by adjoining an algebraic number ζ, i.e., ζ is a root of a rational polynomial. The number ζ is called an algebraic integer if it is root of an *integer* polynomial. The field K is isomorphic to $\mathbb{Q}[x]/\langle f\rangle$ where f is the minimal polynomial of ζ. The set of algebraic integers within K defines a ring R called the ring of integers of K. We also define the ring $K_\mathbb{R} = K \otimes_\mathbb{Q} \mathbb{R} \cong \mathbb{R}[x]/\langle f\rangle$. For an ideal $\mathcal{I}$ of R, we define its norm $N(\mathcal{I})$ as the index of $\mathcal{I}$ in R, i.e., $N(\mathcal{I}) = |R/\mathcal{I}|$. We call a prime integer q unramified in R if all the distinct prime ideal factors of the ideal qR have ramification index 1, that is $qR = \prod_{i\in[\kappa]} \mathfrak{p}_i$ where $\mathfrak{p}_1, \ldots, \mathfrak{p}_\kappa$ are distinct prime ideals of R.

The number field K can be seen as an n-dimensional $\mathbb{Q}$-vector space with basis $\{\zeta^j\}_{j\in[0,n-1]}$, meaning that $a \in K$ can be expressed as $a = \sum_{0\le j<n} a_j\zeta^j$ with $a_j \in \mathbb{Q}$. We can therefore define the coefficient embedding τ such that $\tau(a) = [a_0|\ldots|a_{n-1}]^T$. We sometimes use $\tau_j(a) = a_j$ for simplicity. It then holds that the norms of $\mathbb{R}^n$ induce norms on K (and $K_\mathbb{R}, R$) by $\|a\| := \|\tau(a)\|$. Multiplication in K also maps to a matrix-vector multiplication of the coefficient embeddings as $\tau(ab) = M_\tau(a)\tau(b)$ where M_τ is a ring isomorphism defined by $M_\tau : a \in K \mapsto [\tau(a) \mid \tau(a\zeta) \mid \ldots \mid \tau(a\zeta^{n-1})] \in \mathbb{Q}^{n\times n}$

A popular class of number fields is that of cyclotomic fields. The m-th cyclotomic field is $K_m = \mathbb{Q}(\zeta_m)$ where ζ_m is a primitive m-th root of unity, e.g., $\zeta_m = \exp(i2\pi/m)$. The minimal polynomial, called the m-th cyclotomic polynomial, is $\Phi_m = \prod_{j\in\mathbb{Z}_m^\times}(x - \zeta_m^j)$. It has degree $n = \varphi(m)$. We define the Vandermonde matrix of K_m as $\mathbf{V}_m = [\zeta_m^{jk}]_{j\in\mathbb{Z}_m^\times, k\in[0,n-1]}$. For example, when $m = 2^{\ell+1}$, $\Phi_m = x^n + 1$ with $n = 2^\ell$, and $\mathbf{V}_m = \sqrt{n}\mathbf{U}$ with $\mathbf{U}$ unitary. In that case, we call K_m a power-of-two cyclotomic field. In the latter $M_\tau(a)$ is the nega-circulant matrix with first column $\tau(a)$. In cyclotomic fields, we also define the conjugate of an element a by $a^* = \sigma_{-1}(a)$ where σ_{-1} is the field automorphism of K defined by $\zeta \mapsto \zeta^{-1}$. Conjugation corresponds to transposing M_τ, i.e., $M_\tau(a)^T = M_\tau(a^*)$. As a result, in a power-of-two cyclotomic field of degree n, we have $\tau(a^*) = [a_0 \mid -a_{n-1} \mid \ldots \mid -a_1]^T$.

We extend these notions to vectors and matrices over K. Namely, for $\mathbf{a} \in K^d$, $\tau(\mathbf{a})$ is the concatenation of the coefficient embeddings of its entries. Similarly, $M_\tau(\mathbf{A})$ is the block matrix composed of the $M_\tau([\mathbf{A}]_{i,j})$. Vector and matrix norms are then extended to K^d and $K^{d\times k}$ through these embedding $\tau(\mathbf{a})$ and $M_\tau(\mathbf{A})$ respectively. We also define the conjugate of a vector or matrix by taking the conjugate of each entry and transposing the result, i.e., if $\mathbf{x} = [x_1 \mid \ldots \mid x_d]^T \in K^d$, then $\mathbf{x}^*$ is the row vector $[x_1^* \mid \ldots \mid x_d^*]$.

As we generally work with elements of R_q, we sometimes need to ensure these elements are invertible in the quotient ring R_q. Necessary conditions are provided for example in [39] in cyclotomic rings, where it suffices that q is sufficiently large compared to the ℓ_2 or ℓ_∞ norm of $y \in R_q$. We generalize their invertibility result in cyclotomic rings to be expressed in terms of the ℓ_p norm for an arbitrary p. As R_q is isomorphic to $\mathbb{Z}_q[x]/\langle \Phi_m(x) \rangle$ through $\zeta \mapsto x$, we analyze invertibility in the latter. The proof is provided in the full version [14, Lem. 2.1] for completeness.

Lemma 2.1 **([39, Thm. 1.1] adapted).** *Let $m = \prod_i p_i^{e_i}$ for p_i distinct primes and $e_i \in \mathbb{N}^\times$. Let $z = \prod_i p_i^{f_i}$ for arbitrary $f_i \in [1, e_i]$. Let q be a prime such that $q = 1 \bmod z$ and $ord_m(q) = m/z$. Let $y \in \mathbb{Z}_q[x]/\langle \Phi_m(x) \rangle$ such that there exists $p \in \mathbb{N}^\times$ such that $0 < \|\tau(y)\|_p < \varphi(z)^{\min(1/2, 1/p)} q^{1/\varphi(z)} / \|\mathbf{V}_z\|_2$. Then $y \in (\mathbb{Z}_q[x]/\langle \Phi_m(x) \rangle)^\times$.*

We can also specialize the result in the case of power-of-two cyclotomics akin [39, Cor. 1.2] as follows.

Lemma 2.2 **([39, Cor. 1.2] adapted).** *Let $n \geq \kappa > 1$ be powers of 2 and $q = 2\kappa + 1 \bmod 4\kappa$ a prime. Let $y \in \mathbb{Z}_q[x]/\langle x^n + 1 \rangle$ such that $0 < \|\tau(y)\|_p < \kappa^{\min(0, 1/p - 1/2)} q^{1/\kappa}$ for some $p \in \mathbb{N}^\times$, then $y \in (\mathbb{Z}_q[x]/\langle x^n + 1 \rangle)^\times$.*

2.2 Gaussians

For $s > 0$, we define the centered Gaussian function of parameter s by $\rho_s : \mathbf{x} \in \mathbb{R}^n \mapsto \exp(-\pi \|\mathbf{x}\|_2^2 / s^2)$. We can then define the discrete Gaussian over $\mathbb{Z}^n$ through its probability mass function $\mathcal{D}_{\mathbb{Z}^n, s} = \frac{\rho_s}{\rho_s(\mathbb{Z}^n)} \mathbf{1}_{\mathbb{Z}^n}$, where $\mathbf{1}_{\mathbb{Z}^n}$ is the indicator function of $\mathbb{Z}^n$ and $\rho_s(\mathbb{Z}^n) = \sum_{\mathbf{y} \in \mathbb{Z}^n} \rho_s(\mathbf{y})$. We extend the discrete Gaussian distribution to (vectors of) ring elements as $\mathcal{D}_{R^d, s} = \tau^{-1}(\mathcal{D}_{\mathbb{Z}^{nd}, s})$, i.e., the vector of $\mathbb{Z}^{nd}$ of concatenated coefficient embeddings is sampled from $\mathcal{D}_{\mathbb{Z}^{nd}, s}$, where n denotes the degree of R. We define the smoothing parameter of $\mathbb{Z}^n$, introduced in [45] for arbitrary lattices, as $\eta_\varepsilon(\mathbb{Z}^n) = \min\{s > 0 : \rho_{1/s}(\mathbb{Z}^n) = 1 + \varepsilon\}$ for a given $\varepsilon > 0$. It was recently shown in [28] that $\eta_\varepsilon(\mathbb{Z}^n) \approx \sqrt{\ln(2n/\varepsilon)/\pi}$. We also recall the standard tail bound in ℓ_2 norm from [8, Lem. 1.5]. We only specify it to $\mathbb{Z}^n$ but note it holds for all n-dimensional lattices.

Lemma 2.3 **([8, Lem. 1.5]).** *Let $n \in \mathbb{N}^\times$ and $s > 0$. For all $t \geq 1/\sqrt{2\pi}$, it holds $\mathbb{P}_{\mathbf{x} \sim \mathcal{D}_{\mathbb{Z}^n, s}}[\|\mathbf{x}\|_2 > ts\sqrt{n}] < (t\sqrt{2\pi e} e^{-\pi t^2})^n$.*

2.3 Entropy

For a distribution $\mathcal{X}$ on a support X, we define its min-entropy by $H_\infty(\mathcal{X}) = -\log_2 \max_{x' \in X} \mathbb{P}_{x \sim \mathcal{X}}[x = x']$. Throughout the paper, we interchangeably consider the min-entropy of $\mathcal{X}$ and the min-entropy of a random variable x distributed according to $\mathcal{X}$. We also consider the average predictability through the average conditional min-entropy of distribution $\mathcal{X}$ conditioned on a distribution $\mathcal{Y}$ supported over Y by $\widetilde{H_\infty}(\mathcal{X} \mid \mathcal{Y}) = -\log_2(\mathbb{E}_{y \sim \mathcal{Y}}[\max_{x' \in X} \mathbb{P}_{x \sim \mathcal{X}}[x = x' \mid y]])$. We note that other definitions of conditional entropy are possible, but the average one is better suited for security arguments. We elaborate on this subject in

Sect. 6. By abuse of language, we may use conditional entropy or residual entropy to designate the average conditional min-entropy. We recall the following results of [23] on the conditional entropy, which we use in Sect. 6.2.

Lemma 2.4 ([23, **Lem. 2.2**]). *Let $\mathcal{X}, \mathcal{Y}, \mathcal{Z}$ be random variables. Then*

1. *For any $\delta > 0$, the conditional entropy $H_\infty(\mathcal{X} \mid \mathcal{Y} = y)$ is at least $\widetilde{H_\infty}(\mathcal{X} \mid \mathcal{Y}) - \log_2(1/\delta)$ with probability $1 - \delta$ over the choice of y.*
2. *If $\mathcal{Y}$ takes at most N values, then $\widetilde{H_\infty}(\mathcal{X} \mid \mathcal{Y}) \geq H_\infty(\mathcal{X}) - \log_2 N$ and $\widetilde{H_\infty}(\mathcal{X} \mid \mathcal{Y}, \mathcal{Z}) \geq \widetilde{H_\infty}(\mathcal{X} \mid \mathcal{Z}) - \log_2 N$.*

2.4 Assumptions

We now introduce the *Module Learning With Errors* problem as formalized in [34]. We however leave free the choice of secret and error distributions which is particularly relevant for our work.

Definition 2.1 (M-LWE). *Let R be the ring of integers of a number field of degree n, and d, m, q be in $\mathbb{N}^\times$. Let $\mathscr{D}_s$ be a secret distribution on R^d, and $\mathscr{D}_e$ an error distribution on R^m. The search version of the Module Learning With Errors problem, denoted M-LWE$_{n,d,m,q,\mathscr{D}_s,\mathscr{D}_e}$, asks to recover $\mathbf{s}$ given $\mathbf{A} \hookleftarrow U(R_q^{m\times d})$, and $\mathbf{b} = \mathbf{A}\mathbf{s}+\mathbf{e} \bmod qR$ for $\mathbf{s} \hookleftarrow \mathscr{D}_s$ and $\mathbf{e} \hookleftarrow \mathscr{D}_e$. The advantage of an adversary $\mathcal{A}$ is then Adv$[\mathcal{A}] = \mathbb{P}[\mathcal{A}(\mathbf{A}, \mathbf{b}) = \mathbf{s}]$. The decision version asks to distinguish such pairs $(\mathcal{P}_0)$ $(\mathbf{A}, \mathbf{b} = \mathbf{A}\mathbf{s} + \mathbf{e} \bmod qR)$ from $(\mathcal{P}_1)$ $(\mathbf{A}, \mathbf{u})$ where $\mathbf{u} \hookleftarrow U(R_q^m)$. The adversary's advantage in this case is Adv$[\mathcal{A}] = |\mathbb{P}_{(\mathbf{A},\mathbf{b})\sim\mathcal{P}_0}[\mathcal{A}(\mathbf{A}, \mathbf{b}) = 1] - \mathbb{P}_{(\mathbf{A},\mathbf{u})\sim\mathcal{P}_1}[\mathcal{A}(\mathbf{A}, \mathbf{u}) = 1]|$.*

Our proof, in its computational variant, leverages the *Module Short Integer Solution* problem, formalized in [34], which we extend to arbitrary ℓ_p norms.

Definition 2.2 (M-SIS). *Let R be the ring of integers of a number field of degree n, and d, m, q be in $\mathbb{N}^\times$. Let $p \in [1, \infty]$ and $\beta > 0$. The Module Short Integer Solution problem, denoted M-SIS$^p_{n,d,m,q,\beta}$, asks to find $\mathbf{x} \in R^m$ such that $\mathbf{A}^T\mathbf{x} = \mathbf{0} \bmod qR$ and $0 < \|\mathbf{x}\|_p \leq \beta$ given $\mathbf{A} \hookleftarrow U(R_q^{m\times d})$. The advantage of an adversary is Adv$[\mathcal{A}] = \mathbb{P}[\mathbf{A}^T\mathbf{x} = \mathbf{0} \wedge 0 < \|\mathbf{x}\|_p \leq \beta : \mathbf{x} \leftarrow \mathcal{A}(\mathbf{A})]$.*

We say that a problem P (among search/decision M-LWE and M-SIS) is ε-hard if for all probabilistic polynomial time adversary, Adv$[\mathcal{A}] \leq \varepsilon$. We sometimes refer to ε as the hardness bound of problem P.

2.5 Function Families

Our proof of hardness in Sect. 4 focuses on the security properties of M-LWE when seen as function family. More generally, a function family $\mathcal{F}$ over a set of functions which all have domain X and range Y is simply a probability distribution over F. The M-LWE problem defined in Sect. 2.4 can be interpreted as a function family whose distribution relies on the distribution of $\mathbf{A}$. Moreover, we define another function family, called M-Knap, which is closely related to the M-LWE function family. As all functions can be unambiguously represented by a matrix $\mathbf{A}$, we say that an adversary is given the function f as input when it is given its public representation, i.e., $\mathbf{A}$.

Definition 2.3. *Let $n, d, m, q \in \mathbb{N}^{\times}$, and R be the ring of integers of a number field of degree n, and $X \subseteq R^m$. The M-Knap(n, d, m, q, X) function family is the distribution obtained by sampling a matrix $\mathbf{A} \hookleftarrow U(R_q^{m \times d})$, and outputting $f_{\mathbf{A}}$ defined by $f_{\mathbf{A}}(\mathbf{x}) = \mathbf{A}^T\mathbf{x} \bmod qR$ for all $\mathbf{x} \in X$. The M-LWE(n, d, m, q, X) function family is the distribution obtained by sampling $\mathbf{A} \hookleftarrow U(R_q^{m \times d})$ and outputting $g_{\mathbf{A}}$ defined by $g_{\mathbf{A}}(\mathbf{s}, \mathbf{e}) = \mathbf{A}\mathbf{s} + \mathbf{e} \bmod qR$ for all $(\mathbf{s}, \mathbf{e}) \in R_q^d \times X$.*

We present the security properties we need for arbitrary function families, as well as some useful results which are relevant to our proof. The hardness of the M-LWE problem from Sect. 2.4 can then be expressed as security properties of M-LWE(n, d, m, q, X). Concretely, the one-wayness captures the hardness of the corresponding search problem, while the pseudorandomness captures the hardness of the decision problem.

Definition 2.4. *Let X, Y be two sets, and F be a set of functions from X to Y. Let $\mathcal{F}, \mathcal{G}$ be two function families over F. Let $\mathcal{X}$ be a probability distribution over X, and $\varepsilon \in (0, 1)$.*

- *Indistinguishability. $\mathcal{F}$ and $\mathcal{G}$ are ε-indistinguishable if for all PPT algorithm $\mathcal{A}$, it holds $|\mathbb{P}_{f \sim \mathcal{F}}[\mathcal{A}(f) = 1] - \mathbb{P}_{g \sim \mathcal{G}}[\mathcal{A}(g) = 1]| \leq \varepsilon$.*
- *Collision resistance. $\mathcal{F}$ is ε-collision resistant if for all PPT algorithm $\mathcal{A}$, it holds $\mathbb{P}_{f \sim \mathcal{F}, (x, x') \leftarrow \mathcal{A}(f)}[x \neq x' \wedge f(x) = f(x')] \leq \varepsilon$.*
- *Pseudorandomness. $(\mathcal{F}, \mathcal{X})$ is ε-pseudorandom if for all PPT algorithm $\mathcal{A}$, it holds $|\mathbb{P}_{(f,x) \sim \mathcal{F} \times \mathcal{X}}[\mathcal{A}(f, f(x)) = 1] - \mathbb{P}_{(f,y) \sim \mathcal{F} \times U(Y)}[\mathcal{A}(f, y) = 1]| \leq \varepsilon$.*
- *Second preimage resistance. $(\mathcal{F}, \mathcal{X})$ is ε-second preimage resistant if for all PPT algorithm $\mathcal{A}$, it holds $\mathbb{P}_{(f,x) \sim \mathcal{F} \times \mathcal{X}, x' \leftarrow \mathcal{A}(f,x)}[x \neq x' \wedge f(x) = f(x')] \leq \varepsilon$.*
- *Uninvertibility. $(\mathcal{F}, \mathcal{X})$ is ε-uninvertible if for all PPT algorithm $\mathcal{A}$, it holds that $\mathbb{P}_{(f,x) \sim \mathcal{F} \times \mathcal{X}}[\mathcal{A}(f, f(x)) = x] \leq \varepsilon$.*
- *One-wayness. $(\mathcal{F}, \mathcal{X})$ is ε-one-way if for all PPT algorithm $\mathcal{A}$, it holds that $\mathbb{P}_{(f,x) \sim \mathcal{F} \times \mathcal{X}}[f(\mathcal{A}(f, f(x))) = f(x)] \leq \varepsilon$.*

Each of the probabilities is implicitly reliant on the randomness $\mathcal{A}$ itself.

We now give useful sufficient conditions to ensure some of these security properties. In particular, we extend the results of [44, Lem. 2.4] and [54, Lem. 6] to general distributions, i.e., not limited uniform distributions or unbalanced Bernoulli distributions. We give the proof in the full version [14, Lem. 2.5].

Lemma 2.5 ([54, Lem. 6] adapted). *Let $\mathcal{F}$ be a function family with finite domain X. Let $\mathcal{X}$ be a distribution on X. For $\varepsilon = 2^{-H_\infty(\mathcal{X})}\mathbb{E}_{f \sim \mathcal{F}}[|f(X)|]$, it holds that $(\mathcal{F}, \mathcal{X})$ is ε-uninvertible, even against unbounded adversaries.*

Lemma 2.6 **([44, Lem. 2.2]).** *Let $\mathcal{F}$ be a family of functions computable in polynomial time. Let $\mathcal{X}$ be a distribution on X. If $(\mathcal{F}, \mathcal{X})$ is ε-uninvertible and ε'-second preimage resistant, then it is also $(\varepsilon + \varepsilon')$-one-way.*

Lemma 2.7 **([44, Lem. 2.5]).** *Let $\mathcal{F}$ be a function family with domain X and range Y, and $\mathcal{G}$ be an efficiently sampleable family of efficiently computable functions with domain $X' \supseteq Y$. Let $\mathcal{X}$ be a distribution on X. If $(\mathcal{F}, \mathcal{X})$ is ε-uninvertible, then so is $(\mathcal{G} \circ \mathcal{F}, \mathcal{X})$.*

Lastly, we recall the duality result between the M-LWE and M-Knap function families [43], generalized to the module setting in [13]. We only recall the results we need for our reduction and refer to [13, Lem. 4.1 & 4.2] for a more complete statement.

Lemma 2.8. *Let $n, d, m, k, \ell, q \in \mathbb{N}^\times$, and R be the ring of integers of a number field of degree n, such that q is an unramified prime in R, and $m \geq d + 1$. For any $a, b \in \mathbb{N}^\times$ with $a \geq b$, we define $\delta(a, b) = 1 - \Pr_{\mathbf{A} \sim U(R_q^{b \times a})}[\mathbf{A} R_q^a = R_q^b]$. Let $\mathcal{X}_1, \mathcal{X}_2$ be probability distributions over $X_1 \subseteq R^\ell$ and $X_2 \subseteq R^m$ respectively. If $(M\text{-}LWE(n, k, \ell, q, R^\ell), \mathcal{X}_1)$ is ε_1-pseudorandom, it then holds that $(M\text{-}Knap(n, \ell - k, \ell, q, R^\ell), \mathcal{X}_1)$ is ε_1'-pseudorandom where we have $\varepsilon_1' = 2\delta(\ell, \ell - k) + \varepsilon_1/(1 - \delta(\ell, k))$. Additionally, if $(M\text{-}Knap(n, m - d, m, q, R^m), \mathcal{X}_2)$ is ε_2-one-way, then $(M\text{-}LWE(n, d, m, q, R^m), \mathcal{X}_2)$ is ε_2'-one-way with $\varepsilon_2' = \delta(m, d) + \varepsilon_2/(1 - \delta(m, m - d))$.*

3 Linear Noise Lossiness

In this section, we consider the conditional min-entropy of a random vector $\mathbf{x}$ given a linear evaluation of $\mathbf{x}$, i.e., $\widetilde{H_\infty}(\mathbf{x} \mid \mathbf{M}\mathbf{x} + \mathbf{f})$. More concretely, the matrix $\mathbf{M}$ can be adversarially chosen, while the mask vector $\mathbf{f}$ follows a prescribed distribution. This can be seen as a generalization of the *noise lossiness* notion of [16] which was formulated for $\mathbf{M}$ being the identity matrix $\mathbf{I}$.

The overall goal of [16] is the same as ours: to analyze the conditional min-entropy $\widetilde{H_\infty}(\mathbf{x} \mid \mathbf{M}\mathbf{x} + \mathbf{f})$ for some given matrix $\mathbf{M}$. To do so, they assume that $\mathbf{f}$ follows a Gaussian distribution and, using Gaussian properties, they decompose the mask $\mathbf{f}$ into $\mathbf{M}\mathbf{f}_1 + \mathbf{f}_2$. This decomposition is possible only if the Gaussian parameter of $\mathbf{f}$ is larger than $\|\mathbf{M}\|_2$ times the Gaussian parameter of $\mathbf{f}_1$. Note that in [16], all considered Gaussians $\mathbf{f}, \mathbf{f}_1$ and $\mathbf{f}_2$ are continuous, but the analysis can be generalized to discrete Gaussians using discrete convolution theorems, e.g., [25, Lem. 3] or [29, Thm. 3.1]. Then, they show $\widetilde{H_\infty}(\mathbf{x} \mid \mathbf{M}\mathbf{x} + \mathbf{f}) \geq \widetilde{H_\infty}(\mathbf{x} + \mathbf{f}_1)$, which means it is enough to consider the conditional entropy of $\mathbf{x}$ given $\mathbf{x} + \mathbf{f}_1$. This approach is termed *flooding at the source* and motivated by the idea that it is less costly to hide $\mathbf{x}$ with $\mathbf{f}_1$ than hiding $\mathbf{M}\mathbf{x}$ with $\mathbf{f}$.

We observe that this approach is in general not optimal, and we can in fact generalize their result to directly bound $\widetilde{H_\infty}(\mathbf{x} \mid \mathbf{M}\mathbf{x} + \mathbf{f})$ without relying on a Gaussian decomposition and (loose) inequalities like $\widetilde{H_\infty}(\mathbf{x} \mid \mathbf{M}\mathbf{x} + \mathbf{f}) \geq$

$\widetilde{H_\infty}(\mathbf{x}+\mathbf{f}_1)$. Hence, in our approach, the parameter for $\mathbf{f}$ does not need to be larger than $\|\mathbf{M}\|_2$, which allows for different trade-offs between the size of the mask $\mathbf{f}$ and the amount of entropy left in $\mathbf{x}$. Put differently, we challenge the idea that flooding at the source is most effective.

Even though our proof closely follows the original proof of [16], we think this observation merits some spotlight and might be of independent interest. Due to lack of space, the proofs of this section are deferred to the full version [14, Sec. 3].

Lemma 3.1. *Let $k, n \in \mathbb{N}^\times$ and $\mathbf{M} \in \mathbb{Z}^{n\times k}$ be a matrix. Let $\mathbf{x}$ be a random variable over $X \subseteq \mathbb{Z}^k$, and let $\mathbf{f}$ be a random variable following a discrete distribution χ over $\mathbb{Z}^n$. We denote by $\mathbf{M}X$ the support of $\mathbf{Mx}$, and by Y the support of $\mathbf{Mx}+\mathbf{f}$. It then holds that*

$$\widetilde{H_\infty}(\mathbf{x}|\mathbf{Mx}+\mathbf{f}) \geq H_\infty(\mathbf{x}) - \log_2\left(\sum_{\mathbf{y}\in Y} \max_{\widehat{\mathbf{x}}\in\mathbf{M}X} \mathbb{P}_{\mathbf{f}\sim\chi}[\mathbf{f}=\mathbf{y}-\widehat{\mathbf{x}}]\right).$$

The equality holds when $\mathbf{x}$ follows a uniform distribution. The result also holds true for continuous distributions by replacing the discrete sum with integrals and using density functions.

We then bound the sum using the following lemma, which adapts [16, Lem. 5.4] to a discrete Gaussian mask $\mathbf{f}$. Note that moving to the discrete Gaussian case requires the Gaussian parameter to be above the smoothing parameter of the integer lattice. Combining this bound with Lemma 3.1 then leads to Lemma 3.3 below. We recover [16, Lem. 5.4] by setting $\mathbf{M}=\mathbf{I}$.

Lemma 3.2 ([16, Lem. 5.4] **adapted).** *Let $n \in \mathbb{N}^\times$, and $\sigma \geq \eta_\varepsilon(\mathbb{Z}^n)$ for some $\varepsilon > 0$. Let $\widehat{X} \subseteq \mathbb{Z}^n$ be a bounded set, and define $B = \max_{\widehat{\mathbf{x}}\in\widehat{X}} \|\widehat{\mathbf{x}}\|_2$. Let $\mathbf{f} \sim \mathcal{D}_{\mathbb{Z}^n,\sigma}$. Then, it holds that*

$$\sum_{\mathbf{y}\in\mathbb{Z}^n} \max_{\widehat{\mathbf{x}}\in\widehat{X}} \mathbb{P}_{\mathbf{f}\sim\mathcal{D}_{\mathbb{Z}^n,\sigma}}[\mathbf{f}=\mathbf{y}-\widehat{\mathbf{x}}] \leq (1+\varepsilon)e^{\sqrt{2\pi n}B/\sigma}.$$

Lemma 3.3 (Linear Noise Lossiness). *Let $k, n \in \mathbb{N}^\times$ and $\mathbf{M} \in \mathbb{Z}^{n\times k}$ be a matrix. Let $\sigma \geq \eta_\varepsilon(\mathbb{Z}^n)$ for some $\varepsilon > 0$. Let $\mathbf{x}$ be a random variable over $\mathbb{Z}^k$ such that $\|\mathbf{Mx}\|_2 \leq B$ is always verified. Let $\mathbf{f}$ follow $\mathcal{D}_{\mathbb{Z}^n,\sigma}$. It holds that*

$$\widetilde{H_\infty}(\mathbf{x}|\mathbf{Mx}+\mathbf{f}) \geq H_\infty(\mathbf{x}) - \sqrt{2\pi n}\frac{B}{\sigma}\log_2 e - \log_2(1+\varepsilon).$$

4 M-LWE With General Error Distributions

In this section, we prove the hardness of search M-LWE for *general error distributions* under certain constraints we clarify later on. The high-level proof strategy, albeit generalized to our broader setting, follows the blueprint of [13,44].

It goes as follows: proving hardness of the search M-LWE problem with general bounded error distribution comes down to proving the one-wayness of the corresponding M-LWE function family (Definition 2.3). Instead of doing so directly, we first prove the one-wayness of the related M-Knap function family (Definition 2.3) and then invoke the duality of M-Knap and M-LWE (Lemma 2.8). By Lemma 2.6, one-wayness of M-Knap is implied by its uninvertibility (Sect. 4.1) and its second preimage resistance (Sect. 4.2).

Essentially, our results only require the error distribution to have sufficient min-entropy and to output elements of bounded norm. Previous works on the hardness of M-LWE for *general secret distributions*, e.g., [12,17], did not inherently require any norm bound, which then might be interpreted as an unnecessary requirement in our case. However, because we focus on *error distributions*, this bound is intuitively crucial to ensure hardness. For example, if one considers the pathological case where all the entropy lies in too few coefficients, many samples would be noiseless which may be sufficient to solve this particular M-LWE instance. However, note that in that case, the coefficients containing all the entropy would be extremely big. The latter would then require very large parameters so that our result can apply and ensure the hardness of such an edge M-LWE instance. In particular, it would require an extremely large lattice dimension (or secret dimension) which would essentially compensate for the noiseless equations. Although our result still covers these pathological cases, it does so with very large parameters. For more reasonable cases, one can interpret this norm bound as a safeguard to spread the entropy more evenly and, in a sense, smooth out these extreme edge cases. Typical applications of M-LWE naturally come attached to such norm constraints, e.g., in order to ensure correctness of an encryption scheme. As such, this is a reasonable assumption to make on the error distribution in addition to its min-entropy.

4.1 Uninvertibility

We start by proving the uninvertibility of the M-Knap function family. Actually, we first show it in Lemma 4.1 for a slightly different function family. Then, in a second step, the uninvertiblity of the M-Knap family function is proven in Lemma 4.2 by assuming the hardness of decision M-LWE (with a "standard" error distribution). The slightly different function family is obtained by composing a smaller-dimensional M-Knap with a family $\mathcal{G}$ of linear functions over R. Previous works [13,44] defined this linear function family with a Gaussian distribution in order to connect the result to worst-case to average-case reduction for M-LWE. The distribution $\mathcal{D}$ used to define $\mathcal{G}$ essentially corresponds to the error distribution for which one assumes M-LWE is hard. To give more modularity to our result, we do not fix $\mathcal{D}$ to be a Gaussian so that one can choose the starting M-LWE assumption they deem reasonable. For example, one could reasonably assume M-LWE with bounded uniform noise is hard, which has been well studied from a theoretical and cryptanalytic perspective and used in countless cryptographic applications. The final result would then show that M-LWE with general noise distributions is at least as hard as M-LWE with a bounded uniform noise. We thus start by defining the function family $\mathcal{G}$.

Definition 4.1. *Let n, ℓ, m be in $\mathbb{N}^\times$ such that $m \geq \ell$. Let R be the ring of integers of a number field of degree n. Let $\mathcal{D}$ be a distribution on R^ℓ, and let $X \subseteq R^m$. We define the function family $\mathcal{G}(n, \ell, m, \mathcal{D}, X)$ obtained by sampling the columns of a matrix $\mathbf{Y} \in R^{\ell \times (m-\ell)}$ from $\mathcal{D}$ and outputting $h_\mathbf{Y} : X \to R^\ell$ defined by $\forall \mathbf{x} \in X$, $h_\mathbf{Y}(\mathbf{x}) = [\mathbf{I}_\ell | \mathbf{Y}]\mathbf{x}$.*

We now show that under some norm requirements on $\mathcal{D}$ and the input distribution $\mathcal{X}$ of $\mathcal{G}$, we can show that $(\mathcal{G}(n, \ell, m, \mathcal{D}, X), \mathcal{X})$ is statistically uninvertible, provided $\mathcal{X}$ has sufficient entropy. By composition, Lemma 2.7 gives uninvertibility of M-Knap $\circ\, \mathcal{G}$ which is relevant to later show one-wayness of M-Knap.

Lemma 4.1. *Let n, ℓ, m, d be in $\mathbb{N}^\times$ such that $m \geq \max(d, \ell)$. Let R be the ring of integers of a number field of degree n. Let $\mathcal{D}$ be a distribution on R^ℓ, and, for any $k \in \mathbb{N}^\times$, let $\mathcal{D}^k$ be the distribution over $R^{\ell \times k}$ where all the columns are sampled from $\mathcal{D}$. We also assume that for any[1] $\alpha, \beta \in [1, \infty]$, there exists $B_{\alpha,\beta} \geq 0$ and $p_{\alpha,\beta} \in [0, 1]$ such that*

$$\mathbb{P}_{\mathbf{Y} \sim \mathcal{D}^{m-\ell}}[\|M_\tau([\mathbf{I}_\ell | \mathbf{Y}])\|_{\alpha,\beta} > B_{\alpha,\beta}] \leq p_{\alpha,\beta}.$$

Then, let $X \subseteq R^m$ be a bounded set, and denote by $B_\alpha = \max_{\mathbf{x} \in X} \|\mathbf{x}\|_\alpha$. Let $\mathcal{X}$ be a distribution such that $\operatorname{Supp} \mathcal{X} = X$. We define the function family $\mathcal{F}' =$ M-Knap$(n, m-d, \ell, q, R^\ell) \circ \mathcal{G}(n, \ell, m, \mathcal{D}, X)$. Then, $(\mathcal{F}', \mathcal{X})$ is (statistically) ε'_{inv}-uninvertible for

$$\varepsilon'_{inv} = 2^{-H_\infty(\mathcal{X})} \left(|\mathcal{B}_{\beta,n\ell}(B_{\alpha,\beta} B_\alpha) \cap \mathbb{Z}^{n\ell}| + |X| \cdot p_{\alpha,\beta} \right).$$

Proof. We first bound $\mathbb{E}_{h_\mathbf{Y} \sim \mathcal{G}}[|h_\mathbf{Y}(X)|]$ and use Lemma 2.5 to conclude. Let $h_\mathbf{Y}$ be sampled from $\mathcal{G}(n, \ell, m, \mathcal{D}, X)$. Let $\mathbf{x} \in X$. Then, $h_\mathbf{Y}(\mathbf{x}) = [\mathbf{I}_\ell | \mathbf{Y}]\mathbf{x}$. We then have $\|h_\mathbf{Y}(\mathbf{x})\|_\beta \leq \|[\mathbf{I}_\ell | \mathbf{Y}]\|_{\alpha,\beta} \|\mathbf{x}\|_\alpha$. Because X is bounded and all norms are equivalent on a finitely dimensional vector space, it holds that the bound B_α exists and is finite for any α. By assumption, it then holds that $\|\mathbf{x}\|_\alpha \leq B_\alpha$, and

$$\mathbb{P}_{\mathbf{Y} \sim \mathcal{D}^{m-\ell}}\left[\|M_\tau([\mathbf{I}_\ell | \mathbf{Y}])\|_{\alpha,\beta} > B_{\alpha,\beta}\right] \leq p_{\alpha,\beta}.$$

Hence, with probability at least $1 - p_{\alpha,\beta}$, we have that the ℓ_β norm of $\tau(h_\mathbf{Y}(\mathbf{x}))$ is bounded by $B_{\alpha,\beta} B_\alpha$. The number of integer points in the $n\ell$-dimensional ℓ_β-ball then gives an upper bound on $|h_\mathbf{Y}(X)|$. It means we have

$$|h_\mathbf{Y}(X)| \leq |\mathcal{B}_{\beta,n\ell}(B_{\alpha,\beta} B_\alpha) \cap \mathbb{Z}^{n\ell}| =: K.$$

[1] Recall that all norms are equivalent in finite-dimensional vector spaces. Hence, if there exists $B_{\alpha_0,\beta_0}, p_{\alpha_0,\beta_0}$ for one pair (α_0, β_0), it gives the existence for all pairs (α, β).

We note that if the radius $B_{\alpha,\beta}B_\alpha$ is large enough compared to $n\ell$, the value of K is well approximated by the volume of the ℓ_β-ball, which is

$$\mathrm{Vol}(\mathcal{B}_{\beta,n\ell}(B_{\alpha,\beta}B_\alpha)) = \frac{\left(2B_{\alpha,\beta}B_\alpha \cdot \Gamma\left(\frac{1}{\beta}+1\right)\right)^{n\ell}}{\Gamma\left(\frac{n\ell}{\beta}+1\right)}.$$

We note that we could have trivially chosen $K = |X|$ but this is not tight because $h_{\mathbf{Y}}$ is not injective. We also define $S = \{\mathbf{Y} \in R^{\ell\times(m-\ell)} : \|M_\tau([\mathbf{I}_\ell|\mathbf{Y}])\|_{\alpha,\beta} \leq B_{\alpha,\beta}\}$, and S' its complement in $R^{\ell\times(m-\ell)}$. We then have

$$\begin{aligned}\mathbb{E}\left[|h_{\mathbf{Y}}(X)|\right] &= \sum_{\mathbf{Y}'\in S} \mathbb{P}_{\mathbf{Y}}[\mathbf{Y}=\mathbf{Y}']|h_{\mathbf{Y}'}(X)| + \sum_{\mathbf{Y}'\in S'} \mathbb{P}_{\mathbf{Y}}[\mathbf{Y}=\mathbf{Y}']|h_{\mathbf{Y}'}(X)| \\ &\leq K\cdot \mathbb{P}_{\mathbf{Y}}[\mathbf{Y}\in S] + |X|\cdot \mathbb{P}_{\mathbf{Y}}[\mathbf{Y}\in S'] \\ &\leq K + |X|\cdot p_{\alpha,\beta},\end{aligned}$$

where the first inequality follows from the above calculations and the fact that for $\mathbf{Y}' \in S'$, we have the trivial bound $|h_{\mathbf{Y}'}(X)| \leq |X|$. Lemma 2.5 then yields the $\varepsilon'_{\mathrm{inv}}$-uninvertibility of $\mathcal{G}$, with $\varepsilon'_{\mathrm{inv}} = 2^{-H_\infty(\mathcal{X})}(K+|X|\cdot p_{\alpha,\beta})$. By Lemma 2.7, we thus obtain the $\varepsilon'_{\mathrm{inv}}$-uninvertibility of $\mathcal{F}'$. □

Remark 4.1. The quantity $2^{-H_\infty(\mathcal{X})}|\mathrm{Supp}\,\mathcal{X}|$ is always larger than 1, as we have $|\mathrm{Supp}\,\mathcal{X}| = 2^{H_\infty(U(X))}$. Hence $2^{-H_\infty(\mathcal{X})}|\mathrm{Supp}\,\mathcal{X}| = 2^{H_\infty(U(X))-H_\infty(\mathcal{X})}$. We then use the fact that maximal entropy is achieved for the uniform distribution for a fixed support. As a result, one needs not only to set the bound $B_{\alpha,\beta}$ so that $p_{\alpha,\beta}$ is negligible (e.g., $\leq 2^{-\lambda}$), but also to compensate the entropy difference between $\mathcal{X}$ and $U(X)$.

Our result of Lemma 4.1 is naturally parameterized by (α,β) so as to remain as generic as possible, and cover more distributions $\mathcal{X}$. Certain distributions may be more relevant to analyze in the $\alpha=\infty$ metric than $\alpha=2$ for example. One could even optimize over (α,β) provided that they have an efficient way of computing or approximating $B_{\alpha,\beta}, B_\alpha, p_{\alpha,\beta}$ and the number of integer points in the ℓ_β ball of a given radius. Indeed, a stronger statement would be

$$\varepsilon'_{\mathrm{inv}} \leq 2^{-H_\infty(\mathcal{X})}\cdot \inf_{\alpha,\beta}\left(|\mathcal{B}_{\beta,n\ell}(B_{\alpha,\beta}B_\alpha)\cap \mathbb{Z}^{n\ell}| + |X|\cdot p_{\alpha,\beta}\right).$$

As estimating all these quantities is non trivial for arbitrary values of (α,β), we only give in the full version [14, App. C] a few example parameterizations for α,β (and $\mathcal{D}$), as well as full examples in (1, 2)-norm in [14, App. A & B]. We typically restrict our examples to $\beta\in\{1,2,\infty\}$ for which we know closed-form or close approximations of the number of integer points in the ℓ_β ball[2]. We then

[2] We have $|\mathcal{B}_{1,N}(r)\cap\mathbb{Z}^N| = \sum_{i=0}^{\min(N,\lfloor r\rfloor)} 2^i\binom{N}{i}\binom{\lfloor r\rfloor}{i}$, $|\mathcal{B}_{\infty,N}(r)\cap\mathbb{Z}^N| = (2\lfloor r\rfloor+1)^N$, and $|\mathcal{B}_{2,N}(r)\cap\mathbb{Z}^N| \leq \mathrm{Vol}(\mathcal{B}_{2,N}(r+\sqrt{N}/2))$. When $r\gg N$, we also have $|\mathcal{B}_{p,N}(r)\cap\mathbb{Z}^N| \approx \mathrm{Vol}(\mathcal{B}_{p,N}(r))$.

restrict to the values of α for which we have an expression of $\|\cdot\|_{\alpha,\beta}$. But we again insist that our result can be parameterized differently if needed.

So far, we have proven the uninvertibility of a composition between M-Knap with rank $m-d$ and dimension ℓ and $\mathcal{G}$. However, to eventually prove hardness of M-LWE with rank d and m samples, we would need the uninvertibility of M-Knap with rank $m-d$ and dimension $m > \ell$. We now show that we can obtain the latter by combining Lemma 4.1 with an indistinguishability argument based on M-LWE with error distribution $\mathcal{D}$.

Lemma 4.2. *Let n, k, q, d, m be in $\mathbb{N}^\times$ with $m > d \geq k \geq 1$ and let $\ell = m-d+k$. Let $\mathcal{D}$ be a distribution over R^ℓ, and $X \subseteq R^m$. Assume M-LWE$_{n,k,\ell,q,U(R_q^d),\mathcal{D}}$ is $\varepsilon_{M\text{-}LWE}$-hard. Define the function families $\mathcal{F}' =$ M-Knap$(n, m-d, \ell, q, R^\ell) \circ \mathcal{G}(n, \ell, m, \mathcal{D}, X)$ (as in Lemma 4.1), and $\mathcal{F} =$ M-Knap$(n, m-d, m, q, X)$. If $\mathcal{F}'$ is ε'_{inv}-uninvertible, then $\mathcal{F}$ is ε_{inv}-uninvertible, where*

$$\varepsilon_{inv} = \varepsilon'_{inv} + (m-\ell)\left(2\delta(\ell, ell-k) + \varepsilon_{M\text{-}LWE}/(1-\delta(\ell,k))\right).$$

Proof. First, assuming M-LWE$_{n,k,\ell,q,U(R_q^d),\mathcal{D}}$ is $\varepsilon_{\text{M-LWE}}$-hard entails that the M-LWE function family is $\varepsilon_{\text{M-LWE}}$-pseudorandom. Based on the duality result Lemma 2.8, we get that (M-Knap$(n, m-d, \ell, q, R^\ell), \mathcal{D}$) is $\varepsilon_{\text{rand}}$-pseudorandom with $\varepsilon_{\text{rand}} = 2\delta(\ell, m-d) + \varepsilon_{\text{M-LWE}}/(1-\delta(\ell,k))$ because $m-d = \ell-k$.

Then, it holds that $\mathcal{F}$ and $\mathcal{F}'$ are indistinguishable based on $\varepsilon_{\text{rand}}$. Indeed, assume an adversary $\mathcal{A}$ breaks the $(m-\ell)\varepsilon_{\text{rand}}$-indistinguishability between $\mathcal{F}$ and $\mathcal{F}'$. Take $f_{\mathbf{A}'} \circ h_{\mathbf{Y}}$ according to $\mathcal{F}'$, and $f_{\mathbf{A}}$ according to $\mathcal{F}$. Then $f_{\mathbf{A}'} \circ h_{\mathbf{Y}}$ is the linear map $\mathbf{x}c[\mathbf{A}'^T|\mathbf{A}'^T\mathbf{Y}]\mathbf{x}$. Decomposing $\mathbf{A}^T$ into $[\mathbf{A}_1^T|\mathbf{A}_2^T]$, with $\mathbf{A}_1 \in R_q^{\ell\times(m-d)}$, $\mathbf{A}_2 \in R_q^{(m-\ell)\times(m-d)}$, we have that $f_{\mathbf{A}} = \mathbf{x} \mapsto [\mathbf{A}_1^T|\mathbf{A}_2^T]\mathbf{x}$. By assumption, it means that $\mathcal{A}$ can distinguish $(\mathbf{A}'^T, \mathbf{A}'^T\mathbf{Y} \bmod qR)$ from uniform. By a hybrid argument, it means $\mathcal{A}$ can distinguish $(\mathbf{A}'^T, \mathbf{A}'^T\mathbf{y} \bmod qR)$ for $\mathbf{y} \sim \mathcal{D}$ from uniform with advantage at least $\varepsilon_{\text{rand}}$, thus breaking the $\varepsilon_{\text{rand}}$-pseudorandomness of (M-Knap$(n, m-d, \ell, q, R^\ell), \mathcal{D}$). By assumption, we then have a contradiction, which means that $\mathcal{F}$ and $\mathcal{F}'$ are $(m-\ell)\varepsilon_{\text{rand}}$-indistinguishable.

By indistinguishability, the properties of $\mathcal{F}$ and $\mathcal{F}'$ transfer to one another with an additive loss of $(m-\ell)\varepsilon_{\text{rand}}$. As such, applying Lemma 4.1 yields that $(\mathcal{F}, \mathcal{X})$ is $(\varepsilon'_{\text{inv}} + (m-\ell)\varepsilon_{\text{rand}})$-uninvertible as claimed. □

4.2 Second Preimage Resistance

We now prove the second preimage resistance of the M-Knap function family with respect to an arbitrary distribution. We provide the proof in both statistical and computational hardness regimes to allow for more flexibility depending on the final application.

Lemma 4.3. *Let n, h, q, m be in $\mathbb{N}^\times$ such that q is prime. Let R be the ring of integers of a number field of degree n, and $X \subseteq R^m$. We also define $\mathcal{N} =$* $\max_{\mathbf{x},\mathbf{x}'\in X, \mathbf{x}\neq\mathbf{x}'} N(\langle x_1 - x'_1, \ldots, x_m - x'_m, q\rangle)$. *Let $\mathcal{X}$ be a distribution such that*

Supp $\mathcal{X} = X$. *Then* $(\text{M-Knap}(n,h,m,q,X),\mathcal{X})$ *is* ε_{spr}*-second preimage resistant with respect to unbounded adversaries for*

$$\varepsilon_{spr} = \frac{\mathcal{N}^h}{q^{nh}}(|X|-1).$$

If X *is a bounded set and* $\mathcal{X}$ *is efficiently sampleable,* $(\text{M-Knap}(n,h,m,q,X),\mathcal{X})$ *is also* $\varepsilon_{\text{M-SIS}}$*-second preimage resistant with respect to PPT adversaries provided* $\text{M-SIS}^2_{n,h,m,q,\beta_2}$ *is* $\varepsilon_{\text{M-SIS}}$*-hard for* $\beta_2 = \max\{\|\mathbf{x}-\mathbf{x}'\|_2\,;(\mathbf{x},\mathbf{x}')\in X^2\}$. *The latter statement generalizes to* M-SIS^p *by changing the definition of* β_2 *accordingly.*

Proof. Observing that for any (unbounded) adversaries $\mathcal{A}$, we have

$$\text{Adv}_{\text{spr}}[\mathcal{A}] \le \mathbb{P}_{\substack{\mathbf{A}\hookleftarrow U(R_q^{m\times h})\\ \mathbf{x}\hookleftarrow\mathcal{X}}}[\exists \mathbf{x}''\in X\setminus\{\mathbf{x}\},\ \mathbf{A}^T\mathbf{x}'' = \mathbf{A}^T\mathbf{x} \bmod qR] =: P,$$

by simple inclusion of event and where $\text{Adv}_{\text{spr}}[\mathcal{A}]$ is the advantage of $\mathcal{A}$ in breaking the second-preimage resistance. As P no longer depends on the adversary's behavior or power, we can say that $(\text{M-Knap}(n,h,m,q,X),\mathcal{X})$ is P-second preimage resistant with respect to unbounded adversaries. We now need to estimate or bound P. We then show that for $\mathbf{A}$ uniformly chosen and $\mathbf{x}$ drawn from $\mathcal{X}$, the probability that there exists $\mathbf{x}'\neq\mathbf{x}$ such that $\mathbf{A}^T\mathbf{x}' = \mathbf{A}^T\mathbf{x} \bmod qR$ is less than ε_{spr}. Using the total probability formula and the union bound on $\mathbf{x}''$, we have the following.

$$\begin{aligned}
P &= \sum_{\mathbf{x}'\in X}\mathbb{P}_{\mathbf{x}}[\mathbf{x}=\mathbf{x}']\cdot\mathbb{P}_{\mathbf{A},\mathbf{x}}[\exists\mathbf{x}''\in X\setminus\{\mathbf{x}\},\ \mathbf{A}^T\mathbf{x}''=\mathbf{A}^T\mathbf{x} \bmod qR|\mathbf{x}=\mathbf{x}']\\
&= \sum_{\mathbf{x}'\in X}\mathbb{P}_{\mathbf{x}}[\mathbf{x}=\mathbf{x}']\cdot\mathbb{P}_{\mathbf{A}}[\exists\mathbf{x}''\in X\setminus\{\mathbf{x}'\},\ \mathbf{A}^T(\mathbf{x}''-\mathbf{x}')=\mathbf{0} \bmod qR]\\
&\le \sum_{\mathbf{x}'\in X}\mathbb{P}_{\mathbf{x}}[\mathbf{x}=\mathbf{x}']\sum_{\mathbf{x}''\in X\setminus\{\mathbf{x}'\}}\mathbb{P}_{\mathbf{A}}[\mathbf{A}^T(\mathbf{x}''-\mathbf{x}')=\mathbf{0} \bmod qR].
\end{aligned}$$

Let $\mathbf{x}'\in X$, $\mathbf{x}''\in X\setminus\{\mathbf{x}'\}$. Then, by [41, Lem. 4.4], $\mathbf{A}^T(\mathbf{x}''-\mathbf{x}') \bmod qR$ is uniformly distributed in $(\mathcal{I}_{\mathbf{x}''-\mathbf{x}'}/qR)^h$ over the randomness of $\mathbf{A}$, where $\mathcal{I}_{\mathbf{x}''-\mathbf{x}'} = \langle x_1''-x_1',\ldots,x_m''-x_m',q\rangle$. Hence the probability that $\mathbf{A}^T(\mathbf{x}''-\mathbf{x}') = \mathbf{0} \bmod qR$ is exactly $|\mathcal{I}_{\mathbf{x}''-\mathbf{x}'}/qR|^{-h}$. As $\mathcal{I}_{\mathbf{x}''-\mathbf{x}'}$ and qR are ideals of R, we have $|\mathcal{I}_{\mathbf{x}''-\mathbf{x}'}/qR| = N(qR)/N(\mathcal{I}_{\mathbf{x}''-\mathbf{x}'}) = q^n/N(\mathcal{I}_{\mathbf{x}''-\mathbf{x}'})$. Hence, we have

$$\begin{aligned}
P \le \sum_{\mathbf{x}'\in X}\mathbb{P}_{\mathbf{x}}[\mathbf{x}=\mathbf{x}']\sum_{\mathbf{x}''\in X\setminus\{\mathbf{x}'\}}\frac{N(\mathcal{I}_{\mathbf{x}''-\mathbf{x}'})^h}{q^{nh}} &\le \sum_{\mathbf{x}'\in X}\mathbb{P}_{\mathbf{x}}[\mathbf{x}=\mathbf{x}'](|X|-1)\frac{\mathcal{N}^h}{q^{nh}}\\
&= (|X|-1)\frac{\mathcal{N}^h}{q^{nh}} = \varepsilon_{\text{spr}},
\end{aligned}$$

where the last inequality comes from the definition of $\mathcal{N}$, then giving the first statement.

For the second statement, we simply note that second-preimage resistance is implied by collision-resistance for an efficiently sampleable distribution $\mathcal{X}$. Yet the collision-resistance of M-Knap(n, h, m, q, X) is implied by M-SIS$^p_{n,h,m,q,\beta_p}$ in ℓ_p norm for any $p \geq 1$, and where $\beta_p = \max\{\|\mathbf{x} - \mathbf{x}'\|_p ; (\mathbf{x}, \mathbf{x}') \in X^2\}$. This is obtained directly from [2], but we sketch it here for completeness. Assume an adversary $\mathcal{A}$ breaks the collision-resistance of M-Knap(n, h, m, q, X) with advantage ε. The reduction is given an instance $\mathbf{A} \hookleftarrow U(R_q^{m\times h})$ of M-SIS$^p_{n,h,m,q,\beta_p}$. It sends $\mathbf{A}$ to $\mathcal{A}$ as the description of the function, who then returns $(\mathbf{x}, \mathbf{x}') \in X^2$ such that $\mathbf{A}^T\mathbf{x} = \mathbf{A}^T\mathbf{x}' \bmod qR$ and $\mathbf{x} \neq \mathbf{x}'$. Then $\mathbf{A}^T(\mathbf{x} - \mathbf{x}') = \mathbf{0} \bmod qR$ and $0 < \|\mathbf{x} - \mathbf{x}'\|_p \leq \beta_p$ by definition of β_p, thus solving the M-SIS instance. The reduction thus has advantage ε in solving M-SIS$^p_{n,h,m,q,\beta_p}$. Considering $p = 2$ gives the theorem statement, but we insist it is more general. In particular, if $\varepsilon_{\text{M-SIS},p}$ denotes the hardness bound of M-SIS$^p_{n,h,m,q,\beta_p}$, then $\varepsilon_{\text{spr}} \leq \min_p \varepsilon_{\text{M-SIS},p}$. □

We observe that the statistical bound is most likely not tight. First, the union bound on $\mathbf{x}''$ may be too loose, yielding a daunting factor $|X| - 1$. Second, in many cases, we can ensure $\mathcal{I}_{\mathbf{z}} = R$ (which has norm 1) for all $\mathbf{z}$ by placing minor restrictions on $\mathcal{X}$ (or rather X) and q. A sufficient condition is that at least one of the $x_i - x_i'$ is a unit in R_q. Such a condition can be obtained in cyclotomic rings from Lemma 2.1. For example, if q splits in κ factor in a power-of-two cyclotomic ring, having

$$\max_{\mathbf{x},\mathbf{x}'\in X^2} \min_{\substack{i\in[m] \\ \text{st. } x_i \neq x_i'}} \|x_i - x_i'\|_p < \kappa^{\min(0,1/p-1/2)} q^{1/\kappa},$$

is enough to ensure $\mathcal{N} = 1$. Indeed, let $\mathbf{x} \neq \mathbf{x}'$ be in X, then $0 < \min_i \|x_i - x_i'\|_p < \kappa^{\min(0,1/p-1/2)} q^{1/\kappa}$. Lemma 2.2 then ensures that at least one difference $x_i - x_i'$ is invertible in R_q. Hence $\langle x_i - x_i', q\rangle = R$ and as such $\mathcal{I}_{\mathbf{x}-\mathbf{x}'} = R$ which has norm 1. In such situations, we can thus have $\varepsilon_{\text{spr}} = (|X| - 1)/q^{nh}$. This would require limiting the splitting of q, but it was shown in [20] it is not so damaging in practical cryptographic applications anyway. We note that the bound ε_{spr} does not directly depend on the distribution $\mathcal{X}$ nor $H_\infty(\mathcal{X})$. This is because our proof method (union bound and maximize the norm of $\mathcal{I}_{\mathbf{z}}$) is closer in essence to the collision resistance (which does not depend on the input distribution) than it is to the second-preimage resistance. A finer analysis may lead to a quantity that depends on the entropy though.

The computational bound requires to assume the hardness of M-SIS, which, at first glance, may seem like a circular argument when trying to prove the second-preimage resistance of the M-Knap function family. The main difference lies in the fact that M-SIS, which relates to the collision resistance, is agnostic to the input distribution $\mathcal{X}$, provided the latter is bounded. Although we do not want to assume specific properties of $\mathcal{X}$ to keep our result general, the hypothesis of it being bounded is reasonable in most use cases and applications.

4.3 One-Wayness of the M-LWE Function

Combining Lemma 2.6 to Lemmas 4.2 and 4.3 gives the one-wayness of the M-Knap function family with input distribution $\mathcal{X}$. Combined with the duality results stated in Lemma 2.8, one obtains a reduction from (decision) M-LWE with noise distribution $\mathcal{D}$ to (search) M-LWE with noise distribution $\mathcal{X}$.

Theorem 4.1. *Let λ be a security parameter, and n, d, m, k, q be in $\mathbb{N}^\times$ such that $m > d \geq k \geq 1$ and let $\ell = m - d + k$. Let R be the ring of integers of a number field of degree n. Let $\mathcal{D}$ be a distribution over R^ℓ such that for $\alpha, \beta \in [1, \infty]$ there exists $B_{\alpha,\beta} \geq 0$ and $p_{\alpha,\beta} \in [0,1]$ such that $\mathbb{P}_{\mathbf{Y} \sim \mathcal{D}^{m-\ell}}[\|M_\tau([\mathbf{I}_\ell|\mathbf{Y}])\|_{\alpha,\beta} > B_{\alpha,\beta}] \leq p_{\alpha,\beta}$. Then, let $X \subseteq R^m$ a bounded set, and $\mathcal{X}$ an efficiently sampleable distribution with support X. Denote by $B_\alpha = \max_{\mathbf{x} \in X} \|\mathbf{x}\|_\alpha$, and $\beta_p = \max\{\|\mathbf{x} - \mathbf{x}'\|_p ; (\mathbf{x}, \mathbf{x}') \in X^2\}$ for some $p \in \mathbb{N}^\times$. We further assume that R is unramified above the prime q, and such that $\min_{i \in [\kappa]} N(\mathfrak{p}_i)^{\min(m-d,k)+1} \geq \lambda^{\omega(1)}$, where the $\mathfrak{p}_i$'s are the prime ideal factors of $\langle q \rangle$.*
Then, if decision M-LWE$_{n,k,\ell,q,U(R_q^k),\mathcal{D}}$ is $\varepsilon_{M\text{-}LWE}$-hard and M-SIS$^p_{n,m-d,m,q,\beta_p}$ is $\varepsilon_{M\text{-}SIS}$-hard, it holds that search M-LWE$_{n,d,m,q,U(R_q^d),\mathcal{X}}$ is ε-hard for

$$\varepsilon = \delta(m,d) + \frac{(m-\ell)(2\delta(\ell, m-d) + \varepsilon_{M\text{-}LWE}/(1-\delta(\ell,k))) + \varepsilon'_{inv} + \varepsilon_{M\text{-}SIS}}{1 - \delta(m, m-d)}$$
$$\approx (d-k)\varepsilon_{M\text{-}LWE} + \varepsilon_{M\text{-}SIS} + 2^{-H_\infty(\mathcal{X})}\left(|\mathcal{B}_{\beta,n\ell}(B_{\alpha,\beta}B_\alpha) \cap \mathbb{Z}^{n\ell}| + |X| \cdot p_{\alpha,\beta}\right),$$

where ε'_{inv} as in Lemma 4.1, $\mathcal{B}_{\beta,n\ell}(r)$ is the closed ℓ_β ball of radius r, $\delta(a,b) = 1 - \mathbb{P}_{\mathbf{A} \sim U(R_q^{b \times a})}[\mathbf{A}R_q^a = R_q^b]$, and $\approx$ smoothes out terms negligible in λ.

The formula for ε includes the term in $\varepsilon'_{\text{inv}}$ from Lemma 4.1, which may be difficult to grasp. Concretely, if $\varepsilon_{\text{M-LWE}}$ and $\varepsilon_{\text{M-SIS}}$ are negligible, having ε negligible requires $\mathcal{X}$ to have sufficient entropy to overcome the factor in parenthesis. Assume for simplicity that the bound $B_{\alpha,\beta}$ is enforced[3] in $\mathcal{D}$ so that $p_{\alpha,\beta} = 0$. As mentioned in Sect. 4.1, if the radius r is sufficiently large compared to the dimension N, then $|\mathcal{B}_{\beta,N}(r) \cap \mathbb{Z}^N| \approx \text{Vol}(\mathcal{B}_{\beta,N}(r)) = (2r\Gamma(\beta^{-1}+1))^N / \Gamma(N\beta^{-1}+1)$. With this approximation, the entropy requirement to make ε negligible becomes

$$H_\infty(\mathcal{X}) \gtrsim \lambda + n\ell \log_2\left(2B_{\alpha,\beta}B_\alpha\Gamma(\beta^{-1}+1)\right) - \log_2 \Gamma(n\ell\beta^{-1}+1).$$

Proof. We define $\mathcal{F} = \text{M-Knap}(n, m-d, m, q, X)$. Lemma 4.2 in combination with Lemma 4.1 directly yields the ε_{inv}-uninvertibility of $(\mathcal{F}, \mathcal{X})$, where

$$\varepsilon_{\text{inv}} = \left(2^{-H_\infty(\mathcal{X})}\left(|\mathcal{B}_{\beta,n\ell}(B_{\alpha,\beta}B_\alpha) \cap \mathbb{Z}^{n\ell}| + |X| p_{\alpha,\beta}\right) + (m-\ell)\left(2\delta(\ell, m-d) + \frac{\varepsilon_{\text{M-LWE}}}{1-\delta(\ell,k)}\right)\right).$$

In the computational statement of Lemma 4.3, it holds that $(\mathcal{F}, \mathcal{X})$ is $\varepsilon_{\text{M-SIS}}$-second preimage resistant. Lemma 2.6 then yields that $(\mathcal{F}, \mathcal{X})$ is ε_{ow}-one-way with $\varepsilon_{\text{ow}} = \varepsilon_{\text{inv}} + \varepsilon_{\text{M-SIS}}$. Lemma 2.8 then proves $(\text{M-LWE}(n, d, m, q, X), \mathcal{X})$ is ε-one-way with $\varepsilon = \delta(m,d) + \varepsilon_{\text{ow}}/(1-\delta(m, m-d))$. As one-wayness corresponds to the search variant, we get that search M-LWE$_{n,d,m,q,U(R_q^d),\mathcal{X}}$ is ε-hard.

[3] This comes down to truncating $\mathcal{D}$ to verify the norm bound. Note that this may be enforced at key generation in cryptographic applications, e.g., encryption schemes.

Combining the different expressions of ε_{ow} and ε_{inv} gives the claimed expression of ε from the statement. The final approximation comes from the fact that the $\delta(\cdot,\cdot)$ terms are negligible in λ based on the requirements on q. Indeed, as noted in [13, Lem. 2.6], if the smallest norm N of the prime ideal factors is such that $N^{a-b+1} \geq \lambda^{\omega(1)}$ for $a \geq b$, then $\delta(a,b) \leq \lambda^{-\omega(1)}$. The condition on the $\mathfrak{p}_i$ thus yields that $\delta(m,d), \delta(m,m-d), \delta(\ell,m-d), \delta(\ell,k)$ are negligible. □

Observe that we opted for the computational second preimage resistance using the M-SIS assumption as it is well understood and likely to give better parameters. One can easily use the statistical second preimage resistance from Lemma 4.3 and obtain a similar statement by replacing $\varepsilon_{\text{M-SIS}}$ with $\varepsilon_{\text{spr}} = \mathcal{N}^{m-d}(|X|-1)/q^{n(m-d)}$. We also insist that although we present our result over modules, it also covers the unstructured case by selecting $n = 1$ so that $R = \mathbb{Z}$. This in particular removes certain painstaking subtleties of modules, especially on the duality result of Lemma 2.8 where the $\delta(a,b)$ have a closed-form expression when q is prime, and on the statistical version of Lemma 4.3 which becomes considerably simpler and tighter.

Prior works [13,44,54] deduce a somewhat explicit constraint on the number of samples m. Typically, they require $m = d(1+o(1))$ for very small error (e.g., binary). Reaching $m = 2d$ is possible but takes a toll on other parameters. Unfortunately, one likely cannot reach typical choices of m in cryptographic constructions where one needs at least $O(d \log_2 q)$ samples. Not being able to prove the hardness in such regimes is however not a surprise for unusually small errors as one can possibly obtain subexponential attacks in those regimes. Our result unfortunately suffers from similar constraints, albeit less explicitly. As we do not specify the actual error distribution, the constraint on m does not show up in closed form but rather as the entropy requirement mentioned above. Plugging a specific choice of $\mathcal{X}$ and computing its entropy would then transform the entropy condition into a constraint on m which would also depend on other parameters of the distribution $\mathcal{X}$.

In order to show that our result is applicable to concretely interesting distributions despite its genericity, we provide example parameter choices to prove the hardness of M-LWE with a sparse ternary error in the full version [14, App. B].

5 Hermite Normal Form Transform

At this stage, we have proven that, if $\mathcal{X}$ has sufficient entropy, we can change the error distribution from $\mathcal{D}$ to $\mathcal{X}$ (albeit with different dimensions). But this is still for a secret distribution that is uniform over R_q. We thus use a Hermite Normal Form transformation reduction in order to use $\mathcal{X}$ for *both* the secret and error, i.e., $[\mathbf{s}|\mathbf{e}] \sim \mathcal{X}$. This transform is well-known [6] and quite standard, both from a theoretical standpoint and a practical cryptanalytic aspect. However, it is mostly applied to product distributions, that is $\mathcal{X} = \mathcal{Y}^m$ where all the entries are independently sampled from the same distribution $\mathcal{Y}$ over R. As we target a more general class of distributions, we need to account for this change in the reduction which naturally gives rise to the following variant of HNF-M-LWE which we call *permuted*-HNF-M-LWE. Concretely, it is similar to HNF-M-LWE, i.e., find $\mathbf{x} = [\mathbf{s}|\mathbf{e}] \sim \mathcal{X}'$ given $(\mathbf{A}, [\mathbf{A}|\mathbf{I}]\mathbf{x})$, but for $\mathcal{X}'$ being a random permutation of $\mathcal{X}$.

Definition 5.1 (Permuted HNF). *Let n, d, m, q be in $\mathbb{N}^\times$. Let R be the ring of integers of a number field of degree n, and $\mathcal{X}$ be a distribution supported on a set $X \subseteq R^{m+d}$. The search version of the permuted HNF Module Learning With Errors problem, denoted pHNF-M-LWE$_{n,d,m,q,\mathcal{X}}$, is as follows: Given $\mathbf{A} \hookleftarrow U(R_q^{m\times d})$, and $\mathbf{b} = [\mathbf{A} \mid \mathbf{I}_m] \cdot \mathbf{P} \cdot \mathbf{x} \bmod qR$ for some $\mathbf{x} \hookleftarrow \mathcal{X}$ and $\mathbf{P} \in \{0,1\}^{(m+d)\times(m+d)}$ a random permutation matrix, find $\mathbf{x}$. The decision variant asks to distinguish such pairs $(\mathbf{A}, \mathbf{b} = [\mathbf{A} \mid \mathbf{I}_m] \cdot \mathbf{P} \cdot \mathbf{x} \bmod qR)$ from $(\mathbf{A}, \mathbf{u})$ where $\mathbf{u} \hookleftarrow U(R_q^m)$.*

Remark 5.1. If $\mathcal{X} = \mathcal{Y}^{m+d}$ is a product distribution, identically and independently sampling every entry, $\mathbf{P}\mathbf{x}$ follows exactly the same distribution as $\mathbf{x}$ and we hence recover the standard formulation of M-LWE in Hermite Normal Form [34].

We now show that pHNF-M-LWE with distribution $\mathcal{X}$ is no easier than M-LWE with noise drawn from $\mathcal{X}$, at the expense of reducing the number of samples. The associated reduction loss features the quantity $\delta'(m, d)$ defined as $\mathbb{P}_{(\mathbf{a}_i)_{i\in[m]}\sim U(R_q^d)^m}\,[\nexists S \subseteq [m], |S| = d \wedge (\mathbf{a}_i)_{i\in S}$ are R_q-linearly independent], and introduced in [13]. Because this is a non-standard HNF formulation, we also show that the regular HNF-M-LWE version with distribution $\mathcal{X}$ is also no easier than M-LWE with noise drawn from $\mathcal{X}$, with the same sample constraints, but with a slightly looser reduction (featuring $\delta(d, d)$ defined in Theorem 4.1 instead of $\delta'(m, d)$). As the loss is still acceptable in that case, the latter reduction is still preferable in cases where the distribution $\mathcal{X}$ is not permutation-invariant so as to have a more standard HNF form. We use the notation HNF-M-LWE$_{n,d,m,q,\mathcal{X}}$ for the standard HNF variant, i.e., recovering $\mathbf{x}$ from $[\mathbf{A} \mid \mathbf{I}]\mathbf{x}$ or distinguishing the latter from uniform. We defer the proof to the full version [14, Thm. 5.1].

Theorem 5.1. *Let n, d, m, q be in $\mathbb{N}^\times$, such that $m > d \geq 1$. Let R be the ring of integers of a number field of degree n, and assume that q is prime and unramified in R. Let $\mathcal{D}_s$ be a distribution over R^d and $\mathcal{X}$ a distribution over a set $X \subseteq R^m$. There is a PPT reduction from M-LWE$_{n,d,m,q,\mathcal{D}_s,\mathcal{X}}$ to pHNF-M-LWE$_{n,d,m-d,q,\mathcal{X}}$. More concretely, if $\varepsilon_{M\text{-}LWE}$ and $\varepsilon_{pHNF\text{-}M\text{-}LWE}$ denote the corresponding hardness bounds, it holds that $\varepsilon_{pHNF\text{-}M\text{-}LWE} \leq (1 - \delta'(m, d))^{-1}\varepsilon_{M\text{-}LWE}$. The reduction holds for both the search and decision variants. Similarly, there is a PPT reduction from M-LWE$_{n,d,m,q,\mathcal{D}_s,\mathcal{X}}$ to the regular HNF-M-LWE$_{n,d,m-d,q,\mathcal{X}}$ such that $\varepsilon_{HNF\text{-}M\text{-}LWE} \leq (1 - \delta(d, d))^{-1}\varepsilon_{M\text{-}LWE}$.*

In [13], the authors show the following bound $\delta'(m, d) \leq \delta(d, d)^{\lfloor m/d \rfloor} = (1 - \prod_{0\leq i<d} \prod_{j\in[\kappa]} (1 - N(\mathfrak{p}_j)^{-(d-i)}))^{\lfloor m/d \rfloor}$, where the $\mathfrak{p}_j$ are the κ prime ideal

factors of $\langle q \rangle$. This quantity may not be negligible, but since it only appears multiplicatively, this term does not incur a noticeable security loss for typical parameters. The same holds for the reduction to HNF-M-LWE. Finally, combining Theorem 5.1 with our result of Theorem 4.1, we obtain that HNF-M-LWE$_{n,d,m-d,q,\mathcal{X}}$ (or pHNF-M-LWE$_{n,d,m-d,q,\mathcal{X}}$) is at least as hard as M-LWE$_{n,k,m-d+k,q,U(R_q^k),\mathcal{D}}$, conditioned on all the parameters and distributions constraints of Theorem 4.1 being met. As the HNF reduction consumes d samples, meaningful applications of this reduction would require starting with $m \geq 2d$, meaning one would need to instantiate Theorem 4.1 to reach sufficiently many samples. We mention in Sect. 4.3 that this regime is attainable, and a concrete application can be found in the full version [14, App. A].

6 Hardness of M-LWE with Leakage

Our results from Sects. 4 and 5 prove that under some careful parameter conditions, the search M-LWE problem with $\mathbf{x} = [\mathbf{s}|\mathbf{e}] \sim \mathcal{X}$ remains at least as hard as the standard formulation of M-LWE provided $\mathcal{X}$ is a bounded distribution with sufficient min-entropy. These constraints show that for a given bound and a given min-entropy, the specific shape of the distribution of $\mathbf{x}$ is somewhat irrelevant in the hardness of M-LWE. Additionally, as explored in this section, this allows us to encompass many variants of M-LWE with leakage. If one considers the problem of finding $\mathbf{x} \sim \mathcal{X}$ given $[\mathbf{A} \mid \mathbf{I}]\mathbf{x}$ and some leakage $f(\mathbf{x})$, we can see it as finding $\mathbf{x} \sim \mathcal{X}_f$ given $[\mathbf{A} \mid \mathbf{I}]\mathbf{x}$ where $\mathcal{X}_f$ would be the conditional distribution $\mathcal{X}$ conditioned to some specific value for $f(\mathbf{x})$.

More concretely, for every possible leaked value $c \in f(\operatorname{Supp} \mathcal{X}) =: Y$, one can define the conditional distribution $\mathcal{X}_{f,c}$ as the distribution of $\mathbf{x}$ conditioned on $f(\mathbf{x}) = c$. We could then apply our result to error distribution $\mathcal{X}_{f,c}$ which has entropy $H_\infty(\mathcal{X}_{f,c}) = H_\infty(\mathbf{x} \mid f(\mathbf{x}) = c) = -\log_2 \max_{\mathbf{x}'} \mathbb{P}[\mathbf{x} = \mathbf{x}' \mid f(\mathbf{x}) = c]$. However, this would only give hardness guarantee for a specific value of c. The natural direction would be to take the worst possible value for c, i.e., the one giving the smallest entropy. In that context, it would mean computing the worst-case conditional min-entropy defined by

$$H_\infty(\mathbf{x} \mid f(\mathbf{x})) = \min_{c \in Y} H_\infty(\mathcal{X}_{f,c}) = -\log_2 \max_{\mathbf{x}',c} \mathbb{P}[\mathbf{x} = \mathbf{x}' \mid f(\mathbf{x}) = c].$$

However, assessing the security based on this worst-case conditional min-entropy is too strict. Indeed, if an adversary $\mathcal{A}$ had significant advantage only for leaked values c which happen with negligible probability, it means the overall advantage of $\mathcal{A}$ in breaking the cryptographic scheme would be negligible anyway. It means we can smooth out these corner cases in security arguments, and only deal with values c that happen with non-negligible probability. We note that for these values, it is possible to sample $\mathbf{x}$ a posteriori, i.e., sampling $\mathbf{x}$ such that $f(\mathbf{x}) = c$ for a fixed c, as long as $\mathcal{X}$ is efficiently sampleable and f is efficiently computable. It comes from the requirement that for such c, we may need $\mathcal{X}_{f,c}$ to be efficiently sampleable. For that, the challenger could use a rejection sampling strategy and sample polynomially many $\mathbf{x}$ from $\mathcal{X}$ until it finds one that verifies $f(\mathbf{x}) = c$. As c occurs with non-negligible probability, it would require at most a polynomial number of samples $\mathbf{x}$. We note that the leakage functions we consider in this section satisfy this efficiency requirement.

Nevertheless, because the leaked value $f(\mathbf{x})$ is not under adversarial control (as $\mathbf{x}$ and $f(\mathbf{x})$ are chosen/computed by the challenger), it means that averaging over the value of c suffices for security arguments as explained also in [22, App. B]. We thus consider the average conditional min-entropy $\widetilde{H_\infty}(\mathbf{x} \mid f(\mathbf{x}))$ which quantifies more faithfully the hardness of M-LWE with leakage using the result of previous sections. It is based on the fact that given the leaked value $f(\mathbf{x}) = c$, the predictability of $\mathbf{x}$ by the adversary is at most $\max_{\mathbf{x}'} \mathbb{P}[\mathbf{x} = \mathbf{x}' \mid f(\mathbf{x}) = c]$. On average, the adversary's chance of successfully predicting $\mathbf{x}$ is then $\mathbb{E}_c[\max_{\mathbf{x}'} \mathbb{P}[\mathbf{x} = \mathbf{x}' \mid f(\mathbf{x}) = c]]$. The average conditional min-entropy then corresponds to the bit-security of this average predictability, i.e.,

$$\widetilde{H_\infty}(\mathbf{x} \mid f(\mathbf{x})) = -\log_2 \mathbb{E}_c[\max_{\mathbf{x}'} \mathbb{P}[\mathbf{x} = \mathbf{x}' \mid f(\mathbf{x}) = c]].$$

Remark 6.1. Both the worst-case and average conditional min-entropy can be delicate to estimate or tightly bound in the general case. Nevertheless, we show that certain generic bounds (Lemma 6.1) can still be used to derive meaningful conclusions to apply our hardness result. We also showed that widely used distributions like discrete Gaussians can lead to tighter bounds (Lemma 3.3) in the context of noisy linear leakage. Obtaining better evaluations of this quantity for various distributions and leakage functions then readily improves the hardness guarantees using our result.

In what follows, we apply our result to this average conditional min-entropy in order to obtain an average-case hardness which is sufficient for cryptographic applications. If one desires to deal with specific leaked values c, then we note that it is possible to directly apply our result if one is able to compute $H_\infty(\mathcal{X}_{f,c})$ as described above. One can also determine from the conditional min-entropy that $H_\infty(\mathcal{X}_{f,c})$ is sufficiently large compared to $\widetilde{H_\infty}(\mathbf{x} \mid f(\mathbf{x}))$ to apply the result, with the desired probability over the choice of c, i.e., for values c that are likely to happen as we described above. For that, one can use [23, Lem. 2.2], which is recalled in Item 1 Lemma 2.4, to relate the two quantities.

Overall, if we are further able to show the average conditional min-entropy $\widetilde{H_\infty}((\mathbf{s}, \mathbf{e}) \mid f(\mathbf{s}, \mathbf{e}))$ is above the threshold for the hardness of our reduction, it would in turn provide hardness of M-LWE with leakage function f. We now formalize this with the following M-LWE with leakage assumption.

Definition 6.1 (Leaky-M-LWE). *Let n, d, m, q be in $\mathbb{N}^\times$. Let R be the ring of integers of a number field of degree n, and $\mathcal{X}$ be a distribution supported on a set $X \subseteq R^{m+d}$. Further, let $f \colon X \to Y$ be a function with range Y called the leakage space. The search version of the Leaky Module Learning With Errors problem, denoted as Leaky-M-LWE$_{n,d,m,q,\mathcal{X},f}$, is as follows: Given $\mathbf{A} \hookleftarrow U(R_q^{m\times d})$, $\mathbf{b} = [\mathbf{A} \mid \mathbf{I}_m] \cdot \mathbf{x} \bmod qR$ and $f(\mathbf{x})$ for some $\mathbf{x} \hookleftarrow \mathcal{X}$, find $\mathbf{x}$.*

In this general formulation, we leave unspecified how the function f is defined. One can for instance assume that it is honestly chosen from some distribution, or that the adversary has the right to choose f within some given constraints. Here, the choice of the adversary might even come *after* having seen the matrix $\mathbf{A}$. Observe however that many choices of f yield a totally trivial problem. For example, if f is a linear invertible function, then the leakage allows for recovering $\mathbf{x}$ efficiently. For an arbitrary bijective function f, the problem becomes easy as long as f^{-1} is efficiently computable. As in this case the conditional min-entropy is zero, our reduction does not cover the easy instances.

In the rest of this section we summarize different leakage variants used in the literature and show how our work encompasses them with the Leaky-M-LWE assumption. This demonstrates the full potential of our results. In particular, our work provides the first hardness results for M-LWE with non-linear leakage. As these variants were introduced primarily to improve cryptographic constructions, our framework targets the same applications by providing further confidence in the underlying leakage variants.

6.1 Tailored Approach for Approximate Linear Leakage

We start by looking at a special case of Leaky-M-LWE, where the leakage is a noisy linear equation, often called Hint-M-LWE in the literature. In particular, the leakage function f is defined by $f(\mathbf{x}) = \mathbf{M}\mathbf{x} + \mathbf{f}$ for some adversarially chosen matrix $\mathbf{M} \in R^{k \times m+d}$ and honestly sampled Gaussian noise $\mathbf{f}$. Note that the adversary knows $\mathbf{M}$, but not $\mathbf{f}$[4]. Several works have used these variants to construct more efficient primitives such as functional encryption [40], updatable encryption [31], zero-knowledge proofs [33], threshold signatures [27], or laconic cryptography [24]. However, all existing reductions from standard M-LWE proposed in these works only function for $\mathbf{x}$ coming from a discrete Gaussian distribution. Ours is the first to work for general noise distributions $\mathcal{X}$. Indeed, they essentially study the conditional distribution of $\mathbf{x}$ given $\mathbf{M}\mathbf{x} + \mathbf{f}$. When both $\mathbf{x}$ and $\mathbf{f}$ are Gaussian, convolution theorems akin to [29, Thm. 3.1] can be used to characterize the leakage distribution and in turn the conditional distribution. However, if $\mathbf{x}$ does not follow the prescribed Gaussian distribution, this approach based on convolution fails as the leakage distribution becomes harder to analyze. In our case, instead of studying the conditional distribution, we only look at the conditional entropy, which is all we need to apply our hardness result. This allows for generalizing to different distributions for $\mathbf{x}$ while guaranteeing hardness, which was not known before.

For that, we rely on our generalization of [16] provided in Sect. 3 and Lemma 3.3. It shows that as long as $\mathbf{M}\mathbf{x}$ is bounded by some value B in ℓ_2 norm, one can mask it with a discrete Gaussian of parameter σ resulting in

$$\widetilde{H_\infty}(\mathbf{x} \mid \mathbf{M}\mathbf{x} + \mathbf{f}) \geq H_\infty(\mathbf{x}) - \sqrt{2\pi nk}\frac{B}{\sigma}\log_2 e - \log_2(1+\varepsilon),$$

[4] Previous Extended-LWE assumptions, e.g., [5], considered $\mathbf{M}$ to be (a single row vector) chosen by the challenger from a discrete Gaussian distribution.

provided that $\sigma \geq \eta_\varepsilon(R^k) = \eta_\varepsilon(\mathbb{Z}^{nk})$ ($\approx \sqrt{\ln(2nk/\varepsilon)/\pi}$ by [28]). As we only place a mild requirement on $\|\mathbf{Mx}\|_2$, our approach is then better suited to capture non-Gaussian distributions for $\mathbf{x}$. In particular, if $\sigma \geq B\sqrt{nk}$, then the entropy loss is only $\sqrt{2\pi}\log_2 e + \log_2(1+\varepsilon)$.

This tailored approach is thus the combination of two key ingredients: (1) our generalization of the noise lossiness for better trade-offs, and (2) the fact that we can prove the hardness solely based on evaluating this conditional min-entropy. This opens for different choices of distributions for $\mathbf{x}$ in M-LWE variants with approximate linear leakage. This is for example the case of [50], which constructs a side-channel resistant signature scheme, although we warn that our reduction does not cover the practical parameter regime they consider.

6.2 Leakage with Bounded Support

Although arbitrary leakage functions may be difficult to analyze in general, our approach of abstracting the secret-error distribution comes down to evaluating the residual entropy given the leakage as explained above. We can thus use Lemma 2.4 to obtain a lower bound on said entropy, provided that the range of f is finite and sufficiently small compared (in log) to the initial entropy of $\mathcal{X}$.

Lemma 6.1. *Assuming f takes at most N different values, we have $\widetilde{H_\infty}(\mathbf{x} \mid f(\mathbf{x})) \geq H_\infty(\mathbf{x}) - \log_2 N$. It also holds that*

$$\mathbb{P}_{y \sim f(\mathcal{X})}\left[H_\infty(\mathbf{x} \mid f(\mathbf{x}) = y) \geq H_\infty(\mathbf{x}) - \log_2 N - \log_2(1/\delta)\right] \geq 1 - \delta.$$

Proof. The first statement directly holds from Item 2 of Lemma 2.4. Combined with Item 1, it yields the second claim. □

Remark 6.2. It provides a systematic way of evaluating the hardness of the Leaky-M-LWE problem simply by computing or bounding the size of the leakage space $|Y|$. In the context of arbitrary but bounded-size leakage, an alternative strategy could be to guess the leaked value. More concretely, given a regular M-LWE instance $(\mathbf{A}, \mathbf{b})$, the reduction guesses c such that $f(\mathbf{x}) = c$ and calls the Leaky-M-LWE oracle on $(\mathbf{A}, \mathbf{b}, c)$. This guessing approach is commonly used when no tailored technique is known and entails a reduction security loss that depends on $|Y|$ as well. This is why it is limited to the situations where $|Y|$ is polynomial. Our approach allows us to go beyond polynomial-sized leakage spaces, as long as $H_\infty(\mathbf{x})$ is sufficiently larger than $\log_2|Y|$. More concretely, if we take the example of a leakage with 2^λ possible values with λ the security parameter (e.g., $\lambda = 128$), we only need λ extra bits of entropy to begin with. This can be easily achieved in typical scenarios in lattice-based cryptography (e.g., for $\mathbf{x}$ of dimension 256, going from $\mathbf{x}$ binary to $\mathbf{x}$ ternary gives $256\log_2(3/2) \geq 128$ extra bits of entropy).

Remark 6.3. Notice that this generic approach would give worse results for approximate linear leakage than the tailored one described in Sect. 6.1. Indeed, assume we consider the Gaussian of width σ for $\mathbf{f}$ to be truncated in ℓ_∞ norm at

$t\sigma$ for some $t > 0$. We would have $\|\mathbf{Mx} + \mathbf{f}\|_\infty \leq \|\mathbf{Mx}\|_\infty + t\sigma \leq B_\infty + t\sigma$. Hence, the entropy bound would be $\widetilde{H_\infty}(\mathbf{x} \mid \mathbf{Mx}+\mathbf{f}) \geq H_\infty(\mathbf{x}) - nk\log_2(2(B_\infty + t\sigma)+1)$. As a result, the larger the mask (i.e., larger σ), the more entropy for $\mathbf{x}$ we would need to guarantee hardness, which is counter-intuitive. This demonstrates the looseness of the generic approach in certain use cases. For Hint-M-LWE as defined in the works mentioned in Sect. 6.1, the tailored approach based on Lemma 3.3 then follows the intuition that the larger the mask, the less entropy we need in the first place as the hint would give less and less information on $\mathbf{x}$.

The general approach is most interesting for leakage functions that do not fit the approximate linear hint framework, and for which no prior hardness result was known. We detail below a few concrete examples including exact linear hints, as well as quadratic leakage which, to our knowledge, was not yet tackled by any theoretical hardness result.

6.2.1 Exact Linear Leakage First, we tackle several variants from the so-called Extended-M-LWE family that use exact linear hints without modular reduction, i.e., when f is a linear function over $\mathbb{Z}$ (or R). In that context, the elements constituting the leakage can be assumed short (meaning they do not entail wrap-around modulo q anyway). Examples of such variants have been used to construct functional encryption [1], zero-knowledge proofs [36], side-channel resistant signatures [50], or used in reductions [4,11]. Exact linear hints are typically expressed via $f(\mathbf{x}) = \mathbf{M}\tau(\mathbf{x})$ for a short adversarially chosen $\mathbf{M} \in \mathbb{Z}^{k\times n(m+d)}$. Note that this encompasses leakage over the ring $f(\mathbf{x}) = \mathbf{M}'\mathbf{x}$ by defining $\mathbf{M} = M_\tau(\mathbf{M}')$. We can then bound the cardinal of the support of the leakage space in a similar fashion as in Lemma 4.1 using induced (α, β)-norms.

Lemma 6.2 (Generic Exact Linear Leakage). *The cardinal of the range of f is bounded by* $\min_{\alpha,\beta}|\mathcal{B}_{\beta,k}(B_{\alpha,\beta}B_\alpha) \cap \mathbb{Z}^k|$*, where* $B_{\alpha,\beta} = \|\mathbf{M}\|_{\alpha,\beta}$ *and* $B_\alpha = \max_{\mathbf{x}\in X}\|\mathbf{x}\|_\alpha$.

If the bound exceeds $|X|$, then the residual entropy bound would be $H_\infty(\mathcal{X}) - \log_2|X| \leq 0$ which is vacuous. Reaching this bound of $|X|$ is possible for example if $\ker(\mathbf{M}) = \{\mathbf{0}\}$, i.e., f is injective. It means that f can be inverted and that Leaky-M-LWE$_{n,d,m,q,\mathcal{X},f}$ is easy in this case. It then limits the number of hints k that can be safely given to the adversary. We now explain how Lemma 6.2 helps covering the hardness of the aforementioned works. We distinguish between the adversarially and non-adversarially chosen case.

Adversarial Exact Linear Hints. In both [4,11], the linear function is only on the error part (we thus do not need the HNF transform of Sect. 5) and most importantly adversarial, meaning $\mathbf{M}$ is chosen by the adversary in a certain set. Indeed, [11] considers $f(\mathbf{e}) = \mathbf{z}^T\mathbf{e}$ over the ring for a short adversarially-chosen $\mathbf{z}$. In that case, we can express it as above with $\mathbf{M} = [\mathbf{0} \mid M_\tau(\mathbf{z}^T)] \in \mathbb{Z}^{n\times n(m+d)}$ (the $\mathbf{0}$ part corresponding to the secret part of $\mathbf{x}$). Let us now bound $\|\mathbf{M}\|_{2,\infty}$ as an example. It corresponds to the maximal ℓ_2 norm of the rows.

Yet, the i-th row of $M_\tau(\mathbf{z}^T)$ is the i-th column of $M_\tau(\mathbf{z}^T)^T = M_\tau(\mathbf{z}^{*T})$ which is exactly $\tau(\mathbf{z}^* x^i)$. We then have $B_{2,\infty} = \max_{0\leq i<n} \left\|\mathbf{z}^* x^i\right\|_2$, which simplifies to $\|\mathbf{z}\|_2$ in power-of-two cyclotomic fields. It means the size of the leakage space is bounded by $(2\lfloor \max_{\mathbf{e}} \|\mathbf{e}\|_2 \cdot \max_i \left\|\mathbf{z}^* x^i\right\|_2 \rfloor + 1)^n$, which decreases the min-entropy by at most the logarithm of that. We note that as opposed to [11], our case covers general number fields, and does not restrict the error distribution to a continuous Gaussian. Also, it does not require the explicit construction of a short unimodular matrix as in [11, Lem. 15].

In the general formulation of [4], they define $f(\mathbf{e}) = [\mathrm{Tr}(\langle \mathbf{z}_i , \mathbf{e}\rangle)]_{i\in[k]}$, which is linear by linearity of the field trace and takes values in $\mathbb{Q}^k$. We can write it as $f(\mathbf{e}) = \mathbf{Z}^T \widetilde{\mathbf{V}}^T \widetilde{\mathbf{V}} \tau(\mathbf{e})$, where $\widetilde{\mathbf{V}} = \mathbf{I}_m \otimes \mathbf{V}$, for the Vandermonde matrix $\mathbf{V}$ of the field, and $\mathbf{Z} = [\tau(\mathbf{z}_1) \mid \ldots \mid \tau(\mathbf{z}_k)]$. In the power-of-two cyclotomic case, a standard calculation shows that $[\mathbf{V}^T\mathbf{V}]_{i,j} = 0$ if $i+j \notin \{0, n\}$ and $(-1)^{(i+j)/n} \cdot n$ otherwise. Hence, defining $\mathbf{M} = \mathbf{Z}^T(\mathbf{I}_m \otimes \mathbf{V}^T\mathbf{V})$ yields a matrix in $\mathbb{Z}^{k\times nm}$ which can be used in Lemma 6.2 with an appropriate bound. For example, in the power-of-two cyclotomic case, one gets $\|\mathbf{M}\|_{2,\infty} = n \cdot \max_{i\in[k]} \|\mathbf{z}_i\|_2$.

The set of vectors $\{\mathbf{z}_i\}_{i\in[k]}$ they use in their paper however leads to a much simpler situation. Although they formulate the assumption with the trace, they only use it for adversarial vectors $\mathbf{z}_i$ where each one essentially extracts a single coefficient of $\mathbf{e}$. More concretely, they use $\mathbf{M} = [\mathbf{0} \mid \mathbf{Z}] \in \{0,1\}^{k\times n(m+d)}$ where $\mathbf{Z} \in \{0,1\}^{k\times nm}$ is of rank k and has a single 1 in each row (i.e., up to permutation of the columns, $\mathbf{Z} = [\mathbf{I}_k \mid \mathbf{0}]$). In that case, we can use the (∞,∞)-norm and get $B_{\infty,\infty} = 1$. Hence, the leakage space is directly bounded by $(2\max_{\mathbf{e}} \|\mathbf{e}\|_\infty + 1)^k$. Alternatively, as it comes down to leaking k out of nm coefficients, it may be analyzed differently for specific error distributions. For example, if all the coefficients $\tau_i(\mathbf{e})$ are independently sampled from distributions ψ_i, leaking $\{\tau_i(\mathbf{e})\colon i \in S\}$ then entails that the average and worst-case conditional entropy coincide and equal $\widetilde{H}_\infty(\mathbf{e} \mid f(\mathbf{e})) = H_\infty(\mathbf{e} \mid f(\mathbf{e})) = \sum_{i\in[nm]\setminus S} H_\infty(\psi_i)$. In the case of a discrete Gaussian error for example, this would simply be $H_\infty(\mathcal{D}_{\mathbb{Z}^{nm-k},s}) \geq (nm-k)\log_2 s$.

Non-adversarial Exact Linear Hints. Cryptographic constructions also use the exact linear hints but with a non-adversarial function [1,36,50]. In that case, the matrix $\mathbf{M}$ is controlled by the challenger and follows a prescribed distribution, which can allow for better fine-tuning. In [50], the hints are described as $\mathbf{M}\tau(\mathbf{x})$ which is directly covered by Lemma 6.2. The situation in [1] is exactly the same except they consider the unstructured problem LWE (i.e., when $n = 1$).

In [36], the hint has a slightly different shape than in [4,11], but most importantly does not contain adversarially chosen elements[5]. In their case, the function is $f(\mathbf{x}) = \langle \tau(c\mathbf{x}) , \tau(\mathbf{y})\rangle$, where $\mathbf{y}$ is the mask of $c\mathbf{s}$ in the zero-knowledge proof, and c is the public challenge generated as a hash output. This can then be written as $\mathbf{M}\tau(\mathbf{x})$ with $\mathbf{M} = \tau(\mathbf{y})^T(\mathbf{I}_{m+d} \otimes M_\tau(\mathbf{c})) = \tau(c^*\mathbf{y})^T$. Using the $(2,\infty)$-norm (which comes down to a Cauchy-Schwarz inequality), we have

[5] This was generalized to adversarially chosen c and $\mathbf{y}$ in [55]. Our result can easily handle this case in a similar way as long as c and $\mathbf{y}$ are bounded. In the worst case, they can be considered modulo q, reducing the entropy by at most $\log_2 q$.

$B_{2,\infty} = \|c^*\mathbf{y}\|_2 \leq \eta \cdot t\sigma_2\sqrt{n(d+m)}$, where η is an integer defining the challenge space, and σ_2 is the discrete Gaussian parameter of $\mathbf{y}$ tailcutted at t. The residual entropy is then at least $H_\infty(\mathbf{x}) - \log_2(2\eta t\sigma_2\sqrt{n(d+m)} \cdot \max_{\mathbf{x}\in X} \|\mathbf{x}\|_2 + 1)$. In most cases, this leakage decreases the entropy by at most $\log_2 q$ bits.

6.2.2 Quadratic Leakage Our result also provides a way to prove the hardness of M-LWE beyond linear leakage. Variants of LWE with non-linear hints have been recently introduced, like quadratic leakage in [46, 48] to propose threshold encryption and threshold FHE. In that context, the leakage function is $f(\mathbf{x}) = \mathbf{x}^T\mathbf{F}\mathbf{x} + \mathbf{f}^T\mathbf{x} + f$, possibly with automorphism, or the evalutation thereof. In the threshold PKE construction of [46], the authors introduce the Known-Norm LWE assumption where the adversary learns $f(\mathbf{x}) = \|\mathbf{x}\|_2^2$. This can be generalized to the module setting by giving out $f(\mathbf{x}) = \|\tau(\mathbf{x})\|_2^2$. However, in the structured case, the authors instead generalize the hint to $f(\mathbf{x}) = \langle \mathbf{x}, \mathbf{x} \rangle_{K_\mathbb{R}}$ which corresponds to the autocorrelation (which they call covariance) of $\mathbf{x}$ defined by $\langle \mathbf{x}\, , \mathbf{x} \rangle_{K_\mathbb{R}} = \sum_{i\in[m+d]} x_i^* x_i = \mathbf{x}^*\mathbf{x}$. When K is a cyclotomic field, the conjugate is the automorphism of K defined by $\zeta \mapsto \zeta^{-1}$, which also stabilizes the ring of integers R. It means for $\mathbf{x} \in R^{m+d}$, $f(\mathbf{x}) \in R$. The resulting problem is referred to as Known-Covariance M-LWE (which they only use in the ring setting, i.e., $d = 1$). In power-of-two cyclotomics, we can clearly see it is no harder than the Known-Norm case as the constant coefficient of $\mathbf{x}^*\mathbf{x}$ is $\|\tau(\mathbf{x})\|_2^2$.

The case of Known-Norm M-LWE can be easily handled by guessing $\|\tau(\mathbf{x})\|_2^2$ which is a single (polynomially-bounded) integer, but this method fails for the Known-Covariance M-LWE problem as it would require guessing an entire ring element. Our approach can take over in this setting by bounding the size of the range of f. Using similar bounds as for the exact linear hints, we have $\max_\mathbf{x} \|\mathbf{x}^*\mathbf{x}\|_\infty \leq \max_\mathbf{x} \|M_\tau(\mathbf{x}^*)\|_{2,\infty} \|\mathbf{x}\|_2 = \max_\mathbf{x} \max_i \|\mathbf{x}x^i\|_2 \|\mathbf{x}\|_2$. Focusing on the power-of-two cyclotomic case, we obtain a bound of $\max_\mathbf{x} \|\mathbf{x}\|_2^2$. This would give a leakage space of at most $(2 \max_\mathbf{x} \|\mathbf{x}\|_2^2 + 1)^n$ elements. We however notice that $f(\mathbf{x})$ is self-adjoint, i.e., $f(\mathbf{x})^* = f(\mathbf{x})$. Hence, $\tau_{n/2}(f(\mathbf{x})) = 0$ and for all $i \in [1, n/2-1]$, $\tau_{n-i}(f(\mathbf{x})) = -\tau_i(f(\mathbf{x}))$. Hence, $f(\mathbf{x})$ takes at most $(2B+1)^{n/2}$ values, where $B = \max_\mathbf{x} \|\mathbf{x}\|_2^2$.

As a result, the average conditional min-entropy is at least $\widetilde{H_\infty}(\mathbf{x} \mid \mathbf{x}^*\mathbf{x}) \geq H_\infty(\mathbf{x}) - \frac{n}{2}\log_2(2B+1)$. This could possibly be refined as it appears that although the constant coefficient of $\mathbf{x}^*\mathbf{x}$ is $\|\mathbf{x}\|_2^2$, the other ones tend to be much smaller. Also, we note that this conditional distribution is invariant under permutation as $(\mathbf{P}\mathbf{x})^*(\mathbf{P}\mathbf{x}) = \mathbf{x}^*\mathbf{P}^T\mathbf{P}\mathbf{x} = \mathbf{x}^*\mathbf{x}$. In that case the pHNF-M-LWE and regular HNF-M-LWE coincide.

We give more details on how to instantiate our result to prove the hardness of Known-Covariance M-LWE in the full version [14, App. A]. In particular, we give a parameter set ensuring close to 128 bits of security to show the applicability of our result. Albeit with impractical parameters, it shows that there is nothing fundamentally weak with leaking $\mathbf{x}^*\mathbf{x}$.

6.2.3 Non-algebraic Leakage Our result can also be used to handle non-algebraic leakages contrarily to the ones we covered in the previous sections. A simple example is that of the Extended-M-LWE problem formulated in [37] where $f(\mathbf{x}) = \text{sign}(\langle \tau(c\mathbf{x}), \tau(\mathbf{y})\rangle)$, where $\mathbf{y}$ is a mask for $c\mathbf{x}$ in the zero-knowledge proof, and c is the public challenge obtained as a hash output. This can be seen as a weaker version of the Extended-M-LWE problem from [36] mentioned in Sect. 6.2.1, which now just leaks the sign of $\langle \tau(c\mathbf{x}) , \tau(\mathbf{y})\rangle$ instead of the full inner product. As a result, the leakage space is simply $\{-1, 1\}$ yielding a residual entropy of at least $H_\infty(\mathbf{x}) - 1$. The authors provide a reduction from LWE in the unstructured case which strongly relies on the fact that both c and $\mathbf{y}$ are controlled by the challenger. Our result extends it (albeit most likely loosely) to the structured case of M-LWE and to adversarial $\mathbf{y}$ and c.

More generally, non-algebraic leakage often comes up in side-channel analysis, for example through timing measurements, power traces, or electromagnetic readings. These are generally non-linear in the secret data, and even most likely non-algebraic. Sophisticated machinery is then needed to transform these non-algebraic leakage into information that is more relevant to solving M-LWE (such as randomness bit, hamming weight, etc.). We only mention that our result is general enough to cover these situations, again provided one can lower-bound the average conditional min-entropy. Because leakage incurred by insecure implementations is not easy to model, we leave the application of our result to such use-cases as an interesting research direction. In particular, modeling the leakage exploited in side-channel attacks would provide a deeper understanding of the actual M-LWE assumption underlying such vulnerable systems.

Acknowledgments. We thank the anonymous reviewers for their helpful feedback. This work was supported by the French government through the National Research Agency, under the projects ANR-21-ASTR-0016 *AMIRAL*, ANR-22-PECY-003 *Secure-Compute*, ANR-24-CE48-4293 *HELO* and ANR-25-CE39-4214-01 *RELATE*, by the Austrian Science Fund (FWF) Project J4879-N, by the Bakar Funds and Peder Sather Funds.

References

1. Agrawal, S., Libert, B., Stehlé, D.: Fully secure functional encryption for inner products, from standard assumptions. In: Robshaw, M., Katz, J. (eds.) CRYPTO 2016, Part III. LNCS, vol. 9816, pp. 333–362. Springer, Berlin, Heidelberg (2016). https://doi.org/10.1007/978-3-662-53015-3_12
2. Ajtai, M.: Generating hard instances of lattice problems (extended abstract). In: 28th ACM STOC, pp. 99–108. ACM Press (1996). https://doi.org/10.1145/237814.237838
3. Albrecht, M.R., Player, R., Scott, S.: On the concrete hardness of learning with errors. Cryptology ePrint Archive, Report 2015/046 (2015). https://eprint.iacr.org/2015/046
4. Alperin-Sheriff, J., Apon, D.: Dimension-preserving reductions from LWE to LWR. Cryptology ePrint Archive, Report 2016/589 (2016). https://eprint.iacr.org/2016/589

5. Alperin-Sheriff, J., Peikert, C.: Circular and KDM security for identity-based encryption. In: Fischlin, M., Buchmann, J., Manulis, M. (eds.) PKC 2012. LNCS, vol. 7293, pp. 334–352. Springer, Heidelberg (2012). https://doi.org/10.1007/978-3-642-30057-8_20
6. Applebaum, B., Cash, D., Peikert, C., Sahai, A.: Fast cryptographic primitives and circular-secure encryption based on hard learning problems. In: Halevi, S. (ed.) CRYPTO 2009. LNCS, vol. 5677, pp. 595–618. Springer, Heidelberg (2009). https://doi.org/10.1007/978-3-642-03356-8_35
7. Arora, S., Ge, R.: New algorithms for learning in presence of errors. In: Aceto, L., Henzinger, M., Sgall, J. (eds.) ICALP 2011. LNCS, vol. 6755, pp. 403–415. Springer, Heidelberg (2011). https://doi.org/10.1007/978-3-642-22006-7_34
8. Banaszczyk, W.: New bounds in some transference theorems in the geometry of numbers. Math. Ann. **296**(4), 625–635 (1993)
9. Bos, J.W., et al.: CRYSTALS - Kyber: a CCA-secure module-lattice-based KEM. In: 2018 IEEE European Symposium on Security and Privacy, pp. 353–367. IEEE Computer Society Press (2018). https://doi.org/10.1109/EuroSP.2018.00032
10. Boudgoust, K., Jeudy, C., Roux-Langlois, A., Wen, W.: Towards classical hardness of module-LWE: The linear rank case. In: Moriai, S., Wang, H. (eds.) ASIACRYPT 2020, Part II. LNCS, vol. 12492, pp. 289–317. Springer, Cham (2020). https://doi.org/10.1007/978-3-030-64834-3_10
11. Boudgoust, K., Jeudy, C., Roux-Langlois, A., Wen, W.: On the hardness of module-LWE with binary secret. In: Paterson, K.G. (ed.) CT-RSA 2021. LNCS, vol. 12704, pp. 503–526. Springer, Cham (2021).https://doi.org/10.1007/978-3-030-75539-3_21
12. Boudgoust, K., Jeudy, C., Roux-Langlois, A., Wen, W.: Entropic hardness of module-LWE from module-NTRU. In: Isobe, T., Sarkar, S. (eds.) INDOCRYPT 2022. LNCS, vol. 13774, pp. 78–99. Springer, Cham (2022). https://doi.org/10.1007/978-3-031-22912-1_4
13. Boudgoust, K., Jeudy, C., Roux-Langlois, A., Wen, W.: On the hardness of module learning with errors with short distributions. J. Cryptol. **36**(1), 1 (2023). https://doi.org/10.1007/s00145-022-09441-3
14. Boudgoust, K., Jeudy, C., Tairi, E., Wen, W.: Hardness of M-LWE with general distributions and applications to leaky variants. Cryptology ePrint Archive, Report 2025/1472 (2025). https://eprint.iacr.org/2025/1472
15. Boudgoust, K., Keller, H.: Module learning with errors with truncated matrices. In: Niederhagen, R., Saarinen, M.J.O. (eds.) Post-Quantum Cryptography - 16th International Workshop, PQCrypto 2025, Part I. pp. 255–277. Springer, Cham (2025). https://doi.org/10.1007/978-3-031-86599-2_9
16. Brakerski, Z., Döttling, N.: Hardness of LWE on general entropic distributions. In: Canteaut, A., Ishai, Y. (eds.) EUROCRYPT 2020. LNCS, vol. 12106, pp. 551–575. Springer, Cham (2020). https://doi.org/10.1007/978-3-030-45724-2_19
17. Brakerski, Z., Döttling, N.: Lossiness and entropic hardness for ring-LWE. In: Pass, R., Pietrzak, K. (eds.) TCC 2020, Part I. LNCS, vol. 12550, pp. 1–27. Springer, Cham (2020). https://doi.org/10.1007/978-3-030-64375-1_1
18. Brakerski, Z., Gentry, C., Vaikuntanathan, V.: (Leveled) fully homomorphic encryption without bootstrapping. In: Goldwasser, S. (ed.) ITCS 2012, pp. 309–325. ACM (2012). https://doi.org/10.1145/2090236.2090262
19. Brakerski, Z., Langlois, A., Peikert, C., Regev, O., Stehlé, D.: Classical hardness of learning with errors. In: Boneh, D., Roughgarden, T., Feigenbaum, J. (eds.) 45th ACM STOC. pp. 575–584. ACM Press (2013). https://doi.org/10.1145/2488608.2488680

20. Chung, C.M.M., Hwang, V., Kannwischer, M.J., Seiler, G., Shih, C.J., Yang, B.Y.: NTT multiplication for NTT-unfriendly rings. IACR TCHES **2021**(2), 159–188 (2021). https://doi.org/10.46586/tches.v2021.i2.159-188, https://tches.iacr.org/index.php/TCHES/article/view/8791
21. Del Pino, R., Katsumata, S., Maller, M., Mouhartem, F., Prest, T., Saarinen, M.J.O.: Threshold raccoon: practical threshold signatures from standard lattice assumptions. In: Joye, M., Leander, G. (eds.) EUROCRYPT 2024, Part II. LNCS, vol. 14652, pp. 219–248. Springer, Cham (2024). https://doi.org/10.1007/978-3-031-58723-8_8
22. Dodis, Y., Ostrovsky, R., Reyzin, L., Smith, A.: Fuzzy extractors: how to generate strong keys from biometrics and other noisy data. Cryptology ePrint Archive, Report 2003/235 (2003). https://eprint.iacr.org/2003/235
23. Dodis, Y., Ostrovsky, R., Reyzin, L., Smith, A.: Fuzzy extractors: how to generate strong keys from biometrics and other noisy data. SIAM J. Comput. **38**(1), 97–139 (2008)
24. Döttling, N., Kolonelos, D., Lai, R.W.F., Lin, C., Malavolta, G., Rahimi, A.: Efficient laconic cryptography from learning with errors. In: Hazay, C., Stam, M. (eds.) EUROCRYPT 2023, Part III. LNCS, vol. 14006, pp. 417–446. Springer, Cham (2023). https://doi.org/10.1007/978-3-031-30620-4_14
25. Ducas, L., Galbraith, S., Prest, T., Yu, Y.: Integral matrix gram root and lattice Gaussian sampling without floats. In: Canteaut, A., Ishai, Y. (eds.) EUROCRYPT 2020. LNCS, vol. 12106, pp. 608–637. Springer, Cham (2020). https://doi.org/10.1007/978-3-030-45724-2_21
26. Ducas, L., et al.: CRYSTALS-Dilithium: a lattice-based digital signature scheme. IACR TCHES **2018**(1), 238–268 (2018). https://doi.org/10.13154/tches.v2018.i1.238-268, https://tches.iacr.org/index.php/TCHES/article/view/839
27. Espitau, T., Niot, G., Prest, T.: Flood and submerse: distributed key generation and robust threshold signature from lattices. In: Reyzin, L., Stebila, D. (eds.) CRYPTO 2024, Part VII. LNCS, vol. 14926, pp. 425–458. Springer, Cham (2024). https://doi.org/10.1007/978-3-031-68394-7_14
28. Espitau, T., Wallet, A., Yu, Y.: On gaussian sampling, smoothing parameter and application to signatures. In: Guo, J., Steinfeld, R. (eds.) ASIACRYPT 2023, Part VII. LNCS, vol. 14444, pp. 65–97. Springer, Singapore (2023). https://doi.org/10.1007/978-981-99-8739-9_3
29. Genise, N., Micciancio, D., Peikert, C., Walter, M.: Improved discrete gaussian and subgaussian analysis for lattice cryptography. In: Kiayias, A., Kohlweiss, M., Wallden, P., Zikas, V. (eds.) PKC 2020. LNCS, vol. 12110, pp. 623–651. Springer, Cham (2020). https://doi.org/10.1007/978-3-030-45374-9_21
30. Goldwasser, S., Kalai, Y.T., Peikert, C., Vaikuntanathan, V.: Robustness of the learning with errors assumption. In: Yao, A.C.C. (ed.) ICS 2010, pp. 230–240. Tsinghua University Press (2010)
31. Haidar, C.A., Passelègue, A., Stehlé, D.: Efficient updatable public-key encryption from lattices. In: Guo, J., Steinfeld, R. (eds.) ASIACRYPT 2023, Part V. LNCS, vol. 14442, pp. 342–373. Springer, Singapore (2023). https://doi.org/10.1007/978-981-99-8733-7_11
32. Hoffstein, J., Pipher, J., Silverman, J.H.: NTRU: a ring-based public key cryptosystem. In: Buhler, J.P. (ed.) ANTS 1998. LNCS, vol. 1423, pp. 267–288. Springer, Heidelberg (1998). https://doi.org/10.1007/BFb0054868

33. Kim, D., Lee, D., Seo, J., Song, Y.: Toward practical lattice-based proof of knowledge from hint-MLWE. In: Handschuh, H., Lysyanskaya, A. (eds.) CRYPTO 2023, Part V. LNCS, vol. 14085, pp. 549–580. Springer, Cham (2023). https://doi.org/10.1007/978-3-031-38554-4_18
34. Langlois, A., Stehlé, D.: Worst-case to average-case reductions for module lattices. DCC **75**(3), 565–599 (2015). https://doi.org/10.1007/s10623-014-9938-4
35. Lin, H., Wang, M., Zhuang, J., Wang, Y.: Hardness of module-LWE and ring-LWE on general entropic distributions. Cryptology ePrint Archive, Report 2020/1238 (2020). https://eprint.iacr.org/2020/1238
36. Lyubashevsky, V., Nguyen, N.K.: BLOOM: bimodal lattice one-out-of-many proofs and applications. In: Agrawal, S., Lin, D. (eds.) ASIACRYPT 2022, Part IV. LNCS, vol. 13794, pp. 95–125. Springer, Cham (2022). https://doi.org/10.1007/978-3-031-22972-5_4
37. Lyubashevsky, V., Nguyen, N.K., Seiler, G.: Shorter lattice-based zero-knowledge proofs via one-time commitments. In: Garay, J.A. (ed.) PKC 2021. LNCS, vol. 12710, pp. 215–241. Springer, Cham (2021). https://doi.org/10.1007/978-3-030-75245-3_9
38. Lyubashevsky, V., Peikert, C., Regev, O.: On ideal lattices and learning with errors over rings. In: Gilbert, H. (ed.) EUROCRYPT 2010. LNCS, vol. 6110, pp. 1–23. Springer, Heidelberg (2010). https://doi.org/10.1007/978-3-642-13190-5_1
39. Lyubashevsky, V., Seiler, G.: Short, invertible elements in partially splitting cyclotomic rings and applications to lattice-based zero-knowledge proofs. In: Nielsen, J.B., Rijmen, V. (eds.) EUROCRYPT 2018. LNCS, vol. 10820, pp. 204–224. Springer, Cham (2018). https://doi.org/10.1007/978-3-319-78381-9_8
40. Mera, J.M.B., Karmakar, A., Marc, T., Soleimanian, A.: Efficient lattice-based inner-product functional encryption. In: Hanaoka, G., Shikata, J., Watanabe, Y. (eds.) PKC 2022, Part II. LNCS, vol. 13178, pp. 163–193. Springer, Cham (2022). https://doi.org/10.1007/978-3-030-97131-1_6
41. Micciancio, D.: Generalized compact knapsacks, cyclic lattices, and efficient one-way functions from worst-case complexity assumptions. Cryptology ePrint Archive, Report 2004/286 (2004). https://eprint.iacr.org/2004/286
42. Micciancio, D.: On the hardness of learning with errors with binary secrets. Cryptology ePrint Archive, Report 2018/988 (2018). https://eprint.iacr.org/2018/988
43. Micciancio, D., Mol, P.: Pseudorandom knapsacks and the sample complexity of LWE search-to-decision reductions. In: Rogaway, P. (ed.) CRYPTO 2011. LNCS, vol. 6841, pp. 465–484. Springer, Heidelberg (2011). https://doi.org/10.1007/978-3-642-22792-9_26
44. Micciancio, D., Peikert, C.: Hardness of SIS and LWE with small parameters. In: Canetti, R., Garay, J.A. (eds.) CRYPTO 2013. LNCS, vol. 8042, pp. 21–39. Springer, Heidelberg (2013). https://doi.org/10.1007/978-3-642-40041-4_2
45. Micciancio, D., Regev, O.: Worst-case to average-case reductions based on Gaussian measures. In: 45th FOCS, pp. 372–381. IEEE Computer Society Press (2004). https://doi.org/10.1109/FOCS.2004.72
46. Micciancio, D., Suhl, A.: Simulation-secure threshold PKE from LWE with polynomial modulus. Cryptology ePrint Archive, Report 2023/1728 (2023). https://eprint.iacr.org/2023/1728
47. Mukherjee, A., Aikata, Mert, A.C., Lee, Y., Kwon, S., Deryabin, M., Roy, S.S.: ModHE: modular homomorphic encryption using module lattices potentials and limitations. IACR TCHES **2024**(1), 527–562 (2024). https://doi.org/10.46586/tches.v2024.i1.527-562

48. Passelègue, A., Stehlé, D.: Low communication threshold fully homomorphic encryption. In: Chung, K.M., Sasaki, Y. (eds.) ASIACRYPT 2024, Part I. LNCS, vol. 15484, pp. 297–329. Springer, Singapore (2024). https://doi.org/10.1007/978-981-96-0875-1_10
49. Peikert, C., Pepin, Z.: Algebraically structured LWE, revisited. In: Hofheinz, D., Rosen, A. (eds.) TCC 2019. LNCS, vol. 11891, pp. 1–23. Springer, Cham (2019). https://doi.org/10.1007/978-3-030-36030-6_1
50. del Pino, R., et al.: Raccoon: A Side-Channel Secure Signature Scheme (Specifications) (2023). https://raccoonfamily.org/wp-content/uploads/2023/07/raccoon.pdf
51. del Pino, R., Katsumata, S., Prest, T., Rossi, M.: Raccoon: a masking-friendly signature proven in the probing model. In: Reyzin, L., Stebila, D. (eds.) CRYPTO 2024, Part I. LNCS, vol. 14920, pp. 409–444. Springer, Cham (2024). https://doi.org/10.1007/978-3-031-68376-3_13
52. Regev, O.: On lattices, learning with errors, random linear codes, and cryptography. In: Gabow, H.N., Fagin, R. (eds.) 37th ACM STOC, pp. 84–93. ACM Press (2005). https://doi.org/10.1145/1060590.1060603
53. Stehlé, D., Steinfeld, R., Tanaka, K., Xagawa, K.: Efficient public key encryption based on ideal lattices. In: Matsui, M. (ed.) ASIACRYPT 2009. LNCS, vol. 5912, pp. 617–635. Springer, Berlin, Heidelberg (2009). https://doi.org/10.1007/978-3-642-10366-7_36
54. Sun, C., Tibouchi, M., Abe, M.: Revisiting the hardness of binary error LWE. In: Liu, J.K., Cui, H. (eds.) ACISP 20. LNCS, vol. 12248, pp. 425–444. Springer, Cham (2020). https://doi.org/10.1007/978-3-030-55304-3_22
55. Wang, Z., Lai, Q., Liu, F.H.: Ring/module learning with errors under linear leakage - hardness and applications. In: Tang, Q., Teague, V. (eds.) PKC 2024, Part II. LNCS, vol. 14602, pp. 275–304. Springer, Cham (2024). https://doi.org/10.1007/978-3-031-57722-2_9

IND-CCA Lattice Threshold KEM Under 30 KiB

Katharina Boudgoust[1](✉), Rafaël del Pino[2], Oleksandra Lapiha[3], and Thomas Prest[2]

[1] CNRS, Université Montpellier, LIRMM, Montpellier, France
katharina.boudgoust@lirmm.fr
[2] PQShield, Paris, France
{rafael.del.pino,thomas.prest}@pqshield.com
[3] Royal Holloway University London, London, UK
sasha.lapiha.2021@live.rhul.ac.uk

Abstract. At Asiacrypt'25, Lapiha and Prest proposed a lattice-based IND-CCA threshold key-encapsulation mechanism (TKEM) obtained from a threshold identity-based encryption (TIBE) and a signature scheme. Their construction relies on a variant of the Boneh-Canetti-Halevi-Katz (BCHK) transform, instantiated with a lattice-based TIBE. However it suffers from large ciphertexts at 540 KiB for $\kappa = 128$ bits of security.

We present substantial improvements to their TIBE, resulting in the first concretely efficient lattice-based IND-CCA TKEM, with ciphertexts just under 30 KiB for a threshold $T = 32$, $Q = 2^{45}$ queries, and the same κ.

Our design simplifies the original framework by leveraging the power of random oracles already present in their construction. We further enhance efficiency by adopting approximate computations where appropriate and by replacing module-NTRU trapdoors with NTRU trapdoors, achieving a remarkable eighteenfold reduction in ciphertext size. Finally, leveraging recent developments in secret sharing, we ensure the verifiability of key-extraction shares even in the presence of malicious parties.

1 Introduction

Lattices have emerged as the main mathematical family when it comes to building post-quantum cryptographic schemes. In particular, they allow to build efficient key encapsulation mechanisms (KEMs) and public key encryption schemes (PKEs). In 2022, NIST selected a lattice scheme, Kyber [43], as its main standard ML-KEM [39] for a post-quantum KEM.

While IND-CPA security (indistinguishability under chosen-*plaintext* attacks) constitutes a minimal security baseline for KEMs and PKEs, the standard notion is the stronger IND-CCA security (indistinguishability under chosen-*ciphertext* attacks). Many "natural" PKE constructions achieve IND-CPA security out of the box, but not IND-CCA security. To resolve this issue, generic

S. Bai and E. Persichetti (Eds.): PKC 2026, LNCS 16551, pp. 38–69, 2026.
https://doi.org/10.1007/978-3-032-26731-3_2

compilers have emerged which take as input an IND-CPA scheme, and output an IND-CCA one. The most popular CPA-to-CCA compiler is the Fujisaki-Okamoto transform [24,25], a very efficient transform that only relies on symmetric building blocks, and is used in ML-KEM and the upcoming NIST standard HQC.

Threshold Cryptosystems. Threshold cryptography is a subfield of cryptography in which cryptographic material is split across several parties, who then perform sensitive operations in a distributed manner. In a threshold KEM, the decapsulation key is distributed across N parties, of which at least $T \leq N$ are needed to decapsulate valid ciphertexts. This increases the robustness of the system as well as its resilience to individual users' compromise.

Threshold cryptosystems have many applications. E-voting protocols use them to guarantee tally confidentiality until the close of voting, see for example Cramer et al. [17], or the lattice-based protocol of Aranha et al. [4]. In the blockchain setting, Choudhuri et al. [15] propose them as a way to enhance the privacy of mempools. NIST has released a call for threshold cryptosystems [12], and we expect it will foster more applications.

Building lattice-based threshold KEMs or PKEs has shown to be challenging. While there exist efficient IND-CPA lattice constructions [11,38], achieving IND-CCA security in an efficient manner seems difficult. Indeed, thresholdising the Fujisaki-Okamoto transform requires expensive generic multi-party computation (MPC). Alternative IND-CCA lattice-based threshold constructions have been proposed, usually using heavy machinery such as non-interactive zero-knowledge arguments (NIZKs) [21], threshold fully homomorphic encryption [8] or MPC [16,33]; thus their efficiency is unclear.

A promising CPA-to-CCA compiler is the Boneh-Canetti-Halevi-Katz transform [7,13], or BCHK transform. Boneh, Boyen and Halevi [6] have shown that it enables IND-CCA TPKEs under suitable conditions. To our knowledge, the only BCHK-based lattice threshold construction is due to Lapiha and Prest [34], using a variant of the BCHK transform which they call the BCHK+ transform. However, their ciphertext sizes are prohibitive at 540 KiB.

Our Contributions. Our main contribution is an IND-CCA lattice TKEM which significantly outperforms the Lapiha-Prest construction [34].

The BCHK+ transform requires a threshold identity-based encryption scheme (TIBE) with suitable properties. For a threshold T and a number Q of decryption queries, the TIBE ciphertexts of [34] contain 10 ring elements, for a ring $\mathcal{R}_q = \mathbb{Z}_q[x]/(x^d + 1)$ with q scaling roughly in $\Theta(d^5 \sqrt{QT})$. We design a TIBE that is much simpler and more efficient than the one in [34], requiring only 4 ring elements with q scaling roughly in $\Theta(d^{3/2} \sqrt{QT})$. As a result, for a similar $T = 32$ and $Q = 2^{45}$, our encapsulation key (resp. ciphertexts) is around 6.6 KiB (resp. 30 KiB), which is about 7 times (resp. 18 times) shorter than in [34].

Our second contribution is a TIBE construction which provides robustness for almost identical parameters, although it supports a smaller number of decapsulation queries $Q = 2^{25}$. This feature is underpinned by our use of Vandermonde secret sharing [9], a type of secret sharing that guarantees short shares, as opposed to Shamir secret sharing used by [34]. Using Vandermonde secret sharing allows identifying misbehaving parties via very simple procedures (checking a linear identity and a norm bound). Once again, this construction avoids the use of heavy machinery.

1.1 Technical Overview

The BCHK transform takes as input a signature scheme and a threshold identity-based encryption (TIBE) with suitable properties, and outputs an IND-CCA TKEM. The BCHK+ variant by [34] also adds decapsulation consistency, a property that would otherwise be difficult to obtain in a lattice setting. In [34], the TIBE ciphertexts are 540 KiB and therefore account for an overwhelming portion of the TKEM ciphertext size.

ABB and CHKP-Style Constructions. We first provide a reminder on the ABB [1] and CHKP [14] (H)IBEs, which underpin the TIBE of [34] and ours. In all four works, the master public key is a pseudorandom matrix $\mathbf{A}$ and a uniform vector t. A trapdoor for $\mathbf{A}$ allows, for any identity id, to compute a short preimage $\mathbf{z}$ such that $\mathbf{F}_{\mathsf{id}} \cdot \mathbf{z} \approx t$, where $\mathbf{F}_{\mathsf{id}}$ is a matrix related to $\mathbf{A}$ which embeds id. Encryption computes a ciphertext:

$$\left[\mathbf{u}^T \; v\right] = r \cdot \left[\mathbf{F}_{\mathsf{id}} \; t\right] + \left[\mathbf{e}^T \; e'\right] + \left[0 \; \mathsf{Encode}(\mathsf{msg})\right]. \tag{1}$$

Finally, decryption computes $v - \mathbf{u}^T \cdot \mathbf{z} \approx \mathsf{Encode}(\mathsf{msg})$. [1,14] sample $\mathbf{z}$ using Gaussian sampling, while [34] and we sample $\mathbf{z}$ using noise flooding. This has a big impact on parameters, but is orthogonal to our improvements over [34], so we won't go into more details here.

The [34] TIBE. In [1], we have $\mathbf{F}_{\mathsf{id}} = \left[\mathbf{A}_0 \mid \mathbf{A}_1 + E(\mathsf{id}) \cdot \mathbf{B}\right]$, where $\mathbf{A}_0$ is a (trapdoored) pseudorandom matrix, and $\mathbf{A}_1$ is uniformly random and $\mathbf{B}$ is a gadget matrix. In [34], $\mathbf{F}_{\mathsf{id}} = \left[\mathbf{A}_0 \mid \mathbf{A}_1 + E(\mathsf{id}) \cdot \mathbf{B} \mid \mathbf{A}_2\right]$ is expanded to the right with an additional matrix $\mathbf{A}_2$, and each matrix $\mathbf{A}_i$ is in $\mathcal{R}_q^{1\times 3}$. $\mathbf{A}_0$ embeds a trapdoor à la Eagle/Plover [23,44] (essentially, a $\mathsf{RLWEsample}$), used in the preimage sampling procedure. $\mathbf{A}_2$ is used to embed a module-NTRU trapdoor in the security proof, which allows to simulate the preimages. Therefore the ciphertext in Eq. (1) has $3 \cdot 3 + 1 = 10$ ring elements.

A More Efficient TIBE. In our paper, we take as a starting point a much more efficient TIBE construction, the "ROHIBE" from [14, Section 5.3], then we heavily optimise it.

1. *Simpler embedding.* The main difference of the ROHIBE construction compared to the ABB IBE is that identities are embedded via $\mathbf{F}_{\mathsf{id}} = \left[\mathbf{A}_0 \mid H(\mathsf{id})\right]$, where the matrix $\mathbf{A}_0$ still embeds a Plover trapdoor and H is modelled as

a random oracle. In [1], the identity is embedded as a "tag" of the gadget matrix. The difference of any two tags has to be invertible for preimage sampling to work, hence it requires picking a low-splitting ring that has exponentially many unit elements. As $H(\mathsf{id})$ only requires one ring element, we save two ring elements compared to the embedding $\mathbf{A}_1 + E(\mathsf{id})$ from [34], and do not need any splitting property from the underlying ring.

2. *Fewer matrix blocks.* Our second major design optimisation compared to [34] is that we do not have a matrix $\mathbf{A}_2$. The simpler embedding implies that $H(\mathsf{id})$ can fulfil the role of $\mathbf{A}_2$ and $\mathbf{A}_1 + E(\mathsf{id}) \cdot \mathbf{B}$ at the same time. In the previous construction the matrices $\mathbf{F}_{\mathsf{id}}$ and $\mathbf{F}_{\mathsf{id}'}$ for $\mathsf{id} \neq \mathsf{id}'$ were related by an additive shift so constructing a trapdoor that works for every shift was more complex and incompatible with Hint-LWE leakage. In the current construction each id has its independent matrix extension and its own NTRU trapdoor embedded in $H(\mathsf{id})$. This trapdoor can be used both for Hint-LWE and for the IBE security.
3. *Smaller modulus.* Our simpler design also allows reducing the modulus. Our parameter selection process (Sect. 7) allows taking $q = \Theta(d^{3/2}\sqrt{QT}\log\delta)$, where δ is an upper bound on the probability that decryption fails. Carrying out a similar analysis for the [34] TIBE would result in a much larger $q = \Theta(d^5\sqrt{QT})$. Thus, our construction allows a smaller q, which in turn allows decreasing d, compounding bandwidth gains.
4. *NTRU trapdoors.* As a result of the previous improvements, an NTRU trapdoor becomes tight enough for the reduction to go through. The security of NTRU trapdoors is better-understood than module-NTRU trapdoors, which is especially important in our setting since q is large and therefore overstretched NTRU attacks need to be considered [2,32]. In our parameter regimes such attack do not apply (Sect. 7).
5. *Additional optimisations.* We perform a few more optimisations. Recall that [34] takes $\mathbf{A}_0 = \begin{bmatrix}1 & a_0 & b_0\end{bmatrix} \cdot d_0$, where the role of d_0 was to randomise the first entry of $\mathbf{A}_0$. Instead we simply set $d_0 = 1$ and drop the first coefficient of $\mathbf{A}_0$ when generating a ciphertext.
6. *Bit dropping.* While it is well-known that we can perform heavy bit-dropping on the v part of the ciphertext in Eq. (1), we also notice that we can do the same on two coefficient of $\mathbf{u}$. The reason for that is more subtle: decryption computes $\mathbf{u}^T \cdot \mathbf{z}$, where $\mathbf{z} \in \mathcal{R}^4$ is heavily unbalanced, with the first two coefficients being very large, the third very small, and the last in-between. We adapt the bit-dropping of $\mathbf{u}$ accordingly to gain in ciphertext size without impacting correctness.

To summarise, we save 6 ring elements: 2 in Item 1, 3 in Item 2 and 1 in Item 5. Our modulus q and ring degree d are smaller as well (Item 3) due to the simpler construction, and bit-dropping (Item 6) provides further gains.

Obtaining Share Robustness. Let us recall the joint interactive key extraction of [34]: in the first round, each party i computes their committing value w_i and sends a commitment $\mathsf{cmt}_i = H_{\mathsf{cmt}}(w_i)$ to the other parties. Upon receiving the commitments of the others, everyone reveals in the next round their value w_i.

In the last round, each party computes their response z_i. This response prepares a correct reconstruction by scaling each party's Shamir secret key share by the corresponding Lagrange coefficient. Directly giving out such scalings would be vulnerable to key-recovery attacks.

To mitigate this, [34] copies the strategy of Threshold Raccoon [19] and adds blinding one-time masks m_i, which sum to zero during reconstruction. While simple from a proof perspective, such masks come with two main drawbacks. First, they require the parties to possess mutual secret seeds. And more importantly, they make it difficult to detect which party is misbehaving when a failure occurs during reconstruction. Put differently, a party can simply send garbage in the last round, causing a systematic failure in the combine stage, without ever being caught. This problem has been addressed for Threshold Raccoon by either relying on non-interactive zero-knowledge proof systems [41] or by using different types of secret sharing [9].

In this work, we follow the latter approach and replace the Shamir secret sharing used in [34] by the Vandermonde secret sharing (VSS) [9], a lattice-friendly adaptation of a secret sharing by Desmedt et al. [20]. This technique allows for sharing short values into short shares and with short reconstruction coefficients. The security relies on the Hint-RLWE problem. As the VSS allows for short responses z_i, we can now verify the correctness of each party's response z_i, detecting misbehaving parties. This leads to what we coined extraction share robustness: even if the adversary maliciously generates the key extraction shares, they can not cause the reconstruction of honestly generated ciphertexts to fail. We actually achieve a slightly stronger notion, where this is true even for ciphertexts that are generated with biased randomness.

Note that the security proof of the resulting TIBE now needs to handle the leakage coming from the VSS. To make the proof simpler, we blend the Coset-Hint-RLWE to Hint-RLWE reduction from [34] directly into the security proof. Hence, the Coset-Hint-RLWE now only appears indirectly in our paper.

Stronger Decapsulation Consistency. Finally, we realise that the extraction share robustness of the underlying TIBE allows us to generically reach a stronger notion of decapsulation consistency in the resulting TKEM from the BCHK+ transform compared to [34]. Our notion corresponds to the one defined in [21] in the context of threshold public-key encryption schemes.

Whereas [34] only counted as decapsulation inconsistencies when two unequal but *valid* keys $K \neq K'$ were recovered, we now also count as decapsulation inconsistency when one of the reconstructed keys is *invalid*, i.e. led to $\perp$. Let us try to give some intuition on why robustness of the TIBE and consistency of the TKEM are related. If exactly one of K or K' is equal to $\perp$, we can use the valid key and the BCHK+ transform to recover the underlying message and encryption randomness used to generated the TIBE ciphertext. Then, the shares associated to the other (invalid) key define a forgery for the extraction share robustness game of the underlying TIBE . If neither K nor K' are equal to $\perp$, we fall back to the case considered in [34]. We provide more intuition on the different decapsulation consistency notions in Sect. 6.

2 Preliminaries

We assume familiarity with Landau's asymptotic notations: $O(n)$, o(n), $\omega(n)$, $\Omega(n)$, $a(n) \sim b(n)$, and Knuth's Theta notation $\Theta(n)$. We denote by log the natural logarithm and by $\log_2$ the base 2 logarithm.

Algorithms. To denote the *assign* operation, we use $y := f(x)$ (resp. $y \leftarrow f(x)$) when f is deterministic (resp. randomised). We note **assert** the function that takes a proposition x as input and $\perp$ if x is false, else it does nothing.

Norms. For a vector $\mathbf{x} = (x_0, \ldots, x_{n-1}) \in \mathbb{R}^n$ we define the norms as $\|\mathbf{x}\| := \sqrt{\sum_i x_i^2}$ and $\|\mathbf{x}\|_\infty := \max_i |x_i|$. For a matrix we denote the Gram-Schmidt orthogonalisation of $\mathbf{M} \in \mathbb{R}^{n \times m}$ as matrix $\tilde{\mathbf{M}} \in \mathbb{R}^{n \times m}$ with columns $\tilde{\mathbf{m}}_i$, $i \in [n]$. Then the GS norm of a matrix $\mathbf{M} \in \mathbb{R}^{n \times m}$ is defined as $\|\mathbf{M}\|_{GS} = \max_i \|\tilde{\mathbf{m}}_i\|$.

Set and Distributions. For an integer $N > 0$, we denote $[N] = \{0, \ldots, N-1\}$. We recall that the union $S \cup T$ of two sets writes $S \sqcup T$ when disjoint. For a set S, we denote by $\mathcal{U}(S)$ the *uniform distribution* over S, and write $x \leftarrow S$ as shorthand for $x \leftarrow \mathcal{U}(S)$.

Decomposition Function. For an odd prime q and any positive $\beta < q$, we define the function $\mathsf{Decomp}_\beta : \mathbb{Z}_q \to \mathbb{Z} \times \mathbb{Z}$ in Algorithm 1. We extend it to $\mathcal{R} = \mathbb{Z}[x]/(x^n + 1)$ and its quotient $\mathcal{R}_q = \mathcal{R}/q\mathcal{R}$ by decomposing the elements coefficient-wise. It holds that $\|c_1\|_\infty \leq \beta/2$, $\|c_0\|_\infty \leq \left\lceil \frac{q-1}{2\beta} \right\rceil$ and $\mathbb{E}[c_0] = 0$.

Algorithm 1 $\mathsf{Decomp}_\beta(c) \to (c_0, c_1)$ ▷ Assume $c \in \left\{-\frac{q-1}{2}, \ldots, \frac{q-1}{2}\right\}$.

1: $c_0 := \mathrm{sgn}(c) \cdot \lfloor |c|/\beta \rceil$ ▷ $\mathrm{sgn}(\cdot)$ is the sign function. Round half up.
2: $c_1 := c - c_0 \cdot \beta$
3: **return** (c_0, c_1)

Gaussians and Lattices. For $\Sigma \in \mathbb{R}^{n \times n}$ a positive definite matrix, we denote $\rho_{\sqrt{\Sigma},\mathbf{c}}$ the mass function over $\mathbb{R}^n$ of the Gaussian distribution centered in $\mathbf{c}$:

$$\rho_{\sqrt{\Sigma},\mathbf{c}}(\mathbf{x}) = \exp(-(\mathbf{x} - \mathbf{c})^{\mathrm{T}} \cdot \Sigma^{-1} \cdot (\mathbf{x} - \mathbf{c})/2)$$

When $\sigma \in \mathbb{R}^+$, we note $\rho_\sigma = \rho_{\sqrt{\sigma^2 I},\mathbf{0}}$.

A lattice is a discrete subgroup of $\mathbb{R}^n$. The dual of a lattice Λ, noted $\Lambda^\vee$, is the set $\Lambda^\vee = \{\mathbf{x} \in \mathsf{Span}_\mathbb{R}(\Lambda) \mid \forall \mathbf{v} \in \Lambda, \langle x, v \rangle \in \mathbb{Z}\}$. Discretizing the Gaussian mass function $\rho_{\sqrt{\Sigma},\mathbf{c}}$ over Λ and normalizing its sum to 1, we obtain the discrete Gaussian distribution $D_{\Lambda,\sqrt{\Sigma},\mathbf{c}}$. For any lattice Λ, and any real $\varepsilon > 0$, the smoothing parameter $\eta_\varepsilon(\Lambda)$ is the smallest real $s > 0$ such that $\rho_{1/(\sqrt{2\pi}s)}(\Lambda^\vee) \leq 1+\varepsilon$. For $n > 0$ and the integer lattice $\mathbb{Z}^n$ we have a bound $\eta_\varepsilon(\mathbb{Z}^n) \leq \frac{1}{\sqrt{2\pi}} \cdot \sqrt{\ln(2n\cdot(1+1/\varepsilon))/\pi}$.

Lemma 1 (**[26, Lemma 3.1]**). *For a full-rank matrix* $\mathbf{B} \in \mathbb{R}^{n\times n}$ *and a lattice* $\Lambda = \Lambda(\mathbf{B})$ *we have*

$$\eta_\varepsilon(\Lambda(\mathbf{B})) \leq \|\mathbf{B}\|_{GS} \cdot \eta_\varepsilon(\mathbb{Z}^n)$$

Lemma 2 (**[37] Corollary 7.5**). *For* $k > 1$, *let* $\mathbf{a} \leftarrow \mathcal{R}_q^k$, *let* $\sigma \geq \sqrt{2\pi}\cdot 2d\cdot q^{1/k+2/dk}$. *Then with* $\tilde{\mathbf{a}} = [1\ \mathbf{a}]$, *and* $\mathbf{x} \leftarrow D_{\mathcal{R}^4,\sigma}$*:*

$$\mathrm{SD}(\tilde{\mathbf{a}}^T\mathbf{x}, \mathcal{U}(\mathcal{R}_q)) = 2^{-\Omega(d)}.$$

Lemma 3 (**[26, Corollary 2.8]**). *For* $n > 0$ *and* $\varepsilon \in (0,1)$, *let* $\Lambda' \subseteq \Lambda \subset \mathbb{R}^n$ *be full-rank lattices. Let* $\sigma \geq \eta_\varepsilon(\Lambda')$. *Then*

$$\mathrm{SD}(\mathcal{D}_{\Lambda,\sigma} \bmod \Lambda', \mathcal{U}(\Lambda/\Lambda')) \leq 2\,\varepsilon.$$

Lemma 4 (**Implicit in [14]**). *Let* $\varepsilon \in (0,1/2)$, *and* $n, m_0, m_1 > 0$ *be integers such that* $n < m_0 + m_1$. *Let* $\mathbf{F} = [\mathbf{F}_0 \mid \mathbf{F}_1] \in \mathcal{R}_q^{n\times(m_0+m_1)}$, $\mathbf{t} \in \mathcal{R}_q^n$. *Let* $\mathbf{\Sigma}_0 \in \mathbb{R}^{dm_0\times dm_0}$, $\mathbf{\Sigma}_1 \in \mathbb{R}^{dm_1\times dm_1}$ *be positive definite such that* $s_{\min}(\mathbf{\Sigma}_1) \geq \eta_\varepsilon(\mathbf{F}_1)$. *Denote* $\mathbf{\Sigma} := \begin{bmatrix}\mathbf{\Sigma}_0 & \mathbf{0}\\ \mathbf{0} & \mathbf{\Sigma}_1\end{bmatrix}$. *Then the following distributions are* 2ε*-statistically close:*

$$\mathcal{D}_0 = \{(\mathbf{z},\mathbf{x}) \leftarrow \mathcal{D}_{\Lambda_q^{\mathbf{t}}(\mathbf{F}),\mathbf{\Sigma}}\}$$
$$\mathcal{D}_1 = \{(\mathbf{z},\mathbf{x}) \mid \mathbf{z} \leftarrow \mathcal{D}_{\mathcal{R}^{m_0},\mathbf{\Sigma}_0}, \mathbf{x} \leftarrow \mathcal{D}_{\Lambda_q^{\mathbf{t}-\mathbf{F}_0\mathbf{z}}(\mathbf{F}_1),\mathbf{\Sigma}_1}\}$$

Lemma 5 (**Adapted [40]**). *Let* $m, \mathbf{\Sigma}_0, \mathbf{\Sigma}_1 > 0$, $\varepsilon \leq 1/2$ *s.t.* $\sqrt{\mathbf{\Sigma}_0} \geq \eta_\varepsilon(\mathcal{R}^m)$. *Denote* $\mathbf{\Sigma}_2^{-1} := \mathbf{\Sigma}_0^{-1} + \mathbf{\Sigma}_1^{-1}$ *and assume that* $\sqrt{\mathbf{\Sigma}_2} \geq \eta_\varepsilon(\mathcal{R}^m)$ *and* $\mathbf{x}_i \leftarrow \mathcal{D}_{\mathcal{R}^m,\sqrt{\mathbf{\Sigma}_i}}$, $i \in [2]$. *Then*

$$\mathrm{SD}(\mathbf{x}_0 + \mathbf{x}_1, \mathcal{D}_{\mathcal{R}^m,\sqrt{\mathbf{\Sigma}_0+\mathbf{\Sigma}_1}}) \leq 8\varepsilon.$$

Definition 1 (**NTRU**). *For an integer* q, *a distribution* χ *over* $\mathcal{R}$, *and an algorithm* $\mathcal{A}$, *the advantage of the decisional NTRU problem of* $\mathcal{A}$ *is defined as:*

$$\mathsf{Adv}^{\mathsf{NTRU}}(\mathcal{A}) = \left|\Pr\left[1 \leftarrow \mathcal{A}(f\cdot g^{-1})\right] - \Pr\left[1 \leftarrow \mathcal{A}(h)\right]\right|$$

where $(f,g) \leftarrow \chi^2$ *conditioned on* g *being invertible in* $\mathcal{R}_q$, *and* $h \leftarrow \mathcal{R}_q$. *We say the* $\mathsf{NTRU}_{\chi,q}$ *assumption holds if* $\mathsf{Adv}^{\mathsf{NTRU}}(\mathcal{A})$ *is negligible for all PPT* $\mathcal{A}$.

Lemma 6 (**NTRU Trapdoor quality**). *Let* $\sigma = O(\sqrt{q})$, *there exists a randomised algorithm* $\mathsf{TrapGenNTRU}(1^d, q)$ *that outputs a vector* $\mathbf{a} := [1\ a'] \in \mathcal{R}_q^2$ *and a full rank matrix* $\mathbf{T_a} \in \mathcal{R}^{2\times 2}$, *where* $\mathbf{T_a}$ *is a basis for* $\Lambda_q^\perp(\mathbf{a})$. *Moreover,* $\|\mathbf{T_a}\|_{GS} = O(\sqrt{q})$ *and* a' *is indistinguishable from random based on the* $\mathsf{NTRU}_{\mathcal{D}_\sigma,q}$ *assumption. In practice we can use* $\|\mathbf{T_a}\|_{GS} = 1.17\sqrt{q}$

2.1 Syntax and Security Definitions

We recall relevant cryptographic primitives used in this work.

Definition 2 (Signature). *A signature scheme is a tuple of PPT algorithms* $\mathsf{SIG} = (\mathsf{SIG.Keygen}, \mathsf{SIG.Sign}, \mathsf{SIG.Verify})$ *s.t.:*

1. $\mathsf{SIG.Keygen}(\kappa) \to (\mathsf{sk}, \mathsf{vk})$ *takes as input the security parameter* κ *and outputs a pair of secret key* sk *and verification key* vk.
2. $\mathsf{SIG.Sign}(\mathsf{sk}, \mathsf{msg}) \to \mathsf{sig}$ *takes as input a secret key* sk *and a message* msg *and outputs a signature* sig.
3. $\mathsf{SIG.Verify}(\mathsf{vk}, \mathsf{msg}, \mathsf{sig}) \to b \in \{0,1\}$ *takes as input a verification key* vk*, a message* msg *and a signature* sig *and outputs either* 1 *(meaning accept) or* 0 *(meaning reject).*

Definition 3 ((Q,ε)-sEU-CMA Security). *A signature scheme* SIG *satisfies* (Q,ε)-$\mathsf{sEU\text{-}CMA}$ *if any PPT adversary* $\mathcal{A}$ *that makes at most* Q *signing queries wins* $\mathsf{Exp}^{\mathsf{sEU\text{-}CMA}}_{\mathcal{A},\mathsf{SIG}}(1^\kappa)$ *(see Fig. 1a) with probability at most* ε*. When* $Q = 1$ *we say that* SIG *is an* ε-$\mathsf{sEU\text{-}CMA}$ *one-time signature scheme.*

Definition 4 (IBE with Threshold Key Generation). *An Identity-based Encryption Scheme with Threshold Key Generation is a tuple of PPT algorithms* $\mathsf{TIBE} = (\mathsf{TIBE.Setup}, \mathsf{TIBE.Encrypt}, (\mathsf{TIBE.ShareExtract}_r)_r, \mathsf{TIBE.ShareVerify}, \mathsf{TIBE.Combine})$ *s.t.:*

1. $\mathsf{TIBE.Setup}(1^\kappa) \to (\mathsf{ek}, \{\mathsf{dk}_i\}_{i\in N})$ *takes as input the security parameter. It outputs the encryption key* ek *and* N *decryption key shares* $\{\mathsf{dk}_i\}_{i\in N}$.
2. $\mathsf{TIBE.Encrypt}(\mathsf{ek}, \mathsf{id}, \mathsf{msg}) \to \mathsf{ct}$ *takes as input an encryption key* ek*, identity* id *and message* msg*. It outputs a ciphertext* ct.
3. *For* $r \in \{1, \dots, \mathsf{rounds}\}$, $\mathsf{TIBE.ShareExtract}_r(\mathsf{id}, \mathsf{act}, \mathsf{dk}_i, \{\mathsf{contrib}_{k,j}\}^{k\in\mathsf{act}}_{j<r}) \to \mathsf{contrib}_{i,r}$ *takes as input an identity* id*, the set of active participants* act*, a decryption key share* dk_i *and contributions from previous rounds* $\{\mathsf{contrib}_{k,j}\}^{k\in\mathsf{act}}_{j<r}$*. It outputs a contribution of the current round* $\mathsf{contrib}_{i,r}$.
4. $\mathsf{TIBE.ShareVerify}(\mathsf{ek}, \mathsf{id}, \mathsf{act}, \{\mathsf{contrib}_{j,r}\}_{j,r}, i) \to b \in \{1, \perp\}$ *takes as input an encryption key* ek*, an identity* id*, a set of active participants* act*, their key share contributions* $\{\mathsf{contrib}_{j,r}\}^{j\in\mathsf{act}}_{r\le\mathsf{rounds}}$ *and the index of one party* $i \in \mathsf{act}$*. It outputs either* 1 *(meaning accept) or* $\perp$ *(meaning reject).*
5. $\mathsf{TIBE.Combine}(\mathsf{ek}, \mathsf{ct}, \mathsf{id}, \mathsf{act}, \{\mathsf{contrib}_{i,r}\}_{i,r}) \to \mathsf{msg}/\perp$ *takes as input a set of active participants* act*, their key share contributions* $\{\mathsf{contrib}_{i,r}\}^{i\in\mathsf{act}}_{r\le\mathsf{rounds}}$*, an identity* id *and a ciphertext* ct*. It outputs a message* msg *or an error* $\perp$.

Definition 5 (Decryption Correctness). *A* TIBE *scheme has a* δ*-correct decryption if for every message* msg*, key* $(\mathsf{ek}, \{\mathsf{dk}_i\}_{i\in N})$ *and set* act *of key extractors of size at least* T *over the randomness of the honest encryption, key extraction and decryption algorithms*

$$\Pr_{\mathsf{ct},\mathsf{contrib}}(\mathsf{TIBE.Combine}(\mathsf{ek}, \mathsf{ct}, \mathsf{id}, \mathsf{act}, \mathsf{contrib}) = \mathsf{msg}) \ge 1 - \delta.$$

Here we denote $\mathsf{ct} := \mathsf{TIBE.Encrypt}(\mathsf{ek}, \mathsf{id}, \mathsf{msg})$ *and* $\mathsf{contrib} := \{\mathsf{contrib}_{j,r}\}^{j\in\mathsf{act}}_{r\le\mathsf{rounds}}$ *from the partial key extraction procedure.*

Definition 6 (Extraction Share Correctness). *A* TIBE *scheme has* δ'*-correct extraction shares if for every message* msg*, key* $(\mathsf{ek}, \{\mathsf{dk}_i\}_{i \in N})$*, set* act *of key extractors of size at least* T *and every party* $i \in \mathsf{act}$ *over the randomness of the honest encryption and key extraction algorithms*

$$\Pr_{\mathsf{ct},\mathsf{contrib}}(\mathsf{TIBE}\,.\mathsf{ShareVerify}(\mathsf{ek}, \mathsf{id}, \mathsf{act}, \mathsf{contrib}, i) = 1) \geq 1 - \delta'.$$

Here we denote $\mathsf{ct} := \mathsf{TIBE}\,.\mathsf{Encrypt}(\mathsf{ek}, \mathsf{id}, \mathsf{msg})$ *and* $\mathsf{contrib} := \{\mathsf{contrib}_{j,r}\}_{r \in \mathsf{rounds}}^{j \in \mathsf{act}}$ *from the shared key extraction procedure.*

Definition 7 (Extraction Share Robustness). *Let* TIBE *be a threshold identity-based encryption scheme with* RDistr *beings the distribution of its encryption randomness. Further, let* RSpace *be a set such that* $R \leftarrow \mathsf{RDistr}$ *lies in* RSpace *with overwhelming probability. A* TIBE *scheme is extraction share robust for randomness space* RSpace *if no PPT adversary can win the* Robust *experiment in Fig. 1e with a non-negligible probability. We write* $\mathsf{Adv}_{\mathcal{A},\mathsf{TIBE}}^{\mathsf{Robust}}$ *for the winning probability of adversary* $\mathcal{A}$ *in the* Robust *experiment.*

Definition 8 (γ-spreadness adapted from [27]). *Let* TIBE *be a Threshold IBE scheme defined in Definition 4 and let* $\mathcal{K}, \mathcal{M}, \mathcal{I}, \mathcal{C}$ *denote the sets of valid encryption keys, messages, identities, and ciphertexts respectively. For* $\gamma > 0$ *the* TIBE *is* γ*-spread if for every tuple* $(\mathsf{msg} \in \mathcal{M}, \mathsf{id} \in \mathcal{I}, \mathsf{ek} \in \mathcal{E})$

$$-\log \max_{\mathsf{ct} \in \mathcal{C}} \Pr_{\mathsf{rand}}(\mathsf{ct} = \mathsf{TIBE}\,.\mathsf{Encrypt}(\mathsf{msg}, \mathsf{id}, \mathsf{ek}; \mathsf{rand})) \geq \gamma.$$

Definition 9 (Threshold Key Encapsulation Mechanism). *A threshold key encapsulation mechanism (TKEM) is a tuple of PPT algorithms* $\mathsf{TKEM} = (\mathsf{TKEM}\,.\mathsf{Keygen}, \mathsf{TKEM}\,.\mathsf{Encaps}, (\mathsf{TKEM}\,.\mathsf{ShareDecaps}_r)_r, \mathsf{TKEM}\,.\mathsf{ShareVerify}, \mathsf{TKEM}\,.\mathsf{Combine})$ *s.t.:*

1. $\mathsf{TKEM}\,.\mathsf{Keygen}(1^\kappa) \rightarrow (\mathsf{ek}, \{\mathsf{dk}_i\}_{i \in N})$ *takes as input the security parameter. It outputs the encapsulation key* ek *and* N *decapsulation key shares* $\{\mathsf{dk}_i\}_{i \in N}$.
2. $\mathsf{TKEM}\,.\mathsf{Encaps}(\mathsf{ek}) \rightarrow \mathsf{ct}, K$ *takes as input an encapsulation key* ek*. It outputs a ciphertext* ct *and a session key from the key space* $K \in \mathcal{K}$.
3. *For* $r \in \{1, \ldots, \mathsf{rounds}\}$, $\mathsf{TKEM}\,.\mathsf{ShareDecaps}_r(\mathsf{ct}, \mathsf{act}, \mathsf{dk}_i, \{\mathsf{contrib}_{i,j}\}_{j<r}) \rightarrow \mathsf{contrib}_{i,r}$ *takes as input a ciphertext* ct*, a set of active parties* act*, a decapsulation key share* dk_i *and all contributions by parties in* act *up to the current round* r*. It outputs a contribution* $\mathsf{contrib}_{i,r}$ *for the current round.*
4. $\mathsf{TKEM}\,.\mathsf{ShareVerify}(\mathsf{ek}, \mathsf{ct}, \mathsf{act}, \{\mathsf{contrib}_{j,r}\}_{j,r}, i) \rightarrow b \in \{1, \perp\}$ *takes as input an encapsulation key* ek*, a ciphertext* ct*, a set of active parties* act*, their contributions* $\{\mathsf{contrib}_{j,r}\}_{j \in \mathsf{act}, r \leq \mathsf{rounds}}$ *and the index of one party* $i \in \mathsf{act}$*. It outputs either* 1 *(meaning accept) or* $\perp$ *(meaning reject).*
5. $\mathsf{TKEM}\,.\mathsf{Combine}(\mathsf{ek}, \mathsf{ct}, \mathsf{act}, \{\mathsf{contrib}_{i,r}\}_{i,r}) \rightarrow K/\perp$ *takes as input a ciphertext* ct*, a set of active parties* act *and their contributions* $\{\mathsf{contrib}_{i,r}\}_{i \in \mathsf{act}, r \leq \mathsf{rounds}}$*. It outputs a key* K *or an error message* $\perp$.

Definition 10 (Selective-ID/CCA2 Security). *A* TIBE *(resp. a* TKEM *) scheme achieves selective-ID indistinguishability, selective-ID one-wayness (resp. selective-CCA2 security) if any PPT adversary wins the experiment in Fig. 1b, Fig. 1d (resp. Fig. 1c) with negligible probability. We denote the winning probability of $\mathcal{A}$ as* $\mathsf{Adv}^{\mathsf{sel\text{-}ID\text{-}IND}}_{\mathcal{A},\mathsf{TIBE}}$, $\mathsf{Adv}^{\mathsf{sel\text{-}ID\text{-}OW}}_{\mathcal{A},\mathsf{TIBE}}$ *(resp.* $\mathsf{Adv}^{\mathsf{CCA2}}_{\mathcal{A},\mathsf{TKEM}}$ *).*

2.2 The BCHK+ Transform

We recall in Fig. 2 the BCHK+ transform proven in [34].

Theorem 1 ([34]). *Let* TIBE *be a threshold identity-based encryption from Definition 10. Let $\mathcal{M}$ and* RSpace *denote the message space and randomness space of the* TIBE *, respectively. Let $\mathcal{K}$ be an arbitrary set. Let* SIG *be a one-time signature satisfying* $\varepsilon_{\mathsf{SIG}}$-sEU-CMA *and $G_{\mathsf{fo}} : \{0,1\}^* \to \mathcal{R}$ and $H_{\mathsf{fo}} : \{0,1\}^* \to \mathcal{K}$ be modelled as random oracles. Then* TKEM *as described in Fig. 2 is a CCA-secure TKEM with:*

$$\mathsf{Adv}^{\mathsf{CCA2}}_{\mathcal{A},\mathsf{TKEM}}(\kappa) \leq \varepsilon_{\mathsf{SIG}} + (Q_{G_{\mathsf{fo}}} + Q_{H_{\mathsf{fo}}}) \cdot \mathsf{Adv}^{\mathsf{sel\text{-}ID\text{-}IND}}_{\mathcal{A},\mathsf{TIBE}} + \frac{(Q_{G_{\mathsf{fo}}} + Q_{H_{\mathsf{fo}}})}{|\mathcal{M}|}.$$

2.3 Bounds on Distributions

We use the following results by Lyubashevsky [36] and implications thereof.

Lemma 7 (Lemma 4.3 in [36]). *Let $\mathbf{v} \in \mathbb{R}^d$.*

$$\mathbb{P}[|\langle \mathbf{z}, \mathbf{v} \rangle| > \tau\sigma \|\mathbf{v}\|; \mathbf{z} \leftarrow D_{\mathbb{Z}^d,\sigma}] \leq 2e^{-\tau^2/2}. \tag{2}$$

In particular, if $\tau \geq \sqrt{2(\kappa+1)\log 2}$, then the right side of Eq. (2) is at most $2^{-\kappa}$.

Lemma 8 (Lemma 4.4 in [36], extended). *For any $\tau > 1$ and any lattice $\Lambda \subseteq \mathbb{R}^d$,*

$$\mathbb{P}\left[\|\mathbf{z}\| > \tau\sigma\sqrt{d}; \mathbf{z} \leftarrow D_{\Lambda,\sigma}\right] \leq C^d. \tag{3}$$

where $C = \tau \cdot e^{\frac{1}{2}(1-\tau^2)} < 1$. If $\left(\tau \geq 1 + \frac{\kappa \log 2}{3d}\right)$ **or** *$\left(\tau \geq 1 + \sqrt{\frac{4\,\kappa \log 2}{d}}\right)$, we note that $C^d \leq 2^{-\kappa}$.*

The original formulation of [36, Lemma 4.4] takes $\Lambda = \mathbb{Z}^d$, but we can see that its proof goes through for any lattice $\Lambda \subset \mathbb{R}^d$. Corollary 1 is a direct corollary of Lemma 7.

Corollary 1. *Let $\mathbf{a} \in \mathbb{Z}^d$ be an arbitrary vector. For $\mathbf{x} \leftarrow D_{\mathcal{R}^d,\sigma}$, the following holds with probability at least $1 - 2^{-\kappa}$:*

$$\|\mathbf{a} + \mathbf{x}\|^2 \leq \|\mathbf{a}\|^2 + 2\sqrt{2(\kappa+1)\log 2}\;\|\mathbf{a}\|\;\sigma + \|\mathbf{x}\|^2 \tag{4}$$

$$\sim \|\mathbf{a}\|^2 + \|\mathbf{x}\|^2 \qquad \text{when } \kappa = o(n), \tag{5}$$

Proof. We start from the identity $\|\mathbf{a} + \mathbf{x}\|^2 = \|\mathbf{a}\|^2 + \|\mathbf{x}\|^2 + 2\langle \mathbf{a}, \mathbf{x} \rangle$, then apply Lemma 8 on $\|\mathbf{x}\|$. □

$\mathsf{Exp}^{\mathsf{sEU\text{-}CMA}}_{\mathcal{A},\mathsf{SIG}}(1^\kappa)$

$(\mathsf{sk}, \mathsf{vk}) \leftarrow \mathsf{SIG.Keygen}(1^\kappa)$
$(\mathsf{msg}^*, \mathsf{sig}^*) \leftarrow \mathcal{A}^{\mathsf{SIG.Sign}(\mathsf{sk},\cdot)}(\mathsf{vk})$
Let $\{(\mathsf{msg}_i, \mathsf{sig}_i)\}_{i=0}^{Q-1}$ be the list of $\mathcal{A}$'s oracle queries
return $(\mathsf{SIG.Verify}(\mathsf{vk}, \mathsf{msg}^*, \mathsf{sig}^*) = 1) \wedge (\mathsf{msg}^*, \mathsf{sig}^*) \notin \{(\mathsf{msg}_i, \mathsf{sig}_i)\}_{i=0}^{Q-1}$

(a) The (Q, ε)-sEU-CMA security game

$\mathsf{Exp}^{\mathsf{sel\text{-}ID\text{-}IND}}_{\mathcal{A},\mathsf{TIBE}}(1^\kappa)$

$(\mathsf{id}^*, \mathsf{cor}) \leftarrow \mathcal{A}$
assert $|\mathsf{cor}| = T - 1$
$(\mathsf{ek}, \{\mathsf{dk}_i\}_{i \in N}) \leftarrow \mathsf{TIBE.Setup}(1^\kappa)$
$(\mathsf{msg}_0, \mathsf{msg}_1)$
$\leftarrow \mathcal{A}^{\mathsf{TIBE.ShareExtract}(\cdot,\mathsf{id}),\mathsf{id}\neq\mathsf{id}^*}(\{\mathsf{dk}_i\}_{\mathsf{cor}})$
$b \leftarrow \{0, 1\}$
$\mathsf{ct}^* = \mathsf{TIBE.Encrypt}(\mathsf{ek}, \mathsf{id}^*, \mathsf{msg}_b)$
$b' \leftarrow \mathcal{A}^{\mathsf{TIBE.ShareExtract}(\cdot,\mathsf{id}),\mathsf{id}\neq\mathsf{id}^*}(\{\mathsf{dk}_i\}_{\mathsf{cor}})$
return $(b = b')$

(b) TIBE selective-ID security

$\mathsf{Exp}^{\mathsf{CCA2}}_{\mathcal{A},\mathsf{TKEM}}(1^\kappa)$

$\mathsf{cor} \leftarrow \mathcal{A}$
assert $|\mathsf{cor}| = T - 1$
$(\mathsf{ek}, \{\mathsf{dk}_i\}_{i \in N}) \leftarrow \mathsf{TKEM.Keygen}(1^\kappa)$
$1 \leftarrow \mathcal{A}^{\mathsf{TKEM.ShareDecaps}(\cdot)}(\{\mathsf{dk}_i\}_{\mathsf{cor}})$
$(\mathsf{ct}^*, K_0) = \mathsf{TKEM.Encaps}(\mathsf{ek})$
$K_1 \leftarrow \mathcal{K}$
$b \leftarrow \{0, 1\}$
$b' \leftarrow \mathcal{A}^{\mathsf{TKEM.ShareDecaps}(\mathsf{ct},\cdot),\mathsf{ct}\neq\mathsf{ct}^*}((\mathsf{ct}^*, K_b))$
return $(b = b')$

(c) TKEM selective security

$\mathsf{Exp}^{\mathsf{sel\text{-}ID\text{-}OW}}_{\mathcal{A},\mathsf{TIBE}}(1^\kappa)$

$(\mathsf{id}^*, \mathsf{cor}) \leftarrow \mathcal{A}$
assert $|\mathsf{cor}| = T - 1$
$(\mathsf{ek}, \{\mathsf{dk}_i\}_{i \in N}) \leftarrow \mathsf{TIBE.Setup}(1^\kappa)$
$\mathcal{A}^{\mathsf{TIBE.ShareExtract}(\cdot,\mathsf{id}),\mathsf{id}\neq\mathsf{id}^*}(\{\mathsf{dk}_i\}_{\mathsf{cor}})$
$\mathsf{msg}^* \leftarrow \{0, 1\}^d$
$\mathsf{ct}^* = \mathsf{TIBE.Encrypt}(\mathsf{ek}, \mathsf{id}^*, \mathsf{msg}^*)$
$\mathsf{msg} \leftarrow \mathcal{A}^{\mathsf{TIBE.ShareExtract}(\cdot,\mathsf{id}),\mathsf{id}\neq\mathsf{id}^*}(\{\mathsf{dk}_i\}_{\mathsf{cor}}, \mathsf{ct}^*)$
return $(\mathsf{msg} = \mathsf{msg}^*)$

(d) TIBE Selective-ID One-Way Security

$\mathsf{Exp}^{\mathsf{Robust}}_{\mathcal{A},\mathsf{TIBE}}(1^\kappa)$

$(\mathsf{ek}, \{\mathsf{dk}_i\}_{i \in N}) \leftarrow \mathsf{TIBE.Setup}(1^\kappa)$
$(\mathsf{msg}, \mathsf{id}, \mathsf{rand}, \mathsf{ct}, \mathsf{act}, S) \leftarrow \mathcal{A}(\mathsf{ek}, \{\mathsf{dk}_i\}_{i \in [N]})$
assert $\mathsf{rand} \in \mathsf{RSpace}$
assert $\mathsf{ct} = \mathsf{TIBE.Encrypt}(\mathsf{ek}, \mathsf{id}, \mathsf{msg}; \mathsf{rand})$
for $i \in \mathsf{act}$
  assert $\mathsf{TIBE.ShareVerify}(\mathsf{ek}, \mathsf{act}, S, i)$
return $\mathsf{msg} \neq \mathsf{TIBE.Combine}(\mathsf{ct}, \mathsf{act}, S)$

(e) TIBE Extraction Share Robustness

Fig. 1. Security experiments

TKEM .Keygen(1^κ)

$(\{\mathsf{dk}_i\}_{i\in[N]}, \mathsf{ek}) \leftarrow$ TIBE .Setup(1^κ)
return $(\{\mathsf{dk}_i\}_{i\in[N]}, \mathsf{ek})$

TKEM .Encaps(ek)

$\mathsf{msg} \leftarrow \{0,1\}^d$
$\mathsf{rand} = G_{\mathsf{fo}}(\mathsf{msg})$
$(\mathsf{sk}, \mathsf{vk}) \leftarrow$ SIG.Keygen(1^κ)
id := vk
ct = TIBE .Encrypt(ek, id, msg; rand)
sig $\leftarrow$ SIG.Sign(sk, ct)
$K = H_{\mathsf{fo}}(\mathsf{msg}||\mathsf{ct})$
return (ct, vk, sig), K

TKEM .ShareDecaps$_j$(dk_i, (ct, vk, sig)), $j \le r$

assert SIG.Verify(vk, ct, sig) = 1
$\mathsf{contrib}_{i,j}$ = TIBE .ShareExtract$_j$(dk_i, id = vk)
return $\mathsf{contrib}_{i,j}$

TKEM .ShareVerify(ek, (ct, vk, sig), act, $\{\mathsf{contrib}_{j,r}\}_{j,r}$, i)

assert SIG.Verify(vk, ct, sig) = 1
b = TIBE .ShareVerify(ek, id = vk, act, $\{\mathsf{contrib}_{j,r}\}_{j,r}$, i)
return b

TKEM .Combine($\{\mathsf{contrib}_{i,r}\}_{i\in\mathsf{act}}$, (ct, vk, sig))

assert SIG.Verify(vk, ct, sig) = 1
msg = TIBE .Combine(ct, vk, act, $\{\mathsf{contrib}_{i,r}\}_i$)
$\mathsf{rand} = G_{\mathsf{fo}}(\mathsf{msg})$
assert ct = TIBE .Encrypt(ek, vk, msg; rand)
$K = H_{\mathsf{fo}}(\mathsf{msg}||\mathsf{ct})$
return K

Fig. 2. The BCHK+ transform of [34].

2.4 Hint Ring Learning With Errors

We rely on the Hint-RLWE assumption, introduced by Kim et al. [31]. More specifically, we use a variant by Esgin et al. [23], recalled in Definition 11. While the distribution of the $\mathbf{c}_i$'s in Definition 11 may seem artificial, it is a natural byproduct of the signing procedure used in [23], which we re-use in this work.

Definition 11 (Hint-RLWE). *Let $m > 0$, $Q_1, Q_2 \ge 0$ and q be integers, and $\sigma_{\mathbf{s}}, \sigma_1, \sigma_2 > 0$. Let $\mathbf{a} \leftarrow \mathcal{R}_q^m$. The* Hint-RLWE $^{Q_1,Q_2,\sigma_1,\sigma_2,\beta}_{\mathcal{R},q,m,\sigma_{\mathbf{s}}}$ *problem requires the Adversary to distinguish distributions $\mathcal{D}_{\mathsf{real}}, \mathcal{D}_{\mathsf{ideal}}$ where $\mathbf{s} \leftarrow \mathcal{D}_{\mathcal{R}^{m+1},\sigma_{\mathbf{s}}}$ and:*

$$\mathcal{D}_{\mathsf{real}} = \left\{ \left(\mathbf{a}, \mathbf{b}, \{\mathbf{c}_i, \mathbf{z}_i\}_{i\in[Q_1+Q_2]}\right) \middle| \mathbf{b} = [\mathbf{a}\ \mathbf{I}_m] \cdot \mathbf{s}, \begin{array}{c} \{\mathbf{c}_i, \mathbf{z}_i\}_{i\in[Q_1]} \leftarrow \mathcal{P}_\beta(\mathbf{s}) \\ \{\mathbf{c}_i, \mathbf{z}_i\}_{i\in(Q_1,Q_2]} \leftarrow \mathcal{P}(\mathbf{s}) \end{array} \right\}$$

$$\mathcal{D}_{\mathsf{ideal}} = \left\{ \left(\mathbf{a}, \mathbf{b}, \{\mathbf{c}_i, \mathbf{z}_i\}_{i\in[Q_1+Q_2]}\right) \middle| \mathbf{b} \leftarrow \mathcal{R}_q^m \cdot \mathbf{s}, \begin{array}{c} \{\mathbf{c}_i, \mathbf{z}_i\}_{i\in[Q_1]} \leftarrow \mathcal{P}_\beta(\mathbf{s}) \\ \{\mathbf{c}_i, \mathbf{z}_i\}_{i\in(Q_1,Q_2]} \leftarrow \mathcal{P}(\mathbf{s}) \end{array} \right\}$$

where the distribution $\mathcal{P}_\beta(\mathbf{s})$ is described in Fig. 3 and $\mathcal{P}(\mathbf{s}) = \mathbf{s} + \mathcal{D}_{\mathcal{R}^{m+1},\sigma_2}$.

When the adversary receives no hints ($Q_1 = Q_2 = 0$) in Definition 11, we recover the Ring-LWE problem $\mathsf{RLWE}_{\mathcal{R},q,m,\sigma_{\mathbf{s}}}$. In [23,31] the standard hardness of Hint-RLWE for $Q_1 \ge 1$, and $Q_2 = 0$ is proven. We give a straightforward adaptation of the reduction in Lemma 9. Note that there is a factor 2 in the formula for $\frac{1}{\sigma_0^2}$, which seems to be an artefact of the proof, as is clearly the case when taking $Q = 0$.

$\mathcal{P}_\beta(\mathbf{s})$
$u \leftarrow \mathcal{R}_q$
$(c_0, c_1) := \mathsf{Decomp}_\beta(u)$
$\mathbf{p} \leftarrow \mathcal{D}_{\mathcal{R}^{1+m},\sigma_\mathbf{p}}$
$\mathbf{z} = \mathbf{s} \cdot c_0 + \mathbf{p}$
return $\{(\mathbf{c} = (c_0, c_1), \mathbf{z})\}$

Fig. 3. Hint distribution for Hint-RLWE

Lemma 9 (Theorem 1 and Lemma 2 from [23]). *Assume* $Q_1, Q_2 = \omega(\kappa\, d \log d)^2$, *and let* $B_{\mathsf{hint}} = \frac{Q M^2}{12}$, *where* $M = 2\left\lceil \frac{q-1}{2\beta} \right\rceil + 1$. *Let* $\sigma_0, \sigma_\mathbf{s}, \sigma_1, \sigma_2 > 0$ *such that* $\frac{1}{\sigma_0^2} = 2\left(\frac{1}{\sigma_\mathbf{s}^2} + \frac{B_{\mathsf{hint}}(1+o(1))}{\sigma_1^2} + \frac{Q_2}{\sigma_2^2}\right)$. *If* $\sigma_0 \geq \sqrt{2}\eta_\epsilon(\mathbb{Z}^d)$ *for* $0 < \epsilon \leq 1/2$, *where* $\eta_\epsilon(\mathbb{Z}^d)$ *is the smoothing parameter of* $\mathbb{Z}^d$, *then there is an efficient reduction from* $\mathsf{RLWE}_{\mathcal{R},q,m,\sigma_0}$ *to* $\mathsf{Hint\text{-}RLWE}^{\,Q_1,Q_2,\sigma_1,\sigma_2,\beta}_{\mathcal{R},q,m,\sigma_\mathbf{s}}$ *that reduces the advantage by at most* 4ϵ.

2.5 Short Secret Sharing

We recall the Vandermonde secret sharing (VSS) [9], a lattice-friendly adaptation of a secret sharing by Desmedt et al. [20].

Dictionaries. We recall that a dictionary, or associative array, is a collection of ordered (key, value) pairs with unique keys. We note $\{:\}$ the empty dictionary, and $\mathsf{Dict}\,[k]$ the value of Dict corresponding to the key k. We note $\mathsf{Dict}_1 \cup \mathsf{Dict}_2$ the union of two dictionaries. When a key k is present in both Dict_1 and Dict_2 and $\mathsf{Dict}_1[k], \mathsf{Dict}_2[k]$ are either both sets or both dictionaries, the new value $(\mathsf{Dict}_1 \cup \mathsf{Dict}_2)[k]$ sets as $\mathsf{Dict}_1[k] \cup \mathsf{Dict}_2[k]$.

Lemma 10. *Let* $\varepsilon \in (0, 1/2)$, $m, N, T \geq 1$, $\sigma \geq \sqrt{2}\eta_\epsilon(\mathcal{R}^m)$, $\mathbf{s} \leftarrow D_{\mathcal{R}^m,\sigma}$, *and* $\mathsf{Shares} \leftarrow \mathsf{VandShare}(\mathsf{s}, [N], T)$. *In Algorithm 2, let* $\chi = D_{\mathcal{R}^m,\sigma}$. *For any user* $i \in [N]$ *and any share* $\mathbf{s}^{(\mathsf{idx})} := \mathsf{Shares}[i][\mathsf{idx}]$, *we have* $\mathrm{SD}(\mathbf{s}^{(\mathsf{idx})}, D_{\mathcal{R}^m,\sqrt{k}\cdot\sigma}) \leq (k-1)\cdot 8\varepsilon$ *for a value* $k \in \mathbb{N}, 1 \leq k \leq \log N + 1$ *determined by Algorithm 2.*

3 Improved TIBE Construction From Lattices

Let $\mathsf{H}_{\mathsf{cmt}}(\cdot) : \mathcal{R}_q \to \{0,1\}^{2\kappa}$ and $\mathsf{H}_{\mathsf{id}}(\cdot) : S_{\mathsf{id}} \to \mathcal{R}_q$ be hash functions modelled as random oracles.

Algorithm 2 $\mathsf{VandShare}(\mathbf{s}, \mathcal{P}, T, \mathsf{idx} = \varnothing) \to \mathsf{Dict}$

```
N = |P|
if T = 1 then
    return Dict := {user : {idx : s} | user ∈ P}
else
    Dict = {user : {:} | user ∈ P}, b = ⌊N/2⌋
    Parse P = P_L ⊔ P_R, with P_L the b smallest elements of P
    for k = max(0, T − N + b), ..., min(b, T) do
        idx_L := idx || ":L:" || k,  idx_R := idx || ":R:" || (T − k)
        if k = 0 then
            Dict := Dict ∪ VandShare(s, P_R, T, idx_R)
        else if k = T then
            Dict := Dict ∪ VandShare(s, P_L, T, idx_L)
        else
            s_0 ← χ                                  ▷ This guarantees short shares
            s_1 := (s − s_0) mod q
            Dict_L := VandShare(s_0, P_L, k, idx_L)
            Dict_R := VandShare(s_1, P_R, T − k, idx_R)
            Dict := Dict ∪ Dict_L ∪ Dict_R
    return Dict                               ▷ The values of Dict are also dictionaries.
```

Public Parameters. These include $(\mathbf{A}, t, N, T)$, where N is the overall number of parties in the protocol and T is the threshold on the number of parties required for decryption.

1. The public matrix $\mathbf{A}$ is a matrix with trapdoor *à la* Eagle [44] or Plover [23]. The parameter $\beta \in \mathbb{Z}$ can be set arbitrarily between 2 and $q/2$ and impacts the quality of the trapdoor.

$$\mathbf{A} = \begin{bmatrix} 1 & a & b \end{bmatrix}, \quad \text{where} \quad a \leftarrow \mathcal{R}_q, \quad s, s' \leftarrow \mathcal{D}_{\mathcal{R},\sigma_{\mathbf{s}}}, \\ b = \beta - (a \cdot s + s') \text{ for some } \beta \in \mathbb{Z} \tag{6}$$

2. $t \leftarrow \mathcal{R}_q$ is used as a target for preimage sampling.

Encryption Procedure. In the encryption procedure, the encrypter constructs a public key $\begin{bmatrix} a & b & \mathsf{H}_{\mathsf{id}}(\mathsf{id}) & t \end{bmatrix}$ for the identity id. Then they generate a Lindner-Peikert [35] style ciphertext $(\mathbf{u}, v)$ for this public key and the message msg. This is described in Algorithm 9.

Decryption Procedure. In the decryption procedure, the parties jointly compute a vector $\mathbf{z} = \begin{bmatrix} \mathbf{z}' & x \end{bmatrix}$ such that $\begin{bmatrix} a & b & \mathsf{H}_{\mathsf{id}}(\mathsf{id}) \end{bmatrix} \cdot \mathbf{z} \approx r$, where r is the encryption randomness. They then use $\mathbf{z}$ to perform a Lindner-Peikert style decryption procedure, by computing $v - \mathbf{u}^T \cdot \mathbf{z}'$ and decoding it to recover the message. This is described in Fig. 5.

The TIBE is formally described in Figs. 4 and 5. For clarity of reading, we assume that the state of party i contains (i) the secret key share of i, (ii) all

Algorithm 3 $\mathsf{VandRecover}(\mathcal{P}, \mathsf{act}, \mathsf{idx} = \varnothing) \rightarrow \mathsf{Indices}$

$N = |\mathcal{P}|, T = |\mathsf{act}|$
if $T = 1$ **then**
  return $\mathsf{Indices} := \{\mathsf{user} : \mathsf{idx} \mid \mathsf{user} \in \mathcal{P}\}$
else
  $b = \lfloor N/2 \rfloor$
  Parse $\mathcal{P} = \mathcal{P}_L \sqcup \mathcal{P}_R$, with $\mathcal{P}_L$ the b smallest elements of $\mathcal{P}$
  $\mathsf{act}_L = \mathsf{act} \cap \mathcal{P}_L, \mathsf{act}_R = \mathsf{act} \cap \mathcal{P}_R, k = |\mathsf{act}_L|$
  $\mathsf{idx}_L := \mathsf{idx} \parallel$ `":L:"` $\parallel k$, $\mathsf{idx}_R := \mathsf{idx} \parallel$ `":R:"` $\parallel (T - k)$
  if $k = 0$ **then**
    return $\mathsf{VandRecover}(\mathcal{P}_R, \mathsf{act}_R, \mathsf{idx}_R)$
  else if $k = T$ **then**
    return $\mathsf{VandRecover}(\mathcal{P}_L, \mathsf{act}_L, \mathsf{idx}_L)$
  else
    $\mathsf{Indices}_L := \mathsf{VandRecover}(\mathcal{P}_L, \mathsf{act}_L, \mathsf{idx}_L)$
    $\mathsf{Indices}_R := \mathsf{VandRecover}(\mathcal{P}_R, \mathsf{act}_R, \mathsf{idx}_R)$
    return $\mathsf{Indices} := \mathsf{Indices}_L \sqcup \mathsf{Indices}_R$

contributions of all parties up to the current round, (iii) the values privately generated by i during previous rounds. In order to avoid ROS-style attacks, it is also important to ensure that the participants' views are consistent, by maintaining their internal states and checking it against received contributions, see for example [29, Figure 3]. For clarity of reading, we omit the consistency checks from our description and refer to [29] for more details.

4 TIBE Correctness and Share Robustness

We now study the correctness and share robustness of the TIBE described in Figs. 4 and 5. We start be providing useful equations holding by construction. Let us note $\mathbf{p}^{(i)} = \left[p_0^{(i)}\ p_1^{(i)}\ 0\ p_3^{(i)}\right]^T$, $\mathbf{p} = \sum_i \mathbf{p}^{(i)}$ and $p_j = \sum_{i \in \mathsf{act}} p_j^{(i)}$ for $j \in [4]$. Recall that $b = \beta - \sum_{i \in \mathsf{act}} b$, $\mathbf{s} = \left[\sum_i s^{(i)}\ \sum_i s'^{(i)}\ 1\ 0\right]^{\mathrm{T}}$, $w = \sum_i w^{(i)}$ and $\mathbf{z} = \sum_i \mathbf{z}^{(i)}$. Remember that by construction:

$$\forall\, \mathsf{id}, \left[1\ a\ b\ \mathsf{H}_{\mathsf{id}}(\mathsf{id})\right] \cdot \mathbf{s} = \beta \qquad \text{(Algorithm 4, Line 4)} \qquad (7)$$

$$\forall\, \mathsf{id}, \forall i \in \mathsf{act}, \left[1\ a\ b\ \mathsf{H}_{\mathsf{id}}(\mathsf{id})\right] \cdot \mathbf{s}^{(i)} = b^{(i)} \qquad \text{(Algorithm 5, Line 6)} \qquad (8)$$

$$\forall\, \mathsf{id}, \forall i \in \mathsf{act}, \left[1\ a\ b\ \mathsf{H}_{\mathsf{id}}(\mathsf{id})\right] \cdot \mathbf{p}^{(i)} = w^{(i)} \qquad \text{(Algorithm 10, Line 2)} \qquad (9)$$

$$c_0 \cdot \beta + c_1 = t - w \qquad \text{(Algorithm 12, Line 3)} \qquad (10)$$

4.1 Extraction Share Correctness

We start by proving correctness of the key extraction shares, cf. Definition 6. Due to page constraints, its proof is deferred to the full version of this paper [10].

Algorithm 4 TIBE .KG$(1^\kappa) \rightarrow$ ek, dk

$t, a \leftarrow \mathcal{R}_q \times \mathcal{R}_q$
$(s, s') \leftarrow \mathcal{D}_{\mathcal{R}^2, \sigma_\mathbf{s}}$
$b = \beta - (a \cdot s + s')$
$\mathbf{s} = \begin{bmatrix} s' & s & 1 & 0 \end{bmatrix}^T$ ▷ $\mathbf{s} \in \mathcal{R}^4$, and $\forall$id, $\begin{bmatrix} 1 & a & b & H(\mathsf{id}) \end{bmatrix} \cdot \mathbf{s} = \beta$
return ek $:= (a, b, t)$, dk $:= (s, s')$

Algorithm 5 TIBE .Share(ek, dk) $\rightarrow$ aux, $\{\mathsf{dk}^{(i)}\}_{i \in [N]}$

Shares $\leftarrow$ VandShare$((s, s'), [N], T, \mathsf{idx} = \{\})$
pek := Dict {} ▷ peklists all partial encryption keys (initially empty)
for $i \in [N]$ **do**
  $\mathsf{dk}^{(i)} :=$ Shares$[i]$ ▷ Each user i has a dictionary $\{\mathsf{idx} : \mathbf{s}^{(\mathsf{idx})}\}$of private keys.
  for idx $\in$ Shares$[i]$ **do** ▷ Compute all partial public keys
    pek[idx] $:= b^{(\mathsf{idx})} = a \cdot s^{(\mathsf{idx})} + s'^{(\mathsf{idx})}$
ek $:= (a, b, t, \mathsf{pek})$
return aux := pek, $\{\mathsf{dk}^{(i)}\}_{i \in [N]}$

Algorithm 6 TIBE .Setup$(1^\kappa) \rightarrow$ ek, $\{\mathsf{dk}^{(i)}\}_{i \in [N]}$

$(\mathsf{ek}_0, \mathsf{dk}) \leftarrow$ TIBE .KG(1^κ)
$(\mathsf{ek}_1, \{\mathsf{dk}^{(i)}\}_{i \in [N]}) \leftarrow$ TIBE .Share(ek, dk)
return ek $:= (\mathsf{ek}_0, \mathsf{ek}_1)$, $\{\mathsf{dk}^{(i)}\}_{i \in [N]}$

Algorithm 7 Encode(msg $= (\alpha_0, \ldots, \alpha_{d-1})) \rightarrow M \in \mathcal{R}_q$

return $M = \sum_{i \in [d]} \alpha_i \cdot \lfloor q/2 \rceil \cdot X^i$

Algorithm 8 Decode$(M = \sum_{i \in [d]} \alpha_i \cdot X^i) \rightarrow$ msg $\in \{0,1\}^d / \perp$

return msg $= \sum_{i \in [d]} \lfloor \alpha_i \rceil_q X^i$ ▷

Algorithm 9 TIBE .Encrypt(msg $\in \{0,1\}^d$, id, ek) $\rightarrow$ ct

$(r, \mathbf{e}, e') \leftarrow D_{\mathcal{R}, \sigma_\mathbf{r}} \times D_{\mathcal{R}^3, \sigma_\mathbf{r}} \times D_{\mathcal{R}, \sigma_\mathbf{r}}$
$\begin{bmatrix} \mathbf{u}^T & v \end{bmatrix} := r \cdot \begin{bmatrix} a & b & \mathsf{H}_{\mathsf{id}}(\mathsf{id}) & t \end{bmatrix} + \begin{bmatrix} \mathbf{e}^T & e' \end{bmatrix} + \begin{bmatrix} \mathbf{0}^{1 \times 3} & \mathsf{Encode}(\mathsf{msg}) \end{bmatrix}$ ▷ $\begin{bmatrix} \mathbf{u} \\ v \end{bmatrix} \in \mathcal{R}_q^4$
return ct $:= (\mathbf{u}, v)$

Fig. 4. TIBE algorithms for key generation, encryption and message encoding.

Algorithm 10 TIBE .ShareExtract$_0$(id, act, dk$^{(i)}$, state$^{(i)}$) → contrib$_0^{(i)}$/⊥

$\mathbf{p}^{(i)} \leftarrow D_{\mathcal{R}^2,\sigma_\mathbf{p}} \times \{0\} \times D_{\mathcal{R},\sigma'_\mathbf{p}}$
$w^{(i)} = \left[1 \ a \ b \ \mathsf{H}_{\mathsf{id}}(\mathsf{id})\right] \cdot \mathbf{p}^{(i)}$
$\mathsf{cmt}^{(i)} = \mathsf{H}_{\mathsf{cmt}}(w^{(i)})$
return $\mathsf{contrib}_0^{(i)} := \mathsf{cmt}^{(i)}$

Algorithm 11 TIBE .ShareExtract$_1$(id, act, dk$^{(i)}$, state$^{(i)}$) → contrib$_1^{(i)}$/⊥

return $\mathsf{contrib}_1^{(i)} := w^{(i)}$

Algorithm 12 TIBE .ShareExtract$_2$(id, act, dk$^{(i)}$, state$^{(i)}$) → contrib$_2^{(i)}$/⊥

assert$\{\forall j \in \mathsf{act} \setminus \{i\} : \mathsf{H}_{\mathsf{cmt}}(w^{(j)}) = \mathsf{cmt}^{(j)}\}$
$w := \sum_{j \in \mathsf{act}} w^{(j)}$
$(c_0, c_1) := \mathsf{Decomp}_\beta(t - w)$ ▷ $c_0 \cdot \beta + c_1 = t - w$
$\mathsf{Indices} := \mathsf{VandRecover}([N], \mathsf{act})$ ▷ i is assigned one index Indices$[i]$
$s^{(i)}, s'^{(i)} := \mathsf{dk}^{(i)}\,[\mathsf{Indices}[i]]$
$\mathbf{s}^{(i)} := \left[s'^{(i)} \ s^{(i)} \ 0 \ 0\right]^T$ ▷ $\mathbf{s}^{(i)} \in R^4$ is the partial signing key assigned to i
$\mathbf{z}^{(i)} = \mathbf{p}^{(i)} + c_0 \cdot \mathbf{s}^{(i)}$
return $\mathsf{contrib}_2^{(i)} := \mathbf{z}^{(i)}$

Algorithm 13 TIBE .ShareVerify(ek, id, act, $\{(w^{(j)}, \mathbf{z}^{(j)})\}_{j \in \mathsf{act}}, i$) → $\{1, \perp\}$

$w := \sum_{j \in \mathsf{act}} w^{(j)}$
$(c_0, c_1) := \mathsf{Decomp}_\beta(t - w)$
$\mathsf{Indices} := \mathsf{VandRecover}([N], \mathsf{act})$ ▷ User i is assigned one index Indices$[i]$
$b^{(i)} := \mathsf{pek}[\mathsf{Indices}[i]]$
assert$\{\{\left[1 \ a \ b \ \mathsf{H}_{\mathsf{id}}(\mathsf{id})\right] \cdot \mathbf{z}^{(i)} = w^{(i)} + c_0 \cdot b^{(i)}\}\}$ ▷ Equality
assert$\{\{\left\|\mathbf{z}^{(i)}\right\| \leq B_{\mathsf{ind}}\}\}$ ▷ Shortness
return 1 ▷ Accept if both asserts pass

Algorithm 14 TIBE .Combine(ct, ek, id, act, $\{(w^{(i)}, \mathbf{z}^{(i)})\}_{i \in \mathsf{act}}$) → msg/⊥

for $i \in \mathsf{act}$ **do**
  assert$\{$TIBE .ShareVerify(ek, id, act, $\{(w^{(j)}, \mathbf{z}^{(j)})\}_{j \in \mathsf{act}}, i)\}$
$\mathbf{z} := \left(\sum_{i \in \mathsf{act}} \mathbf{z}^{(i)}\right) + \left[c_1 \ 0 \ c_0 \ 0\right]^T$
$\mathbf{z}' := \left[z_1 \ z_2 \ z_3\right]^T$ ▷ $\mathbf{z}'$ drops the first coefficient of $\mathbf{z}$
return $\mathsf{msg} := \mathsf{Decode}\left(v - \mathbf{u}^T \cdot \mathbf{z}'\right)$

Fig. 5. TIBE algorithms for threshold decryption.

Lemma 11. *Let δ' be the target correctness probability of share verification in Algorithm 13. Given* TIBE *as described in Figs. 4 and 5 with* $\tau \geq 1 + \sqrt{\frac{4 \log \delta'}{3d}}$, $\sigma_{\mathbf{s}} \geq \eta_\epsilon(\mathcal{R}^2)$ *and norm bound* B_{ind} *given as*

$$B_{\mathsf{ind}} = \tau \left(\sqrt{d\,(2\,\sigma_{\mathbf{p}}^2 + {\sigma'_{\mathbf{p}}}^2)} + \frac{d\,q}{2\beta} \cdot \sqrt{2\,d\,(\log N + 1)}\,\sigma_{\mathbf{s}} \right),$$

where d is the ring degree, ($\sigma_{\mathbf{p}}$,$\sigma'_{\mathbf{p}}$) (resp. $\sigma_{\mathbf{s}}$) is the Gaussian width of the masks (resp. secret), q is the modulus, β is the decomposition parameter and N is the number of parties. Then, TIBE *has* $(\log N + 1)\epsilon + \delta' \simeq \delta'$ *extraction share correctness.*

4.2 Decryption Correctness

We now study the decryption correctness of our TIBE , cf. Definition 5. Due to page constraints, its proof is deferred to the full version of this paper [10].

Lemma 12. *Let δ' be the target correctness probability of share verification in Algorithm 13. Given* TIBE *as described in Figs. 4 and 5 with* $\tau \geq 1 + \sqrt{\frac{4(\log \delta' + \log 2)}{2d}}$, $\min(\sigma_{\mathbf{p}}, \sigma_{\mathbf{p}'}) \geq \sqrt{1 + 1/(T-1)} \cdot \eta_\varepsilon(\mathcal{R})$ *and norm bounds B_h and B_r given as*

$$B_h = \tau \sqrt{T\,d\,(2\,\sigma_{\mathbf{p}}^2 + {\sigma'_{\mathbf{p}}}^2)} + \frac{d\,q}{2\,\beta}\left(\tau\sqrt{2\,d}\,\sigma_{\mathbf{s}} + 1\right) + B_1,$$

$$B_r = \sqrt{2(\log \delta' + 1 + \log(8d))}\,\sigma_{\mathbf{r}},$$

where T is the number of parties, d is the ring degree, $\sigma_{\mathbf{p}}$ (resp. $\sigma_{\mathbf{s}}$ and $\sigma_{\mathbf{r}}$) is the Gaussian width of the masks (resp. secret and encryption randomness), q is the modulus, β is the decomposition parameter and B_1 is a norm bound on c_1. Furthermore assume that TIBE *is δ' extraction share correct. If $(B_h + 1) \cdot B_r \leq \lfloor q/4 \rfloor$, then,* TIBE *has* $\delta := T(\delta'+1) + 2 \cdot 2^{-\kappa} + 8\varepsilon \cdot (T-1)$ *decryption correctness.*

We highlight that B_h is mainly impacted by $\sqrt{T}\sigma_{\mathbf{p}}$.

4.3 Extraction Share Robustness

We now analyse whether the TIBE correctly decrypts, even if an adversary can maliciously generated key extraction shares (which still pass the share verification algorithm). Note that we still assume quasi-honestly generated ciphertexts. More concretely, we require the encryption randomness to come from RSpace (where honestly generated randomness lies in RSpace with overwhelming probability). We call this extraction share robustness, as defined in Definition 7.

First, note that our TIBE has $\mathsf{RDistr} = D_{\mathcal{R},\sigma_{\mathbf{r}}} \times D_{\mathcal{R}^{1\times 3},\sigma_{\mathbf{r}}} \times D_{\mathcal{R},\sigma_{\mathbf{r}}}$. By setting $\mathsf{RSpace} = \{(r, \mathbf{e}, e') \in R^{1\times 5} \colon \left\|(r, \mathbf{e}, e')^T\right\|_2 \leq \tau\,\sigma_{\mathbf{r}}\,\sqrt{5d}\}$, for $\tau \geq 1 + \sqrt{\frac{4(\kappa+1)\log 2}{5d}}$ we have by Lemma 8 that honestly sampled encryption randomness from RDistr lies in RSpace with overwhelming probability.

Lemma 13. *Let δ' be the target correctness probability of share verification in Algorithm 13. Given* TIBE *as described in Figs. 4 and 5 with $\tau \geq 1 + \sqrt{\frac{4(\log \delta' + \log 2)}{2d}}$ and norm bounds B_m and B given as*

$$B_m = TB_{\mathsf{ind}} + B_0 + B_1, \text{ and } B = \tau\, \sigma_{\mathbf{r}}\, \sqrt{5d}\, \sigma_{\mathbf{r}},$$

where T is the number of parties, $\sigma_{\mathbf{r}}$ is the Gaussian width of the encryption randomness, B_0 (resp. B_1 and B_{ind}) is a norm bound on c_0 (resp. c_1 and $\mathbf{z}^{(i)}$). Furthermore assume that TIBE *is δ' extraction share correct. If $B \cdot (1 + B_m) \leq \lfloor q/4 \rfloor$, then, the advantage of any PPT adversary $\mathcal{A}$ against the extraction share robustness game for* TIBE *is at most $T(\delta' + 1)$.*

Note that B_m is dominated by $T\sigma_{\mathbf{p}}$, as opposed to $\sqrt{T}\sigma_{\mathbf{p}}$ in the honest case considered for correctness in Lemma 12. Due to page constraints, its proof is deferred to the full version of this paper [10].

Regarding the norm bounds B_0 on c_0 and B_1 on c_1, w.o.p. it holds

$$B_0 = \frac{q}{\beta}\sqrt{\frac{d}{12}}(1 + o(1)), \qquad B_1 = \beta\sqrt{\frac{d}{12}}(1 + o(1)) \tag{11}$$

5 TIBE Security

Before starting with our security proof, we recall the definition of functional simulation of a pair of key generation and sharing algorithms. It is a simplified version of the one in [18], tailored to a trusted setup.

Definition 12 **([18]).** *A key generation and sharing algorithms* KG *and* Share *together with a function oracle* Eval *are called functionally simulatable if there exist efficient functions* SimShare *and* SimEval *s.t. no PPT adversary $\mathcal{A}$ has a non-negligible advantage in the experiment defined in Fig. 6. We denote the advantage of an adversary $\mathcal{A}$ in $\mathsf{Exp}^{\mathsf{KG\text{-}sim}}_{\mathcal{A},\mathsf{KG},\mathsf{Share},\mathsf{Eval}}(1^\kappa)$ as $\mathsf{Adv}^{\mathsf{KG\text{-}sim}}_{\mathcal{A},\mathsf{KG},\mathsf{Share},\mathsf{Eval}}$.*

Lemma 14 **([9, Lemma B.2]).** *Let* KG *and* Share *be as defined in Algorithm 6 and let* $\mathsf{ShareExtract}_i$ *be as in Fig. 5. Then there exists a constant $Q_v = Q_v(T, N, Q_{\mathsf{Dec}})$ (see [5] Theorem 1) such that*

$$\mathsf{Adv}^{\mathsf{KG\text{-}sim}}_{\mathcal{A},\mathsf{KG},\mathsf{Share},\{\mathsf{ShareExtract}_i\}_i} \leq \mathsf{Hint\text{-}RLWE}^{TQ_{dec}+Q_v,\sqrt{\sigma_{\mathbf{p}}^2-\sigma_{\mathbf{p}}'^2},\sigma_{\mathbf{s}},\beta}_{\mathcal{R},q,m,\sigma_{\mathbf{s}}}.$$

Theorem 2. *Let* TIBE *be the scheme defined in Fig. 4 and Fig. 5. Let $\mathcal{R} = \mathbb{Z}[X]/(X^d + 1)$ be a ring of degree d, and q be a prime number. Let $\sigma, \sigma_{\mathbf{s}}, \sigma_{\mathbf{p}}, \sigma'_{\mathbf{p}}, \beta > 0$, $\varepsilon \in (0, 1)$. Suppose that:*

$$\min(\sigma_{\mathbf{p}}, \sigma'_{\mathbf{p}}) > 1.17q^{1/2} \cdot \eta_\varepsilon(R^2). \tag{12}$$

$$(\sigma'_{\mathbf{p}}/\sigma_{\mathbf{p}}) \cdot \sqrt{\sigma_{\mathbf{p}}^2 - \sigma_{\mathbf{p}}'^2} \geq \eta_\varepsilon(\mathcal{R}). \tag{13}$$

$\mathsf{Exp}^{\mathsf{KG\text{-}sim}}_{\mathcal{A},\mathsf{KG},\mathsf{Share},\mathsf{Eval}}(1^\kappa)$

$\mathsf{cor} \leftarrow \mathcal{A}(1^\kappa)$
assert $|\mathsf{cor}| = T - 1$
$(\mathsf{ek}, \mathsf{dk}) \leftarrow \mathsf{KG}(1^\kappa)$, $b \leftarrow \{0, 1\}$
if $b = 0 : \left(\{\mathsf{dk}^{(i)}\}_{i \in [N]}, \mathsf{aux}\right) \leftarrow \mathsf{Share}(\mathsf{dk})$
  $b' \leftarrow \mathcal{A}^{\mathsf{Eval}}\left(\mathsf{ek}, \{\mathsf{dk}^{(i)}\}_{i \in \mathsf{cor}}\right)$
else $\left(\{\mathsf{dk}^{(i)}\}_{i \in \mathsf{cor}}, \mathsf{aux}\right) \leftarrow \mathsf{SimShare}(\mathsf{ek}, \mathsf{cor})$
  $b' \leftarrow \mathcal{A}^{\mathsf{SimEval}}\left(\mathsf{ek}, \{\mathsf{dk}^{(i)}\}_{i \in \mathsf{cor}}\right)$
return $b = b'$

Fig. 6. Security experiment for Functional Simulatability.

Then for any PPT adversary $\mathcal{A}$*:*

$$\begin{aligned}
\mathsf{Adv}^{\mathsf{sel\text{-}ID\text{-}IND}}_{\mathcal{A},\mathsf{TIBE}}(\kappa) \leq {} & (Q_{\mathsf{Dec}} + Q_{\mathsf{H}_{\mathsf{id}}}) \cdot \mathsf{Adv}^{\mathsf{NTRU}_{\mathcal{R},q}}_{\mathcal{A}_1}(\kappa) \\
& + \mathsf{Adv}^{\mathsf{Hint\text{-}RLWE}^{TQ_{dec}+Q_v, \sqrt{\sigma_{\mathbf{p}}^2 - \sigma_{\mathbf{p}}'^2}, \sigma_{\mathbf{s}}, \beta}_{\mathcal{R},q,m,\sigma_{\mathbf{s}}}}_{\mathcal{A}_2}(\kappa) + \mathsf{Adv}^{\mathsf{RLWE}_{\mathcal{R},3,q,\sigma}}_{\mathcal{A}_3}(\kappa) \\
& + Q_{\mathsf{Dec}} \cdot O(\varepsilon) + Q_{\mathsf{Dec}} \cdot (T\, Q_{\mathsf{Dec}} + Q_{H_{\mathsf{cmt}}}) \cdot (q^{-d} + \mathrm{negl}(\kappa)) \\
& + \frac{(Q_{\mathsf{Dec}} + Q_{H_{\mathsf{cmt}}})^2 + Q_{H_{\mathsf{cmt}}} \cdot T \cdot Q_{\mathsf{Dec}}}{2^{2\kappa}}
\end{aligned}$$

where adversaries $\mathcal{A}_3$ *to* $\mathcal{A}_1$ *run in approximately the same time as* $\mathcal{A}$.

Proof. Consider a sequence of hybrids.

Hyb_0 *(*$\mathsf{sel\text{-}ID\text{-}IND}$ *game):* Identical to the real experiment.

Hyb_1 *(Delay* w_h*):* In this second hybrid we postpone sampling the noise $\mathbf{p}^{(i)}$ from TIBE .$\mathsf{ShareExtract}_0$ to the end of TIBE .$\mathsf{ShareExtract}_1$ for one of the honest parties. For each key extraction query $(\mathsf{id}, \mathsf{act})$ of the adversary we pick an arbitrary honest party in act as "last acting" honest party and denote its index as h. Now in TIBE .$\mathsf{ShareExtract}_0$ the party h samples $\mathsf{cmt}_h \leftarrow \{0,1\}^{2\kappa}$. And in TIBE .$\mathsf{ShareExtract}_1$ after every other party in act has revealed their values $\mathbf{w}^{(i)}$ the last honest party samples $\mathbf{p}^{(h)}$ honestly, computes $\mathbf{w}^{(h)} = \left[1\ a\ b\ \mathsf{H}_{\mathsf{id}}(\mathsf{id})\right] \cdot \mathbf{p}^{(h)}$ and programs $\mathsf{H}_{\mathsf{cmt}}(\mathbf{w}^{(h)}) := \mathsf{cmt}_h$. The advantage of the adversary in this hybrid can only increase if $\mathbf{w}^{(h)}$ has been queried to $\mathsf{H}_{\mathsf{cmt}}(\cdot)$ before. However, $\mathbf{w}^{(h)}$ computed above has high entropy since by Lemma 2 over the vector $[1\ a\ H(id)]$, with $\min(\sigma_{\mathbf{p}}, \sigma'_{\mathbf{p}}) \geq \sqrt{2\pi} \cdot 2d \cdot q^{1/3+2/3d}$ we have $\mathrm{SD}(\mathbf{w}^{(h)}, \mathcal{U}(\mathcal{R}_q)) = \mathrm{negl}(\kappa)$. Hence, the probability of querying a fixed $\mathbf{w}^{(h)}$ is bounded by $q^{-d} + \mathrm{negl}(\kappa)$ and the number of queries to $\mathsf{H}_{\mathsf{cmt}}$ is bounded by $T \cdot Q_{\mathsf{Dec}} + Q_{H_{\mathsf{cmt}}}$ where $Q_{H_{\mathsf{cmt}}}$ denotes the number of direct queries to $\mathsf{H}_{\mathsf{cmt}}$ oracle and $T \cdot Q_{\mathsf{Dec}}$ is a bound on queries made by the Challenger when answering the decryption queries. Then by the union, when we apply this change to every decryption query we get

$$\varepsilon_0 - \varepsilon_1 \leq (q^{-d} + \mathrm{negl}(\kappa)) \cdot Q_{\mathsf{Dec}} \cdot (T \cdot Q_{\mathsf{Dec}} + Q_{H_{\mathsf{cmt}}}).$$

Hyb_2 *(Trapdoors in the hash):* In this hybrid we change the answers of the $\mathsf{H}_{\mathsf{id}}(\cdot)$ oracle for all $\mathsf{id} \neq \mathsf{id}^*$. Now on query id instead of sampling a fresh uniformly random value the oracle samples a pair $(h_{\mathsf{id}}, \mathbf{T}_h) \leftarrow \mathsf{TrapGenNTRU}(1^\kappa)$ and replies with $H_{id}(\mathsf{id}) = h_{\mathsf{id}}$. The rest of the experiment is run as before. The total number of queries to $\mathsf{H}_{\mathsf{id}}(\cdot)$ is $Q_{\mathsf{Dec}} + Q_{\mathsf{H}_{\mathsf{id}}}$, hence, the adversary's advantage can only increase as

$$|\varepsilon_1 - \varepsilon_2| \leq (Q_{\mathsf{Dec}} + Q_{\mathsf{H}_{\mathsf{id}}}) \cdot \mathsf{Adv}_{\mathcal{A}_1}^{\mathsf{NTRU}_{\mathcal{R},q}}(\kappa)$$

where $\mathcal{A}_1$ runs in approximately the same time as $\mathcal{A}$.

Hyb_3 *(Hash collisions):* In this hybrid, we ensure that $\mathsf{H}_{\mathsf{cmt}}$ has no collisions and that the adversary cannot find preimages of hashes cmt_i after passing them to the second signing oracle. We introduce a table Cmt that records every cmt sampled in $\mathsf{H}_{\mathsf{cmt}}$ or in TIBE .$\mathsf{ShareExtract}_0$, as well as those passed to the second signing oracle. Whenever a new hash cmt is sampled, we ensure that it was not previously added to Cmt, or the challenger aborts the game. The view of the adversary differs in Hyb_3 if it was previously able to (i) find a pre-image of a cmt_i after passing it to TIBE .$\mathsf{ShareExtract}_1$, or (ii) if a given cmt was sampled twice. We can bound the probability of (i) due to the pre-image resistance of the hash function $\mathsf{H}_{\mathsf{cmt}}$, and with an union bound over all the commits passed by the adversary to TIBE .$\mathsf{ShareExtract}_1$ which gives a bound $Q_{H_{\mathsf{cmt}}} \cdot T \cdot Q_{\mathsf{Dec}} \cdot 2^{-2\kappa}$. As for (ii), we rely on the collision resistance of $\mathsf{H}_{\mathsf{cmt}}$. Since the commitments are sampled uniformly from $\{0,1\}$, we can bound the probability of (ii) by $(Q_{H_{\mathsf{cmt}}} + Q_{\mathsf{Dec}})^2 \cdot 2^{-2\kappa}$ We conclude that,

$$|\varepsilon_2 - \varepsilon_3| \leq \frac{(Q_{\mathsf{Dec}} + Q_{H_{\mathsf{cmt}}})^2 + Q_{H_{\mathsf{cmt}}} \cdot T \cdot Q_{\mathsf{Dec}}}{2^{2\kappa}}$$

Hyb_4 *(Uniform (c_0, c_1)):* In this hybrid, for each decryption we want to set the "challenge" $u = t - w$ to be uniform and then set the honest $\mathbf{z}^{(i)}$ accordingly. We first sample $u \leftarrow \mathcal{R}_q$, and set $\mathbf{w}^{(h)} = t - u - \sum_{i \in \mathsf{act} \setminus h} \mathbf{w}^{(i)}$, as shown in Hyb_1 the distribution of $w^{(h)}$ is close to uniform so this change is statistical. The behaviour of all parties except h is unchanged, party h however needs to still be able to sample $\mathbf{p}^{(h)}$ from the appropriate distribution. Note that sampling $\mathbf{p}^{(h)} \leftarrow D_{\mathcal{R}^2, \sigma_{\mathbf{p}}} \times \{0\} \times D_{\mathcal{R}, \sigma'_{\mathbf{p}}}$ and setting $w^{(h)} = [1\ a\ b\ \mathsf{H}_{\mathsf{id}}(\mathsf{id})] \cdot \mathbf{p}^{(h)}$ is the same as sampling $w^{(h)}$ from the appropriate distribution (statistically close to uniform) and sampling $\mathbf{p}^{(h)} \leftarrow \mathcal{D}_{\Lambda_q^{\mathbf{w}^{(h)}}(\mathbf{F}_{\mathsf{id}}), \mathbf{\Sigma}}$ with $\mathbf{\Sigma} = \mathsf{diag}(\sigma_{\mathbf{p}}, \sigma_{\mathbf{p}}, \sigma'_{\mathbf{p}})$ and $\mathbf{F}_{\mathsf{id}} = [1\ a\ \mathsf{H}_{\mathsf{id}}(\mathsf{id})]$. Using Lemma 4 this is statistically close to sampling $\tilde{\mathbf{p}} = (\mathbf{p}_0^{(h)}, \mathbf{p}_1^{(h)}) \leftarrow \mathcal{D}_{\mathcal{R}^2, \sigma_{\mathbf{p}}}$ and $\mathbf{p}_3^{(h)} \leftarrow \mathcal{D}_{\Lambda_q^{\mathbf{w}^{(h)} - \mathbf{F}\tilde{\mathbf{p}}}(\mathsf{H}_{\mathsf{id}}(\mathsf{id})), \sigma'_{\mathbf{p}}}$, with $\mathbf{F} = [1\ a]$. We want to use the trapdoor introduced in the previous hybrid to sample this preimage, since the trapdoor is for the matrix $[1\ \mathsf{H}_{\mathsf{id}}(\mathsf{id})]$ we consider the following transformation: First sample $\tilde{\mathbf{p}} = (\mathbf{p}_0^{(h)}, \mathbf{p}_1^{(h)}) \leftarrow \mathcal{D}_{\mathcal{R},\sqrt{\sigma_{\mathbf{p}}^2 - {\sigma'_{\mathbf{p}}}^2}} \times \mathcal{D}_{\mathcal{R},\sigma_{\mathbf{p}}}$ then sample $(\mathbf{x}, \mathbf{p}_3^{(h)}) \leftarrow \mathcal{D}_{\Lambda_q^{\mathbf{w}^{(h)} - \mathbf{F}\tilde{\mathbf{p}}}([1\ \mathsf{H}_{\mathsf{id}}(\mathsf{id})]),\sigma'_{\mathbf{p}}}$ and output $(\mathbf{p}_0^{(h)} + \mathbf{x}, \mathbf{p}_1^{(h)}, \mathbf{p}_3^{(h)})$. By Lemma 5, as long as the smoothing condition in Eq. (13) holds, this modification is statistically unnoticeable. The NTRU trapdoor can sample such a distribution according to Lemma 6 if $\sigma_{\mathbf{p}} > \sigma'_{\mathbf{p}} \geq 1.17\sqrt{q}\eta_\epsilon(\mathcal{R}^2)$. Gathering the various bounds, the advantage of the adversary can increase by at most

$$|\varepsilon_3 - \varepsilon_4| \leq (\mathrm{negl}(\kappa) + 2\,\varepsilon) \cdot Q_{\mathsf{Dec}}.$$

Hyb_5 *(Secret Sharing):* Let SimShare and SimShareExtract be as per Lemma 14.

In this hybrid we sample the public key without a trapdoor (i.e. $b \leftarrow \mathcal{R}_q$) and use SimShare to simulate the corrupt key shares. Using Lemma 14 we observe that all honest partial secrets $(s^{(i)}, {s^{(i)}}')$ can be written either as a linear combination of the leaked secrets, or as (s, s') plus a linear combination of the leaked secrets. Meaning that there are $Q_v(T, N)$ hints of the form $\mathbf{s} + \mathbf{r}$ (corresponding to the leakages) and at most $T \cdot Q_{\mathsf{Dec}}$ hints of the form $\mathbf{s} \cdot c + \mathbf{p}$. Since we do not have access to the secret keys, the partial decryption oracles are simulated using the corresponding SimShareExtract. Then by Lemma 14 the advantage changes as

$$|\varepsilon_4 - \varepsilon_5| \leq \mathsf{Adv}^{\mathsf{KG\text{-}sim}}_{\mathcal{A}_2,\mathsf{KG},\mathsf{Share},\{\mathsf{ShareExtract}_i\}_i} \leq \mathsf{Adv}_{\mathcal{A}_2}^{\mathsf{Hint\text{-}RLWE}_{\mathcal{R},q,m,\sigma_{\mathbf{s}}}^{Q_v + TQ_{dec}, \sqrt{\sigma_{\mathbf{p}}^2 - {\sigma'_{\mathbf{p}}}^2}, \sigma_{\mathbf{s}}, \beta}}.$$

Hyb_6 *(Ciphertext RLWE):* Note that now $\mathbf{F}_{\mathsf{id}^*} = [a\ \ b\,\mathsf{H}_{\mathsf{id}}(\mathsf{id}^*)]$ is perfectly random and the experiment can be simulated efficiently. Hence, we apply the RLWE assumption to the challenge ciphertext. As a result, the challenge plaintext is masked by a uniformly random value and the advantage in this experiment is $\varepsilon_5 = 0$. The advantage change can also be bounded as

$$|\varepsilon_5 - \varepsilon_6| \leq \mathsf{Adv}_{\mathcal{A}_3}^{\mathsf{RLWE}_{\mathcal{R},3,q,\sigma_{\mathbf{r}}}}(\kappa).$$

where $\mathcal{A}_3$ runs in approximately the same time as $\mathcal{A}$. □

On Achieving Adaptive Corruptions. In all security notions we consider in this work, the adversary has to decide which $T-1$ parties to corrupt at the very beginning of the game. This is usually called *static* corruptions. Closer to the real world is the concept of *adaptive* corruptions where the adversary can decide during the game which parties they want to corrupt, in particular after already having seen partial key extraction shares. In general, the latter is significantly harder to achieve as it requires the shares of the yet-honest parties given to the adversary during key extraction queries to stay consistent even after the set of corrupted parties changes. Interestingly, we observe that [34] achieves security against adaptive corruptions, without making this explicit in their work. The main reason is that simulating communications of honest parties is very easy thanks to the one-time masks issued by a random oracle.

However, when replacing the masks-with-Shamir-sharing approach by the VSS as done in this work, this argument does not work anymore and we are not able to prove security against adaptive corruptions. Let us give some more intuition on why VSS seems difficult to use in an adaptive corruption context. During the security proof we simulate both the corrupted secret shares and the communication of honest parties during the interactive key extraction procedure. To do the simulation correctly, we need to know which parties are corrupted and which are honest, as it has an impact on where we require RLWE hints. Moreover, in the security proof of VSS, we simulated the honest parties' communication as a function of hints and corrupted key shares. Thus, changing the set of corrupted parties would lead to inconsistent simulation.

If one prioritises security against adaptive corruptions over share robustness, one can modify our scheme as follows (to get closer again to [34]): set $\mathbf{z}^{(i)} = \mathbf{p}^{(i)} + c_0 \cdot \mathbf{s}^{(i)} + m_i$, where m_i a blinding one-time mask. When simulating key extraction shares for honest parties, one simply samples random $\mathbf{z}^{(i)}$, conditioned on the sum of all shares, namely $\mathbf{z}$, to fulfill $\left[1\ a\ b\ \mathsf{H}_{\mathsf{id}}(\mathsf{id})\right] \cdot \mathbf{z} = t$. One can again use the notion of "last acting" honest party to achieve this. This simulation does not reveal the masks m_i. When a honest party later gets corrupted, one can simply program the random oracle that controls the masks m_i according to the honest key share $\mathbf{s}^{(i)}$. Note that this is possible, as m_i changes with every key extraction query.

We leave it as an interesting future work to simultaneously achieve security against adaptive corruptions *and* extraction share robustness for our TIBE .

6 Stronger TKEM Decapsulation Consistency

We now prove that the resulting TKEM from the generic BCHK+ transform of [34] fulfills a stronger decapsulation consistency notion as the one proven in [34], if the starting TIBE additionally fulfills extraction share robustness.

6.1 Definition

In Fig. 7a we recall the decryption consistency experiment used in [34] and in Fig. 7b we recall the decryption consistency notion of [21, Def. A.3], which we are achieving in our work.

Note that the experiment in Fig. 7a leads to a stronger security guarantee than the one in Fig. 7b as the adversary wins even if one of the resulting keys is equal to $\perp$. To accommodate for this change, we require the decryption shares to pass the share verification algorithm.

Another change is that we give out all secret key shares to the adversary, whereas [34, Def. 7] only gives out corrupted key shares and unrestricted access to TKEM .ShareDecaps. In general the latter is weaker than the first. However, this limitation was not needed for the proof of [34], they could have given all secret key shares to the adversary.

$\mathsf{Exp}^{\mathsf{weak\text{-}CD}}_{\mathcal{A},\mathsf{TKEM}}(1^\kappa)$

$\mathsf{cor} \leftarrow \mathcal{A}$
assert $|\mathsf{cor}| = T - 1$
$(\mathsf{ek}, \{\mathsf{dk}_i\}_{i \in N}) \leftarrow \mathsf{TKEM.Keygen}(1^\kappa)$
$(\mathsf{ct}, \mathsf{act}, \mathsf{act}', S, S')$
$\quad \leftarrow \mathcal{A}^{\mathsf{TKEM.ShareDecaps}(\cdot)}(\mathsf{ek}, \{\mathsf{dk}_i\}_{i \in \mathsf{cor}})$
$K = \mathsf{TKEM.Combine}(\mathsf{ct}, \mathsf{act}, S)$
$K' = \mathsf{TKEM.Combine}(\mathsf{ct}, \mathsf{act}', S')$
return $\perp \neq K \neq K' \neq \perp$

(a) [34, Def. 7]

$\mathsf{Exp}^{\mathsf{CD}}_{\mathcal{A},\mathsf{TKEM}}(1^\kappa)$

$(\mathsf{ek}, \{\mathsf{dk}_i\}_{i \in N}) \leftarrow \mathsf{TKEM.Keygen}(1^\kappa)$
$(\mathsf{ct}, \mathsf{act}, \mathsf{act}', S, S')$
$\quad \leftarrow \mathcal{A}(\mathsf{ek}, \{\mathsf{dk}_i\}_{i \in [N]})$
for $i \in \mathsf{act}$
$\quad$ **assert** $\mathsf{TKEM.ShareVerify}(\mathsf{ek}, \mathsf{ct}, \mathsf{act}, S, i)$
for $i \in \mathsf{act}'$
$\quad$ **assert** $\mathsf{TKEM.ShareVerify}(\mathsf{ek}, \mathsf{ct}, \mathsf{act}', S', i)$
$K = \mathsf{TKEM.Combine}(\mathsf{ct}, \mathsf{act}, S)$
$K' = \mathsf{TKEM.Combine}(\mathsf{ct}, \mathsf{act}', S')$
return $K \neq K'$

(b) [21, Def. A.3]

Fig. 7. Security experiments for TKEM Decapsulation Consistency

To give some more intuition on why unrestricted access to TKEM $.\mathsf{ShareDecaps}$ is not as powerful as having the honest secret key shares, we can look at our concrete lattice constructions from Sect. 3: the adversary can query TKEM $.\mathsf{ShareDecaps}$ on the same ciphertext many times, providing them with many short preimages of the same matrix $[1\ a\ b\ H_{\mathsf{id}}(\mathsf{id} = \mathsf{vk})]$ for a fixed target t. This can be seen as a trapdoor for this identity-depending matrix. However, this is not enough to recover honest secret key shares, which are small preimages of the matrix $[1\ a\ b]$.

6.2 Proof

Lemma 15. *Let $G_{\mathsf{fo}}\colon \{0,1\}^* \to \{0,1\}^\kappa$ be modeled as a random oracle and let $Q_{G_{\mathsf{fo}}} \geq 2$ denote the number of queries to it. Let* TKEM *be the scheme obtained as detailed in Fig. 2. If the underlying* TIBE *is γ-spread and extraction share robust, so fulfills the resulting* TKEM *decapsulation consistency. More concretely, for any PPT adversary $\mathcal{A}$ against $\mathsf{Exp}^{\mathsf{CD}}_{\mathcal{A},\mathsf{TKEM}}$ we can build a PPT adversary $\mathcal{B}$ against $\mathsf{Exp}^{\mathsf{Robust}}_{\mathcal{B},\mathsf{TIBE}}$ such that*

$$\mathsf{Adv}^{\mathsf{CD}}_{\mathcal{A},\mathsf{TKEM}} \leq \frac{Q_{F_{\mathsf{fo}}} \cdot (Q_{F_{\mathsf{fo}}} - 1)}{2} 2^{-\gamma} + \mathsf{Adv}^{\mathsf{Robust}}_{\mathcal{B},\mathsf{TIBE}}\,.$$

Proof. Let $\mathcal{B}$ be an adversary in $\mathsf{Exp}^{\mathsf{Robust}}_{\mathcal{B},\mathsf{TIBE}}$ and $\mathcal{A}$ an adversary in $\mathsf{Exp}^{\mathsf{CD}}_{\mathcal{A},\mathsf{TKEM}}$. Upon receiving the public evaluation key ek and all secret key shares $(\mathsf{dk}_i)_{i \in [N]}$, the reduction $\mathcal{B}$ forwards it to $\mathcal{A}$. Now, assume $\mathcal{A}$ wins in $\mathsf{Exp}^{\mathsf{CD}}_{\mathcal{A},\mathsf{TKEM}}$. That is, they output $(\mathsf{ct}, \mathsf{act}, \mathsf{act}', S, S')$ such that all decapsulation shares verify for both (act, S) and (act', S'), and $K \neq K'$, where $K = \mathsf{TKEM}$ $.\mathsf{Combine}(\mathsf{ct}, \mathsf{act}, S)$ and $K' = \mathsf{TKEM}$ $.\mathsf{Combine}(\mathsf{ct}, \mathsf{act}', S')$.

We distinguish two cases. In the first case neither K nor K' equals $\perp$. This is essentially the case considered in [34]. In the second case, exactly one of the keys equals $\perp$.

Case 1) As neither K nor K' equals $\perp$, all assert checks in TKEM .Combine from the BCHK+ transform detailed in Fig. 2 pass. In particular, when running TKEM .Combine, the reduction $\mathcal{B}$ recovers $\mathsf{msg}, \mathsf{msg}'$ where $K = H_{\mathsf{fo}}(\mathsf{msg} \| \mathsf{ct})$ and $K' = H_{\mathsf{fo}}(\mathsf{msg}' \| \mathsf{ct})$ but $\mathsf{msg} \neq \mathsf{msg}'$. At the same time, both messages lead to ct, i.e., $\mathsf{TKEM}\ .\mathsf{Encaps}(\mathsf{ek}, \mathsf{vk}, \mathsf{msg}; G_{\mathsf{fo}}(\mathsf{msg})) = \mathsf{TKEM}\ .\mathsf{Encaps}(\mathsf{ek}, \mathsf{vk}, \mathsf{msg}'; G_{\mathsf{fo}}(\mathsf{msg}')) = \mathsf{ct}$. As done in [34], one can now distinguish two subcases. Either both msg and msg' have already been queried to G_{fo} or one of them has not been queried to G_{fo}. By using the γ-spreadness of TIBE , we can upper bound the probability in both subcases by $\frac{Q_{F_{\mathsf{fo}}} \cdot (Q_{F_{\mathsf{fo}}} - 1)}{2} 2^{-\gamma}$. Note that the argument is purely probabilistic and does not depend on $\mathcal{A}$ having access to only corrupted (as proven in [34]) or all secret key shares (as proven in our work).

Case 2) Without loss of generality, we assume $K' = \perp$ and $K \neq \perp$. As $K \neq \perp$ we know as above that the assert checks in TKEM .Combine passed and hence $K = H_{\mathsf{fo}}(\mathsf{msg} \| \mathsf{ct})$ and $\mathsf{rand} = G_{\mathsf{fo}}(\mathsf{msg})$. The reduction $\mathcal{B}$ then forwards the tuple $(\mathsf{msg}, \mathsf{vk}, \mathsf{rand}, \mathsf{ct}, \mathsf{act}', S')$ as output for the robustness game of the TIBE as defined in Fig. 1e. We now argue that this output is a valid forgery in the robustness game of the TIBE . First, note that $\mathsf{rand} = G_{\mathsf{fo}}(\mathsf{msg})$, with rand following the randomness distribution RDistr and hence lying in RSpace with overwhelming probability. Second, by the winning condition of the decapsulation consistency game, the partial shares of TKEM .ShareVerify have to verify, which implies that the partial shares of TIBE .ShareVerify verify. It also implies that the signature verification passes. Lastly, $\mathsf{TIBE}\ .\mathsf{Combine}(\mathsf{ct}, \mathsf{vk}, \mathsf{act}', S') \neq \mathsf{msg}$. Else $K' = K$, leading to a contraction. □

7 Instantiation

Parameter selection for our scheme with semi-honest correctness (resp. malicious correctness) is performed by ensuring that both Theorem 2 and Lemma 12 (resp. Lemma 13) provide negligible bounds for the adversary's advantage and the decryption failure probability.

Recall from Theorem 2 that the adversary's advantage is upper-bounded as in the equation below. We study each term in one paragraph, then we study correctness, then we conclude.

$$\mathsf{Adv}^{\mathsf{sel\text{-}ID\text{-}IND}}_{\mathcal{A},\mathsf{TIBE}}(\kappa) \leq \overbrace{\mathsf{Adv}_{\mathcal{A}_2}^{\mathsf{Hint\text{-}RLWE}\,{}^{Q_v, Q_M, \sqrt{\sigma_{\mathbf{P}}^2 - \sigma_{\mathbf{P}}'^2}, \sigma_{\mathbf{s}}, \beta}_{\mathcal{R}, q, m, \sigma_{\mathbf{s}}}}(\kappa)}^{\text{ct is pseudorandom}} + \overbrace{\mathsf{Adv}_{\mathcal{A}_3}^{\mathsf{RLWE}_{\mathcal{R},3,q,\sigma_{\mathbf{r}}}}(\kappa)}^{\text{ek is pseudorandom}} \quad (14)$$

$$(Q_H + Q_{\mathsf{Dec}}) \cdot \underbrace{\mathsf{Adv}_{\mathcal{A}_1}^{\mathsf{NTRU}_{\mathcal{R},q}}(\kappa)}_{\text{Embed trapdoor}} + \mathrm{negl}(\kappa). \quad (15)$$

RLWE. The pseudorandomness of the ciphertext ctis quantified by the hardness of $\mathsf{RLWE}_{\mathcal{R},3,q,\sigma_{\mathbf{r}}}$. We can estimate it by using standard tools such as the lattice estimator by Albrecht et al. [3].

Hint-RLWE. Following the reduction of Lemma 9, $\mathsf{Hint\text{-}RLWE}^{Q_v,Q_M,\sqrt{\sigma_{\mathbf{p}}^2-\sigma_{\mathbf{p}}'^2},\sigma_{\mathbf{s}},\beta}_{\mathcal{R},q,m,\sigma_{\mathbf{s}}}$ is no easier than $RLWE_{\mathcal{R},q,1,\sigma_0}$, where $\frac{1}{\sigma_0^2} \le 2\left(\frac{1+Q_v(T,N)}{\sigma_{\mathbf{s}}^2} + \frac{B_{\mathsf{hint}}(1+o(1))}{\sigma_{\mathbf{p}}^2}\right)$, $B_{\mathsf{hint}} = \frac{Q\,d\,M^2}{12}$, $M = 2\left\lceil \frac{q-1}{2\beta} \right\rceil + 1$, and Q_v as in [5] Theorem 1. As typical in other works, we ignore the factor 2 in $1/\sigma_0^2$ which seems to be a proof artefact. We also set $\sigma_{\mathbf{s}} = \Omega(\sqrt{Q_v(T,N)}) = \omega(\sqrt{B_{\mathsf{hint}}} \cdot \sigma_{\mathbf{p}})$, so that it has a negligible influence on σ_0. All in all, we have:

$$\sigma_0 \approx \sigma_{\mathbf{p}}/\sqrt{B_{\mathsf{hint}}} \approx \sigma_{\mathbf{p}}\sqrt{\frac{12}{Q\,d\,M^2}} \approx \sigma_{\mathbf{p}}\frac{\beta}{q}\sqrt{\frac{12}{Q\,n}}. \quad (16)$$

Eq. (16) incentivises us to take $\sigma_{\mathbf{p}}$ large. This condition directly subsumes the one of Theorem 2 are fulfilled. Again, we estimate the hardness of $\mathsf{Hint\text{-}RLWE}_{\mathcal{R},q,\sigma_0}$ using standard tools [3].

NTRU. The multiple instances of NTRUallow us to embed a trapdoor in $H_{\mathsf{id}}(\mathsf{id})$ (one for each identity queried). The hardness of $\mathsf{NTRU}$is well-studied, and tools for estimating it are included in Albrecht et al.'s lattice estimator [3].

Note that our choices of q are very large. This raises the question of whether overstretched NTRU attacks [2,22,32] apply. Our experiments with [3] show that it is not the case. This is not surprising since we can take a large standard deviation σ for the secrets f, g, namely $\sigma \ge \sqrt{q/2n}$ as in Falcon [42]. The state-of-the-art attacks [28] states that on overstretched NTRU attacks become relevant when:

$$0.0058 \cdot \sigma^2 \cdot n^{2.484}/q < 1. \quad (17)$$

In our case, the left side of Eq. (17) is no smaller than $0.0029 \cdot n^{1.484}$, which gives us a comfortable margin.

Correctness. In the semi-honest (resp. malicious) setting, we apply Lemma 12 (resp. Lemma 13) and therefore set our parameters so that their requirements apply. In practice, $B_{\mathsf{ind}} \approx \tau\sqrt{3n}\,\sigma_{\mathbf{p}}$. Note that Lemmas 12 and 13 guarantee decryption correctness with probability at least $1-\delta$. In our case it suffices to set δ to be small (say, 2^{-30}), not negligible. Indeed, the BCHK$^+$ transform guarantees CCA security even in the presence of decryption failures.

Bit Dropping. We may apply bit dropping on four ring elements: the encryption key b, the first ciphertext v, the two last elements of the second ciphertext (u_1, u_2). This has the benefit of decreasing the public key size and ciphertext size. Let us note $\delta_b, \delta_v, \delta_{u_1}, \delta_{u_2}$ the (deterministic) errors incurred by bit-dropping. This error addition has absolutely no negative impact on the security analysis, however it might impact correctness since the decryption equation becomes:

$$v - \mathbf{u} \cdot \mathbf{z}' = \mathsf{Encode}(\mathsf{msg}) + (e' + \delta_v) + r \cdot (z_0 + c_0 \cdot \delta_b) \quad (18)$$
$$- (e_0 \cdot z_1 + (e_1 + \delta_{u_1}) \cdot c_0 + (e_2 + \delta_{u_2}) \cdot p_3) \quad (19)$$

As long as $\|\delta_v + c_0 (r \cdot \delta_b - \delta_{u_1}) - \delta_{u_2} \cdot p_3\|_\infty = o(q)$ w.o.p., then bit-dropping will have a negligible impact on correctness. We note $\nu_b, \nu_{u_1}, \nu_{u_2}, \nu_v$ the bits dropped in b, u_1, u_2, v respectively.

Coefficient Dropping. Since we encapsulate a key of κ bits, we only need to send κ coefficients of v. We can therefore drop the remaining $n - \kappa$ coefficients of v, which further decrease the ciphertext size.

How to Select Parameters. Selecting parameters is a multi-dimensional optimisation process, and it can seem obscure. We explain here our selection process. We recall Hardy's asymptotic notation: $a \asymp b$ is shorthand for $a = \Theta(b)$.

We select $\sigma_\mathbf{r} \asymp \sigma_0 \asymp 1$ (recall that σ_0 is found in the RLWEinstance reduced from Hint-RLWE reduction), as we find that the resulting RLWE instances have κ bits of security against the most common attacks as long as $d \asymp \kappa \cdot \log q$. This seems somewhat optimal, as setting $\sigma_\mathbf{r} = o(1)$ quickly opens the door to hybrid attacks, while setting $\sigma_\mathbf{r} = \omega(1)$ degrades correctness (and similarly for σ_0).

From Eq. (16), this entails $\sigma_\mathbf{p} \asymp \frac{q}{\beta}\sqrt{Q\,d}$ and $\sigma_\mathbf{s} = \omega(1)$. We also require $\sigma_\mathbf{s} = o\left(\frac{\beta}{d\,q\,\sqrt{\log N}}\sigma_\mathbf{p}\right)$, so that $B_\mathsf{ind} \asymp \sqrt{d}\,\sigma_\mathbf{p} \asymp \frac{q\,d}{\beta}\sqrt{Q}$, see the full version [10] for more details.

Next, we set β. Recall that $B_1 \asymp \beta\sqrt{d}$. Setting β as high as possible is good for the Hint-RLWE reduction (see Eq. (16)) but may increase $\|\mathbf{z}\|$, see the full version [10] for more details. We set $B_1 \asymp \sqrt{T}\,B_\mathsf{ind}$ for the honest (that is, no robustness) setting, and $B_1 \asymp T\,B_\mathsf{ind}$ for the robust extraction shares setting, so that B_1 only increases $\|\mathbf{z}\|$ by a constant factor. This gives:

$$\textit{Non-Robust setting:} \quad \beta^2 \asymp q\sqrt{d\,T\,Q} \quad (20)$$
$$\textit{Robust setting:} \quad \beta^2 \asymp q\,T\sqrt{d\,Q} \quad (21)$$

Finally, we study correctness, and seek to minimise q. In the non-robust setting, Lemma 12 guarantee correctness if $q \asymp \sqrt{T}\,B_\mathsf{ind}\,\sqrt{\kappa}\,\sigma_\mathbf{r} \asymp \frac{q\,d}{\beta}\sqrt{Q\,T\,\kappa}$, which implies $\beta \asymp d\sqrt{Q\,T\,\kappa}$. In the robust setting, Lemma 13 guarantee correctness if $q \asymp T\,B_\mathsf{ind}\,\sqrt{d}\,\sigma_\mathbf{r} \asymp \frac{q\,T\,d}{\beta}\sqrt{Q\,d}$, which implies $\beta \asymp d\,T\sqrt{Q\,d}$. In summary:

$$\textit{Non-Robust setting:} \quad \beta^2 \asymp q\sqrt{d\,T\,Q} \asymp d^2\,Q\,T\,\kappa \quad \Rightarrow \quad q \asymp d^{3/2}\,\kappa\sqrt{Q\,T} \quad (22)$$
$$\textit{Robust setting:} \quad \beta^2 \asymp q\,T\sqrt{d\,Q} \asymp d^3\,T^2\,Q \quad \Rightarrow \quad q \asymp d^{5/2}\,T\sqrt{Q} \quad (23)$$

This gives us an asymptotic formula to determine a minimal viable q. We increase d until the underlying RLWEinstances are hard. Finally, bit-dropping has a small impact on correctness as long as $\sigma_{\mathsf{bitdrop}} = O(q/\sqrt{\kappa})$, so we may take $2^{\nu_v} \asymp \sqrt{d}\frac{q}{\beta}2^{\nu_{u_1}} \asymp \sqrt{d}\,q 2^{\nu_{u_2}} \asymp \frac{d\,q}{\beta}2^{\nu_b} \asymp q/\sqrt{\kappa}$.

Parameter Sets. Putting everything together, we obtain parameter sets as detailed in Table 1. The encryption key and ciphertext sizes (in bytes) for our TIBE are given as:

$$|\mathsf{ek}| = (2 \cdot \kappa + d\,(\log q - \nu_b))\,/8 \tag{24}$$

$$|\mathsf{ct}| = (d\,(3 \log q - \nu_{u_1} - \nu_{u_2}) + \kappa(\log q - \nu_v))\,/8 \tag{25}$$

For the TKEM construction, the ciphertext additionally contains a verification key vk and a signature sig. For ML-DSA at NIST security levels 2, and 5, the sum $|\mathsf{vk}| + |\mathsf{sig}|$ is equal to 3732, and 7219, respectively. For Falcon [42] at NIST security levels 1 and 5, the sum $|\mathsf{vk}|+|\mathsf{sig}|$ is equal to 1563, and 3073, respectively.

Table 1. κ is the bit-security, T (resp. Q) is an upper bound on the decryption threshold (resp. number of decryption queries), R = "Extraction Share Robustness", κ_{ek} (resp. κ_{ct}) quantifies the pseudorandomness of the encryption key (resp. ciphertext) in the CoreSVP metric, and $|\mathsf{ek}|$, $|\mathsf{ct}|$ are the sizes in bytes of the TIBE encryption key and ciphertext. Across all parameter sets, we take $T = 32$, $q \approx 2^{50}$, $\sigma_{\mathbf{s}} = 2^{15}$, $\sigma'_{\mathbf{p}} = 2^{27}$ and $\nu_{u_2} = 10$.

Goals				Scheme parameters											Security		Sizes	
κ	R	T	Q	q	d	β	$\sigma_{\mathbf{s}}$	$\sigma_{\mathbf{p}}$	$\sigma'_{\mathbf{p}}$	$\sigma_{\mathbf{r}}$	ν_b	ν_{u_1}	ν_{u_2}	ν_v	κ_{ek}	κ_{ct}	$\lvert\mathsf{ek}\rvert$	$\lvert\mathsf{ct}\rvert$
128	No	32	2^{46}	2^{50}	2048	2^{41}	2^{15}	2^{35}	2^{27}	1	24	29	18	42	128	133	6 688	28 544
128	Yes	32	2^{25}	2^{50}	2048	2^{37}	2^{15}	2^{29}	2^{27}	1	21	27	22	44	132	133	7 456	29 056
256	No	32	2^{46}	2^{50}	4096	2^{40}	2^{15}	2^{36}	2^{27}	1/4	26	30	22	44	263	253	12 352	56 512
256	Yes	32	2^{25}	2^{50}	4096	2^{36}	2^{15}	2^{29}	2^{27}	1/4	22	26	22	44	257	253	14 400	58 560

How to Select Parameters in [34]**.** For comparison, here is a succinct evaluation of [34] with the same methodology we used above. We note that [34] define Gaussians via the notation $\exp(-\pi \cdot \|\mathbf{x}\|^2 / \varsigma^2)$, so their ς correspond to $\sigma\sqrt{2\pi}$. With the notations of [34], we have the following constraints:

1. **Hardness of** RLWE**.** $\mathsf{RLWE}_{R,1,q,\varsigma_{\mathsf{RLWE}}}$ and $\mathsf{RLWE}_{R,7,q,\varsigma}$ need to be hard. Let us take $\varsigma \asymp 1$ and $\varsigma_{\mathsf{RLWE}} \asymp 1$, we can then later set $d = \Omega(\kappa \log q)$ as explained previously. [34] also requires $\varsigma > \eta_\epsilon(R_3)$, but for concrete parameters $\eta_\epsilon(R_3)$ remains small.
2. **Rerandomization.** Equation (10) of [34] requires $\varsigma' \asymp d \cdot \varsigma_{\mathsf{RLWE}} \cdot \varsigma \asymp d$ in order to apply the rerandomization lemma of [30].
3. **Hardness of** Hint-RLWE **.** The hardness of Hint-MLWE requires $\varsigma_0 = \Omega(1)$, therefore we set $\varsigma_a \asymp 1$ and $\varsigma_p \asymp (q/\beta) \cdot \sqrt{Q\,d}$. Maximizing the number of decryption queries Q requires us to take a very large β. There are two other conditions on ς_p, Equations (11) and (12) in [34, Theorem 3], but both are subsumed by the one above.

4. **Correctness.** Finally, correctness is given by [34, Theorem 5], more specifically their Equation (13). The left term of this equation is minimised for $\beta \asymp d^2 \sqrt{qT}\, Q^{1/4}$, in which case Equation (13) of [34] simplifies to $q \asymp d^5 \sqrt{QT}$.

With our methodology, for [34] we obtain the constraint $q \asymp d^5 \sqrt{QT}$. In comparison, our non-robust scheme only requires $q \asymp d^{3/2}\, \kappa \sqrt{QT}$, which is better by a factor $d^{7/2}/\kappa$.

Acknowledgements. We thank the anonymous reviewers as well as Diego F. Aranha for their helpful feedback. Katharina Boudgoust is supported by the French National Research Agency (ANR), under the projects ANR-21-ASTR-0016 AMIRAL, ANR-22-PECY-003 SecureCompute and ANR-25-CE39-4214-01 RELATE. Oleksandra Lapiha was supported by the EPSRC and the UK Government as part of the Centre for Doctoral Training in Cyber Security for the Everyday at Royal Holloway, University of London (EP/S021817/1). Thomas Prest and Rafaël del Pino are supported by the ANR, under the project ANR-25-CE39-4214-01 RELATE.

References

1. Agrawal, S., Boneh, D., Boyen, X.: Efficient Lattice (H)IBE in the Standard Model. In: Gilbert, H. (ed.) EUROCRYPT 2010. LNCS, vol. 6110, pp. 553–572. Springer, Heidelberg (2010). https://doi.org/10.1007/978-3-642-13190-5_28
2. Albrecht, M., Bai, S., Ducas, L.: A Subfield Lattice Attack on Overstretched NTRU Assumptions. In: Robshaw, M., Katz, J. (eds.) CRYPTO 2016. LNCS, vol. 9814, pp. 153–178. Springer, Heidelberg (2016). https://doi.org/10.1007/978-3-662-53018-4_6
3. Albrecht, M.R., Player, R., Scott, S.: On the concrete hardness of Learning with Errors. J. Math. Cryptol. **9**(3), 169–203 (2015)
4. Aranha, D.F., Baum, C., Gjøsteen, K., Silde, T.: Verifiable mix-nets and distributed decryption for voting from lattice-based assumptions. In: Meng, W., Damsgaard Jensen, C., Cremers, C., Kirda, E. (eds.) ACM CCS 2023, pp. 1467–1481. ACM Press (2023)
5. Battagliola, M., Borin, G., Di Crescenzo, G., Meneghetti, A., Persichetti, E.: Enhancing Threshold Group Action Signature Schemes: Adaptive Security and Scalability Improvements. In: Niederhagen, R., Saarinen, MJ.O. (eds.) Post-Quantum Cryptography. PQCrypto 2025. Lecture Notes in Computer Science, vol. 15577. Springer, Cham (2025). https://doi.org/10.1007/978-3-031-86599-2_5
6. Boneh, D., Boyen, X., Halevi, S.: Chosen Ciphertext Secure Public Key Threshold Encryption Without Random Oracles. In: Pointcheval, D. (ed.) CT-RSA 2006. LNCS, vol. 3860, pp. 226–243. Springer, Heidelberg (2006). https://doi.org/10.1007/11605805_15
7. Boneh, D., Canetti, R., Halevi, S., Katz, J.: Chosen-ciphertext security from identity-based encryption. SIAM J. Comput. **36**(5), 1301–1328 (2007)
8. Boneh, D., et al.: Threshold Cryptosystems from Threshold Fully Homomorphic Encryption. In: Shacham, H., Boldyreva, A. (eds.) CRYPTO 2018. LNCS, vol. 10991, pp. 565–596. Springer, Cham (2018). https://doi.org/10.1007/978-3-319-96884-1_19

9. Borin, G., Celi, S., del Pino, R., Espitau, T., Niot, G., Prest, T.: Threshold signatures reloaded: ML-DSA and enhanced raccoon with identifiable aborts. Cryptology ePrint Archive, Paper 2025/1166 (2025)
10. Boudgoust, K., Lapiha, O., del Pino, R., Prest, T.: IND-CCA lattice threshold KEM under 30 KiB. Cryptology ePrint Archive, Paper 2026/021 (2026)
11. Boudgoust, K., Scholl, P.: Simple Threshold (Fully Homomorphic) Encryption from LWE with Polynomial Modulus. In: Guo, J., Steinfeld, R. (eds.) Advances in Cryptology – ASIACRYPT 2023. ASIACRYPT 2023. Lecture Notes in Computer Science, vol. 14438. Springer, Cham (2023). https://doi.org/10.1007/978-981-99-8721-4_12
12. LuÍs, T.A.N., Brandão, Peralta, R.: NIST First Call for Multi-Party Threshold Schemes (2025)
13. Canetti, R., Halevi, S., Katz, J.: Chosen-Ciphertext Security from Identity-Based Encryption. In: Cachin, C., Camenisch, J.L. (eds.) EUROCRYPT 2004. LNCS, vol. 3027, pp. 207–222. Springer, Heidelberg (2004). https://doi.org/10.1007/978-3-540-24676-3_13
14. Cash, D., Hofheinz, D., Kiltz, E., Peikert, C.: Bonsai Trees, or How to Delegate a Lattice Basis. In: Gilbert, H. (ed.) EUROCRYPT 2010. LNCS, vol. 6110, pp. 523–552. Springer, Heidelberg (2010). https://doi.org/10.1007/978-3-642-13190-5_27
15. Choudhuri, A.R., Garg, S., Piet, J., Policharla, G.-V.: Mempool privacy via batched threshold encryption: Attacks and defenses. In: Balzarotti, D., Xu, W. (eds.) USENIX Security 2024. USENIX Association (2024)
16. Cong, K., Cozzo, D., Maram, V., Smart, N.P.: Gladius: LWR Based Efficient Hybrid Public Key Encryption with Distributed Decryption. In: Tibouchi, M., Wang, H. (eds.) ASIACRYPT 2021. LNCS, vol. 13093, pp. 125–155. Springer, Cham (2021). https://doi.org/10.1007/978-3-030-92068-5_5
17. Cramer, R., Gennaro, R., Schoenmakers, B.: A secure and optimally efficient multi-authority election scheme. In: Fumy, W., (ed.) EUROCRYPT'97, vol. 1233, LNCS, pp. 103–118. Springer, Cham (1997)
18. del Pino, R., Espitau, T., Niot, G., Prest, T.: Simple and efficient lattice threshold signatures with identifiable aborts. Cryptology ePrint Archive, Paper 2025/871 (2025)
19. Del Pino, R., Katsumata, S., Maller, M., Mouhartem, F., Prest, T., Saarinen, M.-J.O.: Threshold raccoon: practical threshold signatures from standard lattice assumptions. In: Joye, M., Leander, G., (eds.) EUROCRYPT 2024, Part II, vol. 14652, LNCS, pp. 219–248. Springer, Cham (2024)
20. Desmedt, Y., Di Crescenzo, G., Burmester, M.: Multiplicative non-abelian sharing schemes and their application to threshold cryptography. In: Pieprzyk, J., Safavi-Naini, R. (eds.) ASIACRYPT 1994. LNCS, vol. 917, pp. 19–32. Springer, Heidelberg (1995). https://doi.org/10.1007/BFb0000421
21. Devevey, J., Libert, B., Nguyen, K., Peters, T., Yung, M.: Non-interactive CCA2-Secure Threshold Cryptosystems: Achieving Adaptive Security in the Standard Model Without Pairings. In: Garay, J.A. (ed.) PKC 2021. LNCS, vol. 12710, pp. 659–690. Springer, Cham (2021). https://doi.org/10.1007/978-3-030-75245-3_24
22. Ducas, L., van Woerden, W.: NTRU Fatigue: How Stretched is Overstretched? In: Tibouchi, M., Wang, H. (eds.) ASIACRYPT 2021. LNCS, vol. 13093, pp. 3–32. Springer, Cham (2021). https://doi.org/10.1007/978-3-030-92068-5_1

23. Esgin, M.F., Espitau, T., Niot, G., Prest, T., Sakzad, A., Steinfeld, R.: Plover: masking-friendly hash-and-sign lattice signatures. In: Joye, M., Leander, G. (ed.) EUROCRYPT 2024, Part VII, vol. 14657, LNCS, pp. 316–345. Springer, Cham (2024)
24. Fujisaki, E., Okamoto, T.: How to Enhance the Security of Public-Key Encryption at Minimum Cost. In: Imai, H., Zheng, Y. (eds.) PKC 1999. LNCS, vol. 1560, pp. 53–68. Springer, Heidelberg (1999). https://doi.org/10.1007/3-540-49162-7_5
25. Fujisaki, E., Okamoto, T.: Secure integration of asymmetric and symmetric encryption schemes. J. Cryptol. **26**(1), 80–101 (2013)
26. Gentry, C., Peikert, C., Vaikuntanathan, V.: Trapdoors for hard lattices and new cryptographic constructions. In: Ladner R.E., Dwork, C., (eds.)40th ACM STOC, pp. 197–206. ACM Press (2008)
27. Hofheinz, D., Hövelmanns, K., Kiltz, E.: A Modular Analysis of the Fujisaki-Okamoto Transformation. In: Kalai, Y., Reyzin, L. (eds.) TCC 2017. LNCS, vol. 10677, pp. 341–371. Springer, Cham (2017). https://doi.org/10.1007/978-3-319-70500-2_12
28. Hough, P., Sandsbråten, C., Silde, T.: More efficient lattice-based electronic voting from NTRU. IACR Commun. Cryptol. **1**(4) (2025)
29. Katsumata, S., Reichle, M., Takemure, K.: Adaptively secure 5 round threshold signatures from MLWE/MSIS and DL with rewinding. In: Reyzin, L., Stebila, D. (eds.) CRYPTO 2024, Part VII, vol. 14926, LNCS, pp. 459–491. Springer, Cham (2024). https://doi.org/10.1007/978-3-031-68394-7_15
30. Katsumata, S., Yamada, S.: Partitioning via Non-linear Polynomial Functions: More Compact IBEs from Ideal Lattices and Bilinear Maps. In: Cheon, J.H., Takagi, T. (eds.) ASIACRYPT 2016. LNCS, vol. 10032, pp. 682–712. Springer, Heidelberg (2016). https://doi.org/10.1007/978-3-662-53890-6_23
31. Kim, D., Lee, D., Seo, J., Song, Y.: Toward practical lattice-based proof of knowledge from Hint-MLWE. In: Handschuh, H., Lysyanskaya, A. (eds.) Advances in Cryptology – CRYPTO 2023. CRYPTO 2023. Lecture Notes in Computer Science, vol. 14085. Springer, Cham (2023). https://doi.org/10.1007/978-3-031-38554-4_18
32. Kirchner, P., Fouque, P.-A.: Revisiting Lattice Attacks on Overstretched NTRU Parameters. In: Coron, J.-S., Nielsen, J.B. (eds.) EUROCRYPT 2017. LNCS, vol. 10210, pp. 3–26. Springer, Cham (2017). https://doi.org/10.1007/978-3-319-56620-7_1
33. Kraitsberg, M., Lindell, Y., Osheter, V., Smart, N.P., Talibi Alaoui, Y.: Adding Distributed Decryption and Key Generation to a Ring-LWE Based CCA Encryption Scheme. In: Jang-Jaccard, J., Guo, F. (eds.) ACISP 2019. LNCS, vol. 11547, pp. 192–210. Springer, Cham (2019). https://doi.org/10.1007/978-3-030-21548-4_11
34. Lapiha, O., Prest, T.: A Lattice-Based IND-CCA Threshold KEM from the BCHK+ Transform. In: Hanaoka, G., Yang, B.Y. (eds.) Advances in Cryptology – ASIACRYPT 2025. ASIACRYPT 2025. Lecture Notes in Computer Science, vol. 16247. Springer, Cham (2026). https://doi.org/10.1007/978-981-95-5099-9_15
35. Lindner, R., Peikert, C.: Better Key Sizes (and Attacks) for LWE-Based Encryption. In: Kiayias, A. (ed.) CT-RSA 2011. LNCS, vol. 6558, pp. 319–339. Springer, Heidelberg (2011). https://doi.org/10.1007/978-3-642-19074-2_21
36. Lyubashevsky, V.: Lattice Signatures without Trapdoors. In: Pointcheval, D., Johansson, T. (eds.) EUROCRYPT 2012. LNCS, vol. 7237, pp. 738–755. Springer, Heidelberg (2012). https://doi.org/10.1007/978-3-642-29011-4_43
37. Lyubashevsky, V., Peikert, C., Regev, O.: A Toolkit for Ring-LWE Cryptography. In: Johansson, T., Nguyen, P.Q. (eds.) EUROCRYPT 2013. LNCS, vol. 7881, pp. 35–54. Springer, Heidelberg (2013). https://doi.org/10.1007/978-3-642-38348-9_3

38. Micciancio, D., Suhl, A.: Simulation-secure threshold PKE from LWE with polynomial modulus. IACR Commun. Cryptol. **1**(4), 2 (2024)
39. NIST. FIPS 203: Module-Lattice-Based Key-Encapsulation Mechanism Standard (2024)
40. Peikert, C.: An Efficient and Parallel Gaussian Sampler for Lattices. In: Rabin, T. (ed.) CRYPTO 2010. LNCS, vol. 6223, pp. 80–97. Springer, Heidelberg (2010). https://doi.org/10.1007/978-3-642-14623-7_5
41. del Pino, R., Katsumata, S., Niot, G., Reichle, M., Takemure, K.: Unmasking TRaccoon: A Lattice-Based Threshold Signature with An Efficient Identifiable Abort Protocol. In: Tauman Kalai, Y., Kamara, S.F. (eds.) Advances in Cryptology – CRYPTO 2025. CRYPTO 2025. Lecture Notes in Computer Science, vol 16005. Springer, Cham (2025). https://doi.org/10.1007/978-3-032-01887-8_14
42. Prest, T., et al.: FALCON. Technical report, National Institute of Standards and Technology (2022). https://csrc.nist.gov/Projects/post-quantum-cryptography/selected-algorithms-2022
43. Schwabe, P., et al.: CRYSTALS-KYBER. Technical report, National Institute of Standards and Technology (2022). https://csrc.nist.gov/Projects/post-quantum-cryptography/selected-algorithms-2022
44. Yu, Y., Jia, H., Wang, X.: Compact Lattice Gadget and Its Applications to Hash-and-Sign Signatures. In: Handschuh, H., Lysyanskaya, A. (eds.) Advances in Cryptology – CRYPTO 2023. CRYPTO 2023. Lecture Notes in Computer Science, vol. 14085. Springer, Cham (2023). https://doi.org/10.1007/978-3-031-38554-4_13

BW-KEM: Robust and Versatile MLWE-Based KEM with Barnes-Wall Lattices

Songlin Li[1], Hengchuan Zou[1], Shiyu Shen[2], Yifan Dong[1], and Yunlei Zhao[1](✉)

[1] College of Computer Science and Artificial Intelligence, Fudan University, Shanghai, China
{slli22,hczou23,yfdong24}@m.fudan.edu.cn, ylzhao@fudan.edu.cn
[2] Department of Electrical Engineering, City University of Hong Kong, Hong Kong, China
crypto@sher1e.dev

Abstract. Lattice-based cryptosystems typically employ either direct modulation or its combination with error-correcting codes (ECC) for error correction mechanisms. In this paper, we propose a scalable nested lattice coding framework based on Barnes-Wall lattices that unifies modulation and ECC, enabling efficient and reliable error correction. Our design can serve as a drop-in replacement for direct modulation in lattice-based schemes, significantly improving overall robustness and communication efficiency. By carefully integrating low-dimensional lattice codes into high-dimensional module-lattice-based constructions, we incorporate this technique into MLWE-based key encapsulation mechanism and present an enhanced version of ML-KEM, the NIST-standardized lattice-based KEM. We conduct a detailed analysis of the joint distribution of noise polynomial coefficients, from which we derive a methodology for evaluating the decryption failure rate (DFR) without any independence assumptions on the noise coefficients.

Our scheme, BW-KEM, offers stronger security guarantees, more compact ciphertexts, and significantly reduced DFRs across all security levels compared to ML-KEM. Extensive benchmarking demonstrates that BW-KEM outperforms ML-KEM in key generation and encapsulation, while incurring only marginal overhead in decapsulation. For instance, at the highest security level, BW-KEM achieves a 14-bit and 13-bit improvement in classical and quantum security estimates, respectively, or equivalently, a 16.33% reduction in ciphertext size, while maintaining significantly lower DFRs. These advantages are further complemented by an 8% and 12% acceleration in key generation and encapsulation, respectively, with only a 1% performance loss in decapsulation. Our results suggest that BW-KEM is a promising candidate for practical and quantum-resistant key encapsulation mechanism.

Keywords: Post-quantum cryptography · Lattice-based cryptography · Barnes-Wall lattices · Lattice coding · Error correction

S. Bai and E. Persichetti (Eds.): PKC 2026, LNCS 16551, pp. 70–102, 2026.
https://doi.org/10.1007/978-3-032-26731-3_3

1 Introduction

The rapid advancement of quantum computing in recent years has posed a significant threat to the security of widely deployed public-key cryptographic systems. In response, post-quantum cryptography (PQC) has been systematically explored over the past decades, with the aim of developing cryptosystems that remain secure against quantum adversaries while preserving compatibility with classical computing platforms.

Since 2016, the National Institute of Standards and Technology (NIST) has led an international standardization process to define new post-quantum standards for digital signatures, public-key encryption, and key encapsulation mechanisms [9]. Among the various candidate proposals, lattice-based cryptography has emerged as one of the most promising approaches, due to its efficient cryptographic constructions supported by security reductions to worst-case hardness assumptions.

The module-lattice-based key encapsulation mechanism ML-KEM has been standardized by NIST [40] due to its outstanding overall performance in terms of security, communication bandwidth, and computational efficiency. However, a recent report [30] presented at the NIST Workshop on Guidance for KEMs (February 2025) noted that ML-KEM may not be suitable for all application scenarios. To support cryptographic agility, the report highlights the need for alternative algorithms that offer complementary security assurances, reduced ciphertext sizes, and better adaptability to diverse application requirements. In response, NIST has announced the forthcoming standardization of HQC [1], a code-based KEM intended as a backup to ML-KEM. HQC relies on fundamentally different hardness assumptions, providing resilience in case theoretical or implementation vulnerabilities are found in ML-KEM. Despite these developments, the exceptionally compact ciphertexts achieved by ML-KEM remain unmatched. Existing alternatives have not succeeded in further reducing ciphertext size while maintaining comparable security and computational efficiency. This motivates a natural question: can we redesign certain components within the original ML-KEM framework to improve ciphertext compactness without compromising security and practicality?

In ML-KEM, ciphertext compression is achieved by discarding low-order bits of polynomial coefficients. This introduces additional noise, and the resulting decryption failure rate must remain sufficiently low to avoid secret leakage [14]. Therefore, the extent to which ciphertexts can be compressed is fundamentally constrained by the scheme's error correction capability. ML-KEM relies on direct modulation as its error correction mechanism, whose limited noise tolerance precludes further compression under the current parameter sets. Enhancing this component with a stronger error-correcting strategy offers a promising approach to improving noise tolerance, potentially enabling a more favorable trade-off between ciphertext size and security strength.

Recent research has investigated the integration of linear error-correcting codes (ECC) with modulation schemes to improve noise resilience. Representative approaches include the use of BCH codes [27], polar codes [33,42], LDPC codes [20], and other coding techniques [3,22,35,43]. While such concatenated schemes can enhance error correction performance, they often incur increased algorithmic complexity and heightened susceptibility to side-channel attacks [13]. Moreover, these designs typically suffer from rigid encoding granularity and lack a unified decoding structure, which limits coordination between ECC and modulation and ultimately constrains overall system efficiency [28]. To address these limitations, the concept of *lattice coding* has been extensively studied in information theory over the past few decades [17–19,24]. From the perspective of coset codes, lattice codes provide a natural and elegant integration of linear codes and modulation. This unified framework offers powerful error-correcting capabilities while preserving structural efficiency, making lattice coding a promising foundation for modern cryptographic applications.

Recent works have made promising attempts to explore the integration of lattice codes into cryptographic constructions. Representative efforts include leveraging the Gosset lattice [28,36], the Leech lattice [26,34], and other dimensional lattice codes [26,28,41]. Nevertheless, embedding lattice coding into lattice-based cryptographic schemes poses several nontrivial challenges, as outlined below.

- Firstly, cryptographic algorithms involving secret must operate in constant time to prevent side-channel leakage. However, the additional decoding step introduced by lattice coding may be vulnerable to timing attacks. Therefore, it is crucial to design lattice coding algorithms that eliminate conditional branches and guarantee constant-time execution.
- Secondly, existing designs often exhibit redundancy and dimensional mismatches between the encoded message and the underlying algebraic structures, rendering them unsuitable for module-lattice-based constructions. For instance, encoding a 256-bit message into a vector misaligned with the 256-dimensional ring structure commonly adopted in ML-KEM compromises both efficiency and modularity.
- Moreover, these efforts remain largely theoretical and lack comprehensive evaluations of computational performance. The proposed coding algorithms tend to be complex and impose structural constraints [26,28], raising concerns about their practicality and efficiency in real-world cryptographic applications.
- Furthermore, existing approaches typically assume that the coefficients of the aggregated noise polynomial during decryption are mutually independent when estimating the DFR. However, this assumption does not hold in practice and can result in a significant underestimation of the actual DFR [15].

Recent state-of-the-art works [25,32] have made significant progress toward addressing the aforementioned challenges. In [32], the authors introduced the family of Minal codes, which were specifically tailored to compact ML-KEM. Their analytical framework enables DFR estimation in low-dimensional coding settings without relying explicitly on independence assumptions. However, in parameter selection, this approach yields only marginal improvement in the ciphertext compression of ML-KEM, and an implicit independence assumption is still adopted when choosing coding parameters.

In [25], the authors proposed ciphertext packing and lattice packing techniques to optimize the design of ML-KEM and remove the independence assumption. Their approach achieves notable improvements in ciphertext compression and DFRs, but at the cost of increased computational overhead and larger public key sizes. Although their analysis avoids assuming independence among noise coefficients, it introduces another simplification by treating the polynomial vectors shared across multiple ciphertexts as constants, whose validity warrants further investigation.

Therefore, completely eliminating the independence assumption when employing lattice coding techniques remains an open and nontrivial problem. There is a pressing need to design and analyze lattice coding techniques specifically tailored to the error correction mechanisms of lattice-based cryptographic schemes. Such designs should be robust, lightweight, efficient, and compatible with constant-time implementation requirements, thereby enabling meaningful performance improvements for schemes like ML-KEM without compromising security or practical deployability.

1.1 Our Contributions

To address the limitations of existing error correction mechanisms in lattice-based schemes and to explore the practical potential of lattice coding in cryptographic settings, we propose a novel approach that integrates structured lattice codes into the ML-KEM framework, resulting in a robust and versatile MLWE-based KEM with Barnes-Wall lattices. Our main contributions are summarized as follows:

- We propose a scalable nested lattice coding technique based on Barnes-Wall lattices to enable efficient and reliable error correction. We develop efficient, constant-time encoding and decoding algorithms specifically tailored for cryptographic applications. The scalable structure significantly improves the flexibility and efficiency of incorporating lattice coding into the error correction mechanisms of lattice-based cryptographic schemes. We further provide a complete and formal proof of correctness for the proposed algorithms.
- We integrate our lattice coding technique into a module-lattice-based key encapsulation mechanism, yielding an enhanced variant of ML-KEM. The resulting scheme, BW-KEM, maintains full compatibility with the ML-KEM framework while achieving superior overall performance. Through carefully optimized parameter selection, BW-KEM provides stronger security guarantees, more compact ciphertexts, and substantially lower DFRs across all security levels compared to ML-KEM and its state-of-the-art coded variants.
- We provide a rigorous analysis of BW-KEM, including formal proofs of its correctness and security. Building on our novel error-correcting design, we present a comprehensive error rate analysis combining scalable lattice codes with the MLWE-based KEM framework. We conduct a detailed analysis of the joint distribution of noise polynomial coefficients, from which we derive a methodology for evaluating the DFR without any independence assumptions on the noise coefficients.

- We implement BW-KEM and conduct extensive benchmarking against ML-KEM and its coded variants. Our results demonstrate that BW-KEM outperforms ML-KEM in both key generation and encapsulation, while introducing only a marginal overhead in decapsulation. These results suggest BW-KEM as a promising candidate for practical, quantum-resistant key encapsulation mechanism.

2 Preliminaries

2.1 Notations

Let $\mathbb{Z}$, $\mathbb{R}$ and $\mathbb{C}$ be the sets of rational integers, real numbers and complex numbers, respectively. Let N and q be positive integers. $\mathbb{Z}_q = \mathbb{Z}/q\mathbb{Z} \cong \{0, 1, \ldots, q-1\}$ denotes the residue class modulo q. Let $\mathcal{R}$ and $\mathcal{R}_q$ denote the rings $\mathbb{Z}[x]/(x^N + 1)$ and $\mathbb{Z}_q[x]/(x^N + 1)$, respectively, where $N = 2^{k_0}$ such that $x^N + 1$ is the $2N$-th cyclotomic polynomial. Regular font letters denote elements in $\mathcal{R}$ or $\mathcal{R}_q$, bold lower-case letters represent vectors and bold upper-case letters are matrices. For a vector $\mathbf{v}$ (resp., matrix $\mathbf{A}$), we denote $\mathbf{v}^T$ (resp., matrix $\mathbf{A}^T$) by its transpose. For a polynomial a, we denote by a_i the i-th coefficient associated with the power x^i. For any $x \in \mathbb{R}$, we denote by $\lfloor x \rceil$ the operation of rounding x to the nearest integer, with ties being rounded up.

Modular Reductions. In this work, we extend the definition of modular reduction from $\mathbb{Z}$ to $\mathbb{R}$. For a positive integer q, we define the modular reduction of r under the signed reduction convention as $r' = r \bmod {}^{\pm}q$, where r' is the unique representative of r in the interval $\left[-\frac{q}{2}, \frac{q}{2}\right)$. Similarly, under the standard (non-negative) modular reduction, we define $r' = r \bmod q$, where r' is the unique representative of r in the interval $[0, q)$.

Sizes of Elements. For $\omega \in \mathbb{R}$, its l_∞ norm is denoted as $\|\omega\|_{q,\infty} = |\omega \bmod {}^{\pm}q|$. For an N-dimensional vector $\mathbf{v} = (v_0, \cdots, v_{N-1}) \in \mathbb{R}^N$, we define its l_2 norm as $\|\mathbf{v}\|_{q,2} = \sqrt{\|v_0\|_{q,\infty}^2 + \cdots + \|v_{N-1}\|_{q,\infty}^2}$. If $\omega = \omega_0 + \omega_1 x + \cdots + \omega_{N-1}x^{N-1} \in \mathcal{R}$ or $\mathcal{R}_q$, then its l_2 norm is defined as $\|\omega\|_{q,2} = \sqrt{\|\omega_0\|_{q,\infty}^2 + \cdots + \|\omega_{N-1}\|_{q,\infty}^2}$. Similarly, for $\mathbf{w} = (\omega_1, \cdots, \omega_l) \in \mathcal{R}^l$ or $\mathcal{R}_q^l$, we define its l_2 norm as $\|\mathbf{w}\|_{q,2} = \sqrt{\|\omega_1\|_{q,2}^2 + \cdots + \|\omega_l\|_{q,2}^2}$.

Distributions. For a set S, the notation $x \xleftarrow{\$} S$ denotes that x is sampled uniformly at random from S. If S is a probability distribution, then $x \leftarrow S$ indicates that x is drawn according to the distribution S.

The centered binomial distribution $\mathcal{B}_\eta$, parameterized by a positive integer η, is defined as follows: sample $(a_1, \ldots, a_\eta, b_1, \ldots, b_\eta) \xleftarrow{\$} \{0,1\}^{2\eta}$ and output $\sum_{i=1}^{\eta}(a_i - b_i)$. For an element $f \in \mathcal{R}$, the notation $f \leftarrow \beta_\eta$ indicates that f is generated by independently sampling each coefficient of f from the distribution $\mathcal{B}_\eta$.

Compression and Decompression. We define the compression function $y = \mathsf{Compress}_{q,2^d}(x)$, which maps an element $x \in \mathbb{Z}_q$ to an integer y in the range $\{0, 1, \ldots, 2^d - 1\}$, where the positive integer $d < \lceil \log_2(q) \rceil$. We further define the corresponding decompression function $x' = \mathsf{Decompress}_{2^d,q}(y)$ that outputs an element x' close to the original x. Specifically, these functions are defined as:

$$\mathsf{Compress}_{q,2^d}(x) = \left\lfloor \frac{2^d}{q} \cdot x \right\rceil \bmod 2^d,$$
$$\mathsf{Decompress}_{2^d,q}(y) = \left\lfloor \frac{q}{2^d} \cdot y \right\rceil.$$

The error distribution of $x' - x \bmod {}^{\pm}q$ is nearly uniform over the integers with magnitude at most $\lfloor \frac{q}{2^{d+1}} \rceil$. For a polynomial $\omega \in \mathcal{R}_q$ or a vector $\mathbf{w} \in \mathcal{R}_q^k$, these operations are applied coefficient-wise.

The primary purpose of defining the $\mathsf{Compress}_{q,2^d}$ and $\mathsf{Decompress}_{2^d,q}$ functions is to enable the removal of a certain number of low-order bits from the ciphertext. These discarded bits contribute minimally to the correctness probability of decryption while significantly reducing the overall parameter sizes, thereby improving efficiency in terms of storage and communication overhead.

Extendable Output Function. Let $\mathsf{Sample} : \{0,1\}^* \to \{0,1\}^*$ be an extendable output function, i.e., a deterministic function on bit strings whose output can be extended to arbitrary desired length. We write $y \sim S := \mathsf{Sample}(x)$ to indicate that, given input x, the output y is distributed according to distribution S (or uniformly over a set S). Although this procedure is entirely deterministic, we assume for simplicity that its output distribution is ideal.

2.2 Cryptographic Primitives

Public-Key Encryption. A public-key encryption (PKE) scheme is a tuple of three algorithms $\mathsf{PKE} = (\mathsf{KeyGen}, \mathsf{Enc}, \mathsf{Dec})$ along with a message space $\mathcal{M}$.

- $(\mathsf{pk}, \mathsf{sk}) \leftarrow \mathsf{KeyGen}()$: The key generation algorithm KeyGen outputs a key pair $(\mathsf{pk}, \mathsf{sk})$, where pk also defines a finate randomness space $\mathcal{R} = \mathcal{R}(\mathsf{pk})$ as well as a ciphertext space $\mathcal{C}$.
- $\mathsf{ct} \leftarrow \mathsf{Enc}(\mathsf{pk}, m)$: The encryption algorithm Enc takes as inputs the public key pk and a message $m \in \mathcal{M}$ and outputs a ciphertext ct. If necessary, we make the used randomness of encryption explicit by writing $\mathsf{ct} := \mathsf{Enc}(\mathsf{pk}, m; r)$, where $r \in \mathcal{R}$.
- $m' \leftarrow \mathsf{Dec}(\mathsf{sk}, \mathsf{ct})$: The decryption algorithm Dec, on input sk and a ciphertext ct, deterministically outputs either a message $m' \in \mathcal{M}$ or a special symbol $\perp \notin \mathcal{M}$ to indicate that ct is not a valid ciphertext.

A PKE scheme is $(1-\delta)$-correct if $\mathbb{E}[\max_{m \in \mathcal{M}} \Pr[\mathsf{Dec}(\mathsf{sk}, \mathsf{Enc}(\mathsf{pk}, m)) = m]] \geq 1 - \delta$, where the expectation is taken over $(\mathsf{pk}, \mathsf{sk}) \leftarrow \mathsf{KeyGen}()$ and the probability is taken over the random coins of Enc. The advantage of an adversary $\mathcal{A}$

against indistinguishability under chosen-plaintext attacks (IND-CPA) for PKE is defined as

$$\mathsf{Adv}_{\mathsf{PKE}}^{\mathsf{IND\text{-}CPA}}(\mathcal{A}) := \left|\Pr\left[\mathsf{IND\text{-}CPA}_{\mathsf{PKE}}^{\mathcal{A}} \Rightarrow 1\right] - \frac{1}{2}\right|$$

where game $\mathsf{IND\text{-}CPA}_{\mathsf{PKE}}^{\mathcal{A}}$ is defined in Fig. 1.

Game $\mathsf{IND\text{-}CPA}_{\mathsf{PKE}}^{\mathcal{A}}$	Game $\mathsf{IND\text{-}CCA}_{\mathsf{KEM}}^{\mathcal{A}}$
$(\mathsf{pk}, \mathsf{sk}) \leftarrow \mathsf{KeyGen}()$	$(\mathsf{pk}, \mathsf{sk}) \leftarrow \mathsf{KeyGen}()$
$(m_0, m_1) \leftarrow \mathcal{A}(\mathsf{pk})$	$b \xleftarrow{\$} \{0,1\}$
$b \xleftarrow{\$} \{0,1\}$	$(\mathsf{ct}^*, K_0^*) \leftarrow \mathsf{Encaps}(\mathsf{pk})$
$\mathsf{ct}^* \leftarrow \mathsf{Enc}(\mathsf{pk}, m_b)$	$K_1^* \xleftarrow{\$} \mathcal{K}$
$b' \leftarrow \mathcal{A}(\mathsf{ct}^*)$	$b' \leftarrow \mathcal{A}^{\mathcal{O}_{\text{DECAPS}}}(\mathsf{pk}, \mathsf{ct}^*, K_b^*)$
return $[\![b' = b]\!]$	**return** $[\![b' = b]\!]$

Fig. 1. IND-CPA game for PKE and IND-CCA game for KEM.

Key Encapsulation Mechanism. A key encapsulation mechanism (KEM) scheme consists of three algorithms $\mathsf{KEM} = (\mathsf{KeyGen}, \mathsf{Encaps}, \mathsf{Decaps})$ along with a key space $\mathcal{K}$.

- $(\mathsf{pk}, \mathsf{sk}) \leftarrow \mathsf{KeyGen}()$: The key generation algorithm KeyGen outputs a key pair $(\mathsf{pk}, \mathsf{sk})$, where pk also defines a finate randomness space $\mathcal{R} = \mathcal{R}(\mathsf{pk})$ as well as a ciphertext space $\mathcal{C}$.
- $(\mathsf{ct}, K) \leftarrow \mathsf{Encaps}(\mathsf{pk})$: The encryption algorithm Encaps takes a public key pk and produce a key encapsulation ciphertext ct and a key K.
- $K' \leftarrow \mathsf{Decaps}(\mathsf{sk}, \mathsf{ct})$: The decryption algorithm Decaps, on input sk and a ciphertext ct, deterministically outputs a key $K' \in \mathcal{K}$. If the KEM allows explicit rejection, the output is either a key K' or a special symbol $\perp$ to indicate a rejection.

A KEM scheme is $(1-\delta)$-correct if $\Pr[\mathsf{Decaps}(\mathsf{sk}, \mathsf{ct}) = K : (\mathsf{ct}, K) \leftarrow \mathsf{Encaps}(\mathsf{pk})] \geq 1-\delta$, where the probability is taken over $(\mathsf{pk}, \mathsf{sk}) \leftarrow \mathsf{KeyGen}()$ and the random coins of Encaps. The advantage of an adversary $\mathcal{A}$ against indistinguishability under chosen-ciphertext attacks (IND-CCA) for KEM is defined as

$$\mathsf{Adv}_{\mathsf{KEM}}^{\mathsf{IND\text{-}CCA}}(\mathcal{A}) := \left|\Pr\left[\mathsf{IND\text{-}CCA}_{\mathsf{KEM}}^{\mathcal{A}} \Rightarrow 1\right] - \frac{1}{2}\right|,$$

where game $\mathsf{IND\text{-}CCA}_{\mathsf{KEM}}^{\mathcal{A}}$ is defined in Fig. 1 and the oracle $\mathcal{O}_{\text{DECAPS}}(\mathsf{sk}, \cdot \neq \mathsf{ct}^*)$ returns $\mathsf{Decaps}(\mathsf{sk}, \mathsf{ct})$ for all $\mathsf{ct} \neq \mathsf{ct}^*$.

2.3 Hardness Assumption

Module-LWE. Let l, m be positive integer parameters, and let $\mathcal{D}$ be a distribution over the ring $\mathcal{R}_q$. The (decisional) Module Learning With Errors (MLWE) problem is to distinguish between two types of samples: uniformly random pairs $(\mathbf{a}_i, b_i) \xleftarrow{\$} \mathcal{R}_q^l \times \mathcal{R}_q$, and samples where $\mathbf{a}_i \xleftarrow{\$} \mathcal{R}_q^l$ is uniform and $b_i = \mathbf{a}_i^T \mathbf{s} + e_i$, with a secret $\mathbf{s} \leftarrow \mathcal{D}^l$ shared across all samples and independent noise terms $e_i \leftarrow \mathcal{D}$.

The MLWE problem is assumed to be hard, meaning that for any probabilistic polynomial-time adversary $\mathcal{A}$, its distinguishing advantage is negligible, where $\mathsf{Adv}_{m,l,\mathcal{D}}^{\mathsf{MLWE}}(\mathcal{A}) =$

$$\left| \Pr\left[b' = 1 : \begin{array}{c} \mathbf{A} \xleftarrow{\$} \mathcal{R}_q^{m \times l}; \\ (\mathbf{s}, \mathbf{e}) \leftarrow \mathcal{D}^l \times \mathcal{D}^m; \\ \mathbf{b} = \mathbf{A}\mathbf{s} + \mathbf{e}; \\ b' \leftarrow \mathcal{A}(\mathbf{A}, \mathbf{b}) \end{array} \right] - \Pr\left[b' = 1 : \begin{array}{c} \mathbf{A} \xleftarrow{\$} \mathcal{R}_q^{m \times l}; \\ \mathbf{b} \xleftarrow{\$} \mathcal{R}_q^m; \\ b' \leftarrow \mathcal{A}(\mathbf{A}, \mathbf{b}) \end{array} \right] \right|.$$

3 The Lattice Code

Before introducing our MLWE-based KEM scheme, we first establish the necessary theoretical foundations on Barnes-Wall lattices and lattice coding theory. Subsequently, we propose a simple yet efficient scalable lattice code based on Barnes-Wall lattices, designed to enhance message recovery efficiency while ensuring negligible error probabilities in our scheme.

3.1 Barnes-Wall Lattices

Barnes-Wall lattices are an infinite sequence of full-rank lattices defined for every dimension n that is a power of 2. It is known that Barnes-Wall lattices can be viewed as lattices over the Gaussian integers $\mathbb{G} = \mathbb{Z}[i]$ [31], the construction of which we adopt in this paper.

Definition 1 (Barnes-Wall lattices). *Let $n = 2^k (k \geq 2)$ and $\phi = 1 + i$, the Barnes-Wall lattice of dimension n is defined recursively as*

$$\mathrm{BW}_n = \left\{ [\mathbf{u}, \mathbf{u} + \phi \mathbf{v}] \mid \mathbf{u}, \mathbf{v} \in \mathrm{BW}_{\frac{n}{2}} \right\},$$

with initial condition $\mathrm{BW}_2 = \mathbb{G}$.

Alternatively, the Barnes-Wall lattice can also be defined as lattice over $\mathbb{G}$ generated by the rows of the $(k-1)$-fold Kronecker product $\mathbf{W}_n$:

$$\mathrm{BW}_n = \{ \mathbf{v} \cdot \mathbf{W}_n \mid \mathbf{v} \in \mathbb{G}^{\frac{n}{2}} \}, \mathbf{W}_n = \begin{pmatrix} 1 & 1 \\ 0 & \phi \end{pmatrix}^{\otimes (k-1)} \in \mathbb{C}^{\frac{n}{2} \times \frac{n}{2}}.$$

To obtain the scaled Barnes-Wall lattices is straightforward based on the definition above:

$$\mathrm{BW}_n(\lambda) = \{\lambda \mathbf{v} \cdot \mathbf{W}_n \mid \mathbf{v} \in \mathbb{G}^{\frac{n}{2}}\}, \lambda \in \mathbb{R}^+.$$

Complex numbers and scaled lattices make the definitions more concise, while also enhancing the simplicity and flexibility of subsequent algorithms. The construction can be easily converted to lattices over $\mathbb{Z}$ via the following mapping from $\mathbb{C}^{\frac{n}{2}}$ to $\mathbb{R}^n$:

$$(a_1 + b_1 i, a_2 + b_2 i, \cdots, a_{n/2} + b_{n/2} i) \mapsto (a_1, b_1, a_2, b_2, \cdots, a_{n/2}, b_{n/2}).$$

Under this mapping, the norm and distance notations can be naturally extended. For $n = 2, 4, 8, 16$, the Barnes-Wall lattices are equivalent to $\mathbb{Z}^2$, D_4, E_8, and Λ_{16}, respectively [11]. And these are densest packings in respective dimensions.

The results in [19] can be naturally extended to derive the following lemma concerning scaled Barnes-Wall lattices:

Lemma 1. *Let* $\mathrm{BW}_n(\lambda)$ *be the scaled Barnes-Wall lattice, where* $n = 2^k \geq 2$. *The following properties hold:*

(1) The minimum squared distance satisfies

$$d_{\min}^2(\mathrm{BW}_n(\lambda)) = \frac{n}{2}\lambda^2 = (2\rho(\mathrm{BW}_n(\lambda)))^2,$$

where $\rho(\mathrm{BW}_n(\lambda))$ *denotes the packing radius.*

(2) The fundamental volume is given by $\mathsf{Vol}(\mathrm{BW}_n(\lambda)) = \lambda^n \cdot 2^{\frac{n}{4}(k-1)}$.

(3) The inclusion relation holds: $2^{\lfloor \frac{k}{2} \rfloor}\lambda \cdot \mathbb{G}^{\frac{n}{2}} \subset \mathrm{BW}_n(\lambda)$.

3.2 Scalable Lattice Coding Based on Barnes-Wall Lattices

Definition 2 (Nested lattices). *Two lattices* Λ_c *and* Λ_f *are nested if* $\Lambda_c \subset \Lambda_f$. *The lattice* Λ_c *is referred to as the coarse/shaping lattice, and* Λ_f *as the fine/coding lattice.*

Definition 3 (Nested lattice code). *Let* Λ_c *and* Λ_f *be two lattices with* $\Lambda_c \subset \Lambda_f$ *and let* $\mathcal{P}_c$ *be a fundamental region of* Λ_c. *A nested lattice code* $\mathcal{C}$ *based on the nested lattice pair is defined as* $\mathcal{C} = \Lambda_f \cap \mathcal{P}_c$, *which is a subset of* Λ_f *that forms a complete set of representatives for the quotient group* Λ_f/Λ_c.

When utilizing a nested lattice code $\mathcal{C}$ for message transmission over a noisy channel, the process typically involves the following steps:

- **Encoding:** A lattice labeling process maps each message $\mathbf{m} \in \mathcal{M}$ to a corresponding lattice codeword $\mathbf{w} \in \mathcal{C}$.
- **Lattice Decoding:** Upon receiving the noisy vector $\mathbf{x} = \mathbf{w} + \mathbf{e}$, where $\mathbf{e}$ represents noise, this step employs a certain error-correcting algorithm which treats $\mathbf{x}$ as the input target vector and outputs a lattice vector $\mathbf{w}' \in \mathcal{C}$. Subsequently, a lattice delabeling process maps $\mathbf{w}'$ back to the estimated message $\mathbf{m}'$.

The error-correcting mechanism employed in this work is a Bounded Distance Decoding (BDD) algorithm with radius r. For successful decoding (i.e., ensuring $\mathbf{m}' = \mathbf{m}$), a sufficient condition is that the encoding process is injective and the noise vector lies within the decoding radius r.

In this paper, we consider the coding lattice $\Lambda_f = \mathrm{BW}_n(\lambda)$ and the shaping lattice $\Lambda_c = 2^\tau \lambda \cdot \mathbb{G}^{n/2}$, where $\tau \geq \lfloor \frac{k}{2} \rfloor$. According to Lemma 1, it follows that

$$\Lambda_c \subset 2^{\lfloor \frac{k}{2} \rfloor} \lambda \cdot \mathbb{G}^{n/2} \subset \Lambda_f.$$

Hence, the **scalable nested lattice code**, denoted by $\mathcal{C}_{n,\tau}(\lambda)$, can be defined based on the nested lattice pair $\Lambda_c \subset \Lambda_f$. For the lattice Λ_c, we define $\mathcal{P}_c$ as the fundamental parallelotope corresponding to its standard orthogonal basis. Specifically, it is defined as:

$$\mathcal{P}_c = \{(a_1 + b_1 i, a_2 + b_2 i, \ldots, a_{n/2} + b_{n/2} i) \mid 0 \leq a_j, b_j < 2^\tau \lambda, \forall 1 \leq j \leq n/2\}.$$

Applying Lemma 1, we derive the cardinality of $\mathcal{C}_{n,\tau}(\lambda)$ as

$$|\mathcal{C}_{n,\tau}(\lambda)| = \frac{\mathsf{Vol}(\Lambda_c)}{\mathsf{Vol}(\Lambda_f)} = \frac{\lambda^n \cdot 2^{\tau n}}{\lambda^n \cdot 2^{\frac{n}{4}(k-1)}} = 2^{\tau n - \frac{n}{4}(k-1)}. \quad (1)$$

Next, we present the encoding and decoding procedures for the message space $\mathcal{M} = \{0,1\}^\mu$ and the lattice code $\mathcal{C}_{n,\tau}(\lambda)$. To ensure the injectivity of the encoding map, we impose the condition $|\mathcal{M}| \leq |\mathcal{C}_{n,\tau}(\lambda)|$, which leads to the constraint $\mu \leq \tau n - \frac{n}{4}(k-1)$.

Algorithm 1. $\mathsf{Encode}_{\mathcal{C}_{n,\tau}(\lambda)}(\mathbf{m} \in \{0,1\}^\mu)$

Input: μ-bit string $\mathbf{m} \in \{0,1\}^\mu$, $\mu \leq \tau n - \frac{n}{4}(k-1)$
Output: A lattice code vector $\mathbf{w} \in \mathcal{C}_{n,\tau}(\lambda)$

1: Pad $\mathbf{m}$ with 0's to obtain $\bar{\mathbf{m}}$ with length $\tau n - \frac{n}{4}(k-1)$
2: Divide $\bar{\mathbf{m}}$ into $\frac{n}{2}$ blocks: $\bar{\mathbf{m}} = (\mathbf{m}_0, \mathbf{m}_1, \cdots, \mathbf{m}_{\frac{n}{2}-1})$, such that $\mathbf{m}_j \in \{0,1\}^{2\tau - w_H(j)}$
3: **for** j from 0 to $\frac{n}{2} - 1$ **do**
4: $\quad v_j := \xi_{2\tau - w_H(j)}(\mathbf{m}_j)$
5: **end for**
6: $\mathbf{v} := (v_0, \cdots, v_{\frac{n}{2}-1})$
7: $\mathbf{w} := \lambda \cdot (\mathbf{v}\mathbf{W}_n \bmod 2^\tau)$
8: **return w**

Encoding. The encoding algorithm first pads the message $\mathbf{m}$ to obtain $\bar{\mathbf{m}}$ with length $\tau n - \frac{n}{4}(k-1)$ by appending zeros. Then, in the second step, $\bar{\mathbf{m}}$ is divided into $\frac{n}{2}$ sub-vectors, and each component $\mathbf{m}_j$ is mapped to a Gaussian integer v_j, where $w_H(j)$ denotes the Hamming weight of j. It is straightforward to verify that the total length of $\mathbf{m}_j$ satisfies

$$\sum_{j=0}^{\frac{n}{2}-1} (2\tau - w_H(j)) = \tau n - \frac{n}{4}(k-1),$$

ensuring that the partition is well-defined. The mapping is defined as ξ_l : $\{0,1\}^l \to \mathcal{V}_l$, where $\mathcal{V}_l = \{a + bi \in \mathbb{G} | 0 \le a < 2^{\lceil \frac{l}{2} \rceil}, 0 \le b < 2^{\lfloor \frac{l}{2} \rfloor}\}$. Denote $\boldsymbol{\omega} = (\omega_0, \omega_1, \cdots, \omega_{l-1}) \in \{0,1\}^l$. ξ_l encodes the low $\lceil \frac{l}{2} \rceil$ bits as a, while the remaining bits as b, i.e.,

$$\xi_l : \{0,1\}^l \to \mathcal{V}_l$$

$$\boldsymbol{\omega} = (\omega_0, \omega_1, \cdots, \omega_{l-1}) \mapsto \sum_{j=0}^{\lceil \frac{l}{2} \rceil - 1} \omega_j \cdot 2^j + i \sum_{j=\lceil \frac{l}{2} \rceil}^{l-1} \omega_j \cdot 2^{j - \lceil \frac{l}{2} \rceil}$$

Finally, the encoded vector $\mathbf{w}$ is computed as $\mathbf{w} = \lambda \cdot (\mathbf{v}\mathbf{W}_n \bmod 2^\tau)$, resulting in a vector corresponding to $\mathbf{m}$ in the scalable nested lattice code $\mathcal{C}_{n,\tau}(\lambda)$.

Theorem 1. *The encoding process in Algorithm 1 defines an injective mapping from the message space $\mathcal{M} = \{0,1\}^\mu$ to the lattice code $\mathcal{C}_{n,\tau}(\lambda)$. In particular, when $\mu = \tau n - \frac{n}{4}(k-1)$, the mapping becomes bijective.*

Proof. Denote $\mathcal{V} = \prod_{j=0}^{\frac{n}{2}-1} \mathcal{V}_{2\tau - w_H(j)}$. Based on the definition of ξ_l, it can be observed that the first six steps in Algorithm 1 correspond to partitioning the bit string and converting into a vector $\mathbf{v} \in \mathcal{V}$. Consequently, this procedure defines an injective mapping from the message space $\mathcal{M} = \{0,1\}^\mu$ to the product space $\mathcal{V}$.

Next, we demonstrate that the mapping $\mathbf{v} \mapsto \lambda \cdot (\mathbf{v}\mathbf{W}_n \bmod 2^\tau)$ is injective for $\mathbf{v} \in \mathcal{V}$. Suppose $\lambda \cdot (\mathbf{v}_1\mathbf{W}_n \bmod 2^\tau) = \lambda \cdot (\mathbf{v}_2\mathbf{W}_n \bmod 2^\tau)$, which implies that $(\mathbf{v}_1 - \mathbf{v}_2) \cdot \mathbf{W}_n = 0 \mod 2^\tau$. Let $\tilde{\mathbf{v}} = \mathbf{v}_1 - \mathbf{v}_2 = (\tilde{v}_0, \ldots, \tilde{v}_{\frac{n}{2}-1})$. We prove by induction that $\tilde{v}_j = 0$ for all j.

Suppose $\tilde{v}_0 = \cdots = \tilde{v}_{j-1} = 0$ (this vacuously holds for the base case $j = 0$). We now show that $\tilde{v}_j = 0$. Here we introduce the definition of the ϕ-adic valuation. For any non-zero $x \in \mathbb{G}$, its ϕ-adic valuation, denoted as $\nu_\phi(x)$, is defined as the largest integer α such that ϕ^α divides x (with $\nu_\phi(0) = \infty$).

By Lemma 5 in Appendix A, $\mathbf{W}_n$ is an upper triangular matrix whose j-th diagonal entry is exactly $\phi^{w_H(j)}$. Thus, we obtain $\tilde{v}_j \cdot \phi^{w_H(j)} = 0 \bmod 2^\tau$, which implies that

$$\nu_\phi(\tilde{v}_j \cdot \phi^{w_H(j)}) = \nu_\phi(\tilde{v}_j) + \nu_\phi(\phi^{w_H(j)}) \ge \nu_\phi(2^\tau) = \nu_\phi((-i\phi^2)^\tau) = 2\tau.$$

Then we have $\nu_\phi(\tilde{v}_j) \ge 2\tau - w_H(j) \ge \max(2\tau - 2\lceil w_H(j)/2 \rceil, 2\tau - 2\lfloor w_H(j)/2 \rfloor - 1)$.

Denote $\tilde{v}_j = a_j + b_j i$. According to the definition of $\mathcal{V}_{2\tau - w_H(j)}$, the difference $\tilde{v}_j$ between two coordinates in $\mathcal{V}_{2\tau - w_H(j)}$ is strictly bounded by

$$|a_j| < 2^{\tau - \lfloor w_H(j)/2 \rfloor} \quad \text{and} \quad |b_j| < 2^{\tau - \lceil w_H(j)/2 \rceil}.$$

From $\nu_\phi(\tilde{v}_j) \ge 2\tau - 2\lceil w_H(j)/2 \rceil$, we have $\phi^{2\tau - 2\lceil w_H(j)/2 \rceil} = (-2i)^{\tau - \lceil w_H(j)/2 \rceil}$ divides $\tilde{v}_j$. Thus, both the real and imaginary parts of $\tilde{v}_j$ must be multiples of $2^{\tau - \lceil w_H(j)/2 \rceil}$. In particular, $b_j = 0 \bmod 2^{\tau - \lceil w_H(j)/2 \rceil}$. Given the strict bound on $|b_j|$, this immediately implies $b_j = 0$. Now, we know $\tilde{v}_j = a_j$. Since $\nu_\phi(\tilde{v}_j) \ge$

$2\tau - 2\lfloor w_H(j)/2 \rfloor - 1$, we have $\phi^{2\tau - 2\lfloor w_H(j)/2 \rfloor} = (-2i)^{\tau - \lfloor w_H(j)/2 \rfloor}$ divides $\tilde{v}_j \cdot \phi = a_j + a_j i$. Similarly, we obtain $a_j = 0 \bmod 2^{\tau - \lfloor w_H(j)/2 \rfloor}$, which leads to $a_j = 0$.

Hence, we conclude that $\tilde{v}_j = 0$ for all j, which proves the injectivity of the encoding process. Moreover, when $\mu = \tau n - \frac{n}{4}(k-1)$, we have $|\mathcal{M}| = |\mathcal{C}_{n,\tau}(\lambda)|$, implying that the mapping is bijective. □

Lattice Decoding. Lattice decoding consists of two main sub-processes. The first sub-process involves error correction for a noisy vector $\mathbf{x} = \mathsf{Encode}(\mathbf{m}) + \mathbf{e}$ to recover $\mathsf{Encode}(\mathbf{m})$. This error correction is typically performed using either Maximum Likelihood Decoding (MLD) or Bounded Distance Decoding (BDD).

To the best of our knowledge, the only existing MLD algorithm for Barnes-Wall lattices of arbitrary dimension was proposed by Forney in 1988, which utilizes the trellis representation of BW_n [19]. However, the complexity of this algorithm grows exponentially with the dimension, making it intractable for $n > 32$. Later, Micciancio and Nicolosi [31] proposed the first BDD algorithm for Barnes-Wall lattices that runs in polynomial time. A double-sided version of this decoder was subsequently developed using the squaring construction in [12].

In this paper, we advance the state-of-the-art in BDD for Barnes-Wall lattices. Rather than a straightforward adaptation, we generalize the decoding framework of [12] to propose a novel, scalable BDD algorithm explicitly tailored for $\mathcal{C}_{n,\tau}(\lambda)$, as detailed in Algorithm 2, which significantly enhances both the flexibility and efficiency of the decoding process.

Algorithm 2. $\mathsf{BDD}_{\mathcal{C}_{n,\tau}(\lambda)}(\mathbf{x} \in \mathbb{C}^{n/2})$

Input: A target vector $\mathbf{x} \in \mathbb{C}^{n/2}$
Output: A lattice code vector $\mathbf{w} \in \mathcal{C}_{n,\tau}(\lambda)$

if $n = 2$ **then**
  return $\lambda(\left\lfloor \frac{\mathbf{x}}{\lambda} \right\rceil \bmod 2^{\tau})$
else
  Divide $\mathbf{x} = (\mathbf{x}_1, \mathbf{x}_2)$ such that $\mathbf{x}_1, \mathbf{x}_2 \in \mathbb{C}^{n/4}$
  $\mathbf{y}_1 := \mathsf{BDD}_{\mathcal{C}_{n/2,\tau}(\lambda)}(\mathbf{x}_1)$, $\mathbf{y}_2 := \mathsf{BDD}_{\mathcal{C}_{n/2,\tau}(\lambda)}(\mathbf{x}_2)$
  $\mathbf{z}_1 := \frac{1}{2}\mathsf{BDD}_{\mathcal{C}_{n/2,\tau}(2\lambda)}(2\phi^{-1}(\mathbf{x}_2 - \mathbf{y}_1))$ $(= \mathsf{BDD}_{\mathcal{C}_{n/2,\tau}(\lambda)}(\phi^{-1}(\mathbf{x}_2 - \mathbf{y}_1)))$
  $\mathbf{z}_2 := \frac{1}{2}\mathsf{BDD}_{\mathcal{C}_{n/2,\tau}(2\lambda)}(2\phi^{-1}(\mathbf{x}_1 - \mathbf{y}_2))$ $(= \mathsf{BDD}_{\mathcal{C}_{n/2,\tau}(\lambda)}(\phi^{-1}(\mathbf{x}_1 - \mathbf{y}_2)))$
  $dis_1 := \|\mathbf{y}_1 - \mathbf{x}_1\|^2_{2^{\tau}\lambda,2} + \|\mathbf{y}_1 + \phi\mathbf{z}_1 - \mathbf{x}_2\|^2_{2^{\tau}\lambda,2}$
  $dis_2 := \|\mathbf{y}_2 - \mathbf{x}_2\|^2_{2^{\tau}\lambda,2} + \|\mathbf{y}_2 + \phi\mathbf{z}_2 - \mathbf{x}_1\|^2_{2^{\tau}\lambda,2}$
  if $dis_1 < dis_2$ **then**
    return $(\mathbf{y}_1, \mathbf{y}_1 + \phi\mathbf{z}_1)$
  else
    return $(\mathbf{y}_2 + \phi\mathbf{z}_2, \mathbf{y}_2)$
  end if
end if

One practical implication of the scalability property is illustrated in lines 6–7 of Algorithm 2. Specifically, by scaling $\mathcal{C}_{n/2,\tau}(\lambda)$ to $\mathcal{C}_{n/2,\tau}(2\lambda)$, the computation of $\mathsf{BDD}_{\mathcal{C}_{n/2,\tau}(\lambda)}(\mathbf{x})$ can be reformulated as

$$\mathsf{BDD}_{\mathcal{C}_{n/2,\tau}(\lambda)}(\mathbf{x}) = \frac{1}{2}\mathsf{BDD}_{\mathcal{C}_{n/2,\tau}(2\lambda)}(2\mathbf{x}).$$

This transformation, when combined with the subsequent parameter selection for the cryptographic scheme, ensures that all computations are performed strictly over integers. This avoids operations over dyadic rationals that would otherwise arise from the use of $\phi^{-1} = \frac{1-i}{2}$, thereby eliminating the need for fixed-point or rational arithmetic. Such an integer-only approach is particularly crucial in cryptographic implementations, where it contributes to both efficiency and implementation security.

Lemma 2. *Given a target vector* $\mathbf{x}$ *satisfing* $\mathrm{dist}(\mathbf{x}, \mathcal{C}_{n,\tau}(\lambda)) < r = \sqrt{\frac{n}{8}}\lambda$. *Then* $\mathsf{BDD}_{\mathcal{C}_{n,\tau}(\lambda)}(\mathbf{x})$ *in Algorithm 2 outputs the unique lattice code vector* $\mathbf{w} \in \mathcal{C}_{n,\tau}(\lambda)$ *such that* $\|\mathbf{x} - \mathbf{w}\|_{2^\tau\lambda,2} < r$.

Proof. According to Lemma 1, the packing radius of $\mathrm{BW}_n(\lambda)$ is $\sqrt{\frac{n}{8}}\lambda = r$. Therefore, if there exists a vector $\mathbf{w} \in \mathcal{C}_{n,\tau}(\lambda)$ satisfying $\|\mathbf{x} - \mathbf{w}\|_{2^\tau\lambda,2} < r$, this ensures that $\mathbf{w}$ is the closest lattice codeword to $\mathbf{x}$, thereby guaranteeing uniqueness. It remains to show that $\mathsf{BDD}_{\mathcal{C}_{n,\tau}(\lambda)}(\mathbf{x})$ indeed corresponds to this unique lattice codeword.

We begin by bisecting $\mathbf{w} = (\mathbf{w}_1, \mathbf{w}_2)$. Since $\mathbf{w} \in \mathcal{C}_{n,\tau}(\lambda)$, it follows from Definition 1 that $\mathbf{w}_1, \mathbf{w}_2, \phi^{-1}(\mathbf{w}_2 - \mathbf{w}_1) \in \mathcal{C}_{n/2,\tau}(\lambda)$. We now establish that $\mathbf{w} = \mathsf{BDD}_{\mathcal{C}_{n,\tau}(\lambda)}(\mathbf{x})$ by induction.

For the base case $n = 2$, it is straightforward to verify that the unique lattice vector in $\mathcal{C}_{2,\tau}(\lambda)$ is given by $\lambda(\left\lfloor \frac{\mathbf{x}}{\lambda} \right\rceil \bmod 2^\tau)$. For $n = 2^k \geq 4$, since $\|\mathbf{x} - \mathbf{w}\|^2_{2^\tau\lambda,2} = \|\mathbf{x}_1 - \mathbf{w}_1\|^2_{2^\tau\lambda,2} + \|\mathbf{x}_2 - \mathbf{w}_2\|^2_{2^\tau\lambda,2}$, at least one of the following inequalities must hold:

$$\|\mathbf{x}_1 - \mathbf{w}_1\|^2_{2^\tau\lambda,2} < \frac{n\lambda^2}{16} \quad \text{or} \quad \|\mathbf{x}_2 - \mathbf{w}_2\|^2_{2^\tau\lambda,2} < \frac{n\lambda^2}{16}.$$

- **Case 1:** $\|\mathbf{x}_1 - \mathbf{w}_1\|^2_{2^\tau\lambda,2} < n\lambda^2/16$. Since $\mathrm{dist}(\mathbf{x}_1, \mathcal{C}_{n/2,\tau}(\lambda)) \leq \|\mathbf{x}_1 - \mathbf{w}_1\|_{2^\tau\lambda,2} < \sqrt{n}\lambda/4 = \rho(\mathrm{BW}_{n/2}(\lambda))$, by induction we have $\mathbf{y}_1 = \mathbf{w}_1$ in line 5 of Algorithm 2. Furthermore, since $\|\mathbf{x}_2 - \mathbf{w}_2\|^2_{2^\tau\lambda,2} < n\lambda^2/8$, we obtain that $\|\phi^{-1}(\mathbf{x}_2 - \mathbf{w}_2)\|^2_{2^\tau\lambda,2} < n\lambda^2/16$, which implies that $\|\phi^{-1}(\mathbf{x}_2 - \mathbf{y}_1) - \phi^{-1}(\mathbf{w}_2 - \mathbf{w}_1)\|^2_{2^\tau\lambda,2} < n\lambda^2/16$. Since $\phi^{-1}(\mathbf{w}_2 - \mathbf{w}_1) \in \mathcal{C}_{n/2,\tau}(\lambda)$, the induction hypothesis ensures that $\mathbf{z}_1 = \phi^{-1}(\mathbf{w}_2 - \mathbf{w}_1)$ in line 6.
- **Case 2:** $\|\mathbf{x}_2 - \mathbf{w}_2\|^2_{2^\tau\lambda,2} < n\lambda^2/16$. By a similar argument, we conclude that $\mathbf{y}_2 = \mathbf{w}_2$ and $\mathbf{z}_2 = \phi^{-1}(\mathbf{w}_1 - \mathbf{w}_2)$.

Hence, either $(\mathbf{y}_1, \mathbf{y}_1 + \phi\mathbf{z}_1)$ or $(\mathbf{y}_2 + \phi\mathbf{z}_2, \mathbf{y}_2)$ equals to the unique vector $\mathbf{w}$. After comparing their distance to $\mathbf{x}$, the output of Algorithm 2 satisfies $\mathsf{BDD}_{\mathcal{C}_{n,\tau}(\lambda)}(\mathbf{x}) = \mathbf{w}$, completing the proof. □

Algorithm 3. $\mathsf{Decode}_{\mathcal{C}_{n,\tau}(\lambda)}(\mathbf{x} \in \mathbb{C}^{n/2})$

Input: A target vector $\mathbf{x} \in \mathbb{C}^{n/2}$
Output: μ-bit string $\mathbf{m} \in \{0,1\}^{\mu}$
1: $\mathbf{w} := \mathsf{BDD}_{\mathcal{C}_{n,\tau}(\lambda)}(\mathbf{x})$
2: $\mathbf{v} := \frac{1}{\lambda}\mathbf{w} \cdot \mathbf{W}_n^{-1}$
3: Denote $\mathbf{v} = (v_0, \ldots, v_{\frac{n}{2}-1})$, where $v_j = a_j + b_j i$
4: **for** j from 0 to $\frac{n}{2} - 1$ **do**
5: $\quad b'_j := b_j \bmod 2^{\tau - \lceil w_H(j)/2 \rceil}$
6: $\quad a'_j := a_j - (b_j - b'_j) \bmod 2^{\tau - \lfloor w_H(j)/2 \rfloor}$
7: $\quad v'_j := a'_j + b'_j i$
8: $\quad \mathbf{m}_j := \xi^{-1}_{2\tau - w_H(j)}(v'_j)$
9: **end for**
10: Set $\bar{\mathbf{m}} = (\mathbf{m}_0, \mathbf{m}_1, \ldots, \mathbf{m}_{\frac{n}{2}-1})$ and define $\mathbf{m}$ as the first μ bits of $\bar{\mathbf{m}}$
11: **return m**

The second sub-process serves as the inverse of the encoding procedure, as described in lines 2 to 11 of Algorithm 3. Due to the modulo operation in line 7 of Algorithm 1, it is necessary to adjust the entries of the vector $\mathbf{v}$ to ensure that it belongs to the set $\mathcal{V}$, as defined in the proof of Theorem 1. The following theorem establishes the correctness of the decoding procedure.

Theorem 2 (Correct Decoding Bound). *Let* $\mathbf{m}_0 \in \{0,1\}^{\mu}$ *be a given message, and define* $\mathbf{w}_0 := \mathsf{Encode}_{\mathcal{C}_{n,\tau}(\lambda)}(\mathbf{m}_0)$*. For any* $\mathbf{x} \in \mathbb{C}^{n/2}$*, let* $\mathbf{m} := \mathsf{Decode}_{\mathcal{C}_{n,\tau}(\lambda)}(\mathbf{x})$*. If* $\|\mathbf{x} - \mathbf{w}_0\|_{2^\tau\lambda,2} < \sqrt{\frac{n}{8}}\lambda$*, then* $\mathbf{m} = \mathbf{m}_0$*.*

Proof. From the encoding process in Algorithm 1, let $\mathbf{w}_0 = \lambda \cdot (\mathbf{v}_0\mathbf{W}_n \bmod 2^{\tau})$, where $\mathbf{v}_0 \in \mathcal{V}$ corresponds to $\mathbf{m}_0$. Since $\|\mathbf{x}-\mathbf{w}_0\|_{2^\tau\lambda,2} < \sqrt{\frac{n}{8}}\lambda$, applying Lemma 2 yields $\mathsf{BDD}_{\mathcal{C}_{n,\tau}(\lambda)}(\mathbf{x}) = \mathbf{w}_0$. Thus, when decoding with $\mathbf{x}$ in Algorithm 3, we obtain

$$\mathbf{v} = \frac{1}{\lambda}\mathsf{BDD}_{\mathcal{C}_{n,\tau}(\lambda)}(\mathbf{x}) \cdot \mathbf{W}_n^{-1} = (\mathbf{v}_0\mathbf{W}_n \bmod 2^{\tau}) \cdot \mathbf{W}_n^{-1}. \tag{2}$$

Denote $\mathbf{v} = (v_0, \ldots, v_{\frac{n}{2}-1})$ and $\mathbf{v}' = (v'_0, \ldots, v'_{\frac{n}{2}-1})$ in Algorithm 3, where $\mathbf{v}' \in \mathcal{V}$ corresponds to $\mathbf{m}$. To complete the proof, it suffices to show that $\mathbf{v}' = \mathbf{v}_0$, since this naturally implies $\mathbf{m} = \mathbf{m}_0$ according to the definition of ξ_l.

Recall the ϕ-adic valuation $\nu_\phi(\cdot)$ introduced in the proof of Theorem 1. We first demonstrate that lines 4 to 9 of Algorithm 3 ensure that $\phi^{2\tau - w_H(j)}$ divides $(v_j - v'_j)$, which is equivalent to showing $\nu_\phi(v_j - v'_j) \geq 2\tau - w_H(j)$. Since $v_j - v'_j = (a_j - a'_j - (b_j - b'_j)) + (b_j - b'_j)\phi$ and $\nu_\phi(2) = \nu_\phi(-i\phi^2) = 2$, by the definitions of a'_j and b'_j, we obtain

$$\begin{aligned}\nu_\phi(a_j - a'_j - (b_j - b'_j)) &\geq \nu_\phi(2^{\tau - \lfloor w_H(j)/2 \rfloor}) = 2\tau - 2\lfloor w_H(j)/2 \rfloor, \\ \nu_\phi((b_j - b'_j)\phi) &\geq \nu_\phi(2^{\tau - \lceil w_H(j)/2 \rceil}) + \nu_\phi(\phi) = 2\tau - 2\lceil w_H(j)/2 \rceil + 1.\end{aligned}$$

By the triangle inequality, it follows that

$$\nu_\phi(v_j - v'_j) \geq \min(2\tau - 2\lfloor w_H(j)/2 \rfloor, 2\tau - 2\lceil w_H(j)/2 \rceil + 1) = 2\tau - w_H(j),$$

which implies that $\phi^{2\tau - w_H(j)} \mid (v_j - v'_j)$, as desired.

Then, by Lemma 5 in Appendix A, each entry in the j-th row of $\mathbf{W}_n$ is divisible by $\phi^{w_H(j)}$. Thus each entry of $(\mathbf{v} - \mathbf{v}') \cdot \mathbf{W}_n$ is divisible by $\phi^{2\tau}$,which implies $(\mathbf{v} - \mathbf{v}') \cdot \mathbf{W}_n = 0 \mod 2^\tau$. Therefore, from (2) we deduce $\mathbf{v}'\mathbf{W}_n = \mathbf{v}_0\mathbf{W}_n \mod 2^\tau$. By the injectivity indicated in Theorem 1, it follows that $\mathbf{v}' = \mathbf{v}_0$, which completes the proof. □

4 Construction and Analysis

4.1 The IND-CPA-Secure PKE

Let $\kappa, l, d_\mathbf{u}, d_v$ be positive integer parameters. Let $n = 2^k$ and τ be the parameters of the nested lattices $\mathcal{C}_{n,\tau}(\lambda)$. The message space is defined as $\mathcal{M} = \{0,1\}^{\frac{N}{n}\mu_0}$, where $\mu_0 = \tau n - \frac{n}{4}(k-1)$. Each message $m \in \mathcal{M}$ is represented as a polynomial in $\mathcal{R}$ with binary coefficients. Our public-key encryption scheme BW-PKE is described in Fig. 2.

The scalable lattice coding introduced in Sect. 3.2 is primarily realized through the PolyEncode and PolyDecode procedures. This newly designed error-correction mechanism constitutes the main distinction between BW-PKE and the K-PKE used in ML-KEM [40], and it fully demonstrates the flexibility and efficiency of scalability. In the PolyEncode algorithm, the scaling factor is set to $\frac{q}{2^\tau}$. The input message is divided into $d = \frac{N}{n}$ blocks, each containing μ_0 bits, and each block is encoded via $\mathsf{Encode}_{\mathcal{C}_{n,\tau}(\frac{q}{2^\tau})}$ into n coefficients spaced d positions apart, as shown in line 6 of PolyEncode. The rationale behind this encoding strategy will be further discussed in Sect. 5.1.

In contrast, the decoding procedure first performs a modulus-switching operation on the target polynomial $v' - \mathbf{s}^T\mathbf{u}'$ (line 3 of BW-PKE.Dec), thereby adopting a different scaling factor $\frac{\hat{q}}{2^\tau}$ in the subsequent PolyDecode algorithm, where $\hat{q} = 2^{\lceil \log_2 q \rceil}$. This choice of a power-of-two scaling factor simplifies the arithmetic in the decoding process by enabling efficient bit-shifts and eliminating reliance on fixed-point arithmetic, thus significantly improving both computational efficiency and implementation security. The target polynomial is then similarly divided into d blocks, each consisting of n coefficients, and decoded via $\mathsf{Decode}_{\mathcal{C}_{n,\tau}(\frac{\hat{q}}{2^\tau})}$.

Correctness of the PKE Scheme. We analyze the correctness of BW-PKE by evaluating its decryption error probability. To this end, we first establish the following lemma, which illustrates the flexibility gained from employing distinct scaling factors.

Lemma 3. *It holds that* $w \bmod {}^{\pm}\hat{q} = \frac{\hat{q}}{q}(\frac{q}{\hat{q}}w \bmod {}^{\pm}q)$. *Consequently, we have* $\mathsf{PolyDecode}_{\mathcal{C}_{n,\tau}(\frac{\hat{q}}{2^\tau})}(w \bmod {}^{\pm}\hat{q}) = \mathsf{PolyDecode}_{\mathcal{C}_{n,\tau}(\frac{q}{2^\tau})}(\frac{q}{\hat{q}}w \bmod {}^{\pm}q)$.

BW-PKE.KeyGen()

$\rho, \sigma \xleftarrow{\$} \{0,1\}^{\kappa}$
$\mathbf{A} \sim \mathcal{R}_q^{l \times l} := \mathsf{Sample}(\rho)$
$(\mathbf{s}, \mathbf{e}) \sim \beta_{\eta_1}^l \times \beta_{\eta_1}^l := \mathsf{Sample}(\sigma)$
$\mathbf{t} := \mathbf{A}\mathbf{s} + \mathbf{e}$
return $(\mathsf{pk} := (\mathbf{t}, \rho), \mathsf{sk} := \mathbf{s})$

BW-PKE.Enc($\mathsf{pk} = (\mathbf{t}, \rho), m; r \in \{0,1\}^{\kappa}$)

$\mathbf{A} \sim \mathcal{R}_q^{l \times l} := \mathsf{Sample}(\rho)$
$\mathbf{r} \sim \beta_{\eta_1}^l := \mathsf{Sample}(r)$
$(\mathbf{e}_1, e_2) \sim \beta_{\eta_2}^l \times \beta_{\eta_2} := \mathsf{Sample}(r)$
$\mathbf{u}_0 := \mathbf{A}^T \mathbf{r} + \mathbf{e}_1$
$v_0 := \mathbf{t}^T \mathbf{r} + e_2$
$\mathbf{u} := \mathsf{Compress}_{q, 2^{d_\mathbf{u}}}(\mathbf{u}_0)$
$v := \mathsf{Compress}_{q, 2^{d_v}}(v_0 + \lfloor \mathsf{PolyEncode}(m) \rceil)$
return $c := (\mathbf{u}, v)$

BW-PKE.Dec($\mathsf{sk} = \mathbf{s}, c = (\mathbf{u}, v)$)

$\mathbf{u}' := \mathsf{Decompress}_{2^{d_\mathbf{u}}, q}(\mathbf{u})$
$v' := \mathsf{Decompress}_{2^{d_v}, q}(v)$
$w := \left\lfloor \frac{\hat{q}}{q}(v' - \mathbf{s}^T \mathbf{u}') \right\rceil$
$m' := \mathsf{PolyDecode}(w \bmod {}^{\pm}\hat{q})$
return m'

PolyEncode($m = \sum_{j=0}^{\frac{N}{n}\mu_0 - 1} m_j x^j \in \mathcal{M}$)

for j from 0 to $\frac{N}{n} - 1$ **do**
  $\mathbf{m}_j := (m_{\mu_0 j}, m_{\mu_0 j+1}, \cdots, , m_{\mu_0 j + \mu_0 - 1}) \in \{0,1\}^{\mu_0}$
  $\mathbf{w}_j := \mathsf{Encode}_{\mathcal{C}_{n,\tau}(q/2^{\tau})}(\mathbf{m}_j) \in \mathbb{C}^{n/2}$
  Decompose $\mathbf{w}_j$ into $\mathbf{w}_j = \mathbf{a}_j + \mathbf{b}_j i$, where $\mathbf{a}_j, \mathbf{b}_j \in \mathbb{R}^{n/2}$
  $(a_{j,0}, a_{j,1}, \cdots, a_{j,n/2-1}) := \mathbf{a}_j, (b_{j,0}, b_{j,1}, \cdots, b_{j,n/2-1}) := \mathbf{b}_j$
  $(w_j, w_{j+d}, \cdots, w_{j+(n-1)d}) := (a_{j,0}, b_{j,0}, \cdots, a_{j,n/2-1}, b_{j,n/2-1})$
endfor
$w := \sum_{j=0}^{N-1} w_j x^j$
return w

PolyDecode($w = \sum_{j=0}^{N-1} w_j x^j \in \mathcal{R}_{\hat{q}}$)

for j from 0 to $\frac{N}{n} - 1$ **do**
  $\mathbf{a}_j := (w_j, w_{j+2d}, \cdots, , w_{j+(n-2)d}) \in \mathbb{R}^{n/2}$
  $\mathbf{b}_j := (w_{j+d}, w_{j+3d}, \cdots, , w_{j+(n-1)d}) \in \mathbb{R}^{n/2}$
  $\mathbf{x}_j := \mathbf{a}_j + \mathbf{b}_j i \in \mathbb{C}^{n/2}$
  $\mathbf{m}_j := \mathsf{Decode}_{\mathcal{C}_{n,\tau}(\hat{q}/2^{\tau})}(\mathbf{x}_j) \in \{0,1\}^{\mu_0}$
  $(m_{\mu_0 j}, m_{\mu_0 j+1}, \cdots, , m_{\mu_0 j + \mu_0 - 1}) := \mathbf{m}_j$
endfor
$m := \sum_{j=0}^{\frac{N}{n}\mu_0 - 1} m_j x^j \in \mathcal{M}$
return m

Fig. 2. The description of BW-PKE.

Proof. Since the centered modular reduction $\frac{q}{\hat{q}} w \bmod {}^{\pm}q$ implies the existence of a polynomial $\theta \in \mathbb{Z}[x]/(x^N + 1)$ with integer coefficients such that

$$\frac{q}{\hat{q}} w \bmod {}^{\pm}q = \frac{q}{\hat{q}} w + q\theta,$$

each component of $\frac{q}{\hat{q}} w + q\theta$ lies in the interval $[-\frac{q}{2}, \frac{q}{2})$. Multiplying both sides by $\frac{\hat{q}}{q}$ yields that every component of $w + \hat{q}\theta$ lies in $[-\frac{\hat{q}}{2}, \frac{\hat{q}}{2})$, and hence

$$\begin{aligned} w \bmod {}^{\pm}\hat{q} &= w + \hat{q}\theta \\ &= \frac{\hat{q}}{q}\left(\frac{q}{\hat{q}} w + q\theta\right) \\ &= \frac{\hat{q}}{q}\left(\frac{q}{\hat{q}} w \bmod {}^{\pm}q\right). \end{aligned}$$

Now consider the decoding operation. Scaling the lattice code $\mathcal{C}_{n,\tau}(\frac{\hat{q}}{2^{\tau}})$ and the input $w \bmod {}^{\pm}\hat{q}$ by the same factor $\frac{q}{\hat{q}}$ gives

$$\begin{aligned} m' &= \mathsf{PolyDecode}_{\mathcal{C}_{n,\tau}(\frac{\hat{q}}{2^{\tau}})}(w \bmod {}^{\pm}\hat{q}) \\ &= \mathsf{PolyDecode}_{\mathcal{C}_{n,\tau}(\frac{\hat{q}}{q} \cdot \frac{q}{2^{\tau}})}\left(\frac{\hat{q}}{q}(\frac{q}{\hat{q}} w \bmod {}^{\pm}q)\right) \\ &= \mathsf{PolyDecode}_{\mathcal{C}_{n,\tau}(\frac{q}{2^{\tau}})}\left(\frac{q}{\hat{q}} w \bmod {}^{\pm}q\right). \end{aligned}$$

This completes the proof. □

Based on Lemma 3, we now present the following theorem that formalizes the correctness guarantee of BW-PKE.

Theorem 3. *Let* $\mathbf{s}, \mathbf{e}, \mathbf{r}, \mathbf{e}_1, e_2$ *be random variables distributed as specified in Fig. 2. Let* $\boldsymbol{\epsilon}_\mathbf{u} \leftarrow \phi^l_{d_\mathbf{u}}$ *and* $\epsilon_v \leftarrow \phi_{d_v}$*, where the distribution* ϕ^m_d *over* $\mathcal{R}^m$ *is defined as follows: sample* $\mathbf{x} \xleftarrow{\$} \mathcal{R}^m$ *and output* $\left(\mathbf{x} - \mathsf{Decompress}_{2^d,q}(\mathsf{Compress}_{q,2^d}(\mathbf{x}))\right) \bmod {}^{\pm}q$.

For a polynomial f*, we define its* i*-th block as* $(f)_i = (f_i, f_{i+d}, f_{i+2d}, \dots, f_{i+(n-1)d})$ *for* $i \in \{0, 1, \dots, d-1\}$*. That is, each block comprises* n *coefficients spaced exactly* $d = \frac{N}{n}$ *positions apart. Let* Err *be the error polynomial* $\mathbf{e}^T\mathbf{r} - \mathbf{s}^T(\mathbf{e}_1 + \boldsymbol{\epsilon}_\mathbf{u}) + e_2 + \epsilon_v$*. Denote*

$$\delta = 1 - \Pr\left[\|(\mathsf{Err})_i\|_{q,2} < r_0,\ \forall i\right],$$

where $r_0 = \frac{q\sqrt{2n}}{2^{\tau+2}} - \frac{\sqrt{n}}{2}\left(\frac{q}{\hat{q}} + 1\right)$*. Then* BW-PKE *is* $(1-\delta)$*-correct.*

Proof. According to the BW-PKE.Dec procedure described in Fig. 2, the value of $\mathbf{u}'$ is given by

$$\begin{aligned}\mathbf{u}' &= \mathsf{Decompress}_{2^{d_\mathbf{u}},q}\left(\mathsf{Compress}_{q,2^{d_\mathbf{u}}}(\mathbf{A}^T\mathbf{r} + \mathbf{e}_1)\right)\\ &= \mathbf{A}^T\mathbf{r} + \mathbf{e}_1 + \boldsymbol{\epsilon}_\mathbf{u},\end{aligned}$$

for some $\boldsymbol{\epsilon}_\mathbf{u} \in \mathcal{R}^l$. Similarly, the value of v' is computed as

$$\begin{aligned}v' &= \mathsf{Decompress}_{2^{d_v},q}\left(\mathsf{Compress}_{q,2^{d_v}}(\mathbf{t}^T\mathbf{r} + e_2 + \lfloor \mathsf{PolyEncode}(m) \rceil)\right)\\ &= (\mathbf{A}\mathbf{s} + \mathbf{e})^T\mathbf{r} + e_2 + \lfloor \mathsf{PolyEncode}(m) \rceil + \epsilon_v,\end{aligned}$$

for some $\epsilon_v \in \mathcal{R}$. We may safely assume that $\boldsymbol{\epsilon}_\mathbf{u}$ and ϵ_v follow the distributions $\phi^l_{d_\mathbf{u}}$ and ϕ_{d_v}, respectively, since they both take the form

$$\left(\mathbf{x} - \mathsf{Decompress}_{2^d,q}(\mathsf{Compress}_{q,2^d}(\mathbf{x}))\right) \bmod {}^{\pm}q,$$

where $\mathbf{x}$ is pseudorandom under the hardness assumption of the Module-LWE problem.

Denote $\epsilon_1 = \left\lfloor \frac{\hat{q}}{q}(v' - \mathbf{s}^T\mathbf{u}') \right\rceil - \frac{\hat{q}}{q}(v' - \mathbf{s}^T\mathbf{u}')$, and $\epsilon_2 = \lfloor \mathsf{PolyEncode}(m) \rceil - \mathsf{PolyEncode}(m)$. From Lemma 3, it follows that

$$m' = \mathsf{PolyDecode}_{\mathcal{C}_{n,\tau}\left(\frac{q}{2^\tau}\right)}\left(\frac{q}{\hat{q}}\left\lfloor \frac{\hat{q}}{q}(v' - \mathbf{s}^T\mathbf{u}') \right\rceil \bmod {}^{\pm}q\right).$$

We then derive

$$\begin{aligned}\frac{q}{\hat{q}}\left\lfloor \frac{\hat{q}}{q}(v' - \mathbf{s}^T\mathbf{u}') \right\rceil &= v' - \mathbf{s}^T\mathbf{u}' + \frac{q}{\hat{q}}\epsilon_1\\ &= (\mathbf{A}\mathbf{s} + \mathbf{e})^T\mathbf{r} + e_2 + \lfloor \mathsf{PolyEncode}(m) \rceil + \epsilon_v - \mathbf{s}^T(\mathbf{A}^T\mathbf{r} + \mathbf{e}_1 + \boldsymbol{\epsilon}_\mathbf{u}) + \frac{q}{\hat{q}}\epsilon_1\\ &= \mathsf{PolyEncode}(m) + \mathbf{e}^T\mathbf{r} - \mathbf{s}^T(\mathbf{e}_1 + \boldsymbol{\epsilon}_\mathbf{u}) + e_2 + \epsilon_v + \frac{q}{\hat{q}}\epsilon_1 + \epsilon_2.\end{aligned}$$

Every n coefficients spaced $d = \frac{N}{n}$ positions apart of $\mathsf{PolyEncode}(m)$ (referred to as a *block*) essentially correspond to a lattice code vector in $\mathcal{C}_{n,\tau}(\frac{q}{2^\tau})$. The deviation from the target lattice point is then bounded by

$$\left\|(\mathbf{e}^T\mathbf{r} - \mathbf{s}^T(\mathbf{e}_1 + \boldsymbol{\epsilon}_\mathbf{u}) + e_2 + \epsilon_v)_i\right\|_{q,2} + \frac{q}{\hat{q}}\|(\epsilon_1)_i\|_{q,2} + \|(\epsilon_2)_i\|_{q,2}$$
$$\leq \left\|(\mathbf{e}^T\mathbf{r} - \mathbf{s}^T(\mathbf{e}_1 + \boldsymbol{\epsilon}_\mathbf{u}) + e_2 + \epsilon_v)_i\right\|_{q,2} + \frac{\sqrt{n}}{2}\left(\frac{q}{\hat{q}} + 1\right),$$

since $(\epsilon_1)_i, (\epsilon_2)_i \in (-\frac{1}{2}, \frac{1}{2}]^n$.

According to Theorem 2, decoding succeeds whenever the above deviation is smaller than the packing radius $\frac{q\sqrt{2n}}{2^{\tau+2}}$. Hence, the decryption error probability of $\mathsf{BW\text{-}PKE}$ is

$$1 - \Pr\left[\left\|(\mathbf{e}^T\mathbf{r} - \mathbf{s}^T\mathbf{e}_1 - \mathbf{s}^T\boldsymbol{\epsilon}_\mathbf{u} + e_2 + \epsilon_v)_i\right\|_{q,2} < r_0,\ \forall i\right], \tag{3}$$

where $r_0 = \frac{q\sqrt{2n}}{2^{\tau+2}} - \frac{\sqrt{n}}{2}(\frac{q}{\hat{q}} + 1)$. □

The above provides only the formal statement of correctness. A more comprehensive analysis, including the evaluation methodology for estimating the decryption error rate under concrete parameter settings, will be provided in Sect. 5.

Security of the PKE Scheme. The following theorem establishes the IND-CPA security of $\mathsf{BW\text{-}PKE}$ under the MLWE assumption. The proof is omitted as it straightforwardly follows standard techniques for MLWE-based schemes [8].

Theorem 4 (IND-CPA security of BW-PKE). *For any adversary $\mathcal{A}$ against the IND-CPA security of* $\mathsf{BW\text{-}PKE}$, *there exists an adversary $\mathcal{B}$ such that*

$$\mathsf{Adv}^{\mathsf{IND\text{-}CPA}}_{\mathsf{BW\text{-}PKE}}(\mathcal{A}) \leq 2 \cdot \mathsf{Adv}^{\mathsf{MLWE}}_{l+1,l,\beta_\eta}(\mathcal{B}).$$

4.2 The IND-CCA-Secure KEM

We construct our KEM scheme using $\mathrm{FO}^{\not\perp}_{\mathsf{ID(pk)},m}$, a variant of the Fujisaki-Okamoto (FO) transformation [21,23], designed to achieve strengthened IND-CCA security in the multi-user setting [16], which naturally ensures security in a single-user scenario.

Let $\iota, \gamma \in \mathbb{N}$ be integers. Let $\mathcal{PK}$ denote the public key space of $\mathsf{BW\text{-}PKE}$, $\mathcal{K}$ the key space of $\mathsf{BW\text{-}KEM}$, and $\mathcal{R}$ the randomness space for $\mathsf{BW\text{-}PKE.Enc}$. Let $\mathsf{H} : \{0,1\}^* \to \mathcal{K} \times \mathcal{R}$ be a hash function, where $\mathsf{H}_1(\cdot)$ corresponds to the component mapped into $\mathcal{K}$. Also, let $\mathsf{ID} : \mathcal{PK} \to \{0,1\}^\gamma$ be a fixed-output-length function. The key encapsulation mechanism $\mathsf{BW\text{-}KEM}$ is specified in Fig. 3.

BW-KEM.KeyGen()	BW-KEM.Encaps(pk)	BW-KEM.Decaps((sk, z), c)
$(\mathsf{pk}, \mathsf{sk}) \leftarrow$ BW-PKE.KeyGen()	$m \xleftarrow{\$} \mathcal{M}$	$m' :=$ PKE.Dec(sk, c)
$z \xleftarrow{\$} \{0,1\}^{\iota}$	$(K, r) := \mathsf{H}(\mathsf{ID}(\mathsf{pk}), m)$	$(K', r') := \mathsf{H}(\mathsf{ID}(\mathsf{pk}), m')$
return $(\mathsf{pk}' := \mathsf{pk}, \mathsf{sk}' := (\mathsf{sk}, z))$	$c \leftarrow$ BW-PKE.Enc(pk, $m; r$)	$\tilde{K} := \mathsf{H}_1(\mathsf{ID}(\mathsf{pk}), z, c)$
	return (c, K)	**if** $m' = \perp$ or BW-PKE.Enc(pk, $m'; r'$) $\neq c$
		return $\tilde{K}$
		else return K'

Fig. 3. The description of BW-KEM.

Correctness of the KEM Scheme. It is evident that if BW-PKE is $(1-\delta)$-correct and H is modeled as a random oracle, then BW-KEM is $(1-\delta)$-correct.

Security of the KEM Scheme. Since our KEM scheme is obtained by applying the $\mathrm{FO}^{\not\perp}_{\mathsf{ID}(\mathsf{pk}),m}$ transformation, we leverage the results from [16] to establish the following security theorem. Specifically, we show that BW-KEM achieves IND-CCA security in both the Random Oracle Model (ROM) [5] and the Quantum Random Oracle Model (QROM) [7].

Theorem 5 (IND-CCA security in the (Q)ROM [16]**).** *Let ℓ be the min-entropy of* ID(pk), *i.e., $\ell = \mathsf{H}_\infty(\mathsf{ID}(\mathsf{pk}))$. For any (quantum) adversary $\mathcal{A}$, making at most q_D decapsulation queries, q_H (Q)RO queries, against the IND-CCA security of* BW-KEM, *there exits (quantum) adversary $\mathcal{B}$ against the IND-CPA security of* BW-PKE *(with roughly the same running time), such that:*

- *In the ROM, it holds that* $\mathsf{Adv}^{\mathsf{IND\text{-}CCA}}_{\mathsf{BW\text{-}KEM}}(\mathcal{A}) \leq$
$$2\mathsf{Adv}^{\mathsf{IND\text{-}CPA}}_{\mathsf{BW\text{-}PKE}}(\mathcal{B}) + \frac{2(q_H+1)}{|\mathcal{M}|} + \frac{q_H}{2^{\iota}} + (q_H + q_D)\delta + \frac{1}{2^{\ell}};$$
- *In the QROM, it holds that* $\mathsf{Adv}^{\mathsf{IND\text{-}CCA}}_{\mathsf{BW\text{-}KEM}}(\mathcal{A}) \leq$
$$2\sqrt{q_{HD}\mathsf{Adv}^{\mathsf{IND\text{-}CPA}}_{\mathsf{BW\text{-}PKE}}(\mathcal{B})} + \frac{4q_{HD}}{\sqrt{|\mathcal{M}|}} + \frac{4(q_H+1)}{\sqrt{2^{\iota}}} + 16q_{HD}^2\delta + \frac{1}{|\mathcal{M}|} + \frac{1}{2^{\ell}},$$

where $q_{HD} := q_H + q_D + 1$.

5 Analyzing the DFR Without Independence Assumption

Recalling Theorem 3, the decryption failure rate (DFR) of BW-KEM is expressed as $\delta = 1 - \Pr\left[\|(\mathsf{Err})_i\|_{q,2} < r_0,\ \forall i\right]$, where the noise polynomial is defined as $\mathsf{Err} = \mathbf{e}^T\mathbf{r} - \mathbf{s}^T(\mathbf{e}_1 + \boldsymbol{\epsilon}_{\mathbf{u}}) + e_2 + \epsilon_v$. It is crucial to note that the coefficients arising from the products $\mathbf{e}^T\mathbf{r}$ and $\mathbf{s}^T(\mathbf{e}_1 + \boldsymbol{\epsilon}_{\mathbf{u}})$ are inherently dependent. Ignoring this dependence can lead to a substantial underestimation of the DFR, particularly in contexts where error-correcting codes are employed [15]. To mitigate this issue and ensure a reliable evaluation of the DFR and concrete security, we therefore develop in this section a methodology for estimating the DFR *without* relying on any independence assumptions among the coefficients of the noise polynomial.

5.1 The Joint Distribution of Coefficients in the Noise Polynomial

The successful decoding probability of the i-th block, denoted by $\Pr[\|(\mathsf{Err})_i\|_{q,2} < r_0]$, depends on the joint distribution of the n coefficients within that block. In this section, we characterize the n-dimensional noise distribution by decomposing its joint structure into a sum of simpler and mutually independent components. The main difficulty lies in analyzing the product terms $\mathbf{e}^T\mathbf{r}$ and $\mathbf{s}^T(\mathbf{e}_1 + \boldsymbol{\epsilon}_{\mathbf{u}})$. As a starting point, we establish the following lemma, which considers the fundamental case of a single polynomial multiplication.

Lemma 4. *Let $N = 2^{k_0}$ and $n = 2^k$ be powers of two with $k_0 > k > 1$. Suppose $f, g \in \mathcal{R}_q = \mathbb{Z}_q[x]/(x^N + 1)$ have coefficients drawn independently from distributions ψ_f and ψ_g, respectively. Let $h = f \cdot g \in \mathcal{R}_q$. For each $i \in \{0, 1, \ldots, d-1\}$ with $d = N/n$, define the partial coefficient vector of h*

$$\mathcal{H}_i = (h_i, h_{i+d}, h_{i+2d}, \ldots, h_{i+(n-1)d}),$$

where h_{i+jd} denotes the $(i + jd)$-th coefficient of h for $j = 0, 1, \ldots, n-1$.

Similarly, let $a, b \in \mathbb{Z}_q[y]/(y^n+1)$ have coefficients drawn independently from ψ_a and ψ_b, respectively. Let $c = a \cdot b \in \mathbb{Z}_q[y]/(y^n + 1)$, and denote by $\mathsf{Prod}_{\psi_a,\psi_b}$ the joint distribution of the coefficient vector $(c_0, c_1, \ldots, c_{n-1})$.

If ψ_f is symmetric over $\mathbb{Z}_q$, then each $\mathcal{H}_i$ shares the same distribution and can be expressed as the sum of d independent random variables following $\mathsf{Prod}_{\psi_f,\psi_g}$, namely,

$$\mathcal{H}_i = \sum_{j=0}^{d-1} \mathcal{J}_j, \quad \text{where} \quad \{\mathcal{J}_j\}_{j=0}^{d-1} \overset{\text{i.i.d.}}{\sim} \mathsf{Prod}_{\psi_f,\psi_g}.$$

Proof. We begin by establishing the ring isomorphism between $\mathbb{Z}_q[x]/(x^N + 1)$ and $[\mathbb{Z}_q[y]/(y^n + 1)][x]/(x^d - y)$. We define the mapping

$$\begin{aligned} \mathcal{I} : \mathbb{Z}_q[x]/(x^N + 1) &\to [\mathbb{Z}_q[y]/(y^n + 1)][x]/(x^d - y) \\ \omega(x) &\mapsto \sum_{i=0}^{d-1} \omega^{(i)}(y)x^i, \end{aligned}$$

where $\omega(x) = \omega_0 + \omega_1 x + \cdots + \omega_{N-1}x^{N-1} \in \mathbb{Z}_q[x]/(x^N + 1)$ and $\omega^{(i)}(y) = \sum_{j=0}^{n-1} \omega_{i+jd}y^j \in \mathbb{Z}_q[y]/(y^n + 1)$ for $i = 0, 1, \ldots, d-1$. This mapping groups the coefficients of $\omega(x)$ according to their residue classes modulo d, and thereby produces an element of $[\mathbb{Z}_q[y]/(y^n + 1)][x]/(x^d - y)$.

To prove that $\mathcal{I}$ is a ring isomorphism, we rely on a standard argument from commutative ring theory. Consider the bivariate polynomial ring $\mathbb{Z}_q[x, y]$ and the ideal $I = \langle y^n + 1,\ x^d - y\rangle$. The quotient ring $\mathbb{Z}_q[x, y]/I$ can be evaluated in two equivalent ways. First, eliminating y via the relation $y = x^d$ transforms the generator y^n+1 into $(x^d)^n+1 = x^N+1$, which yields the quotient ring $\mathbb{Z}_q[x]/(x^N+1)$. Alternatively, one may first quotient by $y^n + 1$, obtaining $\mathbb{Z}_q[y]/(y^n + 1)$, and then impose the relation $x^d - y$, resulting in the ring $[\mathbb{Z}_q[y]/(y^n+1)][x]/(x^d-y)$. Hence, we obtain the natural ring isomorphism:

$$\mathbb{Z}_q[x]/(x^N+1) \cong [\mathbb{Z}_q[y]/(y^n+1)][x]/(x^d-y).$$

The mapping $\mathcal{I}$ explicitly realizes this isomorphism by substituting $y = x^d$ and collecting monomials according to their degree modulo d.

Let $f(x) = \sum_{r=0}^{N-1} f_r x^r$ and $g(x) = \sum_{r=0}^{N-1} g_r x^r$ be elements in $\mathbb{Z}_q[x]/(x^N+1)$. Since $\mathcal{I}$ is a ring isomorphism, it strictly preserves multiplication, i.e., $\mathcal{I}(f(x) \cdot g(x)) = \mathcal{I}(f(x)) \cdot \mathcal{I}(g(x))$. Let $h(x) = f(x) \cdot g(x) \in \mathbb{Z}_q[x]/(x^N+1)$. Through the isomorphism, polynomial multiplication in $\mathbb{Z}_q[x]/(x^N+1)$ can be equivalently computed in the quotient ring $[\mathbb{Z}_q[y]/(y^n+1)][x]/(x^d-y)$. Thus, we have the following relation in the mapped ring:

$$\sum_{i=0}^{d-1} h^{(i)}(y)x^i = \left(\sum_{u=0}^{d-1} f^{(u)}(y)x^u\right)\left(\sum_{v=0}^{d-1} g^{(v)}(y)x^v\right).$$

Note that $\mathcal{H}_i = (h_i, h_{i+d}, h_{i+2d}, \ldots, h_{i+(n-1)d})$ coincides exactly with the coefficient vector of $h^{(i)}(y)$. By equating the coefficients of x^i on both sides and reducing any exponents $\geq d$ via the relation $x^d = y$, the coefficient $h^{(i)}(y)$ can be explicitly written as

$$h^{(i)}(y) = \sum_{s=0}^{i} f^{(i-s)}(y) \cdot g^{(s)}(y) + \sum_{s=i+1}^{d-1} \mathcal{S}(f^{(d+i-s)}(y)) \cdot g^{(s)}(y), \tag{4}$$

where $\mathcal{S}(\cdot)$ denotes the cyclic shift operator in $\mathbb{Z}_q[y]/(y^n+1)$ induced by multiplication by y, specifically,

$$\mathcal{S}(\nu(y)) = y \cdot \nu(y) = -\nu_{n-1} + \sum_{j=1}^{n-1} \nu_{j-1}y^j,$$

with $\nu(y) = \sum_{j=0}^{n-1} \nu_j y^j \in \mathbb{Z}_q[y]/(y^n+1)$.

Since $f, g \in \mathcal{R}_q = \mathbb{Z}_q[x]/(x^N+1)$ have coefficients drawn independently from distributions ψ_f and ψ_g, respectively, it can be observed that $h^{(i)}(y)$ in (4) is a sum of d independent polynomials in $\mathbb{Z}_q[y]/(y^n+1)$:

- the first $i+1$ polynomials correspond to the product of two polynomials $c = a \cdot b \in \mathbb{Z}_q[y]/(y^n+1)$, where a and b have coefficients drawn independently from ψ_f and ψ_g, respectively;
- the remaining $d-i-1$ polynomials correspond to a similar product, with a replaced by its cyclic shift $\mathcal{S}(a)$.

Since ψ_f is symmetric, the distribution of $f^{(d+i-s)}(y)$ is invariant under the cyclic shift operator $\mathcal{S}(\cdot)$ in (4). Hence, each $\mathcal{H}_i$ is identically distributed and can be expressed as a sum of d independent random variables following the distribution $\mathsf{Prod}_{\psi_f,\psi_g}$, i.e.,

$$\mathcal{H}_i = \sum_{j=0}^{d-1} \mathcal{J}_j, \quad \text{with} \quad \{\mathcal{J}_j\}_{j=0}^{d-1} \overset{\text{i.i.d.}}{\sim} \mathsf{Prod}_{\psi_f,\psi_g}.$$

□

Now consider the products $\mathbf{e}^T\mathbf{r}$ and $\mathbf{s}^T(\mathbf{e}_1 + \boldsymbol{\epsilon}_\mathbf{u})$ in the noise polynomial Err. As specified in Fig. 2 and Theorem 3, these polynomial vectors are mutually independent, and the components within each vector are independent and identically distributed. Moreover, the distributions of $\mathbf{e}$ and $\mathbf{s}$ are symmetric. Consequently, both products can be regarded as independent sums of l identically distributed polynomial multiplications that follow the structure characterized in Lemma 4. This observation immediately leads to the following corollary, which characterizes the joint distribution of the n coefficients in each block $(\mathsf{Err})_i$. For brevity, its proof is omitted.

Corollary 1. *Let* $\mathsf{Err} = \mathbf{e}^T\mathbf{r} - \mathbf{s}^T(\mathbf{e}_1 + \boldsymbol{\epsilon}_\mathbf{u}) + e_2 + \epsilon_v$ *be defined as in Theorem 3. Define the distribution* φ_d *as follows: sample a random* $x \overset{\$}{\leftarrow} \mathbb{Z}$ *and output* $(x - \mathsf{Decompress}_{2^d,q}(\mathsf{Compress}_{q,2^d}(x))) \bmod {}^{\pm}q$. *Then, for each* $i \in \{0, 1, \dots, d-1\}$ *with* $d = N/n$, *the* n*-dimensional coefficient vector* $(\mathsf{Err})_i$ *follows an identical distribution, which can be expressed as a sum of independent random variables:*

$$(\mathsf{Err})_i = \sum_{j=0}^{ld-1} \mathcal{X}_j + \sum_{j=0}^{ld-1} \mathcal{Y}_j + (e_2)_i + (\epsilon_v)_i,$$

where $\{\mathcal{X}_j\}_{j=0}^{ld-1} \overset{\text{i.i.d.}}{\sim} \mathsf{Prod}_{\mathcal{B}_{\eta_1},\mathcal{B}_{\eta_1}}$ *and* $\{\mathcal{Y}_j\}_{j=0}^{ld-1} \overset{\text{i.i.d.}}{\sim} \mathsf{Prod}_{\mathcal{B}_{\eta_1},\mathcal{B}_{\eta_2}+\varphi_{d_\mathbf{u}}}$. *Moreover,* $(e_2)_i$ *and* $(\epsilon_v)_i$ *are* n*-dimensional coefficient vectors whose components are independently drawn from* $\mathcal{B}_{\eta_2}$ *and* φ_{d_v}, *respectively.*

The above analysis clarifies the rationale behind the encoding polynomial coefficient embedding method illustrated in Fig. 2. To apply Corollary 1 for estimating the DFR of BW-KEM, each μ_0-bit message should be encoded into n coefficients spaced every $\frac{N}{n}$ entries. Since each block $(\mathsf{Err})_i$ follows the same distribution, a union bound on the DFR δ can be derived as

$$\begin{aligned}\delta &= 1 - \Pr\left[\|(\mathsf{Err})_i\|_{q,2} < r_0,\ \forall i\right] \\ &\le \sum_{i=0}^{\frac{N}{n}-1} \Pr\left[\|(\mathsf{Err})_i\|_{q,2} \ge r_0\right] = \frac{N}{n}\Pr\left[\|(\mathsf{Err})_0\|_{q,2} \ge r_0\right].\end{aligned}$$

When n is relatively small, $\Pr\left[\|(\mathsf{Err})_0\|_{q,2} \ge r_0\right]$ can be evaluated directly by computing the corresponding n-dimensional joint distribution. However, as n increases, the computational complexity grows exponentially, making such direct evaluation intractable for $n \ge 8$. To address this challenge, we introduce in the next section a distribution approximation method that enables efficient estimation of the decoding failure rate for larger values of n.

5.2 Asymptotic Approximation of the Noise Distribution for DFR Estimation

The accumulated noise Err that needs to be corrected during decryption consists of two main components: an approximately Gaussian part arising from $\mathbf{e}^T\mathbf{r} - \mathbf{s}^T(\mathbf{e}_1 + \boldsymbol{\epsilon}_\mathbf{u}) + e_2$, and a nearly uniform part resulting from ϵ_v. As n increases, the complexity of directly computing the n-dimensional joint distribution of the product terms $\mathbf{e}^T\mathbf{r}$ and $\mathbf{s}^T(\mathbf{e}_1 + \boldsymbol{\epsilon}_\mathbf{u})$ becomes computationally prohibitive. To overcome this limitation, we introduce an approximation methodology for characterizing the joint distribution of the coefficients.

Note that both product terms can be represented as independent sums of l polynomial multiplications with small-norm coefficients. We establish the following theorem to show that, as lN tends to infinity, the joint distribution of the coefficients converges to a multivariate normal distribution. Furthermore, our analytical framework can be readily generalized to other polynomial rings frequently employed in cryptographic constructions, such as $\mathbb{Z}_q[x]/(x^N - x - 1)$ [6] and $\mathbb{Z}_q[x]/(x^N - x^{N/2} + 1)$ [29].

Theorem 6. *Let* $\mathbf{f} = (\mathbf{f}[0], \mathbf{f}[1], \cdots, \mathbf{f}[l-1])^T$ *and* $\mathbf{g} = (\mathbf{g}[0], \mathbf{g}[1], \cdots, \mathbf{g}[l-1])^T$ *be two independent polynomial vectors, where* $\mathbf{f}[j], \mathbf{g}[j]$ *are polynomials in* $\mathbb{R}[x]/(x^N+1)$ *with coefficients drawn independently from* $\mathcal{N}(0, \sigma_f^2)$ *and* $\mathcal{N}(0, \sigma_g^2)$*, respectively, for* $j = 0, 1, \cdots, l-1$*. Let* $h(x) = \mathbf{f}^T\mathbf{g} = \sum_{j=0}^{l-1} \mathbf{f}[j]\mathbf{g}[j] \in \mathbb{R}[x]/(x^N + 1)$*. For any fixed integers* $0 \le c_1 < c_2 < N$*, as* lN *tends to infinity, the distribution of* $\left(\frac{h_{c_1}}{\sigma_f\sigma_g\sqrt{lN}}, \frac{h_{c_2}}{\sigma_f\sigma_g\sqrt{lN}}\right)$ *converges in distribution to the bivariate standard normal distribution* $\mathcal{N}(\mathbf{0}, \mathbf{I}_2)$*.*

Proof. Let $\phi_{c_1,c_2}(t_1, t_2)$ denote the characteristic function of the random vector $\left(\frac{h_{c_1}}{\sigma_f\sigma_g\sqrt{lN}}, \frac{h_{c_2}}{\sigma_f\sigma_g\sqrt{lN}}\right)$, i.e.,

$$\phi_{c_1,c_2}(t_1, t_2) = \mathbb{E}\left[\exp\left(i\left(t_1\frac{h_{c_1}}{\sigma_f\sigma_g\sqrt{lN}} + t_2\frac{h_{c_2}}{\sigma_f\sigma_g\sqrt{lN}}\right)\right)\right].$$

Denote $\mathbf{f}_j = (\mathbf{f}[j]_0, \mathbf{f}[j]_1, \cdots, \mathbf{f}[j]_{N-1})^T$ and $\mathbf{g}_j = (\mathbf{g}[j]_0, \mathbf{g}[j]_1, \cdots, \mathbf{g}[j]_{N-1})^T$. Let $\mathbf{J}_r$ be a square matrix of order r whose entries are all zeros except those on the anti-diagonal, which are all ones. Define $\mathbf{A}_{c_i} = \mathsf{diag}\{\mathbf{J}_{c_i+1}, -\mathbf{J}_{N-c_i-1}\}$ for $0 \le c_i < N$, i.e.,

$$\mathbf{A}_{c_i} = \begin{pmatrix} \mathbf{J}_{c_i+1} & \mathbf{O} \\ \mathbf{O} & -\mathbf{J}_{N-c_i-1} \end{pmatrix}_{N\times N}, \mathbf{J}_i = \begin{pmatrix} & & 1 \\ & \cdot^{\cdot^{\cdot}} & \\ 1 & & \end{pmatrix}_{i\times i}.$$

It is straightforward to verify that $\mathbf{A}_{c_i}$ satisfies the equation $h_{c_i} = \sum_{j=0}^{l-1} \mathbf{f}_j^T \mathbf{A}_{c_i} \mathbf{g}_j$. Then we obtain

$$t_1\frac{h_{c_1}}{\sigma_f\sigma_g\sqrt{lN}} + t_2\frac{h_{c_2}}{\sigma_f\sigma_g\sqrt{lN}} = \sum_{j=0}^{l-1} \frac{\mathbf{f}_j^T}{\sigma_f}\left(\frac{t_1}{\sqrt{lN}}\mathbf{A}_{c_1} + \frac{t_2}{\sqrt{lN}}\mathbf{A}_{c_2}\right)\frac{\mathbf{g}_j}{\sigma_g}.$$

As $\left(\frac{t_1}{\sqrt{lN}}\mathbf{A}_{c_1} + \frac{t_2}{\sqrt{lN}}\mathbf{A}_{c_2}\right)$ is symmetric, it can be orthogonally diagonalized as $\mathbf{P}^T\mathbf{\Lambda}\mathbf{P}$, where $\mathbf{P}$ is orthogonal and $\mathbf{\Lambda}$ is diagonal. Hence, the characteristic function satisfies

$$\phi_{c_1,c_2}(t_1,t_2) = \mathbb{E}\left[\exp\left(i\sum_{j=0}^{l-1}\frac{(\mathbf{Pf}_j)^T}{\sigma_f}\mathbf{\Lambda}\frac{(\mathbf{Pg}_j)}{\sigma_g}\right)\right] = \prod_{j=0}^{l-1}\mathbb{E}\left[\exp\left(i\frac{(\mathbf{Pf}_j)^T}{\sigma_f}\mathbf{\Lambda}\frac{(\mathbf{Pg}_j)}{\sigma_g}\right)\right].$$

Since $\mathbf{P}$ is orthogonal, it preserves the normal distribution. Thus, $\frac{(\mathbf{Pf}_j)^T}{\sigma_f}\mathbf{\Lambda}\frac{(\mathbf{Pg}_j)}{\sigma_g}$ equals the sum of N scaled products of two independent one-dimensional Gaussian variables.

Suppose $\{\lambda_i\}_{k=0}^{N-1}$ are the eigenvalues of $\left(\frac{t_1}{\sqrt{lN}}\mathbf{A}_{c_1} + \frac{t_2}{\sqrt{lN}}\mathbf{A}_{c_2}\right)$, and let ϕ is the characteristic function of the product of two independent one-dimensional standard Gaussian variables. Since $\phi(t) = (1+t^2)^{-\frac{1}{2}}$ [39], we obtain

$$\phi_{c_1,c_2}(t_1,t_2) = \prod_{j=0}^{l-1}\prod_{k=0}^{N-1}\phi(\lambda_k) = \prod_{j=0}^{l-1}\prod_{k=0}^{N-1}(1+\lambda_k^2)^{-\frac{1}{2}}.$$

Then, for fixed t_1, t_2, we have

$$\ln(\phi_{c_1,c_2}(t_1,t_2)) = -\frac{1}{2}\sum_{j=0}^{l-1}\sum_{k=0}^{N-1}\ln(1+\lambda_k^2) = -\frac{l}{2}\sum_{k=0}^{N-1}(\lambda_k^2 + r_k), \tag{5}$$

where r_k denotes the Lagrange remainder term, satisfying the bound $|r_k| \leq \frac{\lambda_k^4}{2}$. By the Gershgorin Circle Theorem, we obtain $\lambda_k^2 \leq (\frac{2|t_1|}{\sqrt{lN}} + \frac{2|t_2|}{\sqrt{lN}})^2 \leq \frac{4(|t_1|+|t_2|)^2}{lN}$. Hence, the summation of the remainder terms satisfies

$$\left|l\sum_{k=0}^{N-1} r_k\right| \leq l\sum_{k=0}^{N-1}|r_k| \leq l\sum_{k=0}^{N-1}\frac{\lambda_k^4}{2} \leq \frac{8(|t_1|+|t_2|)^4}{lN}. \tag{6}$$

For a square matrix $\mathbf{A}$, let $\mathrm{tr}(\mathbf{A})$ denote the sum of the elements on its main diagonal. From the definition of $\mathbf{A}_{c_i}$, it follows that $\mathrm{tr}(\mathbf{A}_{c_i}^2) = N$ and $\mathrm{tr}(\mathbf{A}_{c_1}\mathbf{A}_{c_2}) = 0$. Thus, for $\sum_{k=0}^{N-1}\lambda_k^2$, we further observe that

$$\begin{aligned}\sum_{k=0}^{N-1}\lambda_k^2 &= \mathrm{tr}\left(\frac{t_1}{\sqrt{lN}}\mathbf{A}_{c_1} + \frac{t_2}{\sqrt{lN}}\mathbf{A}_{c_2}\right)^2 \\ &= \frac{t_1^2}{lN}\mathrm{tr}(\mathbf{A}_{c_1}^2) + \frac{t_2^2}{lN}\mathrm{tr}(\mathbf{A}_{c_2}^2) + \frac{2t_1t_2}{lN}\mathrm{tr}(\mathbf{A}_{c_1}\mathbf{A}_{c_2}) \\ &= (t_1^2+t_2^2)/l.\end{aligned}$$

Combining this equation with (5) and (6), we conclude that as lN tends to infinity, $\phi_{c_1,c_2}(t_1,t_2)$ converges pointwise to $\exp(-(t_1^2+t_2^2)/2)$, which is the characteristic function of the bivariate normal distribution $\mathcal{N}(\mathbf{0},\mathbf{I}_2)$. By Lévy's continuity theorem, we deduce that the random vector $\left(\frac{h_{c_1}}{\sigma_f\sigma_g\sqrt{lN}}, \frac{h_{c_2}}{\sigma_f\sigma_g\sqrt{lN}}\right)$ converges in distribution to $\mathcal{N}(\mathbf{0},\mathbf{I}_2)$. □

Let σ_i $(i = 1, 2)$ denote the standard deviation of the centered binomial distribution B_{η_i}, and let $\sigma_{\epsilon_\mathbf{u}}$ denote the standard deviation of the distribution $\epsilon_\mathbf{u}$. According to Theorem 6, as $lN \to \infty$, the n-dimensional joint distributions of coefficients of $\mathbf{e}^T\mathbf{r}$ and $\mathbf{s}^T(\mathbf{e}_1 + \epsilon_\mathbf{u})$ converge in distribution to the multivariate normal distributions $\mathcal{N}(\mathbf{0}, lN\sigma_1^4\mathbf{I}_n)$ and $\mathcal{N}(\mathbf{0}, lN\sigma_1^2(\sigma_2^2 + \sigma_{\epsilon_\mathbf{u}}^2)\mathbf{I}_n)$, respectively. Let $\sigma^2 = lN\sigma_1^2(\sigma_1^2 + \sigma_2^2 + \sigma_{\epsilon_\mathbf{u}}^2)$. Since the two product terms are independent, we approximate the joint distribution of $(\mathbf{e}^T\mathbf{r} - \mathbf{s}^T(\mathbf{e}_1 + \epsilon_\mathbf{u}))_i$ in $(\mathsf{Err})_i$ by $\mathcal{N}(\mathbf{0}, \sigma^2\mathbf{I}_n)$ when evaluating the DFR under concrete parameter settings. Moreover, we conduct extensive numerical experiments to further confirm the reasonableness of this approximation for our proposed parameter sets, where lN is at least 512. The numerical experiments and test scripts for estimating the DFR of BW-KEM are available at https://github.com/SonglinCrypto/BW-KEM.

6 Security Analysis, Parameter Selection, and Comparative Evaluation

6.1 Core-SVP Hardness

Since the best known attacks against the MLWE problem do not exploit the underlying lattice structure, the hardness of MLWE can be analyzed in terms of the standard LWE problem. For concrete hardness estimation in most practical lattice-based cryptosystems, the primary attacks considered are two BKZ-based [10,37] strategies, namely the primal and the dual attack.

Primal Attack. The primal attack aims to solve the unique-SVP by constructing an instance from the LWE problem. Let $m = (l + 1)n$ denote the number of LWE samples available to the adversary. Given the matrix LWE instance $(\mathbf{A}, \mathbf{b} = \mathbf{A}\mathbf{s} + \mathbf{e}) \in \mathbb{Z}_q^{m \times ln} \times \mathbb{Z}_q^m$, the primal attack constructs a lattice $\Lambda = \{\mathbf{x} \in \mathbb{Z}_q^{m+kn+1} \mid (\mathbf{A} \mid \mathbf{I}_m \mid -\mathbf{b})\mathbf{x} = 0 \mod q\}$ and then applies the BKZ lattice reduction algorithm to find the unique-SVP solution $\mathbf{v} = (\mathbf{s}, \mathbf{e}, 1)$. We refer the reader to [4] for a detailed analysis of the primal attack.

Dual Attack. The dual attack tries to distinguish the matrix LWE instance $(\mathbf{A}, \mathbf{b} = \mathbf{A}\mathbf{s} + \mathbf{e}) \in \mathbb{Z}_q^{m \times ln} \times \mathbb{Z}_q^m$ from a uniformly random sample by identifying a short vector $(\mathbf{v}, \mathbf{w})$ in the dual lattice $\Lambda' = \{(\mathbf{x}, \mathbf{y}) \in \mathbb{Z}_q^m \times \mathbb{Z}_q^{ln} \mid \mathbf{A}^T\mathbf{x} = \mathbf{y} \mod q\}$. Suppose such a vector $(\mathbf{v}, \mathbf{w})$ is found. One then computes $z = \mathbf{v}^T\mathbf{b} = \mathbf{v}^T\mathbf{A}\mathbf{s} + \mathbf{v}^T\mathbf{e} = \mathbf{w}^T\mathbf{s} + \mathbf{v}^T\mathbf{e}$, which is small and approximately Gaussian distributed if $(\mathbf{A}, \mathbf{b})$ corresponds to an LWE sample; otherwise, z is uniformly distributed modulo q. We refer the reader to [2] for a detailed analysis of the dual attack.

Following the simple and conservative methodology of the core-SVP hardness [4], the best known cost of solving the b-dimensional SVP is estimated to be $2^{0.292b}$ in the classical setting and $2^{0.265b}$ in the quantum setting. These cost models are commonly adopted for conservative security estimates of lattice-based schemes. We estimate the classical and quantum core-SVP hardness security of

BW-KEM using the Python script from [4,38]. The concrete results are summarized in Table 2.

6.2 Parameter Sets

We first consider the parameters of the scalable nested lattice code $\mathcal{C}_{n,\tau}(\lambda)$ used in our lattice coding framework. According to the construction of BW-KEM, the length of the shared key is given by $\frac{N}{n}\mu_0$, where $\mu_0 = \tau n - \frac{n}{4}(k-1)$. In our implementation, we fix the parameters as $N = 256$, $n = 32$, and $\tau = 2$, resulting in a 256-bit shared key encapsulated within a 256-dimensional polynomial. The corresponding parameters of $\mathcal{C}_{n,\tau}(\lambda)$ are listed in Table 1.

Table 1. Parameters for $\mathcal{C}_{n,\tau}(\lambda)$.

Scheme	n	τ	μ_0	Coding Lattice	Shaping Lattice
BW-KEM	32	2	32	$\mathrm{BW}_{32}(\frac{q}{4}), \mathrm{BW}_{32}(\frac{\hat{q}}{4})$	$q \cdot \mathbb{G}^{16}, \hat{q} \cdot \mathbb{G}^{16}$

We provide three recommended parameter sets for BW-KEM, namely BW-KEM-512, BW-KEM-768, and BW-KEM-1024, which correspond to NIST security levels 1, 3, and 5, respectively. In addition, for each security level, we offer a '-s' variant as an alternative configuration to support higher security margins when desired. A summary of all parameter sets is provided in Table 2. For all configurations, we fix $N = 256$ and $q = 3329$. The columns labeled "(sec.c, sec.q)" indicate the estimated classical and quantum security levels, respectively. The quantities $|\mathsf{pk}|$, $|\mathsf{ct}|$, and $|K|$ denote the sizes (in bytes) of the public key, ciphertext, and shared key, respectively.

Table 2. Parameter sets of BW-KEM.

Scheme	N	q	l	(η_1, η_2)	d_u	d_v	Primal attack (sec.c,sec.q)	Dual attack (sec.c,sec.q)	δ	$\lvert\mathsf{pk}\rvert$	$\lvert\mathsf{ct}\rvert$	$\lvert K\rvert$
BW-KEM-512	256	3329	2	$(3, 3)$	9	4	$(118, 107)$	$(117, 106)$	$2^{-190.4}$	800	704	32
BW-KEM-512-s	256	3329	2	$(4, 4)$	9	5	$(124, 112)$	$(123, 111)$	$2^{-152.1}$	800	736	32
BW-KEM-768	256	3329	3	$(2, 2)$	9	4	$(183, 166)$	$(181, 164)$	$2^{-226.8}$	1184	992	32
BW-KEM-768-s	256	3329	3	$(3, 3)$	9	6	$(193, 175)$	$(191, 174)$	$2^{-171.2}$	1184	1056	32
BW-KEM-1024	256	3329	4	$(2, 2)$	9	5	$(256, 232)$	$(253, 230)$	$2^{-222.1}$	1568	1312	32
BW-KEM-1024-s	256	3329	4	$(3, 3)$	10	5	$(270, 245)$	$(267, 242)$	$2^{-209.9}$	1568	1440	32

6.3 Comparative Evaluation with Other Schemes

The proposed lattice coding technique substantially enhances the noise tolerance of the error-correction mechanism, thereby enabling greater flexibility in parameter selection. Consequently, BW-KEM achieves more favorable trade-offs between ciphertext size and security compared to existing designs. In our evaluation, the standard parameter sets of ML-KEM are adopted as a reference baseline, and a comprehensive comparison is conducted among BW-KEM, Minal4D [32], and $\mathsf{P}_{t,l}$-Kyber [25], all of which pursue improved trade-offs through refined encoding and noise-management strategies.

Table 3. Comparison between BW-KEM (this work), ML-KEM [40], Minal4D [32] and $\mathsf{P}_{t,l}$-Kyber [25].

NIST Level	**Scheme**	(η_1, η_2)	Requires MLWR?	$\lvert\mathsf{pk}\rvert$	$\lvert\mathsf{ct}\rvert$	Ciphertext compression	δ
I	ML-KEM-512	$(3, 2)$	Yes	800	768	0%	$2^{-138.8}$
	Minal4D-512	$(3, 0)$	Yes	800	736	4.17%	$2^{-125.5}$
	$\mathsf{P}_{t,l}$-Kyber-512	$(3, 2)$	Yes	6176	736	4.17%	$2^{-154.4}$
	BW-KEM-512	$(3, 3)$	**No**	800	704	**8.33%**	$\mathbf{2^{-190.4}}$
III	ML-KEM-768	$(2, 2)$	No	1184	1088	0%	$2^{-164.8}$
	Minal4D-768	$(2, 0)$	Yes	1184	1024	5.88%	$2^{-141.6}$
	$\mathsf{P}_{t,l}$-Kyber-768	$(2, 2)$	No	9248	1024	5.88%	$2^{-175.4}$
	BW-KEM-768	$(2, 2)$	No	1184	992	**8.82%**	$\mathbf{2^{-226.8}}$
V	ML-KEM-1024	$(2, 2)$	No	1568	1568	0%	$2^{-174.8}$
	Minal4D-1024	$(2, 2)$	No	1568	1440	8.16%	$2^{-165.9}$
	$\mathsf{P}_{t,l}$-Kyber-1024	$(2, 2)$	No	12320	1408	10.20%	$2^{-204.8}$
	BW-KEM-1024	$(2, 2)$	No	1568	1312	**16.33%**	$\mathbf{2^{-222.1}}$

As summarized in Table 3, BW-KEM attains the most compact ciphertexts and the lowest DFRs across all security levels. These advantages are achieved without relying on the MLWR assumption, as required in other designs, and without increasing the public key size, as in $\mathsf{P}_{t,l}$-Kyber. By eliminating the MLWR while simultaneously reducing the DFR, BW-KEM demonstrates enhanced robustness and reliability compared with ML-KEM.

Furthermore, for the '-s' parameter variants listed in Table 2, BW-KEM achieves notably higher security margins, improving classical and quantum security estimates by approximately 6–14 and 5–13 bits, respectively, while still outperforming ML-KEM in both ciphertext compactness and decoding reliability.

7 Implementation and Benchmark

The primary implementation difference between our scheme and ML-KEM lies in the newly designed error-correction mechanism. In this section, we first describe several implementation aspects of the proposed lattice coding technique, and then present comprehensive benchmark results, including performance comparisons with ML-KEM, Minal4D, and $\mathsf{P}_{t,l}$-Kyber.

7.1 Lattice Coding

Under the parameter choices of BW-KEM, the scalable lattice coding components implemented include $\mathsf{Encode}_{\mathcal{C}_{32,2}(q/4)}(\mathbf{m} \in \{0,1\}^{32})$ and $\mathsf{Decode}_{\mathcal{C}_{32,2}(\hat{q}/4)}(\mathbf{x} \in \mathbb{G}^{16})$.

In the encoding procedure (Algorithm 1), the core operations consist of splitting the input message $\mathbf{m}$ into a vector $\mathbf{v}$ and computing the vector-matrix product $\mathbf{v}\mathbf{W}_{32} \bmod 4$. To reduce overhead, we restructure the splitting process by embedding it into the precomputed matrix layout, thereby eliminating the need for explicit message parsing. The matrix multiplication is further optimized using lightweight bitwise operations, all implemented in constant time to ensure side-channel resistance.

For the decoding procedure (Algorithm 3), two main subroutines are involved: BDD and delabeling. The BDD subroutine (Algorithm 2) is the most computationally intensive component. To improve performance, we convert the recursive structure into an iterative implementation while preserving correctness. Conditional branches are implemented using constant-time bitwise logic to avoid timing leakage. In the delabeling subroutine, the inverse matrix $\mathbf{W}_{32}^{-1}$ is precomputed in advance. Lines 4–9 of Algorithm 3 are also implemented using efficient bitwise operations.

Overall, our lattice coding implementation is both efficient and constant-time, making it suitable for practical cryptographic deployment while providing resilience against side-channel attacks.

7.2 Performance Benchmark and Comparison

We evaluate the performance of BW-KEM and compare it with ML-KEM, Minal4D, and $\mathsf{P}_{t,l}$-Kyber. The benchmark results are summarized in Table 4, which reports the median cycle counts over 10,000 executions of each KEM implementation. For clearer presentation, the performance of ML-KEM is used as the reference baseline, and the relative performance of the other schemes is also provided for more intuitive comparison. All benchmark tests were conducted on an Intel(R) Core(TM) i7-11700F @ 2.50 GHz with Hyperthreading and TurboBoost disabled. The code was compiled using GNU GCC version 11.4.0 with the following optimization flags: `-Wall -Wextra -Wpedantic -Wmissing-prototypes-Wredundant -decls -Wshadow -Wpointer-arith -O3 -fomit-frame-pointer`.

As shown in Table 4, we compare the benchmark performance of the four schemes across all NIST security levels. Using ML-KEM as the reference baseline, Minal4D achieves moderate ciphertext compression with negligible performance degradation (less than 2%), whereas $\mathsf{P}_{t,l}$-Kyber attains comparable ciphertext

Table 4. Median CPU cycle counts (in kcycles) over 10,000 executions of BW-KEM (this work), ML-KEM [40], Minal4D [32], and $\mathsf{P}_{t,l}$-Kyber [25].

NIST Level	Scheme	KeyGen	Rel. KeyGen	Encaps	Rel. Encaps	Decaps	Rel. Decaps
I	ML-KEM-512	108.8	1.00	125.0	1.00	163.3	1.00
	Minal4D-512	111.0	1.02	126.2	1.01	166.6	1.02
	$\mathsf{P}_{t,l}$-Kyber-512	638.4	5.87	425.4	3.40	529.9	3.25
	BW-KEM-512	97.7	0.90	116.7	0.93	184.8	1.13
III	ML-KEM-768	180.7	1.00	192.9	1.00	242.7	1.00
	Minal4D-768	182.5	1.01	194.8	1.01	247.6	1.02
	$\mathsf{P}_{t,l}$-Kyber-768	947.2	5.24	571.5	2.96	672.6	2.77
	BW-KEM-768	161.5	0.89	180.2	0.93	261.4	1.08
V	ML-KEM-1024	275.8	1.00	295.5	1.00	359.1	1.00
	Minal4D-1024	278.6	1.01	298.5	1.01	362.7	1.01
	$\mathsf{P}_{t,l}$-Kyber-1024	1461.1	5.30	764.7	2.59	887.6	2.47
	BW-KEM-1024	253.0	0.92	260.6	0.88	362.8	1.01

compactness and lower DFRs at the cost of substantially increased computational overhead. In contrast, BW-KEM exhibits highly competitive performance across all security levels. It achieves faster KeyGen and Encaps operations while incurring only a slight performance loss in Decaps relative to ML-KEM.

In particular, BW-KEM reduces the runtime of KeyGen by approximately 8%–11% and that of Encaps by 7%–12% compared to ML-KEM. The minor slowdown observed in Decaps primarily results from the additional lattice decoding operations introduced by our enhanced error-correction mechanism. Nevertheless, this overhead has been effectively mitigated through careful implementation optimization, leading to only a modest slowdown of 1%–13% in decapsulation, with the gap diminishing as the security level increases. For instance, at NIST Level V, BW-KEM achieves substantial reductions in both the DFR and ciphertext size relative to all other schemes (as discussed in Sect. 6.3), at the expense of merely a 1% increase in decapsulation time. Such a minor trade-off is fully acceptable given the notable improvements in ciphertext compactness and robustness.

Acknowledgments. We would like to thank the anonymous reviewers of PKC 2026 for their constructive comments and suggestions. This work was supported by the Special Fund for Key Technologies in Blockchain of Shanghai Scientific and Technological Committee (No.23511100300).

A Properties of the Matrix $\mathbf{W}_n$

Lemma 5. *Let* $\mathbf{W}_n = \begin{pmatrix} 1 & 1 \\ 0 & \phi \end{pmatrix}^{\otimes(k-1)} \in \mathbb{C}^{\frac{n}{2}\times\frac{n}{2}}$ *be the generator matrix of the Barnes-Wall lattice* BW_n*, where* $n = 2^k$ *for* $k \geq 2$*, and* $\phi = 1 + i$*. For any* *index* $j \in \{0, 1, \dots, \frac{n}{2} - 1\}$*, let* $w_H(j)$ *denote the Hamming weight of the binary representation of* j*. Then the following properties hold:*

(1) $\mathbf{W}_n$ *is an upper triangular matrix.*
(2) The j*-th diagonal entry of* $\mathbf{W}_n$ *is exactly* $\phi^{w_H(j)}$*.*
(3) Every entry in the j*-th row of* $\mathbf{W}_n$ *is divisible by* $\phi^{w_H(j)}$*.*

Proof. Denote the base matrix as $\mathbf{B} = \begin{pmatrix} 1 & 1 \\ 0 & \phi \end{pmatrix}$. By definition, $\mathbf{W}_n = \mathbf{B}^{\otimes(k-1)} \in \mathbb{C}^{\frac{n}{2} \times \frac{n}{2}}$. Any row index j and column index c in $\{0, 1, \dots, \frac{n}{2} - 1\}$ can be uniquely represented in binary form as $j = (j_{k-2} \dots j_1 j_0)_2$ and $c = (c_{k-2} \dots c_1 c_0)_2$. By the properties of the Kronecker product, the entry at the j-th row and c-th column of $\mathbf{W}_n$ is given by:

$$(\mathbf{W}_n)_{j,c} = \prod_{l=0}^{k-2} \mathbf{B}_{j_l, c_l}.$$

Property 1: Suppose $j > c$. Then there exists a most significant bit position l such that $j_l = 1$ and $c_l = 0$. For this specific position, the matrix entry $\mathbf{B}_{j_l, c_l} = \mathbf{B}_{1,0} = 0$. Consequently, the entire product evaluates to $(\mathbf{W}_n)_{j,c} = 0$ for any $j > c$. Thus, $\mathbf{W}_n$ is an upper triangular matrix.

Property 2: For the diagonal entries, we have $j = c$, which implies $j_l = c_l$ for all $l \in \{0, \dots, k-2\}$. The j-th diagonal entry is therefore $\prod_{l=0}^{k-2} \mathbf{B}_{j_l, j_l}$. Given $\mathbf{B}_{0,0} = 1$ and $\mathbf{B}_{1,1} = \phi$, each bit $j_l = 1$ contributes a factor of ϕ, while each bit $j_l = 0$ contributes a factor of 1. Since the number of bits where $j_l = 1$ is exactly $w_H(j)$, the diagonal entry is exactly $\phi^{w_H(j)}$.

Property 3: Consider an arbitrary entry $(\mathbf{W}_n)_{j,c}$ in the j-th row. If $(\mathbf{W}_n)_{j,c} = 0$, it is trivially divisible by $\phi^{w_H(j)}$. If $(\mathbf{W}_n)_{j,c} \neq 0$, it must hold that $\mathbf{B}_{j_l, c_l} \neq 0$ for all l. Specifically, for every bit position l where $j_l = 1$, we must have $c_l = 1$ (otherwise $\mathbf{B}_{1,0} = 0$). At these positions, $\mathbf{B}_{j_l, c_l} = \mathbf{B}_{1,1} = \phi$. This means for every 1 in the binary representation of j, the product $\prod_{l=0}^{k-2} \mathbf{B}_{j_l, c_l}$ accumulates a factor of ϕ. Since there are $w_H(j)$ such bits, the overall entry $(\mathbf{W}_n)_{j,c}$ is a multiple of $\phi^{w_H(j)}$. □

References

1. Alagic, G., et al.: Status report on the fourth round of the nist post-quantum cryptography standardization process. (National Institute of Standardsand Technology, Gaithersburg, MD), NIST Internal Report (IR) NIST IR 8545 (2025). http://doi.org/10.6028/NIST.IR.8545
2. Albrecht, M.R.: On dual lattice attacks against small-secret LWE and parameter choices in HElib and SEAL. In: Coron, J.-S., Nielsen, J.B. (eds.) EUROCRYPT 2017. LNCS, vol. 10211, pp. 103–129. Springer, Cham (2017). https://doi.org/10.1007/978-3-319-56614-6_4

3. Alkim, E., Ducas, L., Pöppelmann, T., Schwabe, P.: NewHope without reconciliation. Cryptology ePrint Archive, Report 2016/1157 (2016). https://eprint.iacr.org/2016/1157
4. Alkim, E., Ducas, L., Pöppelmann, T., Schwabe, P.: Post-quantum key exchange - A new hope. In: Holz, T., Savage, S. (eds.) USENIX Security 2016: 25th USENIX Security Symposium, pp. 327–343. USENIX Association, Austin, TX, USA (2016). https://www.usenix.org/conference/usenixsecurity16/technical-sessions/presentation/alkim
5. Bellare, M., Rogaway, P.: Random oracles are practical: a paradigm for designing efficient protocols. In: Denning, D.E., Pyle, R., Ganesan, R., Sandhu, R.S., Ashby, V. (eds.) ACM CCS 93: 1st Conference on Computer and Communications Security, pp. 62–73. ACM Press, Fairfax, Virginia, USA (1993).https://doi.org/10.1145/168588.168596
6. Bernstein, D.J., et al.: NTRU Prime. Technical report, National Institute of Standards and Technology (2020). https://csrc.nist.gov/projects/post-quantum-cryptography/post-quantum-cryptography-standardization/round-3-submissions
7. Boneh, D., Dagdelen, Ö., Fischlin, M., Lehmann, A., Schaffner, C., Zhandry, M.: Random oracles in a quantum world. In: Lee, D.H., Wang, X. (eds.) ASIACRYPT 2011. LNCS, vol. 7073, pp. 41–69. Springer, Heidelberg (2011). https://doi.org/10.1007/978-3-642-25385-0_3
8. Bos, J.W., et al.: CRYSTALS - Kyber: a CCA-secure module-lattice-based KEM. In: 2018 IEEE European Symposium on Security and Privacy, pp. 353–367. IEEE Computer Society Press, London, United Kingdom (2018). https://doi.org/10.1109/EuroSP.2018.00032
9. Chen, L., et al.: Report on post-quantum cryptography. (National Institute of Standardsand Technology, Gaithersburg, MD), NIST Internal Report (IR) NIST IR 8105 (2016). http://doi.org/10.6028/NIST.IR.8105
10. Chen, Y., Nguyen, P.Q.: BKZ 2.0: better lattice security estimates. In: Lee, D.H., Wang, X. (eds.) ASIACRYPT 2011. LNCS, vol. 7073, pp. 1–20. Springer, Heidelberg (2011). https://doi.org/10.1007/978-3-642-25385-0_1
11. Conway, J.H., Sloane, N.J.A.: Sphere Packings, Lattices and Groups, 3rd edn. Springer, New York (1999)
12. Corlay, V., Boutros, J.J., Ciblat, P., Brunel, L.: On the decoding of barnes-wall lattices. In: 2020 IEEE International Symposium on Information Theory (ISIT), pp. 519–524 (2020). https://doi.org/10.1109/ISIT44484.2020.9173976
13. D'Anvers, J.P., Tiepelt, M., Vercauteren, F., Verbauwhede, I.: Timing attacks on error correcting codes in post-quantum schemes. Cryptology ePrint Archive, Report 2019/292 (2019). https://eprint.iacr.org/2019/292
14. D'Anvers, J.P., Vercauteren, F., Verbauwhede, I.: On the impact of decryption failures on the security of LWE/LWR based schemes. Cryptology ePrint Archive, Report 2018/1089 (2018). https://eprint.iacr.org/2018/1089
15. D'Anvers, J.-P., Vercauteren, F., Verbauwhede, I.: The impact of error dependencies on ring/mod-LWE/LWR based schemes. In: Ding, J., Steinwandt, R. (eds.) PQCrypto 2019. LNCS, vol. 11505, pp. 103–115. Springer, Cham (2019). https://doi.org/10.1007/978-3-030-25510-7_6
16. Duman, J., Hövelmanns, K., Kiltz, E., Lyubashevsky, V., Seiler, G.: Faster lattice-based KEMs via a generic Fujisaki-Okamoto transform using prefix hashing. In: Vigna, G., Shi, E. (eds.) ACM CCS 2021: 28th Conference on Computer and Communications Security, pp. 2722–2737. ACM Press, Virtual Event, Republic of Korea (2021). https://doi.org/10.1145/3460120.3484819

17. Erez, U., Zamir, R.: Achieving 1/2 log (1+snr) on the AWGN channel with lattice encoding and decoding. IEEE Trans. Inf. Theory **50**(10), 2293–2314 (2004). https://doi.org/10.1109/TIT.2004.834787
18. Forney, G.D.: Coset codes. i. introduction and geometrical classification. IEEE Trans. Inf. Theory, **34**(5), 1123–1151 (1988). https://doi.org/10.1109/18.21245
19. Forney, G.D.: Coset codes. ii. binary lattices and related codes. IEEE Trans. Inf. Theory **34**(5), 1152–1187 (1988). https://doi.org/10.1109/18.21246
20. Fritzmann, T., Pöppelmann, T., Sepúlveda, J.: Analysis of error-correcting codes for lattice-based key exchange. In: Cid, C., Jacobson, Jr., M.J. (eds.) SAC 2018: 25th Annual International Workshop on Selected Areas in Cryptography. LNCS, vol. 11349, pp. 369–390. Springer, Cham (2019). https://doi.org/10.1007/978-3-030-10970-7_17
21. Fujisaki, E., Okamoto, T.: Secure integration of asymmetric and symmetric encryption schemes. In: Wiener, M. (ed.) CRYPTO 1999. LNCS, vol. 1666, pp. 537–554. Springer, Heidelberg (1999). https://doi.org/10.1007/3-540-48405-1_34
22. Hamburg, M.: Three Bears. Technical report, National Institute of Standards and Technology (2019). https://csrc.nist.gov/projects/post-quantum-cryptography/post-quantum-cryptography-standardization/round-2-submissions
23. Hofheinz, D., Hövelmanns, K., Kiltz, E.: A modular analysis of the Fujisaki-Okamoto transformation. In: Kalai, Y., Reyzin, L. (eds.) TCC 2017. LNCS, vol. 10677, pp. 341–371. Springer, Cham (2017). https://doi.org/10.1007/978-3-319-70500-2_12
24. Liu, L., Yan, Y., Ling, C., Wu, X.: Construction of capacity-achieving lattice codes: polar lattices. IEEE Trans. Commun. **67**(2), 915–928 (2019). https://doi.org/10.1109/TCOMM.2018.2876113
25. Liu, S., Sakzad, A.: Compact lattice-coded (multi-recipient) kyber without CLT independence assumption. In: Hanaoka, G., Yang, B.Y. (eds.) Advances in Cryptology – ASIACRYPT 2025, Part III. Lecture Notes in Computer Science, vol. 16247, pp. 363–395. Springer, Singapore (2025). https://doi.org/10.1007/978-981-95-5099-9_12
26. Liu, S., Sakzad, A.: Lattice codes for CRYSTALS-kyber. Des. Codes Crypt. **93**(8), 3181–3205 (2025). https://doi.org/10.1007/s10623-025-01640-w
27. Lu, X., et al.: LAC. Technical report, National Institute of Standards and Technology (2019). https://csrc.nist.gov/projects/post-quantum-cryptography/post-quantum-cryptography-standardization/round-2-submissions
28. Lyu, S., Liu, L., Ling, C., Lai, J., Chen, H.: Lattice codes for lattice-based PKE. Des. Codes Crypt. **92**(4), 917–939 (2024). https://doi.org/10.1007/s10623-023-01321-6
29. Lyubashevsky, V., Seiler, G.: NTTRU: truly fast NTRU using NTT. IACR Trans. Cryptograph. Hardw. Embed. Syst. **2019**(3), 180–201 (2019). https://doi.org/10.13154/tches.v2019.i3.180-201, https://tches.iacr.org/index.php/TCHES/article/view/8293
30. Mattsson, J.P.: Ml-kem is great! what's missing? NIST Workshop on Guidance for KEMs (2025). https://csrc.nist.gov/Presentations/2025/ml-kem-is-great
31. Micciancio, D., Nicolosi, A.: Efficient bounded distance decoders for barnes-wall lattices. In: 2008 IEEE International Symposium on Information Theory, pp. 2484–2488 (2008). https://doi.org/10.1109/ISIT.2008.4595438
32. Paiva, T.B., Simplício Jr., M.A., Hafiz, S.M., Yildiz, B., Cominetti, E.L., Ogawa, H.S.: Tailorable codes for lattice-based KEMs with applications to compact ML-KEM instantiations. IACR Trans. Cryptograp. Hardw. Embed. Syst. **2025**(3), 139–163 (2025). https://doi.org/10.46586/tches.v2025.i3.139-163

33. Papadopoulos, I., Wang, J.: Polar codes for module-lwe public key encryption: the case of kyber. Cryptography **7**(1) (2023). https://doi.org/10.3390/cryptography7010002, https://www.mdpi.com/2410-387X/7/1/2
34. van Poppelen, A.: Cryptographic decoding of the leech lattice. Cryptology ePrint Archive, Report 2016/1050 (2016). https://eprint.iacr.org/2016/1050
35. Saarinen, M.-J.O.: HILA5: on reliability, reconciliation, and error correction for ring-LWE encryption. In: Adams, C., Camenisch, J. (eds.) SAC 2017. LNCS, vol. 10719, pp. 192–212. Springer, Cham (2018). https://doi.org/10.1007/978-3-319-72565-9_10
36. Saliba, C., Luzzi, L., Ling, C.: Error correction for frodokem using the gosset lattice. arXiv preprint arXiv:2110.01740 (2021)
37. Schnorr, C.P., Euchner, M.: Lattice basis reduction: improved practical algorithms and solving subset sum problems. Math. Program. **66**(2), 181–199 (1994). https://doi.org/10.1007/BF01581144
38. Schwabe, P., et al.: CRYSTALS-KYBER. Technical report, National Institute of Standards and Technology (2020). https://csrc.nist.gov/projects/post-quantum-cryptography/post-quantum-cryptography-standardization/round-3-submissions
39. Simon, M.K.: Probability Distributions Involving Gaussian Random Variables: A Handbook for Engineers. Scientists and Mathematicians. Springer, Heidelberg (2006)
40. of Standards, N.I., Technology: Module-lattice-based key-encapsulation mechanism standard. (Department of Commerce, Washington, D.C.), Federal Information Processing Standards Publication (FIPS) NIST FIPS 203 (2024). https://doi.org/10.6028/NIST.FIPS.203
41. Wang, A., Zheng, Z., Zhao, C., Qiu, Z., Zeng, G., Wang, X.: Scloud+: a lightweight LWE-based KEM without ring/module structure. Cryptology ePrint Archive, Report 2024/1306 (2024). https://eprint.iacr.org/2024/1306
42. Wang, J., Ling, C.: How to construct polar codes for ring-LWE-based public key encryption. Entropy **23**(8) (2021). https://doi.org/10.3390/e23080938, https://www.mdpi.com/1099-4300/23/8/938
43. Zhao, Y., Jin, Z., Gong, B., Sui, G.: KCL (pka OKCN/AKCN/CNKE). Technical report, National Institute of Standards and Technology (2017). https://csrc.nist.gov/projects/post-quantum-cryptography/post-quantum-cryptography-standardization/round-1-submissions

Tight Reductions for SIS-with-Hints Assumptions with Applications to Anonymous Credentials

Ngoc Khanh Nguyen and Jan Niklas Siemer(✉)

King's College London, London, UK
jan.siemer@kcl.ac.uk

Abstract. In this work, we investigate the landscape of emerging lattice-based assumptions tailored for anonymous credentials, focusing on variants of the Short Integer Solution (SIS) problem augmented with auxiliary hints. We provide a tight reduction from the Generalised ISIS_{f_κ} ($\mathrm{GenISIS}_{f_\kappa}$) (Dubois et al., PKC 2025) assumption to its interactive variant $\mathrm{IntGenISIS}_{f_\kappa}$, enabling the construction of proof-friendly signature schemes without incurring the significant efficiency loss observed in prior works. In particular, our results directly apply to the anonymous credential scheme proposed by Bootle et al. (CRYPTO 2023), and circumvent the 4X blow-up in the credential size due to their security loss. We also identify families of functions f for which $\mathrm{GenISIS}_{f_\kappa}$ is as hard as SIS, leading to the first (strongly) unforgeable standard-model signature scheme from SIS without relying on chameleon hash functions.

Moreover, we analyse the "one-more"-type lattice assumptions, showing in particular that Randomised One-More-ISIS (Baldimtsi et al., ASIACRYPT 2024) is at least as hard as standard One-More-ISIS (Agrawal et al., ACM CCS 2022). Further, we inspect different, yet equivalent, variations of Randomised One-More-ISIS which could be of independent interest. Finally, we compare the structural properties of $\mathrm{GenISIS}_{f_\kappa}$ and One-More-ISIS, highlighting both shared techniques and fundamental differences. We believe our results contribute to a clearer understanding of the assumptions underpinning efficient, lattice-based anonymous credential systems.

1 Introduction

Anonymous credentials have become a foundational component in digital identity and e-wallet systems, which are gaining increasing attention from governmental bodies, including several U.S. states [mDL], the European Union [EUD], and the UK [UKD]. With the rapid advancements in quantum computing, there is a growing demand for anonymous credential systems that offer post-quantum security, particularly those based on lattice-based assumptions.

Recent works [BLNS23b, JRS23, AGJ+24, LCL+23] adopt the well-established "signatures with efficient protocols" paradigm introduced by Camenisch and Lysyanskaya [CL03]. This approach relies on three cryptographic primitives:

S. Bai and E. Persichetti (Eds.): PKC 2026, LNCS 16551, pp. 103–135, 2026.
https://doi.org/10.1007/978-3-032-26731-3_4

a commitment scheme, a signature scheme, and a non-interactive zero-knowledge proof of knowledge. Informally, a user $\mathcal{U}$ begins by committing to their attribute vector $\mathbf{m}$ using fresh randomness $\mathbf{r}$ to compute $\mathbf{t} = \mathsf{Com}(\mathbf{m}; \mathbf{r})$, which is then sent to the issuer $\mathcal{I}$[1]. The issuer, using a secret key sk, signs the message $\mathbf{t}$ and returns the signature $\sigma = \mathsf{Sig}(\mathsf{sk}, \mathbf{t})$ to $\mathcal{U}$. To produce an anonymous credential, the user then provides a zero-knowledge proof demonstrating knowledge of the attributes $\mathbf{m}$, randomness $\mathbf{r}$, and signature σ, satisfying

$$\mathsf{Vf}(\mathsf{pk}, \mathsf{Com}(\mathbf{m}; \mathbf{r}), \sigma) = 1.$$

To instantiate this framework efficiently, the signature scheme must be "proof-friendly," meaning it allows efficient proofs of signature possession. This requirement excludes many ROM-secure schemes, such as the NIST-selected Dilithium [DKL+18] and Falcon [FHK+20][2]. One line of works [dPK22, JRS23, LCL+23, AGJ+24, JS24] constructs anonymous credentials and blind signatures using ABB-type standard model signatures [ABB10], which are secure under the well-established (Module-)SIS assumption. However, the underlying signatures are less efficient than their ROM-based counterparts and the anonymous credentials rely on non-tight reductions via complexity leveraging and puncturing strategies, making them less practical overall. These limitations have motivated exploration into signature schemes based on *non-standard* lattice assumptions.

1.1 SIS-with-Hints Assumptions

To support privacy-preserving applications, several works have proposed new lattice assumptions that can be viewed as SIS variants augmented with additional hints.

ISIS_f *Assumption.* Introduced by Bootle et al. [BLNS23b], the ISIS_f assumption has been applied in anonymous credentials [BLNS23b, DKLW25] and direct anonymous attestation [CHE24]. Let $f : [N] \to \mathbb{Z}_q^n$ be an efficiently computable function with domain size $N \in \mathbb{N}$. The ISIS_f assumption states that given a random matrix $\mathbf{A} \leftarrow \mathbb{Z}_q^{n \times m}$ and k hint pairs $(x_i, \mathbf{s}_i) \in [N] \times \mathbb{Z}^m$ such that

$$\mathbf{A}\mathbf{s}_i = f(x_i) \pmod q \quad \text{and} \quad \mathbf{s}_i \text{ is short},$$

it is hard to find a new pair $(x^*, \mathbf{s}^*) \notin \{(x_1, \mathbf{s}_1), \ldots, (x_k, \mathbf{s}_k)\}$ such that $\mathbf{A}\mathbf{s}^* = f(x^*) \pmod q$ and $\mathbf{s}^*$ is also short. Dubois et al. [DKLW25] recently generalised this to the $\mathrm{GenISIS}_{f_\kappa}$ assumption, introducing two key changes: the use of a keyed function $f : \mathcal{K} \times D \to \mathbb{Z}_q^n$ and allowing non-uniform sampling of preimages x_i. [BLNS23b] showed that ISIS_f can be reduced to SIS when f is modeled as a random oracle[3]. However, to maintain proof-friendliness, one must

[1] The user must also prove that $\mathbf{t}$ was correctly formed, but we omit this detail for the sake of the introduction.

[2] As an exception, the work by Beullens et al. [BLNS23a] builds a blind signature scheme by instantiating Falcon with a concrete hash function and running a generic succinct argument [BS23] to prove signature possession.

[3] Additionally, [DKLW25] related the hardness of $\mathrm{GenISIS}_{f_\kappa}$ to the Vanishing SIS assumption [CLM23].

efficiently prove knowledge of f's preimages, highlighting the classic trade-off between security and efficiency.

To construct more efficient proof-friendly signatures, [BLNS23b, DKLW25] introduce a variant called *Interactive* ISIS_f (IntISIS_f). Bootle et al. [BLNS23b] provide a reduction from ISIS_f to IntISIS_f, but with a security loss of $\mathcal{O}(k)$. As shown in their parameter selection, this non-tight reduction significantly impacts performance, increasing credential size by even a factor of four (for $k = 2^{64}$). Hence, it is no surprise the LaZeR library implementation [LSS24] of the anonymous credential system from [BLNS23b] heuristically assumes IntISIS_f is as hard as SIS.

One-More ISIS Assumption. Proposed by Agrawal et al. [AKSY22] for round-optimal blind signatures, the OM-ISIS problem is defined as follows. Given a random matrix $\mathbf{A} \leftarrow \mathbb{Z}_q^{n\times m}$ and a set $T \subset \mathbb{Z}_q^n$ of uniformly random target vectors, an adversary receives $(\mathbf{A}, T)$ and oracle access to a "preimage oracle" O_{pre} that returns a short vector $\mathbf{x} \in \mathbb{Z}^m$ such that $\mathbf{A}\mathbf{x} = \mathbf{y} \pmod q$ for any input $\mathbf{y} \in \mathbb{Z}_q^n$. If the adversary makes k oracle queries and outputs $k+1$ pairwise distinct short vectors

$$\mathbf{s}_1, \ldots, \mathbf{s}_{k+1} \in \mathbb{Z}^m \quad \text{such that} \quad \mathbf{A}\mathbf{s}_i \in T,$$

it wins the OM-ISIS game. Baldimtsi et al. [BCGY24] introduced a variant, rOM-ISIS, enabling the first lattice-based non-interactive blind signature [Han23]. However, it remains unclear whether these assumptions can be reduced to SIS, or even how OM-ISIS and rOM-ISIS relate in terms of hardness.

Ultimately, given the increase of new lattice-based assumptions, it is crucial to understand their interrelations to boost confidence in security of the recent efficient, privacy-preserving constructions.

1.2 Our Contributions

In this work, we explore the relationships between the hardness of recently proposed lattice-based assumptions in the context of anonymous credentials. An overview of our hardness reductions is presented in Fig. 1.

Strong Unforgeable Signatures from $\text{GenISIS}_{f_\kappa}$. We present a new and streamlined framework for constructing signature schemes based on the $\text{GenISIS}_{f_\kappa}$ assumption. Central to our contribution is a *tight reduction* from $\text{GenISIS}_{f_\kappa}$ to $\text{IntGenISIS}_{f_\kappa}$, significantly improving upon the work of [BLNS23b], which incurred a $\mathsf{poly}(\lambda)$ security loss. Our result implies that proof-friendly signature schemes can be instantiated from $\text{GenISIS}_{f_\kappa}$ with minimal or no parameter adjustments. In particular, we avoid the 4X efficiency loss observed in Table 6 of [BLNS23b], demonstrating that the anonymous credential system implemented in LaZeR [LSS24] retains its efficiency under the plain $\text{GenISIS}_{f_\kappa}$ assumption.

Additionally, we identify families of functions f for which $\text{GenISIS}_{f_\kappa}$ is as hard as SIS. Combined with the results of [DKLW25], this yields, to the best of our knowledge, the first strongly unforgeable standard-model signature scheme from SIS that does not rely on chameleon hash functions [KR00, CHKP10, CDJ+25].

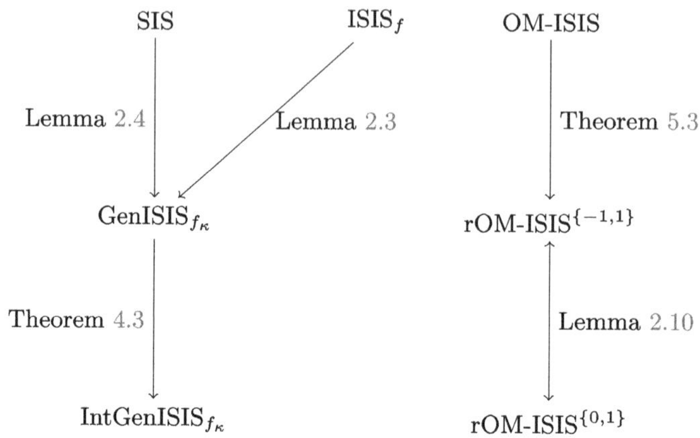

Fig. 1. Overview of our results.

Analysis of the "One-More"-Type Lattice Assumptions. We present the first formal connection between OM-ISIS and its randomised variant. Specifically, we prove that rOM-ISIS is at least as hard as OM-ISIS, thereby enabling the construction of non-interactive blind signature schemes based on the OM-ISIS assumption. Furthermore, we analyse variations of rOM-ISIS in which the additional randomness is sampled from different domains. In particular, we show that the original $\{-1, 1\}$-restriction on the randomness, as used in [BCGY24], yields the same hardness guarantees as the rOM-ISIS variant with $\{0, 1\}$-randomness. This could potentially broaden the applicability and flexibility of the rOM-ISIS assumption in cryptographic constructions.

GenISISf$_{f_\kappa}$ vs OM-ISIS. Some hardness reductions on $\mathrm{GenISIS}_{f_\kappa}$ and OM-ISIS described in Fig. 1 do apply similar techniques (in particular, Theorems 4.3 and 5.3), which include careful entropy-based analysis of adversarial outputs. However, while some structural similarities can be found, ISIS_f and OM-ISIS are fundamentally distinct. In ISIS_f, the adversary is given multiple preimage-target pairs and must produce a *new* one. In contrast, OM-ISIS challenges the adversary to find preimages for *random* targets, while having access to an oracle that produces short preimages for *arbitrary* targets. Hence, establishing a formal connection between these two assumptions remains an intriguing direction for future research.

2 Technical Overview

As we analyse two families of assumptions in our paper, we split the technical overview per family of assumptions and compare them at the end.

2.1 ISIS$_f$ and Its Generalisation

ISIS$_f$ is a versatile problem, which can be used to generically derive constructions for several primitives such as signatures, group signatures, blind signatures, and anonymous credentials. The problem was introduced by Bootle et al. [BLNS23b] to build practical anonymous credentials from lattices. The unique property of the ISIS$_f$ assumption, which makes it so versatile, is the absence of one or multiple target vectors, as known from ISIS. In the case of ISIS$_f$, the function f takes on this part and introduces a more dynamic target, which *in theory* can be chosen by the adversary. Thus, the choice of the function f crucially determines the hardness of an ISIS$_f$ instance. We elaborate on this further in Sect. 4.

Definition 2.1 (ISIS$_f$ - Informal). *Let $f : [N] \rightarrow \mathbb{Z}_q^n$ be a function. In the ISIS$_f$ experiment, the challenger samples a matrix $\mathbf{A} \leftarrow\$ \mathbb{Z}_q^{n\times m}$ uniformly at random along with k hints $(x_i, \mathbf{s}_i)$. The hints are sampled by choosing $x_i \leftarrow\$ [N]$ and $\mathbf{s}_i \leftarrow\$ D_{\mathbb{Z}^m,s}$ under the condition $\mathbf{A} \cdot \mathbf{s}_i = f(x_i)$, which we also denote by $\mathbf{s}_i \leftarrow\$ \mathbf{A}_s^{-1}(f(x_i))$. Given $\mathbf{A}$ and $\{(x_i, \mathbf{s}_i)\}_{i\in[k]}$, the adversary is asked to output a pair $(x^*, \mathbf{s}^*)$. The adversary wins if*

$$\mathbf{A} \cdot \mathbf{s}^* = f(x^*) \wedge 0 < \|\mathbf{s}^*\| \leq \beta \wedge (x^*, \mathbf{s}^*) \notin \{(x_i, \mathbf{s}_i)\}_{i\in[k]}.$$

Intuitively, the ISIS$_f$ assumption states that it is hard to find a new tuple $(x^*, \mathbf{s}^*)$ satisfying $\mathbf{A} \cdot \mathbf{s}^* = f(x^*)$ with short vector $\mathbf{s}^* \in \mathbb{Z}^m$ given a set of solutions. Due to the shape of the equation $\mathbf{A} \cdot \mathbf{s}^* = f(x^*)$, the adversary is required to either break ISIS or to find a preimage for the function f.

Deriving new signatures from more fundamental assumptions by reducing to ISIS$_f$, seems to be hard due to some restrictive choices in the definition of ISIS$_f$. Thus, Dubois et al. [DKLW25] introduced a generalised version of ISIS$_f$ (GenISISf) for this purpose. It lifts two constraints of ISIS$_f$ while retaining the versatility of ISIS$_f$ to derive constructions for several primitives. We highlight the differences to ISIS$_f$ below.

Definition 2.2 (GenISIS$_{f_\kappa}$ - Informal). *Let $f_\kappa : D \rightarrow \mathbb{Z}_q^n$ be a keyed function and let $\chi(D)$ be a distribution over D. In the GenISIS$_{f_\kappa}$ experiment, the challenger samples a key $\kappa \leftarrow\$ \mathcal{K}$ and a matrix $\mathbf{A} \leftarrow\$ \mathbb{Z}_q^{n\times m}$ uniformly along with k hints $(x_i, \mathbf{s}_i)$. The hints are sampled by choosing $x_i \leftarrow\$ \chi(D)$ and $\mathbf{s}_i \leftarrow\$ D_{\mathbb{Z}^m,s}$ under the condition $\mathbf{A} \cdot \mathbf{s}_i = f_\kappa(x_i)$. Given $\mathbf{A}, \kappa$, and $\{(x_i, \mathbf{s}_i)\}_{i\in[k]}$, the adversary is asked to output a pair $(x^*, \mathbf{s}^*)$. The adversary wins if*

$$\mathbf{A} \cdot \mathbf{s}^* = f_\kappa(x^*) \wedge \|\mathbf{s}^*\| \leq \beta \wedge (x^*, \mathbf{s}^*) \notin \{(x_i, \mathbf{s}_i)\}_{i\in[k]}.$$

Other than ISIS$_f$, GenISIS$_{f_\kappa}$ allows x_i to be chosen from any distribution $\chi(D)$ over an arbitrary domain D and introduces a keyed function f_κ instead of a 'static' function f.

To present our first result, we theoretically need to introduce the notion of a Preimage Sampleable Function PSF. However, it is suitable to think of a PSF as a keyed hash function $f'_\kappa : D \to R$, which is invertible with a trapdoor. Inverting the function on a value $y \in R$ results in outputting a preimage $x \in D$ distributed according to some distribution $\chi(D)$ under the condition $f'_\kappa(x) = y$.

Now, we can state our first result. Notice that any ISIS_f instance is also a $\mathrm{GenISIS}_{f_\kappa}$ instance but with size of its keyspace $|\mathcal{K}| = 1$. The following reduction enables a generic transformation from ISIS_f to $\mathrm{GenISIS}_{f_\kappa}$ with a properly keyed function.

Lemma 2.3 (Informal). *Let $\mathcal{F}$ be a collision-resistant PSF with a keyed function $f'_\kappa : D \to R$ and let $\chi(D)$ denote the distribution induced by the PSF. Furthermore, let $g : [N] \to R$ be a bijection. Then, $GenISIS_{f_\kappa}$ with $f_\kappa := f \circ g^{-1} \circ f'_\kappa$ is at least as hard as $ISIS_f$ if f is preimage-resistant.*

The formalised version and proof of Lemma 2.3 can be found in the full version of this paper [NS26, Lemma B.2]. The proof uses the bijection g to map the uniformly distributed part of the hints $x_i \in [N]$ to some set R of the same size. As g is a bijection, the distribution of $r_i = g(x_i)$ stays uniform over R. In the next step, we invert each value $f'^{-1}_\kappa(y_i) = d_i \in D$ for some previously sampled $\kappa \leftarrow\$ \mathcal{K}$, which results in values distributed according to the distribution $\chi(D)$ as the set $\{r_i\}_{i\in[k]}$ was distributed uniformly over R. Furthermore, each hint remains valid as $f_\kappa(d_i) = f \circ g^{-1} \circ f'_\kappa\left((f'_\kappa)^{-1} \circ g(x_i)\right) = f(x_i)$. Thus, the hints are distributed as expected by the $\mathrm{GenISIS}_{f_\kappa}$ adversary. Any $\mathrm{GenISIS}_{f_\kappa}$ solution $(d^*, \mathbf{s}^*) \in D \times \mathbb{Z}^m$, then yields an ISIS_f solution as

$$\mathbf{A} \cdot \mathbf{s}^* = f_\kappa(d^*) = f(g^{-1} \circ f'_\kappa(d^*)).$$

The preimage resistance of f is required for solutions $\mathbf{s}^* = \mathbf{0}$ to be unlikely.

The reduction described above does not only provide a generic transformation from ISIS_f to $\mathrm{GenISIS}_{f_\kappa}$ instances, but it shows that sampling the first part of the hints x_i as a discrete Gaussian in a $\mathrm{GenISIS}_{f_\kappa}$ instance does not decrease the robustness of the corresponding ISIS_f instance. If we choose to use Lemma 2.3 with the PSF introduced in [GPV08], the hints $x_i \in D$ are distributed as a discrete Gaussian. With this observation, we move to the next reduction from SIS to a $\mathrm{GenISIS}_{f_\kappa}$ instance, which requires x_i to be distributed partly discrete Gaussian and partly uniform.

We define a suitable function f_κ to reduce SIS to $\mathrm{GenISIS}_{f_\kappa}$ in the standard model. To sample a key for f_κ, we sample $\ell + 1$ matrices $\mathbf{A}_0, \ldots, \mathbf{A}_\ell \leftarrow\$ \mathbb{Z}_q^{n\times n\lceil\log q\rceil}$ and a vector $\mathbf{u} \leftarrow\$ \mathbb{Z}_q^n$ uniformly. Furthermore, define D as $D := \{0,1\}^\ell \times \{\mathbf{s} \in \mathbb{Z}^{n\lceil\log q\rceil} : \|\mathbf{s}\| \leq s \cdot \sqrt{n\lceil\log q\rceil}\}$, $\kappa = (\mathbf{A}_0, \ldots, \mathbf{A}_\ell, \mathbf{u})$ and

$$f_\kappa : D \to \mathbb{Z}_q^n, (\mathbf{m}, \mathbf{x}) \mapsto \mathbf{A}_\mathbf{m} \cdot \mathbf{x} + \mathbf{u}, \text{ where } \mathbf{A}_\mathbf{m} := \mathbf{A}_0 + \sum_{i\in[\ell]} m_i \cdot \mathbf{A}_i.$$

Lemma 2.4 (Informal). *Let $\beta \in \mathcal{O}\left(\ell(n\log q)^{3/2}\right) \cdot \omega\left(\sqrt{\log(n\lg q)}\right)^4$ and let f_κ be defined as above. Then, $GenISIS_{f_\kappa}$ with f_κ is at least as hard as SIS.*

The formalised version and proof of Lemma 2.4 can be found in the full version of this paper [NS26, Lemma C.1].

We adapt the Strong Existential Unforgeability under *Static* Chosen Message Attacks (sEUF-SCMA) secure signature from [MP12] to $\text{GenISIS}_{f_\kappa}$.[4] The signature scheme described by Micciancio and Peikert provides short preimages $\mathbf{s}_i \in \mathbb{Z}_q^{n \lg q + 2n \lceil \log q \rceil}$ of the matrix $\begin{bmatrix} \bar{\mathbf{A}} & \mathbf{G} - \mathbf{A}\mathbf{R} & \mathbf{A}_\mathbf{m} \end{bmatrix}$ for some uniformly chosen target vector $\mathbf{u} \in \mathbb{Z}_q^n$ as signatures. We move the last part of this matrix into the function f_κ as described above s.t. the function depends on the message $\mathbf{m}$.

To prove the signature and our $\text{GenISIS}_{f_\kappa}$ instance secure, the $\mathbf{G}$-trapdoor moves to the last part of the matrix, i.e., into our function f_κ. Then, the proof uses the lattice-mixing [Boy10] and the prefix [CHKP10] technique to puncture the trapdoor for a specific (set of) message(s). As the proof proceeds similarly to the one of the signature scheme, we focus on the two major differences to the original proof here.

- Originally, there are no messages $\mathbf{m}_i$ in the $\text{GenISIS}_{f_\kappa}$ experiment. As the keyed function f_κ depends on the choice of the message $\mathbf{m} \in \{0,1\}^\ell$, it becomes part of the hints. Thus, a hint in this $\text{GenISIS}_{f_\kappa}$ instance is described by $(x_i = (\mathbf{m}_i, \mathbf{x}_i), \mathbf{s}_i)$, where $\mathbf{x}_i$ and $\mathbf{s}_i$ are distributed discrete Gaussian and $\mathbf{m}_i$ is distributed uniformly random over $\{0,1\}^\ell$.
- In the sEUF-SCMA experiment, the adversary provides the set of distinct messages to sign to the challenger upfront. $\text{GenISIS}_{f_\kappa}$ requires the hints to be distributed according to some distribution $\chi(D)$. As the messages have to be distinct, the probability of a collision induced by $\chi(D)$ needs to be negligible.

The evaluation of these differences suggests that any lattice-based sEUF-SCMA secure signature can be reduced to $\text{GenISIS}_{f_\kappa}$. Furthermore, the reduction presented below implies an efficient technique to make lattice-based sEUF-SCMA signatures generically strong existential unforgeable under *adaptively* chosen message attacks (sEUF-ACMA). The new result presented below should make this transformation a sound competitor compared to the existing technique using chameleon hashes [KR00].

Interactive $\mathit{GenISIS}_{f_\kappa}$. The true potential of the ISIS_f framework stems from the interactive version of ISIS_f. Instances of this problem can be used to generically derive constructions for several primitives such as signatures, group signatures, blind signatures and anonymous credentials. In this paper, we alter the generalised interactive ISIS_f version provided in [DKLW25] slightly to keep reductions for constructions relying on $\text{IntGenISIS}_{f_\kappa}$ as simple as possible.

Definition 2.5 ($\mathbf{IntGenISIS}_{f_\kappa}$ - Informal). *Let $f : \mathcal{K} \times D \to \mathbb{Z}_q^n$ be a keyed function and let $\chi(D)$ be a distribution over D. The $\mathit{IntGenISIS}_{f_\kappa}$ experiment is defined in the following way.*

- *The challenger samples two matrices $\mathbf{A} \leftarrow\$\, \mathbb{Z}_q^{n \times m}, \mathbf{C} \leftarrow\$\, \mathbb{Z}_q^{n \times \ell}$ and a key $\kappa \leftarrow\$\, \mathcal{K}$ uniformly at random and gives them to $\mathcal{A}$.*

[4] Definition and security notions of signatures can be found in Appendix A.2 of the full version [NS26].

- *Then, $\mathcal{A}$ adaptively queries a preimage oracle k-times with short messages $\mathbf{m}_i \in \mathbb{Z}_q^\ell$, which are answered by $(x_i, \mathbf{s}_i)$ sampled as $x_i \leftarrow\$ \chi(D)$ and $\mathbf{s}_i \leftarrow\$ D_{\mathbb{Z}^m,s}$ under the condition $\mathbf{A} \cdot \mathbf{s}_i = f_\kappa(x_i) + \mathbf{C} \cdot \mathbf{m}_i$.*
- *Finally, $\mathcal{A}$ outputs a tuple $(x^*, \mathbf{s}^*, \mathbf{m}^*) \in D \times \mathbb{Z}^m \times \mathbb{Z}^\ell$.*

The adversary wins if $\|\mathbf{m}^*\| \leq \beta_m$ and

$$\mathbf{A} \cdot \mathbf{s}^* = f_\kappa(x^*) + \mathbf{C} \cdot \mathbf{m} \wedge \|\mathbf{s}^*\| \leq \beta_s \wedge (x^*, \mathbf{s}^*, \mathbf{m}^*) \notin \{(x_i, \mathbf{s}_i, \mathbf{m}_i)\}_{i \in [k]}.$$

The interactive version extends $\text{GenISIS}_{f_\kappa}$ by an Ajtai commitment $\mathbf{C} \cdot \mathbf{m} \in \mathbb{Z}_q^n$.

Although the security of constructions is based directly on $\text{IntGenISIS}_{f_\kappa}$, the non-interactive version remains important, as it is typically easier to analyse a non-interactive problem. Bootle et al. [BLNS23b, Theorem 3.3] provide a reduction from ISIS_f to the interactive version of ISIS_f incurring a polynomial loss-factor $\mathcal{O}(k)$. We generalise this theorem to $\text{GenISIS}_{f_\kappa}$ and optimise it by removing the polynomial loss-factor, providing a tight reduction between the problems. Thus, the following theorem prevents a loss of 2^{64} in bit-security for any constructions based on $\text{GenISIS}_{f_\kappa}$, considering the number of preimage queries as 2^{64} as proposed by NIST [NIS].

Theorem 2.6 (Informal version of Theorem 4.3). *Require $\chi(D)$ to have large min-entropy. Any $\mathit{IntGenISIS}_{f_\kappa}$ instance allowing at most k queries is at least as hard as $\mathit{GenISIS}_{f_\kappa}$ handing out $k \cdot T_{\max}$ hints, where $T_{\max} \in \mathit{poly}(\lambda)$ and λ denotes the security parameter.*

In the proof of this theorem, we use several game hops starting with the $\text{IntGenISIS}_{f_\kappa}$ game. The first hop replaces $\mathbf{C}$ by $\mathbf{A} \cdot \mathbf{R}$ for some uniformly chosen $\mathbf{R} \in \{0,1\}^{m \times \ell}$. In the next game hops, we alter the preimage oracle O_{pre}. First, we introduce a loop and introduce the possibility of rejecting samples $(x, \mathbf{A}_s^{-1}(f(x) + \mathbf{C} \cdot \mathbf{m}))$ before outputting one. Next, we ensure that every query generates at most $T_{\max}$ samples before it outputs one. Finally, we use generalised rejection sampling [BTT22] to replace the inversion of matrix $\mathbf{A}$ by $\mathbf{A}_s^{-1}(f(x)) + \mathbf{R} \cdot \mathbf{m}$, where $(x, \mathbf{A}_s^{-1}(f(x))) = (x, \mathbf{s})$ is known from the $k \cdot T_{\max}$ hints provided by $\text{GenISIS}_{f_\kappa}$. Thus, the reduction algorithm is now capable of answering preimage queries correctly with a distribution statistically close to the expected one. However, the recovered $\text{GenISIS}_{f_\kappa}$ solution $(x^*, \mathbf{s}^* - \mathbf{R} \cdot \mathbf{m}^*)$ might collide with an element from the set of hints $\{(x_i, \mathbf{s}_i)\}_{i \in [k \cdot T_{\max}]}$ given to the reduction algorithm as ...

- it does not output all the hints due to rejection sampling, and ...
- O_{pre} does not output $(x_i, \mathbf{s}_i)$ directly (removing it from the space of suitable solutions), but $(x_i, \mathbf{s}_i + \mathbf{R} \cdot \mathbf{m}_i)$ for any queried message $\mathbf{m}_i \in \mathbb{Z}^\ell$. Thus, a solution $(x^*, \mathbf{s}^* - \mathbf{R} \cdot \mathbf{m}^*) = (x_i, \mathbf{s}_i)$ could be a valid $\text{IntGenISIS}_{f_\kappa}$ solution for some $i \in [k \cdot T_{\max}]$, but it would imply an invalid $\text{GenISIS}_{f_\kappa}$ solution.

As the first part of the hints $x_i \in D$ is sampled with large min-entropy, we can upper-bound the probability that the adversary picks a value x^*, which was part of the hints but rejected by O_{pre}, with $k \cdot T_{\max} \cdot 2^{-\omega(\lambda)}$. Therefore, the probability that $\mathcal{A}$ outputs a solution, which reuses a rejected hint, is negligible. Thus, we only need to argue about the case that the adversary reuses a hint output by O_{pre}, i.e., $x^* = x_i$ for some $i \in k \cdot T_{\max}$ and $\mathcal{A}$ has seen $x_i \in D$ as output of a preimage query. To rule out the second case more conveniently, we remove the possibility that any $x \in D$ appears twice in the set of hints. We can upper bound the probability of this scenario due to the large min-entropy of $\chi(D)$ using the birthday bound $k^2 \cdot T_{\max}^2 \cdot 2^{-\omega(\lambda)}$. Thus, the first part x_i of any hint output by O_{pre} can only occur once in the set of hints, which implies that the solution of $\mathcal{A}$ can collide with at most one hint and this hint was output by O_{pre}. Focusing on this case, the condition $(x^*, \mathbf{s}^*, \mathbf{m}^*) \notin \{(x_i, \mathbf{s}_i, \mathbf{m}_i)\}_{i\in[k]}$ then ensures $\mathbf{m}^* \neq \mathbf{m}_i$ as $\mathbf{s}^* = \mathbf{s}_i$ follows immediately otherwise. Since $\mathbf{m}^* \neq \mathbf{m}_i$, there is at least one index $j \in [\ell]$ s.t. $m_j^* \neq m_{i,j}$. We focus on the corresponding column in matrix $\mathbf{C}$ denoted by $\mathbf{c}_j \in \mathbb{Z}_q^\ell$. As the matrix $\mathbf{R}$ is hidden from the adversary, we consider the number of potential preimages $\mathbf{r}_j \in \{0,1\}^m$ s.t. $\mathbf{A} \cdot \mathbf{r}_j = \mathbf{c}_j$. An adapted version of [Lyu12, Lemma 5.2] shows that there at least two preimages $\mathbf{r}_j$ with overwhelming probability. Only one of the two choices for $\mathbf{r}_j$ can potentially cause a collision with the set of hints and the matrix $\mathbf{R} \in \{0,1\}^{m\times\ell}$ is sampled uniformly at random. Thus, the possibility that $(x^*, \mathbf{s}^* - \mathbf{R} \cdot \mathbf{m}^*) \in \{x_i, \mathbf{s}_i\}_{i\in[k\cdot T_{\max}]}$ is at most $\frac{1}{2} - \text{negl}(\lambda)$. This concludes the proof of Theorem 2.6.

Theorem 2.6 yields the first formalisation of the reduction from $\text{GenISIS}_{f_\kappa}$ to $\text{IntGenISIS}_{f_\kappa}$. Furthermore, it tightens the existing proof for ISIS_f in terms of security losses by exploiting conditions rather than probabilities. The reduction satisfies stronger conditions by keeping the 'strong unforgeability flavor' of $\text{IntGenISIS}_{f_\kappa}$, while the interactive version of ISIS_f is closely related to weak unforgeability. Almost all of the techniques used in this proof can be naturally lifted to rings and the reduction trivially applies to the non-generalised ISIS_f context as well. We elaborate on this further in Sect. 4.

2.2 One-More-ISIS and Its Randomised Variant

Alongside ISIS_f, we examine two assumptions called One-More-ISIS (OM-ISIS) and Randomised OM-ISIS (rOM-ISIS). The OM-ISIS assumption was introduced by Agrawal et al. [AKSY22] to build practical, round-optimal lattice-based blind signatures.

Definition 2.7 (One-More-ISIS - Informal). *The challenger samples a matrix $\mathbf{A} \leftarrow\$ \mathbb{Z}_q^{n\times m}$ and a set T of target vectors from $\mathbb{Z}_q^n$ uniformly at random and gives them to $\mathcal{A}$. Then, $\mathcal{A}$ adaptively queries a preimage oracle k-times with arbitrary target vectors $\hat{\mathbf{t}} \in \mathbb{Z}_q^n$, which are answered by $\hat{\mathbf{s}}$ sampled as $\hat{\mathbf{s}} \leftarrow\$ D_{\mathbb{Z}^m,s}$ under the condition $\mathbf{A} \cdot \hat{\mathbf{s}} = \hat{\mathbf{t}}$. Finally, $\mathcal{A}$ outputs a set S of $k+1$ vectors. The adversary wins if for all vectors $\mathbf{s} \in S$ the following holds.*

$$\mathbf{A} \cdot \mathbf{s} \in T \wedge \|\mathbf{s}\| \leq \beta$$

Intuitively, the OM-ISIS notion states that given access to an ISIS solver, it remains hard to compute an additional preimage for a polynomial number of possible ISIS targets. The authors provide an analysis of several attack strategies for OM-ISIS to gain confidence in the assumption [AKSY22, Section 4.5]. To build a non-interactive blind-signature, Baldimtsi et al. [BCGY24] introduce a closely related assumption called rOM-ISIS, which they claim to be more robust. We highlight the differences to OM-ISIS below.

Definition 2.8 (Randomised One-More-ISIS - Informal). *The challenger samples two matrices* $\mathbf{A}, \mathbf{B} \leftarrow\$ \mathbb{Z}_q^{n\times m}$ *and a set* T *of target vectors from* $\mathbb{Z}_q^n$ *uniformly at random and gives them to* $\mathcal{A}$. *Then,* $\mathcal{A}$ *adaptively queries a preimage oracle* k*-times with arbitrary target vectors* $\hat{\mathbf{t}} \in \mathbb{Z}_q^n$, *which are answered by a pair* $(\hat{\mathbf{s}}, \hat{\mathbf{u}})$ *sampled as* $\hat{\mathbf{s}} \leftarrow\$ D_{\mathbb{Z}^m,s}$ *and* $\hat{\mathbf{u}} \leftarrow\$ \{-1,1\}^m$ *under the condition* $\mathbf{A}\cdot\hat{\mathbf{s}}+\mathbf{B}\cdot\hat{\mathbf{u}} = \hat{\mathbf{t}}$. *Finally,* $\mathcal{A}$ *outputs a set* S *of* $k+1$ *pairs* $(\mathbf{s}, \mathbf{u})$. *The adversary wins if for all vectors* $\mathbf{s} \in S$ *the following holds.*

$$\mathbf{A}\cdot\mathbf{s}+\mathbf{B}\cdot\mathbf{u} \in T \wedge \|\mathbf{s}\| \leq \beta \wedge \mathbf{u} \in \{-1,1\}^m$$

The authors state that their assumption is more robust due to the fact that the adversary is not able to select the preimage vector for the challenge. The actual target vector for O_{pre} is $\mathbf{t}-\mathbf{B}\cdot\hat{\mathbf{u}}$, which they claim to be re-randomised due to the random choice of $\hat{\mathbf{u}} \in \{-1,1\}^m$. Baldimtsi et al. [BCGY24] provide some analysis of their assumption, which resembles the analysis of OM-ISIS closely and shows that the restriction of $\hat{\mathbf{u}}$ to $\{-1,1\}$ mostly prevents the previously presented attacks on OM-ISIS. In this paper, we present a reduction from OM-ISIS to rOM-ISIS, which proves that rOM-ISIS is at least as hard as OM-ISIS.

Theorem 2.9 (Informal version of Theorem 5.3). *Let* $m \geq 2n\log q$ *and* $q > 2$. *Randomised One-More-ISIS is at least as hard as One-More-ISIS.*

We prove this theorem by replacing $\mathbf{B} \in \mathbb{Z}_q^{n\times m}$ by $\mathbf{A}\cdot\mathbf{R}$ for some uniformly sampled $\mathbf{R} \leftarrow\$ \{0,1\}^{m\times m}$. This allows us to recover a OM-ISIS solution for the matrix $\mathbf{A} \in \mathbb{Z}_q^{m\times m}$ once $\mathcal{A}$ outputs a rOM-ISIS solution for $\mathbf{A}, \mathbf{B} \in \mathbb{Z}_q^{n\times m}$. The set of targets T can be forwarded to $\mathcal{A}$ without any changes. Preimage queries for vectors $\hat{\mathbf{t}} \in \mathbb{Z}_q^n$ are answered by sampling a vector $\hat{\mathbf{u}} \leftarrow\$ \{-1,1\}^m$ and asking the preimage oracle of OM-ISIS for a preimage $\hat{\mathbf{s}} \in \mathbb{Z}^m$ of $\hat{\mathbf{t}}-\mathbf{B}\cdot\hat{\mathbf{u}}$. Then, the pair $(\hat{\mathbf{s}}, \hat{\mathbf{u}})$ is a suitable and correctly distributed answer to the preimage query. Once $\mathcal{A}$ outputs a valid rOM-ISIS solution as a set of tuples $(\mathbf{s}_i, \mathbf{u}_i)$, the reduction algorithm converts them to short OM-ISIS solutions $\mathbf{s}_i + \mathbf{R}\cdot\mathbf{m}_i$. As any tuple of the rOM-ISIS solution satisfies $\mathbf{A}\cdot\mathbf{s}_i+\mathbf{B}\cdot\mathbf{u}_i \in T$, the converted solution satisfies $\mathbf{A}\cdot(\mathbf{s}_i+\mathbf{R}\cdot\mathbf{u}_i) \in T$ as required. However, the addition of $\mathbf{s}_i$ and $\mathbf{R}\cdot\mathbf{u}_i$ could potentially introduce collisions in the set of solutions. We inspect a potential collision

$$\mathbf{s}_i + \mathbf{R}\cdot\mathbf{u}_i = \mathbf{s}_j + \mathbf{R}\cdot\mathbf{u}_j \Leftrightarrow \mathbf{s}_i - \mathbf{s}_j = \mathbf{R}\cdot(\mathbf{u}_j - \mathbf{u}_i)$$

for some $i \neq j \in [k+1]$. If $\mathbf{u}_i = \mathbf{u}_j$, then $\mathbf{s}_i = \mathbf{s}_j$ follows immediately. This contradicts the winning condition of rOM-ISIS. Therefore, we know $\mathbf{u}_i \neq \mathbf{u}_j$ and apply the same technique as described before. As $\mathbf{u}_i \neq \mathbf{u}_j$, there is an index $c \in [m]$ s.t. $u_{i,c} \neq u_{j,c}$. We consider column $\mathbf{b}_c$ of the matrix $\mathbf{B}$ and the number of preimages $\mathbf{r}_c \in \{0,1\}^m$ in the matrix $\mathbf{R}$ s.t. $\mathbf{A} \cdot \mathbf{r}_c = \mathbf{b}_c$. This time, we require a stronger version of [Lyu12, Lemma 5.2], which we provide in Lemma 3.7. This lemma states that there are at least 2^n preimages with overwhelming probability $1 - 2^n \cdot q^{-n}$. As the examined collision occurs for at most one choice of $\mathbf{R}$ out of the 2^n-many and $\mathbf{R}$ is hidden from $\mathcal{A}$, the probability of picking $\mathbf{R}$ so that this collision occurs is 2^{-n}. We have examined one potential collision, but there could be many within the $k+1$ tuples output by $\mathcal{A}$. We use the union bound to upper bound the probability of a collision in the OM-ISIS solution by $\frac{k \cdot (k+1)}{2} \cdot 2^{-n}$.

It is important to notice that this theorem does not state that rOM-ISIS is strictly harder than OM-ISIS. However, a reduction showing that the assumptions are essentially equivalently robust seems to be prohibited by the constraint $\mathbf{u} \in \{-1,1\}^m$. As we could not find any justification for the choice of $\{-1,1\}$, we assumed that this choice forces an adversary to make their solution dependent on the matrix $\mathbf{B}$. So, we investigated whether rOM-ISIS with a binary constraint $\mathbf{u} \in \{0,1\}^m$ differs from $\mathbf{u} \in \{-1,1\}^m$, because the adversary could potentially set $\mathbf{u} = \mathbf{0}$ in the binary case to make its solutions independent of the matrix $\mathbf{B}$. However, Lemma 2.10 shows that our assumed justification is incorrect. rOM-ISIS with $\mathbf{u} \in \{0,1\}^m$ is exactly as hard as rOM-ISIS with $\mathbf{u} \in \{-1,1\}^m$. We believe that this reduction and the rOM-ISIS version with $\{-1,1\}$ can be of independent interest.

Lemma 2.10 (Informal). *Let $q > 2$ be odd. Then, rOM-ISIS$^{\{0,1\}}$ is as hard as rOM-ISIS$^{\{-1,1\}}$.*

The proof of this lemma is based on the fact that we can transform any vector $\mathbf{v} \in \{-1,1\}^m$ into a vector $\mathbf{u} \in \{0,1\}^m$ and vice versa (if $q > 2$ is odd).

$$\mathbf{u} = 2^{-1} \cdot (\mathbf{v} + \mathbf{1}) \tag{1}$$

$$\Leftrightarrow \mathbf{v} = 2 \cdot \mathbf{u} - \mathbf{1} \tag{2}$$

This transformation is a public operation and as the multiplication of 2 or its inverse can not introduce any collisions, the set of transformed solutions stays valid. Furthermore, we require $q > 2$ to be odd s.t. the distribution of matrix $\mathbf{B} \in \mathbb{Z}_q^{n \times m}$ stays uniform as the reduction algorithm hands $2 \cdot \mathbf{B}$ or $2^{-1} \cdot \mathbf{B}$ to $\mathcal{A}$. In order to apply the public transformation, the reduction algorithms from rOM-ISIS$^{\{0,1\}}$ to rOM-ISIS$^{\{-1,1\}}$ and vice versa have to make several small adjustments, which require control over the target vector for preimage oracles. We omit a detailed description at this point as both reduction algorithms follow immediately from the observation presented above. The formalised version and proof of Lemma 2.10 can be found in the full version [NS26, Lemma D.1].

2.3 Comparison of ISIS$_f$ and One-More-ISIS

As the (keyed) function f can be set arbitrarily for ISIS$_f$ and GenISIS$_{f_\kappa}$, we focus on the initial choice of Bootle et al. [BLNS23b] to compare the assumptions. They set $f(x) = \mathbf{B} \cdot \mathsf{bin}(x)$, where bin denotes the binary encoding of $x \in [N]$. Then, the corresponding IntISIS$_f$ instance shows a lot of similarities to rOM-ISIS with binary vectors $\hat{\mathbf{u}}$. However, there are two differences between the problems.

- The preimage oracle of IntISIS$_f$ does not provide direct control over the target vector due to the multiplication of messages $\mathbf{m}$ by the matrix $\mathbf{C}$, which the rOM-ISIS problem tries to prohibit by 'randomising' the target vector with $\mathbf{B} \cdot \hat{\mathbf{s}}$.
- ISIS$_f$ requests a new solution depending on f while rOM-ISIS asks for a new solution for randomly picked target vectors.

As the rOM-ISIS assumption and ISIS$_f$ assumption crucially rely on the restriction that $\mathsf{bin}(x)$ and $\mathbf{u}$ are binary, we lift this restriction slightly and allow $\mathsf{bin}(x)$ and $\mathbf{u}$ to become any short vector. Under this assumption, the ISIS$_f$ instance becomes trivially insecure and the rOM-ISIS instance becomes a OM-ISIS instance. It follows that the random target vectors of OM-ISIS prevent the trivial attack mounted on the ISIS$_f$ instance.

3 Preliminaries

For a positive integer N, $[N]$ denotes $\{1, \ldots, N\}$. By convention, vectors are in column form and denoted by bold lower-case letters, e.g. $\mathbf{x}$. The i-th component of $\mathbf{x}$ is represented by x_i. Matrices are written as bold capital letters, e.g. $\mathbf{X}$, and their i-th column vector is denoted by $\mathbf{x}_i$. Transposed matrices or vectors are described by $\mathbf{X}^T$. Special matrices are the zero matrix $\mathbf{0}_n$ and the identity matrix $\mathbf{I}_n$ of size n with column vectors $\mathbf{0}$ and unit vectors $\mathbf{e}_i$ respectively. The norm of a vector $\|\cdot\|$ denotes the Euclidean norm $\|\cdot\|_2$ if not specified otherwise. The length of a matrix is defined by the largest norm of its column vectors. Furthermore, let $s_1(\mathbf{X})$ denote the largest singular value of $\mathbf{X}$.

The natural security parameter throughout this paper is λ, and all other quantities are implicit functions of λ. We use standard Landau notation to classify the growth of functions. Denote by $\text{negl}(\lambda)$ an unspecified function that is negligible in λ. Let $\text{poly}(\lambda)$ denote an unspecified function $f(\lambda) \in \mathcal{O}(\lambda^c)$ for some constant c.

If a value x is sampled from some distribution χ, this is denoted by $x \leftarrow\!\$\, \chi$. In some cases, we draw from a finite set X. This denotes sampling uniformly random from this set, which is also described by $U(X)$.

The *statistical distance* between two distributions X and Y over some finite set Ω is defined by $\Delta(X;Y) := \frac{1}{2}\sum_{s\in\Omega} |X(s) - Y(s)|$. Two ensembles of distributions $\{X_\lambda\}$ and $\{Y_\lambda\}$ are *statistically close* if their statistical distance $\Delta(X_\lambda;Y_\lambda)$ is negligible in λ. If two ensembles of distributions are statistically close, they are also *computationally indistinguishable*, i.e., for every ppt algorithm $\mathcal{A}$, $\left|\Pr[\mathcal{A}(1^\lambda, X_\lambda) = 1] - \Pr[\mathcal{A}(1^\lambda, Y_\lambda) = 1]\right| = \text{negl}(\lambda)$.

3.1 Lattices

Since lattices provide the mathematical structure on which the security of all presented problems relies, we dedicate this section to its definition, related structures, and some of their most important properties.

Definition 3.1 (Lattice). *An n-dimensional lattice Λ is an additive subgroup of $\mathbb{R}^n$ and discrete, i.e., for every $\mathbf{x} \in \Lambda$ there exists an n-dimensional ball around $\mathbf{x}$ that contains no other lattice point.*

Throughout this paper, we exclusively consider q-ary lattices over the ring $\mathbb{Z}_q$ for $q \geq 2$, which are usually defined by a matrix $\mathbf{A} \in \mathbb{Z}_q^{n \times m}$ as in Definition 3.2.

Definition 3.2 (q-ary Lattice). *Let $n, m, q \in \mathbb{N}$ with $m \geq n$. Then, define the following q-ary lattice for $\mathbf{A} \in \mathbb{Z}_q^{n \times m}$.*

$$\Lambda_q^{\perp}(\mathbf{A}) := \{\mathbf{e} \in \mathbb{Z}^m : \mathbf{A} \cdot \mathbf{e} = \mathbf{0} \mod q\}$$

Furthermore, let $\Lambda_q^{\mathbf{u}}(\mathbf{A}) := \{\mathbf{e} \in \mathbb{Z}^m : \mathbf{A} \cdot \mathbf{e} = \mathbf{u} \mod q\}$ define a lattice coset for $\mathbf{u} \in \mathbb{Z}_q^n$. Observe that if $\mathbf{t} \in \Lambda_q^{\mathbf{u}}(\mathbf{A})$, then $\Lambda_q^{\mathbf{u}}(\mathbf{A}) = \Lambda_q^{\perp}(\mathbf{A}) + \mathbf{t}$. Hence, $\Lambda_q^{\mathbf{u}}(\mathbf{A})$ denotes a shift of $\Lambda_q^{\perp}(\mathbf{A})$.

One of the two lattice-based assumptions that are considered to be standard assumptions is called Short Integer Solution (SIS). It states that it is hard to find a short non-zero vector in $\Lambda_q^{\perp}(\mathbf{A})$. We define SIS and its inhomogeneous version ISIS in Definition 3.3.

Definition 3.3 ((Inhomogeneous) Short Integer Solution [Ajt96]**).** *Let n, q, β, m be functions of the security parameter λ. The SIS problem and ISIS problem are defined by the experiments described in Fig. 2. For any adversary $\mathcal{A}$, we define*

$$\mathsf{Adv}_{n,q,\beta,m}^{\mathrm{SIS}}(\mathcal{A}) := \Pr\left[\mathrm{Exp}_{n,q,\beta,m}^{\mathrm{SIS}}(\mathcal{A}) \to 1\right]$$
$$\mathsf{Adv}_{n,q,\beta,m}^{\mathrm{ISIS}}(\mathcal{A}) := \Pr\left[\mathrm{Exp}_{n,q,\beta,m}^{\mathrm{ISIS}}(\mathcal{A}) \to 1\right].$$

The $\mathrm{SIS}_{n,q,\beta,m}$ and $\mathrm{ISIS}_{n,q,\beta,m}$ assumptions state that for every ppt adversary $\mathcal{A}$, $\mathsf{Adv}_{n,q,\beta,m}^{\mathrm{SIS}}(\mathcal{A})$ and $\mathsf{Adv}_{n,q,\beta,m}^{\mathrm{ISIS}}(\mathcal{A})$ respectively are negligible.

SIS is considered to be a standard assumption due to a reduction of well-studied worst-case problems on lattices to SIS given in [Ajt96]. Its inhomogeneous version (ISIS) is at least as hard as SIS because any SIS challenge can be transformed into an ISIS challenge by using the last column of $\mathbf{A}$ as target vector $\mathbf{t} \in \mathbb{Z}_q^n$ (and removing that column vector from $\mathbf{A}$). If a ppt adversary was able output a short, suitable solution to ISIS, that solution could be appended by -1 and serve as a solution to the given SIS challenge with marginally larger norm bound.

$\mathrm{Exp}^{\mathrm{SIS}}_{n,q,\beta,m}(\mathcal{A})$	$\mathrm{Exp}^{\mathrm{ISIS}}_{n,q,\beta,m}(\mathcal{A})$
$\mathbf{A} \leftarrow\!\!\$\ \mathbb{Z}_q^{n\times m}$	$\mathbf{A} \leftarrow\!\!\$\ \mathbb{Z}_q^{n\times m}$
$\mathbf{s} \leftarrow \mathcal{A}(\mathbf{A})$	$\mathbf{t} \leftarrow\!\!\$\ \mathbb{Z}_q^{n}$
if $\mathbf{A}\cdot\mathbf{s} = \mathbf{0} \in \mathbb{Z}_q^n \wedge 0 < \|\mathbf{s}\| \leq \beta$	$\mathbf{s} \leftarrow \mathcal{A}(\mathbf{A}, \mathbf{t})$
then return 1	**if** $\mathbf{A}\cdot\mathbf{s} = \mathbf{t} \in \mathbb{Z}_q^n \wedge \|\mathbf{s}\| \leq \beta$
return 0	**then return** 1
	return 0

Fig. 2. The SIS and ISIS experiments.

3.2 Gaussians over Lattices

The previously presented problem highlights that the shortness of vectors is essential for lattice-based problems. Thus, we need to be able to find short vectors efficiently. For this purpose, vectors are usually drawn according to the discrete Gaussian distribution over lattices.

For any Gaussian parameter $s > 0$ and $m \geq 1$, define the Gaussian function on $\mathbb{R}^m$ centered at $\mathbf{c}$ by

$$\forall \mathbf{x} \in \mathbb{R}^m : \rho_{s,\mathbf{c}}(\mathbf{x}) = \exp(-\pi \|\mathbf{x} - \mathbf{c}\|^2 / s^2).$$

The center $\mathbf{c}$ is taken to be $\mathbf{0}$ when omitted.

For any $\mathbf{c} \in \mathbb{R}^m$, real $s > 0$, and m-dimensional lattice Λ, the *discrete Gaussian distribution* over Λ is defined as

$$\forall \mathbf{x} \in \Lambda : D_{\Lambda,s,\mathbf{c}}(\mathbf{x}) = \frac{\rho_{s,\mathbf{c}}(\mathbf{x})}{\rho_{s,\mathbf{c}}(\Lambda)},$$

where the denominator is merely a normalisation factor $\rho_{s,\mathbf{c}}(\Lambda) = \sum_{\mathbf{x}\in\Lambda} \rho_{s,\mathbf{c}}(\mathbf{x})$. Hence, $D_{\Lambda,s,\mathbf{c}}$ is proportional to $\rho_{s,\mathbf{c}}$ for all $\mathbf{x} \in \Lambda$.

Smoothing Parameter. For an n-dimensional lattice Λ and positive real $\epsilon > 0$, the smoothing parameter $\eta_\epsilon(\Lambda)$ is defined to be the smallest positive real $s > 0$ such that $\rho_{1/s}(\Lambda^\vee \setminus \{\mathbf{0}\}) \leq \epsilon$, where $\Lambda^\vee$ defines the dual lattice of Λ [MR04]. The key property of the smoothing parameter is that if $s > \eta_\epsilon(\Lambda)$, then every coset of Λ has roughly equal mass. More precisely, for $s > \eta_\epsilon(\Lambda), \epsilon \in (0, 1)$, and $\mathbf{c} \in \mathbb{R}^n$, then we have [GPV08, Lemma 2.7]

$$\frac{1-\epsilon}{1+\epsilon} \cdot \rho_s(\Lambda) \leq \rho_{s,\mathbf{c}}(\Lambda) \leq \rho_s(\Lambda).$$

This states that the overall density of Λ is almost shift-independent, i.e., the Gaussian blurs out the discrete structure of Λ.

There is a natural bound to $\eta_\epsilon(\Lambda)$ given in Lemma 5.3 of [GPV08] for matrices $\mathbf{A}$ with q prime and $m \geq 2n \lg q$.

Lemma 3.4 (Lemma 5.3 in [GPV08]). *Let $n \in \mathbb{N}$, q be prime, and $m \geq 2n \lg q$. Then, for all but an at most q^{-n} fraction of $\mathbf{A} \in \mathbb{Z}_q^{n \times m}$, we have $\eta_\epsilon(\Lambda_q^\perp(\mathbf{A})) \leq \omega(\sqrt{\log m})$.*

Further, discrete Gaussian distributions often introduce a lot of entropy. We use min-entropy as a metric for entropy.

Definition 3.5 (Min-entropy). *Let χ be some probability distribution over the (finite) set D. Then, the min-entropy of $\chi(D)$ is defined as*

$$H_{\min}(\chi(D)) := -\log\left(\max_{d \in D} \Pr_{x \leftarrow\$ \chi(D)}[x = d]\right).$$

A distribution $\chi(D)$ has large min-entropy if $H_{\min}(\chi(D)) \in \Omega(\lambda)$.

3.3 Other Useful Lemmas

Rejection sampling [Lyu09,Lyu12] is a widely used technique to ensure the zero-knowledge property of many lattice-based (non-)interactive proofs. In this paper, we use a generalised rejection sampling method for ellipsoidal Gaussians proposed in [BTT22, Theorem B.1] and provide a simplified version of the result applied to q-ary lattices in Lemma 3.6.

Lemma 3.6 (Generalised Rejection Sampling [BTT22]). *Take any $\alpha, \beta > 0$ and $\epsilon \leq \frac{1}{2}$. Let $\mathbf{s} \in \mathbb{Z}_q^m$ be such that $\|\mathbf{s}\| \leq \beta, \mathbf{A} \in \mathbb{Z}_q^{n \times m}, \mathbf{w} \in \mathbb{Z}_q^n$ and $\mathbf{t} := \mathbf{A} \cdot \mathbf{s} \in \mathbb{Z}_q^n$. Also, pick $s \geq \max(\alpha\beta, \eta_\epsilon(\Lambda_q^\perp(\mathbf{A})))$. Then, for any*

$$t > 0, \quad M := \exp\left(\frac{1}{2\alpha^2} + \frac{t}{\alpha}\right), \quad \varepsilon := 2\left(\frac{1+\epsilon}{1-\epsilon}\right)\exp\left(-2t^2 \cdot \frac{\pi - 1}{\pi}\right),$$

the statistical distance between distributions RejSamp *and* SimRS *defined in Fig. 3 is at most $\frac{\varepsilon}{2M} + \frac{2\epsilon}{M}$. Moreover, the probability that* RejSamp *outputs something is at least $\frac{1-\varepsilon}{M}\left(1 - \frac{4\epsilon}{(1+\epsilon)^2}\right)$.*

$\mathsf{RejSamp}(\mathbf{A}, \mathbf{s}, \mathbf{t}, \mathbf{w})$	$\mathsf{SimRS}(\mathbf{A}, \mathbf{t}, \mathbf{w})$
if $\mathbf{A} \cdot \mathbf{s} \neq \mathbf{t}$ **then return** $\perp$	$\mathbf{z} \leftarrow\$ \mathbf{A}_s^{-1}(\mathbf{t} + \mathbf{w})$
$\mathbf{y} \leftarrow\$ \mathbf{A}_s^{-1}(\mathbf{w})$	**return** $(\mathbf{A}, \mathbf{t}, \mathbf{w}, \mathbf{z})$ with prob. $\frac{1}{M}$
$\mathbf{z} = \mathbf{y} + \mathbf{s}$	
$p = \frac{D_{\mathbb{Z}^m,s}(\mathbf{z})}{M \cdot D_{\mathbb{Z}^m,s,\mathbf{s}}(\mathbf{z})}$	
return $(\mathbf{A}, \mathbf{t}, \mathbf{w}, \mathbf{z})$ with prob. $\min(p, 1)$	

Fig. 3. Generalised rejection sampling on q-ary lattices.

Furthermore, we require a stronger version of Lemma 5.2 in [Lyu12] for uniform binary vectors, which states that there are at least 2^λ binary preimages of a wide matrix $\mathbf{A} \in \mathbb{Z}_q^{n\times m}$ with high probability.

Lemma 3.7 (Generalisation of [Lyu12, **Lemma 5.2**]**).** *Let matrix* $\mathbf{A} \in \mathbb{Z}_q^{n\times m}, C > 1$ *and* $m > C \cdot n \cdot \log q$. *For uniformly chosen* $\mathbf{r} \leftarrow\$ \{0,1\}^m$ *there are at least* $k+1$ *other* $\mathbf{r}' \in \{0,1\}^m$ *with probability* $1 - k \cdot q^{-(C-1)\cdot n}$ *such that* $\mathbf{A} \cdot \mathbf{r} = \mathbf{A} \cdot \mathbf{r}'$.

Note that Lemma 3.7 states that for uniformly picked $\mathbf{r} \in \{0,1\}^m$, the probability that there are at least 2^n preimages of $\mathbf{A} \cdot \mathbf{r}$ is overwhelming with probability $1 - 2^n \cdot q^{-(C-1)\cdot n}$ for any $q > 2$.

Proof. Define $P_\mathbf{t} := \{\mathbf{r} \in \{0,1\}^m : \mathbf{A} \cdot \mathbf{r} = \mathbf{t}\}$ to be the set of preimages of some vector $\mathbf{t} \in \mathbb{Z}_q^n$.

As the size of the image space is q^n and k is the maximum number of colliding preimages for any element in $\mathbb{Z}_q^n$, the set of preimages with no more than k preimages $S = \{\mathbf{r} \in \{0,1\}^m : |P_{\mathbf{A}\cdot\mathbf{r}}| \leq k\}$ has size strictly less than $k \cdot q^n$. Thus, picking an element uniformly out of set S happens with probability

$$\begin{aligned}\Pr_{\mathbf{r} \leftarrow\$ \{0,1\}^m}[\mathbf{r} \in S] &< \frac{k \cdot q^n}{2^m} \\ &\leq \frac{k \cdot q^n}{q^{Cn}} = \frac{k}{q^{(C-1)n}}.\end{aligned}$$

Thus, the probability of picking an element $\mathbf{r} \in \{0,1\}^m \setminus S$ by choosing uniformly random out of $\{0,1\}^m$ is $\Pr_{\mathbf{r} \leftarrow\$ \{0,1\}^m}[\mathbf{r} \notin S] > 1 - k \cdot q^{-(C-1)\cdot n}$. □

4 Generalised ISIS_f and Its Interactive Version

The ISIS_f framework [BLNS23b] is a versatile framework to generically derive a variety of constructions for primitives such as blind signatures and anonymous credentials directly from an ISIS_f instance. It introduces a function f that removes the requirement of a random target vector as known from ISIS and passes additional hints to the adversary. However, ISIS_f is an ad-hoc assumption and the only known choice for which ISIS_f is proven to be at least as hard as a standard assumption (SIS) is in the random oracle model with $f =$ RO [BLNS23b, Section 3.1.1]. In this case, the ISIS_f instance closely resembles a GPV signature [GPV08].

To rest the hardness of specific ISIS_f instances on other assumptions, Dubois et al. [DKLW25] introduced the Generalised ISIS_{f_κ} ($\mathsf{GenISIS}_{f_\kappa}$) assumption, which relaxes two restrictions of the ISIS_f assumption. The authors reduce a new assumption called Vanishing SIS to $\mathsf{GenISIS}_{f_\kappa}$. Then, they utilise that $\mathsf{GenISIS}_{f_\kappa}$ inherits the versatility of ISIS_f to derive a new family of proof-friendly signatures. We simplify their notion and modify their definition slightly by allowing $\mathbf{s}^* = \mathbf{0}$ to be a suitable solution in Definition 4.1. This condition seemed to be an artifact from the SIS assumption.

The original definition is given in the module setting. Definition 4.1 is the natural translation to the classical setting replacing $\mathcal{R}$ by $\mathbb{Z}$.

Definition 4.1 (GenISIS$_{f_\kappa}$ [DKLW25]). *Let* $\mathrm{pp} = (n, q, m, \beta, s, k)$ *be a tuple of functions of the security parameter* λ. *Furthermore, let* $f : \mathcal{K} \times D \to \mathbb{Z}_q^n$ *be an efficiently computable, keyed function with sets* $\mathcal{K}, D$ *and the distribution* χ *only depending on* λ. *The* Generalised ISIS$_f$ *problem is defined by the experiment in Fig. 4. For any adversary* $\mathcal{A}$, *we define*

$$\mathsf{Adv}_{\mathrm{pp}}^{\mathrm{GenISIS}_{f_\kappa}}(\mathcal{A}) := \Pr\left[\mathrm{Exp}_{\mathrm{pp}}^{\mathrm{GenISIS}_{f_\kappa}}(\mathcal{A}) \to 1\right].$$

The $\mathrm{GenISIS}_f^{\mathrm{pp}}$ *assumption states that for every ppt adversary* $\mathcal{A}$, $\mathsf{Adv}_{\mathrm{pp}}^{\mathrm{GenISIS}_{f_\kappa}}(\mathcal{A})$ *is negligible.*

$\mathrm{Exp}_{\mathrm{pp}}^{\mathrm{GenISIS}_{f_\kappa}}(\mathcal{A})$

$\mathbf{A} \leftarrow\!\!\$\ \mathbb{Z}_q^{n \times m}$
$\kappa \leftarrow\!\!\$\ \mathcal{K}$
for $i \in [k]$ **do**
  $x_i \leftarrow\!\!\$\ \chi(D)$
  $\mathbf{s}_i \leftarrow\!\!\$\ \mathbf{A}_s^{-1}(f_\kappa(x_i))$
$(x^*, \mathbf{s}^*) \leftarrow \mathcal{A}(\kappa, \mathbf{A}, \{(x_i, \mathbf{s}_i)\}_{i \in [k]})$
if $\mathbf{A} \cdot \mathbf{s}^* = f_\kappa(x^*) \wedge \|\mathbf{s}^*\| \leq \beta \wedge (x^*, \mathbf{s}^*) \notin \{(x_i, \mathbf{s}_i)\}_{i \in [k]}$
  then return 1
return 0

Fig. 4. The GenISIS$_{f_\kappa}$ experiment.

GenISIS$_{f_\kappa}$ essentially expects the adversary to either successfully solve ISIS or to calculate a preimage of the function f_κ given k provided hints. Thus, the hardness of a GenISIS$_{f_\kappa}$ instance crucially relies on the choice of the function f_κ. To showcase this, we present a few families of functions, which render GenISIS$_{f_\kappa}$ trivially solvable.

- Additively homomorphic functions imply a trivial solution by adding or subtracting two hints.
- Any form of efficiently invertible function given publically available information enables choosing $\mathbf{s}^* \in \mathbb{Z}^m$ short and finding a preimage of $\mathbf{A} \cdot \mathbf{s}^*$.
- Assume f_κ is a linear function and the domain of f_κ was $\mathbb{Z}_q$, then any hint $(x_i, \mathbf{s}_i)$ can be used to generate a valid GenISIS$_{f_\kappa}$ solution $(-x_i, -\mathbf{s}_i)$.

Hence, the choice of f_κ needs to be non-homomorphic, preimage-resistant, and non-linear or significantly restrict the domain D. In the original paper, Bootle et al. use an ISIS_f instance with $f(x) = \mathbf{B} \cdot \mathsf{bin}(x)$ for some matrix $\mathbf{B}$, where bin denotes the binary decomposition of $x \in [N]$. They call this problem $\text{ISIS}_{\mathsf{bin}}$ and analyse direct lattice reduction as well as exploiting relations on the image space [BLNS23b, Section 3.1.2]. Their assumption crucially relies on the restriction of the domain space, which is virtually $\{0,1\}^{\lceil \log N \rceil}$ picturing $\mathsf{bin}(x)$ as the input.

As stated before, the ISIS_f framework provides generic constructions for several primitives. However, these constructions do not rely on ISIS_f directly, but on its interactive version. We define the interactive version of $\text{GenISIS}_{f_\mathcal{K}}$ and adapt its design to be as simple as possible. In addition to the changes made from ISIS_f to $\text{GenISIS}_{f_\mathcal{K}}$ and in comparison to its definition in [DKLW25], we make the following changes in Definition 4.2.

- We simplify the input to the oracle from $(\mathbf{m}, \mathbf{r}) \in \mathbb{Z}_q^{\ell_m + \ell_r}$ to $\mathbf{m} \in \mathbb{Z}_q^{\ell}$. The adversary has control over $\mathbf{m}$ and $\mathbf{r}$ in the original game as well.
- We remove the condition $0 \neq \mathbf{s}^*$.
- We follow the idea of [DKLW25] to allow for solutions under the same message $\mathbf{m}^*$.

These decisions were made to remove unnecessary restrictions in order to keep reductions to $\text{IntGenISIS}_{f_\mathcal{K}}$ as concise as possible.

Definition 4.2 (Interactive $\text{GenISIS}_{f_\mathcal{K}}$ [DKLW25]). *Define public parameters* $\text{pp} = (n, q, m, \beta_m, \beta_s, s, k, \ell)$ *as a tuple of functions of the security parameter* λ. *Furthermore, let* $f : \mathcal{K} \times D \to \mathbb{Z}_q^n$ *be an efficiently computable, keyed function with sets* $\mathcal{K}, D$ *and the distribution* χ *only depending on* λ. *The* $\text{IntGenISIS}_{f_\mathcal{K}}$ *assumption is defined by the experiment in Fig. 5. For an adversary* $\mathcal{A}$, *we define*

$$\mathsf{Adv}_{\text{pp}}^{\text{IntGenISIS}_{f_\mathcal{K}}}(\mathcal{A}) := \Pr\left[\text{Exp}_{\text{pp}}^{\text{IntGenISIS}_{f_\mathcal{K}}}(\mathcal{A}) \to 1\right].$$

The $\text{IntGenISIS}_f^{\text{pp}}$ *assumption states that for every ppt adversary* $\mathcal{A}$, *its advantage* $\mathsf{Adv}_{\text{pp}}^{\text{IntGenISIS}_{f_\mathcal{K}}}(\mathcal{A})$ *is negligible.*

Usually, it is easier to analyse and reduce problems to non-interactive assumptions. Thus, Bootle et al. [BLNS23b] provided a reduction from ISIS_f to the interactive version of ISIS_f so that the hardness of interactive ISIS_f instances can rely on the hardness of their corresponding ISIS_f instance. However, their reduction has a polynomial loss-factor depending on the number of hints (resp. queries) k. We provide a tight reduction from $\text{IntGenISIS}_{f_\mathcal{K}}$ to $\text{GenISIS}_{f_\mathcal{K}}$ in Theorem 4.3. This reduction removes the polynomial loss-factor of $\frac{1}{3k}$, where k denotes the number of queries to O_{pre}, compared to the original proof in [BLNS23b, Theorem 3.3].

Theorem 4.3 (Optimisation of [BLNS23b, Theorem 3.3]). *Let* $\text{pp} = (n, q, m, \beta_m, \beta_s, s, k, \ell)$ *and* $\text{pp}' = (n, q, m, \beta_s + \sqrt{m} \cdot \beta_m, s, k \cdot T_{\max})$ *be public parameters such that*

$$M := \exp\left(\frac{1}{2\alpha^2} + 1\right) \text{ and } \varepsilon := 2\left(\frac{1+\epsilon}{1-\epsilon}\right)\exp\left(-2\alpha^2 \cdot \frac{\pi - 1}{\pi}\right),$$

$\mathrm{Exp}_{pp}^{\mathrm{IntGenISIS}_{f_\kappa}}(\mathcal{A})$	$O_{\mathrm{pre}}(\mathbf{m} \in \mathbb{Z}^\ell)$
$\mathbf{A} \leftarrow\$ \mathbb{Z}_q^{n\times m}$	**if** $\|\mathbf{m}\| > \beta_m$
$\mathbf{C} \leftarrow\$ \mathbb{Z}_q^{n\times \ell}$	**then return** $\perp$
$\kappa \leftarrow\$ \mathcal{K}$	$x \leftarrow\$ \chi(D)$
$\mathcal{H} = \emptyset$	$\mathbf{s} \leftarrow\$ \mathbf{A}_s^{-1}(f_\kappa(x) + \mathbf{C}\cdot\mathbf{m})$
$(x^*, \mathbf{s}^*, \mathbf{m}^*) \leftarrow \mathcal{A}^{O_{\mathrm{pre}}}(\kappa, \mathbf{A}, \mathbf{C})$	$\mathcal{H} \leftarrow \mathcal{H} \cup \{(x, \mathbf{s}, \mathbf{m})\}$
$b_1 := (x^*, \mathbf{s}^*, \mathbf{m}^*) \notin \mathcal{H} \wedge \|\mathbf{m}^*\| \le \beta_m$	**return** $(x, \mathbf{s})$
$b_2 := \mathbf{A}\cdot\mathbf{s}^* = f_\kappa(x^*) + \mathbf{C}\cdot\mathbf{m}^* \wedge \|\mathbf{s}^*\| \le \beta_s$	
if $b_1 \wedge b_2$	
then return 1	
return 0	

Fig. 5. The $\mathrm{IntGenISIS}_{f_\kappa}$ experiments.

where $\epsilon = \mathrm{negl}(\lambda), \alpha = poly(\lambda)$ *and* $s \ge \max(\alpha\beta_s + \sqrt{m}\cdot\beta_m, \eta_\epsilon(\Lambda_q^\perp(\mathbf{A})))$. *Furthermore, let* $C > 1$ *and* $m \ge Cn\log q$. *Suppose* $\chi(D)$ *has large min-entropy and* $T_{\max}$ *satisfies* $\left(1 - \frac{1}{M}\right)^{T_{\max}} \le 2^{-\lambda}$.

Then, $\mathsf{IntGenISIS}_{f_\kappa}^{\mathrm{pp}}$ *is at least as hard as* $\mathsf{GenISIS}_{f_\kappa}^{\mathrm{pp}'}$, *i.e., for every ppt adversary* $\mathcal{A}$ *against* $IntGenISIS_{f_\kappa}$ *that makes at most* k *queries there is a ppt adversary* $\mathcal{B}$ *against* $GenISIS_{f_\kappa}$ *with*

$$\mathsf{Adv}_{\mathrm{pp}'}^{\mathrm{GenISIS}_{f_\kappa}}(\mathcal{B}) \ge \frac{1}{2}\cdot\mathsf{Adv}_{\mathrm{pp}}^{\mathrm{IntGenISIS}_{f_\kappa}}(\mathcal{A}) - \frac{q^n}{2^m} - 2\cdot\mathsf{StatDist} - \frac{k^2\cdot T_{\max}^2 + k\cdot T_{\max}}{2^{\Omega(\lambda)}},$$

where $\mathsf{StatDist} := \frac{\ell}{2}\cdot\sqrt{q^n/2^m} + k\cdot\left(1-\frac{1}{M}\right)^{T_{\max}} + k\cdot T_{\max}\cdot\left(\frac{\varepsilon}{2M} + \frac{2\epsilon}{M}\right)$.

Proof. Let $\mathcal{A}$ be an arbitrary but fixed ppt algorithm for $\mathrm{IntGenISIS}_{f_\kappa}$ with advantage δ. Assume without loss of generality that $\mathcal{A}$ makes at most k queries. We construct a ppt adversary $\mathcal{B}$ for $\mathrm{GenISIS}_{f_\kappa}$ from $\mathcal{A}$ in Fig. 8. To prove the relation between $\mathcal{A}$ and $\mathcal{B}$, we use a hybrid argument starting with Game_1, which denotes the $\mathrm{IntGenISIS}_{f_\kappa}$ game described in Fig. 5. In the following, define E_i to be the event that $\mathcal{A}$ wins Game_i.

Game_2*:* Instead of choosing the matrix $\mathbf{C}$ uniformly at random, a binary matrix $\mathbf{R} \leftarrow\$ \{0,1\}^{m\times\ell}$ is sampled uniformly and $\mathbf{C}$ is defined by $\mathbf{C} := \mathbf{A}\cdot\mathbf{R}$.

Lemma 4.4. $\Pr[E_2] \ge \Pr[E_1] - \frac{\ell}{2}\cdot\sqrt{q^n/2^m}$.

Proof. As q is prime and $m \ge Cn\log q$, each column of the matrix $\mathbf{C} = \mathbf{A}\cdot\mathbf{R}$ has statistical distance to the uniform distribution $U(\mathbb{Z}_q^n)$ of at most $\frac{1}{2}\cdot\sqrt{q^n/2^m}$ according to the LHL [Reg05, Claim 5.3]. Applying the LHL ℓ-times for each column of the matrix $\mathbf{C}$ yields the result. □

$O_1\ (\mathbf{m} \in \mathbb{Z}^\ell)$	$O_2\ (\mathbf{m} \in \mathbb{Z}^\ell)$	$O_3\ (\mathbf{m} \in \mathbb{Z}^\ell)$
if $\|\mathbf{m}\| > \beta_m$	**if** $\|\mathbf{m}\| > \beta_m$	**if** $\|\mathbf{m}\| > \beta_m$
then return $\perp$	**then return** $\perp$	**then return** $\perp$
$\mathbf{c} = \mathbf{C} \cdot \mathbf{m}$	$\mathbf{c} = \mathbf{C} \cdot \mathbf{m}$	$\mathbf{c} = \mathbf{R} \cdot \mathbf{m}$
while true **do**	**for** ctr $\in [T_{\max}]$ **do**	**for** ctr $\in [T_{\max}]$ **do**
$x \leftarrow\$ \chi(D)$	$x \leftarrow\$ \chi(D)$	$x \leftarrow\$ \chi(D)$
$\mathbf{s} \leftarrow\$ \mathbf{A}_s^{-1}(f_\kappa(x) + \mathbf{c})$	$\mathbf{s} \leftarrow\$ \mathbf{A}_s^{-1}(f_\kappa(x) + \mathbf{c})$	$\bar{\mathbf{s}} \leftarrow\$ \mathbf{A}_s^{-1}(f_\kappa(x))$
$u \leftarrow\$ [0,1)$	$u \leftarrow\$ [0,1)$	$\mathbf{s} = \bar{\mathbf{s}} + \mathbf{c}$
if $u \leq \frac{1}{M}$ **then**	**if** $u \leq \frac{1}{M}$ **then**	$u \leftarrow\$ [0,1)$
$\mathcal{H} \leftarrow \mathcal{H} \cup \{(x, \mathbf{s}, \mathbf{m})\}$	$\mathcal{H} \leftarrow \mathcal{H} \cup \{(x, \mathbf{s}, \mathbf{m})\}$	$p = \frac{D_{\mathbb{Z}^m, s}(\mathbf{s})}{M \cdot D_{\mathbb{Z}^m, s, \mathbf{c}}(\mathbf{s})}$
return $(x, \mathbf{s})$	**return** $(x, \mathbf{s})$	**if** $u \leq \min(p, 1)$ **then**
return $\perp$	**return** $\perp$	$\mathcal{H} \leftarrow \mathcal{H} \cup \{(x, \mathbf{s}, \mathbf{m})\}$
		return $(x, \mathbf{s})$
		return $\perp$

Fig. 6. Preimage oracles O_1 to O_3 used in the hybrid argument.

Game_3*:* In Game_3, the oracle O_{pre} of $\mathcal{A}$ is changed to O_1 defined in Fig. 6.

Lemma 4.5. $\Pr[E_3] = \Pr[E_2]$.

Proof. There is no change in behavior between O_{pre} and O_1 if they are observed as a black box. The oracle O_1 introduces an infinite while-loop[5] and rejects samples with probability $\frac{1}{M}$ before outputting one. O_{pre} outputs the first sample it produces. As the distribution of the samples is the same, the oracles distinguish in runtime only. This can be formalised in the following way.

Let $i^* \in \mathbb{N}$ denote the execution of the while-loop, in which O_1 outputs $(x, \mathbf{s})$. Then, for any input $(\mathbf{m}) \in \{0,1\}^\ell$ and any possible output $(x, \mathbf{s})$, we have:

$$\begin{aligned}
\Pr[(x, \mathbf{s}) \leftarrow O_1(\mathbf{m})] &= \sum_{i=1}^{\infty} \Pr[(x, \mathbf{s}) \leftarrow O_1(\mathbf{m}) \wedge i = i^*] \\
&= \sum_{i=1}^{\infty} \frac{1}{M} \cdot \left(1 - \frac{1}{M}\right)^{i-1} \cdot \Pr[(x, \mathbf{s}) \leftarrow O_{\text{pre}}(\mathbf{m})] \\
&= \Pr[(x, \mathbf{s}) \leftarrow O_{\text{pre}}(\mathbf{m})] .
\end{aligned}$$

□

[5] The infinite while-loop in O_1 leads to a potentially inefficient challenger. Note that the oracle is still expected to execute in polynomial time as long as $M \in \text{poly}(\lambda)$. Furthermore, we could directly hop from Game_2 to Game_4 to keep the challenger polynomial-time. Game_3 is part of the reduction to make the reduction more comprehensible.

Game_4: This game differs from Game_3 by altering the preimage oracle of $\mathcal{A}$ to O_2 defined in Fig. 6.

Lemma 4.6. $\Pr[E_4] \geq \Pr[E_3] - k \cdot \left(1 - \frac{1}{M}\right)^{T_{\max}}$.

Proof. The only difference between O_1 and O_2 is that O_2 aborts after rejecting $T_{\max}$ samples. As the accepting condition is fulfilled with probability $\frac{1}{M}$, the statistical distance between O_2 and O_1 is at most $(1 - \frac{1}{M})^{T_{\max}}$. Therefore, the advantage of $\mathcal{A}$ using at most k queries yields $\Pr[E_4] \geq \Pr[E_3] - k \cdot \left(1 - \frac{1}{M}\right)^{T_{\max}}$. □

Game_5. In this game, we run $\mathcal{A}$ with preimage oracle access to O_3 defined in Fig. 6.

Lemma 4.7. $\Pr[E_5] \geq \Pr[E_4] - k \cdot T_{\max} \cdot \left(\frac{\varepsilon}{2M} + \frac{2\epsilon}{M}\right)$.

Proof. By Lemma 3.6, the statistical distance between $O_2(\mathbf{m})$ and $O_3(\mathbf{m})$ is at most $\frac{\varepsilon}{2M} + \frac{2\epsilon}{M}$. $O_3(\mathbf{m})$ uses rejection sampling at most $T_{\max}$ times per execution and there are k queries. □

At this point, the reduction algorithm is capable of efficiently simulating O_{pre} using O_3 based on the knowledge of at most $k \cdot T_{\max}$ $\text{GenISIS}_{f_\kappa}$ hints $(x_i, \mathbf{s}_i)$ as $\mathbf{s}_i = \mathbf{A}_s^{-1}(f_\kappa(x_i))$. The following game hops are required to ensure the extraction of a valid $\text{GenISIS}_{f_\kappa}$ solution.

Game_6: This challenger algorithm keeps track of all accepted samples in set A and all generated samples in set G.

$$A = \{(x, \mathbf{s} - \mathbf{R} \cdot \mathbf{m}) : x \text{ and } \mathbf{s} \text{ were sent to } \mathcal{A} \text{ by } O_3\}$$
$$G = \{(x, \mathbf{s} - \mathbf{R} \cdot \mathbf{m}) : x \text{ and } \mathbf{s} \text{ were generated while querying } O_3\}$$

Furthermore, an additional, not publically verifiable winning condition $b_3 := (x^*, \mathbf{s}^* - \mathbf{R} \cdot \mathbf{m}^*) \notin G \setminus A$ is introduced.

Lemma 4.8. $\Pr[E_6] \geq \Pr[E_5] - \frac{k \cdot T_{\max}}{2^{\Omega(\lambda)}}$.

Proof. As $\chi(D)$ has large min-entropy, the probability to sample an arbitrary element out of D is at most $2^{-H_{\min}(\chi(D))} \leq 2^{-\Omega(\lambda)}$. As the first part of the hints x is sampled according to $\chi(D)$, the probability that $\mathcal{A}$ hits one of the $k \cdot T_{\max}$ generated samples that it has not seen before is at most $k \cdot T_{\max} \cdot 2^{-\Omega(\lambda)}$. □

Game_7: This game differs from the previous one in the execution of the oracle as it aborts whenever it samples an index $x \in D$ twice. The preimage oracle O_4 is defined in Fig. 7.

Lemma 4.9. $\Pr[E_7] \geq \Pr[E_6] - \frac{k^2 \cdot T_{\max}^2}{2^{\Omega(\lambda)+1}}$.

Proof. Similar to the proof of Lemma 4.8, we use the large min-entropy of $\chi(D)$. As the first part of the hints x is sampled with the large min-entropy of $\chi(D)$, the probability that some index x is sampled twice in k queries is at most $k^2 \cdot T_{\max}^2 \cdot 2^{-\Omega(\lambda)-1}$ due to the birthday bound. □

Game_8: In this game, the previously added, not publically-verifiable winning condition b_3 is replaced by an enclosing condition $b_3 := (x^*, \mathbf{s}^* - \mathbf{R} \cdot \mathbf{m}^*) \notin G$. For convenience, we summarise Game_8 in Fig. 7.

Game_8

$\mathbf{A} \leftarrow\$ \mathbb{Z}_q^{n \times m}$
$\mathbf{R} \leftarrow\$ \{0,1\}^{m \times \ell}$
$\mathbf{C} = \mathbf{A} \cdot \mathbf{R}$
$\kappa \leftarrow\$ \mathcal{K}$
$\mathcal{H} = \emptyset$
$\mathcal{Y} = \emptyset$
$(x^*, \mathbf{s}^*, \mathbf{m}^*) \leftarrow \mathcal{A}^{O_4}(\kappa, \mathbf{A}, \mathbf{C})$
$b_1 := (x^*, \mathbf{s}^*, \mathbf{m}^*) \notin \mathcal{H} \wedge \|\mathbf{m}^*\| \leq \beta_m$
$b_2 := \mathbf{A} \cdot \mathbf{s}^* = f_\kappa(x^*) + \mathbf{C} \cdot \mathbf{m}^* \wedge \|\mathbf{s}^*\| \leq \beta_s$
$b_3 := (x^*, \mathbf{s}^* - \mathbf{R} \cdot \mathbf{m}^*) \notin G$
if $b_1 \wedge b_2 \wedge b_3$
  then return 1
return 0

$O_4\,(\mathbf{m} \in \mathbb{Z}^\ell)$

if $\|\mathbf{m}\| > \beta_m$
  then return $\perp$
$\mathbf{c} = \mathbf{R} \cdot \mathbf{m}$
for ctr $\in [T_{\max}]$ **do**
  $x \leftarrow\$ \chi(D)$
  if $x \in \mathcal{Y}$ **then return** $\perp$
  $\mathcal{Y} \leftarrow \mathcal{Y} \cup \{x\}$
  $\bar{\mathbf{s}} \leftarrow\$ \mathbf{A}_s^{-1}(f_\kappa(x))$
  $\mathbf{s} = \bar{\mathbf{s}} + \mathbf{c}$
  $u \leftarrow\$ [0,1)$
  if $u \leq \min\left(\frac{D_{\mathbb{Z}^m,s}(\mathbf{s})}{M \cdot D_{\mathbb{Z}^m,s,\mathbf{c}}(\mathbf{s})}, 1\right)$ **then**
    $\mathcal{H} \leftarrow \mathcal{H} \cup \{(x, \mathbf{s}, \mathbf{m})\}$
    return $(x, \mathbf{s})$
return $\perp$

Fig. 7. Description of Game_8 and the preimage oracle O_4.

Lemma 4.10. $\Pr[E_8] \geq \frac{1}{2} \cdot \Pr[E_7] - \frac{q^n}{2^m} - \mathsf{StatDist}$, *where*

$$\mathsf{StatDist} := \frac{\ell}{2} \cdot \sqrt{q^n/2^m} + k \cdot \left(1 - \frac{1}{M}\right)^{T_{\max}} + k \cdot T_{\max} \cdot \left(\frac{\varepsilon}{2M} + \frac{2\epsilon}{M}\right).$$

Proof. The difference to the previous winning condition b_3 is that the set of disallowed solutions now also contains all accepted samples A. Thus, we need to analyse solutions output by $\mathcal{A}$ so that $(x^*, \mathbf{s}^* - \mathbf{R} \cdot \mathbf{m}^*) \in A$ only.

Assume the solution of $\mathcal{A}$ is a valid $\mathrm{IntGenISIS}_{f_\kappa}$ solution but it does not satisfy the condition b_3, i.e., there is a hint that was output by $O_3(\mathbf{m})$ as $(x, \mathbf{s} - \mathbf{R} \cdot \mathbf{m}) \in A$. Then, $x^* = x$ follows immediately. Consider the case $\mathbf{m}^* = \mathbf{m}$. Then,

$$\mathbf{s}^* - \mathbf{R} \cdot \mathbf{m}^* = \mathbf{s} - \mathbf{R} \cdot \mathbf{m}$$
$$\overset{\mathbf{m}^* = \mathbf{m}}{\Rightarrow} \mathbf{s}^* = \mathbf{s},$$

which implies that winning condition b_1 is not satisfied and $\mathcal{A}$ has not solved its $\mathrm{IntGenISIS}_{f_\kappa}$ instance correctly.

Thus, we know $x^* = x$ and $\mathbf{m}^* \neq \mathbf{m}$ if b_3 is not satisfied, which implies

$$\mathbf{m}' := \mathbf{m}^* - \mathbf{m} \neq \mathbf{0} \wedge \tag{3}$$

$$\mathbf{s}^* - \mathbf{R} \cdot \mathbf{m}^* = \mathbf{s} - \mathbf{R} \cdot \mathbf{m} \Leftrightarrow \mathbf{s}^* - \mathbf{s} = \mathbf{R} \cdot (\mathbf{m}^* - \mathbf{m}) \tag{4}$$

Using the previous Lemmas 4.4 to 4.7, the statistical distance between Game_1 and Game_5 can be upper-bounded by

$$\mathsf{StatDist} := \frac{\ell}{2} \cdot \sqrt{q^n/2^m} + k \cdot \left(1 - \frac{1}{M}\right)^{T_{\max}} + k \cdot T_{\max} \cdot \left(\frac{\varepsilon}{2M} + \frac{2\epsilon}{M}\right).$$

Thus, the input given to $\mathcal{A}$ in Game_5 is statistically close to the expected input from the $\mathrm{IntGenISIS}_{f_\kappa}$ experiment. This implies that a distinguisher with input from Game_1 or Game_5 could differentiate between the two worlds with at most negligible advantage $\mathsf{StatDist}$. With this in mind, define two distinct matrices $\mathbf{R}, \mathbf{R}' \in \{0,1\}^{m \times \ell}$ s.t. $\mathbf{A} \cdot \mathbf{R} = \mathbf{C} = \mathbf{A} \cdot \mathbf{R}'$. Then, another implication is that a distinguisher with input from Game_5 with either matrix $\mathbf{R}$ or $\mathbf{R}'$ would not be able to tell the difference with more than negligible advantage $2 \cdot \mathsf{StatDist}$.[6] Equation (3) ensures that there is an index $i^* \in [\ell]$ of a non-zero entry in $\mathbf{m}'$, i.e., $m'_{i^*} \neq 0$. Define the set

$$S_{\mathbf{R}} = \{\mathbf{R}' \in \{0,1\}^{m \times \ell} : \mathbf{A} \cdot \mathbf{R} = \mathbf{A} \cdot \mathbf{R}' \wedge \forall i \in [\ell] \setminus \{i^*\} : \mathbf{r}_i = \mathbf{r}'_i\}.$$

Assume there is another matrix $\mathbf{R}' \in S_{\mathbf{R}}$ with $\mathbf{R}' \neq \mathbf{R}$, then

$$\begin{aligned}
\mathbf{r}'_{i^*} \neq \mathbf{r}_{i^*} &\Leftrightarrow \mathbf{r}'_{i^*} \cdot m'_{i^*} \neq \mathbf{r}_{i^*} \cdot m'_{i^*} \\
&\Rightarrow \mathbf{R}' \cdot \mathbf{m}' \neq \mathbf{R} \cdot \mathbf{m}' \\
&\overset{Eq.\ 3\ \&\ 4}{\Leftrightarrow} \mathbf{R}' \cdot (\mathbf{m} - \mathbf{m}^*) \neq \mathbf{s}^* - \mathbf{s} \\
&\Leftrightarrow \mathbf{s} - \mathbf{R}' \cdot \mathbf{m} \neq \mathbf{s}^* - \mathbf{R}' \cdot \mathbf{m}^* \\
&\overset{\text{Lemma 4.9}}{\Rightarrow} (x^*, \mathbf{s}^* - \mathbf{R}' \cdot \mathbf{m}^*) \notin G.
\end{aligned}$$

Thus, if the game had been run with a different matrix $\mathbf{R}'$, the condition b_3 would have been met.

The binary matrix $\mathbf{R}$ is sampled uniformly at random. Therefore, given the matrix $\mathbf{C} = \mathbf{A} \cdot \mathbf{R}$, the probability to choose any matrix $\mathbf{R} \in S_{\mathbf{R}}$ is $\frac{1}{|S_{\mathbf{R}}|}$. Thus, the probability that $\mathcal{A}$ outputs a solution so that condition b_3 is not met is at most $\frac{1}{|S_{\mathbf{R}}|} \Pr[E_7] - \mathsf{StatDist}$. Lemma 3.7 states that with probability at least $1 - \frac{q^n}{2^m}$ there exist at least two matrices in the set $S_{\mathbf{R}}$.

To summarise, the probability that at least two distinct matrices $\mathbf{A} \cdot \mathbf{R} = \mathbf{A} \cdot \mathbf{R}'$ with $\mathbf{R}, \mathbf{R}' \in S_{\mathbf{R}}$ exist is $1 - \frac{q^n}{2^m}$. The probability to choose either one is at

[6] As games Game_1 and Game_5 are statistically close, a reduction can hop from Game_5 with matrix $\mathbf{R}$ to Game_1 and back to Game_5 with matrix $\mathbf{R}'$ within statistical distance $2 \cdot \mathsf{StatDist}$. The added factor for this game hop remains $1 \cdot \mathsf{StatDist}$ as we include the distance for the second hop while adding up the advantages at the end.

least $\frac{1}{2}$ and a difference depending on the choice of $\mathbf{R}$ can only be detected with statistical distance $\mathsf{StatDist}$. Furthermore, only one choice for the matrix $\mathbf{R}$ can result in violating winning condition b_3. Thus, $\Pr[E_8] \geq \frac{1}{2} \cdot \Pr[E_7] - \frac{q^n}{2^m} - \mathsf{StatDist}$. □

The hybrid argument induces the adversary $\mathcal{B}$ against $\mathrm{GenISIS}_{f_\kappa}$ defined in Fig. 8.

$\mathcal{B}(\kappa, \mathbf{A}, \{(x_i, \mathbf{s}_i)\}_{i \in [k \cdot T_{\max}]}, \mathcal{A})$

$\mathbf{R} \leftarrow \{0,1\}^{m \times \ell}$
$\mathbf{B} = \mathbf{A} \cdot \mathbf{R}$
$\mathcal{Y} = \emptyset$
$(x^*, \mathbf{s}^*, \mathbf{m}^*) \leftarrow \mathcal{A}^{O_4}(\kappa, \mathbf{A}, \mathbf{B})$
  // Each call of O_4 in Figure 6 consumes at most $T_{\max}$ hints from $\{(x_i, \mathbf{s}_i)\}_{i \in [k \cdot T_{\max}]}$
if $(x^*, \mathbf{s}^* - \mathbf{R} \cdot \mathbf{m}^*) \notin \{(x_i, \mathbf{s}_i)\}_{i \in [k \cdot T_{\max}]}$
  then return $(x^*, \mathbf{s}^* - \mathbf{R} \cdot \mathbf{m}^*)$
return $\perp$

Fig. 8. Reduction algorithm $\mathcal{B}$ reducing $\mathrm{GenISIS}_{f_\kappa}$ to $\mathrm{IntGenISIS}_{f_\kappa}$.

A correct $\mathrm{IntGenISIS}_{f_\kappa}$ solution of $\mathcal{A}$ yields

$$\begin{aligned} \mathbf{A} \cdot \mathbf{s}^* &= f_\kappa(x^*) + \mathbf{C} \cdot \mathbf{m}^* \\ \Leftrightarrow \mathbf{A} \cdot (\mathbf{s}^* - \mathbf{R} \cdot \mathbf{m}^*) &= f_\kappa(x^*). \end{aligned}$$

The norm of $\mathbf{s}^* - \mathbf{R} \cdot \mathbf{m}^*$ can be upper bounded by $\beta_s + \sqrt{m} \cdot \beta_m$ as $\|\mathbf{s}^*\| \leq \beta_s$ and $\|\mathbf{m}^*\| \leq \beta_m$. Therefore, if $\mathcal{A}^{O_4}$ wins the $\mathrm{IntGenISIS}_{f_\kappa}$ game and the condition $(x^*, \mathbf{s}^* - \mathbf{R} \cdot \mathbf{m}^*) \notin \{(x_i, \mathbf{s}_i)\}_{i \in [k \cdot T_{\max}]}$ holds, then $\mathcal{B}$ outputs a correct $\mathrm{GenISIS}_{f_\kappa}$ solution.

The advantage of $\mathcal{B}$ can be upper bounded by the advantage of $\mathcal{A}$ in the following way.

$$\begin{aligned} \mathsf{Adv}_{pp'}^{GenISIS_{f_\kappa}}(\mathcal{B}) &= \Pr[E_8] \\ &\geq \frac{1}{2} \cdot \Pr[E_7] - \frac{q^n}{2^m} - \mathsf{StatDist} \\ &\geq \frac{1}{2} \cdot \Pr[E_6] - \frac{q^n}{2^m} - \mathsf{StatDist} - \frac{k^2 \cdot T_{\max}^2}{2^{\Omega(\lambda)}} \\ &\geq \frac{1}{2} \cdot \Pr[E_5] - \frac{q^n}{2^m} - \mathsf{StatDist} - \frac{k^2 \cdot T_{\max}^2}{2^{\Omega(\lambda)}} - \frac{k \cdot T_{\max}}{2^{\Omega(\lambda)}} \\ &\geq \frac{1}{2} \cdot \Pr[E_1] - \frac{q^n}{2^m} - 2 \cdot \mathsf{StatDist} - \frac{k^2 \cdot T_{\max}^2 + k \cdot T_{\max}}{2^{\Omega(\lambda)}} \\ &\geq \frac{1}{2} \cdot \delta - \frac{q^n}{2^m} - 2 \cdot \mathsf{StatDist} - \frac{k^2 \cdot T_{\max}^2 + k \cdot T_{\max}}{2^{\Omega(\lambda)}} \end{aligned}$$

□

This reduction can be lifted to rings by borrowing techniques from the original approach [BLNS23b, Theorem 3.3]. The only technique that does not naturally lift to rings is the fact that q is prime, which is only used for the LHL and to ensure that changing the matrix $\mathbf{R} \in \{0,1\}^{m \times \ell}$ removes the potential collision. The latter argument can be resolved (as in [BLNS23b, Theorem 3.3]) by introducing a lower bound for q s.t. the equation $\mathbf{s}^* - \mathbf{s} \neq \mathbf{R}' \cdot (\mathbf{m} - \mathbf{m}^*)$ works over integers.

Generally, this reduction can be modified in several ways to optimise it for specific use-cases. Here are a few examples.

- Choosing the matrix $\mathbf{R}$ with more entropy, e.g. discrete Gaussian, in order to keep the parameter m smaller.
- We use statistical distances for this proof. There are several steps, where Rényi divergence might introduce a smaller loss-factor, e.g. for rejection sampling [JRS24, Theorem 3.1].
- The number of samples for $\text{GenISIS}_{f_\kappa}$ is currently upper-bounded per query and then multiplied by the number of queries. As the upper-bound per query must be (significantly) larger than the expected number of consumed hints per query, there must be a better bound for the number of required $\text{GenISIS}_{f_\kappa}$ hints.
- The constant multiplicative loss-factor of $\frac{1}{2}$ can be swapped for two negligible terms using Lemma 3.7.

Further practical implications of Theorem 4.3 are described in Sect. 2.

5 One-More-ISIS and Its Randomised Variant

In this section, we introduce two assumptions from the family of SIS-with-Hints assumptions. They are called One-More-ISIS (OM-ISIS) and Randomised OM-ISIS (rOM-ISIS). The security guarantees of two round-optimal (non-interactive) blind signatures rely on their hardness. Both assumptions provide a preimage oracle for target vectors $\mathbf{t} \in \mathbb{Z}_q^n$ specified by the adversary. We provide the first reduction from OM-ISIS to rOM-ISIS in Theorem 5.3 to relate the assumptions. We inspect rOM-ISIS further in Appendix D of the full version [NS26].

The OM-ISIS assumption was introduced by Agrawal et al. [AKSY22] to build practical, round-optimal lattice-based blind signatures. Their assumption is inspired by the one-more-RSA assumption by Bellare et al. [BNPS03], and they provide an analysis of several attack strategies for OM-ISIS to gain confidence in the assumption [AKSY22, Section 4.5].

Definition 5.1 (One-More-ISIS [AKSY22]**).** *Let* $\text{pp} = (n, q, m, \beta, s, \ell)$ *be a tuple of functions of the security parameter* λ*. The One-More-ISIS problem is defined by the experiment in Fig. 9. For any adversary* $\mathcal{A}$*, we define*

$$\mathsf{Adv}_{\text{pp}}^{\text{OM-ISIS}}(\mathcal{A}) := \Pr\left[\text{Exp}_{\text{pp}}^{\text{OM-ISIS}}(\mathcal{A}) \to 1\right].$$

The $\text{OM-ISIS}_{\text{pp}}$ *assumption states that for every ppt adversary* $\mathcal{A}$*,* $\mathsf{Adv}_{\text{pp}}^{\text{OM-ISIS}}(\mathcal{A})$ *is negligible.*

$\mathrm{Exp}_{\mathrm{pp}}^{\mathrm{OM-ISIS}}(\mathcal{A})$	$O_{\mathrm{pre}}(\hat{\mathbf{t}} \in \mathbb{Z}_q^n)$
$\mathbf{A} \leftarrow\!\$\ \mathbb{Z}_q^{n\times m}$	$\hat{\mathbf{s}} \leftarrow\!\$\ \mathbf{A}_s^{-1}(\hat{\mathbf{t}})$
$T = \{\mathbf{t}_1, \dots, \mathbf{t}_\ell\} \leftarrow\!\$\ \mathbb{Z}_q^n \times \cdots \times \mathbb{Z}_q^n$	$k \leftarrow k+1$
$k = 0$	**return** $\hat{\mathbf{s}}'$
$\{\mathbf{s}_i\}_{i\in[k+1]} \leftarrow \mathcal{A}^{O_{\mathrm{pre}}}(\mathbf{A}, T)$	
if $\forall i \in [k+1] : \mathbf{A}\cdot\mathbf{s}_i \in T \wedge \|\mathbf{s}_i\| \leq \beta$	
then return 1	
return 0	

Fig. 9. The One-More-ISIS (OM-ISIS) experiment.

The OM-ISIS notion roughly outlines the assumption that, given access to an ISIS solver, it remains hard to compute an additional preimage for a polynomial number of possible ISIS targets. For the construction of a non-interactive blind signature, Baldimtsi et al. [BCGY24] introduced a closely related assumption called rOM-ISIS, which they claim to be more robust. They provide some analysis for their assumption, which resembles the analysis of OM-ISIS closely. We highlight the differences to OM-ISIS below.

Definition 5.2 (Randomised One-More-ISIS [BCGY24]**).** *Let* $\mathrm{pp} = (n, q, m, \beta, s, \ell)$ *be a tuple of functions of the security parameter* λ*. The Randomised OM-ISIS problem is defined by the experiment in Fig. 10. For any adversary* $\mathcal{A}$*, we define*

$$\mathsf{Adv}_{\mathrm{pp}}^{\mathrm{rOM\text{-}ISIS}}(\mathcal{A}) := \Pr\left[\mathrm{Exp}_{\mathrm{pp}}^{\mathrm{rOM-ISIS}}(\mathcal{A}) \to 1\right].$$

The rOM-ISIS$_{\mathrm{pp}}$ *assumption states that for every ppt adversary* $\mathcal{A}$*, its advantage* $\mathsf{Adv}_{\mathrm{pp}}^{\mathrm{rOM\text{-}ISIS}}(\mathcal{A})$ *is negligible.*

Baldimtsi et al. [BCGY24] state that their assumption is more robust due to the fact that the adversary is not able to truly control the preimage vector $\hat{\mathbf{t}}$ since the actual target vector for O_{pre} is $\hat{\mathbf{t}} - \mathbf{B}\cdot\hat{\mathbf{u}}$. As $\hat{\mathbf{u}}$ is a random ± 1 vector, they claim, this randomises the preimage query. The analysis of the authors shows that the restriction of $\hat{\mathbf{u}}$ to $\{-1, 1\}$ prevents one of the previously presented attacks for OM-ISIS, which provides more freedom in parameter selection for their construction. We provide a reduction from OM-ISIS to rOM-ISIS in Theorem 5.3.

Theorem 5.3. *Let* $m \geq C \cdot n \log q$ *with* $C > 1$ *and let* $q > 2$ *be prime. Then,* $\mathrm{rOM\text{-}ISIS}_{n,q,m,\beta,s,\ell}$ *is at least as hard as* $\mathrm{OM\text{-}ISIS}_{n,q,m,\beta+m^{3/2},s,\ell}$*, i.e., for every ppt adversary* $\mathcal{A}$ *against rOM-ISIS there is a ppt adversary* $\mathcal{B}$ *against OM-ISIS with*

$$\mathsf{Adv}_{n,q,m,\beta+m^{3/2},s,\ell}^{\mathrm{OM\text{-}ISIS}}(\mathcal{B}) > \mathsf{Adv}_{n,q,m,\beta,s,\ell}^{\mathrm{rOM\text{-}ISIS}}(\mathcal{A}) - m \cdot (k+1)^2 \cdot 2^n \cdot q^{-(C-1)\cdot n},$$

where $2^n \cdot q^{-(C-1)\cdot n}$ *is negligible due to* $q > 2$ *and* $C > 1$*.*

$\mathrm{Exp}^{\mathrm{rOM-ISIS}}_{\mathrm{pp}}(\mathcal{A})$	$O_{\mathrm{pre}}\left(\hat{\mathbf{t}} \in \mathbb{Z}_q^n\right)$
$\mathbf{A}, \mathbf{B} \leftarrow\!\!\$\ \mathbb{Z}_q^{n\times m}$	$\hat{\mathbf{u}} \leftarrow\!\!\$\ \{-1,1\}^m$
$T = \{\mathbf{t}_1, \dots, \mathbf{t}_\ell\} \leftarrow\!\!\$\ \mathbb{Z}_q^n \times \cdots \times \mathbb{Z}_q^n$	$\hat{\mathbf{s}} \leftarrow\!\!\$\ \mathbf{A}_s^{-1}(\hat{\mathbf{t}} - \mathbf{B}\cdot\hat{\mathbf{u}})$
$k = 0$	$k \leftarrow k+1$
$\{(\mathbf{s}_i, \mathbf{u}_i)\}_{i\in[k+1]} \leftarrow \mathcal{A}^{O_{\mathrm{pre}}}(\mathbf{A}, \mathbf{B}, T)$	**return** $(\hat{\mathbf{s}}, \hat{\mathbf{u}})$
$b_1 := \forall i \in [k+1] : \mathbf{A}\cdot\mathbf{s}_i + \mathbf{B}\cdot\mathbf{u}_i \in T \wedge \lVert\mathbf{s}_i\rVert \leq \beta$	
$b_2 := \forall i \in [k+1] : \mathbf{u}_i \in \{-1,1\}^m$	
if $b_1 \wedge b_2$	
then return 1	
return 0	

Fig. 10. The Randomised One-More-ISIS (rOM-ISIS) experiment.

Proof. Let $\mathcal{A}^{O'_{\mathrm{pre}}}$ be an arbitrary but fixed ppt algorithm for rOM-ISIS with oracle access to O'_{pre} for preimage queries. We construct an adversary $\mathcal{B}$ for OM-ISIS with oracle access to O_{pre} for preimage queries from $\mathcal{A}$ in Fig. 11.

$\mathcal{B}^{O_{\mathrm{pre}}}(\mathbf{A} \in \mathbb{Z}_q^{n\times m}, T \subset \mathbb{Z}_q^n, \mathcal{A})$	$O'_{\mathrm{pre}}(\hat{\mathbf{t}} \in \mathbb{Z}_q^n)$
$\mathbf{R} \leftarrow\!\!\$\ \{0,1\}^{m\times m}$	$\hat{\mathbf{u}} \leftarrow\!\!\$\ \{-1,1\}^m$
$\mathbf{B} = \mathbf{A}\cdot\mathbf{R}$	$\hat{\mathbf{s}} = O_{\mathrm{pre}}(\hat{\mathbf{t}} - \mathbf{B}\cdot\mathbf{u})$
$\{(\mathbf{s}_i, \mathbf{u}_i)\}_{i\in[k+1]} \leftarrow \mathcal{A}^{O'_{\mathrm{pre}}}(\mathbf{A}, \mathbf{B}, T)$	**return** $(\hat{\mathbf{s}}, \hat{\mathbf{u}})$
$S = \{\mathbf{s}_i + \mathbf{R}\cdot\mathbf{u}_i\}_{i\in[k+1]}$	
if $\lvert S\rvert < k+1$ **then**	
return $\perp$	
return S	

Fig. 11. Reduction algorithm $\mathcal{B}$ reducing OM-ISIS to rOM-ISIS.

A single tuple from a correct rOM-ISIS solution $(\mathbf{s}_i, \mathbf{u}_i)$ of $\mathcal{A}$ yields

$$\mathbf{A}\cdot\mathbf{s}_i + \mathbf{B}\cdot\mathbf{u}_i = \mathbf{A}\cdot\mathbf{s}_i + \mathbf{A}\cdot\mathbf{R}\cdot\mathbf{u}_i = \mathbf{A}\cdot(\mathbf{s}_i + \mathbf{R}\cdot\mathbf{u}_i) = \mathbf{t}$$

for some $\mathbf{t} \in T$. Furthermore, the norm bound $\lVert\mathbf{s}_i + \mathbf{R}\cdot\mathbf{u}_i\rVert \leq \lVert\mathbf{s}_i\rVert + \lVert\mathbf{R}\cdot\mathbf{u}_i\rVert \leq \beta + m^{3/2}$ holds for any tuple of a correct rOM-ISIS solution and thus, yields a valid instance in a OM-ISIS solution.

Inspecting multiple tuples, the addition of $\mathbf{s}_i$ and $\mathbf{R}\cdot\mathbf{u}_i$ could potentially lead to collisions in the set S. In this case, the adversary aborts.

We inspect a possible collision between two tuples $(\mathbf{s}_i, \mathbf{u}_i), (\mathbf{s}_j, \mathbf{u}_j)$ with $i \neq j$ so that $\mathbf{s}_i + \mathbf{R} \cdot \mathbf{u}_i = \mathbf{s}_j + \mathbf{R} \cdot \mathbf{u}_j$, which is equivalent to

$$\mathbf{s}_i - \mathbf{s}_j = \mathbf{R} \cdot (\mathbf{u}_j - \mathbf{u}_i)\,. \tag{5}$$

If we assume $\mathbf{u}_i = \mathbf{u}_j$, then $\mathbf{s}_i = \mathbf{s}_j$ follows immediately from the fact that the tuples $(\mathbf{s}_i, \mathbf{u}_i), (\mathbf{s}_j, \mathbf{u}_j)$ output by the adversary $\mathcal{A}$ must be distinct. Therefore, we know that $\mathbf{u}_i \neq \mathbf{u}_j$, which implies that there exists at least one coordinate $c \in [m]$, where $\mathbf{u}_i$ and $\mathbf{u}_j$ differ. Define $\mathbf{u} := \mathbf{u}_j - \mathbf{u}_i$.

We use the same technique as in Lemma 4.10. Define two distinct matrices $\mathbf{R}, \mathbf{R}' \in \{0,1\}^{m \times m}$, which differ in one column only and satisfy $\mathbf{A} \cdot \mathbf{R} = \mathbf{B} = \mathbf{A} \cdot \mathbf{R}'$. Switching from the reduction algorithm $\mathcal{B}$ with matrix $\mathbf{B} = \mathbf{A} \cdot \mathbf{R}$ to the same algorithm with a uniformly chosen matrix $\mathbf{B}$ can be done with statistical distance $\frac{1}{2} \cdot \sqrt{q^n/2^m}$ according to the LHL [Reg05, Claim 5.3]. Switching back to a version of $\mathcal{B}$ with matrix $\mathbf{R}'$ is within the same statistical distance. Thus, there is provably no ppt distinguisher that can distinguish between $\mathcal{B}$ with $\mathbf{R}$ and $\mathbf{R}'$ with more than negligible advantage $\sqrt{q^n/2^m}$.

Lemma 3.7 states that with probability $1 - 2^n \cdot q^{-(C-1)\cdot n}$ there are at least 2^n other matrices

$$\mathbf{R}' = \begin{bmatrix} \mathbf{r}_1 & \dots & \mathbf{r}_{c-1} & \mathbf{r}'_c & \mathbf{r}_{c+1} & \dots & \mathbf{r}_m \end{bmatrix}$$

with $\mathbf{r}'_c \neq \mathbf{r}_c$ satisfying $\mathbf{A} \cdot \mathbf{R} = \mathbf{B} = \mathbf{A} \cdot \mathbf{R}'$. As q is prime, the use of any $\mathbf{R}'$ resolves the collision.

$$\begin{aligned} \mathbf{r}_c \neq \mathbf{r}'_c &\overset{u_c \neq 0}{\Leftrightarrow} \mathbf{r}_c \cdot u_c \neq \mathbf{r}'_c \cdot u_c \\ &\Rightarrow \mathbf{R} \cdot \mathbf{u} \neq \mathbf{R}' \cdot \mathbf{u} \\ &\overset{Eq.\ 5}{\Leftrightarrow} \mathbf{s}_i - \mathbf{s}_j \neq \mathbf{R}' \cdot (\mathbf{u}_j - \mathbf{u}_i) \\ &\Leftrightarrow \mathbf{s}_i - \mathbf{R}' \cdot \mathbf{u}_i \neq \mathbf{s}_j - \mathbf{R}' \cdot \mathbf{u}_j \end{aligned}$$

As the matrix $\mathbf{R}$ is chosen uniformly, the probability to choose the single colliding matrix $\mathbf{R}$ is $\frac{1}{2^n}$. There are at least 2^n matrices $\mathbf{R}, \mathbf{R}'$ with probability $1 - 2^n \cdot q^{-(C-1)\cdot n}$ with $\mathbf{r}_c \neq \mathbf{r}'_c$ as only difference satisfying $\mathbf{A} \cdot \mathbf{R} = \mathbf{A} \cdot \mathbf{R}'$. Furthermore, the choice of $\mathbf{r}_c$ can not be distinguished with more than negligible probability $\sqrt{q^n/2^m} \leq q^{-(C-1)\cdot n}$. Thus, the probability of choosing a matrix $\mathbf{R} \in \{0,1\}^{m \times m}$ s.t. a collision between two arbitrary tuples occurs is at most

$$\Pr_{\mathbf{R} \leftarrow\$ \{\mathbf{R} \in \{0,1\}^{m \times m} : \mathbf{A} \cdot \mathbf{R} = \mathbf{B}\}} [\mathbf{s}_i + \mathbf{R} \cdot \mathbf{u}_i = \mathbf{s}_j + \mathbf{R} \cdot \mathbf{u}_j] < (2^n + 2) \cdot q^{-(C-1)\cdot n}.$$

Note that $2^n \cdot q^{-(C-1)\cdot n}$ is negligible due to $q > 2$ and $C > 1$.

To argue about the probability of collisions in a set with $k+1$ tuples, we use the union bound.

$$\begin{aligned}
&\Pr_{\mathbf{R} \leftarrow\$ \{\mathbf{R}\in\{0,1\}^{m\times m}:\mathbf{A}\cdot\mathbf{R}=\mathbf{B}\}}\left[\exists i,j \in [k+1], i \neq j : \mathbf{s}_i + \mathbf{R}\cdot\mathbf{u}_i = \mathbf{s}_j + \mathbf{R}\cdot\mathbf{u}_j\right] \\
&\leq \sum_{\substack{i,j\in[k+1]\\ i<j}} \Pr_{\mathbf{R} \leftarrow\$ \{\mathbf{R}\in\{0,1\}^{m\times m}:\mathbf{A}\cdot\mathbf{R}=\mathbf{B}\}}\left[\mathbf{s}_i + \mathbf{R}\cdot\mathbf{u}_i = \mathbf{s}_j + \mathbf{R}\cdot\mathbf{u}_j\right] \\
&= \frac{k(k+1)}{2} \cdot \Pr_{\mathbf{R} \leftarrow\$ \{\mathbf{R}\in\{0,1\}^{m\times m}:\mathbf{A}\cdot\mathbf{R}=\mathbf{B}\}}\left[\mathbf{s}_i + \mathbf{R}\cdot\mathbf{u}_i = \mathbf{s}_j + \mathbf{R}\cdot\mathbf{u}_j\right] \\
&< \frac{k(k+1)}{2} \cdot (2^n + 2) \cdot q^{-(C-1)\cdot n} \\
&\leq k(k+1) \cdot 2^n \cdot q^{-(C-1)\cdot n}
\end{aligned}$$

It remains to show that the input of $\mathcal{A}$ is correct. The distributions of $\mathbf{A} \in \mathbb{Z}_q^{n\times m}$ and $T \subset \mathbb{Z}_q^n$ do not differ between OM-ISIS and rOM-ISIS. As q is prime, the matrix $\mathbf{B} = \mathbf{A}\cdot\mathbf{R}$ has statistical distance to the uniform distribution $U(\mathbb{Z}_q^n)$ of at most $\frac{m}{2}\sqrt{q^n/2^m}$ according to the LHL [Reg05, Claim 5.3]. Preimage queries are answered exactly as in the rOM-ISIS experiment. Therefore, the provided distribution of preimages is statistically close to the expected one.

$$\begin{aligned}
&\mathsf{Adv}_{pp}^{rOM\text{-}ISIS}(\mathcal{B}) \\
&> \Pr\left[\mathrm{Exp}_{pp}^{\mathrm{rOM-ISIS}}(\mathcal{A}) = 1 \wedge \left|\{\mathbf{s}_i + \mathbf{R}\cdot\mathbf{u}_i\}_{i\in[k+1]}\right| = k+1 \wedge \mathbf{A}\cdot\mathbf{R} \sim U(\mathbb{Z}_q^n)\right] \\
&\quad - k(k+1)\cdot 2^n \cdot q^{-(C-1)\cdot n} - \frac{1}{2}\sqrt{q^n/2^m} \\
&\geq \mathsf{Adv}_{pp}^{rOM\text{-}ISIS}(\mathcal{A}) - k(k+1)\cdot 2^n \cdot q^{-(C-1)\cdot n} - \frac{m}{2}\sqrt{q^n/2^m}
\end{aligned}$$

□

Note that this reduction can be adapted in similar ways as proposed for Theorem 4.3. An additional optimisation could be introduced by moving from a total bound for $\|\mathbf{R}\cdot\mathbf{u}_i\| \leq m^{3/2}$ to a probabilistic bound as $\mathbf{R} \in \{0,1\}^{m\times m}$ is chosen uniformly at random.

Relationship Between OM-ISIS and rOM-ISIS. Theorem 5.3 shows that rOM-ISIS is at least as hard as OM-ISIS for suitable choices of parameters. However, this does not mean that rOM-ISIS is strictly harder to solve than OM-ISIS. Baldimtsi et al. [BCGY24] point out that the ability to randomise the target vector provides more flexibility for the challenger to answer the preimage query. However, this is always possible - also with discrete Gaussian values as shown in Lemma 2.4. As discrete Gaussians provide more Shannon entropy than binary vectors (as [PR06, Lemma 2.10] shows), this flexibility is inherent in the OM-ISIS assumption and can not be the difference between the two assumptions. Furthermore, choosing the challenge matrix as $\begin{bmatrix}\mathbf{A} & \mathbf{B}\end{bmatrix}$ doubles the width of the challenge matrix, which makes an instance generally easier to solve. Thus, the single property that might induce that rOM-ISIS is more robust than OM-ISIS is the restriction that $\hat{\mathbf{u}} \in \{-1,1\}^m$, which essentially introduces a generalised compact knapsack problem as defined in [Mic07] with $S = \{-1,1\}$. According to Baldimtsi et al. [BCGY24] this restriction prevents the algebraic attacks that were mounted on the OM-ISIS assumption.

As we could not find a justification for the choice of $\{-1,1\}^m$ other than potentially requiring the adversary to make the solutions dependent on the matrix $\mathbf{B}$, we examined an adversary that could potentially output solutions ignoring $\mathbf{B}$ by setting $\mathbf{u}_i = \mathbf{0}$. Thus, the vectors $\hat{\mathbf{u}}$ had to be binary for this scenario. As we show in Lemma 2.10, an adversary is capable of ignoring the matrix $\mathbf{B}$ for its solution by reducing rOM-ISIS with $\hat{\mathbf{u}} \in \{-1,1\}^m$ to rOM-ISIS with $\hat{\mathbf{u}} \in \{0,1\}^m$ and vice versa. This leaves the question about this unusual choice unanswered and provides a slightly more conventional and equivalent version of rOM-ISIS with binary vectors $\hat{\mathbf{u}}$.

6 Comparison of ISIS_f and One-More-ISIS

As the function of ISIS_f and $\mathrm{GenISIS}_{f_\kappa}$ can be set arbitrarily, it is not surprising that one can choose f_κ s.t. it resembles OM-ISIS and rOM-ISIS closely. The initial choice of the function f by Bootle et al. [BLNS23b] was $f(x) = \mathbf{B} \cdot \mathrm{bin}(x)$ with $\mathrm{bin}(x)$ denoting a binary encoding. Comparing ISIS_f with this function f and rOM-ISIS with binary vectors $\hat{\mathbf{u}} \in \{0,1\}^m$ shows a close resemblance. Especially, when you compare the corresponding $\mathrm{IntISIS}_f$ instance

$$\mathbf{A} \cdot \mathbf{s} = \mathbf{B} \cdot \mathrm{bin}(x) + \mathbf{C} \cdot \mathbf{m}$$

with rOM-ISIS. The hardness of both assumptions crucially relies on the fact that the value multiplied by matrix $\mathbf{B}$ is binary. However, a major difference is that the adversary does not have full control over the target vector in $\mathrm{IntISIS}_f$ as its message is multiplied by $\mathbf{C}$ whereas the adversary controls the target vector $\hat{\mathbf{t}}$ in rOM-ISIS completely (disregarding the randomisation argument). From this point of view, the $\mathrm{IntISIS}_f$ instance seems to be more robust than the rOM-ISIS assumption. Nevertheless, the ISIS_f instance is trivially broken if the value multiplied by matrix $\mathbf{B}$ would not be restricted to binary vectors while the rOM-ISIS assumption is not. If rOM-ISIS would not have the restriction to binary vectors $\hat{\mathbf{t}}$, it would be closely related to OM-ISIS, which is not trivially broken due to a second major difference. The winning conditions of ISIS_f and rOM-ISIS seem to be closely related at first glance, but ISIS_f and $\mathrm{GenISIS}_{f_\kappa}$ remove the requirement for random target vectors. The random target vectors in OM-ISIS dampen the effect of the trivial combinatorial attack of adding two hints, which breaks the ISIS_f instance for non-binary vectors $\mathrm{bin}(x)$.

Acknowledgements. We thank Laurens Porzenheim for valuable discussions and literature recommendations that inspired Lemma 2.4, as well as the anonymous reviewers for their constructive feedback. This work was partially funded by the EPSRC Research Council, part of the EPSRC/UKRI Horizon Europe Grant Studentship, Grant Ref: EP/Y02432X/1.

References

[ABB10] Agrawal, S., Boneh, D., Boyen, X.: Efficient lattice (H)IBE in the standard model. In: Gilbert [Gil10], pp. 553–572

[AGJ+24] Argo, S., Güneysu, T., Jeudy, C., Land, G., Roux-Langlois, A., Sanders, O.: Practical post-quantum signatures for privacy. In: Luo et al. (eds.) LLX+24, pp. 1523–1537 (2024)

[Ajt96] Ajtai, M.: Generating hard instances of lattice problems (extended abstract). In: 28th ACM STOC, pp. 99–108. ACM Press (1996)

[AKSY22] Agrawal, S., Kirshanova, E., Stehlé, D., Yadav, A.: Practical, round-optimal lattice-based blind signatures. In: Yin, H., Stavrou, A., Cremers, C., Shi, E. (eds.) ACM CCS 2022, pp. 39–53. ACM Press (2022)

[BCGY24] Baldimtsi, F., Cheng, J., Goyal, R., Yadav, A.: Non-interactive blind signatures: Post-quantum and stronger security. In: Chung, K.-M., Sasaki, Yu. (eds.) ASIACRYPT 2024. Part II, volume 15485 of LNCS, pp. 70–104. Springer, Singapore (2024)

[BLNS23a] Beullens, W., Lyubashevsky, V., Nguyen, N.K., Seiler, G.: Lattice-based blind signatures: short, efficient, and round-optimal. In: Meng, W., Jensen, C.D., Cremers, C., Kirda, E., (eds.) ACM CCS 2023, pp. 16–29. ACM Press (2023)

[BLNS23b] Bootle, J., Lyubashevsky, V., Nguyen, N.K., Sorniotti, A.: A framework for practical anonymous credentials from lattices. In: Handschuh, H., Lysyanskaya, A. (eds.) Advances in Cryptology – CRYPTO 2023. CRYPTO 2023. Lecture Notes in Computer Science, vol 14082. Springer, Cham (2023). https://doi.org/10.1007/978-3-031-38545-2_13

[BNPS03] Bellare, M., Namprempre, C., Pointcheval, D., Semanko, M.: The one-more-RSA-inversion problems and the security of Chaum's blind signature scheme. J. Cryptol. **16**(3), 185–215 (2003)

[Boy10] Boyen, X.: Lattice mixing and vanishing trapdoors: A framework for fully secure short signatures and more. In: Nguyen, P.Q., Pointcheval, D. (eds.) PKC 2010. LNCS, vol. 6056, pp. 499–517. Springer, Berlin, Heidelberg (2010)

[BS23] Beullens, W., Seiler, G.: LaBRADOR: Compact proofs for R1CS from module-SIS. In: Handschuh, H., Lysyanskaya, A. (eds.) CRYPTO 2023. Part V, volume 14085 of LNCS, pp. 518–548. Springer, Cham (2023)

[BTT22] Boschini, C., Takahashi, A., Tibouchi, M.: MuSig-L: lattice-based multi-signature with single-round online phase. In: Dodis, Y., Shrimpton, T. (eds.) Advances in Cryptology – CRYPTO 2022. CRYPTO 2022. Lecture Notes in Computer Science, vol. 13508. Springer, Cham (2022). https://doi.org/10.1007/978-3-031-15979-4_10

[CDJ+25] Clermont, S., Düzlü, S., Janson, C., Porzenheim, L., Struck, P. (2025). Lattice-based sanitizable signature schemes: chameleon hash functions and more. In: Niederhagen, R., Saarinen, MJ.O. (eds.) Post-Quantum Cryptography. PQCrypto 2025. Lecture Notes in Computer Science, vol. 15577. Springer, Cham (2025). https://doi.org/10.1007/978-3-031-86599-2_10

[CHE24] Chen, L., Hough, P., El Kassem, N.: Collaborative, segregated NIZK (CoS-NIZK) and more efficient lattice-based direct anonymous attestation. Cryptology ePrint Archive, Report 2024/864 (2024)

[CHKP10] Cash, D., Hofheinz, D., Kiltz, E., Peikert, C.: Bonsai Trees, or How to Delegate a Lattice Basis. J. Cryptol. **25**(4), 601–639 (2011). https://doi.org/10.1007/s00145-011-9105-2

[CL03] Camenisch, J., Lysyanskaya, A.: A signature scheme with efficient protocols. In: Cimato, S., Galdi, C., Persiano, G. (eds.) SCN 02. LNCS, vol. 2576, pp. 268–289. Springer, Berlin, Heidelberg (2003)

[CLM23] VCini, V., Lai, R.W.F., Malavolta, G.: Lattice-based succinct arguments from vanishing polynomials. In: Handschuh, H., Lysyanskaya, A. (eds.) Advances in Cryptology – CRYPTO 2023. CRYPTO 2023. Lecture Notes in Computer Science, vol. 14082. Springer, Cham (2023). https://doi.org/10.1007/978-3-031-38545-2_3

[DKL+18] Ducas, L., Kiltz, E., Lepoint, T., Lyubashevsky, V., Schwabe, P., Seiler, G., Stehlé, D.: CRYSTALS-Dilithium: a lattice-based digital signature scheme. IACR TCHES **2018**(1), 238–268 (2018)

[DKLW25] Dubois, A., Klooß, M., Lai, R.W.F., Woo, I.K.Y.: Lattice-based proof-friendly signatures from vanishing short integer solutions. In: Jager, T., Pan, J. (eds.) Public-Key Cryptography – PKC 2025. PKC 2025. Lecture Notes in Computer Science, vol. 15674. Springer, Cham (2025). https://doi.org/10.1007/978-3-031-91820-9_15

[dPK22] del Pino, R., Katsumata, S.: A new framework for more efficient round-optimal lattice-based (partially) blind signature via trapdoor sampling. In: Dodis, Y., Shrimpton, T. (eds.) Advances in Cryptology – CRYPTO 2022. CRYPTO 2022. Lecture Notes in Computer Science, vol. 13508. Springer, Cham (2022). https://doi.org/10.1007/978-3-031-15979-4_11

[DS22] Dodis, Y., Shrimpton, T. (eds.): CRYPTO 2022, Part II. LNCS, vol. 13508. Springer, Cham (2022)

[EUD] European Commission. EU Digital Identity Wallets. https://ec.europa.eu/digital-building-blocks/sites/display/EUDIGITALIDENTITYWALLET/EU+Digital+Identity+Wallet+Home

[FHK+20] Fouque, P.-A., et al.: Falcon: Fast-fourier lattice-based compact signatures over NTRU. Technical report (2020). https://falcon-sign.info/falcon.pdf

[Gil10] Gilbert, H. (ed.) EUROCRYPT 2010, vol. 6110, LNCS. Springer, Cham (2010)

[GPV08] Gentry, C., Peikert, C., Vaikuntanathan, V.: Trapdoors for hard lattices and new cryptographic constructions. In: Ladner, R.E., Dwork, C., (eds.) 40th ACM STOC, pp. 197–206. ACM Press (2008)

[Han23] Hanzlik, L.: Non-interactive blind signatures for random messages. In: Hazay, C., Stam, M. (eds.) EUROCRYPT 2023. Part V, volume 14008 of LNCS, pp. 722–752. Springer, Cham (2023)

[HL23] Handschuh, H., Lysyanskaya, A. (eds.): CRYPTO 2023, Part II. LNCS, vol. 14082. Springer, Cham (2023)

[JRS23] Jeudy, C., Roux-Langlois, A., Sanders, O.: Lattice signature with efficient protocols, application to anonymous credentials. In: Handschuh, H., Lysyanskaya, A. (eds.) Advances in Cryptology – CRYPTO 2023. CRYPTO 2023. Lecture Notes in Computer Science, vol. 14082. Springer, Cham (2023). https://doi.org/10.1007/978-3-031-38545-2_12

[JRS24] Jeudy, C., Roux-Langlois, A., Sanders, O.: Phoenix: Hash-and-sign with aborts from lattice gadgets. In: Saarinen, M.-J., Smith-Tone, D. (eds.) Post-Quantum Cryptography - 15th International Workshop. PQCrypto 2024, Part I, pp. 265–299. Springer, Cham (2024)

[JS24] Jeudy, C., Sanders, O.: Improved lattice blind signatures from recycled entropy. Cryptology ePrint Archive, Report 2024/1289 (2024)

[KR00] Krawczyk, H., Rabin, T.: Chameleon signatures. In: NDSS 2000. The Internet Society (2000)

[LCL+23] Lai, Q., Chen, C., Liu, F.-H., Lysyanskaya, A., Wang, Z.: Lattice-based commit-transferrable signatures and applications to anonymous credentials. Cryptology ePrint Archive, Report 2023/766 (2023)

[LLX+24] Luo, B., Liao, X., Xu, J., Kirda, E., Lie, D. (eds.) ACM CCS 2024. ACM Press (2024)

[LSS24] Lyubashevsky, V., Seiler, G., Steuer, P.: The LaZer library: lattice-based zero knowledge and succinct proofs for quantum-safe privacy. In: Luo et al. (eds.) [LLX+24], pp. 3125–3137 (2024)

[Lyu09] Lyubashevsky, V.: Fiat-Shamir with aborts: Applications to lattice and factoring-based signatures. In: Matsui, M. (ed.) ASIACRYPT 2009. LNCS, vol. 5912, pp. 598–616. Springer, Berlin, Heidelberg (2009)

[Lyu12] Lyubashevsky, V.: Lattice Signatures without Trapdoors. In: Pointcheval, D., Johansson, T. (eds.) EUROCRYPT 2012. LNCS, vol. 7237, pp. 738–755. Springer, Heidelberg (2012). https://doi.org/10.1007/978-3-642-29011-4_43

[mDL] American Association of Motor Vehicle Administrators. Mobile Driver License. https://www.aamva.org/topics/mobile-driver-license

[Mic07] Micciancio, D.: Generalized compact knapsacks, cyclic lattices, and efficient one-way functions. Comput. Complex. **16**(4), 365–411 (2007)

[MP12] Micciancio, D., Peikert, C.: Trapdoors for Lattices: Simpler, Tighter, Faster, Smaller. In: Pointcheval, D., Johansson, T. (eds.) EUROCRYPT 2012. LNCS, vol. 7237, pp. 700–718. Springer, Heidelberg (2012). https://doi.org/10.1007/978-3-642-29011-4_41

[MR04] Micciancio, D., Regev,O.: Worst-case to average-case reductions based on Gaussian measures. In: 45th FOCS, pp. 372–381. IEEE Computer Society Press (2004)

[NIS] NIST - National Institute of Standards and Technology, USA. Call for Additional Digital Signature Schemes for the Post-Quantum Cryptography Standardization Process. https://csrc.nist.gov/csrc/media/Projects/pqc-dig-sig/documents/call-for-proposals-dig-sig-sept-2022.pdf

[NS26] Nguyen, N.K., Siemer, J.N.: Tight reductions for SIS-with-hints assumptions with applications to anonymous credentials. Cryptology ePrint Archive, Paper 2026/291 (2026)

[PJ12] Pointcheval, D., Johansson, T. (eds.): EUROCRYPT 2012. LNCS, vol. 7237. Springer, Berlin, Heidelberg (2012)

[PR06] Peikert, C., Rosen, A.: Efficient collision-resistant hashing from worst-case assumptions on cyclic lattices. In: Halevi, S., Rabin, T. (eds.) TCC 2006. LNCS, vol. 3876, pp. 145–166. Springer, Berlin, Heidelberg (2006)

[Reg05] Regev, O.: On lattices, learning with errors, random linear codes, and cryptography. In: Gabow, H.N., Fagin, R., (eds.) 37th ACM STOC, pp. 84–93. ACM Press (2005)

[UKD] UK Department for Science, Innovation & Technology. UK digital identity and attributes trust framework beta version (0.3). https://www.gov.uk/government/publications/uk-digital-identity-and-attributes-trust-framework-beta-version/uk-digital-identity-and-attributes-trust-framework-beta-version

Efficient RLWE Based Chosen-Ciphertext Secure Dual-Receiver Encryption and Sender-Binding KEM in the Standard Model

Laurin Benz[1,2](✉) and Robert Brede[1,2]

[1] Karlsruhe Institute of Technology, Karlsruhe, Germany
{laurin.benz,robert.brede}@kit.edu
[2] KASTEL Security Research Labs, Karlsruhe, Germany

Abstract. Key encapsulation mechanism (KEM) is an often used primitive in communication, closely related to public key encryption (PKE). Dual-receiver encryption (DRE) is another primitive closely related to PKE that allows a sender to encrypt a message to two different receivers. Most applications of DRE need the soundness property which guarantees that both receivers decrypt any ciphertext to the same message. Additionally, IND-CPA security is often not enough and therefore schemes should satisfy a stronger notion like IND-CCA2. Meanwhile, an alternative to IND-CCA2 for KEMs is the IND-SB-CPA security notion which was proven to be strong enough to realize secure channels while in theory enabling the construction of more efficient schemes.

Most IND-CCA2 security proofs rely on the FO transformation, which is only secure in the ROM, and the standard model DREs and KEMs are far from efficient. We fill this gap by providing a sound DRE and a KEM satisfying IND-CCA2 and IND-SB-CPA security respectively. Both schemes are based on RLWE, proven secure in the standard model, and have key sizes of 150 KB and ciphertext sizes of 100 KB, improving upon previous results by a factor of 10x to 100x.

Keywords: Dual-receiver encryption (DRE) · Soundness · Sender-binding key encapsulation mechanism (SB-KEM) · Hybrid Encryption · Ring Learning With Errors (RLWE) · Post-Quantum · IND-CCA2 · Standard Model

1 Introduction

Broadcast encryption (BE) [14], a special form of public key encryption (PKE), allows a sender to encrypt a message to multiple receivers with a single ciphertext. Dual-receiver encryption (DRE) can be seen as a special case of BE for two receivers. While the definition is syntactically simple, Chow, Franklin, and Zhang [11] showed that most applications need the special property "soundness", which guarantees that one receiver can be certain that the other receiver

S. Bai and E. Persichetti (Eds.): PKC 2026, LNCS 16551, pp. 136–166, 2026.
https://doi.org/10.1007/978-3-032-26731-3_5

decrypts the ciphertext to the same message. Additionally, the usual indistinguishability under chosen plaintext attack (IND-CPA) security notion is often not strong enough and instead the more restrictive indistinguishability under adaptive chosen ciphertext attack (IND-CCA2) security, adapted to DRE, is needed. Benz et al. [5] conducted a survey on post-quantum IND-CCA2 secure DRE constructions in the standard model and noticed that all of them lack the soundness property, rendering them useless in applications that require this property [4,8,11–13,26,28].

Furthermore, most IND-CCA2 secure PKE schemes use the well-known Fujisaki-Okamoto (FO) transformation [16] to convert an IND-CPA secure scheme into an IND-CCA2 one. This transformation relies on the Random Oracle Model (ROM), a model where overidealized hash functions are available. While Canetti, Goldreich, and Halevi [10] proved over 20 years ago that there exist schemes which are secure in the ROM, but insecure whenever the random oracle is instantiated, their examples were specifically designed to fail. Recently however, Khovratovich, Rothblum, and Soukhanov [19] presented an attack on the similar Fiat-Shamir transformation [15], using the reliance on the ROM to break a natural proof-system. This motivates further research into secure constructions in the standard model. Recently for example, Hsieh, Waters, and Wu [18] used a special form of pseudorandom generator (PRG) to generically create BE in the standard model, but their scheme only satisfies the BE version of IND-CPA security.

As standard model IND-CCA2 security is hard to achieve and known to be unnecessarily strong for many applications, Beskorovajnov *et al.*. [8] devised a new security notion for PKEs, called indistinguishability under sender-binding chosen plaintext attack (IND-SB-CPA). This notion, which they proved to be between IND-CPA and IND-CCA2, was introduced to enable the construction of smaller, more efficient encryption schemes that are still secure enough to realize secure channels, one of the main uses of IND-CCA2 security. It was also adapted to the key encapsulation mechanism (KEM) framework, resulting in the indistinguishability under sender-binding chosen plaintext attack (IND-SBCPA$_{\text{SB-KEM}}$) security notion [6].

Even though there are many applications for efficient DRE schemes as well as sender-binding key encapsulation mechanisms (SB-KEM), so far the most efficient standard model IND-CCA2 DRE constructions have either key and ciphertext sizes of around 700 MB and 25 KB, or around 120 MB and 100 KB [5]. Also, while the IND-SB-CPA$_{\text{SB-KEM}}$ security notion was introduced to allow for more efficient schemes, the only standard model IND-SB-CPA$_{\text{SB-KEM}}$ KEM prior to this work [6] has worse sizes than the most efficient standard model IND-CCA2 KEMs which in turn have key and ciphertext sizes of around 3 MB and 1 MB, or around 110 MB and 5 KB [29,30].

In this work, we derive a DRE scheme and a SB-KEM based on Ring Learning With Errors (RLWE) satisfying the aforementioned properties. For this, we use a ring version of the trapdoor construction by Micciancio and Peikert [24]. The resulting schemes have key and ciphertext sizes around 150 KB and 100 KB, significantly improving upon previous results. In addition, we prove that RLWE samples are unique under certain conditions, which was shown for LWE by Zhang *et al.* [31] and could be of independent interest.

Outline. In Sect. 2 we introduce notations and primitives needed for our constructions. We also state and prove some new lemmas on the used rings. More specifically, Sect. 2.1 introduces algebraic notation, Sects. 2.2 to 2.4 deal with lattices and RLWE including our new results, while Sect. 2.5 defines all needed cryptographic primitives and their security notions.

We then define our DRE scheme in Sect. 3. Additionally, we prove correctness, soundness and IND-CCA2 security. For this, we adapt the proofs of Benz *et al.*. [5,9,20] to our setting.

The SB-KEM is the focus of Sect. 4. As the scheme is a simplification of our DRE construction, the proofs carry over from Sect. 3.

Finally, in Sect. 5 we give concrete parameters and compare our results to the literature. We also note that using Module Learning With Errors (MLWE) did not improve the parameters, even though the proofs could also be adapted to that setting.

2 Fundamentals

For a matrix S and $p \in [1, \infty)$ we write $\|S\|_p = \max_{\|x\|_p=1} \|Sx\|_p$. For $\alpha \in \mathbb{Z}_q$ we write $\lfloor \alpha \rceil_{q/2}$ for rounding to 0 if $\alpha \mod q \in [-q/4, q/4)$ and $q/2$ otherwise. A function $f : \mathbb{N} \to \mathbb{R}$ is *negligible* if for every $k \in \mathbb{N}$ there is an $n \in \mathbb{N}$ such that for all $x > n : f(x) \leq x^{-k}$. We use the standard big O notations. For a set $\mathbf{S}$ we denote by $x \xleftarrow{\$} \mathbf{S}$ the uniform sampling of an element x from $\mathbf{S}$. For a probability distribution χ, $x \leftarrow \chi$ denotes sampling according to that distribution. Similarly, if P is a probabilistic algorithm, we denote by $y \leftarrow P(x)$ the result of one execution of P with input x. Two distribution ensembles $\mathcal{X}_n, \mathcal{Y}_n (n \in \mathbb{N})$ over set $\mathbf{S}$ are called *statistically indistinguishable* if the statistical distance $\Delta(\mathcal{X}_n, \mathcal{Y}_n) = \sup_{A \subseteq S} |\mathbb{P}[x \in A \mid x \leftarrow \mathcal{X}_n] - \mathbb{P}[y \in A \mid y \leftarrow \mathcal{Y}_n]|$ is negligible in n. The component-wise multiplication of two vectors e, f is denoted by $e \odot f$.

2.1 Algebraic Number Theory

Here, we recall the major definitions of algebraic number theory required for this work. We work with cyclotomic number fields (cyclotomics). The $\tilde{n}$-th cyclotomic is $K = \mathbb{Q}[\zeta]$, where ζ is a primitive $\tilde{n}$-th root of unity. It is isomorph to $\mathbb{Q}[X]/\Phi_{\tilde{n}}$, where $\Phi_{\tilde{n}}$ is the minimal polynomial of ζ, which is also called the $\tilde{n}$-th cyclotomic polynomial. Its ring of integers is always denoted by $R = \mathbb{Z}[X]/\Phi_{\tilde{n}}$ while its degree is denoted by n. For an integer q, we write $R_q = R/qR$ and we always center our elements around 0, such that all coefficients are in the interval $[-q/2, q/2)$. Throughout this work, we will always consider the elements of this ring in their polynomial representation.

There are two different commonly used embeddings for these elements. The first embedding is the coefficient embedding φ, which embeds a polynomial into $\mathbb{Q}$ via the power basis. As $\varphi(R) = \mathbb{Z}^n$, this embedding is especially useful for storing ring elements and performing operations on them. The canonical embedding instead embeds a polynomial into a subset $H \subseteq \mathbb{C}^n$ by evaluating it at each root of $\Phi_{\tilde{n}}$. More specifically, for integers s_1, s_2 with $n = s_1 + 2s_2$ let $H = \{x \in \mathbb{R}^{s_1} \times \mathbb{C}^{2s_2} \mid x_{2j-1+s_1} = \overline{x_{2j+s_1}}, 1 \leq j \leq s_2\}$. The canonical embedding $\sigma := (\sigma_1, ..., \sigma_n) : K \to H$ consists of the embeddings $\sigma_i : h \mapsto h(\zeta_i)$, which evaluate h at the i-th root ζ_i of $\Phi_{\tilde{n}}$, where we reorder the roots in such a way that we end up in H. To draw a random element of R embedded in H we define the space $J := \sigma(R)$.

For vectors of ring elements, we sometimes use a different norm on each ring element than on the whole vector, and the norms we use also depend on the chosen embedding. Hence, for $p, q \in \{2, \infty\}$, $e \in \{\varphi, \sigma\}$ and $x \in R^m$, we define $\left\|[x]_{e,p}\right\|_q := \|(v_1, ..., v_m)\|_q, v_i = \|e(x_i)\|_p$ and we write $\|x\|_{e,p} := \left\|[x]_{e,p}\right\|_p$ for short. For an already canonical embedded element $x \in H$ we abuse notation and also write $\left\|[x]_{e,p}\right\|_q$ for $\left\|\left[\sigma^{-1}(x)\right]_{e,p}\right\|_q$.

Notice that the two embeddings are correlated by the matrix $B_\Lambda = (\zeta_i^{j-1})_{ij}$, where ζ_i is the i-th root of $\Phi_{\tilde{n}}$. Also, the space $(H, +, \odot)$ is isomorph to $(\mathbb{R}^n, +, \cdot)$ via the isomorphism

$$\psi = \begin{pmatrix} I_{s_1} & 0 \\ 0 & \sqrt{2} I_{s_2} \otimes \begin{pmatrix} 1 & 1 \\ -i & i \end{pmatrix} \end{pmatrix}.$$

Note that the multiplication $\cdot$ in $\mathbb{R}^n$ is performed by a matrix multiplication to simulate $\odot$ in H. For $e, f \in H$ we denote by A_e the matrix depending on e that satisfies $\psi(e \odot f) = A_e \cdot \psi(f)$. A concrete definition can be found in the full version. For vectors and matrices over H or $\mathbb{R}^n$, we write $\psi(A)$ or $\psi^{-1}(A)$ for applying the function to each element.

Lyubashevsky, Peikert, and Regev [22] analyzed the fraction of invertible elements in the ring of integers of a cyclotomic after applying a modulo q. Their result is that the fraction is at least polynomial in n and q, as described in the following lemma.

Lemma 1. *([22], Claim 2.25) Consider the $\tilde{n}$-th cyclotomic number field of degree n for some $\tilde{n} \geq 2$. Then for any $q \geq 2$, the fraction of invertible elements in R_q is at least $1/poly(n, \log q)$.*

2.2 Lattices and Gaussian Random Variables

We now recall some basic definitions and lemmas related to lattices and Gaussian distributions.

A lattice $\Lambda \subseteq \mathbb{R}^n$ is a discrete subspace of $\mathbb{R}^n$. As throughout this work we only consider lattices of full-rank, we can alternatively define the lattice as

$\Lambda = \{\sum z_i b_i \mid z_i \in \mathbb{Z}\}$ for a set $B = \{b_1, \ldots, b_n\} \subseteq \mathbb{R}^n$ of linear independent vectors. The set B is then called the basis of Λ. The dual lattice of $\Lambda \subseteq \mathbb{R}^n$ is defined as $\Lambda^\vee = \{x \in \mathbb{R}^n \mid \forall y \in \Lambda : \langle x, y\rangle \in \mathbb{Z}\}$. For a basis B, we denote with $\mathcal{P}_{1/2}(B)$ the origin centered parallelepiped $\mathcal{P}_{1/2}(B) = B \cdot [-1/2, 1/2)^n$. For a modulo q and a vector $a \in R_q^m$, we define $\Lambda_q^\perp(a) := \{x \in R_q^m \mid a^T x = 0 \mod q\}$.

Regarding the Gaussian random variables, we adopt the notation of Genise *et al.*. [17]. The Gaussian function is defined as $\rho : \mathbb{R}^n \to \mathbb{R}, \rho(x) = \exp(-\pi\langle x, x\rangle)$. By normalizing we obtain the Gaussian distribution $\mathcal{D}$. For a matrix $S \in \mathbb{R}^{n\times n}$, the Gaussian distribution $\mathcal{D}_S$ is defined as $\mathcal{D}_S := \sqrt{2\pi}S \cdot \mathcal{D}$. For $s \in \mathbb{R}$, we write $\mathcal{D}_S$ as short for $\mathcal{D}_{sI}$ and denote this by the Gaussian of parameter s. For a lattice $\Lambda \subseteq \mathbb{R}^n$, the discrete Gaussian is defined as the Gaussian restricted to the lattice, meaning $\mathcal{D}_{\Lambda,S}(x) = \mathcal{D}_S(x)/\mathcal{D}_S(\Lambda)$ for $x \in \Lambda$ and 0 otherwise.

Micciancio and Regev [25] introduced the *smoothing parameter* for working with discrete Gaussians.

Definition 1 (Smoothing Parameter). For a lattice $\Lambda \subseteq \mathbb{R}^n$ and positive real $\varepsilon > 0$, the smoothing parameter $\eta_\varepsilon(\Lambda)$ is the smallest real s, such that $\rho(s \cdot \Lambda^\vee) \leq 1 + \varepsilon$.

We use the extension of the smoothing parameter to matrices as in the work by Genise *et al.*. [17]. For any matrix S of full column rank we write $\eta_\varepsilon(\Lambda) \leq S$ if $\eta_\varepsilon(S^+\Lambda) \leq 1$, where S^+ is the pseudoinverse of S.

The tail of a discrete Gaussian can be bounded as follows.

Lemma 2. *Let $t > 1$ and $\Lambda \subseteq \mathbb{R}^n$ be a lattice. Let also $\Sigma \in \mathbb{R}^{n\times n}_{\geq 0}$ be a diagonal matrix and $s = \|\sqrt{\Sigma}\|_2$. Then we have*

$$Pr\left[\|x\|_2 > st\sqrt{n} \mid x \leftarrow \mathcal{D}_{\Lambda,\sqrt{\Sigma}}\right] < \left(e^{\frac{-t^2}{2}} t\sqrt{e}\right)^n,$$

which is negligible in n.

The proof of this is an adaption of a work by Banaszczyk [3, Lemma 1.5(i)], which is shown in the full version.

The next lemma shows that the linear combination of multiple discrete Gaussian distributed variables is again a discrete Gaussian.

Lemma 3. *Consider the $\tilde{n}$-th cyclotomic number field of degree n for some $\tilde{n} \geq 2$, $J \subseteq H$ its embedded ring of integers and $\Lambda = \psi(J) \subseteq \mathbb{R}^n$ the corresponding lattice. Let Σ_f be a positive definite diagonal matrix. For $s_T > 0$, an integer m and $1 \leq i \leq m$, let $t_i \leftarrow \psi^{-1}(\mathcal{D}_{\Lambda,s_T}), e_i \in J$ and $f \leftarrow \psi^{-1}\left(\mathcal{D}_{\Lambda,\sqrt{\Sigma_f}}\right)$. Let $\varepsilon := \varepsilon(n) > 0$ be negligible in n. If $\eta_\varepsilon(\Lambda) \leq \sqrt{2\pi} \cdot A_{e_i}^{-1}\sqrt{\left(\Sigma_f^{-1} + \left(s_T^2 A_{e_i} A_{e_i}^T\right)^{-1}\right)^{-1}}$ for every i, where $e_i \neq 0$ and $\eta_\varepsilon(\Lambda) \leq \sqrt{2\pi} \cdot \sqrt{\Sigma_f}$, then the distribution of*

$$f + \sum_{i=1}^{m} e_i \odot t_i$$

is statistically close to $\psi^{-1}\left(\mathcal{D}_{\Lambda,\sqrt{\Sigma}}\right)$*, where* $\Sigma = \Sigma_f + s_T^2 \sum_{i=1}^{m} A_{e_i} A_{e_i}^T = \Sigma_f + s_T^2 Mul(e)$*, where we define* $e := (e_1, \ldots, e_m)$ *and* $Mul(e) := \sum_{i=1}^{m} A_{e_i} A_{e_i}^T$.

The proof for this is a repeated application of a theorem by Genise *et al.*.[17, Theorem 3] and can be found in the full version.

Another important lemma is the regularity lemma shown by Lyubashevsky, Peikert, and Regev [22], which provides bounds on the variance of a Gaussian distributed x, such that Ax is statistically indistinguishable from uniform, when parts of A are uniformly random. As our Gaussian distribution is scaled up by $\sqrt{2\pi}$ compared to their work, the bound on the parameter of Gaussian is adjusted.

Lemma 4 (*[22]*, **Corollary 7.5).** *Consider the* $\tilde{n}$*-th cyclotomic number field of degree* n *for some* $\tilde{n} \geq 2$*. Let* q *as well as* $z_1 \leq z_2 \leq poly(n)$ *be positive integers. Assume* $A = (I_{z_1}, \bar{A}) \in R_q^{z_1 \times z_2}$*, where* $I_{z_1} \in R_q^{z_1 \times z_1}$ *is the identity matrix and* $\bar{A} \in R_q^{z_1 \times (z_2 - z_1)}$ *is uniformly random. Then with probability* $1 - 2^{-\Omega(n)}$ *over the choices of* $\bar{A}$*, the distribution of* $Ax \in R_q^{z_1}$*, where each coordinate of* $x \in R_q^{z_2}$ *is chosen from a discrete Gaussian distribution of parameter* $r > \sqrt{2\pi^{-1}}n \cdot q^{z_1/z_2 + 2/(nz_2)}$ *over* R*, satisfies that the probability of each of the* q^{nz_1} *possible outcomes is in the interval* $(1 \pm 2^{-\Omega(n)})q^{-nz_1}$ *(and in particular is within statistical distance* $2^{-\Omega(n)}$ *of the uniform distribution over* $R_q^{z_1}$*).*

2.3 Ring LWE and Its Trapdoor

In this paper, we use the decision variant of the Normal Form Ring Learning With Errors (NRLWE) assumption, which is as follows.

Definition 2 (NRLWE). Let λ be the security parameter, $m = m(\lambda), q = q(\lambda) \in \mathbb{Z}$ and $\chi = \chi(\lambda)$ be an error distribution over R_q. The advantage of an adversary $\mathcal{A}$ against the $\text{NRLWE}_{m,q,\chi}$ problem, denoted by $\mathsf{Adv}_{\mathcal{A}}^{\text{NRLWE}_{m,q,\chi}}$ is

$$\mathsf{Adv}_{\mathcal{A}}^{\text{NRLWE}_{m,q,\chi}} := \left|\mathbb{P}\left[\mathcal{A}(a, as + e) = 1\right] - \mathbb{P}\left[\mathcal{A}(a, u) = 1\right]\right|,$$

where $a \leftarrow R_q^m, s \leftarrow \chi, e \leftarrow \chi^m, u \xleftarrow{\$} R_q^m$.

Notice that in contrast to the usual RLWE assumption, the secret is also drawn from the error distribution instead of being uniformly random. Lyubashevsky, Peikert, and Regev [22] showed that NRLWE is as hard as RLWE.

Micciancio and Peiker [24] introduced an efficient method to recover s from $gs + e$, where g is the gadget vector $g = (1, 2, \ldots, 2^{k-1}) \in R_q^k$ for $k = \lceil \log q \rceil$. To recover s from $c = as + e$, one uses a trapdoor for a, which is defined as follows.

Definition 3 (Trapdoor, adapted from [24]). Consider the $\tilde{n}$-th cyclotomic number field of degree n for some $\tilde{n} \geq 2$ and q a modulo. Let $m > k \geq 1$ be integers, $a \in R_q^m$ and $g \in R_q^k$. A g-trapdoor $T \in R^{k \times (m-k)}$ for a is a matrix for which $(T, I_k)a = gh$ for some invertible $h \in R_q$. We refer to h as the tag or label of the trapdoor.

To guarantee correct inversion, one needs a basis of $\Lambda_q^{\perp}(g)$. For a prime $q = \sum_{i=1}^{k} q_i 2^{i-1}$, it can be shown that B_g as follows is such a basis [24, Section 4.2].

$$B_g = \begin{pmatrix} 2 & & & & & q_1 \\ -1 & 2 & & & & q_2 \\ & -1 & & & & q_3 \\ & & \ddots & \ddots & & \vdots \\ & & & -1 & 2 & q_{k-1} \\ & & & & -1 & q_k \end{pmatrix} \in R_q^{k \times k}. \quad (1)$$

Here, each $q_i \in \{0, 1\}$ is interpreted as constant polynomial.

For any $a \in R_q^m$ with a g-trapdoor T, one can recover s, e from $c = as + e$ with the `invert` function described in Fig. 1.

`invert`(T, h, a, c)
$b = (T, I) \cdot c$
Calculate $\hat{s}$ with $b = g\hat{s} + \hat{e}$
$s = h^{-1}\hat{s}$
return $(s, c - as)$

Fig. 1. Invert function.

The `invert` function returns the correct s, if the error $\hat{e} := (T, I_k)e$ is suitable small as stated in the following lemma.

Lemma 5. *Consider the $\tilde{n}$-th cyclotomic number field of degree n for some $\tilde{n} \geq 2$ and q a modulo. Take $m > k$ to be integers, $a \in R_q^m$ and $g \in R_q^k$ the gadget vector above. Let also T be a g-trapdoor for a with tag $h \in R_q$, $s \in R_q$ be a secret and $c = as + e$ for some error $e \in R_q^m$. Finally take either B to be B_g as in Eq. (1) or its Gram-Schmidt orthogonalization. If $(T, I_k)e \in \mathcal{P}_{1/2}(q \cdot B^{-T})$, then* `invert`$(T, h, a, c)$ *returns the correct s.*

Proof. The correctness of the `invert` function relies on the inversion of $g\hat{s} + \hat{e}$ in the second step. More specifically, we have $\hat{e} = (T, I_k)e$ as

$$b = (T, I_k)c = (T, I_k)as + (T, I_k)e = ghs + (T, I_k)e.$$

If $\hat{e} \in \mathcal{P}_{1/2}(q \cdot B^{-T})$, then the correct $\hat{s} = hs$ is calculated [21,24]. As h is invertible, $s = h^{-1}\hat{s}$ is uniquely determined by $\hat{s}$. □

2.4 Uniqueness of RLWE

This chapter proves that under certain conditions, RLWE samples have a unique witness. Zhang *et al.*. [31] showed this property for LWE. We show the uniqueness only for power of two cyclotomics with a very special modulo as these yield nicer structures.

In this section, let $\tilde{n} = 2n > r > 1$ be powers of two and q be some prime with $q = 2r + 1 \mod 4r$. Let $\Phi_{\tilde{n}}$ be the $\tilde{n}$-th cyclotomic polynomial with order n, i.e. $\Phi_{\tilde{n}} = X^n + 1 \equiv f_1 \cdot \ldots \cdot f_r \pmod q$ where $f_i \in \mathbb{Z}_q[X]$ are irreducible in $\mathbb{Z}_q$.

A careful analysis of the decomposition of $\Phi_{\tilde{n}} \mod q$ and the CRT decomposition yields the following probability bound.

The details can be found in the full version.

Lemma 6. *Let $\nu \in R_q \setminus \{0\}$ such that the CRT decomposition of ν is $\pi(\nu) = (\nu_1, \ldots, \nu_r)$ with $\nu_i = \nu \mod f_i \in \{0, 1\}$. Consider the subspace $U := \nu R_q$. Then $\mathbb{P}\left[\|u\|_{\psi,\infty} < q/4 \mid u \xleftarrow{\$} U\right] \leq 2^{-n/r}$.*

With this we can show the uniqueness of RLWE samples.

Lemma 7. *Let $m \geq r \log q + \frac{r\omega(\log n)}{n}$ for some superlogarithmic function $\omega(\log n)$. Then for all but a negligible fraction of $a \in R_q^m$ and for any $b \in R_q^m$, there exists at most one pair $(s, e) \in R_q \times R_q^m$ such that $as + e = b$ and $\|e\|_{\psi,\infty} < q/8$.*

The proof is very similar to the proof from Zhang *et al.* [31, Lemma 6], except that the distribution of $a(s - s')$ is uniform in U^m with U as in Lemma 6.

2.5 Cryptographic Primitives

We now define some cryptographic primitives. If not otherwise noted our definitions in this section are based on a paper by Benz *et al.*. [5].

Our first definition describes a public key encryption scheme which can be used to encrypt a message to two different public keys.

Definition 4 (DRE). A public-key dual-receiver encryption (DRE) scheme $\mathtt{DRE} = (\mathtt{DRE.gen}, \mathtt{DRE.enc}, \mathtt{DRE.dec})$ consists of the following probabilistic polynomial time (PPT) algorithms:

- $\mathtt{DRE.gen}(1^\lambda) \to (pk, sk)$: The randomized *key generation algorithm* outputs a public/secret key pair (pk, sk). We write (pk^R, sk^R) and (pk^S, sk^S) for the key pairs of two independent users.
- $\mathtt{DRE.enc}(pk^R, pk^S, \mathsf{m}) \to \mathsf{c}$: The randomized *encryption algorithm* takes as input two public keys pk^R and pk^S and a message m and outputs a cipher text c.
- $\mathtt{DRE.dec}(sk^i, pk^R, pk^S, \mathsf{c}) \to \mathsf{m}$: The deterministic *decryption algorithm* takes one of the secret keys $sk^i \in \{sk^R, sk^S\}$, two public keys pk^R, pk^S and a ciphertext c and outputs a message m. We write $\mathsf{m}^i = \mathtt{DRE.dec}(sk^i, pk^R, pk^S, \mathsf{c})$.

We also require perfect correctness defined as $\mathtt{DRE.dec}(sk^i, pk^R, pk^S, \mathsf{c}) = \mathsf{m}$ for $(pk^R, sk^R), (pk^S, sk^S) \leftarrow \mathtt{DRE.gen}(1^\lambda)$ and $\mathsf{c} \leftarrow \mathtt{DRE.enc}(pk^R, pk^S, \mathsf{m})$.

The strongest security definition for DRE schemes mimics the IND-CCA2 definition for PKE schemes but additionally allows the adversary to choose for which receiver the decryption oracle is supposed to decrypt a ciphertext.

Definition 5 (IND-CCA2DRE). A DRE scheme satisfies indistinguishability under adaptive chosen ciphertext attack (IND-CCA2$_{\mathrm{DRE}}$), if any PPT algorithm $\mathcal{A}$ wins the IND-CCA2$_{\mathrm{DRE}}$ game in Fig. 2 with probability at most $\frac{1}{2} + \mathtt{negl}(\lambda)$, i. e. the advantage

$$\mathsf{Adv}_{\mathsf{DRE},\mathcal{A}}^{\text{IND-CCA2}_{\text{DRE}}}(\lambda) := \left| \mathbb{P}\left[\mathsf{Exp}_{\mathsf{DRE},\mathcal{A}}^{\text{IND-CCA2}_{\text{DRE}}}(\lambda) = 1\right] - \frac{1}{2} \right| \leq \mathsf{negl}(\lambda).$$

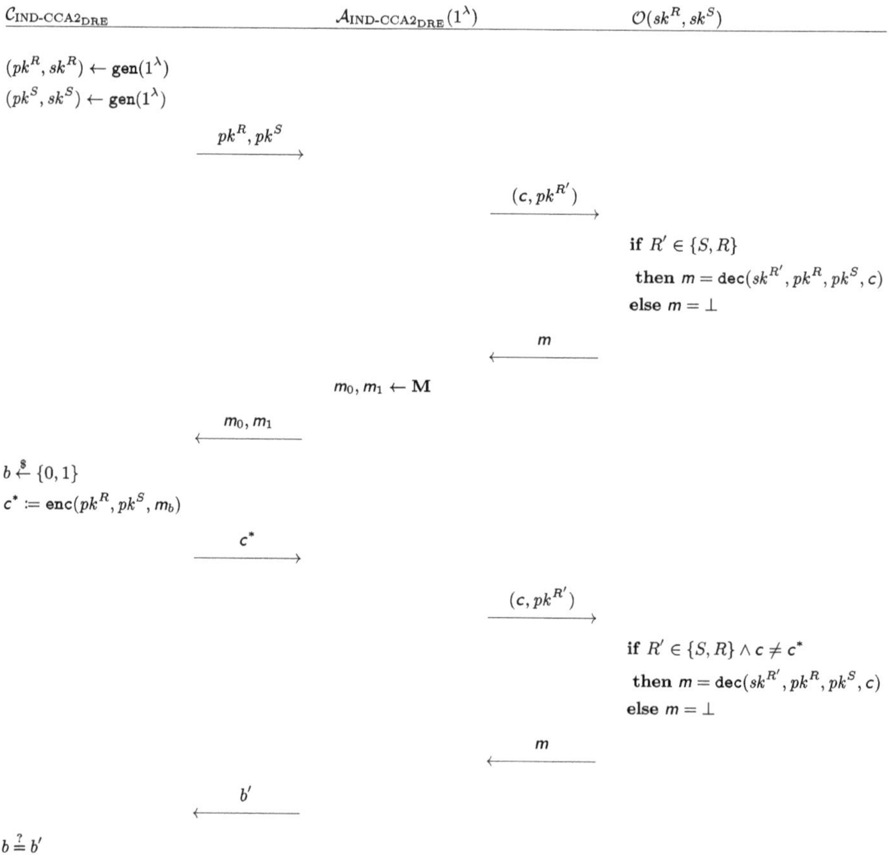

Fig. 2. Depiction of the IND-CCA2$_{\mathrm{DRE}}$ game.

While multiple DRE schemes are defined in the literature, few of them satisfy the important soundess property.

Definition 6 (Soundness for DRE). A DRE scheme DRE is said to be sound, if the advantage $\mathsf{Adv}^{\mathrm{sound}}_{\mathtt{DRE},\mathcal{A}}$ is negligible small, where

$$\mathsf{Adv}^{\mathrm{sound}}_{\mathtt{DRE},\mathcal{A}}(\lambda) := \mathbb{P}\left[\mathtt{DRE.dec}(sk^R, pk^R, pk^S, c) \neq \mathtt{DRE.dec}(sk^S, pk^R, pk^S, c)\right]$$

with $(pk^R, sk^R), (pk^S, sk^S) \leftarrow \mathtt{DRE.gen}(1^\lambda)$ and $c \leftarrow \mathcal{A}(sk^R, sk^S, pk^R, pk^S)$.

We also look at a special version of KEM. Introduced by Benz *et al.*. [6] this adaptation binds ciphertexts to the sender which allows different security notions.

Definition 7 (SB-KEM, [6]). A sender-binding key encapsulation mechanism (SB-KEM) is given by a set of three PPT algorithms $(\mathtt{gen}, \mathtt{enc}, \mathtt{dec})$:

- $\mathtt{gen}(1^\lambda) \to (pk, sk)$: The randomized *key generation algorithm* generates a public/secret key pair.
- $\mathtt{enc}(pk, \mathcal{S}) \to (K, c)$: The randomized *encryption algorithm* takes as input a public key and a sender identity and outputs a symmetric key K and a ciphertext c.
- $\mathtt{dec}(sk, pk, \mathcal{S}, c) \to K$: The deterministic *decryption algorithm* takes as input a public/secret key pair, a sender identity and a ciphertext and returns the symmetric key K.

such that correctness holds, which means $K = \mathtt{dec}(sk, pk, \mathcal{S}, c)$ for honestly generated $(pk, sk) \leftarrow \mathtt{gen}(1^\lambda)$ and $(K, c) \leftarrow \mathtt{enc}(pk, \mathcal{S})$.

The state of the art security definition for a SB-KEM scheme can be seen as a middle ground between IND-CPA and IND-CCA2. This allows for more efficient constructions while still giving most of the benefits of IND-CCA2 like realizing secure channels [6].

Definition 8 (IND-SB-CPA$_{\mathrm{SB-KEM}}$, [6]). A SB-KEM $\Gamma = (\mathtt{gen}, \mathtt{enc}, \mathtt{dec})$ with the set of Party IDs $\mathbf{P}$ satisfies IND-SB-CPA$_{\text{SB-KEM}}$ security, if for any PPT adversary $\mathcal{A}$ the advantage $\mathsf{Adv}^{\text{IND-SB-CPA}_{\text{SB-KEM}}}_{\mathcal{A},\Gamma}(1^\lambda) := \left|\mathbb{P}\left[b = b^*\right] - \frac{1}{2}\right|$ of winning the IND-SB-CPA game shown in Fig. 3 is negligible in λ.

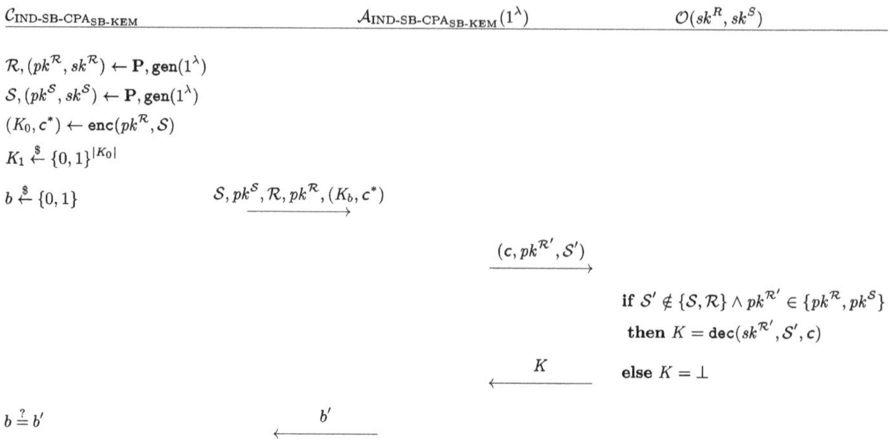

Fig. 3. Depiction of the IND-SB-CPA$_{\text{SB-KEM}}$ game.

Commitment schemes are used in our construction to prevent malicious manipulations of ciphertexts. They can be constructed from many different assumptions with many different properties. See for example the work by Alkadri, Demirel, and El Bansarkhani [2] for more information.

Definition 9 (Commitment scheme). A commitment scheme is a set of three PPT algorithms $\texttt{COM} = (\texttt{COM.gen}, \texttt{COM.com}, \texttt{COM.unveil})$:

- $\texttt{COM.gen}(1^\lambda) \to ck$: The randomized *key generation algorithm* generates a commitment key ck.
- $\texttt{COM.com}(ck, m) \to (c, d)$: The randomized *commitment algorithm* takes as input a commitment key ck and a message m to generate a commitment c together with decommitment information d.
- $\texttt{COM.unveil}(ck, m, c, d) \to \{0,1\}$: The deterministic *unveil algorithm* takes a commitment key ck, a message m, a commitment c and decommitment information d and outputs 1 if (c, d) is a possible output of $\texttt{COM.com}(ck, m)$.

We need a computationally hiding and statistically binding scheme as defined in the following two definitions.

Definition 10 (Hiding). A commitment scheme $\texttt{COM}$ is said to be computationally hiding, if for every PPT attacker $\mathcal{A}$ the advantage

$$\mathsf{Adv}^{\text{Hiding}}_{\texttt{COM},\mathcal{A}} := \left| \mathbb{P}\left[\mathsf{Exp}^{\text{Hiding}}_{\texttt{COM},\mathcal{A}}(1^\lambda)\right] - \frac{1}{2} \right|$$

in the hiding experiment in Fig. 4 is negligible.

$$
\begin{array}{|l|}
\hline
\mathsf{Exp}^{\text{Hiding}}_{\mathtt{COM},\mathcal{A}}(1^\lambda) \\
\hline
ck \leftarrow \mathtt{COM.gen}(1^\lambda) \\
(m_0, m_1, state) \leftarrow \mathcal{A}(1^\lambda, ck, \text{find}) \\
b \xleftarrow{\$} \{0,1\} \\
(c, d) \leftarrow \mathtt{COM.com}(ck, m_b) \\
b' \leftarrow \mathcal{A}(1^\lambda, \text{guess}, state, c) \\
\textbf{return } b \stackrel{?}{=} b' \\
\hline
\end{array}
$$

Fig. 4. Hiding experiment.

Definition 11 (Binding). A commitment scheme COM is said to be statistically binding if there is a negligible function `negl` such that

$$\underset{\substack{ck \leftarrow \mathtt{COM.gen}(1^\lambda) \\ (c,d_0) \leftarrow \mathtt{COM.com}(ck,m_0)}}{\mathbb{P}} \left[\exists (m_1, d_1) \;\middle|\; \begin{array}{l} m_0 \neq m_1, \\ \mathtt{COM.unveil}(ck, m_1, c, d_1) = 1 \end{array} \right] \leq \mathtt{negl}(1^\lambda)\,.$$

As our constructions are defined as hybrid encryption schemes we need symmetric encryption primitives as well. Our security definitions are very weak and yet enough to realize the strong security notions for our constructions.

Definition 12 (SKE). A secret-key encryption (SKE) scheme is a pair of PPT algorithms SKE = (SKE.enc, SKE.dec) with key space $\mathbf{K}_{\mathsf{SKE}}$ and ciphertext space $\mathbf{C}_{\mathsf{SKE}}$ satisfying

- $\mathsf{SKE.enc}(dk, m) \rightarrow c$: The deterministic *encryption algorithm* takes as input a key $dk \in \mathbf{K}_{\mathsf{SKE}}$ and a message m, and outputs a ciphertext c.
- $\mathsf{SKE.dec}(dk, c) \rightarrow m$: The deterministic *decryption algorithm* takes as input a key $dk \in \mathbf{K}_{\mathsf{SKE}}$ and a ciphertext c, and outputs a message m (which may be the special symbol $\perp$)

We require that for all $dk \in \mathbf{K}_{\mathsf{SKE}}$ it holds that

$$m = \mathsf{SKE.dec}(dk, \mathsf{SKE.enc}(dk, m)).$$

As each encryption in the hybrid encryption draws a new symmetric key, we require only one-time indistinguishability.

Definition 13 (OT-IND). A SKE scheme SKE is said to be secure under onetime indistinguishability (OT-IND), if the advantage $\mathsf{Adv}^{\text{OT-IND}}_{\mathsf{SKE},\mathcal{A}}$ of any PPT adversary $\mathcal{A}$ is negligible, where

$$\mathsf{Adv}^{\text{OT-IND}}_{\mathsf{SKE},\mathcal{A}}(\lambda) := \left| \mathbb{P}\left[\mathcal{A}(1^\lambda, \text{guess}, state, \Phi_b) = b\right] - \frac{1}{2} \right| \leq \text{negl}(1^\lambda)$$

with $dk \xleftarrow{\$} \mathbf{K}_{\mathtt{SKE}}, b \xleftarrow{\$} \{0,1\}, \Phi_0 \leftarrow \mathtt{SKE.enc}(dk, m), \Phi_1 \xleftarrow{\$} \mathbf{C}_{\mathtt{SKE}}$ and $(m, state) \leftarrow \mathcal{A}(1^\lambda, \text{mesg})$.

We also require message authentication codes to prevent tampering of the messages.

Definition 14 (MAC). A message authentication code (MAC) scheme MAC with key space $\mathbf{K}_{\mathtt{MAC}}$ consists of the two PPT algorithms MAC = (MAC.sign, MAC.verify), where

- $\mathtt{MAC.sign}(mk, m) \to \tau$: The randomized *signing algorithm* takes as input a signing key $mk \in \mathbf{K}_{\mathtt{MAC}}$ and a message m, and outputs a tag τ.
- $\mathtt{MAC.verify}(mk, m, \tau) \to \{0,1\}$: The deterministic *verification algorithm* takes as input a signing key $mk \in \mathbf{K}_{\mathtt{MAC}}$, a message m and a tag τ, and outputs 1 if τ is a possible output of $\mathtt{MAC.sign}(mk, m)$.

Again, each encryption draws a new key and thus, one-time strongly unforgability is enough.

Definition 15 (OT-SUF). A MAC scheme MAC is one-time strongly unforgeable (OT-SUF) if the advantage $\mathsf{Adv}^{\text{OT-SUF}}_{\mathtt{MAC},\mathcal{A}}$ of any PPT adversary $\mathcal{A}$ is negligible, where

$$\mathsf{Adv}^{\text{OT-SUF}}_{\mathtt{MAC},\mathcal{A}}(\lambda) := \mathbb{P}\left[\begin{matrix}\mathtt{MAC.verify}(mk, \tau') = 1 \\ \tau' \neq \tau\end{matrix} \;\middle|\; \begin{matrix}\tau \leftarrow \mathtt{MAC.sign}(mk, m) \\ \tau' \leftarrow \mathcal{A}(1^\lambda, \text{forge}, \text{state}, \tau)\end{matrix}\right]$$

with $mk \xleftarrow{\$} \mathbf{K}_{\mathtt{MAC}}, (m, state) \leftarrow \mathcal{A}(1^\lambda, \text{sign})$.

A hash function H is used to map an arbitrary input to a specific output format. In our case we only need a very basic property of our hash functions called collision resistance.

Definition 16 (Collision Resistance). A family of hash functions $\{\mathtt{H}_k\}_{k \in \mathbf{K}}$ is said to be collision resistant (CR) if for all PPT algorithms $\mathcal{A}$ the advantage $\mathsf{Adv}^{\text{CR}}_{\mathtt{H},\mathcal{A}}(\lambda)$ is negligibly small, where

$$\mathsf{Adv}^{\text{CR}}_{\mathtt{H},\mathcal{A}}(\lambda) := \mathbb{P}\left[k \xleftarrow{\$} \mathbf{K}, (x, x') \leftarrow \mathcal{A}(1^\lambda, \mathtt{H}_k) : x \neq x' \text{ and } \mathtt{H}(x) = \mathtt{H}(x')\right].$$

We need to look at keyed hash functions, as for every fixed hash function there exists an adversary with a collision hard coded by the pigeonhole principle. Still, in a slight abuse of notation we will speak of a "collision resistant hash function", by which we mean a function sampled uniformly from a collision resistant hash function family.

We also use a key derivation function $\mathtt{KDF} : \{0,1\}^n \to \mathbf{K}$ to generate keys for the SKE- and MAC-schemes from a short seed.

Definition 17 (IND KDF[9]). A key derivation function (KDF) $\texttt{KDF}: \{0,1\}^n \rightarrow \mathbf{K}$ satisfies indistinguishability (IND) security if for all PPT algorithms $\mathcal{A}$ the advantage $\mathsf{Adv}^{\mathrm{IND}}_{\texttt{KDF},\mathcal{A}}(\lambda)$ is negligibly small, where

$$\mathsf{Adv}^{\mathrm{IND}}_{\texttt{KDF},\mathcal{A}}(\lambda) := \left|\mathbb{P}\left[\mathcal{A}\left(1^\lambda, \texttt{KDF}(k)\right) = 1\right] - \mathbb{P}\left[\mathcal{A}\left(1^\lambda, r\right) = 1\right]\right|$$

for $k \xleftarrow{\$} \{0,1\}^n$ and $r \xleftarrow{\$} \mathbf{K}$.

The last primitive we need are full-rank difference encodings which enables us to hide game changes in our hybrid proof later on.

Definition 18 (Full-rank difference encoding [7]). Let $\mathbf{S}$ be a set, R the ring of integers of a number field K and q a modulo. A function $\texttt{FRD}: \mathbf{S} \rightarrow R_q$ is a full rank difference encoding (FRD), if it satisfies the following three properties:

(1) For all $x \in \mathbf{S}$, $\texttt{FRD}(x)$ is invertible
(2) For all $x, y \in \mathbf{S}$ with $x \neq y$, the element $\texttt{FRD}(x) - \texttt{FRD}(y)$ is invertible
(3) $\texttt{FRD}$ is computable in polynomial time

3 DRE Construction

We now turn towards the new DRE construction based on NRLWE.

We describe two variants of the scheme: the *computational variant* and the *statistical variant*. The difference is in the public key, which is either computationally or statistically indistinguishable from uniform. This yields different bounds on the advantage of adversaries on the scheme and different limitations for the parameters.

Let R be the ring of integers with order $n \in \mathbb{N}$ as in Sect. 2, $q \in \mathbb{N}$ a modulo, $J_q = \sigma(R)/q\sigma(R) \subseteq H/qH$ and J_q^* the invertible elements in J_q. Denote with Λ the lattice of the embedded ring $\Lambda := \psi(\sigma(R)) \subseteq \mathbb{R}^n$ and with $B_\Lambda = \{\psi(\sigma(1)), \psi(\sigma(X)), \ldots, \psi(\sigma(X^{n-1}))\} \subseteq \mathbb{R}^n$ the basis of Λ.

Take parameters $l := \lceil \log q \rceil$ and $m \in \mathbb{N}, m \geq 2$. We use the gadget vector $g \in J_q^l$ with its $\texttt{invert}$ function and the Gram-Schmidt orthogonalized basis $\widetilde{B}_g \in R_q^{l\times l}$ of $\Lambda_q^\perp(g)$ as defined in Sect. 2.3. Additional building tools are a commitment scheme $\texttt{COM}$, a SKE $\texttt{SKE}$, a MAC $\texttt{MAC}$, a KDF $\texttt{KDF}$, a hash function $\texttt{H}: \{0,1\}^* \rightarrow \{0,1\}^\nu$ and a FRD $\texttt{FRD}: \{0,1\}^\nu \rightarrow J_q^*$ for some $\nu \in \mathbb{N}$.

For the statistical variant take a $\beta_T > \sqrt{2\pi^{-1}}n \cdot q^{1/m+2/(mn)}$, while for the computational variant choose $\beta_T \in \mathbb{R}$ such that $\mathrm{NRLWE}_{1,q,\chi_2}$ with $\chi_2 = \psi^{-1}(\mathcal{D}_{\Lambda,t\beta_T})$ is hard. Let $t \in \mathbb{R}^+$ be such that for any diagonal matrix $\Sigma \in \mathbb{R}^{n\times n}_{\geq 0}$ we have

$$\delta := \mathbb{P}\left[\|x\|_2 > \|\sqrt{\Sigma}\|_2 \cdot \frac{1}{t} \cdot \sqrt{n} \mid x \leftarrow \mathcal{D}_{\Lambda,\sqrt{\Sigma}}\right] \leq \epsilon(n) \qquad (2)$$

for some negligible function ϵ, which exists by Lemma 2. Finally, take $\alpha \in \mathbb{R}$ with

$$\frac{1}{\alpha} \geq 2\beta_T \left\| \tilde{B}_g^T \right\|_{\varphi,\infty} \cdot \left\| B_\Lambda^{-1} \right\|_2 \cdot \sqrt{nm} \left(\sqrt{nm} + \sqrt{n+1} \right) \text{ and} \tag{3}$$

$$\frac{1}{\alpha} \geq 4 \left\| B_\Lambda^{-1} \right\|_2 \cdot \sqrt{n} \tag{4}$$

such that $q \geq (\sqrt{2\pi} \cdot \alpha t \beta_T \sqrt{m})^{-1} \cdot \sqrt{n} \cdot \omega(\sqrt{\log n})$ for some superlogarithmic function $\omega(\sqrt{\log n})$ and $\text{NRLWE}_{2m,q,\chi_1}$ with $\chi_2 = \psi^{-1}(\mathcal{D}_{\Lambda,tq\alpha})$ is hard.

For a canonically embedded ring element $e = (e_1, \ldots, e_n) \in J$ we write $Mul(e) \in \mathbb{R}^{n \times n}$ for the diagonal matrix with $|e_i|^2$ at the i-th diagonal entry. For a vector v of ring elements we write $Mul(v) := \sum_i Mul(v_i) \in \mathbb{R}^{n \times n}$. Also, calculations with elements in J are performed in J_q.

An overview of the used parameters can be found in Table 1.

Table 1. Overview of the used notation

Symbol	Constraints	Meaning
K	$K = \mathbb{Q}[\zeta]$	The used cyclotomic number field
n	$n \in \mathbb{N}$	The dimension of K
R	$R = \mathbb{Z}[X]/f(X)$	The ring of integers of K
q	$q \in \mathbb{N}$	The used modulo
R_q	$R_q = \mathbb{Z}_q[X]/f(x)$	The ring of the integers of the cyclotomic number field K modulo q
σ	$\sigma : K \to H$	The canonical embedding
φ	$\varphi : K \to \mathbb{Q}^n$	The coefficient embedding
ψ	$\psi : H \to \mathbb{R}^n$	The isomorphism from $H \subseteq \mathbb{C}^n$ to $\mathbb{R}^n$
J_q	$J_q = \sigma(R)/q\sigma(R)$	The canonically embedded ring of integers modulo q
J_q^*	$J_q^* \subseteq J_q$	The invertible elements of J_q
Λ	$\Lambda = \psi(\sigma(R))$	The ring of integers embedded into $\mathbb{R}^n$ interpreted as a lattice
B_Λ	$B_\Lambda \subseteq \mathbb{R}^n$	Basis of Λ
α	$\alpha \in \mathbb{R}$ $\frac{1}{\alpha} \geq 2\beta_T \left\| \tilde{B_g}^T \right\|_{\varphi,\infty} \|B_\Lambda^{-1}\|_2$ $\cdot\sqrt{nm}\left(\sqrt{nm} + \sqrt{n+1}\right)$ $\frac{1}{\alpha} \geq 4 \left\| B_\Lambda^{-1} \right\|_2 \sqrt{n}$	Parameter for the width of the discrete Gaussian of $\bar{s}$ and e_1
β_T	$\beta_T \in \mathbb{R}$	Parameter for the width of the discrete Gaussian for the trapdoor
l	$l = \lceil \log q \rceil$	The dimension of the gadget vector and one of the dimensions of the trapdoor
m	$m \geq 2$	The primary dimension of the keys
g	$g = (1, 2, \ldots, 2^{l-1}) \in J_q^l$	The gadget vector by Micciancio and Peikert [24]
$\tilde{B_g}$	$\tilde{B_g} \in R_q^{l \times l}$	Gram-Schmidt orthogonalization of the basis of $\Lambda_q^\perp(g)$
δ	$\delta = \underset{x \leftarrow \mathcal{D}_{\Lambda,\sqrt{\Sigma}}}{\mathbb{P}} \left[\|x\|_2 > \frac{1}{t}\sqrt{n}\|\sqrt{\Sigma}\|_2 \right]$	Probability for a Gaussian drawn vector to be to large. Should be negligible
t	$t \in \mathbb{R}$	Parameter, such that δ is negligible or small enough
A_e	$A_e \in \mathbb{R}^{n \times n}$	For $e, t \in H$, A_e is the matrix that satisfies $A_e\psi(t) = \psi(e \odot t)$
$Mul(e)$	$Mul(e) \in \mathbb{R}^{n \times n}$	For $e \in J$, $Mul(e)$ is the diagonal matrix with $|e_i|$ on its $i-th$ diagonal entry

We also employ a commitment scheme that was absent in the previous work of Benz *et al.* [5]. This addition is needed because RLWE samples are not unique for commonly used parameters. It can be omitted if the parameters are chosen in such a way that Lemma 7 applies to c_1 of our scheme. Then the used key is uniquely determined by c_1 with overwhelming probability, making the use of COM obsolete. While the resulting parameter sets can be found in the full version, we now focus on the scheme using commitments.

With all this, we can now define the DRE $\texttt{DRE} = (\mathsf{KGen}, \texttt{Enc}, \texttt{Dec})$ in Fig. 5.

$\mathsf{KGen}(1^\lambda)$

- $a_0 \xleftarrow{\$} J_q^*, a' \xleftarrow{\$} J_q^{m-1}, T \leftarrow \psi^{-1}(\mathcal{D}^{l\times m}_{\Lambda,t\beta_T})$
- $ck \leftarrow \texttt{COM.gen}(1^\lambda), a = (a_0, a')$
- **return** $(pk, sk) := ((a, Ta, ck), T)$

$\texttt{Enc}(pk^R, pk^S, m)$

- parse $pk^R = (a^R, a_1^R, ck^R)$
- parse $pk^S = (a^S, a_1^S, ck^S)$
- $k \xleftarrow{\$} \{0,1\}^n$
- $(mk, dk) = \texttt{KDF}(k)$
- $\bar{s} \leftarrow \psi^{-1}(\mathcal{D}_{\Lambda,tq\alpha})$
- $s = \psi^{-1}\left(B_\Lambda\left(\frac{q}{2}\cdot k\right)\right) + \bar{s} \in J_q$
- $(c_0^R, d^R) = \texttt{COM.com}(ck^R, k)$
- $(c_0^S, d^S) = \texttt{COM.com}(ck^S, k)$
- $c_0 = (c_0^R, c_0^S), d = (d^R, d^S)$
- $e_1^R, e_1^S \leftarrow \psi^{-1}(\mathcal{D}^m_{\Lambda,tq\alpha})$
- $c_1 = (a^R s + e_1^R, a^S s + e_1^S)$
- $\Sigma^R = t^2\beta_T^2 Mul(e_1^R)$
  $+ t^2\beta_T^2 m(q\alpha)^2 I_n$
- $\Sigma^S = t^2\beta_T^2 Mul(e_1^S)$
  $+ t^2\beta_T^2 m(q\alpha)^2 I_n$
- $e_2^R \leftarrow \psi^{-1}(\mathcal{D}^l_{\Lambda,\Sigma^R}), e_2^S \leftarrow \psi^{-1}(\mathcal{D}^l_{\Lambda,\Sigma^S})$
- $c_2 = ((a_1^R + g\cdot \texttt{FRD}(\texttt{H}(c_0,c_1)))s + e_2^R,$
  $(a_1^S + g\cdot \texttt{FRD}(\texttt{H}(c_0,c_1)))s + e_2^S)$
- $\Delta = \texttt{SKE.enc}(dk, (m, d))$
- $\tau = \texttt{MAC.sign}(mk, (c_0, c_1, c_2, \Delta))$
- **return** $(c_0, c_1, c_2, \Delta, \tau)$

$\texttt{Dec}(sk^R, pk^R, pk^S, c)$

- parse $sk^R = T$
- parse $pk^R = (a^R, a_1^R, ck^R)$
- parse $pk^S = (a^S, a_1^S, ck^S)$
- parse $c = (c_0^R, c_0^S, c_1^R, c_1^S, c_2^R, c_2^S, \Delta, \tau)$
- $(s, (e_1^R, e_2^R)) = \texttt{invert}(T, \texttt{FRD}(\texttt{H}(c_0, c_1)),$
  $(a^R, (a_1^R + g\cdot\texttt{FRD}(\texttt{H}(c_0,c_1)))), (c_1^R, c_2^R))$
- **if** $\left\|\left[e_1^R\right]_{\sigma,2}\right\|_\infty > q\alpha\sqrt{n}$: **return** $\perp$
- **if** $\left\|\left[e_2^R\right]_{\sigma,2}\right\|_\infty > q\alpha\beta_T\sqrt{n(n+1)m}$:
  return $\perp$
- $e_1^S = c_1^S - a^S s$
- $e_2^S = c_2^S - (a_1^S + g\cdot\texttt{FRD}(\texttt{H}(c_0,c_1)))s$
- **if** $\left\|\left[e_1^S\right]_{\sigma,2}\right\|_\infty > q\alpha\sqrt{n}$: **return** $\perp$
- **if** $\left\|\left[e_2^S\right]_{\sigma,2}\right\|_\infty > q\alpha\beta_T\sqrt{n(n+1)m}$:
  return $\perp$
- $k = \frac{2}{q}\cdot\lfloor B_\Lambda^{-1}\psi(s)\rceil_{q/2}$
- **if** $\left\|\psi(s) - \frac{q}{2}B_\Lambda\cdot k\right\|_2 > q\alpha\sqrt{n}$: **return** $\perp$
- $(mk, dk) = \texttt{KDF}(k)$
- if $\texttt{MAC.verify}(mk, (c_0, c_1, c_2, \Delta), \tau) \neq 1$:
  return $\perp$
- $(m, d = (d^R, d^S)) = \texttt{SKE.dec}(dk, \Delta)$
- **if** $\texttt{COM.unveil}(ck^R, c_0^R, k, d^R) \neq 1 \vee$
  $\texttt{COM.unveil}(ck^S, c_0^S, k, d^S) \neq 1$: **return** $\perp$
- **return** m

Fig. 5. (NRLWE based DRE)

To prove correctness and security we need the following lemma which bounds the smoothing parameter in terms of the Gaussian parameters.

Lemma 8. *For the parameters of the DRE* DRE*,* $\Sigma_f := \Sigma^i \in \mathbb{R}^{n\times n}$, $e = (e_1, \dots e_m) := e_1^i \in J_q^m$ *with* $i \in \{R, S\}$ *and* $\epsilon = \epsilon(n) > 0$ *negligible, it holds that*

$$\eta_\epsilon(\Lambda) \leq \sqrt{2\pi}\sqrt{\Sigma_f},$$
$$\eta_\epsilon(\Lambda) \leq \sqrt{2\pi}t\beta_T\sqrt{m}q\alpha \text{ and}$$
$$\eta_\epsilon(\Lambda) \leq \sqrt{2\pi}A_{e_\nu}^{-1}\sqrt{\left(\Sigma_f^{-1} + (t^2\beta_T^2 A_{e_\nu}A_{e_\nu}^T)^{-1}\right)^{-1}}$$

for $1 \leq \nu \leq m$ *where* $e_\nu \neq 0$.

The proof can be found in the full version.

Theorem 1. *The DRE* DRE *from Fig. 5 is correct with overwhelming probability over the errors.*

Proof. The proof of correctness requires two things. First, `invert` needs to return the correct s. Second, the errors need to be small enough, such that the checks do not fail and k can be recovered from s. The rest follows from the correctness of SKE, MAC and COM. We consider the decryption for R, the decryption for S is analogous.

As stated in Lemma 5, the `invert` function returns the correct s if

$$\sigma^{-1}\left(Te_1^R + e_2^R\right) \in q \cdot \mathcal{P}_{1/2}(\tilde{B_g}^{-T}) \tag{5}$$

holds, where $\tilde{B_g} \in R_q^{l\times l}$ is the Gram-Schmidt orthogonalization of the basis of $\Lambda_q^\perp(g)$. This is equivalent to

$$\left\|\tilde{B_g}^T\sigma^{-1}\left(Te_1^R + e_2^R\right)\right\|_{\varphi,\infty} \leq \frac{q}{2}.$$

By Lemmas 3 and 8 each entry of $Te_1^R + e_2^R \in J_q^l$ is distributed as $\psi^{-1}(\mathcal{D}_{\Lambda,\sqrt{\Sigma}})$, where $\Sigma = t^2\beta_T^2 Mul(e_1^R) + \Sigma^R$. Using the definitions of Σ^R and $Mul(e_1^R)$ and

$$(r_1)^2 := \beta_T^2 \cdot \max_j Mul(e_1^R)_{j,j} \in \mathbb{R}^+$$
$$(r_2)^2 := \beta_T^2 \cdot \max_j Mul(e_1^R)_{j,j} + \beta_T^2 m(q\alpha)^2 \in \mathbb{R}^+$$
$$r^2 := (r_1)^2 + (r_2)^2,$$

it holds that

$$\Sigma \leq t^2r^2I_n,$$

where $\leq$ is on every entry. As each entry of $e_1^R \in J_q^m$ is drawn by a discrete Gaussian, Eq. (2) yields

$$\left|(e_1^R)_{i,j}\right| \leq \left\|(e_1^R)_i\right\|_{\sigma,2} \leq \sqrt{n}q\alpha$$

and thus

$$(r_1)^2 \leq \beta_T^2 mn(q\alpha)^2 \tag{6}$$

$$(r_2)^2 \leq \beta_T^2 mn(q\alpha)^2 + \beta_T^2 m(q\alpha)^2 = \beta_T^2(n+1)m(q\alpha)^2 \tag{7}$$

with overwhelming probability. By Eq. (2) again, each element of $Te_1^R + e_2^R$ has 2-norm at most $r\sqrt{n}$ and therefore

$$\left\|\left[Te_1^R + e_2^R\right]_{\sigma,2}\right\|_\infty \leq r\sqrt{n} \leq \beta_T q\alpha\sqrt{n(2n+1)m}$$

with overwhelming probability. This yields

$$\begin{aligned}\left\|\tilde{B_g}^T \sigma^{-1}(Te_1^R + e_2^R)\right\|_{\varphi,\infty} &\leq \left\|\tilde{B_g}^T\right\|_{\varphi,\infty} \cdot \left\|\left[Te_1^R + e_2^R\right]_{\varphi,2}\right\|_\infty \\ &\leq \left\|\tilde{B_g}^T\right\|_{\varphi,\infty} \cdot \left\|B_\Lambda^{-1}\right\|_2 \cdot \left\|\left[Te_1^R + e_2^R\right]_{\sigma,2}\right\|_\infty \\ &\leq \left\|\tilde{B_g}^T\right\|_{\varphi,\infty} \cdot \left\|B_\Lambda^{-1}\right\|_2 \cdot \beta_T q\alpha\sqrt{n(2n+1)m} \overset{(*)}{\leq} \frac{q}{2}.\end{aligned}$$

The last inequality (*) holds because

$$\begin{aligned}\frac{1}{\alpha} &\overset{(3)}{\geq} 2\beta_T \cdot \left\|\tilde{B_g}^T\right\|_{\varphi,\infty} \cdot \left\|B_\Lambda^{-1}\right\|_2 \cdot \sqrt{nm}\left(\sqrt{nm} + \sqrt{n+1}\right) \\ &\geq 2\beta_T \cdot \left\|\tilde{B_g}^T\right\|_{\varphi,\infty} \cdot \left\|B_\Lambda^{-1}\right\|_2 \cdot \sqrt{n(2n+1)m}.\end{aligned}$$

Thus, the errors are small enough with overwhelming probability so that Eq. (5) holds and `invert` returns the correct s.

The norm checks for e_1^R and e_1^S in the decryption (line 6 and 10) hold by Eq. (2) with overwhelming probability. The norm checks for e_2^R and e_2^S (line 7 and 11) follow from Eqs. (2) and (7).

For the norm on $\bar{s} \in J_q$, by Eq. (2), we have $\|\bar{s}\|_2 \leq q\alpha\sqrt{n}$ with overwhelming probability. This implies two facts. First, the correct seed k can be recovered in line 12 with overwhelming probability as

$$\left\|B_\Lambda^{-1}\bar{s}\right\|_\infty \leq \left\|B_\Lambda^{-1}\bar{s}\right\|_2 \leq \left\|B_\Lambda^{-1}\right\|_2 \cdot \|\bar{s}\|_2 \leq \left\|B_\Lambda^{-1}\right\|_2 \cdot q\alpha\sqrt{n} \overset{(4)}{\leq} \frac{q}{4}.$$

Second, the last norm check in line 13 succeeds with overwhelming probability. $\square$

Having shown the correctness of the scheme we turn towards proving soundness.

Theorem 2. *The DRE* `DRE` *from Fig. 5 is sound as in Definition 6.*

Proof. We need to show that no PPT adversary can produce a cipher c that decrypts to two different messages even given both secret keys. As this means that at least one of the two receivers will decrypt c to some message $m \neq \perp$, we assume without loss of generality that $\mathtt{Dec}(sk^R, pk^R, pk^S, c) \neq \perp$. Thus, we know that the error checks for R succeed and therefore it holds that $c_1^S = a^S s + e_1^S$ for an $e_1^S \in J_q^m$ with $\left\|\left[e_1^S\right]_{\sigma,2}\right\|_\infty \leq q\alpha\sqrt{n}$. Similarly, we know that $c_2^S = (a_1^S + g \cdot \mathtt{FRD}(\mathtt{H}(c_0, c_1)))s)s + e_2^S$ for an $e_2^S \in J_q^l$ with $\left\|\left[e_2^S\right]_{\sigma,2}\right\|_\infty \leq q\alpha\beta_T\sqrt{n(n+1)m}$.

As each entry of T is drawn by a discrete Gaussian, Eq. (2) yields $\left\|[T]_{\sigma,2}\right\|_\infty \leq m\left\|T_{i,j}\right\|_{\sigma,2} \leq m\sqrt{n}\beta_T$ with overwhelming probability and thus

$$\left\|\left[Te_1^S\right]_{\sigma,2}\right\|_\infty \leq \left\|[T]_{\sigma,2}\right\|_\infty \cdot \left\|\left[e_1^S\right]_{\sigma,2}\right\|_\infty \leq \frac{q\sqrt{nm}}{2 \cdot \left\|\tilde{B_g}^T\right\|_{\varphi,\infty} \cdot \left\|B_\Lambda^{-1}\right\|_2 \cdot (\sqrt{nm} + \sqrt{n+1})}.$$

Combining the bounds on e_2^S and α yields

$$\left\|\left[e_2^S\right]_{\sigma,2}\right\|_\infty \leq \frac{q\sqrt{n+1}}{2 \cdot \left\|\tilde{B_g}^T\right\|_{\varphi,\infty} \cdot \left\|B_\Lambda^{-1}\right\|_2 \cdot (\sqrt{nm} + \sqrt{n+1})}.$$

Therefore, S recovers the correct s from `invert` by Lemma 5 as

$$\left\|\tilde{B_g}^T(Te_1^S + e_2^S)\right\|_{\varphi,\infty} \leq \left\|\tilde{B_g}^T\right\|_{\varphi,\infty} \cdot \left\|B_\Lambda^{-1}\right\|_2 \cdot \left\|\left[Te_1^S + e_2^S\right]_{\sigma,2}\right\|_\infty \leq \frac{q}{2}.$$

As all other steps of the decryption depend deterministically on s and the cipher, S recovers the same message m. □

For the security proof we need that the public key is indistinguishable from uniform randomness. For the statistical variant this is statistically true, whereas for the computational variant we need the following Lemma 9.

Lemma 9. *Let $q, m, l, \beta_T, t, a_0, a', a, T, \Lambda$ be as in the* `DRE` *from Fig. 5 and $u \xleftarrow{\$} J_q^m$. Then (a, Ta) is computationally indistinguishable from (a, u) if the $NRLWE_{1,q,\chi}$ assumption holds for $\chi = \psi^{-1}(\mathcal{D}_{\Lambda,t\beta_T})$. Concretely, for any adversary $\mathcal{A}$ on the indistinguishability between (a, Ta) and (a, u), there is an adversary $\mathcal{A}_{NRLWE}$ on $NRLWE_{1,q,\chi}$ with*

$$\mathsf{Adv}_{\mathcal{A}}^{IND}(\lambda) \leq l \cdot \mathsf{Adv}_{\mathcal{A}_{NRLWE}}^{NRLWE_{1,q,\chi}}(\lambda).$$

Proof. First, consider $m = 2$ so that $a' \in J_q$. We use a standard hybrid proof to show that given $(a, b) \in J_q^m \times J_q^l$ no adversary can decide whether $b = u$ or $b = Ta$. In game H_i the first i rows of b are uniformly random while the other rows are $(Ta)_j$. Thus, in the game $G_0 := H_0$ we have $b = Ta$ as in the construction and in $G_1 := H_l$, $b = u$ is completely random. If there is an adversary $\mathcal{A}_i$, which distinguishes game H_{i-1} from H_i, there is an adversary $\mathcal{A}_{NRLWE}$ on $\mathrm{NRLWE}_{1,q,\chi}$ with $\chi = \psi^{-1}(\mathcal{D}_{\Lambda,t\beta_T})$. Given one canonically embedded NRLWE sample $(a_{\mathrm{NRLWE}}, b_{\mathrm{NRLWE}}) \in J_q \times J_q$, $\mathcal{A}_{NRLWE}$ embeds this sample in the i-th row and samples everything else as in game H_i. To do this, it draws $a_0 \xleftarrow{\$} J_q^*$ and sets $a = (a_0, a_0 a_{\mathrm{NRLWE}})^1$ and for b it chooses the vector

$$(u_1, \ldots, u_{i-1}, a_0 b_{\mathrm{NRLWE}}, t_{i+1,1}a_0 + t_{i+1,2}a_0 a_{\mathrm{NRLWE}}, \ldots, t_{l,1}a_0 + t_{l,2}a_0 a_{\mathrm{NRLWE}})^T$$
$$= (u_1, \ldots, u_{i-1}, a_0 b_{\mathrm{NRLWE}}, T(a_0, a')_{[i+1;l]})^T, a' = a_0 a_{\mathrm{NRLWE}},$$

where $T(a_0, a')_{[i+1;l]}$ are the rows $i+1, \ldots, l$ of the resulting vector. Then, $\mathcal{A}_i$ is run with input (a, b). If $b_{\mathrm{NRLWE}} = a_{\mathrm{NRLWE}}s + e$ for some secret $s \in J_q$ and error $e \in J_q$, the i-th row is $a's + a_0 e \sim t_{i,1}a_0 + t_{i,2}a'$ and thus, this simulates game H_{i-1}. If b_{NRLWE} is random instead, it simulates game H_i. Therefore, for any adversary $\mathcal{A}_i$ we have

$$\left|\mathbb{P}\left[\mathcal{A}_i^{H_i}(\lambda) = 1\right] - \mathbb{P}\left[\mathcal{A}_i^{H_{i-1}}(\lambda) = 1\right]\right| \leq \mathsf{Adv}_{\mathcal{A}_{\mathrm{NRLWE}}}^{\mathrm{NRLWE}_{1,q,\chi}}(\lambda).$$

With that, we can bound the advantage of every adversary $\mathcal{A}$ against distinguishing G_0 from G_1 as

$$\begin{aligned}\mathsf{Adv}_{\mathcal{A},G_0,G_1}^{\mathrm{IND}}(\lambda) &= \left|\mathbb{P}\left[\mathcal{A}^{H_l}(\lambda) = 1\right] - \mathbb{P}\left[\mathcal{A}^{H_0}(\lambda) = 1\right]\right| \\ &\leq \sum_{i=1}^{l} \left|\mathbb{P}\left[\mathcal{A}^{H_i}(\lambda) = 1\right] - \mathbb{P}\left[\mathcal{A}^{H_{i-1}}(\lambda) = 1\right]\right| \\ &\leq l \cdot \mathsf{Adv}_{\mathcal{A}_{\mathrm{NRLWE}}}^{\mathrm{NRLWE}_{m,q,\chi}}(\lambda).\end{aligned}$$

As for $m > 2$ the j-th row is $(T(a_0, a'))_j = t_{j,1}a_0 + t_{j,2}a_2 + t_{j,3}a_3 + \cdots + t_{j,m}a_m$ for some $a_2, \cdots, a_m$, and $t_{j,1}a_0 + t_{j,2}a_2$ looks uniform for each j and thus, $T(a_0, a')$ looks uniformly random as claimed. □

Now we turn towards proving the security of our construction by using a series of game hops. We start with the IND-CCA2$_{\mathrm{DRE}}$ game and slowly change parts such that we end up with a scheme where the challenge ciphertext is independent of the chosen challenge messages. Therefore, no adversary can win the resulting game with probability better than $\frac{1}{2}$. Using our previous results we are able to show that no game hop can be detected by an adversary as long as our security assumptions hold. The proof uses some ideas of Benz *et al.*.[5, Theorem 6], Boyen, Izabachène, and Li [9, Theorem 1] and Kiltz, Masny, and Pietrzak [20, Theorem 2], but we have to take some extra precautions.

Theorem 3. *The DRE* `DRE` *from Fig. 5 is IND-CCA2$_{DRE}$-secure if the problem NRLWE$_{2m,q,\chi_1}$ is hard, where $\chi_1 = \psi^{-1}(\mathcal{D}_{\Lambda,tq\alpha})$ and* `COM`, `SKE`, `MAC`, `KDF` *and* `H` *are secure with regards to Definitions 10,11,13 and 15,16. The computational variant also requires that NRLWE$_{1,q,\chi_2}$ for $\chi_2 = \psi^{-1}(\mathcal{D}_{\Lambda,t\beta_T})$ is hard.*

1 Which is distributed as in the `DRE` because a_0 is invertible and a_{NRLWE} is uniform.

Proof. We give an overview of our games: Game 1 to 3 change the decryption oracle in such a way that we can change the public key in Game 4 without being detected. This change in turn allows us to replace c_1^* and c_2^* by randomness in Game 5 and 6, as well as remove k^* from the commitment in c_0^* in Game 7. Finally, we can now replace the symmetric parts by randomness in Game 8 and 9.

Denote by $\mathbb{P}[S_i]$ the probability that the experiment returns 1 in Game i.

Game 0: This game follows the IND-CCA2$_{\text{DRE}}$ game of Fig. 2. The adversary $\mathcal{A}$ gets two independent public keys (pk^R, pk^S) for which it can make decryption queries. We call this phase 1. At one point $\mathcal{A}$ outputs two messages $m_0, m_1 \in \mathbf{M}$ and gets $c^* := \texttt{Enc}(pk^R, pk^S, m_b)$ for $b \xleftarrow{\$} \{0,1\}$. It can now make additional decryption queries in what we call phase 2 as long as the public key is either pk^R or pk^S and $c \neq c^*$. Finally $\mathcal{A}$ outputs b' and wins if $b = b'$.

We thus have

$$\mathbb{P}[S_0] = \mathsf{Adv}_{\mathtt{DRE},\mathcal{A}}^{\text{IND-CCAt-DRE}}(\lambda) + \frac{1}{2}.$$

Game 1: In this game, (c_0^*, c_1^*) are calculated just before the public keys are send to $\mathcal{A}$. As both parts are unavailable to $\mathcal{A}$ until c^* is released, we have

$$\mathbb{P}[S_1] = \mathbb{P}[S_0].$$

Game 2: Now we reject any requests with $\mathtt{H}(c_0, c_1) = \mathtt{H}(c_0^*, c_1^*)$ in phase 1 and $(c_0, c_1) \neq c_0^*, c_1^*$ with $\mathtt{H}(c_0, c_1) = \mathtt{H}(c_0^*, c_1^*)$ in phase 2. As in phase 1, $\mathcal{A}$ does not know anything about $\mathtt{H}(c_0^*, c_1^*)$ it can only make such a query by chance. In phase 2 we can use any adversary returning a query that is now rejected to build an adversary $\mathcal{B}_1$ breaking the collision resistance of the hash function. Therefore, just as in prior works [9, Lemma 4], we have for Q_1 and $X_{\mathtt{H}}$ being the amount of queries in phase 1 and the number of hash values respectively

$$|\mathbb{P}[S_2] - \mathbb{P}[S_1]| \leq \frac{Q_1}{X_{\mathtt{H}}} + \mathsf{Adv}_{\mathtt{H},\mathcal{B}_1}^{\text{CR}}(\lambda).$$

Game 3: In this game the decryption oracle additionally rejects requests with (c_0^*, c_1^*) in phase 2. We can bound the probability by which $\mathcal{A}$ makes such a request by two sub-events[2]

- NoBind: a different $k \neq k^*$ is associated with (c_0^*, c_1^*). For this to return something else than $\perp$, it requires $\texttt{COM.unveil}(ck, (c_0^R)^*, k, d_1) = 1 = \texttt{COM.unveil}(ck, (c_0^R)^*, k^*, d_2)$, but this violates the statistical binding property of the commitment.
- Forge: the same $k = k^*$ is associated with (c_0^*, c_1^*). For a valid query, we have $\texttt{MAC.verify}(mk^*, (c_0^*, c_1^*, c_2, \Delta), \tau) = 1$, where $(mk^*, dk^*) = \texttt{KDF}(k^*)$.

[2] Notice that queries in phase 2 still need to satisfy $c \neq c^*$.

Thus, we can bound the probability by

$$|\mathbb{P}[S_3] - \mathbb{P}[S_2]| \leq \mathbb{P}[\text{Forge}] + \texttt{negl}(\lambda).$$

We show that we can bound the difference between Forge probabilities in the games. For this we define an algorithm $\mathcal{B}_{\mathrm{f}}^i$ that simulates Game i with $\mathcal{A}$ and outputs 1 if $\mathcal{A}$ sends a cipher to the decryption oracle with $(c_2, \Delta) \neq (c_2^*, \Delta^*)$ and $\texttt{MAC.verify}(mk^*, (c_0^*, c_1^*, c_2, \Delta), \tau) = 1$, and a random bit if no such cipher was sent to the decryption oracle. Then we have

$$\begin{aligned}\mathbb{P}\left[\mathcal{B}_{\mathrm{f}}^i = 1\right] &= \mathbb{P}\left[\mathcal{B}_{\mathrm{f}}^i = 1 \mid \text{Forge}_i\right] \cdot \mathbb{P}\left[\text{Forge}_i\right] \\ &\quad + \mathbb{P}\left[\mathcal{B}_{\mathrm{f}}^i = 1 \mid \neg\text{Forge}_i\right] \cdot \mathbb{P}\left[\neg\text{Forge}_i\right] \\ &= \mathbb{P}\left[\text{Forge}_i\right] + \frac{1}{2}(1 - \mathbb{P}\left[\text{Forge}_i\right]) \\ &= \frac{1}{2} + \frac{1}{2} \cdot \mathbb{P}\left[\text{Forge}_i\right]\end{aligned}$$

This yields for $i, j \in \mathbb{N}$:

$$\begin{aligned}\left|\mathbb{P}\left[\text{Forge}_j\right] - \mathbb{P}\left[\text{Forge}_i\right]\right| &= 2 \cdot \left|\mathbb{P}\left[\mathcal{B}_{\mathrm{f}}^j = 1\right] - \mathbb{P}\left[\mathcal{B}_{\mathrm{f}}^i = 1\right]\right| \\ &\leq 2 \cdot \left|\mathbb{P}\left[S_j\right] - \mathbb{P}\left[S_i\right]\right|.\end{aligned}$$

Game 4: Notice that after the last game change, $\mathcal{A}$ is not allowed to make any decryption queries with $(c_0, c_1) = c_0^*, c_1^*$ in either phase. We can use this to change the public key in this game. More specifically, the goal is to change the (a, a_1) part of both parties to $(a, Ta - g \cdot \texttt{FRD}(\texttt{H}(c_0^*, c_1^*)))$ instead of (a, Ta). Here, we have to differentiate between the variants of the scheme's parameter. First, we show how to do this change in the computational variant because it is more instructive.
As Ta is only computational indistinguishable from randomness in this variant, we cannot do the change directly. Instead, we proceed with a series of smaller games, using our sound decryption capabilities to change the public keys of both parties one after another.

Game 4.1 We use sk^R for all decryption queries. Any adversary that can distinguish between Game 3 and 4.1 has to create a ciphertext that decrypts differently depending on whether one uses sk^R or sk^S, thus breaking soundness. As Theorem 2 shows that this can only happen with negligible probability we have

$$|\mathbb{P}[S_{4.1}] - \mathbb{P}[S_3]| \leq \texttt{negl}(\lambda).$$

Game 4.2 We replace a_1^S by a random $u \in J_q^m$. As we don't use sk^S in our decryption oracle anymore we can use Lemma 9 to see that

$$|\mathbb{P}[S_{4.2}] - \mathbb{P}[S_{4.1}]| \leq l \cdot \mathsf{Adv}_{\mathcal{A}_{\text{NRLWE}}}^{\text{NRLWE}_{1,q,\chi_2}}(\lambda).$$

Game 4.3 We replace $a_1^S = u$ by $a_1^S = u - g \cdot \texttt{FRD}(\texttt{H}(c_0^*, c_1^*))$. As u acts as a one time pad we have

$$\mathbb{P}[S_{4.3}] = \mathbb{P}[S_{4.2}].$$

Game 4.4 We further replace $a_1^S = u - g \cdot \texttt{FRD}(\texttt{H}(c_0^*, c_1^*))$ by $a_1^S = T^S a^S - g \cdot \texttt{FRD}(\texttt{H}(c_0^*, c_1^*))$. Once again, Lemma 9 can be used to show that

$$|\mathbb{P}[S_{4.4}] - \mathbb{P}[S_{4.3}]| \leq l \cdot \mathsf{Adv}_{\mathcal{A}_{\mathrm{NRLWE}}}^{\mathrm{NRLWE}_{1,q,\chi_2}}(\lambda)$$

Game 4.5 We now use sk^S for all decryption queries. To see that the decryption oracle can still handle all the same queries, notice that for a valid $c = (c_0, c_1, c_2, \Delta, \tau)$ we have

$$\begin{aligned} c_2^S &= (a_1^S + g \cdot \texttt{FRD}(\texttt{H}(c_0, c_1)))s + e_2^S \\ &= (T^S a^S + g(\texttt{FRD}(\texttt{H}(c_0, c_1)) - \texttt{FRD}(\texttt{H}(c_0^*, c_1^*))))s + e_2^S. \end{aligned}$$

As $\texttt{FRD}(\texttt{H}(c_0, c_1)) - \texttt{FRD}(\texttt{H}(c_0^*, c_1^*))$ is invertible for all $\texttt{H}(c_0, c_1) \neq \texttt{H}(c_0^*, c_1^*)$, and such queries were already rejected before, we can use the trapdoor to decrypt all valid queries. Also, as in Game 4.1, the soundness property makes sure that the difference between using sk^R or sk^S is negligible, and so

$$|\mathbb{P}[S_{4.5}] - \mathbb{P}[S_{4.4}]| \leq \texttt{negl}(\lambda).$$

Game 4.6 We now apply the changes of Games 4.2–4.4 to sk^R. As before, this yields

$$|\mathbb{P}[S_{4.6}] - \mathbb{P}[S_{4.5}]| \leq 2l \cdot \mathsf{Adv}_{\mathcal{A}_{\mathrm{NRLWE}}}^{\mathrm{NRLWE}_{1,q,\chi_2}}(\lambda) + \texttt{negl}(\lambda)$$

This finishes the public key change in the computational variant. In the statistical variant each row of Ta is statistically indistinguishable from uniform by Lemma 4 with $z_1 = 1$ and $z_2 = m$. Therefore, we can skip Game 4.2–4.4 and Game 4.6 but otherwise use the same arguments.
To summarize, after Game 4 we have:

$$(pk, sk) = ((a, Ta - g \cdot \texttt{FRD}(\texttt{H}(c_0^*, c_1^*))), T),$$

and we reject all queries with $\texttt{H}(c_0, c_1) = \texttt{H}(c_0^*, c_1^*)$.

Game 5: This game changes c_1^*, c_2^* for both parties. Instead of drawing them honestly, we draw $\bar{c}_1^* \stackrel{\$}{\leftarrow} J_q^m$ for each party and set $c_1^* = \bar{c}_1^* + a \cdot \psi^{-1}(B_\Lambda(q/2 \cdot k))$. For c_2^* we draw $\bar{e} \leftarrow \psi^{-1}(\mathcal{D}^l_{\Lambda, t\beta_T q\alpha\sqrt{m}})$ and set $c_2^* = Tc_1^* + \bar{e}$, also for each party.
Assume that there is an adversary that can distinguish both games. We use it to build an adversary $\mathcal{B}_2$ against the $\mathrm{NRLWE}_{2m,q,\chi_1}$ assumption[3] that receives

[3] We need $2m$ to split the vectors for both parties.

the canonically embedded samples $(a_{\mathrm{NRLWE}}, b_{\mathrm{NRLWE}}) = ((a^R_{\mathrm{NRLWE}}, a^S_{\mathrm{NRLWE}}), (b^R_{\mathrm{NRLWE}}, b^S_{\mathrm{NRLWE}})) \in J_q^{2m} \times J_q^{2m}$. By Lemma 1, we can assume that both a^i_{NRLWE} have an invertible element
and without loss of generality we can assume that both a^i_{NRLWE} have the invertible element at the first position[4].
The adversary $\mathcal{B}_2$ simulates Game 5 with $a = a_{\mathrm{NRLWE}}$, while still generating honest secret keys. It also sets $(\bar{c}_1^R)^* = b^R_{\mathrm{NRLWE}}$ and $(\bar{c}_1^S)^* = b^S_{\mathrm{NRLWE}}$ instead of drawing it randomly.
If b_{NRLWE} is random, then this perfectly simulates Game 5. If $b_{\mathrm{NRLWE}} = a_{\mathrm{NRLWE}}x + y$ for some $x \leftarrow \chi_1, y \leftarrow \chi_1^{2m}$ instead, then it simulates Game 4, as

$$\begin{aligned} c_1^* &= b_{\mathrm{NRLWE}} + a_{\mathrm{NRLWE}} \cdot \psi^{-1}\left(B_\Lambda\left(\frac{q}{2}\cdot k\right)\right) \\ &= a_{\mathrm{NRLWE}}\left(x + \psi^{-1}\left(B_\Lambda\left(\frac{q}{2}\cdot k\right)\right)\right) + y \sim as + e \end{aligned} \tag{8}$$

and

$$\begin{aligned} c_2^* &= Tc_1^* + \bar{e} \overset{(8)}{\sim} T(as+e) + \bar{e} = Tas + Te + \bar{e} \\ &= (a_1 + g \cdot \mathtt{FRD}(\mathtt{H}(c_0^*, c_1^*)))s + Te + \bar{e} \overset{(*)}{\sim} (a_1 + g \cdot \mathtt{FRD}(\mathtt{H}(c_0^*, c_1^*)))s + \tilde{e}. \end{aligned}$$

For $(*)$ to hold, we need that $Te + \bar{e} = \tilde{e}$ is distributed as e_2^i. By Lemma 3, $Te + \bar{e}$ is distributed as $\psi^{-1}(\mathcal{D}^l_{\Lambda,\sqrt{\Sigma}})$ with $\Sigma = t^2\beta_T^2 Mul(e_1^i) + t^2\beta_T^2 m(q\alpha)^2$, which is the distribution of e_2^i. The bounds on the smoothing parameter hold by Lemma 8. Therefore we have

$$|\mathbb{P}[S_5] - \mathbb{P}[S_4]| \leq \mathsf{Adv}_{\mathcal{B}_2}^{\mathrm{NRLWE}_{2m,q,\chi_1}}.$$

Game 6: We now choose c_1^* completely random. As $\bar{c}_1^*$ acted as a one-time pad, the adversary cannot distinguish this and hence

$$\mathbb{P}[S_6] = \mathbb{P}[S_5].$$

Game 7: The next change is to make the commitment independent of k^*. We achieve this by changing $c_0^* = (\mathtt{COM.com}(ck^i, k^*, r^i))_{i\in\{R,S\}}$ to $c_0^* = (\mathtt{COM.com}(ck^i, k', r^i))_{i\in\{R,S\}}$ with random $k' \overset{\$}{\leftarrow} \{0,1\}^n$ over two games. A straightforward reduction shows for an adversary $\mathcal{B}_3$ on the hiding game

$$|\mathbb{P}[S_7] - \mathbb{P}[S_6]| \leq 2 \cdot \mathsf{Adv}_{\mathtt{COM},\mathcal{B}_3}^{\mathrm{Hiding}}.$$

Game 8: In this game, we change mk^*, dk^* to random. As k^* is not used anymore, this reduces to the indistinguishability from the KDF as in the works of Boyen, Izabachène, and Li [9, Lemma 6]. Additionally, as the MAC

[4] Otherwise reorder a_{NRLWE} and b_{NRLWE} such that an invertible element is at the first position.

key is now random, the Forge probability can be directly reduced to the forgery game of the $\mathtt{MAC}$ and thus

$$|\mathbb{P}[S_8] - \mathbb{P}[S_7]| \leq \mathsf{Adv}^{\mathrm{IND}}_{\mathtt{KDF},\mathcal{B}_4}(\lambda)$$
$$\mathbb{P}[\mathrm{Forge}_8] \leq \mathsf{Adv}^{\mathrm{OT\text{-}SUF}}_{\mathtt{MAC},\mathcal{B}_5}(\lambda).$$

This also bounds $\mathbb{P}[\mathrm{Forge}_3]$ and hence $|\mathbb{P}[S_3] - \mathbb{P}[S_2]|$ by a negligible function using the arguments in Game 3.

Game 9: Finally, we can change Δ^* to random. As dk^* is random, any adversary $\mathcal{B}_6$ that distinguishes this breaks the SKE indistinguishability, and thus

$$|\mathbb{P}[S_9] - \mathbb{P}[S_8]| \leq \mathsf{Adv}^{\mathrm{OT\text{-}IND}}_{\mathtt{SKE},\mathcal{B}_6}(\lambda).$$

We now have a game with a ciphertext independent of the chosen value b. Using our assumptions we thus see that

$$\mathsf{Adv}^{\mathrm{IND\text{-}CCAt\text{-}DRE}}_{\mathrm{DRE},\mathcal{A}}(\lambda) \leq \mathtt{negl}(\lambda).$$

□

4 SB-KEM Construction

We now construct a SB-KEM from the same ingredients. So choose $R, n, q, m, l, \beta_T, t, \Lambda, B_\Lambda, g, \tilde{B}_g, J_q, J_q^*$ as for the DRE scheme from Sect. 3. The only difference is the bound α, which changes to

$$\frac{1}{\alpha} \geq 2\beta_T \cdot \left\| \tilde{B_g}^T \right\|_{\varphi,\infty} \cdot \left\| B_\Lambda^{-1} \right\|_2 \cdot \sqrt{n(2n+1)m}$$

as no soundness is required for the SB-KEM. For the computational variant, a double trapdoor similar to the work of Kiltz, Masny, and Pietrzak [20] is required, doubling the cipher size. While the resulting sizes can be found in Sect. 5, we only describe the statistical variant in this section.

Additional building blocks are again a key derivation function $\mathtt{KDF}$ and a FRD $\mathtt{FRD} : \mathbf{P} \to J_q^*$, where $\mathbf{P}$ is the set of parties.

Figure 6 shows the definition of the SB-KEM $\mathtt{KEM} = (\mathsf{KGen}, \mathtt{Enc}, \mathtt{Dec})$.

Theorem 4. *The SB-KEM* $\mathtt{KEM}$ *from Fig. 6 is correct with overwhelming probability over the errors* $e_1, e_2, \bar{s}$.

The proof is the same as for Theorem 1.

Theorem 5. *The SB-KEM* $\mathtt{KEM}$ *from Fig. 6 is IND-SB-CPA*$_{SB-KEM}$ *given that* $NRLWE_{m,q,\chi}$ *is hard, where* $\chi = \psi^{-1}(\mathcal{D}_{\Lambda,tq\alpha})$ *and the* $\mathtt{KDF}$ *satisfies Definition 17.*

The proof is very similar to Theorem 3 except half of the games can be omitted. Games 1–3 can be omitted as the security game already does not accept these queries. Also Game 7–9 can be done in one game, where we replace the key k with randomness, reducing this game hop straight to the KDF indistinguishability game.

$\mathsf{KGen}(1^\lambda)$

$a_0 \leftarrow J_q^*, a' \leftarrow J_q^{m-1}, T \leftarrow \psi^{-1}(\mathcal{D}^{l\times m}_{\Lambda,t\beta_T})$

$a = (a_0, a')$

return $(pk, sk) := ((a, Ta), T)$

$\mathtt{Enc}(pk, \mathcal{S})$

parse $pk = (a, a_1)$

$k \leftarrow \{0,1\}^n$

$\bar{s} \leftarrow \psi^{-1}(\mathcal{D}_{\Lambda,tq\alpha})$

$e_1 \leftarrow \psi^{-1}(\mathcal{D}^m_{\Lambda,tq\alpha})$

$s = \psi^{-1}\left(B_\Lambda\left(\frac{q}{2}\cdot k\right)\right) + \bar{s} \in J_q$

$c_1 = as + e_1$

$\Sigma = t^2\beta^2 Mul(e_1)$
$+ t^2\beta^2 m(q\alpha)^2 I_n$

$e_2 \leftarrow \psi^{-1}(\mathcal{D}^l_{\Lambda,\sqrt{\Sigma}})$

$c_2 = (a_1 + g\cdot \mathtt{FRD}(\mathcal{S}))s + e_2$

$K = \mathtt{KDF}(k)$

return $(K, c) := (K, (c_1, c_2))$

$\mathtt{Dec}(sk, pk, \mathcal{S}, c)$

parse $pk = (a, a_1)$

parse $sk = T$

parse $c = (c_1, c_2)$

$(s, (e_1, e_2)) = \mathtt{invert}(T, \mathtt{FRD}(\mathcal{S}),$
$(a, (a_1 + g\cdot \mathtt{FRD}(\mathcal{S}))), (c_1, c_2))$

if $\left\|[e_1]_{\sigma,2}\right\|_\infty > q\alpha\sqrt{n}$: **return** $\perp$

if $\left\|[e_2]_{\sigma,2}\right\|_\infty > q\alpha\beta_T\sqrt{n(n+1)m}$:
return $\perp$

$k = \frac{2}{q}\lfloor B_\Lambda^{-1}\psi(s)\rceil_{q/2}$

if $\left\|\psi(s) - \frac{q}{2}B_\Lambda\cdot k\right\|_2 > q\alpha\sqrt{n}$: **return** $\perp$

$K = \mathtt{KDF}(k)$

return K

Fig. 6. RLWE based SB-KEM

5 Parameter Sets

The computations are performed in the polynomial representation instead of the canonical embedding to avoid complex numbers. Hence, the discrete Guassians have to be translated to the coefficent embedding. For $2n$-cyclotomics, where n is a power of two, the Gaussians simply translate to the coefficent embedding with a scaling of $\frac{1}{\sqrt{n}}$ as shown by Lyubashevsky, Peikert, and Regev [22]. For the modulo q we choose a prime with $q = 2r + 1 \mod 4r$, for $r = 16$, as Bert *et al.*. [7] showed a FRD for these parameters.

The construction requires that the bound of a vector sampled from a discrete Gaussian is not too large with overwhelming probability as described in Eq. (2). For concrete parameters we choose to have $\delta \leq 2^{-\lambda}$, where λ is the security parameter. Using the bound from Lemma 2, we obtain the values for t depending on n and λ summarized in Table 2. The values for t are determined such that they best fit the security level λ which the parameter sets achieve.

Table 2. The values for t depending on the dimension n and λ to achieve $\delta \leq 2^{-\lambda}$

n	λ	t
512	90	0.731
1024	157	0.745
1024	165	0.74
2048	192	0.79

The norm $\left\|\tilde{B_g}^T\right\|_{\varphi,\infty}$ was determined numerically and yielded $\left\|\tilde{B_g}^T\right\|_{\varphi,\infty} = 4$ for any q and n. For B_Λ^{-1} it can be shown that $\left\|B_\Lambda^{-1}\right\|_2 = \frac{1}{n}\left\|B_\Lambda\right\|_2 = \frac{1}{\sqrt{n}}$, based on the fact that B_Λ contains n orthogonal vectors of length $\sqrt{n}$ [22,24].

To estimate the hardness of NRLWE, we use the lattice estimator [1], a tool frequently used to estimate the hardness of LWE instances. Concretely, we use commit "5ba00f5" and the cost model "MINZOV" [23].

The parameter sets for the DRE and the KEM are shown in Table 3 and Table 4, respectively. The parameters $\gamma_T := \frac{1}{\sqrt{n}} t\beta_T$ and $\gamma_e := \frac{1}{\sqrt{n}} tq\alpha$ are the parameters of the Gaussian distribution in the coefficient embedding for T and the errors, respectively. More specifically, each coefficient of the polynomial is drawn independently from a Gaussian distribution with that width. The "C/S" column specifices whether the parameter set is in the computational (C) or statistical (S) variant. The column "λ" specifices the bit security. For t we use the values from Table 2, which ensure $\delta \leq 2^{-\lambda}$. For example, for $n = 1024$ all parameter sets with $\lambda \leq 157$ use $t = 0.745$, while the others use $t = 0.74$.

Table 3. Parameter Sets for the DRE

n	q ($\lceil \log_2 q \rceil$)	m	γ_T	γ_e	C/S	λ	size(pk)	size(sk)	size(c)
512	0xF3d21 (20)	2	1.29	1.29	C	84	28.2 KB	51.2 KB	56.4 KB
1024	0xF69A1 (20)	2	0.79	0.79	C	155	56.3 KB	102 KB	112.6 KB
1024	0x31F7E1 (22)	2	1.42	1.42	C	157	67.6 KB	124 KB	135.2 KB
1024	0x7884418FD21 (43)	2	2048	2513	C	138	247 KB	473 KB	494 KB
1024	0x4dd796487d61 (47)	6	3987	5306	S	132	318 KB	1.7 MB	638 KB
2048	0x1F24D205A1 (37)	7	1073	10.1	S	192	416 KB	2.45 MB	833 KB

Table 4. Parameter Sets for the SB-KEM

n	q ($\lceil \log_2 q \rceil$)	m	γ_T	γ_e	C/S	λ	size(pk)	size(sk)	size(c)
512	0xF3d21 (20)	2	1.69	1.7	C	87	28.2 KB	51.2 KB	56.4 KB
1024	0xF69A1 (20)	2	1.027	1.027	C	162	56.3 KB	102 KB	112.6 KB
1024	0x31F7E1 (22)	2	1.85	1.85	C	163	67.6 KB	124 KB	135.2 KB
1024	0x3c7d313b5a5 (42)	2	2048	2148	C	144	237 KB	452 KB	473 KB
1024	0x3ac62ca642e1 (46)	6	3804	10240	S	143	306 KB	1.62 MB	306 KB
2048	0x1F24D205A1 (37)	6	1976	15.3	S	192	407 KB	2.1 MB	407 KB

We now turn towards comparing our constructions to the existing literature. The only existing IND-SB-CPA$_{\text{SB-KEM}}$ secure SB-KEM by Benz *et al.*. [6] has no concrete parameters but we estimate their size to be much worse than the most efficient standard model post-quantum KEMs, which is why we compare our construction to those instead. To the best of our knowledge, the currently most efficient post-quantum KEMs in the standard model are the Learning Parity with Noise (LPN)-based construction by Xu and Li [29] and the RLWE-based construction by Yang, Ma, and Zhang [30]. As representative for KEMs in the ROM, Kyber [27] is used as it has been standardized recently. Table 5 shows the parameters of the different KEMs. While our scheme is worse than Kyber, it is significantly better than existing non-ROM KEMs by improving the public and secret key compared to the LPN-based or the ciphertext size compared to the RLWE-based scheme.

Table 5. Comparison of the key sizes for our construction with existing post-quantum KEMs.

Scheme	λ	pk	sk	c
Kyber512 [27]	128	0.8 KB	1.632 KB	0.768 KB
Kyber768 [27]	192	1.184 KB	2.4 KB	1.088 KB
LPN-based [29]	128	50.78 MB	62.50 MB	4.54 KB
RLWE-based [30]	80	1.923 MB	0.96 MB	1.280 MB
Ours	87	28.2 KB	51.5 KB	56.4 KB
Ours	164	56.3 KB	102 KB	112.6 KB

With regards to our DRE scheme, there are, to the best of our knowledge, only two sound post-quantum IND-CCA2$_{\text{DRE}}$ DRE schemes, both by Benz *et al.*. [5]. One is LPN based, while the other is LWE based. We compare ourselves to their parameters though we note that they chose a very small Gaussian width for the LWE errors which makes the scheme far less secure than claimed. The results can be found in Table 6.

Table 6. Comparison of the key sizes for our construction with existing post-quantum IND-CCA2$_{\text{DRE}}$ DREs.

Scheme	λ	pk	sk	c
LWE-based [5]	"256"	61.45MB	58.49MB	91.45KB
LPN-based [5]	256	351.13MB	351.13MB	26.5KB
Ours	157	56.3KB	102KB	112.6KB

6 Conclusion

In this work, we constructed efficient RLWE based DRE and SB-KEM schemes. Both are IND-CCA2 secure in the standard model. The resulting sizes are a significant improvement on the best currently known constructions in the literature.

We also want to mention that in the process of developing this paper we implemented a proof of concept of the resulting SB-KEM which can be found on Gitlab[5]. This shows the accessibility of the scheme, making it usable in applications.

Finally, we note that our sizes can probably be improved even further by using compression tactics, which could push the schemes into the regime of ROM based PKEs. This is left as a further research topic.

Acknowledgements. We thank the PKC 2025 anonymous reviewers for their valuable feedback. We also thank Michael Klooß for his valuable input and Wasilij Beskorovajnov for his part in kickstarting our research. This work was funded by the Topic Engineering Secure Systems of the Helmholtz Association (HGF) and supported by KASTEL Security Research Labs, Karlsruhe.

References

1. Albrecht, M.R., Player, R., Scott, S.: On the concrete hardness of learning with errors. J. Math. Cryptol. **9**(3), 169–203 (2015). https://doi.org/10.1515/jmc2015-0016
2. Alkadri, N.A., Demirel, D., El Bansarkhani, R.: Post-quantum commitment schemes. HNO **9**, 32 (2015)
3. Banaszczyk, W.: New bounds in some transference theorems in the geometry of numbers. Math. Ann. **296**, 625–635 (1993)
4. Bellare, M., Rogaway, P.: Optimal asymmetric encryption. In: De Santis, A. (ed.) Advances in Cryptology – EUROCRYPT'94. LNCS, vol. 950, pp. 92–111. Springer, Heidelberg (1995). https://doi.org/10.1007/BFb0053428
5. Benz, L., Beskorovajnov, W., Eilebrecht, S., Gröll, R., Müller, M., MüllerQuade, J.: Chosen-ciphertext secure dual-receiver encryption in the standard model based on post-quantum assumptions. In: Tang, Q., Teague, V. (eds.) PKC 2024: 27th International Conference on Theory and Practice of Public Key Cryptography, Part IV. LNCS, vol. 14604, pp. 257–288. Springer, Heidelberg (2024). https://doi.org/10.1007/978-3-031-57728-4_9
6. Benz, L., Beskorovajnov, W., Eilebrecht, S., Müller-Quade, J., Ottenhues, A., Schwerdt, R.: Sender-binding key encapsulation. In: Boldyreva, A., Kolesnikov, V. (eds.) PKC 2023: 26th International Conference on Theory and Practice of Public Key Cryptography, Part I. LNCS, vol. 13940, pp. 744–773. Springer, Heidelberg (2023). https://doi.org/10.1007/978-3-031-31368-4_26

[5] https://gitlab.kit.edu/robert.brede/rlwe-sb-kem.

7. Bert, P., Eberhart, G., Prabel, L., Roux-Langlois, A., Sabt, M.: Implementation of lattice trapdoors on modules and applications. In: Cheon, J.H., Tillich, J.-P. (eds.) Post-Quantum Cryptography - 12th International Workshop, PQCrypto 2021, pp. 195–214. Springer, Cham (2021). https://doi.org/10.1007/978-3-030-81293-5_11
8. Beskorovajnov, W., Gröll, R., Müller-Quade, J., Ottenhues, A., Schwerdt, R.: A new security notion for PKC in the standard model: weaker, simpler, and still realizing secure channels. In: IACR International Conference on Public-Key Cryptography, pp. 316–344 (2022)
9. Boyen, X., Izabachène, M., Li, Q.: Secure hybrid encryption in the standard model from hard learning problems. In: Cheon, J.H., Tillich, J.-P. (eds.) PostQuantum Cryptography - 12th International Workshop, PQCrypto 2021, pp. 399– 418. Springer, Cham (2021). https://doi.org/10.1007/978-3-030-81293-5_21
10. Canetti, R., Goldreich, O., Halevi, S.: The random oracle methodology, revisited. J. ACM (JACM) **51**(4), 557–594 (2004)
11. Chow, S.S.M., Franklin, M.K., Zhang, H.: Practical dual-receiver encryption - soundness, complete non-malleability, and applications. In: Benaloh, J. (eds.) Topics in Cryptology – CT-RSA 2014. LNCS, vol. 8366, pp. 85–105. Springer, Heidelberg (2014). https://doi.org/10.1007/978-3-319-04852-9_5
12. Damgård, I., Hofheinz, D., Kiltz, E., Thorbek, R.: Public-key encryption with non-interactive opening. In: Malkin, T. (ed.) Topics in Cryptology – CT-RSA 2008. LNCS, vol. 4964, pp. 239–255. Springer, Heidelberg (2008). https://doi.org/10.1007/978-3-540-79263-5_15
13. Dodis, Y., Katz, J., Smith, A., Walfish, S.: Composability and on-line deniability of authentication. In: Reingold, O. (ed.) TCC 2009: 6th Theory of Cryptography Conference. LNCS, vol. 5444, pp. 146–162. Springer, Heidelberg (2009). https://doi.org/10.1007/978-3-642-00457-5_10
14. Fiat, A., Naor, M.: Broadcast encryption. In: Stinson, D.R. (ed.) Advances in Cryptology – CRYPTO'93. LNCS, vol. 773, pp. 480–491. Springer, Heidelberg (1994). https://doi.org/10.1007/3-540-48329-2_40
15. Fiat, A., Shamir, A.: How to prove yourself: practical solutions to identification and signature problems. In: Odlyzko, A.M. (ed.) Advances in Cryptology – CRYPTO'86, volume 263 of Lecture Notes in Computer Science, Santa Barbara, CA, USA, pp. 186–194. Springer Berlin Heidelberg, Germany (1987). https://doi.org/10.1007/3-540-47721-7_12
16. Fujisaki, E., Okamoto, T.: Secure integration of asymmetric and symmetric encryption schemes. In: Wiener, M. (ed.) CRYPTO 1999. LNCS, vol. 1666, pp. 537–554. Springer, Heidelberg (1999). https://doi.org/10.1007/3-540-48405-1_34
17. Genise, N., Micciancio, D., Peikert, C., Walter, M.: Improved discrete Gaussian and Subgaussian analysis for lattice cryptography. In: Kiayias, A., Kohlweiss, M., Wallden, P., Zikas, V. (eds.) PKC 2020: 23rd International Conference on Theory and Practice of Public Key Cryptography, Part I. LNCS, vol. 12110, pp. 623–651. Springer, Heidelberg (2020). https://doi.org/10.1007/978-3-030-45374-9_21
18. Hsieh, Y.-C., Waters, B., Wu, D.J.: A generic approach to adaptively-secure broadcast encryption in the plain model. In: Fehr, S., Fouque, P.-A. (eds.) Advances in Cryptology – EUROCRYPT 2025, Part III. LNCS, vol. 15603, pp. 336–365. Springer, Heidelberg (2025). https://doi.org/10.1007/978-3-031-91131-6_12
19. Khovratovich, D., Rothblum, R.D., Soukhanov, L.: How to prove false statements: practical attacks on fiat-Shamir. In: Kalai, Y.T., Kamara, S.F. (eds.) Advances in Cryptology – CRYPTO 2025, Part VI. LNCS, vol. 16005, pp. 3–26. Springer, Heidelberg (2025). https://doi.org/10.1007/978-3-032-01887-8_1

20. Kiltz, E., Masny, D., Pietrzak, K.: Simple chosen-ciphertext security from low-noise LPN. In: Krawczyk, H. (ed.) PKC 2014: 17th International Conference on Theory and Practice of Public Key Cryptography. LNCS, vol. 8383, pp. 1–18. Springer, Heidelberg (2014). https://doi.org/10.1007/978-3-642-54631-0_1
21. Lai, R.W., Cheung, H.K., Chow, S.S.: Trapdoors for ideal lattices with applications. In: Information Security and Cryptology, pp. 239–256. Springer International Publishing, Cham (2014)
22. Lyubashevsky, V., Peikert, C., Regev, O.: A toolkit for Ring-LWE cryptography. In: Johansson, T., Nguyen, P.Q. (eds.) Advances in Cryptology – EUROCRYPT 2013. LNCS, vol. 7881, pp. 35–54. Springer, Heidelberg (2013). https://doi.org/10.1007/978-3-642-38348-9_3
23. MATZOV. Report on the security of LWE: improved dual lattice attack (2022). https://zenodo.org/records/6412487. Accessed 24 Aug 2024
24. Micciancio, D., Peikert, C.: Trapdoors for lattices: simpler, tighter, faster, smaller. In: Pointcheval, D., Johansson, T. (eds.) Advances in Cryptology – EUROCRYPT 2012. LNCS, vol. 7237, pp. 700–718. Springer, Heidelberg (2012). https://doi.org/10.1007/978-3-642-29011-4_41
25. Micciancio, D., Regev, O.: Worst-case to average-case reductions based on gaussian measures. SIAM J. Comput. **37**(1), 267–302 (2007). https://doi.org/10.1137/S0097539705447360
26. Noh, G., Hong, D., Kwon, J.O., Jeong, I.R.: A strong binding encryption scheme from lattices for secret broadcast. IEEE Commun. Lett. **16**(6), 781–784 (2012)
27. N.I. of Standards and Technology: Module-Lattice-Based Key-Encapsulation Mechanism Standard. Federal Information Processing Standards Publication (2024). https://doi.org/10.6028/NIST.FIPS.203
28. Unger, N., Goldberg, I.: Improved strongly deniable authenticated key exchanges for secure messaging. Proc. Priv. Enhancing Technol. **2018**(1), 21–66 (2018). https://doi.org/10.1515/popets-2018-0003
29. Xu, S., Li, X.: Chosen-ciphertext secure key encapsulation mechanism in the standard model. IEEE Access **9**, 13683–13690 (2021). https://doi.org/10.1109/ACCESS.2021.3051047
30. Yang, X., Ma, W., Zhang, C.: Efficient chosen ciphertext secure key encapsulation mechanism in standard model over ideal lattices. Int. J. Comput. Math. **94**(5), 866–883 (2017). https://doi.org/10.1080/00207160.2016.1149578
31. Zhang, J., Yu, Yu., Fan, S., Zhang, Z.: Improved lattice-based CCA2-secure PKE in the standard model. Sci. China Inf. Sci. **63**(8), 1–22 (2020). https://doi.org/10.1007/s11432-019-9861-3

Improved Reduction from RLWE to MP-LWE

Rahinatou Yuh Njah Epouse Nchiwo[1] and Alice Pellet-Mary[2](✉)

[1] Aalto University, Espoo, Finland
rahinatou.njahepousenchiwo@aalto.fi
[2] Univ Bordeaux, CNRS, Inria, Bordeaux INP, IMB, UMR 5251, Talence, France
alice.pellet-mary@math.u-bordeaux.fr

Abstract. The Middle Product Learning With Errors (MP-LWE) problem was introduced in 2017 by Rosca, Sakzad, Steinfeld, and Stehlé (Crypto 2017). In their work and in a follow up work by Rosca, Stehlé, and Wallet (Eurocrypt 2018), the authors proved that MP-LWE is at least as hard as the Ring LWE problem over the field $\mathbb{Q}[x]/f(x)$, for an exponentially large class of polynomials f (with fixed degree and bounded coefficients). A few years later, Peikert and Pepin gave a new reduction from Ring LWE to MP-LWE (Journal of Cryptology 2024). This new reduction improved the results of Rosca et al. by increasing the set of polynomials f for which the reduction holds. However, even though the sets of polynomials covered by both reductions have exponential size, they remain negligible among the set of all polynomials of fixed degree and bounded coefficients.

In this work, we provide a refined analysis of the reduction of Rosca et al. Our new analysis shows that the reduction of Rosca et al. actually covers a much larger class of polynomials than what was known before, containing (experimentally) at least 90% of all polynomials of fixed degree and bounded coefficients.

1 Introduction

Structured lattices have been widely used over the past decade to construct efficient post-quantum cryptographic primitives. Among the structured lattice assumptions frequently used, one can cite for instance the Ring/Module Learning With Errors (LWE) problem [SSTX09,LPR10,BGV14,LS15], the Ring/Module Short Integer Solution (SIS) problem [LM06,PR06,LS15], or the NTRU problem [HPS06]. These examples, which cover most of the structured lattice-based constructions, all rely on the choice of some irreducible polynomial f, defining a number field $K = \mathbb{Q}[x]/f(x)$ (the structured lattices considered are then modules of this number field). This means that there exists as many Ring LWE (/Module LWE / Ring SIS / Module SIS / NTRU) problems as there are irreducible

S. Bai and E. Persichetti (Eds.): PKC 2026, LNCS 16551, pp. 167–196, 2026.
https://doi.org/10.1007/978-3-032-26731-3_6

polynomials / number fields.[1] A natural question is then to relate the hardness of the Ring LWE problem for a polynomial f_1 with the hardness of the Ring LWE problem for another polynomial f_2: are there weak polynomials (leading to easy Ring LWE problems)? Or stronger polynomials? This question is still open, and we know very little about it.

A first step towards understanding the hardness of a structured lattice problem for multiple choices of polynomials was achieved by Lyubashevsky in 2016 [Lyu16]. In his work, the author introduced the $R^{<n}$-SIS problem, which is a structured lattice problem (hence enabling the construction of asymptotically fast and compact primitives) and is at least as hard as the Polynomial-SIS_f problem[2] for an *exponentially large* family of polynomials f. It is important to note that the $R^{<n}$-SIS problem does not depend on the choice of a polynomial: it is a single problem, and not a family of problems like the Polynomial-SIS_f problems. The reduction hence shows that if an attacker can solve the $R^{<n}$-SIS problem, then they can solve many Polynomial-SIS_f problems, for exponentially many polynomials f. While this does not answer the mathematical question of comparing the hardness of Polynomial-SIS for different polynomials, this gives a pretty nice answer to the cryptographic preoccupation of finding a structured lattice problem with strong security guarantees.

The result of Lyubashevsky was later adapted to LWE by Rosca at al. in 2017 [RSSS17]. In their article, the authors introduced the so-called Middle-Product Learning With Errors problem (MP-LWE). This is a structured variant of LWE, which the authors used to construct an asymptotically efficient and compact public key encryption scheme. In terms of security, the authors proved that an efficient attacker against the MP-LWE problem could be used to construct efficient attackers against the Polynomial LWE_f problem for an exponentially large family of polynomials f. Let us emphasize that the MP-LWE problem (like the $R^{<n}$-SIS problem) does not rely on the choice of a polynomial f. Hence, we obtain a *single* problem, which is hard as long as *at least one* of the Polynomial-LWE_f problem is hard for a polynomial f covered by the reduction. A year later, Rosca, Stehlé and Wallet proved that the Ring LWE_f and the Polynomial LWE_f problems are equivalent for an exponentially large class of polynomials f [RSW18]. Combining these two results provides a proof that the MP-LWE problem is at least as hard as the Ring LWE_f problem for an exponentially large set of polynomials. The point of combining the two reductions was to base the hardness of the MP-LWE problem on the hardness of the Ring LWE problem, which is better understood than that of the Polynomial LWE problem.

Since its introduction in 2017, the MP-LWE problem has been used to construct multiple cryptographic constructions [Hir18, BDH+20, LVV19, LDSP20, FLA23, DAZ19, LSW+23, YYZW22], it has led to a submission to the

[1] Multiple irreducible polynomials may define the same number fields (up to isomorphism). Depending on the structured problem considered, the problem may depend on the choice of the polynomial or only on the choice of the number field. For simplicity in this introduction, we ignore the discrepancy between number fields and defining polynomials.

[2] This problem can be considered as a variant of the Ring-SIS_f problem.

NIST [SSZ19,SSZ17], and a deterministic variant of the problem (similar to the learning with rounding problem) has been proposed [BBD+19]. On the security side, a new reduction from Ring LWE to MP-LWE was described by Peikert and Pepin in [PP24]. This new reduction allows to prove the hardness of the MP-LWE problem from the hardness of Ring LWE_f for an even larger class of polynomials as what was proven in [RSSS17,RSW18]. Even though the class of polynomials covered by the reductions from [RSSS17,RSW18] and [PP24] are both exponentially large, they cover only a negligible proportion of the set of all polynomials with fixed degree and bounded coefficients. More precisely, both classes require the polynomials f to have a fixed degree m, their coefficients bounded by some quantity B (polynomial in m) *and* they require that a constant fraction cm of the coefficients of the polynomials are equal to 0 (for some contant $c > 0$). These sets of polynomials hence only cover a negligible fraction of the set of all polynomials of degree m and coefficients bounded by B (they cover at most B^{-cm} of it, which tends to 0 exponentially quickly when m tends to infinity). The main question that motivated our work is then the following: can we prove the hardness of MP-LWE from the hardness of Ring LWE_f over a significantly larger set of polynomials? Ideally, we would like to obtain a reduction covering the set of all irreducible polynomials of degree m and coefficients polynomially bounded.

Our Contributions. In this work, we prove hardness of the MP-LWE problem from the hardness of the Ring LWE_f problem for a family of polynomials f which experimentally covers at least 90% of all irreducible polynomials of degree m with coefficients bounded by some $B = \text{poly}(m)$. More precisely, we introduce some quantity $D(f)$, which depends on the polynomial f (the exact definition of $D(f)$ is given in Definition 4.2 but is not needed for this introduction). We computed this quantity $D(f)$ experimentally on many random polynomials, for varying degrees m and coefficients bound B, and we observed that at least 90% of the random polynomials we generated satisfy $D(f) \leq m$. On the other hand, we also proved the following theorem.

Theorem 1.1 (Informal, see Corollary 5.5**).** *If* $B = \text{poly}(m)$, *then* MP-LWE *is at least as hard as Ring* LWE_f *for any irreducible monic polynomial* f *of degree* m, *coefficients bounded by* B, *and satisfying* $D(f) \leq m$.

This theorem, combined with our experimental results on $D(f)$, provides a very large family of Ring LWE_f problems that can serve as foundation for the security of MP-LWE.

A natural question arising then is the following: maybe $D(f) \leq m$ for *all* polynomials f, and not just for $\geq 90\%$ of them? We answer this question by the negative: we exhibit two families of polynomials (the Bugeaud-Mignotte polynomials [BM04,BM10] and the shifted cyclotomic polynomials) for which $D(f)$ grows exponentially with the degree m of f. Hence, Theorem 1.1 does not cover all irreducible polynomials of degree m with polynomially bounded coefficients. These counter-examples also explain why we did not manage to prove a polynomial upper bound on $D(f)$ for all polynomials f.

Technical Details. To obtain our result, we follow the reduction from Ring LWE_f to MP-LWE from [RSSS17,RSW18], but we provide a tighter analysis for the last steps of the reduction. More precisely, the reduction from [RSSS17,RSW18] is obtained with multiple steps, going via some intermediate algorithmic problems. The intermediate steps of the reduction are depicted in Fig. 1. The precise definition of the different algorithmic problems appearing on the figure is not needed for this introduction. The important observation is that all these algorithmic problems are parameterized by some parameter $\alpha \geq 0$, which measure the noise rate. For $\alpha = 0$, there is no noise and the problems are easy to solve. On the other hand, for $\alpha \geq 1$, the problems are provably intractable. Each reduction in the chain from (dual) Ring LWE to MP-LWE increases the noise rate α. In order to have a meaningful reduction, we must ensure that this increase is not too large, otherwise we would end up reducing to an untractable problem.

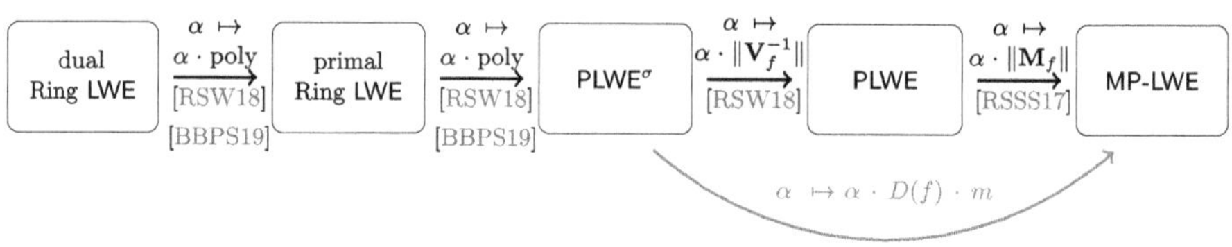

Fig. 1. Known reductions from (dual) Ring LWE to MP-LWE are shown in black. Our improved analysis is shown in red. The two reductions on the left assume that $B = \mathrm{poly}(\deg(f))$ (where B is a bound on the coefficients of f). (Color figure online)

Let us analyze the successive steps of this reduction in more details. If $B = \mathrm{poly}(m)$, the first two steps only increase the noise rate by a polynomial factor, which is considered to be fine (in full generality, the increase is of the order of $\mathrm{poly}(m, B)$). We note that the original results from [RSW18] did not allow to prove a polynomial noise rate increase for these two reductions, but combining their reduction with a more recent result from [BBPS19] now allows us to prove it.

The costly steps are the last two steps, which increase the noise rate respectively by the norm of the inverse Vandermonde matrix associated to f (denoted by $\mathbf{V}_f^{-1}$) and the norm of a matrix $\mathbf{M}_f$ associated to f (the authors proved in [RSSS17] that $\|\mathbf{M}_f\| \leq m \cdot \mathrm{EF}(f)$, where $\mathrm{EF}(f)$ is the so-called expansion factor of f). These two quantities are usually very large when f is chosen randomly. Our central observation, which led to our improved analysis, is as follows. The large increase of the noise rate in each of the last two steps of the reduction is due to a distortion of the error of the LWE samples, which can be very large in some directions of the space. However, this distortion is usually very skewed: some directions are expanded while others are contracted. The works of [RSSS17] and [RSW18] analyzed the two distortions independently, hence they had to provide for each of them an upper bound that was larger than the "maximum" of each distortion. However, when analyzing the two distortion together, we noticed that they actually compensate one another. This is depicted in Fig. 2 below. Said differently, if we analyze the two steps of the reduction at the same time (going directly from PLWE^σ to $\mathsf{MP\text{-}LWE}$), then the distortion applied to the errors can be bounded by a significantly smaller upper bound. This is what we do in our refined analysis: we prove that the total distortion between PLWE^σ and $\mathsf{MP\text{-}LWE}$ is upper bounded by some quantity which we call $D(f)$. At a high level, this quantity $D(f)$ is approximately equal to $\|\mathbf{V}_f^{-1}\mathbf{M}_f\|$. By comparison, combining the two analyses from [RSSS17] and [RSW18] would give an upper bound $\|\mathbf{V}_f^{-1}\| \cdot \|\mathbf{M}_f\|$ on the noise growth. Since the spectral norm of matrices is sub-multiplicative, the bound on the noise growth obtained by our analysis is always at least as good as the one obtained by combining [RSSS17, RSW18].

Combining this new analysis with the known reduction from (dual) Ring LWE to PLWE^σ from [RSW18] (and using the more recent improvements from [BBPS19]), we obtain Theorem 1.1.

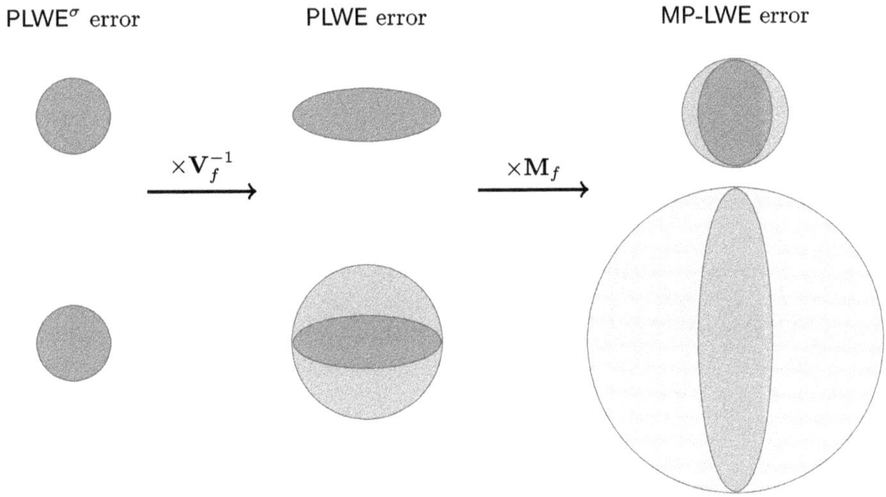

Fig. 2. The figure illustrates how the two distortions compensate one another. On the first line, we over-estimate the skewed error by a spherical error only after performing the two distortions (the over-estimated spherical error is shown in lighter blue on the right part of the picture). On the second line, we overestimate the skewed errors by a spherical error after each distortion, which leads to a larger over-estimation after the two distortions (each over-estimated error is shown in lighter blue compared to the previous one). (Color figure online)

It then only remains to analyze the quantity $D(f)$. Unfortunately, we were not able to prove that this quantity remains small for all polynomials f. As a matter of fact, we were even able to exhibit two families of polynomials for which we proved that $D(f)$ grows exponentially with the degree of the polynomial (the first family is the so-called Bugeaud-Mignotte polynomials [BM04, BM10], and the second family consists of shifted cyclotomic polynomials).[3] On the positive side, we experimentally observed that the quantity $D(f)$ seems small for almost all random polynomials: the Bugeaud-Mignotte polynomials and the shifted cyclotomic polynomials are rare exceptions. The experiments seem to indicate that $D(f)$ remains (on average) constant when the size of the polynomial's coefficient increase, and grows at most linearly with the degree when it tends to infinity.[4]

Comparison with Previous Works. As explained above, our new analysis refines the one of [RSSS17,RSW18], by reducing the bound on the noise growth of the critical steps. As a result, our analysis is always at least as good as theirs, meaning that the set of polynomials covered by our analysis contains the set of polynomials covered by their analysis.

The comparison with the reduction from [PP24] is a bit more subtle. The techniques used in the [PP24] reduction are significantly different from the ones used in the reduction from [RSSS17,RSW18], and we do not know whether they can be unified. Our improved analysis relies on techniques used in the reduction from [RSSS17,RSW18] and it does not seem that similar ideas would improve the analysis of the reduction from [PP24].

Regarding the sets of polynomials covered by both reductions, it was previously thought that the reduction from [PP24] covered more polynomials than the one from [RSSS17,RSW18]. Our new analysis shows that this is actually not the case: the set of polynomials covered by the reduction from [RSSS17,RSW18] (with our analysis) is much larger in size than the set of polynomials covered by the reduction from [PP24]. However, it is important to note that our set of polynomials does not contain all the polynomials covered by the [PP24] reduction. Indeed, the Bugeaud-Mignotte polynomials that are not covered by our analysis were covered by the reduction from [PP24]. A more detailed comparison between the two works is provided in Sect. 6.

Open Problems. As explained above, our new analysis of the reduction covers most polynomials, but not all polynomials. An interesting question would be to see if we can have a reduction from Ring LWE_f to MP-LWE for all polynomials.[5]

Another open question we identified would be to obtain a reduction from Ring LWE to MP-LWE subsuming both reductions from [RSSS17,RSW18] and

[3] The Bugeaud-Mignotte polynomials were already used in [RSW18] as examples of polynomials for which the norm of the inverse Vandermonde $\|\mathbf{V}_f^{-1}\|$ grows exponentially fast. Therefore, these polynomials are not covered by our improved analysis, nor by the previous analysis of [RSSS17,RSW18].

[4] The code we used to obtain all the experimental results displayed in this article is available at https://plmlab.math.cnrs.fr/apelletm/code-mplwe.

[5] Here, it might be interesting to remember that the Ring LWE problem depends on the choice of a number field, rather than the choice of a polynomial. If, for each number field, we can find a defining polynomial that is covered by our reduction, then this would be sufficient to obtain a reduction from all possible Ring LWE problems to MP-LWE.

from [PP24]. Indeed, as explained above, both reductions use significantly different approaches, and achieve non-comparable results. Being able to unify the two reductions could be a first step towards obtaining a reduction that works for all polynomials.

2 Preliminaries

For completeness and notation purposes, we begin by recalling the definition of some mathematical structures needed in the definition of RLWE, PLWE and MP-LWE and, moreover, relevant in the proof of our main theorem. Some additional preliminaries on lattices, which are not needed in the core of the article, are available in the full version [NP26].

Probability and Gaussian Distributions. If D is a probability distribution, we will use the notation $x \leftarrow D$ to indicate that x is sampled from the distribution D, and $x \sim D$ to indicate that x is a random variable whose probability distribution is equal to D.

For $H \subseteq \mathbb{R}^m$ or $H \subseteq \mathbb{C}^m$ a real vector space, we denote by $\mathcal{N}_{H,\mathbf{\Sigma}}$, a continuous Gaussian distribution of covariance matrix $\mathbf{\Sigma}$ (which should be symmetric definite positive), for the norm induced by the ℓ_2 norm over $\mathbb{R}^m$ or $\mathbb{C}^m$. If $\mathbf{\Sigma} = \sigma^2 \cdot I_n$ for some $n > 0$ and $\sigma > 0$, then we will abuse notations and simply write $\mathcal{N}_{H,\sigma}$ instead of $\mathcal{N}_{H,\sigma^2 I_n}$. We will use the following property about distortion of multivariate Gaussian distributions. A proof of this result can be found in [Tab21].

Lemma 2.1. *Let $m \geq d$ be integers and $\mathbf{\Sigma} \in \mathbb{R}^{m\times m}$ be symmetric definite positive. Let $\mathbf{M} \in \mathbb{R}^{d\times m}$ be of rank d. Then $\mathbf{\Sigma}' := \mathbf{M}\mathbf{\Sigma}\mathbf{M}^T \in \mathbb{R}^{d\times d}$ is symmetric definite positive, and if $X \sim \mathcal{N}_{\mathbb{R}^m,\mathbf{\Sigma}}$, then $\mathbf{M}X \sim \mathcal{N}_{\mathbb{R}^d,\mathbf{\Sigma}'}$.*

Structured Matrices. We recall the definitions of some structured matrices that are useful in the upcoming sections.

Definition 2.2 (Rot matrix). *For a polynomial of degree m and $a \in \mathbb{Z}[x]$, we define the $Rot_f^d(a) \in \mathbb{R}^{d\times m}$ for any $d > 0$ to be the matrix whose ith row is the coefficient of the polynomial $(x^{i-1}a) \mod f$, $i \in [1, \ldots, d]$. When $m = d$, we simply write $Rot_f(a)$.*

Definition 2.3 (Hankel matrix). *The Hankel matrix $\mathbf{M}_f \in \mathbb{R}^{m\times m}$ is defined as the matrix whose entries $(\mathbf{M}_f)_{i,j}$, are given by the constant coefficient of the polynomial $x^{i+j-2} \mod f$, for any $i, j \in [1, \ldots, m]$.*

Given a ring R and $k > 0$, we denote by $R^{<k}[x]$ the set of polynomials in $R[x]$ with degree $< k$. The lemma below allows us to express the Hankel matrix using the Rotational matrix.

Lemma 2.4 ([RSSS17, **Lemma** 2.4]). *For any $a \in R^{<m}[x]$ and $\mathbf{a} = (a_0, \ldots, a_{m-1})^T$ its coefficient vector, we have $\mathbf{M}_f\mathbf{a} = Rot_f(a) \cdot (1, 0, \ldots, 0)^T$.*

The *spectral norm* of a matrix $\mathbf{A} \in \mathbb{C}^{m \times n}$, denoted $|||\mathbf{A}|||$, is the largest singular value of $\mathbf{A}$. Explicitly,

$$|||\mathbf{A}||| = \sqrt{\lambda_{\max}(\mathbf{A}^*\mathbf{A})} = \sigma_{\max(\mathbf{A})}$$

where $\mathbf{A}^*$ is the conjugate transpose of $\mathbf{A}$. The Frobenius norm of the same matrix $\mathbf{A}$ is defined as $\|\mathbf{A}\|_F = \sqrt{\sum_i^m \sum_i^n |\mathbf{A}_{i,j}|^2}$. The Frobenius and spectral norms are related via the following inequalities

$$|||\mathbf{A}||| \leq \|\mathbf{A}\|_F \leq \sqrt{\mathrm{rk}(\mathbf{A})} \cdot |||\mathbf{A}|||. \tag{1}$$

Interpolation Polynomials. We will use Lagrange interpolation polynomials, and some property about their constant coefficient.

Definition 2.5 (Lagrange polynomials). *Let $\alpha_1, \ldots, \alpha_m$ be distinct complex numbers. For any $1 \leq i \leq m$, we denote by L_i the following Lagrange basis polynomial (associated to the α_j's)*

$$L_i = \prod_{j \neq i} \frac{x - \alpha_j}{\alpha_i - \alpha_j}$$

that satisfies $L_i(\alpha_i) = 1$ and $L_i(\alpha_j) = 0$ if $j \neq i$.

Lemma 2.6. *Let $f \in \mathbb{Z}[x]$ be a monic irreducible polynomial of degree m and $\alpha_1, \ldots, \alpha_m$ be its complex roots. Let L_i be a Lagrange basis polynomial associated to the α_j's, (see Definition 2.5). Then the constant coefficient of L_i is*

$$L_i(0) = \frac{-f_0}{\alpha_i \cdot f'(\alpha_i)},$$

where f_0 is the constant coefficient of f.

Proof. Note first that since f is irreducible, then its roots α_j's are all distinct, and so the Lagrange polynomial L_i is well-defined. Note also that the irreducibility of f implies that $f_0 \neq 0$ and that all the roots α_j's are non zero. By definition of L_i, we have that

$$L_i(0) = (-1)^{m-1} \cdot \prod_{j \neq i} \frac{\alpha_j}{\alpha_i - \alpha_j}.$$

Now, since f is monic and has complex roots $\alpha_1, \ldots, \alpha_m$, then $f = \prod_{j=1}^m (x - \alpha_j)$. In particular, it holds that $\prod_{j=1}^m \alpha_j = (-1)^m \cdot f_0$, which implies that $\prod_{j \neq i} \alpha_j = (-1)^m \cdot f_0 \alpha_i^{-1}$ (recall that $\alpha_i \neq 0$). We also have, for all k, $f'(\alpha_k) = \prod_{j \neq k}(\alpha_k - \alpha_j)$. Plugging this in the equation above leads the desired formula $L_i(0) = -\frac{f_0}{\alpha_i \cdot f'(\alpha_i)}$. □

Number Fields. For a field K, with $\mathbb{Q} \subset K$, we say that K is a field extension of $\mathbb{Q}$ denoted $K/\mathbb{Q}$. The field K can be seen as a vector space over $\mathbb{Q}$. The degree of this field extension is the dimension of K as a vector space of $\mathbb{Q}$. If this extension is finite, it is called a *number field.* In this article, K will always refer to a number field of finite degree m. A number field K of degree m can always be expressed as the quotient ring $\mathbb{Q}[x]/(f(x))$ for some monic irreducible polynomial $f(x) \in \mathbb{Z}[x]$ of degree m (which is called a defining polynomial of K). We denote by Δ_K the (absolute value of the) discriminant of the field K. We will denote $K_{\mathbb{R}} = K \otimes_{\mathbb{Q}} \mathbb{R} \simeq \mathbb{R}[x]/f(x)$ (where f is a defining polynomial of K), which is a ring and an $\mathbb{R}$-vector space, but not a field (unless f has degree 1 or 2 and is irreducible in $\mathbb{R}[x]$).

An element $\alpha \in K$ is called an algebraic integer if it is the root of a nonzero monic polynomial with integer coefficients. The set of all algebraic integers in a number field K forms a ring structure called the *ring of integers* which is denoted $\mathcal{O}_K$. If $\mathcal{O}_K = \mathbb{Z}[\alpha]$, we say that the field K is *monogenic.* A subring $\mathcal{O} \subset \mathcal{O}_K$ is an *order* of K if it is a $\mathbb{Z}$-module with finite rank m.

Embeddings. An embedding of a number field K to the complex field $\mathbb{C}$, is an homomorphism of fields $\sigma : K \to \mathbb{C}$. If $\sigma(K) \subseteq \mathbb{R}$, we say σ is a real embedding. It is a complex embedding if $\sigma(K) \nsubseteq \mathbb{R}$, which comes in conjugate pairs. A field K of degree m admits m distinct embeddings from K to $\mathbb{C}$, which we will denote $\sigma_1, \ldots, \sigma_m$. We denote by $\tau(\cdot)$ the *canonical embedding* which maps the number field into $\mathbb{C}^m$ as:

$$\begin{aligned} \tau : K &\to \mathbb{C}^m \\ \alpha &\mapsto \sigma_1(\alpha), \ldots, \sigma_m(\alpha) \end{aligned}$$

Also, we denote $T_f(\cdot)$ as the *coefficient embedding* which maps an element of a number field $K = \mathbb{Q}[x]/(f(x))$ to its coefficient vector with respect to the $\mathbb{Q}$-basis $(1, x, \ldots, x^{m-1})$:

$$\begin{aligned} T_f : K &\longrightarrow \mathbb{Q}^m, \\ \sum_{i=0}^{m-1} a_i x^i &\mapsto (a_0, \ldots, a_{m-1}). \end{aligned}$$

The coefficient embedding can be defined for any number field K, using the isomorphism $K \simeq \mathbb{Q}[x]/f(x)$ for some defining polynomial f. Note however that it will depend on the choice of a defining polynomial f, as well as the choice of an isomorphism between K and $\mathbb{Q}[x]/f(x)$.

Definition 2.7 (Vandermonde matrix). *The Vandermonde matrix of the complex roots $\alpha_1, \alpha_2, \ldots, \alpha_n \in \mathbb{C}$ of the polynomial f, is defined as*

$$\mathbf{V}_f = \begin{bmatrix} 1 & \alpha_1 & \cdots & \alpha_1^{n-1} \\ 1 & \alpha_2 & \cdots & \alpha_2^{n-1} \\ \vdots & \vdots & \ddots & \vdots \\ 1 & \alpha_n & \cdots & \alpha_n^{n-1} \end{bmatrix}$$

Remark 2.8. We can move from one embedding to another through the Vandermonde matrix by the relation

$$\tau(x) = \mathbf{V}_f T_f(x).$$

Ideals. An integral ideal of K is a subset $I \subseteq \mathcal{O}_K$ which is stable by addition and multiplication by elements of $\mathcal{O}_K$. A fractional ideal of K is a subset $J \subset K$ of the form $J = xI$ for some integral ideal I and $x \in \mathbb{Q}$. The algebraic norm of a non-zero integral ideal is $\mathcal{N}(I) := [\mathcal{O}_K : I]$, which is the cardinality of the (finite) set $\mathcal{O}_K/I$. And the algebraic norm of a fractional ideal $J = xI$ is defined as $\mathcal{N}(xI) = x^m \mathcal{N}(I)$. In this article, we will be interested by two particular ideals: the conductor ideal and the different ideal.

Let $\mathcal{O}$ be an order of K (in this work, we will always consider $\mathcal{O} = \mathbb{Z}[x]/f(x)$). The conductor of the order $\mathcal{O}$ is defined by $\mathcal{C}_{\mathcal{O}} := \{x \in K : x\mathcal{O}_K \subseteq \mathcal{O}\}$. This is an integral ideal of K. For a monic irreducible polynomial $f \in \mathbb{Z}[x]$ of degree m, we denote by Δ_f the absolute value of the discriminant of f, i.e., $\Delta_f = |\mathrm{Res}(f, f')| = \prod_{i \neq j}(\alpha_i - \alpha_j) \in \mathbb{Z}$ where $\alpha_1, \ldots, \alpha_m$ are the complex roots of f. If $K = \mathbb{Q}[x]/f(x)$ is the number field defined by f, the discriminant of f is simply $\Delta_f = \mathcal{N}(f'(x))$, where $\mathcal{N}$ is the algebraic norm over K. This quantity is related to the norm of the conductor ideal of the order $\mathbb{Z}[x]/f(x)$ via the following equation (see, e.g., [Sut16, Th. 12.22])

$$\Delta_f = \mathcal{N}(\mathcal{C}_{\mathbb{Z}[x]/f(x)})\Delta_K.$$

From the definition of Δ_f as the resultant of f and f', we can see that $\Delta_f \leq \|f\|^{m-1} \cdot \|f'\|^m \leq m^m \cdot \|f\|^{2m-1}$, where $\|f\|$ refers to the Euclidean norm of the vector of coefficients of f.

The different ideal of the number field K is another ideal that we will consider in this work. We denote it by $(\mathcal{O}_K^\vee)^{-1}$. We will not need to know the precise definition of this ideal, but simply that it is an integral ideal of K whose algebraic norm is equal to the discriminant of the field K, i.e., $\mathcal{N}((\mathcal{O}_K^\vee)^{-1}) = \Delta_K$ (see, e.g., [Con09, Theorem 4.8]).

Finally, we will use in Sect. 5.1 the following result which states that, in any fractional ideal I and for any prime integer $q \in \mathbb{Z}$ sufficiently large, there exists a small element t in I with tI^{-1} coprime to $q\mathcal{O}_K$ and where t is almost as short as the shortest non-zero element of I. In Sects. 5.1 and 5.2 we will use this lemma with the conductor ideal and the different ideal respectively. Historically, a similar result was first proven in [RSW18, Th. 3.1], but with a larger upper bound on t, which depended on q. An improved version was then proven [BBPS19, Lemma 2.36], which removed the dependency in q. The version we recall below is a slight adaptation from the one of [BBPS19] (where we made the constant explicit and changed the infinity norm for the Euclidean norm). A proof is available in the full version [NP26] for completeness.

Lemma 2.9. *Let K be a number field of degree m, and let $\mathcal{O}_K$ be its ring of integers. Let $q \geq 8m$ be a prime integer and let I be any fractional ideal of K.*

Then there exists a non-zero element $t \in I$ with tI^{-1} coprime to $q\mathcal{O}_K$ satisfying

$$\|\tau(t)\| \leq 8m^2 \cdot \Delta_K^{2/m} \cdot \mathcal{N}(I)^{1/m}.$$

Variants of LWE. In this work, we will consider multiple structured variants of LWE, which we define now. We start by defining the primal and dual RLWE problems.

Definition 2.10 (primal-RLWE/dual-RLWE). *Let $f \in \mathbb{Z}[x]$ be a degree m irreducible monic polynomial and $K = \mathbb{Q}[x]/f(x)$. Let $q \geq 2$ be an integer and χ be a probability distribution on $\tau(K_{\mathbb{R}}) \subset \mathbb{C}^m$.*

Let $s \in \mathcal{O}_K/q\mathcal{O}_K$ (resp. $s \in \mathcal{O}_K^\vee/q\mathcal{O}_K^\vee$). The primal-$\mathsf{RLWE}_{f,q,\chi}$ distribution (resp. dual-$\mathsf{RLWE}_{f,q,\chi}$ distribution) with parameters f, q and χ, denoted by $A_{f,q,\chi,s}$ (resp. $A^\vee_{f,q,\chi,s}$) is the distribution obtained by sampling $a \leftarrow \mathcal{U}(\mathcal{O}_K/q\mathcal{O}_K)$ and $e \in K_{\mathbb{R}}$ such that $\tau(e) \sim \chi$ and outputting $(a,b) \in \mathcal{O}_K/q\mathcal{O}_K \times K_{\mathbb{R}}/q\mathcal{O}_K$ (resp. $(a,b) \in \mathcal{O}_K/q\mathcal{O}_K \times K_{\mathbb{R}}/q\mathcal{O}_K^\vee$) where $b = as + e \bmod q$.

The decision primal-$\mathsf{RLWE}_{f,q,\chi}$ (resp. decision dual-$\mathsf{RLWE}_{f,q,\chi}$) problem with parameters f, q and χ consists in distinguishing between a sampler from $A_{f,q,\chi,s}$ (resp. $A^\vee_{f,q,\chi,s}$) and a uniform sampler over $\mathcal{O}_K/q\mathcal{O}_K \times K_{\mathbb{R}}/q\mathcal{O}_K$ (resp. $\mathcal{O}_K/q\mathcal{O}_K \times K_{\mathbb{R}}/q\mathcal{O}_K^\vee$), with non-negligible probability over the random choice of $s \leftarrow \mathcal{U}(\mathcal{O}_K/q\mathcal{O}_K)$ (resp. $s \leftarrow \mathcal{U}(\mathcal{O}_K^\vee/q\mathcal{O}_K^\vee)$).

When $\chi = \mathcal{N}_{\tau(K_{\mathbb{R}}),\alpha q}$ is a Gaussian distribution over $\tau(K_{\mathbb{R}})$ with parameter αq for some $\alpha \in (0,1)$, we will simplify the notations and replace the subscript χ by the subscript α in the notations above (i.e., we will write $\mathsf{RLWE}_{f,q,\alpha}$ instead of $\mathsf{RLWE}_{f,q,\chi}$).

We now define the PLWE problem and its variant PLWE^σ which was defined in [RSW18, Definition 4.1]. The two definitions differ only in the choice of the embedding (τ vs T_f) used to define the error distribution.

Definition 2.11 (PLWE/PLWE$^\sigma$)**.** *Let $f \in \mathbb{Z}[x]$ be a degree m irreducible monic polynomial. Define $\mathcal{O} = \mathbb{Z}[x]/f(x)$ and $K = \mathbb{Q}[x]/f(x)$. Let $q \geq 2$ be an integer, and χ be a probability distribution over $T_f(K_{\mathbb{R}}) = \mathbb{R}^n$ (resp. over $\tau(K_{\mathbb{R}})$).*

Let $s \in \mathcal{O}$. The PLWE *(resp. PLWE^σ) distribution with parameters f, q, χ and s, denoted by $\mathcal{B}_{f,q,\chi,s}$ (resp. $\mathcal{B}^\sigma_{f,q,\chi,s}$) is the distribution obtained by sampling $a \leftarrow \mathcal{U}(\mathcal{O}/q\mathcal{O})$ and $e \in K_{\mathbb{R}}$ such that $T_f(e) \sim \chi$ (resp. $\tau(e) \sim \chi$) and outputting $(a,b) \in \mathcal{O}/q\mathcal{O} \times K_{\mathbb{R}}/q\mathcal{O}$ where $b = as + e \bmod q$.*

The decision $\mathsf{PLWE}_{f,q,\chi}$ (resp. $\mathsf{PLWE}^\sigma_{f,q,\chi}$) problem with parameters f, q and χ consists in distinguishing between a sampler from $\mathcal{B}_{f,q,\chi,s}$ (resp. $\mathcal{B}^\sigma_{f,q,\chi,s}$) and a uniform sampler over $\mathcal{O}/q\mathcal{O} \times K_{\mathbb{R}}/q\mathcal{O}$, with non-negligible probability over the random choice of $s \leftarrow \mathcal{U}(\mathcal{O}/q\mathcal{O})$.

Remark 2.12. We observe that PLWE and PLWE^σ only differ in the geometry of the error e. Also, by the relation $\tau(e) = \mathbf{V}_f T_f(e)$, we have $\mathsf{PLWE}^\sigma_{f,q,\mathbf{V}_f \cdot \chi} = \mathsf{PLWE}_{f,q,\chi}$

We now define the middle product learning with errors problem (MP-LWE). Before that, let us define the middle product of two polynomials.

Definition 2.13 (Middle product). *Let R be a ring and $a \in R^{<d_a}[x], b \in R^{<d_b}[x]$ where $d_a > 0$ and $d_b > 0$, satisfying $d_a + d_b - 1 = d + 2k$ for some d and k. The middle product of a and b of size d and denoted by $a \odot_d b$, is given by the map*

$$\odot_d : R^{<d_a}[x] \times R^{<d_b}[x] \longrightarrow R^{<d}[x]$$
$$(a,b) \mapsto a \odot_d b = \left\lfloor \frac{(a \cdot b) \mod x^{k+d}}{x^k} \right\rfloor$$

The middle product of two polynomials a and b, returns the middle coefficients of the polynomial product ab.

Remark 2.14. Unless stated otherwise, if χ is a distribution over R^d, we will also interpret it as a distribution over $R^{<d}[x]$

Definition 2.15 (MP-LWE). *Let $n, d > 0$, $q \geq 2$ be integers, and χ be a probability distribution over $\mathbb{R}^{<d}[x]$.*

Let $s \in \mathbb{Z}_q^{<n+d-1}[x]$. The MP-LWE distribution with parameters n, d, q, χ and s, denoted by $\mathcal{C}_{q,n,d,\chi}$ is the distribution obtained by sampling $a \leftarrow \mathcal{U}(\mathbb{Z}_q^{<n}[x])$ and $e \leftarrow \chi$ and outputting $(a,b) \in \mathbb{Z}_q^{<n}[x] \times \mathbb{R}_q^{<d}[x]$ where $b = a \odot_d s + e \bmod q$.

The decision $\mathsf{MP\text{-}LWE}_{q,n,d,\chi}$ problem with parameters n, d, q and χ consists in distinguishing between a sampler from $\mathcal{C}_{q,n,d,\chi}$ and a uniform sampler over $\mathbb{Z}_q^{<n}[x] \times \mathbb{R}_q^{<d}[x]$, with non-negligible probability over the random choice of $s \leftarrow \mathcal{U}(\mathbb{Z}_q^{<n+d-1}[x])$.

Similarly to the RLWE case, we use the simpler notation $\mathsf{MP\text{-}LWE}_{q,n,d,\alpha}$ (resp. $\mathsf{PLWE}^{\sigma}_{f,q,\alpha}$) when the distribution χ is of the form $\mathcal{N}_{\mathbb{R}^d,\alpha q}$ (resp. $\mathcal{N}_{\tau(K_{\mathbb{R}}),\alpha q}$).

A lot of reductions between the problems defined above have already been proven in the literature. In this article, we will use the two following results from [RSSS17].

Lemma 2.16 ([RSSS17, **Lemma** 3.7]). *Let $n \geq m \geq d > 0$, $q \geq 2$, and χ a distribution over $\mathbb{R}^m$. Then there exists a ppt reduction from $\mathsf{PLWE}_{f,q,\chi}$ for any monic $f \in \mathbb{Z}[x]$ with constant coefficient coprime with q and degree $m \in [d,n]$, to $\mathsf{MP\text{-}LWE}_{q,n,d,\mathbf{J}\cdot\mathbf{M}_f^d\cdot\chi}$. Here, the matrix $\mathbf{M}_f^d$ is the one obtained by keeping only the first d rows of M_f, and $\mathbf{J} \in \mathbb{Z}^{d\times d}$ is the one with 1's on the anti-diagonal and 0's everywhere else.*

Lemma 2.17 ([RSSS17, **Lemma** 3.8]). *Let $n, d > 0$, $q \geq 2$. Let $\sigma' > 0$. Let $\mathbf{\Sigma}_0 \in \mathbb{R}^{d\times d}$ be symmetric definite positive matrix with $|||\mathbf{\Sigma}_0||| < (\sigma')^2$. Then there exists a ppt reduction from $\mathsf{MP\text{-}LWE}_{\ q,n,d,\mathcal{N}_{\mathbb{R}^d,\mathbf{\Sigma}_0}}$ to $\mathsf{MP\text{-}LWE}_{\ q,n,d,\mathcal{N}_{\mathbb{R}^d,\sigma'}}$*

3 Reduction from PLWE^{σ} to MP-LWE

In this section, we present our improved analysis of the reduction from PLWE^{σ} to MP-LWE. Most of the technical results needed for this analysis were already proven in [RSSS17], and in particular in the proof of their Lemma 3.7 (recalled as Lemma 2.16 in preliminaries). Our improved analysis is obtained by instantiating this lemma with a different distribution than the one used in [RSSS17]. Overall, we obtain the following result.

Theorem 3.1. *Let $n \geq d > 0$ be integers. Let $f \in \mathbb{Z}[x]$ be a monic irreducible polynomial of degree $m \in [d, n]$. Let $q \geq 2$ coprime with the constant coefficient of f, and let $\chi = \mathcal{N}_{K_\mathbb{R}, \mathbf{\Sigma}}$, where $\mathbf{\Sigma}$ is a symmetric positive definite matrix. There is a* ppt *reduction from decision* $\mathsf{PLWE}^{\sigma}_{f,q,\chi}$ *to decision* $\mathsf{MP\text{-}LWE}_{q,n,d,\alpha}$ *where* $\alpha = 1/q \cdot \sqrt{|||\mathbf{\Sigma}|||} \cdot \left|\left|\left|\mathbf{M}_f^d \cdot \mathbf{V}_f^{-1}\right|\right|\right|$.

In the next section, we will analyze in more details the quantity $\left|\left|\left|\mathbf{M}_f^d \cdot \mathbf{V}_f^{-1}\right|\right|\right|$ appearing in the loss of the approximation factor. We observe that, in the proof of this theorem, we naturally obtain a reduction from PLWE^{σ} to an $\mathsf{MP\text{-}LWE}$ problem with non-spherical gaussian error distribution. In order to obtain a simple final statement, we overestimate this error distribution by a spherical gaussian distribution (with parameter αq). We decided to state our result with a spherical gaussian distribution because this is the one that is most likely to be used in constructions. However, if one wants to combine our reduction with another reduction from $\mathsf{MP\text{-}LWE}$ to another problem, then they may get better bounds by using the intermediate $\mathsf{MP\text{-}LWE}$ problem with non-spherical gaussian error distribution (its covariance matrix $\mathbf{\Sigma}_0$ can be recovered from the proof below).

Proof. Let us define the distribution $\chi' = \mathbf{V}_f^{-1}\chi$. Recall from Remark 2.12 that $\mathsf{PLWE}^{\sigma}_{f,q,\chi}$ is just $\mathsf{PLWE}_{f,q,\chi'}$. Instantiating Lemma 2.16 with the distribution χ', we obtain a polynomial time reduction from decision $\mathsf{PLWE}^{\sigma}_{f,q,\chi} = \mathsf{PLWE}_{f,q,\chi'}$ to decision $\mathsf{MP\text{-}LWE}_{q,n,d,\mathbf{J}\cdot\mathbf{M}_f^d\cdot\chi'}$, where $\mathbf{M}_f^d$ and $\mathbf{J}$ are as defined in Lemma 2.16.

Since χ is a Gaussian distribution of parameter Σ, and since $\mathbf{J} \cdot \mathbf{M}_f^d \cdot \mathbf{V}_f^{-1} \in \mathbb{R}^{d \times m}$, we know from Lemma 2.1 that $\mathbf{J} \cdot \mathbf{M}_f^d \cdot \chi' = \mathcal{N}_{\mathbb{R}^d, \mathbf{\Sigma}_0}$, where

$$\mathbf{\Sigma}_0 = \mathbf{J} \cdot \mathbf{M}_f^d \cdot \mathbf{V}_f^{-1} \cdot \mathbf{\Sigma} \cdot (V_f^{-1})^T \cdot (\mathbf{M}_f^d)^T \cdot \mathbf{J}^T.$$

Taking the spectral norm of $\mathbf{\Sigma}_0$ gives us,

$$\begin{aligned} |||\mathbf{\Sigma}_0||| &= \left|\left|\left|(\mathbf{J} \cdot \mathbf{M}_f^d \cdot \mathbf{V}_f^{-1}) \cdot \mathbf{\Sigma} \cdot (\mathbf{J} \cdot \mathbf{M}_f^d \cdot \mathbf{V}_f^{-1})^T\right|\right|\right| \\ &\leq |||\mathbf{J}|||^2 \cdot \left|\left|\left|\mathbf{M}_f^d \cdot \mathbf{V}_f^{-1}\right|\right|\right|^2 \cdot |||\mathbf{\Sigma}||| \\ &\leq \left|\left|\left|\mathbf{M}_f^d \cdot \mathbf{V}_f^{-1}\right|\right|\right|^2 \cdot |||\mathbf{\Sigma}|||, \end{aligned}$$

where in the first inequality we used the sub-multiplicaticity of the spectral norm and its invariance by transposition; and in the second inequality we used the fact that $|||\mathbf{J}||| = 1$.

Finally, using Lemma 2.17 and the upper bound on $|||\mathbf{\Sigma}_0|||$ obtained above, we conclude that there exists a p.p.t. reduction from $\mathsf{MP\text{-}LWE}_{q,n,d,\mathcal{N}_{\mathbb{R}^d,\mathbf{\Sigma}_0}}$ to

MP-LWE$_{q,n,d,\alpha}$, where $\alpha = \frac{1}{q} \cdot \left|\left|\left| \mathbf{M}_f^d \cdot \mathbf{V}_f^{-1} \right|\right|\right| \cdot \sqrt{|||\boldsymbol{\Sigma}|||}$. Combining both reductions finishes the proof. □

4 Bound on the Quantity $||\mathbf{M}_f^d \cdot \mathbf{V}_f^{-1}||$

In the previous section, we saw that the reduction from PLWE$^\sigma$ to MP-LWE has a loss which depends on the quantity $\left|\left|\left| \mathbf{M}_f^d \cdot \mathbf{V}_f^{-1} \right|\right|\right|$. In this section, we study this quantity more thoroughly. In the first subsection, we give a simple formula for the coefficients of the matrix $\mathbf{M}_f \cdot \mathbf{V}_f^{-1}$, and we derive from this an upper bound on its matrix norm, depending only on simple quantities. We then report on numerical experiments which seem to indicate that the upper bound (and so the quantity $\left|\left|\left| \mathbf{M}_f^d \cdot \mathbf{V}_f^{-1} \right|\right|\right|$) are small for almost all random polynomials (of a fixed degree and coefficients bounded by some B). Finally, we also provide specially chosen counter-examples, for which we can prove that the quantity $\left|\left|\left| \mathbf{M}_f^d \cdot \mathbf{V}_f^{-1} \right|\right|\right|$ is (exponentially) large. These counter-examples only represent a negligible proportion of all irreducible polynomials of a given degree with coefficients bounded by B, which explains why we do not detect them in our experiments using uniformly random polynomials. The existence of such polynomials with exponentially large $\left|\left|\left| \mathbf{M}_f^d \cdot \mathbf{V}_f^{-1} \right|\right|\right|$ explains why we cannot hope to prove theoretically that this quantity remains small for all polynomials.

Summing up, experimental results seem to indicate that the quantity $\left|\left|\left| \mathbf{M}_f^d \cdot \mathbf{V}_f^{-1} \right|\right|\right|$ remains a small polynomial for most random polynomials with bounded coefficients (e.g., at least 90% of random polynomials with coefficients in $[-B, B]$ satisfy $\left|\left|\left| \mathbf{M}_f^d \cdot \mathbf{V}_f^{-1} \right|\right|\right| \leq \sqrt{dm} \cdot m$), but for some specific choices of polynomials, this quantity can grow exponentially with the degree.

4.1 Theoretical Upper Bound

In this section, we first prove a lemma that provides a description of the coefficients of the matrix $\mathbf{M}_f\mathbf{V}_f^{-1}$ as a function of the roots of f.

Lemma 4.1. *Let f be a monic irreducible polynomial of degree m, and let $\mathbf{M}_f$ and $\mathbf{V}_f$ be as defined in Definitions 2.3 and 2.7, respectively. Let $1 \leq i, j \leq m$, then, the (i,j)-th coefficient of the matrix $\mathbf{M}_f\mathbf{V}_f^{-1}$ is given by the formula*

$$(\mathbf{M}_f\mathbf{V}_f^{-1})_{i,j} = \frac{-f_0 \cdot \alpha_j^{i-2}}{f'(\alpha_j)}.$$

Proof. Let us fix some $i, j \in \{1, \ldots, m\}$ and compute $(\mathbf{M}_f\mathbf{V}_f^{-1})_{i,j}$.

Let $\alpha_1, \ldots, \alpha_m$ be the complex roots of f, and let L_j be the j'th Lagrange polynomial associated to the α_k's (as defined in Definition 2.5). By definition of $\mathbf{V}_f$, the vector $\mathbf{a}$ consisting of the coefficients of L_j is the j-th column of $\mathbf{V}_f^{-1}$

(because $\mathbf{V}_f \mathbf{a} = \mathbf{e}_j$, the j-th vector of the canonical basis of $\mathbb{R}^m$). So, computing $\mathbf{M}_f \boldsymbol{a}$ allows us to compute the j-th column of the matrix $\mathbf{M}_f \mathbf{V}_f^{-1}$. In other words, the coefficient $(\mathbf{M}_f \mathbf{V}_f^{-1})_{i,j}$ is simply the i'th coefficient of $\mathbf{M}_f \boldsymbol{a}$. Lemma 2.4 tells us that if $\mathbf{a}$ is a vector formed by the coefficients of a polynomial $a(x)$ of degree $< m$, then $\mathbf{M}_f \mathbf{a} = Rot_f(a)(1, 0, \ldots, 0)^T$. Applying this result to the polynomial $a = L_j$, we get

$$\mathbf{M}_f \mathbf{a} = Rot_f(a) \begin{pmatrix} 1 \\ 0 \\ \vdots \\ 0 \end{pmatrix} = Rot_f(L_j) \begin{pmatrix} 1 \\ 0 \\ \vdots \\ 0 \end{pmatrix}.$$

Using the fact that $(\mathbf{M}_f \mathbf{V}_f^{-1})_{i,j} = (\mathbf{M}_f \boldsymbol{a})_i$ and the equation above, it only remains to compute the first coefficient of the i'th row of $Rot_f(L_j)$.

By Definition 2.2, the i-th row of the matrix $Rot_f(L_j)$ consists of the coefficients of the polynomial $x^{i-1} L_j \bmod f$. Let us call $Q_{i,j}$ this polynomial, that is, $Q_{i,j} = x^{i-1} L_j \bmod f$ and $\deg(Q_{i,j}) < m$. In order to prove our lemma, it only remains to prove that $Q_{i,j} = \alpha_j^{i-1} L_j$. Indeed, we have seen that $(\mathbf{M}_f \mathbf{V}_f^{-1})_{i,j}$ is equal to the constant coefficient of $Q_{i,j}$. Moreover, we know from Lemma 2.6 that $L_j(0) = \frac{-f_0}{\alpha_j \cdot f'(\alpha_j)}$. Hence, if we have the equality of polynomials, we will obtain that

$$(\mathbf{M}_f \mathbf{V}_f^{-1})_{i,j} = Q_{i,j}(0) = \alpha_j^{i-1} \cdot \frac{-f_0}{\alpha_j \cdot f'(\alpha_j)} = \frac{-f_0 \cdot \alpha_j^{i-2}}{f'(\alpha_j)},$$

as desired. Let us then prove the equality $Q_{i,j} = \alpha_j^{i-1} L_j$. Both polynomials have degree $< m$, so to prove their equality, it suffices to prove that they coincide at m distinct inputs. Let us evaluate them at the roots $\alpha_1, \ldots, \alpha_m$ of f. If $k \neq j$, we get $Q_{i,j}(\alpha_k) = (x^{i-1} L_j)(\alpha_k) = \alpha_k^{i-1} L_j(\alpha_k) = 0 = (\alpha_j^{i-1} L_j)(\alpha_k)$, where in the first equality we used the fact that $Q_{i,j} = x^{i-1} L_j \bmod f$ and $f(\alpha_k) = 0$, and for the last two equalities we used the fact that $L_j(\alpha_k) = 0$ for all $k \neq j$. For $k = j$, we obtain $Q_{i,j}(\alpha_j) = (x^{i-1} L_j)(\alpha_j) = \alpha_j^{i-1} L_j(\alpha_j)$. Hence, we see that for all $k \in \{1, \ldots, m\}$, it holds that $Q_{i,j}(\alpha_k) = (\alpha_j^{i-1} L_j)(\alpha_k)$, as desired. This concludes the proof. □

This lemma motivates the definition of the following quantity $D(f)$, which will give us a simpler upper bound on the quantity $\left|\left|\left| \mathbf{M}_f^d \cdot \mathbf{V}_f^{-1} \right|\right|\right|$.

Definition 4.2 ($D(f)$). *Let $f \in \mathbb{Z}[x]$ be a monic irreducible polynomial of degree $m > 0$, and f_0 be the constant coefficient of f. We define the quantity $D(f)$ as follows:*

$$D(f) = \max_{\alpha \text{ complex root of } f} \left| \frac{f_0 \max(|\alpha|^{-1}, |\alpha|^{m-2})}{f'(\alpha)} \right|.$$

Corollary 4.3. *For any monic irreducible polynomial f of degree m and any $d \le m$, it holds that*

$$\left|\left|\left|\mathbf{M}_f^d \cdot \mathbf{V}_f^{-1}\right|\right|\right| \le \sqrt{dm} \cdot D(f)$$

$$\text{and, if } d = m, \quad \left|\left|\left|\mathbf{M}_f^d \cdot \mathbf{V}_f^{-1}\right|\right|\right| \ge D(f).$$

Proof. For the upper bound, let us observe that for any root α_j of f, and any $1 \le i \le m$, it holds that $|\alpha_j|^{i-2} \le \max(|\alpha_j|^{-1}, |\alpha_j|^{m-2})$ (the function $x \mapsto |\alpha_j|^x$ is either increasing or decreasing, depending on whether $|\alpha_j| \ge 1$ or not). Using this observation, the definition of $D(f)$, and Lemma 4.1, we see that $|(\mathbf{M}_f^d \cdot \mathbf{V}_f^{-1})_{i,j}| \le D(f)$ for any $1 \le i \le d$ and $1 \le j \le m$. Using the relation between the operator norm and the Frobenius norm (see preliminaries), we conclude that $\left|\left|\left|\mathbf{M}_f^d \cdot \mathbf{V}_f^{-1}\right|\right|\right| \le \|\mathbf{M}_f^d \cdot \mathbf{V}_f^{-1}\|_F \le \sqrt{dm} \cdot D(f)$ as desired.

For the lower bound, we show that at least one coefficient of $\mathbf{M}_f^d \cdot \mathbf{V}_f^{-1}$ has its absolute value equal to $D(f)$ (when $d = m$). Let j be such that α_j maximizes the quantity $\left|\frac{f_0 \max(|\alpha|^{-1}, |\alpha|^{m-2})}{f'(\alpha)}\right|$. In other words, $D(f) = \left|\frac{f_0 \max(|\alpha_j|^{-1}, |\alpha_j|^{m-2})}{f'(\alpha_j)}\right|$. Then using Lemma 4.1, we have that either $|(\mathbf{M}_f^d \cdot \mathbf{V}_f^{-1})_{1,j}| = D(f)$ if $|\alpha_j| \le 1$, or $|(\mathbf{M}_f^d \cdot \mathbf{V}_f^{-1})_{m,j}| = D(f)$ if $|\alpha_j| \ge 1$ (here we use that $d = m$, so that we can take $i = m$). We conclude that

$$\left|\left|\left|\mathbf{M}_f^d \cdot \mathbf{V}_f^{-1}\right|\right|\right| \ge \max_{i,j} |(\mathbf{M}_f^d \cdot \mathbf{V}_f^{-1})_{i,j}| \ge D(f),$$

as desired. □

This lemma says that, when $d = m$, the quantity $D(f)$ is a good approximation of the quantity $\left|\left|\left|\mathbf{M}_f^d \cdot \mathbf{V}_f^{-1}\right|\right|\right|$ (up to a small polynomial factor). In the rest of the article, we will hence phrase our results in terms of the quantity $D(f)$, rather than the quantity $\left|\left|\left|\mathbf{M}_f^d \cdot \mathbf{V}_f^{-1}\right|\right|\right|$. The reason we introduce the quantity $D(f)$ in this section is because we hope that this quantity might be easier to analyze theoretically than the quantity $\left|\left|\left|\mathbf{M}_f^d \cdot \mathbf{V}_f^{-1}\right|\right|\right|$. Indeed, the definition of $D(f)$ only involves the roots and derivative of the polynomial f, which seems easier to analyze. Moreover, $D(f)$ seems related to some mathematical object called the Mahler measure. For a monic polynomial f of degree m, the Mahler measure is given by

$$M(f) = \prod_{i=1}^{m} \max(1, |\alpha_i|).$$

In [Mah64], it was proven that for any complex root α of f

$$\frac{\max(1, |\alpha|)^{m-2}}{|f'(\alpha)|} \le \frac{(\sqrt{m} - 1)^{m-1} \cdot M(f)^{m-2}}{\sqrt{|\Delta(f)|}},$$

where $\Delta(f)$ is the discriminant of f. If all the roots of f have absolute values at least 1, then the left hand side of the above equation is very similar to our definition of $D(f)$, and so one may hope that this equation could be helpful to theoretically prove an upper bound on the quantity $D(f)$ for a large class of polynomials f. Unfortunately, we did not manage to exploit this formula to obtain theoretical proofs of smallness of $D(f)$. This is why we instead provide numerical experiments that seem to indicate that $D(f)$ is small for a large class of polynomials. We let open the question of using the Mahler measure (or any other tool) to formally prove that $D(f)$ is small for almost all polynomials of fixed degree and bounded coefficients. Note that the counter-examples that we provide in Sect. 4.3 prevent us from proving that $D(f)$ is small for all polynomials.

4.2 Experimental Average-Case Upper Bound

In this section, we build an empirical argument for bounding the quantity $D(f)$. The code we used for the experiments is available here. We show that for random polynomials f with coefficients bounded by some $B > 0$, then the quantity $D(f)$ remains very small, even when the degree of f increases, or when the bound B increases. Since $\left|\left|\left|\mathbf{M}_f^d \cdot \mathbf{V}_f^{-1}\right|\right|\right| \leq \sqrt{dm} \cdot D(f)$ (see Corollary 4.3), this also provides an upper bound on the quantity $\left|\left|\left|\mathbf{M}_f^d \cdot \mathbf{V}_f^{-1}\right|\right|\right|$.

In our experiment, we picked some integer $B > 0$ and degree m, and sampled multiple uniformly random monic irreducible polynomials f of degree m and with coefficients uniformly distributed in $[-B, B]$. For each of these polynomials, we computed the quantity $D(f)$. For each pair (m, B), we sampled between 20 and 1000 random polynomials. We show the observed values for $D(f)$ in Figs. 3 and 4. In the first figure, we display the quantity $D(f)$ as a function of the degree m of the polynomial, whereas in the second one we display $D(f)$ as a function of the bound B. The boxes contain 50% of the random inputs (between the first and the third quartile), while the whiskers contain 80% of the inputs (between the first and the ninth decile). One can observe from these experimental results that the quantity $D(f)$ seems rather constant, and independent of the bound B or the degree m. An assumption such as "$D(f) \leq m$" seems pretty safe, at least for 90% of the random polynomials sampled during the experiments (which corresponds to the maximum of the top whisker).

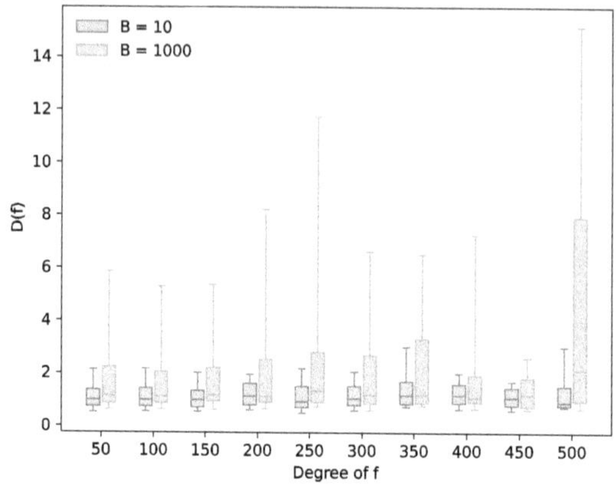

Fig. 3. The quantity $D(f)$ as a function of the degree of f for random polynomials with coefficients in $[-B, B]$. The boxes correspond to the interval $(0.25, 0.75)$ and the whiskers correspond to $(0.1, 0.9)$.

4.3 Counter-Examples: Polynomials with Large $\|\mathbf{M}_f \mathbf{V}_f^{-1}\|$

In this section, we describe two families of polynomials for which the quantity $\left|\left|\left|\mathbf{M}_f^d \mathbf{V}_f^{-1}\right|\right|\right|$ grows exponentially quickly (either with the degree m of f, or with d). Since $D(f) \geq \left|\left|\left|\mathbf{M}_f^d \mathbf{V}_f^{-1}\right|\right|\right|$, this shows that there is no hope to be able to prove a polynomial upper bound on $D(f)$ for all polynomials of fixed degree and bounded coefficients.

Recall that $D(f)$ is defined by

$$D(f) = \max_{\alpha \text{ complex root of } f} \left| \frac{f_0 \max(|\alpha|^{-1}, |\alpha|^{m-2})}{f'(\alpha)} \right|.$$

If we want to make this quantity exponentially large, we can either make $|f'(\alpha)|$ exponentially small; or make $|\alpha| \geq 2$ (for example) while ensuring that $|f'(\alpha)|$ is not exponentially small. In our first counter-example, we consider the Bugeaud-Mignotte polynomials. These polynomials have two roots that are exponentially close to one another, and so for one of these roots, the quantity $|f'(\alpha)|$ becomes exponentially small (recall that for a monic polynomial f, it holds that $|f'(\alpha)| = \prod_{\substack{\alpha' \text{ root of f} \\ \alpha' \neq \alpha}} |\alpha' - \alpha|$). This leads to an exponentially large $D(f)$. For our second family of counter-examples, we consider a shifted cyclotomic polynomial $f(x) = \Phi_p(x-3)$ (where Φ_p is the p-th cyclotomic polynomial). This polynomial has large roots (≥ 2 in absolute value), while keeping the nice properties of the cyclotomic polynomial which make the quantity $|f'(\alpha)|$ not too small. This also leads to an exponentially large $D(f)$.

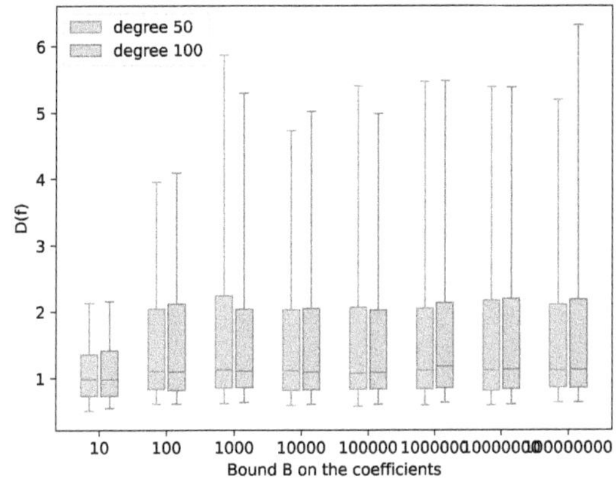

Fig. 4. The quantity $D(f)$ as a function of the bound B for random polynomials with coefficients in $[-B, B]$. The boxes correspond to the interval $(0.25, 0.75)$ and the whiskers correspond to $(0.1, 0.9)$.

Bugeaud-Mignotte Polynomials. Let us first consider the family of Bugeaud-Mignotte polynomials [BM04,BM10]. These polynomials were already used in [RSW18, Appendix E] as counter-examples for their reduction from RLWE to PLWE. The Bugeaud-Mignotte polynomials we consider in this section are of the form

$$g_{m,a} = x^m - 2(ax-1)^2,$$

for some $a \in \mathbb{Z}_{\geq 2}$. They have the property to have two roots exponentially close to one another (close to $1/a$), which makes them good candidate to have a $D(f)$ growing to infinity exponentially quickly. This is what we prove in the following lemma.

Proposition 4.4. *Let $m \geq d \geq 1$ be integers, with $m \geq 6$. Let $a \in \mathbb{Z}_{\geq 2}$ and $f = g_{m,a} = x^m - 2(ax-1)^2$ be a Bugeaud-Mignotte polynomial. Then*

$$\left|\left|\left|\mathbf{M}_f^d \mathbf{V}_f^{-1}\right|\right|\right| \geq a^{\Omega(m)},$$

where the constant in the $\Omega(\cdot)$ is absolute (in particular, it does not depend on a nor m).

This lemma says that for a Bugeaud-Mignotte polynomial, the quantity $\left|\left|\left|\mathbf{M}_f^d \mathbf{V}_f^{-1}\right|\right|\right|$ tends to infinity exponentially quickly in both m and $\log(a)$ (which corresponds to our $\log(B)$ in the case of random polynomials).

Proof. For any matrix $\mathbf{M}$, the operator norm $|||\mathbf{M}|||$ of $\mathbf{M}$ is at least as large as the absolute value of the largest coefficient of $\mathbf{M}$. Hence, to prove the Lemma, it suffices to find a coefficient of the matrix $\mathbf{M}_f^d \mathbf{V}_f^{-1}$ whose absolute value is at least $a^{\Omega(m)}$.

Using Lemma 4.1, we know that the (i,j)-th coefficient of $\mathbf{M}_f^d\mathbf{V}_f^{-1}$ satisfies

$$|(\mathbf{M}_f^d\mathbf{V}_f^{-1})_{i,j}| = \left|\frac{f_0 \cdot \alpha_j^{i-2}}{f'(\alpha_j)}\right|,$$

where α_j range over the complex roots of f. Choosing $i = 1$ and observing that $|f_0| = 2$ for our polynomial, we obtain

$$|(\mathbf{M}_f^d\mathbf{V}_f^{-1})_{1,j}| = \left|\frac{2 \cdot \alpha_j^{-1}}{f'(\alpha_j)}\right|.$$

Let us now choose a good root α_j of f. Using [RSW18, Lemma E.1], we know that f has two roots in the disc centered at $1/a$ and radius $1/a^{m/2}$. Note that [RSW18, Lemma E.1] requires $a > (1 + 2^{1-m/2})^{m/2}$, which is satisfied in our case since we imposed $m \geq 6$ and $a \geq 2$. Let us choose s such that the root α_s is one of the two roots inside the above mentioned disc, i.e., $\alpha_s = \frac{1}{a} + \varepsilon$ for some $|\varepsilon| \leq a^{-m/2}$. Using the fact that $m \geq 6$ and that $a \geq 2$, we see that $|\alpha_s| \leq \frac{1}{a} \cdot (1 + a^{1-m/2}) \leq \frac{1}{a} \cdot (5/4) \leq 5/8$. Hence, we have

$$|(\mathbf{M}_f^d\mathbf{V}_f^{-1})_{1,s}| = \left|\frac{2 \cdot \alpha_s^{-1}}{f'(\alpha_s)}\right| \geq \left|\frac{1}{f'(\alpha_s)}\right|.$$

It only remains to compute an upper bound on $|f'(\alpha_s)|$. The derivative of f is $f'(x) = mx^{m-1} - 4a(ax - 1)$. Evaluating as α_s, we obtain

$$\begin{aligned}
|f'(\alpha_s)| &= |m \cdot \alpha_s^{m-1} - 4a(a \cdot \alpha_s - 1)| \\
&\leq |m \cdot \alpha_s^{m-1}| + |4a(a \cdot \alpha_s - 1)| \\
&\leq m \cdot \left(\tfrac{5}{4a}\right)^{m-1} + |4a(a \cdot (1/a + \varepsilon) - 1)| \\
&\leq m \cdot \left(\tfrac{5}{4a}\right)^{m-1} + 4a^2 \cdot \varepsilon \\
&\leq m \cdot \left(\tfrac{5}{4a}\right)^{m-1} + 4a^{2-m/2} \\
&\leq \frac{1}{a^{\Omega(m)}}.
\end{aligned}$$

Combining everything, we obtain the desired lower bound on $\left|\left|\left|\mathbf{M}_f^d\mathbf{V}_f^{-1}\right|\right|\right|$. □

Shifted Cyclotomic Polynomials. In this subsection, we describe another family of polynomials for which the quantity $\left|\left|\left|\mathbf{M}_f^d \cdot \mathbf{V}_f^{-1}\right|\right|\right|$ increases exponentially quickly with the degree: shifted cyclotomic polynomials of prime conductor. The reason for which the quantity $\left|\left|\left|\mathbf{M}_f^d \cdot \mathbf{V}_f^{-1}\right|\right|\right|$ explodes for these polynomials is not due to a very small denominator as for the Bugeaud-Mignotte polynomials, but to an exponentially large numerator, together with a not-so-large denominator, which does not compensate the numerator. More formally, we prove the following result.

Proposition 4.5. *Let $f(x) = \Phi_p(x-3)$ be a shifted cyclotomic polynomial where p is prime and Φ_p is the p-th cyclotomic polynomial (so that $m := \deg(f) = p-1$). Let $1 \le d \le m$ be an integer. Then*

$$\left|\left|\left|\mathbf{M}_f^d \cdot \mathbf{V}_f^{-1}\right|\right|\right| \ge \frac{2^{d-2}}{p^2}.$$

Note that the polynomial $\Phi_p(x-3)$ is irreducible because $\Phi_p(x)$ is (if we had $\Phi_p(x-3) = f_1(x)f_2(x)$, then we would have $\Phi_p(x) = f_1(x+3)f_2(x+3)$, contradicting the irreducibility of Φ_p). Also note that here, contrary to the previous case, the quantity $\left|\left|\left|\mathbf{M}_f^d \cdot \mathbf{V}_f^{-1}\right|\right|\right|$ only grows exponentially with d and not with m. So to get an exponentially large lower bound, we need to assume that d tends to infinity with m, for instance taking $d = c \cdot m$ for some constant $c \in (0,1)$.

Proof. As for the proof of Proposition 4.4, we prove this result by giving a lower bound on the absolute value of one coefficient of the matrix. This time, we take $i = d$ (the last row of the matrix), and any column j (for instance $j = 1$). Using Lemma 4.1, we have

$$\begin{aligned}\left|\left|\left|\mathbf{M}_f^d \cdot \mathbf{V}_f^{-1}\right|\right|\right| &\ge |(\mathbf{M}_f^d \cdot \mathbf{V}_f^{-1})_{d,1}| \\ &\ge \left|\frac{f_0 \cdot \alpha_1^{d-2}}{f'(\alpha_1)}\right|,\end{aligned}$$

where α_1 is any root of f. By definition of $f(x) = \Phi_p(x-3)$, we know that $\alpha_1 = \zeta + 3$ for ζ a root of Φ_p. Hence, $|\alpha_1| \ge 3 - |\zeta| \ge 2$. Moreover, since f has integer coefficients (because Φ_p has) and its constant coefficient is not 0 (because 0 is not a root of f), we know that $|f_0| \ge 1$. Overall, we obtain

$$\left|\left|\left|\mathbf{M}_f^d \cdot \mathbf{V}_f^{-1}\right|\right|\right| \ge \frac{2^{d-2}}{|f'(\alpha_1)|}.$$

To prove the proposition, it only remains to show that $|f'(\alpha_1)|$ is bounded from above by p^2. By definition of f, we know that $f'(x) = \Phi_p'(x-3) = \sum_{k=1}^{p-1} k(x-3)^{k-1}$ (here, we use the fact that $\Phi_p(x) = \sum_{k=0}^{p-1} x^k$ since p is prime). Evaluating this as $x = \alpha_1 = \zeta + 3$, we obtain

$$\begin{aligned}|f'(\alpha_1)| = \left|\sum_{k=1}^{p-1} k \cdot (\alpha_1 - 3)^{k-1}\right| &= \left|\sum_{k=1}^{p-1} k \cdot \zeta^{k-1}\right| \\ &\le \sum_{k=1}^{p-1} k \cdot |\zeta|^{k-1} = \sum_{k=1}^{p-1} k \le p^2.\end{aligned}$$

Combining everything, we obtain $\left|\left|\left|\mathbf{M}_f^d \cdot \mathbf{V}_f^{-1}\right|\right|\right| \ge \frac{2^{d-2}}{p^2}$ as desired. □

5 Reduction from RLWE to MP-LWE

In the previous section, we described an improved analysis for the reduction from PLWE^σ to MP-LWE. However, the hardness of the PLWE^σ problem is less understood than the hardness of the RLWE problem. So in this section, our objective is to state a reduction from the hardness of primal/dual RLWE to MP-LWE. To do so, we simply combine the reduction from the previous section with known reductions from primal/dual RLWE to PLWE^σ (using results from [Pei16, RSW18, BBPS19]).

In the first subsections, we recall the known reductions from primal/dual RLWE to PLWE^σ, obtained by combining results from prior works [Pei16, RSW18, BBPS19]. We then conclude this section by combining the reductions from primal/dual RLWE to PLWE^σ and the reduction from PLWE^σ to MP-LWE from Sect. 3, in order to obtain the full reduction.

5.1 Reduction from Primal RLWE to PLWE^σ

Let us first recall the reduction from primal RLWE to PLWE^σ. This reduction was proven in [RSW18, Section 4.1]. The reduction relies on the existence of a small element t in the conductor ideal $\mathcal{C}_\mathcal{O}$ of the order $\mathcal{O} = \mathbb{Z}[x]/f(x)$, coprime to the modulus q. The authors of [RSW18] gave an upper bound on the size of such t in their Theorem 3.1, however, as we said in preliminaries, better bounds have been proven in the follow-up work [BBPS19] (see Lemma 2.9). Hence, we combine below the reduction from [RSW18, Section 4.1] with the better bound from [BBPS19] in order to obtain a tighter reduction from primal RLWE to PLWE^σ. The proof is available in the full version [NP26].

Theorem 5.1 (Combining results from [RSW18, BBPS19]). *Let $f \in \mathbb{Z}[x]$ be a monic irreducible polynomial of degree m. Let $K = \mathbb{Q}[x]/f(x)$ be the number field with defining polynomial f and let $\mathcal{O} = \mathbb{Z}[x]/f(x)$ be an order of K, and $\mathcal{C}_\mathcal{O}$ be its conductor ideal. Let $\alpha \in (0,1)$ be a real number and $q \geq 8m$ be a prime integer such that $q\mathcal{O}_K$ is coprime with $\mathcal{C}_\mathcal{O}$. Then there exists a (non-uniform) polynomial time reduction from decision primal $\mathsf{RLWE}_{f,q,\alpha}$ to decision $\mathsf{PLWE}^\sigma_{f,q,\mathcal{N}_{\tau(K_\mathbb{R}),\mathbf{\Sigma}}}$, where $\mathbf{\Sigma}$ is a symmetric positive definite matrix satisfying*

$$\sqrt{|||\mathbf{\Sigma}|||} \leq \alpha q \cdot (64 m^4 \cdot \Delta_K^{4/m} \cdot \mathcal{N}(\mathcal{C}_\mathcal{O})^{2/m}).$$

5.2 Reduction from Dual RLWE to PLWE^σ

Let us now recall the known reduction from dual RLWE to PLWE^σ. The idea of the reduction is to combine a reduction from dual RLWE to primal RLWE (due to [Pei16, Se. 2.3.2] and reformulated in [RSW18, Th. 2.13]), with the reduction from primal RLWE to PLWE^σ from the previous subsection. The proof is available in the full version [NP26].

Theorem 5.2 (Combining results from [RSW18,BBPS19,Pei16]**).** *Let $f \in \mathbb{Z}[x]$ be a monic irreducible polynomial of degree m. Let $K = \mathbb{Q}[x]/f(x)$ be the number field with defining polynomial f and let $\mathcal{O} = \mathbb{Z}[x]/f(x)$ be an order of K, and $\mathcal{C}_{\mathcal{O}}$ be its conductor ideal. Let $\alpha \in (0,1)$ be a real number and $q \geq 8m$ be a prime integer such that $q\mathcal{O}_K$ is coprime to $\mathcal{C}_{\mathcal{O}}$. Then there exists a (non-uniform) polynomial time reduction from decision dual $\mathsf{RLWE}_{f,q,\alpha}$ to decision $\mathsf{PLWE}^{\sigma}_{f,q,\mathcal{N}_{\tau(K_{\mathbb{R}}),\mathbf{\Sigma}}}$, where $\mathbf{\Sigma}$ is a symmetric positive definite matrix satisfying*

$$\sqrt{|||\mathbf{\Sigma}|||} \leq \alpha q \cdot (512 m^6 \cdot \Delta_K^{7/m} \cdot \mathcal{N}(\mathcal{C}_{\mathcal{O}})^{2/m}).$$

5.3 Combining the Reductions

We can now combine the reductions from Sects. 5.1 and 5.2 with the reduction from Sect. 3 in order to obtain our main result: a reduction from primal/dual RLWE to MP-LWE. We state this result in two different ways: first, we state in Theorem 5.3 a reduction from RLWE_f for *any* polynomial f to the MP-LWE problem, where the parameters of the MP-LWE problem depend on some quantities related to f. This formulation has the advantage of being very precise, and shows what quantities impact the tightness of the reduction. In a second statement (Corollary 5.5), we phrase the result the other way around: we fix some parameters for the MP-LWE problem, and we explicit a class of polynomials f for which there is a reduction from primal/dual RLWE_f to MP-LWE with these parameters. This formulation has the advantage of providing instances of MP-LWE that are as hard as RLWE_f for large classes of polynomials f, which was the main goal of the introduction of the MP-LWE problem.

Theorem 5.3. *Let $f \in \mathbb{Z}[x]$ be a monic irreducible polynomial of degree m and $K = \mathbb{Q}[x]/f(x)$ be the number field defined by f. Let $\mathcal{O} = \mathbb{Z}[x]/f(x)$ be an order of K, and $\mathcal{C}_{\mathcal{O}}$ be the conductor ideal of this order. Let n, d be positive integers such that $d \leq m \leq n$. Let $q \geq 8m$ be a prime integer which does not divide the constant coefficient of f nor $\mathcal{N}(\mathcal{C}_{\mathcal{O}})$. Let $\alpha \in (0,1)$ be a real number. There is a* ppt *(non-uniform) reduction from decision primal/dual $\mathsf{RLWE}_{f,q,\alpha}$ to decision $\mathsf{MP\text{-}LWE}_{q,n,d,\alpha'}$ where*

$$\alpha' = \begin{cases} \alpha \cdot 64\sqrt{md} \cdot m^4 \cdot \Delta_K^{4/m} \cdot \mathcal{N}(\mathcal{C}_{\mathcal{O}})^{2/m} \cdot D(f) & for\ primal\text{-}\mathsf{RLWE}, \\ \\ \alpha \cdot 512\sqrt{md} \cdot m^6 \cdot \Delta_K^{7/m} \cdot \mathcal{N}(\mathcal{C}_{\mathcal{O}})^{2/m} \cdot D(f) & for\ dual\text{-}\mathsf{RLWE}. \end{cases}$$

Proof. First, we prove the reduction from dual RLWE. Theorem 5.2 gives us a reduction from decision dual $\mathsf{RLWE}_{f,q,\alpha}$ to decision $\mathsf{PLWE}^{\sigma}_{f,q,\mathcal{N}_{\tau(K_{\mathbb{R}}),\mathbf{\Sigma}}}$, where

$$\sqrt{|||\mathbf{\Sigma}|||} \leq \alpha q \cdot (512 m^6 \cdot \Delta_K^{7/m} \cdot \mathcal{N}(\mathcal{C}_{\mathcal{O}})^{2/m}).$$

And Theorem 3.1 combined with Corollary 4.3, establish a probabilistic polynomial time reduction from decision $\mathsf{PLWE}^{\sigma}_{f,q,\mathcal{N}_{\tau(K_{\mathbb{R}}),\mathbf{\Sigma}}}$ to the decision $\mathsf{MP\text{-}LWE}_{q,n,d,\alpha'}$ where $\alpha' = 1/q \cdot \sqrt{|||\mathbf{\Sigma}|||} \cdot \sqrt{md} \cdot D(f)$. We get,

$$\alpha' \leq \alpha \cdot (512 \cdot m^6 \cdot \Delta_K^{7/m} \cdot \mathcal{N}(\mathcal{C}_{\mathcal{O}})^{2/m}) \cdot \sqrt{md} \cdot D(f).$$

Now we prove the reduction from primal RLWE. By Theorem 5.1, we get a reduction from decision primal $\mathsf{RLWE}_{f,q,\alpha}$ to $\mathsf{PLWE}^{\sigma}_{f,q,\mathcal{N}_{\tau(K_{\mathbb{R}}),\boldsymbol{\Sigma}}}$, where

$$\sqrt{|||\boldsymbol{\Sigma}|||} \leq \alpha q \cdot (64m^4 \cdot \Delta_K^{4/m} \cdot \mathcal{N}(\mathcal{C}_{\mathcal{O}})^{2/m}).$$

By Theorem 3.1 and Corollary 4.3, we get ppt reduction from decision $\mathsf{PLWE}^{\sigma}_{f,q,\mathcal{N}_{\tau(K_{\mathbb{R}}),\boldsymbol{\Sigma}}}$ to the decision $\mathsf{MP\text{-}LWE}_{q,n,d,\alpha'}$ where $\alpha' = 1/q \cdot \sqrt{|||\boldsymbol{\Sigma}|||md} D(f)$. We get,

$$\alpha' \leq \alpha \cdot (64m^4 \cdot \Delta_K^{4/m} \cdot \mathcal{N}(\mathcal{C}_{\mathcal{O}})^{2/m}) \cdot \sqrt{md} \cdot D(f).$$

Hence, we deduce our result. □

We can rephrase this theorem by fixing a noise parameter α' for the MP-LWE instance, and obtaining a set of all polynomials f that are covered by the reduction. In order to simplify the statement, we observe that for a prime integer q, the condition "q does not divide $\mathcal{N}(\mathcal{C}_{\mathcal{O}})$" is implied by the condition "q does not divide Δ_f". Let us then define the following set of polynomials.

Definition 5.4. *Let $0 < d \leq n$ be integers, and $q \geq 2$ be a prime integer. Let $\gamma > 0$ be some real number. We define the set of admissible polynomials $\mathrm{Adm}_{d,n,q,B,\gamma}$ as the set of all monic irreducible polynomials with degree $m \in [d, n]$, with coefficients in $[-B, B]$, whose constant coefficient and discriminant are both coprime with q, and satisfying*

$$D(f) \leq \gamma.$$

Numerical experiments from Sect. 4.2 seem to indicate that when $\gamma \geq n$, then the set of admissible polynomials $\mathrm{Adm}_{d,n,q,B,\gamma}$ contains at least 90% of all monic irreducible polynomials of degree $\leq m$ with coefficients bounded by B. We can now state the following corollary to Theorem 5.3.

Corollary 5.5. *Let $0 < d \leq n$ be integers and $q \geq 8n$ be a prime number. Let $B > 0$ be an integer. Let $\alpha, \alpha' > 0$ be real numbers such that $\alpha' \geq \alpha \cdot 64 \cdot n^{14} \cdot B^8$ (resp. $\alpha' \geq \alpha \cdot 512 \cdot n^{22} \cdot B^{14}$).*

Then, $\mathsf{MP\text{-}LWE}_{d,n,q,\alpha'}$ is at least as hard as primal $\mathsf{RLWE}_{f,q,\alpha}$ (resp. dual $\mathsf{RLWE}_{f,q,\alpha}$) for all admissible polynomials $f \in \mathrm{Adm}_{d,n,q,B,n}$.

Note that if we take $B = \mathrm{poly}(n)$ in the Corollary, then α' can be taken as small as $\alpha \cdot \mathrm{poly}(n)$. Hence, for such B's, we obtain a reduction from primal/dual RLWE to MP-LWE with a polynomial loss for $\geq 90\%$ of the polynomials of degree in $[d, n]$ with coefficients bounded by B (where the 90% is based on numerical experiments) .

Proof. Let f be an admissible polynomial in $\mathrm{Adm}_{d,n,q,B,n}$ and let us call m its degree. Then, by definition of $\mathrm{Adm}_{d,n,q,B,n}$, we know that $D(f) \leq n$. We also know that the coefficients of f are bounded in absolute value by B, hence $\|f\| \leq \sqrt{m}B$ and so $\Delta_f^{1/m} \leq m^2 B^2$ (see preliminaries). From preliminaries, we also know that $\Delta_K^{1/m} \cdot \mathcal{N}(\mathcal{C}_\mathcal{O})^{1/m} = \Delta_f^{1/m}$, where $\mathcal{O} = \mathbb{Z}[x]/f(x)$. Finally, using the inequalities $d \leq m \leq n$, we obtain that for f in $\mathrm{Adm}_{d,n,q,B,n}$, it holds that

$$64\sqrt{md} \cdot m^4 \cdot \Delta_K^{4/m} \cdot \mathcal{N}(\mathcal{C}_\mathcal{O})^{2/m} \cdot D(f) \leq 64 \cdot n^{14} \cdot B^8$$
$$512\sqrt{md} \cdot m^6 \cdot \Delta_K^{7/m} \cdot \mathcal{N}(\mathcal{C}_\mathcal{O})^{2/m} \cdot D(f) \leq 512 \cdot n^{22} \cdot B^{14}.$$

Let us now verify that the conditions required to apply Theorem 5.3 to f are satisfied. First, q is coprime with the constant coefficient of f by definition of $\mathrm{Adm}_{d,n,q,B,n}$. Moreover, q is coprime with Δ_f by definition of $\mathrm{Adm}_{d,n,q,B,n}$, which implies that q is coprime with $\mathcal{N}(\mathcal{C}_\mathcal{O})$ (since $\mathcal{N}(\mathcal{C}_\mathcal{O})$ divides Δ_f, see preliminaries). Moreover, $q \geq 8n \geq 8m$ by assumption. Hence, we can apply Theorem 5.3 to f, to obtain a probabilistic polynomial time reduction from primal/dual $\mathsf{RLWE}_{f,q,\alpha}$ to $\mathsf{MP\text{-}LWE}_{q,n,d,\alpha'}$ with

$$\alpha' = \begin{cases} \alpha \cdot 64\sqrt{md} \cdot m^4 \cdot \Delta_K^{4/m} \cdot \mathcal{N}(\mathcal{C}_\mathcal{O})^{2/m} \cdot D(f) & \textit{for primal-}\mathsf{RLWE}, \\ \\ \alpha \cdot 512\sqrt{md} \cdot m^6 \cdot \Delta_K^{7/m} \cdot \mathcal{N}(\mathcal{C}_\mathcal{O})^{2/m} \cdot D(f) & \textit{for dual-}\mathsf{RLWE}. \end{cases}$$

Using the inequalities proven just above concludes the proof. □

6 Comparison with Peikert-Pepin [PP24]

The analysis of the reduction from RLWE to MP-LWE that we described in the previous sections improves the results from [RSSS17] and [RSW18], by following the same strategy, and optimizing some steps. In [PP24], Peikert and Pepin also proposed a reduction from RLWE to MP-LWE, but following a different strategy. In this section, we compare our analysis of the reduction from [RSSS17,RSW18] with the reduction from Peikert and Pepin. We show that our reduction achieves a smaller noise growth than theirs for most polynomials. But we also show that there exist some polynomials for which Peikert-Pepin's reduction gives better results than ours.

6.1 Recalling the Reduction from Peikert-Pepin

We first recall the reduction from RLWE to MP-LWE obtained by the authors of [PP24]. Their reduction requires that the number field K is monogenic, i.e., that $\mathcal{O}_K = \mathbb{Z}[x]/f(x)$.[6]

Theorem 6.1 (Adapted from [PP24, Cor. 5.5]). *Let $d \leq n$ be positive integers. Let f be a monic irreducible polynomial of degree d and let $K = \mathbb{Q}[x]/f(x)$ be the field generated by f. Assume that $\mathcal{O}_K = \mathbb{Z}[x]/f(x)$. Let $q > 0$ be an integer and $\alpha \in (0,1)$. Then, there is a* ppt *reduction from* $\mathsf{RLWE}_{f,q,\alpha}$ *to* $\mathsf{MP\text{-}LWE}_{q,n,d,\alpha'}$, *where $\alpha' = \alpha \cdot |||\mathbf{V}_f|||$.*

[6] Their statement actually covers a more general regime: they show a reduction from Order-LWE to MP-LWE for any monogenic order. Since we are interested in this work with RLWE, we instantiate their reduction to this specific case.

Proof We simply instantiated [PP24, Cor. 5.5] with the order $\mathcal{O} = \mathcal{O}_K$, in the case where $\mathcal{O}_K = \mathbb{Z}[x]/f(x)$, and adapted the phrasing to our notation. With our notations, $\mathcal{O}$ admits as power basis $(1, x, \ldots, x^{d-1})$ and the matrix $\mathbf{P}$ (from [PP24, Cor. 5.5]) associated to this power basis is simply $\mathbf{V}_f\mathbf{V}_f^T$. □

Peikert and Pepin also gave in [PP24, Lemma 5.6] an example of a set of polynomials achieving a polynomial noise growth. We recall this set here. For $d, B > 0$ integers and $c \in (0, 1)$, we define $\mathrm{Adm}^{PP}_{d,B,c}$ the set of all monic irreducible polynomials f of degree d of the form

$$f(x) = x^d + g(x),$$

where $g(x)$ is a polynomial of degree at most $(1 - c)d$ and has coefficients in $[-B, B]$. The authors then proved that for a constant c and a polynomially bounded B, the noise growth of Theorem 6.1 remains polynomially bounded. More precisely, then proved the following result.

Lemma 6.2 ([PP24, Lemma 5.6]). *Let $d, B > 0$ be integers, and $c \in (0, 1)$. For any $f \in \mathrm{Adm}^{PP}_{d,B,c}$ such that $\mathbb{Z}[x]/f(x)$ is maximal in $\mathbb{Q}[x]/f(x)$, there is a* ppt *reduction from* $\mathsf{RLWE}_{f,q,\alpha}$ *to* $\mathsf{MP\text{-}LWE}_{q,n,d,\alpha'}$ *where* $\alpha' = \alpha \cdot d \cdot (dB)^{1/c}$.

In order to have a similar noise growth as in our Corollary 5.5, let us fix for instance $c = 1/14$.

6.2 Comparison

Let us now compare Theorems 5.3 and 6.1. A first observation is that there are some small constraints that differ a bit in the two statements: we require that the modulus q is coprime with the constant coefficient of f and the discriminant of f, whereas [PP24] has no restriction on q; on the other hand [PP24] requires that the degree of f is exactly d whereas we allow the degree to be any $m \in [d, n]$. These differences are quite minor however, and the main difference between the two statements lies is in the noise growth (i.e., how larger α' is compared to α). This is what we will compare in this section.

First of all, let's consider the set of admissible polynomials $\mathrm{Adm}^{PP}_{d,B,1/14}$ from [PP24] and $\mathrm{Adm}_{d,d,B,d}$ from our Definition 5.4 (we take $n = d$ to ease the comparison). We have already argued that our set $\mathrm{Adm}_{d,d,B,d}$ contains experimentally at least 90% of all monic irreducible polynomials of degree d and coefficients bounded by B. On the other hand, the set $\mathrm{Adm}^{PP}_{d,B,1/14}$ contains at most a proportion $B^{-d/14}$ of all monic irreducible polynomials of degree d and coefficients bounded by B (since it requires $d/14$ coefficients of the polynomial to be equal to 0), a proportion that goes to 0 exponentially fast as d goes to infinity. Our set of admissible polynomials is hence arguably larger than the one from [PP24].

Still, we would like to emphasize that even if our set $\mathrm{Adm}_{d,d,B,d}$ is larger than the set $\mathrm{Adm}^{PP}_{d,B,1/14}$, it does not contain it fully. Indeed, the set $\mathrm{Adm}^{PP}_{d,B,1/14}$ contains the Bugeaud-Mignotte polynomials $g_{d,a} = x^d - 2(ax-1)^2$, whereas we have seen in Sect. 4.2 that these polynomials do not belong to our set of admissible polynomials.

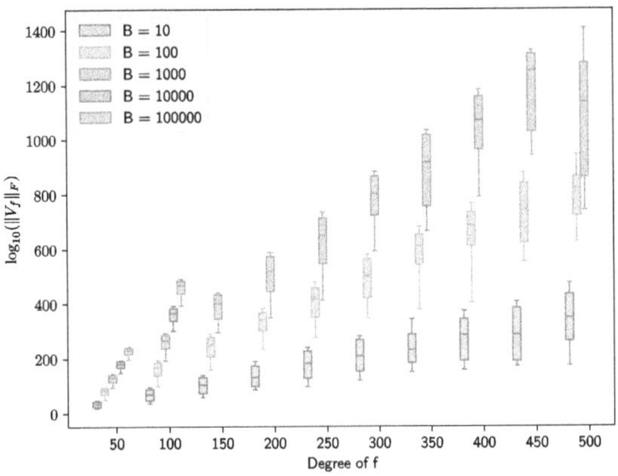

Fig. 5. The quantity $\log_{10}(\|\mathbf{V}_f\|_F)$ as a function of the degree of f for random polynomials with coefficients in $[-B, B]$. The boxes correspond to the interval $(0.25, 0.75)$ and the whiskers correspond to $(0.1, 0.9)$.

Once we have compared the set of admissible polynomials from [PP24] with our set of admissible polynomials, we can also wonder whether the restrictions on the set from [PP24] are an artifact of their proof or not. In other words: if we take a random polynomial f, does it have a small $|||\mathbf{V}_f|||$ (and hence induces a small noise growth in Theorem 6.1) with good probability? We performed experiments to test this, and observed that random polynomials f are very likely to have a very large $|||\mathbf{V}_f|||$, growing exponentially quickly with the degree of f. The results of our experiments are shown in Fig. 5. Note that the vertical axis of this figure is in log scale. We computed the Frobenius norm of the matrix $\mathbf{V}_f$ instead of the spectral norm, because it was easier to compute, but recall that the two quantities are within a factor $\sqrt{d}$, so the change only has a very limited impact on the actual values. One can see on Fig. 5 that at least 90% of the randomly tested polynomials have a norm of the Vandermonde matrix which grows exponentially with the degree of the polynomial. Hence, the set of admissible polynomials for [PP24] does not seem to contain a non-negligible proportion of all polynomials with bounded coefficients.

We also computed the Frobenius norm of the Vandermonde matrix $\|\mathbf{V}_f\|_F$ for random Bugeaud-Mignotte polynomials, and we observed that, in this case, the norm of the Vandermonde matrix increases only polynomially (and even linearly) with the degree of f, as was expected (see Fig. 6). The code used for both experiments is available at https://plmlab.math.cnrs.fr/apelletm/code-mplwe.

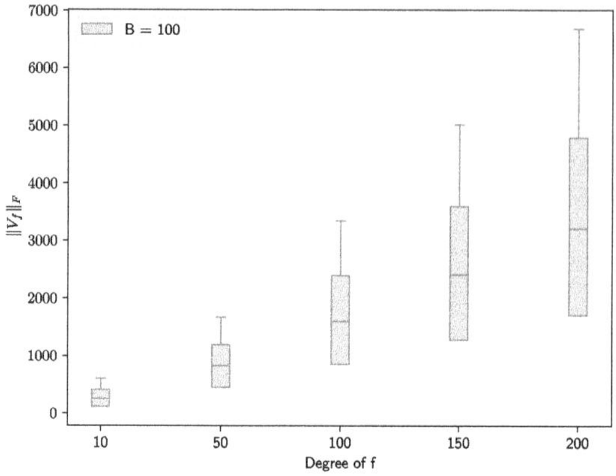

Fig. 6. The quantity $\|\mathbf{V}_f\|_F$ as a function of the degree of f for random Bugeaud-Mignotte polynomials with coefficients in $[-100, 100]$. The boxes correspond to the interval $(0.25, 0.75)$ and the whiskers correspond to $(0.1, 0.9)$.

Acknowledgments. The authors would like to warmly thank Alexandre Wallet, who suggested that we look at the Bugeaud-Mignotte polynomials for our counter-examples. We are also grateful to Wenwen Xia, for noticing a sign mistake in Lemma 4.1, as well as Damien Stehlé, Aurel Page, and Camilla Hollanti for helpful discussions. Finally, we would like to thank the reviewers of TCC'25 and PKC'26 for their constructive comments. Alice Pellet-Mary is supported by the TOTORO ANR grant (ANR-23-CE48-0002) and by the France 2030 program, managed by the French National Research Agency (ANR-22-PETQ-0008 PQ-TLS). Rahinatou Yuh Njah Nchiwo is supported in part by a PhD scholarship from the Magnus Ehrnrooth Foundation, Finland, and by the Vilho, Yrjö and Kalle Väisälä Fund, and in part by Business Finland Co-innovation Consortium Grant (#BFRK/473/31/2024, PI C. Hollanti) and by Research Council of Finland Grant (#351271, PI C. Hollanti). The support from the Foundation for Aalto University Science and Technology toward a research visit to the University of Bordeaux is also gratefully acknowledged.

References

[BBD+19] Bai, S., Boudgoust, K., Das, D., Roux-Langlois, A., Wen, W., Zhang, Z.: Middle-product learning with rounding problem and its applications. In: Galbraith, S.D., Moriai, S. (eds.) ASIACRYPT 2019. LNCS, vol. 11921, pp. 55–81. Springer, Cham (2019). https://doi.org/10.1007/978-3-030-34578-5_3

[BBPS19] Bolboceanu, M., Brakerski, Z., Perlman, R., Sharma, D.: Order-LWE and the hardness of ring-LWE with entropic secrets. In: Galbraith, S.D., Moriai, S. (eds.) ASIACRYPT 2019. LNCS, vol. 11922, pp. 91–120. Springer, Cham (2019). https://doi.org/10.1007/978-3-030-34621-8_4

[BDH+20] Bai, S., et al.: MPSign: a signature from small-secret middle-product learning with errors. In: Kiayias, A., Kohlweiss, M., Wallden, P., Zikas, V. (eds.)

PKC 2020. LNCS, vol. 12111, pp. 66–93. Springer, Cham (2020). https://doi.org/10.1007/978-3-030-45388-6_3
[BGV14] Brakerski, Z., Gentry, C., Vaikuntanathan, V.: (Leveled) fully homomorphic encryption without bootstrapping. ACM Trans. Comput. Theory (TOCT) **6**(3), 1–36 (2014)
[BM04] Bugeaud, Y., Mignotte, M.: On the distance between roots of integer polynomials. Proc. Edinb. Math. Soc. **47**(3), 553–556 (2004)
[BM10] Bugeaud, Y., Mignotte, M.: Polynomial root separation. Int. J. Number Theory **6**(03), 587–602 (2010)
[Con09] Conrad, K.: The different ideal. Expository papers/Lecture notes (2009). http://www.math.uconn.edu/kconrad/blurbs/gradnumthy/different.pdf
[DAZ19] Das, D., Au, M.H., Zhang, Z.: Ring signatures based on middle-product learning with errors problems. In: Buchmann, J., Nitaj, A., Rachidi, T. (eds.) AFRICACRYPT 2019. LNCS, vol. 11627, pp. 139–156. Springer, Cham (2019). https://doi.org/10.1007/978-3-030-23696-0_8
[FLA23] Fan, J., Lu, X., Au, M.H.: Adaptively secure identity-based encryption from middle-product learning with errors. In: Australasian Conference on Information Security and Privacy, pp. 320–340. Springer, Cham (2023)
[Hir18] Hiromasa, R.: Digital signatures from the middle-product LWE. In: Baek, J., Susilo, W., Kim, J. (eds.) ProvSec 2018. LNCS, vol. 11192, pp. 239–257. Springer, Cham (2018). https://doi.org/10.1007/978-3-030-01446-9_14
[HPS06] Hoffstein, J., Pipher, J., Silverman, J.H.: NTRU: a ring-based public key cryptosystem. In: Buhler, J.P. (ed.) ANTS 1998. LNCS, vol. 1423, pp. 267–288. Springer, Heidelberg (1998). https://doi.org/10.1007/BFb0054868
[LDSP20] Le, H.Q., Duong, D.H., Susilo, W., Pieprzyk, J.: Trapdoor delegation and HIBE from middle-product LWE in standard model. In: Conti, M., Zhou, J., Casalicchio, E., Spognardi, A. (eds.) ACNS 2020. LNCS, vol. 12146, pp. 130–149. Springer, Cham (2020). https://doi.org/10.1007/978-3-030-57808-4_7
[LM06] Lyubashevsky, V., Micciancio, D.: Generalized compact knapsacks are collision resistant. In: Bugliesi, M., Preneel, B., Sassone, V., Wegener, I. (eds.) ICALP 2006. LNCS, vol. 4052, pp. 144–155. Springer, Heidelberg (2006). https://doi.org/10.1007/11787006_13
[LPR10] Lyubashevsky, V., Peikert, C., Regev, O.: On ideal lattices and learning with errors over rings. In: Gilbert, H. (ed.) EUROCRYPT 2010. LNCS, vol. 6110, pp. 1–23. Springer, Heidelberg (2010). https://doi.org/10.1007/978-3-642-13190-5_1
[LS15] Langlois, A., Stehlé, D.: Worst-case to average-case reductions for module lattices. Des. Codes Crypt. **75**(3), 565–599 (2015)
[LSW+23] Lin, H., Sun, S.-F., Wang, M., Liu, J.K., Wang, W.: Shorter linkable ring signature based on middle-product learning with errors problem. Comput. J. **66**(12), 2974–2989 (2023)
[LVV19] Lombardi, A., Vaikuntanathan, V., Vuong, T.D.: Lattice trapdoors and IBE from middle-product LWE. In: Hofheinz, D., Rosen, A. (eds.) TCC 2019. LNCS, vol. 11891, pp. 24–54. Springer, Cham (2019). https://doi.org/10.1007/978-3-030-36030-6_2
[Lyu16] Lyubashevsky, V.: Digital signatures based on the hardness of ideal lattice problems in all rings. In: Cheon, J.H., Takagi, T. (eds.) ASIACRYPT 2016. LNCS, vol. 10032, pp. 196–214. Springer, Heidelberg (2016). https://doi.org/10.1007/978-3-662-53890-6_7

[Mah64] Mahler, K.: An inequality for the discriminant of a polynomial. Michigan Math. J. **11**(3), 257–262 (1964)

[NP26] Nchiwo, R.Y.N., Pellet-Mary, A.: Improved reduction from RLWE to MP-LWE. Cryptology ePrint Archive (2026)

[Pei16] Peikert, C.: How (not) to instantiate ring-LWE. In: Zikas, V., De Prisco, R. (eds.) SCN 2016. LNCS, vol. 9841, pp. 411–430. Springer, Cham (2016). https://doi.org/10.1007/978-3-319-44618-9_22

[PP24] Peikert, C., Pepin, Z.: Algebraically structured LWE, revisited. J. Cryptol. **37**(3), 28 (2024)

[PR06] Peikert, C., Rosen, A.: Efficient collision-resistant hashing from worst-case assumptions on cyclic lattices. In: Halevi, S., Rabin, T. (eds.) TCC 2006. LNCS, vol. 3876, pp. 145–166. Springer, Heidelberg (2006). https://doi.org/10.1007/11681878_8

[RSSS17] Roşca, M., Sakzad, A., Stehlé, D., Steinfeld, R.: Middle-product learning with errors. In: Katz, J., Shacham, H. (eds.) CRYPTO 2017. LNCS, vol. 10403, pp. 283–297. Springer, Cham (2017). https://doi.org/10.1007/978-3-319-63697-9_10

[RSW18] Rosca, M., Stehlé, D., Wallet, A.: On the ring-LWE and polynomial-LWE problems. In: Nielsen, J.B., Rijmen, V. (eds.) EUROCRYPT 2018. LNCS, vol. 10820, pp. 146–173. Springer, Cham (2018). https://doi.org/10.1007/978-3-319-78381-9_6

[SSTX09] Stehlé, D., Steinfeld, R., Tanaka, K., Xagawa, K.: Efficient public key encryption based on ideal lattices. In: Matsui, M. (ed.) ASIACRYPT 2009. LNCS, vol. 5912, pp. 617–635. Springer, Heidelberg (2009). https://doi.org/10.1007/978-3-642-10366-7_36

[SSZ17] Steinfeld, R., Sakzad, A., Zhao, R.K.: Titanium: proposal for a NIST post-quantum public-key encryption and KEM standard. NIST PQC Round **1**(4), 12 (2017)

[SSZ19] Steinfeld, R., Sakzad, A., Zhao, R.K.: Practical MP-LWE-based encryption balancing security-risk versus efficiency. Des. Codes Crypt. **87**(12), 2847–2884 (2019)

[Sut16] Sutherland, A.: The different and the discriminant. Lecture notes: Number theory I, Fall 2016. Lecture 12 (2016). https://math.mit.edu/classes/18.785/2016fa/LectureNotes12.pdf

[Tab21] Taboga, M.: Linear combinations of normal random variables, lectures on probability theory and mathematical statistics (2021). Online appendix. https://www.statlect.com/probability-distributions/normal-distribution-linear-combinations

[YYZW22] Yang, N., Yang, S., Zhao, Y., Wu, W.: Inner product encryption from middle-product learning with errors. In: International Symposium on Security and Privacy in Social Networks and Big Data, pp. 94–113. Springer, Cham (2022)

Signature Schemes

Batched & Non-interactive Blind Signatures from Lattices

Foteini Baldimtsi[1,2], Rishab Goyal[3], and Aayush Yadav[1(✉)]

[1] George Mason University, Fairfax, USA
{foteini,ayadav5}@gmu.edu
[2] Mysten Labs, Palo Alto, USA
[3] University of Wisconsin – Madison, Madison, USA
rishab@cs.wisc.edu

Abstract. Non-interactive blind signatures (NIBS; EUROCRYPT '23) allow a signer to asynchronously generate presignatures for a recipient, ensuring that only the intended recipient can extract a "blinded" signature for a random message.

We introduce a new generalization called non-interactive *batched* blind signatures (NIBBS). Our goal is to reduce the computation and communication costs for signers and receivers, by batching multiple blind signature queries. More precisely, we define the property of 'succinct communication' which requires that the communication cost from signer to receiver be *independent* of the batch size. NIBBS is very suitable for large-scale deployments requiring only minimal signer-side effort.

We design a NIBBS scheme and prove its security based on the hardness of lattice assumptions (in the random oracle model). When instantiated with the low-depth PRF candidate "Crypto Dark Matter" (TCC '18) and the succinct lattice-based proof system for rank-1 constraint systems (CRYPTO '23), our final signature size is 308 KB with < 1 KB communication.

Keywords: blind signatures · non-interactive protocols · batched protocols · lattice-based cryptography

1 Introduction

Blind signatures are a special class of digital signatures that enable a receiver to obtain a signature on a message without revealing the message to the signer. They were introduced by Chaum [Cha83] as a building block for private e-cash. The idea was that a bank, acting as the signer, signs a coin's serial number and some other useful information without seeing it, so that when the coin is later spent, the bank cannot link it to any specific user. Since then, blind signatures have emerged as an attractive tool across a variety of applications. These include e-voting [CGT06], anonymous credentials [PZ13,BL13,FHS15,DGS+18], direct anonymous attestation [BCC04], and cryptocurrency mixers [HBG16,HAB+17].

S. Bai and E. Persichetti (Eds.): PKC 2026, LNCS 16551, pp. 199–234, 2026.
https://doi.org/10.1007/978-3-032-26731-3_7

Blind signatures are typically formalized as a two-party protocol between a *signer* (holding a secret key sk) and a *receiver* (holding a message μ and signer's verification key vk). In blind signatures, signing is an *interactive* process—the recipient sends a "blinded" message to the signer, and the signer responds with a signature on the blinded message. The recipient then locally "un-blinds" the signature and outputs the final message-signature pair (μ, σ) which can be verified using vk. The two central security properties are *blindness* (the signer learns nothing about μ and cannot link the transcripts of protocol executions to the signatures that it created) and *one-more unforgeability* (if the receiver is granted Q signatures, it cannot produce $Q+1$ or more distinct valid signatures) [JLO97].

Non-interactive Blind Signatures. Blind signatures are inherently interactive protocols, making *two-move* protocols *round-optimal.* However, the two-move barrier holds only if the message to be signed is selected by the receiver. In many applications, this is not the case! For instance, in e-cash, coins are simply signatures on random coin IDs. Thus, a natural question is whether we can design *non-interactive* blind signatures, when the messages are random strings.

This was studied in the groundbreaking work of Hanzlik [Han23]. Clearly, a non-interactive blind signature (NIBS) will lead to *minimal round complexity* (just one-move, from signer to receiver). Hanzlik pointed out that NIBS could readily replace standard blind signatures in any application where the message choice was unimportant and could be random/unstructured. Interestingly, there are many such applications beyond e-cash. For instance, NIBS can be used for anonymous token systems (à la Privacy Pass [DGS+18]), lottery systems [Han23] and cryptocurrency airdrops [BCGY24], where coins are distributed by creating and publishing a pre-signature, enabling users to privately obtain the final signatures (coins). Among these, anonymous token systems stand out as a particularly compelling application, given the growing industry interest[1] and the ongoing standardization efforts through IETF [IET25b].

Batching Non-interactive Blind Signatures. In many applications, users require *multiple tokens at once* rather than a single token each time they contact the issuer. For instance, this happens in Privacy Pass [DGS+18], which was originally proposed for anonymous authentication in content delivery networks (CDNs). In light of many such emerging applications, the concept of batching in (interactive) blind signatures was recently introduced by Hanzlik, Loss and Wagner [HLW23]. The importance of batched token issuance is equally reflected in ongoing standardization efforts, such as a recent IETF draft [IET25a], which proposes batched issuance techniques for privacy-preserving tokens.

Somewhat unfortunately, the [HLW23] construction only offers amortized cost benefits in the interactive setting. This does not come as a surprise given that, in regular blind signatures, the messages are selected by the receiver, and for each message the signer has to compute a separate response. Thus, the com-

[1] Major technology companies have been actively developing such systems, including Google's Private State Tokens [Goo25] and Cloudflare's Privacy Pass [MRFH25].

munication complexity (both, Receiver → Signer and Signer → Receiver) scales linearly with the batch size.

Our observation is that *batching* makes significantly more sense in the non-interactive setting. In NIBS, a receiver/client could simply specify the number of tokens/signatures it wants (say N), and the signer could (potentially) issue a single pre-signature that can be "un-blinded" to obtain N blind signatures. Since each blind signature is supposed to be associated to a random message, we could hope to keep the communication cost to be *sub-linear* (and ideally constant) with respect to the batch size. As such, NIBS already eliminates the need for back-and-forth communication between signer and receiver, and we believe a batched variant would significantly bring down computation and communication costs, enabling large-scale deployments with minimal signer-side effort.

The major question that inspires this work is thus:

> $\mathcal{Q}$. *Can we design a practical batched NIBS scheme with provable security, while keeping communication cost independent of batch size?*

Our Results. In this work, we introduce the concept of *batching* in NIBS and define the notion of non-interactive batched blind signatures (NIBBS). We provide a practical and post-quantum NIBBS construction, based on hardness of lattice problems.

Taking the batch size to be 1, our NIBBS scheme also gives the first concretely efficient post-quantum secure NIBS scheme. Prior to this work, the known post-quantum constructions either required a relaxed notion of blindness [BCGY24] or gave up concrete efficiency [BCGY24, ZCH25]. In other words, we did not have a candidate construction for NIBS that was *practical and post-quantum.* We summarize our contributions below:

1. **Formalizing and constructing non-interactive batched blind signatures.** We formally introduce the notion of batching in NIBS. We then provide a NIBBS construction and prove it secure under the hardness of the randomized one-more ISIS assumption [BCGY24] (and other standard lattice assumptions [Ajt96, Reg05]) in the random oracle model [BR94]. Notably, the communication cost of our scheme is independent of the batch size, and at just under 1 KB, is nearly optimal. Current conservative estimates put the size of a single blind signature to be around 308 KB, depending on the parameter choices. We also present an alternate construction from the ISIS_f assumption [BLNS23b] that bypasses some of the technical shortcomings of the previous approach.
2. **Practical-ish post-quantum NIBS.** Using the same instantiation, we also obtain the first concretely efficient post-quantum (non-batched) NIBS scheme that is provably secure under the same set of assumptions. As with the batched scheme, the overall communication is minimal (< 1 KB), and our estimate puts the size of the final blind signature to be between slightly smaller at 306 KB.

1.1 Related Work

Since the introduction of blind signatures, numerous schemes have been designed based on various number-theoretic assumptions. Some constructions are based in the plain model [GRS+11,BFPV13,GG14,Gha17], while many practical schemes rely on idealized models for their security proofs [PS96,PS00,Abe01,Bol03, BL13,FHS15,HKL19,KLR21,KLX22,CAHL+22,TZ22,CATZ24]. We also have generic constructions due to Juels et al. [JLO97] and Fischlin [Fis06], who developed the first generic blind signature scheme achieving optimal round complexity.

In recent years, several round-optimal schemes from lattices have been proposed [LNP22a,dPK22,AKSY22,BLNS23a]. Lyubashevsky et al. [LNP22a] introduced a scheme using one-time signatures under Module-SIS and Module-LWE assumptions, but it supports only a bounded number of signatures per key, with each signature around 150 KB. Del Pino and Katsumata [dPK22] adapted Fischlin's paradigm for unbounded signatures, reducing the size to 102 KB. Agrawal et al. [AKSY22] used lattice-based NIZKs to shrink signature size to 45 KB and transcript size to 1 KB relying on the one-more ISIS assumption [AKSY22]. Beullens et al. [BLNS23a] improved this by shifting costly computation to the receiver, reducing the signature size to 22 KB but increasing the first message to several hundred kilobytes. Most recently, Jeudy and Sanders [JS24] showed that it was possible to reuse randomness from commitments to mask pre-signature, achieving a 41 KB signature size, but with faster signing than previous works.

Table 1. Communication and signature sizes of practical batched blind signature schemes (in kilobytes). Communication is given for batches of N messages. Horizontal line through a row indicates that the number is common across all batch sizes.

Scheme	Post-quantum secure	#Moves	Communication $N=4$	$N=16$	$N=256$	$\lvert\sigma\rvert$
[HLW23]	✗	3	67.92–175.88	206.72–588.32	2982.4–8837.12	9.41–13.98
This work (NIBBS, §5)	✓	1	——	0.74	——	308.78

Non-interactivity. The notion of non-interactive blind signatures (NIBS) was introduced by Hanzlik [Han23], who proposed a generic construction using verifiable random functions, digital signatures, and dual-mode non-interactive witness indistinguishable proofs, proving security in the random oracle model (RO). Hanzlik also developed a practical NIBS scheme based on signatures on equivalence classes [HS14,FHS19], with security proven in the generic group model (GGM). All schemes in [Han23] were proved to satisfy weak blindness. Building on this, Baldimtsi et al. [BCGY24] identified limitations in the original definitional framework [Han23], proposing an improved framework with stronger security definitions. They presented two new constructions: a generic paradigm using circuit-private leveled homomorphic encryption (LHE) and a simpler approach based on general-purpose non-interactive zero-knowledge (NIZK) proofs. Additionally, they introduced a practical lattice-based NIBS scheme under a new randomized one-more-ISIS (rOM-ISIS) assumption, though it only satisfied the weaker security properties from the original framework.

Recently, Zhang, et al. [ZCH25] gave a construction for lattice-based NIBS in the random oracle model by partially instantiating the generic VRF construction of [Han23] and proved blindness under the weaker definitions. This construction was proven insecure by a concurrent work [GKK+25], who also gave an updated construction which is claimed to to be secure under the rOM-ISIS assumption. We do not include this work in our comparisons as it does not give concrete estimates, however we note that the specific VRF instantiation that the authors propose [EKS+21] yields a scheme with highly limited reusability as [EKS+21] only supports up to 5 VRF evaluations under the same key. This can be circumvented with the lattice-based VRF of Esgin, et al. [ESLR23] at the cost of two additional proofs of hash computations, which leads us to believe that our scheme is concretely more efficient.

Finally, Hanzlik, et al. [HPZ25] recently proposed a generic construction using garbled circuits, which can be instantiated to support pre-signature issuance on standard RSA public keys.

Table 2. Comparison of state-of-the-art practical lattice-based blind signatures, all sizes in kilobytes. R → S indicates the total communication from the recipient to the signer (similarly S → R. [BCGY24] is omitted from the list as it does not achieve full blindness.

		Communication		
Scheme	**Assumption**	R → S	S → R	$\lvert\sigma\rvert$
[AKSY22]	OM-ISIS	0.96	0.56	45
[BLNS23a]	MLWE, MSIS	∼ 50	∼ 60	22
[JS24]	MLWE, MSIS	8.73	50.89	41.12
This work (NIBS)	rOM-ISIS	—	0.68	306.18

Batching. The concept of batching in blind signatures was introduced by Hanzlik, et al. [HLW23]. Their main result was a concurrently secure round-optimal blind signature based on cut-and-choose. In addition, they introduced a formal model for batched blind signatures, and proposed a batching technique for their scheme in order to achieve reduced (amortized) communication complexity.

We give a comparison of our NI$\underline{\text{B}}$BS scheme with other batched blind signatures in Table 1 and of our NIBS scheme with other state-of-the-art lattice-based blind signatures in Table 2.

2 Technical Overview

We introduce a new generalization for NIBS, that we call non-interactive *batched* blind signatures (NIBBS). Briefly, the goal in NIBBS is to provide a new capability by allowing a receiver to derive an entire batch of (blind) message-signature pairs from a single pre-signature. As suggested earlier, this drastically reduces the overall communication size between signer and receiver for applications where a receiver needs more than one blind signature.

Formalizing NIBBS. For simplicity, consider a globally fixed batch size N. Syntactically, a NIBBS scheme (similar to NIBS) consists of the following algorithms: the Setup algorithm generates the system's global public parameters pp, which serves as a common reference string (CRS); two key generation algorithms $\mathsf{KeyGen}_S \rightarrow (\mathsf{sk}, \mathsf{vk})$ for the signer and $\mathsf{KeyGen}_R \rightarrow (\mathsf{sk}_R, \mathsf{pk}_R)$ for the receiver; using the secret key sk, the signer runs the randomized Issue algorithm for any receiver's public key pk_R to compute a pre-signature psig and a nonce nonce, which represents (a portion of) the signer's randomness; finally, the receiver's Obtain algorithm outputs N message-signature pairs $[\![\mu, \sigma]\!] := \{(\mu_1, \sigma_1), (\mu_2, \sigma_2), \ldots, (\mu_N, \sigma_N)\}$.

Baldimtsi, et al. [BCGY24] introduced the notion of reusability for NIBS. Informally, it requires that a signer be able to issue multiple distinct pre-signatures (leading to multiple distinct message-signature pairs) for the *same* receiver public key pk_R. Clearly, without reusability a NIBS would be somewhat ineffectual. As with standard NIBS, we define reusability in the batched setting to guarantee that a signer is able to issue multiple pre-signatures to the same receiver public key pk_R, and further that the receiver can obtain N distinct final message-signature pairs for each pre-signature.

In terms of security, NIBBS should satisfy the properties of *one-more unforgeability* and *blindness*. One-more unforgeability in the NIBBS context is a natural extension of the same property for NIBS. Namely, the adversary, after seeing Q pre-signatures for receiver public keys of its choice, must produce $(NQ+1)$ valid signatures.

Blindness ensures that a final signature cannot be linked to its corresponding pre-signature. However, since the receiver now obtains an entire batch of signatures from a single pre-signature, we must ensure that our definition not only captures the unlinkability between signatures from different batches, but also between signatures *within* the same batch. To that end, we define two security notions—*inter-batch blindness* and *intra-batch blindness*. For the inter-batch blindness experiment, the changes from the non-batched setting are minimal. Specifically, the adversary is given access to the Obtain oracle with respect to two different receiver secret keys, sk_{R_0} and sk_{R_1}, and outputs two pairs of $(\mathsf{psig}_b, \mathsf{nonce}_b)_{b \in \{0,1\}}$. The key difference in the batched setting is that the challenger now runs the Obtain algorithm on each $(\mathsf{psig}_b, \mathsf{nonce}_b)$, and provides the adversary with two batches of message-signature pairs, $[\![\mu, \sigma]\!]_{\hat{b}}$ and $[\![\mu, \sigma]\!]_{1-\hat{b}}$ for a random bit $\hat{b}$. The adversary's goal remains to correctly map each batch to their corresponding pre-signature, i.e., to guess the bit $\hat{b}$.

For intra-batch blindness, the adversary is given access to the Obtain oracle with respect to a single receiver secret key, sk_R, and outputs two pairs of $(\mathsf{psig}_b, \mathsf{nonce}_b)_{b\in\{0,1\}}$ along with a "permutation" map, φ. The challenger runs the Obtain algorithm on each $(\mathsf{psig}_b, \mathsf{nonce}_b)$ and provides the adversary with the resulting $2N$ message-signature pairs, either in the original order if the random bit $\hat{b} = 0$, or permuted according to φ otherwise. Once again, the goal of the adversary is to correctly guess $\hat{b}$. Importantly, this ensures that an adversary cannot link final signatures to their respective batches, thus giving us the aforementioned "intra"-batch blindness property.

Constructing NI$\underline{\text{B}}$BS. The starting point for our design is the generic template for NIBS given in [BCGY24]. The core idea is as follows: the receiver's public key pk_R is set as a commitment to a pseudorandom function (PRF) key K, while sk_R is set to be K along with the opening randomness for the commitment. To issue a pre-signature, the signer samples a random string r and signs $\mathsf{pk}_R||r$, sending both the (pre)signature as well as the random nonce r. At the other end, the receiver computes the message μ as a PRF evaluation of r under key K, and the corresponding signature as a proof of knowledge of a pre-signature on $\mathsf{pk}_R||r$ such that pk_R is a commitment to K and μ is a PRF evaluation of r under K.

The binding property of the commitment scheme ensures that, with high probability, the receiver computes a single signature for a given pre-signature and nonce pair, then by NIZK soundness[2] and unforgeability of the underlying signature scheme, we can prove one-more unforgeability of NIBS. Blindness for this design follows from simpler reductions to the (multi-theorem) zero-knowledge property of NIZKs and commitment hiding security.

As it turns out, this NIBS template can be quite naturally generalized to support *batching*. In particular, instead of evaluating the PRF on nonce r, the receiver evaluates it on $r||\mathsf{i}$ for each $\mathsf{i} \in [N]$, thus obtaining N distinct messages, and their corresponding signatures. In order to guarantee unforgeability, the statement for the ith batch must additionally require that $\mathsf{i} \leqslant N$, with i as part of the witness.

Lattice-Based Instantiation. We now explain how to instantiate the generic approach essentially starting from the template of [AKSY22, BCGY24]. Let the vector $\mathbf{k}$ of small norm be the receiver's secret PRF key. Then, for a random vector $\mathbf{u}$, and public matrix $\mathbf{C}$, the receiver's public key pk_R is given by $\mathbf{t} := \mathbf{C} \cdot \mathbf{k} + \mathsf{H}(\mathbf{u})$.

Given $\mathbf{t}$, the signer with public verification key matrices $\mathbf{A}$ and $\mathbf{B}$ can now create a pre-signature by (pre-)signing $\mathbf{t}$ along with a short random nonce vector $\mathbf{r}$ by using trapdoor lattice sampling [GPV08] (see also [AKSY22, BLNS23a, BCGY24]) to sample a short preimage $\mathbf{s}$ with respect to $\mathbf{A}$ such that $\mathbf{A}\cdot\mathbf{s}+\mathbf{B}\cdot\mathbf{r} = \mathbf{t}$ and send, both, pre-signature $\mathbf{s}$ and nonce $\mathbf{r}$ to the receiver.

---

[2] To be more precise, this requires the stronger knowledge soundness, which can be generically achieved in the CRS model by relying on public-key encryption.

On receiving the pre-signature and nonce pair, the receiver can compute N random messages as the PRF evaluation $\mu_i := \mathsf{F}_{\mathbf{k}}\left(\mathbf{r}||\vec{i}\right)$ (where $\vec{i}$ is the binary representation of $i \in [N]$), and the corresponding signatures as the NIZK proof π_i stating that, given $\mathbf{A}, \mathbf{B}, \mathbf{C}$ and μ_i, there exist vectors $\mathbf{k}, \mathbf{u}, \mathbf{s}$ and $\mathbf{r}$, and integer i such that $\mathbf{A} \cdot \mathbf{s} + \mathbf{B} \cdot \mathbf{r} = \mathbf{C} \cdot \mathbf{k} + \mathsf{H}(\mathbf{u})$, $\mu_i = \mathsf{F}_{\mathbf{k}}\left(\mathbf{r}||\vec{i}\right)$, $i \in [N]$ and $\|\mathbf{k}\|, \|(\mathbf{s}, \mathbf{r})\|$ are short.

A technical limitation for such Fischlin-style approaches is that the NIZK must be straight-line extractable. Fortunately, we can utilize the folklore "encryption-to-the-sky" trick and have the receiver encrypt its secrets using public key encryption. In particular, this allows a challenger, holding the secret decryption key $\mathsf{sk}_{\mathsf{PKE}}$, to extract all the secrets in a straight-line manner. Let ψ_i be the encryption of the witness to the relation under public key $\mathsf{pk}_{\mathsf{PKE}}$, sampled during setup, and let ρ_i denote the encryption randomness. Then, each NIZK must also prove correct computation of ψ_i where ψ_i and $\mathsf{pk}_{\mathsf{PKE}}$ are part of the instance, and ρ_i of the witness. Importantly, the final signature must now also include ψ_i.

Estimating Efficiency. Efforts to construct practically efficient (non-) interactive blind signature schemes from hard lattices assumptions [AKSY22, BLNS23a, BCGY24] have largely relied on the use of the NIZK proof system of Lyubashevsky, et al. [LNP22b] which produces very short proofs for affine relations. It is therefore crucial in these works that the entire NIZK relation is also composed of affine equations (and norm bounds). Thus, in order to build practical lattice-based NI<u>B</u>BS, we would need to be able to specify the lattice-instantiation explicitly in linear terms. However, for the security of the protocol we need to be able to prove that the final (public) message μ_i was computed as a PRF evaluation of $(\mathbf{r}||\vec{i})$ with key $\mathbf{k}$ where, in particular, $\mathbf{r}$ and $\mathbf{k}$ are hidden as part of the witness of the NIZK (otherwise, blindness can be trivially broken).

This underpins the core technical hurdle in instantiating the generic template for NI<u>B</u>BS via affine relations in order to apply the [LNP22b] framework. Namely, that all popular approaches for designing secure PRFs from lattice-based assumptions require very high degree computations in the inputs and PRF keys [BPR12, BLMR13, BP14]. This technical tension suggests that any natural attempt in instantiating the generic template using practical lattice-based NIZKs will ultimately fail[3].

We remark that for many existing lattice-based PRFs [BPR12, BLMR13, BP14], their evaluation can be segmented into $\sim \lambda$ incremental checks of degree-1 (or 2) such that by linking all $O(\lambda)$ checks together, it can be proven using the [LNP22b] framework that the PRF was correctly computed (this approach

[3] This is in part why Baldimtsi et al. [BCGY24] could only design lattice-based NIBS with *very weak security* [Han23]. They simply omitted the PRF computation entirely, and replaced it with a random linear function. They proved that as long as blindness is only desired against at most two signatures, then their NIBS are secure. Moreover, they suggested that one could easily break blindness of their lattice-based NIBS protocol if an attacker learns as few as *three* blind signatures.

was used in [ADDS21, AG24]). Unfortunately, the family of lattice-based PRFs involve rounding down the final computation (modulo q), to a lower modulus p such that q/p is superpolynomial in the security parameter; an artifact of the reduction from the learning with rounding (LWR) assumption, on which they rely, to the learning with errors (LWE) assumption. Consequently, the modulus for the NIZK proof system, which itself has to be greater than q for soundness, is rather large in practice.

Given, these challenges inherent in instantiating the protocol, we make two crucial design choices intended to make our final approach practical. Firstly, we instantiate our scheme with the Crypto Dark Matter PRF candidate [BIP+18] which can be computed by depth-3 arithmetic circuit. Secondly, we use the lattice-based general purpose SNARK LaBRADOR [BS23] which provides compact proofs for rank-1 constraint systems (R1CS) to avoid any dependence on [LNP22b][4].

In Sect. 5.2, we provide concrete instantiation of parameters for our NI$\underline{\text{B}}$BS construction. The estimated sizes of the pre-signature and the final blind signatures are provided in Tables 1 and 2. Our estimates are not based on aggressive calculations, nor assume any non-standard software optimization tricks. We simply provide our estimates as a proof-of-concept to show practical feasibility of NI$\underline{\text{B}}$BS, and we believe that our framework will serve as an important stepping stone for future research in lattice-based (non-interactive) batched blind signatures.

Remark 2.1 (Fully dynamic batching)**.** While our above exposition considers a fixed batch size N, our approach is much more general. In particular, we can design NI$\underline{\text{B}}$BS with truly dynamic batch sizes. For instance, consider that each receiver–when it contacts a signer–provides a (user-specific) batch size N to the signer. Now to handle such adaptive batch sizes, we make a small adjustment to the pre-signature computation. Instead of creating a (standard) digital signature for just the receiver's public key $\mathsf{pk}_R := \mathbf{t}$, it can create the signature for $\mathsf{pk}_R || N$. Now, during the final blind signature generation, the receiver treats N as part of the NP witness. This readily gives us NI$\underline{\text{B}}$BS with fully dynamic batch size. In the main body, we consider static batch sizes for ease of exposition, however our ideas can be easily generalized as explained here.

3 Preliminaries

Notation. We use λ to denote the security parameter. We use $\leftarrow_\$$ to denote the output of a randomized algorithm and $\leftarrow$ to denote output of a deterministic algorithm. We denote the set of all positive integers up to n as $[n] := \{1, \ldots, n\}$ and the set of all non-negative integers up to n as $[0, n] := \{0\} \cup [n]$.

Following common convention, we use lowercase bold-face letters to denote vectors and uppercase bold-face letters for matrices. For a vector $\mathbf{x}$, x_i denotes its ith element. For a vector $\mathbf{x}$, we write its ℓ_2 norm as $\|\mathbf{x}\|_2$, often dropping the subscript and writing it simply as $\|\mathbf{x}\|$. We write the ℓ_∞ norm of $\mathbf{x}$ as $\|\mathbf{x}\|_\infty$.

[4] LaBRADOR can be made zero-knowledge with a small overhead (cf. [BS23]).

We write polynomials $u(X)$ in indeterminate X simply as u when it is clear from context. In all that follows, $\mathbb{Z}$ is the set of integers, and $\mathbb{Z}_q$ denotes the set of integers modulo q. For a power of two d, we denote by $\mathcal{R}$ the ring $\mathbb{Z}[X]/(X^d+1)$. We write the ring $\mathbb{Z}_q[X]/(X^d+1) \cong \mathcal{R}/q\mathcal{R}$ as $\mathcal{R}_{q,d}$. When the degree is omitted from the subscript, it is assumed to be the fixed protocol parameter d.

Decomposition Gadget. We will utilize a suitable "gadget" matrix $\mathbf{G} \in \mathbb{Z}_q^{n\times n\cdot\ell}$, such that there exists a deterministic inverse function $\mathbf{G}^{-1} : \mathbb{Z}_q^n \to \mathbb{Z}^{n\cdot\ell}$, with a "short" image and $\mathbf{G}\cdot\mathbf{G}^{-1}(\mathbf{x}) = \mathbf{x}$ for any $\mathbf{x} \in \mathbb{Z}_q^n$. A typical example is $\mathbf{G} = \mathbf{I}_n \otimes \left[2^0\ 2^1\ \cdots\ 2^{\ell-1}\right]$ with $\mathbf{G}^{-1}(\mathbf{x})$ defined such that each of its ℓ entries has $\{0,1\}$ coefficients. More simply, $\mathbf{G}^{-1}$ may be viewed as the (entry-wise) binary decomposition function.

Vectorization. The vectorization operation $\mathsf{Vec} : \mathbb{Z}^{n\times m} \to \mathbb{Z}^{nm}$ is a linear algebraic transformation which maps an $n\times m$ matrix to a unique vector of dimension nm. Let $\mathbf{e}_i$ be the ith canonical basis vector for the m-dimensional space, then for a row-major vectorization, it holds that[5] $\mathsf{Vec}(\mathbf{X}) = \sum_{i=1}^{m} (\mathbf{e}_i \otimes \mathbf{I}_n)\,\mathbf{X}\mathbf{e}_i$.

3.1 Randomness Extraction

The min-entropy of a random variable X is defined as $\mathbf{H}_\infty(X) := -\log_2(\max_x \Pr[X = x])$. Let $\Delta(X,Y)$ denote the statistical distance between two random variables X and Y. Below we state the Leftover Hash Lemma (LHL) from [HILL99,DRS04,DRS04].

Lemma 3.1 (Leftover hash lemma). *Let $\mathcal{H} = \{h : X \to Y\}$ be a universal hash family, then for any random variable W taking values in X, the following holds*

$$\Delta\left((h, h(W)), (h, U_Y)\right) \leqslant \frac{1}{2}\sqrt{2^{-\mathbf{H}_\infty(W)}\cdot|Y|},$$

where U_Y denotes uniform distribution over Y.

In our security proofs, we make use of a corollary following from the previous lemma.

Corollary 3.2 *Let $\ell > m\cdot n\log q + \omega(\log n)$, q a prime, and m, n are positive integers. Let $\mathbf{R}$ be an $k\times m$ matrix chosen as per distribution $\mathcal{X}$, where $k = k(n)$ is polynomial in n and $\mathbf{H}_\infty(\mathcal{X}) = \ell$. Let $\mathbf{A}$ and $\mathbf{B}$ be matrices chosen uniformly in $\mathbb{Z}_q^{n\times k}$ and $\mathbb{Z}_q^{n\times m}$, respectively. Then the statistical distance between the following distributions is negligible in n.*

$$\{(\mathbf{A}, \mathbf{A}\cdot\mathbf{R})\} \approx_s \{(\mathbf{A}, \mathbf{B})\}$$

[5] Moreover, for $\mathbf{x} \in \mathbb{Z}^{nm}$ the inverse vectorization is given by $\mathsf{Vec}^{-1}(\mathbf{x}) := \left(\mathsf{Vec}(\mathbf{I}_m)^\top \otimes \mathbf{I}_n\right)\cdot(\mathbf{I}_m \otimes \mathbf{x})$.

3.2 Lattice Preliminaries

Given positive integers n, m, q and a matrix $\mathbf{A} \in \mathbb{Z}_q^{n \times m}$, we let $\Lambda_q^{\perp}(\mathbf{A})$ denote the m-dimensional lattice

$$\{\mathbf{x} \in \mathcal{R}^m \ : \ \mathbf{A} \cdot \mathbf{x} = \mathbf{0} \pmod q\} \ .$$

For $\mathbf{t} \in \mathbb{Z}_q^n$, we let $\Lambda_q^{\mathbf{t}}(\mathbf{A})$ denote the coset $\{\mathbf{x} \in \mathcal{R}^m \ : \ \mathbf{A} \cdot \mathbf{x} = \mathbf{t} \pmod q\}$.

Discrete Gaussians. Let $\mathfrak{s}$ be any positive real number. The discrete Gaussian distribution $\mathfrak{D}_{\mathcal{R}^m, \mathfrak{s}}$ on $\mathcal{R}^m$ with parameter $\mathfrak{s}$ is defined by

$$\rho_{\mathcal{R}^m, \mathfrak{s}}(\mathbf{x}) = \frac{\mathsf{exp}(-\left\|\mathbf{x}\right\|^2/2\mathfrak{s}^2)}{\sum_{\mathbf{z} \in \mathcal{R}^m} \mathsf{exp}(-\left\|\mathbf{z}\right\|^2/2\mathfrak{s}^2)} \ .$$

The following lemma shows that if the parameter $\mathfrak{s}$ of a discrete Gaussian distribution is small, then any vector drawn from this distribution will be short (with high probability).

Lemma 3.3 ([MR04, Lemma 4.4]). *Let m, n, q be positive integers with $m > n$, $q \geqslant 2$. Then for $\mathfrak{s} = \tilde{\Omega}(n)$ and any m-dimensional lattice $\mathcal{L} = \Lambda_q^{\perp}(\mathbf{A})$,*

$$\Pr\left[\|\mathbf{x}\| > \mathfrak{s}\sqrt{m} \ : \ \mathbf{x} \leftarrow_{\$} \mathfrak{D}_{\mathcal{L}, \mathfrak{s}}\right] \leqslant \mathsf{negl}(n) \ .$$

Lattice Trapdoors. "Lattices with trapdoors" are statistically indistinguishable from randomly chosen lattices, but have certain trapdoors that allow efficient solutions to hard lattice problems [Ajt96, GPV08]. More formally, for lattice parameters n, m, q with $m \geqslant O(n \log q)$, a trapdoor lattice sampler consists of algorithms $\mathsf{TrapGen}$ and $\mathsf{SamplePre}$ with the following syntax[6]:

- $\mathsf{TrapGen}(1^n, 1^m, q) \to (\mathbf{A}, \mathbf{T_A})$. The lattice generation algorithm is a randomized algorithm that takes as input the matrix dimensions n, m, modulus q, and outputs a matrix $\mathbf{A} \in \mathbb{Z}_q^{n \times m}$ together with a trapdoor $\mathbf{T_A}$.
- $\mathsf{SamplePre}(\mathbf{A}, \mathbf{T_A}, \mathbf{t}, \mathfrak{s}) \to \mathbf{s}$. The presampling algorithm takes as input a matrix $\mathbf{A}$, trapdoor $\mathbf{T_A}$, a vector $\mathbf{t} \in \mathbb{Z}_q^n$ and a parameter $\mathfrak{s} \in \mathbb{R}_{>0}$ (which determines the length of the output vectors). It outputs a vector $\mathbf{s} \in \mathbb{Z}_q^m$ such that $\mathbf{A} \cdot \mathbf{s} = \mathbf{t}$ and $\|\mathbf{s}\| \leqslant \mathfrak{s}\sqrt{m}$.

Furthermore, these algorithms must satisfy the following properties:

i. **Well-distributedness of matrix.** The following distributions are statistically indistinguishable:

$$\{\mathbf{A} \ : \ (\mathbf{A}, \mathbf{T_A}) \leftarrow_{\$} \mathsf{TrapGen}(1^n, 1^m, q)\} \approx_{\mathsf{s}} \left\{\mathbf{A} \ : \ \mathbf{A} \leftarrow_{\$} \mathbb{Z}_q^{n \times m}\right\} \ .$$

[6] In certain places, we may choose to omit the trapdoor generation step and instead opt for the more succinct notation $\mathbf{s} \leftarrow_{\$} \mathbf{A}_{\mathfrak{s}}^{-1}(\mathbf{t})$ instead.

ii. **Preimage sampling.** For all $(\mathbf{A}, \mathbf{T}_{\mathbf{A}}) \leftarrow_{\$} \mathsf{TrapGen}(1^n, 1^m, q)$, if $\mathfrak{s} = \omega\left(\sqrt{n \log q \cdot \log m}\right)$, then the following distributions are statistically indistinguishable:

$$\left\{\mathbf{s} : \mathbf{t} \leftarrow_{\$} \mathbb{Z}_q^n, \mathbf{s} \leftarrow_{\$} \mathsf{SamplePre}(\mathbf{A}, \mathbf{T}_{\mathbf{A}}, \mathbf{t}, \mathfrak{s})\right\} \approx_{\mathsf{s}} \mathfrak{D}_{\mathcal{R}^m, \mathfrak{s}} \quad .$$

These properties are satisfied by the gadget-based trapdoor lattice sampler of [MP12] for parameters m such that $m = \Omega(n \log q)$. This was specifically shown for the case of module lattices in [BEP+21, Lemma 4] and [BEP+21, Theorem 4].

3.3 Hardness Assumptions

Definition 3.4 (rOM-ISIS [BCGY24]). Let $q, n, m, \mathfrak{s}, \mathfrak{B}$ be functions of security parameter λ. Consider the following experiment:

i. The challenger uniformly samples two matrices $\mathbf{A}, \mathbf{B} \in \mathbb{Z}_q^{n \times m}$, and sends $\mathbf{A}, \mathbf{B}$ to adversary $\mathcal{A}$.

ii. $\mathcal{A}$ adaptively makes queries of the following types to the challenger, in any order.
   - **Syndrome queries.** $\mathcal{A}$ requests for a challenge vector, to which the challenger replies with a uniformly sampled vector $\mathbf{t} \leftarrow_{\$} \mathbb{Z}_q^n$. We denote the set of received vectors by $\mathcal{S}$.
   - **Preimage queries.** $\mathcal{A}$ queries a vector $\hat{\mathbf{t}} \in \mathbb{Z}_q^n$, to which the challenger replies with a short vector $\hat{\mathbf{s}} \in \mathbb{Z}_q^m$ and a ± 1 vector $\hat{\mathbf{r}} \in \mathbb{Z}_2^m$ such that $\mathbf{A} \cdot \hat{\mathbf{s}} + \mathbf{B} \cdot \hat{\mathbf{r}} = \hat{\mathbf{t}}$ and $\|\hat{\mathbf{s}}\| \leqslant \mathfrak{s}\sqrt{m}$. Let Q denote the total number of preimage queries.

iii. Finally, $\mathcal{A}$ outputs $Q+1$ tuples of the form $\{(\mathbf{s}_j, \mathbf{r}_j, \mathbf{t}_j)\}_{j \in [Q+1]}$. $\mathcal{A}$ wins if

$$\forall j \in [Q+1], \quad \mathbf{A} \cdot \mathbf{s}_j + \mathbf{B} \cdot \mathbf{r}_j = \mathbf{t}_j, \quad \|\mathbf{s}_j\| \leqslant \mathfrak{B}, \ \mathbf{r}_j \in \mathbb{Z}_2^m \text{ and } \mathbf{t}_j \in \mathcal{S} \quad .$$

The $\mathsf{rOM\text{-}ISIS}_{q,n,m,\mathfrak{s},\mathfrak{B}}$ assumption states that for every PPT adversary $\mathcal{A}$, the probability that $\mathcal{A}$ wins is $\mathsf{negl}(\lambda)$.

3.4 Cryptographic Building Blocks

We recall the standard cryptographic building blocks that will be essential to this work.

3.4.1 Pseudorandom Functions

A pseudorandom function (PRF) $\mathsf{F} : \{0,1\}^\lambda \times \{0,1\}^\lambda \to \{0,1\}^\lambda$ is a keyed function[7], that takes a λ-bit key as input, and on input $x \in \{0,1\}^\lambda$, it outputs a value $y = \mathsf{F}_K(x)$. *(Throughout the paper, we use $\mathsf{F}_K(x)$ as a shorthand for PRF evaluation.)*

Definition 3.5 (Pseudorandomness). *A PRF F is said to be secure if for every stateful* PPT *adversary $\mathcal{A}$, there exists a negligible function $\mathsf{negl}(\cdot)$ such that for all λ, the following holds:*

$$\Pr\left[b = \mathcal{A}^{O_{K,b}(\cdot)}(1^\lambda) \ : \ K \leftarrow_{\$} \{0,1\}^\lambda,\ b \leftarrow_{\$} \{0,1\}\right] \leqslant \frac{1}{2} + \mathsf{negl}(\lambda),$$

where oracle $O_{K,b}$ is defined as $\mathsf{F}_K(\cdot)$ if $b = 0$, otherwise it is defined as a random function from $\{0,1\}^\lambda \to \{0,1\}^\lambda$.

Crypto Dark Matter PRF. Boneh, et al. [BIP+18] gave a novel strong PRF candidate which can be computed via a depth-3 $\mathsf{ACC}^0\,[p,q]$ circuit for primes $p < q$. As stated in the overview, this bypasses the supposed PRF barrier [BBKK18] and gives a simple, low-depth PRF $\mathsf{F} : \mathbb{Z}_p^{n' \times \ell m'} \times \mathbb{Z}_p^m \to \mathbb{Z}_q^n$, for $\ell = \lceil \log_p(q) \rceil$, defined as follows:

$$\mathsf{F}_{\mathbf{K}}(\mathbf{x}) := \mathbf{Y}_1 \cdot \left(\mathbf{K} \cdot \mathbf{G}^{-1}\left(\mathbf{Y}_0 \cdot \mathbf{x} \bmod q\right) \bmod p\right) \bmod q\ ,$$

where $\mathbf{K} \in \mathbb{Z}_p^{n' \times m'}$ is the secret PRF key, $\mathbf{x} \in \mathbb{Z}_p^m$ is the input, $\mathbf{Y}_0 \in \mathbb{Z}_q^{m' \times m}$ and $\mathbf{Y}_1 \in \mathbb{Z}_q^{n \times n'}$ $(n < n')$ are fixed public matrices and $\mathbf{G}^{-1}$ is the decomposition gadget which maps $\mathbb{Z}_q^{m'} \to \mathbb{Z}_q^{\ell m'}$.

Security. The security of the PRF is known to degrade when the key $\mathbf{K}$ is chosen to be a circulant matrix (instead of random) [CCKK22]. Aside from this, the scheme has held up to the recent cryptanalytic scrutiny [BIP+18, DGH+21] where the best attacks require exponential time and memory.

3.5 Public Key Encryption

A public key encryption (PKE) scheme PKE consists of the following polynomial-time algorithms.

- $\mathsf{Setup}(1^\lambda) \to (\mathsf{pk}, \mathsf{sk})$. The setup algorithm takes as input the security parameter λ, and outputs a public-secret key pair $(\mathsf{pk}, \mathsf{sk})$.
- $\mathsf{Enc}(\mathsf{pk}, m) \to c$. The encryption algorithm takes as input a public key pk and a message m, and outputs a ciphertext c.
- $\mathsf{Dec}(\mathsf{sk}, c) \to m$. The decryption algorithm takes as input a secret key sk and a ciphertext c, and outputs a message m.

[7] For simplicity, we fix the key space, input space, and output space to be λ-bit strings, but this is not essential to the definition.

The scheme satisfies correctness if for all λ, m, $(\mathsf{pk},\mathsf{sk}) \leftarrow_\$ \mathsf{Setup}(1^\lambda)$, and every ciphertext $c \leftarrow_\$ \mathsf{Enc}(\mathsf{pk}, m)$, we have that $\mathsf{Dec}(\mathsf{sk}, c) = m$. Further, the standard IND-CPA security notion is defined as follows.

Definition 3.6 (IND-CPA). *A public key encryption scheme* PKE *is IND-CPA secure if for every stateful* PPT *adversary* $\mathcal{A}$*, there exists a negligible functions* $\epsilon(\cdot)$*, such that for every* $\lambda \in \mathbb{N}$

$$\Pr\left[\mathcal{A}(c) = b : \begin{array}{r} (\mathsf{pk},\mathsf{sk}) \leftarrow_\$ \mathsf{Setup}(1^\lambda) \\ b \leftarrow_\$ \{0,1\} \\ (m_0, m_1) \leftarrow \mathcal{A}(\mathsf{pk}) \\ c \leftarrow_\$ \mathsf{Enc}(\mathsf{pk}, m_b) \end{array}\right] \leqslant \frac{1}{2} + \mathsf{negl}(\lambda).$$

3.6 Non-interactive Zero-Knowledge

A non-interactive zero-knowledge (NIZK) proof system NIZK for relation $\mathcal{R}$ consists of the following polynomial time algorithms:

- $\mathsf{Setup}(1^\lambda) \to \mathsf{crs}$. The setup algorithm takes as input the security parameter λ, and outputs a common reference string crs.
- $\mathsf{Prove}(\mathsf{crs}, \mathfrak{x}, \mathfrak{w}) \to \pi$. The prover algorithm takes as input the crs, an instance $\mathfrak{x} \in \mathcal{L}_{\mathcal{R}}$, and a witness $\mathfrak{w}$. It outputs a proof π.
- $\mathsf{Verify}(\mathsf{crs}, \mathfrak{x}, \pi) \to 0/1$. The verification algorithm takes as input the crs, an instance $\mathfrak{x}$, and a proof π. It outputs either 1 (accept) or 0 (reject).

Definition 3.7 (Non-interactive zero-knowledge). *A NIZK proof system* NIZK *must satisfy the following properties:*

i. **Completeness.** *For every* $\lambda \in \mathbb{N}$*, crs* $\mathsf{crs} \leftarrow_\$ \mathsf{Setup}(1^\lambda)$*, any instance* $\mathfrak{x} \in \mathcal{L}_{\mathcal{R}}$ *with corresponding witness* $\mathfrak{w}$*,*

$$\Pr\left[\mathsf{Verify}(\mathsf{crs}, \mathfrak{x}, \pi) = 1 \ : \ \pi \leftarrow_\$ \mathsf{Prove}(\mathsf{crs}, \mathfrak{x}, \mathfrak{w})\right] = 1.$$

ii. **Soundness.** *For every stateful* PPT *adversary* $\mathcal{A}$*, there exists a negligible function* $\mathsf{negl}(\cdot)$ *such that for all* $\lambda \in \mathbb{N}$*,*

$$\Pr\left[\begin{array}{l} \mathsf{Verify}(\mathsf{crs}, \mathfrak{x}, \pi) = 1 \\ \nexists \mathfrak{w} \ : \ (\mathfrak{x}, \mathfrak{w}) \in \mathcal{R} \end{array} : \begin{array}{r} \mathsf{crs} \leftarrow_\$ \mathsf{Setup}(1^\lambda) \\ (\mathfrak{x}, \pi) \leftarrow \mathcal{A}(1^\lambda, \mathsf{crs}) \end{array}\right] \leqslant \mathsf{negl}(\lambda) \ .$$

iii. **(Multi-theorem) zero-knowledge.** *There exists a stateful* PPT *simulator* $\mathcal{S}$ *such that for every stateful* PPT *adversary* $\mathcal{A}$*, there exists a negligible function* $\mathsf{negl}(\cdot)$ *such that for all* $\lambda \in \mathbb{N}$*,*

$$\Pr\left[\begin{array}{l} \mathcal{A}\left(\{\pi_{i,b}\}_i\right) = b \\ \wedge\ \forall i \in [\ell] \ : \ (\mathfrak{x}_i, \mathfrak{w}_i) \in \mathcal{R} \end{array} : \begin{array}{r} b \leftarrow_\$ \{0,1\} \\ \mathsf{crs}_0 \leftarrow_\$ \mathsf{Setup}(1^\lambda) \\ \mathsf{crs}_1 \leftarrow_\$ \mathcal{S}(1^\lambda) \\ \{\mathfrak{x}_i, \mathfrak{w}_i\}_{i \in [\ell]} \leftarrow \mathcal{A}(1^\lambda, \mathsf{crs}_b) \\ \forall i \in [\ell] \ : \ \pi_{i,0} \leftarrow_\$ \mathsf{Prove}(\mathsf{crs}_0, \mathfrak{x}_i, \mathfrak{w}_i) \\ \{\pi_{i,1}\}_i \leftarrow_\$ \mathcal{S}(\mathsf{crs}_1, \{\mathfrak{x}_i\}_i) \end{array}\right] \leqslant \frac{1}{2} + \mathsf{negl}(\lambda) \ .$$

Argument of Knowledge. *A NIZK proof system* NIZK *is an argument of knowledge (NIZKAoK) if it additionally satisfies the following extraction property:*

iv. **Knowledge extraction.** *There exists a* PPT *extractor* $\mathcal{E}$ *such that for every stateful* PPT *adversary* $\mathcal{A}$, *there exists a negligible function* $\mathsf{negl}(\cdot)$ *such that for all* $\lambda \in \mathbb{N}$,

$$\Pr\left[\begin{array}{l}\mathsf{Verify}(\mathsf{crs}, \mathfrak{x}, \pi) = 1 \\ \wedge\ (\mathfrak{x}, \mathfrak{w}) \notin \mathcal{R}\end{array} : \begin{array}{r}\tau \leftarrow_{\$} \{0,1\}^{\lambda} \\ \mathsf{crs} \leftarrow \mathcal{E}(1^{\lambda}; \tau) \\ (\mathfrak{x}, \pi) \leftarrow \mathcal{A}(1^{\lambda}, \mathsf{crs}) \\ \mathfrak{w} \leftarrow \mathcal{E}(\tau, \mathfrak{x}, \pi)\end{array}\right] \leqslant \mathsf{negl}(\lambda) \quad ,$$

where τ *denotes the randomness used for running the setup algorithm with* $\mathcal{E}$, *and we assume without any loss of generality that* $|\tau| = \lambda$.

Straight-Line Knowledge Extraction. In our security proofs, we make regular use of straight-line extraction (i.e., a non-rewinding extractor). These can be constructed generically using PKE by encrypting the witness under a shared public encryption key and sending the ciphertext along with the NIZK proof. Importantly, the NIZK proof itself must contain a proof of well-formedness of the ciphertext.

3.7 Non-interactive Blind Signatures

In a non-interactive blind signature scheme, a signer issues a random *pre-signature* psig to any receiver with public key pk_R, so that the receiver can extract a blind signature σ for a random message μ using its secret key sk_R. Formally, a NIBS consists of the following polynomial-time algorithms:

- $\mathsf{Setup}(1^{\lambda}) \rightarrow \mathsf{pp}$. On input the security parameter λ, the global setup algorithm outputs a set of public parameters pp. All algorithms take pp as an input, but we usually omit it as an explicit input for brevity.
- $\mathsf{KeyGen}_S(\mathsf{pp}) \rightarrow (\mathsf{sk}, \mathsf{vk})$. On input pp, the signer's key generation algorithm samples a public (verification)-secret key pair $(\mathsf{sk}, \mathsf{vk})$.
- $\mathsf{KeyGen}_R(\mathsf{pp}) \rightarrow (\mathsf{sk}_R, \mathsf{pk}_R)$. On input pp, the receiver's key generation algorithm samples a public-secret key pair $(\mathsf{sk}_R, \mathsf{pk}_R)$.
- $\mathsf{Issue}(\mathsf{sk}, \mathsf{pk}_R) \rightarrow (\mathsf{psig}, \mathsf{nonce})$. The signer's issuance algorithm takes as input the signer's secret key sk as well as a receiver's public key pk_R. It then outputs a pre-signature psig along with nonce which represents (a portion of) the signer's random coins.
- $\mathsf{Obtain}(\mathsf{sk}_R, \mathsf{vk}, (\mathsf{psig}, \mathsf{nonce})) \rightarrow (\mu, \sigma)/\bot$. The receiver's blind signature extraction algorithm takes as input the receiver's secret key sk_R as an input, along with a verification key vk and pre-signature-nonce pair $(\mathsf{psig}, \mathsf{nonce})$, and outputs a message-signature pair (μ, σ) or aborts and outputs $\bot$.

- $\mathsf{Verify}(\mathsf{vk}, \mu, \sigma) \rightarrow 0/1$. The signature verification algorithm that takes as input a verification key vk and message-signature pair (μ, σ), and outputs 1 (accept) or 0 (reject).

Furthermore, a NIBS scheme NIBS must satisfy the following properties:

i. **Correctness.** For every security parameter $\lambda \in \mathbb{N}$, $\mathsf{pp} \leftarrow\!\$\, \mathsf{Setup}(1^\lambda)$, $(\mathsf{sk}, \mathsf{vk}) \leftarrow\!\$\, \mathsf{KeyGen}_S(\mathsf{pp})$, $(\mathsf{sk}_R, \mathsf{pk}_R) \leftarrow\!\$\, \mathsf{KeyGen}_R(\mathsf{pp})$,

$$\Pr[\mathsf{Verify}(\mathsf{vk}, \mathsf{Obtain}(\mathsf{sk}_R, \mathsf{vk}, \mathsf{Issue}(\mathsf{sk}, \mathsf{pk}_R))) = 1] = 1 \quad ,$$

where the probability is taken over the randomness of Issue and Obtain.

ii. **Reusability.** There exists a negligible function $\mathsf{negl}(\cdot)$ such that for every $\lambda \in \mathbb{N}$,

$$\Pr\left[\begin{array}{l} \mathsf{nonce}_0 = \mathsf{nonce}_1 \\ \vee\ \mu_0 = \mu_1 \end{array} : \begin{array}{r} \mathsf{pp} \leftarrow\!\$\, \mathsf{Setup}(1^\lambda) \\ (\mathsf{sk}, \mathsf{vk}) \leftarrow\!\$\, \mathsf{KeyGen}_S(\mathsf{pp}) \\ (\mathsf{sk}_R, \mathsf{pk}_R) \leftarrow\!\$\, \mathsf{KeyGen}_R(\mathsf{pp}) \\ \forall b \in \{0,1\} : \qquad\qquad\qquad\qquad \\ (\mathsf{psig}_b, \mathsf{nonce}_b) \leftarrow\!\$\, \mathsf{Issue}(\mathsf{sk}, \mathsf{pk}_R) \\ (\mu_b, \sigma_b) \leftarrow\!\$\, \mathsf{Obtain}(\mathsf{sk}_R, \mathsf{vk}, (\mathsf{psig}_b, \mathsf{nonce}_b)) \end{array}\right] \leqslant \mathsf{negl}(\lambda) \quad .$$

iii. **One-more unforgeability.** For every *stateful, admissible* PPT adversary $\mathcal{A}$, there exists a negligible function $\mathsf{negl}(\cdot)$ such that for every $\lambda \in \mathbb{N}$,

$$\Pr\left[\begin{array}{l} \bigwedge_{i \in [Q+1]} \mathsf{Verify}(\mathsf{vk}, \mu_i, \sigma_i) = 1 \\ \bigwedge_{i \neq j \in [Q+1]} \mu_i \neq \mu_j \end{array} : \begin{array}{r} \mathsf{pp} \leftarrow\!\$\, \mathsf{Setup}(1^\lambda) \\ (\mathsf{sk}, \mathsf{vk}) \leftarrow\!\$\, \mathsf{KeyGen}_S(\mathsf{pp}) \\ \{(\mu_i, \sigma_i)\}_{i=1}^{Q+1} \leftarrow\!\$\, \mathcal{A}^{O_{\mathsf{sk}}(\cdot)}(\mathsf{vk}) \end{array}\right] \leqslant \mathsf{negl}(\lambda) \quad ,$$

where oracle O_{sk} takes as input a receiver's public key $\mathsf{pk}_{R^{(i)}}$, and outputs a pre-signature-nonce pair $(\mathsf{psig}^{(i)}, \mathsf{nonce}^{(i)})$ by running $\mathsf{Issue}(\mathsf{sk}, \mathsf{pk}_{R^{(i)}})$, and $\mathcal{A}$ is *admissible* iff $\mathcal{A}$ makes at most Q queries to O_{sk}.

iv. **Receiver blindness.** For every *stateful, admissible* PPT adversary $\mathcal{A}$, there exists a negligible function $\mathsf{negl}(\cdot)$ such that for every $\lambda \in \mathbb{N}$,

$$\Pr\left[\begin{array}{l} \mathcal{A}^{O_{\mathsf{sk}_{R_0},\mathsf{sk}_{R_1}}(\cdot,\cdot,\cdot)}(\mu_{\hat{b}}, \sigma_{\hat{b}}, \mu_{1-\hat{b}}, \sigma_{1-\hat{b}}) = \hat{b} : \\ \hfill \mathsf{pp} \leftarrow\!\$\, \mathsf{Setup}(1^\lambda),\ \hat{b} \leftarrow\!\$\, \{0,1\}, \\ \hfill \forall b \in \{0,1\} : \ (\mathsf{sk}_{R_b}, \mathsf{pk}_{R_b}) \leftarrow\!\$\, \mathsf{KeyGen}_R(\mathsf{pp}) \\ \hfill (\mathsf{vk}, (\mathsf{psig}_b, \mathsf{nonce}_b)_{b \in \{0,1\}}) \leftarrow\!\$\, \mathcal{A}^{O_{\mathsf{sk}_{R_0},\mathsf{sk}_{R_1}}(\cdot,\cdot,\cdot)}(\mathsf{pk}_{R_0}, \mathsf{pk}_{R_1}) \\ \hfill \forall b \in \{0,1\} \ : \ (\mu_b, \sigma_b) \leftarrow\!\$\, \mathsf{Obtain}(\mathsf{sk}_{R_b}, \mathsf{vk}, (\mathsf{psig}_b, \mathsf{nonce}_b)) \end{array}\right] \leqslant \frac{1}{2} + \mathsf{negl}(\lambda) \quad ,$$

where oracle $O_{\mathsf{sk}_{R_0},\mathsf{sk}_{R_1}}$, on the ith query $\left(b^{(i)}, \mathsf{vk}^{(i)}, \left(\mathsf{psig}^{(i)}, \mathsf{nonce}^{(i)}\right)\right)$, outputs $\mathsf{Obtain}(\mathsf{sk}_{R_{b^{(i)}}}, \mathsf{vk}^{(i)}, (\mathsf{psig}^{(i)}, \mathsf{nonce}^{(i)}))$. That is, $O_{\mathsf{sk}_{R_0},\mathsf{sk}_{R_1}}$ provides $\mathcal{A}$ oracle access to the Obtain algorithm w.r.t. $\mathsf{sk}_{R_0}, \mathsf{sk}_{R_1}$. We say that $\mathcal{A}$ is admissible iff:

a. $\sigma_0, \sigma_1 \neq \perp$ (i.e., Obtain algorithm does not abort), and

b. $\mathsf{nonce}_0 \neq \mathsf{nonce}^{(i)}$ and $\mathsf{nonce}_1 \neq \mathsf{nonce}^{(i)}$ for all i. (That is, $\mathcal{A}$ cannot make an Obtain query with nonce value to be either of the challenge nonce values.)

v. **Nonce blindness.** For every *stateful, admissible* PPT adversary $\mathcal{A}$, there exists a negligible function $\mathsf{negl}(\cdot)$ such that for every $\lambda \in \mathbb{N}$,

$$\Pr\left[\begin{array}{r} \mathcal{A}^{O_{\mathsf{sk}_R}(\cdot,\cdot)}(\mu_{\hat{b}}, \sigma_{\hat{b}}, \mu_{1-\hat{b}}, \sigma_{1-\hat{b}}) = \hat{b} : \\ \mathsf{pp} \leftarrow \mathsf{Setup}(1^\lambda),\ (\mathsf{sk}_R, \mathsf{pk}_R) \leftarrow \mathsf{KeyGen}_R(\mathsf{pp}) \\ (\mathsf{vk}, (\mathsf{psig}_b, \mathsf{nonce}_b)_{b\in\{0,1\}}) \leftarrow \mathcal{A}^{O_{\mathsf{sk}_R}(\cdot,\cdot)}(\mathsf{pk}_R),\ \hat{b} \leftarrow \{0,1\} \\ \forall b \in \{0,1\}\ :\ (\mu_b, \sigma_b) \leftarrow \mathsf{Obtain}(\mathsf{sk}_R, \mathsf{vk}, (\mathsf{psig}_b, \mathsf{nonce}_b)) \end{array}\right] \leqslant \frac{1}{2} + \mathsf{negl}(\lambda) \ ,$$

where oracle O_{sk_R}, on the ith query $\left(\mathsf{vk}^{(i)}, \left(\mathsf{psig}^{(i)}, \mathsf{nonce}^{(i)}\right)\right)$, outputs $\mathsf{Obtain}(\mathsf{sk}_R, \mathsf{vk}^{(i)}, (\mathsf{psig}^{(i)}, \mathsf{nonce}^{(i)}))$. That is, O_{sk_R} provides $\mathcal{A}$ oracle access to the Obtain algorithm w.r.t. sk_R. We say that $\mathcal{A}$ is admissible iff:

a. $\sigma_0, \sigma_1 \neq \perp$ (i.e., Obtain algorithm does not abort), and

b. $\mathsf{nonce}_0 \neq \mathsf{nonce}^{(i)}$ and $\mathsf{nonce}_1 \neq \mathsf{nonce}^{(i)}$ for all i. (That is, $\mathcal{A}$ cannot make an Obtain query with nonce value to be either of the challenge nonce values.)

4 Non-interactive Batched Blind Signatures

A non-interactive *batched* blind signature (NIBBS) scheme extends a standard NIBS scheme so that, given a single random pre-signature psig, a receiver with public key pk_R can extract $N \in \mathbb{N}$ blind signatures $\sigma_1, \sigma_2, \ldots, \sigma_N$ for the corresponding random messages $\mu_1, \mu_2, \ldots, \mu_N$ using its secret key sk_R. Formally, a NIBBS consists of the following polynomial-time algorithms:

- $\mathsf{Setup}(1^\lambda, N) \rightarrow \mathsf{pp}$. On input the security parameter λ and a batch size N, the global setup algorithm outputs a set of public parameters pp. All algorithms take pp as an input, but we usually omit it as an explicit input for brevity.
- $\mathsf{KeyGen}_S(\mathsf{pp}) \rightarrow (\mathsf{sk}, \mathsf{vk})$. On input pp, the signer's key generation algorithm samples a public (verification)-secret key pair $(\mathsf{sk}, \mathsf{vk})$.
- $\mathsf{KeyGen}_R(\mathsf{pp}) \rightarrow (\mathsf{sk}_R, \mathsf{pk}_R)$. On input pp, the receiver's key generation algorithm samples a public-secret key pair $(\mathsf{sk}_R, \mathsf{pk}_R)$.
- $\mathsf{Issue}(\mathsf{sk}, \mathsf{pk}_R) \rightarrow (\mathsf{psig}, \mathsf{nonce})$. The signer's issuance algorithm takes as input the signer's secret key sk as well as a receiver's public key pk_R. It then outputs a pre-signature psig along with nonce which represents (a portion of) the signer's random coins.
- $\mathsf{Obtain}(\mathsf{sk}_R, \mathsf{vk}, (\mathsf{psig}, \mathsf{nonce})) \rightarrow [\![\mu, \sigma]\!]/\perp$. The receiver's blind signature extraction algorithm takes as input the receiver's secret key sk_R, along with a verification key vk and pre-signature-nonce pair (psig, nonce), and outputs N message-signature pairs $[\![\mu, \sigma]\!] := \{(\mu_1, \sigma_1), (\mu_2, \sigma_2), \ldots, (\mu_N, \sigma_N)\}$ or aborts and outputs $\perp$.

- $\mathsf{Verify}(\mathsf{vk}, \mu, \sigma) \rightarrow 0/1$. The signature verification algorithm that takes as input a verification key vk and message-signature pair (μ, σ), and outputs 1 (accept) or 0 (reject).

Furthermore, in addition to the standard notion of correctness, a NIBS scheme with batching must satisfy the following properties:

i. **Succinct communication.** For $\lambda \in \mathbb{N}$, there exists a polynomial $\mathsf{poly}(\lambda)$ such that $|\mathsf{psig}|, |\mathsf{nonce}| \leqslant \mathsf{poly}(\lambda)$.
ii. **Reusability.** There exists a negligible function $\mathsf{negl}(\cdot)$ such that for every $\lambda \in \mathbb{N}$,

$$\Pr\left[\begin{array}{l}\mathsf{nonce}_0 = \mathsf{nonce}_1 \\ \bigvee_{\mathsf{i,j} \in [N]} \mu_{\mathsf{i},0} = \mu_{\mathsf{j},1}\end{array} : \forall b \in \{0,1\} : \begin{array}{r}\mathsf{pp} \leftarrow\!\$\, \mathsf{Setup}(1^\lambda) \\ (\mathsf{sk}, \mathsf{vk}) \leftarrow\!\$\, \mathsf{KeyGen}_S(\mathsf{pp}) \\ (\mathsf{sk}_R, \mathsf{pk}_R) \leftarrow\!\$\, \mathsf{KeyGen}_R(\mathsf{pp}) \\ (\mathsf{psig}_b, \mathsf{nonce}_b) \leftarrow\!\$\, \mathsf{Issue}(\mathsf{sk}, \mathsf{pk}_R) \\ [\![\mu, \sigma]\!]_b \leftarrow\!\$\, \mathsf{Obtain}(\mathsf{sk}_R, \mathsf{vk}, (\mathsf{psig}_b, \mathsf{nonce}_b))\end{array}\right] \leqslant \mathsf{negl}(\lambda) \ .$$

iii. **One-more unforgeability.** For every *stateful, admissible* PPT adversary $\mathcal{A}$, there exists a negligible function $\mathsf{negl}(\cdot)$ such that for every $\lambda \in \mathbb{N}$,

$$\Pr\left[\begin{array}{l}\bigwedge_{i \in [NQ+1]} \mathsf{Verify}(\mathsf{vk}, \mu_i, \sigma_i) = 1 \\ \bigwedge_{i \neq j \in [NQ+1]} \mu_i \neq \mu_j\end{array} : \begin{array}{r}\mathsf{pp} \leftarrow\!\$\, \mathsf{Setup}(1^\lambda) \\ (\mathsf{sk}, \mathsf{vk}) \leftarrow\!\$\, \mathsf{KeyGen}_S(\mathsf{pp}) \\ \{(\mu_i, \sigma_i)\}_{i=1}^{NQ+1} \leftarrow\!\$\, \mathcal{A}^{O_{\mathsf{sk}}(\cdot)}(\mathsf{vk})\end{array}\right] \leqslant \mathsf{negl}(\lambda) \ ,$$

where oracle O_{sk} takes as input a receiver's public key $\mathsf{pk}_{R^{(j)}}$, and outputs a pre-signature-nonce pair $(\mathsf{psig}^{(j)}, \mathsf{nonce}^{(j)})$ by running $\mathsf{Issue}(\mathsf{sk}, \mathsf{pk}_{R^{(j)}})$, and $\mathcal{A}$ is *admissible* iff $\mathcal{A}$ makes at most Q queries to O_{sk}.
iv. **Inter-batch blindness.** For every *stateful, admissible* PPT adversary $\mathcal{A}$, there exists a negligible function $\mathsf{negl}(\cdot)$ such that for every $\lambda \in \mathbb{N}$,

$$\Pr\left[\begin{array}{l}\mathcal{A}^{O_{\mathsf{sk}_{R_0}, \mathsf{sk}_{R_1}}(\cdot,\cdot,\cdot)}([\![\mu, \sigma]\!]_{\hat{b}}, [\![\mu, \sigma]\!]_{1-\hat{b}}) = \hat{b} : \\ \hfill \mathsf{pp} \leftarrow\!\$\, \mathsf{Setup}(1^\lambda),\ \hat{b} \leftarrow\!\$\, \{0,1\}, \\ \hfill \forall b \in \{0,1\} : \ (\mathsf{sk}_{R_b}, \mathsf{pk}_{R_b}) \leftarrow\!\$\, \mathsf{KeyGen}_R(\mathsf{pp}) \\ \hfill (\mathsf{vk}, (\mathsf{psig}_b, \mathsf{nonce}_b)_{b \in \{0,1\}}) \leftarrow\!\$\, \mathcal{A}^{O_{\mathsf{sk}_{R_0}, \mathsf{sk}_{R_1}}(\cdot,\cdot,\cdot)}(\mathsf{pk}_{R_0}, \mathsf{pk}_{R_1}) \\ \hfill \forall b \in \{0,1\} \ : \ [\![\mu, \sigma]\!]_b \leftarrow\!\$\, \mathsf{Obtain}(\mathsf{sk}_{R_b}, \mathsf{vk}, (\mathsf{psig}_b, \mathsf{nonce}_b))\end{array}\right] \leqslant \frac{1}{2} + \mathsf{negl}(\lambda) \ ,$$

where oracle $O_{\mathsf{sk}_{R_0}, \mathsf{sk}_{R_1}}$, on the jth query $\left(b^{(j)}, \mathsf{vk}^{(j)}, \left(\mathsf{psig}^{(j)}, \mathsf{nonce}^{(j)}\right)\right)$, outputs $\mathsf{Obtain}(\mathsf{sk}_{R_{b^{(j)}}}, \mathsf{vk}^{(j)}, (\mathsf{psig}^{(j)}, \mathsf{nonce}^{(j)}))$. That is, $O_{\mathsf{sk}_{R_0}, \mathsf{sk}_{R_1}}$ provides $\mathcal{A}$ oracle access to the Obtain algorithm w.r.t. $\mathsf{sk}_{R_0}, \mathsf{sk}_{R_1}$. We say that $\mathcal{A}$ is admissible iff:
   a. For all $\mathsf{i} \in [N]$ and $b \in \{0,1\}$, $\sigma_{\mathsf{i},b} \neq \perp$ (i.e., Obtain algorithm does not abort), and
   b. $\mathsf{nonce}_0 \neq \mathsf{nonce}^{(j)}$ and $\mathsf{nonce}_1 \neq \mathsf{nonce}^{(j)}$ for all j. (That is, $\mathcal{A}$ cannot make an Obtain query with nonce value to be either of the challenge nonce values.)

v. **Intra-batch blindness.** For every *stateful, admissible* PPT adversary $\mathcal{A}$, there exists a negligible function $\mathsf{negl}(\cdot)$ such that for every $\lambda \in \mathbb{N}$,

$$\Pr\left[\begin{array}{c} \mathcal{A}^{O_{\mathsf{sk}_R}(\cdot,\cdot)}\left(\left\{\left(\mu_{\varphi_{\hat{b}}(i,b)}, \sigma_{\varphi_{\hat{b}}(i,b)}\right)\right\}_{\substack{i\in[N]\\ b\in\{0,1\}}}\right) = \hat{b} : \\ \mathsf{pp} \leftarrow_{\$} \mathsf{Setup}(1^\lambda),\ (\mathsf{sk}_R, \mathsf{pk}_R) \leftarrow_{\$} \mathsf{KeyGen}_R(\mathsf{pp}), \hat{b} \leftarrow_{\$} \{0,1\} \\ \varphi_0 := \iota,\ (\mathsf{vk}, (\mathsf{psig}_b, \mathsf{nonce}_b)_{b\in\{0,1\}}, \varphi_1) \leftarrow \mathcal{A}^{O_{\mathsf{sk}_R}(\cdot,\cdot)}(\mathsf{pk}_R) \\ \forall b \in \{0,1\}\ :\ [\![\mu, \sigma]\!]_b \leftarrow_{\$} \mathsf{Obtain}(\mathsf{sk}_R, \mathsf{vk}, (\mathsf{psig}_b, \mathsf{nonce}_b)) \end{array}\right] \leqslant \frac{1}{2} + \mathsf{negl}(\lambda)\ ,$$

where φ_0 and φ_1 are bijective permutation maps in $[N] \times \{0,1\} \to [N] \times \{0,1\}$ with φ_0, in particular, being the identity map ι; and oracle O_{sk_R}, on the jth query $\left(\mathsf{vk}^{(j)}, \left(\mathsf{psig}^{(j)}, \mathsf{nonce}^{(j)}\right)\right)$, outputs $\mathsf{Obtain}(\mathsf{sk}_R, \mathsf{vk}^{(j)}, (\mathsf{psig}^{(j)}, \mathsf{nonce}^{(j)}))$. That is, O_{sk_R} provides $\mathcal{A}$ oracle access to the Obtain algorithm w.r.t. sk_R. We say that $\mathcal{A}$ is admissible iff:

a. φ_1 is a valid permutation map in $[N] \times \{0,1\} \to [N] \times \{0,1\}$.
b. For all $\mathrm{i} \in [N]$ and $b \in \{0,1\}$, $\sigma_{\mathrm{i},b} \neq \perp$ (i.e., Obtain algorithm does not abort), and
c. $\mathsf{nonce}_0 \neq \mathsf{nonce}^{(j)}$ and $\mathsf{nonce}_1 \neq \mathsf{nonce}^{(j)}$ for all j. (That is, $\mathcal{A}$ cannot make an Obtain query with nonce value to be either of the challenge nonce values.)

5 Lattice-Based NI$\underline{\text{B}}$BS

Let $N \in \mathbb{N}$ be the batch size, and let parameters $n, m, n', m', \mathfrak{s}, \mathfrak{B} = \mathfrak{s}\sqrt{m}, \mathfrak{B}_N = (\mathfrak{s} + n'm_N)\sqrt{m}$, and positive integer q be functions of the security parameter λ such that the randomized one-more ISIS instance $\mathsf{rOM\text{-}ISIS}_{q,n,m,\mathfrak{s},\mathfrak{B}_N}$ is hard. These parameters must satisfy the following constraints:

$$n = \mathsf{poly}(\lambda),\ n' > n,\ m > n\log q + \Theta(\lambda),\ n'm_N > n\log q + \Theta(\lambda)\ . \quad (1)$$

This construction relies on a hash function $\mathsf{H} : \mathbb{Z}_2^\lambda \to \mathbb{Z}_q^n$ (modeled as a random oracle), a lattice trapdoor $\mathcal{T} = (\mathcal{T}.\mathsf{TrapGen}, \mathcal{T}.\mathsf{SamplePre})$, a public key encryption scheme $\mathsf{PKE} = (\mathsf{PKE.KeyGen}, \mathsf{PKE.Enc}, \mathsf{PKE.Dec})$ and a NIZK proof system $\mathsf{NIZK} = (\mathsf{NIZK.Setup}, \mathsf{NIZK.Prove}, \mathsf{NIZK.Verify})$ for relation $\mathcal{R}^{\mathsf{NI\underline{B}BS}}$, defined as follows:

Relation $\mathscr{R}^{\mathsf{NI\underline{B}BS}}$

Instance: Each instance $\mathfrak{x}$ is interpreted as matrices $\mathbf{A}, \mathbf{B}, \mathbf{C}, \mathbf{Y}_0$ and $\mathbf{Y}_1$, a PKE public key $\mathsf{pk}_{\mathsf{PKE}}$, a message vector μ and ciphertext ψ.

Witness: Witness $\mathfrak{w}$ consists of secret vectors $\mathbf{k}, \mathbf{u}, \mathbf{s}, \mathbf{r}$ and $\mathbf{i}$, and PKE randomness ρ.

Membership: $\mathfrak{w}$ is a valid witness for $\mathfrak{x}$ if the following are satisfied:

▷ $\mathbf{A} \cdot \mathbf{s} + \mathbf{B} \cdot \mathbf{r} = \mathbf{C} \cdot \mathbf{k} + \mathsf{H}(\mathbf{u})$

▷ $\mu = \mathbf{Y}_1 \cdot \left(\mathsf{Vec}^{-1}(\mathbf{k}) \cdot \mathbf{G}^{-1} \left(\mathbf{Y}_0 \cdot \begin{bmatrix} \mathbf{r} \\ \mathbf{i} \end{bmatrix} \bmod 3 \right) \bmod 2 \right) \bmod 3$

▷ $\psi = \mathsf{PKE.Enc}\left(\mathsf{pk}_{\mathsf{PKE}}, \mathbf{k}||\mathbf{u}||\mathbf{s}||\mathbf{r}||\mathbf{i}\ ;\ \rho\right)$

▷ $||\mathbf{s}|| \leqslant \mathfrak{B}, \quad \mathbf{k} \in \mathbb{Z}_2^{n' m_N}, \quad \mathbf{r} \in \mathbb{Z}_2^{m}, \quad \mathbf{i} \in \mathbb{Z}_2^{m_N - m'}$.

5.1 Construction

We are now ready to describe our lattice-based NI$\underline{\text{B}}$BS scheme.

- $\mathsf{Setup}(1^\lambda, N) \to \mathsf{pp}$. The public parameter setup algorithm computes n, m, n', $m', \mathfrak{s}, q$ from the security parameter λ. It then sets $m_N = m' + \lceil \log_2(N) \rceil$, and samples matrices $\mathbf{Y}_0 \leftarrow_\$ \mathbb{Z}_3^{\frac{m_N}{2} \times (m + m_N - m')}$, $\mathbf{Y}_1 \leftarrow_\$ \mathbb{Z}_3^{n \times n'}$ and $\mathbf{C} \leftarrow_\$ \mathbb{Z}_q^{n \times n' m_N}$. It then runs the key generation algorithm of PKE and generates the corresponding public and secret key pair as

$$(\mathsf{pk}_{\mathsf{PKE}}, \mathsf{sk}_{\mathsf{PKE}}) \leftarrow_\$ \mathsf{PKE.KeyGen}(1^\lambda) .$$

  Next, it generates $\mathsf{crs}_{\mathsf{NIZK}} \leftarrow_\$ \mathsf{NIZK.Setup}(1^\lambda)$ and outputs

$$\mathsf{pp} := \left(1^\lambda, n, m, n', m_N, \mathfrak{s}, q, N, \mathsf{pk}_{\mathsf{PKE}}, \mathsf{crs}_{\mathsf{NIZK}}, \mathbf{Y}_0, \mathbf{Y}_1, \mathbf{C}\right) .$$

  The public parameters are fixed once and for all.

- $\mathsf{KeyGen}_S(\mathsf{pp}) \to (\mathsf{sk}, \mathsf{vk})$. The signer's key generation algorithm runs the lattice trapdoor setup to obtain

$$(\mathbf{T}_\mathbf{A}, \mathbf{A}) \leftarrow_\$ \mathcal{T}.\mathsf{TrapGen}(1^\lambda, n, m, q) .$$

  It also samples a matrix $\mathbf{B} \leftarrow_\$ \mathbb{Z}_q^{n \times m}$, then outputs the signer's secret signing key $\mathsf{sk} := \mathbf{T}_\mathbf{A}$ and verification key $\mathsf{vk} := (\mathbf{A}, \mathbf{B})$.

- $\mathsf{KeyGen}_R(\mathsf{pp}) \to (\mathsf{sk}_R, \mathsf{pk}_R)$. The receiver's key generation algorithm samples the PRF key $\mathbf{K} \leftarrow_\$ \mathbb{Z}_2^{n' \times m_N}$ and a random vector $\mathbf{u} \leftarrow_\$ \mathbb{Z}_2^\lambda$. It then vectorizes $\mathbf{K}$ as $\mathbf{k} := \mathsf{Vec}(\mathbf{K})$, and computes

$$\mathbf{t} := \mathbf{C} \cdot \mathbf{k} + \mathsf{H}(\mathbf{u}) .$$

  Finally, it sets the receiver's secret key as $\mathsf{sk}_R := (\mathbf{K}, \mathbf{u})$ and the public key as $\mathsf{pk}_R := \mathbf{t}$, and outputs them.

- $\mathsf{Issue}(\mathsf{sk}, \mathsf{pk}_R) \to (\mathsf{psig}, \mathsf{nonce})$. Given the receiver's public key $\mathsf{pk}_R =: \mathbf{t}$, the signer's pre-signature issuance algorithm samples a random vector $\mathbf{r} \leftarrow_\$ \mathbb{Z}_2^m$ and, using the secret signing key $\mathsf{sk} =: \mathbf{T_A}$, it computes

$$\mathbf{s} \leftarrow_\$ \mathcal{T}.\mathsf{SamplePre}\left(\mathbf{A}, \mathbf{T_A}, \mathbf{t} - \mathbf{B} \cdot \mathbf{r}, \mathfrak{s}\right),$$

 and outputs the pre-signature, $\mathsf{psig} := \mathbf{s}$ and the nonce, $\mathsf{nonce} := \mathbf{r}$.

- $\mathsf{Obtain}(\mathsf{sk}_R, \mathsf{vk}, \mathsf{psig}, \mathsf{nonce}) \to [\![\mu, \sigma]\!]$. The receiver's signature obtainment algorithm first parses sk_R as $(\mathbf{K}, \mathbf{u})$ and then, for $\mathsf{vk} =: (\mathbf{A}, \mathbf{B})$, $\mathsf{psig} =: \mathbf{s}$, and $\mathsf{nonce} =: \mathbf{r}$, it checks if

$$\mathbf{A} \cdot \mathbf{s} + \mathbf{B} \cdot \mathbf{r} \stackrel{?}{=} \mathbf{C} \cdot \mathsf{Vec}(\mathbf{K}) + \mathsf{H}(\mathbf{u}) \ \wedge\ \|\mathbf{s}\| \stackrel{?}{\leqslant} \mathfrak{B} \ \wedge\ \mathbf{r} \stackrel{?}{\in} \mathbb{Z}_2^m .$$

 If any check fails it aborts and outputs $\perp$. Otherwise, for each $\mathfrak{i} \in [N]$, it computes the message $\mu_\mathfrak{i}$ as

$$\mu_\mathfrak{i} := \mathbf{Y}_1 \cdot \left(\mathbf{K} \cdot \mathbf{G}^{-1}\left(\mathbf{Y}_0 \cdot \begin{bmatrix} \mathbf{r} \\ \mathbf{g}^{-1}(\mathfrak{i}) \end{bmatrix} \bmod 3\right) \bmod 2\right) \bmod 3 ,$$

 where, $\mathbf{g}^{-1} : \mathbb{Z}_N \to \mathbb{Z}_2^{\log_2(N)}$ ($\log_2(N) = m_N - m'$) is the binary decomposition gadget.
 With this, it now generates the corresponding ciphertext as

$$\psi_\mathfrak{i} \leftarrow \mathsf{PKE.Enc}\left(\mathsf{pk}_{\mathsf{PKE}}, \mathbf{k}\|\mathbf{u}\|\mathbf{s}\|\mathbf{r}\|\mathbf{g}^{-1}(\mathfrak{i})\ ;\ \rho_\mathfrak{i}\right)$$

 from uniformly sampled randomness $\rho_\mathfrak{i}$. It then generates the NIZK proof

$$\pi_\mathfrak{i} \leftarrow_\$ \mathsf{NIZK.Prove}\begin{pmatrix} \mathsf{crs}_{\mathsf{NIZK}}, \mathfrak{x}_\mathfrak{i} := (\mathbf{A}, \mathbf{B}, \mathbf{C}, \mathbf{Y}_0, \mathbf{Y}_1, \mathsf{pk}_{\mathsf{PKE}}, \mu_\mathfrak{i}, \psi_\mathfrak{i}), \\ \mathfrak{w}_\mathfrak{i} := (\mathbf{k}, \mathbf{u}, \mathbf{s}, \mathbf{r}, \mathbf{g}^{-1}(\mathfrak{i}), \rho_\mathfrak{i}) \end{pmatrix},$$

 Finally, it outputs $[\![\mu, \sigma]\!] := \{(\mu_1, \sigma_1 := (\psi_1, \pi_1)), \ldots, (\mu_N, \sigma_N := (\psi_N, \pi_N))\}$.

- $\mathsf{Verify}(\mathsf{vk}, \mu, \sigma) \to 0/1$. The signature verification algorithm parses σ as (ψ, π) and outputs 1 (accept) if

$$\mathsf{NIZK.Verify}\left(\mathsf{crs}_{\mathsf{NIZK}}, \mathfrak{x} := (\mathbf{A}, \mathbf{B}, \mathbf{C}, \mathbf{Y}_0, \mathbf{Y}_1, \mathsf{pk}_{\mathsf{PKE}}, \mu, \psi), \pi\right) = 1 ,$$

 and 0 (reject) otherwise.

Security. We now state our main theorem concerning the security of our NIBBS scheme.

Theorem 5.1. *Let $N \in \mathbb{N}$ be the batch size, and let parameters $n, m, n', m', \mathfrak{s}, \mathfrak{B} = \mathfrak{s}\sqrt{m}, \mathfrak{B}_N = (\mathfrak{s} + n'm_N)\sqrt{m}$, and positive integer q be functions of the security parameter λ satisfying (1) such that the randomized one-more ISIS instance $\mathsf{rOM\text{-}ISIS}_{q,n,m,\mathfrak{s},\mathfrak{B}_N}$ is hard.*

If $\mathsf{F}_\mathbf{K}$ is a pseudorandom function, NIZK is a NIZK for $\mathcal{R}^{\mathsf{NIBBS}}$ and PKE is an IND-CPA secure encryption scheme then construction 5 is a secure non-interactive batched blind signature scheme.

Proof of Theorem. We prove the correctness, succinctness (of communication), reusability, one-more unforgeability, and inter- and intra-batch blindness of our scheme. The theorem will accordingly follow.

Correctness. By correctness of trapdoor sampling, $\mathbf{s}$ is a valid preimage of $(\mathbf{t}-\mathbf{B}\cdot\mathbf{r})$ with respect to $\mathbf{A}$ such that $\|\mathbf{s}\| \leqslant \mathfrak{B}$ and $\mathbf{r} \in \mathbb{Z}_2^m$. Since it further holds, by construction, that $\mathsf{Vec}(\mathbf{K}) \in \mathbb{Z}_2^{n' m_N}$, and for each $\mathrm{i} \in [N]$, $\mu_\mathrm{i} = \mathsf{F}_\mathbf{K}(\mathbf{r}\|\mathbf{g}^{-1}(\mathrm{i}))$, it follows from correctness of PKE and completeness of NIZK, that each π_i is a valid proof for $\mathscr{R}^{\mathsf{NI\underline{B}BS}}$. Consequently, construction 5 is correct.

Succinct Communication. This follows straightforwardly from the construction as the size of both $\mathbf{s} \in \mathbb{Z}^m$ and $\mathbf{r} \in \mathbb{Z}_2^m$ is independent of N.

Next, we consider the following lemmas concerning the reusability, one-more unforgeability, as well as inter- and intra-batch blindness of the protocol. We provide the detailed proofs in the full version of this article.

Lemma 5.2 (Reusability). *Suppose* $\mathsf{F}_\mathbf{K}$ *is a pseudorandom function. Then, construction 5 is reusable.*

Proof. For $b \in \{0,1\}$, let $(\mathbf{s}_{(b)}, \mathbf{r}_{(b)})$ be the pre-signature and nonce pairs given to a receiver with $\mathsf{pk}_R := \mathbf{t}$, then one can check that

$$\Pr\left[\mathbf{r}_{(0)} = \mathbf{r}_{(1)} \vee \left(\bigvee_{\mathrm{i},\mathrm{j}\in[B]} \mu_{\mathrm{i},0} = \mu_{\mathrm{j},1}\right)\right] \leqslant$$
$$\sum_{\mathrm{i},\mathrm{j}\in[N]} \Pr\left[\mathsf{F}_\mathbf{K}\left(\begin{bmatrix}\mathbf{r}_{(0)}\\ \mathbf{g}^{-1}(\mathrm{i})\end{bmatrix}\right) = \mathsf{F}_\mathbf{K}\left(\begin{bmatrix}\mathbf{r}_{(1)}\\ \mathbf{g}^{-1}(\mathrm{j})\end{bmatrix}\right)\right] + \mathsf{negl}(\lambda) .$$

Now, if with non-negligible probability, $\mathsf{F}_\mathbf{K}\left(\begin{bmatrix}\mathbf{r}_{(0)}\\ \mathbf{g}^{-1}(\mathrm{i})\end{bmatrix}\right) = \mathsf{F}_\mathbf{K}\left(\begin{bmatrix}\mathbf{r}_{(1)}\\ \mathbf{g}^{-1}(\mathrm{j})\end{bmatrix}\right)$ for any $\mathrm{i},\mathrm{j} \in [N]$ and for uniform choice of $\mathbf{r}_{(b)}$, then clearly $\mathsf{F}_\mathbf{K}$ is distinguishable from a random function, which would contradict our assumption. It follows that the above probability must be negligible, and consequently the construction is reusable. □

Lemma 5.3 (One-more unforgeability). *Suppose the* $\mathsf{rOM\text{-}ISIS}_{q,n,m,\mathfrak{s},\mathfrak{B}_N}$ *problem is hard and* NIZK *is sound. Then, construction 5 is one-more unforgeable.*

Pf. sketch. The proof of one-more unforgeability follows via a reduction to the $\mathsf{rOM\text{-}ISIS}$ assumption. The reduction sets $\mathbf{C} := \mathbf{A}_\top \cdot \mathbf{R}$ for $\mathbf{R}$ a uniformly chosen binary matrix. The fact that this change is indistinguishable to an adversary can be shown via the leftover hash lemma (Corollary 3.2). Then, whenever the adversary makes a query for the hash of some value $\mathbf{u}$, the reduction queries the $\mathsf{rOM\text{-}ISIS}$ oracle for a syndrome $\mathbf{h}$ and programs the random oracle such that $\mathsf{H}(\mathbf{u}) := \mathbf{h}$. When the adversary outputs its (one-more) forgeries, the reduction extracts $(\mathbf{k}_j, \mathbf{u}_j, \mathbf{s}_j, \mathbf{r}_j)$ from each proof π_j. With high probability, the adversary must have queried each $\mathbf{u}_j$ to the random oracle such that $\mathbf{h}_j = \mathsf{H}(\mathbf{u}_j)$ so that each $\mathbf{h}_j$ is in the set $\mathcal{S}$. So that $\mathbf{h}_j = \mathbf{A} \cdot (\mathbf{s}_j - \mathbf{R} \cdot \mathbf{k}_i) + \mathbf{B} \cdot \mathbf{r}_j$. Consequently, at least one of $(\mathbf{s}_i - \mathbf{R} \cdot \mathbf{k}_i)$ is a valid rOM-ISIS solution. □

Lemma 5.4 (Inter-batch blindness). *Suppose the* $\mathsf{F}_{\mathbf{K}}$ *is a pseudorandom function,* NIZK *is a multi-theorem zero-knowledge proof system and* PKE *is* IND-CPA *secure. Then, construction 5 is inter-batch blind.*

Pf. sketch. To prove batch receiver blindness, we will have the challenger simulate its NIZK proof, and then compute the encryptions ψ_{i}'s as encryptions of $\mathbf{0}$ for each receiver. These changes can be shown to be indistinguishable to an adversary by the zero-knowledge of the NIZK proof system, and IND-CPA security of the the public key encryption scheme respectively. Next, leveraging the leftover hash lemma (Corollary 3.2), we can have the challenger sample each receiver public key $\mathbf{t}$ uniformly. Notice, at this stage, that the adversary learns no information about the receiver and blindness follows. □

Lemma 5.5 (Intra-batch blindness). *Suppose the* $\mathsf{F}_{\mathbf{K}}$ *is a pseudorandom function,* NIZK *is multi-theorem zero-knowledge proof system and* PKE *is* IND-CPA *secure. Then, construction 5 is intra-batch blind.*

Pf. sketch. The proof of batch nonce blindness is quite similar to the previous proof—the challenger simulates its NIZK proof, then computes the encryptions ψ_{i}'s as encryptions of $\mathbf{0}$, and then leveraging the leftover hash lemma (Corollary 3.2), the challenger samples each receiver public key $\mathbf{t}$ uniformly. Since the adversary learns no information about the receiver, blindness follows. □

5.2 Instantiation

In this section, we propose concrete parameters to instantiate our NI<u>B</u>BS protocol and provide rough estimates for the size of the final signature. In choosing our parameters, we aim for 128-bit classical security.

Preimage Sampling Paramters. We instantiate the trapdoor generation and preimage sampling procedures using NTRU lattices over the Falcon-512 ring $\mathcal{R}_{\mathsf{F}} := \mathcal{R}_{q_{\mathsf{F}}, d_{\mathsf{F}}}$, where $q_{\mathsf{F}} = 12289$ and $d_{\mathsf{F}} = 512$. . The other parameters are computed as prescribed in [PFH+22, §2.6]). Concretely,

$$\mathfrak{s} = \frac{1.17}{\pi}\sqrt{q_{\mathsf{F}} \cdot \log\left(4d_{\mathsf{F}} \cdot \left(1 + \sqrt{\lambda \cdot 2^{64}}\right)/2\right)} \approx 2^{7.37} \text{ and } \mathfrak{B} = 1.1 \cdot \mathfrak{s}\sqrt{2d_{\mathsf{F}}}\ .$$

PRF Parameters. We carry over the parameters from [ADDG24] for our desired security level so that $n = 82$ and $n', m_N = 256$ (so that $m' = m_N - \lceil \log_2(B) \rceil$), except we set $m = 1024$ for sufficient rOM-ISIS hardness. Note that, since the final message is in $\mathbb{Z}_3^n$, the final message space is sufficiently large $(2^{\Theta(\lambda)})$.

Receiver Keys. Let $\mathsf{Coeff} : \mathbb{Z}[X]/(X^d+1) \to \mathbb{Z}^d$ be the canonical coefficient map, and $\mathsf{Coeff}^{-1} : \mathbb{Z}^d \to \mathbb{Z}[X]/(X^d+1)$ be its inverse. Then, the PRF key $\mathbf{K} \in \mathbb{Z}_2^{n' \times m_N}$ can be interpreted as $n'm_N/d_\mathsf{F} = 128$ polynomials $(k_1, \ldots, k_{128}) = \mathsf{Coeff}^{-1}(\mathsf{Vec}(\mathbf{K}))$. For $u \leftarrow\!\!\$\ \{0,1\}^{256}$, the receiver's public key $t \in \mathcal{R}_\mathsf{F}$ is then given as

$$t := \sum_{j=1}^{128} c_j \cdot k_j + \mathsf{H}(u) \bmod q_\mathsf{F} \ ,$$

where $\mathsf{H} : \{0,1\}^{256} \to \mathcal{R}_\mathsf{F}$ is a secure hash function such as SHA-3-256 and $c_i \in \mathcal{R}_\mathsf{F}$ are sampled during protocol setup.

Pre-signature Issuance. Given a receiver public key $t \in \mathcal{R}_\mathsf{F}$, the signer first samples the nonce vector $\mathbf{r} \leftarrow\!\!\$\ \mathbb{Z}_2^m$, and then decomposes it into $m/d = 2$ polynomials $(r_1, r_2) = \mathsf{Coeff}^{-1}(\mathbf{r})$. The signer then uses its NTRU secret trapdoor to sample short polynomials $s_1, s_2 \in \mathcal{R}_\mathsf{F}$ with respect to $a \in \mathcal{R}_\mathsf{F}$ such that

$$a \cdot s_1 + s_2 + b \cdot r_1 + r_2 = t \bmod q_\mathsf{F} \ ,$$

for $b \in \mathcal{R}_\mathsf{F}$ a part of the signer's verification key. The presignature is then s_1 and the nonce is $\mathbf{r}$ (the receiver can recover s_2 on its own). An important change, following the template of [AKSY22] is that we use rejection sampling to keep the ℓ_∞ norm of (s_1, s_2) to be at most $\lceil 4.15 \cdot \mathfrak{s} \rceil = 688$ for compatibility with the encryption scheme. Using, this bound, we get that the size of the signer's message is at most 0.62 KB for the presignature and an additional 0.12 KB for the nonce.

Blind Signature Generation. The receiver encrypts 133 polynomials in $\mathcal{R}_\mathsf{F}$—$\{k_j\}_{j\in[128]}, r_1, r_2, s_1$, along with u and i (as constant coefficients) using the Regev style public key encryption scheme from [LPS10] over $\mathcal{R}_{q_\mathsf{PKE}, d_\mathsf{F}}$. Thus, the rank of the plaintext space is 133, which is the main source of inefficiency in our final signature, as the required PKE modulus is $q_\mathsf{PKE} = 210596593 \approx 2^{27.6}$. Consequently, the ciphertext size is 231.53 KB, and can be brought down to around 214.78 KB by dropping lower order bits [SAB+22].

Unfortunately, the Falcon parameters do not satisfy the necessary conditions for the use of the modular Johnson-Lindenstrauss projections [BS23, Lemma 2.2] (also see [AAB+24]). So, we must lift the signature verification equation to a larger modulus ring $\mathcal{R}_{q_\mathsf{L}, d_\mathsf{F}}$ for modulus $q_\mathsf{L} > q_\mathsf{F}$. To simplify our final estimates, we set it to be as close as possible to the original LaBRADOR modulus 2^{32}. Now, we can lift the signature verification check directly to $\mathcal{R}$ (modulo nothing) so that

$$a \cdot s_1 + s_2 + b \cdot r_1 + r_2 + q_\mathsf{F}\delta = \sum_{j=1}^{128} c_j \cdot k_j + \mathsf{H}(u) \in \mathcal{R} \ , \qquad (2)$$

where the modular wraparound $\delta \in \mathcal{R}_{q_\mathsf{L}, d_\mathsf{F}}$ must now be made part of the witness. For appropriately bounded δ, if (2) holds over $\mathcal{R}$, it must hold over $\mathcal{R}_{q_\mathsf{L}, d_\mathsf{F}}$.

Further, to be compatible with the degree of the polynomial-ring in LaBRADOR, i.e., $d_{\mathsf{L}} = 64$, we use a reduced degree polynomial-ring. Note that the constraints over the larger ring $\mathcal{R}_{\mathsf{F}}$ can be reformulated as constraints over any sub-ring of degree d/c for some constant c. Specifically, the encryption scheme is instantiated over $\mathcal{R}_{q_{\mathsf{F}},d_{\mathsf{L}}}$ where $(\mathcal{R}_{q_{\mathsf{F}},d_{\mathsf{L}}}^{d_{\mathsf{F}}/d_{\mathsf{L}}} =)\ \mathcal{R}_{q_{\mathsf{F}},d_{\mathsf{L}}}^{8} \cong \mathcal{R}_{\mathsf{F}}$ and this bijection preserves the norms [LNPS21].

The receiver must prove knowledge of the polynomials satisfying the relation $\mathcal{R}^{\mathsf{NI\underline{B}BS}}$ with respect to the instantiation discussed in this section. In total, we approximate that the overall relation involves $\approx 2^{19.5}$ R1CS constraints (Table 3), which gives a proof size of 58 KB using LaBRADOR (cf. [BS23, § 7.1]). However, this only accounts for the SNARK without the additional zero-knowledge property. The LaBRADOR paper gives limited guidance on how to make the protocol zero-knowledge, but the main idea is to deploy a NIZK proof system at an intermediate level of the LaBRADOR recursion (so that the witness is already quite small). This involves some overhead required for blinding the outer commitments up to the NIZK level, masking the Johnson-Lindenstrauss projection and some additional garbage polynomials. In particular, for a binary-R1CS with 2^{20} constraints, using the lattice-based NIZK proof system for linear relations [LNP22b], the overhead is about 11 KB (cf. [BS23, § 6]). Since a single R1CS constraint can be expressed in no more than $\log_2^2(q_{\mathsf{L}}) \approx 2^{10}$ constraints, and given the slow order of growth of the LaBRADOR proofs, a very rough estimate puts the overhead for 2^{20} (general) R1CS constraints at about 36 KB, although with the right instantiation, we expect the actual overhead to be a few kilobytes lower. Nevertheless, with full zero-knowledge, the signature size is $58 + 36 + 214.78 = 308.78$ KB.

Table 3. Approximate R1CS constraint count.

Component	**#Constraints**
Hash computation (SHA-3-256)	27000
Signature verification [PFH+22]	68609
PRF computation [BIP+18]	286000
PKE computation [LPS10]	273408
ℓ_2-norm bounds	73019
Binary coefficient checks	66560
Total	**794596**

We sketch out our calculations of the number of constraints in the following section. These estimates are somewhat conservative, and further optimizations and reductions in the proof size may be possible. In particular, using SNARK-friendly hash functions [AGR+16] can also significantly reduce the number of constraints, leading to modest savings in the proof size.

Remark 5.6 (Instantiation of lattice-based NIBS). Our scheme can also readily be used as a standard (non-batched) NIBS. The main distinction is the absence of the index $\mathfrak{i}$ which allows for a few minor optimizations. In particular, the signer can now precompute $\mathbf{G}^{-1}(\mathbf{Y}_0 \cdot \mathbf{r} \bmod 3)$ and send the resulting $\tilde{\mathbf{r}} \in \mathbb{Z}_3^{256}$. This increases the size of the signer's message by just 0.06 KB. On the other hand, it reduces the receiver's computation time, as well as the final signature size by 2.6 KB (1.6 KB ciphertext and 1 KB proof) to 306.18 KB after compression. Furthermore, and as we show in Sect. 6, one can entirely do away with the hash computation if one is willing to rely on the recently proposed ISIS_f assumption [BLNS23b].

5.3 Estimating R1CS Constraint Count

In this section, we sketch out our computation of the number of R1CS constraints shown in Table 3.

Hash Computation. Standard SHA-3-256 circuits require extensive bit-level constraints. According to zk-SNARK benchmarks, SHA-3-256 for a short input (like 128 bits) costs $\sim 27,000$ constraints[8].

Signature Verification. Recall that the relation we are interested in is

$$a \cdot s_1 + s_2 + b \cdot r_1 + r_2 + q_{\mathsf{F}}\delta = \sum_{j=1}^{128} c_j \cdot k_j + \mathsf{H}(u) \ ,$$

where $a, b, c_1, \ldots, c_{128}$ are public polynomials and $s_1, s_2, r_1, r_2, d, k_1, \ldots, k_{128}, u$ are secret witness polynomials. Now, for each multiplication of public and secret polynomials, we need one R1CS constraint per coefficient. Thus, for $a \cdot s_1$, s_2, $b \cdot r_1$, r_2, and $q_F \cdot d$, each contributes 512 constraints, resulting in a total of 2,560 constraints for the left-hand side. On the right-hand side, each term $c_j \cdot k_j$ requires 512 constraints for the multiplication of their coefficients, resulting in 65536 constraints for the entire sum. Additionally, u, being a secret polynomial, contributes 512 constraints. Together, the right-hand side contributes 66048 constraints. Finally, we need one additional R1CS constraint to enforce the equality between the left-hand side and the right-hand side of the equation. Adding all of these constraints together, we get a total of 68609 R1CS constraints.

PRF Computation. To compute the R1CS constraints for the given check, we will break down the individual operations. First, we compute $\mathbf{Y}_0 \cdot \begin{bmatrix} \mathbf{r} \\ \mathbf{g}^{-1}(\mathfrak{i}) \end{bmatrix}$, where $\mathbf{Y}_0 \in \mathbb{Z}_3^{128 \times (1024+\kappa_N)}$ for $\kappa_N = \lceil \log_2(N) \rceil$ is a public matrix and $\begin{bmatrix} \mathbf{r} \\ \mathbf{g}^{-1}(\mathfrak{i}) \end{bmatrix} \in \mathbb{Z}_2^{1024+\kappa_N}$ is part of the witness. The multiplication requires $(1024 + \kappa_N)$ operations, resulting in as many constraints. Next, the inverse gadget decomposition $\mathbf{G}^{-1}$ maps the resulting vector from $\mathbb{Z}_3^{128} \to \mathbb{Z}_2^{256}$, by expanding each of the

[8] https://tinyurl.com/eth-research-sha-const.

128 entries of the input vector into its (2-bit) binary representation. Thus, each of the 128 elements introduces two binary variables, resulting in a total of 256 constraints for the $\mathbf{G}^{-1}$ operation. We then apply the vectorization operation Vec^{-1} to $\mathsf{Coeff}(k_1, \ldots, k_{128})$. The Vec^{-1} operation transforms a vector in $\mathbb{Z}_2^{65536}$ into a matrix in $\mathbb{Z}_2^{256\times 256}$. This transformation involves matrix multiplication and the Kronecker product of identity matrices, which essentially reshapes the vector into a matrix. Since the result is a 256×256 matrix, and each element in the matrix corresponds to a constraint in the R1CS, the operation introduces 65536 constraints. The resulting matrix and vector are then multiplied to give a new vector in $\mathbb{Z}_2^{256}$. For each element of the resulting vector, the matrix-vector multiplication involves a dot product of a row of the 256×256 matrix with the 256-dimensional vector. Each of these dot products requires 256 scalar multiplications, followed by a summation. Since we have a total of 256 elements in the resulting vector, the operations for this matrix-vector multiplication contributes to $256 \cdot 256 = 65536$ constraints. Finally, we multiply the result with $\mathbf{Y}_1 \in \mathbb{Z}_3^{82\times 256}$. The total number of operations for this matrix-vector multiplication is $82 \cdot 256 = 20992$ and as many constraints. Summing all of these contributions, the total number of R1CS constraints is $283392 + 128 \cdot \kappa_N$. For $N \leqslant 2^{20}$, this value is bounded from above by 286000.

PKE Computation. The proof of computation of the encryption of $\mathbf{m} \in \mathcal{R}_{q_{\mathsf{PKE}},d_{\mathsf{F}}}^{133}$ according to [LPS10] requires proving

$$\psi_1 = a_1 \cdot s + e_1 \text{ and } \boldsymbol{\psi}_2 = \mathbf{a}_2 \cdot s + \mathbf{e}_2 + p \cdot \mathbf{m} \ ,$$

for ciphertexts $(\psi_1, \boldsymbol{\psi}_2) \in \mathcal{R}_{q_{\mathsf{PKE}},d_{\mathsf{F}}} \times \mathcal{R}_{q_{\mathsf{PKE}},d_{\mathsf{F}}}^{133}$, public polynomial $a_1 \in \mathcal{R}_{q_{\mathsf{PKE}},d_{\mathsf{F}}}$ and polynomial vector $\mathbf{a}_2 \in \mathcal{R}_{q_{\mathsf{PKE}},d_{\mathsf{F}}}^{133}$ and witness $(s, e_1, \mathbf{e}_2, \mathbf{m}) \in \mathcal{R}_{q_{\mathsf{PKE}},d_{\mathsf{F}}} \times \mathcal{R}_{q_{\mathsf{PKE}},d_{\mathsf{F}}} \times \mathcal{R}_{q_{\mathsf{PKE}},d_{\mathsf{F}}}^{133} \mathcal{R}_{q_{\mathsf{PKE}},d_{\mathsf{F}}}^{133}$.

To enforce the first relation, we need to compute multiply a public polynomial with a secret polynomial. This requires 512 R1CS constraints, one per coefficient; and the addition of a secret polynomial to this product involves another 512 constraints. For the second relation, we notice that each polynomial-vector multiplication requires 512 constraints for each of the 133 entries in the vector, leading to $133 \cdot 512 = 68096$ constraints, and the scalar multiplication also contributes 68096 constraints. Finally, adding up the three vectors contributes $2 \cdot 68096 = 136192$ constraints. The total number of R1CS constraints required to enforce both equations is therefore $1024 + 4 \cdot 68096 = 273408$.

ℓ_2-norm Bound. For any polynomial, computing the square of each coefficient requires 512 multiplication constraints, summing these squares adds 511 constraints, and enforcing that the resulting sum is less than or equal to some (public) bound requires approximately 64 constraints via bit-decomposition and range checking. Therefore, each polynomial contributes roughly $512 + 511 + 64 = 1087$ R1CS constraints, and since we need to perform this check for polynomials s_1, s_2, δ, s and e_1, and polynomial vector $\mathbf{e}_2$, the total number of constraints is $4 \cdot 1087 + 133 \cdot 512 + 511 + 64 = 73019$.

Binary Coefficient Checks. Checking that the coefficients of polynomials $k_1, k_2, \ldots, k_{128}, r_1$ and r_2 are binary, can be done by ensuring that for each coefficient x, the equation $x \cdot (1 - x) = 0$ holds, which requires one R1CS constraint per coefficient. Since each of the polynomials has 512 coefficients, the total number of R1CS constraints is $512 \cdot 130 = 66560$.

6 Lattice-Based NI$\underline{\text{B}}$BS from ISIS_f

A minor drawback of our construction 5 is that it requires proving the computation of the hash function in the NIZK proof. Aside from the computational overhead, this additionally necessitates a somewhat strong assumption, since the proof of unforgeability also requires modeling the hash function as a random oracle. While not unusual in practice (see for example [BLNS23a]), this approach may be unsatisfactory for provable security. In this section, we give an alternate construction that is secure under the recently proposed ISIS_f assumption [BLNS23b] which does not require this stronger assumption concerning the random oracle. We begin by recalling the ISIS_f assumption [BLNS23b]:

Definition 6.1 (ISIS$_f$ [BLNS23b]). *Let $q, n, m, \mathfrak{s}, \mathfrak{B}$ be functions of security parameter λ. Also let $f : \mathcal{D} \to \mathbb{Z}_q^n$ be a function on some input domain $\mathcal{D}$ and for $\mathbf{A} \leftarrow_\$ \mathbb{Z}_q^{n \times m}$, let $\mathcal{O}_{\mathbf{A},f}$ be an oracle that chooses a random input $\alpha \in \mathcal{D}$ and outputs $(\mathbf{s}, \alpha)$ for $\mathbf{s} \in \mathbb{Z}_q^m$ such that $\mathbf{s} \leftarrow_\$ \mathbf{A}_{\mathfrak{s}}^{-1}(f(\alpha))$. Given $(\mathbf{A}, f)$ and access to $\mathcal{O}_{\mathbf{A},f}$, the ISIS_f problem asks to find $(\mathbf{s}', \alpha') \in \mathbb{Z}_q^m \times \mathcal{D}$, such that $\mathbf{A} \cdot \mathbf{s}' = f(\alpha')$, $\mathbf{s}' \neq \mathbf{s}$ and $\|\mathbf{s}'\| \leqslant \mathfrak{B}$.*

Let $N \in \mathbb{N}$ be the batch size, and let parameters $n, m, n', m', \mathfrak{s}, \mathfrak{B} = \mathfrak{s}\sqrt{m}$, and positive integer q be functions of the security parameter λ satisfying the constraints in (1). By $f : [2^m] \to \mathbb{Z}_q^n$ we denote a linear map characterizing the ISIS_f. We give a NI$\underline{\text{B}}$BS construction that is secure under the ISIS_f assumption.

This construction relies on a lattice trapdoor $\mathcal{T} = (\mathcal{T}.\mathsf{TrapGen}, \mathcal{T}.\mathsf{SamplePre})$, a public key encryption scheme $\mathsf{PKE} = (\mathsf{PKE.KeyGen}, \mathsf{PKE.Enc}, \mathsf{PKE.Dec})$ and NIZK proof systems $\mathsf{NIZK}_1 = (\mathsf{NIZK}_1.\mathsf{Setup}, \mathsf{NIZK}_1.\mathsf{Prove}, \mathsf{NIZK}_1.\mathsf{Verify})$, $\mathsf{NIZK}_2 = (\mathsf{NIZK}_2.\mathsf{Setup}, \mathsf{NIZK}_2.\mathsf{Prove}, \mathsf{NIZK}_2.\mathsf{Verify})$ respectively for relations $\mathcal{R}_1^{\mathsf{NI\underline{B}BS},\mathsf{ISIS}_f}$ and $\mathcal{R}_2^{\mathsf{NI\underline{B}BS},\mathsf{ISIS}_f}$, defined as follows:

Relation $\mathcal{R}_1^{\mathsf{NI\underline{B}BS},\mathsf{ISIS}_f}$

Instance: Each instance $\mathfrak{x}$ is interpreted as polynomial matrices $\mathbf{C}_0$ and $\mathbf{C}_1$, an encryption public key $\mathsf{pk}_{\mathsf{PKE}}$, a polynomial vector $\mathbf{t}$ and a ciphertext ϕ.

Witness: Witness $\mathfrak{w}$ consists of secret polynomial vectors $\mathbf{k}$ and $\mathbf{u}$, and the encryption randomness ν.

Membership: $\mathfrak{w}$ is a valid witness for $\mathfrak{x}$ if the following are satisfied:

- $\phi = \mathsf{PKE.Enc}(\mathsf{pk}_{\mathsf{PKE}}, \mathbf{k}||\mathbf{u}; \nu)$
- $\mathbf{t} = \mathbf{C}_0 \cdot \mathbf{k} + \mathbf{C}_1 \cdot \mathbf{u}$
- $\mathbf{k}, \mathbf{u} \in \mathbb{Z}_2^{n'mN}$

Relation $\mathscr{R}_2^{\mathsf{NI\underline{B}BS},\mathsf{ISIS}_f}$

Instance: Each instance $\mathfrak{x}$ is interpreted as matrices $\mathbf{A}, \mathbf{B}, \mathbf{C}_0, \mathbf{C}_1, \mathbf{Y}_0$ and $\mathbf{Y}_1$, a linear map f, a PKE public key $\mathsf{pk}_{\mathsf{PKE}}$, a message vector μ and ciphertext ψ.

Witness: Witness $\mathfrak{w}$ consists of secret vectors $\mathbf{k}, \mathbf{u}, \mathbf{s}$ and $\mathbf{i}$, integer α and PKE randomness ρ.

Membership: $\mathfrak{w}$ is a valid witness for $\mathfrak{x}$ if the following are satisfied:

- ▷ $\mathbf{A} \cdot \mathbf{s} = \mathbf{C}_0 \cdot \mathbf{k} + \mathbf{C}_1 \cdot \mathbf{u} + f(\alpha)$
- ▷ $\mu = \mathbf{Y}_1 \cdot \left(\mathsf{Vec}^{-1}(\mathbf{k}) \cdot \mathbf{G}^{-1}\left(\mathbf{Y}_0 \cdot \begin{bmatrix} f(\alpha) \\ \mathbf{i} \end{bmatrix} \bmod 3\right) \bmod 2\right) \bmod 3$
- ▷ $\psi = \mathsf{PKE.Enc}\left(\mathsf{pk}_{\mathsf{PKE}}, \mathbf{k}||\mathbf{u}||\mathbf{s}||\mathbf{i}||\alpha \ ; \ \rho\right)$
- ▷ $\|\mathbf{s}\| \leqslant \mathfrak{B}, \quad \alpha \in [2^m], \quad \mathbf{k}, \mathbf{u} \in \mathbb{Z}_2^{n' m_N}, \quad \mathbf{i} \in \mathbb{Z}_2^{m_N - m'}.$

6.1 Construction

We are now ready to describe our lattice-based NI$\underline{\text{B}}$BS scheme.

- $\mathsf{Setup}(1^\lambda, N) \to \mathsf{pp}$. The public parameter setup algorithm computes $n, m, n', m', \mathfrak{s}, q$ from the security parameter λ as well as the linear map f. It then sets $m_N = m' + \lceil \log_2(N) \rceil$, and samples matrices $\mathbf{Y}_0 \leftarrow_{\$} \mathbb{Z}_3^{\frac{m_N}{2} \times (m + m_N - m')}$, $\mathbf{Y}_1 \leftarrow_{\$} \mathbb{Z}_3^{n \times n'}$ and $\mathbf{C}_0, \mathbf{C}_1 \leftarrow_{\$} \mathbb{Z}_q^{n \times n' m_N}$. It then runs the key generation algorithm of PKE and generates the corresponding public and secret key pair as

$$(\mathsf{pk}_{\mathsf{PKE}}, \mathsf{sk}_{\mathsf{PKE}}) \leftarrow_{\$} \mathsf{PKE.KeyGen}(1^\lambda) \ .$$

  Next, it generates $\mathsf{crs}_{\mathsf{NIZK}_1} \leftarrow_{\$} \mathsf{NIZK}_1.\mathsf{Setup}(1^\lambda)$ and $\mathsf{crs}_{\mathsf{NIZK}_2} \leftarrow_{\$} \mathsf{NIZK}_2.\mathsf{Setup}(1^\lambda)$ and outputs

$$\mathsf{pp} := \left(1^\lambda, n, m, n', m_N, \mathfrak{s}, q, N, f, \mathsf{pk}_{\mathsf{PKE}}, \mathsf{crs}_{\mathsf{NIZK}_1}, \mathsf{crs}_{\mathsf{NIZK}_2}, \mathbf{Y}_0, \mathbf{Y}_1, \mathbf{C}_0, \mathbf{C}_1\right) \ .$$

  The public parameters are fixed once and for all.

- $\mathsf{KeyGen}_S(\mathsf{pp}) \to (\mathsf{sk}, \mathsf{vk})$. The signer's key generation algorithm is the same as in construction 5.
- $\mathsf{KeyGen}_R(\mathsf{pp}) \to (\mathsf{sk}_R, \mathsf{pk}_R)$. The receiver's key generation algorithm samples the PRF key $\mathbf{K} \leftarrow_{\$} \mathbb{Z}_2^{n' \times m_N}$ and a random vector $\mathbf{u} \leftarrow_{\$} \mathbb{Z}_2^{n' m_N}$. It then vectorizes $\mathbf{K}$ as $\mathbf{k} := \mathsf{Vec}(\mathbf{K})$, and computes an Ajtai commitment

$$\mathbf{t} := \mathbf{C}_0 \cdot \mathbf{k} + \mathbf{C}_1 \cdot \mathbf{u} \ .$$

  Next, it generates a ciphertext,

$$\phi \leftarrow \mathsf{PKE.Enc}\left(\mathsf{pk}_{\mathsf{PKE}}, \mathbf{k}||\mathbf{u}\ ;\ \nu\right)$$

from uniformly sampled randomness ν and the NIZK proof

$$\tau \leftarrow_{\$} \mathsf{NIZK}_1.\mathsf{Prove}\left(\mathsf{crs}_{\mathsf{NIZK}_1}, \mathfrak{x} := (\mathbf{C}_0, \mathbf{C}_1, \mathsf{pk}_{\mathsf{PKE}}, \mathbf{t}, \phi), \mathfrak{w} := (\mathbf{k}, \mathbf{u}, \nu)\right) ,$$

It then sets the receiver's secret key as $\mathsf{sk}_R := (\mathbf{K}, \mathbf{u})$, the public key as $\mathsf{pk}_R := (\mathbf{t}, \phi, \tau)$ and outputs them.

- $\mathsf{Issue}(\mathsf{sk}, \mathsf{pk}_R) \rightarrow (\mathsf{psig}, \mathsf{nonce})$. Given the receiver's public key $\mathsf{pk}_R =: (\mathbf{t}, \phi, \tau)$, the signer's pre-signature issuance algorithm first checks if

$$\mathsf{NIZK}_1.\mathsf{Verify}(\mathsf{crs}_{\mathsf{NIZK}_1}, \mathfrak{x} := (\mathbf{C}_0, \mathbf{C}_1, \mathsf{pk}_{\mathsf{PKE}}, \mathbf{t}, \phi), \tau) \stackrel{?}{=} 1 ,$$

otherwise it aborts and outputs $\perp$. It then samples a random integer $\alpha \leftarrow_{\$} [2^m]$ and, using the secret signing key $\mathsf{sk} =: \mathbf{T}_{\mathbf{A}}$, it computes

$$\mathbf{s} \leftarrow_{\$} \mathcal{T}.\mathsf{SamplePre}\left(\mathbf{A}, \mathbf{T}_{\mathbf{A}}, \mathbf{t} + f(\alpha), \mathfrak{s}\right),$$

and outputs the pre-signature, $\mathsf{psig} := \mathbf{s}$ and the nonce, $\mathsf{nonce} := \alpha$.

- $\mathsf{Obtain}(\mathsf{sk}_R, \mathsf{vk}, \mathsf{psig}, \mathsf{nonce}) \rightarrow [\![\mu, \sigma]\!]$. The receiver's signature obtainment algorithm first parses sk_R as $(\mathbf{K}, \mathbf{u})$ and then, for $\mathsf{vk} =: (\mathbf{A}, \mathbf{B})$, $\mathsf{psig} =: \mathbf{s}$, and $\mathsf{nonce} =: \alpha$, it checks if

$$\mathbf{A} \cdot \mathbf{s} \stackrel{?}{=} \mathbf{C}_0 \cdot \mathsf{Vec}(\mathbf{K}) + \mathbf{C}_1 \cdot \mathbf{u} + f(\alpha)\ \wedge\ \|\mathbf{s}\| \stackrel{?}{\leqslant} \mathfrak{B}\ \wedge\ \alpha \stackrel{?}{\in} [2^m] .$$

If any check fails it aborts and outputs $\perp$. Otherwise, for each $\mathfrak{i} \in [N]$, it computes the message $\mu_{\mathfrak{i}}$ as

$$\mu_{\mathfrak{i}} := \mathbf{Y}_1 \cdot \left(\mathbf{K} \cdot \mathbf{G}^{-1}\left(\mathbf{Y}_0 \cdot \begin{bmatrix} f(\alpha) \\ \mathbf{g}^{-1}(\mathfrak{i}) \end{bmatrix} \bmod 3\right) \bmod 2\right) \bmod 3 ,$$

where, $\mathbf{g}^{-1} : \mathbb{Z}_N \rightarrow \mathbb{Z}_2^{\log_2(N)}$ ($\log_2(N) = m_N - m'$) is the binary decomposition gadget.
With this, it now generates the corresponding ciphertext as

$$\psi_{\mathfrak{i}} \leftarrow \mathsf{PKE.Enc}\left(\mathsf{pk}_{\mathsf{PKE}}, \mathbf{k}||\mathbf{u}||\mathbf{s}||\mathbf{g}^{-1}(\mathfrak{i})||\alpha\ ;\ \rho_{\mathfrak{i}}\right)$$

from uniformly sampled randomness $\rho_{\mathfrak{i}}$. It then generates the NIZK proof

$$\pi_{\mathfrak{i}} \leftarrow_{\$} \mathsf{NIZK}_2.\mathsf{Prove}\left(\begin{matrix}\mathsf{crs}_{\mathsf{NIZK}_2}, \mathfrak{x}_{\mathfrak{i}} := (\mathbf{A}, \mathbf{B}, \mathbf{C}_0, \mathbf{C}_1, \mathbf{Y}_0, \mathbf{Y}_1, f, \mathsf{pk}_{\mathsf{PKE}}, \mu_{\mathfrak{i}}, \psi_{\mathfrak{i}}), \\ \mathfrak{w}_{\mathfrak{i}} := (\mathbf{k}, \mathbf{u}, \mathbf{s}, \mathbf{g}^{-1}(\mathfrak{i}), \alpha, \rho_{\mathfrak{i}})\end{matrix}\right) ,$$

Finally, it outputs $[\![\mu, \sigma]\!] := \{(\mu_1, \sigma_1 := (\psi_1, \pi_1)), \ldots, (\mu_N, \sigma_N := (\psi_N, \pi_N))\}$.

- $\mathsf{Verify}(\mathsf{vk}, \mu, \sigma) \to 0/1$. The signature verification algorithm parses σ as (ψ, π) and outputs 1 (accept) if

$$\mathsf{NIZK}_2.\mathsf{Verify}\left(\mathsf{crs}_{\mathsf{NIZK}_2}, \mathfrak{x} := \left(\mathbf{A}, \mathbf{B}, \mathbf{C}_0, \mathbf{C}_1, \mathbf{Y}_0, \mathbf{Y}_1, f, \mathsf{pk}_{\mathsf{PKE}}, \mu_{\mathfrak{i}}, \psi_{\mathfrak{i}}\right), \pi\right) = 1 ,$$

and 0 (reject) otherwise.

Security. We now state our main theorem concerning the security of our NI$\underline{\text{B}}$BS scheme.

Theorem 6.2. *Let $N \in \mathbb{N}$ be the batch size, and let parameters $n, m, n', m', \mathfrak{s}, \mathfrak{B} = \mathfrak{s}\sqrt{m}$, and positive integer q be functions of the security parameter λ such that (1) is satisfied, and the ISIS_f and $\mathsf{SIS}_{q,n,2n'm_N,\sqrt{2n'm_N}}$ problems are hard for an appropriately chosen function $f : [2^m] \to \mathbb{Z}_q^n$.*

If NIZK_1 is a NIZK for $\mathcal{R}_1^{\mathsf{NI\underline{B}BS},\mathsf{ISIS}_f}$, NIZK_2 is a NIZK for $\mathcal{R}_2^{\mathsf{NI\underline{B}BS},\mathsf{ISIS}_f}$ and PKE is an $\mathsf{IND\text{-}CPA}$ secure encryption scheme then, construction 6 is a secure non-interactive batched blind signature scheme.

Due to space consraints, we prove the lemmas concerning the one-more unforgeability, and inter- and intra-batch of the protocol in the full version of this article.

Acknowledgements. Foteini Baldimtsi and Aayush Yadav were supported by NSF award 2143287. Rishab Goyal was supported by a gift from the Stellar Development Foundation.

References

[AAB+24] Aardal, M.A., Aranha, D.F., Boudgoust, K., Kolby, S., Takahashi, A.: Aggregating falcon signatures with LaBRADOR. In: Reyzin, L., Stebila, D. (eds.) CRYPTO 2024, Part I. LNCS, vol. 14920, pp. 71–106. Springer, Cham (2024)

[Abe01] Abe, M.: A secure three-move blind signature scheme for polynomially many signatures. In: Pfitzmann, B. (ed.) EUROCRYPT 2001. LNCS, vol. 2045, pp. 136–151. Springer, Heidelberg (2001). https://doi.org/10.1007/3-540-44987-6_9

[ADDG24] Albrecht, M.R., Davidson, A., Deo, A., Gardham, D.: Crypto dark matter on the torus - oblivious PRFs from shallow PRFs and TFHE. In: Joye, M., Leander, G. (eds.) EUROCRYPT 2024, Part VI. LNCS, vol. 14656, pp. 447–476. Springer, Cham (2024)

[ADDS21] Albrecht, M.R., Davidson, A., Deo, A., Smart, N.P.: Round-optimal verifiable oblivious pseudorandom functions from ideal lattices. In: Garay, J.A. (ed.) PKC 2021. LNCS, vol. 12711, pp. 261–289. Springer, Cham (2021). https://doi.org/10.1007/978-3-030-75248-4_10

[AG24] Albrecht, M.R., Gur, K.D.: Verifiable oblivious pseudorandom functions from lattices: practical-ish and thresholdisable. In: Chung, K.-M., Sasaki, Y. (eds.) ASIACRYPT 2024, Part IV. LNCS, vol. 15487, pp. 205–237. Springer, Singapore (2024)

[AGR+16] Albrecht, M., Grassi, L., Rechberger, C., Roy, A., Tiessen, T.: MiMC: efficient encryption and cryptographic hashing with minimal multiplicative complexity. In: Cheon, J.H., Takagi, T. (eds.) ASIACRYPT 2016. LNCS, vol. 10031, pp. 191–219. Springer, Heidelberg (2016). https://doi.org/10.1007/978-3-662-53887-6_7

[Ajt96] Ajtai, M.: Generating hard instances of lattice problems (extended abstract). In: 28th ACM STOC, Philadephia, PA, USA, 22–24 May 1996, pp. 99–108. ACM Press (1996)

[AKSY22] Agrawal, S., Kirshanova, E., Stehlé, D., Yadav, A.: Practical, round-optimal lattice-based blind signatures. In: Yin, H., Stavrou, A., Cremers, C., Shi, E. (eds.) ACM CCS 2022, Los Angeles, CA, USA, 7–11 November 2022, pp. 39–53. ACM Press (2022)

[BBKK18] Barak, B., Brakerski, Z., Komargodski, I., Kothari, P.K.: Limits on low-degree pseudorandom generators (or: sum-of-squares meets program obfuscation). In: Nielsen, J.B., Rijmen, V. (eds.) EUROCRYPT 2018. LNCS, vol. 10821, pp. 649–679. Springer, Cham (2018). https://doi.org/10.1007/978-3-319-78375-8_21

[BCC04] Brickell, E.F., Camenisch, J., Chen, L.: Direct anonymous attestation. In: Atluri, V., Pfitzmann, B., McDaniel, P. (eds.) ACM CCS 2004, Washington, DC, USA, 25–29 October 2004, pp. 132–145. ACM Press (2004)

[BCGY24] Baldimtsi, F., Cheng, J., Goyal, R., Yadav, A.: Non-interactive blind signatures: post-quantum and stronger security. In: Chung, K.-M., Sasaki, Y. (eds.) ASIACRYPT 2024, Part II. LNCS, vol. 15485, pp. 70–104. Springer, Singapore (2024)

[BEP+21] Bert, P., Eberhart, G., Prabel, L., Roux-Langlois, A., Sabt, M.: Implementation of lattice trapdoors on modules and applications. In: Cheon, J.H., Tillich, J.-P. (eds.) PQCrypto 2021 2021. LNCS, vol. 12841, pp. 195–214. Springer, Cham (2021). https://doi.org/10.1007/978-3-030-81293-5_11

[BFPV13] Blazy, O., Fuchsbauer, G., Pointcheval, D., Vergnaud, D.: Short blind signatures. J. Comput. Secur. **21**(5), 627–661 (2013)

[BIP+18] Boneh, D., Ishai, Y., Passelègue, A., Sahai, A., Wu, D.J.: Exploring crypto dark matter. In: Beimel, A., Dziembowski, S. (eds.) TCC 2018. LNCS, vol. 11240, pp. 699–729. Springer, Cham (2018). https://doi.org/10.1007/978-3-030-03810-6_25

[BL13] Baldimtsi, F., Lysyanskaya, A.: Anonymous credentials light. In: Sadeghi, A.-R., Gligor, V.D., Yung, M. (eds.) ACM CCS 2013, Berlin, Germany, 4–8 November 2013, pp. 1087–1098. ACM Press (2013)

[BLMR13] Boneh, D., Lewi, K., Montgomery, H., Raghunathan, A.: Key homomorphic PRFs and their applications. In: Canetti, R., Garay, J.A. (eds.) CRYPTO 2013. LNCS, vol. 8042, pp. 410–428. Springer, Heidelberg (2013). https://doi.org/10.1007/978-3-642-40041-4_23

[BLNS23a] Beullens, W., Lyubashevsky, V., Nguyen, N.K., Seiler, G.: Lattice-based blind signatures: short, efficient, and round-optimal. In: Meng, W., Jensen, C.D., Cremers, C., Kirda, E. (eds.) ACM CCS 2023, Copenhagen, Denmark, 26–30 November 2023, pp. 16–29. ACM Press (2023)

[BLNS23b] Bootle, J., Lyubashevsky, V., Nguyen, N.K., Sorniotti, A.: A framework for practical anonymous credentials from lattices. In: Handschuh, H., Lysyanskaya, A. (eds.) CRYPTO 2023, Part II. LNCS, vol. 14082, pp. 384–417. Springer, Cham (2023)

[Bol03] Boldyreva, A.: Threshold signatures, multisignatures and blind signatures based on the gap-Diffie-Hellman-group signature scheme. In: Desmedt, Y.G. (ed.) PKC 2003. LNCS, vol. 2567, pp. 31–46. Springer, Heidelberg (2003). https://doi.org/10.1007/3-540-36288-6_3

[BP14] Banerjee, A., Peikert, C.: New and improved key-homomorphic pseudorandom functions. In: Garay, J.A., Gennaro, R. (eds.) CRYPTO 2014. LNCS, vol. 8616, pp. 353–370. Springer, Heidelberg (2014). https://doi.org/10.1007/978-3-662-44371-2_20

[BPR12] Banerjee, A., Peikert, C., Rosen, A.: Pseudorandom functions and lattices. In: Pointcheval, D., Johansson, T. (eds.) EUROCRYPT 2012. LNCS, vol. 7237, pp. 719–737. Springer, Heidelberg (2012). https://doi.org/10.1007/978-3-642-29011-4_42

[BR94] Bellare, M., Rogaway, P.: Entity authentication and key distribution. In: Stinson, D.R. (ed.) CRYPTO 1993. LNCS, vol. 773, pp. 232–249. Springer, Heidelberg (1994). https://doi.org/10.1007/3-540-48329-2_21

[BS23] Beullens, W., Seiler, G.: LaBRADOR: compact proofs for R1CS from module-SIS. In: Handschuh, H., Lysyanskaya, A. (eds.) CRYPTO 2023, Part V. LNCS, vol. 14085, pp. 518–548. Springer, Cham (2023)

[CAHL+22] Chairattana-Apirom, R., Hanzlik, L., Loss, J., Lysyanskaya, A., Wagner, B.: PI-cut-choo and friends: compact blind signatures via parallel instance cut-and-choose and more. In: Dodis, Y., Shrimpton, T. (eds.) CRYPTO 2022, Part III. LNCS, vol. 13509, pp. 3–31. Springer, Cham (2022)

[CATZ24] Chairattana-Apirom, R., Tessaro, S., Zhu, C.: Pairing-free blind signatures from CDH assumptions. In: Reyzin, L., Stebila, D. (eds.) CRYPTO 2024, Part I. LNCS, vol. 14920, pp. 174–209. Springer, Cham (2024)

[CCKK22] Cheon, J.H., Cho, W., Kim, J.H., Kim, J.: Adventures in crypto dark matter: attacks, fixes and analysis for weak pseudorandom functions. DCC **90**(8), 1735–1760 (2022)

[CGT06] Canard, S., Gaud, M., Traoré, J.: Defeating malicious servers in a blind signatures based voting system. In: Di Crescenzo, G., Rubin, A. (eds.) FC 2006. LNCS, vol. 4107, pp. 148–153. Springer, Heidelberg (2006). https://doi.org/10.1007/11889663_11

[Cha83] Chaum, D.: Blind signature system. In: Chaum, D. (ed.) CRYPTO 1983, Santa Barbara, CA, USA, p. 153. Plenum Press, New York (1983)

[DGH+21] Dinur, I., et al.: MPC-friendly symmetric cryptography from alternating moduli: candidates, protocols, and applications. In: Malkin, T., Peikert, C. (eds.) CRYPTO 2021. LNCS, vol. 12828, pp. 517–547. Springer, Cham (2021). https://doi.org/10.1007/978-3-030-84259-8_18

[DGS+18] Davidson, A., Goldberg, I., Sullivan, N., Tankersley, G., Valsorda, F.: Privacy pass: bypassing internet challenges anonymously. PoPETs **2018**(3), 164–180 (2018)

[dPK22] del Pino, R., Katsumata, S.: A new framework for more efficient round-optimal lattice-based (partially) blind signature via trapdoor sampling. In: Dodis, Y., Shrimpton, T. (eds.) CRYPTO 2022, Part II. LNCS, vol. 13508, pp. 306–336. Springer, Cham (2022)

[DRS04] Dodis, Y., Reyzin, L., Smith, A.: Fuzzy extractors: how to generate strong keys from biometrics and other noisy data. In: Cachin, C., Camenisch, J.L. (eds.) EUROCRYPT 2004. LNCS, vol. 3027, pp. 523–540. Springer, Heidelberg (2004). https://doi.org/10.1007/978-3-540-24676-3_31

[EKS+21] Esgin, M.F., et al.: Practical post-quantum few-time verifiable random function with applications to algorand. In: Borisov, N., Diaz, C. (eds.) FC 2021. LNCS, vol. 12675, pp. 560–578. Springer, Heidelberg (2021). https://doi.org/10.1007/978-3-662-64331-0_29

[ESLR23] Esgin, M.F., Steinfeld, R., Liu, D., Ruj, S.: Efficient hybrid exact/relaxed lattice proofs and applications to rounding and VRFs. In: Handschuh, H., Lysyanskaya, A. (eds.) CRYPTO 2023, Part V. LNCS, vol. 14085, pp. 484–517. Springer, Cham (2023)

[FHS15] Fuchsbauer, G., Hanser, C., Slamanig, D.: Practical round-optimal blind signatures in the standard model. In: Gennaro, R., Robshaw, M. (eds.) CRYPTO 2015. LNCS, vol. 9216, pp. 233–253. Springer, Heidelberg (2015). https://doi.org/10.1007/978-3-662-48000-7_12

[FHS19] Fuchsbauer, G., Hanser, C., Slamanig, D.: Structure-preserving signatures on equivalence classes and constant-size anonymous credentials. J. Cryptol. **32**(2), 498–546 (2019)

[Fis06] Fischlin, M.: Round-optimal composable blind signatures in the common reference string model. In: Dwork, C. (ed.) CRYPTO 2006. LNCS, vol. 4117, pp. 60–77. Springer, Heidelberg (2006). https://doi.org/10.1007/11818175_4

[GG14] Garg, S., Gupta, D.: Efficient round optimal blind signatures. In: Nguyen, P.Q., Oswald, E. (eds.) EUROCRYPT 2014. LNCS, vol. 8441, pp. 477–495. Springer, Heidelberg (2014). https://doi.org/10.1007/978-3-642-55220-5_27

[Gha17] Ghadafi, E.: Efficient round-optimal blind signatures in the standard model. In: Kiayias, A. (ed.) FC 2017. LNCS, vol. 10322, pp. 455–473. Springer, Cham (2017). https://doi.org/10.1007/978-3-319-70972-7_26

[GKK+25] Ganguly, A., Karmakar, A., Kundu, S., Pal, D., Sarkar, S.: Revisiting lattice-based non-interactive blind signature. Cryptology ePrint Archive, Paper 2025/1848 (2025)

[Goo25] Google. Private state tokens (2025). https://developers.google.com/privacy-sandbox/protections/private-state-tokens. Accessed 2 May 2025

[GPV08] Gentry, C., Peikert, C., Vaikuntanathan, V.: Trapdoors for hard lattices and new cryptographic constructions. In: Ladner, R.E., Dwork, C. (eds.) 40th ACM STOC, Victoria, BC, Canada, 17–20 May 2008, pp. 197–206. ACM Press (2008)

[GRS+11] Garg, S., Rao, V., Sahai, A., Schröder, D., Unruh, D.: Round optimal blind signatures. In: Rogaway, P. (ed.) CRYPTO 2011. LNCS, vol. 6841, pp. 630–648. Springer, Heidelberg (2011). https://doi.org/10.1007/978-3-642-22792-9_36

[HAB+17] Heilman, E., Alshenibr, L., Baldimtsi, F., Scafuro, A., Goldberg, S.: TumbleBit: an untrusted bitcoin-compatible anonymous payment hub. In: NDSS 2017, San Diego, CA, USA, 26 February–1 March 2017. The Internet Society (2017)

[Han23] Hanzlik, L.: Non-interactive blind signatures for random messages. In: Hazay, C., Stam, M. (eds.) EUROCRYPT 2023, Part V. LNCS, vol. 14008, pp. 722–752. Springer, Cham (2023)

[HBG16] Heilman, E., Baldimtsi, F., Goldberg, S.: Blindly signed contracts: anonymous on-blockchain and off-blockchain bitcoin transactions. In: Clark, J., Meiklejohn, S., Ryan, P.Y.A., Wallach, D., Brenner, M., Rohloff, K. (eds.) FC 2016. LNCS, vol. 9604, pp. 43–60. Springer, Heidelberg (2016). https://doi.org/10.1007/978-3-662-53357-4_4

[HILL99] Håstad, J., Impagliazzo, R., Levin, L.A., Luby, M.: A pseudorandom generator from any one-way function. SIAM J. Comput. **28**(4), 1364–1396 (1999)

[HKL19] Hauck, E., Kiltz, E., Loss, J.: A modular treatment of blind signatures from identification schemes. In: Ishai, Y., Rijmen, V. (eds.) EUROCRYPT 2019. LNCS, vol. 11478, pp. 345–375. Springer, Cham (2019). https://doi.org/10.1007/978-3-030-17659-4_12

[HLW23] Hanzlik, L., Loss, J., Wagner, B.: Rai-choo! Evolving blind signatures to the next level. In: Hazay, C., Stam, M. (eds.) EUROCRYPT 2023, Part V. LNCS, vol. 14008, pp. 753–783. Springer, Cham (2023)

[HPZ25] Hanzlik, L., Paracucchi, E., Zanotto, R.: Non-interactive blind signatures from RSA assumption and more. In: Fehr, S., Fouque, P.-A. (eds.) Advances in Cryptology – EUROCRYPT 2025, pp. 365–394. Springer, Cham (2025)

[HS14] Hanser, C., Slamanig, D.: Structure-preserving signatures on equivalence classes and their application to anonymous credentials. In: Sarkar, P., Iwata, T. (eds.) ASIACRYPT 2014. LNCS, vol. 8873, pp. 491–511. Springer, Heidelberg (2014). https://doi.org/10.1007/978-3-662-45611-8_26

[IET25a] IETF. Batched token issuance protocol (2025). https://datatracker.ietf.org/doc/html/draft-ietf-privacypass-batched-tokens-04. Accessed 2 May 2025

[IET25b] IETF. Privacy pass (privacypass) (2025). https://datatracker.ietf.org/wg/privacypass/about/. Accessed 2 May 2025

[JLO97] Juels, A., Luby, M., Ostrovsky, R.: Security of blind digital signatures. In: Kaliski, B.S. (ed.) CRYPTO 1997. LNCS, vol. 1294, pp. 150–164. Springer, Heidelberg (1997). https://doi.org/10.1007/BFb0052233

[JS24] Jeudy, C., Sanders, O.: Improved lattice blind signatures from recycled entropy. Cryptology ePrint Archive, Report 2024/1289 (2024)

[KLR21] Katz, J., Loss, J., Rosenberg, M.: Boosting the security of blind signature schemes. In: Tibouchi, M., Wang, H. (eds.) ASIACRYPT 2021. LNCS, vol. 13093, pp. 468–492. Springer, Cham (2021). https://doi.org/10.1007/978-3-030-92068-5_16

[KLX22] Kastner, J., Loss, J., Xu, J.: On pairing-free blind signature schemes in the algebraic group model. In: Hanaoka, G., Shikata, J., Watanabe, Y. (eds.) PKC 2022, Part II. LNCS, vol. 13178, pp. 468–497. Springer, Cham (2022)

[LNP22a] Lyubashevsky, V., Nguyen, N.K., Plancon, M.: Efficient lattice-based blind signatures via gaussian one-time signatures. In: Hanaoka, G., Shikata, J., Watanabe, Y. (eds.) PKC 2022, Part II. LNCS, vol. 13178, pp. 498–527. Springer, Cham (2022)

[LNP22b] Lyubashevsky, V., Nguyen, N.K., Plançon, M.: Lattice-based zero-knowledge proofs and applications: shorter, simpler, and more general. In: Dodis, Y., Shrimpton, T. (eds.) CRYPTO 2022, Part II. LNCS, vol. 13508, pp. 71–101. Springer, Cham (2022)

[LNPS21] Lyubashevsky, V., Nguyen, N.K., Plancon, M., Seiler, G.: Shorter lattice-based group signatures via "almost free" encryption and other optimizations. In: Tibouchi, M., Wang, H. (eds.) ASIACRYPT 2021. LNCS, vol. 13093, pp. 218–248. Springer, Cham (2021). https://doi.org/10.1007/978-3-030-92068-5_8

[LPS10] Lyubashevsky, V., Palacio, A., Segev, G.: Public-key cryptographic primitives provably as secure as subset sum. In: Micciancio, D. (ed.) TCC 2010. LNCS, vol. 5978, pp. 382–400. Springer, Heidelberg (2010). https://doi.org/10.1007/978-3-642-11799-2_23

[MP12] Micciancio, D., Peikert, C.: Trapdoors for lattices: simpler, tighter, faster, smaller. In: Pointcheval, D., Johansson, T. (eds.) EUROCRYPT 2012. LNCS, vol. 7237, pp. 700–718. Springer, Heidelberg (2012). https://doi.org/10.1007/978-3-642-29011-4_41

[MR04] Micciancio, D., Regev, O.: Worst-case to average-case reductions based on Gaussian measures. In: 45th FOCS, Rome, Italy, 17–19 October 2004, pp. 372–381. IEEE Computer Society Press (2004)

[MRFH25] Meunier, T., Rubin, C.D., Faz-Hernández, A.: Privacy pass: upgrading to the latest protocol version (2025). https://blog.cloudflare.com/privacy-pass-standard. Accessed 2 Feb 2025

[PFH+22] Prest, T., et al.: FALCON. Technical report, National Institute of Standards and Technology (2022). https://csrc.nist.gov/Projects/post-quantum-cryptography/selected-algorithms-2022

[PS96] Pointcheval, D., Stern, J.: Provably secure blind signature schemes. In: Kim, K., Matsumoto, T. (eds.) ASIACRYPT 1996. LNCS, vol. 1163, pp. 252–265. Springer, Heidelberg (1996). https://doi.org/10.1007/BFb0034852

[PS00] Pointcheval, D., Stern, J.: Security arguments for digital signatures and blind signatures. J. Cryptol. **13**(3), 361–396 (2000)

[PZ13] Paquin, C., Zaverucha, G.: U-prove cryptographic specification v1.1 (revision 3). Technical report, Microsoft Corporation (2013)

[Reg05] Regev, O.: On lattices, learning with errors, random linear codes, and cryptography. In: Gabow, H.N., Fagin, R. (eds.) 37th ACM STOC, Baltimore, MA, USA, 22–24 May 2005, pp. 84–93. ACM Press (2005)

[SAB+22] Schwabe, P., et al.: CRYSTALS-KYBER. Technical report, National Institute of Standards and Technology (2022). https://csrc.nist.gov/Projects/post-quantum-cryptography/selected-algorithms-2022

[TZ22] Tessaro, S., Zhu, C.: Short pairing-free blind signatures with exponential security. In: Dunkelman, O., Dziembowski, S. (eds.) EUROCRYPT 2022, Part II. LNCS, vol. 13276, pp. 782–811. Springer, Cham (2022)

[ZCH25] Zhang, H., Chen, X., Huang, Q.: Lattice-based non-interactive blind signature schemes in the random oracle model. In: Liu, J.K., Chen, L., Sun, S.-F., Liu, X. (eds.) Provable and Practical Security, pp. 289–308. Springer, Singapore (2025)

Scalable Two-Round n-Out-of-n and Multi-signatures from Lattices in the Quantum Random Oracle Model

Qiqi Lai[1], Feng-Hao Liu[2], Yang Lu[1], Haiyang Xue[3], Yong Yu[1], and Yuan Chen[4](✉)

[1] School of Artificial Intelligence and Computer Science, Shaanxi Normal University, Xi'an, China
{laiqq,luyang,yuyong}@snnu.edu.cn
[2] Washington State University, Pullman, WA, USA
feng-hao.liu@wsu.edu
[3] Singapore Management University, Singapore, Singapore
[4] State Key Laboratory of Integrated Services Networks, Xidian University, Xi'an, China
yuanchen@xidian.edu.cn

Abstract. In this paper, we construct the first asymptotically efficient two-round n-out-of-n and multi-signatures from lattices in the quantum random oracle model (QROM), using the Fiat-Shamir with Aborts (FSwA) paradigm. Our protocols can be viewed as the improvements on the two-round protocols by Damgård et al. (JoC 2022).

From a technical perspective, the simulation of QROM and the efficient reduction from breaking underlying assumption to forging signatures are the essential challenges to achieving efficient QROM security for the previously related works. In order to conquer the former one, we adopt the quantum-accessible pseudorandom function (QPRF) to simulate QROM. Particularly, we show that there exists a QPRF that is both invertible and programmable, which can simulate QROM with the same properties. Moreover, we use QPRF as an intermediate tool to successfully simulate QROM whose output is separable, even against a quantum adversary. For the latter challenge, we tweak and apply the online extractability by Unruh (Eurocrypt 2015).

1 Introduction

Due to the applications in the decentralized scenarios, decentralized signatures have recently received wide attentions. *Multi-signature* (MS) and *Threshold signature* (TS) are two similar classes of decentralized signatures.

In a nutshell, MS allows a group of n users, each holding signing key pairs $(\mathsf{sk}_i, \mathsf{pk}_i)$, to collectively sign the same message and obtain a succinct signature. On the other hand, TS involves a particular key generation process (regardless of distributed or trusted one), which split the secret key sk into n shares handed out to different participants, such that a message can only be signed if t or

S. Bai and E. Persichetti (Eds.): PKC 2026, LNCS 16551, pp. 235–268, 2026.
https://doi.org/10.1007/978-3-032-26731-3_8

more participants agree to do so. The special case of n-out-of-n signature is achieved by setting $t = n$, which is also called as *distributed signature* (DS).

Although these two primitives are quite similar, MS is different from DS in several ways: (i) there is no particular key generation, as each participant generates their own key pairs; (ii) the group of participants is dynamically formed from certain sets; (iii) the verification process does not rely on a fixed public key, but rather on the list or aggregation of the corresponding public keys.

State-of-the-Art of Multi/Threshold Signature. Numerous recent studies have focused on Schnorr-type schemes, such as the threshold version of ECDSA, threshold Schnorr, and multi-signing of Schnorr. However, Schnorr-type constructions are vulnerable to quantum attacks, it is crucial to investigate the multi and threshold signatures of post-quantum alternatives. Significant attentions have been directed towards lattice-based signatures, including Dilithium [21] and Raccoon [17].

Dilithium is based on the "Fiat-Shamir with Aborts" (FSwA) technique of Lyubashevsky's signature [35], which employs rejection sampling to guarantee security. Raccoon is also considered as a variant of the Lyubashevsky's signature, which employs Rényi divergence argument to get rid of rejection sampling. However, unlike Schnorr, thresholding Dilithium or Raccoon presents greater challenges due to the adoption of small distributions. Several schemes with other technique routes have been proposed, but they either rely on costly primitives, such as fully homomorphic encryption(FHE) in [1,5,26], or fail to achieve comparable efficiency and full security based on standard assumptions [24].

Damgård et al. [13] address the challenge by using homomorphic trapdoor commitment (HTDC) schemes as a building block. They proposed DS and MS in both two-round and three-round settings, denoted as $\mathsf{DS}_2/\mathsf{MS}_2$ and $\mathsf{DS}_3/\mathsf{MS}_3$, respectively. Notably, their DS_2 and MS_2 are the first lattice-based two-round schemes. Subsequently, MulSig-L by Boschini et al. [8] and DualMS by Chen [10] improved upon MS_2. Compared with MS_2, MulSig-L does not rely on additional lattice-based HTDC and benefits from preprocessing in the first round. DualMS further enhances the construction by utilizing a trapdoor-free "dual signing simulation" technique, resulting in much better efficiency.

Recently, there are several interesting advancements on TS from lattice assumptions.[1] del Pino et al. [16] proposed a three-round thresholdized version of Raccoon, named TRaccoon, without relying on any heavy primitives such as FHE or HTDC. In order to further reduce the round complexity, several offline-online two-round TS protocols have been constructed [7,9,22]. All these protocols in [7,9,22] still require a trusted dealer to generate secret shares. Recently, [14,39] propose a novel distributed key generation with short share protocols over lattices, which can compile the standard Fiat-Shamir with/without abort signature into the threshold variants.

[1] There are also other related works considering adaptive security [29] and robustness [23], but they require four/five rounds. In this paper, we just focus on the construction of two/three-round protocols.

Common problems in Lattice-Based Setting. All these two-round protocols can only been proven to be secure in the classical random oracle model (ROM), through using the currently known techniques. For post-quantum cryptographic constructions in the ROM, we need to further consider that the quantum adversary might conduct arbitrary superposition queries to ROM, which is further called QROM and first proposed by Boneh et al. in [4]. Currently, only three-round DS and MS in [13,24] achieve security in the QROM by utilizing the technique of lossy identification [30]. The QROM security for all known existing two-round schemes, including $\mathsf{DS}_2/\mathsf{MS}_2$, MulSig-L, DualMS, and recently proposed TS protocols in [9,22,22], remains an open problem.

1.1 Our Goals

Therefore, the motivation of this paper is to design asymptotically efficient two-round MS and DS from lattices in the QROM.

(**Main Goal 1**) Design efficient two-round DS from lattices in the QROM.

(**Main Goal 2**) Design efficient two-round MS from lattices in the QROM, especially with key aggregation property.

1.2 Our Contributions

This work aims at the above two main goals and makes the following three major contributions.

Contribution 1. We construct the first FSwA-style two-round DS_2 signature from lattices in the QROM, which can be viewed as the significant improvement on two-round protocol by Damgård et al. in [13]. Compared with [13], a notable feature is that our protocol is exactly two-round, i.e., each party performs an independent abort and still outputs a signature in exactly two rounds with polynomial modulus. This makes our schemes significantly more scalable. From the perspective of technique, such exactly two-round is obtained through embedding the protocol challenge in a cut-and-choose way, instead of employing other kinds of Fiat-Shamir without abort techniques, such as noise flooding techniques [1,22,26] or relying on Hint-MLWE assumption [7,9]. We believe our technique for such exactly two-round should be of independently theoretical interest.

For the security proof of our new construction, we leverage the tweaked online extractability technology by Unruh [40] and our newly modified QPRF (which is introduced as the independent technique contribution in the following Contribution 3). Besides, our construction has much lower security loss, as we use online extractability instead of usual rewinding method. Particularly, we improve the adversary's advantage for forging a signature from $\Theta(\varepsilon_{\mathsf{MSIS}}^{1/2})$ or $\Theta(\varepsilon_{\mathsf{MSIS}}^{1/4})$ to $\Theta(\varepsilon_{\mathsf{MSIS}})$, where $\varepsilon_{\mathsf{MSIS}}$ denotes the hardness of the underlying MSIS assumption.

Contribution 2. We construct the first FSwA-style two-round MS from lattices in the QROM, which has the same properties (i.e., exactly two-round, lower security loss, and polynomial modulus) as the above mentioned n-out-of-n signature. However, compared with n-out-of-n signature, there is an additional obstacle in the security proof. In order to conquer it, we prove the security in the key-verification model, rather than the plain public key model. In the key-verification model, we use as an additional building block a multi-proof straight-line extractable non-interactive zero knowledge proof of knowledge (NIZKPoK). Although such NIZKPoK will induce many more overheads, it gives another nice property, key aggregation.

Contribution 3. As a technical contribution, we make essential modifications on the direct QPRF construction in [42], which was originally proposed by Banerjee, Peikert, and Rosen in [3], such that it becomes an invertible variant. Besides, we show that the invertible QPRF is adaptively programmable even against efficient quantum adversary conducting superposition queries.

With such QPRF, we can prove the security of our two-round protocols in the QROM. Particularly, we can efficiently simulate the adversary's view even without the real secret key, and then efficiently reduce the security of our constructions to the underlying assumptions. We believe such a new QPRF should be of independent interest.

Overall, we list the comparisons with the most related works in Table 1.

Table 1. Comparison with previous TS, MS, DS. The column "Reduc. Appro." indicates the security reduction approach. For two rows TRaccoon and Ringtail, we use "-" to represent the corresponding reduction approach. This is because TRaccoon and Ringtail prove unforgeability directly based on SelfTargetMSIS, rather than much weaker assumption MSIS. However, from the perspective of hardness reduction, we still need to use the rewinding to establish the reduction between SelfTargetMSIS and MSIS.

	QROM	Round	Scalable	Reduc.-Appro.	Assumptions
MS_3 [24]	✓	3	×	Lossy	MLWE,rMLWE
DS_3 [13]+[24]	✓	3	×	Lossy	MLWE
DS_2 [13]	×	2	×	Rewinding	MLWE,MSIS
MS_2 [13]	×	2	×	Rewinding	MLWE,MSIS
MulSig-L [8]	×	2	×	Rewinding	MLWE,MSIS
DualMS [10]	×	2	×	Rewinding	MLWE,MSIS
TRaccoon [16]	×	3	✓	-	SelfTargetMSIS,PRF, Hint-MLWE
TS_2 [22]	×	2	✓	Rewinding	AOM-MLWE
TSL [9]	×	2	✓	Rewinding	MSIS
Ringtail [7]	×	2	✓	-	SelfTargetMSIS,PRF, Hint-MLWE,MLWE,
Our QDS_2	✓	2	✓	Online-Extractability	MLWE,MSIS
Our QMS_2	✓	2	✓	Online-Extractability	MLWE,MSIS

2 Technical Overview

In this section, we present an overview of our techniques. In fact, our intuition is quite simple: analyze the essential obstacles to proving the existing two-round signatures to be secure in the QROM, then overcome them to achieve the desired security relying on the MLWE, MSIS and DSPR assumptions.

2.1 Recall the Existing Protocol in [13]

To present our techniques in a natural way, we first recall Damgård et al.'s elegant two-round distributed n-out-of-n protocol, called DS_2, in [13].[2] The protocols in [13] are based on Dilithium signature scheme [21], and thus work over cyclotomic rings $R = \mathbb{Z}[X]/(f(X))$ and $R_q = \mathbb{Z}_q[X]/(f(X))$, where N is a power of 2, and $f(X) = X^N + 1$ is the $2N$-th cyclotomic polynomial. *For simplicity, here we just consider the case of 2 parties, which can be naturally generalized to the case of n-party setting.* We describe the detailed key and signature generations of DS_2 in [13] in the following Fig. 1.

KeyGen of DS_2 executed by $P_2(\mathsf{pp})$

Sample $\mathbf{A}_2 \xleftarrow{\$} R_q^{k\times\ell}$, compute $g_2 \leftarrow \mathsf{H}_1(\mathbf{A}_2, 2)$

$\xleftrightarrow{g_1, g_2}$

$\xleftrightarrow{\mathbf{A}_1, \mathbf{A}_2}$

Check $g_1 \stackrel{?}{=} \mathsf{H}_1(\mathbf{A}_1, 1)$
If YES, compute $\mathbf{A} = \mathbf{A}_1 + \mathbf{A}_2$
and set $\hat{\mathbf{A}} = [\mathbf{A}, \mathbf{I}] \in R_q^{k\times(\ell+k)}$
Sample $\boldsymbol{s}_2 \xleftarrow{\$} S_\beta^{\ell+k}$, compute $\boldsymbol{t}_2 := \hat{\mathbf{A}} \cdot \boldsymbol{s}_2$,
$g_2' \leftarrow \mathsf{H}_2(\boldsymbol{t}_2, 2)$

$\xleftrightarrow{g_1', g_2'}$

$\xleftrightarrow{\boldsymbol{t}_1, \boldsymbol{t}_2}$

Check $g_1' \stackrel{?}{=} \mathsf{H}_2(\boldsymbol{t}_1, 1)$
If YES, set $\boldsymbol{t} = \boldsymbol{t}_1 + \boldsymbol{t}_2$

DS_2 executed by $P_2(\boldsymbol{s}_2, \mathsf{pk} := (\mathbf{A}, \boldsymbol{t}), \mu)$

$\boldsymbol{y_2} \xleftarrow{\$} D^{\ell+k}$; $\boldsymbol{w_2} \leftarrow \hat{\mathbf{A}}\boldsymbol{y_2} \bmod q$
$\mathsf{ck} \leftarrow \mathsf{H}_3(\mu, \mathsf{pk})$

$\mathsf{com}_2 \leftarrow \mathsf{Commit}_{\mathsf{ck}}(\boldsymbol{w_2}, r_2)$

$\xleftrightarrow{\mathsf{com}_1, \mathsf{com}_2}$

$c \leftarrow \mathsf{H}_0(\mathsf{com}_1 + \mathsf{com}_2, \mu, \mathsf{pk})$
$\boldsymbol{z_2} \leftarrow c\boldsymbol{s_2} + \boldsymbol{y_2}$
If RejSamp $(c\boldsymbol{s_2} + \boldsymbol{z_2}) = 0$;
$(\boldsymbol{z_2}, \boldsymbol{r_2}) \leftarrow (\perp, \perp)$

$\xleftrightarrow{(\boldsymbol{z_1}, \boldsymbol{r_1}), (\boldsymbol{z_2}, \boldsymbol{r_2})}$

If $\boldsymbol{z_1} = \perp \vee \boldsymbol{z_2} = \perp$: restart
Output $(\mathsf{com}_1 + \mathsf{com}_2, \boldsymbol{z_1} + \boldsymbol{z_1}, r_1 + r_2)$
as a signature

Fig. 1. Simple description of DS_2 Protocol in [13]. Here, we just describe the behaviors of P_2 for saving space, due to the fact that the computations and communications of P_1 are symmetrically equivalent to these of P_2.

Security Analysis of DS_2. In order to establish the security reduction for DS_2, there are the following important items needed to be considered:

1. For the key generation, the simulator utilizes the invertible (or called pre-image extractable in certain previous papers) and programmable properties of classical ROM (H_1 and H_2) to recover the adversary's key before programming the honest user's key, and thus embed the MSIS challenge into the public key of DS_2.
2. For the signature queries, the simulator employs a HTDC scheme to enable the successful simulation of signatures. Moreover, in order to obtain security against concurrent attacks, we need to use the output of H_3 as the commitment key ck, i.e., $\mathsf{ck} \leftarrow \mathsf{H}_3(\mu, \mathsf{pk})$.

[2] Here, we just focus on the DS_2 construction, as most of the techniques can be easily extended to the setting of multi-signature.

3. For the reduction from solving hard problems to forging signature, the simulator needs to simulate H_3 such that its output is separable, i.e., for each input pair (μ, pk), H_3 gets one of two different types of outputs according to certain independent Bernoulli distribution, i.e., gets the normal commitment key ck (i.e., $\mathsf{ck} \leftarrow \mathsf{H}_3(\mu, \mathsf{pk})$) for the probability p and the trapdoor commitment key tck (i.e., $\mathsf{tck} \leftarrow \mathsf{H}_3(\mu, \mathsf{pk})$) for the probability $(1-p)$, where $p \in (0, 1)$. Particularly, the uniformity of ck and tck allows the adversary to use ck for the challenge message μ^*, but use tck for all the signature generation queries, with a non-negligible probability. Then, assuming the binding property of the HTDC scheme with normal key ck, the simulator can solve an underlying MSIS problem, through using rewinding technique.

2.2 Enhancing the Security of DS_2 into the QROM

We know that there are two main parts for the security proof of DS_2: the efficient simulations of random oracles and the efficient reduction through rewinding. Thus, for QROM security, we need to ensure all the proof techniques have the corresponding counterparts for QROM and quantum adversaries.

Simulation of QROM. We need to consider how to simulate QROM efficiently, such that not only it can be both invertible and programmable, but also its output space is separable, following the proof strategy of [13]. Up until now, there are two types of simulation approaches for QROM: stateless simulation (e.g. quantum-secure pseudorandom functions [4,42] and $2Q$-wise independent functions [43]), and stateful simulation (e.g. the compressed oracle [19,32,44]).

Among them, the compressed oracle is a powerful simulation technique, which supports both inversion and reprogramming [18,19,32]. However, it seems that we can not apply the compressed oracle to directly achieve the desired separable property, due to the inconsistency between the commitment key space S_{ck} of tck and the output of compressed oracle.

Particularly, the existing compressed oracle and its variants just support random functions with the following different ranges: uniform distribution over $\{0,1\}^n$ [32], uniform distribution over abelian groups [11], and non-uniform distribution over $\{0,1\}^n$ but all outputs are independently sampled [12]. But, tck in the known instantiation of HTDC scheme is the structured matrix, whose distribution is clearly not compatible with the above mentioned compressed oracle techniques in [11,12,32].

On the other hand, we can not use stateless simulations, such as QPRF, to directly output tck. This is because for each input pair (μ, pk), $\mathsf{H}_3(\mu, \mathsf{pk})$ should output either tck or ck relying on certain independent randomness, according to the proof strategy of [13]. However, when dealing with superposition queries, these stateless simulations do not have sufficient randomness for all possible input pairs.

Based on the current state of art, we need to improve the existing simulation approaches, such that the resulting QROM satisfies the separable property. Notice that the technical details of the compressed oracle [44] are relatively

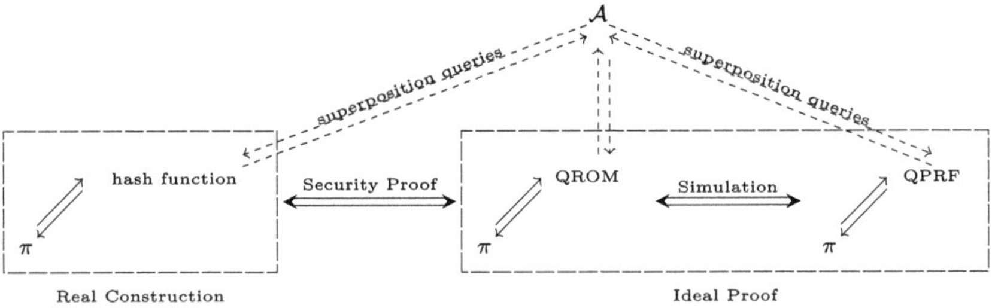

Fig. 2. Illustration of the high-level idea of using QPRF. Clearly, such QPRF is only used in the ideal security proof. In the real constructions, it will be replaced with a good hash function, such as SHA-256. And thus, the instantiation of QPRF will not affect the practical efficiency of our QDS_2 or QMS_2.

more complicated. One always needs additional investigations on the related backgrounds. So, as the main technical challenge in this paper, we want to ask

Is there a stateless simulation approach for QROM, *which is not only both invertible and programmable, but also its output is separable?*

In this paper, our answer is positive. Particularly, our choice is QPRF [42]. We illustrate the high-level idea for using QPRF in the security proof in Fig. 2. Of course, we require the concrete instantiation of QPRF is both invertible *and* programmable, even against quantum adversaries, which are significantly non-trivial. As far as we know, it seems that this is the first time to consider how to program and invert QPRF simultaneously in the literature, even the invertible property for PRF has been defined previously in [6,27]. We believe such QPRF is of independent interest, and can be used on other applications, such as PIR [27].

More precisely, we choose to use the following direct construction of QPRF in [3,42]: for a key $\mathsf{k} := (\{a_i\}_{i\in[\bar{m}]}, \{s_i\}_{i\in[\bar{\ell}]}) \in \mathcal{K}$ and input $x := (x_1, \ldots, x_{\bar{\ell}}) \in \{0,1\}^{\bar{\ell}}$, let

$$\mathsf{QPRF}_{\mathsf{k}}(x) = \mathsf{QPRF}_{\{a_i\},\{s_i\}}(x_1, \ldots, x_{\bar{\ell}}) = \left\lfloor (a_1, \ldots, a_{\bar{m}}) \cdot \prod_{i=1}^{\bar{\ell}} s_i^{x_i} \right\rceil_{\bar{p}}, \tag{1}$$

where $\bar{p}, \bar{q}, \bar{m}, \bar{\ell}$ are integers such that $\bar{q} > \bar{p}$, a_i is chosen from a ring $\bar{R}_{\bar{q}} = \mathbb{Z}_{\bar{q}}[X]/(X^{\bar{N}}+1)$, s_i is chosen from a small distribution χ over $\bar{R}$, $(a_1, \ldots, a_{\bar{m}})\cdot s = (a_1 \cdot s, \ldots, a_{\bar{m}} \cdot s)$, and $\lfloor \cdot \rceil_{\bar{p}}$ denotes rounding ring elements from $R_{\bar{q}}$ to $R_{\bar{p}}$.[3] For certain parameter settings, such QPRF can be proven to be secure, just as in Theorem 4.3. Below, we sketch how to prove the properties of (1).

[3] Here, we use the bar notation to distinguish the notations of QPRF from those of the protocols DS, MS, QDS, QMS. Particularly, the parameter setting of QPRF is independent of $\mathsf{QDS}_2, \mathsf{QMS}_2$ protocols in this paper. And thus, the modulus of our protocols is still considered to be polynomial, regardless of the modulus of QPRF.

Inversion. For the invertible property of QPRF, it is essentially non-trivial. This is because the pseudorandomness of QPRF implicitly implies the one-way property, and it should be impossible to invert the input from certain QPRF output value. But, the situation might be quite different, when the simulator just uses it to simulate QROM. Here the simulator holds the secret key for QPRF, and the adversary can only get outputs through querying the simulator. Even with such new application scenario in our security proof, all existing known QPRFs, including the above (1), still do not satisfy our requirement of inversion.

As one of our significant technical contribution, we tweak the direct QPRF in [42], through (i) embedding a MP trapdoor [37] in the vector $\boldsymbol{a}^\top = (a_1, \dots, a_{\bar{m}})$; (ii) choosing the specific ring structure such that the small ring element are invertible over $\bar{R}_{\bar{q}}$. Notice that, such a modification will not affect the security of the direct QPRF, as the ring-based learning with errors (RLWE) assumption still holds. Moreover, we can invert such QPRF, i.e., get $\boldsymbol{x}$ from $\boldsymbol{y}^\top = \mathsf{QPRF}(\boldsymbol{x}) \in \bar{R}_{\bar{p}}^{\bar{m}} = (\mathbb{Z}_{\bar{p}}[X]/(X^{\bar{N}}+1))^{\bar{m}}$, in the following way: (i) with the MP trapdoor in $\boldsymbol{a}^\top$, we can first get $\hat{s}_0 = \prod_{i=1}^{\ell} s_i^{x_i}$ from $\boldsymbol{y}^\top$, through using the inversion algorithm for the ring-based learning with rounding (RLWR) problem; (ii) in order to determine $x_1 = 0$ or 1, we directly compute $\hat{s}_1 = s_1^{-1} \cdot \hat{s}_0$. Notice that if $x_1 = 1$, then $\hat{s}_1 = \prod_{i=2}^{\ell} s_i^{x_i}$, whose norm should be upper bounded by certain value B with overwhelming probability. Otherwise, $\hat{s}_1 = s_1^{-1} \cdot \prod_{i=2}^{\ell} s_i^{x_i}$, whose norm will be larger than B with overwhelming probability, according to the decisional small polynomial rate (DSPR) assumption [34]. The detailed inversion algorithm and the related proof are given in Algorithm 1 and Theorem 4.7, respectively.

Reprogramming. In order to prove the reprogrammable property for QPRF, we resort to the existing adaptive programming result and technique for random function in [25,40]. The high level technique route can be described as follows:

$$\mathsf{QPRF}_k(\cdot) \overset{(i)}{\approx} \boxed{\mathsf{RF}(\cdot) \approx \mathsf{RF}'(\cdot)} \overset{(ii)}{\approx} \mathsf{QPRF}'_k(\cdot). \tag{2}$$

Here, we use the box to indicate the existing result about the adaptive programming for random functions in [25,40]. $\mathsf{RF}(\cdot)$ denotes a random function. $\mathsf{RF}'(\cdot)$ and $\mathsf{QPRF}'_k(\cdot)$ denote the programmed functions at certain points. Below, we just need to consider how to prove the steps (i) and (ii) in the above (2).

At the first glance, it seems that the standard security of QPRF, i.e., *oracle indistinguishability* in [42], is sufficient. However, there is still a tiny mismatching! This is because for the box part in the above (2), the adversary not only accesses RF as an oracle, but also takes as input certain pairs $(x, \mathsf{RF}(x))$, where x has sufficient entropy. As a result, it is necessary to introduce a "seemingly" strong definition, oracle-and-input indistinguishability, for QPRF as in Definition 3.7. Furthermore, as a justification of such strong security notion, we show that it can be derived from standard oracle indistinguishability in Lemma 3.8.

The separable property. Just as analyzed above, we can not make QPRF directly output either ck or tck. In order to conquer this challenge, we employ QPRF as an intermediate tool, i.e., use the output of QPRF as randomness to invoke the corresponding key generation algorithm CGen or TCGen. Particularly, we conduct in the following way: (1) choose a specific key $\mathsf{k}_3 \xleftarrow{\$} \mathcal{K}$; (2) divide the output of $\mathsf{QPRF}_{\mathsf{k}_3}(\mu, \mathsf{pk})$ into two parts: $ra_1 \in \{0,1\}^{\ell_{ra_1}}$ and $ra_2 \in \{0,1\}^{\ell_{ra_2}}$;[4] (3) if the number of 1 in ra_1 is larger than certain value num, then we compute $(\mathsf{tck}, \mathsf{td}) \leftarrow \mathsf{Eqv\text{-}TCGen}(\mathsf{cpp}_{\mathsf{Eqv}}, ra_2)$, and return tck as the output of H_3, i.e., define $\mathsf{tck} \leftarrow \mathsf{H}_3(\mu, \mathsf{pk})$; otherwise, compute $\mathsf{ck} \leftarrow \mathsf{Eqv\text{-}CGen}(\mathsf{cpp}_{\mathsf{Eqv}}, ra_2)$, return ck, i.e., define $\mathsf{ck} \leftarrow \mathsf{H}_3(\mu, \mathsf{pk})$. Here, num is set to separate tck and ck with certain probability. $\mathsf{cpp}_{\mathsf{Eqv}}$ are public parameter, and $\mathsf{Eqv\text{-}TCGen}$ and $\mathsf{Eqv\text{-}CGen}$ are two modes of HTDC scheme.

In this case, as the above simulation for H_3 is stateless and a fixed function, we can easily define another fixed function H'_3, such that it always returns the corresponding td, i.e., define $\mathsf{td} \leftarrow \mathsf{H}'_3(\mu, \mathsf{pk})$. According to the pseudorandomness of QPRF, the above simulation for H_3 can not be distinguished by the efficient quantum adversary.

Notice that the above partitioning argument inherently lead to a security loss linear in the number of signing queries. In [38], Pan and Wagner have successfully remove such reduction loss through using pseudorandom matching/path technique. But, there are still other technical obstacles to instantiate their elegant approaches in the lattice-based settings. We leave it as future work.

FURTHERMORE EFFICIENCY CONSIDERATION. Up until now, we have successfully obtained the desired QPRF in theory, which can simulate QROM satisfying inversion, reprogramming and separation. However, after analyzing the left hand side of Fig. 1 deeply, we find the efficiency bottleneck of KeyGen protocol is in its second round, i.e., all participants needs to interactively send their own matrix $\mathbf{A}_u \in R_q^{k\times\ell}$. It is preferable to reduce such communication overhead.

Here, our general idea is to introduce another random oracle H'_1. And each participant's random matrix $\mathbf{A}_u$ is generated as $\mathbf{A}_u \leftarrow \mathsf{H}'_1(s_u)$, where $s_u \xleftarrow{\$} \{0,1\}^{l_1^*}$ is a random seed. In this case, the participants just need to interactively send the $\mathsf{H}_1(s_u)$ and s_u, rather than $\mathsf{H}_1(\mathbf{A}_u)$ and $\mathbf{A}_u$. Clearly, s_u is significantly shorter than $\mathbf{A}_u$. Particularly, our modified protocol is described in Fig. 3.

For Security Reduction of DS_2. One of essential obstacles to proving the QROM security of DS_2 is the application of rewinding technique. Although there are several works [31–33] that have solved the dilemma on quantum rewinding for the underlying $\mathsf{Dilithium}$ signature scheme [21], these elegant techniques can not be applied to the QROM security of DS_2. This is because all above mentioned techniques require the underlying Σ-protocol to satisfy the collapsing property. But, our Σ-protocol does not satisfy it, due to the usage of equivocal commitment scheme. Up until now, we still do not know how to construct commitment schemes with both equivocal and collapse-binding properties

Another widely used approach of obtaining lattice-based distributed signatures in the QROM is the lossy ID technique [13,24,30], which can obtain much tighter security proof. One implicit but crux point in this lossy ID technique

[4] Particularly, we define $\mathsf{QPRF}_{\mathsf{k}_3}(\cdot) : \{0,1\}^{l_3^*} \rightarrow (\{0,1\}^{l_{ra_1}} \times \{0,1\}^{l_{ra_2}})$, and compute $(ra_1, ra_2) = \mathsf{QPRF}_{\mathsf{k}_3}(\mu, \mathsf{pk})$, where μ denotes the signing message, pk is the generated public key by KeyGen.

is that there should be statistical security in the simulated experiment. However, the HTDC scheme used in the DS_2 protocol just inherently satisfies computational binding, and do not satisfy the essential requirement of lossy technique. Thus, it seems that we need new techniques for proving the QROM security.

2.3 New Idea: Online Extractability Allowing Security Proof in the QROM.

Online extractability is another reasonable candidate direction to achieve security in the QROM. We notice an existing online extractability technique by Pino and Katsumata in [15].[5] However, their online extractability technique relies heavily on a primitive called extractable linear homomorphic commitment, which is seemingly inherently not compatible with the equivocation property required for DS_2 in Fig. 1. Thus, it is still not clear how to directly apply this online extractability technique to our desired settings.

Fortunately, inspired by Pino and Katsumata's online extractability technique, we have one crucial observation: the party P_2 might directly generate more than one response $\boldsymbol{z}_{2,j}$ with respect to the same vector $\boldsymbol{w}_2 = \mathbf{A} \cdot \boldsymbol{y}_2$, where each different $\boldsymbol{z}_{2,j}$ is computed with different challenge $c_{2,j}$. I.e., $\boldsymbol{z}_{2,j} = \boldsymbol{y}_2 + c_{2,j} \cdot \boldsymbol{s}_2$ and $\boldsymbol{z}_{2,j'} = \boldsymbol{y}_2 + c_{2,j'} \cdot \boldsymbol{s}_2$. Based on this, given one forged signature, if we can find two valid responses for two different challenges, we can extract the witness through using the special soundness extractor of the underlying Σ-protocol.

Of course, in order to avoid the trivial extractability from normal valid signature, we need to first hide all different responses by certain hash function, i.e., just send out $h_{2,j} = \mathsf{H}(\boldsymbol{z}_{2,j})$ rather than sending all $\boldsymbol{z}_{2,j}$ in clear.[6] Then, we can use the idea of cut-and-choose to decide which $\boldsymbol{z}_{2,j}$ will be disclosed. Notice that if the value j is randomly chosen, we can easily prove its soundness. More importantly, such a new cut-and-choose proof idea provide a chance to allow each

Modified KeyGen Protocol of QDS_2

Sample $s_2 \xleftarrow{\$} \{0,1\}^{\ell_2^*}$, compute $g_2 \leftarrow \mathsf{H}_1(s_2, 2)$

$\xleftrightarrow{g_1, g_2}$

$\xleftrightarrow{s_1, s_2}$

Check $g_1 \stackrel{?}{=} \mathsf{H}_1(s_1, 1)$

If YES, compute $\mathbf{A}_u = \mathsf{H}_1'(s_u)$, $\mathbf{A} = \mathbf{A}_1 + \mathbf{A}_2$, and set $\hat{\mathbf{A}} = [\mathbf{A}, \mathbf{I}] \in R_q^{k \times (\ell+k)}$

Sample $\boldsymbol{s}_2 \xleftarrow{\$} S_\beta^{\ell+k}$, compute $\boldsymbol{t}_2 := \hat{\mathbf{A}} \cdot \boldsymbol{s}_2$, $g_2' \leftarrow \mathsf{H}_2(\boldsymbol{t}_2, 2)$

$\xleftrightarrow{g_1', g_2'}$

$\xleftrightarrow{\boldsymbol{t}_1, \boldsymbol{t}_2}$

Check $g_1' \stackrel{?}{=} \mathsf{H}_2(\boldsymbol{t}_1, 1)$, If YES, set $\boldsymbol{t} = \boldsymbol{t}_1 + \boldsymbol{t}_2$

Fig. 3. Simple description of our modified KeyGen protocol for QDS_2 Protocol. Similar to Fig. 1, we just describe the behaviors of P_2 for saving space.

[5] In their paper, such a property is named as straight-line extractability.

[6] The other one desired property of such a hash function H is collision resistance, which details are deferred to the security proof in Sect. 5.2.

participant conducting rejection sampling independently, which is the essential idea to make our protocols to be exactly two-round and scalable.

In fact, the above analysis is matched with the essential idea of Unruh in [40]. Notice that in [18], Don et al. further propose a much better technique to improve the framework of [40]. However, such an improvement can not apply to our distributed signatures.

One More Subtlety. Even almost all security targets for two-round protocols have been achieved, there is still one subtlety: the hash function used to hide the responses $\boldsymbol{z}_j$. Here, as we consider for the case of all parties cooperating to sign message μ, we require it to satisfy the linear homomorphic property. Besides, we also need such a hiding function to have binding and trapdoor-inversion properties, for the reason of security proof. It is a technical challenge to obtain these desired properties for the hiding function in a sufficiently efficient way. Fortunately, we observe that all the responses $\boldsymbol{z}_j$ follows from the discrete Gaussian distribution, which means all $\boldsymbol{z}_j$ are small vectors. Based on this significant property, we can utilize the hermite normal form MLWE to instantiate the hiding function with all desired properties.

Particularly, given an uniform matrix $\mathbf{A}_{\mathsf{Inv}} \in R_q^{m' \times (\ell+k)}$ and its trapdoor $\mathbf{T}_{\mathbf{A}_{\mathsf{Inv}}} \in R^{m' \times m'}$, we first sample an error vector $\boldsymbol{r}_j \leftarrow \chi^{m'}$, and then compute $\widetilde{\mathsf{com}}_j = \mathbf{A}_{\mathsf{Inv}} \cdot \boldsymbol{z}_j + \boldsymbol{r}_j \in R_q^{m'}$, where the dimension of $\boldsymbol{z}_j$ is $(\ell + k)$. Clearly, for the adversary without $\mathbf{T}_{\mathbf{A}_{\mathsf{Inv}}}$, $\widetilde{\mathsf{com}}_j$ is computationally distinguishable from uniform, according to the $\mathsf{MLWE}_{q,(\ell+k),m',\chi}$ assumption. But, with $\mathbf{T}_{\mathbf{A}_{\mathsf{Inv}}}$, the simulator can efficiently extract $\boldsymbol{z}_j$ from $\widetilde{\mathsf{com}}_j$, through using the inversion algorithm for MLWE in [37]. Besides, as $\boldsymbol{z}_j, \boldsymbol{r}_j$ are small vectors, the binding of $\widetilde{\mathsf{com}}_j$ follows clearly from the $\mathsf{MSIS}_{q,m',(\ell+k+m'),\beta}$ assumption with respect to $[\mathbf{A}_{\mathsf{Inv}}, \mathbf{I}_{m'}]$, where $\mathbf{I}_{m'}$ is the identity matrix in $R_q^{m' \times m'}$, and $\|(\boldsymbol{z}_j, \boldsymbol{r}_j)\| \leq \beta$.

Putting All Above Ingredients Together. We present our main two-round protocol QDS_2 in Fig. 4. Below, we slightly analyze QDS_2. Compared with the sign protocol in the right hand side of Fig. 1, there are several differences deriving some extra round advantages. We notice that the real challenge for our QDS_2 is J output by the random oracle H_5. And the challenges $\{c_j\}_{j \in [m]}$ outputted by H_0 are just required to be different from each other, rather than ensuring enough soundness for the underlying Σ-protocol.[7] In this case, the parties in QDS_2 first run the rejection sampling algorithm, and then interactively send transcripts, in contrast to the reverse order in the previous DS_2 in [13]. With this particular feature, the outcome of each party's rejection sampling will not affect other parties. And regardless of the number of parties in the system, the whole distributed signature protocol will output the correct signature, after exactly two round interactions. This makes our QDS_2 has the incomparable advantage

[7] Here is another difference, that is c_j does not depend on any $\boldsymbol{w}_j^{(2)}$. But this will not affect our security, due to the following two reasons: (1) the output distribution of rejection sampling algorithms is still simulateable; (2) for the underlying Σ-protocol, the adversary can not forge the valid responses with respect to two different challenges c_{j_1}, c_{j_2}, with $j_1 \neq j_2$.

QDS_2 executed by $P_2(\mathsf{sk} := \boldsymbol{s}_2, \mathsf{pk} := (\mathbf{A}, \boldsymbol{t}), \mu)$

i. $\mathsf{ck} \leftarrow \mathsf{H}_3(\mu, \mathsf{pk}), \mathbf{A}_{\mathsf{Inv}} \leftarrow \mathsf{H}_4(\mu, \mathsf{pk})$

ii. $\boldsymbol{y}_2 \leftarrow D_\sigma^{\ell+k}, \boldsymbol{w}_2 = \hat{\mathbf{A}} \cdot \boldsymbol{y}_2 \mod q$

iii. For $j = 1$ to m, conduct as follows:

$$\begin{cases} A. & c_j \leftarrow \mathsf{H}_0(\mu, j, \mathsf{pk}, \mathsf{ck}, \mathsf{ck}') \\ B. & \boldsymbol{z}_{2,j} = c_j \cdot \boldsymbol{s}_2 + \boldsymbol{y}_2 \\ C. & \text{run} \quad \mathsf{Rej}(\boldsymbol{z}_{2,j}, c_j \cdot \boldsymbol{s}_2, \sigma) \rightarrow b_{2,j} \end{cases}$$

iv. If $b_{2,j} = 0$ for certain $j \in [m]$, then go to Step(ii)

v. Sample $\boldsymbol{r}_2$ and compute $\mathsf{com}_2 \leftarrow \mathsf{Eqv.Commit}_{\mathsf{ck}}(\boldsymbol{w}_2; \boldsymbol{r}_2)$

vi. Sample $\boldsymbol{r}'_{2,j}$ and compute $\widetilde{\mathsf{com}}_{2,j} = \mathbf{A}_{\mathsf{Inv}} \cdot \boldsymbol{z}_{2,j} + \boldsymbol{r}'_{2,j}$

$$\xleftrightarrow{\left(\mathsf{com}_1, \{\widetilde{\mathsf{com}}_{2,j}\}_{j\in[m]}\right), \left(\mathsf{com}_2, \{\widetilde{\mathsf{com}}_{2,j}\}_{j\in[m]}\right)}$$

vii. $\mathsf{com} = \mathsf{com}_1 + \mathsf{com}_2, \widetilde{\mathsf{com}}_j = \widetilde{\mathsf{com}}_{1,j} + \widetilde{\mathsf{com}}_{2,j}$
$J \leftarrow \mathsf{H}_5(\mathsf{pk}, \mu, \mathsf{com}, \{c_j\}, \{\widetilde{\mathsf{com}}_j\})$

$$\xleftrightarrow{(\boldsymbol{z}_{1,J}, \boldsymbol{r}_1, \boldsymbol{r}'_{1,J}), (\boldsymbol{z}_{2,J}, \boldsymbol{r}_2, \boldsymbol{r}'_{2,J})}$$

viii. Output $\mathsf{Sig} := \left(\mathsf{com}, \boldsymbol{r} = \boldsymbol{r}_1 + \boldsymbol{r}_2, \{\widetilde{\mathsf{com}}_j\}, \{\boldsymbol{z}_J = \boldsymbol{z}_{1,J} + \boldsymbol{z}_{2,J}\}, \{\boldsymbol{r}'_J = \boldsymbol{r}'_{1,J} + \boldsymbol{r}'_{2,J}\}\right)$
as a signature

Fig. 4. Our Two-Round n-out-of-n Distributed Signature Protocol

on the round complexity over other related two-round FSwA-style distributed signature protocols.

In order to ensure the domain of J is large enough, we might need to set the parameter m in Fig. 4 to be at least equivalent to 2^λ, where λ is the security parameter. This will clearly cause the construction to be useless. In order to overcome this obstacle, we can first set a relative small value for m (e.g. $m = 2$), and then conduct the parallelization to the current protocol for t times (e.g. $t = \lambda$). The detailed QDS_2 are presented in Fig. 8.

2.4 Two-Round Multi-signature in the QROM

Similar to [13], we can also convert the above QDS_2 into a two-round multi-signature QMS_2, where our QMS_2 has the nice property of key aggregation. However, after applying all above mentioned techniques, there is still one reduction gap from the fully secure multi-signature. Particularly, through using the above online extractability technique, we can solve the MSIS problem with respect to $[\hat{\mathbf{A}}, \sum_{i\in|L|} a_{j_i} \boldsymbol{t}_{j_i}]$ from the forged signature Sig^* output by the adversary, where $a_{j_i} = \mathsf{H}_{\mathsf{agg}}(L, \boldsymbol{t}_{j_i})$, $\mathsf{H}_{\mathsf{agg}}(\cdot,\cdot)$ is a random oracle, and L is the set of participants in the current running of QMS_2. Without loss of generality, for multi-signature protocol, we suppose the j_1-th participant is honest and all others are corrupted together by the adversary. In this case, we should use the reduction algorithm to solve the MSIS problem with respect to $[\hat{\mathbf{A}}, \boldsymbol{t}_{j_1}]$, rather than $[\hat{\mathbf{A}}, \sum_{i\in|L|} a_{j_i} \boldsymbol{t}_{j_i}]$. And it seems to be an inherent obstacle for obtaining solutions of MSIS with respect to $[\hat{\mathbf{A}}, \boldsymbol{t}_{j_1}]$, from that of $[\hat{\mathbf{A}}, \sum_{i\in|L|} a_{j_i} \boldsymbol{t}_{j_i}]$.

In order to conquer this dilemma, we try to enhance the multi-signature protocol into the key-verification model, where we require each participant to publish a multi-proof straight-line extractable NIZKPoK on his/her secret key sk_j with respect to the corresponding public key pk_j. Then, through using the extractability property of NIZKPoK, we can patch the above mentioned reduction gap, and thus obtain a provably secure multi-signature protocol in the key-verification model. In practice, one participant might want to ensure that the public keys of all his parters are well-formed, before joining into one multi-party protocol. And thus, we believe such a key-verification model is reasonable, even it implicitly implies slightly many more overheads. The formal and detailed protocol of our two-round multi-signature is presented in Sect. 6.

2.5 Future Directions

In this paper, we only focus on the feasibility of constructing the asymptotically efficient two-round n-out-of-n and multi-signature protocols in the QROM, rather than striving for concrete efficiency. In order to obtain much better concrete efficiency, it is necessary to use more efficient building blocks. Particularly, we can use the more efficient trapdoor-equivocal vector commitment scheme, which can compress many vectors $\boldsymbol{w}_i$ into one short commitment. One of reasonable candidates of such vector commitment scheme has been proposed in [41]. We treat proposing much more practical commitment schemes and further optimizing the efficiency our QROM secure two-round protocols as interesting directions for future work.

Notice that MulSig-L in [8] and DualMS in [10] can be viewed as significant improvements on MS_2 in [13]. Thus, one might hope to apply our new techniques to [8,10], which will derive more efficient two-round QMS_2. But, it seems that the double-forking technique used in [8,10] is inherently not compatible with our online extractability technique. Of course, if we abandon the key-aggregation property in [8,10], i.e., just use one-forking in the security proof, it is possible to leverage our techniques to obtain QROM security. But, we still need further analyses. We leave it as an interesting future direction.

3 Preliminaries

Due to space limit, we defer the detailed descriptions on the notations, backgrounds on discrete gaussian distribution, definitions on underlying assumptions such as MSIS, MLWE, DSPR, and rejection sampling together with the signature scheme Dilithium to the full version of this paper.

3.1 Quantum Computation and Quantum Random Oracle Model

In this Section, we recall several basic results on Quantum Computation and Quantum Random Oracle Model.

Fact 3.1 (Fact 1 in [42]). *For any classical efficiently computable function f, we can efficiently implement it by a quantum computer. Moreover, f can be implemented as an oracle which can be queried on quantum superpositions.*

Definition 3.2 (Quantum Random Oracle, QROM). *Given sets $\mathcal{X}$ and $\mathcal{Y}$, let $\mathcal{Y}^{\mathcal{X}}$ be the set of all functions $\mathsf{H} : \mathcal{X} \to \mathcal{Y}$. The quantum random oracle model (QROM) is a security model, in which any adversary $\mathcal{A}$ gets hash values from the random oracle by querying the oracle on quantum superpositions. Moreover, for a random hash function $\mathsf{H} \in \mathcal{Y}^{\mathcal{X}}$, we write $\mathcal{A}^{|\mathsf{H}\rangle}$ to denote that $\mathcal{A}$ can query the random oracle H in superpositions.*

There are several ways to simulate QROM. Here, we recall techniques of replacing the random oracle with quantum-secure pseudorandom function (called QPRF, defined in Sect. 3.2).

Fact 3.3 ([4,42]). *For any sets $\mathcal{X}$ and $\mathcal{Y}$, we can use quantum-secure pseudorandom function to efficiently simulate quantum random oracle from $\mathcal{X}$ to $\mathcal{Y}$, when considering efficient quantum adversary.*

3.2 Quantum-Secure Pseudorandom Function

Definition 3.4 (PRF [42]). *A pesudorandom function is a function $\mathsf{PRF} : \mathcal{K} \times \mathcal{X} \to \mathcal{Y}$, where $\mathcal{K}, \mathcal{X}, \mathcal{Y}$ are the key-space, domain and range, respectively. Implicitly, the settings of $\mathcal{K}, \mathcal{X}, \mathcal{Y}$ depend on the security parameter λ. Given any pair $(\mathsf{k}, x) \in \mathcal{K} \times \mathcal{X}$, there exists $y \in \mathcal{Y}$, which can be written as $y = \mathsf{PRF}_{\mathsf{k}}(x)$.*

Definition 3.5 (Classical Security). *A pseudorandom function PRF is classical security, if no efficient quantum adversary $\mathcal{A}$ making classical queries can distinguish between a truly random function and the function $\mathsf{PRF}_{\mathsf{k}}$ for a random $\mathsf{k} \in \mathcal{K}$. More formally, for any efficient quantum adversary $\mathcal{A}$, there exists a negligible function $\varepsilon = \varepsilon(\lambda)$ such that $\left| \Pr_{\mathsf{k} \xleftarrow{\$} \mathcal{K}}[\mathcal{A}^{\mathsf{PRF}_{\mathsf{k}}}(\cdot) = 1] - \Pr_{O \xleftarrow{\$} \mathcal{Y}^{\mathcal{X}}}[\mathcal{A}^{O}(\cdot) = 1] \right| < \varepsilon$, where $\mathcal{Y}^{\mathcal{X}}$ denotes the class of all functions from $\mathcal{X}$ to $\mathcal{Y}$.*

Notice that in Definition 3.5, we only allow $\mathcal{A}$ to conduct classical queries. Below, we generalize the definition to allow $\mathcal{A}$ to conduct quantum queries, i.e., directly query one superposition of all $x \in \mathcal{X}$ each time. Such quantum secure pseudorandom functions are called Quantum Pseudorandom Functions, or QPRF.

Definition 3.6 (Quantum Security). *A pseudorandom function PRF is quantum security, if no efficient quantum adversary $\mathcal{A}$ making quantum queries can distinguish between a truly random function and the function $\mathsf{PRF}_{\mathsf{k}}$ for a random $\mathsf{k} \in \mathcal{K}$. More formally, for any efficient quantum adversary $\mathcal{A}$, there exists a negligible function $\varepsilon = \varepsilon(\lambda)$ such that $\left| \Pr_{\mathsf{k} \xleftarrow{\$} \mathcal{K}}[\mathcal{A}^{|\mathsf{PRF}_{\mathsf{k}}\rangle}(\cdot) = 1] - \Pr_{O \xleftarrow{\$} \mathcal{Y}^{\mathcal{X}}}[\mathcal{A}^{|O\rangle}(\cdot) = 1] \right| < \varepsilon$.*

In fact, the above security in Definitions 3.5 and 3.6 are called as Oracle-Indistinguishability, as in [42]. In this paper, we need to use the following "seemingly" strong quantum security: Oracle-and-input indistinguishability.

Definition 3.7 (Strong Quantum Security). *A* QPRF *is strong quantum security, if no efficient quantum adversary $\mathcal{A}$ making quantum queries and taking several random input-output pairs as input can distinguish between a truly random function and the function* $\mathsf{PRF_k}$ *for a random* $\mathsf{k} \in \mathcal{K}$. *More formally, for any efficient quantum adversary $\mathcal{A}$, there exists a negligible function $\varepsilon = \varepsilon(\lambda)$ such that*

$$\Big| \Pr_{(\mathsf{k},x_1,\ldots,x_n) \xleftarrow{\$} \mathcal{K}\times\mathcal{X}^n}\left[\mathcal{A}^{|\mathsf{PRF_k}\rangle}\left((x_i, \mathsf{PRF_k}(x_i))_{i\in[n]}\right) = 1\right] - \Pr_{(O,x_1,\ldots,x_n) \xleftarrow{\$} \mathcal{Y}^{\mathcal{X}}\times\mathcal{X}^n}\left[\mathcal{A}^{|O\rangle}\left((x_i, O(x_i))_{i\in[n]}\right) = 1\right] \Big| < \varepsilon.$$

Lemma 3.8 (Oracle-and-input Indistinguishability). *If one* PRF *satisfies the standard quantum security as in Definition 3.6, then such* PRF *also satisfies the strong quantum security as in Definition 3.7.*

Due to space limitation, the proof of this lemma is deferred to the full version of this paper.

3.3 Trapdoor Homomorphic Commitment Scheme

In this section, we recall the notion of trapdoor commitment scheme, called Eqv-Trapdoor Commitment Scheme (Eqv-TCOM). Particularly, for Eqv-TCOM, td is used to equivocate a commitment to an arbitrary message. Of course, the commitment scheme always satisfies the hiding and binding properties. Below, we present the syntaxes for Eqv-trapdoor commitment scheme.

Definition 3.9 (Eqv-Trapdoor Commitment Scheme [13]). *A trapdoor commit-
ment scheme* Eqv-TCOM *consists of seven algorithms* (CSetup, CGen, Commit, Open, TCGen, Eqv-TCommit, Eqv) *as follows.*

- $\mathsf{CSetup}(1^\lambda) \to \mathsf{cpp}$: *The setup algorithm takes the security parameter λ as input, and outputs a public parameter* cpp *defining sets $S_{\mathsf{ck}}, S_{\mathsf{msg}}, S_r, S_{\mathsf{com}}$, and S_{td} and the distribution $\mathcal{D}(S_r)$ from which the randomness is sampled.*
- $\mathsf{CGen}(\mathsf{cpp}) \to \mathsf{ck}$: *The key generation algorithm takes* cpp *as input, and outputs a commitment key from S_{ck}.*
- $\mathsf{Commit_{ck}}(\mathsf{msg}; \mathsf{Rand}) \to \mathsf{com}$: *The commit algorithm takes as input a message* $\mathsf{msg} \in S_{\mathsf{msg}}$ *and randomness* $\mathsf{Rand} \in S_r$, *and outputs commitment* $\mathsf{com} \in S_{\mathsf{com}}$.
- $\mathsf{Open_{ck}}(\mathsf{com}, \mathsf{Rand}, \mathsf{msg}) \to b$: *The opening algorithm outputs $b = 1$ if the input tuple is valid, and $b = 0$ otherwise.*
- $\mathsf{TCGen}(\mathsf{cpp}) \to (\mathsf{tck}, \mathsf{td})$: *The trapdoor key generation algorithm takes* cpp *as input, and outputs* $\mathsf{tck} \in S_{\mathsf{ck}}$ *and the trapdoor* $\mathsf{td} \in S_{\mathsf{td}}$.

- $\mathsf{Eqv\text{-}TCommit}_{\mathsf{tck}}(\mathsf{td}) \rightarrow \mathsf{com}$: *The trapdoor commit algorithm takes* $\mathsf{tck}, \mathsf{td}$ *as input, and outputs a commitment* $\mathsf{com} \in S_{\mathsf{com}}$.
- $\mathsf{Eqv}_{\mathsf{tck}}(\mathsf{td}, \mathsf{com}, \mathsf{msg}) \rightarrow \mathsf{Rand}$: *The equivocation algorithm takes as input* $(\mathsf{td}, \mathsf{com}, \mathsf{msg})$, *outputs randomness* $\mathsf{Rand} \in S_r$, *such that* $\mathsf{Open}_{\mathsf{tck}}(\mathsf{com}, \mathsf{Rand}, \mathsf{msg}) \rightarrow 1$.

A usual commitment scheme COM is a special case of Eqv-TCOM: it only consists of CSetup, CGen, Commit, and Open. Due to space limitation, we defer the formal presentations of the correctness, hiding, binding, key uniformness, additive homomorphism, and its detailed instantiations to the full version of this paper.

3.4 n-Out-of-n Signature and Multi-signature

Definition 3.10 (Two-Round DS Protocol). *A two-round distributed signature protocol* DS_2 *consists of the following algorithms.*

- $\mathsf{Setup}(1^\lambda) \rightarrow \mathsf{pp}$: *The setup algorithm takes a security parameter* λ *as input, and outputs a public parameter* pp.
- $\mathsf{Gen}_j(\mathsf{pp}) \rightarrow (\mathsf{sk}_j, \mathsf{pk})$ *for every* $j \in [n]$: *The interactive key generation algorithm that is run by party* P_j. *Each* P_j *runs the protocol on the public parameter* pp *as input. At the end of the protocol,* P_j *obtains a secret key share* sk_j *and public key* pk.
- $\mathsf{Sign}_1(\mathsf{pp}, \mathsf{sid}, \mathsf{sk}_j, \mathsf{pk}, \mu) \rightarrow \{\mathsf{msg}_1, \mathsf{st}_1\}$: *The first round of interactive signing algorithm is run by party* P_j. *Each* P_j *takes as inputs an session ID* sid, *a pair of signing key and public key* $(\mathsf{sk}_j, \mathsf{pk})$, *and a message* μ. *It outputs a protocol message* msg_j *and a state* st_j.
- $\mathsf{Sign}_2(\mathsf{sid}, \mathsf{st}_j, \{\mathsf{msg}_i\}_{i \in [n] \setminus \{j\}}) \rightarrow \mathsf{Sig}_j$: *The second round of interactive signing algorithm is run by party* P_j. *Each* P_j *takes as inputs an session ID* sid, *a state information* st_j *(including a secret key share and all private contributions from the first round) and a set of protocol messages* $\{\mathsf{msg}_i\}_{i \in [n] \setminus \{j\}}$. *It outputs a partial signature* Sig_j.
- $\mathsf{SAgg}(\mathsf{sid}, \{\mathsf{Sig}_1, \ldots, \mathsf{Sig}_n\}) \rightarrow \mathsf{Sig}$: *The signature aggregation algorithm (which can be run by each of the participants in distributed signature protocol or the third party) takes as inputs an session ID* sid, *a set of partial signature* $\{\mathsf{Sig}_1, \ldots, \mathsf{Sig}_n\}$. *It outputs a final signature* $\widehat{\mathsf{Sig}}$.
- $\mathsf{Ver}(\mathsf{pp}, \mathsf{pk}, \mu, \widehat{\mathsf{Sig}}) \rightarrow b$: *The verification algorithm takes as inputs the public parameter* pp, *the public key* pk, *a message* μ, *and a signature* $\widehat{\mathsf{Sig}}$. *It outputs* $b = 1$ *if the signature is valid; Otherwise* $b = 0$.

Definition 3.11 (Two-Round MS Protocol in the Key-Verification Model). *A two-round multi-signature protocol* MS_2 *in the key-verification model consists of the following algorithms.*

- $\mathsf{Setup}(1^\lambda) \rightarrow \mathsf{pp}$: *The set up algorithm that outputs a public parameter* pp *on a security parameter* λ *as input.*

- $\mathsf{Gen}(\mathsf{pp}) \rightarrow (\mathsf{sk}, \mathsf{pk}, \pi)$: *Given a public parameter* pp *as input, the non-interactive key generation algorithm outputs a key pair* $(\mathsf{sk}, \mathsf{pk})$, *together with an* NIZKPoK *proof of validity of the public key* pk, *denoted as* π.
- $\mathsf{KAgg}(L) \rightarrow \mathsf{apk}$: *Given a set of public keys* $L = \{\mathsf{pk}_1, \ldots, \mathsf{pk}_n\}$, *the key aggregation algorithm outputs an aggregated public key* apk.
- $\mathsf{Sign}_1(\mathsf{pp}, \mathsf{sid}, \mathsf{sk}_j, \mathsf{pk}_j, \mu, L) \rightarrow \{\mathsf{msg}_j, \mathsf{st}_j\}$: *The first stage of interactive signing algorithm is run by party* P_j. *Each* P_j *takes as inputs an session ID* sid, *a pair of signing key and public key* $(\mathsf{sk}_j, \mathsf{pk}_j)$, *a message* μ, *and a set of co-signers public keys* L, *and outputs a state* st_j *as output and a protocol message* msg_j.
- $\mathsf{Sign}_2(\mathsf{sid}, \mathsf{st}_j, \{\mathsf{msg}_i\}_{i \in [n] \setminus \{j\}}) \rightarrow \mathsf{Sig}_j$: *The second stage of interactive signing algorithm is run by party* P_j. *Each* P_j *takes as inputs an session ID* sid, *a state information* st *and a set of protocol messages* $\{\mathsf{msg}_i\}_{i \in [n] \setminus \{j\}}$, *and outputs a partial signature* Sig_j.
- $\mathsf{SAgg}(\mathsf{sid}, \{\mathsf{Sig}_1, \ldots, \mathsf{Sig}_n\}) \rightarrow \widehat{\mathsf{Sig}}$: *The signature aggregation algorithm (which can be run by each of the participants in multi-signature protocol or the third party) takes as inputs an session ID* sid, *a set of partial signature* $\{\mathsf{Sig}_1, \ldots, \mathsf{Sig}_n\}$, *and outputs a final multi-signature* $\widehat{\mathsf{Sig}}$.
- $\mathsf{Ver}(\mathsf{pp}, \widehat{\mathsf{Sig}}, \mu, \mathsf{apk}) \rightarrow b$: *The verification algorithm that takes* pp, *a signature, a message, and a set of public keys and outputs* $b = 1$ *if the signature is valid. Otherwise* $b = 0$.
- $\mathsf{KVer}(\mathsf{pp}, \mathsf{pk}, \pi) \rightarrow b$: *The key verification algorithm that takes as input* pp, pk, *and a proof* π, *and outputs* $b = 1$ *if* pk *is a valid public key. Otherwise* b=*0*.

Notice that in order to prove the security of our MS_2 against quantum access adversary, we redefine the multi-signature protocol in a more stronger model, i.e., the key-verification model as in [20]. Compared with the plain public key model, this model additionally asks every participant to prove the knowledge of secret key, i.e., publish a NIZKPoK of the used secret key. In this paper, we just focus on how to design the multi-signature protocol itself, since there are existing efficient multi-proof straight-line extractable NIZKPoK protocols for MSIS in the QROM [15,28], which can be used in a black-box way.

Due to space limitation, we defer the formal security notions for n-out-of-n signature and multi-signature to the full version of this paper.

4 Simulation of Quantum Random Oracle

In this section, we consider how to simulate QROM through using Quantum secure PRF (QPRF), such that it can be programmable, invertible and separable. Particularly, we notice that the direct QPRF construction in [3,42], can be used to simulate QROM, according to [4,42]. Thus, one target of this section is to show that for any efficient quantum adversary conducting superposition queries, the above mentioned direct QPRF construction can be reprogrammable and invertible. The other target of this section is to use QPRF as an intermediate tool to simulate QROM satisfying the separable property.

Below, we first recall a ring-based variant of concrete construction of QPRF in [3,42]. Then we define a new "injective mode" for such a QPRF, which is computationally close to the original "normal mode", following from the RLWE assumption. Furthermore, for such "injective mode" QPRF, we present an efficient algorithm, which could invert successfully with certain parameter settings. Moreover, with the same parameter settings, we show that such QPRF is reprogrammable, i.e., any efficient adversary can not distinguish whether the value $\mathsf{QPRF}_{\mathsf{k}}(x)$ has been redefined or not, when x has sufficient entropy. Finally, we formally define the separable property for random oracle, and show how to simulate QROM with such property, through using QPRF as an intermediate tool.

Besides, we add bar symbol for the variables in this section, in order to indicate that the parameters are locally defined and independent of other parts in this paper.

Construction 4.1 (Direct QPRF in [3,42]). *Let $\bar{p}, \bar{q}, \bar{d}, \bar{m}, \bar{N}, \bar{\ell}$ be integers with $\bar{q} > \bar{p}$, $\bar{d} = \lceil \log \bar{q} \rceil$, and $\bar{m} = \bar{d} + 2$. Let $\bar{R} = \mathbb{Z}[X]/(X^{\bar{N}} + 1)$ be a $2\bar{N}$-th cyclotomic ring with $\bar{N}$ being power of 2 and $\bar{R}_{\bar{q}} = \bar{R}/\bar{q}\bar{R}$. Let χ be a small distribution over $\bar{R}$. We define $\mathsf{QPRF} : \mathcal{K} \times \{0,1\}^{\bar{\ell}} \rightarrow \bar{R}_{\bar{p}}^{1\times\bar{m}}$ as follows:*

For a key $\mathsf{k} := (\{a_i\}_{i\in[\bar{m}]}, \{s_i\}_{i\in[\bar{\ell}]}) \in \mathcal{K}$ and input $x := (x_1, \ldots, x_{\bar{\ell}}) \in \{0,1\}^{\bar{\ell}}$, let $\mathsf{QPRF}_{\mathsf{k}}(x) = \mathsf{QPRF}_{\{a_i\},\{s_i\}}(x_1, \ldots, x_{\bar{\ell}}) = \left\lfloor (a_1, \ldots, a_{\bar{m}}) \cdot \prod_{i=1}^{\ell} s_i^{x_i} \right\rceil_p$, where $a_i \leftarrow \bar{R}_q$, $s_i \leftarrow \chi$.

Remark 4.2. *Notice that if $\bar{q}$ is chosen such that $X^{\bar{N}} + 1$ splits into very few irreducible factors modulus $\bar{q}$, and χ is concentrated on 'small' elements, then each independent $s_i \leftarrow \chi$ is invertible over $\bar{R}_{\bar{q}}$, according to Corollary 1.2 in [36].*

For the security of the above Construction 4.1, we have the following theorem.

Theorem 4.3 (Generalization of Theorem 6.1 in [42]). *Let $\chi = D_{\bar{R},\bar{r}}$ be a small distribution over $\bar{R}$, where all coefficients of each polynomial are chosen independently from $D_{\mathbb{Z},\bar{r}}$. Let $\bar{q} \geq \bar{p} \cdot \bar{\ell} \cdot (\bar{r} \cdot \sqrt{2(\bar{N} + \bar{\ell})} \cdot \omega(\sqrt{\log(\bar{N} + \bar{\ell})}))^{\bar{\ell}} \cdot \bar{N}^{\omega(1)}$. Let QPRF be as in Construction 4.1. If the $\mathsf{RLWE}_{\bar{q},1,\bar{m},\chi}$ holds, then Construction 4.1 is a secure QPRF.*

Generally, the proof idea of this theorem is quite similar to that of Theorem 6.1 in [42], except with the replacement of matrices from $D_{\mathbb{Z},\bar{r}}^{n\times n}$ with ring elements from $\chi = D_{\bar{R},\bar{r}}$. In this case, we can still show the security of QPRF through using RLWE. Here, due to space limitation, we defer the detailed proof to the full version.

4.1 Inversion of Construction 4.1

In this section, we show that if the vector $\boldsymbol{a} \in \bar{R}_{\bar{q}}^{\bar{m}}$ is generated together with the trapdoor $\mathbf{T}$ as in [37] and each $s_i \leftarrow \chi$ is invertible over $\bar{R}_{\bar{q}}$, then QPRF in

Construction 4.1 can be inverted efficiently. Basically, this is due to the fact that Construction 4.1 is corresponding to the ring learning with rounding (RLWR) problem, which can be inverted efficiently with the related trapdoor.

Particularly, we have the following formal theorems on the RLWR.

Lemma 4.4 (Trapdoors for RLWR [2,37]). *For any* $\bar{N} \geq 1, \bar{q} \geq 2$, $\bar{d} = \lceil \log \bar{q} \rceil$, $\bar{m} = \bar{d} + 2$, $\bar{p} \geq 3 \cdot \sqrt{\bar{m}\bar{N}} \cdot (\sqrt{2\bar{N}} + \sqrt{\bar{d}\bar{N}})$, *there exist the following two efficient algorithms* (TrapGen, RLWRInvert).

TrapGen$(1^{\bar{N}}, \bar{q}, \bar{m}, \bar{d})$: *A* PPT *algorithm which on input positive integers* $\bar{N}, \bar{q}, \bar{m}, \bar{d}$, *first samples a vector* $(a_1, a_2) \in \bar{R}_{\bar{q}}^2$ *and trapdoor* $\mathbf{T} \in S_1^{2\times\bar{d}}$, *where* $\bar{R}_{\bar{q}} = \mathbb{Z}_{\bar{q}}[X]/(X^{\bar{N}} + 1)$. *Furthermore, the algorithm computes* $(a_3, \ldots, a_{\bar{m}}) = (a_1, a_2)\mathbf{T} + \boldsymbol{g}^\top$, *where* $\boldsymbol{g}^\top = (1, 2, \ldots, 2^{\bar{d}-1})$. *In this case,* $\boldsymbol{a}^\top = (a_1, \ldots, a_{\bar{m}})^\top$ *is computationally close to uniform over* $R_q^{\bar{m}}$, *according to the* $\mathsf{RLWE}_{q,1,1,S_1}$ *assumption. Clearly, it holds* $\boldsymbol{a}^\top \cdot \begin{bmatrix} -\mathbf{T} \\ \mathbf{I}_{\bar{d}\times\bar{d}} \end{bmatrix} = \boldsymbol{g}^\top$, *where* $\mathbf{I}_{\bar{d}\times\bar{d}} \in \bar{R}_{\bar{q}}^{\bar{d}\times\bar{d}}$ *is an identity matrix.*

RLWRInvert$(\mathbf{T}, \boldsymbol{a}, \boldsymbol{b})$: *An algorithm taking as input* $(\boldsymbol{a}, \mathbf{T})$ *output by* TrapGen $(1^{\bar{N}}, q, \bar{m}, \bar{d})$, *and some value* $\boldsymbol{b} \in R_{\bar{p}}^{\bar{m}}$ *such that* $\boldsymbol{b}^\top = \lfloor \boldsymbol{a}^\top \cdot s \rceil_{\bar{p}}$ *for some* $s \in \bar{R}_{\bar{q}}$, *outputs* s.

Due to space limitation, we defer the detailed proof to the full version.

Based on the above result in Lemma 4.4, we can define the following *injective mode* for Construction 4.1, which is almost identical to Construction 4.1 except that $\mathbf{A}$ is generated from the algorithm TrapGen.

Construction 4.5 (Injective mode of Construction 4.1). *Let* $\bar{p}, \bar{q}, \bar{d}, \bar{m}, \bar{N}, \bar{\ell}$ *be integers with* $\bar{q} > \bar{p}$, $\bar{d} = \lceil \log \bar{q} \rceil$, *and* $\bar{m} = \bar{d}+2$. *Let* $\bar{R} = \mathbb{Z}[X]/(X^{\bar{N}}+1)$ *be a* $2\bar{N}$*-th cyclotomic ring with* $\bar{N}$ *being power of 2 and* $\bar{R}_{\bar{q}} = \bar{R}/\bar{q}\bar{R}$. *Let* $\chi = D_{\bar{R},\bar{r}}$ *be a small distribution over* $\bar{R}$. *We define* QPRF : $\mathcal{K} \times \{0,1\}^{\bar{\ell}} \to \bar{R}_{\bar{p}}^{1\times\bar{m}}$ *as follows:*

For a key $\mathsf{k} := (\{a_i\}_{i\in[\bar{m}]}, \{s_i\}_{i\in[\bar{\ell}]}) \in \mathcal{K}$ *and input* $x := (x_1, \ldots, x_{\bar{\ell}}) \in \{0,1\}^{\bar{\ell}}$, *let* $\mathsf{QPRF}_{\mathsf{k}}(x) = \mathsf{QPRF}_{\{a_i\},\{s_i\}}(x_1, \ldots, x_{\bar{\ell}}) = \left\lfloor (a_1, \ldots, a_{\bar{m}}) \cdot \prod_{i=1}^{\bar{\ell}} s_i^{x_i} \right\rceil_{\bar{p}}$, *where the vector* $\boldsymbol{a} \in R_{\bar{q}}^{\bar{m}}$ *is generated through running the algorithm* TrapGen$(1^{\bar{N}}, \bar{q}, \bar{m}, \bar{d})$, *i.e.,* $(\boldsymbol{a}, \mathbf{T}) \leftarrow$ TrapGen$(1^{\bar{N}}, \bar{q}, \bar{m}, \bar{d})$, *and* $s_i \leftarrow \chi$.

Clearly, for the adversary without the trapdoor matrix $\mathbf{T}$, this injective mode is computationally close to the original *normal mode* in Construction 4.1. Besides, Theorem 4.3 should be still set up in the injective mode, for the adversary without the trapdoor $\mathbf{T}$.

Lemma 4.6 (Indistinguishability of Normal/Injective modes). *For the adversary* $\mathcal{A}$ *without the trapdoor* $\mathbf{T}$ *of the vector* $\boldsymbol{a}$, *if the* $\mathsf{RLWE}_{\bar{q},1,1,S_1}$ *assumption holds, then Constructions 4.1 and 4.5 are computational indistinguishability, even* $\mathcal{A}$ *queries the functions in a superposition for any polynomial times.*

Due to space limit, we defer the detailed proof to the full version.

Below, we describe the concrete invert algorithm for Inj-QPRF.

Algorithm 1: Efficient algorithm $\mathsf{Invert}^{O_{\mathsf{RLWRInvert}}}(\mathbf{T}, \{a_i\}, \{s_i\}, \{b_i\})$ for inverting the function $\mathsf{Inj\text{-}QPRF}_{\{a_i\},\{s_i\}}(x_1, ..., x_{\bar{\ell}})$

Input: An oracle $O_{\mathsf{RLWRInvert}}$ for inverting $\lfloor (a_1, \ldots, a_{\bar{m}}) \cdot s \rceil_{\bar{p}}$, when $\bar{p}$ is large enough.
- PRFKey : vector $\boldsymbol{a} = (a_1, \ldots, a_{\bar{m}})^\top \in \bar{R}_{\bar{q}}^{1\times \bar{m}}$ and $\{s_i\}_{i\in[\bar{\ell}]}$;
- Trapdoor $\mathbf{T} \in \bar{R}^{2\times \bar{d}}$ for $(a_1, \ldots, a_{\bar{m}})$;
- Vector $\boldsymbol{b} = \left\lfloor \boldsymbol{a}^\top \cdot \prod_{i=1}^{\bar{\ell}} s_i^{x_i} \right\rceil_{\bar{p}}$ for any $x_i \leftarrow \{0, 1\}$.

Output: The vector $x = (x_1, ..., x_{\bar{\ell}}) \in \{0, 1\}^{\bar{\ell}}$.
1. Get $s \leftarrow O_{\mathsf{RLWRInvert}}(\mathbf{T}, \boldsymbol{a}, \boldsymbol{b})$, s.t. $\boldsymbol{b} = \lfloor \boldsymbol{a}^\top \cdot s \rceil_{\bar{p}}$, where $s \in \bar{R}_{\bar{q}}$;
2. Set $\hat{s} = s$, if $\|\hat{s}\| \geq r^{\bar{\ell}} \cdot (2\bar{N})^{\bar{\ell}/2}$, return $\perp$;
3. Set $s'_0 = \hat{s}$, for $i = 1, ..., (\bar{\ell} - 1)$, conduct the following steps:
   (i) Compute s_i^{-1}, set $s'_i = s_i^{-1} \cdot s'_{i-1}$, where the computation is conducted over $\bar{R}_{\bar{q}}$.
   (ii) If $\|s'_i\| \leq (\bar{r}\sqrt{2\bar{N}})^{\bar{\ell}-i}$, set $x_i = 1$; Otherwise set $x_i = 0$;
4. Check if $s'_{\bar{\ell}-1} = s_{\bar{\ell}}$, set $x_{\bar{\ell}} = 1$; Otherwise set $x_{\bar{\ell}} = 0$;

return $\boldsymbol{x} = (x_1, ..., x_{\bar{\ell}})$.

Theorem 4.7. *For some $\boldsymbol{a} \in R_{\bar{q}}^{\bar{m}}$ and integers $\bar{p}, \bar{q}, \bar{d}, \bar{N}, \bar{m}$ such that $\bar{q} \geq \bar{p}\cdot\bar{\ell}\cdot(\bar{r}\cdot\sqrt{2(\bar{N}+\bar{\ell})}\cdot\omega(\sqrt{\log(\bar{N}+\bar{\ell})}))^{\bar{\ell}}\cdot\bar{N}^{\omega(1)} \geq \left(\bar{r}\cdot\sqrt{2\bar{N}}\right)^{\bar{\ell}}$, $\bar{d} = \lceil \log \bar{q} \rceil$, and $\bar{m} = \bar{d}+2$ and $\bar{p} \geq 3\cdot\sqrt{\bar{m}\bar{N}}\cdot(\sqrt{2\bar{N}}+\sqrt{\bar{d}\bar{N}})$, suppose the oracle $O_{\mathsf{RLWRInvert}}$ in Algorithm 1 correctly invert $\lfloor \boldsymbol{a}^\top \cdot s \rceil_{\bar{p}}$ for any $s \in \bar{R}_{\bar{q}}$. Then, for any invertible $s_i \in \bar{R}_{\bar{q}}$, Algorithm 1 correctly inverts $\mathsf{Inj\text{-}QPRF}_{\boldsymbol{a},\{s_i\}} = \left\lfloor \boldsymbol{a}^\top \cdot \prod_{i=1}^{\bar{\ell}} s_i^{x_i} \right\rceil_{\bar{p}}$, assuming the $\mathsf{DSPR}_{\bar{q},\bar{R},\chi}$ assumption.*

Due to space limitation, we defer the detailed proof to the full version.

4.2 Adaptive Programming for QPRF in Construction 4.1

In this section, we need to prove that when using the QPRF to simulate QROM, we can conduct adaptive programming similar to the results in [25,40], which is needed for the security proof of our two-round protocols in the QROM. Particularly, we show that even when conducting quantum queries, an efficient quantum adversary can not distinguish whether the value $\mathsf{QPRF}_{\mathsf{k}}(x)$ in Construction 4.1 has been redefined or not, where x has sufficient entropy. Overall, the result of this section can be viewed as a generalization of the existing results in [25,40].

Theorem 4.8 (QPRF programming, adaptive) *Let $\mathsf{QPRF} : \mathcal{K}\times(\mathcal{X}_1, \mathcal{X}_2) \rightarrow \mathcal{Y}$ be a quantum secure pseudorandom function for certain sets $\mathcal{K}, \mathcal{X}_1, \mathcal{X}_2, \mathcal{Y}$. For a random key $\mathsf{k} \xleftarrow{\$} \mathcal{K}$, consider the following adaptive reprogramming games:*

Let $\mathcal{A}$ be any efficient adversary conducting q_1 times quantum queries to QPRF and q_2 times reprogramming queries as defined in the above Fig. 5. Then the distinguishing advantage of $\mathcal{A}$ is bounded by

$$\left|\Pr(\mathsf{Repro}_0^{\mathcal{A}} = 1) - \Pr(\mathsf{Repro}_1^{\mathcal{A}} = 1)\right| \leq \frac{3q_2}{2}\sqrt{q_1/|\mathcal{X}_1|} + 2\varepsilon_{\mathsf{QPRF}},$$

GAME Repro_b	$\mathsf{Reprogram}(x_2)$
1: $\mathcal{O}_0 := \mathsf{QPRF}_k(\cdot,\cdot)$	
2: $\mathcal{O}_1 := \mathcal{O}_0$	1: $(x_1, y) \xleftarrow{\$} X_1 \times Y$
3: $b' \leftarrow A^{\vert\mathcal{O}_b\rangle,\mathsf{Reprogram}}$	2: $\mathcal{O}_1 := \mathcal{O}_1^{(x_1 \Vert x_2)\mapsto y}$
4: **return** b'	3: **return** x_1

Fig. 5. Adaptive reprogramming games Repro_b for QPRF, with $b \in \{0, 1\}$

where $\varepsilon_{\mathsf{QPRF}}$ *is the probability for the efficient quantum adversary to distinguish* QPRF *and random function.*

Due to space limit, we defer the detailed proof to the full version.

4.3 Separation of QROM

In this section, we first formally define the separable property for random oracle, and then analyze the essential challenge for such property when against adversary conducting superposition queries. Finally, we show that how to overcome such obstacle through using QPRF in Construction 4.1.

Definition 4.9 (Separation of ROM). *Given a random oracle* $\mathsf{H} : \mathcal{X} \to \mathcal{Y}$, *we say it is separable, if for each query on* $x \in \mathcal{X}$, *there exists an independent Bernoulli random variable* X *satisfying* $\Pr(X = 1) = p$, *such that* $\mathsf{H}(x)$ *returns the random sample from one of two different but public sampling distributions* Y_1, Y_2 *supported over* $\mathcal{Y}$, *according to the value of* X, *i.e.,*

$$\mathsf{H}(x) := \begin{Bmatrix} y' & \textit{if } X = 1 \\ y'' & \textit{if } X = 0 \end{Bmatrix}$$

where $y' \leftarrow Y_1, y'' \leftarrow Y_2$.

For classical ROM. In the case of classical random oracle, such separable property can be obtained through simulating H in a lazy sampling way. Particularly, the simulator first initialize an empty table HT. Then, when receiving the adversary's query x, if $\mathsf{HT}[x] = \perp$, then the simulator sets $\mathsf{HT}[x]$ in the following way: (i) generates an independent Bernoulli $X \in \{0, 1\}$; (ii) if $X = 1$, samples $y_1 \leftarrow Y_1$ with ra_2 as running randomness. Otherwise, samples $y_2 \leftarrow Y_2$ with ra_2 as running randomness; (iii) stores y_1 or y_2 in tables $\mathsf{HT}[x]$. If $\mathsf{HT}[x] \neq \perp$, then the simulator directly returns $\mathsf{HT}[x]$ as the value of $\mathsf{H}(x)$.

For QROM. In the case of QROM, it seems that there is an essential challenge for the above lazy sampling simulation approach. Particularly, for compressed oracle and its variants, we need to ensure the compatibility between the distributions Y_1, Y_2 and the output distribution of compressed oracle. Unfortunately, the existing instantiations on lattice-based homomorphic HTDC are not compatible. On the other hand, we can not directly use the stateless simulations neither, as they do not have sufficient randomness for all possible inputs.

In order to overcome the above obstacles, we propose the following simulation algorithm through using QPRF.

Theorem 4.10. *Assume* QPRF *exists, the above simulation for* QROM *in Fig. 6 satisfies the separable property.*

Due to space limitation, we defer the detailed proof to the full version.

5 Two Round n-Out-of-n Threshold Signature from Lattices in the QROM

In this section, we present one of our main constructions: two-round n-out-of-n threshold signature, which is provably secure based on MSIS, MLWE and DSPR in the QROM. Below, we first describe our protocol in Sect. 5.1, and then prove the correctness and the security of unforgeability in Sect. 5.2.

1. For any input $x \in \mathcal{X}$, invoke $\mathsf{QPRF}_{\mathsf{k}}(x) : \mathcal{X} \rightarrow (\{0,1\}^{l_{ra_1}} \times \{0,1\}^{l_{ra_2}})$, where $\mathsf{k} \xleftarrow{\$} \mathcal{K}$, and l_{ra_1}, l_{ra_2} are the bit-lengths of two parts of outputs.
2. Compute $(ra_1, ra_2) = \mathsf{QPRF}_{\mathsf{k}}(x)$.
3. If the number of 1 in ra_1 is more than num, then sample $y_1 \leftarrow Y_1$ through using ra_2 as running randomness, i.e., running the sample algorithm $y_1 \leftarrow \mathsf{Sample}_1(ra_2)$, return y_1 as $\mathsf{H}(x)$. Here, num is set to make $\Pr[\|ra_1\|_1 > num] = p$.
4. Otherwise, compute $y_2 \leftarrow Y_2$ through using ra_2 as the running randomness, i.e., running the sample algorithm $y_2 \leftarrow \mathsf{Sample}_2(ra_2)$, return y_2 as $\mathsf{H}(x)$.

Fig. 6. Simulation of QROM $\mathsf{H} : \mathcal{X} \rightarrow \mathcal{Y}$ with the separable property through using QPRF

Table 2. Parameters of Our Two Round n-out-of-n Threshold Signature

Parameter	Description
n	Number of parties
N	A power of two defining the degree of $f(X)$
$f(X) = X^N + 1$	The $2N$-th cyclotomic polynomial
q	Prime modulus
$R = \mathbb{Z}[X]/(f(X))$	Cyclotomic ring
$R_q = \mathbb{Z}_q[X]/(f(X))$	Ring
k, m'	The height of random matrices $\mathbf{A}$ and $\mathbf{A}_{\mathsf{Inv}}$, respectively
ℓ	The width of random matrices $\mathbf{A}$
$B = \sigma\sqrt{2N(\ell + k)}$	The upper bound of $\Vert \boldsymbol{z}_{i,J_i}^{(u)} \Vert$
$B_n = \sqrt{n}B$	The upper bound of $\Vert \boldsymbol{z}_{i,J_i} \Vert$, with $\boldsymbol{z}_{i,J_i} = \sum_{u=1}^{n} \boldsymbol{z}_{i,J_i}^{(u)}$
$C = \{c \in R : \Vert c \Vert_\infty = 1 \wedge \Vert c \Vert_1 = \kappa\}$	Challenge space where $\lvert C \rvert = \binom{N}{n} 2^\kappa$
$\mathcal{M}$	Message space
κ	The ℓ_1-norm of challenge $c \in C$
$S_\eta = \{x \in R : \Vert x \Vert_\infty \leq \eta\}$	Set of small secrets
m, t	Iteration parameters for Sign protocol
$T = \kappa\eta\sqrt{m \cdot N(\ell + k)}$	The upper bound of $\Vert (c_{i,j}\boldsymbol{s}_n)_{j\in[m]} \Vert$
α	Parameter defining σ and M, according to rejection sampling
$\sigma = \alpha T$	Standard deviation of the Gaussian distribution of $\boldsymbol{y}_i^{(n)}$
$M = \exp\left(\sqrt{\frac{2(\lambda+1)}{\log e}} \cdot \frac{1}{\alpha} + \frac{1}{2\alpha^2}\right)$	The expected number of restarts until Rej output 1
$\mathsf{cpp}_{\mathsf{Eqv}}$	Public parameters for commitment scheme, honestly
	generated by $\mathsf{Eqv\text{-}CSetup}$
$l_0, l_1, l_1' = k \cdot \ell \cdot N \cdot \log q, l_2, l_5 = t \log m$	Output bit lengths of random oracles
	$\mathsf{H}_0, \mathsf{H}_1, \mathsf{H}_1', \mathsf{H}_2, \mathsf{H}_5$
$l_0^* = \log(m \cdot t \cdot \lvert\mathcal{M}\rvert) + k \cdot N \cdot \log q \cdot (\ell + 1)$	Input bit lengths of random oracles H_0, where $\mathsf{Eqv}\text{-}S_{\mathsf{ck}}$
$+ \log \lvert \mathsf{Eqv}\text{-}S_{\mathsf{ck}} \rvert + \log(q \cdot m' \cdot (\ell + k))$	is specified by $\mathsf{cpp}_{\mathsf{Eqv}}$
l_1^*	Input bit lengths of random oracles $\mathsf{H}_1, \mathsf{H}_1'$
$l_2^* = k \cdot N \cdot \log q + \log n$	Input bit lengths of random oracles H_2
$l_3^* = l_4^* = \log \lvert\mathcal{M}\rvert + k \cdot N \cdot \log q \cdot (\ell + 1)$	Input bit lengths of random oracles $\mathsf{H}_3, \mathsf{H}_4$
$l_5^* = k \cdot N \cdot \log q \cdot (\ell + 1) + \log \lvert\mathcal{M}\rvert$	Input bit lengths of random oracles H_5, where $\mathsf{Eqv}\text{-}S_{\mathsf{com}}$
$+t \log \lvert \mathsf{Eqv}\text{-}S_{\mathsf{com}} \rvert + mt \log(2N\kappa(q \cdot m' \cdot (\ell + k)))$	is specified by $\mathsf{cpp}_{\mathsf{Eqv}}$

5.1 Construction

Generally, our protocol can be viewed as enhancing the security of the existing protocol by Damgård et al. in [13] from classical ROM into the QROM, through leveraging the tweaked online extractability framework by Unruh in [40] and our modified QPRF in Construction 4.5. Similar to [13], we need to use as a building block an additively HTDC scheme Eqv-TCOM with uniform keys.

Particularly, our construction is formally specified in Figs. 7, 8, 9. Here, as all players have the same role, we just describe the n-th player's behavior. In order to help the readers to understand our construction more easily, we go over the high-level ideas for each step as follows.

Parameter Setup. According to Definition 3.10, the algorithm $\mathsf{QDS}_2.\mathsf{Setup}$ should be invoked by a trusted party, and outputs a set of public parameters as

Protocol $\mathsf{QDS}_2.\mathsf{Gen}_n(\mathsf{pp})$:
The protocol is parameterized by public parameters described in Table 2 and relies on the random oracles: $\mathsf{H}_1 : \{0,1\}^{l_1^*} \to \{0,1\}^{l_1}$, $\mathsf{H}'_1 : \{0,1\}^{l_1^*} \to \{0,1\}^{l'_1}$, $\mathsf{H}_2 : \{0,1\}^{l_2^*} \to \{0,1\}^{l_2}$.

Matrix Generation

1. Sample a random seed $s_n \in \{0,1\}^{l_1^* - \log n}$, and generate a random oracle commitment $g_n \leftarrow \mathsf{H}_1(s_n, n)$. Send out g_n.
2. Upon receiving g_u for all $u \in [n-1]$, send out the seed s_n.
3. Upon receiving s_u for all $u \in [n-1]$:
   (a) If $\mathsf{H}_1(s_u, u) \neq g_u$ for some u, then send out $\perp$.
   (b) Otherwise compute $\mathbf{A}_u = \mathsf{H}'_1(s_u, u)$ for all $u \in [n]$. And set public random matrix $\overline{\mathbf{A}} := [\mathbf{A}|\mathbf{I}] \in R_q^{k\times(\ell+k)}$, where $\mathbf{A} := \sum_{u\in[n]} \mathbf{A}_u$.

Key Pair Generation

1. Sample a secret key shares $\boldsymbol{s}_n \stackrel{\$}{\leftarrow} S_\eta^{\ell+k}$ and compute a public key share $\boldsymbol{t}_n := \overline{\mathbf{A}}\boldsymbol{s}_n$, respectively, and generate a random oracle commitment $g'_n \leftarrow \mathsf{H}_2(\boldsymbol{t}_n, n)$. Send out g'_n.
2. Upon receiving g'_u for all $u \in [n-1]$, send out $\boldsymbol{t}_n$.
3. Upon receiving $\boldsymbol{t}_u$ for all $u \in [n-1]$:
   (a) If $\mathsf{H}_2(\boldsymbol{t}_u, u) \neq g'_u$ for some u then send out $\perp$.
   (b) Otherwise set a combined public key $\boldsymbol{t} := \sum_{u\in[n]} \boldsymbol{t}_u$.

If the protocol does not abort, P_n obtain $(\mathsf{sk}_n, \mathsf{pk}) = (\boldsymbol{s}_n, (\mathbf{A}, \boldsymbol{t}))$ as local output.

Fig. 7. Gen Protocol of Our Two-Round n-out-of-n Threshold Signature Scheme

in Table 2. Notice that most of our parameters follow from those of [13], except with the following case:

- As we want to generalize the framework of Unruh in [40] into the threshold setting, it is necessary to replace the random oracle for hashing the vector $\boldsymbol{z}_j$ as an additively homomorphic trapdoor-inversion function indexed by the matrix $\mathbf{A}_{\mathsf{Inv}} \in R_q^{m'\times(\ell+k)}$. Particularly, such function is defined to be $\mathsf{Inv\text{-}H}(\boldsymbol{z}_j) := \mathbf{A}_{\mathsf{Inv}} \cdot \boldsymbol{z}_j + \boldsymbol{r}_j$, where $\boldsymbol{r}_j$ is randomly sampled from the same small distribution as that of $\boldsymbol{z}_j$. Thus, we need to set the dimensions of $\mathbf{A}_{\mathsf{Inv}}$ accordingly, ensuring the function $\mathsf{Inv\text{-}H}$ to satisfy both binding and hiding properties. Moreover, with the corresponding trapdoor $\mathbf{T}_{\mathbf{A}_{\mathsf{Inv}}} \in R^{m'\times m'}$, it should be efficient to get $\boldsymbol{z}_j$ from $\mathsf{Inv\text{-}H}(\boldsymbol{z})$.

Key Generation. The key generation algorithm $\mathsf{QDS}_2.\mathsf{Gen}$ almost follows that of [13], except that we introduce another random oracle H'_1 as the randomness generator. Particulary, in order to interactively generate a random matrix $\mathbf{A} \in R_q^{k\times\ell}$ in a secure way, the n-th participant employs the following random oracle commitments: first choose his random seed $s_n \stackrel{\$}{\leftarrow} \{0,1\}^{l_1^*}$, then compute and send out $g_n \leftarrow \mathsf{H}_1(s_n, n)$. Then with s_u for all $u \in [n]$, any one can generate the random matrix $\mathbf{A}_u \stackrel{\$}{\leftarrow} H'_1(s_u, u)$. Due to the uniform distribution of s_n, the input of H'_1 has sufficient entropy. And thus we can reprogram H'_1 in the security proof. Notice that in this case, the participants just need to send out the seed $s_u \in \{0,1\}^{l_2^*}$, rather than $\mathbf{A}_u \in R_q^{k\times\ell}$, in the public channel. Clearly, this will significantly reduce the communication overhead of our construction.

Signature Generation. One important point for the $\mathsf{QDS}_2.\mathsf{Sign}_n$ algorithm in Fig. 8 is the iterations at (1.a) of **Signature generation**. With these steps, we can realize online extractability, according to [40]. And thus, we can

Protocol $\mathsf{QDS}_2.\mathsf{Sign}_n(sid, \mathsf{sk}_n, \mathsf{pk}, \mu)$

The protocol is parameterized by public parameters described in Table 2 and relies on the random oracles $\mathsf{H}_0 : \{0,1\}^{l_0^*} \to C$, $\mathsf{H}_3 : \{0,1\}^{l_3^*} \to \mathsf{Eqv}\text{-}S_{\mathsf{ck}}$, $\mathsf{H}_4 : \{0,1\}^{l_4^*} \to R_q^{m' \times (\ell+k)}$ and $\mathsf{H}_5 : \{0,1\}^{l_5^*} \to \{0,1\}^{l_5}$. The protocol assumes that $\mathsf{QDS}_2.\mathsf{Gen}_n(\mathsf{pp})$ has been previously invoked.

Inputs

1. P_n receives a unique sessions ID sid, $\mathsf{sk}_n = \boldsymbol{s}_n$, $\mathsf{pk} = (\mathbf{A}, \boldsymbol{t})$ and message $\mu \in M$ as input.
2. P_n verifies that sid has not been used before (if it has been, the protocol is not executed).
3. P_n locally computes per-message commitment keys $\mathsf{ck} \leftarrow \mathsf{H}_3(\mu, \mathsf{pk})$, $\mathbf{A}_{\mathsf{Inv}} \leftarrow \mathsf{H}_4(\mu, \mathsf{pk})$.

Signature Generation P_n works as follows:

1. $\mathsf{Sign}_1(\mathsf{pp}, \mathsf{sid}, \mathsf{sk}_n, \mathsf{pk}, \mu)$: Upon receiving message μ, conduct the first round interaction as follows.
   (a) for $i = 1$ to t; conduct as follows.
      i. Sample $\boldsymbol{y}_i^{(n)} \leftarrow D_\sigma^{\ell+k}$ and compute $\boldsymbol{w}_i^{(n)} := \overline{\mathbf{A}}\boldsymbol{y}_i^{(n)}$, with $\overline{\mathbf{A}} := [\mathbf{A}|\mathbf{I}] \in R_q^{k\times(\ell+k)}$.
      ii. for $j = 1$ to m; conduct as follows:
         A. Derive challenges $c_{i,j} \leftarrow \mathsf{H}_0(i, j, \mu, \mathsf{pk}, \mathsf{ck}, \mathbf{A}_{\mathsf{Inv}})$.
         B. Compute signature shares $\boldsymbol{z}_{i,j}^{(n)} = c_{i,j}\boldsymbol{s}_n + \boldsymbol{y}_i^{(n)}$.
         C. Run the rejection sampling $\mathsf{Rej}(\boldsymbol{z}_{i,j}^{(n)}, c_{i,j}\boldsymbol{s}_n, \sigma) \to \{0,1\}$.
      iii. If the above rejection sampling algorithm outputs 0 for certain $j \in [m]$, then go to the Step i.
   (b) Compute $\widetilde{\mathsf{com}}_{i,j}^{(n)} \leftarrow \mathsf{Inv}\text{-}\mathsf{H}(\boldsymbol{z}_{i,j}^{(n)}) = \mathbf{A}_{\mathsf{Inv}} \cdot \boldsymbol{z}_{i,j}^{(n)} + \boldsymbol{r}_{i,j}^{\prime(n)}$ where $\boldsymbol{r}_{i,j}^{\prime(n)} \leftarrow D_\sigma^{m'}$ for all $(i,j) \in [t] \times [m]$.
   (c) Compute $\mathsf{com}_i^{(n)} \leftarrow \mathsf{Eqv}\text{-}\mathsf{Commit}_{\mathsf{ck}}(\boldsymbol{w}_i^{(n)}, r_i^{(n)})$ with $r_i^{(n)} \xleftarrow{\$} \mathsf{Eqv}\text{-}S_r$.
   (d) Set $\mathsf{st}_n := (\mathsf{sk}_n, \{\boldsymbol{r}_{i,j}^{\prime(n)}, r_i^{(n)}, \boldsymbol{z}_{i,j}^{(n)}\}_{i\in[t],j\in[m]})$.
   (e) Send out $\mathsf{msg}_n := (\{\mathsf{com}_i^{(n)}\}_{i\in[t]}, \{\widetilde{\mathsf{com}}_{i,j}^{(n)}\}_{i\in[t],j\in[m]})$.
2. $\mathsf{Sign}_2(\mathsf{sid}, \mathsf{st}_n, \{\mathsf{msg}_u\}_{u\in[n-1]})$: Upon receiving $\mathsf{msg}_u := (\{\mathsf{com}_i^{(u)}\}_{i\in[t]}, \{\widetilde{\mathsf{com}}_{i,j}^{(u)}\}_{i\in[t],j\in[m]})$ for all $u \in [n-1]$, compute the signature shares as follows.
   (a) Set $\mathsf{com}_i := \sum_{u\in[n]} \mathsf{com}_i^{(u)}$ and $\widetilde{\mathsf{com}}_{i,j} := \sum_{u\in[n]} \widetilde{\mathsf{com}}_{i,j}^{(u)}$ for all $i \in [t], j \in [m]$.
   (b) Get challenges $J_1||...||J_t \leftarrow \mathsf{H}_5(\mathsf{pk}, \mu, \{\mathsf{com}_i\}_{i\in[t]}, \{c_{i,j}\}_{i\in[t],j\in[m]}, \{\widetilde{\mathsf{com}}_{i,j}\}_{i\in[t],j\in[m]})$.
   (c) Send out $\mathsf{Sig}_n := (\{\mathsf{com}_i^{(n)}\}_{i\in[t]}, \{\widetilde{\mathsf{com}}_{i,j}^{(n)}\}_{i\in[t],j\in[m]}, \{\boldsymbol{z}_{i,J_i}^{(n)}\}_{i\in[t]}, \{r_i^{(n)}\}_{i\in[t]}, \{\boldsymbol{r}_{i,J_i}^{\prime(n)}\}_{i\in[t]})$.
3. $\mathsf{SAgg}(\mathsf{sid}, \{\mathsf{Sig}_1, \ldots, \mathsf{Sig}_n\})$: Upon receiving $\mathsf{Sig}_u := (\mathsf{com}_i^{(u)}, \widetilde{\mathsf{com}}_{i,j}^{(u)}, \{\boldsymbol{z}_{i,J_i}^{(u)}\}_{i\in[t]}, \{r_i^{(u)}\}_{i\in[t]}, \{\boldsymbol{r}_{i,J_i}^{\prime(u)}\}_{i\in[t]})$ for all $u \in [n]$, compute the combined signature as follows.
   (a) Set $\mathsf{com}_i := \sum_{u\in[n]} \mathsf{com}_i^{(u)}$ and $\widetilde{\mathsf{com}}_{i,j} := \sum_{u\in[n]} \widetilde{\mathsf{com}}_{i,j}^{(u)}$ for all $i \in [t], j \in [m]$.
   (b) Compute $\boldsymbol{z}_i := \sum_{u\in[n]} \boldsymbol{z}_{i,J_i}^{(u)}$, $r_i := \sum_{u\in[n]} r_i^{(u)}$ and $\boldsymbol{r}_i' := \sum_{u\in[n]} \boldsymbol{r}_{i,J_i}^{\prime(u)}$ for all $i \in [t]$.
   (c) If the protocol does not abort, P_n obtains the final signature:
   $\widehat{\mathsf{Sig}} := (\{\mathsf{com}_i\}_{i\in[t]}, \{\widetilde{\mathsf{com}}_{i,j}\}_{i\in[t],j\in[m]}, \{\boldsymbol{z}_i\}_{i\in[t]}, \{r_i\}_{i\in[t]}, \{\boldsymbol{r}_i'\}_{i\in[t]})$ as local output.

Fig. 8. Sign Protocol of Our Two-Round n-out-of-n Threshold Signature Scheme

circumvent the essential obstacle, rewinding, for the security proof of signature in the QROM. The other crucial point is the computation of $c_{i,j}$, i.e., $c_{i,j} \leftarrow \mathsf{H}_0(i, j, \mu, \mathsf{pk}, \mathsf{ck}, \mathsf{ck}')$. In fact, this step has at least three significance:

- For fixed i and different j and j', $c_{i,j} \neq c_{i,j'}$. This is necessary for successful extractability through using the extractor Ext (presented in full version, due to space limitation), according to [40].
- The computation of $c_{i,j}$ does not rely on $\mathsf{com}_i^{(u)}$ or $\boldsymbol{w}_i^{(u)}$. And thus, for each $(i,j) \in [t] \times [m]$, all participants will use the same challenge $c_{i,j}$ for the related individual running of underlying Dilithium signature scheme. Clearly, only with such condition, $\{\boldsymbol{z}_{i,J_i}\}_{i\in[t]}$ in the final signature can be verified successfully with respect to public key $(\mathbf{A}, \boldsymbol{t})$, according to the step (2.c) of the algorithm $\mathsf{QDS}_2.\mathsf{Ver}$ in Fig. 9.
- Although each challenge $c_{i,j} \leftarrow \mathsf{H}_0(i, j, \mu, \mathsf{pk}, \mathsf{ck}, \mathsf{ck}')$ remains to be unchanged across all different participants, it does not affect the simulation of the transcript $(\boldsymbol{w}_i^{(n)}, c_{i,J_i}, \boldsymbol{z}_{i,J_i})$. Particularly, we first sample $\boldsymbol{z}_{i,J_i}$ from the desired

Algorithm $\mathsf{QDS}_2.\mathsf{Ver}((\{\mathsf{com}_i\}_{i\in[t]}, \{\widetilde{\mathsf{com}}_{i,j}\}_{i\in[t],j\in[m]}, \{\boldsymbol{z}_i\}_{i\in[t]}, \{r_i\}_{i\in[t]}, \{\boldsymbol{r}'_i\}_{i\in[t]}), \mu, \mathsf{pk})$
Upon receiving a message μ, signature $(\{\mathsf{com}_i\}_{i\in[t]}, \{\widetilde{\mathsf{com}}_{i,j}\}_{i\in[t],j\in[m]}, \{\boldsymbol{z}_i\}_{i\in[t]}, \{r_i\}_{i\in[t]}, \{\boldsymbol{r}'_i\}_{i\in[t]})$ and combined public key $\mathsf{pk} := (\mathbf{A}, \boldsymbol{t})$ works as follows:

1. Generate commitment keys $\mathsf{ck} \leftarrow \mathsf{H}_3(\mu, \mathsf{pk})$, $\mathbf{A}_{\mathsf{Inv}} \leftarrow \mathsf{H}_4(\mu, \mathsf{pk})$, derive $c_{i,j} \leftarrow \mathsf{H}_0(i, j, \mu, \mathsf{pk}, \mathsf{ck}, \mathsf{ck}')$ for all $i \in [t], j \in [m]$ and compute $J_1||...||J_t \leftarrow \mathsf{H}_5(\mathsf{pk}, \mu, \{\mathsf{com}_i\}_{i\in[t]}, \{c_{i,j}\}_{i\in[t],j\in[m]}, \{\widetilde{\mathsf{com}}_{i,j}\}_{i\in[t],j\in[m]})$.
2. Perform the checks as follows:
   (a) for $i = 1$ to t do:
      Check that $c_{i,1}, ..., c_{i,m}$ pairwise distinct.
   (b) for $i = 1$ to t do:
      Check that $||\boldsymbol{z}_i|| \leq B_n$.
   (c) for $i = 1$ to t do:
      Reconstruct $\boldsymbol{w}_i := \overline{\mathbf{A}}\boldsymbol{z}_i - c_{i,J_i}\boldsymbol{t}$, and check $\mathsf{Eqv\text{-}Open}_{\mathsf{ck}}(\mathsf{com}_i, r_i, \boldsymbol{w}_i) = 1$.
   (d) for $i = 1$ to t do:
      Check $\widetilde{\mathsf{com}}_{i,J_i} = \mathbf{A}_{\mathsf{Inv}} \cdot \boldsymbol{z}_i + \boldsymbol{r}'_i$.

If all checks succeed then return 1, otherwise, return 0.

Fig. 9. Ver Algorithm of Our Two-Round n-out-of-n Threshold Signature Scheme

distribution, and then compute $\boldsymbol{w}_i^{(n)} = \overline{\mathbf{A}}\boldsymbol{z}_{i,J_i}^{(n)} - c_{i,J_i}\boldsymbol{t}_n$. Finally, with the help of the trapdoor-equivocation commitment scheme Eqv-TCOM, we can derive the related randomness $r_i^{(n)} \leftarrow \mathsf{Eqv}_{\mathsf{tck}}(\mathsf{td}, \mathsf{com}_i^{(n)}, \boldsymbol{w}_i^{(n)})$. This simulation is crucial to the Game 6 in the proof of Theorem 5.2.

Verification. Thanks to the linearity of the underlying signature scheme, and additive homomorphism of Eqv-TCOM and $\mathsf{Inv\text{-}H}(\boldsymbol{z})$ with respect to both message and randomness, the verifier just need to verify the sum of signature shares, i.e., $\sum_{u=1}^{n} \mathsf{Sig}_u$, where Sig_u is the signature share from each participant.

5.2 Correctness and Security

Theorem 5.1 (Correctness) *For public parameters as in Table 2, two-round threshold n-out-of-n signature* $\mathsf{QDS}_2 = (\mathsf{Setup}, (\mathsf{Gen}_u)_{u\in[n]}, (\mathsf{Sign}_u)_{u\in[n]}, \mathsf{Ver})$ *in Figs. 7, 8, 9 satisfies the correctness. In other words, suppose the underlying Dilithium scheme is correct, and the trapdoor commitment scheme* Eqv-TCOM *and the trapdoor-inversion function* Inv-H *are correct and additively homomorphic, then a valid generated signatures will be accepted by the verification algorithm, except with a negligible probability.*

Due to space limitation, we defer the detailed proof of this theorem to the full version. Below, we focus on the security of our QDS_2 construction.

Theorem 5.2 *Suppose that the trapdoor commitment scheme* Eqv-TCOM *is hiding, biding, additively homomorphic, and has a secure equivocation trapdoor, uniform keys and uniform commitment. Particularly, the output of* $\mathsf{Eqv\text{-}TCommit}_{\mathsf{tck}}(\mathsf{td})$ *has sufficient bit-length ϑ. And suppose there exists* QPRF *that can be programmable and invertible simultaneously under* $\mathsf{DSPR}_{\bar{q},\bar{R},\chi}$ *assumption. For any quantum polynomial-time adversary $\mathcal{A}$ that initiates a single key generation protocol by querying* $\mathcal{O}_{\mathsf{Gen}}(\cdot,\cdot)$*, initiates Q_s signature generation protocols by querying* $\mathcal{O}_{\mathsf{Sign}_1}(\cdot,\cdot), \mathcal{O}_{\mathsf{Sign}_2}(\cdot,\cdot)$ *with* sid*, and makes Q_h quantum superpositions queries to random oracle* $\mathsf{H}_0, \mathsf{H}_1, \mathsf{H}'_1, \mathsf{H}_2, \mathsf{H}_3, \mathsf{H}_4, \mathsf{H}_5$*, the protocol* QDS_2 *of Figs. 7,*

8, 9 is QDS-UF-CMA *secure under* $\mathsf{MSIS}_{q,k,k+\ell+1,\beta}$ *and* $\mathsf{MLWE}_{q,\ell,k,\eta}$ *assumptions in the* QROM*, where* $\beta = 2\sqrt{B_n^2 + \kappa}$*. Concretely, using other parameters specified in Table 2, the advantage of* $\mathcal{A}$ *is bounded as follows.*

$$\begin{aligned}\mathbf{Adv}^{\mathsf{UF\text{-}CMA}}_{\mathsf{QDS}_2}(\mathcal{A}) \le\ & 2\varepsilon_{\mathsf{Inj\text{-}QPRF}} + 5\varepsilon_{\mathsf{QPRF}} + e(Q_h + Q_s + 1)\Big[(Q_h + Q_s)\cdot t\cdot \varepsilon_{\mathsf{td}} \\ & + 2(Q_h + Q_s)\cdot \varepsilon_{\mathsf{QPRF}} + \frac{3Q_s}{2}\sqrt{Q_s + Q_h}2^{\frac{-t\cdot\vartheta}{2}} + 2\varepsilon_{\mathsf{QPRF}} + t\cdot Q_s\cdot(m-1) \\ & \cdot \mathbf{Adv}_{\mathsf{MLWE}_{q,(\ell+k),m',\chi}} + t\cdot Q_s\cdot \varepsilon_{\mathsf{Rej}} + \frac{3}{2}\sqrt{Q_h}(2^{-\frac{l_1^*}{2}} + 2^{-\frac{kN\log q}{2}}) \\ & + 4(\varepsilon_{\mathsf{QPRF}} + \varepsilon_{\mathsf{Inj\text{-}QPRF}}) + \mathbf{Adv}_{\mathsf{MLWE}_{q,\ell,k,\eta}} + 2(Q_h+1)2^{-(t\log m)/2} + \varepsilon_{bind} \\ & + \mathbf{Adv}_{\mathsf{MSIS}_{q,k,k+\ell+1,\beta}}\Big]\end{aligned}$$

Here, $\varepsilon_{\mathsf{QPRF}}$ *denotes the advantage for an efficient quantum adversary distinguishing* QROM *and* QPRF *in Construction 4.1, where* $\varepsilon_{\mathsf{QPRF}} = \mathbf{Adv}_{\mathsf{RLWE}_{\bar{q},1,\bar{m},\chi}}$ *with* $\chi = D_{\bar{R},\bar{r}}$*.* $\varepsilon_{\mathsf{Inj\text{-}QPRF}}$ *denotes the advantage distinguishing injective* QPRF *in Construction 4.5 from the direct Construction 4.1,where* $\varepsilon_{\mathsf{Inj\text{-}QPRF}} = \mathbf{Adv}_{\mathsf{RLWE}_{\bar{q},1,1,S_1}} + \mathsf{DSPR}_{\bar{q},\bar{R},\chi}$*.* $\varepsilon_{\mathsf{td}}$ *is the statistical distances of true commitment key for* Eqv-TCOM *and the uniform.* $\varepsilon_{\mathsf{Rej}}$ *is the statistical distances of the output distribution of rejection sampling algorithm and the ideal distribution.* ε_{bind} *are the advantages of breaking* Eqv-TCOM*, for any efficient quantum adversary. Moreover, all these values are negligible according to the related instantiations in this paper.*

Due to space limitation, we defer the proof of this theorem to the full version.

6 Two Round Multi-signature from Lattices in the QROM

In this section we describe our two-round multi-signature QMS_2 in the key-verification model. We remark that with the help of the multi-proof straight-line extractable NIZKPoK in the key generation stage, our QMS_2 can be proven secure relying on essentially the same idea as QDS_2. And the main difference from n-out-of-n signature is that, the protocol does not require interactive key generation any more, and instead for each signing execution a party receives a set of public keys Ł together with a message to be signed. Particularly, our construction of two-round multi-signature $\mathsf{QMS}_2 = (\mathsf{Setup}, \mathsf{Gen}, \mathsf{KVer}, \mathsf{KAgg}, \mathsf{Sign}, \mathsf{Ver})$ is formally specified in Figs. 10, 11, 12. As the number of participants may change for each signing attempt, in this section we define n to be the maximum number of signers allowed in a single execution of signing protocol. Without loss of generality, we assume that each signer assign the index n to itself, and consider other signers' indices as $1, ..., (n'-1)$, where $n' = |Ł| \le n$. Due to space limitation, we defer the formal definition of the multi-proof straight-line extractable NIZKPoK systems to full version, which can be instantiated in the QROM as in [15,28].

Algorithm $\mathsf{QMS}_2.\mathsf{Gen}(\mathsf{pp})$

Given as inputs the public matrix $\overline{\mathbf{A}} := [\mathbf{A}|\mathbf{I}] \in R_q^{k\times(\ell+k)}$ together with the common reference string CRS of the used multi-proof NIZKPoK system Π, the Algorithm conducts the following steps:

1. Sample a secret key shares $\boldsymbol{s}_n \xleftarrow{\$} S_\eta^{\ell+k}$ and compute a public key share $\boldsymbol{t}_n := \overline{\mathbf{A}}\boldsymbol{s}_n$;
2. Run $\Pi.\mathsf{Prove}(\mathsf{CRS}, \overline{\mathbf{A}}, \boldsymbol{t}_n, \boldsymbol{s}_n)$ to output a NIZKPoK proof π_n as an appendix of public key.
3. Output $(\mathsf{sk}_n, \mathsf{pk}_n) = (\boldsymbol{s}_n, (\boldsymbol{t}_n, \pi_n))$ as local output.

Algorithm $\mathsf{QMS}_2.\mathsf{KVer}(\mathsf{pp}, \mathsf{pk}_n)$

Given $\mathsf{pp}, \mathsf{pk}_n$ as input, the algorithm conducts the following steps:

1. Parse $\mathsf{pk}_n := (\boldsymbol{t}_n, \pi_n)$, where $\boldsymbol{t}_n \in R_q^k$ and π_n is a proof of NIZKPoK system Π;
2. Runs $\Pi.\mathsf{Verify}(\mathsf{CRS}, \overline{\mathbf{A}}, \boldsymbol{t}_n, \pi_n)$ to output 1 if π_n is a valid proof; Otherwise output 0.

Algorithm $\mathsf{QMS}_2.\mathsf{KAgg}(\mathsf{pp}, \text{Ł})$

Given pp and the public key set $\text{Ł} := \{\mathsf{pk}_1, \ldots, \mathsf{pk}_{(n'-1)}, \mathsf{pk}_n\}$ as input, the algorithm conducts the following steps:

1. Parse each public key $\mathsf{pk}_j \in \text{Ł}$ as $\mathsf{pk}_j := (\boldsymbol{t}_j, \pi_j)$, and run $\mathsf{QMS}_2.\mathsf{KVer}(\mathsf{pp}, \mathsf{pk}_j)$. If all public keys pass the key verification algorithm $\mathsf{QMS}_2.\mathsf{KVer}(\cdot,\cdot)$, then conduct the following steps; Otherwise, abort.
2. For $j \in [n'-1]$, compute $a_i := \mathsf{H}_{\mathsf{agg}}(\text{Ł}, \boldsymbol{t}_j)$, and compute $a_n := \mathsf{H}_{\mathsf{agg}}(\text{Ł}, \boldsymbol{t}_n)$;
3. Compute and return $\tilde{\boldsymbol{t}} = \sum_{j=1}^{n'-1} a_j \cdot \boldsymbol{t}_j + a_n \cdot \boldsymbol{t}_n$.

Fig. 10. Gen, KVer, KAgg algorithms of Our Two-Round Multi-Signature Scheme

6.1 Construction

As the construction and proof of QMS_2 is almost same to these of QDS_2, below we highlight the differences in red color.

Given a multi-proof straight-line extractable NIZKPoK system $\Pi = (\Pi.\mathsf{Setup}, \Pi.\mathsf{Prove}, \Pi.\mathsf{Verify}))$ for $\mathcal{L}_{B,q}$, we make a brief overview of our QMS_2 scheme as follows.

- The Setup works just like the one for QDS_2, but it additionally outputs a matrix $\overline{\mathbf{A}} = [\mathbf{A}|\mathbf{I}] \in R_q^{k\times(\ell+k)}$ as part of public parameters, so we assume that $\overline{\mathbf{A}}$ is generated by a trusted third party. And the input lengths of QROM is changed and we show these as follows.
  - $l_0^* = \log(m \cdot t \cdot |\mathcal{M}|) + k \cdot N \cdot \log q \cdot (n+1) + \log|\mathsf{Eqv}\text{-}S_{\mathsf{ck}}| + \log|\mathsf{Inv}\text{-}S_{\mathsf{ck}}|$
  - $l_3^* = l_4^* = \log|\mathcal{M}| + n \cdot k \cdot N \cdot \log q$
  - $l_5^* = nk \cdot N \log q + \log|\mathcal{M}| + t \log|\mathsf{Eqv}\text{-}S_{\mathsf{com}}| + mt \log(2N\kappa|\mathsf{Inv}\text{-}S_{\mathsf{com}}|)$

  Besides, the Setup algorithm runs $\Pi.\mathsf{Setup}$ to output the common string reference CRS.
- The Gen, KVer, KAgg algorithms are formally specified in Fig. 10.
- The signing protocol Sign and verification Ver are described in Figs. 12 and 11. The main differences from QDS_2.Sign and QDS_2.Ver is that at the beginning stages of QDS_2.Sign and QDS_2.Ver, each participant need to first verify the well-formedness of other participant's public keys.

6.2 Correctness and Security

As the correctness of QMS2 is quite similar to that of Theorem 5.1, here we omit it for simplicity. Below, we just focus on the security. Similar to QDS_2 in Sect. 5, we show that our QMS_2 is UF-CMA secure.

Theorem 6.1 *Suppose that the trapdoor commitment scheme* $\mathsf{Eqv\text{-}TCOM}$ *is hiding, biding, additively homomorphic, and has a secure equivocation trapdoor, uniform keys and uniform commitment. Particularly, the output of* $\mathsf{Eqv\text{-}TCommit}_{\mathsf{tck}}(\mathsf{td})$ *has sufficient bit-length* ϑ. *Suppose* $\Pi = (\Pi.\mathsf{Setup}, \Pi.\mathsf{Prove}, \Pi.\mathsf{Verify}))$ *is a multi-proof straight-line extractable* NIZKPoK *system for* $\mathcal{L}_{B,q}$, *just as defined in the full version of this paper. And suppose there exists* QPRF *that can be programmable and invertible simultaneously. For any quantum polynomial-time adversary* $\mathcal{A}$ *that initiates a single key generation protocol by querying* $\mathcal{O}_n^{\mathsf{QMS}_2}$ *with* $sid = 0$, *initiates* Q_s *signature generation protocols by querying* $\mathcal{O}_n^{\mathsf{QMS}_2}$ *with* $sid \neq 0$, *and makes* Q_h *quantum superpositions queries to random oracle* $\mathsf{H}_0, \mathsf{H}_3, \mathsf{H}_4, \mathsf{H}_5$, *the protocol* QMS_2 *of Figs. 10, 12, 11 is* QMS-SUF-CMA *secure under* $\mathsf{MSIS}_{q,k,k+\ell+1,\beta}$ *and* $\mathsf{MLWE}_{q,\ell,k,\eta}$ *assumptions in the* QROM, *where* $\beta = \sqrt{(2B_n)^2 + 4\kappa^2 + \eta^2(4\kappa^2 \cdot (\ell + k))}$. *Concretely, using other parameters specified in Table 2, the advantage of* $\mathcal{A}$ *is bounded as follows.*

Protocol $\mathsf{QMS}_2.\mathsf{Ver}(\{\mathsf{com}_i\}_{i\in[t]}, \{\widetilde{\mathsf{com}}_{i,j}\}_{i\in[t],j\in[m]}, \{\boldsymbol{z}_i\}_{i\in[t]}, \{\boldsymbol{r}_i\}_{i\in[t]}, \{\boldsymbol{r}'_i\}_{i\in[t]}), \mu, \mathrm{Ł})$

Upon receive a message μ, signature $\widehat{\mathsf{Sig}} = (\{\mathsf{com}_i\}_{i\in[t]}, \{\widetilde{\mathsf{com}}_{i,j}\}_{i\in[t],j\in[m]}, \{\boldsymbol{z}_i\}_{i\in[t]}, \{\boldsymbol{r}_i\}_{i\in[t]}, \{\boldsymbol{r}'_i\}_{i\in[t]})$, and a set of public keys Ł, if $|\mathrm{Ł}| > n$ then reject the signature. Otherwise work as follows:

1. Check public key in Ł, i.e., run Π.Verify algorithm. If there exist certain $(\boldsymbol{t}_j, \pi_j) \in \mathrm{Ł}$ such that $\Pi.\mathsf{Verify}(\mathsf{CRS}, \bar{\mathbf{A}}, \boldsymbol{t}_j, \pi_j) = 0$, then send out $\perp$. Otherwise, conduct the following steps.
2. Run the algorithm to $\mathsf{QMS}_2.\mathsf{KAgg}(\mathsf{pp}, \mathrm{Ł})$ to generate the aggregated key $\mathsf{apk} := \tilde{\boldsymbol{t}}$.
3. Generate commitment keys $\mathsf{ck} \leftarrow \mathsf{H}_3(\mu, \mathrm{Ł})$ and $\mathbf{A}_{\mathsf{Inv}} \leftarrow \mathsf{H}_4(\mu, \mathrm{Ł})$, Compute challenges $c_{i,j} \leftarrow \mathsf{H}_0(i, j, \mu, \mathsf{ck}, \mathbf{A}_{\mathsf{Inv}}, \mathrm{Ł})$ Then Compute $J_1||...||J_t \leftarrow \mathsf{H}_5(\mathrm{Ł}, \mu, \{\mathsf{com}_i\}_{i\in[t]}, \{c_{i,j,u}\}_{i\in[t],j\in[m],u\in[n']}, \{\widetilde{\mathsf{com}}_{i,j}\}_{i\in[t],j\in[m]})$, where $n' = |\mathrm{Ł}|$.
4. Perform the checks as follows:
   (a) for $i = 1$ to t do:
      Check that $c_{i,1}, ..., c_{i,m}$ pairwise distinct.
   (b) for $i = 1$ to t do:
      check that $||z_i|| \leq B_n$.
   (c) for $i = 1$ to t do:
      Reconstruct $\boldsymbol{w}_i := \overline{\mathbf{A}}\boldsymbol{z}_i - c_{i,J_i}\tilde{t}$, check $\mathsf{Eqv\text{-}Open}_{\mathsf{ck}}(\mathsf{com}_i, r_i, \boldsymbol{w}_i) = 1$.
   (d) for $i = 1$ to t do:
      Check $\widetilde{\mathsf{com}}_{i,J_i} = \mathbf{A}_{\mathsf{Inv}} \cdot \boldsymbol{z}_i + \boldsymbol{r}'_i$.

If all checks succeed then return 1, otherwise, return 0.

Fig. 11. Ver Algorithm of Our Two-Round Multi-Signature Scheme

Protocol $\mathsf{QMS}_2.\mathsf{Sign}(sid, \mathsf{sk}_n, \mathsf{pk}_n, \mu, \text{Ł})$

The protocol is parameterized by public parameters described in Table 2 and matrix $\overline{\mathbf{A}}$, and relies on the random oracles $\mathsf{H}_0 : \{0,1\}^{l_0^*} \to C$, $\mathsf{H}_3 : \{0,1\}^{l_3^*} \to \mathsf{Eqv}\text{-}S_{\mathsf{ck}}$, $\mathsf{H}_4 : \{0,1\}^{l_4^*} \to \mathsf{Inv}\text{-}S_{\mathsf{ck}}$ and $\mathsf{H}_5 : \{0,1\}^{l_5^*} \to \{0,1\}^{l_5}$. The protocol assumes that $\mathsf{QMS}_2.\mathsf{Gen}(\mathsf{pp})$ has been previously invokes. If a party halts with $\perp$ at any point, then all $\mathsf{Sign}(sid, \mathsf{sk}_n, \mathsf{pk}_n, \mu, \text{Ł})$ executions are aborted.

Inputs

1. P_n receives a unique sessions ID sid, $\mathsf{sk}_n = \boldsymbol{s}_n$, $\mathsf{pk} = \boldsymbol{t}_n$ and message $\mu \in M$ as input and a list of public keys Ł as input. If $n' := |\text{Ł}| > n$ or $\boldsymbol{t}_n \notin \text{Ł}$ or $\Pi.\mathsf{Verify}(\mathsf{CRS}, \bar{\mathbf{A}}, \boldsymbol{t}_j, \pi_j) = 0$ for certain $(\boldsymbol{t}_j, \pi_j) \in \text{Ł}$, then send out $\perp$. Otherwise parse Ł as $\{\boldsymbol{t}_1, \ldots \boldsymbol{t}_{n'-1}, \boldsymbol{t}_n\}$.
2. P_n runs the algorithm to $\mathsf{QMS}_2.\mathsf{KAgg}(\mathsf{pp}, \text{Ł})$ to generate the aggregated key $\mathsf{apk} := \tilde{\boldsymbol{t}}$.
3. P_n verifies that sid has not been used before (if it has been, the protocol is not executed).
4. P_n locally computes a per-message commitment key $\mathsf{ck} \leftarrow \mathsf{H}_3(\mu, \text{Ł})$, $\mathbf{A}_{\mathsf{Inv}} \leftarrow \mathsf{H}_4(\mu, \mathsf{pk})$.

Signature Generation P_n works as follows:

1. $\mathsf{Sign}_1(\mathsf{pp}, \mathsf{sid}, \mathsf{sk}_n, \mathsf{pk}_n, \mu, \text{Ł})$: Upon receiving message μ and public key set Ł, conduct the first round interaction as follows.
   (a) Compute the aggerate coefficient $a_n := \mathsf{H}_{\mathsf{agg}}(\text{Ł}, \boldsymbol{t}_n)$.
   (b) for $i = 1$ to t; conduct as follows:
      i. Sample $\boldsymbol{y}_i^{(n)} \leftarrow D_\sigma^{\ell+k}$ and compute $\boldsymbol{w}_i^{(n)} := \overline{\mathbf{A}}\boldsymbol{y}_i^{(n)}$.
      ii. for $j = 1$ to m, conduct as follows:
         A. Derive challenges $c_{i,j} \leftarrow \mathsf{H}_0(i, j, \mu, \mathsf{ck}, \mathbf{A}_{\mathsf{Inv}}, \text{Ł})$.
         B. Computes signature shares $\boldsymbol{z}_{i,j}^{(n)} = a_n c_{i,j} \boldsymbol{s}_n + \boldsymbol{y}_i^{(n)}$.
         C. Run the rejection sampling $\mathsf{Rej}(\boldsymbol{z}_{i,j}^{(n)}, a_n c_{i,j} \boldsymbol{s}_n, \sigma) \to \{0,1\}$.
      iii. If the above rejection sampling algorithm outputs 0 for certain $j \in [m]$, then send out $\perp$, and go to the step i.
   (c) Compute $\widetilde{\mathsf{com}}_{i,j}^{(n)} \leftarrow \mathsf{Inv}\text{-}\mathsf{H}(\boldsymbol{z}_{i,j}^{(n)}) = \mathbf{A}_{\mathsf{Inv}} \cdot \boldsymbol{z}_{i,j}^{(n)} + \boldsymbol{r}_{i,j}^{\prime(n)}$ where $\boldsymbol{r}_{i,j}^{\prime(n)} \leftarrow D_\sigma^{m'}$ for all $(i,j) \in [t] \times [m]$.
   (d) Compute $\mathsf{com}_i^{(n)} \leftarrow \mathsf{Eqv}\text{-}\mathsf{Commit}_{\mathsf{ck}}(\boldsymbol{w}_i^{(n)}, r_i^{(n)})$ with $r_i^{(n)} \xleftarrow{\$} \mathsf{Eqv}\text{-}S_r$.
   (e) Set $\mathsf{st}_n := (sk_n, \{\boldsymbol{r}_{i,j}^{\prime(n)}, r_i^{(n)}, \boldsymbol{z}_{i,j}^{(n)}\}_{i\in[t],j\in[m]})$.
   (f) Send out $\mathsf{msg}_n := (\{\mathsf{com}_i^{(n)}\}_{i\in[t]}, \{\widetilde{\mathsf{com}}_{i,j}^{(n)}\}_{i\in[t],j\in[m]})$.
2. $\mathsf{Sign}_2(\mathsf{sid}, \mathsf{st}_1, \{\mathsf{msg}_2, \ldots, \mathsf{msg}_n\})$: Upon receiving $\mathsf{msg}_u := (\{\mathsf{com}_i^{(u)}\}_{i\in[t]}, \{\widetilde{\mathsf{com}}_{i,j}^{(n)}\}_{i\in[t],j\in[m]})$ for all $u \in [n'-1]$, conduct the second round interaction as follows.
   (a) For each $u \in [n'-1]$, derive per-user challenges $c_{i,j} \leftarrow \mathsf{H}_0(i, j, \mu, \mathsf{ck}, \mathsf{ck}', \text{Ł})$ where $i \in [t], j \in [m]$. Set $\mathsf{com}_i := \sum_{u\in[n'-1]} \mathsf{com}_i^{(u)} + \mathsf{com}_i^{(n)}$ and $\widetilde{\mathsf{com}}_{i,j} := \sum_{u\in[n'-1]} \widetilde{\mathsf{com}}_{i,j}^{(u)} + \widetilde{\mathsf{com}}_{i,j}^{(n)}$ for all $i \in [t], j \in [m]$.
   (b) Get challenges $J_1||\ldots||J_t \leftarrow \mathsf{H}_5(\text{Ł}, \mu, \{\mathsf{com}_i\}_{i\in[t]}, \{c_{i,j}\}_{i\in[t],j\in[m]}, \{\widetilde{\mathsf{com}}_{i,j}\}_{i\in[t],j\in[m]})$.
   (c) Send out $\mathsf{Sig}_n := (\{\mathsf{com}_i^{(n)}\}_{i\in[t]}, \{\widetilde{\mathsf{com}}_{i,j}^{(n)}\}_{i\in[t],j\in[m]}, \{\boldsymbol{z}_{i,J_i}^{(n)}\}_{i\in[t]}, \{r_i^{(n)}\}_{i\in[t]}, \{\boldsymbol{r}_{i,J_i}^{\prime(n)}\}_{i\in[t]})$.
3. $\mathsf{SAgg}(\mathsf{sid}, \{\mathsf{Sig}_1, \ldots, \mathsf{Sig}_n\})$: Upon receiving $\mathsf{Sig}_u := (\mathsf{com}_i^{(u)}, \widetilde{\mathsf{com}}_{i,j}^{(u)}, \{\boldsymbol{z}_{i,J_i}^{(u)}\}_{i\in[t]}, \{r_i^{(u)}\}_{i\in[t]}, \{\boldsymbol{r}_{i,J_i}^{\prime(u)}\}_{i\in[t]})$ for all $u \in [n'-1]$, compute the combined signature as follows:
   (a) Set $\mathsf{com}_i := \sum_{u\in[n]} \mathsf{com}_i^{(u)}$ and $\widetilde{\mathsf{com}}_{i,j} := \sum_{u\in[n]} \widetilde{\mathsf{com}}_{i,j}^{(u)}$ for all $i \in [t], j \in [m]$.
   (b) Compute $\boldsymbol{z}_{i,J_i} := \sum_{u\in[n'-1]} \boldsymbol{z}_{i,J_i}^{(u)} + \boldsymbol{z}_{i,J_i}^{(n)}$, $r_i := \sum_{u\in[n'-1]} r_i^{(u)} + r_i^{(n)}$ and $r'_{i,J_i} := \sum_{u\in[n'-1]} r_{i,J_i}^{\prime(u)} + r_{i,J_i}^{\prime(n)}$ for all $i \in [t]$.
   (b) If the protocol does not abort, P_n obtains a signature: $\widehat{\mathsf{Sig}} := (\{\mathsf{com}_i\}_{i\in[t]}, \{\widetilde{\mathsf{com}}_{i,j}\}_{i\in[t],j\in[m]}, \{\boldsymbol{z}_{i,J_i}\}_{i\in[t]}, \{r_i\}_{i\in[t]}, \{r'_{i,J_i}\}_{i\in[t]})$ as local output.

Fig. 12. Sign Protocol of Our Two-Round Multi-Signature Scheme

$$\begin{aligned}\mathbf{Adv}_{\mathsf{QMS}_2}^{\mathsf{UF\text{-}CMA}}(\mathcal{A}) \leq\, & 2\varepsilon_{\mathsf{Inj\text{-}QPRF}} + 5\varepsilon_{\mathsf{QPRF}} + e(Q_h + Q_s + 1)\Big[(Q_h + Q_s) \cdot t \cdot \varepsilon_{\mathsf{td}} \\ & + 2(Q_h + Q_s) \cdot \varepsilon_{\mathsf{QPRF}} + \frac{3Q_s}{2}\sqrt{Q_s + Q_h}2^{\frac{-t\cdot\vartheta}{2}} + 2\varepsilon_{\mathsf{QPRF}} + t \cdot Q_s \cdot (m-1) \\ & \cdot \mathbf{Adv}_{\mathsf{MLWE}_{q,(\ell+k),m',\chi}} + t \cdot Q_s \cdot (\varepsilon_{\mathsf{Rej}} + \varepsilon_{\mathsf{td}}) + \frac{3}{2}\sqrt{Q_h}(2^{-\frac{l_1^*}{2}} + 2^{-\frac{kN\log q}{2}}) \\ & + 4(\varepsilon_{\mathsf{QPRF}} + \varepsilon_{\mathsf{Inj\text{-}QPRF}}) + \mathbf{Adv}_{\mathsf{MLWE}_{q,\ell,k,\eta}} + 2(Q_h + 1)2^{-(t\log m)/2} + \varepsilon_{bind} \\ & + \mathbf{Adv}_{\mathsf{MSIS}_{q,k,k+\ell+1,\beta}}\Big]\end{aligned}$$

Due to space limit, we defer the analysis to the full version.

Acknowledgements. We would like to thank the anonymous reviewers of PKC 2026 for their insightful advices. Qiqi Lai is supported by the National Natural Science Foundation of China (62172266, 62436004, 62372317), the Key Research and Development Program of Shaanxi under Grant 2024GXZDCYL- 01-15. Feng-Hao Liu is supported by NSF Career Award CNS-2402031. Any opinions, findings, and conclusions or recommendations expressed in this material are those of the author(s) and do not necessarily reflect the views of the sponsors.

References

1. Agrawal, S., Stehlé, D., Yadav, A.: Round-optimal lattice-based threshold signatures, revisited. In: Bojanczyk, M., Merelli, E., Woodruff, D.P. (eds.) ICALP 2022. LIPIcs, vol. 229, pp. 8:1–8:20. Schloss Dagstuhl (2022)
2. Alwen, J., Krenn, S., Pietrzak, K., Wichs, D.: Learning with rounding, revisited. In: Canetti, R., Garay, J.A. (eds.) CRYPTO 2013, Part I. LNCS, vol. 8042, pp. 57–74. Springer, Heidelberg (2013). https://doi.org/10.1007/978-3-642-40041-4_4
3. Banerjee, A., Peikert, C., Rosen, A.: Pseudorandom functions and lattices. In: Pointcheval, D., Johansson, T. (eds.) EUROCRYPT 2012. LNCS, vol. 7237, pp. 719–737. Springer, Heidelberg (2012). https://doi.org/10.1007/978-3-642-29011-4_42
4. Boneh, D., Dagdelen, Ö., Fischlin, M., Lehmann, A., Schaffner, C., Zhandry, M.: Random oracles in a quantum world. In: Lee, D.H., Wang, X. (eds.) ASIACRYPT 2011. LNCS, vol. 7073, pp. 41–69. Springer, Heidelberg (2011). https://doi.org/10.1007/978-3-642-25385-0_3
5. Boneh, D., et al.: Threshold cryptosystems from threshold fully homomorphic encryption. In: Shacham, H., Boldyreva, A. (eds.) CRYPTO 2018. LNCS, vol. 10991, pp. 565–596. Springer, Cham (2018). https://doi.org/10.1007/978-3-319-96884-1_19
6. Boneh, D., Kim, S., Wu, D.J.: Constrained keys for invertible pseudorandom functions. In: Kalai, Y., Reyzin, L. (eds.) TCC 2017. LNCS, vol. 10677, pp. 237–263. Springer, Cham (2017). https://doi.org/10.1007/978-3-319-70500-2_9
7. Boschini, C., Kaviani, D., Lai, R.W.F., Malavolta, G., Takahashi, A., Tibouchi, M.: Ringtail: practical two-round threshold signatures from learning with errors. Cryptology ePrint Archive, Report 2024/1113 (2024)
8. Boschini, C., Takahashi, A., Tibouchi, M.: MuSig-L: lattice-based multi-signature with single-round online phase. In: Dodis, Y., Shrimpton, T. (eds.) CRYPTO 2022, Part II. LNCS, vol. 13508, pp. 276–305. Springer, Cham (2022). https://doi.org/10.1007/978-3-031-15979-4_10
9. Chairattana-Apirom, R., Tessaro, S., Zhu, C.: Partially non-interactive two-round lattice-based threshold signatures. Cryptology ePrint Archive, Report 2024/467 (2024)
10. Chen, Y.: DualMS: efficient lattice-based two-round multi-signature with trapdoor-free simulation. In: Handschuh, H., Lysyanskaya, A. (eds.) CRYPTO 2023, Part V. LNCS, vol. 14085, pp. 716–747. Springer, Cham (2023). https://doi.org/10.1007/978-3-031-38554-4_23

11. Chung, K.-M., Fehr, S., Huang, Y.-H., Liao, T.-N.: On the compressed-oracle technique, and post-quantum security of proofs of sequential work. In: Canteaut, A., Standaert, F.-X. (eds.) EUROCRYPT 2021, Part II. LNCS, vol. 12697, pp. 598–629. Springer, Cham (2021). https://doi.org/10.1007/978-3-030-77886-6_21
12. Czajkowski, J., Majenz, C., Schaffner, C., Zur, S.: Quantum lazy sampling and game-playing proofs for quantum indifferentiability. Cryptology ePrint Archive, Report 2019/428 (2019)
13. Damgård, I., Orlandi, C., Takahashi, A., Tibouchi, M.: Two-round n-out-of-n and multi-signatures and trapdoor commitment from lattices. J. Cryptol. **35**(2), 14 (2022)
14. del Pino, R., Espitau, T., Niot, G., Prest, T.: Simple and efficient lattice threshold signatures with identifiable aborts. Cryptology ePrint Archive, Report 2025/871 (2025)
15. del Pino, R., Katsumata, S.: A new framework for more efficient round-optimal lattice-based (partially) blind signature via trapdoor sampling. In: Dodis, Y., Shrimpton, T. (eds.) CRYPTO 2022, Part II. LNCS, vol. 13508, pp. 306–336. Springer, Cham (2022). https://doi.org/10.1007/978-3-031-15979-4_11
16. Del Pino, R., Katsumata, S., Maller, M., Mouhartem, F., Prest, T., Saarinen, M.-J.O.: Threshold raccoon: practical threshold signatures from standard lattice assumptions. In: Joye, M., Leander, G. (eds.) EUROCRYPT 2024, Part II. LNCS, vol. 14652, pp. 219–248. Springer, Cham (2024). https://doi.org/10.1007/978-3-031-58723-8_8
17. del Pino, R., Prest, T., Rossi, M., Saarinen, M.O.: High-order masking of lattice signatures in quasilinear time. In: 44th IEEE Symposium on Security and Privacy, SP 2023, San Francisco, CA, USA, 21–25 May 2023, pp. 1168–1185. IEEE (2023)
18. Don, J., Fehr, S., Majenz, C., Schaffner, C.: Efficient NIZKs and signatures from commit-and-open protocols in the QROM. In: Dodis, Y., Shrimpton, T. (eds.) CRYPTO 2022, Part II. LNCS, vol. 13508, pp. 729–757. Springer, Cham (2022). https://doi.org/10.1007/978-3-031-15979-4_25
19. Don, J., Fehr, S., Majenz, C., Schaffner, C.: Online-extractability in the quantum random-oracle model. In: Dunkelman, O., Dziembowski, S. (eds.) EUROCRYPT 2022, Part III. LNCS, vol. 13277, pp. 677–706. Springer, Cham (2022). https://doi.org/10.1007/978-3-031-07082-2_24
20. Drijvers, M., et al.: On the security of two-round multi-signatures. In: 2019 IEEE Symposium on Security and Privacy, pp. 1084–1101. IEEE Computer Society Press (2019)
21. Ducas, L., Kiltz, E., Lepoint, T., Lyubashevsky, V., Schwabe, P., Seiler, G., Stehlé, D.: CRYSTALS-Dilithium: a lattice-based digital signature scheme. IACR TCHES **2018**(1), 238–268 (2018)
22. Espitau, T., Katsumata, S., Takemure, K.: Two-round threshold signature from algebraic one-more learning with errors. In: Reyzin, L., Stebila, D. (eds.) CRYPTO 2024, Part VII. LNCS, vol. 14926, pp. 387–424. Springer, Cham (2024). https://doi.org/10.1007/s00145-025-09549-2
23. Espitau, T., Niot, G., Prest, T.: Flood and submerse: distributed key generation and robust threshold signature from lattices. In: Reyzin, L., Stebila, D. (eds.) CRYPTO 2024, Part VII. LNCS, vol. 14926, pp. 425–458. Springer, Cham (2024). https://doi.org/10.1007/978-3-031-68394-7_14
24. Fukumitsu, M., Hasegawa, S.: A lattice-based provably secure multisignature scheme in quantum random oracle model. In: Nguyen, K., Wu, W., Lam, K.Y., Wang, H. (eds.) ProvSec 2020. LNCS, vol. 12505, pp. 45–64. Springer, Cham (2020). https://doi.org/10.1007/978-3-030-62576-4_3

25. Grilo, A.B., Hövelmanns, K., Hülsing, A., Majenz, C.: Tight adaptive reprogramming in the QROM. In: Tibouchi, M., Wang, H. (eds.) ASIACRYPT 2021. LNCS, vol. 13090, pp. 637–667. Springer, Cham (2021). https://doi.org/10.1007/978-3-030-92062-3_22
26. Gür, K.D., Katz, J., Silde, T.: Two-round threshold lattice-based signatures from threshold homomorphic encryption. In: Saarinen, M.-J., Smith-Tone, D. (eds.) PQCrypto 2024, Part II. LNCS, vol. 14772, pp. 266–300. Springer, Cham (2024). https://doi.org/10.1007/978-3-031-62746-0_12
27. Hoover, A., Patel, S., Persiano, G., Yeo, K.: Plinko: single-server PIR with efficient updates via invertible PRFs. Cryptology ePrint Archive, Report 2024/318 (2024)
28. Katsumata, S.: A new simple technique to bootstrap various lattice zero-knowledge proofs to QROM secure NIZKs. In: Malkin, T., Peikert, C. (eds.) CRYPTO 2021, Part II. LNCS, vol. 12826, pp. 580–610. Springer, Cham (2021). https://doi.org/10.1007/978-3-030-84245-1_20
29. Katsumata, S., Reichle, M., Takemure, K.: Adaptively secure 5 round threshold signatures from MLWE/MSIS and DL with rewinding. In: Reyzin, L., Stebila, D. (eds.) CRYPTO 2024, Part VII. LNCS, vol. 14926, pp. 459–491. Springer, Cham (2024). https://doi.org/10.1007/978-3-031-68394-7_15
30. Kiltz, E., Lyubashevsky, V., Schaffner, C.: A concrete treatment of Fiat-Shamir signatures in the quantum random-oracle model. In: Nielsen, J.B., Rijmen, V. (eds.) EUROCRYPT 2018. LNCS, vol. 10822, pp. 552–586. Springer, Cham (2018). https://doi.org/10.1007/978-3-319-78372-7_18
31. Lai, R.W.F., Malavolta, G., Spooner, N.: Quantum rewinding for many-round protocols. In: Kiltz, E., Vaikuntanathan, V. (eds.) TCC 2022, Part I. LNCS, vol. 13747, pp. 80–109. Springer, Cham (2022). https://doi.org/10.1007/978-3-031-22318-1_4
32. Liu, Q., Zhandry, M.: Revisiting post-quantum Fiat-Shamir. In: Boldyreva, A., Micciancio, D. (eds.) CRYPTO 2019. LNCS, vol. 11693, pp. 326–355. Springer, Cham (2019). https://doi.org/10.1007/978-3-030-26951-7_12
33. Lombardi, A., Ma, F., Spooner, N.: Post-quantum zero knowledge, revisited or: how to do quantum rewinding undetectably. In: 63rd FOCS, pp. 851–859. IEEE Computer Society Press (2022)
34. López-Alt, A., Tromer, E., Vaikuntanathan, V.: On-the-fly multiparty computation on the cloud via multikey fully homomorphic encryption. In: Karloff, H.J., Pitassi, T. (eds.) 44th ACM STOC, pp. 1219–1234. ACM Press (2012)
35. Lyubashevsky, V.: Lattice signatures without trapdoors. In: Pointcheval, D., Johansson, T. (eds.) EUROCRYPT 2012. LNCS, vol. 7237, pp. 738–755. Springer, Heidelberg (2012). https://doi.org/10.1007/978-3-642-29011-4_43
36. Lyubashevsky, V., Seiler, G.: Short, invertible elements in partially splitting cyclotomic rings and applications to lattice-based zero-knowledge proofs. In: Nielsen, J.B., Rijmen, V. (eds.) EUROCRYPT 2018. LNCS, vol. 10820, pp. 204–224. Springer, Cham (2018). https://doi.org/10.1007/978-3-319-78381-9_8
37. Micciancio, D., Peikert, C.: Trapdoors for lattices: simpler, tighter, faster, smaller. In: Pointcheval, D., Johansson, T. (eds.) EUROCRYPT 2012. LNCS, vol. 7237, pp. 700–718. Springer, Heidelberg (2012). https://doi.org/10.1007/978-3-642-29011-4_41
38. Pan, J., Wagner, B.: Chopsticks: fork-free two-round multi-signatures from non-interactive assumptions. In: Hazay, C., Stam, M. (eds.) EUROCRYPT 2023, Part V. LNCS, vol. 14008, pp. 597–627. Springer, Cham (2023). https://doi.org/10.1007/978-3-031-30589-4_21

39. Pino, R.D., Niot, G.: Finally! A compact lattice-based threshold signature. In: Jager, T., Pan, J. (eds.) PKC 2025, Part III. LNCS, vol. 15676, pp. 169–199. Springer, Cham (2025). https://doi.org/10.1007/978-3-031-91826-1_6
40. Unruh, D.: Non-interactive zero-knowledge proofs in the quantum random oracle model. In: Oswald, E., Fischlin, M. (eds.) EUROCRYPT 2015. LNCS, vol. 9057, pp. 755–784. Springer, Heidelberg (2015). https://doi.org/10.1007/978-3-662-46803-6_25
41. Wee, H., Wu, D.J.: Succinct vector, polynomial, and functional commitments from lattices. In: Hazay, C., Stam, M. (eds.) EUROCRYPT 2023, Part III. LNCS, volume 14006, pp. 385–416. Springer, Cham (2023). https://doi.org/10.1007/978-3-031-30620-4_13
42. Zhandry, M.: How to construct quantum random functions. In: 53rd FOCS, pp. 679–687. IEEE Computer Society Press (2012)
43. Zhandry, M.: Secure identity-based encryption in the quantum random oracle model. In: Safavi-Naini, R., Canetti, R. (eds.) CRYPTO 2012. LNCS, vol. 7417, pp. 758–775. Springer, Berlin, Heidelberg (2012). https://doi.org/10.1007/978-3-642-32009-5_44
44. Zhandry, M.: How to record quantum queries, and applications to quantum indifferentiability. In: Boldyreva, A., Micciancio, D. (eds.) CRYPTO 2019, Part II. LNCS, vol. 11693, pp. 239–268. Springer, Cham (2019). https://doi.org/10.1007/978-3-030-26951-7_9

Threshold Blind Signatures from CDH

Michael Reichle(✉) and Zoé Reinke

ETH Zurich, Zurich, Switzerland
{michael.reichle,zoe.reinke}@inf.ethz.ch

Abstract. Blind signatures are a versatile cryptographic primitive with many applications, especially in privacy-preserving technologies. Threshold blind signature schemes (TBS) enhance blind signatures with a signing procedure distributed among up to n signers to reduce the risk attached to the compromise of the secret key.

So far, TBS constructions over groups rely on strong assumptions, e.g., the algebraic group model (AGM) or interactive assumptions. In this work, we propose two TBS based on the computational Diffie-Hellman assumption (CDH) in the ROM:

- The first TBS over pairing-free groups without the AGM.
- The first round-optimal TBS over pairing-based groups that does not rely on interactive assumptions.

The starting point for both constructions is the pairing-based signature scheme derived from Boneh-Boyen IBE (Eurocrypt'04), and their recent blind signature variants by Katsumata et al. (Asiacrypt'23) and Klooß et al. (Asiacrypt'24) based on the decisional Diffie-Hellman assumption (DDH). We first remove the reliance on DDH in their schemes, then provide careful adaptations to the threshold setting.

1 Introduction

Blind signatures are cryptographic building blocks involving two parties called the signer and the user. The signer is in possession of a key pair $(\mathsf{sk}, \mathsf{vk})$, while the user holds a message m for which he wants to obtain a signature verifying under the signer's public key vk. The signer and the user run an interactive signing protocol, after which the signer should not have learnt the message m and the user should not be able to forge signatures. These two properties are called blindness and one-more unforgeability (OMUF). More formally, blindness guarantees that the signer is not able to link any message-signature pair to the issuing signing session. OMUF ensures that the user cannot compute more valid signatures for distinct messages than the number of completed signing sessions. Blind Signatures were developed in the context of electronic cash by Chaum [14], and have since found wide applications in privacy-preserving technologies.

Threshold blind signatures (TBS) are interactive protocols that keep the properties of blindness and OMUF, but distribute the signing process among multiple signers. In TBS schemes, the user interacts with $t+1$-out-of-n signers to obtain a valid signature. Importantly, OMUF ensures that even if the user

S. Bai and E. Persichetti (Eds.): PKC 2026, LNCS 16551, pp. 269–301, 2026.
https://doi.org/10.1007/978-3-032-26731-3_9

colludes with up to t malicious signers, it remains hard to forge signatures. Threshold blind signature schemes can be used for the same purposes as blind signature schemes, but have the advantage that they diminish the risk attached to compromised secret keys.

Blind Signatures in Pairing-Free Groups. Blind signature schemes over pairing-free groups are widely standard with many known tradeoffs (e.g., [1,4,12, 13,20,24–26,35]). The first blind signature scheme in pairing-free groups was proposed by Pointcheval and Stern [35] in the random oracle model (ROM). Later, a construction achieving partial blindness was given by Abe and Okamoto [4]. Partial blindness allows the signer and user to agree on a common public message τ which is signed in conjunction with the hidden message m. While these constructions and later works following their template [24,25] are elegant, their security was proven in the ROM under the restriction that at most $\mathsf{polylog}(\lambda)$-many signing sessions are concurrently opened, where λ denotes the security parameter. Indeed, afterwards efficient attacks were discovered against [4,35] in the concurrent setting [6,40].

Subsequently, several blind signatures with unlimited concurrency were proposed [1,16,20,26,38]. However, their security is only proven in both the ROM and the algebraic group model (AGM). It remained an open problem to construct blind signatures in pairing-free groups with unlimited concurrency, but without resorting to the AGM, until the work by Chairattana-Apirom et al. [13], hereafter denoted CTZ. CTZ presents two schemes:

- An efficient blind signature with constant signature and communication size under an interactive $\mathsf{CT\text{-}CDH}$ assumption (and in a slightly weaker model).
- A blind signature proven secure under the CDH assumption. However, the communication and signature size linearly depends on λ.

Subsequently, Klooß et al. [29] proposed a pairing-free blind signature scheme with constant signature size and linear communication size proven secure under a decisional assumption, namely DDH. This construction was later optimized by Klooß and Reichle to achieve both constant signature and communication size [28]. Also, Brandt et al. [11] provide a scheme with an (almost) tight security proof with constant signature and communication under DDH. However, the tightness comes at the cost of larger concrete sizes. In summary, while significant progress in this area was made in recent years, to this date no *efficient, concurrently secure* pairing-free blind signature scheme proven secure under a search assumption in the ROM (without the AGM or interactive assumptions) has been proposed.[1]

Threshold Blind Signatures in Pairing-Free Groups. In comparison to blind signatures, threshold blind signatures only recently gained more attention of the cryptographic community. The first blind threshold signature scheme for pairing-free groups, Snowblind [16] based on [38], relies on the AGM. Recently,

[1] A concurrent work [30] constructs efficient blind signatures from the discrete logarithm assumption in the ROM. We compare our work to theirs in Sect. 1.3.

Lehmann et al. [32] revisited the security definitions of TBS and proposed a hierarchy of security notions for OMUF. Also, [32] gives a variant of Snowblind [16] that satisfies the strongest security notion in their hierarchy, namely OMUF-3. There is no known TBS construction in pairing-free groups that does not rely on the AGM to date.

Blind Signatures in Pairing-Friendly Groups. Over pairing-friendly groups, there are many constructions relying on algebraic models or interactive assumptions [2,8,18,19,21,22]. Also, several constructions in the ROM from standard assumptions are known [3,7,12,23]. The most efficient construction is given by [27] proven secure in the ROM under DDH, with signatures consisting of 2 group elements.

Threshold Blind Signatures in Pairing-Friendly Groups. The first TBS schemes are based on pairings, introduced by Vo et al. [39] and Kuchta and Manulis [31] . Later, [32] gives variants that satisfy the stronger security notion OMUF-3. However, all constructions rely on an interactive variant of CDH.

Our Goal. In this paper, we develop *efficient* threshold blind signatures that are provably secure in only the ROM under the CDH assumption.

1.1 Our Contribution

We propose two threshold blind signatures, namely TBS and pTBS, proven secure under the CDH assumption in the ROM. Both constructions satisfy OMUF-3, the strongest notion in [32]'s hierarchy and are concretely efficient:[2]

- Our scheme TBS is over pairing-free groups and has signatures that consist of 10 group and scalar elements, while communication is linear in the security parameter λ for both schemes. For $\lambda = 128$, this corresponds to 320 Byte signatures. In comparison, the only known blind signature proven under CDH in the ROM, namely CTZ-3 [13], has signatures of size 10.5 KB.[3]
- Our scheme pTBS is over pairing-friendly groups and has signatures that consist of 2 group elements, i.e., pTBS preserves the signature size of the state of the art [27] in the threshold setting.

A comparison between our threshold blind signature schemes and other group-based constructions with OMUF-3 is given in Table 1.

Both our schemes are based on the signature derived from Boneh-Boyen IBE [9], hereafter BB[4], which is secure under CDH. In more detail, our scheme pTBS is based on the blind signature [27], itself based on BB, of which we

[2] We adapt OMUF-3 to partial blindness and consider forgeries for distinct messages, i.e., we do not consider strong unforgeability. Also, we note that our scheme pTBS is proven under an analogue of CDH over pairings.

[3] A concurrent work constructs blind signatures from DLog (cf. Footnote 1).

[4] We note that there is another signature scheme by Boneh-Boyen [10]. These are distinct schemes.

Table 1. We compare threshold blind signatures over groups that satisfy OMUF-3. Here, BOMDH refers to the interactive bilinear one-more Diffie-Hellman assumption. Schemes above (resp. below) the line rely on pairing-free (reps. pairing-friendly) groups.

Scheme	Assumption	Model	Moves	Total Communication	Signature
SB+ [16,32]	DLog	AGM,ROM	7	$\Theta(t^2)(\lambda + \mathbb{G} + \mathbb{Z}_p)$	$1\mathbb{G} + 2\mathbb{Z}_p$
TBS (cf. Section 4)	CDH	ROM	6	$\Theta(\lambda + t)(\lambda + \mathbb{G} + \mathbb{Z}_p)$	$2\mathbb{G} + 8\mathbb{Z}_p$
tBlindBLS-3 [32,39]	BOMDH	ROM	2	$(t + 2) \cdot \mathbb{G}$	$1\mathbb{G}$
pTBS (cf. Section 5)	CDH	ROM	2	$\Theta(\lambda + t)(\lambda + \mathbb{G} + \mathbb{Z}_p)$	$2\mathbb{G}$

provide a careful threshold adaptation. Our scheme TBS is based on [29], itself an adaptation of [27] without pairings. For the latter, we note that [29] crucially relies on the DDH assumption in their security argument. We first propose a blind signature BS that we prove secure under CDH, then adapt it to the threshold setting.

1.2 Technical Overview

First, let us discuss our pairing-free scheme. Our starting point is the blind signature scheme presented by [29]. Recall that their scheme is secure in the ROM under the DDH assumption over a pairing-free group $\mathbb{G}$ of prime-order p. We employ additive notation for $\mathbb{G}$. We will briefly present the main characteristics of their construction that are relevant for our work. Then, we describe our techniques to remove the reliance on the DDH assumption in [29] and to build a threshold version of our scheme.

Starting Point. The blind signature scheme from [29] is based on a digital signature scheme derived from Boneh-Boyen's IBE [9]. That is, a BB signature σ consists of two group elements $S = (S_1, S_2)$, where S_1 and S_2 are of the following form:

$$S_1 = uV + s(\overline{m}U + H), \qquad S_2 = sG. \tag{1}$$

Here, G is a generator for $\mathbb{G}$, the element $u \in \mathbb{Z}_p$ forms the secret key, and $U = uG \in \mathbb{G}$, $H \in \mathbb{G}$ and $V \in \mathbb{G}$ are part of the public key. Also, $\overline{m} = \mathsf{H}(m)$ is the hash of the message m to be signed with randomness $s \xleftarrow{\$} \mathbb{Z}_p$. Verification of this signature relies on pairings. However, as observed in [29], this reliance can be removed by using a Σ-protocol to prove that $\mathbf{S} = (S_1, S_2)$ is of the above form.

In order to turn this scheme into a blind signature scheme, the signing process is split among a user and a signer. For the purpose of hiding the (hashed) message from the signer, the user sends the signer a Pedersen commitment [34] C to $\overline{m}$ along with a proof π_{Ped} certifying that the user knows an opening for commitment C. The signer then homomorphically generates a blinded BB (pre-) signature $\mathbf{T}$ on the commitment C, from which the user derives a valid signature $\mathbf{S}$ by eliminating the commitment's randomness implicitly contained in $\mathbf{T}$.

For blindness, the user rerandomizes $\mathbf{S}$. Further, the signer issues a proof that $\mathbf{T}$ is well-formed via an appropriate Σ-protocol. The user then adapts the Σ-protocol transcript to show that $\mathbf{S}$ is distributed as in Eq. (1) by leveraging linear properties of the Σ-protocol, randomizes the transcripts, and lastly compiles them into a non-interactive proof π via Fiat-Shamir.[5] The signature consists of the randomized BB signature $\mathbf{S}$ and the randomized proof π.

To facilitate the proof of one-more unforgeability, the proof π is implemented as an OR-proof for the statement that given a tuple $\mathbf{D} = (D_1, D_2, D_3)$ it holds that

1. either the BB signature $\mathbf{S}$ is well-formed, i.e., satisfies Eq. (1), or
2. the tuple $\mathbf{D}$ forms a valid DDH tuple.

Roughly, the first statement enforces that the adversary is forced to provide well-formed signatures, whereas the second statement serves as a simulation trapdoor in the OMUF proof. Further, the tuple $\mathbf{D}$ allows to achieve partial blindness by deriving $\mathbf{D}$ from a random oracle evaluated on the common message τ. As noted before, the blind signature by [29] sketched above is secure in the ROM under the DDH assumption.

Towards a CDH-Based Blind Signature. We aim to prove the scheme by [29] secure under the CDH assumption. To this end, we first replace the second statement of the OR-proof (i.e., $\mathbf{D}$ is a valid DDH tuple) with a statement claiming knowledge of the discrete logarithm of a value $W = \mathsf{H}_{\mathsf{DLog}}(\tau)$ which again is derived by hashing the common message τ. This modification eliminates the DDH tuple from the scheme, similar to [13].

However, this change alone is not enough to prove security under CDH. In order to understand the issue, let us give a high-level overview of the OMUF proof by [29]. Recall that in the OMUF game, the adversary obtains access to a signing oracle and is asked to provide $\ell+1$ valid signatures for distinct messages, while only finishing up to ℓ signing sessions. Note that the pre-signature $\mathbf{T}$ (from which the user derives a BB signature $\mathbf{S}$) is revealed to the user *before* the signing session is finalized. However, the proof strategy by [29] relies on the puncturing strategy from BB: the adversary is forced to provide a forgery for a message m^* for which the verification key vk is punctured. That is, the game can issue signatures for any message $m \neq m^*$ and the signature on m^* which is provided by the adversary allows to solve CDH. By the pigeon-hole principle, the adversary will never *finalize* a signing session where m^* is committed in the Pedersen commitment C with sufficient probability. It is still possible though that an *incomplete* session requires simulating a BB pre-signature $\mathbf{T}$ for m^* which is not possible if the verification key vk is punctured. Under the DDH assumption, the BB pre-signatures $\mathbf{T}$ look random as long as the corresponding session is never finished. As this is true for sessions with m^*, it is sufficient to simply send a random tuple $\mathbf{T}$ in this case.

Hiding T via Pedersen Commitments. As we aim to avoid the DDH assumption, we cannot argue in this manner. Instead, we randomize the pre-signatures

[5] These steps are closely interwoven in their execution.

$\mathbf{T}$ sent by the signer via linearly homomorphic commitments for $\mathbb{Z}_p$. First, we observe that the second element T_2 of a BB pre-signature $\mathbf{T} = (T_1, T_2)$ is already uniform. Therefore, it suffices to hide T_1 until the signing session is finished. To do so, we let the signer send $T_{\$,1} = T_1 + dG$ to the user *along with* a Pedersen commitment $C_S = \mathsf{Com}(d, r)$, instead of sending T_1 in plain. In the last message of the signing session, the signer opens the commitment C_S. Observe that now, the BB pre-signature $\mathbf{T}_\$ = (T_{\$,1}, T_2)$ simply consists of two uniform group elements until C_S is opened. Further, as Pedersen commitments are statistically hiding, we can argue that unfinished signing sessions leak no information.

An additional detail is that in order to blind the proof π, the user must know the BB signature $\mathbf{S}$ as it is part of the statement proven by π. As the user needs to randomize π already in the second round, but learns $\mathbf{S}$ only in the very last move, this causes an issue. To resolve this, we let the user also blind the proof π with the randomized term $S_{\$,1}$. All statements are linear, therefore it is possible to recover an appropriate Fiat-Shamir proof π in the end (at the cost of a second Pedersen commitment).

Before we continue, we note that employing commitments to avoid leaking critical information from unfinished signing sessions is not new to our work. Chairattana-Apirom et al. [13] employ homomorphic commitments with a special equivocation property and Brandt et al. [11] employ homomorphic dual-mode commitments for this purpose. Neither choice is an option for us. The equivocation property in [13] relies on the underlying signature having a specific form which is not the case for BB signatures. On the other hand, the dual-mode commitments in [11] rely on DDH.

We observe that in our case, any linear commitment that is binding and hiding under CDH is sufficient. Concretely, we use Pedersen for efficiency and the signature consists of only an additional 3 $\mathbb{Z}_p$ elements (after some optimizations) compared to [29].

Complications due to Partial Blindness. Similar to [29], our scheme satisfies partial blindness which leads to further complications in the OMUF proof. To understand the issue, recall that partial blindness allows the adversary to finish arbitrarily-many sessions for common messages τ that are distinct to the forgeries' common message τ^*. In particular, that means the simulation must provide BB pre-signatures for arbitrary messages within signing sessions with common messages $\tau \neq \tau^*$. Again, under DDH it is possible to simulate these sessions by outputting random tuples $\mathbf{T}$.

However, in our case, this is not possible as we want to avoid DDH. We observe that, for $m = m^*$ with $\tau \neq \tau^*$, the game might have to open the commitment C_S to the pre-signatures $\mathbf{T}$ in the last move of the protocol, de-randomizing the random looking pre-signature $\mathbf{T}_\$$. The game therefore has to send correctly distributed BB pre-signatures $\mathbf{T}$ for m^* if $\tau \neq \tau^*$. As vk is punctured for message m^* however, the game is not able to compute $\mathbf{T}_\$$ honestly via the secret key and the proof fails. To resolve this issue, we decouple signing sessions with distinct common messages τ by leveraging the symmetry in BB signatures. Roughly, observe that the signer can either issue valid signatures via v *or* u, the DLog of V

or U, respectively. We cannot choose a τ-dependent U as its discrete logarithm u forms the signing key (which must work for every common message τ). However, we can choose V based on the common message τ which allows us to simulate BB signatures *even* for the punctured message m^*. We refer to the main body for more details.

Ensuring that S is Well-formed. Recall that we replaced the DDH tuple $\mathbf{D}$ with a random group element W. In [29], the tuple $\mathbf{D}$ serves as a "toggle" for the proof π. That is, if $\mathbf{D}$ is a DDH tuple, then the game can simulate the proof π via the discrete logarithms in $\mathbf{D}$. Otherwise, if $\mathbf{D}$ is not a DDH tuple, then the adversary must provide valid BB signatures $\mathbf{S}$. Under the DDH assumption, [29] show that the adversary must provide valid BB signatures in its forgeries, even when the game simulates the BB pre-sigantures and uses the $\mathbf{D}$-branch of the OR-proof π, allowing to solve CDH.

We cannot employ this argument, as we want to avoid reliance on DDH. Instead, we ensure that the adversary provides valid BB forgeries via a forking-based argument, following the proof strategy by [13]. That is, if the BB forgeries are invalid, then we show that the adversary must break the DLog assumption (either by breaking binding of the homomorphic commitment or by computing the discrete logarithm w of W). In summary, the protocol looks as follows:

1. The user sends a Pedersen commitment C to $\overline{m} = \mathsf{H}(m)$ and a proof π that certifies knowledge of an opening of C.
2. The signer computes a BB pre-signature $\mathbf{T} = (T_1, T_2)$ from the commitment C and masks T_1 via $T_{\$,1} = T_1 + dG$ over $\mathbb{G}$ with a random mask dG. The signer commits to d in a homomorphic commitment C_S, and sends $(\mathbf{T}_\$, C_S)$ to the user, where $\mathbf{T}_\$ = (T_{\$,1}, T_2)$. Also, the signer initiates a Σ-protocol proof that either $\mathbf{T}$ is well-formed or it knows the discrete logarithm of $W = \mathsf{H}_{\mathsf{DLog}}(\tau)$.
3. The user computes a masked BB signature $\mathbf{S}_\$$ from $(T_{1,\$}, T_2)$, where the first term is still additively masked by dG. Next, the user randomizes the commitment C_S, the blinding factor d committed in C_S and the obtained BB signature in $\mathbf{S}_\$$. Then, the user adapts and blinds the (incomplete) Σ-protocol transcript for the signature $\mathbf{S}_\$$, following the techniques in [29], and compiles the transcript via Fiat-Shamir. It blinds the obtained challenge c and sends the blinded c to the signer.
4. The signer computes the Σ-protocol response z and outputs z and an opening for C_S.
5. The user finally derives an actual BB signature $\mathbf{S}$ by removing the masking term dG from $\mathbf{S}_\$$. He then adapts and blinds the final part of the Σ-protocol transcript and outputs the randomized Fiat-Shamir proof π, BB signature $\mathbf{S}$, commitment C_S and opening (d, r) for C_S.

With these adaptations, we can show security of our blind signature under CDH. Also, blindness follows similar to [29] as the Pedersen commitment and the masking term d are rerandomized by the user.

Towards a Threshold Signing Protocol. Finally, let us describe how to construct a threshold blind signature TBS based on our blind signature. To distribute signing among $t+1$-out-of-n parties, a natural first step is to distribute the signing key for the BB signature $\mathbf{T}$. That is, the key generation algorithm computes n Shamir shares u_i of secret key u, whereby any subset of $t+1$ shares allows to linearly reconstruct u. To issue a BB signature in a distributed manner, each signer issues a partial signature following Eq. (1), that is, it sets

$$(T_{1,i}, T_{2,i}) = (\lambda_i u_i V + s_i(\overline{m}U + H), T_2 = s_i G), \tag{2}$$

where λ_i is the i-th Lagrange coefficient for the chosen set $\mathcal{S}$ of signers and $s_i \overset{\$}{\leftarrow} \mathbb{Z}_p$. As above, we can leverage the linearity of BB to (partially) sign a commitment C to obtain a partial pre-signature $\mathbf{T}_i$. Additionally, each signer $i \in \mathcal{S}$ issues a Σ-protocol proving that its partial signature $\mathbf{T}_i$ on C is well-formed or it knows the discrete logarithm of $W = \mathsf{H}_{\mathsf{DLog}}(\tau)$. To ensure unforgeability under CDH, the tuple $\mathbf{T}_i$ is again blinded to $\mathbf{T}_{\$,i} = \mathbf{T}_i + (d_i G, 0)$ and the randomness d_i is committed in a Pedersen commitment $C_{\mathcal{S},i}$. As the Σ-protocol and the BB signature are linear, the user simply adds up the partial signatures and Σ-protocol transcripts to obtain a blind signature, following the blinding steps outlined above.

Proving Security. As an issued TBS signature is distributed exactly as in our non-threshold variant BS, we show blindness of TBS leveraging blindness of BS. Showing unforgeability is more involved. Here, in order for our overall proof strategy to work, we must always be able to simulate one of the two branches of the OR-proof and, further, we must be able to switch freely between both modes of simulation, while retaining soundness of the OR-proof. To achieve this, we employ a commit-and-open protocol for the challenge of the DLog-branch of the Σ-protocol: each signer i commits to the challenge $c_{1,i}$ it employs for simulating the DLog-branch in cm_i, then opens cm_i to $c_{1,i}$ after receiving $(\mathsf{cm}_j)_j$ from the other signers j. This gives the simulator enough leverage to program the aggregated challenge $c_1 = \sum_j c_{1,j}$ in the signing protocol, allowing to simulate either branch of the OR-proof later on. Further, we show that revealing partial signatures retains unforgeability, i.e., even given access to a signing oracle for partial signatures, it remains hard to forge BB signatures if *no* partial signature for the forgery's message was issued.

However, another complication arises since partial signatures may leak additional information in *incomplete* signing sessions. Recall that in $\mathsf{OMUF\text{-}3}$ (cf. [32]), such incomplete sessions do not count towards the number of forgeries the adversary $\mathcal{A}$ must supply; in some sense such sessions may give "free" information to $\mathcal{A}$. Here, the leaked information is non-trivial: if signer i opens its commitment $C_{\mathcal{S},i}$ to blinding term d_i in the last round, it is possible to recompute $\mathbf{T}_i = \mathbf{T}_{\$,i} - (d_i G, 0)$, from which $\mathcal{A}$ can recompute a partial BB signature $\mathbf{S}_i$ (cf. Eq. (2)). This is possible, even if another honest signer i' in the session did not yet complete the session. As a consequence, the simulator must supply correctly distributed partial BB pre-signatures even for sessions with m^*. This conflicts with the puncturing of vk on m^*.

To remedy this, we can employ a masking techqniue, as in [32, $\mathsf{tBlindBLS}$-3, Figure 3]: the signer's last round message is masked with a zero share Δ_i

derived from evaluation(s) of a pseudorandom function (PRF) with pairwise-shared seeds. This ensures that the final round does not leak anything beyond the aggregated response. Here, it is important that the PRF is evaluated on fresh input. We therefore evaluate it on the tuple $(c_{1,j})_j$: since an honest signer's challenge $c_{1,i}$ has high min-entropy, the tuple must be fresh in each session. In our scheme TBS, we mask the signer's *full* message in the last round, including the Σ-protocol response z_i (similar to, e.g., [17,32]) and the opening for $C_{S,i}$ (similar to [33]).

With these modifications, we can follow the proof strategy of our (non-threshold) blind signature, carefully adapting the proof to the distributed setting. Note that instead of applying the masking-based technique directly, we could employ the generic transformation proposed by [32, Figure 5] to obtain OMUF-3 security. However, this would increase the number of rounds by 1 and communication in the last round by a factor $t + 1$.

Let us remark that our techniques to thresholdize BS do not rely on any specific structure of BS. Applying the above modifications (i.e., commit-and-open for the challenge and masking the full response) to other AGM-free blind signatures (e.g., [11,28]), combined with our proof technique (i.e., using the commit-and-open protocol to control the honest Σ-protocol branch), likely yields AGM-free threshold blind signatures with other efficiency/security tradeoffs.

Our Pairing-Based Variant. Our pairing-based scheme pTBS is derived from the pairing-based blind signature by [27] proven under DDH—which is also based on BB and the basis for [29]. Roughly, the structure of the signatures is (almost) as in Eq. (1) and blind issuance also relies on signing a user's commitment C to message m via BB. As above, the user supplies a proof π_{Ped} to ascertain well-formedness of C. Here, it is simple to obtain a scheme based on CDH: we replace the DDH-based proof system in [27] with the one from [29]. To issue signatures in a threshold manner, each signer signs the user's commitment C with its partial key as in Eq. (2). Note that the scheme is round-optimal, as the pairing allows for verification (therefore no Σ-protocol must be issued). However, proving unforgeability in the threshold setting is more subtle.

As before, partial signatures may leak additional information without having completed a full singing session. Again, we can employ masking to remedy this: each signer masks its partial signature $\mathbf{T}_i$ with a zero share Δ_i. Here, the PRF-input based on which Δ_i is derived cannot have high min-entropy as the input must be (1) consistent across all signers and (2) established without communication (to retain round-optimality). Therefore, as in [32, tBlindBLS-3], we evaluate the PRF on the user's message (C, π_{Ped}) to be signed.

Note that there is a subtlety since the PRF-input might not be fresh in different signing sessions: On repeated input (C, π), the same mask Δ_i is reused as it is dervied deterministically from (C, π). However, the output $\mathbf{T}_i$ might differ (as signing is randomized). Therefore, the adversary may learn, e.g., differences of partial signatures $\mathbf{T}_i$ on message m^* by cancelling out the masks Δ_i. It seems difficult to both puncture the verification key and simulatenously, handle the simulation of partial signatures in a consistent manner. Our idea is to instead *derandomize* signing: each signer i computes its randomness for the partial signature $\mathbf{T}_i$ based on a PRF-evaluation on (C, π), i.e., the same input that is used to generate the zero-shares. Therefore, on repeated queries, the adversary learns no additional information. On fresh queries, the zero share Δ_i again conceals partial signatures, which allows us to prove security of pTBS. Note that as [32, tBlindBLS-3] is based on BLS, this subtle issue does not appear in their proof (as BLS is already deterministic).

1.3 Concurrent Work

The concurrent work [30] constructs blind signatures in the ROM from DLog. We give a brief comparison with our construction BS (cf. Section 3):

- *Efficiency.* In terms of efficiency, both constructions are comparable. The communication is dominated by some proof sent by the user, and signatures are $6\mathbb{Z}_p$ elements (compared to $8\mathbb{Z}_p$ and $2\mathbb{G}$ elements in our construction).
- *Assumptions.* Both constructions are based on a standard search assumption over groups. However, DLog is a weaker assumption than CDH.
- *Techniques.* We obtain our construction by adapting [29] and carefully hiding information from incomplete sessions via homomorphic commitments to avoid DDH. Conceptually, we show that [29] is provable under CDH with minor adaptations. In contrast, [30] builds on [28] and replaces the underlying Σ-protocol in [28] with a Σ-protocol that enables a proof based on DLog instead of DDH.

The focus of our work is threshold blind signatures from BB. While we believe that our approach also allows to thresholdize works like [28,30], this is out of scope.

2 Preliminaries

Notation. The security parameter is denoted by λ. Throughout, $\mathbb{G}$ denotes a group of prime order p and $G \in \mathbb{G}$ denotes a generator of $\mathbb{G}$. We use additive notation and denote group elements like G with uppercase letters, while scalars $x \in \mathbb{Z}_p$ are denoted by lowercase letters. Vectors of group elements and vectors of scalars are denoted by bold letters (e.g., $\mathbf{G}$ or $\mathbf{x}$). We denote by $y \leftarrow \mathcal{A}(x)$ a probabilistic algorithm $\mathcal{A}$ running with input x and producing output y. To express that a value v is assigned to a variable x, we write $x := v$. Also, $x \xleftarrow{\$} \mathcal{D}$ means that x is sampled uniformly at random from set $\mathcal{D}$, if $\mathcal{D}$ is a set, and that x is sampled from distribution $\mathcal{D}$, if $\mathcal{D}$ is a distribution. For an interactive protocol run by parties A and B on inputs in_A and in_B respectively, we use the notation $A(\mathsf{in}_A) \longleftrightarrow B(\mathsf{in}_B)$. To express that an interactive protocol is run by a set of parties $\mathcal{S}$ each running an instantiation of algorithm A with respective inputs in_{A_i} and a party running a different algorithm B with input in_B, we write $\{A(\mathsf{in}_{A_i})\}_{i \in \mathcal{S}} \longleftrightarrow B(\mathsf{in}_B)$. In specifications of algorithms, we write **req**C to state that, if the condition C is not satisfied, the algorithm returns $\perp$. To signify, in a specification of a game, that the game returns 0 if a condition C is met, we write **abort if** C.

2.1 Assumptions and Information-Theoretical Tools

Denote by GrGen a PPT algorithm that on input 1^λ returns a group description $\mathcal{G} = (\mathbb{G}, p, G)$, where p is the prime order of $\mathbb{G}$ and $G \in \mathbb{G}$ is a generator. Additionally, let $\mathsf{PGen}(1^\lambda)$ denote a PPT algorithm that on input 1^λ, outputs $(\mathbb{G}_1, \mathbb{G}_2, \mathbb{G}_T, e, G_1, G_2)$, where $\mathbb{G}_1, \mathbb{G}_2$ and $\mathbb{G}_T$ are cyclic groups of prime order p, G_1 and G_2 generate $\mathbb{G}_1$ and $\mathbb{G}_2$, respectively, and $e : \mathbb{G}_1 \times \mathbb{G}_2 \to \mathbb{G}_T$ is a bilinear mapping.

Assumptions. The DLog assumption expresses that given a group $\mathbb{G}$, a generator G and a uniform group element $X \in \mathbb{G}$, it is hard to compute x such that $X = xG$. The CDH assumption states that given group $\mathbb{G}$, generator G and group elements $A = aG$ and $B = bG$, it is hard to compute $C = abG$. We denote by $\mathsf{co\text{-}DLog}$ and $\mathsf{co\text{-}CDH}$ their natural analogues over pairings. We give formal definitions in the full version [36].

Forking Lemma. We will make use of the Forking Lemma introduced by [5]. Roughly, it ensures that if an event occurs with good probability, then with good probability (albeit for a square-root loss) the event will also occur if the adversary is run again with changed random oracle outputs as inputs. A formal definition is given in the full version [36].

Shamir Secret Sharing. Our threshold blind signature schemes employ Shamir secret sharing [37], which is based on polynomial interpolation, to compute secret key shares sk_i for all signing parties. A formal definition is given in the full version [36].

2.2 Blind Signatures

We define (partially) blind signatures and their desired security properties. The definitions are taken and adapted from [29].

Definition 1 (Partially Blind Signature Scheme). *A partially blind signature scheme with message space $\mathcal{M}$ and common message space $\mathcal{T}$ is a tuple of PPT algorithms* $\mathsf{BS} = (\mathsf{Setup}, \mathsf{KeyGen}, \mathsf{Signer}, \mathsf{User}, \mathsf{Verify})$ *with the following syntax:*

- $\mathsf{Setup}(1^\lambda)$*: takes as input security parameter λ and returns public parameters* par. *These are given as input to all other algorithms implicitly.*
- $\mathsf{KeyGen}()$*: outputs a pair of keys* $(\mathsf{vk}, \mathsf{sk})$. *We assume that* sk *includes* vk *implicitly.*
- $\mathsf{Signer}(\mathsf{sk}, \tau) \longleftrightarrow \mathsf{User}(\mathsf{vk}, m, \tau)$*:* Signer *takes as input a secret key* sk *and common message $\tau \in \mathcal{T}$.* User *takes as input a key* vk*, a message $m \in \mathcal{M}$ and common message $\tau \in \mathcal{T}$. After the execution,* User *returns a signature σ and we write* $\sigma \leftarrow \langle \mathsf{Signer}(\mathsf{sk}, \tau), \mathsf{User}(\mathsf{vk}, m, \tau) \rangle$.

- $\mathsf{Verify}(\mathsf{vk}, m, \tau, \sigma)$: *is deterministic and takes as input public key* vk*, message* $m \in \mathcal{M}$*, a common message* $\tau \in \mathcal{T}$*, and a signature* σ*, and outputs* $b \in \{0,1\}$.

Note that (plain) blind signatures are a special case of partially blind signatures where $|\mathcal{T}| = 1$. Blind signatures should satisfy three properties, namely correctness, one-more unforgeability and blindness. Intuitively, these three properties give the following guarantees: Correctness entails that whenever a user and a signer correctly run the signing protocol with a correctly generated key pair $(\mathsf{vk}, \mathsf{sk})$ on a message $m \in \mathcal{M}$ and a common message $\tau \in \mathcal{T}$, the generated signature should successfully verify for vk, τ and m. One-more unforgeability guarantees that the user is not able to generate valid signatures on its own without interacting with the signer, even after having successfully completed several signing sessions with the signer. Lastly, blindness ensures that the signer is not able to map a run of the interactive signing protocol to a message-signature pair (m, σ) output by the user. Note that it is easy to recover formal definitions from the corresponding notions of threshold blind signatures defined in Sect. 2.6. For completeness, we provide formal definitions in the full version [36].

2.3 Proof Systems

Relations and Σ-Protocols. We define NP-relations and Σ-Protocols, following the definitions from [29].

Definition 2 (NP-Relation and Language). *Let* $\mathsf{R} \subseteq \{0,1\}^* \times \{0,1\}^*$ *be a binary relation. We say that* R *is an* NP-relation*, if there is a polynomial* p *such that* R *can efficiently be decided and for every* $(\mathbb{x}, \mathbb{w}) \in \mathsf{R}$*, we have* $|\mathbb{w}| \leq p(|\mathbb{x}|)$*. We denote by* $\mathscr{L}_\mathsf{R} = \{\mathbb{x} \in \{0,1\}^* \mid \exists \mathbb{w} \text{ s.t. } (\mathbb{x}, \mathbb{w}) \in \mathsf{R}\}$ *the language induced by* R.

Definition 3 (Σ-Protocol). *Let* R *be an NP-relation. A* Σ*-protocol for relation* R *with challenge space* $\mathcal{C}$ *is a tuple of PPT algorithms* $\Sigma = (\mathsf{Init}, \mathsf{Resp}, \mathsf{Verify})$ *such that*

- $\mathsf{Init}(\mathbb{x}, \mathbb{w})$: *given a statement* $\mathbb{x} \in \mathscr{L}_\mathsf{R}$ *and a witness* $\mathbb{w}$*, outputs a first flow message (i.e., commitment)* A *and a state* st*, where we assume* st *includes* $(\mathbb{x}, \mathbb{w})$,
- $\mathsf{Resp}(\mathsf{st}, c)$: *given a state* st *and a challenge* $c \in \mathcal{C}$*, deterministically outputs a third flow message (i.e., response)* z,
- $\mathsf{Verify}(\mathbb{x}, A, c, z)$: *given a statement* $\mathbb{x} \in \mathscr{L}_\mathsf{R}$*, a commitment* A*, a challenge* $c \in \mathcal{C}$*, and a response* z*, deterministically outputs a bit* $b \in \{0,1\}$.

We call the tuple (A, c, z) *the* transcript *and say that it is* valid for $\mathbb{x}$ *if* $\mathsf{Verify}(\mathbb{x}, A, c, z)$ *outputs 1. When the context is clear, we simply say it is valid and omit* $\mathbb{x}$.

Σ-Protocols for NP-relations should satisfy three properties, namely correctness, special honest-verifier zero-knowledge (HVZK) and special soundness, defined below.

Definition 4 (Correctness). *Let* R *be an NP-relation and* $\Sigma = (\mathsf{Init}, \mathsf{Resp}, \mathsf{Verify})$ *be a* Σ*-protocol for* R*. We say* Σ *is* correct, *if for all* $(\mathbb{x}, \mathbb{w}) \in \mathsf{R}$, $(A, \mathsf{st}) \leftarrow \mathsf{Init}(\mathbb{x}, \mathbb{w})$, $c \in \mathcal{C}$, *and* $z \leftarrow \mathsf{Resp}(\mathsf{st}, c)$, *it holds that* $\mathsf{Verify}(\mathbb{x}, A, c, z) = 1$.

Definition 5 (Special HVZK). *Let* R *be an NP-relation and* $\Sigma = (\mathsf{Init}, \mathsf{Resp}, \mathsf{Verify})$ *be a* Σ*-protocol for* R*. We say that* Σ *is* special honest-verifier zero-knowledge *(HVZK), if there exists a PPT zero-knowledge simulator* Sim *such that for any (potentially unbounded) adversary* $\mathcal{A}$*, it holds that for any* $(\mathbb{x}, \mathbb{w}) \in \mathsf{R}$ *and* $c \in \mathcal{C}$ *that* $D_{\mathsf{real}} = D_{\mathsf{sim}}$ *for*

$$D_{\mathsf{real}} := \{(A, c, z) \mid A \leftarrow \mathsf{Init}(\mathbb{x}, \mathbb{w}), z \leftarrow \mathsf{Resp}(\mathsf{st}, c)\},$$
$$D_{\mathsf{sim}} := \{(A, c, z) \mid (A, z) \leftarrow \mathsf{Sim}(\mathbb{x}, c)\}.$$

In this work, we write HVZK for short.

Definition 6 (Special Soundness). *Let* R *be an NP-relation and* $\Sigma = (\mathsf{Init}, \mathsf{Resp}, \mathsf{Verify})$ *be a* Σ*-protocol for* R*. We say that* Σ *is* (2-)special sound, *if there exists a* deterministic *PT extractor* Ext *such that given two valid transcripts* $\{(A, c_b, z_b)\}_{b \in \{0,1\}}$ *for statement* $\mathbb{x}$ *with* $c_0 \neq c_1$*, along with* $\mathbb{x}$*, outputs a witness* $\mathbb{w}$ *such that* $(\mathbb{x}, \mathbb{w}) \in \mathsf{R}$.

We additionally define the property of (perfect) randomizability [28]. Looking ahead, we follow the rerandomization procedure in Lemma 1 as in [28] in our blind signature construction. This specific randomization procedure allows to issue Fiat-Shamir proofs in a blind manner, whereas Definition 7 and Corollary 1 facilitate the blindness proof.

Definition 7 ((Perfect) Randomizable Transcripts). *Let* Σ *be a* Σ*-protocol for relation* R *with challenge space* $\mathcal{C}$*, and suppose* Σ *is HVZK. Let* Rand *be an efficient randomization algorithm such that* $\mathsf{Rand}(\mathbb{x}, (A, c, z))$*, given a valid transcript* (A, c, z) *for* $\mathbb{x}$*, outputs a new valid transcript for* $\mathbb{x}$*. We say* Σ *has randomizable transcripts (resp. strongly randomizable transcripts) if a* Rand *exists such that for all* $\mathbb{x} \in \mathscr{L}_{\mathsf{R}}$ *(resp. all* $\mathbb{x}$*) and all accepting* $\pi^* = (A^*, c^*, z^*)$*, the distributions*

$$D_{\mathsf{SHVZK}} := \{(\mathbb{x}, (A, c, z)) | c \xleftarrow{\$} \mathcal{C}; (A, z) \leftarrow \mathsf{Sim}(x, c)\}$$
$$D_{\mathsf{Rand}} := \{(\mathbb{x}, (A, c, z)) | (A, c, z) \leftarrow \mathsf{Rand}(x, \pi^*)\}$$

are identical.

We also recall the following corollary from [28].

Corollary 1. *Suppose* Σ *is a* Σ*-protocol for relation* R *which is HVZK and has randomizable transcripts. Then for all* $(\mathbb{x}, \mathbb{w}) \in \mathsf{R}$ *and all accepting* $\pi^* = (A^*, c^*, z^*)$*, the following distributions are identical:*

$$D_{\mathsf{Real}} := \{(\mathbb{x}, (A, c, z)) | A, \mathsf{st} \leftarrow \mathsf{Init}(\mathbb{x}, \mathbb{w}); c \xleftarrow{\$} \mathcal{C}; z \leftarrow \mathsf{Resp}(\mathsf{st}, c)\}$$
$$D_{\mathsf{SHVZK}} := \{(\mathbb{x}, (A, c, z)) | c \xleftarrow{\$} \mathcal{C}; (A, z) \leftarrow \mathsf{Sim}(\mathbb{x}, c)\}$$
$$D_{\mathsf{Rand}} := \{(\mathbb{x}, (A, c, z)) | (A, c, z) \leftarrow \mathsf{Rand}(\mathbb{x}, \pi^*)\}.$$

Non-interactive Proof System. Our blind signature scheme will also use straightline-extractable non-interactive zero-knowledge proofs as a building block. The definitions below follow [29].

Definition 8 (Non-Interactive Proof System). *A* non-interactive proof system *(NIPS) for NP-relation* R *using a random oracle* H *is a pair* $\mathsf{NIPS} = (\mathsf{Prove}, \mathsf{Ver})$ *of PPT algorithms with access to a random oracle, where*

- $\mathsf{Prove}^{\mathsf{H}}(\mathbb{x}, \mathbb{w})$*: generates a proof* π *given* $(\mathbb{x}, \mathbb{w}) \in \mathsf{R}$.
- $\mathsf{Ver}^{\mathsf{H}}(\mathbb{x}, \pi)$*: verifies a proof* π *for statement* $\mathbb{x}$ *and outputs* 0 *or* 1.

We are interested in NIPS that satisfy three properties, namely correctness, witness-indistinguishability and knowledge soundness. Roughly, correctness guarantees that any proof π computed for a statement $\mathbb{x}$ and a witness $\mathbb{w}$ should successfully verify for $\mathbb{x}$ with probability close to 1. Informally, witness-indistinguishability expresses that it should be hard for an adversary to tell which witness $\mathbb{w}$ was used to compute a certain proof for a statement $\mathbb{x}$. Lastly, knowledge soundness means that there exists an algorithm called the extractor that successfully computes a witness for a given statement $\mathbb{x}$, when provided with $\mathbb{x}$, a proof for $\mathbb{x}$ and all adversarial random oracle queries made during the computation of the proof as inputs. A NIPS is relaxed knowledge sound if the extractor computes the witness only for a relaxed relation $\tilde{\mathsf{R}} \supsetneq \mathsf{R}$, where $\tilde{\mathsf{R}}$ is called the knowledge relation. Formal definitions are given in the full version [36].

2.4 Pseudorandom Function

A pseudorandom function is a function $F : \mathcal{K} \times \mathcal{X} \to \mathcal{Y}$ such that $F(k, \cdot)$ is indistinguishable from a random function $f : \mathcal{X} \to \mathcal{Y}$ for random $k \xleftarrow{\$} \mathcal{K}$. We refer to the full version [36] for a formal definition.

2.5 Commitment Schemes

We define commitment schemes. For simplicity, we follow the convention that to verify the commitment c, we check that $c = \mathsf{Commit}(\mathsf{CK}, m, r)$ holds. Therefore, we sometimes refer to r as opening. Note that this convention ensures correctness by definition.

Definition 9 (Commitment Scheme). *A (non-interactive) commitment scheme with message space* $\mathcal{M}$ *and randomness space* $\mathcal{R}$ *is a tuple of PPT algorithms* $\mathsf{Com} = (\mathsf{Setup}, \mathsf{Commit})$ *with the following syntax:*

- $\mathsf{Setup}(1^\lambda)$*: takes as input security parameter* λ *and returns a public commitment key* CK.
- $\mathsf{Commit}(\mathsf{CK}, m, r)$*: takes as input public commitment key* CK*, a message* $m \in \mathcal{M}$*, and (explicit) randomness* $r \in \mathcal{R}$*, and returns commitment* c.

When the public commitment key CK is obvious from the context, we sometimes omit the parameter CK from Commit as input.

We consider commitment schemes that are perfectly hiding and computationally binding. Intuitively, the hiding property ensures that the commitment c does not leak any information about the committed message m, while the binding property expresses that it is hard to open c to two distinct messages. We also require Com to be linearly homomorphic, and write $a \cdot \mathsf{Commit}(m, r) = \mathsf{Commit}(a{\cdot}m, a{\cdot}r)$, $\mathsf{Commit}(m_1, r_1) + \mathsf{Commit}(m_2, r_2) = \mathsf{Commit}(m_1+m_2, r_1+r_2)$. Formal definitions are given in the full version [36].

2.6 Threshold Blind Signatures

We introduce threshold blind signatures, following the definitions from [32].

Definition 10 (Threshold Blind Signature). *A threshold (partially) blind signature scheme with message space* $\mathcal{M}$ *and common message space* $\mathcal{T}$ *is a tuple of PPT algorithms* $\mathsf{TBS} = (\mathsf{Setup}, \mathsf{KeyGen}, \mathsf{ISign}, \mathsf{USign}, \mathsf{Verify})$ *such that:*

- $\mathsf{Setup}(1^\lambda)$*: takes as input security parameter* λ *and returns public parameters* par*. These are given as input to all other algorithms implicitly.*
- $\mathsf{KeyGen}(n, t+1)$*: takes as input the number of signers* n *as well as the threshold* $t+1$ *and outputs the public key* vk *representing the set of all signers, the set* $\{\mathsf{sk}_i\}_{i\in[n]}$ *of secret keys for each individual signer as well as additional auxiliary information* aux*, which may be used by the user and the signers in the course of the signing protocol, but which is not necessary for signature verification.*
- $\{\mathsf{ISign}(k, \mathsf{sk}_k, \mathsf{aux}, \mathsf{ctx}, \tau)\}_{k\in\mathcal{S}} \longleftrightarrow \mathsf{USign}(\mathsf{vk}, \mathsf{aux}, m, \mathcal{S}, \tau)$*: is an* r *round interactive protocol between a set* $\mathcal{S}$ *of signers running the signing algorithm* ISign *and one party running the user algorithm* USign*. The* j*-th round signer algorithm* ISign_j *takes as input signer index* k*, secret key share* sk_k*, auxiliary information* aux*, context data* ctx *and common message* $\tau \in \mathcal{T}$*. The* j*-th round user algorithm* USign_j *takes as input a key* vk*, a message* $m \in \mathcal{M}$*, auxiliary information* aux*, a set of signers* $\mathcal{S}$ *and common message* $\tau \in \mathcal{T}$*. After the execution,* USign *returns a signature* σ *and we write* $\sigma \leftarrow \langle\{\mathsf{ISign}(k, \mathsf{sk}_k, \mathsf{aux}, \mathsf{ctx}, \tau)\}_{k\in\mathcal{S}}, \mathsf{USign}(\mathsf{vk}, \mathsf{aux}, m, \mathcal{S}, \tau)\rangle$*. We omit initial inputs in later rounds and assume these are passed on in the state.*
  More formally, we use the following notation to describe the interactive signing protocol, where ISign_j *and* USign_j *describe the* j*-th round of the algorithms* ISign *and* USign*, respectively:*

$$
\begin{aligned}
(\mathsf{st}_0^U, \mathsf{pm}_0^U) &\leftarrow \mathsf{TBS.USign}_0(\mathsf{vk}, \mathsf{aux}, m, \mathcal{S}, \tau),\\
(\mathsf{st}_{1,i}^I, \mathsf{pm}_{1,i}^I) &\leftarrow \mathsf{TBS.ISign}_1(i, \mathsf{sk}_i, \mathsf{aux}, \mathsf{ctx}, \tau, \mathsf{pm}_0^U),\\
(\mathsf{st}_1^U, \mathsf{pm}_1^U) &\leftarrow \mathsf{TBS.USign}_1(\mathsf{st}_0^U, \{\mathsf{pm}_{1,i}^I\}_{i\in\mathcal{S}})\\
(\mathsf{st}_{j,i}^I, \mathsf{pm}_{j,i}^I) &\leftarrow \mathsf{TBS.ISign}_j(i, \mathsf{st}_{j-1,i}^I, \mathsf{pm}_{j-1}^U),\\
(\mathsf{st}_j^U, \mathsf{pm}_j^U) &\leftarrow \mathsf{TBS.USign}_j(\mathsf{st}_{j-1}^U, \{\mathsf{pm}_{j,i}^I\}_{i\in\mathcal{S}})\\
(\mathsf{ssid}, \mathcal{S}', \mathsf{pm}_{r,i}^I) &\leftarrow \mathsf{TBS.ISign}_r(i, \mathsf{st}_{r-1i}^I, \mathsf{pm}_{r-1}^U),\\
\sigma/\bot &\leftarrow \mathsf{TBS.USign}_r(\mathsf{st}_{r-1}^U, \{\mathsf{pm}_{r,i}^I\}_{i\in\mathcal{S}}).
\end{aligned}
$$

– $\mathsf{TBS.Verify}(\mathsf{vk}, m, \tau, \sigma)$: *takes as input public key* vk, *message* $m \in \mathcal{M}$, *common message* $\tau \in \mathcal{T}$, *and signature* σ, *and deterministically outputs bit* b.

Threshold blind signatures should satisfy correctness, blindness and one-more unforgeability. Analogously to blind signatures, correctness states that a signature derived from an honest protocol execution verifies and blindness ensures that the signers cannot link the derived signature to the issuing signing session. For one-more unforgeability, we follow the strongest notion OMUF-3 in [32]'s hierarchy except for two modifications: (1) we do not consider *strong* unforgeability, i.e., in our notion the adversary wins if it provides forgeries for ℓ pairwise-distinct messages, and (2) we generalize the definitions to partial blindness. Roughly, OMUF-3 states that it is hard for an adversary to forge ℓ signatures on distinct messages with common message τ after *completing* at most $\ell - 1$ signing sessions with τ. Here, a session only counts as complete if all honest signing parties have been invoked for the final round with shared post-fix session identifier ssid, shared context ctx and shared set of honest co-signers $\mathcal{S}_{\mathsf{hon}}$.

As alluded to above, we make two slight adjustments to the definition of OMUF-3 from [32]. First, we introduce a common message τ and thus generalize the definitions to the setting of threshold partially blind signatures. Secondly, we slightly harden the winning conditions of the OMUF-3 experiment by letting the adversary win whenever he outputs the required number of ℓ valid message-signature pairs and all ℓ messages are pairwise distinct (instead of only demanding that all ℓ message-signature pairs are pairwise distinct).

Definition 11 (Correctness of a Threshold Blind Signature). *A threshold (partially) blind signature scheme* TBS *is correct with correctness error* γ_{err} *if for all allowable* $1 \le t < n$, *for all* $\mathcal{S} \subseteq [n]$ *such that* $t < |\mathcal{S}| \le n$, *all* $m \in \mathcal{M}$, $\tau \in \mathcal{T}$ *it holds that for* $\mathsf{in}_i = (i, \mathsf{sk}_i, \mathsf{aux}, \mathsf{ctx}, \tau)$ *and* $\mathsf{in}_U = (\mathsf{vk}, \mathsf{aux}, m, \mathcal{S}, \tau)$ *that*

$$\Pr[\sigma \leftarrow \langle\{\mathsf{ISign}(\mathsf{in}_i)\}_{i\in\mathcal{S}}, \mathsf{USign}(\mathsf{in}_U)\rangle : \mathsf{TBS.Verify}(\mathsf{vk}, \sigma, m) = 1] \ge 1 - \gamma_{\mathsf{err}}.$$

Definition 12 (OMUF-3). *Let* $\mathsf{TBS} = (\mathsf{Setup}, \mathsf{KeyGen}, \mathsf{ISign}, \mathsf{USign}, \mathsf{Verify})$ *be a threshold blind signature scheme. We consider the game given in Fig. 1a and denote by* $\mathsf{AdvTOMUF}_{\mathcal{A},n,t}^{\mathsf{TBS},3}(\lambda)$ *the probability that the game outputs* 1. *We say*

$\mathsf{Exp}^{\mathsf{OMUF}}_{\mathsf{TBS},\mathcal{A}}(1^\lambda)$

$\mathsf{par} \leftarrow \mathsf{Setup}(1^\lambda)$
$S_1, \ldots, S_r := \emptyset$
$\mathsf{ES}_3[\cdot] := \emptyset$
$\mathsf{EI}_3[\cdot,\cdot] := \emptyset$
$\mathcal{C} \leftarrow \mathcal{A}(n,t)$
if $|\mathcal{C}| > t$ **then return** 0
$(\mathsf{vk}, (\mathsf{sk}_i)_{i\in[n]}, \mathsf{aux}) \leftarrow \mathsf{KeyGen}(n,t)$
$(\tau^*, \ell, (m_k^*, \sigma_k^*)_{k\in[\ell]}) \leftarrow \mathcal{A}^{\mathcal{O}^{\mathsf{Signer}}(\cdot)}(\mathsf{vk}, (\mathsf{sk}_i)_{i\in\mathcal{C}}, \mathsf{aux})$
if $\ell \le |\mathsf{ES}_3[\tau^*]|$ **then return** 0
return $\forall k \in [\ell] : \begin{pmatrix} \mathsf{Verify}(\mathsf{vk}, \sigma_k^*, m_k^*) = 1 \\ \wedge \forall j \in [\ell] \setminus \{k\} : m_k^* \neq m_j^* \end{pmatrix}$

$\mathcal{O}^{\mathsf{Signer}}(j, \mathsf{sid}, i, \mathsf{ctx}^{\mathsf{sid}}, \tau^{\mathsf{sid}}, \mathsf{pm}^{\mathsf{U}}_{j-1})$

return $\bot$ **if** $(i, \mathsf{sid}) \in S_j$
return $\bot$ **if** $j > 1 \wedge (i, \mathsf{sid}) \notin S_1, \ldots, S_{j-1}$
$S_j := S_j \cup \{(i, \mathsf{sid})\}$
if $j = 1$ **then**
  $(\mathsf{st}_1^{(\mathsf{S},i)}, \mathsf{pm}_1^{(\mathsf{S},i)}) \leftarrow \mathsf{ISign}_1(i, \mathsf{sk}_i, \mathsf{aux}, \mathsf{ctx}^{\mathsf{sid}}, \tau^{\mathsf{sid}}, \mathsf{pm}_0^{\mathsf{U}})$
else
  $(\mathsf{st}_j^{(\mathsf{S},i)}, \mathsf{pm}_j^{(\mathsf{S},i)}) \leftarrow \mathsf{ISign}_j(i, \mathsf{st}_{j-1}^{(\mathsf{S},i)}, \mathsf{pm}_{j-1}^{\mathsf{U}})$
if $j = r$ **then**
  parse $(\mathsf{ssid}_i^{\mathsf{sid}}, \mathcal{S}_i^{\mathsf{sid}}) := \mathsf{st}_{r-1}^{(\mathsf{S},i)}$
  $\mathcal{S}_{\mathsf{hon}} := \mathcal{S}_i^{\mathsf{sid}} \setminus \mathcal{C}$
  $\mathsf{EI}_3[\mathsf{ssid}_i^{\mathsf{sid}}, \mathcal{S}_{\mathsf{hon}}] := \mathsf{EI}_3[\mathsf{ssid}_i^{\mathsf{sid}}, \mathcal{S}_{\mathsf{hon}}] \cup \{i\}$
  if $\mathcal{S}_{\mathsf{hon}} \subseteq \mathsf{EI}_3[\mathsf{ssid}_i^{\mathsf{sid}}, \mathcal{S}_{\mathsf{hon}}]$ **then**
    $\mathsf{ES}_3[\tau] := \mathsf{ES}_3[\tau] \cup \{\mathsf{ssid}_i^{\mathsf{sid}}\}$
  return $(\mathsf{pm}_r^{(\mathsf{S},i)}, \mathsf{ssid}_i^{\mathsf{sid}}, \mathcal{S}_i)$
return $\mathsf{pm}_j^{(\mathsf{S},i)}$

$\mathsf{Exp}^{\mathsf{blind}}_{\mathsf{TBS},\mathcal{A}}(1^\lambda)$

$\mathsf{par} \leftarrow \mathsf{Setup}(1^\lambda)$
$b \xleftarrow{\$} \{0,1\}$
$S_1, \ldots, S_r := \emptyset$
$b' \leftarrow \mathcal{A}^{\mathcal{O}^{\mathsf{User}_0}(\cdot), \ldots, \mathcal{O}^{\mathsf{User}_r}(\cdot)}()$
return $b = b'$

$\mathcal{O}^{\mathsf{User}_0}(\mathsf{sid}, \mathsf{vk}^{\mathsf{sid}}, \mathsf{aux}^{\mathsf{sid}}, \tau^{\mathsf{sid}}, m_0^{\mathsf{sid}}, m_1^{\mathsf{sid}}, \mathcal{S}_0^{\mathsf{sid}}, \mathcal{S}_1^{\mathsf{sid}})$

return $\bot$ **if** $\mathsf{sid} \in S_1$
$S_1 := S_1 \cup \{\mathsf{sid}\}$
$(\mathsf{st}_{0,0}^{\mathsf{U}}, \mathsf{pm}_{0,0}^{\mathsf{U}}) \leftarrow \mathsf{USign}_0(\mathsf{vk}^{\mathsf{sid}}, \mathsf{aux}^{\mathsf{sid}}, m_b^{\mathsf{sid}}, \mathcal{S}_0^{\mathsf{sid}}, \tau^{\mathsf{sid}})$
$(\mathsf{st}_{1,0}^{\mathsf{U}}, \mathsf{pm}_{1,0}^{\mathsf{U}}) \leftarrow \mathsf{USign}_0(\mathsf{vk}^{\mathsf{sid}}, \mathsf{aux}^{\mathsf{sid}}, m_{1-b}^{\mathsf{sid}}, \mathcal{S}_1^{\mathsf{sid}}, \tau^{\mathsf{sid}})$
return $(\mathsf{pm}_{0,0}^{\mathsf{U}}, \mathsf{pm}_{1,0}^{\mathsf{U}})$

$\mathcal{O}^{\mathsf{User}_j}(\mathsf{sid}, (\mathsf{pm}_{0,j}^{(\mathsf{S},i)})_{i\in\mathcal{S}_0^{\mathsf{sid}}}, (\mathsf{pm}_{1,j}^{(\mathsf{S},i)})_{i\in\mathcal{S}_1^{\mathsf{sid}}})$

return $\bot$ **if** $\mathsf{sid} \in S_j \wedge \mathsf{sid} \notin S_{j-1}$
$S_j := S_j \cup \{\mathsf{sid}\}$
$(\mathsf{st}_{0,j}^{\mathsf{U}}, \mathsf{pm}_{0,j}^{\mathsf{U}}) \leftarrow \mathsf{USign}_j(\mathsf{st}_{0,j-1}^{\mathsf{U}}, (\mathsf{pm}_{0,j}^{(\mathsf{S},i)})_{i\in\mathcal{S}_0^{\mathsf{sid}}})$
$(\mathsf{st}_{1,j}^{\mathsf{U}}, \mathsf{pm}_{1,j}^{\mathsf{U}}) \leftarrow \mathsf{USign}_j(\mathsf{st}_{1,j-1}^{\mathsf{U}}, (\mathsf{pm}_{1,j}^{(\mathsf{S},i)})_{i\in\mathcal{S}_1^{\mathsf{sid}}})$
return $(\mathsf{pm}_{0,j}^{\mathsf{U}}, \mathsf{pm}_{1,j}^{\mathsf{U}})$

$\mathcal{O}^{\mathsf{User}_r}(\mathsf{sid}, (\mathsf{pm}_{0,r}^{(\mathsf{S},i)})_{i\in\mathcal{S}_0^{\mathsf{sid}}}, (\mathsf{pm}_{1,r}^{(\mathsf{S},i)})_{i\in\mathcal{S}_1^{\mathsf{sid}}})$

return $\bot$ **if** $\mathsf{sid} \in S_r \wedge \mathsf{sid} \notin S_{r-1}$
$S_r := S_r \cup \{\mathsf{sid}\}$
$\sigma_b^{\mathsf{sid}} \leftarrow \mathsf{USign}_r(\mathsf{st}_{0,r-1}^{\mathsf{U}}, (\mathsf{pm}_{0,r}^{(\mathsf{S},i)})_{i\in\mathcal{S}_0^{\mathsf{sid}}})$
$\sigma_{1-b}^{\mathsf{sid}} \leftarrow \mathsf{USign}_r(\mathsf{st}_{1,r-1}^{\mathsf{U}}, (\mathsf{pm}_{1,r}^{(\mathsf{S},i)})_{i\in\mathcal{S}_1^{\mathsf{sid}}})$
if $\sigma_0^{\mathsf{sid}} = \bot \vee \sigma_1^{\mathsf{sid}} = \bot$ **then return** $(\bot, \bot)$
return $(\sigma_0^{\mathsf{sid}}, \sigma_1^{\mathsf{sid}})$

Fig. 1. Security experiments for TBS.

that TBS *is 3-one-more unforgeable if, for all PPT adversaries* $\mathcal{A}$*, and* $n, t \in \mathbb{N}$ *such that* $t < n$

$$\mathsf{AdvTOMUF}^{\mathsf{TBS}}_{\mathcal{A}}(\lambda) = \mathrm{negl}(\lambda).$$

Definition 13 (Partial Blindness of a Threshold Blind Signature Scheme). *Let* $\mathsf{TBS} = (\mathsf{Setup}, \mathsf{KeyGen}, \mathsf{ISign}, \mathsf{USign}, \mathsf{Verify})$ *be a threshold blind signature scheme. We consider the game given in Fig. 1b and denote by* $\mathsf{Adv}^{\mathsf{blind\text{-}t}}_{\mathcal{A},\mathsf{TBS}}(\lambda)$ *the difference between the probability that the game with* $b = 0$ *outputs* 1 *and the probability that the game with* $b = 1$ *outputs* 1*. We say that* TBS *satisfies partial blindness if for all PPT adversaries* $\mathcal{A}$*, and* $n, t \in \mathbb{N}$ *such that* $t < n$*, it holds that*

$$\mathsf{AdvTPBlind}^{\mathsf{TBS}}_{\mathcal{A}}(\lambda) = \mathrm{negl}(\lambda).$$

3 Pairing-Free Blind Signature from CDH

Now, we present our blind signature BS proven under CDH. This scheme will serve as a basis for our threshold blind signature TBS in Sect. 4. We refer to Sect. 1 for a high-level overview of our scheme. To begin, let us establish some convenient notation similar to [29].

3.1 Notation and Preparations

We introduce two maps $\phi^{\mathsf{BB}}_{G,V}\colon \mathbb{G}\times\mathbb{Z}_p^2 \to \mathbb{G}^3$ and $\phi^{\mathsf{DLog}}_{G}\colon \mathbb{Z}_p \to \mathbb{G}$ that are defined as follows:

$$\phi^{\mathsf{BB}}_{G,V}(X,(s,u)) = \begin{pmatrix} u\cdot V + s\cdot X \\ s\cdot G \\ u\cdot G \end{pmatrix}, \tag{3}$$

where $X = \overline{m}U + H$ and $V \in \mathbb{G}$, and

$$\phi^{\mathsf{DLog}}_{G}(w) = wG. \tag{4}$$

We note that map $\phi^{\mathsf{BB}}_{G,V}$ establishes that the image is a valid BB signature (cf. Eq. (1)), while map ϕ^{DLog}_{G} expresses a "knowledge of DLog" statement. We also note that maps ϕ^{DLog}_{G} and $\phi^{\mathsf{BB}}_{G,V}(X,\cdot)$ are linear, when value X is fixed. When values G and V are clear from the context, we will write $\phi_0(X,(s,u))$ and $\phi_1(w)$ for short. For map ϕ_0, we define relation $\mathsf{R_{bb}}$ and induced language $\mathscr{L}_{\mathsf{bb}}$:

$$\mathsf{R_{bb}} := \{(\mathbb{x}_0, \mathbb{w}_0) \mid \mathbf{S} = \phi_0(X,(s,u))\},$$

where $\mathbb{x}_0 = (G,V,X,\mathbf{S}) \in \mathbb{G}^6$ and $\mathbb{w}_0 = (s,u) \in \mathbb{Z}_p^2$. Analogously, for map ϕ_1, we define relation $\mathsf{R_{dlog}}$ and induced language $\mathscr{L}_{\mathsf{dlog}}$:

$$\mathsf{R_{dlog}} := \{(\mathbb{x}_1, \mathbb{w}_1) \mid W = \phi_1(w)\},$$

where $\mathbb{x}_1 = (G,W) \in \mathbb{G}^2$ and $\mathbb{w}_1 = w \in \mathbb{Z}_p$. For the relations $\mathsf{R_{bb}}$ and $\mathsf{R_{dlog}}$, we define the Σ-protocols $\Sigma_0 = (\mathsf{Init}_0, \mathsf{Resp}_0, \mathsf{Verify}_0)$ and $\Sigma_1 = (\mathsf{Init}_1, \mathsf{Resp}_1, \mathsf{Verify}_1)$, respectively, with challenge space $\mathbb{Z}_p$. We denote the HVZK simulators of Σ_0 and Σ_1 by Sim_0 and Sim_1, respectively. Instantiations of Σ_0 and Σ_1 are given below.

Instantiation of the Σ-protocols. We can instantiate both Σ_0 and Σ_1 with a standard Schnorr-type Σ-protocol with challenge space $\mathbb{Z}_p$ for the relation of statements $\mathbb{x} = \mathbf{T}$ and witnesses $\mathbb{w} = \mathbf{w}$ with $\phi(\mathbf{w}) = \mathbf{T}$, where $\phi\colon \mathbb{Z}_p^{\omega} \to \mathbb{G}^{\kappa}$ is a linear map. Concretely, such a Σ-protocol looks as follows:

Σ-protocol $\Sigma = (\mathsf{Init}, \mathsf{Resp}, \mathsf{Verify})$ for R_{ϕ} with $\mathbb{x} = (\phi, \mathbf{T})$ and $\mathbb{w} = \mathbf{w}$

- $\mathsf{Init}(\mathbb{x}, \mathbb{w})$:
  1. Sample $\mathbf{r} \xleftarrow{\$} \mathbb{Z}_p^{\omega}$ and set $\mathbf{A} := \phi(\mathbf{r})$.
  2. Output commitment $\mathbf{A}$ and state $\mathsf{st} := (\mathbf{w}, \mathbf{r})$.

- $\mathsf{Resp}(\mathrm{st}, c)$: Output $\mathbf{z} := c \cdot \mathbf{w} + \mathbf{r}$,
- $\mathsf{Verify}(\mathbb{x}, A, c, z)$: Output 1 if $\mathbf{A} = \phi(z) - c \cdot \mathbf{T}$ and 0 otherwise.

It is well-known that the generic Σ-protocol satisfies useful properties (cf. [28]).

Lemma 1 (Properties of the generic Σ-protocol Σ). *The above generic Σ-protocol Σ is correct, special sound, HVZK and efficient. Additionally, it is strongly randomizable. More concretely*

- $\mathsf{Sim}(\mathbf{T}, c)$ *samples* $\mathbf{z} \xleftarrow{\$} \mathbb{Z}_p^\omega$, *sets* $\mathbf{A} = c \cdot \mathbf{T} - \phi(\mathbf{z})$ *and outputs* $(\mathbf{A}, \mathbf{z})$.
- $\mathsf{Rand}(\mathbf{T}, (\mathbf{A}^*, c^*, \mathbf{z}^*))$ *samples* $c' \xleftarrow{\$} \mathbb{Z}_p$ *and* $\mathbf{z}' \xleftarrow{\$} \mathbb{Z}_p^\omega$ *and outputs*

$$(\mathbf{A}, c, \mathbf{z}) = (\mathbf{A}^* - c'\mathbf{T} + \phi(\mathbf{z}'), c^* + c', \mathbf{z}^* + \mathbf{z}').$$

NIPS for Pedersen Openings. We define relations $\mathsf{R}_{\mathsf{Ped}}$ and $\tilde{\mathsf{R}}_{\mathsf{Ped}}$ as follows:

$$\mathsf{R}_{\mathsf{Ped}} := \{(\mathbb{x}, \mathbb{w}) \mid C = \overline{m}U + tG\}, \text{ where } \mathbb{x} = (C, U, G), \ \mathbb{w} = (\overline{m}, t), \quad (5)$$

$$\tilde{\mathsf{R}}_{\mathsf{Ped}} := \{(\mathbb{x}, \mathbb{w}) \mid \mathbb{w}G = U \vee (\mathbb{x}, \mathbb{w}) \in \mathsf{R}_{\mathsf{Ped}}\}, \quad \text{where } \mathbb{x} = (C, U, G). \quad (6)$$

We denote by $\mathsf{NIPS}_{\mathsf{Ped}} = (\mathsf{NIPS}_{\mathsf{Ped}}.\mathsf{Prove}^{\mathsf{H}_{\mathsf{Ped}}}, \mathsf{NIPS}_{\mathsf{Ped}}.\mathsf{Ver}^{\mathsf{H}_{\mathsf{Ped}}})$ a NIPS for relation $\mathsf{R}_{\mathsf{Ped}}$ that is statistically witness-indistinguishable and online-extractable for relation $\tilde{\mathsf{R}}_{\mathsf{Ped}}$. $\mathsf{NIPS}_{\mathsf{Ped}}$ has access to random oracle $\mathsf{H}_{\mathsf{Ped}} : \{0,1\}^* \to \mathcal{Y}_{\mathsf{Ped}}$ with image space $\mathcal{Y}_{\mathsf{Ped}}$. A suitable instantiation is given in [29, Section C].

Furthermore, $\mathsf{Com} = (\mathsf{Com.Setup}, \mathsf{Com.Commit})$ denotes a linearly homomorphic commitment scheme. Looking ahead, we require that Com is perfectly hiding and computationally binding. If clear by context, we abbreviate $\mathsf{Com.Commit}$ as Com. A suitable instantiation for Com are Pedersen commitments.

Random Oracles. Our scheme is in the random oracle model. For readability, we define several random oracles and give a brief overview here.

- $\mathsf{H}_{\mathsf{M}} : \{0,1\}^* \to \mathbb{Z}_p$ is used to hash the messages m.
- $\mathsf{H}_{\Sigma} : \{0,1\}^* \to \mathbb{Z}_p$ is used to compile Σ_0 and Σ_1 into an OR-proof via Fiat-Shamir.
- $\mathsf{H}_{\mathsf{Ped}} : \{0,1\}^* \to \mathcal{Y}_{\mathsf{Ped}}$ is the random oracle for $\mathsf{NIPS}_{\mathsf{Ped}}$.
- $\mathsf{H}_{\mathsf{DLog}} : \{0,1\}^* \to \mathbb{G}$ is used to derive the element W for the DLog proof Σ_1.
- $\mathsf{H}_{\mathsf{V}} : \{0,1\}^* \to \mathbb{G}$ is used to derive a part of the BB verification key.

3.2 Construction

Our signature scheme BS is given in Fig. 2 and Fig. 3. It allows to issue signatures of the form (S_1, S_2, π), where (S_1, S_2) is a BB signature and π is a Fiat-Shamir proof of the disjunctive relation $\mathsf{R}_{\mathsf{bb}} \cup \mathsf{R}_{\mathsf{dlog}}$. The latter is an OR-proof guaranteeing that either the signature (S_1, S_2) is well-formed or that the discrete logarithm of $\mathsf{H}_{\mathsf{DLog}}(\tau) = W$ is known. The OR-proof is instantiated by additive secret sharing of the challenge of Σ_0 and Σ_1 for R_{bb} and $\mathsf{R}_{\mathsf{dlog}}$, respectively, following the well-known techniques by [15].

$\mathsf{Setup}(1^\lambda)$	$\mathsf{Verify}(\mathsf{vk}, m, \tau, \sigma)$
$(\mathbb{G}, p, G) \leftarrow \mathsf{GrGen}(1^\lambda)$	**parse** $(S_1, S_2, \pi, (d_1, r_1), (d_2, r_2)) = \sigma$
$\mathsf{par}_{\mathsf{Com}} \leftarrow \mathsf{Com.Setup}(1^\lambda)$	**parse** $(\mathbf{A}_0, A_1, c, c_0, \mathbf{z}_0, z_1) = \pi$
$\mathsf{par} := ((\mathbb{G}, p, G), \mathsf{par}_{\mathsf{Com}})$	$\mathbf{S} := (S_1, S_2, U), \overline{m} := \mathsf{H}_{\mathsf{M}}(m), X := \overline{m}U + H$
return par	$\mathbf{S}_\$:= \mathbf{S} + (d_1 G, 0, 0)^\top$
$\mathsf{KeyGen}()$	$\mathbf{A}_{\$,0} := \mathbf{A}_0 - (d_2 G, 0, 0)^\top$
$u \xleftarrow{\$} \mathbb{Z}_p, U := uG$	$C_S := \mathsf{Com.Commit}(d_1, r_1)$
$H \xleftarrow{\$} \mathbb{G}$	$C_{A_0} := \mathsf{Com.Commit}(d_2, r_2)$
return $\mathsf{vk} := (G, U, H), \mathsf{sk} := u$	$\mathbb{x}_0^C := (G, V, X, \mathbf{S}_\$)$
	$W := \mathsf{H}_{\mathsf{DLog}}(\tau)$, $\mathbb{x}_1 := (G, W)$
	$c := \mathsf{H}(\mathbb{x}_0^C, \mathbf{A}_{\$,0}, \mathbb{x}_1, A_1, m, C_S, C_{A_0}, \mathsf{par}_{\mathsf{Com}})$
	$c_1 := c - c_0$
	if $\mathsf{Verify}_0(\mathbb{x}_0, \mathbf{A}_0, c_0, \mathbf{z}_0) = 0$ **return** 0
	if $\mathsf{Verify}_1(\mathbb{x}_1, A_1, c_1, z_1) = 0$ **return** 0
	return 1

Fig. 2. The algorithms Setup, KeyGen and Verify belonging to scheme BS. Differences to the DDH-reliant scheme from [29] are highlighted in grey .

In order to ensure that we can prove OMUF for our scheme BS, we let the signer issue a masked signature tuple $\mathbf{T}_\$^* = (S_1 + d_1 G, S_2)$ as well as a commitment C_S to value d_1 in the second move of our scheme. We let the signer reveal d_1 as well as the corresponding commitment randomness r only in the last round. This ensures that unfinished sessions do not reveal the BB signature (S_1, S_2) and the commitment ensures the tuple $(C_S, \mathbf{T}_\$^*)$ determines (S_1, S_2) *computationally.* Looking ahead, the latter property is required for (computational) soundness of the proof π.

As a consequence, the user does not know the actual signature tuple (S_1, S_2) which is required to derive the joint challenge of the Σ-protocols via H_Σ. Neither can the user blind the first flow of the Σ-protocol $\mathbf{A}_0^*$ at this point, as this requires knowledge of the signature tuple. Therefore, the user computes these values homomorphically, i.e., it sets up masked signatures $(S_{\$,1}, S_{\$,2})$ and masked commitment $\mathbf{A}_{\$,0}$ that still contain the masking term $d_1 G$. These values and the masking term $d_1 G$ are then blinded, similar to [29]. Then, the user derives the joint Σ-protocol challenge on the masked values $\mathbf{A}_{\$,0}$ and $(S_{\$,1}, S_{\$,2})$, as well as the commitment C_S and C_{A_0} which determine the randomized masking terms d_1 and d_2.

As verification of signatures σ generated by BS involves recomputing the joint challenge c, it is necessary to include the openings (d_1, r_1) and (d_2, r_2) for the commitments C_S and C_{A_0} in the final signature σ.

$\mathsf{ISign}_1(\mathsf{sk}, \tau, C, \pi_{\mathsf{Ped}})$

$\mathbb{x}_{\mathsf{Ped}} := (C, U, G)$

$\textbf{req } \mathsf{NIPS}_{\mathsf{Ped}}.\mathsf{Ver}^{\mathsf{H}_{\mathsf{Ped}}}(\mathbb{x}_{\mathsf{Ped}}, \pi_{\mathsf{Ped}}) = 1$

$s^* \xleftarrow{\$} \mathbb{Z}_p; \quad \mathbb{w}_0 := (s^*, \mathsf{sk})$

$d_1^*, r_1^* \xleftarrow{\$} \mathbb{Z}_p$

$X_C := C + H; \quad W := \mathsf{H}_{\mathsf{DLog}}(\tau)$

$\mathbf{T}^* := \phi_0(X_C, \mathbb{w}_0); \quad \mathbf{T}_\$^* := \mathbf{T}^* + (d_1^* G, 0, 0)^\top$

$C_S^* := \mathsf{Com}(d_1^*, r_1^*)$

$\mathbb{x}_0^t := (G, V, X_C, \mathbf{T}^*); \quad \mathbb{x}_1 := (G, W)$

$c_1^* \xleftarrow{\$} \mathbb{Z}_p; \quad (A_1^*, z_1^*) \leftarrow \mathsf{Sim}_1(\mathbb{x}_1, c_1^*)$

$(\mathbf{A}_0^*, \mathsf{st}_0) \leftarrow \mathsf{Init}_0(\mathbb{x}_0^t, \mathbb{w}_0)$

$\textbf{return } (\mathbf{T}_\$^*, \mathbf{A}_0^*, A_1^*, C_S^*)$

$\mathsf{ISign}_2(c^*)$

$c_0^* := c^* - c_1^*$

$\mathbf{z}_0^* \leftarrow \mathsf{Resp}_0(\mathsf{st}_0, c_0^*)$

$\textbf{return } (\mathbf{z}_0^*, z_1^*, c_0^*, d_1^*, r_1^*)$

$\mathsf{USign}_2(\mathbf{z}_0^*, z_1^*, c_0^*, d_1^*, r_1^*)$

$\textbf{req } \mathbf{A}_0^* = \phi_0(X_C, \mathbf{z}_0^*) - c_0^*(\mathbf{T}_\$^* - (d_1^* G, 0, 0)^\top)$
$\qquad = \phi_0(X_C, \mathbf{z}_0^*) - c_0^* \mathbf{T}^*$

$\textbf{req } A_1^* = \phi_1(\mathbf{z}_1^*) - c_1^* W$

$\textbf{req } C_S^* = \mathsf{Com}(d_1^*, r_1^*)$

$c_0 := c_0^* + c_0'; \quad c_1 := c_1^* + c_1' \quad /\!/ \; c = c_0 + c_1$

$\mathbf{z}_0 := \mathbf{z}_0^* + \mathbf{z}_0' + c_0^* \cdot (s', 0)$

$z_1 := z_1^* + z_1'$

$d_1 := d_1^* + d_1'; r_1 := r_1^* + r_1'$

$d_2 := c_0' d_1 + d_2'; r_2 := c_0' r_1 + r_2'$

$\mathbf{S} := \mathbf{S}_\$ - (d_1 G, 0, 0)^\top$

$\mathbf{A}_0 := \mathbf{A}_{\$,0} + (d_2 G, 0, 0)^\top$

$\pi := (\mathbf{A}_0, A_1, c, c_0, \mathbf{z}_0, z_1)$

$\sigma_{\mathsf{bb}} := (S_1, S_2, \pi, (d_1, r_1), (d_2, r_2))$

$\textbf{return } \sigma_{\mathsf{bb}}$

$\mathsf{USign}_0(\mathsf{vk}, m, \tau)$

$t \xleftarrow{\$} \mathbb{Z}_p; \quad \overline{m} := \mathsf{H}_{\mathsf{M}}(m),$

$C := \overline{m} U + tG$

$\mathbb{x}_{\mathsf{Ped}} := (C, U, G); \quad \mathbb{w}_{\mathsf{Ped}} := (\overline{m}, t)$

$\pi_{\mathsf{Ped}} \leftarrow \mathsf{NIPS}_{\mathsf{Ped}}.\mathsf{Prove}^{\mathsf{H}_{\mathsf{Ped}}}(\mathbb{x}_{\mathsf{Ped}}, \mathbb{w}_{\mathsf{Ped}})$

$\textbf{return } (C, \pi_{\mathsf{Ped}})$

$\mathsf{USign}_1(\mathbf{T}_\$^*, \mathbf{A}_0^*, A_1^*, C_S^*)$

$s' \xleftarrow{\$} \mathbb{Z}_p;$

$c_0', c_1' \xleftarrow{\$} \mathbb{Z}_p;$

$\mathbf{z}_0' \xleftarrow{\$} \mathbb{Z}_p^2; \quad z_1' \xleftarrow{\$} \mathbb{Z}_p$

$d_1', r_1', d_2', r_2' \xleftarrow{\$} \mathbb{Z}_p$

$X := \overline{m} U + H = X_C - tG$

$\mathbf{S}_\$:= \mathbf{T}_\$^* - (t \cdot T_{\$,2}^*, 0, 0)^\top + \phi_0(X, (s', 0)) + (d_1' G, 0, 0)^\top$
$\qquad = \mathbf{S} + ((d_1^* + d_1')G, 0, 0)^\top$

$\mathbf{A}_{\$,0} := \mathbf{A}_0^* - (t \cdot A_{0,2}^*, 0, 0)^\top + \phi_0(X, \mathbf{z}_0') - c_0' \mathbf{S}_\$ - (d_2' G, 0, 0)^\top$
$\qquad = \mathbf{A}_0 - ((c_0'(d_1^* + d_1') + d_2')G, 0, 0)^\top$

$C_S := C_S^* + \mathsf{Com}(d_1', r_1') = \mathsf{Com}(d_1^* + d_1', r_1^* + r_1')$

$C_{A_0} := c_0' C_S + \mathsf{Com}(d_2', r_2')$
$\qquad = \mathsf{Com}(c_0'(d_1^* + d_1') + d_2', c_0'(r_1^* + r_1') + r_2')$

$A_1 := A_1^* + \phi_1(z_1') - c_1' W = A_1^* + z_1' G - c_1' W$

$\mathbb{x}_0^C := (G, V, X, \mathbf{S}_\$); \quad \mathbb{x}_1 := (G, W)$

$c := \mathsf{H}_\Sigma(\mathbb{x}_0^C, \mathbf{A}_{\$,0}, \mathbb{x}_1, A_1, m, C_S, C_{A_0}, \mathsf{par}_{\mathsf{Com}})$

$c^* := c - c_0' - c_1'$

$\textbf{return } c^*$

Fig. 3. The interactive signing protocol executed by the signer and the user in scheme BS. Algorithms ISign_1 and ISign_2 are executed by the signer, algorithms USign_0, USign_1 and USign_2 are executed by the user. Differences to the DDH-reliant scheme from [29] are highlighted in grey. The Σ-protocols and statements are blinded as in [29], except that some operations are performed with masked $\mathbf{T}_\$^*$. Note that we write Com short for Com.Commit. We leave the state implicit for readability.

Optimizations. The performance of our scheme BS can be improved via 2 natural optimizations. The numbers reported in Sect. 1 assume the following changes are made.

1. The values $\mathbf{A}_0, A_1$ are omitted from the proof π as these values can be reconstructed from the remaining transcript of π. We note that these are not omitted in the formal construction as it simplifies notation in the security analysis.

2. We can further reduce the signature size by one $\mathbb{Z}_p$ element. Instead of committing to d_1 and d_2 in separate commitments, we can commit to d_1 and d_2 in a single multi-Pedersen commitment of the form $C_S = d_1G_1 + d_2G_2 + rG$. Therefore, only a single opening value r is required. As we only require that d_1 and d_2 are computationally fixed by C_S, it is straightforward to adapt the proof accordingly.

3.3 Security Analysis

We give an overview of our security analysis. In particular, we show correctness, one-more unforgeability and blindness. Due to space limitations, we only provide proof sketches. Formal proofs for all statements are given in the full version [36].

Correctness. It is easy but tedious to verify that the scheme is correct.

Theorem 1 (Correctness). *BS is correct with error γ_{err}, where γ_{err} is the correctness error of $\mathsf{NIPS}_{\mathsf{Ped}}$.*

One-more Unforgeability. We show that BS is one-more unforgeable. As discussed in Sect. 1.2, we follow the proof strategy by [29] but manage to remove the reliance on DDH in their argument. We refer to Sect. 1.2 for an overview of the puncturing-based proof strategy of [29]. Let us briefly discuss how our modifications allow to prove security under CDH in more detail.

Simulation Strategy for BB Signatures. We must be able to simulate BB (pre-)signatures $\mathbf{T}^*$ issued by the signer. As our goal is to puncture the BB verification key for a specific message $\overline{m}^*$, this turns out to be non-trivial. Here, $\overline{m}^*$ is the hash of a message for which the adversary provides a forgery but never finishes a signing session with the forgeries' common message τ^*. Note that $\overline{m}^*$ is guessed by the reduction in advance which is required for puncturing.[6]
Given the punctured setup, it remains easy to sign any message *not* equal to $\overline{m}^*$. However, the adversary might still query $\overline{m}^*$ in *some* sessions which we refer to as "challenge" sessions hereafter. These challenge sessions are all sessions where the Pedersen commitment C commits to $\overline{m}^*$ which can be tested by extracting from π_{Ped}. Therefore, we can identify whether any given signing session corresponds to a challenge session or not in the reduction. Let us explain how to simulate $\mathbf{T}^*$ in challenge sessions.
In [29], a DDH-based argument allows to randomize all such pre-signatures $\mathbf{T}^*$ which suffices for simulation. In our case, we cannot afford this argument as we wish to avoid decisional assumptions. However, as the signer now masks $\mathbf{T}^*$ with a random value d_1 and the commitment Com is hiding, we can argue

[6] This guess is correct with sufficient probability following the argument by [29] based on the pigeon-hole principle: There are only $k-1$ finished sessions on common message τ^* and but k forgeries. We refer to Game 9 in the proof in the full version [36] for more details. .

that we can randomize all *unfinished* challenge sessions. In particular, we know that no session is finished if $\overline{m}^*$ is extracted from π_{Ped} and the common message τ is the forgery's common message τ^* (which can be guessed in advance). Therefore, by sending a random tuple $(\mathbf{T}^*_{\$}, C^*_S)$, we can simulate such unfinished sessions as described in Sect. 1.2.
However, we must *also* simulate sessions where $\overline{m}^*$ is extracted *and* $\tau \neq \tau^*$. These sessions might be finished and if so, reveal a BB pre-signature $\mathbf{T}^*$ for $\overline{m}^*$ in plain (as the user can remove the masking term). Therefore, we must issue well-distributed pre-signatures $\mathbf{T}^*$. However, the verification key is punctured for $\overline{m}^*$ and simulation fails.
To resolve this issue, the crucial observation is that there are *two* ways to issue BB signatures due to symmetry in their structure:

$$S_1 = uV + s(\overline{m}U + H), \qquad S_2 = sG.$$

Roughly, it is hard to compute signatures (without the signing key u) because $u \cdot V = uv \cdot G$ forms a CDH tuple. But we can compute (S_1, S_2) by knowing *either* the discrete logarithm u of U *or* the discrete logarithm v of V. If we choose V differently for each common message τ (e.g., by deriving $V_\tau = \mathsf{H}_\mathsf{V}(\tau)$ as in BS), then we can embed elements V_τ with known logarithm into H_V. This allows to sign *any* message, even if the remaining verification key is punctured. This crucially relies on the structure of (S_1, S_2) and the fact that puncturing is compatible with this observation. To argue security, we embed a CDH challenge in the forgery's V_{τ^*} and puncture the verification key accordingly. As discussed above, for the forgeries' τ^* we can leverage the commitment's hiding property to simulate challenge sessions instead. In total, we can now simulate *all* sessions and the forgery for $\overline{m}^*$ yields a BB signature $\mathbf{S}$ for the punctured verification key, allowing to solve CDH.

Enforcing Well-Formedness. As signatures contain an OR-proof that either the BB signature $\mathbf{S}$ is valid (i.e., well-formed according to the above equation) or the discrete logarithm of W is known, we have to ensure that the adversary indeed provides us with valid BB signatures. To do so, in contrast to [29], we must rely on a forking-based argument to avoid the DDH assumption, following the proof technique by [13].

Theorem 2 (One-More Unforgeability). *For any PPT adversary $\mathcal{A}$ causing at most Q random oracle queries and finishing at most $k-1$ signing sessions, there exist reductions $\mathcal{A}_{\mathsf{KS}}, \mathcal{A}_{\mathsf{DL}}, \mathcal{A}_{\mathsf{Bnd}}$ and $\mathcal{A}_{\mathsf{CDH}}$ having a runtime similar to $\mathcal{A}$ such that*

$$\mathsf{AdvOMUF}^{\mathsf{BS}}_{\mathcal{A}}(\lambda) \leq \frac{Q^2}{p} + \mathsf{AdvKS}^{\mathsf{NIPS}_{\mathsf{Ped}}, \tilde{\mathsf{R}}_{\mathsf{Ped}}}_{\mathcal{A}_{\mathsf{KS}}}(\lambda) + \mathsf{AdvDL}^{\mathsf{GrGen}}_{\mathcal{A}_{\mathsf{DL}}}(\lambda) +$$
$$Q^2 \cdot \left(k \cdot \left(\sqrt{Q_{\mathsf{H}_\Sigma}(\mathsf{AdvDL}^{\mathsf{GrGen}}_{\mathcal{A}_{\mathsf{DL}}}(\lambda) + \mathsf{AdvBnd}^{\mathsf{Com}}_{\mathcal{A}_{\mathsf{Bnd}}}(\lambda))} + \frac{Q_{\mathsf{H}_\Sigma}}{p}\right) + \mathsf{AdvCDH}^{\mathsf{GrGen}}_{\mathcal{A}_{\mathsf{CDH}}}(\lambda)\right).$$

Blindness. Blindness follows as the commitment C_S is randomomized and the user blinds the signature and proofs as in [29]. We follow the techniques from [28, Theorem 4.7] for a more compact proof. An important point is that we must rely on a forking-based argument, similar to [13], to ensure that the issued BB signatures are well-formed. This is crucial: if the adversary $\mathcal{A}$ finds a way to issue and identify misformed BB signatures $\mathbf{S}$, then $\mathcal{A}$ could issue a well-formed signature in one signing session and a misformed signature in the other session, breaking blindness. However, the signer issues an interactive Σ-protocol proof of well-formedness for $\mathbf{T}^*$ which allows to deduce that the derived signature $\mathbf{S}$ is well-formed, else the signer must know the discrete logarithm of $W = \mathsf{H}_{\mathsf{DLog}}(\tau)$. Alternatively, we could let the signer prove well-formedness of $\mathbf{T}^*$ with a separate NIPS as in [13].

Theorem 3 (Blindness). *For any PPT adversary $\mathcal{A}$ causing at most Q random oracle queries and starting at most k signing sessions, there exist reductions $\mathcal{A}_{\mathsf{WI}}$ and $\mathcal{A}_{\mathsf{DL}}, \mathcal{A}_{\mathsf{Bnd}}$, where $\mathcal{A}_{\mathsf{DL}}, \mathcal{A}_{\mathsf{Bnd}}$ have running time roughly that of $\mathcal{A}$, such that*

$$\mathsf{AdvPBlind}^{\mathsf{BS}}_{\mathcal{A}}(\lambda) \le 2kQ \cdot \left(\mathsf{AdvWI}^{\mathsf{NIPS},\tilde{\mathsf{R}}_{\mathsf{Ped}}}_{\mathcal{A}_{\mathsf{WI}}}(Q,\lambda) + \frac{1+Q}{p} + \sqrt{Q(\mathsf{AdvDL}^{\mathsf{GrGen}}_{\mathcal{A}_{\mathsf{DL}}}(\lambda) + \mathsf{AdvBnd}^{\mathsf{Com}}_{\mathcal{A}_{\mathsf{Bnd}}}(\lambda))} \right).$$

4 Pairing-Free Threshold Blind Signature from CDH

Here, we describe how to enhance our blind signature BS with a threshold signing procedure. We denote the resulting threshold blind signature by TBS. As we base our construction on the blind signature BS, we employ the same notation and building blocks. We refer to Sect. 3.1 for an overview.

More Preparations. Let us define the PPT algorithm $\mathsf{IssueShares}$. On input of value $u \in \mathbb{Z}_p$, number of signers n and threshold $t+1$, the algorithm $\{(i, u_i)\}_{i\in[n]} \leftarrow \mathsf{IssueShares}(u, n, t+1)$ computes n Shamir's shares $\{u_i\}_{i\in[n]}$ of value u, of which $t+1$ will allow to reconstruct value u. See the full version [36] for a formal definition. The Lagrange coefficient belonging to the key share of signer k for signing set $\mathcal{S}$ is written as $\lambda_k^{\mathcal{S}}$. If the signing set $\mathcal{S}$ is clear from the context, we may omit it. Also, let $\mathsf{H}_{\mathsf{com}} : \{0,1\}^* \to \mathbb{G}$ denote another hash function and let $\mathsf{F}_{\mathsf{msk}}$ be a PRF that maps from $\{0,1\}^*$ to $\mathbb{Z}_p^4$ with key space $\mathcal{K}_{\mathsf{msk}}$.

4.1 Construction

We give our threshold blind signature scheme TBS in Figs. 4 and 5. On a high level, we let each signer generate a partial BB signature via its share u_i and employ a commit-and-open protocol to derive the challenge for the simulated Σ-protocol Σ_1. Looking ahead, the latter enables us to switch simulation of Σ_1 and Σ_0 in the OMUF proof.

Overview. Let us give a brief description of our scheme TBS. KeyGen generates n shares $\{u_i\}_{i\in[n]}$ of secret key u, $t+1$ of which are necessary to reconstruct u. Each signing party i receives one secret key share.

Signing Protocol. To initiate a signing session, the user again commits in C to $\overline{m} = \mathsf{H_M}(m)$ as in our non-threshold blind signature BS. The user sends C and an opening proof π_{Ped} to the signers.

To sign the commitment C, each signer k computes a partial BB signature $\mathbf{T}_k^* = \phi_0(X_C, (s_k^*, \lambda_k u_k))$ via its share u_k for $X_C = C + H$. As before, the partial signature $\mathbf{T}_k^*$ is masked via $\mathbf{T}_{\$,k}^* = \mathbf{T}_k^* + (d_{1,k}^*, 0, 0)^\mathsf{T}$. Note that each signer chooses its own mask $d_{1,k}^*$ and commits to $d_{1,k}^*$ in $C_{S,k}^*$. Then, signer k initiates a Σ_0 proof via $\mathbf{A}_{0,k}^* \leftarrow \mathsf{Init}_0$ to prove statement $\mathbb{x}_{0,k} = (G, V, X_C, \mathbf{T}_k^*)$ via witness $\mathbb{w}_{0,k} = (s_k^*, \lambda_k u_k)$ and computes a simulated Σ_1 transcript $(A_{1,k}^*, c_{1,k}^*, z_{1,k}^*)$ for the statement $\mathbb{x}_1 = (G, W)$ with challenge $c_{1,k}^* \in \mathbb{Z}_p$. The challenge $c_{1,k}^* = \mathsf{H_{com}}(k, c_{1,k}^*)$ is committed to in cm_k^c via $\mathsf{H_{com}}$.

As in BS, the masked (partial) signature $\mathbf{T}_{\$,k}^*$, the Σ-protocol commitments $\mathbf{A}_{0,k}^*$ and $A_{1,k}^*$ and the commitment $C_{S,k}^*$ are sent to the user. In addition, each signer k also sends the challenge commitment cm_k^c.

Upon receiving all signer messages, the user sums up the $t+1$ randomized partial signatures $\mathbf{T}_{\$,i}^*$, the $t+1$ commitments $C_{S,i}^*$, and the $t+1$ Σ_0 and Σ_1 commitments $\mathbf{A}_{0,i}^*$ and $A_{1,i}^*$, respectively. Due to linearity, these resulting values form a valid BS signer response which is then blinded by the user as in BS. Also, the user derives the blinded challenge c^* as in BS and forwards it to all signers.

In response, the signers open their challenge commitments $c_{1,k}^*$ and forward their opening to the user. The user sums up the challenges $c_{1,i}^*$ to derive the challenge c_1^* for Σ_1 and forwards the individual challenges to the signers. The signers then verify whether $c_{1,i}^*$ is indeed a correct opening for cm_i^c. If so, each signer derives the challenge c_1^* for Σ_1 (as above) and the challenge $c_0^* = c^* - c_1^*$ for Σ_0. Finally, each signer sends their opening $(d_{1,k}^*, r_{1,k}^*)$ for $C_{S,k}^*$ and the honest and simulated Σ-protocol responses $\mathbf{z}_{0,k}^*$ and $z_{1,k}^*$ for Σ_0 and Σ_1, respectively, to the user.

Again, by linearity, it suffices to sum up the openings and the Σ-protocol responses to obtain a valid BS signer response. Then, the user derives its signature as in BS.

Verification. As described above, signatures issued by TBS are of the same form as BS signatures and verification is identical.

4.2 Security Analysis

We show correctness, one-more unforgeability and blindness. We refer to the full version [36] for formal proofs.

Correctness. As alluded to above, the correctness of TBS follows from correctness of BS, and from the linearity of the commitment Com and the Σ-protocols.

Theorem 4 (Correctness). *TBS is correct with error γ_{err}, where γ_{err} is the correctness error of $\mathsf{NIPS_{Ped}}$.*

Setup(1^λ)

$(\mathbb{G}, p, G) \leftarrow \mathsf{GrGen}(1^\lambda)$
$\mathsf{par}_{\mathsf{Com}} \leftarrow \mathsf{Com.Setup}(1^\lambda)$
$\mathsf{par} := ((\mathbb{G}, p, G), \mathsf{par}_{\mathsf{Com}})$
return par

Verify$(\mathsf{vk}, m, \tau, \sigma)$

// Verification as in BS (cf. Section 3)
return $\mathsf{BS.Verify}(\mathsf{vk}, m, \tau, \sigma)$

KeyGen$(n, t+1)$

$u \xleftarrow{\$} \mathbb{Z}_p; \quad U := uG$
$\{(i, u_i)\}_{i \in [n]} \leftarrow \mathsf{IssueShares}(u, n, t+1)$
$(w_{i,j})_{(i,j) \in [n]^2, i<j} \xleftarrow{\$} \mathcal{K}_{\mathsf{msk}}^{n(n-1)/2}$
$\forall_{i,j \in [n], i>j} w_{i,j} := w_{j,i}$
$H \xleftarrow{\$} \mathbb{G}$
$\mathsf{vk} := (G, U, H)$
for $i \in [n]$ **do**
  $\mathsf{sk}_i := u_i$
return $(\mathsf{vk}, \{\mathsf{sk}_i\}_{i \in [n]})$

Fig. 4. The algorithms Setup, KeyGen and Verify belonging to scheme TBS. Differences to blind signature scheme BS due to translation into the threshold setting are highlighted in grey .

One-More Unforgeability. First, we show that partial signing is compatible with the puncturing strategy, i.e., partial signatures $\mathbf{T}_k^*$ can be simulated for message $m \neq m^*$ while the verification key is punctured for m^*, as shown in the full version [36]. Then, we carefully follow the proof strategy of BS (cf. Section 3.3) to argue one-more unforgeability, namely OMUF-3.

We note that the commit-and-open protocol to establish c_1^* is crucial to employ witness indistinguishability of the OR-proof. That is, the simulation can control the agreed upon challenge c_1^* *after* seeing the user's challenge c^* by programming the honest openings $c_{1,k}^*$ for cm_k^c. This allows to simulate either Σ_0 or Σ_1 at will, and to generate the other with the corresponding witness. Furthermore, we leverage the PRF-based masking to argue that unless some session is completed (i.e., all honest signers in $\mathcal{S}$ execute ISign_3 with the same ssid), the response in ISign_3 looks random in the view of the signer. This is important as partial signatures cannot be simulated for the message m^* for which vk is punctured.

Theorem 5 (OMUF-3). *Let p be the order of group $\mathbb{G}$. For any PPT adversary $\mathcal{A}$ making at most Q random oracle queries and finishing at most $k-1$ signing sessions, there exist reductions $\mathcal{A}_{\mathsf{KS}}, \mathcal{A}_{\mathsf{DL}}, \mathcal{A}_{\mathsf{Bnd}}$ and $\mathcal{A}_{\mathsf{CDH}}$ having a runtime similar to $\mathcal{A}$ such that*

$$\mathsf{AdvTOMUF}_{\mathcal{A}}^{\mathsf{TBS}}(\lambda) \leq \frac{2Q^2}{p} + \mathsf{AdvKS}_{\mathcal{A}_{\mathsf{KS}}}^{\mathsf{NIPS}_{\mathsf{Ped}}, \tilde{\mathsf{R}}_{\mathsf{Ped}}}(\lambda) + \mathsf{AdvDL}_{\mathcal{A}_{\mathsf{DL}}}^{\mathsf{GrGen}}(\lambda) +$$
$$Q^2 \cdot \left(k \cdot \left(\sqrt{Q(\mathsf{AdvDL}_{\mathcal{A}_{\mathsf{DL}}}^{\mathsf{GrGen}}(\lambda) + \mathsf{AdvBnd}_{\mathcal{A}_{\mathsf{Bnd}}}^{\mathsf{Com}}(\lambda))} + \frac{Q}{p}\right) + \mathsf{AdvCDH}_{\mathcal{A}_{\mathsf{CDH}}}^{\mathsf{GrGen}}(\lambda)\right).$$

$\mathsf{ISign}_1(k, \mathsf{sk}_k, \mathsf{aux} := \bot, \mathsf{ctx}, \tau, (C, \pi_{\mathsf{Ped}}, \mathcal{S}))$

$\textbf{return } \bot \textbf{ if } k \notin \mathcal{S}$

$\mathbb{x}_{\mathsf{Ped}} := (C, U, G)$

$\textbf{req } \mathsf{NIPS}_{\mathsf{Ped}}.\mathsf{Ver}^{\mathsf{H}_{\mathsf{Ped}}}(\mathbb{x}_{\mathsf{Ped}}, \pi_{\mathsf{Ped}}) = 1$

$s_k^* \xleftarrow{\$} \mathbb{Z}_p; \quad \mathbb{w}_{0,k} := (s_k^*, \mathsf{sk}_k = \lambda_k u_k)$

$d_{1,k}^*, r_{1,k}^* \xleftarrow{\$} \mathbb{Z}_p$

$X_C := C + H; \quad W := \mathsf{H}_{\mathsf{DLog}}(\tau)$

$\mathbf{T}_k^* := \phi_0(X_C, \mathbb{w}_{0,k}); \quad \mathbf{T}_{\$,k}^* := \mathbf{T}_k^* + (d_k^* G, 0, 0)^\mathsf{T}$

$C_{S,k}^* := \mathsf{Com.Commit}(d_{1,k}^*, r_{1,k}^*)$

$\mathbb{x}_{0,k}^t := (G, V, X_C, \mathbf{T}_k^*); \quad \mathbb{x}_1 := (G, W)$

$(\mathbf{A}_{0,k}^*, \mathsf{st}_{0,k}) \leftarrow \mathsf{Init}_0(\mathbb{x}_{0,k}^t, \mathbb{w}_{0,k})$

$c_{1,k}^* \xleftarrow{\$} \mathbb{Z}_p; \quad \mathsf{cm}_k^c := \mathsf{H}_{\mathsf{cm}}(k, c_{1,k}^*)$

$(A_{1,k}^*, z_{1,k}^*) \leftarrow \mathsf{Sim}_1(\mathbb{x}_1, c_{i,k}^*)$

$\textbf{return } (\mathbf{T}_{\$,k}^*, \mathbf{A}_{0,k}^*, A_{1,k}^*, C_{S,k}^*, \mathsf{cm}_k^c)$

$\mathsf{ISign}_2(k, (c^*, \{\mathsf{cm}_i^c\}_{i \in \mathcal{S}}))$

$\textbf{return } c_{1,k}^*$

$\mathsf{ISign}_3(k, \{c_{1,i}^*\}_{i \in \mathcal{S}})$

$\mathsf{ssid} := (\mathsf{ctx}, \mathcal{S}, (c_{1,i}^*)_{i \in \mathcal{S}})$

$\textbf{for } i \in \mathcal{S} \textbf{ do}$

$\quad \textbf{return } \bot \textbf{ if } \mathsf{cm}_i^c \neq \mathsf{H}_{\mathsf{cm}}(i, c_{1,i}^*)$

$c_1^* := \sum_{i \in \mathcal{S}} c_{1,i}^*; \quad c_0^* := c^* - c_1^*$

$\Delta_k \leftarrow \sum_{j \in \mathcal{S}, j<k} \mathsf{F}_{\mathsf{msk}, w_{k,j}}(\mathsf{ssid}) - \sum_{j \in \mathcal{S}, j>k} \mathsf{F}_{\mathsf{msk}, w_{k,j}}(\mathsf{ssid})$

$\mathbf{z}_{0,k}^* \leftarrow \mathsf{Resp}_0(\mathsf{st}_{0,k}, c_0^*)$

$\tilde{\mathbf{z}}_{0,k}^* := \mathbf{z}_{0,k}^* + (\Delta_{k,1}, \Delta_{k,2})$

$\tilde{d}_{1,k}^* := d_{1,k}^* + \Delta_{k,3}; \quad \tilde{r}_{1,k}^* := r_{1,k}^* + \Delta_{k,4}$

$\textbf{return } (\mathsf{ssid}, \mathcal{S}, (\tilde{\mathbf{z}}_{0,k}^*, z_{1,k}^*, \tilde{d}_{1,k}^*, \tilde{r}_{1,k}^*))$

$\mathsf{USign}_0(\mathsf{vk}, \mathsf{aux} := \bot, m, \mathcal{S}, \tau)$

$(C, \pi_{\mathsf{Ped}}) \leftarrow \mathsf{BS.USign}_0(\mathsf{vk}, m, \tau)$

$\textbf{return } (C, \pi_{\mathsf{Ped}}, \mathcal{S})$

$\mathsf{USign}_1(\{\mathbf{T}_{\$,i}^*, \mathbf{A}_{0,i}, A_{1,i}, C_{S,i}^*, \mathsf{cm}_i^c\}_{i \in \mathcal{S}})$

$\mathbf{T}_\$^* := \sum_{i \in \mathcal{S}} \mathbf{T}_{\$,i}^* \quad C_S^* := \sum_{i \in \mathcal{S}} C_{S,i}^*$

$\mathbf{A}_0^* := \sum_{i \in \mathcal{S}} \mathbf{A}_{0,i}^*; \quad A_1^* := \sum_{i \in \mathcal{S}} A_{1,i}^*$

$c^* \leftarrow \mathsf{BS.USign}_1(\mathbf{T}_\$^*, \mathbf{A}_0^*, A_1^*, C_S^*)$

$\textbf{return } (c^*, \{\mathsf{cm}_i^c\}_{i \in \mathcal{S}})$

$\mathsf{USign}_2(\{c_{1,i}^*\}_{i \in \mathcal{S}})$

$c_1^* := \sum_{i \in \mathcal{S}} c_{1,i}^*$

$\textbf{return } \{c_{1,i}^*\}_{i \in \mathcal{S}}$

$\mathsf{USign}_3(\{c_{0,i}^*, \tilde{\mathbf{z}}_{0,i}^*, z_{1,i}^*, \tilde{d}_{1,i}^*, \tilde{r}_{1,i}^*\}_{i \in \mathcal{S}})$

$c_0^* := c^* - c_1^*$

$\mathbf{z}_0^* := \sum_{i \in \mathcal{S}} \tilde{\mathbf{z}}_{0,i}^*; \quad z_1^* := \sum_{i \in \mathcal{S}} z_{1,i}^*$

$d_1^* := \sum_{i \in \mathcal{S}} \tilde{d}_{1,i}^*; \quad r_1^* := \sum_{i \in \mathcal{S}} \tilde{r}_{1,i}^*$

$\sigma \leftarrow \mathsf{BS.USign}_2(c_0^*, \mathbf{z}_0^*, z_1^*, d_1^*, r_1^*)$

$\textbf{return } \sigma$

Fig. 5. The interactive signing protocol executed by the signing parties and the user in scheme TBS. Algorithms ISign_1, ISign_2 and ISign_3 are executed by the signers, algorithms USign_0, USign_1, USign_2 and USign_3 are executed by the user. We leave the user and signer states implicit for readability. Notable differences to blind signature scheme BS are highlighted in grey .

Blindness. As the user either forwards messages between signers or computes its output as in BS after aggregating the signers' messages, blindness follows immediately.

Theorem 6 (Blindness). *For any adversary* $\mathcal{A}$ *on blindness of scheme* TBS *there exists an adversary* $\mathcal{A}_{\mathsf{BS}}$ *on blindness of scheme* BS *having runtime similar to* $\mathcal{A}$*, such that*

$$\mathsf{AdvTPBlind}_{\mathcal{A}}^{\mathsf{TBS}}(\lambda) \leq \mathsf{AdvPBlind}_{\mathcal{A}_{\mathsf{BS}}}^{\mathsf{BS}}(\lambda).$$

5 Pairing-Based Threshold Blind Signature from CDH

We now describe our pairing-based threshold blind signature pTBS. Our scheme pTBS is based on [27], which itself is based on BB, similar to BS and TBS. We do not consider partial blindness here, as compared to our previous schemes, it would require a structural change on BB. At the cost of an additional group element in the signature, we believe that achieving partial blindness is possible with the modifications from [27, Section 7.2].

Preparations. As in Sects. 3 and 4, we employ a random oracle $\mathsf{H}_{\mathsf{M}} : \{0,1\}^* \leftarrow \mathbb{Z}_p$ to preprocess the message. Also, we employ a proof system $\mathsf{NIPS}_{\mathsf{Ped}} = (\mathsf{NIPS}_{\mathsf{Ped}}.\mathsf{Prove}^{\mathsf{H}_{\mathsf{Ped}}}, \mathsf{NIPS}_{\mathsf{Ped}}.\mathsf{Ver}^{\mathsf{H}_{\mathsf{Ped}}})$ with random oracle $\mathsf{H}_{\mathsf{Ped}}$ for relation $\mathsf{R}_{\mathsf{Ped}}$, as defined in Sect. 3. Analogously to Sect. 4, $\mathsf{IssueShares}$ is a PPT algorithm computing n Shamir's shares $\{u_i\}_{i\in[n]}$ of value u on input $(n, t+1)$, of which $t+1$ are necessary to reconstruct value u.

Note that $\mathsf{F}_{\mathsf{msk}}$ now denotes a PRF with key space $\mathcal{K}_{\mathsf{msk}}$ that maps from $\{0,1\}^*$ to $\mathbb{G}_1$, again employed to mask the individual signer messages. In addition, we employ a PRF $\mathsf{F}_{\mathsf{rnd}}$ with key space $\mathcal{K}_{\mathsf{rnd}}$ that maps from $\{0,1\}^*$ to $\mathbb{Z}_p$ to derandomize each signer.

5.1 Construction

Our pairing-based threshold blind signature scheme pTBS is given in Fig. 6. The issued signatures $\sigma = (\sigma_0, \sigma_1)$ in pTBS follow the structure

$$\sigma_0 = \mathsf{bb\text{-}sk} + r \cdot (m \cdot U_1 + H_1), \quad \sigma_1 = rG_1,$$

where $(\mathbb{G}_1, \mathbb{G}_2, \mathbb{G}_T, e, G_1, G_2) \leftarrow \mathsf{PGen}(1^\lambda)$ are pairing-friendly groups, and $U_1 = \alpha G_1$ and $H_1 = \gamma G_1$ and $\mathsf{bb\text{-}sk} = \alpha\beta G_1$. Notably, the structure of σ can be verified via the pairing e and additional elements $U_2 = \alpha G_2, H_2 = \gamma G_2$ and $V = \alpha\beta \cdot e(G_1, G_2)$ specified in the public key.

Overview. As in our scheme TBS, the signers receive linear shares $\mathsf{bb\text{-}sk}_i$ of the secret key $\mathsf{bb\text{-}sk}$ during key generation.

The signing protocol is initiated by the user sending a Pedersen commitment C to the message, along with a proof π_{Ped} of opening knowledge, to the signers. Each signer k then uses their share $\mathsf{bb\text{-}sk}_k$ of sk to compute a partial signature σ_k^* on C. As in TBS, signer k masks their partial signature σ_k^* with a zero share Δ_k. Importantly, the partial signature is derived deterministically via $\mathsf{F}_{\mathsf{rnd}}$.

Finally, the user obtains a valid signature to its message m by linearly combining all $t+1$ partial signatures and removing the remaining randomness introduced by C from the resulting signature σ.

$\mathsf{Setup}(1^\lambda)$

$(\mathbb{G}_1, \mathbb{G}_2, \mathbb{G}_T, e, G_1, G_2) \leftarrow \mathsf{PGen}(1^\lambda)$
$\mathsf{par} := (\mathbb{G}_1, \mathbb{G}_2, \mathbb{G}_T, e, G_1, G_2)$
$\mathbf{return}\ \mathsf{par}$

$\mathsf{KeyGen}(n, t+1)$

$\alpha, \beta, \gamma \xleftarrow{\$} \mathbb{Z}_p$
$U_1 := \alpha G_1, U_2 := \alpha G_2, H_1 := \gamma G_1$
$H_2 := \gamma G_2, V := \alpha\beta \cdot e(G_1, G_2)$
$\{\beta_i\}_{i \in [n]} \leftarrow \mathsf{IssueShares}(\beta, n, t+1)$
$\{w_{i,j}\}_{i,j \in [n], i<j} \xleftarrow{\$} \mathcal{K}_{\mathsf{msk}}^{n(n-1)/2}$
$\forall_{i,j \in [n], i>j} w_{i,j} := w_{j,i}$
$\{w_i\}_{i \in [n]} \xleftarrow{\$} \mathcal{K}_{\mathsf{rnd}}^n$
$\mathsf{bb\text{-}sk}_i := \beta_i \alpha G_1$
$\mathsf{sk}_i := (\mathsf{bb\text{-}sk}_i, \{w_{i,j}\}_{j \in [n] \setminus \{i\}}, w_i)$
$\mathsf{vk} := (U_1, U_2, H_1, H_2, V)$
$\mathbf{return}\ (\{\mathsf{sk}_i\}_{i \in [n]}, \mathsf{vk})$

$\mathsf{Verify}(\mathsf{vk}, m, \sigma)$

$\overline{m} := \mathsf{H_M}(m)$
$\mathbf{req}\ \ e(\sigma_0, G_2) = V + e(\sigma_1, \overline{m}U_2 + H_2)$
$\mathbf{return}\ 1$

$\mathsf{USign}_0(\mathsf{vk}, \mathsf{aux} := \bot, m, \mathcal{S}, \tau := \bot)$

$\overline{m} := \mathsf{H_M}(m)$
$t \xleftarrow{\$} \mathbb{Z}_p, C := \overline{m}U_1 + tG_1$
$\mathbb{x}_{\mathsf{Ped}} := (C, U_1, G_1), \mathbb{w}_{\mathsf{Ped}} := (\overline{m}, t)$
$\pi_{\mathsf{Ped}} \leftarrow \mathsf{NIPS_{Ped}.Prove}^{\mathsf{H_{Ped}}}(\mathbb{x}_{\mathsf{Ped}}, \mathbb{w}_{\mathsf{Ped}})$
$\mathbf{return}\ (\mathcal{S}, C, \pi_{\mathsf{Ped}})$

$\mathsf{ISign}_1(k, \mathsf{sk}_k, \mathsf{aux} := \bot, \mathsf{ctx}, \tau := \bot, (\mathcal{S}, C, \pi_{\mathsf{Ped}}))$

$\mathbf{return}\ \bot\ \mathbf{if}\ k \notin \mathcal{S}$
$\mathbf{req}\ \ \mathsf{NIPS_{Ped}.Ver}^{\mathsf{H_{Ped}}}(\mathbb{x}_{\mathsf{Ped}}, \pi_{\mathsf{Ped}}) = 1$
$\mathsf{ssid} := (\mathsf{ctx}, \mathcal{S}, C, \pi_{\mathsf{Ped}})$
$r_k \xleftarrow{\$} \mathsf{F}_{\mathsf{rnd}, w_k}(\mathsf{ssid}), \quad \sigma^*_{k,1} := r_k G_1$
$\Delta_k \leftarrow \sum_{j \in \mathcal{S}, j<k} \mathsf{F}_{\mathsf{msk}, w_{k,j}}(\mathsf{ssid}) - \sum_{j \in \mathcal{S}, j>k} \mathsf{F}_{\mathsf{msk}, w_{k,j}}(\mathsf{ssid})$
$\sigma^*_{k,0} := \lambda_k \cdot \mathsf{bb\text{-}sk}_k + r_k(H_1 + C) + \Delta_k$
$\sigma^*_k := (\sigma^*_{k,0}, \sigma^*_{k,1})$
$\mathbf{return}\ (\mathsf{ssid}, \mathcal{S}, \sigma^*_k)$

$\mathsf{USign}_1(\{\sigma^*_i\}_{i \in \mathcal{S}})$

$\sigma^* = (\sigma^*_0, \sigma^*_1) := \left(\sum_{i \in \mathcal{S}} \sigma^*_{i,0}, \sum_{i \in \mathcal{S}} \sigma^*_{i,1}\right)$
$\mathbf{req}\ \ e(\sigma^*_0, G_2) = V + e(\sigma^*_1, \overline{m}U_2 + tG_2 + H_2)$
$r' \xleftarrow{\$} \mathbb{Z}_p$
$\sigma := (\sigma^*_0 - t \cdot \sigma^*_1 + r'(\overline{m}U_1 + H_1), \sigma^*_1 + r'G_1)$
$\mathbf{return}\ \sigma$

Fig. 6. Our pairing-based TBS scheme pTBS based on [27]. Algorithm ISign_1 is executed by the signers, algorithms USign_0 and USign_1 are executed by the user. We leave the user and signer states implicit for readability. Notable differences to the blind signature from [27] due to translation into the threshold setting are highlighted in grey .

5.2 Security Analysis

We show correctness, one-more unforgeability and blindness. We refer to the full version [36] for formal proofs.

Correctness. Again, correctness is immediate.

Theorem 7 (Correctness). pTBS *is correct with error* γ_{err}, *where* γ_{err} *is the correctness error of* $\mathsf{NIPS_{Ped}}$.

One-More Unforgeability. The argument is based on puncturing BB signatures. Roughly, we let the simulation guess an $\mathsf{H_M}$ query such that its input m^* appears in the forgeries, yet is never extracted from π_{Ped} in *finished* sessions. Also, we show that partial BB signatures can be simulated even with a verification key vk punctured for m^*. Together, this breaks CDH.

An important but subtle detail of the proof is that as in TBS, partial signatures may leak information. In particular, we cannot sign for extracted m^* with punctured setup, but incomplete sessions may leak information on such partial signatures σ_i^* on m^*. This is solved by masking partial signatures σ_i^* with zero shares Δ_i. It is important to note that Δ_i cannot be derived from high min-entropy input here, as signers must agree on the input without interaction. Therefore, the zero share Δ_i may appear in more than one session, in which case it does not mask the partial signatures as desired. This is where deterministic signing is important: if Δ_i appears more than once, the derived partial signature is identical, and therefore such sessions leak no additional information.

Theorem 8 (OMUF-3)**.** *Let p be the order of group $\mathbb{Z}_p$. For any PPT adversary $\mathcal{A}$ making at most Q_{M} random oracle queries, there exist reductions $\mathcal{A}_{\mathsf{KS}}, \mathcal{A}_{\mathsf{DL}}$ and $\mathcal{A}_{\mathsf{CDH}}$ having a runtime similar to $\mathcal{A}$ such that*

$$\begin{aligned}\mathsf{AdvTOMUF}_{\mathcal{A}}^{\mathsf{pTBS}}(\lambda) \leq &\mathsf{AdvKS}_{\mathcal{A}_{\mathsf{KS}}}^{\mathsf{NIPS}_{\mathsf{Ped}},\tilde{\mathsf{R}}_{\mathsf{Ped}}}(\lambda) + \mathsf{AdvDL}_{\mathcal{A}_{\mathsf{DL}}}^{\mathsf{PGen}}(\lambda) + \\ &\frac{Q_{\mathsf{M}}^2}{p} + Q_{\mathsf{M}} \cdot \mathsf{AdvCDH}_{\mathcal{A}_{\mathsf{CDH}}}^{\mathsf{PGen}}(\lambda).\end{aligned}$$

Blindness. Blindness follows as in [27].

Theorem 9 (Blindness). *For any PPT adversary $\mathcal{A}$ causing at most Q random oracle queries there exists a reduction $\mathcal{A}_{\mathsf{WI}}$ such that*

$$\mathsf{AdvTPBlind}_{\mathcal{A}}^{\mathsf{pTBS}}(\lambda) \leq 2 \cdot \mathsf{AdvWI}_{\mathcal{A}_{\mathsf{WI}}}^{\mathsf{NIPS},\tilde{\mathsf{R}}_{\mathsf{Ped}}}(Q, \lambda).$$

References

1. Abe, M.: A secure three-move blind signature scheme for polynomially many signatures. In: Pfitzmann, B. (ed.) EUROCRYPT 2001. LNCS, vol. 2045, pp. 136–151. Springer, Heidelberg (2001). https://doi.org/10.1007/3-540-44987-6_9
2. Abe, M., Fuchsbauer, G., Groth, J., Haralambiev, K., Ohkubo, M.: Structure-preserving signatures and commitments to group elements. In: Rabin, T. (ed.) CRYPTO 2010. LNCS, vol. 6223, pp. 209–236. Springer, Heidelberg (2010). https://doi.org/10.1007/978-3-642-14623-7_12
3. Abe, M., Jutla, C.S., Ohkubo, M., Roy, A.: Improved (almost) tightly-secure simulation-sound QA-NIZK with applications. In: Peyrin, T., Galbraith, S. (eds.) ASIACRYPT 2018. LNCS, vol. 11272, pp. 627–656. Springer, Cham (2018). https://doi.org/10.1007/978-3-030-03326-2_21
4. Abe, M., Okamoto, T.: Provably secure partially blind signatures. In: Bellare, M. (ed.) CRYPTO 2000. LNCS, vol. 1880, pp. 271–286. Springer, Heidelberg (2000). https://doi.org/10.1007/3-540-44598-6_17

5. Bellare, M., Neven, G.: Multi-signatures in the plain public-key model and a general forking lemma. In: Juels, A., Wright, R.N., De Capitani di Vimercati, S. (eds.) ACM CCS 2006, pp. 390–399. ACM Press (2006). https://doi.org/10.1145/1180405.1180453
6. Benhamouda, F., Lepoint, T., Loss, J., Orrù, M., Raykova, M.: On the (in)security of ROS. In: Canteaut, A., Standaert, F.-X. (eds.) EUROCRYPT 2021. LNCS, vol. 12696, pp. 33–53. Springer, Cham (2021). https://doi.org/10.1007/978-3-030-77870-5_2
7. Blazy, O., Fuchsbauer, G., Pointcheval, D., Vergnaud, D.: Short blind signatures. J. Comput. Secur. **21**(5), 627–661 (2013)
8. Boldyreva, A.: Threshold signatures, multisignatures and blind signatures based on the Gap-Diffie-Hellman-group signature scheme. In: Desmedt, Y.G. (ed.) PKC 2003. LNCS, vol. 2567, pp. 31–46. Springer, Heidelberg (2003). https://doi.org/10.1007/3-540-36288-6_3
9. Boneh, D., Boyen, X.: Efficient selective-ID secure identity-based encryption without random oracles. In: Cachin, C., Camenisch, J.L. (eds.) EUROCRYPT 2004. LNCS, vol. 3027, pp. 223–238. Springer, Heidelberg (2004a). https://doi.org/10.1007/978-3-540-24676-3_14
10. Boneh, D., Boyen, X.: Short signatures without random oracles. In: Cachin, C., Camenisch, J.L. (eds.) EUROCRYPT 2004. LNCS, vol. 3027, pp. 56–73. Springer, Heidelberg (2004b). https://doi.org/10.1007/978-3-540-24676-3_4
11. Brandt, N., Hofheinz, D., Klooß, M., Reichle, M.: Tightly-secure blind signatures in pairing-free groups. Cryptology ePrint Archive, Report 2024/2075 (2024). https://eprint.iacr.org/2024/2075
12. Chairattana-Apirom, R., Hanzlik, L., Loss, J., Lysyanskaya, A., Wagner, B.: PI-cut-choo and friends: compact blind signatures via parallel instance cut-and-choose and more. In: Dodis, Y., Shrimpton, T. (eds.) CRYPTO 2022, Part III. LNCS, vol. 13509, pp. 3–31. Springer, Cham (2022). https://doi.org/10.1007/978-3-031-15982-4_1
13. Chairattana-Apirom, R., Tessaro, S., Zhu, C.: Pairing-free blind signatures from CDH assumptions. In: Reyzin, L., Stebila, D. (eds.) CRYPTO 2024, Part I. LNCS, vol. 14920, pp. 174–209. Springer, Cham (2024). https://doi.org/10.1007/978-3-031-68376-3_6
14. Chaum, D.: Blind signatures for untraceable payments. In: Chaum, D., Rivest, R.L., Sherman, A.T. (eds.) CRYPTO 1982, pp. 199–203. Plenum Press, New York (1982). https://doi.org/10.1007/978-1-4757-0602-4_18
15. Cramer, R., Damgård, I., Schoenmakers, B.: Proofs of partial knowledge and simplified design of witness hiding protocols. In: Desmedt, Y.G. (ed.) CRYPTO 1994. LNCS, vol. 839, pp. 174–187. Springer, Heidelberg (1994). https://doi.org/10.1007/3-540-48658-5_19
16. Crites, E.C., Komlo, C., Maller, M., Tessaro, S., Zhu, C.: Snowblind: a threshold blind signature in pairing-free groups. In: Handschuh, H., Lysyanskaya, A. (eds.) CRYPTO 2023, Part I. LNCS, vol. 14081, pp. 710–742. Springer, Cham (2023). https://doi.org/10.1007/978-3-031-38557-5_23
17. Del Pino, R., Katsumata, S., Maller, M., Mouhartem, F., Prest, T., Saarinen, M.J.O.: Threshold raccoon: Practical threshold signatures from standard lattice assumptions. In: Joye, M., Leander, G. (eds.) EUROCRYPT 2024, Part II. LNCS, vol. 14652, pp. 219–248. Springer, Cham (2024). https://doi.org/10.1007/978-3-031-58723-8_8

18. Fuchsbauer, G., Hanser, C., Kamath, C., Slamanig, D.: Practical round-optimal blind signatures in the standard model from weaker assumptions. In: Zikas, V., De Prisco, R. (eds.) SCN 2016. LNCS, vol. 9841, pp. 391–408. Springer, Cham (2016). https://doi.org/10.1007/978-3-319-44618-9_21
19. Fuchsbauer, G., Hanser, C., Slamanig, D.: Practical round-optimal blind signatures in the standard model. In: Gennaro, R., Robshaw, M. (eds.) CRYPTO 2015. LNCS, vol. 9216, pp. 233–253. Springer, Heidelberg (2015). https://doi.org/10.1007/978-3-662-48000-7_12
20. Fuchsbauer, G., Plouviez, A., Seurin, Y.: Blind schnorr signatures and signed ElGamal encryption in the algebraic group model. In: Canteaut, A., Ishai, Y. (eds.) EUROCRYPT 2020. LNCS, vol. 12106, pp. 63–95. Springer, Cham (2020). https://doi.org/10.1007/978-3-030-45724-2_3
21. Fuchsbauer, G., Wolf, M.: Concurrently secure blind Schnorr signatures. In: Joye, M., Leander, G. (eds.) EUROCRYPT 2024, Part II. LNCS, vol. 14652, pp. 124–160. Springer, Cham (2024). https://doi.org/10.1007/978-3-031-58723-8_5
22. Ghadafi, E.: Efficient round-optimal blind signatures in the standard model. In: Kiayias, A. (ed.) FC 2017. LNCS, vol. 10322, pp. 455–473. Springer, Cham (2017). https://doi.org/10.1007/978-3-319-70972-7_26
23. Hanzlik, L., Loss, J., Wagner, B.: Rai-choo! Evolving blind signatures to the next level. In: Hazay, C., Stam, M. (eds.) EUROCRYPT 2023, Part V. LNCS, vol. 14008, pp. 753–783. Springer, Cham (2023). https://doi.org/10.1007/978-3-031-30589-4_26
24. Hauck, E., Kiltz, E., Loss, J.: A modular treatment of blind signatures from identification schemes. In: Ishai, Y., Rijmen, V. (eds.) EUROCRYPT 2019. LNCS, vol. 11478, pp. 345–375. Springer, Cham (2019). https://doi.org/10.1007/978-3-030-17659-4_12
25. Kastner, J., Loss, J., Xu, J.: The Abe-Okamoto partially blind signature scheme revisited. In: Agrawal, S., Lin, D. (eds.) ASIACRYPT 2022, Part IV. LNCS, vol. 13794, pp. 279–309. Springer, Cham (2022). https://doi.org/10.1007/978-3-031-22972-5_10
26. Kastner, J., Loss, J., Xu, J.: On pairing-free blind signature schemes in the algebraic group model. In: Hanaoka, G., Shikata, J., Watanabe, Y. (eds.) PKC 2022, Part II. LNCS, vol. 13178, pp. 468–497. Springer, Cham (2022). https://doi.org/10.1007/978-3-030-97131-1_16
27. Katsumata, S., Reichle, M., Sakai, Y.: Practical round-optimal blind signatures in the ROM from standard assumptions. In: Guo, J., Steinfeld, R. (eds.) ASIACRYPT 2023, Part II. LNCS, vol. 14439, pp. 383–417. Springer, Singapore (2023). https://doi.org/10.1007/978-981-99-8724-5_12
28. Klooß, M., Reichle, M.: Blind signatures from proofs of inequality. In: Kalai, Y.T., Kamara, S.F. (eds.) CRYPTO 2025, Part VI. LNCS, vol. 16005, pp. 157–189. Springer, Cham (2025). https://doi.org/10.1007/978-3-032-01887-8_6
29. Klooß, M., Reichle, M., Wagner, B.: Practical blind signatures in pairing-free groups. In: Chung, K.M., Sasaki, Y. (eds.) ASIACRYPT 2024, Part I. LNCS, vol. 15484, pp. 363–395. Springer, Singapore (2024). https://doi.org/10.1007/978-981-96-0875-1_12
30. Klooß, M., Lai, R.W.F., Reichle, M.: Blind signatures from arguments of inequality. Cryptology ePrint Archive, Paper 2025/1886 (2025). https://eprint.iacr.org/2025/1886
31. Kuchta, V., Manulis, M.: Rerandomizable threshold blind signatures. In: Yung, M., Zhu, L., Yang, Y. (eds.) INTRUST 2014. LNCS, vol. 9473, pp. 70–89. Springer, Cham (2015). https://doi.org/10.1007/978-3-319-27998-5_5

32. Lehmann, A., Nazarian, P., Özbay, C.: Stronger security for threshold blind signatures. In: Fehr, S., Fouque, P.A. (eds.) EUROCRYPT 2025, Part II. LNCS, vol. 15602, pp. 335–364. Springer, Cham (2025). https://doi.org/10.1007/978-3-031-91124-8_12
33. Niot, G., Reichle, M., Takemure, K.: Adaptively-secure three-round threshold schnorr from DL. Cryptology ePrint Archive, Paper 2025/1941 (2025). https://eprint.iacr.org/2025/1941
34. Pedersen, T.P.: Non-interactive and information-theoretic secure verifiable secret sharing. In: Feigenbaum, J. (ed.) CRYPTO 1991. LNCS, vol. 576, pp. 129–140. Springer, Heidelberg (1992). https://doi.org/10.1007/3-540-46766-1_9
35. Pointcheval, D., Stern, J.: Security arguments for digital signatures and blind signatures. J. Cryptol. **13**(3), 361–396 (2000). https://doi.org/10.1007/s001450010003
36. Reichle, M., Reinke, Z.: Threshold blind signatures from CDH. Cryptology ePrint Archive, Paper 2025/1798 (2025). https://eprint.iacr.org/2025/1798
37. Shamir, A.: How to share a secret. Commun. Assoc. Comput. Mach. **22**(11), 612–613 (1979). https://doi.org/10.1145/359168.359176
38. Tessaro, S., Zhu, C.: Short pairing-free blind signatures with exponential security. In: Dunkelman, O., Dziembowski, S. (eds.) EUROCRYPT 2022, Part II. LNCS, vol. 13276, pp. 782–811. Springer, Cham (2022). https://doi.org/10.1007/978-3-031-07085-3_27
39. Vo, D.L., Zhang, F., Kim, K.: A new threshold blind signature scheme from pairings. In: SCIS2003, pp. 233–238. SCIS (2003)
40. Wagner, D.: A generalized birthday problem. In: Yung, M. (ed.) CRYPTO 2002. LNCS, vol. 2442, pp. 288–304. Springer, Heidelberg (2002). https://doi.org/10.1007/3-540-45708-9_19

On Post-quantum Signature with Message Recovery from Hash-and-Sign in QROM

Bohang Chen, Shuai Han(✉), and Shengli Liu

School of Computer Science, Shanghai Jiao Tong University, Shanghai 200240, China
{bohang0918,dalen17,slliu}@sjtu.edu.cn

Abstract. Post-quantum signatures have been suffering from their inefficiency compared to traditional signatures. To reduce space consumption, a promising approach is to design signature schemes with message recovery, which can embed part of the message into the signature without increasing its length. A notable example is the PSS-R signature scheme (probabilistic signature scheme with recovery) proposed by Bellare and Rogaway (EUROCRYPT 1996) in the classical ROM (random oracle model). However, there were few works considering post-quantum signature schemes with message recovery.

In this work, we study the design of post-quantum signature scheme with message recovery in the QROM (quantum ROM). Specifically, we adapt the classic PSS-R signature scheme to the post-quantum setting and prove its security in the QROM. Our security proof is conceptually similar to the original proof of PSS-R, but faces challenges in QROM when we need to reprogram two random oracles with correlated inputs/outputs. To address these issues, we extend the tight adaptive reprogramming theorem (Grilo et al., ASIACRYPT 2021) and the measure-and-reprogram theorem (Don et al., CRYPTO 2020) to our setting, to support reprogramming two oracles successively, where the input to one oracle depends on the other oracle's output. With these extended proof techniques, we provide the first security proof of a PSS-R-like signature scheme with message recovery in the QROM.

Keywords: Post-quantum security · digital signature · message recovery · QROM

1 Introduction

Post-quantum Signatures with Message Recovery. We revisit a type of signature with message recovery adapted from hash-and-sign schemes in the post-quantum setting. Signature with message recovery is an enhancement of signature schemes that packs some part of the message into the signature, saving space for applications that require a large number of signatures stored (e.g. blockchain applications), or run in a memory-sensitive environment (e.g. IoT applications). A notable example of such signature schemes is the PSS-R scheme (probabilistic signature scheme with recovery) proposed by Bellare and Rogaway [3].

S. Bai and E. Persichetti (Eds.): PKC 2026, LNCS 16551, pp. 302–333, 2026.
https://doi.org/10.1007/978-3-032-26731-3_10

Up to now, there have been few works considering post-quantum signature schemes with message recovery. Among them, del Pino et al. [15] proposed a post-quantum signature scheme with message recovery for a preliminary version of Falcon [9], by modifying a previous hash-and-sign signature scheme in [7] and achieving message recovery with a similar construction to PSS-R. With message recovery, the total size of a message and its signature in (the preliminary version of) Falcon can be reduced by up to 250 bytes. However, they only provided a security proof under the classical random oracle model (ROM), leaving a gap when taking the oracle's quantum accessibility into account.

In this work, we consider the post-quantum adaptation of the PSS-R scheme [3], which was originally instantiated under number-theoretic assumptions such as RSA, and was proved in the classical ROM.

Security of Signature in QROM. The gap between security in the classical ROM and quantum ROM (QROM) has been studied for years, with many works trying to bridge the gap in a generic way [2,4,6,11,16,17].

In particular, Yamakawa and Zhandry [16] provided a lifting theorem, which can translate an adversary in some specific kinds of games that have access to only the classical random oracle, to another one that has access to the quantum random oracle. For digital signatures, based on such lifting theorem, they proved that with certain properties, the EUF-CMA security (existential unforgeability under chosen message attacks) of a digital signature scheme in the ROM can be lifted to the EUF-CMA security in the QROM directly.

However, it is hard to lift the security of the PSS-R signature scheme [3] to QROM via the lifting theorem [16], since the PSS-R scheme does not meet the requirements of the lifting theorem. More precisely, the main problem is that the PSS-R scheme [3] makes use of two random oracles successively, and the query for one oracle depends on the output from the other oracle. This makes it hard to develop a method to simulate the signing oracle by only non-adaptively reprogramming the random oracle, as required by the lifting theorem [16]. Besides, their theorem does not state the concrete security loss of lifting, making it hard to quantify the tightness of such reduction.

Therefore, to provide a security proof for the PSS-R signature scheme [3] under QROM with concrete security loss, one may need to resort to more fundamental techniques such as the tight adaptive reprogramming technique introduced by Grilo et al. [11] and/or the measure-and-reprogram technique introduced by Don et al. [6], and build the security proof from scratch.

However, the techniques in [6,11] remain unsuitable for proving the security of the PSS-R scheme [3] under QROM. Specifically, the tight adaptive reprogramming technique in [11] cannot be used to reprogram two random oracles where the input to one oracle depends on the output from the other oracle, as is the case with the PSS-R scheme. Moreover, the measure-and-reprogram technique in [6] focuses on reprogramming a single random oracle, and can hardly be used to reprogram two random oracles simultaneously.

This makes the post-quantum adaptation of PSS-R even more challenging. It is interesting to ask the following question:

How to adapt the PSS-R signature scheme under QROM based on post-quantum assumptions?

Our Contributions. In this work, we answer the above question in the affirmative.

- *Generalized PSS-R from preimage sampleable function.* To adapt the PSS-R scheme [3] under post-quantum assumptions, we generalize it by proposing a generic construction of signature schemes with message recovery based on a preimage sampleable function (PSF) [10], which was known to have many post-quantum instantiations.
- *Security proof under QROM.* As our main contribution, we prove the EUF-CMA security of our generalized PSS-R signature scheme under QROM, and show its concrete security loss. To this end, we extend the tight adaptive reprogramming technique in [11] and the measure-and-reprogram technique in [6] to support the reprogramming of two random oracles where the input for one oracle depends on the output from the other oracle, as is the case of the PSS-R and our schemes.

  With our extended techniques, our security proof under QROM goes with two main steps. First, we reduce the EUF-NMA security (existential unforgeability under no message attacks, i.e., without signing oracle) of our scheme to the EUF-CMA security, by using the extended tight adaptive reprogramming technique. Then, we prove the EUF-NMA security based on the properties of PSF, by using the extended measure-and-reprogram technique. We refer to Sect. 4 for more details.

  To the best of our knowledge, this yields the *first* security proof under QROM for (variants of) the PSS-R scheme.

From a technical perspective, our extensions of the techniques in [6,11] are non-trivial, as explained below.

- *Extended tight adaptive reprogramming technique.* To support the reprogramming of two random oracles, we first extend the tight adaptive reprogramming technique [11] in a more quantum-friendly way by establishing a superposition-controlled reprogramming lemma (i.e., Lemma 2), so that we can control the position of the random oracle to be reprogrammed with quantum superposition, rather than with a classical variable from a distribution as was done in [11]. Then, we apply our Lemma 2 to the quantum representation of the reprogramming game involving two random oracles to erase the reprogramming of the two oracles one by one, even if the input for one oracle depends on the output from the other oracle. This shows that the reprogramming of the two oracles is unnoticeable to a quantum adversary (i.e., Theorem 5). We refer to Sect. 3 for more details.
  We note that our extension is non-trivial, as their technique [11] doesn't imply our theorem even in a white-box way (see Subsect. 3.1 for more explanations).
- *Extended measure-and-reprogram technique.* The second extension is a reformulation of the measure-and-reprogram technique [6] to handle the case where

two random oracles are involved. While this may appear analogous to the situation considered by the measure-and-reprogram theorem for multiple queries to a single random oracle with enforced extraction order (i.e., [6, Theorem 7]), it is actually quite different since we deal with two random oracles. Therefore, we adapt their theorem to our setting and give a concrete bound. We refer to Theorem 3 in Subsect. 2.4 for more details.

Instantiations and Comparison with Falcon. By instantiating the PSF following the Falcon signature's approach [9], we can obtain a concrete signature scheme with message recovery via our generic construction. Specifically, we use the NTRU-Lattice [12] for a trapdoor, and use the fast Fourier sampling [8] to sample the preimage. This results in the *first* post-quantum signature scheme supporting message recovery in QROM.

Below we compare our scheme with Falcon-512 [9] to show the advantage of message recovery.

- When instantiating our scheme with the PSF and the parameters from Falcon-512 [9], our signature scheme has 1252 bytes signature size, where we can embed 787 bytes message into the signature.[1]
- The Falcon-512 signature scheme has a signature size of 666 bytes, which does not support message embedding.

So with our signature scheme, for a message of size $\ell_m \geq 787$ bytes, we can embed 787 bytes into the signature, so that the total size of the message and its signature is $\ell_m - 787 + 1252 = \ell_m + 465$ bytes; while for messages of size $\ell_m < 787$ bytes, we can embed the whole message into the signature, so that the total size of the message and its signature is 1252 bytes.

In comparison, for Falcon-512, the total size of the message and signature is $\ell_m + 666$ bytes regardless of the message length ℓ_m.

This shows that our signature scheme with message recovery has an advantage over Falcon-512 for messages of size $\ell_m \geq 586$ bytes (so that both $\ell_m + 465$ and $1252 \leq \ell_m + 666$). Compared to Falcon-512 (whose signature is 666 bytes), our scheme can save up to 201 bytes of space, cutting the total space overhead of the signature by approximately 30% .

We note that our advantage holds even if the messages are hashed to short digests, as is done in many concrete deployment scenarios. The point is that even if the signatures are generated w.r.t. short digests (say $H(m)$), one still needs to store the entire message (say m). With our scheme, one can parse $m = (m_1, m_2)$, and generate a signature σ over $m_1||H(m)$, in which case one only needs to store (m_2, σ), thus saving the space for storing m_1. This approach achieves our claimed advantage.

[1] Jumping ahead, our generic construction is shown in Fig. 5 in Sect. 4, and here we instantiate the set $\mathcal{Y} = \mathcal{Y}_1 \times \mathcal{Y}_2 \times \mathcal{Y}_3$ with $\mathcal{Y}_1 = \{0,1\}^{320}$, $\mathcal{Y}_2 = \mathcal{M}_1 = \{0,1\}^{787\times 8}$ and $\mathcal{Y}_3 = \{0,1\}^{320}$, instantiate the PSF $\mathsf{PSF} = (\mathsf{TrapGen}, \mathsf{SampleDom}, \mathsf{SamplePre})$ with the one involved in Falcon-512 [9], and instantiate the hash functions H and G similar to the ones used in Falcon-512 [9].

More Related Works. Among recent progress on QROM proof techniques, two lines of work are particularly relevant to our technical approach.

Specifically, Pan and Zeng [14] discussed the computational version of the adaptive reprogramming technique, but its direct application to statistical settings like ours would incur a substantial security loss.

Concurrently, Cojocaru et al. [5] developed the coherent measure-and-reprogram technique. Their improvement replaces a standard measurement with a coherent operation that writes the result into a separate quantum register. Although this method does not directly apply to our use case, its core insight—delaying the irreversible collapse of a quantum register to harness superposition—is conceptually similar to our extension of the adaptive reprogramming lemma.

More Discussions. Finally, we note that our established superposition-controlled reprogramming lemma (i.e., Lemma 2) might have broader applications beyond serving merely as a tool for proving the adaptive reprogramming theorem for two random oracles. Our Lemma 2 allows reprogramming controlled by quantum superposition, instead of a classical distribution. This provides better compatibility with quantum operation, and convinces us of its plausible application to security proofs in a fully quantum setting, where both the cryptographic system and the adversary are assumed to have quantum power. We leave it as future work to find such applications.

2 Preliminaries

Let $\lambda \in \mathbb{N}$ denote the security parameter throughout the paper. If x is defined by y or the value of y is assigned to x, we write $x := y$. For $n \in \mathbb{N}$, define $[n] := \{1, 2, ..., n\}$. For a set $\mathcal{X}$, denote by $x \leftarrow \mathcal{X}$ the procedure of sampling x from $\mathcal{X}$ uniformly at random. If $\mathcal{D}$ is a distribution, $x \leftarrow \mathcal{D}$ means that x is sampled according to $\mathcal{D}$. All our algorithms are probabilistic unless stated otherwise. We use $y \leftarrow \mathcal{A}(x)$ to define the random variable y obtained by executing algorithm $\mathcal{A}$ on input x. We also use $y \leftarrow \mathcal{A}(x; r)$ to make explicit the random coins r used in the probabilistic computation. "PPT" abbreviates probabilistic polynomial-time. Denote by negl some negligible function. For two sets $\mathcal{X}$ and $\mathcal{Y}$, we denote the collection of all functions from $\mathcal{X}$ to $\mathcal{Y}$ as $\mathcal{Y}^{\mathcal{X}}$. In our security proofs, we use $\Pr_i$ to denote the probability of the event that game G_i returns 1.

2.1 Digital Signature

Definition 1 (Digital Signature). *A digital signature scheme over message space $\mathcal{M}$ consists of three PPT algorithms $\mathsf{SIG} = (\mathsf{KeyGen}, \mathsf{Sign}, \mathsf{Vrfy})$:*

- $(vk, sk) \leftarrow \mathsf{KeyGen}(1^\lambda)$*: This algorithm takes as input the security parameter 1^λ, outputting a verification key vk and a signing key sk.*
- $\sigma \leftarrow \mathsf{Sign}(sk, m)$*: This algorithm takes as input a signing key sk and a message $m \in \mathcal{M}$, outputting a signature σ for the message.*

- $0/1 \leftarrow \mathsf{Vrfy}(vk, m, \sigma)$: *This is a deterministic algorithm that takes as input a verification key* vk, *a message* m *and a signature* σ, *outputting a bit indicating whether the signature is valid.*

In some memory sensitive applications, we may want to use a digital signature scheme with message recovery, which supports embedding some part of the message (say m_1) into the signature, so that only the remaining part of the message (say m_2) is needed in the verification of the signature.

Definition 2 (Digital Signature with Message Recovery). *A digital signature scheme with message recovery over message space* $\mathcal{M} = \mathcal{M}_1 \times \mathcal{M}_2$ *consists of three PPT algorithms* $\mathsf{SIG} = (\mathsf{KeyGen}, \mathsf{Sign}, \mathsf{Vrfy})$:

- $(vk, sk) \leftarrow \mathsf{KeyGen}(1^\lambda)$ *and* $\sigma \leftarrow \mathsf{Sign}(sk, m)$: *These algorithms work as per the ordinary digital signature scheme in Definition 1.*
- $(0, \perp)/(1, m_1') \leftarrow \mathsf{Vrfy}(vk, m_2, \sigma)$: *This is a deterministic algorithm that takes as input a verification key* vk, *the second part* $m_2 \in \mathcal{M}_2$ *of a message and a signature* σ, *outputting* $(0, \perp)$ *if the signature is invalid, and outputting* $(1, m_1' \in \mathcal{M}_1)$ *if the signature is valid.*

The **correctness** property requires that for any $(vk, sk) \leftarrow \mathsf{KeyGen}(1^\lambda)$ and any $m = (m_1, m_2) \in \mathcal{M}$, it holds that

$$\Pr\left[\mathsf{Vrfy}(vk, m_2, \sigma) = (1, m_1) : \sigma \leftarrow \mathsf{Sign}(sk, m)\right] = 1 - \mathsf{negl}(\lambda).$$

Below we define the EUF-CMA security (existential unforgeability under chosen message attacks) and EUF-NMA security (existential unforgeability under no message attacks) for digital signature with message recovery.

Definition 3 (EUF-CMA Security). *A digital signature scheme with message recovery* SIG *over message space* $\mathcal{M} = \mathcal{M}_1 \times \mathcal{M}_2$ *is* EUF-CMA *secure, if for any PPT adversary* $\mathcal{A}$, *it holds that* $\mathsf{Adv}^{\mathsf{EUF\text{-}CMA}}_{\mathsf{SIG},\mathcal{A}} := \Pr[\mathsf{Exp}^{\mathsf{EUF\text{-}CMA}}_{\mathsf{SIG},\mathcal{A}} = 1] \leq \mathsf{negl}(\lambda)$, *where the experiment* $\mathsf{Exp}^{\mathsf{EUF\text{-}CMA}}_{\mathsf{SIG},\mathcal{A}}$ *is shown in Fig. 1.*

Definition 4 (EUF-NMA Security). *A digital signature scheme with message recovery* SIG *over message space* $\mathcal{M} = \mathcal{M}_1 \times \mathcal{M}_2$ *is* EUF-NMA *secure, if for any PPT adversary* $\mathcal{A}$, *it holds that* $\mathsf{Adv}^{\mathsf{EUF\text{-}NMA}}_{\mathsf{SIG},\mathcal{A}} := \Pr[\mathsf{Exp}^{\mathsf{EUF\text{-}NMA}}_{\mathsf{SIG},\mathcal{A}} = 1] \leq \mathsf{negl}(\lambda)$, *where the experiment* $\mathsf{Exp}^{\mathsf{EUF\text{-}NMA}}_{\mathsf{SIG},\mathcal{A}}$ *is shown in Fig. 1.*

2.2 Preimage Sampleable Function

Below we recall the definition of preimage sampleable function (PSF) from [10].

Definition 5 (Preimage Sampleable Function [10]). *A collection of preimage sampleable functions consists of three PPT algorithms* $\mathsf{PSF} = (\mathsf{TrapGen}, \mathsf{SampleDom}, \mathsf{SamplePre})$:

$\mathsf{Exp}^{\mathsf{EUF\text{-}CMA}}_{\mathsf{SIG},\mathcal{A}}$:	$\mathsf{Exp}^{\mathsf{EUF\text{-}NMA}}_{\mathsf{SIG},\mathcal{A}}$:	$\textsc{Sign}(m = (m_1, m_2))$:
$\mathcal{S} := \emptyset$ $(vk, sk) \leftarrow \mathsf{KeyGen}(1^\lambda)$ $(m_2^*, \sigma^*) \leftarrow \mathcal{A}^{\textsc{Sign}(\cdot)}(vk)$ $(b, m_1^*) \leftarrow \mathsf{Vrfy}(vk, m_2^*, \sigma^*)$ Return $(m_1^*, m_2^*) \notin \mathcal{S} \wedge b = 1$	$(vk, sk) \leftarrow \mathsf{KeyGen}(1^\lambda)$ $(m_2^*, \sigma^*) \leftarrow \mathcal{A}(vk)$ $(b, m_1^*) \leftarrow \mathsf{Vrfy}(vk, m_2^*, \sigma^*)$ Return $b = 1$	$\sigma \leftarrow \mathsf{Sign}(sk, m)$ $\mathcal{S} := \mathcal{S} \cup \{(m_1, m_2)\}$ Return σ

Fig. 1. The EUF-CMA experiment $\mathsf{Exp}^{\mathsf{EUF\text{-}CMA}}_{\mathsf{SIG},\mathcal{A}}$ (left) and the EUF-NMA experiment $\mathsf{Exp}^{\mathsf{EUF\text{-}NMA}}_{\mathsf{SIG},\mathcal{A}}$ (middle) for digital signature with message recovery, where the oracle Sign (right) is used in the former experiment.

- $(a, t) \leftarrow \mathsf{TrapGen}(1^\lambda)$: *This algorithm takes as input the security parameter* 1^λ, *outputting 'a' as the description of a trapdoor function* $f_a \colon \mathcal{X} \to \mathcal{Y}$ *(for some sets* $\mathcal{X}$ *and* $\mathcal{Y}$ *depending on* λ*) and 't' as a trapdoor for* f_a.
- $x \leftarrow \mathsf{SampleDom}(1^\lambda)$: *This algorithm takes as input the security parameter* 1^λ, *sampling an element* x *from some distribution* $\mathcal{D}_x$ *over* $\mathcal{X}$.
- $x \leftarrow \mathsf{SamplePre}(y, t)$: *This algorithm takes as input* $y \in \mathcal{Y}$ *and the trapdoor* t *for* f_a, *outputting an element* $x \in \mathcal{X}$.

Fixing $(a, t) \leftarrow \mathsf{TrapGen}(1^\lambda)$, we require a preimage sampleable function PSF to satisfy the following properties:

- **Image Distribution**: For $x \leftarrow \mathsf{SampleDom}(1^\lambda)$, $f_a(x)$ follows the uniform distribution over $\mathcal{Y}$.
- **Preimage Sampling Correctness**: For any $y \in \mathcal{Y}$, $x \leftarrow \mathsf{SamplePre}(y, t)$ satisfies $f_a(x) = y$.
- **Preimage Sampling Distribution**: For any $y \in \mathcal{Y}$, $x \leftarrow \mathsf{SamplePre}(y, t)$ follows the distribution $\mathcal{D}_x$ conditioned on $f_a(x) = y$.
- **Preimage Min-entropy**: For every $y \in \mathcal{Y}$, the conditional probability,

$$p_{\max} := \max_{x' \in \mathcal{X}} \Pr_x \left[x = x' \mid f_a(x) = y \right] = 2^{-\omega(\log \lambda)},$$

  where the probability is over $x \leftarrow \mathsf{SampleDom}(1^\lambda)$.
- **Collision Resistance**: For any PPT adversary $\mathcal{A}$, it holds that

$$\mathsf{Adv}^{\mathsf{CR}}_{\mathsf{PSF},\mathcal{A}} := \Pr\left[x \neq x' \wedge f_a(x) = f_a(x') \right] \leq \mathsf{negl}(\lambda),$$

  where the probability is over $(a, t) \leftarrow \mathsf{TrapGen}(1^\lambda)$ and $(x, x') \leftarrow \mathcal{A}(a)$.

2.3 Quantum Computation

We rely on the common notation as in [13] for quantum computation. For completeness, we provide an introduction to the notations that we use.

Let $\mathcal{H}$ be a finite-dimensional complex Hilbert space, representing the state space of a quantum system. We represent the vectors in $\mathcal{H}$ and its dual space with the standard bra-ket notation.

Let X be a quantum register with its state space being $\mathcal{H}_X$. We use the register's name as subscripts for vectors and operators. Specifically, we denote $|\cdot\rangle_X$ and $\langle\cdot|_X$ for vectors in $\mathcal{H}_X$ and its dual space, respectively. We also denote U_X for operators acting on $\mathcal{H}_X$. If the operator is a density operator, it will be describing the state of register X. If there are multiple registers' names written in the subscripts, it represents vectors or operators of a multi-register system.

For multi-register systems, the state space is the tensor product of the single-register spaces with an implicitly fixed register order. To simplify notation, we use subscripts to permute registers as needed, and the displayed tensor-product order is immaterial. Furthermore, for an operator U, we may omit some registers' subscripts when it acts as identity on those registers within the multi-register system.

For a Hilbert space $\mathcal{H}$ of dimension d, we mainly work on the computational basis $|0\rangle, |1\rangle, \cdots, |d-1\rangle$. We also utilize the Fourier basis $|\phi_0\rangle, |\phi_1\rangle, \cdots, |\phi_{d-1}\rangle$ given by $|\phi_i\rangle \stackrel{\text{def}}{=} \mathcal{F}|i\rangle$, where $\mathcal{F}$ is the operator of Quantum Fourier Transform (QFT) [13, Chapter 5]. Nevertheless, among the vectors in the Fourier basis, we only need to note the form of $|\phi_0\rangle$, which is the "uniform state" $|\phi_0\rangle \stackrel{\text{def}}{=} \frac{1}{\sqrt{d}}\sum_{i=0}^{d-1}|i\rangle$.

Our quantum systems always employ binary encoding. When we say a register X contains a superposition over a finite non-empty set $\mathcal{X}$, we mean the register X contains $\lceil \log_2 |\mathcal{X}| \rceil$ qubits, and each element $x \in \mathcal{X}$ is encoded as a binary string of the same length within X.

Quantum Gates. Let us introduce some well-known quantum gates. One is the CNOT gate and its extension. The ordinary $\mathsf{CNOT}_{X,Y}$ gate is a unitary acting on two qubits and does $\mathsf{CNOT}_{X,Y}|b_1\rangle_X|b_2\rangle_Y = |b_1\rangle_X|b_2 \oplus b_1\rangle_Y$, for all $b_1, b_2 \in \{0,1\}$ where $\oplus$ denotes the XOR operation and the former qubit is called the control bit. We may also use $\mathsf{CNOT}_{X,Y}$ to denote its multi-qubit version, acting on two registers X and Y, each of n qubits. The multi-qubit $\mathsf{CNOT}_{X,Y}$ gate applies single-qubit $\mathsf{CNOT}_{X,Y}$ gates for n times, the i-th time on the i-th qubit of X and Y with X's qubit always being the control bit.

Another is the SWAP gate, acting on two registers X and Y that share the same state space $\mathcal{H}_X$. The $\mathsf{SWAP}_{X,Y}$ gate does $\mathsf{SWAP}_{X,Y}|x_1\rangle_X|x_2\rangle_Y = |x_2\rangle_X|x_1\rangle_Y$ for all $x_1, x_2 \in \mathcal{X}$. Intuitively, the SWAP gate's action is equivalent to swapping the two registers physically.

Useful Metrics. We now introduce some useful metrics that help us analyze the quantum system. We introduce the fidelity and the trace distance, both to describe the similarity between two quantum states.

The *fidelity* of two quantum states (in density operator form) ρ and σ is defined as $F(\rho,\sigma) = \operatorname{tr}\left(\sqrt{\rho^{1/2}\sigma\rho^{1/2}}\right)$, where tr denotes the trace of an operator. For pure states $|\psi\rangle$ and $|\phi\rangle$, the fidelity can be written in a simpler form as $F(|\psi\rangle\langle\psi|, |\phi\rangle\langle\phi|) = |\langle\psi|\phi\rangle|$.

The *trace distance* of two quantum states ρ and σ is defined as $D(\rho,\sigma) = \frac{1}{2}\operatorname{tr}(|\rho-\sigma|)$, where $|\rho-\sigma| \stackrel{\text{def}}{=} \sqrt{(\rho-\sigma)^\dagger(\rho-\sigma)}$.

The trace distance is closely related to distinguishing two quantum states. It is shown that for all possible measurement D, the probability of distinguishing two quantum states ρ and σ is upper bounded by trace distance [13, Chapter 9], i.e.,

$$|\Pr[\mathsf{D}(\rho) = 1] - \Pr[\mathsf{D}(\sigma) = 1]| \leq D(\rho, \sigma).$$

In our analysis, we will use fidelity to bound the trace distance, using the inequality $D(\rho, \sigma) \leq \sqrt{1 - F(\rho, \sigma)^2}$ in [13, Chapter 9].

2.4 Quantum Random Oracle

A quantum random oracle extends the classical random oracle by allowing quantum access to the oracle. Formally, for finite non-empty sets $\mathcal{X}$ and $\mathcal{Y}$, a quantum random oracle first samples a function $H \leftarrow \mathcal{Y}^{\mathcal{X}}$ uniformly at random. Then, it answers each query by applying a unitary on quantum registers X and Y, where X contains a superposition over $\mathcal{X}$ and Y contains a superposition over $\mathcal{Y}$. This unitary maps the transformation $|x\rangle_X |y\rangle_Y \rightarrow |x\rangle_X |y \oplus H(x)\rangle_Y$ for all $x \in \mathcal{X}$ and $y \in \mathcal{Y}$.

Following Grilo et al. [11], our formulation of the adaptive reprogramming relies on the superposition oracle [17].

The superposition oracle is a way to simulate the quantum random oracle with a quantum circuit (inefficiently), with an internal register F serving as a truth table. The internal register F can be split into slots of registers denoted by F_x for $x \in \mathcal{X}$, corresponding to the value of $H(x)$. It works as follows:

- At the beginning of the simulation, the simulator prepares its internal register F, such that the state of F_x is $|\phi_0\rangle_{F_x}$ for all $x \in \{0,1\}^n$.
- On a quantum random oracle query $|x\rangle_X |y\rangle_Y$, the simulator applies a unitary,

$$\mathcal{O}_{XYF}^{(H)} \stackrel{\text{def}}{=} \sum_{x \in \{0,1\}^n} |x\rangle\langle x|_X \otimes \mathsf{CNOT}_{F_x, Y}$$

To understand how this simulation works, we can treat the superposition oracle as storing the uniform superposition of all possible truth tables of the random oracle in its internal register F, and looking up the table to answer random oracle queries.

At first glance, adding a measurement of F right after the preparation of the uniform state seems to be necessary, so that the simulation lines up with the ordinary description of a quantum random oracle, where H is sampled uniformly from $\mathcal{X} \rightarrow \mathcal{Y}$ at the beginning of the simulation.

However, this is unnecessary, as in the quantum gate $\mathcal{O}_{XYF}^{(H)}$, the register F always acts as a control register, thus $\mathcal{O}_{XYF}^{(H)}$ commutes with a measurement acting on F. Therefore, we can always postpone the measurement of F to the end of the simulation, or even ignore it equivalently, and the simulation is still perfect.

The superposition oracle is useful especially when we need to reprogram the random oracle on certain positions, as it allows us to formulate the reprogramming process simply by replacing the original register within F with a fresh uniform random state, as was done in [11].

When we need an efficient simulation of the random oracle, we use the compressed oracle technique, which is also introduced in [17]. This allows us to simulate the quantum random oracle with polynomial-sized registers and within polynomial time.

To analyze such replacements properly, we need the following lemma:

Lemma 1 (Decomposition of Superposition Oracle's State [1,11]). *Let $|\gamma\rangle_{AF}$ be the joint adversary-oracle state after an adversary has made q queries to a superposition oracle with register F. Then, the state can be decomposed as,*

$$|\gamma\rangle_{AF} = \sum_{\substack{S\subset\mathcal{X}\\ |S|\leq q}} \beta_S\,|\gamma^{(S)}\rangle_{AF_S} \otimes \left(|\phi_0\rangle^{\otimes|\mathcal{X}\setminus S|}\right)_{F_{\mathcal{X}\setminus S}},$$

where F_S for $S \subset \mathcal{X}$ denotes the combination of registers F_x for all $x \in S$, and $|\gamma^{(S)}\rangle_{AF_S}$ are vectors such that $\langle\phi_0|_{F_x}|\gamma^{(S)}\rangle_{AF_S} = 0$ for all $x \in S$.

Another important result is the optimality of Grover Search theorem in the language of quantum random oracle.

Theorem 1 (Optimality of Grover Search [17], adapted). *For any adversary $\mathcal{A}$ making q quantum queries to a random oracle $H : \mathcal{X} \to \mathcal{Y}$, the probability of finding the preimage of an arbitrary $y \in \mathcal{Y}$ is given by*

$$\Pr\left[H(x) = y : x \leftarrow \mathcal{A}^H(y)\right] \leq \left(\sqrt{\tfrac{(q+1)^2}{|\mathcal{Y}|}} + \sqrt{\tfrac{1}{|\mathcal{Y}|}}\right)^2 = \tfrac{(q+2)^2}{|\mathcal{Y}|}.$$

A crucial tool for our analysis is the measure-and-reprogram theorem as follows.

Theorem 2 (Measure and Reprogram, single input [6]). *Let $\mathcal{X}_0, \mathcal{X}_1$ be finite non-empty sets. There exists a black-box polynomial-time 2-stage quantum algorithm $\mathcal{S}$ such that, for an arbitrary oracle quantum algorithm $\mathcal{A}$ that makes q queries to a uniform random $H : \mathcal{X}_0 \to \mathcal{X}_1$ and that outputs some $x \in \mathcal{X}_0$ and a (possibly quantum) output z, the algorithm $\mathcal{S}^{\mathcal{A}}$ works as follows:*

- *In the first stage, it takes the initial input, and outputs some $x \in \mathcal{X}_0$.*
- *In the second stage, it takes some $\Theta \in \mathcal{X}_1$ as an additional input, and outputs the final output (x, z).*

Then, for uniform random $\Theta \leftarrow \mathcal{X}_1$, for any $x^\circ \in \mathcal{X}_0$ and any (possibly quantum) predicate V:

$$\begin{aligned}&\Pr_{\Theta}\left[x = x^\circ \wedge V(x, \Theta, z) : (x, z) \leftarrow \langle \mathcal{S}^{\mathcal{A}}, \Theta\rangle\right]\\ &\qquad\qquad \geq \tfrac{1}{(2q+1)^2}\cdot \Pr_H\left[x = x^\circ \wedge V(x, H(x), z) : (x, z) \leftarrow \mathcal{A}^H\right].\end{aligned}$$

We consider the case of applying measure-and-reprogram to two successive oracle queries ($h^{(x)} = H(x), g^{(x)} = G(h^{(x)})$) with two functions $H : \mathcal{X}_0 \to \mathcal{X}_1$ and $G : \mathcal{X}_1 \to \mathcal{X}_2$. In this case, we must reprogram two different oracles in an enforced order (i.e., reprogram oracle G after reprogramming H). The following theorem shows an adaptation of the theorem in [6] to our setting.

Theorem 3 (Measure and Reprogram, two oracles). *Let $\mathcal{X}_0, \mathcal{X}_1$ and $\mathcal{X}_2$ be finite non-empty sets. There exists a black-box polynomial-time 3-stage quantum algorithm $\mathcal{S}$ such that, for an arbitrary oracle quantum algorithm $\mathcal{A}$ that makes q_H queries to a uniform random $H : \mathcal{X}_0 \to \mathcal{X}_1$ and q_G queries to a uniform random $G : \mathcal{X}_1 \to \mathcal{X}_2$, and that outputs $x_H \in \mathcal{X}_0$ and a (possibly quantum) output z, the algorithm $\mathcal{S}^{\mathcal{A}}$ works as follows:*

- *In the first stage, it takes the initial input, and outputs some $x_H \in \mathcal{X}_0$.*
- *In the second stage, it takes some $\Theta_H \in \mathcal{X}_1$ as an additional input, and outputs some $x_G \in \mathcal{X}_1$.*
- *In the third stage, it takes some $\Theta_G \in \mathcal{X}_2$ as an additional input, and outputs the final output (x_H, z).*

Moreover, it satisfies the following properties. Let $\mathcal{A}$ be an arbitrary oracle quantum algorithm that outputs $x_H \in \mathcal{X}_0$ and a (possibly quantum) auxiliary output z. Then, for uniform random $\Theta_H \leftarrow \mathcal{X}_1$ and $\Theta_G \leftarrow \mathcal{X}_2$, for any $x^\circ \in \mathcal{X}_0$ and for any predicate V:

$$\begin{aligned}&\Pr_{\Theta_H,\Theta_G}\left[x_H = x^\circ \wedge V(x_H, \Theta_H, \Theta_G, z) : (x_H, z) \leftarrow \left\langle \mathcal{S}^{\mathcal{A}}, \Theta_H, \Theta_G \right\rangle\right] \\ &\geq \tfrac{1}{(2\max\{q_H, q_G\}+1)^4} \cdot \Pr_{H,G}\left[x = x^\circ \wedge V\left(x_H, h^{(x)}, g^{(x)}, z\right) : (x_H, z) \leftarrow \mathcal{A}^{H,G}\right] - \varepsilon_{x^\circ},\end{aligned}$$

where $h^{(x)} \stackrel{\text{def}}{=} H(x)$, $g^{(x)} \stackrel{\text{def}}{=} G(h^{(x)})$, and $\sum_{x^\circ \in \mathcal{X}_0} \varepsilon_{x^\circ} = \frac{1}{|\mathcal{X}_1|}$.

Although adapted from the original theorem for multiple input measure-and-reprogram with enforced extraction order (Theorem 7 in [6]), our result differs in the sense that we are dealing with two random oracles at once. Therefore, we provide a proof of the theorem here.

Intuitively, the proof first applies Theorem 2 twice on both oracles respectively. At this point, it is not guaranteed that the two oracles are reprogrammed in our desired order. Therefore, we then carefully analyze the probability of the event that G is reprogrammed before H is reprogrammed, and exclude the occurrence of this event to complete the proof.

Proof (Theorem 3). Consider an intermediate adversary $\mathcal{A}_+^{H,G}$ that calls $\mathcal{A}$ to obtain $(x_H, z) \leftarrow \mathcal{A}^{H,G}$, and then queries $x_G := y'_H := H(x_H)$, $y'_G := G(x_G)$ before outputting $(x_H, x_G, y'_H, y'_G, z)$.

We first reprogram the oracle H. To do this, we consider two new predicates

$$V'(x_H, x_G, y_H, y_G, z) = [V(x_H, y_H, y_G, z) \wedge x_G = y_H],$$

and,

$$V''(x_H, x_G, y_H, y_G, z) = [V'(x_H, x_G, y_H, y_G, z) \wedge y_G = G(y_H)].$$

Note that computing $G(y_H)$ with the predicate is possible in this case, as we can w.l.o.g use the compressed oracle technique [17] to simulate G, and output the oracle G's internal states (which is of polynomial size) within z when we are reprogramming the oracle H.

Clearly, for any $x_H^\circ \in \mathcal{X}_0$,

$$\begin{aligned}
&\Pr\left[x_H = x_H^\circ \wedge V(x_H, h^{(x_H)}, g^{(x_H)}, z) = 1 : (x_H, z) \leftarrow \mathcal{A}^{H,G}\right]\\
=&\Pr\left[x_H = x_H^\circ \wedge V''(x_H, x_G, h^{(x_H)}, g^{(x_H)}, z) = 1 : (x_H, x_G, y'_G, z) \leftarrow \mathcal{A}_+^{H,G}\right]\\
=&\Pr\left[x_H = x_H^\circ \wedge V''(x_H, x_G, h^{(x_H)}, y'_G, z) = 1 : (x_H, x_G, y'_G, z) \leftarrow \mathcal{A}_+^{H,G}\right].
\end{aligned}$$

By Theorem 2, there exists a two-stage simulator $\mathcal{S}_1$ such that,

$$\begin{aligned}
&\Pr\left[x_H = x_H^\circ \wedge V''(x_H, x_G, \Theta_H, y'_G, z) = 1 : (x_H, x_G, y'_G, z) \leftarrow \left\langle \mathcal{S}_1^{\mathcal{A}_+^G}, \Theta_H \right\rangle\right]\\
\geq&\frac{1}{(2q_H+1)^2}\Pr\left[x_H = x_H^\circ \wedge V'(x_H, x_G, h^{(x_H)}, y'_G, z) = 1 : (x_H, x_G, y'_G, z) \leftarrow \mathcal{A}_+^{H,G}\right]
\end{aligned}$$

As $V''(x_H, x_G, \Theta_H, y'_G, z) = 1$ indicates $y'_G = G(\Theta_H) = G(x_G)$, we also have,

$$\begin{aligned}
&\Pr\left[x_H = x_H^\circ \wedge V'(x_H, x_G, \Theta_H, G(x_G), z) = 1 : (x_H, x_G, y'_G, z) \leftarrow \left\langle \mathcal{S}_1^{\mathcal{A}_+^G}, \Theta_H \right\rangle\right]\\
\geq&\Pr\left[x_H = x_H^\circ \wedge V''(x_H, x_G, \Theta_H, y'_G, z) = 1 : (x_H, x_G, y'_G, z) \leftarrow \left\langle \mathcal{S}_1^{\mathcal{A}_+^G}, \Theta_H \right\rangle\right].
\end{aligned}$$

Let $\mathcal{B}^G$ be an adversary that samples Θ_H and calls $\left\langle \mathcal{S}_1^{\mathcal{A}_+^G}, \Theta_H \right\rangle$ to obtain (x_H, x_G, y'_G, z). We make $(x_H, x_G, y'_G, z, \Theta_H)$ to be $\mathcal{B}$'s output. Now, we can apply Theorem 2 to reprogram the oracle G, treating $\mathcal{B}$ as the algorithm $\mathcal{A}$ in Theorem 2. Therefore, for any $x_G^\circ \in \mathcal{X}_1$,

$$\begin{aligned}
&\Pr\left[(x_H, x_G) = (x_H^\circ, x_G^\circ) \wedge V'(x_H, x_G, \Theta_H, \Theta_G, z) = 1 : (x_H, x_G, y'_G, z, \Theta_H) \leftarrow \left\langle \mathcal{S}_2^{\mathcal{B}^G}, \Theta_G \right\rangle\right]\\
\geq&\frac{1}{(2q_G+1)^2}\Pr\left[(x_H, x_G) = (x_H^\circ, x_G^\circ) \wedge V'(x_H, x_G, \Theta_H, G(x_G), z) = 1 : (x_H, x_G, y'_G, z, \Theta_H) \leftarrow \mathcal{B}^G\right].
\end{aligned}$$

With all above, we found that,

$$\begin{aligned}
&\Pr\left[(x_H, x_G) = (x_H^\circ, x_G^\circ) \wedge V'(x_H, x_G, \Theta_H, \Theta_G, z) = 1 : (x_H, x_G, y'_G, z, \Theta_H) \leftarrow \left\langle \mathcal{S}_2^{\mathcal{B}^G}, \Theta_G \right\rangle\right]\\
\geq&\frac{1}{(2q_G+1)^2(2q_H+1)^2}\Pr\left[(x_H, x_G) = (x_H^\circ, x_G^\circ) \wedge V(x_H, h^{(x_H)}, g^{(x_H)}, z) = 1 : (x_H, z) \leftarrow \mathcal{A}^{H,G}\right].
\end{aligned}$$

Summing over all $x_G^\circ \in \mathcal{X}_1$, we obtain,

$$\Pr\left[x_H = x_H^\circ \wedge V'(x_H, x_G, \Theta_H, \Theta_G, z) = 1 : (x_H, x_G, y_G', z, \Theta_H) \leftarrow \left\langle \mathcal{S}_2^{\mathcal{B}^G}, \Theta_G \right\rangle\right]$$
$$\geq \frac{1}{(2q_G+1)^2(2q_H+1)^2} \Pr\left[x_H = x_H^\circ \wedge V(x_H, h^{(x_H)}, g^{(x_H)}, z) = 1 : (x_H, z) \leftarrow \mathcal{A}^{H,G}\right].$$

At this point, we are just one step away from completing the proof. Considering the running procedure of $\mathcal{S}_2^{\mathcal{B}}$ as a whole, we can interpret it as a 3-stage simulator. Θ_H and Θ_G are given as input in the second and third stage, but the order is not determined. We reformulate this simulator to make the order explicit with an indicator bit b.

Specifically, we view the entire procedure of $\mathcal{S}_2^{\mathcal{B}}$ as a three-stage simulator $\mathcal{S} = (\mathcal{S}^1, \mathcal{S}^2, \mathcal{S}^3)$.

Stage $\mathcal{S}_1$ chooses a bit $b \in \{0,1\}$ that fixes the output order and then outputs

$$x_0 \stackrel{\text{def}}{=} \begin{cases} x_H & \text{if } b = 0, \\ x_G & \text{if } b = 1. \end{cases}$$

Stage $\mathcal{S}_2$ is given the matching reprogrammed value of x_0 (i.e., Θ_H if $b = 0$, and Θ_G if $b = 1$) as input and outputs the other element:

$$x_1 \stackrel{\text{def}}{=} \begin{cases} x_G & \text{if } b = 0, \\ x_H & \text{if } b = 1. \end{cases}$$

Stage $\mathcal{S}_3$ receives the remaining reprogrammed value (i.e., Θ_G if $b = 0$, and Θ_H if $b = 1$) and returns the final output (x_H, x_G, y_G', z).

In our theorem, we require that the simulator reprograms the oracle H before reprogramming the oracle G. This is equivalent to requiring $b = 0$ in the above reformulation.

By the total probability theorem, for $(x_H, x_G, y_G', z) \leftarrow \langle \mathcal{S}, \Theta_H, \Theta_G \rangle$,

$$\begin{aligned} &\Pr[x_H = x_H^\circ \wedge V'(x_H, x_G, \Theta_H, \Theta_G, z) = 1] \\ &= \Pr[V'(x_H, x_G, \Theta_H, \Theta_G, z) = 1 \mid b = 0] \Pr[b = 0] \\ &\qquad + \Pr[V'(x_H, x_G, \Theta_H, \Theta_G, z) = 1 \mid b = 1] \Pr[b = 1] \end{aligned} \tag{1}$$

Note when $b = 1$, Θ_H is given to $\mathcal{S}$ after x_G is returned. In this case, to make $V'(x_H, x_G, \Theta_H, \Theta_G, z) = 1$, we need to make $\Theta_H = x_G$. As Θ_H is sampled uniformly, independent of the already fixed x_G, we have that for $(x_H, x_G, y_G', z) \leftarrow \langle \mathcal{S}, \Theta_H, \Theta_G \rangle$,

$$\begin{aligned} &\Pr[x_H = x_H^\circ \wedge V'(x_H, x_G, \Theta_H, \Theta_G, z) = 1 \mid b = 1] \\ &\qquad \leq \Pr[x_H = x_H^\circ \wedge x_G = \Theta_H \mid b = 1] = \frac{\Pr[x_H = x_H^\circ \mid b = 1]}{|\mathcal{X}_1|} \end{aligned} \tag{2}$$

Finally, with (1) and (2), we conclude that for $(x_H, x_G, y'_G, z) \leftarrow \langle \mathcal{S}, \Theta_H, \Theta_G \rangle$,

$$\begin{aligned}
&\Pr[x_H = x_H^\circ \wedge V'(x_H, x_G, \Theta_H, \Theta_G, z) = 1 \wedge b = 0] \\
\geq &\Pr[x_H = x_H^\circ \wedge V'(x_H, x_G, \Theta_H, \Theta_G, z) = 1] \\
&\qquad - \Pr[V'(x_H, x_G, \Theta_H, \Theta_G, z) = 1 \mid b = 1] \Pr[b = 1] \\
\geq &\Pr[x_H = x_H^\circ \wedge V'(x_H, x_G, \Theta_H, \Theta_G, z) = 1] \\
&\qquad - |\mathcal{X}_1|^{-1} \Pr[x_H = x^\circ \mid b = 1]
\end{aligned}$$

Finally, by the definition of V', we have that

$$\begin{aligned}
&\Pr[x_H = x_H^\circ \wedge V'(x_H, x_G, \Theta_H, \Theta_G, z) = 1 \wedge b = 0] \\
= &\Pr[x_H = x_H^\circ \wedge x_G = \Theta_H \wedge V(x_H, \Theta_H, \Theta_G, z) = 1 \wedge b = 0] \\
\leq &\Pr[x_H = x_H^\circ \wedge V(x_H, \Theta_H, \Theta_G, z) = 1 \wedge b = 0]
\end{aligned}$$

Now, we define a new simulator $\mathcal{S}'$ that follows the same procedure as $\mathcal{S}$ but aborts immediately when $b = 1$ and packs x_G, y'_G into z. With $\mathcal{S}'$, we finally obtain the conclusion,

$$\begin{aligned}
&\Pr[x_H = x_H^\circ \wedge V(x_H, \Theta_H, \Theta_G, z) = 1 : (x_H, z) \leftarrow \langle \mathcal{S}', \Theta_H, \Theta_G \rangle] \\
= &\Pr[x_H = x_H^\circ \wedge V(x_H, \Theta_H, \Theta_G, z) = 1 \wedge b = 0 : (x_H, z) \leftarrow \langle \mathcal{S}', \Theta_H, \Theta_G \rangle] \\
\geq &\Pr[x_H = x_H^\circ \wedge V'(x_H, x_G, \Theta_H, \Theta_G, z) = 1] - |\mathcal{X}_1|^{-1} \Pr[x_H = x^\circ \mid b = 1] \\
\geq &\tfrac{1}{(2q_G+1)^2(2q_H+1)^2} \Pr\left[x_H = x_H^\circ \wedge V(x_H, h^{(x_H)}, g^{(x_H)}, z) = 1 : (x_H, z) \leftarrow \mathcal{A}^{H,G}\right] \\
&\qquad - |\mathcal{X}_1|^{-1} \Pr[x_H = x_H^\circ \mid b = 1]
\end{aligned}$$

This completes the proof of Theorem 3. □

3 Extended Adaptive Reprogramming

In this section, we extend the tight adaptive reprogramming theorem in [11] to handle two random oracles.

We first recall the tight adaptive reprogramming theorem in [11].

Theorem 4 (Adaptive Reprogramming[11]). *Let $\mathcal{X}, \mathcal{Y}$ be finite sets, and D be a distinguisher in the game defined in Fig. 2. Let D query the reprogram oracle R times and let q_r denote the number of queries to the random oracle $|\mathsf{O}_b\rangle$ between the $(r-1)$-th and r-th query to the reprogram oracle. By $p^{(r)}$ we denote the distribution p in the input of the r-th query to the reprogram oracle. Furthermore, by $p_{\mathcal{X}}^{(r)}$ we denote the marginal distribution of x, according to $p^{(r)}$. We also define,*

$$p_{\max}^r := \mathrm{E} \max_x p_{\mathcal{X}}^{(r)}(x),$$

where the expectation is taken over the behavior of D until its r-th query to the reprogram oracle. Then,

where the expectation is taken over the behavior of D *until its* r*-th query to the reprogram oracle. Then,*

$$\left|\Pr\left[\mathsf{REPRO}_1^{\mathsf{D}} = 1\right] - \Pr\left[\mathsf{REPRO}_0^{\mathsf{D}} = 1\right]\right| \leq \sum_{r=1}^{R}\left(\sqrt{\hat{q_r} p_{\max}^{(r)}} + \frac{1}{2}\hat{q_r} p_{\max}^{(r)}\right),$$

where $\hat{q_r} = \sum_{i=1}^{r} q_i$.

Our goal is to extend Theorem 4 to support reprogramming two oracles successively, in which case the query for one oracle depends on the output of the other oracle. The theorem is stated as follows:

GAME $\mathsf{REPRO}_b^{\mathsf{D}}$	$\mathsf{REPROGRAM}(p)$
$\mathsf{O}_0 \leftarrow \mathcal{Y}^{\mathcal{X}}$	$(x, x') \leftarrow p$
$\mathsf{O}_1 := \mathsf{O}_0$	$y \leftarrow \mathcal{Y}$
$b' \leftarrow \mathsf{D}_b^{\lvert \mathsf{O}_b \rangle, \mathsf{REPROGRAM}}$	$\mathsf{O}_b := \mathsf{O}_b^{x \to y}$
Return b'	Return (x, x')

Fig. 2. The adaptive reprogramming game.

Theorem 5 (Adaptive Reprogramming, Extended). *Let* $\mathcal{X}, \mathcal{Y}, \mathcal{Z}$ *be finite sets with* $\mathcal{X} = \mathcal{X}_1 \times \mathcal{X}_2$*, and* D *be a distinguisher in the game defined in Fig. 3. Let* D *query the reprogram oracle* R *times and let* q_{H_r} *and* q_{G_r} *denote the number of queries to the random oracles* $\lvert \mathsf{O}_{H_b} \rangle$ *and* $\lvert \mathsf{O}_{G_b} \rangle$*, respectively, between the* $(r-1)$*-th and* r*-th query to the reprogram oracle.*

$$\left|\Pr\left[\mathsf{REPRO}_1^{\mathsf{D}} = 1\right] - \Pr\left[\mathsf{REPRO}_0^{\mathsf{D}} = 1\right]\right| \leq \sum_{r=1}^{R}\left(\sqrt{2\hat{q}_{H_r}|\mathcal{X}_2|^{-1}} + \sqrt{2\hat{q}_{G_r}|\mathcal{Y}|^{-1}}\right)$$

where $\hat{q}_{H_r} = \sum_{i=1}^{r} q_{H_i}$ *and* $\hat{q}_{G_r} = \sum_{i=1}^{r} q_{G_i}$.

GAME $\mathsf{REPRO}_b^{\mathsf{D}}$	$\mathsf{REPROGRAM}(x_1)$
$\mathsf{O}_{H_0} \leftarrow \mathcal{Y}^{\mathcal{X}}$	$x_2 \leftarrow \mathcal{X}_2$
$\mathsf{O}_{G_0} \leftarrow \mathcal{Z}^{\mathcal{Y}}$	$y \leftarrow \mathcal{Y}$
$\mathsf{O}_{H_1} := \mathsf{O}_{H_0}$	$z \leftarrow \mathcal{Z}$
$\mathsf{O}_{G_1} := \mathsf{O}_{G_0}$	$\mathsf{O}_{H_1} := \mathsf{O}_{H_1}^{(x_1, x_2) \to y}$
$b' \leftarrow \mathsf{D}_b^{\lvert \mathsf{O}_{H_b} \rangle, \lvert \mathsf{O}_{G_b} \rangle, \mathsf{REPROGRAM}}$	$\mathsf{O}_{G_1} := \mathsf{O}_{G_1}^{y \to z}$
Return b'	Return x_2

Fig. 3. The adaptive reprogramming game for reprogramming two oracles successively.

Remark 1 (Reprogramming the Random Oracle as a Man-in-the-Middle). Although we write the theorem as if the challenger has full control over the random oracle, it is worth noting that it doesn't have to own the random oracle to do the reprogramming. In fact, the challenger as a man in the middle between the adversary and the oracle is already enough to reprogram the random oracle.

Specifically, let H be the original random function. When reprogramming H to $H^{x \to y}$, the challenger can query the original random oracle H on x, and keep the classical $\Delta y_x \stackrel{\text{def}}{=} y \oplus H(x)$ locally. Then the challenger constructs a quantum gate, denoted by U_{Δ_x}. When it acts on a state $|x'\rangle |y'\rangle$ for $x' \in \mathcal{X} \setminus \{x\}$, it does nothing. When it acts on the state $|x\rangle |y'\rangle$, it turns $|x\rangle |y'\rangle$ to $|x\rangle |y' \oplus \Delta y_x\rangle$.

Upon an RO query from the adversary after the reprogramming, whose input is $|x'\rangle_X |y'\rangle_Y$, the challenger first applies the x-controlled gate U_{Δ_x}, then, it sends $\mathsf{U}_{\Delta_x} |x'\rangle_X |y'\rangle_Y$ to the original random oracle H. It is easy to verify that the resulting transform is identical to an ordinary reprogrammed oracle.

In this section, we will provide a proof for Theorem 5 with a new lemma, the superposition-controlled reprogramming lemma (cf. Lemma 2). In some sense, this lemma is an adaptation of the tight adaptive reprogramming theorem in [11] to allow the reprogramming controlled by a quantum superposition state, instead of a classical variable from a distribution.

Before giving the proof, we will first show why Theorem 4 (i.e., the original tight adaptive reprogramming theorem) cannot be directly extended to meet our demand of adaptively reprogramming two oracles successively, even if we use it in a white-box way.

3.1 Limitations of the Tight Adaptive Reprogramming Theorem [11]

At first glance, the formulation of Theorem 5 is very similar to the statement of Theorem 4, except that we have to reprogram two random oracles successively. So we initially expected that applying their theorem twice to reprogram the two oracles one by one would be enough to prove our theorem. Specifically, we may first use their theorem to reprogram H oracle, with the required min-entropy from $x_2 \leftarrow \mathcal{X}_2$. Then, we may use the theorem again to reprogram G oracle, with the required min-entropy from $y := H(x_1, x_2)$.

However, such an approach is not correct. When using their theorem statement literally to reprogram oracle G, we have to treat the description of oracle H as a part of the distinguisher's view to match the theorem's description. In this case, we cannot conclude that the value of $H(m\|r)$ (which is y sampled in the previous reprogram procedure of H in this case) is statistically uniform, as the distinguisher can access the oracle H at will.

We then try to open the black-box and use the superposition oracle to describe the random oracle's behavior, attempting to follow their proof strategy to improve the theorem. Their proof includes a crucial step, which is to take the expectation of some metrics of the entire system (including the internal states of the random oracle to be reprogrammed) over the input distribution p. During their proof, the variable x from $(x, x') \leftarrow p$ is treated as a fresh random variable outside of the system.

However, in our use of the theorem, our desired entropy source $y := H(x_1, x_2)$ when reprogramming the oracle G is in fact a part of the system. If we follow their proof strategy, we will still have to show how this coupling between y and the system affects the theorem's analysis. If the reprogramming process becomes more complicated, such coupling will become more difficult to analyze.

At this point, we realized that the original tight adaptive reprogramming theorem formulation is hard to extend to a case with a more complicated reprogramming process. Therefore, we decided to re-prove their theorem with a more general formulation.

Our approach to dealing with the issue is rooted in the observation that the theorem requires unconditional min-entropy (or, min-entropy from the view of the entire system) rather than min-entropy in some party's view. This requirement is not so desirable in the presence of multiple oracles. Therefore, we take advantage of quantum computation to keep the random variables in their quantum superposition, preserving their entropy, instead of using classical random values as in [11]. To do this, we develop a more fundamental lemma, Lemma 2, which can reprogram the oracle given an appropriate superposition state which controls the position to be reprogrammed, instead of a classical distribution.

3.2 Superposition-Controlled Reprogramming

Let $\mathcal{A}$ be a quantum algorithm with access to a superposition random oracle $|H\rangle_F$, where $H : \mathcal{X} \to \mathcal{Y}$. Let X and Z denote two working registers of $\mathcal{A}$, where X contains a superposition over $\mathcal{X}$ and Z contains the remaining workspace state. Let q denote the number of $\mathcal{A}$'s queries to the random oracle. Let the system state after $\mathcal{A}$ terminates be $|\gamma_0\rangle_{XZF}$.

We consider the following quantum gate RE acting on $|\gamma_0\rangle_{XZF} \otimes |\phi_0\rangle_W$:

$$\mathsf{RE} = \sum_{x \in \mathcal{X}} |x\rangle\langle x|_X \otimes \mathsf{SWAP}_{F_x,W}.$$

Intuitively, RE reprograms F_x with a fresh uniformly random state by swapping F_x and the new register W, where the reprogrammed position x is controlled by the register X.

Then we have the following lemma:

Lemma 2 (Superposition-controlled reprogramming). *For any $\mathcal{A}$ that makes q queries to the superposition oracle and outputs $|\gamma_0\rangle_{XZF}$ such that X is separable from ZF, i.e., $|\gamma_0\rangle_{XZF} = |x\rangle_X \otimes |\gamma\rangle_{ZF}$, and for any (unbounded) quantum distinguisher* D,

$$\left|\Pr\left[\mathsf{D}(|\gamma_0\rangle_{XZF} \otimes |\phi_0\rangle_W) = 1\right] - \Pr\left[\mathsf{D}\left(\mathsf{RE}\left(|\gamma_0\rangle_{XZF} \otimes |\phi_0\rangle_W\right)\right) = 1\right]\right| \leq \sqrt{2q\alpha_{\max}^2},$$

where $\alpha_{\max} = \max_{x' \in \mathcal{X}} |\langle x' \rangle\, x_X|$ and $|\phi_0\rangle_W$ is the uniform superposition as defined in Subsect. 2.3.

Proof. We prove the lemma by computing the fidelity between the states before and after the reprogramming. We first write the state in a form that makes the action of RE explicit.

We can represent the state $|\gamma\rangle_{XZF}$ as a sum of tensor-product states with amplitudes $\{\alpha_x\}_{x\in\mathcal{X}}$:

$$\begin{aligned}|\gamma_0\rangle_{XZF}\otimes|\phi_0\rangle_W &= \sum_{x\in\mathcal{X}}\alpha_x|x\rangle_X\otimes|\gamma\rangle_{ZF}\otimes|\phi_0\rangle_W \\ &= \sum_{x\in\mathcal{X}}\alpha_x|x\rangle_X\otimes\sum_{\substack{S\subset\mathcal{X}\\|S|\le q}}\beta_S|\gamma^{(S)}\rangle_{ZF_S}\left(|\phi_0\rangle^{\otimes|\mathcal{X}\setminus S|}\right)_{F_{\mathcal{X}\setminus S}}\otimes|\phi_0\rangle_W.\end{aligned}$$

The decomposition over registers Z and F in the second equation is given by Lemma 1, where we recall that $|\gamma^{(S)}\rangle_{ZF_S}$ satisfies $\langle\phi_0|_{F_x}|\gamma^{(S)}\rangle_{ZF_S}=0$ for all $x\in S$. To make the effect of swapping explicit, we further expand the state in the Fourier basis $\{\phi_0,\phi_1,\cdots,\phi_{|\mathcal{Y}|-1}\}$ of register F_x.

$$|\psi\rangle\stackrel{\text{def}}{=}|\gamma\rangle_{XZF}\otimes|\phi_0\rangle_W=\sum_{x\in\mathcal{X}}\alpha_x|x\rangle_X\otimes$$
$$\Bigg(\underbrace{\sum_{\substack{S\subset\mathcal{X}\\|S|\le q,\,x\in S}}\beta_S\sum_{i=1}^{|\mathcal{Y}|-1}|\phi_i\rangle\langle\phi_i|_{F_x}|\gamma^{(S)}\rangle_{ZF_S}\left(|\phi_0\rangle^{\otimes|\mathcal{X}\setminus S|}\right)_{F_{\mathcal{X}\setminus S}}\otimes|\phi_0\rangle_W+}_{\stackrel{\text{def}}{=}|\psi_{x,0}\rangle_{ZFW}}$$
$$\underbrace{\sum_{\substack{S\subset\mathcal{X}\\|S|\le q,\,x\notin S}}\beta_S|\gamma^{(S)}\rangle_{ZF_S}\left(|\phi_0\rangle^{\otimes|\mathcal{X}\setminus S|}\right)_{F_{\mathcal{X}\setminus S}}\otimes|\phi_0\rangle_W}_{\stackrel{\text{def}}{=}|\psi_{x,1}\rangle_{ZFW}}\Bigg).$$

We note that the summation over i starts from 1 instead of 0 because the $i=0$ term vanishes due to the property $\langle\phi_0|_{F_x}|\gamma^{(S)}\rangle_{ZF_S}=0$ for all $x\in S$.

Now we apply RE to the state and get

$$|\psi'\rangle\stackrel{\text{def}}{=}\mathsf{RE}\left(|\gamma_0\rangle_{XZF}\otimes|\phi_0\rangle_W\right)=\sum_{x\in\mathcal{X}}\alpha_x|x\rangle_X\otimes$$
$$\Bigg(\underbrace{\sum_{\substack{S\subset\mathcal{X}\\|S|\le q,x\in S}}\beta_S\sum_{i=1}^{|\mathcal{Y}|-1}|\phi_0\rangle\langle\phi_i|_{F_x}|\gamma^{(S)}\rangle_{ZF_S}\left(|\phi_0\rangle^{\otimes|\mathcal{X}\setminus S|}\right)_{F_{\mathcal{X}\setminus S}}\otimes|\phi_i\rangle_W+}_{\stackrel{\text{def}}{=}|\psi'_{x,0}\rangle_{ZFW}}$$
$$\underbrace{\sum_{\substack{S\subset\mathcal{X}\\|S|\le q,x\notin S}}\beta_S|\gamma^{(S)}\rangle_{ZF_S}\left(|\phi_0\rangle^{\otimes|\mathcal{X}\setminus S|}\right)_{F_{\mathcal{X}\setminus S}}\otimes|\phi_0\rangle_W}_{\stackrel{\text{def}}{=}|\psi'_{x,1}\rangle_{ZFW}}\Bigg).$$

Here we define some new notations $|\psi\rangle, |\psi'\rangle$ and $|\psi_{x,0}\rangle, |\psi_{x,1}\rangle, |\psi'_{x,0}\rangle, |\psi'_{x,1}\rangle$ in the equation above to make our following presentation more compact. We further denote $\langle\phi_i|_{F_x} |\gamma^{(S)}\rangle_{ZF_S}$ as $|\gamma^{(S)}_{x,i}\rangle_{ZF_{S\setminus x}}$, so that we can write $|\psi_{x,0}\rangle$ and $|\psi'_{x,0}\rangle$ as

$$|\psi_{x,0}\rangle = \sum_{\substack{S\subset\mathcal{Y}\\|S|\leq q, x\in S}} \beta_S \sum_{i=1}^{|\mathcal{Y}|-1} |\phi_i\rangle_{F_x} |\gamma^{(S)}_{x,i}\rangle_{ZF_{S\setminus x}} \left(|\phi_0\rangle^{\otimes|\mathcal{X}\setminus S|}\right)_{F_{\mathcal{X}\setminus S}} |\phi_0\rangle_W$$

$$|\psi'_{x,0}\rangle = \sum_{\substack{S\subset\mathcal{X}\\|S|\leq q, x\in S}} \beta_S \sum_{i=1}^{|\mathcal{Y}|-1} |\phi_0\rangle_{F_x} |\gamma^{(S)}_{x,i}\rangle_{ZF_{S\setminus x}} \left(|\phi_0\rangle^{\otimes|\mathcal{X}\setminus S|}\right)_{F_{\mathcal{X}\setminus S}} |\phi_i\rangle_W$$

With these notations and the explicit representation of the state vectors, we are now getting into computing the fidelity of the two states.

$$\begin{aligned} F(|\psi\rangle\langle\psi|, |\psi'\rangle\langle\psi'|) = |\langle\psi\rangle\,\psi'| &= \left|\sum_{x\in\mathcal{X}} |\alpha_x|^2 \langle x\rangle\, x_X \cdot \left(\left(\langle\psi_{x,0}| + \langle\psi_{x,1}|\right)\left(|\psi'_{x,0}\rangle + |\psi'_{x,1}\rangle\right)\right)\right| \\ &= \left|\sum_{x\in\mathcal{X}} |\alpha_x|^2 \langle\psi_{x,1}\rangle\,\psi'_{x,1}\right|. \end{aligned} \tag{3}$$

We omit the vanishing terms $\langle\psi_{x,0}|\psi'_{x,1}\rangle$, $\langle\psi_{x,1}|\psi'_{x,0}\rangle$ and $\langle\psi_{x,0}|\psi'_{x,0}\rangle$ in (3). We show that the inner product in one of the registers is zero for the vanishing terms. For $\langle\psi_{x,0}|\psi'_{x,1}\rangle$, we have $\langle\psi_{x,0}|_{ZFW}\,|\phi_0\rangle_{F_x} = 0$, in which the projection of $\psi'_{x,1}$ onto the register F_x is $|\phi_0\rangle_{F_x}$. Similarly, we have $\langle\phi_0|_W\,|\psi'_{x,0}\rangle_{ZFW} = 0$, which indicates $\langle\psi_{x,1}|\psi'_{x,0}\rangle = 0$ and $\langle\psi_{x,0}|\psi'_{x,0}\rangle = 0$.

For the leftover term , we have

$$\begin{aligned} F(|\psi\rangle\langle\psi|, |\psi'\rangle\langle\psi'|) &= \left|\sum_{x\in\mathcal{X}} |\alpha_x|^2 \langle\psi_{x,1}\rangle\,\psi'_{x,1}\right| = \sum_{x\in\mathcal{X}} |\alpha_x|^2 \sum_{\substack{S\subset\mathcal{X}\\|S|\leq q, x\in S}} |\beta_S|^2 \\ &= \sum_{\substack{S\subset\mathcal{X}\\|S|\leq q}} |\beta_S|^2 \sum_{x\in\mathcal{X}\setminus S} |\alpha_x|^2 \geq \sum_{\substack{S\subset\mathcal{X}\\|S|\leq q}} |\beta_S|^2 \cdot (1 - q\alpha^2_{\max}) = 1 - q\alpha^2_{\max}. \end{aligned}$$

Finally, we can bound the probability with fidelity by

$$\begin{aligned} &\left|\Pr\left[\mathsf{D}(|\gamma_0\rangle_{XZF} \otimes |\phi_0\rangle_W) = 1\right] - \Pr\left[\mathsf{D}\big(\mathsf{RE}\left(|\gamma_0\rangle_{XZF} \otimes |\phi_0\rangle_W\right)\big) = 1\right]\right| \\ &= D(|\psi\rangle\langle\psi|, |\psi'\rangle\langle\psi'|) \leq \sqrt{1 - F(|\psi\rangle\langle\psi|, |\psi'\rangle\langle\psi'|)^2} \leq \sqrt{1 - (1 - q\alpha^2_{\max})^2} \\ &= \sqrt{2q\alpha^2_{\max} - q^2\alpha^4_{\max}} \leq \sqrt{2q\alpha^2_{\max}}, \end{aligned}$$

where the (in)equalities in the second line are from the properties of the two metrics mentioned in Subsect. 2.3.

This completes the proof of Lemma 2. □

With Lemma 2, we can restate Theorem 4 as follows:

Theorem 6 (Adaptive Reprogramming [11, **Theorem 1**], **Restated)** *Let the symbols be the same as defined in Theorem 4. Then, for the game defined in Fig. 2,*

$$\left|\Pr\left[\mathsf{REPRO}_1^{\mathsf{D}} = 1\right] - \Pr\left[\mathsf{REPRO}_0^{\mathsf{D}} = 1\right]\right| \leq \sum_{r=1}^{R} \sqrt{2\hat{q}_r p_{\max}^{(r)}}.$$

Comparing Theorem 6 with Theorem 4 (i.e. the original theorem in [11]), our bound does not include the linear term $\hat{q}_r p_{\max}^{(r)}$ but has a larger factor up to $\sqrt{2}$ times in the leading square root term $\sqrt{\hat{q}_r p_{\max}^{(r)}}$. This might be because our lemma (Lemma 2) allows the distinguisher to be given the quantum superposition $|x\rangle_X$, whereas [11] requires a measured classical x. Nevertheless, using our theorem does not increase the security loss bound in the main application results (i.e., Proposition 1 and Proposition 2 of [11]), and our result still provides a tight bound up to constant factors.

As the proof shares the same idea with that of Theorem 5 and the conclusion is similar to the original theorem in [11], we omit the proof here.

3.3 Proof of Extended Adaptive Reprogramming Theorem

Now we present the proof of Theorem 5. The idea of the proof is to simulate all the classical random sampling in the game with quantum circuits, and then apply Lemma 2 to each step.

GAME $\mathsf{G}_{r.0}$-$\mathsf{G}_{r.3}$

- $\mathsf{O}_H \leftarrow \mathcal{Y}^{\mathcal{X}}$
- $\mathsf{O}_G \leftarrow \mathcal{Z}^{\mathcal{Y}}$
- $b' \leftarrow \mathsf{D}_b^{|\mathsf{O}_G\rangle, |\mathsf{O}_H\rangle, \mathsf{REPROGRAM}}$
- Return b'

$\mathsf{REPROGRAM}_{r+1}(x_1)$ $\mathsf{G}_{r.0}$-$\mathsf{G}_{r.3}$

- Prepare $|x_1\rangle_{X_1}$
- Prepare $\left|\phi_0^{(\mathcal{X}_2)}\right\rangle_{X_2}$, $\left|\phi_0^{(\mathcal{Y})}\right\rangle_Y$, $\left|\phi_0^{(\mathcal{Z})}\right\rangle_Z$
- Measure X_2 // $\mathsf{G}_{r.0}$
- Apply RE_{YF_GZ} // $\mathsf{G}_{r.0}$-$\mathsf{G}_{r.1}$
- Apply RE_{XF_HY} // $\mathsf{G}_{r.0}$-$\mathsf{G}_{r.2}$
- Measure X_2 // $\mathsf{G}_{r.1}$-$\mathsf{G}_{r.3}$
- Return register X_2

$\mathsf{REPROGRAM}_j(x_1)$ $j \leq r$

- Prepare $\left|\phi_0^{(\mathcal{X}_2)}\right\rangle_{X_2}$
- Measure X_2
- Return register X_2

$\mathsf{REPROGRAM}_j(x_1)$ $j > r+1$

- Prepare $|x_1\rangle_{X_1}$
- Prepare $\left|\phi_0^{(\mathcal{X}_2)}\right\rangle_{X_2}$, $\left|\phi_0^{(\mathcal{Y})}\right\rangle_Y$, $\left|\phi_0^{(\mathcal{Z})}\right\rangle_Z$
- Measure X_2
- Apply RE_{YF_GZ}
- Apply RE_{XF_HY}
- Return register X_2

Fig. 4. The games $\mathsf{G}_{r.0}$ to $\mathsf{G}_{r.3}$ for the proof of Theorem 5, where $r = 0, 1, 2, \cdots, R-1$, and $\mathsf{REPROGRAM}_j$ denotes the j-th query to the $\mathsf{REPROGRAM}$ oracle.

Proof (Theorem 5). Following the proof of the original theorem in [11], we start with the superposition oracle version of the game in Fig. 3. We let G_0 be the superposition oracle version of the original game $\mathsf{REPRO}_1^{\mathsf{D}}$. For those familiar with superposition oracle, it is easy to see that the game is identical to the game $\mathsf{REPRO}_1^{\mathsf{D}}$ in Fig. 3, so we omit the details of game transition to G_0 here. For completeness, we provide the details of game transition to G_0 in Appendix A.

Now we use game transitions to prove the theorem. For $r = 1, 2, \cdots, R$, we let game G_r proceed the same as G_0, except that for the first r queries to the $\mathsf{REPROGRAM}$ oracle, it only returns a fresh uniform random $x_r \in \mathcal{X}_1$ and does nothing else (i.e., does not reprogram the oracles), as shown in Fig. 4.

We see that for $r = 0, 1, \cdots, R-1$, the difference between G_r and G_{r+1} lies only in the $(r+1)$-th query to the $\mathsf{REPROGRAM}$ oracle. We now use another sequence of games, from $\mathsf{G}_{r.0}$ to $\mathsf{G}_{r.3}$, to bound the distinguishability between the game G_r and G_{r+1}.

Game $\mathsf{G}_{r.0}$. This game is the same as G_r. We only define this game for consistency of the notation.

Game $\mathsf{G}_{r.1}$. In this game, the measurement of X_2 in the $(r+1)$-th query to the $\mathsf{REPROGRAM}$ oracle is moved to the end of the reprogramming function. We note that in the operator RE_{XF_HY}, register X is only used as control bits, thus RE_{XF_HY} commutes with the measurement of X_2. This gives us $\Pr_{r.1} = \Pr_{r.0}$.

Game $\mathsf{G}_{r.2}$. In this game, we do not apply RE_{YF_GZ} anymore. We note that before RE_{YF_GZ} is applied in Game G_3, the register Y is separable from the other part of the system. To apply Lemma 2, we need to ensure that the internal register F_G is accessed only through the oracle queries.

Luckily this is the case, as the $\mathsf{REPROGRAM}$ oracle queries prior to the $(r+1)$-th query now do nothing to the oracle G due to the previous game transitions. Moreover, prior to the $(r+1)$-th oracle query to $\mathsf{REPROGRAM}$ we see that there are only $\hat{q}_{G_{r+1}}$ queries to the oracle G. Finally, recalling that register Y is in the state $|\phi_0^{(\mathcal{Y})}\rangle_Y = \sum_{y\in\mathcal{Y}} \sqrt{|\mathcal{Y}|^{-1}}\, |y\rangle_Y$, we conclude from Lemma 2 that, $|\Pr_{r.2} - \Pr_{r.1}| \le \sqrt{2\hat{q}_{G_{r+1}}|\mathcal{Y}|^{-1}}$.

Game $\mathsf{G}_{r.3}$. In this game, we do not apply RE_{XF_HY} anymore. Similarly, before RE_{XF_HY} is applied in Game G_4, the register X is separable from the other part of the system and X is in the state $|x_1\rangle_{X_1} |\phi_0^{(\mathcal{X}_2)}\rangle_{X_2} = |x_1\rangle_{X_1} \otimes \sum_{x_2\in\mathcal{X}_2} \sqrt{|\mathcal{X}_2|^{-1}}\, |x_2\rangle_{X_2}$. Moreover, prior to the r-th oracle query to $\mathsf{REPROGRAM}$, the oracle H is accessed only through oracle queries (instead of accessing its internal states directly), and there are only $\hat{q}_{H_{r+1}}$ such queries to H. We conclude from Lemma 2 that, $|\Pr_{r.3} - \Pr_{r.2}| \le \sqrt{2\hat{q}_{H_{r+1}}|\mathcal{X}_2|^{-1}}$.

At the end of this game sequence, we delete the unused registers in the game $\mathsf{G}_{r.3}$, and find that the game is identical to the game G_{r+1}. This shows that,

$$|\Pr_{r+1} - \Pr_r| = |\Pr_{r.3} - \Pr_{r.0}| \le \sqrt{2\hat{q}_{H_{r+1}}|\mathcal{X}_2|^{-1}} + \sqrt{2\hat{q}_{G_{r+1}}|\mathcal{Y}|^{-1}}.$$

Now, consider the final game G_R, in which none of the $\mathsf{REPROGRAM}$ calls reprogram the random oracles H or G anymore. That is to say that G_R is identical to the game REPRO_0, where the distinguisher D is given random oracles that are never reprogrammed. Therefore, we sum up the previous results and conclude that,

$$\left|\Pr\left[\mathsf{REPRO}_1^{\mathsf{D}}=1\right]-\Pr\left[\mathsf{REPRO}_0^{\mathsf{D}}=1\right]\right| \le \sum_{r=0}^{R-1} |\Pr_{r+1}-\Pr_r| \le \sum_{r=1}^{R}\left(\sqrt{2\hat{q}_{H_r}|\mathcal{X}_2|^{-1}}+\sqrt{2\hat{q}_{G_r}|\mathcal{Y}|^{-1}}\right).$$

This completes the proof of Theorem 5. □

4 Generic Construction of Signature Scheme with Message Recovery

In this section, we present a generic construction of signature schemes with message recovery from preimage sampleable function, and prove its EUF-CMA security in the QROM. This scheme is a post-quantum adaptation of the PSS-R scheme proposed by Bellare and Rogaway [3].

Let $\mathcal{M}=\mathcal{M}_1\times\mathcal{M}_2$ be the message space. We require the following building blocks to construct the scheme:

- A preimage sampleable function PSF = (TrapGen, SampleDom, SamplePre) with a preimage space $\mathcal{X}$ and an image space $\mathcal{Y}=\mathcal{Y}_1\times\mathcal{Y}_2\times\mathcal{Y}_3$, where $\mathcal{Y}_2=\{0,1\}^{l_2}\supseteq\mathcal{M}_1$ and $\mathcal{Y}_3=\{0,1\}^{l_3}$ for some positive integers $l_2,l_3\in\mathbb{N}$.
- Two hash functions $H:\mathcal{M}_1\times\mathcal{M}_2\times\mathcal{Y}_3\to\mathcal{Y}_1$ and $G:\mathcal{Y}_1\to\mathcal{Y}_2\times\mathcal{Y}_3$, where G can be further partitioned into two hash functions $G_1:\mathcal{Y}_1\to\mathcal{Y}_2$ and $G_2:\mathcal{Y}_1\to\mathcal{Y}_3$ such that $G(\omega)=G_1(\omega)\|G_2(\omega)$ holds for all $\omega\in\mathcal{Y}_1$.

With the above building blocks, we present the signature scheme with message recovery in Fig. 5. It is straightforward to check the correctness of the signature scheme based on the preimage sampling correctness of PSF.

$\mathsf{KeyGen}(1^\lambda)$:	$\mathsf{Sign}(sk=t, m=(m_1,m_2))$:	$\mathsf{Vrfy}(vk=a, m_2, \sigma)$:
$(a,t)\leftarrow\mathsf{TrapGen}(1^\lambda)$	$r\leftarrow\mathcal{Y}_3$	$\omega'\|M'\|R' := f_a(\sigma)$
$vk := a$	$\omega := H(m_1\|m_2\|r)$	$m_1' := M'\oplus G_1(\omega')$
$sk := t$	$M := m_1\oplus G_1(\omega)$	$r' := R'\oplus G_2(\omega')$
Return (vk, sk)	$R := r\oplus G_2(\omega)$	If $H(m_1'\|m_2\|r')=\omega'$ then
	$\sigma\leftarrow\mathsf{SamplePre}(\omega\|M\|R, t)$	return $(1, m_1')$
	Return σ	else return $(0,\perp)$

Fig. 5. Generic construction of signature scheme with message recovery from preimage sampleable function.

Theorem 7 (EUF-CMA **security**). *If* PSF *is a collision-resistant preimage sampleable function and H, G are modeled as quantum accessible random oracles,* *then the signature scheme in Fig. 5 is* EUF-CMA *secure. Specifically, for any PPT adversary* $\mathcal{A}$ *against the* EUF-CMA *security of the scheme that makes* q_H *and* q_G *queries to the oracles* H *and* G*, respectively, and makes* q_S *queries to the signing oracle* SIGN*, there exists a PPT adversary* $\mathcal{B}$ *against the collision-resistance of* PSF*, such that*

$$\mathsf{Adv}^{\mathsf{CR}}_{\mathsf{PSF},\mathcal{B}} \geq \frac{1-p_{max}}{(2\max\{q_H,q_G+1\}+1)^4} \cdot \mathsf{Adv}^{\mathsf{EUF\text{-}CMA}}_{\mathsf{SIG},\mathcal{A}} - \frac{(1-p_{max})q_S(q_H+q_S+2)^2}{(2\max\{q_H,q_G+1\}+1)^4|\mathcal{Y}_1|} - \frac{(1-p_{max})q_S}{(2\max\{q_H,q_G+1\}+1)^4}\left(\sqrt{\frac{2q_H}{|\mathcal{Y}_3|}}+\sqrt{\frac{2q_G}{|\mathcal{Y}_1|}}\right) - \frac{1-p_{max}}{|\mathcal{Y}_1|},$$

where p_{max} *is the preimage min-entropy parameter of* PSF *defined in Subsect. 2.2.*

To prove this theorem, we break it down into two lemmas. First, in Lemma 3, we show the reduction from EUF-NMA to EUF-CMA by using our extended adaptive reprogramming theorem (i.e., Theorem 5). Then in Lemma 4, we prove the EUF-NMA security of the scheme based on the collision-resistance of PSF by using our extended measure-and-reprogram theorem (i.e., Theorem 3).

Lemma 3 (**EUF-NMA to EUF-CMA**)**.** *For any PPT adversary* $\mathcal{A}$ *against the* EUF-CMA *security of the scheme in Fig. 5, there exists a PPT adversary* $\mathcal{B}$ *against the* EUF-NMA *security, such that*

$$\left|\mathsf{Adv}^{\mathsf{EUF\text{-}NMA}}_{\mathsf{SIG},\mathcal{B}} - \mathsf{Adv}^{\mathsf{EUF\text{-}CMA}}_{\mathsf{SIG},\mathcal{A}}\right| \leq q_S\left(\sqrt{2q_H|\mathcal{Y}_3|^{-1}}+\sqrt{2q_G|\mathcal{Y}_1|^{-1}}\right)+\frac{q_S(q_H+q_S+2)^2}{|\mathcal{Y}_1|}.$$

Proof. We use game transitions to prove the lemma. See Fig. 6 for the description of the games.

Game G_0. This is the original EUF-CMA game for signature scheme with message recovery (cf. Figure 1).

Game G_1. This game reprograms the two random oracles H and G. To show the indistinguishability, we construct a simulator with Theorem 5 such that O_{H_b} and O_{G_b} are set to the oracles H and G respectively. Specifically, our simulator simulates the game G_{-1} except that we sample r using the REPROGRAM oracle, i.e., $r \leftarrow \mathsf{REPROGRAM}(m_1\|m_2)$. Clearly, if we are given O_{H_0} and O_{G_0}, this simulation is identical to the game G_{-1}. If we are given O_{H_1} and O_{G_1}, this simulation is identical to the game G_0. Therefore, the indistinguishability follows from Theorem 5 that $|\Pr_0 - \Pr_{-1}| \leq q_S\left(\sqrt{2q_H|\mathcal{Y}_3|^{-1}}+\sqrt{2q_G|\mathcal{Y}_1|^{-1}}\right)$.

Game G_2. In this game, we switch the first input to the SamplePre algorithm from $\omega\|M\|R$ to $\omega^*\|M^*\|R^*$, where the starred variables are the intermediate values sampled for reprogramming in G_{-1}. In fact, as the oracles H and G are already reprogrammed, we can see that,

$$\begin{aligned}\omega &= H(m_1\|m_2\|r) = \omega^*,\\ M &= m_1 \oplus G_1(\omega) = m_1 \oplus M^* \oplus m_1 = M^*,\\ R &= r \oplus G_2(\omega) = r \oplus R^* \oplus r = R^*.\end{aligned}$$

Game G_0-G_5

$\mathcal{S} := \emptyset$

$\mathcal{W} := \emptyset$ //G_3-G_5

$(vk, sk) \leftarrow \mathsf{KeyGen}(1^\lambda)$

$(m_2', \sigma') \leftarrow \mathcal{A}^{\textsc{Sign}(\cdot), H, G}(vk)$

$\omega' \| M' \| R' := f_a(\sigma^*)$

$m_1' := M' \oplus G_1(\omega')$

$r' := R' \oplus G_2(\omega')$

If $(m_1', m_2') \in \mathcal{S}$ then Return 0

If $\omega' \in \mathcal{W}$ then Return 0 //G_3-G_5

Return $\omega' = H(m_1' \| m_2' \| r')$

$\textsc{Sign}(m = (m_1, m_2))$ G_0-G_5

$r \leftarrow \mathcal{Y}_3$

$\sigma^* \leftarrow \mathsf{SampleDom}(1^\lambda)$ //G_4-G_5

$\omega^* \| M^* \| R^* := f_a(\sigma^*)$ //G_4-G_5

$\omega^* \leftarrow \mathcal{Y}_1$ //G_1-G_3

$M^* \leftarrow \mathcal{Y}_2,\ R^* \leftarrow \mathcal{Y}_3$ //G_1-G_3

$H := H^{m_1 \| m_2 \| r \to \omega^*}$ //G_1-G_5

$G := G^{\omega^* \to (M^* \oplus m_1) \| (R^* \oplus r)}$ //G_1-G_5

$\omega := H(m_1 \| m_2 \| r)$ //G_0-G_1

$M := m_1 \oplus G_1(\omega)$ //G_0-G_1

$R := r \oplus G_2(\omega)$ //G_0-G_1

$\sigma \leftarrow \mathsf{SamplePre}(\omega \| M \| R, t)$ //G_0-G_1

$\sigma \leftarrow \mathsf{SamplePre}(\omega^* \| M^* \| R^*, t)$ //G_2-G_4

$\mathcal{S} := \mathcal{S} \cup \{(m_1, m_2)\}$

$\mathcal{W} := \mathcal{W} \cup \{\omega^*\}$ //G_3-G_5

Return σ //G_0-G_4

Return σ^* //G_5

Fig. 6. The game transition for the reduction from EUF-NMA to EUF-CMA (Lemma 3).

This indicates that G_0 is identical to G_{-1}, i.e., $\Pr_0 = \Pr_{-1}$.

Game G_3. In this game, we add an aborting condition to the game, i.e., if ω' is equal to any of the ω^* sampled in the game, we abort the game and return 0. This game is identical to G_{-1} as long as the Bad event $\omega' \in \mathcal{W} \wedge (m_1', m_2') \notin \mathcal{S} \wedge \omega' = H(m_1' \| m_2' \| r')$ does not happen.

Let H° be the un-reprogrammed version of H, we will bound the probability of the Bad event with the optimality of Grover Search with random oracle H° as shown in Theorem 1. Consider an adversary $\mathcal{B}_s$ who obtains some $y \in \mathcal{Y}_1$, and is searching for a preimage x such that $H^\circ(x) = y$. Let $\mathcal{B}_s$ simulates the game G_0 with the adversary $\mathcal{A}$ in G_0, except that,

1. When $\mathcal{B}_s$ needs to reprogram the random oracle H, it does the reprogramming as a man-in-the-middle between H° and $\mathcal{A}$ following the method described in Remark 1.
2. $\mathcal{B}_s$ samples $t \leftarrow [q_S]$ and replaces ω^* with y in the t-th query to the $\textsc{Sign}$ oracle.
3. $\mathcal{B}_s$ returns $m_1' \| m_2' \| r'$ directly before checking whether $(m_1', m_2') \in \mathcal{S}$.

As y is chosen uniformly, the view to $\mathcal{A}$ provided by $\mathcal{B}_s$ is identical to that of $\mathcal{A}$ in the real game of G_0. We then have that,

$$
\begin{aligned}
\Pr[\mathsf{Bad}] &= \Pr[\omega' \in \mathcal{W} \wedge (m_1', m_2') \notin \mathcal{S} \wedge \omega' = H(m_1' \| m_2' \| r')] \\
&\leq \Pr[\omega' \in \mathcal{W} \wedge (m_1', m_2') \notin \mathcal{S} \wedge \omega' = H^\circ(m_1' \| m_2' \| r')] && (4) \\
&= q_S \Pr[\omega' = y \wedge (m_1', m_2') \notin \mathcal{S} \wedge \omega' = H^\circ(m_1' \| m_2' \| r')] && (5) \\
&\leq q_S \Pr[\omega' = y \wedge \omega' = H^\circ(m_1' \| m_2' \| r')] .
\end{aligned}
$$

The inequality (4) in the second line follows from that $m_1'\|m_2'\|r'$ is not a reprogrammed position of oracle H as $(m_1', m_2') \notin \mathcal{S}$.

For the equation (5) in the third line, we recall that one of the $\omega^* \in \mathcal{W}$ is replaced by an identically distributed element y, and the probability of each element to be replaced is equal. Therefore, there is $\frac{1}{q_S}$ probability that the resulting ω' happens to be y.

As $\mathcal{B}_s$ queries H° for $q_H + q_S$ times (q_H times from $\mathcal{A}$ and q_S times from the reprogramming process within SIGN), by Theorem 1, we can bound its probability of finding such x' by,

$$\Pr\left[\omega' = y \wedge \omega' = H^\circ(x') : x' \leftarrow \mathcal{B}_s(y)\right] \leq \frac{(q_H + q_S + 2)^2}{|\mathcal{Y}_1|}.$$

We finally conclude that,

$$|\Pr_0 - \Pr_{-1}| \leq \Pr[\mathsf{Bad}] \leq \frac{q_S(q_H + q_S + 2)^2}{|\mathcal{Y}_1|}.$$

Game G_4. In this game, we no longer sample ω^*, M^*, and R^* directly. Instead, we sample σ^* from $\mathsf{SampleDom}(1^\lambda)$ and then parse ω^*, M^*, and R^* from $f_a(\sigma^*)$. By the image distribution property of PSF introduced in Subsect. 2.2, the distribution of $f_a(\sigma^*)$ in G_0 is uniform. Therefore, ω^*, M^*, and R^* in G_0 are perfectly indistinguishable from those sampled from a uniform distribution in G_{-1}. This then concludes that $\Pr_0 = \Pr_{-1}$.

Game G_5. In this game, we change the output of SIGN oracle from σ to σ^*. Due to the preimage sampling distribution property of PSF, the distribution of σ follows D_x conditioned on $f_a(\sigma) = \omega^*\|M^*\|R^*$, which is exactly the same distribution as the posterior distribution of σ^* when fixing $f_a(\sigma^*) = \omega^*\|M^*\|R^*$. This indicates that $(\sigma^*, \omega^*\|M^*\|R^*)$ in this game is perfectly indistinguishable from $(\sigma, \omega^*\|M^*\|R^*)$. This proves that $\Pr_0 = \Pr_{-1}$.

We can now translate an adversary $\mathcal{A}$ in G_0 to an adversary $\mathcal{B}$ against the EUF-NMA security such that $\mathsf{Adv}^{\mathsf{EUF\text{-}NMA}}_{\mathsf{SIG},\mathcal{B}} \geq \Pr_0$.

Specifically, denote the un-reprogrammed random oracles by H° and G°, let $\mathcal{B}$ work as follows:

- On input the verification key vk from the challenger $\mathcal{C}$ of the EUF-NMA game, $\mathcal{B}$ passes vk to $\mathcal{A}$.
- On $\mathcal{A}$'s query to the SIGN oracle, $\mathcal{B}$ simulates the SIGN oracle as in G_0, and passes the output to $\mathcal{A}$. This simulation contains the step of reprogramming the random oracles H and G. We note that, although $\mathcal{B}$ does not control the random oracles, it can still complete the reprogramming process as a man-in-the-middle between $\mathcal{C}$ and $\mathcal{A}$, as shown in Remark 1.
- On $\mathcal{A}$'s query to the random oracles H or G, $\mathcal{B}$ does as shown in Remark 1 to answer the query.
- On $\mathcal{A}$'s outputting the message-signature pair (m_2', σ'), it outputs (m_2', σ') to the challenger $\mathcal{C}$ of the EUF-NMA game.

We see that $\mathcal{B}$'s simulation provides a view to $\mathcal{A}$ that is identical to $\mathcal{A}$'s view in G_0, and we will show that the output of $\mathcal{B}$ is a valid signature as long as $\mathcal{A}$'s output wins the simulated G_0.

Consider the case where $\mathcal{A}$'s output wins the simulated G_0. As $(m_1', m_2') \notin \mathcal{S}$, we know immediately that for any $r \in \mathcal{Y}_3$, $m_1' \| m_2' \| r$ is not a reprogrammed position of oracle H. Moreover, as $\omega' \notin \mathcal{W}$, we also know ω' is not a reprogrammed position of oracle G. Therefore, $H(m_1' \| m_2' \| r') = H^\circ(m_1' \| m_2' \| r')$ and $G(\omega') = G^\circ(\omega')$. As (m_2', σ') passes the signature verification with the queried values $H(m_1' \| m_2' \| r')$ and $G(\omega')$, it also passes the signature verification with the original random oracles H° and G°.

This shows that $\mathcal{B}$ forges a valid signature in the EUF-NMA game with probability at least $\mathsf{Adv}^{\mathsf{EUF\text{-}NMA}}_{\mathsf{SIG},\mathcal{B}} \geq \Pr_0$.

Finally, with all the game transitions above, we conclude that,

$$\left|\mathsf{Adv}^{\mathsf{EUF\text{-}NMA}}_{\mathsf{SIG},\mathcal{B}} - \mathsf{Adv}^{\mathsf{EUF\text{-}CMA}}_{\mathsf{SIG},\mathcal{A}}\right| \leq q_S \left(\sqrt{2q_H|\mathcal{Y}_3|^{-1}} + \sqrt{2q_G|\mathcal{Y}_1|^{-1}}\right) + \frac{q_S(q_H+q_S+2)^2}{|\mathcal{Y}_1|}.$$

This completes the proof of Lemma 3. □

Lemma 4 (EUF-NMA Security). *For any PPT adversary $\mathcal{A}$ against the* EUF-NMA *security of the scheme that makes q_H and q_G queries to the oracles H and G, respectively, there exists a PPT adversary $\mathcal{B}$ against the collision resistance of* PSF, *such that*

$$\mathsf{Adv}^{\mathsf{CR}}_{\mathsf{PSF},\mathcal{B}} \geq \frac{1-p_{max}}{(2\max\{q_H,q_G+1\}+1)^4} \cdot \mathsf{Adv}^{\mathsf{EUF\text{-}NMA}}_{\mathsf{SIG},\mathcal{A}} - \frac{1-p_{max}}{|\mathcal{Y}_1|}.$$

Proof. Let $\mathcal{A}$ be an adversary in the EUF-NMA game of the scheme in Fig. 5. To construct $\mathcal{B}$ against the collision resistance of PSF, we first construct an intermediate adversary $\mathcal{A}_+$ as shown in Fig. 7. On input the description of an instance a of PSF, $\mathcal{A}_+$ interprets a as the signature's vk, and outputs the signature σ^* with corresponding $x' := m_1' \| m_2' \| r'$ under the help of $\mathcal{A}$.

$\mathcal{A}_+(a)$
$vk := a$
$(m_2', \sigma') \leftarrow \mathcal{A}^{H,G}(vk)$
$\omega' \| M' \| R' := f_a(\sigma')$
$m_1' := M' \oplus G_1(\omega')$
$r' := R' \oplus G_2(\omega')$
$x' := m_1' \| m_2' \| r'$
Return (x', σ')

Fig. 7. The intermediate adversary $\mathcal{A}_+$ constructed from the EUF-NMA adversary $\mathcal{A}$.

We consider a predicate $V(x', (y_H, y_G), \sigma')$ which outputs 1 *iff* $\omega' = y_H$ and $(m_1' \| r') \oplus G(\omega') = (M' \| R')$, where $\omega' \| M' \| R' := f_a(\sigma^*)$. This is the predicate version of the signature verification. Specifically, denote $h^{(x')} = H(x')$ and

$g^{(x')} = G(h^{(x')})$, if (m'_2, σ') returned by $\mathcal{A}$ is a valid signature, then $V(x', (h^{(x')}, g^{(x')}), \sigma') = 1$, and vice versa.

Therefore, by the definition of $\mathcal{A}$ and $\mathcal{A}_+$, for some fixed $(a,t) \leftarrow \mathsf{TrapGen}(1^\lambda)$,

$$\Pr\left[V(x', (h^{(x')}, g^{(x')}), \sigma') = 1 : (x', \sigma') \leftarrow \mathcal{A}_+(a)\right] = \mathsf{Adv}^{\mathsf{EUF\text{-}NMA}}_{\mathsf{SIG},\mathcal{A}}.$$

According to Theorem 3 (by treating $\mathcal{A}_+$ as the algorithm $\mathcal{A}$ in Theorem 3) and summing over all $x^\circ \in \mathcal{X}_0$, we know that there exists a simulator $\mathcal{S}$ such that,

$$\begin{aligned}&\Pr\left[V(x', (\Theta_H, \Theta_G), \sigma') = 1 : (x', \sigma') \leftarrow \langle \mathcal{S}^{\mathcal{A}_+}, \Theta_H, \Theta_G \rangle\right]\\ &\geq \tfrac{1}{(2\max\{q_H, q_G+1\}+1)^4} \cdot \Pr\left[V(x', (h^{x'}, g^{x'}), \sigma') = 1 : (x', \sigma') \leftarrow \mathcal{A}_+(a)\right] - \tfrac{1}{|\mathcal{Y}_1|}.\end{aligned}$$

Now, we use the statistical property of the preimage sampleable function to replace the Θ_H and Θ_G. Specifically, we first sample $\sigma^* \leftarrow \mathsf{SampleDom}(1^\lambda)$ and then write $\omega^* \| M^* \| R^* := f_a(\sigma^*)$. Upon the simulator's outputting $x' = m'_1 \| m'_2 \| r'$ in the first stage, we compute $\Theta'_H := \omega^*$ and $\Theta'_G := (M^* \oplus m'_1) \| (R^* \oplus r')$, and replace Θ_H and Θ_G with Θ'_H and Θ'_G respectively. With the preimage sampling distribution property of PSF, we have that,

$$\begin{aligned}&\Pr\left[V(x', (\Theta_H, \Theta_G), \sigma') = 1 : (x', \sigma') \leftarrow \langle \mathcal{S}^{\mathcal{A}_+}, \Theta_H, \Theta_G \rangle\right]\\ &\qquad = \Pr\left[V(x', (\Theta'_H, \Theta'_G), \sigma') = 1 : (x', \sigma') \leftarrow \langle \mathcal{S}^{\mathcal{A}_+}, \Theta'_H, \Theta'_G \rangle\right].\end{aligned}$$

We will show that σ' and σ^* are very likely to be a pair of collision for the PSF if the simulator's output passed the predicate V.

In fact, it's easy to see $f_a(\sigma^*) = f_a(\sigma')$ from the fact that $V(x', \Theta'_H, \Theta'_G, \sigma') = 1$. Furthermore, as replacing Θ_H and Θ_G with Θ'_H and Θ'_G does not give away any information about the signature σ^* other than $f_a(\sigma^*)$, σ^* still satisfies the distribution $\mathcal{D}_x$ conditioned on $f_a(\sigma^*) = f_a(\sigma')$ under the simulator $\mathcal{S}$'s view.

This implies that, for $(x', \sigma') \leftarrow \langle \mathcal{S}^{\mathcal{A}_+}, \Theta'_H, \Theta'_G \rangle$,

$$\Pr\left[\sigma' = \sigma^* \mid f_a(\sigma') = f_a(\sigma^*)\right] \leq \max_{\sigma''} \Pr\left[\sigma^* = \sigma'' \mid f_a(\sigma') = f_a(\sigma^*)\right] \leq p_{\max}.$$

Therefore, for $(x', \sigma') \leftarrow \langle \mathcal{S}^{\mathcal{A}_+}, \Theta'_H, \Theta'_G \rangle$, we conclude that,

$$\begin{aligned}&\Pr\left[\sigma' \neq \sigma^* \wedge f_a(\sigma') = f_a(\sigma^*)\right]\\ &= \Pr\left[\sigma' \neq \sigma^* \mid f_a(\sigma') = f_a(\sigma^*)\right] \Pr\left[f_a(\sigma') = f_a(\sigma^*)\right]\\ &\geq \Pr\left[\sigma' \neq \sigma^* \mid f_a(\sigma') = f_a(\sigma^*)\right] \Pr\left[V(x', \Theta'_H, \Theta'_G, \sigma') = 1\right]\\ &\geq (1 - p_{\max}) \cdot \Pr\left[V(x', \Theta'_H, \Theta'_G, \sigma') = 1\right]\\ &\geq \tfrac{1 - p_{\max}}{(2\max\{q_H, q_G+1\}+1)^4} \cdot \mathsf{Adv}^{\mathsf{EUF\text{-}NMA}}_{\mathsf{SIG},\mathcal{A}} - \tfrac{1 - p_{\max}}{|\mathcal{Y}_1|}.\end{aligned}$$

Finally, we are ready to show our constructed adversary $\mathcal{B}$ against the collision resistance of PSF. $\mathcal{B}$ runs the simulator $\mathcal{S}^{\mathcal{A}_+}$ and prepares the inputs Θ'_H and Θ'_G with the sampled $\sigma^* \leftarrow \mathsf{SampleDom}(1^\lambda)$ in the way mentioned above. Upon the simulator's outputting x', σ', $\mathcal{B}$ outputs (σ^*, σ') as a collision of the PSF. With the above analysis, we conclude that,

$$\mathsf{Adv}^{\mathsf{CR}}_{\mathsf{PSF},\mathcal{B}} \geq \frac{1-p_{\max}}{(2\max\{q_H,q_G+1\}+1)^4} \cdot \mathsf{Adv}^{\mathsf{EUF\text{-}NMA}}_{\mathsf{SIG},\mathcal{A}} - \frac{1-p_{\max}}{|\mathcal{Y}_1|}.$$

This completes the proof of Lemma 4. □

Finally, we conclude that Theorem 7 follows directly from combining Lemma 3 and Lemma 4, and this shows the EUF-CMA security of our scheme in the QROM.

Acknowledgments. The authors sincerely appreciate the reviewers' valuable comments and helpful suggestions. The authors also thank You Lyu for insightful discussions during the early stages of this research. The authors were partially supported by National Natural Science Foundation of China (62522212, 62572295, 62372292), National Key R&D Program of China (2025YFA1017100), and National Cryptologic Science Fund of China (2025NCSF01009).

A Quantum Representation of Game $\mathsf{REPRO}^{\mathsf{D}}_1$ in Theorem 5

In this appendix, we provide the missing transition from the ordinary formulation of Theorem 5 to its superposition oracle form, which is the one we use as the starting point in the proof. We will see the equivalence between the two formulations, as the following claim shows.

Claim. The game G_0 in Fig. 4 is perfectly indistinguishable from the game $\mathsf{REPRO}^{\mathsf{D}}_1$ in Fig. 3.

Proof. It suffices to show the claim in the case where $R = 1$, which means the challenger only queries the REPROGRAM oracle once. For $R > 1$, a similar reasoning of hybrid argument as was done in the proof of Theorem 5 will work.

Game $\mathsf{REPRO}_b^{\mathsf{D}}$	$\mathsf{REPROGRAM}(x_1)$ H_0-H_5
$\mathsf{O}_{H0} \leftarrow \mathcal{Y}^{\mathcal{X}}$	Prepare $\lvert x_1\rangle_{X_1}$
$\mathsf{O}_{G0} \leftarrow \mathcal{Z}^{\mathcal{X}}$	Prepare $\left\lvert\phi_0^{(\mathcal{X}_2)}\right\rangle_{X_2}, \left\lvert\phi_0^{(\mathcal{Y})}\right\rangle_{Y}, \left\lvert\phi_0^{(\mathcal{Z})}\right\rangle_{Z}$
$\mathsf{O}_{H1} := \mathsf{O}_{H0}$	Measure X_2, Y, Z //H_0
$\mathsf{O}_{G1} := \mathsf{O}_{G0}$	Prepare $\lvert 0\rangle_{Y'}, \lvert 0\rangle_{Z'}$ //H_1-H_5
$b' \leftarrow \mathsf{D}_b^{\lvert\mathsf{O}_{Gb}\rangle,\lvert\mathsf{O}_{Hb}\rangle,\mathsf{REPROGRAM}}$	Measure X_2 //H_1-H_5
Return b'	Apply $\mathsf{CNOT}_{YY'}$, $\mathsf{CNOT}_{ZZ'}$ //H_1
	Apply RE_{YF_GZ}
	Apply RE_{XF_HY}
	Apply $\sum_{x\in\mathcal{X}} \lvert x\rangle\langle x\rvert_X \otimes \mathsf{CNOT}_{F_{Hx}Y'}$ //H_2
	Apply $\sum_{y\in\mathcal{Y}} \lvert y\rangle\langle y\rvert_{Y'} \otimes \mathsf{CNOT}_{F_{Gy}Z'}$ //H_2
	Apply O_H on input registers XY' //H_3-H_4
	Apply O_G on input registers $Y'Z'$ //H_3
	Return register X_2

Fig. 8. Game transitions from the game REPRO_1^D in Fig. 3 to the game G_0 in Fig. 4

We consider the game transition shown in Fig. 8.

Game H_0. It is the same game as the original game in Fig. 3, but represents all the classical procedures in a quantumly simulated way, and samples random variables by preparing and measuring corresponding quantum states. The game is identical to the game $\mathsf{REPRO}_1^{\mathsf{D}}$ in Fig. 3.

Game H_1. This game uses the purified measurement technique, copying the registers X_2, Y, Z to X_2', Y', Z' using CNOT gates. This is perfectly indistinguishable from measuring the registers X_2, Y, Z with respect to their computational basis if the extra registers X_2', Y', Z' are all hidden from the other parts of the quantum circuit, as the view of the distinguisher would, when represented by density operators, be the same.

Game H_2. We try to postpone the purified measurement to after the RE gates. It is trivial that $\mathsf{CNOT}_{X_2X_2'}$ commutes with both RE_{YF_GZ} and RE_{XF_HY} and that $\mathsf{CNOT}_{YY'}$ is commutable with RE_{YF_GZ}.

For the following calculations, we heavily use the fact that two quantum gates commute if, 1) both gates act on disjoint sets of registers or, 2) all registers accessed by both gates are used as control registers in both gates.

To move $\mathsf{CNOT}_{ZZ'}$ after RE_{YF_GZ}, we have,

$$\begin{aligned}
&\mathsf{RE}_{XF_HY} \circ \mathsf{RE}_{YF_GZ} \circ \mathsf{CNOT}_{ZZ'}\\
=&\mathsf{RE}_{XF_HY} \circ \sum_{y\in\mathcal{Y}} \lvert y\rangle\langle y\rvert_Y \otimes (\mathsf{SWAP}_{F_{Gy},Z} \circ \mathsf{CNOT}_{F_{Gy}Z'})\\
=&\mathsf{RE}_{XF_HY} \circ \sum_{y\in\mathcal{Y}} \lvert y\rangle\langle y\rvert_Y \otimes (\mathsf{CNOT}_{F_{Gy}Z'} \circ \mathsf{SWAP}_{F_{Gy},Z})\\
=&\mathsf{RE}_{XF_HY} \circ \left(\sum_{y\in\mathcal{Y}} \lvert y\rangle\langle y\rvert_Y \otimes \mathsf{CNOT}_{F_{Gy}Z'}\right) \circ \mathsf{RE}_{YF_GZ}.
\end{aligned}$$

As the purified measurement of Y register has already been applied, and the register Y acts as a control register in the RE_{YF_GZ} gate, the system state can be decomposed as

$$\sum_{y\in\mathcal{Y}} c_y \left|yy\right\rangle_{YY'} \otimes \left|\psi_y\right\rangle_{XZX'Z'F_H},$$

for some coefficient $c_y \in \mathbb{C}$ and vectors $\left|\psi_y\right\rangle_{ZX'Z'F_H}$. In other words, the registers Y and Y' are still entangled, and contain the same element when measuring to the computational basis.

This means we can rewrite $\sum_{y\in\mathcal{Y}} |y\rangle\langle y|_Y \otimes \mathsf{CNOT}_{F_{Gy}Z'}$ to $\sum_{y\in\mathcal{Y}} |y\rangle\langle y|_{Y'} \otimes \mathsf{CNOT}_{F_{Gy}Z'}$. With this representation, we have that,

$$\begin{aligned}
&\mathsf{RE}_{XF_HY} \circ \mathsf{RE}_{YF_GZ} \circ \mathsf{CNOT}_{ZZ'}\\
=&\mathsf{RE}_{XF_HY} \circ \left(\sum_{y\in\mathcal{Y}} |y\rangle\langle y|_{Y'} \otimes \mathsf{CNOT}_{F_{Gy}Z'}\right) \circ \mathsf{RE}_{YF_GZ}\\
=&\left(\sum_{y\in\mathcal{Y}} |y\rangle\langle y|_{Y'} \otimes \mathsf{CNOT}_{F_{Gy}Z'}\right) \circ \mathsf{RE}_{XF_HY} \circ \mathsf{RE}_{YF_GZ}.
\end{aligned}$$

To move $\mathsf{CNOT}_{YY'}$ after RE_{XF_HY}, we have,

$$\begin{aligned}
\mathsf{RE}_{XF_HY} \circ \mathsf{CNOT}_{YY'} &= \sum_{x\in\mathcal{X}} |x\rangle\langle x|_X \otimes (\mathsf{SWAP}_{F_{Hx},Y} \circ \mathsf{CNOT}_{YY'})\\
&= \sum_{x\in\mathcal{X}} |x\rangle\langle x|_X \otimes (\mathsf{CNOT}_{F_{Hx}Y'} \circ \mathsf{SWAP}_{F_{Hx},Y})\\
&= \left(\sum_{x\in\mathcal{X}} |x\rangle\langle x|_X \otimes \mathsf{CNOT}_{F_{Hx}Y'}\right) \circ \mathsf{RE}_{XF_HY}.
\end{aligned}$$

With the above calculations, we show that the game H_2 is perfectly indistinguishable from the game H_1, i.e., $\Pr_2 = \Pr_1$.

Game H_3. We find that the controlled CNOT gates share the same expression as QRO queries, thus we use the QRO query to represent them instead. This is a literal translation, so this game is identical to the previous game, i.e., $\Pr_3 = \Pr_2$.

Game H_4. In this game, we do not query the random oracle G on the registers Y' and Z'. As Y' and Z' are internal registers hidden from the distinguisher, removing this does not affect the distinguisher's view. Therefore, $\Pr_4 = \Pr_3$.

Game H_5. In this game, we do not query the random oracle H on the registers X and Y'. As X is measured, and Y' is an internal register hidden from the distinguisher, this also doesn't affect the distinguisher's view. Therefore $\Pr_5 = \Pr_4$

Now we can see that H_5 in Fig. 8 is identical to G_0 in Fig. 4, and this completes the proof of our claim. □

References

1. Alagic, G., Majenz, C., Russell, A., Song, F.: Quantum-access-secure message authentication via blind-unforgeability. In: Canteaut, A., Ishai, Y. (eds.) EUROCRYPT 2020. LNCS, vol. 12107, pp. 788–817. Springer, Cham (2020). https://doi.org/10.1007/978-3-030-45727-3_27
2. Ambainis, A., Hamburg, M., Unruh, D.: Quantum security proofs using semi-classical oracles. In: Boldyreva, A., Micciancio, D. (eds.) CRYPTO 2019. LNCS, vol. 11693, pp. 269–295. Springer, Cham (2019). https://doi.org/10.1007/978-3-030-26951-7_10
3. Bellare, M., Rogaway, P.: The exact security of digital signatures-how to sign with RSA and Rabin. In: Maurer, U. (ed.) EUROCRYPT 1996. LNCS, vol. 1070, pp. 399–416. Springer, Heidelberg (1996). https://doi.org/10.1007/3-540-68339-9_34
4. Boneh, D., Dagdelen, Ö., Fischlin, M., Lehmann, A., Schaffner, C., Zhandry, M.: Random oracles in a quantum world. In: Lee, D.H., Wang, X. (eds.) ASIACRYPT 2011. LNCS, vol. 7073, pp. 41–69. Springer, Heidelberg (2011). https://doi.org/10.1007/978-3-642-25385-0_3
5. Cojocaru, A., Garay, J.A., Liu, Q., Song, F.: Improved quantum lifting by coherent measure-and-reprogram. In: Chung, K.M., Sasaki, Y. (eds.) Advances in Cryptology – ASIACRYPT 2024, Part IX. Lecture Notes in Computer Science, vol. 15492, pp. 158–184. Springer, Singapore, Kolkata, India (2024). https://doi.org/10.1007/978-981-96-0947-5_6
6. Don, J., Fehr, S., Majenz, C.: The measure-and-reprogram technique 2.0: multi-round fiat-shamir and more. In: Micciancio, D., Ristenpart, T. (eds.) CRYPTO 2020. LNCS, vol. 12172, pp. 602–631. Springer, Cham (2020). https://doi.org/10.1007/978-3-030-56877-1_21
7. Ducas, L., Lyubashevsky, V., Prest, T.: Efficient identity-based encryption over NTRU lattices. In: Sarkar, P., Iwata, T. (eds.) ASIACRYPT 2014. LNCS, vol. 8874, pp. 22–41. Springer, Heidelberg (2014). https://doi.org/10.1007/978-3-662-45608-8_2
8. Ducas, L., Prest, T.: Fast fourier orthogonalization. In: Proceedings of the 2016 ACM International Symposium on Symbolic and Algebraic Computation, pp. 191–198 (2016)
9. Fouque, P.A., et al.: Falcon: fast-fourier lattice-based compact signatures over NTRU. Submission to the NIST's Post-quantum Cryptography Standardization Process **36**(5), 1–75 (2018)
10. Gentry, C., Peikert, C., Vaikuntanathan, V.: Trapdoors for hard lattices and new cryptographic constructions. In: Ladner, R.E., Dwork, C. (eds.) 40th Annual ACM Symposium on Theory of Computing, pp. 197–206. ACM Press, Victoria, BC, Canada (2008). https://doi.org/10.1145/1374376.1374407
11. Grilo, A.B., Hövelmanns, K., Hülsing, A., Majenz, C.: Tight adaptive reprogramming in the QROM. In: Tibouchi, M., Wang, H. (eds.) ASIACRYPT 2021. LNCS, vol. 13090, pp. 637–667. Springer, Cham (2021). https://doi.org/10.1007/978-3-030-92062-3_22
12. Hoffstein, J., Howgrave-Graham, N., Pipher, J., Silverman, J.H., Whyte, W.: NTRUSign: digital signatures using the NTRU lattice. In: Joye, M. (ed.) CT-RSA 2003. LNCS, vol. 2612, pp. 122–140. Springer, Heidelberg (2003). https://doi.org/10.1007/3-540-36563-X_9
13. Nielsen, M.A., Chuang, I.L.: Quantum Computation and Quantum Information: 10th Anniversary Edition. Cambridge University Press (2010)

14. Pan, J., Zeng, R.: Selective opening security in the quantum random oracle model, revisited. In: Tang, Q., Teague, V. (eds.) PKC 2024: 27th International Conference on Theory and Practice of Public Key Cryptography, Part III. Lecture Notes in Computer Science, vol. 14603, pp. 92–122. Springer, Cham, Switzerland, Sydney, NSW, Australia (2024). https://doi.org/10.1007/978-3-031-57725-3_4
15. del Pino, R., Lyubashevsky, V., Pointcheval, D.: The whole is less than the sum of its parts: constructing more efficient lattice-based AKEs. In: Zikas, V., De Prisco, R. (eds.) SCN 2016. LNCS, vol. 9841, pp. 273–291. Springer, Cham (2016). https://doi.org/10.1007/978-3-319-44618-9_15
16. Yamakawa, T., Zhandry, M.: Classical vs quantum random oracles. In: Canteaut, A., Standaert, F.-X. (eds.) EUROCRYPT 2021. LNCS, vol. 12697, pp. 568–597. Springer, Cham (2021). https://doi.org/10.1007/978-3-030-77886-6_20
17. Zhandry, M.: How to record quantum queries, and applications to quantum indifferentiability. In: Boldyreva, A., Micciancio, D. (eds.) CRYPTO 2019. LNCS, vol. 11693, pp. 239–268. Springer, Cham (2019). https://doi.org/10.1007/978-3-030-26951-7_9

Revisiting the Concrete Security of Falcon-Type Signatures

Huiwen Jia[1,2], Shiduo Zhang[3], Yang Yu[3,4,5](✉), and Chunming Tang[1,2]

[1] School of Mathematics and Information Science, Key Laboratory of Information Security,Guangzhou University, Guangzhou, China
{hwjia,ctang}@gzhu.edu.cn
[2] Guangzhou Center for Applied Mathematics, Guangzhou University, Guangzhou, China
[3] Institute for Advanced Study, Tsinghua University, Beijing, China
{zsd,yu-yang}@mail.tsinghua.edu.cn
[4] Zhongguancun Laboratory, Beijing, China
[5] State Key Laboratory of Cryptography and Digital Economy Security, Beijing, China

Abstract. Falcon is a selected signature scheme in the NIST post-quantum standardization. It is an efficient instantiation of the GPV framework over NTRU lattices. While the GPV framework comes with an elegant security proof in theory, Falcon had no formal proof involving concrete parameters for a long time. Until recently, Fouque et al. initiate the concrete security analysis of Falcon-type signatures. They give a formal proof of Falcon$^+$, a minor modification of Falcon, in the random oracle model, whereas they claim that Falcon$^+$-512 barely achieves the claimed 120-bit security for plain unforgeability. Furthermore, they show that standard reductions for strong unforgeability are vacuous for Falcon parameters, necessitating the introduction of a new, non-standard assumption.

In this work, we revisit the concrete security analysis of Falcon-type signatures and present positive results. We develop improved analytic tools by leveraging the profile of the NTRU trapdoor bases. This eliminates the security loss for both Falcon$^+$-512 and Falcon$^+$-1024 in the case of plain unforgeability. We also apply our new analysis to the recent weak-smoothness variant Falcon^{ws} (Zhang et al. Asiacrypt 2025) that admits smaller parameters than Falcon under a non-standard assumption. As a result, we propose new parameters for Falcon^{ws} allowing for provable security under standard assumptions and signature size 17.8% (resp. 12.8%) smaller than that of Falcon-512 (resp. Falcon-1024) simultaneously. Moreover, we give a refined strong unforgeability security proof by replacing the worst-case analysis with a probabilistic analysis, which leads to a substantial increase in concrete security. Based on this, we show that by using a tighter Gaussian sampler, e.g. the one in Falcon^{ws}, Falcon-type signatures can achieve concrete security for strong unforgeability closely consistent with the claimed security level while keeping the compact size.

S. Bai and E. Persichetti (Eds.): PKC 2026, LNCS 16551, pp. 334–363, 2026.
https://doi.org/10.1007/978-3-032-26731-3_11

Keywords: FALCON · Rényi Divergence · Security Proof · Lattice-Based Cryptography

1 Introduction

FALCON [PFH+22] is one of three digital signature algorithms selected by NIST for post-quantum cryptography (PQC) standardization. It offers excellent efficiency, particularly a significant advantage in terms of size, among them. FALCON is based on the celebrated GPV framework for lattice-based hash-and-sign signatures [GPV08] and adopts a set of efficiency-oriented designs, e.g. the nearly-optimal NTRU trapdoor [DLP14], a ring-efficient Gaussian sampler [DP16] and well-analyzed parameters [Pre17]. The security assumptions of FALCON are standard computational hard problems over NTRU lattices, which have been extensively studied. With the post-quantum standardization and migration underway, it is crucial to investigate the security of FALCON not only in a pure algorithmic cryptanalysis sense, but also with respect to provable security.

The GPV framework is quite elegant from a theoretical standpoint. It has a tight and arguably easy security proof in both the random oracle model (ROM) [GPV08] and the quantum random oracle model (QROM) [BDF+11], in contrast with Fiat-Shamir type constructions, e.g. another NIST winning signature scheme Dilithium [LDK+22]. However, such security analysis becomes complicated when it comes to concrete parameters: some arguments in the original proof could even be invalidated. The concrete security analysis of FALCON remains largely unexplored for quite a long time, despite FALCON being selected for standardization.

Until recently, Fouque et al. present the first concrete security analysis of FALCON-type signatures [FGdG+26]. To do so, they introduce a minor but crucial modification of FALCON, termed FALCON$^+$, in which the signing algorithm picks a fresh salt within the repeat loop until a preimage with a norm below the bound β is found. This modification allows for a formal proof in the ROM. By leveraging elaborate Rényi arguments and recent proof techniques [BRTZ24], some concrete security bounds of FALCON$^+$ are calculated. Unfortunately, their results still do not provide compelling evidence to support the concrete security of FALCON-type signatures. In the case of plain unforgeability, while they confirmed the claimed security level for the FALCON-1024 parameter set, they showed a loss of 7 bits in provable security for FALCON$^+$-512. Crucially, in the case of strong unforgeability, their analysis reveals that the traditional reduction from the Short Integer Solution (SIS) problem with norm 2β is trivial for FALCON parameters. To circumvent this, they reduced strong unforgeability to a second-preimage version of the inhomogeneous SIS problem (t-$\mathcal{R}$-SPISIS)[1]. Consequently, the security guarantee for strong unforgeability relies on the non-standard assumption that t-$\mathcal{R}$-SPISIS is as hard as standard SIS.

[1] The t-$\mathcal{R}$-SPISIS problem was introduced in a major revision of [FGdG+26] published on November 6, 2025. This updated version includes two additional authors (Fouque and de Groote). The old version 20250226:153603 is cited as [GJK24] in this work.

The standardization also promoted the exploration of the design space to improve various aspects of PQC schemes. A number of FALCON variants and modifications have emerged [CPS+20, EFG+22, ETWY22, ENS+23, LTYZ25] in the past few years. Very recently, Zhang et al. propose a variant of FALCON in [ZJR+25] achieving smaller size and higher security. Their FALCON variant works with the so-called weak smoothness condition in which the closeness parameter associated with $\eta_\epsilon(\mathbb{Z}^n)$ is $\epsilon = O(1)$, hence we refer to it as FALCON^{WS}. The overly large ϵ of FALCON^{WS} forbids the original GPV security proof: the adversary cannot program the RO, as the simulated syndrome is no longer statistically indistinguishable from uniform. To address this issue, Zhang et al. resorted to one additional non-standard hardness assumption to ensure the simulated syndrome is computationally indistinguishable from uniform. While they conducted some cryptanalysis on the new assumption to claim no impact on the concrete security, removing such a non-standard assumption while maintaining the gain in size could be an interesting problem.

1.1 Our Contributions

In this work, we revisit the security analysis of FALCON-type signatures. We obtain some positive results. Our contributions are mainly threefold.

Sharper Security Bounds Using the NTRU Basis Profile. We present a refined concrete security analysis for FALCON that significantly tightens the provable bit security. Unlike the prior worst-case analysis in [FGdG+26], which conservatively estimated the Rényi loss for all possible bases, our approach incorporates the geometric profile of each specific basis generated by FALCON's key generation. This basis-aware evaluation yields instance-specific security bounds that are substantially tighter in practice. In our extensive evaluation over 1,000 distinct basis instances, the Rényi loss are bounded by 0.2 bits in all cases. An overview of the provable bit security is shown in Table 1. Notice that the larger security margin of FALCON$^+$-1024 compensates for the 8 bits Rényi losses. In fact, our analysis shows that the resulting Rényi loss for FALCON+-1024 is below 0.2 bits as well.

Table 1. Provable bit security levels of plain unforgeability for FALCON.

Scheme	[FGdG+26]	Ours
FALCON$^+$-512	113	120
FALCON$^+$-1024	256	256

On the Provable Security of FALCON^{WS}. To improve the bandwidth efficiency of FALCON, Zhang et al. [ZJR+25] proposed a compact variant FALCON^{WS}, where the closeness parameter $\epsilon = O(1) \gg 1/\sqrt{Q_s \lambda}$ for the maximum number of signing queries Q_s and security parameter λ. While this approach significantly improves bandwidth and security, their security proof relies on a non-standard assumption. Furthermore, the Rényi divergence-based analysis from [FGdG+26] becomes ineffective here, as the large ϵ causes the Rényi loss from the RO simulation to grow prohibitively. Removing this non-standard assumption remains an open challenge. In this work, we address this challenge by a refined smoothing parameter bound. We establish the maximum permissible value of ϵ that preserves provable security under standard assumptions, albeit in a setting that differs from that of [ZJR+25]. The resulting parameter sets achieve a balanced trade-off between bandwidth and security. A comparative summary of our new parameter sets against prior designs is provided in Table 2.

Table 2. Comparison of FALCON variants in sizes (byte) and bit security.

	PK Size	Sig. Size	Standard Assumption
FALCON^{+}-512	897	666	✓
FALCON^{WS}-512	640	474	×
Ours	704	547	✓
FALCON^{+}-1024	1793	1280	✓
FALCON^{WS}-1024	1408	979	×
Ours	1536	1115	✓

Refined Analysis of Strong Unforgeability. As shown in [GJK24], the original 2β norm bound incurred a 25-bit loss for FALCON^{+}-512, while rendering the security guarantee for FALCON^{+}-1024 void since $2\beta > q$. The updated version in [FGdG+26] circumvents this problem by adopting a non-standard assumption. We introduce a refined norm bound of $\sqrt{2}\beta$, motivated by the high likelihood of near-orthogonality between the forgery and simulated signature in the ROM. This modification reduces the security loss and enables strong unforgeability for both security levels. We further tighten the reduction by co-optimizing ϵ and the auxiliary parameter L, a technique originating from [BRTZ24] and employed in [FGdG+26], for which we present an optimized strategy for its selection. As summarized in Table 3, our approach significantly improves the concrete strong unforgeability of FALCON compared to [GJK24, FGdG+26]. In addition, we propose new parameter sets for FALCON^{WS} that achieve SUF-CMA security under standard assumptions. See Table 4 for more details.

Table 3. Comparison of provable bit security of strong unforgeability for FALCON$^+$.

	FALCON$^+$-512	FALCON$^+$-1024	Standard Assumption
[GJK24]	89	—	√
[FGdG+26]	113	256	×
Ours	107	251	√

Table 4. Comparison of provable bit security of strong unforgeability for our revised FALCON^{WS} and FALCON$^+$.

	PK Size	Sig. Size	Security	Standard Assumption
FALCON$^+$-512	897	666	113	×
FALCON^{WS}-512 with SUF	768	576	114	√
FALCON$^+$-1024	1793	1280	256	×
FALCON^{WS}-1024 with SUF	1664	1179	265	√

Our scripts are open-source for checking or extension purposes, available at https://github.com/hwjia4github/Concrete-Security-of-Falcon-type-Signatures/.

2 Preliminaries

Let $\mathbb{R}$, $\mathbb{Z}$ and $\mathbb{N}$ denote the set of real numbers, integers and natural numbers respectively. Vectors (resp. matrices) are denoted by bold lowercase (resp. uppercase) letters. For a distribution D, we write $z \leftarrow D$ when the random variable z is sampled from D. For a real-valued function f and a countable set S, we write $f(S) = \sum_{x \in S} f(x)$ assuming this sum is absolutely convergent. Let ln denote the natural logarithm.

2.1 Linear Algebra and Lattices

Let b_i (resp. $\mathbf{b}_i$) denote the i-th coordinate (resp. column) of $\mathbf{b}$ (resp. $\mathbf{B}$). Given $\mathbf{u}, \mathbf{v} \in \mathbb{R}^n$, their inner product is $\langle \mathbf{u}, \mathbf{v} \rangle = \sum_{i=0}^{n-1} u_i v_i$. Let $\|\mathbf{v}\| = \sqrt{\langle \mathbf{v}, \mathbf{v} \rangle}$ be the ℓ_2-norm of $\mathbf{v}$.

Let $\mathbf{B} = [\mathbf{b}_0, \cdots, \mathbf{b}_{n-1}] \in \mathbb{R}^{m \times n}$ be a matrix of rank n. The Gram-Schmidt Orthogonalization (GSO) of $\mathbf{B}$ is the unique matrix $\tilde{\mathbf{B}} = [\tilde{\mathbf{b}}_0, \cdots, \tilde{\mathbf{b}}_{n-1}] \in \mathbb{R}^{m \times n}$ such that $\mathbf{B} = \tilde{\mathbf{B}}\mathbf{U}$ where $\tilde{\mathbf{b}}_i$'s are pairwise orthogonal and $\mathbf{U}$ is upper-triangular with 1 on its diagonal. Let $\|\mathbf{B}\|_{GS} = \max_i \|\tilde{\mathbf{b}}_i\|$.

A lattice Λ generated by a basis $\mathbf{B}$ is $\Lambda = \Lambda(\mathbf{B}) = \{\mathbf{Bz} \mid \mathbf{z} \in \mathbb{Z}^n\}$. The dual lattice of Λ is $\Lambda^* = \{\mathbf{w} \in \text{span}(\Lambda) \mid \langle \mathbf{x}, \mathbf{w} \rangle \in \mathbb{Z}, \forall \mathbf{x} \in \Lambda\}$. Many lattice-based schemes use a specific family of lattices known as q-ary lattice. Given $\mathbf{A} \in \mathbb{Z}_q^{n\times m}$, let $\Lambda_q^{\perp}(\mathbf{A}) = \{\mathbf{x} \in \mathbb{Z}^m \mid \mathbf{Ax} = \mathbf{0} \bmod q\}$. Each $\mathbf{u} \in \mathbb{Z}_q^n$ defines a lattice coset $\Lambda_{\mathbf{u}}^{\perp}(\mathbf{A}) = \{\mathbf{x} \in \mathbb{Z}^m \mid \mathbf{Ax} = \mathbf{u} \bmod q\}$.

2.2 NTRU

Let $\mathcal{R} = \mathbb{Z}[X]/(X^n + 1)$ with $n = 2^k$ be a power-of-2 cyclotomic ring and $\mathcal{R}_q = \mathcal{R}/q\mathcal{R}$ for a modulus $q \in \mathbb{N}$. For $f = \sum_{i=0}^{n-1} f_i X^i \in \mathcal{R}$, its ℓ_2-norm is $\|f\| = \sqrt{\sum_i f_i^2}$. Similarly, we write $\|(f,g)\| = \sqrt{\|f\|^2 + \|g\|^2}$ for $f, g \in \mathcal{R}$.

A NTRU lattice is a free module of rank 2 over $\mathcal{R}$ defined by $h \in \mathcal{R}_q$ as

$$\Lambda_{h,q} = \{(u,v) \in \mathcal{R}^2 \mid u + vh = 0 \bmod q\}.$$

In a typical NTRU-based scheme, the public key is $h = f^{-1}g \bmod q$ for short $f, g \in \mathcal{R}$ while (f,g) is used as the secret key. Two NTRU bases are of special interest:

$$\mathbf{B}_h = \begin{bmatrix} -h & q \\ 1 & 0 \end{bmatrix} \quad \text{and} \quad \mathbf{B}_{f,g} = \begin{bmatrix} g & G \\ -f & -F \end{bmatrix}$$

where $G, F \in \mathcal{R}$ such that $fG - gF = q$ and $\mathbf{B}_{f,g}$ is also called the NTRU trapdoor basis. In particular, FALCON uses a high-quality NTRU trapdoor such that $\|B_{f,g}\|_{GS} \le 1.17\sqrt{q}$.

2.3 Gaussians

Let $\rho_s(\mathbf{x}) = \exp(-\pi \cdot \|\mathbf{x}\|^2/s^2)$ with $\mathbf{x} \in \mathbb{R}^n$ be the Gaussian function of width s. The width s is actually the scaled standard deviation of the corresponding Gaussian, i.e. $s = \sigma\sqrt{2\pi}$, where σ represents the standard deviation. We omit the subscript s if $s = 1$. Let $\rho_{s,\mathbf{c}}(\mathbf{x}) = \rho_s(\mathbf{x} - \mathbf{c})$ for a center $\mathbf{c} \in \mathbb{R}^n$.

The *discrete Gaussian* on a lattice Λ with center $\mathbf{c}$ and width s is defined by the probability function

$$D_{\Lambda,s,\mathbf{c}}(\mathbf{x}) = \frac{\rho_{s,\mathbf{c}}(\mathbf{x})}{\rho_{s,\mathbf{c}}(\Lambda)} \propto \rho_{s,\mathbf{c}}(\mathbf{x})$$

for $\mathbf{x} \in \Lambda$. The discrete Gaussian on $\Lambda + \mathbf{c}$, for $\mathbf{c} \in \mathrm{span}(\Lambda)$, is defined by

$$D_{\Lambda+\mathbf{c},s}(\mathbf{x}) = \frac{\rho_s(\mathbf{x})}{\rho_s(\Lambda + \mathbf{c})}$$

for $\mathbf{x} \in \Lambda + \mathbf{c}$. Let $\eta_\epsilon(\Lambda) = \min\{s > 0 \mid \rho_{1/s}(\Lambda^*) \le 1 + \epsilon\}$ be the *smoothing parameter* of the lattice Λ with respect to the closeness parameter $\epsilon \in (0,1)$. We write $\overline{\eta_\epsilon}(\mathbb{Z}^m) = \sqrt{\ln(2m(1+1/\epsilon))/\pi}$ that is a tight upper bound of $\eta_\epsilon(\mathbb{Z}^m)$.

Lemma 1 ([MR07], Implicit in Lemma 4.4). *For any lattice Λ, $\mathbf{c} \in \mathrm{span}(\Lambda)$ and $s \ge \eta_\epsilon(\Lambda)$, it holds that $\rho_{s,c}(\Lambda) \in [\frac{1-\epsilon}{1+\epsilon}, 1] \cdot \rho_s(\Lambda)$.*

Lemma 2 ([GPV08]). *Let Λ be an m-dimensional lattice with a basis $\mathbf{B}$, then*

$$\eta_\epsilon(\Lambda) \leq \|\mathbf{B}\|_{GS} \cdot \overline{\eta_\epsilon}(\mathbb{Z}^m).$$

Lemma 3 (Min-Entropy of Gaussian[GJK24]**).** *Let $n \in \mathbb{N}, \Lambda = \mathbb{Z}^n, \epsilon \in (0, 1/2)$ and $s \geq \eta_\epsilon(\Lambda) > 2$. Then for any $c \in \mathbb{R}^n$ and $x \in \Lambda$, $D_{\Lambda,s,c}(\mathbf{x}) \leq \frac{1}{2^{n-1}}$.*

Lemma 4 ([Ban95]). *Let Λ be a lattice and let $\mathbf{u}$ be an arbitrary vector in $\mathbb{R}^m$. Then*

$$\sum_{\substack{\mathbf{x}\in\Lambda+\mathbf{u} \\ \|\mathbf{x}\|_\infty \geq t}} e^{-\pi\|\mathbf{x}\|^2} < 2e^{-\pi t^2} \sum_{\mathbf{x}\in\Lambda} e^{-\pi\|\mathbf{x}\|^2}.$$

Lemma 5 ([Ban93]). *For each $c \geq (2\pi)^{-1/2}$, one has*

1. $\rho(\Lambda \backslash c\sqrt{n}B_m) < (c\sqrt{2\pi e}e^{-\pi c^2})^m \rho(\Lambda)$
2. $\rho((\Lambda + \mathbf{u}) \backslash c\sqrt{m}B_m) < 2(c\sqrt{2\pi e}e^{-\pi c^2})^m \rho(\Lambda)$ *for any* $\mathbf{u} \in \mathbb{R}^m$

where B_m denote the open unit ball in $\mathbb{R}^m$.

2.4 Rényi Divergence

Definition 1 (Rényi Divergence). *Let P, Q be two distributions such that* $\mathrm{Supp}(P) \subseteq \mathrm{Supp}(Q)$*. For $a \in (1, +\infty)$, the Rényi divergence of order a is*

$$R_a(P \,||\, Q) = \left(\sum_{x\in\mathrm{Supp}(P)} \frac{P(x)^a}{Q(x)^{a-1}} \right)^{\frac{1}{a-1}}.$$

In particular, the Rényi divergence of order $+\infty$ is

$$R_\infty(P \,||\, Q) = \max_{x\in\mathrm{Supp}(P)} \frac{P(x)}{Q(x)}.$$

The Rényi divergence is a closeness measure between distributions. It leads to tighter bounds in many typical cryptographic usecases compared to the statistical distance-based arguments, as verified in [BLL+15,Pre17].

Lemma 6 ([BLL+15,Pre17]). *For two distributions P, Q, two families of distributions $(P_i)_i, (Q_i)_i$ and any function f, the Rényi divergence verifies the following properties:*

- ***Data processing inequality.*** $R_a(P^f \,||\, Q^f) \leq R_a(P \,||\, Q)$.
- ***Multiplicativity.*** $R_a\left(\prod_i P_i \,||\, \prod_i Q_i\right) = \prod_i R_a(P_i \,||\, Q_i)$.
- ***Probability preservation.*** *For any event $E \subseteq \mathrm{Supp}(Q)$ and $a \in (1, +\infty)$,*

$$Q(E) \geq P(E)^{a/(a-1)}/R_a(P \,||\, Q),$$

$$Q(E) \geq P(E)/R_\infty(P \,||\, Q).$$

Lemma 7 (Optimal Rényi Order[FGdG+26]**).** *For* $\lambda \in \mathbb{N}$, *let* $\mathcal{E}_1, \mathcal{E}_2$ *be two events such that* $\Pr[\mathcal{E}_1] \geq 2^{-\lambda}$. *Assume that for any* $Q \in \mathbb{N}$ *and* $a \in (1, \infty)$ *the Rényi divergence between two arbitrary distributions is at most* $R_a \in [1, \infty)$, *and*

$$\Pr[\mathcal{E}_2] \leq R_a^Q \cdot \Pr[\mathcal{E}_1]^{\frac{a-1}{a}} \quad \forall a > 1.$$

Then

$$-\log(\Pr[\mathcal{E}_2]) \leq -\log(\Pr[\mathcal{E}_1]) - \min_{a>1} \left\{ Q \log R_a + \frac{\lambda}{a} \right\}.$$

Definition 2 (Relative Error[MW17]**).** *Let* $\mathcal{P}$ *and* $\mathcal{Q}$ *be two discrete probability distributions over the same countable set* $\mathcal{X}$. *The relative error of* $\mathcal{P}$ *and* $\mathcal{Q}$ *is defined as*

$$\delta_{RE}(\mathcal{P}, \mathcal{Q}) = \max_{x \in \mathsf{sup}(\mathcal{P})} \frac{|\mathcal{P}(x) - \mathcal{Q}(x)|}{\mathcal{P}(x)}.$$

Lemma 8 (Relative Error Lemma [Pre17]**).** *Let* $\mathcal{P}$ *and* $\mathcal{Q}$ *be two discrete probability distributions such that* $\sup(\mathcal{P}) = \sup(\mathcal{Q})$ *and* $\delta_{RE} > 0$. *Then for all* $a \in (1, +\infty)$

$$R_a(\mathcal{P} \,||\, \mathcal{Q}) \lesssim 1 + \frac{a\delta_{RE}^2}{2}.$$

3 FALCON-Type Signatures

This paper mainly investigates the concrete security analysis of FALCON$^+$ introduced by [FGdG+26] that is a minor modification of FALCON with a formal proof and FALCON^{WS} introduced by [ZJR+25] that is a recent variant of FALCON achieving better compactness. Let us first briefly recall FALCON$^+$ and FALCON^{WS}.

3.1 FALCON$^+$

A FALCON-type signature scheme is a NTRU-based instantiation of the GPV hash-and-sign framework [GPV08] over $\mathcal{R} = \mathbb{Z}[X]/(X^n + 1)$ with $n = 2^k$. Its secret key sk, generated by TpdGen, is a NTRU trapdoor basis $\mathbf{B}_{f,g}$ of well-bounded Gram-Schmidt norms. The signing procedure is in essence preimage Gaussian sampling, denoted PreSmp, over some coset of $\Lambda_{h,q}$ determined by the hash of message, salt and public key. A valid signature is a short Gaussian vector in the coset. Therefore the scheme is specified by the following parameters.

- the basis quality parameter $\alpha > 1$ such that $\|\mathbf{B}_{f,g}\|_{GS} \leq \alpha\sqrt{q}$;
- the Gaussian width $s = \alpha\sqrt{q} \cdot \overline{\eta_\epsilon}(\mathbb{Z}^{2n})$ and the corresponding standard deviation $\sigma = s/\sqrt{2\pi}$;
- the signature norm bound $\beta = \tau \cdot \sigma\sqrt{2n}$ for some $\tau \approx 1$.

$\mathsf{Sign}^+(\mathsf{sk}, \mathsf{m})$	$\mathsf{Verify}(\mathsf{pk}, \mathsf{m}, \mathsf{sig})$
repeat	$c = \mathsf{H}(\mathsf{pk}, \mathsf{r}, \mathsf{m}) \in \mathcal{R}_n$
$\quad \mathsf{r} \leftarrow \{0,1\}^k$	$s_1 = c - s_2 h \bmod q$
$\quad c = \mathsf{H}(\mathsf{pk} = h, \mathsf{r}, \mathsf{m})$	**if** $\|(s_1, s_2)\| \leq \beta$
$\quad (s_1, s_2) \leftarrow \mathsf{PreSmp}^+(\mathsf{sk}, s, (c, 0))$	$\quad$ accept
until $\|(s_1, s_2)\| \leq \beta$	**else**
return $(\mathsf{sig} = (\mathsf{r}, s_2))$	$\quad$ reject

Fig. 1. High level procedure of FALCON$^+$.

FALCON$^+$ is the first FALCON-type signature scheme with provable security. Compared to FALCON, FALCON$^+$ picks a random salt refreshing the lattice coset within the loop of Gaussian sampling. With this minor modification, the reduction in the security proof can program the RO with a fresh, potentially "large" preimage without being forced to use a conditional distribution. The signing and verification procedure is described on a high level in Fig. 1.

FALCON$^+$ uses the same parameters as FALCON: $n = 512$ (resp. 1024) for NIST security level I (resp. V) and the modulus $q = 12289$. The basis quality parameter $\alpha = 1.17$ and the signature norm bound $\beta = \tau\sigma\sqrt{2n}$ with a fixed tailcut factor $\tau = 1.1$. The closeness parameter is set according to the Rényi divergence-based argument [Pre17] as $\epsilon = 1/\sqrt{Q_s \cdot \lambda}$, where $Q_s = 2^{64}$ is the maximal number of signing queries and $\lambda = 128$ or 256 is the security parameter. The preimage sampler PreSmp^+ is implemented with the FFO sampler [DP16] that is a ring-efficient Klein-GPV sampler.

The provable security of FALCON$^+$ is based on the following hardness assumptions.

Definition 3 ($\mathcal{R}$-SIS, t-$\mathcal{R}$-ISIS)**.** *The Ring Short Integer Solution problem and the Ring Inhomogeneous Short Integer Solution problem relative to the* NTRU *trapdoor algorithm* TpdGen *with parameters* $m, q > 0$ *and* $\alpha, B > 0$ *are defined via the games* $\mathcal{R}$-SIS *and* t-$\mathcal{R}$-ISIS *in Fig. 2. The advantages of* A *is defined as*

$$\mathsf{Adv}^{\mathcal{R}\text{-}\mathsf{SIS}}_{m,q,\alpha,B,\mathsf{A}} = \Pr[\mathcal{R}\text{-}\mathsf{SIS}_{m,q,\alpha,B}(\mathsf{A}) \Rightarrow 1],$$
$$\mathsf{Adv}^{t\text{-}\mathcal{R}\text{-}\mathsf{ISIS}}_{m,q,\alpha,B,\mathsf{A}} = \Pr[t\text{-}\mathcal{R}\text{-}\mathsf{ISIS}_{m,q,\alpha,B}(\mathsf{A}) \Rightarrow 1].$$

By Rényi divergence-based arguments, the security proofs in the Random Oracle Model (ROM) of FALCON$^+$ are presented in [FGdG+26]: the strong unforgeability is reduced to $\mathcal{R}$-SIS while the plain unforgeability is reduced to t-$\mathcal{R}$-ISIS. Theorem 1 offers a characterization of the plain unforgeability of FALCON$^+$ and a detailed account of core issues we are concerned.

Theorem 1 (Unforgeability, [FGdG+26]**).** *For any adversary* A *against the* **UF-CMA** *security of* COREFALCON$^+$ *running in time* t_{A}*, making at most* Q_s

Game $\mathcal{R}\text{-}\mathsf{SIS}_{m,q,\alpha,B}(\mathsf{A})$

for $i \in [m]$ **do**
  $(h_i, \cdot, \cdot) \leftarrow \mathsf{TpdGen}(q, \alpha)$
$(u, v_1, \ldots, v_m) \leftarrow \mathsf{A}(h_1, \ldots, h_m)$
return $[\![u + \sum_i h_i \cdot v_i = 0 \wedge \|(u, v_1, \ldots, v_m)\| \leq B]\!]$

Game $t\text{-}\mathcal{R}\text{-}\mathsf{ISIS}_{m,q,\alpha,B}(\mathsf{A})$

for $i \in [m]$ **do**
  $(h_i, \cdot, \cdot) \leftarrow \mathsf{TpdGen}(q, \alpha)$
for $j \in [t]$ **do**
  $c_j \leftarrow \mathcal{R}_q$
$(j, u, v_1, \ldots, v_m) \leftarrow \mathsf{A}(h_1, \ldots, h_m, c_1, \ldots, c_t)$
return $[\![u + \sum_i h_i \cdot v_i = c_j \wedge \|(u, v_1, \ldots, v_m)\| \leq B]\!]$

Fig. 2. Games defining $\mathcal{R}\text{-}\mathsf{SIS}_{m,q,\alpha,B}$ and $\text{-}\mathcal{R}\text{-}\mathsf{ISIS}_{m,q,\alpha,B}$

signing queries and Q_{H} *RO queries, there exist adversary* B *against* $(Q_{\mathsf{H}}+1)$-$\mathcal{R}$-ISIS *running in time* $t_{\mathsf{B}} \approx t_{\mathsf{A}}$ *such that for all* $C_s \in \mathbb{N}^{\geq 1}$ *and* $a_u, a_p \in \mathbb{R}^{>1}$ *it holds*

$$\mathsf{Adv}^{Q_s\text{-}\mathbf{UF\text{-}CMA}}_{\mathrm{FALCON}^+,\mathsf{A}} \leq \left(r_u^{C_s} \cdot \left(r_p^{C_s} \cdot \mathsf{Adv}^{(Q_{\mathsf{H}}+1)\text{-}\mathcal{R}\text{-}\mathbf{ISIS}}_{1,q,\alpha,\beta,\mathsf{B}} \right)^{\frac{a_p-1}{a_p}} \right)^{\frac{a_u-1}{a_u}} + \sum_{i=0}^{Q_s} \binom{C_s}{i} (1 - p_{\mathsf{PreSmp}^+,\beta})^{C_s - i} (p_{\mathsf{PreSmp}^+,\beta})^i + \frac{Q_s(C_s + Q_{\mathsf{H}})}{2^k},$$

where

$p_{\mathsf{PreSmp}^+,\beta} = \max_{(\mathbf{B},\cdot)\in\mathsf{TpdGen}, c\in\mathcal{R}_q} \Pr_{(s_1,s_2)\leftarrow\mathsf{PreSmp}^+(\mathbf{B},s,(c,0))}[\|(s_1,s_2)\|_2 \leq \beta]$,
$r_u = \max_{(\cdot,h)\in\mathsf{TpdGen}} R_{a_u}(\mathcal{P} \,\|\, \mathcal{Q}_h)$ *with* $\mathcal{P} = \mathcal{U}(\mathcal{R}_q)$ *and* $\mathcal{Q}_h$ *the distribution of* $s_1 + s_2 \cdot h \mod q$*, where* $s_1, s_2 \sim D_{\mathcal{R},s}$
$r_p = \max_{(\mathbf{B},\cdot)\in\mathsf{TpdGen}, c\in\mathcal{R}_q} R_{a_p}(\mathsf{PreSmp}^+(\mathbf{B}, s, (c, 0)) \,\|\, \mathcal{D}_{\Lambda(\mathbf{B}),s,(c,0)})$.

Security Reduction Losses in FALCON$^+$. In Theorem 1, $\mathsf{Adv}^{(Q_{\mathsf{H}}+1)\text{-}\mathcal{R}\text{-}\mathbf{ISIS}}_{1,q,\alpha,\beta,\mathsf{B}}$ is the advantage against the underlying ISIS problem, and r_p and r_u are the Rényi divergences with respect to the underlying sampler and RO simulation, respectively. Note that the first term in $\mathsf{Adv}^{(Q_{\mathsf{H}}+1)\text{-}\mathcal{R}\text{-}\mathbf{ISIS}}_{1,q,\alpha,\beta,\mathsf{B}}$ indicates that there are two sources of security losses in the concrete security of FALCON$^+$.

1. *The loss from preimage sampler*: The actual preimage sampler PreSmp^+ usually does not output a perfect Gaussian $D_{\Lambda(\mathbf{B}),s,(c,0)}$. The Rényi divergence between the real preimage distribution and the ideal one is bounded by

$r_p = R_{a_p}(\mathsf{PreSmp}^+ \| D_{\Lambda(\mathbf{B}),s,(c,0)}) \leq 1 + 2a_p\epsilon^2$. The term r_p is exponentiated by C_s, the maximal number of the calls of PreSmp^+ (including repetitions). Then the multiplicative factor $r_p^{C_s}$ of $\mathsf{Adv}_{1,q,\alpha,\beta,\mathsf{B}}^{(Q_\mathsf{H}+1)\text{-}\mathcal{R}\text{-}\mathbf{ISIS}}$ indicates that the sampler incurs $l_p = C_s \cdot \log_2(r_p)$ bits of security loss.

2. *The loss from RO Simulation*: In the security proof, the simulator must answer RO queries $\mathsf{H}(\mathsf{pk}, \mathsf{r}, \mathsf{m})$ without knowing the trapdoor. It does so by programming the RO output as $c = s_1 + s_2 h \bmod q$ with $s_1, s_2 \leftarrow D_{\mathcal{R},s}$. The distribution $\mathcal{Q}_h$ of these programmed outputs is not perfectly uniform over $\mathcal{R}_q$. The term $r_u = R_{a_u}(\mathcal{U}(\mathcal{R}_q) \| \mathcal{Q}_h) \approx 1 + \frac{2a_u\epsilon^2}{(1-\epsilon)^2}$ quantifies the Rényi divergence between the ideal uniform distribution and this simulated distribution. It is exponentiated by C_s as well, thus the RO simulation incurs $l_u = C_s \cdot \log_2(r_u)$ bits of security loss.

As claimed in [FGdG+26], the total security loss in the plain unforgeability analysis from two Rényi arguments was approximately 7 bits for FALCON$^+$-512 and 8 bits for FALCON$^+$-1024. A closely matching loss profile was observed in the strong unforgeability setting, although the underlying SIS problem becomes substantially easier in the security proof for strong unforgeability.

3.2 FALCON^{WS}

To further improve the bandwidth efficiency, the recent work [ZJR+25] introduces a FALCON variant FALCON^{WS} working with the so-called weak smoothness condition, i.e. $\epsilon = O(1)$. This leads to a much smaller Gaussian width $s = \alpha\sqrt{q} \cdot \eta_\epsilon(\mathbb{Z}^{2n})$, which allows smaller parameters and higher forgery security.

The preimage distribution output by the original Klein-GPV sampler will have a significant discrepancy from the ideal Gaussian under the weak smoothness condition. To address this issue, [ZJR+25] exploits the rejection sampling to rectify the sampling error (Step 5 in Fig. 3). By this, the preimage in FALCON^{WS} exactly follows the ideal Gaussian, which actually eliminates the Rényi loss from the sampler in the security proof.

$\mathsf{PreSmp}^{\mathsf{WS}}(\mathsf{sk}, s, (c, 0))$ with weak smoothness

1: $\mathbf{v} \leftarrow \mathbf{0}, \mathbf{c}' \leftarrow \mathbf{c}, \Delta \leftarrow 1$
2: **for** $i = n-1, \cdots, 0$
3: $\quad c_i'' \leftarrow \langle \mathbf{c}', \tilde{\mathbf{b}}_i \rangle / \|\tilde{\mathbf{b}}_i\|^2, s_i \leftarrow s/\|\tilde{\mathbf{b}}_i\|$
4: $\quad z_i \leftarrow D_{\mathbb{Z},s_i,c_i''}$
5: $\quad \Delta \leftarrow \Delta \cdot \dfrac{\rho_{s_i,c_i''}(\mathbb{Z})}{\rho_{s_i}(\mathbb{Z})}$
6: $\quad \mathbf{c}' \leftarrow \mathbf{c}' - z_i \mathbf{b}_i, \mathbf{v} \leftarrow \mathbf{v} + z_i \mathbf{b}_i$
7: **return** $\mathbf{v}$ with probability Δ otherwise restart

Fig. 3. Preimage sampler used in FALCON^{WS}.

However, as noted before, there is another source of reduction loss from the RO simulation. The use of an excessively large ϵ in FALCON^{WS} would drastically amplify this loss, which invalidates the security reduction. To build a theoretical security proof, [ZJR+25] introduces an additional non-standard hardness assumption to guarantee computational indistinguishability of the simulated syndrome from uniform. While they gave some cryptanalytic results to show that the new assumption does not degrade concrete security, removing such an extra assumption would be much more reassuring.

4 Sharper Security Bounds Using the NTRU Basis Profile

In this section, we leverage the profile of the trapdoor basis to improve the Rényi divergence-based security arguments for the GPV framework. Specifically, we present *basis-specific* Rényi divergence bounds for both the Klein-GPV sampler [GPV08] and the RO simulation in the GPV security proof. By applying the new analysis to FALCON$^+$, we can eliminate the 7 bits of security loss for the FALCON$^+$-512 parameter set claimed in [FGdG+26].

4.1 Basis-Specific Rényi Analysis of the Klein-GPV Sampler

The closeness error between the output distribution by the trapdoor sampler and the ideal Gaussian is a primary source of the security loss in the GPV framework. The Klein-GPV sampler, adopted by FALCON, reduces the high-dimensional lattice Gaussian sampling to a sequence of one-dimensional integer Gaussian samplings with varying parameters. The Gaussian width at each iteration is $s_i = s/\|\tilde{\mathbf{b}}_i\|$ inversely proportional to the Gram-Schmidt norm of the NTRU trapdoor. The Klein-GPV sampler requires all s_i's are greater than $\eta_\epsilon(\mathbb{Z}) \approx \sqrt{\ln(2(1+1/\epsilon)}$ for a small closeness parameter ϵ, which gives a Rényi divergence bound for the signature distribution and Gaussian.

The existing Rényi analysis is based on the almost shift invariant property of integer Gaussians with width greater than the smoothing parameter. Let $\epsilon_i > 0$ such that $s_i = \sqrt{\ln(2(1+1/\epsilon_i))/\pi} \geq \eta_{\epsilon_i}(\mathbb{Z})$. We observe that ϵ_i is highly sensitive to $\|\tilde{\mathbf{b}}_i\|$: ϵ_i, i.e. the sampling error at the i-th iteration, can be significantly smaller than the global ϵ with $\|\tilde{\mathbf{b}}_i\|$ decreasing. The Rényi divergence bound can therefore be improved by taking all s_i's into account. To this end, we present a refined Rényi analysis using a basis-specific metric

$$\delta_{\mathbf{B},s} = \prod_{i=1}^{m} \frac{1+\epsilon_i}{1-\epsilon_i} - 1.$$

Theorem 2 (Basis-Specific Relative Error of the Klein-GPV Sampler). *For any basis* $\mathbf{B} \in \mathbb{Z}^{m \times m}$, $s \geq \|\mathbf{B}\|_{GS} \cdot \eta_\epsilon(\mathbb{Z}^m)$ *with* $\epsilon \in (0,1)$ *and any target* $\mathbf{t} \in \mathbb{Z}^m$, *the relative error of the Klein-GPV Sampler* $\mathsf{PreSmp}(\mathbf{B}, s, \mathbf{t})$ *is bounded by*

$$\delta_{RE}(\mathsf{PreSmp}(\mathbf{B}, s, \mathbf{t}), D_{\mathcal{L}(\mathbf{B}),s,\mathbf{t}}) \leq \delta_{\mathbf{B},s}.$$

Proof. As detailed in [GPV08], the probability that the Klein-GPV Sampler $\mathsf{PreSmp}(\mathbf{B}, s, \mathbf{t})$ outputs a vector $\mathbf{v}$ is proportional to $\prod_{i=1}^{m} \frac{1}{\rho_{s_i,c_i}(\mathbb{Z})} \cdot \rho_{s,\mathbf{c}}(\mathbf{v})$, where $s_i = s/\|\tilde{\mathbf{b}}_i\|$ and some real c_i. Since each $s_i \geq \eta_{\epsilon_i}(\mathbb{Z})$ for some ϵ_i, Lemma 1 shows that $\rho_{s_i,c_i}(\mathbb{Z}) \in [\frac{1-\epsilon_i}{1+\epsilon_i}, 1] \cdot \rho_{s_i}(\mathbb{Z})$. The claimed bound follows immediately. □

Corollary 1 (Basis-Specific Rényi Divergence of the Klein-GPV Sampler). *Under the same conditions as Theorem 2, for any $a > 1$, the Rényi divergence is bounded by*

$$R_a\left(\mathsf{PreSmp}(\mathbf{B}, s, \mathbf{t}), D_{\mathcal{L}(\mathbf{B}),s,\mathbf{t}}\right) \lesssim 1 + \frac{a\delta_{\mathbf{B},s}^2}{2}.$$

Remark 1. The key advancement in our analysis is its basis-specific nature. Instead of using the worst-case lower bound as in [Pre17], our results are tailored to *each specific basis* $\mathbf{B}$. This enables tighter bounds in practice, as we leverage the actual geometric properties of $\mathbf{B}$ rather than conservative worst-case estimates. Our experimental evaluation validates the efficacy of this analytical approach in achieving a tight security reduction.

4.2 Basis-Specific Rényi Analysis of the RO Simulation

This subsection addresses the Rényi loss from the RO simulation through a refined analysis of the smoothing parameter that accounts for the geometric profile of the lattice basis. Building on this tighter bound and a more detailed treatment of the relative error in the original analysis of [FGdG+26], we obtain significantly improved bounds for the Rényi loss in the RO simulation.

Theorem 3. *Let $\mathbf{B} \in \mathbb{Z}^{m\times m}$ be a basis of the lattice Λ and $\alpha_i = \frac{\|\mathbf{B}\|_{GS}}{\|\tilde{\mathbf{b}}_i\|}$. Let $s = \|\mathbf{B}\|_{GS} \cdot \sqrt{\ln(2m(1+1/\epsilon))/\pi}$, then*

$$\rho_{1/s}(\Lambda^*\backslash\mathbf{0}) \leq \frac{\sum_{i=0}^{m-1} 2\left(\frac{\epsilon}{2\,m(1+\epsilon)}\right)^{\alpha_i^2}}{1-\sum_{i=0}^{m-1} 2\left(\frac{\epsilon}{2\,m(1+\epsilon)}\right)^{\alpha_i^2}}.$$

Defining the right side of the inequality as ϵ', then $\eta_{\epsilon'}(\Lambda) \leq \|\mathbf{B}\|_{GS} \cdot \sqrt{\ln(2m(1+1/\epsilon))/\pi}$.

Proof. Note that for the dual lattice Λ^*, the reverse order GSO of dual basis $\tilde{\mathbf{B}}^*$ satisfies $\tilde{\mathbf{b}}_i^* = \frac{\tilde{\mathbf{b}}_i}{\|\tilde{\mathbf{b}}_i\|^2}$. Then let us consider the fundamental parallelepiped (scaled)

$$\mathcal{P}(\tilde{\mathbf{B}}^*) = \{\tilde{\mathbf{B}}^*\mathbf{x} \mid \mathbf{x} \in \mathbb{R}^n, \forall i : -1 < x_i < 1\}.$$

Obviously, there are no other lattice points of Λ^* inside $\mathcal{P}(\tilde{\mathbf{B}}^*)$ except the zero point $\mathbf{0}$. Denote $\mathcal{Q}_i = \left\{\mathbf{x} \in \mathbb{R}^m \mid \left|\langle \mathbf{x}, \frac{\tilde{\mathbf{b}}_i^*}{\|\tilde{\mathbf{b}}_i^*\|}\rangle\right| \geq \|\tilde{\mathbf{b}}_i^*\|\right\}$. It follows from Lemma 2.4 in [Ban95] that

$$\rho_{1/s}\left(\Lambda^* \cap \mathcal{Q}_i\right) < 2e^{-\pi s^2\|\tilde{\mathbf{b}}_i^*\|^2}\rho_{1/s}\left(\Lambda^*\right).$$

Notice that $\Lambda^*\backslash\mathcal{P}(\tilde{\mathbf{B}}^*) = \Lambda^* \cap (\mathcal{Q}_0 \cup \cdots \cup \mathcal{Q}_{m-1}) = \cup_{i=0}^{m-1}(\Lambda^* \cap \mathcal{Q}_i)$ then

$$\begin{aligned}\rho_{1/s}(\Lambda^*\backslash\mathbf{0}) = \rho_s\left(\Lambda^*\backslash\mathcal{P}(\tilde{\mathbf{B}}^*)\right) &\leq \sum_{i=0}^{m-1} \rho_s(\Lambda^* \cap \mathcal{Q}_i) \\ &< 2\rho_{1/s}(\Lambda^*) \sum_{i=0}^{m-1} e^{-\pi s^2 \|\tilde{\mathbf{b}}_i^*\|^2} \\ &= 2\rho_{1/s}(\Lambda^*) \sum_{i=0}^{m-1} e^{-\pi\left(\|\mathbf{B}\|_{GS}\cdot\sqrt{\ln(2\,m(1+1/\epsilon))/\pi}\right)^2\cdot\frac{1}{\|\mathbf{b}_i^*\|^2}} \\ &= \sum_{i=0}^{m-1} 2\left(\frac{\epsilon}{2\,m(1+\epsilon)}\right)^{\alpha_i^2} \cdot \rho_{1/s}(\Lambda^*).\end{aligned}$$

Rearranging terms, we can get the upper bound estimate for $\rho_{1/s}(\Lambda^*\backslash\mathbf{0})$. □

Remark 2. In FALCON, the Gaussian width s for preimage sampling is set with respect to closeness parameter ϵ. However, our basis-specific analysis reveals that it corresponds to a significantly smaller effective parameter ϵ'. As shown later, the exponent of ϵ' is approximately 5 bits smaller than that of the original ϵ.

Next, we observe a potential for improvement in the original analysis of Lemma 8 in [FGdG+26], which bounds the relative error between the uniform distribution $\mathcal{U}(\mathcal{R}_q)$ and the simulated distribution $\mathcal{Q}_h$ by a factor derived from $\frac{1+\epsilon}{1-\epsilon}$. This value implicitly overlooks a critical subtlety: the ϵ terms in the numerator and denominator actually correspond to two distinct closeness parameters with significantly different magnitudes.

Theorem 4. (Refined Uniformity Bound, adapted from Lemma 8 of [FGdG+26]). *Let Λ, Λ' be m-dimensional full-rank lattices with $\Lambda' \subseteq \Lambda$. Then for any $a \in (1,\infty)$, $\epsilon \in (0, \frac{1}{2})$, any $s \geq \eta_\epsilon(\Lambda')$, and any $\mathbf{c} \in \mathbb{R}^n$,*

$$R_a\left(\mathcal{U}(\Lambda/\Lambda')\|D_{\Lambda/\Lambda',s,\mathbf{c}}\right) \lesssim 1 + \frac{a\delta^2}{2},$$

where $\delta = (\epsilon + \epsilon')/(1-\epsilon)$.

Proof. The quotient group Λ/Λ' is defined as the additive group of cosets $\mathbf{x} + \Lambda', \mathbf{x} \in \Lambda$. Sampling from a discrete Gaussian over this quotient group we obtain that for any $\mathbf{x} \in \Lambda$

$$D_{\Lambda/\Lambda',s,\mathbf{c}}(x) = \frac{\rho_{s,\mathbf{c}}(\mathbf{x} + \Lambda')}{\rho_{s,\mathbf{c}}(\Lambda)}.$$

Notice that since $s \geq \eta_\epsilon(\Lambda')$ and $\Lambda' \subset \Lambda$, there exists $\epsilon' \ll \epsilon$ such that $s \geq \eta_{\epsilon'}(\Lambda)$. As a consequence, we get

$$\frac{\mathcal{U}(|\Lambda/\Lambda'|)(\mathbf{x})}{D_{\Lambda/\Lambda',s,\mathbf{c}}(\mathbf{x})} \in \left[\frac{1-\epsilon}{1+\epsilon'}, \frac{1+\epsilon'}{1-\epsilon}\right].$$

Applying Lemma 8 with $\delta = (\epsilon + \epsilon')/(1-\epsilon)$, we complete the proof. □

Remark 3. In [FGdG+26], the relative error is bounded by $2\epsilon/(1-\epsilon)$, leading to a Rényi divergence upper bound of $1+2a\epsilon^2/(1-\epsilon)^2$. In contrast, our analysis employs a tighter bound of $\delta = (\epsilon+\epsilon')/(1-\epsilon)$, where the term ϵ' is negligible for the FALCON parameters (for example, $\epsilon' = 2^{-782250}$). Consequently, the relative error in our work is effectively halved compared to theirs, resulting in a Rényi divergence bound that is approximately four times tighter (since the bound depends quadratically on the error).

In summary, by combining a basis-specific analysis of the smoothing parameter with a more refined treatment of the relative error, our experimental results show that the resulting Rényi loss from the RO simulation becomes numerically comparable to that originating from the sampler. See Table 5 for more details.

4.3 Analysis and Experimental Results for FALCON$^+$

The GSO Profile of NTRU Trapdoor Bases. It is known that $\|\tilde{\mathbf{b}}_{2i}\| = \|\tilde{\mathbf{b}}_{2i+1}\|$ for each FALCON trapdoor basis. As per the symplecticity of NTRU [GHN06], it holds that $\|\tilde{\mathbf{b}}_i\| * \|\tilde{\mathbf{b}}_{2n-i}\| = q$ and this indicates that $\|\tilde{\mathbf{b}}_i\| \in [\sqrt{q}/1.17, 1.17\sqrt{q}]$. Figure 4 shows the average profile of FALCON trapdoor bases.

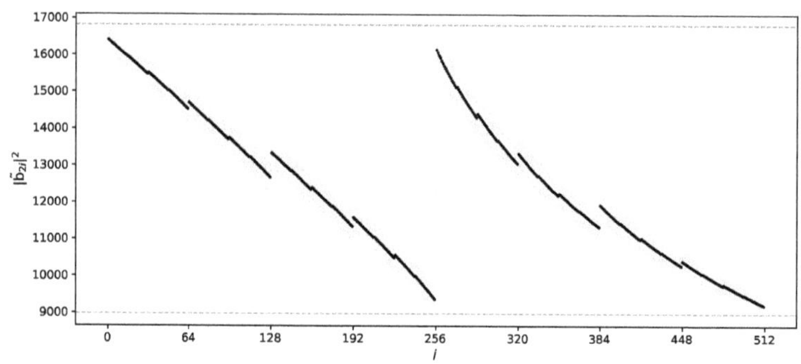

Fig. 4. The black scatter points represent the mean of $\|\tilde{\mathbf{b}}_{2i}\|^2$ for the 1,000 random FALCON-512 basis, and the gray area represents the standard deviation. The values of the two horizontal dashed lines are $(1.17\sqrt{q})^2$ and $(\sqrt{q}/1.17)^2$.

Rényi Divergence Estimation of the Klein-GPV Sampler. Based on our improved analysis in Corollary 1 and the characterization of the NTRU basis profile, we present a conservative estimate of the optimization achieved. Note that in Theorem 2,

$$s_i = s/\|\tilde{\mathbf{b}}_i\| = \alpha_i \cdot \sqrt{\ln(2(1+1/\epsilon))/\pi} > \sqrt{\ln(2(1+1/\epsilon^{\alpha_i^2}))/\pi} \geq \eta_{\epsilon_i'}(\mathbb{Z}^n)$$

for $\epsilon'_i = \epsilon^{\alpha_i^2}$. As a result, the relative error between $\mathsf{PreSmp}(\mathbf{B}, s, \mathbf{t})$ and $D_{\mathcal{L}(\mathbf{B}),s,\mathbf{t}}$ is bounded by

$$\delta_{\mathbf{B},s} = \prod_{i=1}^{2n} \frac{1+\epsilon'_i}{1-\epsilon'_i} - 1 \approx 2\sum_{i=1}^{2n} \epsilon'_i.$$

We derive a heuristic estimate via integral approximation as follows:

$$\begin{aligned} 2\sum_{i=1}^{2n} \epsilon'_i &= 4\sum_{i=0}^{n-1} \epsilon^{\alpha_{2i}^2} \\ &\approx \epsilon \cdot \frac{4n}{1.17^4 - 1} \int_0^{1.17^4-1} \epsilon^x \, dx \\ &= \frac{4n\epsilon}{1.17^4 - 1} \cdot \frac{1 - \epsilon^{1.17^4-1}}{|\ln \epsilon|} \\ &\approx \frac{4n\epsilon}{0.87|\ln \epsilon|}. \end{aligned} \tag{1}$$

Recall that $\delta_{\mathbf{B},s} = \prod_{i=1}^{m} \frac{1+\epsilon_i}{1-\epsilon_i} - 1$ is a basis-specific metric. Compared to the original relative error $\delta = \left(\frac{1+\epsilon}{1-\epsilon}\right)^{2n} - 1 \approx 4n\epsilon$, we improve by a factor of $\delta/\delta_{\mathbf{B},s} \approx 0.87|\ln \epsilon| \approx 21.4$ for FALCON, implying that the actual relative error caused by the sampling algorithm is about 4.4 bits lower than previously estimated. The experimental results are shown in Fig. 5: The relative error obtained from tests on 1,000 sets of random FALCON bases is smaller than the estimate from Eq. 1, which implies a smaller Rényi divergence.

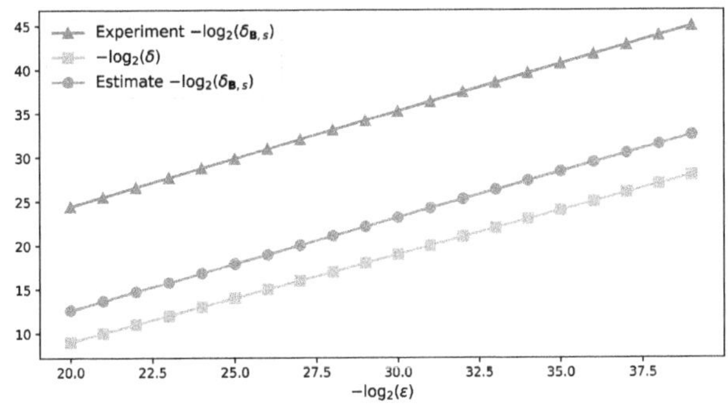

Fig. 5. The experiment $\delta_{\mathbf{B},s}$ comes from the mean of $\delta_{\mathbf{B},s}$ for the 1,000 random FALCON-512 basis.

Rényi Divergence Estimation of the RO Simulation. With the knowledge of the NTRU trapdoor profile, one can use Theorem 3 to estimate ϵ' in

$\eta_{\epsilon'}(\Lambda_{NTRU}) \leq 1.17\sqrt{q} \cdot \sqrt{\ln(4n(1+1/\epsilon))/\pi}$ that corresponds to the Gaussian width s in FALCON. We also give a heuristic estimate using integral approximation as follows:

$$\begin{aligned}\sum_{i=0}^{2n-1} 2\left(\frac{\epsilon}{4n(1+\epsilon)}\right)^{\alpha_i^2} &= 4\sum_{i=0}^{n-1}\left(\frac{\epsilon}{4n(1+\epsilon)}\right)^{\alpha_{2i}^2} \\ &\approx \frac{\epsilon}{n(1+\epsilon)} \cdot \frac{n}{1.17^4-1}\int_0^{1.17^4-1}\left(\frac{\epsilon}{4n(1+\epsilon)}\right)^x dx \\ &= \frac{\epsilon}{1+\epsilon} \cdot \frac{1}{1.17^4-1} \cdot \frac{1-\left(\frac{\epsilon}{4n(1+\epsilon)}\right)^{1.17^4-1}}{\left|\ln\left(\frac{\epsilon}{4n(1+\epsilon)}\right)\right|} \\ &\approx \frac{1.15\epsilon}{|\ln(\epsilon/4n)|}.\end{aligned} \tag{2}$$

Then by Theorem 3, it follows that ϵ' is about $\frac{1.15}{|\ln(\epsilon/4n)|}$ times smaller than ϵ in width s. As shown in Fig. 6, the relative error obtained from testing 1,000 sets of random FALCON bases closely matches the estimate derived from Eq. 4.3, validating the accuracy of our estimation method. We present the numbers associated with FALCON for a straightforward comparison:

- for FALCON-512: $\eta_{2^{-40.9}}(\Lambda_{NTRU}) \leq 1.17\sqrt{q} \cdot \sqrt{\ln(4n(1+2^{35.5}))/\pi}$
- for FALCON-1024: $\eta_{2^{-41.2}}(\Lambda_{NTRU}) \leq 1.17\sqrt{q} \cdot \sqrt{\ln(4n(1+2^{36}))/\pi}$

Experiments on FALCON Bases. We conducted extensive experiments to validate the effectiveness of our basis-specific analysis. As shown in Table 5, our improved analysis achieves a Rényi loss of 0.077 bits in average and the maximal loss among 1,000 random FALCON instances is less than 0.2 bits.

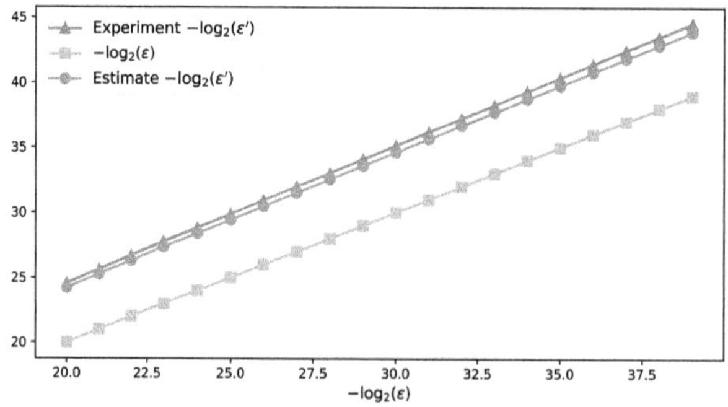

Fig. 6. The experiment ϵ' comes from the mean of ϵ' for the 1,000 random FALCON-512 basis. The estimate ϵ' is set as $\frac{1.15\epsilon}{|\ln(\epsilon/4n)|}$.

Table 5. Comparisons of the bit losses (in bits) achieved by [FGdG+26] and our analysis. The item A/B represents the mean and the maximum measured over 1,000 FALCON instances.

	$loss_p$		$loss_u$	
	[FGdG+26]	Ours	[FGdG+26]	Ours
FALCON$^+$-512	3.29	0.03854/0.09312	3.14	0.03852/0.09299
FALCON$^+$-1024	3.14	0.04563/0.08663	3.46	0.04561/0.08658

4.4 Refined Concrete Security of FALCON$^+$

Putting everything together, we get a refined concrete security assessment of FALCON$^+$. The resulting Rényi losses under our basis-specific analysis are summarized in Table 6, along with the bounds from [FGdG+26] for comparison.

Table 6. Concrete security of FALCON$^+$ for plain unforgeability. For FALCON$^+$-1024, the bit security estimates by both [FGdG+26] and ours are 256, which are actually determined by the term $\frac{Q_s(C_s+Q_{\mathrm{H}})}{2^k}$ in Theorem 1. For this, we also include the bit security ignoring that term in the bracket.

	FALCON$^+$-512		FALCON$^+$-1024	
Parameter	[FGdG+26]	Ours	[FGdG+26]	Ours
Degree of $\mathcal{R}$	512		1024	
Bit security for t-$\mathcal{R}$-**ISIS**	120		278	
Max Signing queries, Q_s	2^{64}		2^{64}	
Max repetitions, C_s	$2^{64}+2^{50}$		$2^{64}+2^{36}$	
Rényi Order, a_p	72.96	2577.30	157.05	6417.73
Rényi Order, a_u	69.64	2573.91	153.28	6413.92
Bits lost from $r_p^{C_s}$, $loss_p$	3.29	0.09312	3.54	0.08663
Bits lost from $r_u^{C_s}$, $loss_u$	3.14	0.093	3.46	0.08658
Final bit security	113.17	119.81	256 (271)	256 (277.82)

Remark 4. Note that the security loss values for our analysis in Table 6 correspond to the maximum measured over 1,000 instances. This constitutes a conservative estimate, and we are therefore confident that for the majority of FALCON trapdoor bases, the actual reduction loss will not exceed the reported values. For a completely proven assurance, one can add some checks in the key generation to guarantee the used basis achieving the security bounds.

5 On the Provable Security of FALCON^{WS}

Despite its better compactness and higher bit security, the lack of a formal proof based on standard assumptions is seen as a major limitation of FALCON^{WS}.

Driven by this, we investigate how large the closeness parameter ϵ can be to allow for a formal proof relying exclusively on standard hardness assumptions while maintaining the advantage of FALCON^{WS} in terms of size. To this end, we extend the Rényi divergence-based analysis in [FGdG+26] to the weak smoothness setting and present a security proof for FALCON^{WS}. Building upon the improved analysis of the RO simulation, i.e. a tighter bound on the smoothing parameter of NTRU lattices (Theorem 3), together with a key lemma in [ZJR+25] (Lemma 9), we figure out the maximal ϵ allowing for a formal proof solely on standard assumptions. As a result, we present new parameters for FALCON^{WS} to support provable security on standard assumption while offering 17.8% (resp. 12.8%) smaller signature sizes compared to FALCON-512 (resp. FALCON-1024).

Theorem 5 characterizes the plain unforgeability of FALCON^{WS}, in which the Rényi term $r_p^{C_s} = 1$ due to the use of the rejection sampling.

Theorem 5 (Unforgeability of FALCON^{WS}**, Adapted from**[FGdG+26]**).** *For any adversary* A *against the* **UF-CMA** *security of* FALCON^{WS} *running in time* t_{A}*, making at most* Q_s *signing queries and* Q_{H} *RO queries, there exist adversary* B *against* $(Q_{\mathsf{H}}+1)$-$\mathcal{R}$-**ISIS** *running in time* $t_{\mathsf{B}} \approx t_{\mathsf{A}}$ *such that for all* $C_s \in \mathbb{N}^{\geq 1}$ *and* $a_u, a_p \in \mathbb{R}^{>1}$ *it holds*

$$\mathsf{Adv}^{Q_s\text{-}\mathbf{UF\text{-}CMA}}_{\text{FALCON}^+,\mathsf{A}} \leq \left(r_u^{C_s} \cdot \mathsf{Adv}^{(Q_{\mathsf{H}}+1)\text{-}\mathcal{R}\text{-}\mathbf{ISIS}}_{1,q,\alpha,\beta,\mathsf{B}}\right)^{\frac{a_u-1}{a_u}}$$
$$+\sum_{i=0}^{Q_s}\binom{C_s}{i}(1-p_{\mathsf{PreSmp},\beta})^{C_s-i}(p_{\mathsf{PreSmp},\beta})^i + \frac{Q_s(C_s+Q_{\mathsf{H}})}{2^k},$$

where

$p_{\mathsf{PreSmp},\beta} = \max_{(\mathbf{B},\cdot)\in\mathsf{TpdGen},c\in\mathcal{R}_q} \Pr_{(s_1,s_2)\leftarrow\mathsf{PreSmp}(\mathbf{B},s,(c,0))}[\|(s_1,s_2)\|_2 \leq \beta]$,
$r_u = \max_{(\cdot,h)\in\mathsf{TpdGen}} R_{a_u}(\mathcal{P} \,\|\, \mathcal{Q}_h)$ *with* $\mathcal{P} = \mathcal{U}(\mathcal{R}_q)$ *and* $\mathcal{Q}_h$ *the distribution of* $s_1 + s_2 \cdot h \mod q$*, where* $s_1, s_2 \sim D_{\mathcal{R},s}$
$r_p = \max_{(\mathbf{B},\cdot)\in\mathsf{TpdGen},c\in\mathcal{R}_q} R_{a_p}(\mathsf{PreSmp}(\mathbf{B},s,(c,0)) \,\|\, \mathcal{D}_{\Lambda(\mathbf{B}),s,(c,0)})$.

As per Theorem 5, for the original FALCON^{WS}-512 and FALCON^{WS}-1024 proposed in [ZJR+25], the security loss becomes prohibitively large. To get provably secure parameters, it suffices to consider the Rényi loss $r_u = R_{a_u}(\mathcal{U}(\mathcal{R}_q) \,\|\, \mathcal{Q}_h)$ from RO simulation. Lemma 9 shows a generic bound on the Rényi divergence.

Lemma 9 ([ZJR+25]). *Let* Λ *and* Λ' *be full-rank lattices with* $\Lambda' \subseteq \Lambda$*. For any* $a \in (1,\infty)$*,* $\epsilon \in (0,1)$*, and* $s \in \mathbb{R}$ *such that* $\sqrt{2}s \geq \eta_\epsilon(\Lambda')$ *and* $s \geq \sqrt{2}\cdot\eta_{\epsilon'}(\Lambda)$*, it holds that*

$$R_a(\mathcal{U}(\Lambda/\Lambda') \,\|\, D_{\Lambda,s,\mathbf{c}} \bmod \Lambda') \lesssim 1 + \frac{a(\epsilon+4\epsilon')}{2}.$$

Applying Lemma 9 on $\Lambda = \mathbb{Z}^{2n}$ and $\Lambda_{h,q}$ along with FALCON^{WS} parameters, the term ϵ' is sufficiently small to be safely ignored, and the corresponding values of ϵ are computed to be 2^{-82} for FALCON^{WS}-512 and 2^{-84} for FALCON^{WS}-1024, respectively. This results in a tighter bound for the Rényi divergence with respect to the RO simulation.

To optimize the overall Rényi loss term in Theorem 5, we propose to increase the value of ϵ under the constraint that the resulting security loss remains bounded by a predefined threshold. Then, by leveraging the basis-specific smoothing parameter analysis introduced in Theorem 3, we are able to determine the actual (larger) ϵ that equivalently satisfies the required condition from the previous step.

Table 7 shows the experimental results on 1,000 instances under different ϵ. Since rejection sampling eliminates the security loss from the sampler and simultaneously enhances the concrete security of the underlying $\mathcal{R}$-ISIS problem, the forgery security maintains redundancy. Consequently, for FALCON^{WS}-512 we select $\epsilon = 2^{-23.5}$, corresponding to a security loss of approximately 11 bits, while for FALCON^{WS}-1024 we choose $\epsilon = 2^{-21.5}$, yielding a security loss of about 45 bits. These parameter sets allows for a formal security proof solely on standard assumptions.

Table 7. Bit loss $loss_u$ from $r_u^{C_s}$. Numbers are measured over 1,000 instances. The term (A, B) represents the maximum and mean of security loss respectively.

ϵ of $\eta_\epsilon(\mathbb{Z}^{2n})$	FALCON^{WS}-512	FALCON^{WS}-1024
$2^{-21.5}$	(48.50, 24.20)	(44.60, 27.60)
$2^{-22.5}$	(23.55, 11.56)	(21.68, 13.25)
$2^{-23.3}$	(13.22, 6.41)	(10.54, 6.36)

Table 8 shows our new parameter set for FALCON^{WS} with provable security. The provably secure FALCON^{WS} removes the additional non-standard assumption required by original FALCON^{WS}. Compared to FALCON, it reduces 20% (resp. 13.7%) bandwidth (public key plus signature) for the NIST level I (resp. V).

Table 8. New parameter sets for FALCON^{WS} with provable security.

Parameter	Description	NIST-I	NIST-V
n	Degree of ring $\mathcal{R}$	512	1024
q	Modulus	2048	4096
ϵ	Closeness parameter	$2^{-23.3}$	$2^{-21.5}$
σ	Standard deviation	58.11	81.21
τ	Tailcut rate	1.1	
β	Max. signature norm bound	2045.45	4042.91
$\lvert\mathsf{pk}\rvert$	PK size in bytes	704	1536
$\lvert\mathsf{sig}\rvert$	Estimated signature size in bytes	547	1115
λ	Key Rec. / Forg. security	134 / 128	273 / 295
a_p	Optimal Rényi order of sampler	—	—
a_u	Optimal Rényi order of RO simulation	19.43	13.24
$loss_p$	Bits lost from $r_p^{C_s}$	0	
$loss_u$	Bits lost from $r_u^{C_s}$	13	44.6
Final bit security		115	250

6 Refined Analysis of Strong Unforgeability

The analysis in [GJK24] indicates that FALCON offers no meaningful security guarantee for strong unforgeability. This limitation stems directly from that the original security proof relies on a reduction to the $\mathcal{R}$-SIS problem with a solution norm bound 2β. This bound comes from the triangle inequality:

$$\|(s_1^* - s_1, s_2^* - s_2)\| \leq \|(s_1^*, s_2^*)\| + \|(s_1, s_2)\| \leq 2\beta$$

for the forgery signature (s_1^*, s_2^*) and the simulated signature (s_1, s_2). While this bound is always correct, it is overly pessimistic and leads to severe consequences for concrete security:

- For FALCON$^+$-512, this yields a security loss of approximately 25 bits compared to plain unforgeability (with bound β)
- For FALCON$^+$-1024, the value 2β exceeds the modulus q, rendering the corresponding $\mathcal{R}$-SIS instance trivial and the security guarantee meaningless.

This issue was resolved in the updated version [FGdG+26] by introducing a non-standard assumption. In contrast, we improve the concrete security analysis for strong unforgeability by deriving a tighter norm bound and a parameter optimization method.

6.1 A Tighter Norm Bound

We propose a refined, probabilistic analysis that replaces the worst-case bound of 2β with a tighter, average-case bound of $\sqrt{2}\beta$. The rationale stems from the concentration of measure phenomena in high-dimensional spaces, which implies that randomly chosen vectors are, with high probability, nearly orthogonal.

Lemma 10. *Let $\mathcal{L} \subset \mathbb{R}^m$ be a lattice, $s \geq \eta_\epsilon(\mathcal{L})$ with $0 < \epsilon < 1$, $\beta := \tau\sqrt{m}\frac{s}{\sqrt{2\pi}}$ and $c > 0$ with $\tau^2(c^2-1) > 1$. Given $\mathbf{w} \in \mathcal{L}+\mathbf{t}$ with $\|\mathbf{w}\| \leq \beta$, let $\mathbf{v} \leftarrow D_{\mathcal{L}+\mathbf{t},s}$. Then for any $0 < \alpha < \frac{\tau^2\cdot(c^2-1)-1}{2}$,*

$$\Pr[\|\mathbf{v}-\mathbf{w}\| \leq c\beta] \geq 1 - \left(2e^{-\frac{\alpha^2 m}{2\cdot\tau^2}} + 2\left(\left((c^2-1)\cdot\tau^2 - 2\alpha\right)e\right)^{m/2} \cdot e^{-\frac{\left((c^2-1)\cdot\tau^2-2\alpha\right)m}{2}}\right)\cdot\frac{1+\epsilon}{1-\epsilon}$$

Proof. For any $t > 0$, it holds that

$$\begin{aligned}\Pr[\|\mathbf{v}-\mathbf{w}\| \geq c\cdot\beta] &= \Pr[\|\mathbf{v}-\mathbf{w}\|^2 \geq c^2\cdot\beta^2] \\ &= \Pr[\|\mathbf{v}\|^2 - 2\langle\mathbf{v},\mathbf{w}\rangle + \|\mathbf{w}\|^2 \geq c^2\cdot\beta^2] \\ &\leq \Pr[\|\mathbf{v}\|^2 - 2\langle\mathbf{v},\mathbf{w}\rangle \geq (c^2-1)\cdot\beta^2] \\ &= \Pr[\|\mathbf{v}\|^2 - 2\langle\mathbf{v},\mathbf{w}\rangle \geq (c^2-1)\cdot\beta^2 \wedge \langle\mathbf{v},\mathbf{w}\rangle \leq -t] \\ &\quad + \Pr[\|\mathbf{v}\|^2 - 2\langle\mathbf{v},\mathbf{w}\rangle \geq (c^2-1)\cdot\beta^2 \wedge \langle\mathbf{v},\mathbf{w}\rangle l \geq -t] \\ &\leq \Pr[\langle\mathbf{v},\mathbf{w}\rangle l \leq -t] + \Pr[\|\mathbf{v}\|^2 \geq (c^2-1)\cdot\beta^2 - 2t].\end{aligned}$$

By Lemma 4,

$$\Pr[\langle \mathbf{v}, \mathbf{w}\rangle l \leq -t] \leq \Pr[|\langle \mathbf{v}, \mathbf{w}\rangle| \geq t] \leq 2e^{-\pi \frac{t^2}{\|\mathbf{w}\|^2 s^2}} \cdot \frac{\rho_s(\Lambda)}{\rho_s(\Lambda + \mathbf{t})} \leq 2e^{-\pi \frac{t^2}{\|\mathbf{w}\|^2 s^2}} \cdot \frac{1+\epsilon}{1-\epsilon}.$$

By Lemma 5, for $\left(c^2 - 1\right) \cdot \beta^2 - 2t > \frac{ms^2}{2\pi}$ it follows that

$$\Pr[\|\mathbf{v}\|^2 \geq \left(c^2 - 1\right) \cdot \beta^2 - 2t] \leq 2C^m \cdot \frac{\rho_s(\Lambda)}{\rho_s(\Lambda + \mathbf{w})} \leq 2C^m \cdot \frac{1+\epsilon}{1-\epsilon}.$$

with $C = \sqrt{\frac{(c^2-1)\cdot\beta^2-2t}{ms^2}}\sqrt{2\pi e} \cdot e^{-\pi \frac{(c^2-1)\cdot\beta^2-2t}{ms^2}}$. By setting $t = \alpha \cdot \frac{ms^2}{2\pi}$ for any $0 < \alpha < \frac{\tau^2\cdot(c^2-1)-1}{2}$, then

$$\begin{aligned}
\Pr[\|\mathbf{v} - \mathbf{w}\| \geq c \cdot \beta] &\leq \Pr[\langle \mathbf{v}, \mathbf{w}\rangle l \leq -t] + \Pr[\|\mathbf{v}\|^2 \geq \left(c^2 - 1\right) \cdot \beta^2 - 2t] \\
&\leq \left(2e^{-\pi \frac{t^2}{\|\mathbf{w}\|^2 s^2}} + 2C^m\right) \cdot \frac{1+\epsilon}{1-\epsilon} \\
&\leq \left(2e^{-\frac{\alpha^2 m}{2\cdot\tau^2}} + 2\left(\left((c^2-1)\cdot\tau^2 - 2\alpha\right)e\right)^{m/2} \cdot e^{-\frac{\left((c^2-1)\cdot\tau^2-2\alpha\right)m}{2}}\right) \cdot \frac{1+\epsilon}{1-\epsilon}.
\end{aligned}$$

□

Theorem 6 (Strong Unforgeability, Adapted from[GJK24]). *For any adversary* A *against the* **SUF-CMA** *security of* FALCON$^+$ *running in time* t_A*, making at most* Q_s *signing queries and* Q_H *RO queries, there exist adversary* B *against* $\mathcal{R}$-**SIS** *running in time* $t_\mathsf{B} \approx t_\mathsf{A}$ *such that for all* $C_s \in \mathbb{N}^{\geq 1}$, $L \in [Q_\mathsf{H} + 1]$ *and* $a_u, a_p \in \mathbb{R}^{>1}$ *it holds*

$$\begin{aligned}
\mathsf{Adv}^{Q_s\text{-}\mathbf{SUF\text{-}CMA}}_{\text{COREFALCON}^+,\mathsf{A}} \leq& \frac{(Q_\mathsf{H}+1)}{L \cdot p_{\mathsf{PreSmp},\beta}} \left(r_u^{C_s+L} \cdot \left(r_p^{C_s+1} \cdot \left(\frac{1}{t} \cdot \mathsf{Adv}^{\mathcal{R}\text{-}\mathbf{SIS}}_{1,q,\alpha,c\beta,\mathsf{B}} + \frac{1}{2^{n-1}}\right)\right)^{\frac{a_p-1}{a_p}}\right)^{\frac{a_u-1}{a_u}} \\
&+ \sum_{i=0}^{Q_s} \binom{C_s}{i} (1 - p_{\mathsf{PreSmp},\beta})^{C_s - i} (p_{\mathsf{PreSmp},\beta})^i + \frac{Q_s(C_s + Q_\mathsf{H})}{2^k},
\end{aligned}$$

where

t is the lower bound established in Lemma 10,
$p_{\mathsf{PreSmp},\beta} = \max_{(\mathbf{B},\cdot)\in\mathsf{TpdGen}, c\in\mathcal{R}_q} \Pr_{(s_1,s_2)\leftarrow\mathsf{PreSmp}(\mathbf{B},s,(c,0))}[\|(s_1, s_2)\|_2 \leq \beta]$,
$r_u = R_{a_u}(\mathcal{P} \,\|\, \mathcal{Q}_h)$ *with* $\mathcal{P} = \mathcal{U}(\mathcal{R}_q)$ *and* $\mathcal{Q}_h$ *the distribution of* $s_1 + s_2 \cdot h$ mod q, *where* $s_1, s_2 \sim D_{\mathcal{R},s}$ *and* $(\cdot, h) \in \mathsf{TpdGen}$
$r_p = R_{a_p}(\mathsf{PreSmp}(\mathbf{B}, s, (c, 0)) \,\|\, \mathcal{D}_{\Lambda(\mathbf{B}),s,(c,0)})$ *with* $(\mathbf{B}, \cdot) \in \mathsf{TpdGen}$.

Proof. The proof largely follows Theorem 1 in [GJK24], with two modifications. First, the Rényi divergences r_p and r_u are defined relative to the specific public key h, rather than using their upper bounds as in [GJK24]. Second, we adjust the reduction from the $\mathcal{R}$-SIS problem to Game G_8 in the final step.

Consider the sequence of games defined in Fig. 7.

Game G_0. This is the strong unforgeability game for CoreFalcon$^+$ so by definition we have $\Pr[G_0^{\mathsf{A}} \Rightarrow 1] = \mathsf{Adv}^{Q_s\text{-}\mathbf{SUF\text{-}CMA}}_{\textsc{CoreFalcon}^+,\mathsf{A}}$.

Game G_1. This game is identical to the previous one, except that it aborts if the overall number of sampled preimages in the signing oracle, i.e. including potential repetitions, exceeds threshold C_s.

Claim. For $p_{\mathsf{PreSmp},\beta} = \max_{c \in \mathcal{R}_q} \Pr_{(s_1,s_2) \leftarrow \mathsf{PreSmp}(\mathbf{B},s,(c,0))}[\|(s_1,s_2)\|_2 \leq \beta]$ it holds that

$$\left|\Pr[G_0^{\mathsf{A}} \Rightarrow 1] - \Pr[G_1^{\mathsf{A}} \Rightarrow 1]\right| \leq \sum_{i=0}^{Q_s} \binom{C_s}{i} (1 - p_{\mathsf{PreSmp},\beta})^{C_s - i} (p_{\mathsf{PreSmp},\beta})^i.$$

Proof. To proof the claim, we model the experiment using a binomial distributed random variable $X \sim B(C_s, p_{\mathsf{PreSmp},\beta})$, i.e. we have C_s Bernoulli trials and success probability $p_{\mathsf{PreSmp},\beta}$. A trial corresponds to sampling a preimage using PreSmp in the signing oracle and the trial succeeds if the norm is sufficiently small, i.e. $\|(s_1,s_2)\|_2 \leq \beta$. Hence, the random variable, counting the overall number of successes in the Bernoulli trials, tells us the number of signing queries we are able to answer. Since we need to answer Q_s signing queries, we are interested in the CDF for value Q_s, i.e. $\Pr[X < Q_s]$ which is exactly the claim.

□

Game G_2. This game is identical to the previous one except that it aborts in the signing oracle Sgn if there already exists a query to the RO on the same public key, salt r, and message m. To ease the depiction in further hybrids, we define a new RO H' maintaining the same set $\mathcal{H}$ as H but aborting in case of a query on the same input as a previous query. Oracle H' is then called within the signing oracle instead of H.

Claim. $\left|\Pr[G_1^{\mathsf{A}} \Rightarrow 1] - \Pr[G_2^{\mathsf{A}} \Rightarrow 1]\right| \leq \frac{Q_s(C_s+Q_{\mathsf{H}})}{2^k}$.

Proof. The salt r is chosen uniformly at random from $\{0,1\}^k$ for each signing query. The total number of elements in $\mathcal{H}$ is at most $C_s + Q_{\mathsf{H}}$, as at most one element is added per query to H and there are C_s implicit queries via Sgn and Q_{H} direct ones. Thus, the probability that the freshly chosen salt was part of a previous query is at most $\frac{C_s+Q_{\mathsf{H}}}{2^k}$. For Q_s queries to the signing oracle Sgn, we obtain the claimed bound. □

Game G_3. This game is identical to the previous one except that the game computes a preimage of c^* with respect to h using the preimage sampler PreSmp with trapdoor $\mathbf{B}$. If the norm of the resulting preimage (s_1', s_2') is larger than β, the game aborts.

Claim. $\Pr[G_2^{\mathsf{A}} \Rightarrow 1] = (p_{\mathsf{PreSmp},\beta})^{-1} \cdot \Pr[G_3^{\mathsf{A}} \Rightarrow 1]$

Proof. The probability that the abort does not trigger is $p_{\mathsf{PreSmp},\beta}$. Since the preimage is computed after adversary A outputs their forgery and the winning condition is not affected by (s_1', s_2'), the abort event is independent of A's winning probability. Hence we can apply the multiplicative difference lemma to obtain the statement. □

Games $G_0 - G_7$

$\mathcal{H}, \mathcal{Q} \leftarrow \emptyset$
$cnt, l \leftarrow 0$
choose random $\mathcal{S} \subset [Q_{\mathsf{H}} + 1]$ such that $|\mathcal{S}| = L$ // $G_4 - G_7$
$(\mathbf{B}, h) \leftarrow \mathsf{Gen}$
$(\mathsf{m}^*, \mathsf{sig}^*) \leftarrow \mathsf{A}^{\mathsf{Sgn}(\cdot), \mathsf{H}(\cdot,\cdot,\cdot)}(h)$
parse $\mathsf{sig}^* \to (\mathsf{r}^*, s_2^*)$
$c^* \leftarrow \mathsf{H}(h, \mathsf{r}^*, \mathsf{m}^*)$ // $G_3 - G_7$
$(s_1', s_2') \leftarrow \mathsf{PreSmp}(\mathbf{B}, s, (c^*, 0))$ // $G_3 - G_7$
$(s_1', s_2') \leftarrow D_{\Lambda(\mathbf{B}), s, (c^*, 0)}$ // $G_6 - G_7$
find (s_1', s_2') *s.t.* $(c^*, h, \mathsf{r}^*, \mathsf{m}^*, \cdot, s_1', s_2') \in \mathcal{H}$ // G_7
if $\|(s_1, s_2)\| > \beta$ // $G_3 - G_7$
  abort // $G_3 - G_7$
find l^* *s.t.* $(c^*, h, \mathsf{r}^*, \mathsf{m}^*, l^*, \cdot, \cdot) \in \mathcal{H}$ // $G_4 - G_7$
if $l^* \notin \mathcal{S} \wedge l^* \neq \bot$ // $G_4 - G_7$
  abort // $G_4 - G_7$
$s_1^* = c^* - s_2^* \cdot h \bmod q$
return $[\![\mathsf{Verify}(h, \mathsf{m}^*, \mathsf{sig}^*) = 1 \wedge (\mathsf{m}^*, \mathsf{sig}^*) \notin \mathcal{Q}]\!]$

Oracle $\mathsf{Sgn}(\mathsf{m})$

repeat
  $cnt \leftarrow cnt + 1$ // $G_1 - G_7$
  if $cnt > C_s$ // $G_1 - G_7$
    abort // $G_1 - G_7$
  $\mathsf{r} \leftarrow \{0,1\}^k$
  $c = \mathsf{H}(h, \mathsf{r}, \mathsf{m})$ // $G_0 - G_1$
  $(c, s_1, s_2) \leftarrow \mathsf{H}'(h, \mathsf{r}, \mathsf{m})$ // $G_2 - G_7$
  $(s_1, s_2) \leftarrow \mathsf{PreSmp}(\mathsf{sk}, s, (c, 0))$ // $G_0 - G_5$
  $(s_1, s_2) \leftarrow D_{\Lambda(\mathbf{B}), s, (c, 0)}$ // G_6
until $\|(s_1, s_2)\| \leq \beta$
$\mathsf{sig} \leftarrow (\mathsf{r}, s_2)$
$\mathcal{Q} \leftarrow \mathcal{Q} \cup \{(\mathsf{m}, \mathsf{sig})\}$
return sig

Oracle $\mathsf{H}'(h, \mathsf{r}, \mathsf{m})$

if $\exists\, c$ *s.t.* $(c, h, \mathsf{r}, \mathsf{m}, \cdot, \cdot, \cdot) \in \mathcal{H}$
  abort
$c \leftarrow \mathcal{R}_q$
$(s_1, s_2) \leftarrow (\bot, \bot)$
$s_1, s_2 \leftarrow D_{\mathcal{R}, s}$ // $G_5 - G_7$
$c \leftarrow s_1 + s_2 \cdot h \bmod q$ // $G_5 - G_7$
$\mathcal{H} \leftarrow \mathcal{H} \cup \{(c, h, \mathsf{r}, \mathsf{m}, \bot, s_1, s_2)\}$
return (c, s_1, s_2)

Oracle $\mathsf{H}(h, \mathsf{r}, \mathsf{m})$

if $\exists\, c$ *s.t.* $(c, h, \mathsf{r}, \mathsf{m}, \cdot, \cdot, \cdot) \in \mathcal{H}$
  return c
$c \leftarrow \mathcal{R}_q$
$(s_1, s_2) \leftarrow (\bot, \bot)$
$l \leftarrow l + 1$
if $l \in \mathcal{S}$ // $G_5 - G_7$
  $s_1, s_2 \leftarrow D_{\mathcal{R}, s}$ // $G_5 - G_7$
  $c \leftarrow s_1 + s_2 \cdot h \bmod q$ // $G_5 - G_7$
$\mathcal{H} \leftarrow \mathcal{H} \cup \{(c, h, \mathsf{r}, \mathsf{m}, l, s_1, s_2)\}$
return c

Fig. 7. Games for the proof of Theorem 6.

Game G_4. This game is identical to the previous one except for the following changes. For a fixed integer $L \in [Q_\mathsf{H}+1]$, we choose a random subset $\mathcal{S} \subset [Q_\mathsf{H}]$ with $|\mathcal{S}| = L$. For every query to H, we record the query number l and the game abort if the the RO query of the forgery corresponds to a query to H and the query number l^* is not in S.

Claim. $\Pr[G_3^\mathsf{A} \Rightarrow 1] = \frac{Q_\mathsf{H}+1}{L} \cdot \Pr[G_4^\mathsf{A} \Rightarrow 1]$

Proof. First note that the probability of an abort is independent of the winning probability in G_3 since set $\mathcal{S}$ is not used anywhere else and hence does not influence the winning probability. The game does not abort if the challenge RO query corresponds to a signing query (case $l^* = \perp$) but only to a direct RO query. Since $\mathcal{S}$ is of fixed size L, we can apply the multiplicative difference lemma and obtain the claim. □

Game G_5. This game is the same as the previous one, except that the RO H' no longer returns a uniformly random element $c \leftarrow \mathcal{R}_q$. Instead, it computes c as follows: It samples two elements s_1, s_2 from $D_{\mathcal{R},s}$. Then, c is computed as $c = s_1 + s_2 \cdot h \mod q$, where h is the public key. For future use, s_1, s_2, along with the input and output to the RO, are stored in $\mathcal{H}$. This procedure is also applied in H if the query number l is in $\mathcal{S}$.

Claim. For $h \in \mathcal{R}$, let $\mathcal{P} = \mathcal{U}(\mathcal{R}_q)$ and $\mathcal{Q}_h$ be the distribution of $s_1 + s_2 \cdot h \mod q$ where $s_1, s_2 \leftarrow D_{\mathcal{R},s}$. Then, for any $a_u \in (1, \infty)$,

$$\Pr[G_4^\mathsf{A} \Rightarrow 1] \leq \left(R_{a_u}(\mathcal{P} \,||\, \mathcal{Q}_h)^{C_s} \cdot \Pr[G_5^\mathsf{A} \Rightarrow 1]\right)^{\frac{a_u-1}{a_u}}$$

Proof. Define two underlying distributions for a $(Q+1)$-tuple of random variables $(c_0 = (\mathbf{B}, h), c_1, \ldots, c_Q)$.

$\bar{\mathcal{P}}$	$\bar{\mathcal{Q}}$
$(\mathbf{B}, h) \xleftarrow{s} \mathsf{TpdGen}$	$(\mathbf{B}, h) \xleftarrow{s} \mathsf{TpdGen}$
for $i \in [Q]$	**for** $i \in [Q]$
$\quad c_i \xleftarrow{s} \mathcal{R}_q$	$\quad (s_1, s_2) \leftarrow D_{\mathcal{R},s}$
return $((\mathbf{B}, h), c_1, \ldots, c_Q)$	$\quad c_i = s_1 + s_2 \cdot h \mod q$
	return $((\mathbf{B}, h), c_1, \ldots, c_Q)$

These distributions describe the underlying distributions of G_4 and G_5. By the data processing inequality it holds that, for any $a \in (1, \infty)$,

$$R_a(G_4 \,||\, G_5) \leq R_a(\bar{\mathcal{P}} \,||\, \bar{\mathcal{Q}}).$$

Let the marginal distribution of c_i be denoted by $\bar{\mathcal{P}}_i$ ($\bar{\mathcal{Q}}_i$ resp.) and the distribution of c_i conditioned on $c_{<i} = (c_0, \ldots, c_{i-1})$ as $\bar{\mathcal{P}}_{i|c_{<i}}$ ($\bar{\mathcal{Q}}_{i|c_{<i}}$ resp.). Since the distribution of $c_0 = (\mathbf{B}, h)$ is the same for $\bar{\mathcal{P}}$ and $\bar{\mathcal{Q}}$, it holds that

$$R_a(\bar{\mathcal{P}}_0 \,||\, \bar{\mathcal{Q}}_0) = 1.$$

For the conditional distributions, note that random variable c_i is independent of the previous random variables $c_1, \ldots, c_{i-1}$. However, c_i might depend on h and thus on random variable $c_0 = (\mathbf{B}, h)$. Hence for all $i \in [Q+1]$,

$$\begin{aligned} R_a(\bar{\mathcal{P}}_{i|c_{<i}} \,||\, \bar{\mathcal{Q}}_{i|c_{<i}}) &= R_a(\bar{\mathcal{P}}_{i|(c_0,\ldots,c_{i-1})} \,||\, \bar{\mathcal{Q}}_{i|(c_0,\ldots,c_{i-1})}) \\ &= R_a(\mathcal{P} \,||\, \bar{\mathcal{Q}}_{i|c_0}) \\ &= R_a(\mathcal{P} \,||\, \mathcal{Q}_h), \end{aligned}$$

where $\mathcal{P} = \mathcal{U}(R_q)$ and $\mathcal{Q}_h$ the distribution of $s_1 + s_2 \cdot h \mod q$ where $s_1, s_2 \leftarrow D_{R,s}$. Note that h does not occur in distribution $\mathcal{P}$ because the individual random variables c_i (for $i \geq 1$) are independent of h. It then follows that

$$R_a(\bar{\mathcal{P}} \,||\, \bar{\mathcal{Q}}) \leq R_a(\mathcal{P} \,||\, \mathcal{Q}_h)^Q.$$

Finally, we obtain

$$\Pr[G_5^{\mathsf{A}} \Rightarrow 1] \geq \frac{\Pr[G_4^{\mathsf{A}} \Rightarrow 1]^{\frac{a}{a-1}}}{R_a(G_4 \,||\, G_5)} \geq \frac{\Pr[G_4^{\mathsf{A}} \Rightarrow 1]^{\frac{a}{a-1}}}{R_a(\mathcal{P} \,||\, \mathcal{Q}_h)^Q}.$$

The claim follows by setting $Q = C_s$ due to at most C_s queries from Sgn to the RO.

Game G_6. This game is identical to the previous one except that the output of the preimage sampler $\mathsf{PreSmp}(\mathbf{B}, s, (c, 0))$ is replaced by a Gaussian over the same lattice, standard deviation and center, namely $D_{\Lambda(\mathbf{B}),s,(c,0)}$.

Claim. For distributions $\mathsf{PreSmp} = \mathsf{PreSmp}(\mathbf{B}, s, (c, 0))$, $D = D_{\Lambda(\mathbf{B}),s,(c,0)}$, and $a_p \in (1, \infty)$ it holds that

$$\Pr[G_5^{\mathsf{A}} \Rightarrow 1] \leq \left(R_{a_p}(\mathsf{PreSmp} \,||\, D)^{C_s} \cdot \Pr[G_6^{\mathsf{A}} \Rightarrow 1]\right)^{\frac{a_p-1}{a_p}}.$$

Proof. The claim follows analogously to Game G_5.

Game G_7. This game is identical to the previous one except that s_1, s_2 are not sampled from a Gaussian distribution centred at $(c, 0)$ as before. Instead, the preimage of c that was sampled in the RO is used.

Claim. $\Pr[G_6^{\mathsf{A}} \Rightarrow 1] = \Pr[G_7^{\mathsf{A}} \Rightarrow 1]$.

Proof. We need to show that the distributions of the games are the same. The RO output c is the same in both games. In G_6, the signing oracle outputs $(s_1, s_2) \sim D_{\Lambda(\mathbf{B}),s,(c,0)}$. Since $\Lambda(\mathbf{B})$ is the NTRU lattice for h and q and the distribution is shifted by $(c, 0)$ the output is distributed according to a Gaussian $D_{\mathcal{R},s}$ conditioned on $s_1 + s_2 \cdot h = c \mod q$. The output distribution in Game G_7 is a Gaussian $D_{\mathcal{R},s}$ as well where the condition $s_1 + s_2 \cdot h = c \mod q$ is fulfilled by construction.

Game G_8. This game is identical to the previous one except that the game aborts if s_1^*, s_2^* corresponding to the adversary's output equals the preimage with which the challenge RO output c^* was computed and the message/signature pair is not in $\mathcal{Q}$.

Claim. $|\Pr[G_7^{\mathsf{A}} \Rightarrow 1] - \Pr[G_8^{\mathsf{A}} \Rightarrow 1]| \leq \frac{1}{2^{n-1}}$.

Proof. We distinguish two cases: first, the adversary queried the signing oracle corresponding to c^*, i.e., a signing query to m^* output $(r^*, \cdot)$ and $\mathsf{H}(h, r^*, m^*) = c^*$. In this case, the abort event cannot trigger because if the preimages are the same, the signature must be the same as well. Second, if the signing oracle was not queried corresponding to c^*, the adversary does not have any information about the preimages of c^* except that they are Gaussian distributed. Hence, we obtain the claimed upper bound by using the min-entropy of a sample from a Gaussian distribution conditioned on c^* from Lemma 3.

Reduction from $\mathcal{R}$-**SIS** to G_8. We now can reduce $\mathcal{R}$-**SIS** to Game G_8.

Claim. There exists an adversary B against $\mathcal{R}$-SIS such that

$$\Pr[G_8^{\mathsf{A}} \Rightarrow 1] \leq \frac{1}{t} \cdot \mathsf{Adv}_{1,q,\alpha,c\beta,\mathsf{B}}^{\mathcal{R}\text{-}\mathbf{SIS}},$$

where t is the lower bound established in Lemma 10.

Proof. Due to the changes in the previous games, adversary B can perfectly simulate the game for adversary A against G_8 without having the secret key for h. Assume that A wins the strong unforgeability game G_8, i.e. the forgery verifies and the tuple (m^*, sig^*) was not queried before. It implies that the output $(s_1^* - s_1', s_2^* - s_2')$ of adversary B fulfills the following conditions. First, it holds that

$$(s_1^* - s_1') + (s_2^* - s_2')h = 0.$$

Second, it cannot equal 0 due to the changes in G_8. Third, by Lemma 10, $\Pr[E] > t$, where E denote the event that $\|(s_1^* - s_1', s_2^* - s_2')\| \leq c\beta$. Then we have

$$\begin{aligned} \mathsf{Adv}_{1,q,\alpha,c\beta,\mathsf{B}}^{\mathcal{R}\text{-}\mathbf{SIS}} &= \Pr[\mathsf{B} \text{ solves } \mathcal{R}\text{-}\mathbf{SIS}] = \Pr[G_8^{\mathsf{A}} \Rightarrow 1 \wedge E] \\ &= \Pr[G_8^{\mathsf{A}} \Rightarrow 1] \cdot \Pr[E] \\ &\geq \Pr[G_8^{\mathsf{A}} \Rightarrow 1] \cdot t. \end{aligned}$$

This completes the proof. □

Remark 5. If we fix $\tau = 1.1$ and $c = \sqrt{2}$, then for Falcon-512, $\epsilon = 2^{-35.5}, \alpha = 0.055$ and the computed probability lower bound is 0.2627, meaning at most 2 bits of security loss for our tighter norm bound $\sqrt{2}\beta$. Similarly, for Falcon-1024, $\epsilon = 2^{-36}, \alpha = 0.062$ and the computed probability lower bound is 0.867, meaning at most 1 bits of security loss. With this new bound, we can obviously improve the SUF-CMA security. More importantly, the new bound satisfies $\sqrt{2}\beta < q$, which renders the strong unforgeability guarantee for Falcon-1024 meaningful. The estimated SUF-CMA security of Falcon with bound $\sqrt{2}\beta$ is shown is Table 9.

Table 9. SUF-CMA security of FALCON.

	FALCON-512	FALCON-1024
SUF-CMA	107	251

Remark 6. Building upon the refined Rényi divergence analysis established in Sect. 4, we demonstrate that increasing ϵ can also enhance the SUF-CMA security of FALCON. However, even with our improved analysis in Theorem 2, the Rényi loss term r_p grows rapidly with ϵ, limiting the extent to which ϵ can be increased. Consequently, the resulting security improvement remains modest, where $\epsilon \approx 2^{-32}$. In the next subsection, we present a $\text{FALCON}^{\text{WS}}$ variant specifically optimized for SUF-CMA security. Since its sampler introduces no Rényi loss, this variant offers greater flexibility in parameter adjustment,

6.2 New $\text{FALCON}^{\text{WS}}$ Parameters with SUF-CMA Security

Directly tightening the norm bound from 2β to $\sqrt{2}\beta$ already provides an obvious enhancement for FALCON-type signature's strong unforgeability. In this subsection we present a new parameter set for $\text{FALCON}^{\text{WS}}$ with SUF-CMA security.

In addition to the refined Rényi divergence analysis established in Sect. 4 and the tighter norm bound of $\sqrt{2}\beta$, we further observe that the Rényi loss in Theorem 6 is not optimal for FALCON parameters. Specifically, we can further tighten the reduction by co-optimizing ϵ and the auxiliary parameter L, a technique originating from [BRTZ24] and employed in [FGdG+26], for which we present an optimized strategy for its selection.

Our approach aims to balance the multiplicative factor in the security reduction:

$$\frac{Q_{\mathsf{H}}}{L} \cdot r_u^{C_s+L} \cdot r_p^{C_s}.$$

By carefully increasing ϵ, we drive this factor close to Q_{H}, thereby ensuring that the first and last terms in the advantage expression $\mathsf{Adv}^{Q_s\text{-}\mathbf{SUF\text{-}CMA}}_{\text{COREFALCON}^+,\mathsf{A}}$ become nearly optimal under concrete parameter settings. This optimization allows us to achieve a tight security proof while maintaining practical signature size and security levels, as demonstrated in our experimental evaluation in Table 10.

Remark 7. It should be noted that although the security loss $loss_u$ for both parameter sets significantly exceeds 1 bit, we emphasize that this reduction loss does not ultimately compromise the overall security guarantee. This is because the multiplicative prefactor Q_{H}/L of the first term in $\mathsf{Adv}^{Q_s\text{-}\mathbf{SUF\text{-}CMA}}_{\text{COREFALCON}^+,\mathsf{A}}$ effectively compensates for approximately $\log(L) = 55$ or 56 bits of security. That is, through careful parameter tuning, we ensure that the value of the first term in the advantage expression $\mathsf{Adv}^{Q_s\text{-}\mathbf{SUF\text{-}CMA}}_{\text{COREFALCON}^+,\mathsf{A}}$ remains strictly smaller than the third one, thereby rendering the observed reduction loss inconsequential to the final security level.

Table 10. A FALCON^{WS} variant targeting SUF-CMA security.

Parameter	Description	NIST-I	NIST-V
n	Degree of ring $\mathcal{R}$	512	1024
q	Modulus	4096	8192
ϵ	Closeness parameter	$2^{-21.5}$	
σ	Standard deviation	79.993	114.86
τ	Tailcut rate	1.1	
$\sqrt{2}\beta$	Max. signature norm bound	3982.1	8085.8
$\lvert \mathsf{pk} \rvert$	PK size in bytes	768	1664
$\lvert \mathsf{sig} \rvert$	Estimated signature size in bytes	576	1179
λ	Key Rec. / Strong Forg.	134 / 114	273 / 265
L	Number of programmed RO queries	2^{55}	2^{56}
a_p	Optimal Rényi order of sampler	—	—
a_u	Optimal Rényi order of RO simulation	5.23	12.55
$loss_p$	Bits lost from $r_p^{C_s}$	0	
$loss_u$	Bits lost from $r_u^{C_s}$	45.52	42.29
Final bit security		114	265

Acknowledgments. We would like to thank the anonymous reviewers for helpful comments and suggestions. This work is supported by the National Cryptologic Science Fund of China (2025NCSF01004), the National Natural Science Foundation of China (12441104, 12571572, 62502259), Beijing Natural Science Foundation (L254054) and the Guangzhou Science and Technology Plan Project (2025A03J0121). Fundamental and Interdisciplinary Disciplines Breakthrough Plan of the Ministry of Education of China (JYB2025XDXM114).

References

[Ban93] Banaszczyk, W.: New bounds in some transference theorems in the geometry of numbers. Math. Ann. **296**(1), 625–635 (1993)

[Ban95] Banaszczyk, W.: Inequalities for convex bodies and polar reciprocal lattices in R^n. Discrete Comput. Geometry **13**, 217–231 (1995)

[BDF+11] Boneh, D., Dagdelen, O., Fischlin, M., Lehmann, A., Schaffner, C., Zhandry, M.: Random oracles in a quantum world. In: ASIACRYPT (2011)

[BLL+15] Bai, S., Langlois, A., Lepoint, T., Stehlé, D., Steinfeld, R.: Improved security proofs in lattice-based cryptography: using the Rényi divergence rather than the statistical distance. In: ASIACRYPT (2015)

[BRTZ24] Bellare, M., Riepel, D., Tessaro, S., Zhang, Y.: Count corruptions, not users: improved tightness for signatures, encryption and authenticated key exchange. In: ASIACRYPT (2024)

[CPS+20] Chuengsatiansup, C., Prest, T., Stehlé, D., Wallet, A., Xagawa, K.: Mod-Falcon: compact signatures based on module-NTRU lattices. In: ASI-ACCS 20

[DLP14] Ducas, L., Lyubashevsky, V., Prest, T.: Efficient identity-based encryption over NTRU lattices. In: ASIACRYPT (2014)

[DP16] Ducas, L., Prest, T.: Fast fourier orthogonalization. In: ISSAC (2016)

[EFG+22] Espitau, T., et al.: A simpler, parallelizable, maskable variant of falcon. In: EUROCRYPT, Mitaka (2022)

[ENS+23] Espitau, T., Quyen Nguyen, T.T., Sun, C., Tibouchi, M., Wallet, A.: Antrag: annular NTRU trapdoor generation - making mitaka as secure as falcon. In: ASIACRYPT (2023)

[ETWY22] Espitau, T., Tibouchi, M., Wallet, A., Yu, Y.: Shorter hash-and-sign lattice-based signatures. In: CRYPTO (2022)

[FGdG+26] Fouque, P., Gajland, P., de Groote, H., Janneck, J., Kiltz, E.: A closer look at falcon. Eurocrypt 2026 (to appear)

[GHN06] Gama, N., Howgrave-Graham, N., Nguyen, P.Q.: Symplectic lattice reduction and NTRU. In: EUROCRYPT (2006)

[GJK24] Gajland, P., Janneck, J., Kiltz, E.: A closer look at falcon. Cryptology ePrint Archive, Paper 2024/1769, version 20250226:153603 (2024)

[GPV08] Gentry, C., Peikert, C., Vaikuntanathan, V.: Trapdoors for hard lattices and new cryptographic constructions. In: STOC (2008)

[LDK+22] Lyubashevsky, V., et al.: CRYSTALS-DILITHIUM. Technical report, National Institute of Standards and Technology (2022). https://csrc.nist.gov/Projects/post-quantum-cryptography/selected-algorithms-2022

[LTYZ25] Lin, X., Tibouchi, M., Yu, Y., Zhang, S.: Do not disturb a sleeping falcon - floating-point error sensitivity of the falcon sampler and its consequences. In: EUROCRYPT (2025)

[MR07] Micciancio, D., Regev, O.: Worst-case to average-case reductions based on gaussian measures. SIAM J. Comput. **37**(1), 267–302 (2007)

[MW17] Micciancio, D., Walter, M.: Gaussian sampling over the integers: efficient, generic, constant-time. In: CRYPTO (2017)

[PFH+22] Prest, T., et al.: FALCON. Technical report, National Institute of Standards and Technology (2022). https://csrc.nist.gov/Projects/post-quantum-cryptography/selected-algorithms-2022

[Pre17] Prest, T.: Sharper bounds in lattice-based cryptography using the Rényi divergence. In: ASIACRYPT (2017)

[ZJR+25] Zhang, S., Jia, H., Ran, D., Yu, Y., Yu, Y., Wang, X.: GPV preimage sampling with weak smoothness and its applications to lattice signatures. In: ASIACRYPT (2025)

Optimized G+G Signature

Renjie Jin , Shuoqu Jian, and Longjiang Qu(✉)

College of Science, National University of Defense Technology, Changsha 410073, China
ljqu_happy@hotmail.com

Abstract. At ASIACRYPT 2023, Devevey, Passelègue and Stehlé proposed the G+G signature, which is designed based on the Fiat-Shamir transform without rejection sampling technique. However, the optimization of the G+G signature have not been studied as extensively as those of Lyubashevsky-type signatures.

The contribution of this work is the integration of the Asymmetric Learning with Errors (ALWE) problem into the key generation phase of the G+G signature. We present a more precise estimation method for the largest singular value of the secret key and introduce a new non-spherical Gaussian distribution to characterize the signature distribution. Experimental results demonstrate that, under parameters ensuring the same security level, our optimized G+G variant reduces the signature size by approximately 25%.

Keywords: Lattice signature · Asymmetric LWE · Discrete Gaussian

1 Introduction

Lattice-based cryptography stands as one of the most pivotal cryptographic primitives in the post-quantum era. Among its core components, lattice-based signatures have emerged as a central research topic. Currently, existing lattice-based signature schemes can be broadly categorized into two classes based on their design paradigms: Hash-and-Sign [11] and the Fiat-Shamir transform [14]. The former heavily relies on discrete Gaussian sampling over lattice cosets, with major advancements typically arising from improvements in lattice trapdoors and optimizations of Gaussian samplers [2,9,19]. The latter, primarily employing the rejection sampling technique [6,15] to support the compactness of signature size, achieves optimization mainly through enhancements in the underlying source distribution [3] and the application of rejection strategies [10]. In 2023, Devevey et al. [5] proposed a rejection-free Fiat-Shamir signature, which is regarded as a promising new direction in this branch, particularly as the so-called "noise flooding" technique fails to produce signatures with compact parameters. However, the construction of G+G signatures remains high-level. While its signature size is competitive compared to known schemes [2,6,7,19], there is significant room for improvement since the underlying spherical Gaussian distribution is not the optimal distribution for constructing signatures with compact size.

S. Bai and E. Persichetti (Eds.): PKC 2026, LNCS 16551, pp. 364–392, 2026.
https://doi.org/10.1007/978-3-032-26731-3_12

1.1 Our Contributions

In this work, we integrate the *Asymmetric Learning with Errors* (ALWE) problem into the key setting of the G+G signature, leveraging the asymmetry of key distribution combined with signature truncation techniques to output signatures with smaller size. Specifically, we propose new method for estimating the largest singular values of the secret key and introduce a new type of non-spherical Gaussian distribution to achieve fine-grained control over Gaussian parameters. Experimental results demonstrate that the size of our new optimized signature is reduced by approximately 25% compared to the original G+G signature (at the same security level). Moreover, we analyze the security of the ALWE problem using an enhanced security evaluation model to ensure the practical security of the new signature scheme.

1.2 Technique Overview

Our goal is to optimize the size of the G+G signature. Specifically, we seek to do this without modifying the idea of signing processing, so as to preserve the original security reduction. To this end, we transform the signature distribution from a spherical Gaussian to a non-spherical one. In G+G signature [5], the secret key $\mathbf{S} \leftarrow (\mathbf{I}_l \mid \mathbf{S}_1^\top \mid \mathbf{S}_2^\top)^\top \in \mathbb{Z}^{k\times l}$, where $(\mathbf{S}_1, \mathbf{S}_2) \hookleftarrow \chi^{(k-m-l)\times \ell} \times \chi^{m\times l}$ and χ is a probability distribution. Let $\sigma, s \geq 0$ and define $\Sigma(\mathbf{S}) : \mathbb{Z}^{k\times \ell} \to \mathbb{R}^{k\times k}$ as

$$\Sigma(\mathbf{S}) : \mathbf{S} \mapsto \sigma^2 \mathbf{I}_k - 4\, s^2 \mathbf{S}\mathbf{S}^\top.$$

The signature follows the distribution $\mathcal{D}_{\mathbb{Z}^k,\sigma}$, where the parameter σ is chosen such that $\Sigma(\mathbf{S})$ is publicly sampleable and while maintaining sufficient "smoothness" over the lattice $2\mathbf{S}\mathbb{Z}^k$ to enable signature simulation in the security reduction. Therefore, the lower bound for σ is critically determined by the largest singular value of $\mathbf{S}$. Consequently, optimizing the structure of $\mathbf{S}$ to reduce this bound serves as an effective approach for minimizing the signature size.

Step 1: Asymmetric Secret Key Setting.
We sample $(\mathbf{S}_1, \mathbf{S}_2) \hookleftarrow \chi_1^{(k-m-l)\times \ell} \times \chi_2^{m\times l}$ where χ_1, χ_2 are the same distribution but have different standard deviations, with χ_1 being the narrower one. At this point, the key pair is set as follows

$$\begin{aligned} \mathsf{pk} :&= \mathbf{A} \leftarrow (q\mathbf{J} - 2\mathbf{B} \mid 2\mathbf{A}_1 \mid 2\mathbf{I}_m) \in \mathbb{Z}_{2q}^{m\times k}, \\ \mathsf{sk} :&= \mathbf{S} \leftarrow (\mathbf{I}_l \mid \mathbf{S}_1^\top \mid \mathbf{S}_2^\top)^\top \in \mathbb{Z}^{k\times l}, \end{aligned}$$

where $\mathbf{B} \leftarrow \mathbf{A}_1\mathbf{S}_1 + \mathbf{S}_2 \bmod q$ and $\mathbf{J}$ is a gadget. The security of the keys is guaranteed by the computational indistinguishability between the ALWE distribution [20] and the uniform distribution.

Step 2: New Signature Distribution: A New Non-spherical Gaussian.
We compress the signature distribution from a spherical Gaussian into a non-spherical one with a well-defined shape. The primary goal is to eliminate the

redundancy in the standard deviation inherent in the original spherical Gaussian distribution of G+G signature, enabling further compression of the signature size along certain dimensions. Specifically, our improvement lies in the construction of the covariance matrix $\Sigma(\mathbf{S})$, we set

$$\Sigma(\mathbf{S}) = \begin{bmatrix} \sigma_1^2 \cdot \mathbf{I}_l & & \\ & \sigma_2^2 \cdot \mathbf{I}_{k-m-l} & \\ & & \sigma_3^2 \cdot \mathbf{I}_m \end{bmatrix} - 4\,s^2 \left[\mathbf{I}_l, \mathbf{S}_1^\top, \mathbf{S}_2^\top\right]^\top \left[\mathbf{I}_l, \mathbf{S}_1, \mathbf{S}_2\right].$$

Our goal is to find lower bounds for σ_i $(i = 1, 2, 3)$ ensuring the positive semi-definiteness of $\Sigma(\mathbf{S})$[1]. Notably, the structure of $\mathbf{S}\mathbf{S}^\top$ allows for a significant reduction in σ_1, which is tied to the identity matrix component. This analysis requires examining the impact of $\mathbf{S}_1$ and $\mathbf{S}_2$—sampled from the same distribution with varying parameters—on the singular values.

Remark 1. From the perspective of reducing the value of σ_1 in $\Sigma(\mathbf{S})$, the ellipsoidal Gaussian distribution proposed in [13] has already achieved this. The purpose of employing an asymmetrically distributed secret key in this work is to further optimize the ellipsoidal Gaussian distribution, which requires integrating the signature truncation technique introduced by Bai et al. [1]. By narrowing the distribution width of $\mathbf{S}_1$ while increasing the distribution parameter of $\mathbf{S}_2$, we can ensure the security of the secret key. Meanwhile, by leveraging the signature truncation technique, we can effectively reduce the size of the G+G signature. This will be discussed in more detail later.

Step 3: Bound on the Largest Singular Value of S. The structure of our secret key $\mathbf{S}$ makes directly estimating the largest singular value of $\mathbf{S}\mathbf{S}^\top$ challenging. Therefore, we opt to transform the problem into the context of an ellipsoidal Gaussian distribution. Specifically, we introduce a scaling factor $t := \sigma_2/\sigma_3$ between σ_2 and σ_3, and systematically explore a limited range of values for t through experimental means. This approach allows us to approximate simulate the target non-spherical Gaussian parameters $(\sigma_1, \sigma_2, \sigma_3)$ using the ellipsoidal Gaussian parameters $(\sigma_1, \sigma_2, \sigma_2/t)$. Concretely, for the simulatability of signature we require

$$\Sigma(\mathbf{S}) = \begin{bmatrix} \sigma_1^2 \cdot \mathbf{I}_l & & \\ & \sigma_2^2 \cdot \mathbf{I}_{k-m-l} & \\ & & \sigma_3^2 \cdot \mathbf{I}_m \end{bmatrix} - 4\,s^2\mathbf{S}\mathbf{S}^\top \geq 4\,s^2\mathbf{S}\mathbf{S}^\top.$$

Here, $\Sigma(\mathbf{S}) \geq 4s^2\mathbf{S}\mathbf{S}^\top$ implies that $\Sigma(\mathbf{S}) - 4s^2\mathbf{S}\mathbf{S}^\top$ is a positive semi-definite matrix. A routine calculation shows that

$$\begin{bmatrix} \sigma_1^{-2} \cdot \mathbf{I}_l & & \\ & \sigma_2^{-2} \cdot \mathbf{I}_{k-m-l} & \\ & & \sigma_3^{-2} \cdot \mathbf{I}_m \end{bmatrix} \cdot \mathbf{S}\mathbf{S}^\top < (8\,s^2)^{-1}\mathbf{I}_k.$$

[1] Indeed, we should also determine the lower bounds for σ_i that ensure $\Sigma(\mathbf{S})$ is smooth over the lattice $2\mathbf{S}\mathbb{Z}^k$.

Setting $t = \sigma_2/\sigma_3$, we obtain

$$\begin{bmatrix} \sigma_1^{-1} \cdot \mathbf{I}_l & & \\ & \sigma_2^{-1} \cdot \mathbf{I}_{k-m-l} & \\ & & \sigma_3^{-1} \cdot \mathbf{I}_m \end{bmatrix} \sqrt{\mathbf{S}\mathbf{S}^\top} = \mathrm{diag}(\sigma_1^{-1}\mathbf{I}_l, \sigma_2^{-1}\mathbf{S}_1^\top, \sigma_2^{-1} \cdot t \cdot \mathbf{S}_2^\top)^\top.$$

Defining $\mathbf{S}_{\text{new}} = (\mathbf{S}_1^\top, t \cdot \mathbf{S}_2^\top)$, we deduce that

$$\begin{bmatrix} \sigma_1^{-1} \cdot \mathbf{I}_l & & \\ & \sigma_2^{-1} \cdot \mathbf{I}_{k-m-l} & \\ & & \sigma_3^{-1} \cdot \mathbf{I}_m \end{bmatrix} \sqrt{\mathbf{S}\mathbf{S}^\top} = \begin{pmatrix} \sigma_1^{-1}\mathbf{I}_l & \\ & \sigma_2^{-1}\mathbf{I}_{k-l} \end{pmatrix} (\mathbf{I}_l, \mathbf{S}_{\text{new}}^\top)^\top.$$

Experimental results indicate that exploring only a small range of values for t is sufficient to estimate the largest singular value of $\mathbf{S}\mathbf{S}^\top$ with reasonable accuracy.

Step 4: Truncate the Signature. Based on the public key setting of G+G signature, during signature verification, the portion corresponding to $\mathbf{S}_1$ occupies the high-order bits of the signature, while $\mathbf{S}_2$ occupies the low-order bits. We can typically truncate the lower bits of the signature, storing the information of the low-order bits in the form of a hint, and subsequently recover them in the verification algorithm. According to the structure of our secret key, $\mathbf{S}_1$ has a narrower distribution, while $\mathbf{S}_2$ has a wider distribution. Truncating the signature segment corresponding to $\mathbf{S}_2$ neither compromises the security of the signature scheme nor increases its size - instead, it further reduces the signature size relative to LWE-based secret key settings.

1.3 Related Work

Lattice Signatures. The first secure lattice-based signature scheme following the Hash-and-Sign paradigm was introduced by Gentry, Peikert, and Vaikuntanathan [11]. Their seminal work systematically resolved the issue of secret key leakage in prior trapdoor sampling techniques. Subsequently, Micciancio and Peikert [16] proposed the notion of gadget-based trapdoors, which substantially enhanced the efficiency of lattice-based trapdoor mechanisms while offering practical implementability and inherent parallelism. Chen et al. [2] generalized exact gadget trapdoors to an approximate variant, enabling its use in practical lattice signature schemes. Espitau et al. [9] proposed the range Asymmetric Numeral Systems (rANS) encoding mechanism as a means of signature compression, tackling the size reduction problem from a distinct perspective. Jia et al. [13] and Yu et al. [19] further optimized gadget trapdoors and preimage samplers to achieve near-optimal performance, with the latter presenting the most compact construction under this paradigm to date.

Lattice-based signatures following the Fiat-Shamir paradigm were first introduced by Lyubashevsky [14], who proposed the signature scheme on lattices using rejection sampling techniques. Later, Lyubashevsky [15] further refined this approach by employing Gaussian distributions, establishing a general framework for signature simulation based on rejection sampling mechanisms. Ducas et al. [6] proposed an efficient bimodal Gaussian distribution, which reduced rejection rates while optimizing signature size. The work of Devevey et al. [3,4] not only revealed potential issues in the security analysis of rejection sampling in Lyubashevsky-type signatures but also demonstrated that the bimodal Gaussian distribution is the optimal source distribution for such schemes. Subsequently, they proposed a rejection-free Fiat-Shamir signature [5] based on Gaussian convolution techniques, while a comprehensive security analysis opens up new possibilities for efficiency improvements in this signature paradigm. Recently, Gartner [10] achieved significant signature size reduction through an iterative rejection sampling strategy, resulting in the most compact Fiat-Shamir signature construction to date.

Roadmap. This paper is organized as follows. Section 2 introduces the necessary definitions and foundational results. Section 3 presents an analysis of the G+G signature scheme and introduces its optimized construction. Section 4 concludes the paper. Related details for evaluating the hardness of asymmetric problems are provided in the Appendix.

2 Notations and Preliminaries

We fixed some marks throughout the paper. Assuming $\mathbb{R}$ denotes the field of real numbers, $\mathbb{Z}$ denotes the ring of integers. For positive integer q, $\mathbb{Z}/q\mathbb{Z}$ denotes the ring of integers modulo q. Let $[n] := \{1, \cdots, n\}$. We denote by the negligible function $f(n)$ (or $negl(n)$), if it decreases faster than the reciprocal of any polynomial function $g(n)$. Assuming $\log n$ denotes the logarithm to the base 2. Matrices and vectors are represented using bold fonts, for example, matrix $\mathbf{A}$ and vector $\mathbf{a}$. The notation $(\mathbf{A} \mid \mathbf{B})$ and $(\mathbf{A}, \mathbf{B})$ both denote matrix concatenation. We use $\sigma_1(\mathbf{A})$ to denote the largest singular value of $\mathbf{A}$. For vectors $\mathbf{a}, \mathbf{b}$, denote by $\mathbf{a}^\top \mathbf{b}$ (or $< \mathbf{a}, \mathbf{b} >$) the Euclidean inner product of $\mathbf{a}$ and $\mathbf{b}$. For a set of vectors $\mathbf{B} := \{\mathbf{b}_1, \cdots, \mathbf{b}_t\}$ in $\mathbb{R}^m$, denote by $||\mathbf{b}_i||$ the l_2-norm of $\mathbf{b}_i$ $(1 \leq i \leq t)$ and

$$||\mathbf{B}|| := \max_{i \in \{1, \cdots, t\}} ||\mathbf{b}_i||$$

the l_2-norm of the matrix $\mathbf{B}$.

Let $\mathcal{C}$ be a PPT (probabilistic polynomial time) algorithm. $\mathbf{t} \leftarrow \mathcal{C}(\mathbf{s})$ means that the random variable $\mathbf{t}$ is the output of $\mathcal{C}$ with input $\mathbf{s}$ and some random values. Write vector $\mathbf{s} \hookleftarrow \mathcal{D}$ if $\mathbf{s}$ is sampled from $\mathcal{D}$ at random with distribution $\mathcal{D}$. $\mathbf{s} \sim \mathcal{D}$ denotes that $\mathbf{s}$ follows the distribution $\mathcal{D}$. We use $\mathcal{U}(\mathbb{Z}_q)$ to represent the uniform distribution over $\mathbb{Z}_q$. We denote $\Sigma > 0$ ($\Sigma \geq 0$) when a symmetric matrix $\Sigma \in \mathbb{R}^{m \times m}$ is (semi-) positive definite, i.e., $\mathbf{x}^t \Sigma \mathbf{x} > 0$ ($\mathbf{x}^t \Sigma \mathbf{x} \geq 0$) for all nonzero $\mathbf{x} \in \mathbb{R}^m$. We write $\Sigma_1 \geq \Sigma_2$ if $\Sigma_1 - \Sigma_2 \geq 0$.

2.1 Lattice and Discrete Gaussian

Given a linearly independent vectors set $\mathbf{S} := \{\mathbf{s}_1, \mathbf{s}_2, \cdots, \mathbf{s}_n\} \subset \mathbb{R}^m$, define lattice $\Lambda(\mathbf{S})$ generated from $\mathbf{S}$ as

$$\Lambda(\mathbf{S}) := \left\{ \mathbf{x} \in \mathbb{R}^m \mid \mathbf{x} = \sum_{i=1}^{n} d_i \mathbf{s}_i \text{ where } d_i \in \mathbb{Z} \right\}.$$

When $n = m$, we call the lattice a full-rank lattice.

For positive integer q and public matrix $\mathbf{S} \in \mathbb{Z}_q^{n \times m}$, define the following q-ary lattices and a lattice coset:

$$\Lambda_q(\mathbf{S}) := \{\mathbf{x} \in \mathbb{Z}^m \mid \exists \mathbf{t} \in \mathbb{Z}_q^n \ s.t. \ \mathbf{S}^\top \mathbf{t} = \mathbf{x} \ (\text{mod } q)\},$$

$$\Lambda_q^\perp(\mathbf{S}) := \{\mathbf{x} \in \mathbb{Z}^m \mid \mathbf{S}\mathbf{x} = \mathbf{0} \ (\text{mod } q)\},$$
$$\Lambda_q^\mathbf{u}(\mathbf{S}) := \{\mathbf{x} \in \mathbb{Z}^m \mid \mathbf{S}\mathbf{x} = \mathbf{u} \ (\text{mod } q)\}.$$

We introduce the definition of Gaussian function $\rho(\mathbf{x}) = \exp(-\pi\langle \mathbf{x}, \mathbf{x}\rangle)$ maps from $\mathbb{R}^n$ to $(0, 1]$ where $\mathbf{x} \in \mathbb{R}^n$. Given an invertible matrix $\mathbf{A} \in \mathbb{R}^{n \times n}$, the Gaussian function associate with $\mathbf{A}$ is defined as

$$\rho_\mathbf{A}(\mathbf{x}) = \exp(-\pi \mathbf{x}^\top \Sigma^{-1} \mathbf{x}),$$

where $\Sigma = \mathbf{A}\mathbf{A}^\top$. For a lattice Λ with dimension n, the discrete Gaussian distribution over Λ is defined as:

$$\mathcal{D}_{\Lambda, \sqrt{\Sigma}, \mathbf{c}}(\mathbf{x}) := \frac{\rho_{\sqrt{\Sigma}}(\mathbf{x})}{\rho_{\sqrt{\Sigma}}(\Lambda + \mathbf{c})},$$

where $\mathbf{c} \in \text{span}(\Lambda)$. In this work, we use σ to denote the standard deviation of a discrete Gaussian distribution and omit $\mathbf{c}$ if $\mathbf{c} = \mathbf{0}$. Unless otherwise specified, let $\mathcal{D}_{\mathbb{Z}^{n \times m}, \sigma}$ denote the distribution obtained by independently sampling m integer vectors from $\mathcal{D}_{\mathbb{Z}^n, \sigma}$ and viewing them as the columns of a matrix in $\mathbb{Z}^{n \times m}$.

Definition 1 (Smooth Parameter). *For lattice Λ and any real $\epsilon > 0$, the smoothing parameter $\eta_\epsilon(\Lambda)$ is the smallest real $\sigma > 0$ such that $\rho(\sigma \cdot \Lambda^*) \leq 1 + \epsilon$ where Λ^* is the dual lattice of Λ.*

2.2 Lattice Assumptions

We introduce LWE problem, which is proposed by Regev [17]. LWE problem is typically defined by parameters n, m, q, and χ. Among these parameters, χ is usually instantiated as a discrete Gaussian distribution.

Definition 2 (LWE). *Let $n, m, q > 0$ be integers. For secret $\mathbf{s} \in \mathbb{Z}_q^n$, the LWE distribution over $\mathbb{Z}_q^n \times \mathbb{Z}_q$ is defined as $A_{\mathbf{s},\alpha} := (\mathbf{a}, \mathbf{a}^\top \mathbf{s} + e)$ where $\mathbf{a} \leftarrow \mathcal{U}(\mathbb{Z}_q^n)$ and $e \hookleftarrow \chi_\alpha$ with standard deviation α.*

- *Search-LWE$_{n,m,q,\chi}$: Given m independent samples from $A_{\mathbf{s},\alpha}$, find* $\mathbf{s}$.
- *Decision-LWE$_{n,m,q,\chi}$: Given m independent samples either chosen from $A_{\mathbf{s},\alpha}$ or $\mathcal{U}(\mathbb{Z}_q^n \times \mathbb{Z}_q)$, distinguish which is the case.*

Definition 3 ([20],Asymmetric-LWE(ALWE)). *Let $n, m, q, \alpha_1, \alpha_2 > 0$ be integers with $\alpha_1 \neq \alpha_2$. Suppose $\mathbf{A} \leftarrow \mathcal{U}(\mathbb{Z}_q^{n\times m})$, $\mathbf{s} \hookleftarrow \chi_{\alpha_1}^m$ and $\mathbf{e} \hookleftarrow \chi_{\alpha_2}^n$.*

- *Search-ALWE$_{n,m,q,\alpha_1,\alpha_2}$: Given sample $(\mathbf{A}, \mathbf{A}\mathbf{s} + \mathbf{e}) \in \mathbb{Z}_q^{n\times m} \times \mathbb{Z}_q^n$, find* $\mathbf{s}$.
- *Decision-ALWE$_{n,m,q,\alpha_1,\alpha_2}$: Distinguish $(\mathbf{A}, \mathbf{A}\mathbf{s} + \mathbf{e})$ and uniform over $\mathbb{Z}_q^{n\times m} \times \mathbb{Z}_q^n$.*

Moreover, we can similarly define the asymmetric Module-LWE (AMLWE) problem by extending this asymmetric setting to the module lattice case. Nonetheless, the relationship below holds for our parameter choices with respect to all known solving algorithms despite the absence of a general proof

$$\mathrm{LWE}_{n,m,q,\min(\alpha_1,\alpha_2)} \preceq \mathrm{ALWE}_{n,m,q,\alpha_1,\alpha_2} \preceq \mathrm{LWE}_{n,m,q,\max(\alpha_1,\alpha_2)}.$$

We introduce Short Integer Solution (SIS) and Inhomogeneous SIS (ISIS) problems.

Definition 4 (SIS and ISIS). *Let n, m, q be positive integers and real $\beta > 0$. We introduce the following two problems:*

- *SIS$_{n,m,q,\beta}$: Given a uniformly random matrix $\mathbf{A} \in \mathbb{Z}_q^{n\times m}$, find a non-zero vector $\mathbf{x} \in \mathbb{Z}^m$ which satisfies $\mathbf{A}\mathbf{x} = \mathbf{0} \mod q$ and $\|\mathbf{x}\| < \beta$.*
- *ISIS$_{n,m,q,\beta}$: Given a uniformly random matrix $\mathbf{A} \in \mathbb{Z}_q^{n\times m}$, a uniformly random $\mathbf{u} \in \mathbb{Z}_q^n$, find a vector $\mathbf{x} \in \mathbb{Z}^m$ which satisfies $\mathbf{A}\mathbf{x} = \mathbf{u} \mod q$ and $\|\mathbf{x}\| < \beta$.*

Definition 5 ([20], Asymmetric-SIS (ASIS) and Asymmetric-ISIS (AISIS)). *Let n, m_1, m_2, q be positive integers and $\beta_1, \beta_2 > 0$ be distinct real numbers. We introduce the following two problems:*

- *ASIS$_{n,m_1,m_2,q,\beta_1,\beta_2}$: Given a uniformly random matrix $\mathbf{A} \in \mathbb{Z}_q^{n\times(m_1+m_2)}$, find a non-zero vector $\mathbf{x} := (\mathbf{x}_1, \mathbf{x}_2) \in \mathbb{Z}^{m_1} \times \mathbb{Z}^{m_2}$ which satisfies $\mathbf{A}\mathbf{x} = \mathbf{0} \mod q$ and $\|\mathbf{x}_1\| < \beta_1$, $\|\mathbf{x}_2\| < \beta_2$.*
- *AISIS$_{n,m_1,m_2,q,\beta_1,\beta_2}$: Given a uniformly random matrix $\mathbf{A} \in \mathbb{Z}_q^{n\times(m_1+m_2)}$, a uniformly random $\mathbf{u} \in \mathbb{Z}_q^n$, find a vector $\mathbf{x} := (\mathbf{x}_1, \mathbf{x}_2) \in \mathbb{Z}^{m_1} \times \mathbb{Z}^{m_2}$ which satisfies $\mathbf{A}\mathbf{x} = \mathbf{u} \mod q$ and $\|\mathbf{x}_1\| < \beta_1$, $\|\mathbf{x}_2\| < \beta_2$.*

We can similarly define the asymmetric Module-SIS (AMSIS) problem by extending this asymmetric setting to the module lattice case. It is straightforward to observe that ASIS$n, m_1, m_2, q, \beta_1, \beta_2$ is at least as hard as $\mathrm{SIS}_{n,m_1+m_2,q,\max(\beta_1,\beta_2)}$. Specifically, we have:

$$\mathrm{SIS}_{n,m_1+m_2,q,\max(\beta_1,\beta_2)} \preceq \mathrm{ASIS}_{n,m_1,m_2,q,\beta_1,\beta_2} \preceq \mathrm{SIS}_{n,m_1+m_2,q,\min(\beta_1,\beta_2)}.$$

2.3 Digital Signature

A *digital signature scheme* is defined by a triple of probabilistic polynomial-time (PPT) algorithms $(\mathsf{KeyGen}, \mathsf{Sign}, \mathsf{Verify})$ satisfying:

- $\mathsf{KeyGen}(1^\lambda) \to (\mathsf{pk}, \mathsf{sk})$: Takes a security parameter λ as input and outputs a public key pk and a secret key sk.
- $\mathsf{Sign}(\mathsf{sk}, \mu) \to \sigma$: Takes the secret key sk and a message μ as input, and outputs a signature σ.
- $\mathsf{Verify}(\mathsf{pk}, \mu, \sigma) \to \{0, 1\}$: Takes the public key pk, a message μ, and a signature σ as input, and outputs 1 if the signature is valid, or 0 otherwise.

Security Model: Existential Unforgeability Under Chosen-Message Attacks (EUF-CMA). A digital signature scheme achieves *EUF-CMA security* if for PPT adversary $\mathcal{A}$, the advantage $\mathsf{Adv}_{\mathcal{A}}^{\mathsf{EUF-CMA}}(\lambda)$ in the following game is negligible in the security parameter λ:

- **Setup:** The challenger runs $(\mathsf{pk}, \mathsf{sk}) \leftarrow \mathsf{KeyGen}(1^\lambda)$ and gives pk to $\mathcal{A}$.
- **Signing Queries:** $\mathcal{A}$ may adaptively query the signing oracle on messages $\mu_1, \ldots, \mu_Q$. For each query μ_i, the challenger returns $\sigma_i \leftarrow \mathsf{Sign}(\mathsf{sk}, \mu_i)$.
- **Forgery:** $\mathcal{A}$ outputs a forgery (μ^*, σ^*).
- **Success:** $\mathcal{A}$ wins if:
  - $\mathsf{Verify}(\mathsf{pk}, \mu^*, \sigma^*) = 1$,
  - and μ^* was not previously queried to the signing oracle.

The scheme is EUF-CMA secure if:

$$\mathsf{Adv}_{\mathcal{A}}^{\mathsf{EUF-CMA}}(\lambda) = \Pr[\mathcal{A} \text{ wins}] \leq \mathsf{negl}(\lambda).$$

Modulus Rounding. We utilize rounding to diminish the dimensions of public keys and signatures. Let $v \in \mathbb{N}\backslash\{0\}$. Any integer $x \in \mathbb{Z}$ can be uniquely expressed as:

$$x = 2^v \cdot x_+ + x_-, \quad (x_+, x_-) \in \mathbb{Z} \times [-2^{v-1}, 2^{v-1} - 1],$$

the method essentially involves separating the lower-order bits from the higher-order ones. We define the function $[\cdot]_v : \mathbb{Z} \to \mathbb{Z}$ such that $[x]_v = \lfloor x/2^v \rceil = x_+$, where $\lfloor \cdot \rceil : \mathbb{R} \to \mathbb{Z}$ denotes the rounding operator. More specifically, the "rounding half-up" method is used, where $[x] = \lfloor x + 0.5 \rfloor$ and half-way values are rounded up. With a slight abuse of notation, when $q > 2^v$, we extend $[\cdot]_v$ to accept inputs in $\mathbb{Z}_q$, assuming the output is an element in $\mathbb{Z}_{q_v}$, where $q_v = \lfloor q/2^v \rceil$. Formally, we define:

$$[\cdot]_v : \mathbb{Z}_q \mapsto \mathbb{Z}_{q_v} = \mathbb{Z}_{\lfloor q/2^v \rceil} \text{ such that } [x]_v = \lfloor x/2^v \rceil \mod q_v = (x)_+ \mod q_v$$

where $x \in \mathbb{Z}_q$ is assumed to have a representative integer in $\{0, \ldots, q-1\}$. The function $[\cdot]_v$ naturally extends to vectors component-wise.

We also recall a useful lemma from [8] to bound the offset introduced by rounding.

Lemma 1. *Let v, q be positive integers such that $q > 2^v, v \geq 4$, and set $q_v = \lfloor q/2^v \rceil$. Moreover, assume that $q_v = \lfloor q/2^v \rfloor$, i.e., q can be decomposed as $q = 2^v \cdot q_v + q_\perp$ with $q_\perp \in [0, 2^{v-1} - 1]$. Then, for any $x \in \mathbb{Z}_q$, we have*

$$|x - 2^v \cdot [x]_v| \leq 2^v - 1$$

Moreover, for any $\mathbf{x}, \boldsymbol{\delta} \in \mathbb{Z}_q^n$, we have

$$\|2^v \cdot (\lfloor \mathbf{x} + \boldsymbol{\delta} \rceil_v - \lfloor \mathbf{x} \rceil_v)\| \leq \|2^v \cdot \lfloor \boldsymbol{\delta} \rceil_v \mod q\| + \|\mathbf{1}\| \cdot 2^v$$

3 Asymmetric G+G: More Compact Signature Scheme Based on Asymmetric LWE

In this section, we propose an efficient variant of the G+G signature that achieves a smaller signature size by leveraging the signature truncation technique from [1]. Specifically, we introduce ALWE in the key generation algorithm. Through an analysis of the largest singular value of the covariance matrix of the perturbation vector, we (experimentally) derive tighter lower bounds for the Gaussian parameters, which allow us to further reduce the standard deviation of the signature distribution, resulting in a more compact signature.

Description of G+G Scheme. We first introduce the G+G protocol as well as some notations. Let $m \geq \ell > 0, k > m + \ell$ and $\mathbf{J} := (\mathbf{I}_m \mid \mathbf{0}^{m \times (k-m)})$. Let χ be probability distribution over $\mathbb{Z}$. Define the challenge space $\mathcal{C} \subseteq \mathbb{Z}_2^\ell$. Let $\sigma, s \geq 0$ and define $\boldsymbol{\Sigma}(\mathbf{S}) : \mathbb{Z}^{k \times \ell} \to \mathbb{R}^{k \times k}$ as

$$\Sigma(\mathbf{S}) : \mathbf{S} \mapsto \sigma^2 \mathbf{I}_k - 4\, s^2 \mathbf{S}\mathbf{S}^\top.$$

The scheme is also parametrized by an odd modulus q and an acceptance bound γ. The G+G identification protocol is described in Fig. 1.

Note that the standard deviation of the signature distribution largely depends on the covariance matrix $\Sigma(\mathbf{S})$. We first begin by analyzing the largest singular value of the secret key $\mathbf{S}$. For ease of analysis, the key is denoted as $\mathbf{S} := (\mathbf{S}_1^\top \mid \mathbf{S}_2^\top \mid \mathbf{S}_3^\top)^\top$. The covariance matrix can be written as

$$\Sigma(\mathbf{S}) = \begin{pmatrix} \Sigma_{11} & \Sigma_{12} & \Sigma_{13} \\ \Sigma_{21} & \Sigma_{22} & \Sigma_{23} \\ \Sigma_{31} & \Sigma_{32} & \Sigma_{33} \end{pmatrix} \quad \text{where } \Sigma_{ij} = \begin{cases} \sigma^2 \mathbf{I}_l - 4\, s^2 \mathbf{S}_1 \mathbf{S}_1^\top & i = j = 1; \\ \sigma^2 \mathbf{I}_{k-m-l} - 4\, s^2 \mathbf{S}_2 \mathbf{S}_2^\top & i = j = 2; \\ \sigma^2 \mathbf{I}_m - 4\, s^2 \mathbf{S}_3 \mathbf{S}_3^\top & i = j = 3; \\ -4\, s^2 \mathbf{S}_i \mathbf{S}_j^\top & i \neq j. \end{cases}$$

The Gaussian parameter σ critically influences both signature size and verification bound—the former being a key performance metric in signature schemes, and the latter a decisive factor for security against forgery attacks. To enhance both security and efficiency, we propose optimizing the Gaussian sampling by replacing the spherical Gaussian with a non-spherical distribution under otherwise identical conditions.

$\mathsf{lGen}(1^\lambda)$

1 : $\mathbf{A}_1 \hookleftarrow \mathcal{U}(\mathbb{Z}_q^{m\times(k-m-l)})$

2 : $(\mathbf{S}_1, \mathbf{S}_2) \hookleftarrow \chi^{(k-m-l)\times \ell} \times \chi^{m \times l}$

3 : $\mathbf{B} \leftarrow \mathbf{A}_1\mathbf{S}_1 + \mathbf{S}_2 \bmod q$

4 : $\mathbf{A} \leftarrow (q\mathbf{J} - 2\mathbf{B}|2\mathbf{A}_1|2\mathbf{I}_m) \in \mathbb{Z}_{2q}^{m\times k}$

5 : $\mathbf{S} \leftarrow (\mathbf{I}_l|\mathbf{S}_1^\top|\mathbf{S}_2^\top)^\top \in \mathbb{Z}^{k\times l}$

6 : $\mathrm{vk} \leftarrow \mathbf{A}, \mathrm{sk} \leftarrow \mathbf{S}$

7 : **return** (vk, sk)

$\mathsf{Prover}(\mathbf{A}, \mathbf{S})$		$\mathsf{Verifier}(\mathbf{A})$
$\mathbf{y} \hookleftarrow \mathcal{D}_{\mathbb{Z}^k, \sqrt{\Sigma(\mathbf{S})}}$ $\mathbf{w} \leftarrow \mathbf{Ay} \mod q$		
	$\xrightarrow{\mathbf{w}}$	
		$\mathbf{c} \hookleftarrow U(\mathcal{C})$
	$\xleftarrow{\mathrm{c}}$	
$\mathbf{k} \hookleftarrow \mathcal{D}_{\mathbb{Z}^l, s, -c/2}$ $\mathbf{z} \leftarrow \mathbf{y} + \mathbf{Sc} + 2\mathbf{Sk}$		
	$\xrightarrow{\mathbf{z}}$	
		Accept if $\mathbf{Az} = \mathbf{w} + q\mathbf{Jc} \mod 2q$ and$\|\mathbf{z}\| \le \gamma$

Fig. 1. G+G Protocol

Asymmetric LWE in the Key Generation. Our idea, initially proposed in [20], is simple and intuitive, though its application to the analysis of G+G signature is somewhat more involved. In simple terms, we need to modify the distributions of $\mathbf{S}_1, \mathbf{S}_2$ in the second step of the $\mathsf{lGen}(1^\lambda)$ algorithm such that they differ—namely, by *narrowing* the distribution of $\mathbf{S}_1$ while *widening* that of $\mathbf{S}_2$. For specific modifications, refer to Fig. 2. As the following analysis shows, such a adjustment not only maintains the security of the signature but also significantly reduces the signature size.

IGen'(1^λ)

1 : $\mathbf{A}_1 \hookleftarrow \mathcal{U}(\mathbb{Z}_q^{m\times(k-m-l)})$

2 : $(\mathbf{S}_1, \mathbf{S}_2) \hookleftarrow {\chi_1}^{(k-m-l)\times\ell} \times {\chi_2}^{m\times l}$ $\triangleright$ χ_1 is narrower while χ_2 is wider

3 : $\mathbf{B} \leftarrow \mathbf{A}_1\mathbf{S}_1 + \mathbf{S}_2 \bmod q$

4 : $\mathbf{A} \leftarrow (q\mathbf{J} - 2\mathbf{B}|2\mathbf{A}_1|2\mathbf{I}_m) \in \mathbb{Z}_{2q}^{m\times k}$

5 : $\mathbf{S} \leftarrow (\mathbf{I}_l|\mathbf{S}_1^\top|\mathbf{S}_2^\top)^\top \in \mathbb{Z}^{k\times l}$

6 : $\mathrm{vk} \leftarrow \mathbf{A}, \mathrm{sk} \leftarrow \mathbf{S}$

7 : **return** (vk, sk)

Fig. 2. Modified key generation algorithm

3.1 Analysis of Distribution Convolution

In this section, we analyze the general case where the last two components of the secret key $\mathbf{S} := (\mathbf{I}_l, \mathbf{S}_1, \mathbf{S}_2)$ are drawn from the same distribution but with different parameters. W.L.O.G., we assume that these two components of the $\mathbf{S}$ are sampled from discrete Gaussian distributions with different standard deviations $\hat{\sigma}_1, \hat{\sigma}_2$ since in the subsequent analysis, we only require the standard deviations of these probability distributions and will not involve further distributional properties.

In the following analysis, assume $\mathbf{S}_1 \hookleftarrow \mathcal{D}_{\mathbb{Z}^{(k-m-l)\times l}, \hat{\sigma}_1}$ and $\mathbf{S}_2 \hookleftarrow \mathcal{D}_{\mathbb{Z}^{m\times l}, \hat{\sigma}_2}$. Therefore, the distribution of the perturbation vector $\mathbf{y}$ in the signature has changed, and the modified covariance matrix is given by

$$\Sigma(\mathbf{S}) = \begin{bmatrix} \sigma_1^2 \cdot \mathbf{I}_l & & \\ & \sigma_2^2 \cdot \mathbf{I}_{k-m-l} & \\ & & \sigma_3^2 \cdot \mathbf{I}_m \end{bmatrix} - 4\, s^2 \left[\mathbf{I}_l, \mathbf{S}_1^\top, \mathbf{S}_2^\top\right]^\top [\mathbf{I}_l, \mathbf{S}_1, \mathbf{S}_2].$$

The final output signature $\mathbf{z}$ follows the distribution $\mathcal{D}_{\mathbb{Z}^k, \sqrt{\Sigma}}$ where $\Sigma = \sigma_1^2 \cdot \mathbf{I}_l \oplus \sigma_2^2 \cdot \mathbf{I}_{k-m-l} \oplus \sigma_3^2 \cdot \mathbf{I}_m$. We now only need to analyze the relationship between the largest singular values of $\mathbf{S}_1$ and $\mathbf{S}_2$ and the Gaussian parameters σ_1, σ_2, and σ_3, in order to select specific and appropriate distributions for $\mathbf{S}_1$ and $\mathbf{S}_2$ such that the standard deviation of the signature $\mathbf{z}$ distribution is minimized. To ensure the correctness of sampling the perturbation vector $\mathbf{y}$, we require its covariance matrix $\boldsymbol{\Sigma}(\mathbf{S})$ to "smooth out" the lattice $2\mathbf{S}\mathbb{Z}^k$, i.e., $\Sigma(\mathbf{S}) \geq r^2\mathbf{I}_k$ where $r := \eta_\epsilon(2\mathbf{S}\mathbb{Z}^k)$ is the smooth parameter. Starting from this condition, the following matrix should be positive semi-definite

$$\Sigma_1 = \begin{bmatrix} \sigma_1^2 \cdot \mathbf{I}_l & & \\ & \sigma_2^2 \cdot \mathbf{I}_{k-m-l} & \\ & & \sigma_3^2 \cdot \mathbf{I}_m \end{bmatrix} - 8\, s^2 \left[\mathbf{I}_l, \mathbf{S}_1^\top, \mathbf{S}_2^\top\right]^\top [\mathbf{I}_l, \mathbf{S}_1, \mathbf{S}_2] \geq 0.$$

In the following, we address the problem of estimating the largest singular value of the secret key matrix. This is essential to ensure the positive definiteness condition holds while achieving more optimal parameters σ_1, σ_2, and σ_3.

Bounds on Singular Values of Secret Key S. Due to the nonlinearity of singular values, deriving an upper bound for $\mathbf{S} = (\mathbf{I}_l \mid \mathbf{S}_1^\top \mid \mathbf{S}_2^\top)^\top$ would be non-trivial. Intuitively, the largest singular value of $\mathbf{S}$ determines the lower bound for the standard deviation of the signature distribution. To make the analysis tractable, we transform the non-spherical Gaussian case into an ellipsoidal Gaussian scenario, reducing the problem to the setting studied by Jia et al. [13].

Our core idea is to introduce a scaling factor t between σ_2 and σ_3 to reduce the number of free variables. This approach is motivated by the inherent proportionality we observe between σ_2 and σ_3. By exploring t within a bounded range, we obtain a sufficiently accurate estimation for our experimental goals, despite its potential suboptimality. A routine calculation shows that

$$\begin{bmatrix} \sigma_1^{-2} \cdot \mathbf{I}_l & & \\ & \sigma_2^{-2} \cdot \mathbf{I}_{k-m-l} & \\ & & \sigma_3^{-2} \cdot \mathbf{I}_m \end{bmatrix} \cdot \mathbf{S}\mathbf{S}^\top < (8\,s^2)^{-1}\mathbf{I}_k.$$

Setting $t = \sigma_2/\sigma_3$, we obtain

$$\begin{bmatrix} \sigma_1^{-1} \cdot \mathbf{I}_l & & \\ & \sigma_2^{-1} \cdot \mathbf{I}_{k-m-l} & \\ & & \sigma_3^{-1} \cdot \mathbf{I}_m \end{bmatrix} \sqrt{\mathbf{S}\mathbf{S}^\top} = \mathrm{diag}(\sigma_1^{-1}\mathbf{I}_l, \sigma_2^{-1}\mathbf{S}_1^\top, \sigma_2^{-1} \cdot t \cdot \mathbf{S}_2^\top)^\top.$$

Defining $\mathbf{S}_{\text{new}} = (\mathbf{S}_1^\top, t \cdot \mathbf{S}_2^\top)$, we deduce that

$$\begin{bmatrix} \sigma_1^{-1} \cdot \mathbf{I}_l & & \\ & \sigma_2^{-1} \cdot \mathbf{I}_{k-m-l} & \\ & & \sigma_3^{-1} \cdot \mathbf{I}_m \end{bmatrix} \sqrt{\mathbf{S}\mathbf{S}^\top} = \begin{pmatrix} \sigma_1^{-1}\mathbf{I}_l & \\ & \sigma_2^{-1}\mathbf{I}_{k-l} \end{pmatrix} (\mathbf{I}_l, \mathbf{S}_{\text{new}}^\top)^\top.$$

To address potential inaccuracies in singular value upper bound estimation, we follow established evaluation methods by generating a large number of random samples and computing the median singular value. In practice, we first estimate the parameter t, then compute $\sigma_1(\mathbf{S}_{\text{new}})$ via random sampling, enabling accurate singular value estimation.

Comparison with Known Gaussian-Type Distributions. At the high-level, the distribution of the signature $\mathbf{z}$ can fall into three categories: spherical Gaussian, ellipsoidal Gaussian, and the non-spherical Gaussian proposed in this work. These three cases correspond to the G+G scheme, the hash-and-sign signature scheme in [13], and our G+G variant, respectively. Moreover, our proposed distribution offers greater parametric flexibility and represents the most general case. By setting $\sigma_1 \neq \sigma_2 = \sigma_3$, the distribution reduces to an ellipsoidal Gaussian; if all σ_i are identical, it simplifies to a spherical Gaussian.

This highlights the potential of the distribution proposed in this work, as it allows us to freely adjust the *allocation* of standard deviations to meet the requirements of efficient signature scheme construction. Particularly in the context where most Fiat-Shamir type signatures nowadays employ the signature truncation technique introduced in [1], including NIST standardized signatures such as ML-DSA, extensive studies have confirmed that signature truncation does not compromise the security of the scheme, nor does it affect the integrity of the security reduction. This enables us to increase the standard deviation σ_2 while reducing σ_1, ensuring the security of the secret key (from public key) while fully truncating the part of the signature corresponding to $\mathbf{S}_2$, thereby achieving shorter signature sizes. Simultaneously, as $\mathbf{S}_1$ becomes sparser, the signature size reaches an even high level.

Indeed, if we aim to find the "narrowest" possible distribution for $\mathbf{z}$, the spherical Gaussian is not the optimal choice, as it requires the standard deviation σ of the signature distribution to satisfy $\sigma > \sqrt{8} \cdot \sigma_1(\mathbf{S}) \cdot s$, as demonstrated in the G+G scheme. While replacing the spherical Gaussian with an ellipsoidal Gaussian represents a significant improvement, it still lacks sufficient parametric flexibility in essence. In the aforementioned calculations regarding σ_i, our objective is to minimize σ_1 and σ_2 at the cost of a slight increase in σ_3, which is more compatible with signature truncation techniques. The asymmetric distribution introduced in this paper is the key to making our non-spherical distribution more efficient than the elliptical Gaussian distribution.

At this point, an intuitive question remains: *Is the concept of "three distinct standard deviations" the optimal scenario for the G+G signature scheme?* Based on current lattice-based signature constructions leveraging LWE and its variants, the answer appears to be affirmative. In fact, this structure is inherently dictated by the structure of the public key. Whether in compact hash-and-sign signature [19] or in G+G signature, the public key structure typically comprises an identity matrix, a uniformly random matrix, and a pseudorandom matrix embedding the secret key. This corresponds to the secret key being partitioned into three components aligned with the public-key structure, and introducing a fourth component seems unnecessary. Therefore, excessive optimization beyond this may yield diminishing gains.

Security of ALWE Problem. In [12,20], the authors experimentally discussed the computational complexity of solving the ALWE and LWE problems under known attacks by leveraging standard deviations. Furthermore, in the NIST-standardized key encapsulation algorithm ML-KEM, its parameter set ML-KEM-512 also employs asymmetric parameters, meaning its key security relies on the ALWE problem as well. This work follows the same consideration. When deriving the minimum standard deviation of the signature distribution, the upper bound of σ_3 is determined using known results, which simultaneously ensures that σ_2 is not too small to cause non-zero elements in the secret key $\mathbf{S}_1$ from becoming overly sparse.

In Fig. 3, we analyze the relationship between the bit security of ALWE and LWE under certain attacks (the attack methods for evaluating ALWE are provided in the Appendix, we also taken into account the latest attack [18] and its asymmetric variants) and the standard deviations of the secret distribution

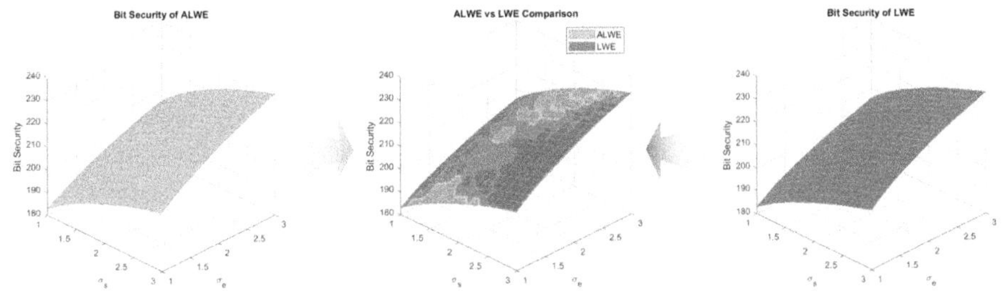

Fig. 3. Comparison of Bit Security between LWE and ALWE

σ_s and noise distribution σ_e, respectively. The leftmost plot illustrates the relationship between the complexity of directly solving the ALWE problem using the plain attack and the standard deviations of **s** and **e**. The rightmost plot is derived by transforming the ALWE problem into an LWE problem via the complexity formula from the work [20], i.e.,

$$\mathrm{ALWE}_{n,m,q,\sigma_s,\sigma_e} \approx \mathrm{LWE}_{n,m,q,\sqrt{\sigma_s \cdot \sigma_e}},$$

followed by analysis with the primal attack[2]. In this way, we can compare the security of LWE with that of ALWE by converting LWE security into ALWE security. For clarity, in our three-dimensional coordinate system, the x-axis and y-axis represent the standard deviations, while the z-axis indicates the concrete bit security. To facilitate a more intuitive comparison, we superimpose the two plots and present a top-view surface plot for contrast. The results show no significant difference in security between ALWE and LWE under primal attack, provided that appropriate parameters are selected.

Impact on the Provable Security. The existential unforgeability of the G+G signature relies on the following properties of the underlying identification scheme: completeness, commitment recoverability, the HVZK property, key indistinguishability, and lossy soundness. Among these, key indistinguishability and lossy soundness are guaranteed by the hardness of the MLWE and MSIS problems, respectively. In this work, we replace MLWE and MSIS with the AMLWE and AMSIS problems. Crucially, the AMLWE distribution retains the same essential characteristics as the MLWE distribution—namely, it remains computationally indistinguishable from the uniform distribution. Therefore, with appropriately chosen AMLWE and AMSIS parameters, the security reduction of the G+G identification scheme established by Devevey et al. remains valid. As a result, our variant of the G+G signature still satisfies existential unforgeability.

---

[2] In our tests, the relationship holds with equality. Indeed, according to the results from [12], achieving equality is both meaningful and justified.

3.2 Optimized G+G: An Experimental Perspective

In this section, we evaluate the efficiency and security of an optimized variant of G+G by considering key recovery attacks and signature forgery attacks, which are typically examined in signature security assessments. We first present the optimized version of G+G signature. Subsequently, we conduct a comprehensive evaluation of the variant's signatures and provide a detailed comparison with the original G+G scheme.

We introduce the module version of new G+G signature variant in Fig. 4 as well as some notations. Let $m > 0, k > m + 1$ and $l = 1$. Set $\mathbf{j} = (\eta^*, 0, \cdots, 0) \in \mathcal{R}^m$ where $\eta^* = 1 - x^{n/2}$, $\eta = 1 + x^{n/2}$ and satisfy $\eta \cdot \eta^* = 2 \mod 1 + x^n$. Denote by $\chi_\zeta := \{x \in \mathcal{R} \mid ||x||_\infty \leq \zeta\}$, the challenge space is $\mathcal{R}/\eta^*\mathcal{R}$.

$\mathsf{KeyGen}(1^\lambda)$

$\mathbf{A}_1 \leftarrow\!\!\$\, \mathcal{U}(\mathcal{R}_q^{m\times(k-m-1)})$

$(\mathbf{s}_1, \mathbf{s}_2) \hookleftarrow \chi_{\zeta_1}^{(k-m-1)} \times \chi_{\zeta_2}^{m}$

$\mathbf{b} := \mathbf{A}_1\mathbf{s}_1 + \mathbf{s}_2$ $\quad \triangleright$ LWE sample $\mathbf{b} \in \mathcal{R}_q^m$

$\mathbf{A} \leftarrow (q\mathbf{j} - 2\mathbf{b} \mid 2\mathbf{A}_1 \mid 2\mathbf{I}_m) \in \mathcal{R}_{2q}^{m\times k}$

$\mathbf{s} \leftarrow (1 \mid \mathbf{s}_1^\top \mid \mathbf{s}_2^\top)^\top \in \mathcal{R}^k$

$\mathsf{vk} \leftarrow \mathbf{A}, \mathsf{sk} \leftarrow \mathbf{s}$

return $(\mathsf{vk}, \mathsf{sk})$

$\mathsf{Sign}(\mathbf{A}, \mathbf{s}, \mu)$

$\mathbf{y} \leftarrow \mathcal{D}_{\mathcal{R}^k, \Sigma(\mathbf{s})}$

$\mathbf{w} := \mathbf{A}\mathbf{y} \mod 2q$ $\quad \triangleright$ Compute commitment $\mathbf{w} \in \mathcal{R}_{2q}^m$

$c \leftarrow H(\mu, \mathbf{w})$

$u \leftarrow \mathcal{D}_{\mathcal{R}, s, -\eta^* c/2}$

$\mathbf{z} \leftarrow \mathbf{y} + (c + \eta u)\mathbf{s}$

return $(\mathbf{z}, \mathbf{c})$

$\mathsf{Verify}(\mathbf{A}, \mu, \mathbf{z}, \mathbf{c})$

$\mathbf{w} \leftarrow \mathbf{A}\mathbf{z} - q\mathbf{c}\mathbf{j} \mod 2q$

if $\mathbf{c} = H(\mathbf{w}, \mu)$

and $||\mathbf{z}|| \leq \gamma$ **then**

  return 1

end if

return 0

Fig. 4. The new G+G variant signature

Table 1. Parameter Settings for the G+G Variant signature

Parameter	Set-I	Set-II
q	65537	65537
n	256	256
$(m, k-m)$	$(3,4)$	$(4,5)$
(ζ_1, ζ_2)	(1,2)	(1,3)
s	14.22	14.22
$(\sigma_1, \sigma_2, \sigma_3)$	(40,485,762)	(41,575,986)
β	28864	36907

Table 2. Comparison with the G+G scheme

Schemes	Parameter Comparison I		Parameter Comparison II	
	Set-I	G+G-120 bits	Set-II	G+G-180 bits
Public key size (Bytes)	1472	1472	1952	1952
Signature size with rANS (Bytes)	1216	1677	1584	2143
BKZ block-size b to break (A)MSIS	510	461	707	633
Classical bit-cost	148	134	206	185
Quantum bit-cost	135	118	187	162
BKZ block-size b to break (A)MLWE	461	415	719	610
Classical bit-cost	134	121	209	178
Quantum bit-cost	118	106	190	156

The method for evaluating the parameter security of the *Asymmetric SIS* (ASIS) problem[3] is provided in the Appendix. When assessing security, we adopt conventional attack methods for the parameters of the original G+G signature, consistent with the evaluation approach used for ML-DSA signature.

Comparison of parameter size. In Table 3, we propose the parameter selections for the G+G variant signature and accordingly present the results of several main parameters. By controlling parameters n, m, and k to align with the G+G signature, we ensure consistent overall security levels while facilitating more straightforward comparison. In Table 2, we compare the two selected parameter sets with the 120-bit and 180-bit security parameters from the G+G signature scheme. The comparison includes public key size, signature size, and their security against signature forgery attacks and key recovery attacks. The signature size estimation employs the rANS encoding technique. Here, we also need to use the relevant techniques proposed or employed in [5] to further optimize our scheme, by truncating the signature when outputting it, which simultaneously

[3] Although the evaluation methods provided in the Appendix are targeted at the plain ALWE/ASIS problems, their extension to the assessment of AMLWE/AMSIS problems is natural.

affects the upper bound β for signature verification. Similarly, during the sampling of $\mathbf{s}_1, \mathbf{s}_2$, we need to perform some repeated loop operations to obtain high-quality secret key, and we keep the acceptance rate consistent with G+G at 0.5. The results show that the signature sizes in our two parameter sets have improved by approximately 25% compared to the G+G signature.

Table 3. Parameter Settings for the G+G Variant signature

Parameter	Set-I	Set-II
q	65537	65537
n	256	256
$(m, k-m)$	$(3,4)$	$(4,5)$
(ζ_1, ζ_2)	(1,3)	(2,3)
s	14.22	14.22
$(\sigma_1, \sigma_2, \sigma_3)$	(42,524,974)	(50,897,1025)
β	30982	44055
Public key size (Bytes)	992	1312
Signature size with rANS (Bytes)	1243	1636
BKZ block-size b to break (A)MSIS	488	691
Classical bit-cost	142	202
Quantum bit-cost	125	177
TSM block-size b to break (A)MLWE	501	692
Classical bit-cost	146	202
Quantum bit-cost	128	177

4 Conclusion

This paper proposed an optimized G+G signature by incorporating asymmetric LWE and a new non-spherical Gaussian distribution. We provided an experimental largest singular value analysis of the secret key matrix, which collectively enable a signature size reduction of about 25% at the same security level. A question worth studying is: Is there a more specific analytical approach to the hardness of asymmetric LWE/SIS problems?

Acknowledgments. We thank the anonymous reviewers of PKC 2026 for their insightful comments and constructive suggestions. This work was supported by National Natural Science Foundation of China (Grant No. 12525115), Natural Science Foundation of Hunan Province (Grant No. 2026JJ60006,2026JJ90267).

A Appendix

Security Estimation Approaches for ALWE and ASIS Problems[4]. We first convert the AMLWE problem into the ALWE problem, then extend LWE solving methods to ALWE. Since any other bounded centrally symmetric distribution can be viewed as a subgaussian distribution with certain parameters, for ease of analysis and without loss of generality, we only consider the ALWE problem where the secret vector $\mathbf{s} \leftarrow \mathcal{D}_{\mathbb{Z}^n,\sigma_1}$ and the error vector $\mathbf{e} \leftarrow \mathcal{D}_{\mathbb{Z}^m,\sigma_2}$, with each component of $\mathbf{s}$ and $\mathbf{e}$ drawn from subgaussian distributions with standard deviations σ_1 and σ_2, respectively. Our goal is to compute and output $\mathbf{s} \in \mathbb{Z}_q^n$ given problem samples $(\mathbf{A}, \mathbf{b} = \mathbf{As} + \mathbf{e}) \in \mathbb{Z}_q^{m\times n} \times \mathbb{Z}_q^m$.

Currently, the main method for solving SIS is BKZ and its variants for lattice basis reduction. Since such algorithms do not have advantages when solving RSIS and MSIS problems compared to standard SIS, the literature often converts RSIS or MSIS problems into standard SIS problems for analysis. Specifically, we first convert the AMSIS[1] problem[5] into the ASIS[1] problem, then extend SIS solving methods to ASIS. Formally, we consider the ASIS problem where, given an ASIS[1] problem instance $\mathbf{A} = (\mathbf{A}_1 \| \mathbf{A}_2) \in \mathbb{Z}_q^{n\times(m_1+m_2-n)}$, the goal is to a non-zero solution $\mathbf{x}^\top = (\mathbf{x}_1^\top, \mathbf{x}_2^\top)$ satisfying $\|\mathbf{x}_1\|_1 \leq \beta_1$, $\|\mathbf{x}_2\|_1 \leq \beta_2$, and $\mathbf{A}_1\mathbf{x}_1 + \mathbf{A}_2\mathbf{x}_2 = \mathbf{0} \mod q$, where $\mathbf{x}_1 \in \mathbb{Z}^{m_1}$, $\mathbf{x}_2 \in \mathbb{Z}^{m_2}$.

A.1 Primal Attacks on ALWE and Their Variants

The basic idea of primal attacks is to transform the ALWE problem into solving an appropriate Bounded Distance Decoding (BDD) or Shortest Vector Problem (SVP) on a lattice through embedding. The main difference among various primal attacks lies in the embedding method. We consider the following primal attacks and their variants on the $\text{ALWE}_{n,m,q,\sigma_1,\sigma_2}$ problem.

Traditional Primal Attack. The traditional primal attack uses Kannan embedding to convert the LWE solving problem into finding a unique shortest vector problem (uSVP) on a lattice. First, define the lattice

$$\mathbf{\Lambda} = \{\mathbf{y} \in \mathbb{Z}^m : \mathbf{y} = \mathbf{Ax} \mod q, \mathbf{x} \in \mathbb{Z}_q^n\},$$

where the dimension of $\mathbf{\Lambda}$ is $d = m$. When m is sufficiently larger than n, matrix $\mathbf{A}$ has n linearly independent rows with high probability. Without loss of generality, assume the first n rows of $\mathbf{A}$ are linearly independent (otherwise, we can permute linearly independent rows to the front), and let $\mathbf{A}_1 \in \mathbb{Z}_q^{n\times n}$ be

[4] Our evaluation method is consistent with that of the Aigis-Sig signature scheme, i.e., a generalized version of the hardness problem evaluation approach in [20]. For the self-completeness of this paper, we elaborate on the evaluation method here.

[5] The AMSIS problem under the ℓ_1-norm.

the submatrix of the first n rows, i.e., $\mathbf{A} = \begin{pmatrix} \mathbf{A}_1 \\ \mathbf{A}_2 \end{pmatrix}$. Denote $\mathbf{A}_1^{-1} \in \mathbb{Z}_q^{n\times n}$ as the inverse of $\mathbf{A}_1$, and let $\mathbf{A}' = \begin{pmatrix} \mathbf{I}_n \\ \mathbf{A}_2\mathbf{A}_1^{-1} \end{pmatrix}$, then we have

$$\mathbf{\Lambda} = \{\mathbf{y} : \mathbf{y} = \mathbf{A}\mathbf{x} \mod q, \mathbf{x} \in \mathbb{Z}_q^n\} = \{\mathbf{y} : \mathbf{y} = \mathbf{A}'\mathbf{x} \mod q, \mathbf{x} \in \mathbb{Z}_q^n\} \subseteq \mathbb{Z}^m,$$

and the following matrix

$$\mathbf{B} = \begin{pmatrix} \mathbf{I}_n & \mathbf{0} \\ \mathbf{A}_2\mathbf{A}_1^{-1} & q\mathbf{I}_{m-n} \end{pmatrix} \in \mathbb{Z}^{m\times m}$$

forms a basis for lattice $\mathbf{\Lambda}$. It is easy to verify that $\det(\mathbf{\Lambda}) = q^{m-n}$. From $\mathbf{b} = \mathbf{A}\mathbf{s} + \mathbf{e} \mod q$, we know that the distance from vector b to lattice $\mathbf{\Lambda}$ is $\|\mathbf{e}\|$. If we can find the lattice point $\mathbf{u} \in \mathbf{\Lambda}$ closest to $\mathbf{b}$, then with high probability we have $\mathbf{e} = \mathbf{b} - \mathbf{u}$. In other words, the problem of solving for vector $\mathbf{e}$ can be transformed into a Bounded Distance Decoding (BDD) problem on lattice $\mathbf{\Lambda}$, which can be solved using the nearest plane algorithm. Furthermore, using Kannan embedding, the BDD problem can be converted into a uSVP problem. Specifically, consider the lattice $\mathbf{\Lambda}'$ generated by the column vectors of the following matrix $\mathbf{B}'$:

$$\mathbf{B}' = \begin{pmatrix} \mathbf{I}_n & \mathbf{0} & \\ \mathbf{A}_2\mathbf{A}_1^{-1} & q\mathbf{I}_{m-n} & \mathbf{b} \\ \mathbf{0} & \mathbf{0} & t \end{pmatrix} \in \mathbb{Z}^{(m+1)\times(m+1)},$$

where $t \in \mathbb{Z}$ is an adjustable parameter. Theoretically, taking $t = \|\mathbf{e}\|$ achieves good results, but practical experiments show that $t = 1$ works better, so we typically choose $t = 1$. In this case, with very high probability, $\mathbf{v} = (\mathbf{e}^\top, 1)^\top \in \mathbb{Z}^{m+1}$ is the unique shortest vector in lattice $\mathbf{\Lambda}'$. Therefore, we can solve for the error vector $\mathbf{e} \in \mathbb{Z}^m$ by solving the uSVP problem on lattice $\mathbf{\Lambda}'$, and then recover the secret key $\mathbf{s} \in \mathbb{Z}_q^n$ by solving the linear equation system, i.e., computing $\mathbf{A}\mathbf{s} = \mathbf{b} - \mathbf{e} \mod q$. Moreover, since each component of vector $\mathbf{e}$ is drawn from the subgaussian distribution $\mathcal{D}_{\mathbb{Z}^m,\sigma_2}$, we have $\|\mathbf{v}\| \approx \|\mathbf{e}\| \approx \sigma_2\sqrt{m}$, i.e., $\mathbf{v}$ has relatively short length.

Primal Attack: Variant 1. When $\sigma_1 = \sigma_2$, this attack algorithm is currently the most effective primal attack method. Define the lattice

$$\mathbf{\Lambda} = \{\mathbf{v} = (\mathbf{x}^\top, \mathbf{y}^\top, z)^\top \in \mathbb{Z}^{n+m+1} : (\mathbf{A}\|\mathbf{I}_m\| - \mathbf{b})\mathbf{v} = \mathbf{0} \mod q\},$$

it is easy to verify that the matrix

$$\mathbf{B} = \begin{pmatrix} \mathbf{I}_n & \mathbf{0} & 0 \\ -\mathbf{A} & q\mathbf{I}_m & \mathbf{b} \\ \mathbf{0} & \mathbf{0} & 1 \end{pmatrix} \in \mathbb{Z}^{(m+n+1)\times(m+n+1)}$$

forms a basis for lattice $\mathbf{\Lambda}$. Clearly, the dimension of lattice $\mathbf{\Lambda}$ is $d = m + n + 1$. Furthermore, we have $\det(\mathbf{\Lambda}) = q^m$, and $\mathbf{v} = (\mathbf{s}^\top, \mathbf{e}^\top, 1)^\top \in \mathbb{Z}^{n+m+1}$ is a short vector in lattice $\mathbf{\Lambda}$. Therefore, we can recover vector $\mathbf{s} \in \mathbb{Z}_q^m$ by solving the (u)SVP problem on lattice $\mathbf{\Lambda}$. Moreover, since each component of vectors $\mathbf{s}$ and $\mathbf{e}$ is drawn from subgaussian distributions $\mathcal{D}_{\mathbb{Z}^n,\sigma_1}$ and $\mathcal{D}_{\mathbb{Z}^m,\sigma_2}$, respectively, we have $\|\mathbf{v}\| \approx \sqrt{\sigma_1^2 n + \sigma_2^2 m}$.

Primal Attack: Variant 2. This attack algorithm is a further variant of the primal attack. When $\sigma_1 \neq \sigma_2$ and the values of σ_1 and σ_2 are not significantly different, this variant primal attack algorithm is more effective. Formally, let $c = \sigma_2/\sigma_1$. Define the lattice

$$\mathbf{\Lambda} = \left\{ \mathbf{v} = \begin{pmatrix} c\mathbf{x} \\ \mathbf{y} \\ \sigma_2 z \end{pmatrix} \in \mathbb{R}^{n+m+1} : (\mathbf{A}\|\mathbf{I}_m\| - b)\mathbf{u} = \mathbf{0} \mod q, \mathbf{u} = \begin{pmatrix} \mathbf{x} \\ \mathbf{y} \\ z \end{pmatrix} \in \mathbb{Z}^{n+m+1} \right\},$$

then the following matrix

$$\mathbf{B} = \begin{pmatrix} c\mathbf{I}_n & \mathbf{0} & 0 \\ -\mathbf{A} & q\mathbf{I}_m & b \\ \mathbf{0} & \mathbf{0} & \sigma_2 \end{pmatrix} \in \mathbb{R}^{(n+m+1)\times(n+m+1)}$$

forms a basis for lattice $\mathbf{\Lambda}$. Clearly, the dimension of lattice $\mathbf{\Lambda}$ is $d = m + n + 1$. Furthermore, we have $\det(\mathbf{\Lambda}) = \sigma_2 c^n q^m$, and $\mathbf{v} = (c\mathbf{s}^\top, \mathbf{e}^\top, \sigma_2)^\top \in \mathbb{R}^{m+n+1}$ is a short vector in lattice $\mathbf{\Lambda}$. Therefore, we can recover the secret key $\mathbf{s}$ by solving the (u)SVP problem on lattice $\mathbf{\Lambda}$. Moreover, since each component of vectors $\mathbf{s}$ and $\mathbf{e}$ is drawn from subgaussian distributions $\mathcal{D}_{\mathbb{Z}^n,\sigma_1}$ and $\mathcal{D}_{\mathbb{Z}^m,\sigma_2}$, respectively, we have $\|\mathbf{v}\| \approx \sigma_2\sqrt{n + m + 1}$.

Intuitively, the idea of this variant attack algorithm is to scale each component of the target short vector to the same magnitude, thereby achieving better attack results. In fact, practical experiments show that (u)SVP solving algorithms on lattices do tend to output short vectors with balanced component values.

Computational Cost Evaluation Model for Primal Attacks. Currently, the most effective method for solving the SVP is the BKZ-b lattice basis reduction algorithm and its variants. Given a basis of a d-dimensional lattice as input, such algorithms transform the lattice basis reduction problem into a shortest vector problem in a $b < d$ dimensional sublattice, and continuously improve the quality of the input d-dimensional lattice basis (i.e., reduce the norm of vectors in the basis) by repeatedly solving the shortest vector problem in different b-dimensional sublattices. Depending on the algorithm, the actual BKZ-b algorithm typically calls the shortest vector solving algorithm for b-dimensional lattices $O(d)$ times. Therefore, the computational cost of the BKZ-b lattice basis reduction algorithm is mainly determined by the computational cost of the shortest vector solving algorithm for b-dimensional lattices.

Usually, we assume that running the BKZ-b algorithm to reduce the basis $\mathbf{B} \in \mathbb{Z}^{d\times d}$ of a d-dimensional lattice produces a reduced basis satisfying the Geometric Series Assumption (GSA) (this is optimal from the attacker's perspective). Let the resulting reduced basis be $\hat{\mathbf{B}} = (\hat{\mathbf{b}}_1, \ldots, \hat{\mathbf{b}}_d)$, then we have

$$\|\hat{\mathbf{b}}_1\| = \delta^d \det(\mathbf{\Lambda})^{1/d},$$
$$\|\hat{\mathbf{b}}_i^*\| = \delta^{-2d(i-1)/(d-1)}\|\hat{\mathbf{b}}_1\|,$$

where $\delta = ((\pi b)^{1/b} \cdot b/2\pi e)^{1/2(b-1)}$, and $\hat{\mathbf{B}}^* = (\hat{\mathbf{b}}_1^*, \ldots, \hat{\mathbf{b}}_d^*)$ is the Gram-Schmidt orthogonalization matrix of $\hat{\mathbf{B}}$ (i.e., $\hat{\mathbf{b}}_1 = \hat{\mathbf{b}}_1^*$). Specifically, research shows that when the projection of the target unique shortest vector $\mathbf{v}$ in the space spanned by the last b orthogonal vectors $(\hat{\mathbf{b}}_{d-b+1}^*, \ldots, \hat{\mathbf{b}}_d^*)$ has norm less than $\|\hat{\mathbf{b}}_{d-b+1}^*\|$, the BKZ-$b$ lattice basis reduction algorithm will be able to recover vector $\mathbf{v}$.

For a unique shortest vector $\mathbf{v}$ with norm $\ell = \|\mathbf{v}\|$, the norm of its projection in the space spanned by the last b orthogonal vectors $(\hat{\mathbf{b}}_{d-b+1}^*, \ldots, \hat{\mathbf{b}}_d^*)$ is approximately $\ell\sqrt{b/d}$, assuming that the values of $\mathbf{v}$ on each projection component are approximately equal. In this case, the computational cost of primal attack algorithms and their variants is mainly determined by the minimum b value satisfying the inequality

$$\ell\sqrt{b/d} \leq \delta^{(-d^2+2db-d)/(d-1)} \det(\mathbf{\Lambda})^{1/d}.$$

We directly use the complexity of the b-dimensional sublattice SVP solving algorithm to very conservatively estimate the complexity of solving the unique shortest vector in a d-dimensional lattice (since the latter requires running the b-dimensional sublattice SVP solving algorithm many times as a subroutine). Furthermore, we use $\text{cost}_b = 2^{0.292b}$ and $\text{cost}_b = 2^{0.265b}$ to characterize the complexity of classical and quantum algorithms for solving the shortest vector in b-dimensional lattices, respectively.

A.2 Dual Attacks on ALWE and Their Variants

Dual attacks first transform the LWE problem into an SIS problem, then use the solution to the SIS problem to transform the LWE solving problem into distinguishing between a subgaussian distribution and the uniform distribution over $\mathbb{Z}_q^n$ with certain parameters. We consider the following dual attack algorithms and their variants on the $\text{ALWE}_{n,m,q,\sigma_1,\sigma_2}$ problem.

Traditional Dual Attack. Since traditional dual attacks only consider the error distribution of the LWE problem, such attack methods do not actually distinguish between ALWE and LWE problems, i.e., they directly treat ALWE as LWE. Specifically, when $\sigma_1 \gg \sigma_2$, traditional dual attacks are more effective. Formally, let

$$\mathbf{\Lambda} = \{\mathbf{x} \in \mathbb{Z}^m : \mathbf{A}^\top \mathbf{x} = \mathbf{0} \mod q\},$$

then the dimension of $\mathbf{\Lambda}$ is $d = m$. When m is sufficiently larger than n, matrix $\mathbf{A}$ has n linearly independent columns with high probability. Without loss of generality, assume the first n columns of $\mathbf{A}^\top$ are linearly independent (otherwise, we can permute linearly independent columns to the front), and let $\mathbf{A}_1 \in \mathbb{Z}_q^{n\times n}$ be the submatrix of the first n columns, i.e., $\mathbf{A}^\top = (\mathbf{A}_1 \| \mathbf{A}_2) \in \mathbb{Z}_q^{n\times m}$. Denote $\mathbf{A}_1^{-1} \in \mathbb{Z}_q^{n\times n}$ as the inverse of $\mathbf{A}_1$, and let $\mathbf{A}' = (\mathbf{I}_n \| \mathbf{A}_1^{-1}\mathbf{A}_2)$, then we have

$$\mathbf{\Lambda} = \{\mathbf{x} \in \mathbb{Z}^m : \mathbf{A}^\top \mathbf{x} = \mathbf{0} \mod q\} = \{\mathbf{x} \in \mathbb{Z}^m : \mathbf{A}'\mathbf{x} = \mathbf{0} \mod q\},$$

and the matrix

$$\mathbf{B} = \begin{pmatrix} q\mathbf{I}_n & -\mathbf{A}_1^{-1}\mathbf{A}_2 \\ \mathbf{0} & \mathbf{I}_{m-n} \end{pmatrix} \in \mathbb{Z}^{m\times m}$$

forms a basis for lattice $\mathbf{\Lambda}$. Clearly, $\det(\mathbf{\Lambda}) = q^n$. First, the traditional dual attack finds a short vector $\mathbf{v} \in \mathbb{Z}^m$ satisfying $\mathbf{A}^\top \mathbf{v} = \mathbf{0} \mod q$ from the m-dimensional lattice $\mathbf{\Lambda}$ with basis $\mathbf{B}$ (i.e., solving the SIS problem). Then, the attack algorithm computes $\mathbf{u} = \langle \mathbf{v}, \mathbf{b} \rangle = \langle \mathbf{v}, \mathbf{e} \rangle \mod q$ and uses known algorithms to distinguish $\mathbf{u}$ from elements drawn from the uniform distribution over $\mathbb{Z}_q$. Specifically, if $\ell = \|\mathbf{v}\|$ is relatively small, then $\langle \mathbf{v}, \mathbf{e} \rangle$ has a relatively small value, and element $\mathbf{u}$ can be roughly viewed as following a subgaussian distribution with standard deviation $\ell\sigma_2$. In this case, there exist effective algorithms that can distinguish $\mathbf{u}$ from the uniform distribution over $\mathbb{Z}_q$ with probability $4\exp(-2\pi^2\tau^2)$, where $\tau = \ell\sigma_2/q$.

Clearly, for the ALWE problem, the larger the value of σ_2, the larger the value of $\ell\sigma_2$, and thus the smaller the probability of distinguishing $\mathbf{u}$ from elements drawn from the uniform distribution over $\mathbb{Z}_q$. Therefore, intuitively, the larger the value of σ_2, the more difficult it is for traditional dual attack algorithms to attack ALWE.

Dual Attack: Variant 1. Define the lattice

$$\mathbf{\Lambda} = \{(\mathbf{x}^\top, \mathbf{y}^\top)^\top \in \mathbb{Z}^{m+n} : \mathbf{A}^\top \mathbf{x} = \mathbf{y} \mod q\},$$

then the dimension of lattice $\mathbf{\Lambda}$ is $d = m+n$. When m is sufficiently larger than n, matrix $\mathbf{A}^\top$ has n linearly independent columns with high probability. Without loss of generality, assume the first n columns of $\mathbf{A}^\top$ are linearly independent (otherwise, we can permute linearly independent columns to the front), and let $\mathbf{A}_1 \in \mathbb{Z}_q^{n\times n}$ be the submatrix of the first n columns, i.e., $\mathbf{A}^\top = (\mathbf{A}_1 \| \mathbf{A}_2) \in \mathbb{Z}_q^{n\times m}$. Denote $\mathbf{A}_1^{-1} \in \mathbb{Z}_q^{n\times n}$ as the inverse of $\mathbf{A}_1$, and let $\mathbf{A}' = (\mathbf{I}_n \| \mathbf{A}_1^{-1}\mathbf{A}_2)$, then we have

$$\mathbf{\Lambda} = \{(\mathbf{x}^\top, \mathbf{y}^\top)^\top : \mathbf{A}^\top \mathbf{x} = \mathbf{y} \mod q\} = \{(\mathbf{x}^\top, \mathbf{y}^\top)^\top : \mathbf{A}'\mathbf{x} = \mathbf{A}_1^{-1}\mathbf{y} \mod q\},$$

and the matrix

$$\mathbf{B} = \begin{pmatrix} q\mathbf{I}_n & -\mathbf{A}_1^{-1}\mathbf{A}_2 & \mathbf{A}_1^{-1} \\ \mathbf{0} & \mathbf{I}_{m-n} & \mathbf{0} \\ \mathbf{0} & \mathbf{0} & \mathbf{I}_n \end{pmatrix} \in \mathbb{Z}^{(m+n)\times(m+n)}$$

forms a basis for lattice $\mathbf{\Lambda}$. Clearly, $\det(\mathbf{\Lambda}) = q^n$. First, this variant dual attack finds a short vector $\mathbf{v} = (\mathbf{x}^\top, \mathbf{y}^\top)^\top \in \mathbb{Z}^{m+n}$ satisfying $\mathbf{A}^\top \mathbf{x} = \mathbf{y} \mod q$ from the $m+n$-dimensional lattice $\mathbf{\Lambda}$ with basis $\mathbf{B}$. Then, the attack algorithm computes

$$u = \langle \mathbf{x}, \mathbf{b} \rangle = \langle \mathbf{y}, \mathbf{s} \rangle + \langle \mathbf{x}, \mathbf{e} \rangle \mod q,$$

and uses known algorithms to distinguish $\mathbf{u}$ from elements drawn from the uniform distribution over $\mathbb{Z}_q$. Specifically, if $\ell = \|\mathbf{v}\|$ is relatively small, then both $\langle \mathbf{y}, \mathbf{s} \rangle$ and $\langle \mathbf{x}, \mathbf{e} \rangle$ have relatively small values. Furthermore, assuming that each component of $\mathbf{v}$ has roughly the same magnitude, element $u = \langle \mathbf{y}, \mathbf{s} \rangle + \langle \mathbf{x}, \mathbf{e} \rangle$ can be viewed as following a subgaussian distribution with standard deviation $\ell\sqrt{\frac{\sigma_1^2 m+\sigma_2^2 n}{m+n}}$. In this case, there exist effective algorithms that can distinguish u from the uniform distribution over $\mathbb{Z}_q$ with probability $4\exp(-2\pi^2\tau^2)$, where $\tau = \ell\sqrt{\frac{\sigma_1^2 m+\sigma_2^2 n}{m+n}}/q$.

Dual Attack: Variant 2. When $\sigma_1 \neq \sigma_2$ but σ_1 and σ_2 are not significantly different, this variant dual attack is more effective for solving ALWE problems. Formally, let $c = \frac{\sigma_2}{\sigma_1}$, and define the lattice

$$\mathbf{\Lambda} = \{(\mathbf{x}^\top, \mathbf{y}^\top/c)^\top \in \mathbb{R}^{m+n} : \mathbf{A}^\top \mathbf{x} = \mathbf{y} \mod q, \mathbf{x} \in \mathbb{Z}^m, \mathbf{y} \in \mathbb{Z}^n\},$$

then the dimension of lattice $\mathbf{\Lambda}$ is $d = m+n$. When m is sufficiently larger than n, matrix $\mathbf{A}^\top$ has n linearly independent columns with high probability. Without loss of generality, assume the first n columns of $\mathbf{A}^\top$ are linearly independent (otherwise, we can permute linearly independent columns to the front), and let $\mathbf{A}_1 \in \mathbb{Z}_q^{n\times n}$ be the submatrix of the first n columns, i.e., $\mathbf{A}^\top = (\mathbf{A}_1 \| \mathbf{A}_2) \in \mathbb{Z}_q^{n\times m}$. Denote $\mathbf{A}_1^{-1} \in \mathbb{Z}_q^{n\times n}$ as the inverse of $\mathbf{A}_1$, and let $\mathbf{A}' = (\mathbf{I}_n \| \mathbf{A}_1^{-1}\mathbf{A}_2)$, then we have

$$\mathbf{\Lambda} = \{(\mathbf{x}^\top, \mathbf{y}^\top/c)^\top : \mathbf{A}^\top \mathbf{x} = \mathbf{y} \mod q\} = \{(\mathbf{x}^\top, \mathbf{y}^\top/c)^\top : \mathbf{A}'\mathbf{x} = \mathbf{A}_1^{-1}\mathbf{y} \mod q\},$$

and the matrix

$$\mathbf{B} = \begin{pmatrix} q\mathbf{I}_n & -\mathbf{A}_1^{-1}\mathbf{A}_2 & \mathbf{A}_1^{-1} \\ \mathbf{0} & \mathbf{I}_{m-n} & \mathbf{0} \\ \mathbf{0} & \mathbf{0} & \frac{1}{c}\mathbf{I}_n \end{pmatrix} \in \mathbb{R}^{(m+n)\times(m+n)}$$

forms a basis for lattice $\mathbf{\Lambda}$. Clearly, $\det(\mathbf{\Lambda}) = (q/c)^n$. First, this variant dual attack finds a short vector $\mathbf{v} = (\mathbf{x}^\top, \hat{\mathbf{y}}^\top)^\top \in \mathbb{R}^{m+n}$ satisfying $\mathbf{A}^\top \mathbf{x} = c\hat{\mathbf{y}} \mod q$ from the $(m+n)$-dimensional lattice $\mathbf{\Lambda}$ with basis $\mathbf{B}$. Then, the attack algorithm computes

$$u = \langle \mathbf{x}, \mathbf{b} \rangle = c \cdot \langle \hat{\mathbf{y}}, \mathbf{s} \rangle + \langle \mathbf{x}, \mathbf{e} \rangle \mod q,$$

and uses known algorithms to distinguish u from elements drawn from the uniform distribution over $\mathbb{Z}_q$. Specifically, if $\ell = \|\mathbf{v}\|$ is relatively small, then both $c \cdot \langle \hat{\mathbf{y}}, \mathbf{s} \rangle$ and $\langle \mathbf{x}, \mathbf{e} \rangle$ have relatively small values, and element $u = c \cdot \langle \hat{\mathbf{y}}, \mathbf{s} \rangle + \langle \mathbf{x}, \mathbf{e} \rangle$

can be roughly viewed as following a subgaussian distribution with standard deviation $\ell\sigma_2$. In this case, there exist effective algorithms that can distinguish $\mathbf{u}$ from the uniform distribution over $\mathbb{Z}_q$ with probability $4\exp(-2\pi^2\tau^2)$, where $\tau = \ell\sigma_2/q$.

Finally, it should be noted that this variant dual attack does not care about the magnitude relationship between σ_1 and σ_2. In fact, we can also use $c' = \sigma_1/\sigma_2$ for the corresponding dual attack, but this dual attack is equivalent to using coefficient $c = \sigma_2/\sigma_1$ under our computational cost evaluation model.

Dual Attack: Variant 3. This algorithm is similar to the dual attack algorithm in Variant 2, with the main difference being the choice of c. Formally, let $c = \frac{\sigma_2}{\sigma_1}\sqrt{\frac{m}{n}}$. This variant dual attack first computes a short vector $\mathbf{v} = (\mathbf{x}^\top, \hat{\mathbf{y}}^\top)^\top \in \mathbb{R}^{m+n}$ satisfying $\mathbf{A}^\top\mathbf{x} = c\hat{\mathbf{y}} \mod q$. Then, the attack algorithm computes

$$u = \langle \mathbf{x}, b\rangle = c \cdot \langle \hat{\mathbf{y}}, \mathbf{s}\rangle + \langle \mathbf{x}, \mathbf{e}\rangle \mod q,$$

and uses known algorithms to distinguish u from elements drawn from the uniform distribution over $\mathbb{Z}_q$. Specifically, if $\ell = \|\mathbf{v}\|$ is relatively small, then both $c \cdot \langle \hat{\mathbf{y}}, \mathbf{s}\rangle$ and $\langle \mathbf{x}, \mathbf{e}\rangle$ have relatively small values, and element $u = c \cdot \langle \hat{\mathbf{y}}, \mathbf{s}\rangle + \langle \mathbf{x}, \mathbf{e}\rangle$ can be roughly viewed as following a subgaussian distribution with standard deviation $\ell\sigma_2\sqrt{\frac{2m}{m+n}}$. In this case, there exist effective algorithms that can distinguish $\mathbf{u}$ from the uniform distribution over $\mathbb{Z}_q$ with probability $4\exp(-2\pi^2\tau^2)$, where $\tau = \ell\sigma_2\sqrt{\frac{2m}{m+n}}/q$.

Similarly, we can also use coefficient $c' = \frac{\sigma_1}{\sigma_2}\sqrt{\frac{n}{m}}$ for the corresponding dual attack, but this case is equivalent to using coefficient $c = \frac{\sigma_2}{\sigma_1}\sqrt{\frac{m}{n}}$ under our computational cost evaluation model.

Computational Cost Evaluation Model for Dual Attacks. The computational cost of dual attacks and their variants mainly consists of the cost of solving the short vector problem and the cost of converting the distinguishing advantage of solving the ALWE problem into a computational advantage (where the latter requires the distinguishing advantage to be at least greater than $1/2$). For the cost of solving the short vector problem, we will use the model from primal attacks, i.e., running BKZ-b to reduce the basis of a d-dimensional lattice, we will obtain a short vector $\mathbf{v}$ with norm $\ell = \|\mathbf{v}\| = \delta^d \det(\mathbf{\Lambda})^{1/d}$. Substituting this into the previous analysis, we obtain the advantage of distinguishing the ALWE problem as $\epsilon = 4\exp(-2\pi^2\tau^2)$, where τ is uniquely determined by ℓ and the specific dual attack algorithm. To make the final distinguishing advantage greater than $1/2$, we will need $1/\epsilon^2$ short vectors. Considering that each run of the sieving algorithm can produce approximately $2^{0.2075b}$ short vectors, the entire attack needs to be repeated approximately $R = 1/\max(1, 1/(2^{0.2075b}\epsilon^2))$ times.

Similar to the computational cost model for primal attacks, we will use the complexity of the b-dimensional sublattice SVP solving algorithm to very conservatively estimate the complexity of solving the shortest vector in a d-dimensional lattice (since the latter requires running the b-dimensional sublattice SVP solving algorithm many times as a subroutine). Furthermore, we will use $\text{cost}_b = 2^{0.292b}$ and $\text{cost}_b = 2^{0.265b}$ to characterize the complexity of classical and quantum algorithms for solving the shortest vector in b-dimensional lattices, respectively. Under this conservative model, the final complexity of dual attacks is

$$1/\max(1, 1/(2^{0.2075b} \cdot 16\exp(-4\pi^2\tau^2))) \cdot \text{cost}_b,$$

where τ is uniquely determined by b and the specific dual attack algorithm.

A.3 Attacks on ASIS and Their Variants

Compared to solving the infinity norm (A)SIS problem, BKZ and its variant lattice basis reduction algorithms are usually more suitable for solving the Euclidean norm (A)SIS problem. Specifically, for the ASIS problem ASIS^1 corresponding to the four parameter sets chosen by the Aigis signature scheme, although the target vector $\mathbf{x} = \begin{pmatrix} \mathbf{x}_1 \\ \mathbf{x}_2 \end{pmatrix} \in \mathbb{Z}^{m_1+m_2}$ satisfies $\|\mathbf{x}\|_1 \leq \max(\beta_1, \beta_2) < q$ (and $(\mathbf{I}_n\|\mathbf{A})\mathbf{x} = \mathbf{0} \mod q$), its Euclidean norm may be $\|\mathbf{x}\|_2 > q$. In other words, although the Euclidean norm of the trivial solution $\mathbf{u} = (q, 0, \ldots, 0)^\top$ may be smaller than the norm of the target vector, i.e., $\|\mathbf{u}\|_2 < \|\mathbf{x}\|_2$, its infinity norm is greater than our requirement, i.e., $\|\mathbf{u}\|_1 > \max(\beta_1, \beta_2)$. This means that directly using BKZ lattice basis reduction algorithms to solve the infinity norm (A)SIS problem will encounter certain difficulties. Therefore, we adopt the infinity norm SIS problem solving model from [21]. Furthermore, based on the inequality $\|\mathbf{x}\|_1 \leq \|\mathbf{x}\|_2$, we can also transform the infinity norm SIS problem into a Euclidean norm SIS problem, and then solve the infinity norm SIS problem by solving the Euclidean norm SVP problem. Next, we will refer to these two attack algorithms as the infinity norm attack algorithm and the Euclidean norm attack algorithm, respectively, and evaluate the complexity of solving ASIS^1 by considering them and their variants.

Traditional Euclidean Norm Attack. This class of attack algorithms is the ordinary SVP solving method. Formally, define

$$\mathbf{\Lambda} = \{\mathbf{x} \in \mathbb{Z}^{m_1+m_2} : (\mathbf{I}_n\|\mathbf{A})\mathbf{x} = \mathbf{0} \mod q\}.$$

Then the matrix

$$\mathbf{B} = \begin{pmatrix} q\mathbf{I}_n & \mathbf{0} \\ -\mathbf{A} & \mathbf{I}_{m_1+m_2-n} \end{pmatrix} \in \mathbb{Z}^{(m_1+m_2)\times(m_1+m_2)}$$

forms a basis for lattice $\mathbf{\Lambda}$. The dimension of lattice $\mathbf{\Lambda}$ is $d = m_1 + m_2$ and $\det(\mathbf{\Lambda}) = q^n$. To ensure that the solution to the Euclidean norm ASIS problem is also a solution to the infinity norm ASIS problem, the norm of the target vector $\mathbf{x} \in \mathbb{Z}^d$ must satisfy $\|\mathbf{x}\|_2 \leq \beta = \min(\beta_1, \beta_2)$. Therefore, the complexity of this attack algorithm is the complexity of running the BKZ-b lattice basis reduction algorithm to find a vector $\mathbf{x}$ satisfying $\|\mathbf{x}\|_2 \leq \beta = \min(\beta_1, \beta_2)$.

Euclidean Norm Attack: Variant 1. This class of attack algorithms hopes to achieve better attack results by balancing the values of each component in the target vector. Formally, let $c = \beta_2/\beta_1$, and define the lattice

$$\mathbf{\Lambda} = \left\{ \mathbf{x} = \begin{pmatrix} c\mathbf{x}_1 \\ \mathbf{x}_2 \end{pmatrix} \in \mathbb{R}^{m_1+m_2} : (\mathbf{I}_n \| \mathbf{A})\mathbf{v} = \mathbf{0} \mod q, \mathbf{v} = \begin{pmatrix} \mathbf{x}_1 \\ \mathbf{x}_2 \end{pmatrix} \in \mathbb{Z}^{m_1+m_2} \right\}.$$

Then the matrix

$$\mathbf{B} = \begin{pmatrix} c\mathbf{I}_{m_1} & \mathbf{0} \\ \mathbf{0} & \mathbf{I}_{m_2} \end{pmatrix} \begin{pmatrix} q\mathbf{I}_n & -\mathbf{A} \\ \mathbf{0} & \mathbf{I}_{m_1+m_2-n} \end{pmatrix} \in \mathbb{R}^{(m_1+m_2)\times(m_1+m_2)}$$

forms a basis for lattice $\mathbf{\Lambda}$. The dimension of lattice $\mathbf{\Lambda}$ is $d = m_1 + m_2$ and $\det(\mathbf{\Lambda}) = c^{m_1} q^n$. Clearly, by solving for a vector $\mathbf{x} = (c\mathbf{x}_1^\top, \mathbf{x}_2^\top)^\top \in \mathbb{R}^{m_1+m_2}$ in lattice $\mathbf{\Lambda}$ with Euclidean norm less than β_2, we can obtain the solution $(\mathbf{x}_1^\top, \mathbf{x}_2^\top)^\top \in \mathbb{Z}^{m_1+m_2}$ to the ASIS problem. Therefore, the complexity of this method is the complexity of running the BKZ-b lattice basis reduction algorithm to find a vector $\mathbf{x}$ satisfying $\|\mathbf{x}\|_2 \leq \beta = \beta_2$.

Finally, it should be noted that this variant Euclidean norm attack does not care about the magnitude relationship between β_1 and β_2. In fact, we can also use $c' = \beta_1/\beta_2$ for the corresponding Euclidean norm attack, but this variant attack is equivalent to using coefficient $c = \beta_2/\beta_1$ under our computational cost evaluation model.

Computational Cost Evaluation Model for Euclidean Norm Attacks. Let $\delta = ((\pi b)^{1/b} \cdot b/2\pi e)^{1/2(b-1)}$. Running the BKZ-$b$ algorithm to reduce the basis $\mathbf{B} \in \mathbb{Z}^{d\times d}$ of a d-dimensional lattice will yield a lattice vector satisfying $\|\mathbf{x}\|_2 \approx \delta^d \det(\mathbf{\Lambda})^{1/d}$. Clearly, when the inequality

$$\delta^d \det(\mathbf{\Lambda})^{1/d} \leq \beta$$

holds, we can successfully obtain a solution to the ASIS problem using the Euclidean norm attack algorithm. Similar to the computational cost model for primal attacks on ALWE, we will use the complexity of the b-dimensional sublattice SVP solving algorithm to very conservatively estimate the complexity of solving the shortest vector in a d-dimensional lattice (since the latter requires running the b-dimensional sublattice SVP solving algorithm many times as a subroutine). Furthermore, we will use $\text{cost}_b = 2^{0.292b}$ and $\text{cost}_b = 2^{0.265b}$ to characterize the complexity of classical and quantum algorithms for solving the shortest vector in b-dimensional lattices, respectively.

Traditional Infinity Norm Attack. Define

$$\mathbf{\Lambda} = \{\mathbf{x} \in \mathbb{Z}^{m_1+m_2} : (\mathbf{I}_n \| \mathbf{A})\mathbf{x} = \mathbf{0} \mod q\}.$$

Then the matrix

$$\mathbf{B} = \begin{pmatrix} q\mathbf{I}_n & -\mathbf{A} \\ \mathbf{0} & \mathbf{I}_{m_1+m_2-n} \end{pmatrix} \in \mathbb{Z}^{(m_1+m_2)\times(m_1+m_2)}$$

forms a basis for lattice $\mathbf{\Lambda}$. Clearly, the dimension of lattice $\mathbf{\Lambda}$ is $d = m_1 + m_2$ and $\det(\mathbf{\Lambda}) = q^n$.

Running the BKZ-b basis reduction algorithm with matrix $\mathbf{B}$ as input, we obtain a reduced basis $\hat{\mathbf{B}} \in \mathbb{Z}^{d\times d}$. Let $\hat{\mathbf{B}}^* = (\hat{\mathbf{b}}_1^*, \ldots, \hat{\mathbf{b}}_d^*)$ be the Gram-Schmidt orthogonalization matrix of $\hat{\mathbf{B}}$, and $\ell_i = \log_2(\|\hat{\mathbf{b}}_i^*\|)$, then there exist integers $1 \le i \le j \le d$ such that:

- For the first i vectors, we have $\ell_1 = \ell_2 = \cdots = \ell_i = \log_2 q$;
- For the middle $j - i$ vectors, we have $\ell'_j = \log_2 q + s \cdot (j' - i)$, where $j' \in \{i+1, \ldots, j\}$, $s = -\frac{1}{b-1}\log_2\left(\frac{b}{2\pi e}(\pi b)^{1/b}\right) < 0$, and $(j-i)(i+j+1) = -\frac{2(n-j)\log_2 q}{s}$;
- For the last $d - j$ vectors, we have $\ell_{j+1} = \ell_{j+2} = \cdots = \ell_d = 0$.

Although the BKZ-b lattice basis reduction algorithm cannot directly guarantee that the short vector found satisfies the solution to the ASIS problem. However, with the reduced basis $\hat{\mathbf{B}} \in \mathbb{Z}^{d\times d}$ as input, we can obtain $(4/3)^{b/2}$ vectors with complexity equivalent to solving a b-dimensional lattice SVP problem, such that the Euclidean norm of the projection vectors of these vectors in the space spanned by the first i basis vectors is approximately $2^{\ell_{i+1}}$. By modeling the distribution of these $(4/3)^{b/2}$ vectors (see the computational cost evaluation model section), we can estimate the probability that this algorithm can find an ASIS solution among these $(4/3)^{b/2}$ vectors. Dividing the computational cost of the BKZ-b lattice basis reduction algorithm by this probability yields the overall computational complexity of this attack algorithm.

The Variant of Infinity Norm Attack. Define

$$\mathbf{\Lambda} = \{\mathbf{x} \in \mathbb{Z}^{m_1+m_2} : (\mathbf{I}_n \| \mathbf{A})\mathbf{x} = \mathbf{0} \mod q\}.$$

Then the matrix

$$\mathbf{B} = \begin{pmatrix} q\mathbf{I}_n & -\mathbf{A} \\ \mathbf{0} & \mathbf{I}_{m_1+m_2} \end{pmatrix} \in \mathbb{Z}^{(m_1+m_2)\times(m_1+m_2)}$$

forms a basis for lattice $\mathbf{\Lambda}$. Clearly, the dimension of lattice $\mathbf{\Lambda}$ is $d = m_1+m_2$ and $\det(\mathbf{\Lambda}) = q^n$. Randomize matrix $\mathbf{B}$ to obtain $\mathbf{B}'$ such that $\mathbf{B}'$ does not contain trivial vectors $q\mathbf{e}_i$, where $\mathbf{e}_i$ is the i-th unit vector. Then run the BKZ-b basis reduction algorithm with matrix $\mathbf{B}'$ as input to obtain a reduced basis $\hat{\mathbf{B}} \in \mathbb{Z}^{d\times d}$. Let $\hat{\mathbf{B}}^* = (\hat{\mathbf{b}}_1^*, \ldots, \hat{\mathbf{b}}_d^*)$ be the Gram-Schmidt orthogonalization matrix of $\hat{\mathbf{B}}$, and $\ell_i = \log_2(\|\hat{\mathbf{b}}_i^*\|)$, then there exists an integer $1 \le j \le d$ such that:

- For the first j vectors, we have $\ell_{j'} = -s \cdot (j - j' + 1)$, where $j' \in \{1, \ldots, j\}$, $s = -\frac{1}{b-1}\log_2\left(\frac{b}{2\pi e}(\pi b)^{1/b}\right) < 0$, and $j(j+1) = -\frac{2n\log_2 q}{s}$;
- For the last $d - j$ vectors, we have $\ell_{j+1} = \ell_{j+2} = \cdots = \ell_d = 0$.

Furthermore, with the reduced basis $\hat{\mathbf{B}} \in \mathbb{Z}^{d\times d}$ as input, we can obtain $(4/3)^{b/2}$ vectors with complexity equivalent to solving a b-dimensional lattice SVP problem, such that the Euclidean norm of these vectors is approximately

2^{ℓ_1}. By modeling the distribution of these $(4/3)^{b/2}$ vectors (see the computational cost evaluation model section), we can estimate the probability that this algorithm can find an ASIS solution among these $(4/3)^{b/2}$ vectors. Dividing the computational cost of the BKZ-b lattice basis reduction algorithm by this probability yields the overall computational complexity of this attack algorithm.

References

1. Bai, S., Galbraith, S.D.: An improved compression technique for signatures based on learning with errors. In: Benaloh, J. (ed.) Topics in Cryptology - CT-RSA 2014. Lecture Notes in Computer Science, vol. 8366, pp. 28–47. Springer (2014). https://doi.org/10.1007/978-3-319-04852-9_2
2. Chen, Y., Genise, N., Mukherjee, P.: Approximate trapdoors for lattices and smaller hash-and-sign signatures. In: Galbraith, S.D., Moriai, S. (eds.) Advances in Cryptology - ASIACRYPT 2019. Lecture Notes in Computer Science, vol. 11923, pp. 3–32. Springer (2019). https://doi.org/10.1007/978-3-030-34618-8_1
3. Devevey, J., Fallahpour, P., Passelègue, A., Stehlé, D.: A detailed analysis of Fiat-Shamir with aborts. In: Handschuh, H., Lysyanskaya, A. (eds.) Advances in Cryptology - CRYPTO 2023. Lecture Notes in Computer Science, vol. 14085, pp. 327–357. Springer (2023). https://doi.org/10.1007/978-3-031-38554-4_11
4. Devevey, J., Fawzi, O., Passelègue, A., Stehlé, D.: On rejection sampling in Lyubashevsky's signature scheme. In: Agrawal, S., Lin, D. (eds.) Advances in Cryptology - ASIACRYPT 2022. Lecture Notes in Computer Science, vol. 13794, pp. 34–64. Springer (2022). https://doi.org/10.1007/978-3-031-22972-5_2
5. Devevey, J., Passelègue, A., Stehlé, D.: G+G: a Fiat-Shamir lattice signature based on convolved gaussians. In: Guo, J., Steinfeld, R. (eds.) Advances in Cryptology - ASIACRYPT 2023. Lecture Notes in Computer Science, vol. 14444, pp. 37–64. Springer (2023). https://doi.org/10.1007/978-981-99-8739-9_2
6. Ducas, L., Durmus, A., Lepoint, T., Lyubashevsky, V.: Lattice signatures and bimodal gaussians. In: Canetti, R., Garay, J.A. (eds.) Advances in Cryptology - CRYPTO 2013. Lecture Notes in Computer Science, vol. 8042, pp. 40–56. Springer (2013). https://doi.org/10.1007/978-3-642-40041-4_3
7. Ducas, L., et al.: Crystals-Dilithium: a lattice-based digital signature scheme. IACR Trans. Cryptogr. Hardw. Embed. Syst. **2018**(1), 238–268 (2018). https://doi.org/10.13154/TCHES.V2018.I1.238-268
8. Espitau, T., Katsumata, S., Takemure, K.: Two-round threshold signature from algebraic one-more learning with errors. In: Reyzin, L., Stebila, D. (eds.) Advances in Cryptology - CRYPTO 2024. Lecture Notes in Computer Science, vol. 14926, pp. 387–424. Springer (2024). https://doi.org/10.1007/978-3-031-68394-7_13
9. Espitau, T., Tibouchi, M., Wallet, A., Yu, Y.: Shorter hash-and-sign lattice-based signatures. In: Dodis, Y., Shrimpton, T. (eds.) Advances in Cryptology - CRYPTO 2022. Lecture Notes in Computer Science, vol. 13508, pp. 245–275. Springer (2022). https://doi.org/10.1007/978-3-031-15979-4_9
10. Gärtner, J.: Compact lattice signatures via iterative rejection sampling. In: Kalai, Y.T., Kamara, S.F. (eds.) Advances in Cryptology - CRYPTO 2025. Lecture Notes in Computer Science, vol. 16000, pp. 514–547. Springer (2025). https://doi.org/10.1007/978-3-032-01855-7_17

11. Gentry, C., Peikert, C., Vaikuntanathan, V.: Trapdoors for hard lattices and new cryptographic constructions. In: Dwork, C. (ed.) ACM Symposium on Theory of Computing, Victoria, British Columbia, Canada, 17–20 May 2008, pp. 197–206. ACM (2008). https://doi.org/10.1145/1374376.1374407
12. Hu, Y., Dong, S., Dong, X.: Analysis on AIGIS-enc: asymmetrical and symmetrical. IET Inf. Secur. **15**(2), 147–155 (2021). https://doi.org/10.1049/ISE2.12009
13. Jia, H., Hu, Y., Tang, C.: Lattice-based hash-and-sign signatures using approximate trapdoor, revisited. IET Inf. Secur. **16**(1), 41–50 (2022). https://doi.org/10.1049/ISE2.12039
14. Lyubashevsky, V.: Fiat-Shamir with aborts: applications to lattice and factoring-based signatures. In: Matsui, M. (ed.) Advances in Cryptology - ASIACRYPT 2009. Lecture Notes in Computer Science, vol. 5912, pp. 598–616. Springer (2009). https://doi.org/10.1007/978-3-642-10366-7_35
15. Lyubashevsky, V.: Lattice signatures without trapdoors. In: Pointcheval, D., Johansson, T. (eds.) Advances in Cryptology - EUROCRYPT 2012. Lecture Notes in Computer Science, vol. 7237, pp. 738–755. Springer (2012). https://doi.org/10.1007/978-3-642-29011-4_43
16. Micciancio, D., Peikert, C.: Trapdoors for lattices: simpler, tighter, faster, smaller. In: Pointcheval, D., Johansson, T. (eds.) Advances in Cryptology - EUROCRYPT 2012. Lecture Notes in Computer Science, vol. 7237, pp. 700–718. Springer (2012). https://doi.org/10.1007/978-3-642-29011-4_41
17. Regev, O.: On lattices, learning with errors, random linear codes, and cryptography. In: Gabow, H.N., Fagin, R. (eds.) ACM Symposium on Theory of Computing, pp. 84–93. ACM (2005). https://doi.org/10.1145/1060590.1060603
18. Xia, W., Wang, L., Wang, G., Gu, D., Wang, B.: A refined hardness estimation of LWE in two-step mode. In: Tang, Q., Teague, V. (eds.) Public-Key Cryptography - PKC 2024. Lecture Notes in Computer Science, vol. 14603, pp. 3–35. Springer (2024). https://doi.org/10.1007/978-3-031-57725-3_1
19. Yu, Y., Jia, H., Wang, X.: Compact lattice gadget and its applications to hash-and-sign signatures. In: Handschuh, H., Lysyanskaya, A. (eds.) Advances in Cryptology - CRYPTO 2023. Lecture Notes in Computer Science, vol. 14085, pp. 390–420. Springer (2023). https://doi.org/10.1007/978-3-031-38554-4_13
20. Zhang, J., Yu, Y., Fan, S., Zhang, Z., Yang, K.: Tweaking the asymmetry of asymmetric-key cryptography on lattices: KEMS and signatures of smaller sizes. In: Kiayias, A., Kohlweiss, M., Wallden, P., Zikas, V. (eds.) Public-Key Cryptography - PKC 2020. Lecture Notes in Computer Science, vol. 12111, pp. 37–65. Springer (2020). https://doi.org/10.1007/978-3-030-45388-6_2

Cryptanalysis

Two Is All It Takes: Asymptotic and Concrete Improvements for Solving Code Equivalence

Alessandro Budroni[1(✉)], Andre Esser[1], Ermes Franch[2], and Andrea Natale[3]

[1] Technology Innovation Institute, Abu Dhabi, UAE
{alessandro.budroni,andre.esser}@tii.ae
[2] University of Bergen, Bergen, Norway
ermes.franch@uib.no
[3] COSIC, KU Leuven, Leuven, Belgium
andrea.natale@esat.kuleuven.be

Abstract. The Linear Code Equivalence (LCE) problem asks, for two given linear codes $\mathcal{C}, \mathcal{C}'$, to find a monomial $\mathbf{Q}$ mapping $\mathcal{C}$ into $\mathcal{C}'$. Algorithms solving LCE crucially rely on a (heuristic) subroutine, which recovers the secret monomial from $\Omega(\log n)$ pairs of codewords $(\mathbf{v}_i, \mathbf{w}_i) \in \mathcal{C} \times \mathcal{C}'$ satisfying $\mathbf{w}_i = \mathbf{v}_i\mathbf{Q}$. We greatly improve on this known bound by giving a constructive algorithm that provably recovers the secret monomial from any *two* pairs of such codewords for fields of sufficiently large prime order q. Furthermore, we demonstrate that in practice this algorithm remains effective even for small prime fields. We then show that this reduction in the number of required pairs enables the design of a more efficient algorithm for solving the LCE problem. Our asymptotic analysis shows that this algorithm outperforms previous approaches for a wide range of parameters. Our concrete analysis reveals significant improvements as well. Most notably, in the context of the LESS signature scheme, a second-round contender in the ongoing NIST standardization effort, we achieve bit security reductions of up to 24 bits.

1 Introduction

Code-based cryptography remains a strong contender for the next post-quantum digital signature standard. Historically, most code-based signature schemes have based their security on the Syndrome Decoding Problem (SDP) [13,16,18,27,29]. While the SDP is well studied and provides a solid security foundation, its conservative nature often comes at the price of larger signatures, larger public keys, or

Supported by the Deutsche Forschungsgemeinschaft (DFG, German Research Foundation) Project-ID MA 2536/12.
Supported by the Research Council of Norway (No. 311646/O70).
Part of this work was conducted during Andrea Natale's internship at the Technology Innovation Institute, UAE.

S. Bai and E. Persichetti (Eds.): PKC 2026, LNCS 16551, pp. 395–427, 2026.
https://doi.org/10.1007/978-3-032-26731-3_13

slower signing and verification. In recent years, a promising alternative emerged with the LESS signatures scheme [10], which is based on the *Linear Code Equivalence* (LCE) problem. The collective improvements established over the past years [3,7,14,22] have positioned LESS as a strong candidate [1] in the ongoing second round of the NIST standardization process for post-quantum digital signatures [20]. Furthermore, due to its compatibility with the cryptographic group action framework, the LCE problem has served as the foundation of a variety of digital signature schemes with advanced functionalities, including threshold [5,6], ring [2], and identity-based [2] signatures.

The Linear Code Equivalence problem is defined as follows: Given two $\mathbb{F}_q$-linear $[n, k]$ codes $\mathcal{C}, \mathcal{C}'$, find a monomial $\mathbf{Q}$ that maps $\mathcal{C}$ into $\mathcal{C}'$, i.e., $\mathcal{C}' = \mathcal{C}\mathbf{Q}$. The best algorithms for solving LCE rely on the computation of low-weight codewords $\mathbf{v} \in \mathcal{C}$, $\mathbf{w} \in \mathcal{C}'$ in both codes [4,9,19]. Among the found codewords, the algorithms then identify pairs of codewords equivalent under the secret monomial, i.e., codewords satisfying $\mathbf{w}_i = \mathbf{v}_i\mathbf{Q}$. Once enough such pairs have been identified, the secret monomial can be recovered in polynomial time. A central question that arises is

How many such pairs are required to recover $\mathbf{Q}$ *in* polynomial time?

The currently best known (heuristic) algorithm for recovering $\mathbf{Q}$ from such information in polynomial time requires $\Omega(\log n)$ pairs of equivalent codewords [4,9].[1] Note that this algorithm retrieves the secret monomial solely from the information provided by those pairs of equivalent codewords (or 2-dimensional subcodes). In such a scenario, a single pair of codewords cannot be sufficient to recover $\mathbf{Q}$ in polynomial time, as for two codewords of same weight, there usually exist exponentially many monomials $\mathbf{Q}'$ satisfying the relation $\mathbf{w} = \mathbf{v}\mathbf{Q}'$.

However, generally, the searched monomial is uniquely determined by the equivalence relationship $\mathcal{C}' = \mathcal{C}\mathbf{Q}$. By combining the code structure with the information provided by the pairs of equivalent codewords, we introduce a new algorithm that recovers the secret monomial from only *two* pairs of such codewords and prove it to run in polynomial-time whenever the field size is large enough. As a second main contribution, we then build on this result to overcome a central bottleneck in previous algorithms relying on finding low-weight codewords, resulting in the fastest known algorithm for solving LCE for most parameters. Most notably, the new algorithm reduces security levels for suggested parameter sets of the LESS signature scheme by up to 24 bits.

Related Work. For solving the LCE problem, there exist two main approaches: algorithms following the above concept of computing low-weight codewords in the underlying codes [4,9,19] and a recently introduced meet-in-the-middle technique relying on *canonical forms* [14]. The latter has attracted increased attention since its introduction, with recent results improving its success probability [21] as well as the range of applicable parameters [8]. Notably, the algorithm's

[1] More precisely, this algorithm require pairs of equivalent 2-dimensional subcodes.

complexity is (almost) independent of the field size, obtaining a time complexity of roughly $2^{c(R)n}$, where c is a constant depending on the code rate $R = k/n$. For large choices of q, this algorithm becomes the fastest known algorithm to solve LCE. However, with respect to suggested parameters, algorithms relying on finding low-weight codewords remain yet superior.

An early algorithm by Leon [19] computes all low-weight codewords in both codes and recovers the secret monomial from the resulting sets provided that those sets are sufficiently large. Beullens [9] improved upon Leon's approach by increasing the weight of the codewords and computing only a subset of them for each code. More precisely, Beullens concentrates on finding small support 2-dimensional subcodes, i.e., codes generated by pairs of codewords with a small joint support. He then defines a criterion, called Lex, to identify equivalent subcodes and, eventually, relies on a heuristic algorithm recovering the secret monomial from $\Omega(\log n)$ equivalent pairs. Most recently, Barenghi, Biasse, Santini and Persichetti (BBPS) [4] improved on Beullens' algorithm by modifying the subroutine to find small support subcodes, while relying on the same post-processing to recover the secret monomial.

1.1 Our Contribution

In this work we combine both of the above approaches to design a faster algorithm for LCE. Therefore we first build on the concept of canonical forms to prove a fundamental result on the number of pairs of equivalent codewords required to reconstruct the secret monomial, after which we show how to leverage this new subroutine within the codeword-search framework. In the following we provide more technical details on these two contributions.

Recovering the Secret Monomial from Two Pairs of Equivalent Codewords. We prove the following fundamental result on the recovery of the secret monomial of an LCE instance from two pairs of equivalent codewords

Theorem 1 (Informal). *From two pairs of equivalent codewords the secret monomial* $\mathbf{Q}$ *can be recovered in time*

$$\tilde{\mathcal{O}}\left(2^{\varepsilon/2}n^4\right), \quad \text{where } \varepsilon = \mathcal{O}\left(\tfrac{n}{q} + \log q\right).$$

In order to prove Theorem 1 we build on a recent result by Chou, Persichetti and Santini [14] which recovers the secret monomial from two (information) sets $I, J \subset [n]$ with $|I| = |J| = k$ that are mapped to each other via the monomial action, i.e., $\pi(i) \in J$ for $i \in I$, where π is the permutation that defines the monomial action. In order to find two such *colliding* sets I, J, we show how to extract a subset sum problem instance from the support pattern of two equivalent codewords, whose solution corresponds to such colliding sets. From those sets we then recover $\mathbf{Q}$ in time $\tilde{\mathcal{O}}(n^4)$ via a recent variant of [14] due to Nowakowski

[21] that obtains high success probability already for small field sizes $q \geq 7$. The subset sum instance itself is defined via a (multi-) set of input integers S and target k, i.e., we are looking for a subset $S' \subseteq S$ such that $\sum_{s \in S'} s = k$. For the derived instance, it holds $|S| = \mathcal{O}(n)$ and $\sum_{s \in S} s = n$ which implies that the instance can be solved efficiently via dynamic programming (if a solution exist). In case no exact solution for target k but only for target $k - \varepsilon$ exists, we show how to extend this solution to the desired sets via an enumeration procedure that requires to test $\mathcal{O}\left(2^{\frac{\varepsilon}{2}}\right)$ candidates. We then establish an upper bound on the approximation quality ε that can be achieved, leading to Theorem 1.

Note that Theorem 1 proves the recovery of the secret monomial from two pairs of equivalent codewords to be polynomial-time whenever the field size is $q = \Omega\left(\frac{n}{\log n}\right)$. Note that for parameters suggested in the LESS NIST submission we have $q = 127$ and $n \in \{252, 400, 548\}$ and therefore those arguably already fall into the polynomial-time regime. However, we further quantify this by providing a full implementation and comprehensive experimental evidence.

Using our implementation we successfully recover the secret monomial from two pairs of equivalent codewords within minutes for all LESS parameter sets with empirical success probability one over thousands of experiments. Furthermore, we extend our experiments to larger code length up to $n = 2^{19}$ to observe the asymptotic behavior of the algorithm. This confirms that the analysis around Theorem 1 is rather conservative. Namely, the required field size to enter the polynomial-time regime, i.e., the regime where an *exact* solution to the subset sum instance for target k exists ($\varepsilon = 0$) and, hence, enumeration is avoided, seems to only scale as $q = \Omega(\log n)$, maximizing as $q = 41$ for $n = 2^{19}$ in our experiments.

A Faster Algorithm Solving LCE. As a second contribution, we build on Theorem 1 to design a faster algorithm for solving LCE. Conceptually, the algorithm follows the standard paradigm of low-weight codeword search: we construct two lists L_1 and L_2 of fixed weight codewords from $\mathcal{C}$ and $\mathcal{C}'$, with list sizes chosen to guarantee the existence of at least two pairs of equivalent codewords between them. The algorithm then constructs all pairs of codewords from both lists, i.e., $V = L_1 \times L_1$ and $W = L_2 \times L_2$. In the last step the algorithm searches for potentially equivalent pairs between V and W and initiates the re-construction of the secret monomial for each found candidate.

Observe that the overall efficiency of this approach hinges on the fact that two pairs of equivalent codewords suffice for monomial reconstruction. Since $|V| = |W| = N^2$, where $|L_1| = |L_2| = N$, the general case where c pairs are needed requires lists V', W' of size $|V'| = |W'| = N^c$. Given that N grows exponentially, any non-constant c leads to super-exponential complexity. To avoid this, prior work bypassed the explicit construction of V' and W', instead aiming to identify c equivalent codeword pairs between V and W directly. However, this requires that all $c = \Omega(\log n)$ candidates identified as potentially equivalent are indeed equivalent with high probability. To achieve this, prior work introduced additional constraints. Namely, Beullens [9] enforces that the support of the codewords largely overlaps by focusing on 2-dimensional subcodes, while

Table 1. Bit complexity estimates for suggested LESS parameters.

	Previous	This work
LESS-I	139	**127**
LESS-III	214	**195**
LESS-V	290	**266**

BBPS generalized to smaller, but still lower bounded, support intersections [4]. In summary, both algorithms remain constraint by the high value of c, which leads to suboptimal parameter choices, which we mitigate by relying on the new algorithm achieving $c = 2$.

We then provide further practical speedups, such as the exploitation of the existence of scalar multiples of the solution to reduce the initial list size and the introduction of a new, more efficient *compatibility criterion* outperforming Beullens' Lex function. Overall, applied to the parameters suggested in the LESS signature NIST second-round submission, the improved algorithm leads to a bit security reduction of up to 24 bits (compare to Table 1). With respect to other parameters throughout the literature, we even achieve bit security reductions of up to 42 bits.

We then turn to the asymptotic analysis of the algorithm, providing the first such analysis for a codeword finding based approach dating past Leon's algorithm. In this context we also analyze a commonly known lower bound for algorithms following this paradigm. In particular, we find that this lower bound converges to the complexity of the canonical forms algorithm *from below*, highlighting the potential of codeword-finding based algorithm's even for large values of q. Motivated by our experimental results, we first analyze the case where $q = \omega(1)$ grows with n, leading to a time complexity expressed as a function of the code rate R. For example, for rate $R = \frac{1}{2}$, the complexity of our algorithm is $2^{cn+o(n)}$ with $c \in \left[\frac{2}{3}, \frac{4}{5}\right]$ depending on the size of q. In comparison, Leon's algorithm achieves $c = 1$ in this regime, while the canonical forms approach attains $c = \frac{1}{2}$, suggesting that the new algorithm falls short of the canonical forms approach.

However, this stands in clear contrast to the concrete analysis which shows that the new algorithm remains largely superior to the canonical forms approach even for cryptographic sized instances. This discrepancy goes back to the extremely slow convergence of the minimum distance of a random linear code to its asymptotic limit of $n-k$ (used in the analysis) when q grows in n, motivating a pre-asymptotic analysis, where we treat q as a constant. We show that this setting accurately reflects the concrete performance of the algorithm already for small q and, in particular, for instances of cryptographic relevance.

Artifacts. We provide all source code used to conduct the practical experiments and to compute the asymptotic and concrete complexity estimates is available at the git repository [11].

Outline. In Sect. 2, we define necessary notation as well as fundamentals, and give a formal definition of the LCE problem. In Sect. 3, we introduce our new algorithm for solving LCE from only two pairs. Subsequently, in Sect. 4, we present the new algorithm for solving LCE and its concrete analysis along with a comparison to the state of the art. Finally, in Sect. 5, we provide the asymptotic treatment of the algorithm's complexity.

2 Preliminaries

For any $n \in \mathbb{N}$, we let $[n] := \{1, \ldots, n\}$. We denote matrices with capital bold letters and vectors with lower case bold letters. All vectors are row-vectors if not stated otherwise. For a vector $\mathbf{v}$ we denote by $\mathsf{sort}(\mathbf{v})$ the vector obtained by sorting the entries of $\mathbf{v}$ lexicographically. For a matrix $\mathbf{A} \in \mathbb{F}_q^{n \times n}$, we refer to its entry in the i-th row and j-th column by $\mathbf{A}(i, j)$. Given a set of indices $I \subseteq [n]$ we denote with $\mathbf{v}_I$ the projection of the length-n vector $\mathbf{v}$ onto the indices in I. We extend this to matrices by letting $\mathbf{M}_I$ be the submatrix formed by the columns of $\mathbf{M}$ indexed by I. We define $\mathsf{GL}_n(\mathbb{F}_q)$ as the linear group of invertible matrices, $\mathsf{Perm}_n(\mathbb{F}_q)$ as the set of permutation matrices, and $\mathsf{Mono}_n(\mathbb{F}_q)$ as the set of monomial matrices, i.e., matrices $\mathbf{Q} = \mathbf{DP}$ with $\mathbf{D}$ being a full-rank diagonal matrix and $\mathbf{P} \in \mathsf{Perm}_n(\mathbb{F}_q)$. In addition, when referring to a permutation matrix $\mathbf{P}$, we use the notation $\pi(i) = j$ meaning that j is the only index such that $\mathbf{P}(j, i) \neq 0$. We say a probability p is *high* if $p = 1 - o(1)$.

Linear Code Equivalence. An $[n, k]$ linear code $\mathcal{C}$ over $\mathbb{F}_q$ is a subspace of dimension k of $\mathbb{F}_q^n$. $\mathcal{C}$ can be represented via a basis $\mathbf{G} \in \mathbb{F}_q^{k \times n}$ called *generator matrix* or a *parity-check matrix* $\mathbf{H} \in \mathbb{F}_q^{n-k \times n}$ satisfying $\mathbf{Hc} = \mathbf{0}$ if and only if $\mathbf{c} \in \mathcal{C}$. We refer to n as the *length* of $\mathcal{C}$ and to the quantity $R := k/n$ as the *code rate*. We say that $I \subset [n]$, with $|I| = k$, is an *information set* of $\mathcal{C}$ if $\mathsf{rank}(\mathbf{G}_I) = k$.

Given a codeword $\mathbf{c} \in \mathcal{C}$, we define its support $\mathrm{Supp}\mathbf{c} := \{i \in [n] : c_i \neq 0\}$ as the set of indices corresponding to its nonzero entries. The Hamming weight $\mathrm{wt}(\mathbf{c}) = |\mathrm{Supp}\mathbf{c}|$ of $\mathbf{c}$ is the size of its support. We denote by N_w the number of codewords of fixed weight w in $\mathcal{C}$, which for random codes is known to be of expected size

$$N_w = \binom{n}{w} \frac{(q-1)^w}{q^{n-k}}.$$

The minimum distance $\min(\{\mathrm{wt}\mathbf{c} \mid \mathbf{c} \in \mathcal{C} \setminus \{0\}\})$ of a linear code is defined as the minimum weight over all its nonzero codewords. For large n, the minimum distance of a random $[n, k]$ linear code over $\mathbb{F}_q$ is known to meet the Gilbert-Varshamov bound, which is the smallest w satisfying $N_w \geq 1$. We denote this w by w_{GV}. Furthermore, we define the relative weight coefficient $\omega_{\text{GV}} := w_{\text{GV}}/n$.

Below, we formally define the linear code equivalence problem, which we refer to as LCE problem throughout this work.

Definition 1 (Linear Code Equivalence (LCE)**).** *Given two $[n, k]$ linear codes $\mathcal{C}, \mathcal{C}'$ over $\mathbb{F}_q$ with generator matrices $\mathbf{G}$ and $\mathbf{G}'$, respectively, the* Linear Code Equivalence (LCE) *problem asks to find a monomial $\mathbf{Q} \in \mathsf{Mono}_n(\mathbb{F}_q)$ such that there exists a matrix $\mathbf{S} \in \mathsf{GL}_n(\mathbb{F}_q)$ satisfying $\mathbf{G}' = \mathbf{SGQ}$. We call $(\mathcal{C}, \mathcal{C}')$ an* instance *of the* LCE *problem.*

We generally consider random instances of LCE, where $\mathbf{G}$ and $\mathbf{Q}$ are sampled uniformly at random. Those instances are known to be solvable in (heuristic) polynomial time for $q < 5$ [25], while believed to be hard for any $q \geq 5$ [26]. The special case $\mathbf{Q} \in \mathsf{Perm}_n(\mathbb{F}_q)$ is known as the *Permutation Code Equivalence* (PCE) problem, to which our results apply analogously. If a solution exists for two codes $\mathcal{C}, \mathcal{C}'$, we call them *equivalent* and write $\mathcal{C}' = \mathcal{C}\mathbf{Q}$. Motivated by cryptographic constructions, we restrict to LCE instances with a unique solution $\mathbf{Q}$ (up to scalars). We focus on code rates $R \leq \frac{1}{2}$, since solving LCE at rate R is equivalent to solving it at $1 - R$ via their dual codes. Furthermore, unless otherwise specified, in the following sections we assume that the underlying codes are random linear codes and that, for any fixed weight w, the weight-w codewords of a code are uniformly distributed among all vectors of weight w over the same field.

Our analysis makes use of the following result for the complexity of computing fixed-weight codewords in a given linear code.

Lemma 1 (Prange's ISD complexity[23]**).** *The cost of computing m of the N_w codewords of weight w in a random $[n, k]$ linear code is $\tilde{\mathcal{O}}\left(\frac{m}{N_w}\binom{n}{w}/\binom{n-k}{w}\right)$.*

Furthermore, letting $h(x) := -x\log_2 x - (1-x)\log_2(1-x)$ denote the binary entropy function, we use the following standard approximation of binomial coefficients

$$\frac{2^{h(\frac{k}{n})n}}{n+1} \leq \binom{n}{k} \leq 2^{h(\frac{k}{n})n}. \tag{1}$$

Canonical Forms. Chou, Persichetti, and Santini introduced the notion of *canonical forms* in [14] to show that it suffices to find two information sets I, J for $\mathcal{C}, \mathcal{C}'$ *colliding* under $\mathbf{Q}$, i.e., that are sent to each other by $\mathbf{Q}$, to recover the monomial in polynomial time, as we summarize in the following.

Theorem 2. *Let $\mathbf{G}, \mathbf{G}'$ be generator matrices of two equivalent $[n, k]$ linear codes $\mathcal{C}, \mathcal{C}'$ over $\mathbb{F}_q$, for $q \geq 7$, with respect to a monomial matrix $\mathbf{Q}$ and let π be the underlying permutation. Let I and J be colliding information sets of $\mathcal{C}$ and $\mathcal{C}'$, respectively, i.e., $\pi(i) \in J$, for every $i \in I$. Then there exists a polynomial-time algorithm* $\mathsf{CF\text{-}RecoverMonomial}(\mathbf{G}, \mathbf{G}', I, J)$ *that recovers $\mathbf{Q}$ with probability $1 - \mathcal{O}(n^{-1})$.*

For a proof of the above, see [14, Proposition 10] and [21, Lemma 3.4]. Generally the time complexity of CF-RecoverMonomial is dominated by the computation of canonical forms which is known to lie in $\mathcal{O}(n^3)$ [7]. Nowakowski [21] introduces slight overheads to guarantee high success probability already for constant field sizes $q \geq 7$. We therefore account for this algorithm conservatively with $\tilde{\mathcal{O}}(n^4)$ in our analysis.

The Subset Sum Problem. In our analysis we make use of a reduction to the subset sum problem. We refer to this problem as SSP and it is defined as follows.

Definition 2 (Subset Sum Problem). *Let $m \in \mathbb{N}$ and let $S = \{a_1, \ldots, a_m\}$ be a multiset with $a_i \in \mathbb{N}$. Given a target $b \in \mathbb{N}$, the* Subset Sum Problem *with input (S, b) asks to find a subset $S' \subseteq S$ such that $\sum_{s \in S'} s = b$. If such a subset S' exists, we say that the instance admits an* exact solution.

When no exact solution exists, we might consider approximate solutions, which we define as exact solutions for target $b - \varepsilon$, for some $\varepsilon > 0$. Note that while the Subset Sum Problem is NP-complete, several algorithms exist to solve it in practice, including a classical dynamic programming approach that runs in pseudo-polynomial time.

3 Solving LCE Given Two Equivalent Codeword Pairs

In this section, we introduce an algorithm that recovers the monomial transformation from only two pairs of equivalent codewords. The algorithm builds on Theorem 2, in particular, that for the recovery of the monomial it suffices to recover two *colliding information sets* $I \subset [n]$ in $\mathcal{C}$ and $J \subset [n]$ in $\mathcal{C}'$ such that $\pi(i) \in J$ for any $i \in I$, where π is the secret permutation $\mathbf{P}$ defining the monomial.

Let us start by formally defining the notion of *equivalent codewords.*

Definition 3 (Equivalent Codewords). *Let $\mathcal{C}, \mathcal{C}'$ be two $[n, k]$ linear codes over $\mathbb{F}_q$, equivalent under some monomial transformation $\mathbf{Q} \in \mathsf{Mono}_n(\mathbb{F}_q)$ and let $\mathbf{v} \in \mathcal{C}$ and $\mathbf{w} \in \mathcal{C}'$ be two nonzero codewords. We say that $(\mathbf{v}, \mathbf{w})$ is a pair of* equivalent *codewords with respect to $\mathcal{C}, \mathcal{C}'$ if $\mathbf{w} = \mathbf{v}\mathbf{Q}$.*

In the following, the codes $\mathcal{C}$ and $\mathcal{C}'$ are usually clear from the context, hence, we drop the term *with respect to $\mathcal{C}, \mathcal{C}'$.*

3.1 Basic Idea: Reduction to SSP

Let $\mathcal{C}, \mathcal{C}'$ be two equivalent $[n, k]$ linear codes $\mathcal{C}, \mathcal{C}'$ via a monomial $\mathbf{Q} \in \mathsf{Mono}_n(\mathbb{F}_q)$, and let $(\mathbf{v}_1, \mathbf{w}_1), (\mathbf{v}_2, \mathbf{w}_2) \in \mathcal{C} \times \mathcal{C}'$ be two pairs of equivalent codewords of weight w. In the following we leverage the information on the support of the codewords, $\mathbf{v}_i, \mathbf{w}_i$ to identify two colliding information sets I, J for $\mathcal{C}$ and $\mathcal{C}'$

respectively. Recall that this implies that I gets mapped into J via the monomial $\mathbf{Q}$, which suffices to recover $\mathbf{Q}$ via Theorem 2.

Refining the SSP *Instance.* Let $I_i := \mathrm{Supp}\mathbf{v}_i \subset [n]$ and $J_i := \mathrm{Supp}\mathbf{w}_i \subset [n]$, for $i = 1, 2$. We have that

$$|I_1 \cap I_2| =: \ell, \quad |I_1 \setminus I_2| = |I_2 \setminus I_1| = w - \ell, \quad \big|[n] \setminus I_1 \cup I_2\big| = n - 2w + \ell. \quad (2)$$

The sizes for the sets corresponding to J_1, J_2 are analogous. Most importantly, since zero (resp. non-zero) entries of $\mathbf{v}_1, \mathbf{v}_2$ are mapped to zero (resp. non-zero) entries of $\mathbf{w}_1, \mathbf{w}_2$ by $\mathbf{Q}$, we know that the indices in $I_1 \cap I_2$ are mapped into the indices in $J_1 \cap J_2$, those of $I_1 \setminus I_2$ into $J_1 \setminus J_2$ and similarly for the remaining sets. The goal is to combine the sets from Eq. 2 to obtain the desired information sets for $\mathcal{C}$ and correspondingly for $\mathcal{C}'$. This problem is a subset sum problem with input integers $\{w - \ell, w - \ell, n - 2w + \ell, \ell\}$ and target k, i.e., we are searching for a sum of input integers that sums up to k. Note that this instance could be easily solved via dynamic programming as all given integers are of polynomial size. However, the small set of input integers makes it unlikely that this instance has a solution. In the following, we therefore exploit the additional information given by the support intersection of the two pairs to obtain a refined subset sum instance with a larger input set containing smaller integers.

Let $I_{\text{int}} := I_1 \cap I_2$ and $J_{\text{int}} := J_1 \cap J_2$. As already observed, a monomial $\mathbf{Q}$ with $\mathbf{w}_t = \mathbf{v}_t\mathbf{Q}$ must map the indices in I_{int} into the indices in J_{int}. This implies that for any $i \in I_{\text{int}}$ there exists a $j \in J_{\text{int}}$ such that

$$\mathbf{w}_1(j) = \alpha_{i,j} \cdot \mathbf{v}_1(i) \quad \text{and} \quad \mathbf{w}_2(j) = \alpha_{i,j} \cdot \mathbf{v}_2(i) \quad \text{for some } \alpha_{i,j} \in \mathbb{F}_q^*, \qquad (3)$$

where $\alpha_{i,j} = \mathbf{Q}(i,j)$. Note that this implies that $\frac{\mathbf{v}_1(i)}{\mathbf{v}_2(i)} = \frac{\mathbf{w}_1(j)}{\mathbf{w}_2(j)}$. This allows us to group the indices in I_{int} and J_{int} into equivalence classes labeled by their quotient $\frac{\mathbf{v}_1(i)}{\mathbf{v}_2(i)}$, respectively $\frac{\mathbf{w}_1(j)}{\mathbf{w}_2(j)}$, with the permutation acting exclusively between the indices contained in equivalence classes sharing the same label. More precisely, let

$$F_c^{\mathbf{v}_1,\mathbf{v}_2} := \{i \in I_{\text{int}} \mid \mathbf{v}_1[i]/\mathbf{v}_2[i] = c\} \qquad (4)$$

for $c \in \mathbb{F}_q^*$, and let $F_c^{\mathbf{w}_1,\mathbf{w}_2}$ be analogously defined for the set J_{int} and vectors $\mathbf{w}_i$. Then, for every $i \in F_c^{\mathbf{v}_1,\mathbf{v}_2}$ it holds $\pi(i) \in F_c^{\mathbf{w}_1,\mathbf{w}_2}$. In turn, we obtain a refined subset sum instance with input integers being the multiset

$$S = \{w - \ell, w - \ell, n - 2w + \ell\} \cup D, \qquad (5)$$

where D is the multiset defined as

$$D := \big\{|F_c^{\mathbf{v}_1,\mathbf{v}_2}| \colon c \in \mathbb{F}_q^*\big\} \setminus \{0\}. \qquad (6)$$

Any solution to the subset sum instance with input set S from Eq. 5 and target k, can be uniquely mapped to a pair of sets $I, J \subset [n]$ of size $|I| = |J| = k$ describing indices in $\mathcal{C}, \mathcal{C}'$ satisfying $\pi(i) \in J$ for $i \in I$. Therefore, we simply translate the integers of the subset sum solution $S' \subset S$ back into the sets

Algorithm 1. SSP-RecoverMonomial($\mathbf{G}, \mathbf{G}', (\mathbf{v}_1, \mathbf{w}_1), (\mathbf{v}_2, \mathbf{w}_2)$)

Input: $\mathbf{G}, \mathbf{G}' \in \mathbb{F}_q^{k \times n}$ generators of $\mathcal{C}, \mathcal{C}'$ respectively. Two pairs of equivalent codewords $(\mathbf{v}_1, \mathbf{w}_1), (\mathbf{v}_2, \mathbf{w}_2) \in \mathcal{C} \times \mathcal{C}'$ of Hamming weight w.
Output: A monomial $\mathbf{Q}$ such that $\mathcal{C}' = \mathcal{C}\mathbf{Q}$ or $\perp$

Construct the set S from Eq. (5) from $(\mathbf{v}_1, \mathbf{w}_1), (\mathbf{v}_2, \mathbf{w}_2)$
Compute (approximate) solution $S' \subset S$ to SSP instance (S, k), i.e., $\sum_{s \in S'} s = k - \delta$, $\delta \geq 0$
$K \leftarrow$ `indices`$(S', \mathbf{v}_1, \mathbf{v}_2)$ and $K' \leftarrow$ `indices`$(S', \mathbf{w}_1, \mathbf{w}_2)$
if $|K| = k$ **then**
  $\mathbf{Q} \leftarrow$ CF-RecoverMonomial($\mathbf{G}, \mathbf{G}', K, K'$)
  if $\mathbf{Q} \neq \perp$ **then**
    Return $\mathbf{Q}$
else if $|K| < k$ **then**
  Choose a non-empty set $F_c^{\mathbf{v}_1, \mathbf{v}_2}$ such that $F_c^{\mathbf{v}_1, \mathbf{v}_2} \cap K = \emptyset$, for any $c \in \mathbb{F}_q^*$
  Choose $I^* \subset F_c^{\mathbf{v}_1, \mathbf{v}_2}$ with $|I^*| = \delta$ and let $\tilde{K} \leftarrow K \cup I^*$
  Derive $F_c^{\mathbf{w}_1, \mathbf{w}_2} \subseteq J_1 \cap J_2$, the corresponding set to $F_c^{\mathbf{v}_1, \mathbf{v}_2}$ in $\mathcal{C}'$
  for $J^* \subset F_c^{\mathbf{w}_1, \mathbf{w}_2}$ with $|J^*| = \delta$ **do**
    $\tilde{K}' \leftarrow K' \cup J^*$
    $\mathbf{Q} \leftarrow$ CF-RecoverMonomial($\mathbf{G}, \mathbf{G}', \tilde{K}, \tilde{K}'$)
    if $\mathbf{Q} \neq \perp$ **then**
      Return $\mathbf{Q}$
Return $\perp$

from which they originate. We denote this conversion by `indices`$(\cdot)$, i.e., $I =$ `indices`$(S', \mathbf{v}_1, \mathbf{v}_2)$ and $J =$ `indices`$(S', \mathbf{w}_1, \mathbf{w}_2)$. Now, as long as I forms an information set in $\mathcal{C}$ (or analogously J in $\mathcal{C}'$) we can recover the secret monomial via Theorem 2.

We give a pseudocode of the procedure that recovers the secret monomial from two equivalent codeword pairs in Algorithm 1. Note that, in case the subset sum instance does not admit a solution for target k but only for target $k - \varepsilon$ for some $\varepsilon > 0$, we introduce an enumeration procedure to extend the sets to size k. More precisely, we extend I by elements from $F_c^{\mathbf{v}_1, \mathbf{v}_2}$ and J by elements from $F_c^{\mathbf{w}_1, \mathbf{w}_2}$ for some c such that these sets are not yet included in I, J, i.e., $F_c^{\mathbf{v}_1, \mathbf{v}_2} \cap I = F_c^{\mathbf{w}_1, \mathbf{w}_2} \cap J = \emptyset$. In the following, we first prove bounds on the approximation quality, i.e., we upper bound ε, after which we prove the correctness and complexity of the algorithm (in dependence on ε).

3.2 On the Existence of a Subset Sum Solution in Algorithm1

In the following we lower-bound the necessary field size to ensure that the subset sum instance defined by the input set S from Eq. (5) and target k admits an approximate solution and give an upper bound on the achievable approximation error.

Therefore, consider the following, not necessarily optimal, strategy for constructing a solution. Starting from any of the obtainable sums disregarding the set D, i.e., starting with $s \in \{0, w-\ell, 2w-2\ell, n-2w+\ell, n-w, n-\ell\}$ we add elements from set D until we either exactly reach k or the addition of any further element from D leads to a value larger than k. With this strategy, we obtain an (approximate) solution if $s \leq k \leq s+\ell$, since $|D| = \ell$. If we restrict our attention to $s = n-2w+\ell$, we obtain the following condition

$$n-2w+\ell \leq k \leq n-2w+2\ell.$$

In the following, we show that this strategy already leads to an approximate solution for *constant* q with an approximation error that is roughly bounded by the average size μ of elements in D.

The Information Set Constraint. Recall that to eventually reconstruct the solution via Theorem 2 we require that the k indices corresponding to the subset sum solution form an information set in $\mathcal{C}$. Since the input integer $n-2w+\ell$ corresponds to the set $[n] \setminus I_1 \cup I_2$, this set alone cannot represent an information set, as it does not include any elements from the support of $\mathbf{v}_1$ or $\mathbf{v}_2$. It follows that the columns of the generator matrix of $\mathcal{C}$ indexed by this set can have a rank at most $k-2$. We therefore must ensure to include at least two more indices, one in $\mathrm{Supp}\mathbf{v}_1$ and one in $\mathrm{Supp}\mathbf{v}_2$ to obtain an information set. In the following, we enforce the stricter criterium of including at least two elements from D (originating from the support intersection) when constructing the colliding information sets. In the context of Algorithm 1 this translates into[2]

$$n-2w+\ell+\min(D) < k \leq n-2w+2\ell.$$

Then, by conservatively bounding $\min(D)$ with the expected size μ of the elements in D, we obtain the condition

$$n-2w+\ell+\mu < k \leq n-2w+2\ell. \tag{7}$$

The following proposition shows that the set of indices obtained via Eq. (7) is an information set with probability analogous to a random set of k indices.

Proposition 1. *Let K be the set of k indices resulting from the union of the indices in $[n] \setminus I_1 \cup I_2$ and two distinct subsets $F_c^{\mathbf{v}_1,\mathbf{v}_2}$, $F_{c'}^{\mathbf{v}_1,\mathbf{v}_2}$ of $I_1 \cap I_2$ (see Eq. (4)). Then K is an information set for $\mathcal{C}$ with probability*

$$\prod_{i=1}^{k-2}(1-q^{-i}).$$

[2] For *approximate* solutions this ensures that at least one element from D is included, but then the enumeration procedure within Algorithm 1 ensures that at least one more index from the support intersection is included.

Proof. The code $\mathcal{C}$ admits a generator matrix $\mathbf{G}$ whose last two rows are the low-weight codewords $\mathbf{v}_1, \mathbf{v}_2$. As the code is uniform over all codes of dimension k containing $\mathbf{v}_1, \mathbf{v}_2$, the matrix formed by the first $k-2$ rows of $\mathbf{G}$ can be seen as uniformly drawn from $\mathbb{F}_q^{(k-2)\times n}$.[3]

Let $\mathbf{M}$ be the $k \times k$ submatrix of $\mathbf{G}$ formed by the columns indexed by K. The set K is an information set if and only if $\mathbf{M}$ is full rank. By construction, K contains $n-2w+\ell$ indices from $[n] \setminus I_1 \cup I_2$, corresponding to the zero entries of $\mathbf{v}_1$ and $\mathbf{v}_2$, and $s := k - n + 2w - \ell \geq 2$ indices arising from the support intersection of the two codewords. It follows that there exists a combination of the rows of $\mathbf{M}$ that puts it in the following block form

$$\mathbf{M} = \left(\begin{array}{c|c} \mathbf{A} & \mathbf{B} \\ \hline \mathbf{0}_{2,k-s} & \mathbf{C} \end{array}\right) \quad \in \mathbb{F}_q^{k\times k},$$

where $\mathbf{A} \in \mathbb{F}_q^{(k-2)\times(k-s)}$, $\mathbf{B} \in \mathbb{F}_q^{(k-2)\times s}$, $\mathbf{C} \in \mathbb{F}_q^{2\times s}$, and $\mathbf{0}_{2,k-s} \in \mathbb{F}_q^{2\times(k-s)}$, with $s \geq 2$. Since K contains at least two subsets $F_c^{\mathbf{v}_1,\mathbf{v}_2}$ and $F_{c'}^{\mathbf{v}_1,\mathbf{v}_2}$ of indices coming from the support intersection of $\mathbf{v}_1$ and $\mathbf{v}_2$, the matrix $\mathbf{C}$ has rank 2. After a suitable column permutation, we can write $\mathbf{C} = (\mathbf{C}' \mid \tilde{\mathbf{C}})$ where $\tilde{\mathbf{C}} \in \mathbb{F}_q^{2\times 2}$ is invertible and contains one column with index in $F_c^{\mathbf{v}_1,\mathbf{v}_2}$ and one with index in $F_{c'}^{\mathbf{v}_1,\mathbf{v}_2}$. Resorting its columns, we have that $\mathbf{M}$ is full rank if

$$\mathbf{M}' = \left(\begin{array}{c|c|c} \mathbf{A} & \mathbf{B}' & \tilde{\mathbf{B}} \\ \hline \mathbf{0}_{2,k-s} & \mathbf{C}' & \tilde{\mathbf{C}} \end{array}\right) \quad \in \mathbb{F}_q^{k\times k}$$

is full rank. Since $\tilde{\mathbf{C}}$ is invertible, $\mathbf{M}'$ has the same rank as:

$$\mathbf{M}'' = \left(\begin{array}{c|c|c} \mathbf{A} & \mathbf{B}'' & \mathbf{0}_{k-2,2} \\ \hline \mathbf{0}_{2,k-s} & \mathbf{0}_{2,s-2} & \mathbf{I}_2 \end{array}\right) \quad \in \mathbb{F}_q^{k\times k},$$

where $\mathbf{B}'' = \mathbf{B}' - \tilde{\mathbf{B}}\tilde{\mathbf{C}}^{-1}\mathbf{C}'$. Thus,

$$\mathsf{rank}(\mathbf{M}) = \mathsf{rank}(\mathbf{M}'') = \mathsf{rank}(\mathbf{A} \mid \mathbf{B}'') + 2,$$

which shows that $\mathbf{M}$ is full rank k if and only if $[\mathbf{A} \mid \mathbf{B}''] \in \mathbb{F}_q^{(k-2)\times(k-2)}$ is full rank. The matrix $[\mathbf{A}|\mathbf{B}']$ is a selection of some columns from the upper part of $\mathbf{G}$ which is a uniform random matrix in $\mathbb{F}_q^{(k-2)\times n}$, as $\tilde{\mathbf{B}}\tilde{\mathbf{C}}^{-1}\mathbf{C}'$ does not depend on $\mathbf{B}'$, the matrix $\mathbf{B}'' = \mathbf{B}' - \tilde{\mathbf{B}}\tilde{\mathbf{C}}^{-1}\mathbf{C}'$ is also a uniform matrix. Then we can treat $[\mathbf{A}|\mathbf{B}'']$ as a uniformly random matrices n $\mathbb{F}_q^{(k-2)\times(k-2)}$, which leads to

$$\Pr[\mathsf{rank}(\mathbf{M}) = k] = \Pr[\mathsf{rank}([\mathbf{A} \mid \mathbf{B}'']) = k-2] = \prod_{i=1}^{k-2} \left(1 - q^{-i}\right)$$

□

[3] Actually, the first $k-2$ rows are linearly independent and avoid the space generated by $\mathbf{v}_1, \mathbf{v}_2$. Hence, they are not exactly uniformly distributed; however, the distance between the two distribution is exponentially small in n.

Notice that, given a $k \times n$ matrix chosen uniformly at random, the probability of a random set of k indices being an information set is $\prod_{i=1}^{k}(1-q^{-i}) < \prod_{i=1}^{k-2}(1-q^{-i})$.

On the Distribution of ℓ and D. Modeling the codewords $\mathbf{v}_i$ as uniformly distributed over the set of all weight-w words, the support intersection size ℓ follows a hypergeometric distribution with population size n, w success states (support size of the first codeword), and sample size w (support size of the second codeword), that is

$$\Pr[\ell = c] = \frac{\binom{w}{c}\binom{n-w}{w-c}}{\binom{n}{w}},$$

and the expected value of ℓ is $\mathbb{E}[\ell] = w^2/n$.

The elements of D are then following a binomial distribution with ℓ trials and success probability $p = \frac{1}{q-1}$ conditioned to only positive values (by definition, there are only non-zero values in D). The mean of this distribution is $\mu = \frac{\ell p}{\tau} \approx \ell p$, since $\tau := \Pr[X > 0] = 1 - (1-p)^{\ell}$ quickly converges to 1.

Necessary Field Size to Obtain an Approximate Solution. We now show that satisfying inequality (7) leads to a lower bound on the required field size. However, for any constant rate $R \leq 1/2$, this lower bound is a (small) constant as we show in the following lemma.

Lemma 2. (SSP Approximation Exists for Constant Field Size). *Let $n \in \mathbb{N}$ be the code length, and let the rate $R \leq 1/2$ be constant. Then, there exists a constant q_0 such that for any $q \geq q_0$, and w such that $w_{GV} \leq w < \frac{(q-1)n}{q}$, the inequality in Eq. 7 is satisfied with probability at least $1/2$ over the choice of the codewords $\mathbf{v}_1, \mathbf{v}_2$.*

Proof. Recall that ℓ follows a hyper-geometric distribution with $p = \frac{w}{n} = \omega$ and $w = \omega n$ trials. Let us assume $\ell \geq \mathbb{E}[\ell] = w^2/n$, which happens with probability at least 1/2. Now, by substituting $w = \omega n$, $k = Rn$ and $\mu = \ell/(q-1)$ into Eq. 7 and dividing by n we obtain

$$1 - 2\omega + \frac{\ell}{n}\left(1 + \frac{1}{q-1}\right) < R \leq 1 - -2\omega + \frac{2\ell}{n}. \tag{8}$$

Using a standard tail bound for the hypergeometric distribution [15] of ℓ we get

$$\Pr[\ell \geq (\omega + \varepsilon)\omega n] \leq e^{-2\varepsilon^2 \omega n} \quad \text{for any } \varepsilon \geq 0.$$

Conditioning the tail bound with $\ell \geq \omega^2 n$ and letting $\epsilon := \frac{\varepsilon}{\omega}$ we have

$$\Pr\left[\ell \geq (1+\epsilon)\omega^2 n \mid \ell \geq \omega^2 n\right] = \frac{\Pr\left[\ell \geq (1+\epsilon)\omega^2 n\right]}{\Pr[\ell \geq \omega^2 n]} \leq 2e^{-2\epsilon^2\omega^3 n}.$$

This ensure that $\omega^2 n \leq \ell < (1+\epsilon)\omega^2 n\}$ with $1/2 - o(1)$.

To prove that Ineq. 8 holds for all ℓ in this range, we substitute ℓ with $(1+\epsilon)\omega^2 n$ in the lower bound and with $\omega^2 n$ in the upper bound, which leads to

$$1 - 2\omega + \omega^2(1+\epsilon)\left(1 + \frac{1}{q-1}\right) < R \leq 1 - -2\omega + 2\omega^2. \tag{9}$$

Note that the right inequality is trivially satisfied as $-2\omega + 2\omega^2 = 2\omega(\omega - 1) \geq -\frac{1}{2}$ for $0 \leq \omega \leq 1$ and hence

$$1 - 2\omega + 2\omega^2 \geq \frac{1}{2} \geq R.$$

Consider the left side of Ineq. 9 if we define $\epsilon' = \epsilon + \frac{1+\epsilon}{q-1}$, using $1 - 2\omega + \omega^2 = (1-\omega)^2$, this inequality can be rewritten as

$$(1-\omega)^2 + \omega^2\epsilon' < R.$$

The derivative of $(1-\omega)^2 + \omega^2\epsilon'$ is $-2(1-\omega) + 2\omega\epsilon' = 2(\omega(1+\epsilon') - 1)$ which means the function is decreasing in ω for $0 \leq \omega \leq \frac{1}{1+\epsilon'}$. Therefore, if the inequality holds for the smallest value of $\omega = \omega_{\mathrm{GV}}$ it also holds for all ω wit $\omega_{\mathrm{GV}} \leq \omega \leq \frac{1}{1+\epsilon'}$. Furthermore, as $\epsilon' \geq \frac{1}{q-1}$ we have that $\omega \leq \frac{1}{1+\epsilon'} < \frac{q-1}{q}$, which is given by the statement, it therefore suffices to concentrate on $\omega = \omega_{\mathrm{GV}}$.

The value of ω_{GV} is determined as the smallest ω for which $h_q(\omega) > 1 - R$ then $R > 1 - h_q(\omega_{\mathrm{GV}})$, where h_q is the q-ary entropy function. The left-hand side of Eq. (9) can be rewritten as

$$(1-\omega_{\mathrm{GV}})^2 + \omega_{\mathrm{GV}}^2\epsilon' < 1 - h_q(\omega_{\mathrm{GV}}) < R,$$

from which we get the simpler expression

$$\omega_{\mathrm{GV}}(2 - \omega_{\mathrm{GV}}(1+\epsilon')) > h_q(\omega_{\mathrm{GV}}). \tag{10}$$

For $q \to \infty$ we have that $h_q(\omega_{\mathrm{GV}}) \to \omega_{\mathrm{GV}}$ and $\epsilon' \to \epsilon$ which transforms the above inequality into

$$\omega_{\mathrm{GV}}(1 - \omega_{\mathrm{GV}}(1+\epsilon)) > 0,$$

which is true for all w_{GV} in the considered range $0 < \omega_{\mathrm{GV}} < \frac{1}{1+\epsilon} < \frac{q-1}{q}$. This implies that there exists a q_0, not depending on n, such that the inequality is satisfied for any $q \geq q_0$. □

Lemma 2 shows that a constant field size q_0 is sufficient to ensure that we can obtain an approximate solution to the SSP instance by starting from the set $[n] \setminus I_1 \cup I_2$ and then adding at least two elements from D. While the lemma does not directly state the value of q_0, we can determine an upperbound on this constant as the smallest q satisfying (compare to Eq. (10))

$$\omega_{\mathrm{GV}}\left(2 - \omega_{\mathrm{GV}}\left(1 + \frac{1}{q-1}\right)\right) > h_q(\omega_{\mathrm{GV}}). \tag{11}$$

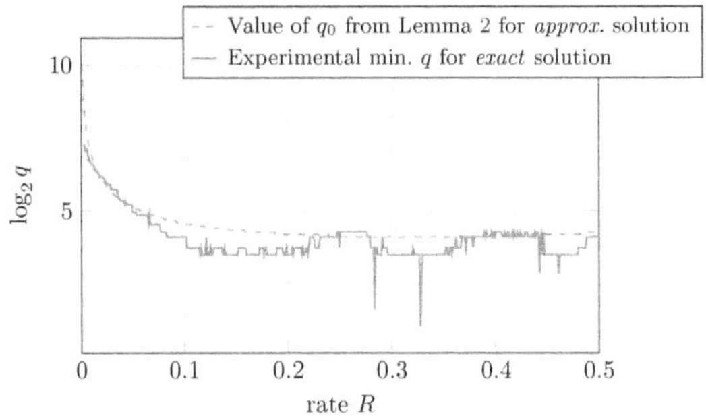

Fig. 1. Lowerbound on q_0 from Eq. 11 vs. The experimentally observed minimal q allowing an exact solution to the SSP instance for 10/10 trials, $n = 1024$.

We illustrate the constant q_0 in Fig. 1 as a function of the rate (dashed line). It can be observed that for rates approaching zero q_0 grows, but already for rates around $R = 0.05$ a field size of $q \approx 31$ is sufficient to obtain an approximate solution.

Note that the analysis is rather conservative, as in the context of Lemma 2 it is only considered to start from the set $[n] \setminus I_1 \cup I_2$, while any other set, i.e., $I_1 \setminus I_2, I_2 \setminus I_1, \emptyset$ or any combination of the sets is also a valid starting choice. Furthermore, the analysis essentially assumes that the elements in D are all matching their expectation, while any variance leading to smaller values in D increases the probability of the subset sum instance admitting an exact solution. For these reasons, the subset sum instance for the q_0 from Lemma 2 can in many practical cases already be solved exactly. We give more details on this in Sect. 3.4, where we provide comprehensive experiments on the procedure. For now we proceed with the *provable* approximation quality.

On the Approximation Quality of the Solution. Lemma 2 proves that already for constant field size we can expect to find an approximate solution, i.e., a subset sum solution for target $k - \varepsilon$ for some $\varepsilon \geq 0$. The following lemma quantifies the approximation quality by providing an upper bound on ε in dependence on the weight w of the codewords and the field size q.

Lemma 3 (SSP Approximation Error). *Let $n \in \mathbb{N}$ sufficiently large, $k = Rn$ for constant $R \leq 1/2$. Let $q > q_0$ for the constant q_0 from Lemma 2, and $w < \frac{(q-1)n}{q}$. Then, with probability at least $\frac{1}{2} - o(1)$ over the choice of the codewords $\mathbf{v}_1, \mathbf{v}_2$, the subset sum instance with input set S as in Eq. (5) and target $k - \varepsilon$ admits a solution, where $\varepsilon \leq (1+\delta)\frac{2w^2}{(q-1)n} + \log q$ for any constant $\delta > 0$.*

Proof. Again consider the approximate solution constructed by starting from the set $[n] \setminus I_1 \cup I_2$ and then adding elements from the set D until the addition of any further element leads to exceeding k. According to Lemma 2, for the made choice of q, this strategy leads to an approximate solution $k - \varepsilon'$ with probability $1/2 - o(1)$. Clearly, we have that $\varepsilon' \leq \max(D)$. Now observe that the value of $\max(D)$ can be modeled as the maximum load of a bin when throwing $m = \ell$ balls (the elements in the support intersection) into $n = q - 1$ bins (the possible quotients in $\mathbb{F}_q^*$). It is well known (see for example [28, Chapter 5]) that for the maximum load $\max(D)$ it holds with high probability that

$$\max(D) = \begin{cases} \mu + \mathcal{O}(\sqrt{\mu \ln n}), & \mu = \Omega(\ln n) \\ \mathcal{O}\left(\frac{\ln n}{\ln \ln n}\right), & \mu = \Theta(1), \end{cases}$$

where $\mu = \mathbb{E}[d] = \frac{m}{n}$, with $d \in D$. Now observe that $\varepsilon = (1 + \delta)\mu + \log n$ is an upper bound for both cases for any constant $\delta > 0$. Furthermore, Raab and Steger [24] have shown that the intermediate regime smoothly transitions between the two behaviors resulting in ε being an upper bound for all μ, yielding $\varepsilon' \leq \max(D) \leq \varepsilon$

Now observe that Lemma 2 conditions on $\ell \geq \mathbb{E}[\ell] = \frac{w^2}{n}$ which happens with probability $\Pr[\ell \geq \mathbb{E}[\ell]] \geq 1/2$, implying

$$\mathbb{E}[\ell \mid \ell \geq \mathbb{E}[\ell]] \leq \frac{\mathbb{E}[\ell]}{\Pr[\ell \geq \mathbb{E}[\ell]]} \leq 2\mathbb{E}[\ell] = \frac{2w^2}{n}.$$

In turn, the expected bin load satisfies

$$\mu = \frac{\mathbb{E}[\ell \mid \ell \geq 1/2]}{q-1} \leq \frac{2\mathbb{E}[\ell]}{q-1} = \frac{2w^2}{n(q-1)}.$$

Substituting $\mu \leq \frac{2w^2}{n}$ and $n = q - 1$ into ε yields the statement. □

Note that the approximation error given in Lemma 3 is about $\varepsilon = \mathcal{O}\left(\frac{n}{q} + \log q\right)$, since $w = \Theta(n)$.

3.3 The Complexity of Algorithm 1

We now provide an analysis of the running time of Algorithm 1. Recall that in case the subset sum instance admits an exact solution for target k the algorithm recovers the secret monomial in a straightforward fashion via Theorem 2. In cases where only approximate solutions for target $k-\varepsilon$ exist, an enumeration procedure is used to still recover the secret monomial, whose running time depends on the approximation quality ε. The following theorem states the running time of Algorithm 1 in dependence on n and ε.

Theorem 3. *Let $\mathbf{G}, \mathbf{G}' \in \mathbb{F}_q^{k \times n}$ be generator matrices of two random equivalent codes $\mathcal{C}, \mathcal{C}'$ via a secret monomial $\mathbf{Q} \in \mathsf{Mono}_n(\mathbb{F}_q)$, $q \geq q_0$ be a prime, where q_0 is the constant from Lemma 2, and $(\mathbf{v}_1, \mathbf{w}_1), (\mathbf{v}_2, \mathbf{w}_2) \in \mathcal{C} \times \mathcal{C}'$ be two pairs of equivalent codewords of Hamming weight w. Then Algorithm 1 on input $\mathbf{G}, \mathbf{G}'$ and $(\mathbf{v}_i, \mathbf{w}_i)$, for $i = 1, 2$, recovers the secret monomial $\mathbf{Q}$ with probability at least $0.47 - o(1)$ in time $\tilde{\mathcal{O}}(2^{\varepsilon} n^4)$, where ε is defined as in Lemma 3.*

Proof. Lemma 2 guarantees that there exists an (approximate) solution to the SSP instance (S, k) such that the corresponding sets K, K' satisfy $|K| = |K'| = k - \delta$ with probability about 1/2 for q being a sufficiently large constant. We already argued that the sets of indices K and K' for $\mathcal{C}$ and $\mathcal{C}'$ collide, i.e., they are mapped to each other via the secret monomial $\mathbf{Q}$. If the SSP instance is solved exactly, i.e., $|K| = |K'| = k$, then K and K' can be input to CF-RecoverMonomial to compute the secret monomial $\mathbf{Q}$. In case those sets form information sets in $\mathcal{C}$ and $\mathcal{C}'$, CF-RecoverMonomial has been shown to succeed in recovering the secret monomial with high probability $1 - \mathcal{O}(n^{-1})$ when $q \geq 7$ [21], while numerical analysis shows that $q_0 \geq 19$ for all code rates (see Fig. 1). Furthermore, note that Eq. (7) ensures that for $|K| = k$ at least two distinct subsets of indices $F_c^{\mathbf{v}_1,\mathbf{v}_2}, F_{c'}^{\mathbf{v}_1,\mathbf{v}_2}$ are included in K, and, hence, the probability of K being an information set is at least $\prod_{i=0}^{k-2}(1 - q_0^{-i})$ according to Proposition 1. The total probability of success is then at least $\frac{1}{2}\left(1 - \mathcal{O}(n^{-1})\right)\prod_{i=0}^{k-2}(1 - q_0^{-i}) > \frac{1}{2} \cdot 0.94 - o(1) = 0.47 - o(1)$ since $q_0 \geq 19$.

If, on the other hand, the SSP instance is not solved exactly, but instead we have $|K| = k - \delta < k$, the algorithm completes K via bruteforce to form an information set. The brute-force step chooses one of the sets $F_c^{\mathbf{v}_1,\mathbf{v}_2}$, derived from the codeword support intersection of $\mathbf{v}_1, \mathbf{v}_2$, that is not included in K, i.e., $F_c^{\mathbf{v}_1,\mathbf{v}_2} \cap K = \emptyset$. In line 10, an arbitrary subset $I^* \subset F_c^{\mathbf{v}_1,\mathbf{v}_2}$ of size δ is chosen, and the set $\tilde{K} = K \cup I^*$ is constructed, so that $|\tilde{K}| = k$. Subsequently, the algorithm constructs the set $\tilde{K}' = K' \cup J^*$ for every $J^* \subset F_c^{\mathbf{w}_1,\mathbf{w}_2}$ of size $|J^*| = \delta$, where $F_c^{\mathbf{w}_1,\mathbf{w}_2}$ is the set of indices of $\mathcal{C}'$ corresponding to $F_c^{\mathbf{v}_1,\mathbf{v}_2}$. For each trial, the algorithm attempts to recover $\mathbf{Q}$ via CF-RecoverMonomial with input sets $\tilde{K}$ and $\tilde{K}'$. Note that we already know that the indices in $F_c^{\mathbf{v}_1,\mathbf{v}_2}$ are mapped to those in $F_c^{\mathbf{w}_1,\mathbf{w}_2}$. This implies that there must be a set $J^* \subset F_c^{\mathbf{w}_1,\mathbf{w}_2}$ such that I^* is mapped into J^*. Since the algorithm exhaustively iterates over all J^* this set is found. For the correct choice of J^*, CF-RecoverMonomial returns $\mathbf{Q}$ again with probability $\left(1 - \mathcal{O}(n^{-1})\right)\prod_{i=0}^{k-2}(1 - q^{-i})$ as long as K (or equivalently K') form information sets in $\mathcal{C}$ (and $\mathcal{C}'$). Similar to the case $|K| = k$, Proposition 1 applies because $\tilde{K}$ contains both the set $I^* \subset F_c^{\mathbf{v}_1,\mathbf{v}_2}$ and at least one other set $F_{c'}^{\mathbf{v}_1,\mathbf{v}_2}$ (by Eq. 7) with $c \neq c'$. The proof of Proposition 1 then follows analogously, by considering I^* in place of $F_c^{\mathbf{v}_1,\mathbf{v}_2}$.

The running time of Algorithm 1 is dominated by the brute-force search over $F_c^{\mathbf{w}_1,\mathbf{w}_2}$ and the attempt to reconstruct $\mathbf{Q}$ for each guess. The number of possible sets J^* is $\binom{|F_c^{\mathbf{w}_1,\mathbf{w}_2}|}{\delta}$. This term is maximized when $|F_c^{\mathbf{w}_1,\mathbf{w}_2}| = \max(D)$ and $\delta = \max(D)/2$ as $\binom{\max(D)}{\max(D)/2} \leq 2^{\max(D)}$, while Lemma 3 shows that $\max(D) \leq \varepsilon$. Knowing that the time complexity of CF-RecoverMonomial is $\tilde{\mathcal{O}}(n^4)$ results in the stated running time. □

In the full version of this paper [12, Appendix B], we show how to further improve this running time to $\tilde{\mathcal{O}}\left(2^{\frac{\varepsilon}{2}} n^4\right)$ by leveraging a meet-in-the-middle strategy that exploits the intrinsics of canonical forms.

Recall that Lemma 3 bounds $\varepsilon = \mathcal{O}\left(\frac{n}{q} + \log q\right)$. This implies that for $q = \Omega\left(\frac{n}{\log n}\right)$ the running time in Theorem 3 is polynomial in n. On the other hand for constant q the running time might be exponential. Moreover, in the intermediate regime, i.e., q growing in n but $q = o\left(\frac{n}{\log n}\right)$, the algorithm's running time is bounded to be subexponential.

However, the analysis concentrates on a specific subset sum solution and makes further conservative assumptions on the distribution on the elements in D. For these reasons, we observe far better results in practice, achieving polynomial time complexity even for small choices of q as we demonstrate in the following section.

3.4 Practical Experiments

We provide a full implementation of the algorithm reconstructing the secret monomial from two equivalent codeword pairs. Therefore, given two pairs of equivalent codewords $(\mathbf{v}_1, \mathbf{w}_1), (\mathbf{v}_2, \mathbf{w}_2)$ we construct the input set S from Eq. (5) and then compute a solution for target k if it exists. When constructing the solution S', we ensure that $|S' \cap D| \geq 2$ such that the probability of K forming an information set is at least the one of random sets (see Proposition 1).

In our experiments, if not stated otherwise, we fix $w = w_{\mathrm{GV}}$ to the smallest possible value of w, which seems to constitute the worst case. Note that for this w on average the size of the intersection $\ell := |I_1 \cap I_2|$ is minimized and, in turn, $|[n] \setminus I_1 \cup I_2| = n - 2w + \ell$ is maximized.

Necessary Field Size and Approximation Quality in Practice. In Fig. 1 we additionally report for every rate the smallest value of q that led to an *exact* solution of the subset sum instance in 10 out of 10 trials for $n = 1024$ (solid blue line). As can be observed, this q is often smaller or only marginally larger than the bound given by Lemma 2 required for an *approximate* solution (dashed line in Fig. 1). We also experimentally confirm the hypothesis that w_{GV} constitutes the worst weight: A change to $w = \lfloor 1.1 \cdot w_{\mathrm{GV}} \rceil$ leads to lower required values of q.

However, as intuition suggests, the smallest field size q required for an exact solution to exist grows in n, in contrast to the value from Lemma 2, which is constant. In Fig. 2, we report the smallest value of q required to obtain an exact solution in 10 out of 10 trials as a function of n for different rates. While we observe that the value is slowly increasing in n, in the range of parameters investigated, the dependence seems only logarithmic. This would imply the polynomial regime for Algorithm 1 starts from $q = \Omega(\log n)$ rather than from $q = \Omega\left(\frac{n}{\log n}\right)$.

Distribution of Obtainable Subset Sums. If the polynomial-regime indeed starts from $q = \Omega(\log n)$, this would imply that the subset sums obtained via

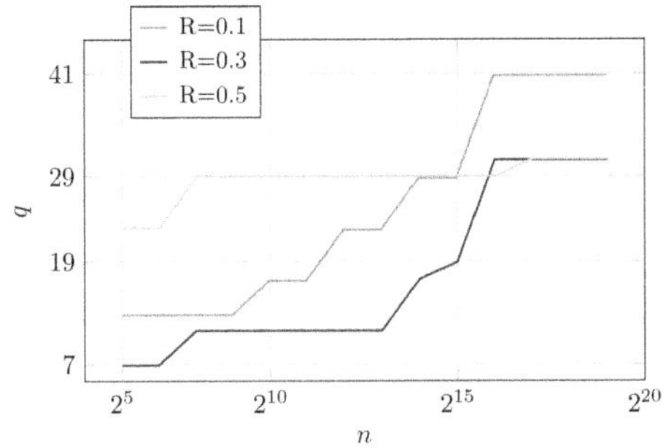

Fig. 2. Smallest prime q leading to exact solutions to the SSP instances from Algorithm 1 in 10 out of 10 trials.

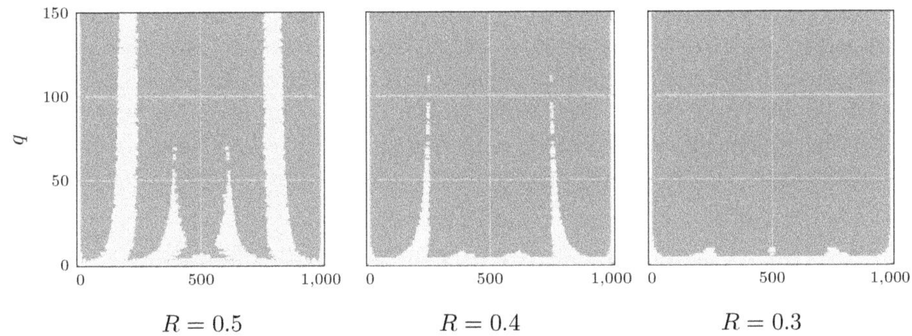

Fig. 3. Distribution of subset sums from S (Eq. (5)) with $n = 1000$, $w = w_{GV}$. Green areas represent obtainable sums, gray areas not obtainable subset sums.

sums of elements from D distribute densely in $[\ell]$: The total number of subset sums is $2^{|D|} \sim 2^{q-1}$ and for $q = \Omega(\log n)$ the average gap between obtainable sums becomes $\frac{\sum_{d \in D} d}{2^{|D|}} \sim \frac{\ell}{2^{q-1}} = \mathcal{O}(1)$, as $\ell = \Theta(n)$. Our experiments confirm that the density of the distribution of obtainable subset sums from the set S defining the subset sum instance quickly grows in q. We illustrate the reachable sums in $[n]$ in Fig. 3. Observe, that for smaller rates the sums distribute more evenly, which stems from the higher weight w_{GV} in those cases and the correspondingly larger value of ℓ.

Experiments on LESS Parameters. We also provide extensive experiments on parameters suggested in the LESS signature scheme. In particular, we are able to recover the secret monomial from two pairs of equivalent codewords of weight w_{GV} on average in less than 1, 3 and 8 min for LESS-I, -III and -V parameters respectively with empirical success probability close to one. Note that in all trials the subset sum instances admitted *exact* solutions for target k. Therefore the only failure originated from the extracted sets K, K' not forming information sets in $\mathcal{C}, \mathcal{C}'$ which happens with probability about $1/q = \frac{1}{127} \approx 0.008$. We

Table 2. Empirical time (in seconds) and success probability on LESS parameters.

	(n, k, q)	w	success rate	Time SSP	Time CF
LESS-I	$(252, 126, 127)$	107	0.9916	0.02	36.1
		96	0.9920	0.02	35.7
LESS-III	$(400, 200, 127)$	167	0.9929	0.04	151
		148	0.9922	0.03	152
LESS-V	$(548, 274, 127)$	226	0.9928	0.05	423
		202	0.9914	0.05	423

averaged for each parameter set over 10,000 experiments. In Table 2 we give the full details on those experiments. We also performed a similar experiment with slightly higher values of w motivated by the application given in Sect. 4.1, on which the algorithm, as expected, performs similarly well. Those experiments also show that the time to actually solve the subset sum instance is negligible.

4 A New Algorithm Solving Code Equivalence

In the following, we propose a new algorithm for solving LCE, following the codeword-search paradigm, that achieves significant concrete and asymptotic improvements over the state of the art. At the core of the proposed algorithm lies the observation from the previous section that two pairs of equivalent codewords are sufficient to recover the secret monomial for sufficiently large q.

High Level Description. The algorithm first, similarly to other algorithms based on low-weight codeword finding, computes two sufficiently large lists of weight w codewords in both codes, where w is an optimization parameter. After the construction of those lists, pairs of codewords are formed. We then define a criterion to check the compatibility of pairs with respect to monomial transformations, where pairs are deemed compatible if there exists any monomial transformation (not necessarily $\mathbf{Q}$) between them. Eventually, for each pair of codewords found to be compatible, we initiate the reconstruction of the secret monomial via Algorithm 1. As shown in the previous section, this reconstruction is successful whenever the two codeword pairs were indeed equivalent under the searched monomial $\mathbf{Q}$ for sufficiently large fields. We summarize this procedure in Algorithm 2.

Analysis of Algorithm 2. We first establish the following theorem, stating the complexity of Algorithm 2 in dependence on the used subroutines. Subsequently, we provide a concrete instantiation of the Compatible-Pairs subroutine.

Algorithm 2. Solving LCE

Input: $\mathbf{G}, \mathbf{G}' \in \mathbb{F}_q^{k \times n}$

Output: $\mathbf{Q} \in \mathsf{Mono}_n(\mathbb{F}_q)$ with $\mathbf{G} = \mathbf{S}\mathbf{G}'\mathbf{Q}$ for some invertible $\mathbf{S} \in \mathbb{F}_q^{k \times k}$ or $\perp$

```
choose w and N optimally
Compute a list L1 of codewords of weight w in G, with |L1| = N
Compute a list L2 of codewords of weight w in G', with |L2| = N
Construct V = L1 × L1 and W = L2 × L2 containing pairs of codewords
Z ← Compatible-Pairs(V, W)
for ((v1, w1), (v2, w2)) ∈ Z do
    Q ← SSP-RecoverMonomial(G, G', (v1, w1), (v2, w2))
    if Q ≠⊥ then
        Return Q
Return ⊥
```

In the following analyses we use the number of field operations as a measure for time complexity and the number of field elements that need to be stored as a memory unit. We denote by $T_{\mathsf{ISD}}^{n,k,w,q}$ the time to find a weight-w codeword in an $[n, k]$ linear code over $\mathbb{F}_q$, while by T_{Sub} and p_{Sub} we refer to the time complexity and the success probability of a subroutine Sub.

Theorem 4. (Complexity of Algorithm2). *Let $n \in \mathbb{N}$, $k = Rn$ for constant rate R, $w \leq n - k$, and $q \geq q_0$ be a prime, where q_0 is the constant from Lemma 2. Then Algorithm 2 solves the* LCE *problem with probability at least $\frac{p_{\mathsf{SSP\text{-}RecoverMonomial}} \cdot p_{\mathsf{Compatible\text{-}Pairs}}}{2}$ in expected time and memory*

$$T = 2N \cdot T_{\mathsf{ISD}}^{n,k,w} + T_{\mathsf{Compatible\text{-}Pairs}} + |Z| \cdot T_{\mathsf{SSP\text{-}RecoverMonomial}} \quad \text{and} \quad M = \tilde{\mathcal{O}}\left(N + |Z|\right).$$

Proof. Let us fix $N = \sqrt{2N_w}$. The time complexity of the algorithm splits into the time complexity to compute two lists of weight-w codewords of size $|L_i| = N$, the time to construct the list $|Z|$ via Compatible-Pairs and the time complexity to apply the SSP-RecoverMonomial function to each element $v \in Z$. Adding those terms, leads to the stated running time. The memory complexity is dominated by the size of the lists V, W and Z resulting in the stated memory complexity since $|V| = |W| = N$.[4]

For the correctness note that if there are at least two codewords $\mathbf{v}_1, \mathbf{v}_2 \in L_1$ and two codewords $\mathbf{w}_1, \mathbf{w}_2 \in L_2$ with $\mathbf{w}_i = \mathbf{v}_i\mathbf{Q}$ the algorithm succeeds with probability $p_{\mathsf{Compatible\text{-}Pairs}} \cdot p_{\mathsf{SSP\text{-}RecoverMonomial}}$. Therefore it remains to show that for $|L_i| = \sqrt{2N_w}$ such pairs exist in the lists L_i with probability at least $\frac{1}{2}$. Note that for any $\mathbf{c} \in \mathcal{C}$ there is exactly one $\mathbf{w} \in \mathcal{C}'$ such that $\mathbf{c} = \mathbf{w}\mathbf{Q}$ for the searched monomial. Therefore we expect that there are $\frac{|L_1 \times L_2|}{N_w} = 2$ equivalent

[4] Here we conveniently assume that none of the subroutines consumes a higher memory, which is generally the case.

codewords between the two lists. Moreover this number is closely approximated by a binomial distribution with sample size $|L_1 \times L_2| = 2N_w$ and probability N_w^{-1}. For this distribution we know that $\Pr[X \geq \mathbb{E}[X]] \geq 1/2$. □

Note that in line 7 of Algorithms 2, 1 is also called on non-equivalent pairs, not matching its input definition. This is generally not an issue, as such pairs produce non-corresponding sets of indices in line 3, leading to failure in recovering $\mathbf{Q}$ and causing the algorithm to return $\perp$.

Identifying Compatible Codewords. In the following we derive a criterion to determine efficiently if two pairs of codewords can be mapped via a monomial transformation. Eventually, this criterion leads to an instantiation of the Compatible-Pairs function in Algorithm 2. More precisely, given two pairs of codewords $(\mathbf{v}_1, \mathbf{w}_1), (\mathbf{v}_2, \mathbf{w}_2) \in \mathcal{C} \times \mathcal{C}'$, we say that those pairs are *compatible* if there exists a monomial transformation $\mathbf{Q}'$ such that $\mathbf{v}_1 = \mathbf{w}_1\mathbf{Q}'$ and $\mathbf{v}_2 = \mathbf{w}_2\mathbf{Q}'$, for some $\mathbf{Q}' \in \mathsf{Mono}_n(\mathbb{F}_q)$. Note that, unlike equivalent pairs (see Definition 3), such a monomial $\mathbf{Q}'$ does not necessarily define a linear equivalence between $\mathcal{C}$ and $\mathcal{C}'$, i.e., it is not guaranteed to solve the code equivalence problem. However, any pair of equivalent codewords must necessarily be compatible according to this definition. We summarize this property in the following.

Definition 4. (Compatible Pairs). *Let $\mathcal{C}, \mathcal{C}'$ be two $[n, k]$ codes over $\mathbb{F}_q$. We call two pairs of codewords $(\mathbf{v}_1, \mathbf{w}_1)$, $(\mathbf{v}_2, \mathbf{w}_2)$ with $\mathbf{v}_i \in \mathcal{C}$ and $\mathbf{w}_i \in \mathcal{C}'$* compatible *if and only if there exists a monomial $\mathbf{Q} \in \mathsf{Mono}_n(\mathbb{F}_q)$ such that*

$$\mathbf{w}_1 = \mathbf{v}_1\mathbf{Q} \quad \textit{and} \quad \mathbf{w}_2 = \mathbf{v}_2\mathbf{Q}.$$

In Sect. 3.1, we already observed that a suitable monomial has to map indices in I_{int} to indices in J_{int}, where $I_{\text{int}} = \text{Supp}\mathbf{v}_1 \cap \text{Supp}\mathbf{v}_2$ and $J_{\text{int}} = \text{Supp}\mathbf{w}_1 \cap \text{Supp}\mathbf{w}_2$ are the respective support intersections. Therefore compatibility implies that for every $i \in I_{\text{int}}$ there exists a $j \in J_{\text{int}}$ satisfying (compare to Eq. (3))

$$\frac{\mathbf{v}_1(i)}{\mathbf{v}_2(i)} = \frac{\mathbf{w}_1(j)}{\mathbf{w}_2(j)},$$

which translates into a simple criterion to check compatibility of pairs.

Lemma 4 (Compatibility Criterion). *Two pairs of codewords $(\mathbf{v}_1, \mathbf{w}_1)$ and $(\mathbf{v}_2, \mathbf{w}_2)$ of same Hamming weight $\text{wt}(\mathbf{v}_i) = \text{wt}(\mathbf{w}_i) = w$ are compatible if and only if the entries of $\mathbf{v}_{\text{comp}}$ and $\mathbf{w}_{\text{comp}}$ generate the same multiset, where*

$$\mathbf{v}_{\text{comp}} := \left(\frac{\mathbf{v}_1(i)}{\mathbf{v}_2(i)}\right)_{i \in I} \quad \textit{and} \quad \mathbf{w}_{\text{comp}} := \left(\frac{\mathbf{w}_1(j)}{\mathbf{w}_2(j)}\right)_{j \in J}$$

with $I = \mathit{Supp}\mathbf{v}_1 \cap \mathit{Supp}\mathbf{v}_2$ and $J = \mathit{Supp}\mathbf{w}_1 \cap \mathit{Supp}\mathbf{w}_2$.

Proof. The proof is given in the full version of the paper [12, Appendix C]. □

An Algorithm for Finding Compatible Pairs. Lemma 4 now easily turns into an algorithm to instantiate the Compatible-Pairs function in Algorithm 2: For each element $(\mathbf{v}_1, \mathbf{v}_2) \in V$ (resp. $(\mathbf{w}_1, \mathbf{w}_2) \in W$) we compute the corresponding labels $\mathbf{v}_{\text{comp}}$ (resp. $\mathbf{w}_{\text{comp}}$). Finally we compute elements between the lists satisfying equality with respect to the multiset of the labels via a sort-and-match procedure. We summarize this procedure in Algorithm 3 and its complexity in Lemma 5. The time complexity is essentially linear in the sizes of V, W and Z.

Algorithm 3. Compatible-Pairs(V, W)

Input: lists $V, W \subset \mathbb{F}_q^n \times \mathbb{F}_q^n$ with $V = \{(\mathbf{v}_1, \mathbf{v}_2) \mid \text{wt}(\mathbf{v}_1) = \text{wt}(\mathbf{v}_2) = w\}$ and $W = \{(\mathbf{w}_1, \mathbf{w}_2) \mid \text{wt}(\mathbf{w}_1) = \text{wt}(\mathbf{w}_2) = w\}$

Output: list $Z = \{((\mathbf{v}_1, \mathbf{w}_1), (\mathbf{v}_2, \mathbf{w}_2)) \mid \mathbf{v}_i \in V, \mathbf{w}_i \in W \wedge (\mathbf{v}_1, \mathbf{w}_1)$ and $(\mathbf{v}_2, \mathbf{w}_2)$ are compatible$\}$

1: $V' \leftarrow \{(\mathsf{sort}(\mathbf{v}_{\text{comp}}), (\mathbf{v}_1, \mathbf{v}_2)) \in (\mathbb{F}_q^*)^\ell \times V \mid \ell \geq w^2/n\}$
2: $W' \leftarrow \{(\mathsf{sort}(\mathbf{w}_{\text{comp}}), (\mathbf{w}_1, \mathbf{w}_2)) \in (\mathbb{F}_q^*)^\ell \times W \mid \ell \geq w^2/n\}$
3: $Z \leftarrow \{((\mathbf{v}_1, \mathbf{w}_1), (\mathbf{v}_2, \mathbf{w}_2)) \mid (\mathbf{x}, \mathbf{v}_1, \mathbf{v}_2) \in V' \wedge (\mathbf{x}, \mathbf{w}_1, \mathbf{w}_2) \in W'\}$
4: **Return** Z

Lemma 5 (Finding Compatible Pairs). *Algorithm 3 runs in expected time and memory*

$$(\ell + 2n)\big(|V| + |W|\big) + 4n \cdot |V \times W| \cdot \frac{(w^2/n)!}{(q-1)^{w^2/n}},$$

and returns any compatible pair between V *and* W *with probability at least* $1/2$.

Proof. The proof is given in the full version of the paper [12, Appendix C]. □

4.1 Concrete Complexity of Algorithm 2

In this section, we begin by presenting a practical improvement of Algorithm 3, followed by a concrete analysis of Algorithm 2.

Exploiting Scalar Multiples. By exploiting the existence of scalar multiples of the solution we are able to decrease the initial list size from $\sqrt{2N_w}$ to

$$N = \sqrt{\frac{2N_w}{q-1}}, \tag{12}$$

without reducing the success probability of Algorithm 2. This requires an adaptation of Algorithm 3 to still find all pairs, compatible up to a scalar, resulting in a slightly increased time complexity. We provide the full details on this improvement, including the pseudocode and proofs in the full version of the paper [12, Appendix D.1].

The Concrete Algorithm. Consider the instantiation of Algorithm 2 using a starting list size N as specified in Eq. (12) and where the Compatible-Pairs function is instantiated via the corresponding adaptation of Algorithm 3 (see the full version of the paper for the formal instantiation [12, Algorithm 6]).

Theorem 5 (Concrete Complexity of Algorithm2). *Let $n, k, w \in \mathbb{N}$, with $w < n - k$, and let $q \geq q_0$ be a prime, where q_0 is the constant from Lemma 2. Then the* LCE *problem can be solved in expected time*

$$0.47^{-1} \cdot \left(2T_{\mathrm{ISD}}^{n,k,q,w} \cdot \sqrt{\frac{2N_w}{q-1} + \frac{4N_w(\ell + 2n)}{\sqrt{q-1}}} + 2^{\varepsilon/2} n^4 \cdot \frac{16(N_w)^2 (w^2/n)!}{(q-1)^{w^2/n+1}} \right)$$

and expected memory $M_{\mathrm{ISD}}^{n,k,q,w} + \frac{2N_w(\ell+2n)}{\sqrt{q-1}} + \frac{4(N_w)^2(w^2/n)!}{(q-1)^{w^2/n+1}}$, where $T_{\mathrm{ISD}}^{n,k,q,w}$ (resp. $M_{\mathrm{ISD}}^{n,k,q,w}$) is the expected time (resp. memory) complexity for finding a weight-w codeword in an $[n, k]$ linear code over $\mathbb{F}_q$ and ε is as defined in Lemma 3.

Proof. The proof is given in the full version of the paper [12, Appendix D.2]. □

Concrete Comparison. In the following we provide a comparison to the sate of the art. In line with our experiments from Sect. 3.4 for the considered parameters, we assume in the following that an exact solution to the subset sum instance exists, i.e., that $\varepsilon = 0$ in Theorem 5. For the estimation of the bitcomplexity of LEON [19], BEULLENS [9], BBPS [4] as well as $T_{\mathrm{ISD}}^{n,k,q,w}$ in Theorem 5 we rely on the *CryptographicEstimators* library [17][5]. Our estimations closely follow the cost model implemented in this library, ensuring a consistent and fair comparison. We provide a complexity formula for $T_{\mathrm{ISD}}^{n,k,q,w}$ in the full version of the paper [12, Appendix D.3]. For the CF-MITM [14] we use the following formula, representing actually a lower bound for the algorithm's complexity

$$T_{\mathsf{CF}} = \mathcal{O}\left(k^2 \cdot n \sqrt{\binom{n}{k}} \right) = \tilde{\mathcal{O}}\left(2^{h(k/n)n/2} \right). \tag{13}$$

Application to LESS Parameters. The scheme provides three parameter sets for different security categories, which all use $q = 127$ and rate $\frac{1}{2}$. We refer to those as LESS-I ($n = 252$), LESS-III ($n = 400$) and LESS-V ($n = 548$).

In Fig. 4, we compare the concrete time complexity of Algorithm 2 given in Theorem 5 against other known algorithms for varying q. In this comparison we fix $n = 252$ (left) and $n = 400$ (right), and the code rate to $\frac{1}{2}$, i.e., to the choices made for LESS-I and LESS-III. It can observed that Algorithm 2 obtains the lowest time complexity. Furthermore we again observe the mild dependence of CF-MITM on the value q. As known, BEULLENS improves upon LEON only for large fields.

[5] available at https://github.com/Crypto-TII/CryptographicEstimators.

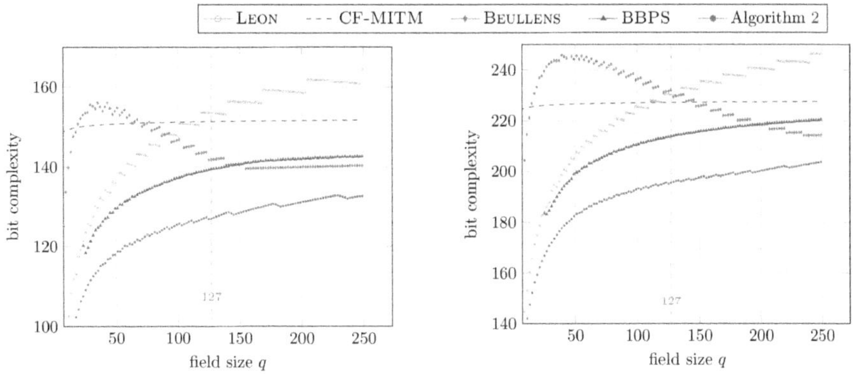

Fig. 4. Bitcomplexity of LCE for $n = 252$ (left) and $n = 400$ (right) with rate 0.5.

Table 3. Bitcomplexity estimates to solve LCE for suggested LESS parameters.

	CF-MITM	LEON	BEULLENS	BBPS	Algorithm 2
LESS-I	151	153	142	139	**127** (107)
LESS-III	227	230	232	214	**195** (167)
LESS-V	302	307	324	290	**266** (226)

We provide in Table 3 the bitcomplexity estimates of all different algorithms for LESS parameters, where the number in parenthesis denotes the optimal value for w. We observe a bitcomplexity reduction by 12 (LESS-I), 19 (LESS-III) and 24 (LESS-V) bits compared to the best previous algorithm, which is for all parameters the BBPS algorithm. We note that while these new bit security estimates lie below the NIST thresholds of 143, 207 and 272, they do not violate the security argument made in the LESS NIST submission. The proposed parameter sets were selected under the rationale that any codeword search expected to yield at least one equivalent pair must still require a computational effort of at least 128, 192, and 256 bits, respectively, matching the AES key-lengths. However, the proposed algorithm drastically decreases the security margin by reducing the gap between constructive algorithms and the used lower bound. Applied to other parameters in the literature we achieve improvements up to 42 bits (see [12, Appendix D.4]).

5 Asymptotic Analysis of Algorithm 2

In the following, we first study the asymptotic behavior of Algorithm 2 for q growing with n. While this analysis suggests an improvement over Leon's algorithm, it still falls short of the CF-MITM algorithm. However, we observe that this asymptotic behavior is only achieved for unrealistically large $q > 2^{100}$, far beyond cryptographic relevance. This mismatch motivates the study for constant q, which yields a close approximation of the algorithm's concrete behavior already for small fields.

Let us first derive an asymptotic runtime formula from Theorem 4, which serves as a basis for the analyses. Note that from Lemma 1 it follows that $\sqrt{N_w} \cdot T_{\mathrm{ISD}}^{n,k,q,w} = \tilde{\mathcal{O}}\left(\frac{\binom{n}{w}}{\binom{n-k}{w}\sqrt{N_w}}\right)$. Furthermore, as Algorithm1 runs in time about $T_{\textsf{SSP-RecoverMonomial}} = 2^{\varepsilon}$, we have $T_{\textsf{SSP-RecoverMonomial}}|Z| = \tilde{\mathcal{O}}(2^{\varepsilon} \cdot T_{\textsf{Compatible-Pairs}})$ as Z is the output of the Compatible-Pairs function. Eventually, the asymptotic runtime of Algorithm 2 summarizes as

$$T = \tilde{\mathcal{O}}\left(\max\left(\frac{\binom{n}{w}}{\binom{n-k}{w}\sqrt{N_w}}, 2^{\varepsilon} \cdot T_{\textsf{Compatible-Pairs}}\right)\right). \tag{14}$$

5.1 Asymptotic for Non-constant q

In the following, we analyze the runtime expression from Eq. (14), optimizing it over the choice of the weight w, or more precisely over the corresponding number of codewords N_w. When $q = \mathcal{O}(n)$ grows in n, the minimum distance $w_{\min}$ of a random q-ary linear code with constant rate asymptotically satisfies $w_{\min} = n - k + \delta$, where $\delta = o(n)$. At this weight, the number of codewords is constant, i.e., $N_{w_{\min}} = \Theta(1)$.

At the other extreme, for weight $w = n - k$, the number of codewords is $N_{n-k} = \Theta\left(\binom{n}{n-k}\right)$. Since N_w increases monotonically with w, varying w over the interval $[w_{\min}, n-k]$ allows us to interpolate between these two extremes—gradually increasing N_w up to $\mathcal{O}\left(\binom{n}{n-k}\right)$. In contrast, the effect of increasing w on the term $\binom{n}{w}/\binom{n-k}{w}$ is only subexponential within this range. In fact, using Stirling's approximation, we have

$$\frac{\binom{n}{w_{\min}}}{\binom{n-k}{w_{\min}}} = \binom{n}{n-k}^{1+o(1)}.$$

Furthermore Lemma 3 shows that $\varepsilon = \mathcal{O}\left(\frac{n}{q}\right)$ and, hence, $\tilde{\mathcal{O}}(2^{\varepsilon} \cdot T_{\textsf{Compatible-Pairs}}) = T_{\textsf{Compatible-Pairs}}^{1+o(1)}$ for any q that grows with n. Thus, for $w \in [w_{\min}, n-k]$, the total runtime from Theorem 4 further simplifies to

$$T = \max\left(\frac{\binom{n}{n-k}}{\sqrt{N_w}}, T_{\textsf{Compatible-Pairs}}\right)^{1+o(1)}. \tag{15}$$

The following theorem now states the running time of Algorithm 2 where Compatible-Pairs is instantiated via Algorithm 3.

Theorem 6 (Asymptotic for Non-Constant Field Size). *Let $n \in \mathbb{N}$, $k = Rn$ for constant $R \in [0,1]$ and $q = c_q n$ be prime for $c_q = \mathcal{O}(1)$ and $c_q \gg \frac{1}{n}$. Then Algorithm 2 runs in expected time*

$$T = \max\left(\binom{n}{n-k}^{4/5} \cdot \beta^{\frac{(1-R)^2 n}{5}}, \binom{n}{n-k}^{2/3}\right)^{1+o(1)}, \text{ where } \beta := \min\left(1, \frac{(1-R)^2}{c_q \cdot e}\right).$$

Proof. The proof is given in the full version of the paper [12, Appendix E.1]. □

Note that the running time of Algorithm 2 interpolates between the two end-points $\binom{n}{n-k}^{4/5+o(1)} = 2^{4h(1-R)/5n+o(n)}$ and $\binom{n}{n-k}^{2/3+o(1)} = 2^{2h(1-R)/3n+o(n)}$, depending on the size of q, where we approximate binomials via Eq. (1).

Lower Bound for Codeword-Finding-Based Approaches. Note that a general lower bound for codeword-finding-based approaches (in the style of Algorithm 2) is obtained by making the optimistic assumptions that (1) the secret monomial can be reconstructed from a *single* pair of equivalent codewords in negligible time and (2) that this pair of codewords can be found in time linear in $|L_1| = \mathcal{O}\left(\sqrt{N_w}\right)$. Then minimizing the expression in Eq. (15) over the choice of N_w leads to $N_w = \binom{n}{n-k}^{\frac{1}{2} \pm o(1)}$ with a corresponding running time of

$$T_{\text{Lower}} = \binom{n}{n-k}^{\frac{1}{2} \pm o(1)}. \tag{16}$$

Note that this matches the complexity of the CF-MITM algorithm (compare to Eq. (13)) up to second order terms, when moving to the dual instance.

Comparison to Other Approaches and Section 4.1. Recall that Leon's algorithm, requires to find all codewords of minimum weight and therefore achieves a running time (see Lemma 1) of

$$T_{\text{LEON}} = \tilde{\mathcal{O}}\left(\binom{n}{w_{\min}} \Big/ \binom{n-k}{w_{\min}}\right) = \binom{n}{n-k}^{1+o(1)} = 2^{h(1-R)n+o(n)}. \tag{17}$$

In summary, the different algorithms achieve asymptotic exponents $c = \log_{\binom{n}{n-k}} T$ (for q growing in n) of

$$c_{\text{LEON}} = 1, \quad c_{\text{new}} \in [2/3, 4/5], \quad c_{\text{Lower}} = c_{\text{CF-MITM}} = 1/2,$$

suggesting that Algorithm 2 does not improve on CF-MITM. However, this stands in clear contrast to the concrete estimates from the previous section. Moreover, the concrete runtime exponent for all LESS parameter sets, obtained as $c = \frac{\log T}{n}$ with T given in Theorem 5, satisfies $c < 0.51 < 2/3h(1-R) = 2/3$ (compare to Table 3). Therefore, even for cryptographic-sized instances, and even though c includes many polynomial factors and second order terms, the concrete runtime exponent stays far below the asymptotic result from Theorem 6.

This is explained by the extremely slow convergence of the minimum weight $w_{\min}$ to its asymptotic limit of $n-k$, used in the analysis. For example, using LESS parameters, i.e., $q = 127$ and rate $R = 1/2$, the minimum weight lies around $w_{\min} = 0.365n$ rather than the asymptotic value of $n/2 - o(n)$. Furthermore, even for q as large as 2^{20}, the minimum weight of a random linear q-ary $[n, n/2]$ code is only about $0.45n$, for $q = 2^{100}$ it reaches $0.49n$. This motivates the following study of a pre-asymptotic regime, where we treat q as a constant while still assuming the recovery of the monomial remains negligible. Note that while Theorem 3 actually yields an exponential complexity for this regime, our experiments have shown that already small values of q suffice to enter the polynomial-time regime. Furthermore, we find this analysis to closely approximates the observed concrete complexity behavior.

5.2 Asymptotic for Constant q

We again start from Eq. (14). However, note that for fixed q the running time of *Algorithm* 3 becomes $T_{\mathsf{Compatible\text{-}Pairs}} = \tilde{\mathcal{O}}\left(N_w^2\right)$, since the upper bound on Z given in Lemma 5 becomes trivial implying $Z = \Theta(N_w^2)$.

Lemma 6 (Size of Z for Constant q). *Let $n \in \mathbb{N}$. For any constant q the expected size of Z in Algorithm 2 is $\mathbb{E}\left[|Z|\right] = \frac{|V \times W|}{\mathrm{poly}(\ell)}$.*

Proof. The proof is given in the full version of the paper [12, Appendix E.3]. □

We now express the complexity of Algorithm 2 as a function $2^{\vartheta(R,q,\omega)n}$, with $\vartheta(R, q, \omega)$ being a constant that depends on the code rate R, the chosen relative weight ω, where $w = \omega n$ as well as the field size q using a straightforward application of Lemma 1. We provide its proof in the full version of the paper [12, Appendix E.2]. In those statements for correctness we include ε, while as discussed previously, we assume in the subsequent comparison $\varepsilon = o(n)$

Corollary 1 (Runtime Exponent of Algorithm 2). *Let $n \in \mathbb{N}$, $k = Rn$, $w = \omega n$ for constants $\omega, R \in [0, 1]$ and q be a constant prime integer. Then Algorithm 2 runs in expected time $T = \tilde{\mathcal{O}}\left(2^{\vartheta n}\right)$ with*

$$\vartheta = \max\left(h(\omega) - (1-R)h\left(\frac{\omega}{1-R}\right) - \frac{\gamma}{2},\ 2\gamma + \log\frac{\varepsilon}{n}\right)$$

where $\gamma = h(\omega) + \omega\log(q-1) - (1-R)\log q$ and ε as defined in Lemma 3.

For a given rate R and field size q we choose ω to minimize the expression ϑ from Corollary 1. Usually this is the case for an ω balancing both factors in the maximum, i.e., an ω satisfying $h(\omega) - (1-R)h\left(\frac{\omega}{1-R}\right) - \frac{\gamma}{2} = 2\gamma$.

Before comparing the three analyses, we state the following corollary about the running time of Corollary 1 under the assumption that the $\mathsf{Compatible\text{-}Pairs}$ subroutine runs in linear time $T_{\mathsf{Compatible\text{-}Pairs}} = \tilde{\mathcal{O}}\left(N_w\right)$, changing the second term in the maximum from $2\gamma + \log\frac{\varepsilon}{n}$ to $\gamma + \log\frac{\varepsilon}{n}$.

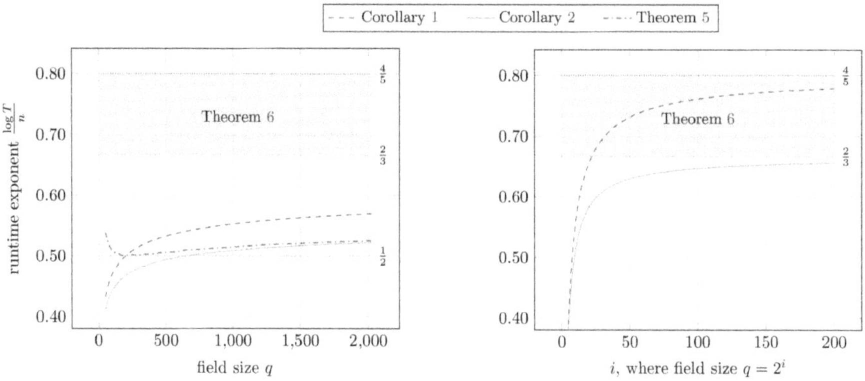

Fig. 5. Asymptotic and concrete runtime exponents where $q = k = \frac{n}{2}$.

Corollary 2 (Optimistic Runtime Exponent of Algorithm2). *Let $n \in \mathbb{N}$, $k = Rn$, $w = \omega n$ for constants $\omega, R \in [0,1]$ and q be a constant integer. Then assuming $T_{\textsf{Compatible-Pairs}} = \tilde{\mathcal{O}}(N_w)$, Algorithm 2 runs in expected time $T = \tilde{\mathcal{O}}(2^{\vartheta n})$ with*

$$\vartheta = \max\left(h(\omega) - (1-R)h\left(\frac{\omega}{1-R}\right) - \frac{\gamma}{2},\ \ \gamma + \log\frac{\varepsilon}{n}\right)$$

where $\gamma = h(\omega) + \omega\log(q-1) - (1-R)\log q$ and ε as defined in Lemma 3.

Comparison to Previous Analysis. In Fig. 5 (on the left) we illustrate the runtime exponent of Algorithm 2 from Corollary 1 (blue dashed line), the optimistic exponent from Corollary 2 as well as the concrete runtime exponent obtained from Theorem 5 (green dash dotted line) for rate $R = \frac{q}{n} = \frac{1}{2}$. For comparison, we also highlight in gray the region in which the asymptotic exponent according to Theorem 6 lies (*i.e.*, the interval $[2/3, 4/5]$).

We observe that the concrete exponent generally lies between the result of Corollaries 1 and 2, with a quick convergence to the latter for increasing q. This convergence is due to the fact that, even if polynomial, the hidden factors in the output list size in Lemma 6 are of order $\Theta(n^q)$ (see the corresponding proof), and therefore quickly affect the concrete complexity even for fixed q. This shows that Corollary 2 closely approximates the concrete behavior of Algorithm 2.

In the same figure on the right, we can see that Corollary 1 and Corollary 2 align well with Theorem 6. Namely, for large $q > 2^{100}$ those variants converge to the exponents $\frac{2}{3}$ and $\frac{4}{5}$ as stated in Theorem 6 when q grows with n.

Comparison to Existing Techniques. Now, that we established Corollaries 1 and 2 as solid upper and lower bounds for the complexity of Algorithm 2, we

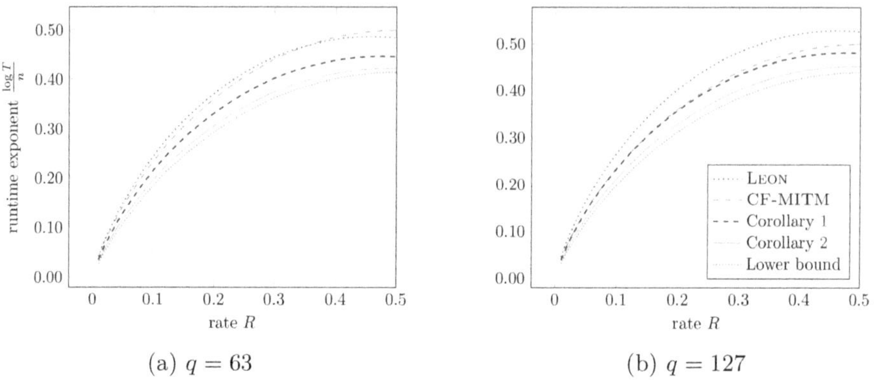

Fig. 6. Runtime exponent of different algorithms as a function of the rate R for different choices of q.

compare them against existing techniques. More precisely we compare against the running time of LEON from Eq. (17) and CF-MITM from Eq. (13) as well as the theoretical lower bound for codeword-finding-based approaches from Eq. (16) for constant q.[6] For constant q the corresponding runtime exponents are

$$c_{\text{Lower}} = \max\left(h(\omega) - (1-R)h\left(\frac{\omega}{1-R}\right) - \frac{\gamma}{2},\ \gamma/2\right), \quad \omega \in [\omega_{\text{GV}}, 1-R]$$

similar to the results of Corollaries 1 and 2 (note the $\gamma/2$ in the max) and

$$c_{\text{LEON}} = h(\omega) - (1-R)h\left(\frac{\omega}{1-R}\right) \quad \text{and} \quad c_{\text{CF-MITM}} = \frac{h(R)}{2}.$$

Comparison for Fixed q. In Fig. 6 we compare the different runtime exponents for fixed $q \in \{63, 127\}$. Here we restrict to rates $R \leq 1/2$ since solving LCE with code rate R is equivalent to solving LCE with code rate $1 - R$.

We observe that across all code rates, Algorithm 2 achieves the smallest runtime exponent among any constructive algorithm. Moreover, for smaller values of q, the runtime exponent approaches the lower bound, whereas for larger q, it begins to diverge. This divergence is related to the fast growth of N_w as q increases, since the difference between the lower bound and the complexity given in Theorem 4 is a factor of $(N_w)^{3/2}$ in the second term of the maximum.

Comparison in the (q, R) Space. In general, the time complexity of Algorithm 2 increases with q, while the runtime of the canonical forms approach remains independent of the field size. This suggests that, for sufficiently large q, the canonical forms method eventually outperforms Algorithm 2. However, for rate 1/2, this break-even point requires $q > 200$ with respect to the (upper) bound

[6] For BEULLENS and BBPS no asymptotic analyses have been provided.

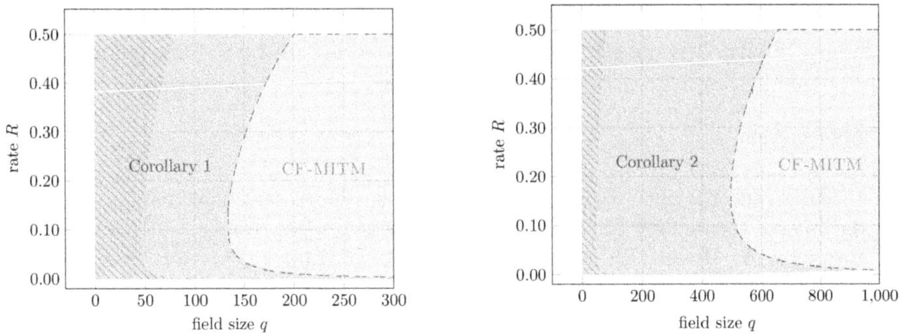

Fig. 7. Partition of the (q, R) space by optimal algorithms.

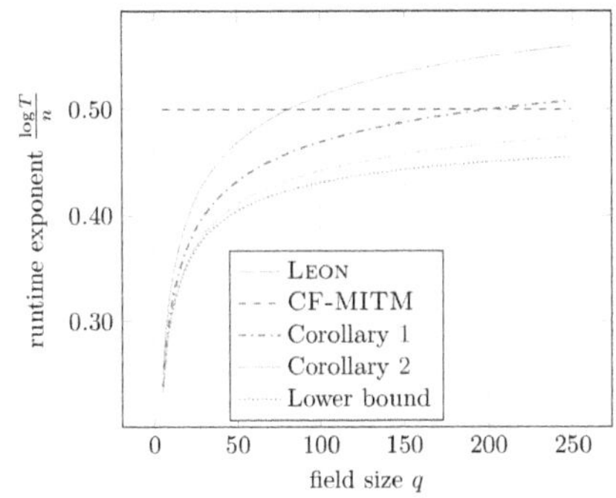

Fig. 8. Runtime exponents for fixed rate $R = \frac{1}{2}$ as a function of the field size q.

from Corollary 1 and $q > 650$ with respect to the (lower) bound from Corollary2. Note that we find the practical break even point following the analysis from Sect. 4.1 to require even higher $q \geq 1550$. In the case of Leon's algorithm, the break-even point is already reached at $q = 81$ (asymptotic) and $q = 98$ (concrete). Figure 7 classifies the (q, R) space by optimal algorithms, where for Algorithm 2 we use the upper bound from Corollary 1 (left) and lower bound from Corollary 2 (right). Here, Algorithm 2 obtains the lowest runtime exponent in the entire green area, while the striped area corresponds to the regime, where Leon's algorithm is favorable to CF-MITM.

Comparison for the Worst Case Rate. As can be observed from Fig. 6, the maximum runtime exponent for all algorithms is obtained at rate $R = 0.5$. For this reason cryptographic constructions, including the LESS signature scheme, usually resort to this choice for the code rate. To quantify the improvement for this specific choice, we compare in Fig. 8 the runtime exponent of the different approaches for fixed rate $R = 0.5$ as a function of q. As observed earlier, the runtime exponent of CF-MITM is constant in q. The intersections of the runtime exponents of Leon, the upper bound from Corollary 1 and the lower bound from Corollary 2 with this constant lie at $q = 81$, $q = 202$ and $q = 658$, respectively.

References

1. Baldi, M., et al.: LESS (version 2.0). Technical report, National Institute of Standards and Technology (2025). https://www.less-project.com/
2. Barenghi, A., Biasse, J.F., Ngo, T., Persichetti, E., Santini, P.: Advanced signature functionalities from the code equivalence problem. Int. J. Comput. Math. Comput, Syst. Theory **7**(2), 112–128 (2022)
3. Barenghi, A., Biasse, J.F., Persichetti, E., Santini, P.: LESS-FM: fine-tuning signatures from the code equivalence problem. In: Cheon, J.H., Tillich, J.P. (eds.) Post-Quantum Cryptography - 12th International Workshop, PQCrypto 2021, pp. 23–43. Springer, Cham (2021). https://doi.org/10.1007/978-3-030-81293-5_2
4. Barenghi, A., Biasse, J.F., Persichetti, E., Santini, P.: On the computational hardness of the code equivalence problem in cryptography. Adv. Math. Commun. **17**(1), 23–55 (2023)
5. Battagliola, M., Borin, G., Di Crescenzo, G., Meneghetti, A., Persichetti, E.: Enhancing threshold group action signature schemes: adaptive security and scalability improvements. In: Niederhagen, R., Saarinen, M.J.O. (eds.) Post-Quantum Cryptography - 16th International Workshop, PQCrypto 2025, Part I, pp. 129–161. Springer, Cham (2025). https://doi.org/10.1007/978-3-031-86599-2_5
6. Battagliola, M., Borin, G., Meneghetti, A., Persichetti, E.: Cutting the GRASS: threshold GRoup action signature schemes. In: Oswald, E. (ed.) CT-RSA 2024. LNCS, vol. 14643, pp. 460–489. Springer, Cham (2024). https://doi.org/10.1007/978-3-031-58868-6_18
7. Beckwith, L., Esser, A., Persichetti, E., Santini, P., Zweydinger, F.: Less is even more: optimizing digital signatures from code equivalence. IACR Trans. Cryptographic Hardware Embedded Syst. **2025**(4), 386–408 (2025)
8. Bennett, H., et al.: Asymptotic improvements to provable algorithms for the code equivalence problem. Cryptology ePrint Archive, Paper 2025/187 (2025). https://eprint.iacr.org/2025/187
9. Beullens, W.: Not enough LESS: an improved algorithm for solving code equivalence problems over F_q. In: Dunkelman, O., Jacobson, Jr., M.J., O'Flynn, C. (eds.) SAC 2020. LNCS, vol. 12804, pp. 387–403. Springer, Cham (2020). https://doi.org/10.1007/978-3-030-81652-0_15
10. Biasse, J.-F., Micheli, G., Persichetti, E., Santini, P.: LESS is more: code-based signatures without syndromes. In: Nitaj, A., Youssef, A. (eds.) AFRICACRYPT 2020. LNCS, vol. 12174, pp. 45–65. Springer, Cham (2020). https://doi.org/10.1007/978-3-030-51938-4_3
11. Budroni, A., Esser, A., Franch, E., Natale, A.: Accompanying repository. https://github.com/AlessandroBudroni/Two-Is-All-It-Takes
12. Budroni, A., Esser, A., Franch, E., Natale, A.: Two is all it takes: asymptotic and concrete improvements for solving code equivalence. Cryptology ePrint Archive, Report 2025/227 (2025). https://eprint.iacr.org/2025/227
13. Cayrel, P.-L., Véron, P., El Yousfi Alaoui, S.M.: A zero-knowledge identification scheme based on the Q-ARY syndrome decoding problem. In: Biryukov, A., Gong, G., Stinson, D.R. (eds.) SAC 2010. LNCS, vol. 6544, pp. 171–186. Springer, Heidelberg (2011). https://doi.org/10.1007/978-3-642-19574-7_12

14. Chou, T., Persichetti, E., Santini, P.: On linear equivalence, canonical forms, and digital signatures. Designs, Codes Crypto. (2025). https://doi.org/10.1007/s10623-025-01576-1
15. Chvátal, V.: The tail of the hypergeometric distribution. Discret. Math. **25**(3), 285–287 (1979)
16. Debris-Alazard, T., Sendrier, N., Tillich, J.-P.: Wave: a new family of trapdoor one-way preimage sampleable functions based on codes. In: Galbraith, S.D., Moriai, S. (eds.) ASIACRYPT 2019. LNCS, vol. 11921, pp. 21–51. Springer, Cham (2019). https://doi.org/10.1007/978-3-030-34578-5_2
17. Esser, A., Verbel, J.A., Zweydinger, F., Bellini, E.: SoK: cryptographicestimators - a software library for cryptographic hardness estimation. In: Zhou, J., Quek, T.Q.S., Gao, D., Cárdenas, A.A. (eds.) ASIACCS 2024. ACM Press (2024). https://doi.org/10.1145/3634737.3645007
18. Feneuil, T., Joux, A., Rivain, M.: Syndrome decoding in the head: shorter signatures from zero-knowledge proofs. In: Dodis, Y., Shrimpton, T. (eds.) CRYPTO 2022, Part II. LNCS, vol. 13508, pp. 541–572. Springer, Cham (2022). https://doi.org/10.1007/978-3-031-15979-4_19
19. Leon, J.: Computing automorphism groups of error-correcting codes. IEEE Trans. Inf. Theory **28**(3), 496–511 (1982). https://doi.org/10.1109/TIT.1982.1056498
20. National Institute of Standards and Technology: Post-quantum cryptography: Digital signature schemes. Round 2 Additional Signatures (2023). https://csrc.nist.gov/projects/pqc-dig-sig/round-2-additional-signatures
21. Nowakowski, J.: An improved algorithm for code equivalence. In: Post-Quantum Cryptography: 16th International Workshop, PQCrypto 2025, Taipei, Taiwan, April 8–10, 2025, Proceedings, Part I. pp. 71–103. Springer-Verlag, Berlin, Heidelberg (2025). https://doi.org/10.1007/978-3-031-86599-2_3
22. Persichetti, E., Santini, P.: A new formulation of the linear equivalence problem and shorter LESS signatures. In: Guo, J., Steinfeld, R. (eds.) ASIACRYPT 2023, Part VII. LNCS, vol. 14444, pp. 351–378. Springer, Singapore (2025). https://doi.org/10.1007/978-981-99-8739-9_12
23. Prange, E.: The use of information sets in decoding cyclic codes. IRE Trans. Inf. Theory **8**(5), 5–9 (1962)
24. Raab, M., Steger, A.: balls into bins—a simple and tight analysis. In: International Workshop on Randomization and Approximation Techniques in Computer Science, pp. 159–170. Springer (1998)
25. Sendrier, N.: Finding the permutation between equivalent linear codes: the support splitting algorithm. IEEE Trans. Inf. Theory **46**(4), 1193–1203 (2000)
26. Sendrier, N., Simos, D.E.: The hardness of code equivalence over and its application to code-based cryptography. In: Gaborit, P. (ed.) Post-Quantum Cryptography - 5th International Workshop, PQCrypto 2013, pp. 203–216. Springer, Heidelberg (2013). https://doi.org/10.1007/978-3-642-38616-9_14
27. Stern, J.: A new identification scheme based on syndrome decoding. In: Stinson, D.R. (ed.) CRYPTO'93. LNCS, vol. 773, pp. 13–21. Springer, Heidelberg (1994). https://doi.org/10.1007/3-540-48329-2_2
28. Upfal, E., Mitzenmacher, M.: Probability and Computing. Cambridge University Press, Cambridge, England (2005)
29. Véron, P.: Improved identification schemes based on error-correcting codes. Appl. Algebra Eng. Commun. Comput. **8**, 57–69 (1997)

Security Analysis on UOV Families with Odd Characteristics: Using Symmetric Algebra

Yi Jin[1], Yuansheng Pan[1], Xiaoou He[1], Boru Gong[1](✉), and Jintai Ding[2]

[1] CCB Fintech Co., Ltd, Shanghai, China
jinyi6259@gmail.com, kimozu1995@gmail.com, hexiaoou26@gmail.com, gongboru@gmail.com

[2] Xi'an Jiaotong-Liverpool University, Suzhou, China
jintai.ding@gmail.com

Abstract. UOV and its variants have been submitted to NIST's PQC Standardization Project. Security analysis against UOV families (*i.e.*, UOV and its variants) are typically categorized into key-recovery attacks and forgery attacks, with the XL algorithm serving as one of the most significant methods for mounting key-recovery attacks. Recently, Ran introduced a novel key-recovery attack against UOV families that could be seen as an XL attack using exterior algebra; nevertheless, this key-recovery attack is applicable only when the underlying field of UOV instances is of characteristic 2.

In this work, we address this limitation by generalizing Ran's approach, and our contributions are three-fold. First, we generalize the notion of exterior algebra and propose the notion of *p-reduced symmetric algebra* over *any* field, which is essentially symmetric algebra when the characteristic p of the underlying field is 0 and is exterior algebra when $p = 2$. Moreover, ased upon the well-studied property of the reduced symmetric algebra, we generalize Ran's attack from characteristic 2 to fields of any characteristic following essentially the same approach; As a result, our attack applies to all recommended QR-UOV instances submitted to the NIST PQC standardization project. Finally, analysis on these attacks also implies the connection between the characteristic p and the concrete hardness of UOV instances, which is helpful for choosing parameter sets for UOV families.

Keywords: MPKC · UOV · XL Algorithm · Symmetric Algebra

1 Introduction

Digital signature schemes are fundamental to cybersecurity, as they provide authenticity, integrity, and non-repudiation for digital communications. Classic digital signature schemes are usually based on the hardness of certain problems in number theory, and they have played a very important role in network security for decades. Moreover, the emergence of quantum computing has intensified

S. Bai and E. Persichetti (Eds.): PKC 2026, LNCS 16551, pp. 428–454, 2026.
https://doi.org/10.1007/978-3-032-26731-3_14

research into post-quantum cryptography (PQC), particularly following Shor's algorithm [26], which threatens traditional cryptographic systems. As such, NIST launched the PQC Standardization Project in the 2010 s, aiming to standardize quantum-resistant algorithms. Recently, NIST issued a call for additional digital signature proposals to be considered in the PQC standardization process in September 2022 [20], with primary interest in additional general-purpose signature schemes that are not based on structured lattices; for certain applications, NIST is also interested in signature schemes that have short signatures and fast verification speed.

1.1 UOV and Its Variants

The multivariate public key cryptosystems (MPKC) are a family of candidate post quantum cryptographic schemes that usually have short signatures and fast verification speed, and the security of these cryptosystems in MPKC are firmly connected to the computational hardness of solving multivariate polynomial equation systems. The idea of MPKC dates back to 1980 s, and many leading cryptographers built various types of MPKCs. Compared with other types of post-quantum counterparts, multivariate-based digital signature schemes (*e.g.*, UOV and its variants) usually offer signatures whose lengths are comparable to those classic ones [11].

The Unbalanced Oil and Vinegar (UOV) digital signature scheme was first proposed in 1999 [22]. It leverages the hash-and-sign paradigm underpinned by a trapdoored multivariate quadratic map. Its origin could be traced back to Patarin's groundbreaking linearization equations attack [21] in 1995 against the Matsumoto-Imai cryptosystem [19]. Following this innovative stride, Patarin ingeniously repurposed the attack's underlying principle into the design of the Oil and Vinegar signature scheme (OV) [22] in 1997. However, an invariant subspace attack [17] cracked the *balanced* version of this scheme in 1998. Kipnis, Patarin, and Goubin promptly introduced the original UOV. Over two decades, UOV has withstood rigorous cryptanalytic scrutiny, which validates its robust security and consistent reliability.

As a classic multivariate-based scheme, UOV has drawn significant attention over the past decades. Researchers have proposed variants of UOV to improve its efficiency and security properties. Notable examples include MAYO [7], QR-UOV [14], SNOVA [28]. These variants, along with the original UOV scheme, were submitted to NIST's PQC Project in response to the call for additional digital signature schemes. All four candidates successfully advanced to the second round of the PQC process.

1.2 Previous Works

Security analysis against *UOV families* (*i.e.*, UOV and its variants) is usually carried out by listing all the known critical attacks that may influence its concrete hardness estimation result. Historically, those attacks are usually classified into two types: (1) the *key-recovery attacks* that aim to recover the secret key from the given public key, *e.g.*, the Kipnis-Shamir attack [17,23], the intersection attack [4] and the MinRank attack [1,4,5,15,27]; (2) the *forgery attacks* that aim to forge a message/signature pair passing the verification test, *e.g.*, the collision attacks against the hash function, and the direct attack. It is worth noting that XL algorithm is an important method widely used in most attacks against UOV.

Recently, Ran [24] proposed a key-recovery attack against those UOV instances whose underlying (finite) fields are of characteristic $p = 2$. This wedge product attack is based on the observation that when $p = 2$, the public key of a UOV instance in polar form could be seen as a specific subspace of an exterior algebra. Although wedge product attack outperforms those existing key-recovery attacks in terms of many recommended instances of UOV [8], MAYO [7] and SNOVA [29], it is not applicable to QR-UOV [14] due to its constraint on the characteristic, *i.e.*, $p = 2$.

Recently, Hung Le *et al.* [18] extended Ran's wedge product attack to SNOVA [29] by fully utilizing its block-ring structure. Specifically, they derived a more conservative as well as a less conservative heuristic formula to estimate the cost of wedge product attack against SNOVA, which was confirmed via experiments. Using the more conservative formula, this attack outperforms the previous best known key-recovery counterparts for almost all of the current SNOVA parameters [29] submitted to the second round of NIST Additional Call for Digital Signatures, breaking 5 of the 10.

1.3 Contributions in This Work

As mentioned previously, Ran's wedge product attack [24] is applicable to those UOV instances whose underlying field is of characteristic $p = 2$. To generalize Ran's wedge product attack so that it can be applied to those UOV instances with *odd* characteristic, it is natural to consider the algebraic structure of UOV. It is routine to see that the polar form the UOV public key could be seen as an alternating form when $p = 2$, which leads us to define a new generalized form for all characteristics, *i.e.*, the p-reduced symmetric form, that coincides with the alternating form in the case of $p = 2$. The set of p-reduced symmetric forms corresponds to the p-reduced symmetric algebra. With this observation in mind, we generalize Ran's attack [24], and conduct a further security analysis against UOV families (*i.e.*, UOV and its variants). Our contribution in this work is three-fold, as the following indicates.

First and foremost, we propose a new algebra, *i.e.*, the reduced symmetric algebra, over *any* field of characteristic p. This new algebra could be seen as a natural generalization of the exterior algebra used in Ran's wedge product attack [24]. The strength of this new algebra lies in the facts: (1) when $p = 0$, this algebra is essentially the symmetric algebra; (2) when $p = 2$, this algebra is essentially the exterior algebra; (3) what interests us most is that this algebra is also well-defined for every *odd* characteristic p. This new algebra may be of independent interest in the realm of commutative algebra. Please refer to Sect. 3 for full details.

Moreover, we construct a new attack by fully utilizing the properties of the reduced symmetric algebra, and it is essentially a key-recovery attack against *all* UOV instances. On the one hand, when $p = 2$, our key-recovery attack is equivalent to Ran's wedge product attack [24]. On the other hand, compared with Ran's wedge product attack [24], the strength of our new attack lies in the fact that it is also applicable to UOV instances with *odd* characteristics, *e.g.*, those recommended QR-UOV instances [14]. Please refer to Sects. 4 and 5 for full details.

Our final contribution lies in the connection between the characteristic p of the underlying field $\Bbbk$ in a UOV instance and the concrete hardness of that UOV instance. Previous works in MPKC show that for a UOV instance, the order q of its underlying (finite) field $\Bbbk$ is firmly connected to its concrete hardness, and a larger order usually results in a more secure UOV instance, *provided other parameters remain unchanged*; however, the characteristic $p = \mathsf{char}(\Bbbk)$ was usually not taken into the consideration of the concrete hardness analysis of UOV in the past. By contrast, analysis in Sect. 5 shows that our new attack runs faster when the characteristic p of the underlying field $\Bbbk$ of UOV gets smaller. Conversely, this implies that choosing a larger characteristic p helps increase the (concrete) hardness of UOV; for instance, a UOV instance with $\Bbbk = \mathbb{F}_{79}$ is, in general, more secure than a similar UOV instance with $\Bbbk = \mathbb{F}_{81}$. Please refer to Sect. 5 for full details.

1.4 Organization of This Work

The work is organized as follows. Section 2 specifies the notations/conventions used in this work, as well as some preliminary definitions/arguments in MPKC and algebra. In Sect. 3, a new algebra, *i.e.*, the p-reduced symmetric algebra, is defined that can reveal the hidden structure in the UOV problem and could be seen as a generalization of the exterior algebra used in Ran's attack [24]. In Sect. 4, we first reformulate the UOV problem, and then construct our key-recovery attack based upon the p-reduced symmetric algebra that can solve UOV instances with *odd* characteristics as well as UOV instances with characteristic 2; the time complexity of our new attack is also conducted. In Sect. 5 we carry out the bit-cost estimation of recommended QR-UOV instances using our new attack, analyze the relation between its performance and the choice of characteristics, and compare the performance of our new attack with those of its key-recovery counterparts. We conclude this work in Sect. 6 with implications of our contributions for UOV security and future research directions.

2 Preliminaries

2.1 Notations

For any positive integer k, let $[k]$ denote the index set $\{1, 2, \ldots, k\}$, and let Perm_k be the set of permutations on $[k]$. Let $\mathbb{F}_q$ be the finite field with $q = p^e$ elements, where e is a positive integer, and let $\Bbbk$ be a (possibly infinite) field of characteristic $p \geq 0$. We denote vectors over $\Bbbk$ by bold lowercase letters, *e.g.*, $\mathbf{x}$, and matrices over $\Bbbk$ by bold uppercase letters, *e.g.*, $\mathbf{M}$.

The notion of the multi-set is necessary for our description. In this work, a multi-subset of the indexing set is denoted by bold lowercase letters, *e.g.*, $\mathbf{i}, \mathbf{j}$. To avoid ambiguity with standard sets, we use double curly braces to denote multi-sets. Let $\mathcal{I}_{n,d} := \{\mathbf{i} = \{\{i_1, \ldots, i_d\}\} \mid i_j \in [n]\}$ denote the class of all multi-subsets of the indexing set $[n]$ with cardinality d; Moreover, given the field characteristic $p \in \{0, 2, 3, \ldots\}$, the constrained index set $\mathcal{I}_{n,d}^{\leq p}$ is defined as

$$\mathcal{I}_{n,d}^{\leq p} := \begin{cases} \{\mathbf{i} \in \mathcal{I}_{n,d} \mid m_{\mathbf{i}}(k) \leq p \text{ for all } k \in [n]\} & \text{if } p > 0, \\ \mathcal{I}_{n,d} & \text{if } p = 0, \end{cases}$$

where $m_{\mathbf{i}}(k)$ represents the multiplicity of the index k in the multi-subset $\mathbf{i}$.

Throughout this work, let W be a vector space over $\Bbbk$ and we write W^d for the d-fold Cartesian product of W. Let $W^* = \{f : W \to \Bbbk \mid f \text{is} \Bbbk\text{−linear}\}$ denote the dual space of W. For a finite-dimensional vector space W, if $\{\mathbf{e}_1, \ldots, \mathbf{e}_n\}$ is a $\Bbbk$-basis for W, its dual basis is denoted by $\{\mathbf{e}_1^*, \ldots, \mathbf{e}_n^*\}$ satisfying $\mathbf{e}_i^*(\mathbf{e}_j) = \delta_{i,j}$, where $\delta_{\cdot,\cdot}$ is the Kronecker delta function.

2.2 UOV Families and the UOV Problem

The UOV problem is essential for the security of all UOV families (*i.e.*, UOV and its variants). Here we redefine the UOV problem in terms of the polar form.

UOV Families. In UOV as well as its variants, the public key consists of a system of homogeneous multivariate quadratic polynomials $\mathcal{P} = (p_1, \ldots, p_m)$ over $\mathbb{F}_q$ in n variables. These polynomials are well constructed such that there exists a o-dimensional subspace $O \subseteq \mathbb{F}_q^n$, called the *oil space*, which serves as the secret key and satisfies that $p_i(\mathbf{x}) = 0$ for $\mathbf{x} \in O, i \in [m]$.

The security of UOV families is firmly connected to the computational hardness of the *UOV problem* that asks to recover the oil space O, given the public key $\mathcal{P}$.

We define the *vinegar space* as the $v := n - o$ dimensional subspace $V \subseteq \mathbb{F}_q^n$ which is the orthogonal complement of the oil space with respect to the standard inner product.

Polar Form. For a (homogeneous) quadratic polynomial $p(\mathbf{x})$ over $\mathbb{F}_q$ in n indeterminates, its *polar form* is defined as

$$q(\mathbf{x}, \mathbf{y}) := p(\mathbf{x} + \mathbf{y}) - p(\mathbf{x}) - p(\mathbf{y}) + p(\mathbf{0}).$$

In essence the polar form is a symmetric 2-form [6]; in particular, for the special case $\text{char}(\mathbb{F}_q) = 2$, this form is additionally alternating [24].

Similarly, for a system of multivariate (homogeneous) quadratic polynomials $\mathcal{P} = (p_1, \ldots, p_m)$ over finite fields $\mathbb{F}_q$ in n indeterminates, we can define its *polar form* as $\mathcal{Q} := (q_1, \ldots, q_m)$. In this work, every multivariate quadratic polynomial is assumed to be homogeneous.

The Oil Space is Totally Isotropic. Here we generalize the notion of totally isotropic subspaces for bilinear forms [23,25]. Let $\mathcal{P}$ denote a system of multivariate quadratic polynomials over $\mathbb{F}_q$ in n indeterminates, and let $\mathcal{Q}$ be its associated polar form. A subspace $W \subseteq \mathbb{F}_q^n$ is called *totally isotropic* for $\mathcal{Q}$ if $\mathcal{Q}(\mathbf{x}, \mathbf{y}) = \mathbf{0}$ for all $\mathbf{x}, \mathbf{y} \in W$. For UOV and its variants, the secret oil space O essentially forms a totally isotropic subspace of the public key. We formalize this property as follows:

Proposition 1. *Let $\mathcal{P}$ be a UOV public key over $\mathbb{F}_q$ in n variables, and let $\mathcal{Q}$ be its polar form.*

1. *When* $\operatorname{char}(\mathbb{F}_q)$ *is odd, an o-dimensional subspace $W \subseteq \mathbb{F}_q^n$ is an oil space for $\mathcal{P}$ if and only if W is a totally isotropic subspace of $\mathcal{Q}$.*
2. *When* $\operatorname{char}(\mathbb{F}_q) = 2$ *and $v < \frac{o-1}{2}m$, this equivalence holds with overwhelming probability.*

The equivalence in the odd characteristic case is immediate, as $\mathcal{Q}(\mathbf{x}, \mathbf{x}) = 2\mathcal{P}(\mathbf{x})$ inherently ensures $\mathcal{P}(\mathbf{x}) = \mathbf{0}$ when $\mathcal{Q}$ vanishes on W. When $\operatorname{char}(\mathbb{F}_q) = 2$, $\mathcal{Q}$ is alternating and no longer algebraically bounds the squared terms. However, finding an o-dimensional totally isotropic subspace for $\mathcal{Q}$ requires satisfying $m\binom{o}{2}$ equations. Since we need ov variables to determine an o-dimensional subspace in $\mathbb{F}_q^{v+o}$, the system is strictly overdetermined when $v < \frac{o-1}{2}m$. Under the generic behavior of UOV central maps, the planted oil space is the unique solution with overwhelming probability.

Hence, solving the UOV problem is equivalent to finding an o-dimensional totally isotropic subspace of the polar form $\mathcal{Q}$.

2.3 Key Recovery Attacks for UOV Families

In this subsection we list several key recovery attacks/tools against UOV families, *i.e.*, the XL algorithm(s), the reconciliation attack, and Ran's attack.

XL Algorithm. The XL algorithm is a method for solving systems of multivariate quadratic equations. It serves as a core subroutine in many key-recovery attacks against UOV families.

The XL algorithm [10], named for e**X**tended **L**inearization, originates from the idea to linearize the given system by regarding each monomial as one variable, and then use linear algebra to the coefficient matrix of the linearized system. The most effective improvements of XL are Wiedemann XL (WXL) [31], and the hybrid approaches [3,30].

Roughly speaking, for a system of m multivariate quadratic equations in n indeterminates over the finite fields $\mathbb{F}_q$, when the *degree bound* $D \geq 2$ is sufficiently large, the plain XL algorithm has time complexity

$$\mathcal{O}\left(\binom{n+D}{D}^{\omega}\right),$$

where $2 \leq \omega < 3$ is the exponent of matrix multiplication. Similarly, the time complexity of the WXL variant is

$$\mathcal{O}\left(\binom{n+2}{2} \cdot \binom{n+D}{D}^2\right),$$

where D denotes the least d such that the coefficient of z^d in $\frac{(1-z^2)^m}{(1-z)^{n+1}}$ does not exceed d, *i.e.*,

$$D := \min\left\{d : \mathrm{coef}\left(\frac{(1-z^2)^m}{(1-z)^{n+1}}, z^d\right) \leq d\right\}.$$

And the XL has time complexity

$$\mathcal{O}\left(q^k \cdot \binom{n-k+D}{D}^\omega\right) \text{and} \mathcal{O}\left(q^k \cdot \binom{n-k+2}{2} \cdot \binom{n-k+D}{D}^2\right)$$

using plain XL and WXL respectively where D denotes the least d such that the coefficient of z^d in $\frac{(1-z^2)^m}{(1-z)^{n-k+1}}$ does not exceed d itself, *i.e.*,

$$D := \min\left\{d : \mathrm{coef}\left(\tfrac{(1-z^2)^m}{(1-z)^{n-k+1}}, z^d\right) \leq d\right\}.$$

Reconciliation Attack. Reconciliation attack [12] aims to recover a vector $\mathbf{o}$ in oil space O by solving the polynomial system $\mathcal{P}(\mathbf{o}) = \mathbf{0}$ which can be done by XL algorithm. Given that $\dim(O) = o$, imposing o generic affine constraints on $\mathbf{o}$ typically yields a unique solution in O. When $n - o \leq m$, the constrained system $\mathcal{P}(\mathbf{o}) = \mathbf{0}$ becomes an overdetermined system of m equations in fewer than m variables, making it efficiently solvable and superior to direct attacks. When $n - o > m$, we solve for $\mathbf{o}_i \in O$ by constructing an overdetermined system:

$$\begin{cases} \mathcal{P}(\mathbf{o}_i) = \mathbf{0}, & 1 \leq i \leq k, \\ \mathcal{Q}(\mathbf{o}_i, \mathbf{o}_j) = \mathbf{0}, & 1 \leq i < j \leq k \end{cases}$$

where Q encodes P's polar form. However, this strategy introduces $k(n-o)$ variables and $m\binom{k+1}{2}$ equations, rendering it generally less efficient than direct attack when k exceeds a small threshold.

Ran's Wedge Product Attack. Recently Ran [24] proposed a key-recovery attack against those UOV instances whose underlying field is of characteristic 2. It is based upon the connection between properties of the UOV polar form and those of exterior algebra, and improves the cost estimates of several UOV recommended instances in UOV, MAYO and SNOVA whose underlying field is of characteristic 2.

Recall that in UOV and its variants, the public key is the system of multivariate quadratic polynomial $\mathcal{P} = (p_1, ..., p_m)$ over the finite field $\mathbb{F}_q$ in n

indeterminates, and its secret key is the oil space $O \subseteq \mathbb{F}_q^n$ of dimension o. Let $V = \langle \mathbf{v}_1, \ldots, \mathbf{v}_v \rangle$ denote the *vinegar space*, *i.e.*, the $v := n - o$ dimensional subspace of $\mathbb{F}_q^n$ that is the orthogonal complement of O with respect to the standard inner product. And let $\mathcal{V} = \mathbf{v}_1 \wedge \cdots \wedge \mathbf{v}_v$ be its associated v-wedge. Ran defined a map [24]

$$\mathcal{M} : \bigwedge^{v} \mathbb{F}_q^n \longrightarrow \left(\bigwedge^{v+2} \mathbb{F}_q^n \right)^m$$
$$\alpha \longmapsto (\alpha \wedge q_1, \ldots, \alpha \wedge q_m)$$

where $q_1, \ldots, q_m$ are polar forms of the public key. Notice that $\mathcal{M}$ is basically a linear map from $\mathbb{F}_q^{\binom{n}{v}}$ to $\mathbb{F}_q^{m\binom{n}{v+2}}$. Moreover, the matrix corresponding $\mathcal{M}$ can be viewed as a Macaulay matrix on exterior algebra. It is routine to see that $\mathcal{V}$ lies in the kernel of $\mathcal{M}$; moreover, if the kernel of $\mathcal{M}$ is of dimension 1, it is precisely $\mathbb{F}_q\mathcal{V}$ and hence we can determine the vinegar space using every nonzero element in the kernel. And Ran has made perfect rank prediction for a large number of different (non-trivial) parameter sets as

$$\text{rank}(\mathcal{M}) = \sum_{i=0}^{\lfloor \frac{o}{2} \rfloor} (-1)^i \binom{m+i-1}{i} \binom{v+o}{v+2i}$$

except for two exceptions which can be avoided by adding requirements to parameters [24].

2.4 Graded Frobenius Algebra

Here we introduce graded Frobenius algebra, which is a finite dimensional $\mathbb{N}$-graded $\Bbbk$-algebra. Jumping ahead, the p-reduced symmetric algebra with $p > 0$ to be defined in Sect. 3 is the graded Frobenius algebra.

Definition 2. (Graded Frobenius Algebra). *Let $A = \bigoplus_{i=0}^{u} A_i$ be a finite-dimensional $\mathbb{N}$-graded $\Bbbk$-algebra. A is called a* ***graded Frobenius algebra*** *if there exists a homogeneous linear map $\varepsilon : A \to \Bbbk$ of degree $-u$ (the* ***counit****) such that the bilinear form*

$$\langle a, b \rangle := \varepsilon(a \cdot b)$$

is non-degenerate, i.e., *for any homogeneous $a \neq 0$, $\exists b$ with $\langle a, b \rangle \neq 0$.*

Proposition 3. *Let $A = \bigoplus_{i=0}^{u} A_i$ be a graded Frobenius algebra over a field $\Bbbk$. For any degree d, the graded components A_d and A_{u-d} are mutually dual vector spaces with* $\dim A_d = \dim A_{u-d}$.

Proof. By the definition of a graded Frobenius algebra, there exists a homogeneous linear map $\varepsilon : A \to \Bbbk$ (of degree $-u$) inducing a non-degenerate bilinear form $\langle a, b \rangle = \varepsilon(ab)$. Consider the linear map $\phi : A_{u-d} \to (A_d)^*$ defined by $\phi(w)(v) = \langle v, w \rangle$. For any nonzero $w \in A_{u-d}$, non-degeneracy guarantees the existence of $a \in A$ such that $\varepsilon(aw) \neq 0$. Decomposing a into homogeneous components $\sum_i a_i$, the homogeneity of ε implies that only the $a_d \in A_d$ term satisfies $\varepsilon(a_d w) \neq 0$ (since for $i \neq d$ we have $\varepsilon(a_i w) = 0$ with $\deg \varepsilon = -u$), proving ϕ is injective. Similarly, we can construct an injection $\psi : A_d \to (A_{u-d})^*$. As A_d and A_{u-d} are finite-dimensional, the injectivity combined with dimension comparison $\dim A_{u-d} \leq \dim(A_d)^* = \dim A_d \leq \dim(A_{u-d})^* = \dim A_{u-d}$ immediately yields $\dim A_d = \dim A_{u-d}$, with ϕ and ψ being isomorphisms. □

3 p-Reduced Symmetric Algebra

In this section, we propose the definition of the p-reduced symmetric algebra.

The motivation for this new algebra stems from analyzing the polar forms associated with UOV public keys. Specifically, while the polar form is an alternating form in characteristic $p = 2$, we observe that more generally, it possesses the p-reduced property for any characteristic p. This observation is the primary reason for defining the p-reduced symmetric algebra, as it is the appropriate structure to study the entire set of these p-reduced forms.

The p-reduced symmetric algebra could be seen as a generalization of the exterior algebra. As we shall see in Sect. 4, the notion of the p-reduced symmetric algebra enables us to generalize Ran's wedge product attack.

3.1 Symmetric Form and p-Reduced Symmetric Algebra

We start by recalling the symmetric and alternating d-form and then defining p-reduced symmetric d-form as a generalization of polar forms so that we have multiplication operation between forms. Moreover, we present p-reduced algebra and interpret the polar form as a degree-2 element in the p-reduced symmetric algebra. Jumping ahead, our new algebra is *graded* which is similar to the polynomial rings.

Symmetric d-form. We shall define the p-reduced property for symmetric form.

First of all, let's review the definition of symmetric and alternating d-form. Let W be a vector space over $\Bbbk$. A *d-form* on W is a $\Bbbk$-multilinear map $f : W^d \to \Bbbk$. And a d-form f is called *symmetric* if for each $i \in [d-1]$ and $\mathbf{x}_1, \ldots, \mathbf{x}_d \in W$ satisfying

$$f(\mathbf{x}_1, \ldots, \mathbf{x}_i, \mathbf{x}_{i+1}, \ldots, \mathbf{x}_d) = f(\mathbf{x}_1, \ldots, \mathbf{x}_{i+1}, \mathbf{x}_i, \ldots, \mathbf{x}_d).$$

What's more, a d-form f is called *alternating* if for each $i \in [d-1]$ and $\mathbf{x}_1, \ldots, \mathbf{x}_d \in W$ satisfying

$$f(\mathbf{x}_1, \ldots, \mathbf{x}_i, \mathbf{x}_{i+1}, \ldots, \mathbf{x}_d) = 0 \text{ when } \mathbf{x}_i = \mathbf{x}_{i+1}.$$

As a consequence, an alternating d-form has the following property (skew-symmetric):

$$f(\mathbf{x}_1, \ldots, \mathbf{x}_i, \mathbf{x}_{i+1}, \ldots, \mathbf{x}_d) = -f(\mathbf{x}_1, \ldots, \mathbf{x}_{i+1}, \mathbf{x}_i, \ldots, \mathbf{x}_d)$$

which is actually an equivalent definition if and only if $\mathrm{char}(\mathbb{k}) \neq 2$.

We remark that in characteristic 2, alternating d-forms are symmetric, since swapping two arguments does not change the sign.

We now define the multiplication operation between symmetric forms (on the same vector space W).

Definition 4. *For a symmetric d-form f of W and a symmetric ℓ-form g of W, their product is defined to be a map $f \odot g$ from $W^{d+\ell}$ to $\mathbb{k}$ as:*

$$(f \odot g)(\mathbf{x}_1, ..., \mathbf{x}_{d+\ell}) := \sum_{\sigma} f(\mathbf{x}_{\sigma(1)}, ..., \mathbf{x}_{\sigma(d)}) \cdot g(\mathbf{x}_{\sigma(d+1)}, ..., \mathbf{x}_{\sigma(d+\ell)}),$$

where σ ranges from all permutations over the index set $[d+\ell]$ such that $\sigma(1) < \cdots < \sigma(d)$ and $\sigma(d+1) < \cdots < \sigma(d+\ell)$.

It is routine to verify that the product $f \odot g$ is a symmetric $(d+\ell)$-form of W.

For characteristic $p > 0$, consider a symmetric d-form f $(0 < d < p)$ and a $(p-d)$-form g. Evaluating their product $f \odot g$ at p identical vectors $\mathbf{x}$ yields:

$$f \odot g(\mathbf{x}_1 = \mathbf{x}, \ldots, \mathbf{x}_p = \mathbf{x}) = \binom{p}{d} f(\mathbf{x}, \ldots, \mathbf{x}) g(\mathbf{x}, \ldots, \mathbf{x}) = 0.$$

Here, the equality $\binom{p}{d} = 0$ holds in the field of characteristic p. This property motivates the following definition of p-reduced forms:

Definition 5 (p-reduced Symmetric d-form). *Let $d \geq 0$. A symmetric d-form $f \colon W^d \to \mathbb{k}$ is said to be* p-reduced *if $f(\mathbf{x}_1, \ldots, \mathbf{x}_d) = 0$ whenever $\mathbf{x}_1 = \cdots = \mathbf{x}_p$ and $d \geq p > 0$.*

It is easy to verify that the multiplication $\odot$ defined in Definition 4 preserves the p-reduced property.

When $p = 0$, all symmetric d-forms are p-reduced. When $p = 2$, they coincide with alternating d-forms in characteristic 2 (Fig. 1).

Henceforth, the p-reduced symmetric d-form will be abbreviated as the (symmetric) d-form.

p-Reduced Symmetric Algebra. Recall that the symmetric algebra of W is

$$\mathrm{Sym}(W) = \mathbb{k} \oplus W \oplus W^{\otimes 2} \oplus \cdots / C,$$

where C is the ideal generated by the set $\{\mathbf{x} \otimes \mathbf{y} - \mathbf{y} \otimes \mathbf{x} \mid \mathbf{x}, \mathbf{y} \in W\}$. What interests us most is a *special* quotient algebra.

Definition 6. *The* p-reduced symmetric algebra *of W, is defined as the quotient algebra*

$$\overline{\mathrm{Sym}(W)} := \mathrm{Sym}(W)/I,$$

where I is the (graded) ideal generated by $\left\{\overline{\mathbf{x}^{\otimes p}} \in \mathrm{Sym}(W) : \mathbf{x} \in W\right\}$ when $p > 0$, and $I = \{0\}$ when $p = 0$.

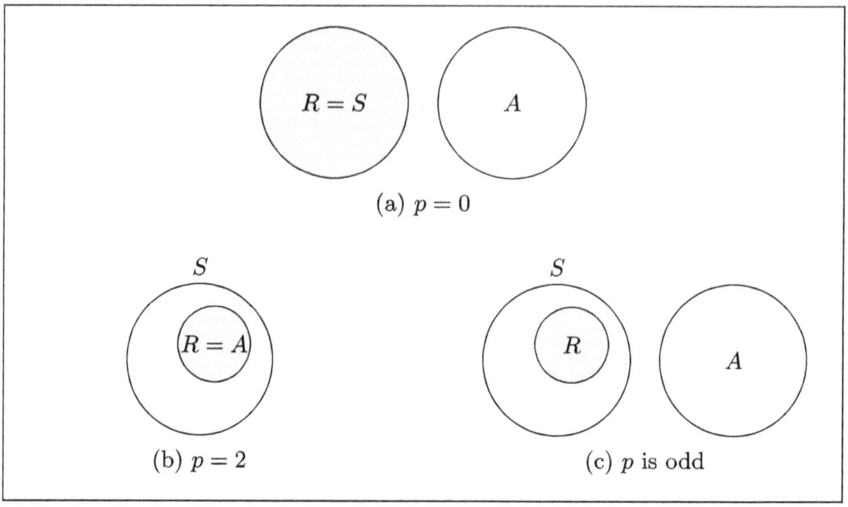

Fig. 1. Relationships between the sets of alternating forms (A), symmetric forms (S), and p-reduced symmetric forms (R) under different field characteristics.

Remark 7. First, when $p = 0$, the p-reduced symmetric algebra coincides with the symmetric algebra. Moreover, the 2-reduced symmetric algebra is essentially the exterior algebra that plays an important role in Ran's attack [24].

In the following, we denote the multiplication in the p-reduced symmetric algebra, inherited from the tensor algebra, by $\odot$, and its d-th homogeneous component by $\bigodot^d W$, so that

$$\overline{\mathrm{Sym}(W)} = \bigoplus_{d \geq 0} \bigodot^d W$$

With respect to a fixed basis $\{\mathbf{e}_1, \dots, \mathbf{e}_n\}$ of W, we define the standard basis for each $\bigodot^d W$ as:

$$\{\mathbf{e}_{i_1} \odot \mathbf{e}_{i_2} \odot \cdots \odot \mathbf{e}_{i_d} \;:\; \mathbf{i} = \{\{i_1, \dots, i_d\}\} \in \mathcal{I}_{n,d}^{\leq p}\}.$$

We adopt the shorthand notation $\mathbf{x}^{\odot c} := \mathbf{x}^c$ for $c \geq 1$, and define $\mathbf{x}^0 := 1_{\mathbb{k}}$. Since $\overline{\mathrm{Sym}(W)}$ is commutative, we can equivalently denote the basis elements in the power form $\odot_{j \in [n]} \mathbf{e}_j^{m_{\mathbf{i}}(j)}$, where $m_{\mathbf{i}}(j)$ is the multiplicity of $\mathbf{e}_j$ in the product $\mathbf{e}_{i_1} \odot \cdots \odot \mathbf{e}_{i_d}$.

Lemma 8. *Let $n = \dim_{\mathbb{k}} W$. The p-reduced symmetric algebra of W is isomorphic to the quotient polynomial algebra $\mathbb{k}[x_1, \dots, x_n]/(x_1^p, \dots, x_n^p)$.*

Proof. Fix a basis $\{\mathbf{e}_1, \dots, \mathbf{e}_n\}$ of W. The desired isomorphism is explicitly given by mapping $\mathbf{e}_i \mapsto x_i$ for $i = 1, \dots, n$.

The set of all symmetric d-forms, $d \geq 0$, on a $\Bbbk$-vector space W naturally forms a graded algebra under the multiplication defined in Definition 4, and admits a canonical isomorphism to the p-reduced symmetric algebra. More precisely:

Theorem 9. *Let* $\dim_{\Bbbk} W = n < \infty$. *There exists a graded algebra isomorphism:*

$$\bigoplus_{d\geq 0}\{p\text{-reduced symmetric } d\text{-forms on } W\} \cong \overline{\mathrm{Sym}(W)}.$$

Proof. Let n be the dimension of W over $\Bbbk$. The isomorphism is constructed as follows: for each degree $d \geq 0$, define a map Φ_d sending generators $\mathbf{e}_{i_1} \odot \cdots \odot \mathbf{e}_{i_d} \in \bigodot^d W$ to the symmetric d-form

$$(\mathbf{x}_1, \ldots, \mathbf{x}_d) \longmapsto \sum_{\sigma \in \mathrm{Perm}_d} \prod_{k=1}^{d} \mathbf{e}^*_{i_k}(\mathbf{x}_{\sigma(k)}),$$

which extends linearly to the full space. It is straightforward to verify that $\Phi_d(\mathbf{e}_{i_1} \odot \cdots \odot \mathbf{e}_{i_d})$ satisfies all the conditions of a symmetric d-form and the map $\oplus_{d\geq 0}\Phi_d$ preserves the multiplication defined in Definition 4. The inverse map Ψ_d takes a symmetric d-form f to the element

$$\sum_{\mathfrak{i} \in \mathcal{I}^{\leq p}_{n,d}} \frac{f(\mathbf{e}_{i_1}, \ldots, \mathbf{e}_{i_d})}{\prod_{k\in[n]} m_{\mathfrak{i}}(k)!} \mathbf{e}_{i_1} \odot \cdots \odot \mathbf{e}_{i_d}$$

Note that under the p-reduction condition, we need not worry about $m_{\mathfrak{i}}(k)! = 0$ in $\Bbbk$ when $p > 0$, since $f(\mathbf{e}_{i_1}, \ldots, \mathbf{e}_{i_d}) = 0$ whenever any $m_{\mathfrak{i}}(k) > p$. □

Corollary 10. *Under the isomorphism in Theorem 9, we interpret the polar form as a degree-2 element in the p-reduced symmetric algebra. For a polar form* $q(\mathbf{x}, \mathbf{y}) = \sum_{1\leq i,j\leq n} a_{ij}x_i y_j$ *with* $a_{ij} = a_{ji}$, *its image under* Ψ_2 *is given by:*

$$\Psi_2(q) \overset{Theorem 9}{=} \sum_{1\leq i<j\leq n} a_{i,j}\mathbf{e}_i \odot \mathbf{e}_j + \sum_{i=1}^{n} \frac{a_{i,i}}{2!}\mathbf{e}_i \odot \mathbf{e}_i \qquad \in \overline{\mathrm{Sym}(\mathbb{F}_q^n)}_2$$

$$\overset{Lemma 8}{\leftrightarrow} \sum_{1\leq i<j\leq n} a_{i,j}x_i x_j + \sum_{i=1}^{n} \frac{a_{i,i}}{2!}x_i^2 \qquad \in \mathbb{F}_q[x_1, \ldots, x_n]/(x_1^p, \ldots, x_n^p)$$

where $\{\mathbf{e}_1, \ldots, \mathbf{e}_n\}$ *is the standard basis of* $\mathbb{F}_q^n$.

Remark 11. For the polar form q of a homogeneous quadratic polynomial $p \in \mathbb{F}_q[x_1, \ldots, x_n]$, we have $\Psi_2(q) = \bar{p} \in \mathbb{F}_q[x_1, \ldots, x_n]/(x_1^p, \ldots, x_n^p)$.

Permanent Minor. Recall that the determinant of a square matrix of order d plays a key role in Ran's attack [24], and it essentially corresponds to a specially alternating d-form from W^d to $\Bbbk$. In this work, to establish its analogue in the context of the p-reduced symmetric algebra, we define the permanent minor as the unsigned counterpart of the determinant minor. Note that when $p = 2$, this construction reduces to the determinant minor.

Definition 12 (Permanent Minor). *Let* $\dim_{\Bbbk} W = n < \infty$*, and let* $\mathbf{i} = \{i_1, \ldots, i_d\} \in \mathcal{I}_{n,d}$ *where* $d \geq 1$*. Then the* permanent minor *of* W *relative to a fixed basis* $\{\mathbf{e}_1, \ldots, \mathbf{e}_n\}$ *and the* multi-set $\mathbf{i}$ *is the multilinear map* $\mathrm{Per}_{\mathbf{i}}^{\{\mathbf{e}_1,\ldots,\mathbf{e}_n\}} : W^d \to \Bbbk$ *defined by*

$$\mathrm{Per}_{\mathbf{i}}^{\{\mathbf{e}_1,\ldots,\mathbf{e}_n\}}(\mathbf{x}_1, \mathbf{x}_2, \ldots, \mathbf{x}_d) = \sum_{\sigma \in \mathrm{Perm}_d} \mathbf{e}_{i_1}^*(\mathbf{x}_{\sigma(1)})\mathbf{e}_{i_2}^*(\mathbf{x}_{\sigma(2)}) \cdots \mathbf{e}_{i_d}^*(\mathbf{x}_{\sigma(d)}).$$

The integer d *is called the* order *of the permanent minor.*

We note that the superscript $\mathbf{e}_1, \ldots, \mathbf{e}_n$ of $\mathrm{Per}_{\mathbf{i}}^{\mathbf{e}_1,\ldots,\mathbf{e}_n}$ is typically omitted when the basis is clear from the context. The permanent minor $\mathrm{Per}_{\mathbf{i}}$ is exactly the symmetric d-form $\mathbf{e}_{i_1} \odot \mathbf{e}_{i_2} \odot \cdots \odot \mathbf{e}_{i_d} \in \overline{\mathrm{Sym}(W)}_d$. Consequently, the set of non-zero permanent minors of order d constitutes a $\Bbbk$-basis for $\overline{\mathrm{Sym}(W)}_d$.

In particular, when $d = n$ and $\mathbf{i} = \{1, 2, ..., n\}$, this specific permanent minor is defined as

$$\mathrm{Per}_{\mathbf{i}}(\mathbf{x}_1, \ldots, \mathbf{x}_n) = \sum_{\sigma} \mathbf{e}_1^*(\mathbf{x}_{\sigma(1)})\mathbf{e}_2^*(\mathbf{x}_{\sigma(2)}) \cdots \mathbf{e}_n^*(\mathbf{x}_{\sigma(n)}),$$

which is equivalent to the notion of the *permanent* of a square matrix [9].

3.2 Duality

In this section, we first compute the dimension of the d-th homogeneous component $\overline{\mathrm{Sym}(W)}_d$. We then show that $\overline{\mathrm{Sym}(W)}$ is a graded Frobenius algebra. This algebraic structure allows us to exploit the duality properties necessary for analyzing the XL algorithm.

Proposition 13. *Let* $p = \mathrm{char}(\Bbbk) > 0$*. Also let* $n = \dim_{\Bbbk} W$ *with* $\{\mathbf{e}_1, ..., \mathbf{e}_n\}$ *being a* $\Bbbk$*-basis for* W*. Then the* p*-reduced symmetric algebra* $\overline{\mathrm{Sym}(W)}$ *is a finite-dimensional graded* $\Bbbk$*-algebra with the following properties:*

(1) Top degree component:
- *The algebra is supported in degrees* 0 *through* $n(p-1)$*.*
- $\dim \overline{\mathrm{Sym}(W)}_{n(p-1)} = 1$*, generated by the product* $(\odot_{i=1}^n \mathbf{e}_i^{p-1})$*.*

(2) Hilbert series:

$$H_{\overline{\mathrm{Sym}(W)}}(t) = \frac{(1-t^p)^n}{(1-t)^n} = (1 + t + \cdots + t^{p-1})^n$$

(3) Dimension formula: For each $d \geq 0$*,*

$$\dim \overline{\mathrm{Sym}(W)}_d = \sum_{j=0}^{\min(n, \lfloor d/p \rfloor)} (-1)^j \binom{n}{j} \binom{d - jp + n - 1}{n-1}$$

This formula counts degree d *monomials where each variable has exponent* $< p$*.*

Proof. By Lemma 8, we have the algebra isomorphism $\overline{\mathrm{Sym}(W)} \cong \Bbbk[x_1, \ldots, x_n]/(x_1^p, \ldots, x_n^p)$. Since the sequence $(x_1^p, \ldots, x_n^p)$ is regular, the Hilbert series of $\overline{\mathrm{Sym}(W)}$ is equal to $\frac{(1-t^p)^n}{(1-t)^n}$ Consequently, statements (1) and (3) follow directly from this Hilbert series computation combined with property (2). □

Theorem 14. *Let* $n = \dim_{\Bbbk} W$. *The p-reduced symmetric algebra* $\overline{\mathrm{Sym}(W)}$ *is a graded Frobenius algebra.*

Proof. By Proposition 13 we have $\overline{\mathrm{Sym}(W)} = \bigoplus_{i=0}^{u} \overline{\mathrm{Sym}(W)}_i$, where $u = n(p-1)$. Fix a basis $\{\mathbf{e}_1, \ldots, \mathbf{e}_n\}$ of W.

Define a homogeneous linear map $\varepsilon : \overline{\mathrm{Sym}(W)} \to \Bbbk$ of degree $-u$ by setting:

$$\varepsilon\left(k \cdot \mathbf{e}_1^{p-1} \odot \cdots \odot \mathbf{e}_n^{p-1}\right) = k \quad \text{and} \quad \varepsilon(x) = 0 \text{ for } \deg x < u.$$

This induces a bilinear form $\langle x, y \rangle := \varepsilon(x \odot y)$.

To verify non-degeneracy, take any non-zero $x \in \overline{\mathrm{Sym}(W)}$ and let $x_d = \sum_\alpha k_\alpha \mathbf{e}_1^{\alpha_1} \odot \cdots \odot \mathbf{e}_n^{\alpha_n}$ (where $|\alpha| = \sum \alpha_i = d$) be its non-zero homogeneous component. For each monomial term $k_\alpha e^\alpha$ in x_d, define the dual monomial:

$$y_\alpha := \mathbf{e}_1^{p-1-\alpha_1} \odot \cdots \odot \mathbf{e}_n^{p-1-\alpha_n} \in \overline{\mathrm{Sym}(W)}_{u-d}.$$

Then $\langle x, y_\alpha \rangle = k_\alpha \neq 0$ for at least one α, since $x_d \neq 0$. Thus $\overline{\mathrm{Sym}(W)}$ satisfies the condition of a graded Frobenius algebra. □

4 Solving the UOV Problem Using p-Reduced Symmetric Algebra

We now utilize the reduced symmetric algebra introduced in the previous section to develop a corresponding XL algorithm for solving the UOV problem. Our approach builds upon the polar form-based UOV problem formulation presented in Sect. 2.2, which follows a framework similar to Ran's attack.

4.1 Macaulay Matrix on p-Reduced Symmetric Algebra

The XL algorithm was designed to solve a system of multivariate polynomials with a unique solution over finite fields. It constructs the Macaulay matrix in a given degree and solves the resultant system using sparse matrix methods. The Macaulay matrix thus plays a central role in the algorithm, and its definition could refer to [10].

Here we first generalize the definition of the Macaulay matrix from the polynomial ring to a locally finite $\mathbb{N}$-graded $\Bbbk$-algebra $A = \bigoplus_{i \geq 0} A_i$.[1]

[1] Recall that an $\mathbb{N}$-graded $\Bbbk$-algebra is locally finite if each graded component A_i is a finite-dimensional vector space over $\Bbbk$, *i.e.*, $\dim_{\Bbbk} A_i < \infty$ for all $i \geq 0$.

Given an ordered basis for each A_i as well as a graded ideal $I = \bigoplus_j I_j := (f_1, \dots, f_m)$ where each f_i is homogeneous element in A, we define the *Macaulay matrix* $\mathbf{M}_d$ over degree d related to I

$$\mathbf{M}_d := \begin{array}{c} \\ f'_1 \\ \vdots \\ f'_\ell \end{array} \begin{array}{c} \begin{array}{ccc} e_1 & \cdots & e_h \end{array} \\ \begin{pmatrix} a_{1,1} & \cdots & a_{1,h} \\ \vdots & \ddots & \vdots \\ a_{\ell,1} & \cdots & a_{\ell,h} \end{pmatrix} \end{array}$$

The columns of $\mathbf{M}_d$ are indexed by the ordered basis $(e_1, \dots, e_h)$ of A_d. The rows are indexed by the sequence $(f'_1, \dots, f'_\ell)$, which consists of the degree-d homogeneous elements from the set

$$\{f_i e_j \ : \ e_j \text{ is a basis element of } A_{d-\deg f_i},\ i \in [m]\}$$

arranged in lexicographical order with respect to the indices (i, j). The entry $a_{i,j}$ is the coefficient of e_j in f'_i.

For the UOV problem, the set of polar forms $\mathcal{Q} = \{q_1, \dots, q_m\}$, where each q_i is a symmetric 2-form, generates a graded ideal $I = (q_1, \dots, q_m)$ within the locally finite algebra $\mathrm{Sym}(\mathbb{F}_q^n) \cong \mathbb{F}_q[x_1, \dots, x_n]/(x_1^p, \dots, x_n^p)$. To solve the UOV problem, we consider the kernel of the Macaulay matrix $\mathbf{M}_d$.

We give a toy example to show $\mathbf{M}_3$. Consider $\mathbb{F}_9$-space $V = \mathbb{F}_9^3$, take $d = 3$, $m = 2$. Let $\mathbf{e}_1 = (1, 0, 0)$, $\mathbf{e}_2 = (0, 1, 0)$ and $\mathbf{e}_3 = (0, 0, 1)$ be a standard basis of $\mathbb{F}_9^3$. For the homogeneous quadratic form $p_k(\mathbf{x}) = \sum_{i \leq j} a_{i,j}^{(k)} x_i x_j$, its polar form can be rewritten as 2-form $\sum_{i \leq j} a_{i,j}^{(k)} \mathbf{e}_i \odot \mathbf{e}_j$. Then a Macaulay matrix on the 3-form is

$$\begin{array}{c} \\ q_1 \odot \mathbf{e}_1 \\ q_1 \odot \mathbf{e}_2 \\ q_1 \odot \mathbf{e}_3 \\ q_2 \odot \mathbf{e}_1 \\ q_2 \odot \mathbf{e}_2 \\ q_2 \odot \mathbf{e}_3 \end{array} \begin{array}{c} \begin{array}{ccccccc} \mathbf{e}_1 \odot \mathbf{e}_1 \odot \mathbf{e}_2 & \mathbf{e}_1 \odot \mathbf{e}_1 \odot \mathbf{e}_3 & \mathbf{e}_1 \odot \mathbf{e}_2 \odot \mathbf{e}_2 & \mathbf{e}_1 \odot \mathbf{e}_2 \odot \mathbf{e}_3 & \mathbf{e}_1 \odot \mathbf{e}_3 \odot \mathbf{e}_3 & \mathbf{e}_2 \odot \mathbf{e}_2 \odot \mathbf{e}_3 & \mathbf{e}_2 \odot \mathbf{e}_3 \odot \mathbf{e}_3 \end{array} \\ \begin{pmatrix} a_{1,2}^{(1)} & a_{1,3}^{(1)} & a_{2,2}^{(1)} & a_{2,3}^{(1)} & a_{3,3}^{(1)} & 0 & 0 \\ a_{1,1}^{(1)} & 0 & a_{1,2}^{(1)} & a_{1,3}^{(1)} & 0 & a_{2,3}^{(1)} & a_{3,3}^{(1)} \\ 0 & a_{1,1}^{(1)} & 0 & a_{1,2}^{(1)} & a_{1,3}^{(1)} & a_{2,2}^{(1)} & a_{2,3}^{(1)} \\ a_{1,2}^{(2)} & a_{1,3}^{(2)} & a_{2,2}^{(2)} & a_{2,3}^{(2)} & a_{3,3}^{(2)} & 0 & 0 \\ a_{1,1}^{(2)} & 0 & a_{1,2}^{(2)} & a_{1,3}^{(2)} & 0 & a_{2,3}^{(2)} & a_{3,3}^{(2)} \\ 0 & a_{1,1}^{(2)} & 0 & a_{1,2}^{(2)} & a_{1,3}^{(2)} & a_{2,2}^{(2)} & a_{2,3}^{(2)} \end{pmatrix} \end{array}.$$

Kernel of $\mathbf{M}_d$. For isotropic subspace O in the UOV problem, for any $\mathbf{o}_1, \dots, \mathbf{o}_d \in O$, $p_k(\mathbf{o}_i, \mathbf{o}_j) = 0$, for $k \in [m], i, j \in [d]$. Then, for every f in the standard basis of $\mathrm{Sym}(\mathbb{F}_q^n)_{d-2}$, we have

$$(f \odot p_k)(\mathbf{o}_1, \dots, \mathbf{o}_d) = \sum_{\mathbf{i} \in \mathcal{I}_{n,d}^{\leq p}} c_{\mathbf{i}} \mathbf{e}_{i_1} \odot \cdots \odot \mathbf{e}_{i_d}(\mathbf{o}_1, \dots, \mathbf{o}_d) = 0.$$

Since the vector $(c_{\mathbf{i}})_{\mathbf{i} \in \mathcal{I}_{n,d}^{\leq p}}$ forms a row of the degree-d Macaulay matrix, it follows that the sequence of all permanent minors of degree d, *i.e.*, $(\mathbf{e}_{i_1} \odot \cdots \odot \mathbf{e}_{i_d}(\mathbf{o}_1, \dots, \mathbf{o}_d))_{\mathbf{i} \in \mathcal{I}_{n,d}^{\leq p}}$, lies in the kernel of the Macaulay matrix.

Consider an element $\mu = \sum_{\mathbf{j}\in\mathcal{I}_{n,d}^{\leq p}} \mu_{\mathbf{j}}\mathbf{e}_{j_1}\odot\cdots\odot\mathbf{e}_{j_d} \in \overline{\mathrm{Sym}(\mathbb{F}_q^n)}_d$. This element defines a map:

$$\mu \mapsto (\mathbf{e}_{i_1}\odot\cdots\odot\mathbf{e}_{i_d}(\mu))_{\mathbf{i}\in\mathcal{I}_{n,d}^{\leq p}}$$

where the component $\mathbf{e}_{i_1}\odot\cdots\odot\mathbf{e}_{i_d}(\mu)$ is given by:

$$\mathbf{e}_{i_1}\odot\cdots\odot\mathbf{e}_{i_d}(\mu) := \sum_{\mathbf{j}\in\mathcal{I}_{n,d}^{\leq p}} \mu_{\mathbf{j}}\mathbf{e}_{i_1}\odot\cdots\odot\mathbf{e}_{i_d}(\mathbf{e}_{j_1},\ldots,\mathbf{e}_{j_d})$$

This mapping is well-defined. Moreover, the map is an injection. Thus, the set of resulting coordinate vectors is isomorphic to the original space:

$$\left\{(\mathbf{e}_{i_1}\odot\cdots\odot\mathbf{e}_{i_d}(\mu))_{\mathbf{i}} : \mu\in\overline{\mathrm{Sym}(O)}_d\right\} \cong \overline{\mathrm{Sym}(O)}_d$$

Hence, if the dimension of $\overline{\mathrm{Sym}(O)}_d$ is equal to the dimension of $\mathrm{Ker}\mathbf{M}_d$, then the vector in kernel $\mathbf{M}_d$ always lies in $\overline{\mathrm{Sym}(O)}_d$.

4.2 XL Algorithm on p-Reduced Symmetric Algebra

Now we give the XL algorithm on $\overline{\mathrm{Sym}(V)}$. Later in Sect. 4.3 we show how to find a parameter D such that the XL algorithm works.

Algorithm 1. XL algorithm on $\overline{\mathrm{Sym}(V)}$

Input: A sequence of symmetric 2-forms $\{f_i \in \overline{\mathrm{Sym}(\mathbb{F}_q^n)}_2 : i\in[m]\}$ with an isotropic subspace $O\subseteq\mathbb{F}_q^n$ of dimension o and a degree bound D, $2\leq D\leq o(p-1)$.

Output: $\mathbf{x},\mathbf{y}\in\mathbb{F}_q^n$ such that $f_i(\mathbf{x},\mathbf{y})=0$, for all $i\in[m]$.

1: Compute the set $\{\alpha_j\odot f_i : \alpha_j$ comes from basis of $\overline{\mathrm{Sym}(V)}_{D-2}, i\in[m]\}$ and construct its Macaulay matrix $\mathbf{M}_D$ using the basis of D-form.
2: Compute the reduced row echelon form of the Macaulay matrix $\mathbf{M}_D$.
3: Check if the dimension of the kernel equals $\overline{\mathrm{Sym}(O)}_D$, if not, then fail.
4: Solve for a permanent minors vector in the kernel space under some linear constraints.
5: Using this vector, we will show it is easy to get vectors in O.

Let $\mathbf{o}_1,\ldots,\mathbf{o}_o\in\mathbb{F}_q^n$ be a basis of O such that the lower $o\times o$ block of the matrix $(\mathbf{o}_1,\ldots,\mathbf{o}_o)$ is the identity matrix, and let $v=n-o$. For any $\mathbf{o}_{i_1}\odot\cdots\odot\mathbf{o}_{i_d}\in\overline{\mathrm{Sym}(O)}_d$ and any multi-index $\mathbf{j}=\{\{j_1,\ldots,j_d\}\}$ with $v+1\leq j_k\leq n$, the permanent $\mathrm{Per}_{\mathbf{j}}(\mathbf{o}_{i_1}\odot\cdots\odot\mathbf{o}_{i_d})$ evaluates to a constant:

$$\mathrm{Per}_{\mathbf{j}}(\mathbf{o}_{i_1}\odot\cdots\odot\mathbf{o}_{i_d}) = \begin{cases}\prod_{k\in[n]} m_{\mathbf{j}}(k)! & \text{if } \mathbf{j}=\{\{i_1+v,\ldots,i_d+v\}\},\\ 0 & \text{otherwise.}\end{cases}$$

By constraining these constants within $\text{Ker}\mathbf{M}_d$, we obtain a vector consisting of all permanent minors of $(\mathbf{o}_{i_1}, \dots, \mathbf{o}_{i_d})$ in $\text{Ker}\mathbf{M}_d$. We can then compute the entries of $\mathbf{o}_{i_k}$ for each $k \in [d]$. Specifically, let $\mathbf{j}'$ be the multiset obtained by replacing the element $i_k + v$ in $\{\{i_1 + v, \dots, i_d + v\}\}$ with any $l \in [v]$. We have

$$\text{Per}_{\mathbf{j}'}(\mathbf{o}_{i_1} \odot \cdots \odot \mathbf{o}_{i_d}) = o_{i_k,l} \prod_{x \in [n]} m_{\mathbf{i}}(x)!$$

A toy example for solving $\mathbf{o}_i \in O$ using permanent minors. For $\mathbf{o}_1 = (a_1 a_2, 1, 0)$, $\mathbf{o}_2 = (b_1, b_2, 0, 1)$ is a basis of O and $(\mathbf{o}_1, \mathbf{o}_1, \mathbf{o}_2)$ is

$$\begin{pmatrix} a_1 & a_1 & b_1 \\ a_2 & a_2 & b_2 \\ 1 & 1 & 0 \\ 0 & 0 & 1 \end{pmatrix}$$

we have $\text{Per}_{\{\{1,3,4\}\}} = 2a_1$, $\text{Per}_{\{\{1,3,3\}\}} = 2b_1$, $\text{Per}_{\{\{2,3,4\}\}} = 2a_2$ and $\text{Per}_{\{\{2,3,3\}\}} = 2b_2$, then we can compute $\mathbf{o}_1$ and $\mathbf{o}_2$.

4.3 Complexity Analysis

In this subsection, we analyze the bit cost / complexity of our algorithm.

Parameter D. First we show how to choose a parameter D in XL algorithm on $\overline{\text{Sym}(V)}$ as

$$D := \min\left\{2 \le d \le o(p-1) : \dim \text{Ker}\mathbf{M}_d \le \dim \overline{\text{Sym}(O)}_d\right\}. \tag{1}$$

Recall that dimension of the d-space $\overline{\text{Sym}(O)}_d$ is easy to obtain by the *dimension formula* stated in Proposition 13.

In the following, we estimate $\dim \text{Ker}\mathbf{M}_d$. By definition of Macaulay matrix $\mathbf{M}_d$ of degree d, for $d \ge 0$, we have

$$\begin{aligned} \dim \text{Ker}\mathbf{M}_d &= \dim_{\mathbb{F}_q} \overline{\text{Sym}(\mathbb{F}_q^n)}_d - \dim_{\mathbb{F}_q}(f_1, \dots, f_m)_d \\ &= \dim_{\mathbb{F}_q} \left(\overline{\text{Sym}(\mathbb{F}_q^n)}/(f_1, \dots, f_m)\right)_d \\ &= \dim_{\mathbb{F}_q} \left(\mathbb{F}_q[x_1, \dots, x_n]/(x_1^p, \dots, x_n^p, f_1, \dots, f_m)\right)_d \end{aligned}$$

To compute the dimension of the quotient algebra at an arbitrary degree d, we consider both the semi-regularity conjecture and the Hilbert series of semi-regular sequences in the p-reduced algebra. The definition of semi-regular sequences and the proof of their Hilbert series properties in the p-reduced symmetric algebra naturally generalize those for Boolean algebras.

Theorem 15 ([2]). *The quadratic forms sequence $(f_1, \dots, f_m)$ is D-semi-regular in*

$$\mathbb{F}_q[x_1, \dots, x_n]/(x_1^p, \dots, x_n^p)$$

if and only if the Hilbert series of $\mathbb{F}_q[x_1, \ldots, x_n]/(x_1^p, \ldots, x_n^p, f_1, \ldots, f_m)$ *is given by:*

$$\left[\frac{(1+t+t^2+\cdots+t^{p-1})^n}{(1+t^2+\cdots+t^{2(p-1)})^m}\right]_D. \tag{2}$$

Conjecture 16. The public key $(p_1, \ldots, p_m)$ of UOV instance $(n, o, m, q = p^e)$ is a D-semi-regular sequence on p-reduced symmetric algebra $\mathbb{F}_q[x_1, \ldots, x_n]/(x_1^p, \ldots, x_n^p)$ with very high probability, where D to be the first d for which

$$\dim_{\mathbb{F}_q}\left(\mathbb{F}_q[x_1, \ldots, x_n]/(x_1^p, \ldots, x_n^p, p_1, \ldots, p_m)\right)_d \leq \dim_{\mathbb{F}_q}\left(\mathbb{F}_q[x_1, \ldots, x_o]/(x_1^p, \ldots, x_o^p)\right)_d.$$

The conjecture is a heuristic assumption, we don't have a theoretical proof. We test it for some UOV parameters. The actual $\dim \mathrm{Ker}\mathbf{M}_d$ is equal to the coefficient of t^d of the truncated Hilbert series (2) when $d < D$ and the actual $\dim \mathrm{Ker}\mathbf{M}_D$ is equal to $\dim \overline{\mathrm{Sym}(O)}_D$ (Table 1).

Table 1. Experimental results and our prediction of the dimension of $\mathrm{Ker}(\mathbf{M}_d)$ in various cases. The values of d shown in boldface indicate when it reaches our target D as defined in Formula (1).

$d < p = 7$.

(n, o, m, q, p)	d	actual $\dim(\ker \mathbf{M}_d)$	predicted $\dim(\ker \mathbf{M}_d)$	$\dim\left(\overline{\mathrm{Sym}(O)}_d\right)$
(6, 3, 6, 7, 7)	3	20	20	10
	4	15	15	15
(6, 3, 7, 7, 7)	3	14	14	10
	4	15	0	15
(8, 4, 8, 7, 7)	4	70	70	35
	5	56	56	56
(8, 4, 9, 7, 7)	4	42	42	35
	5	56	0	56
(8, 4, 10, 7, 7)	3	40	40	20
	4	35	15	35
(10, 5, 10, 7, 7)	5	252	252	126
	6	210	210	210
(10, 5, 11, 7, 7)	5	132	132	126
	6	210	0	210
(10, 5, 12, 7, 7)	4	121	121	70
	5	126	22	126

$d \geq p = 3$.

(n, o, m, q, p)	d	actual $\dim(\ker \mathbf{M}_d)$	predicted $\dim(\ker \mathbf{M}_d)$	$\dim\left(\overline{\mathrm{Sym}(O)}_d\right)$
(6, 3, 6, 9, 3)	3	14	14	7
	4	6	-21	6
(6, 3, 7, 9, 3)	3	8	8	7
	4	6	-36	6
(8, 4, 6, 9, 3)	4	65	65	19
	5	16	-48	16
(8, 4, 7, 9, 3)	4	35	35	19
	5	16	-112	16
(8, 4, 8, 9, 3)	3	48	48	16
	4	19	6	19
(10, 5, 7, 9, 3)	5	192	192	51
	6	45	-335	45
(10, 5, 8, 9, 3)	5	52	52	51
	6	45	-586	45
(10, 5, 9, 9, 3)	4	156	156	45
	5	51	-78	51

Cost Estimate. By applying XL algorithm with Wiedemann algorithm [16], the cost of our attack is

$$\min_{1 \leq o' \leq o} \mathrm{cost}_{o',D} = \min_{1 \leq o' \leq o} 3(2r^2 + r)\binom{n'+1}{2}\left(\dim \overline{\mathrm{Sym}(\mathbb{F}_q^{n'})}_D - \dim \overline{\mathrm{Sym}(O')}_D + 1\right)^2$$

where $n' = v + o'$ and $r = \log_2 q$. Notice that, in order to achieve a speed-up, during the cost estimation, we project a UOV instance (n, o, m, q) down to (n', o', m, q) with $o' < o$, and let O' denote the corresponding o'-dimensional totally isotropic space. In particular, by applying the dimension formula, we obtain an explicit expression for the cost as:

$$\min_{1\le o'\le o} 3(2r^2+r)\binom{n'+1}{2}\Big(\sum_{j=0}^{\min\left(n',\left\lfloor \frac{D}{p}\right\rfloor\right)} (-1)^j\binom{n'}{j}\binom{D-jp+n'-1}{n'-1} - \sum_{j=0}^{\min\left(o',\left\lfloor \frac{D}{p}\right\rfloor\right)} (-1)^j\binom{o'}{j}\binom{D-jp+o'-1}{o'-1}+1\Big)^2. \quad (3)$$

If no D satisfies (1), then for all $2\le d\le o(p-1)$, we have $\overline{\mathrm{Sym}(O)}_d \subsetneq \mathrm{Ker}\mathbf{M}_d$. In this case, we must search within $\mathrm{Ker}\mathbf{M}_d$ for elements lying in $\overline{\mathrm{Sym}(O)}_d$. Then the cost becomes:

$$\min_{\substack{1\le o'\le o\\ 2\le D\le o'(p-1)}} \mathrm{cost}_{o',D}+q^{\dim \mathrm{Ker}\mathbf{M}_D-\dim \overline{\mathrm{Sym}(O')}_D}$$

4.4 From Duality View

Let $\mathcal{A}: V_1\to V_2$ be a linear map between finite-dimensional vector spaces, and let $\mathcal{A}^*: V_2^*\to V_1^*$ be its dual map. With respect to dual bases, the matrix of $\mathcal{A}^*$ is the transpose of the matrix of $\mathcal{A}$.

Consider the linear map

$$\left(\bigodot^{d-2}\mathbb{F}_q^n\right)^m \to \bigodot^{d}\mathbb{F}_q^n,$$
$$(\mu_1,\dots,\mu_m)\mapsto \sum_{i\in[m]}\mu_i\odot q_i.$$

It is straightforward to verify that, the Macaulay matrix $\mathbf{M}_d$ on the p-reduced symmetric algebra is the transpose of the representation matrix of this linear map in the standard bases. In Theorem 14, we show $\overline{\mathrm{Sym}(\mathbb{F}_q^n)}$ is a graded Frobenius algebra, then by Proposition 3, we have $\bigodot^{d}\mathbb{F}_q^n$ and $\bigodot^{u-d}\mathbb{F}_q^n$ are mutually dual spaces, where $u=n(p-1)$. Then we can view $\mathbf{M}_d$ as the matrix corresponding with linear map for $2\le d\le n(p-1)$:

$$\mathcal{M}_d: \bigodot^{n(p-1)-d}\mathbb{F}_q^n \to \left(\bigodot^{n(p-1)-(d-2)}\mathbb{F}_q^n\right)^m$$
$$\mu\mapsto(\mu\odot q_1,\dots,\mu\odot q_m)$$

Setting $d=o(p-1)$, let $V=\langle \mathbf{v}_1,\dots,\mathbf{v}_v\rangle$ be the vinegar space, and let

$$\mathcal{V}=\mathbf{v}_1^{p-1}\odot\cdots\odot\mathbf{v}_v^{p-1}\in\overline{\mathrm{Sym}(V)}$$

be its highest degree element. We have $\mathcal{V} \in \mathrm{Ker}\mathcal{M}_d$ because $q_i \in \mathbb{F}_q^n \odot V$, as shown in [24]. Following [24], we also require $v < 2m$ to prevent elements in the ideal $(\odot_{i\in[m]} q_i^{p-1})$ from appearing in the kernel of $\mathcal{M}_d$.

5 Performance

Recall that as a generalization of Ran's attack [24], our attack depicted in Algorithm 1 can handle not only UOV instances with characteristic $p = 2$, but also those UOV instances with *odd* characteristic. For instance, in Sect. 5.2 we shall use our new attack to analyze the hardness of 12 recommended QR-UOV instances presented in [14].

Nevertheless, our new attack means more than that. Previous works in MPKC show that for a UOV instance, the order q of its underlying field $\mathbb{k} = \mathbb{F}_q$ is firmly connected to its concrete hardness, and a larger order usually results in a more secure UOV instance, *provided other parameters remain unchanged*; however, the characteristic $p = \mathrm{char}(\mathbb{k})$ was usually not taken into the consideration of the concrete hardness analysis of UOV in the past. In Sect. 5.3 we show that our new attack runs faster when the characteristic p of the underlying field $\mathbb{k}$ of UOV gets smaller. Conversely, this implies that choosing a larger characteristic p may help increase the (concrete) hardness of UOV; for instance, a UOV instance with $\mathbb{k} = \mathbb{F}_{79}$ is, in general, more secure than a similar UOV instance with $\mathbb{k} = \mathbb{F}_{81}$.

5.1 Algebraic Analysis for the Speed-up

The main difference between the new attack and existing attacks against UOV (and its variants) lies in the ideal being studied. Existing attacks analyze the ideal:

$$(p_1, \ldots, p_m) \subseteq \mathbb{F}_q[x_1, \ldots, x_n]/(x_1^q - x_1, \ldots, x_n^q - x_n).$$

Conversely, our new attack studies the ideal:

$$(p_1, \ldots, p_m) \subseteq \mathbb{F}_q[x_1, \ldots, x_n]/(x_1^p, \ldots, x_n^p).$$

Roughly speaking, the new attacks operate within a quotient ring of a much smaller size. This reduction in the ring's size is what explains the significant speed-up compared to existing methods. In particular, the case $p = 2$ yields the most significant improvement. This difference in the underlying structure also explains why the efficiency of the new attack is p-sensitive–the speed advantage diminishes as the characteristic p increases.

Table 2. Bit-cost estimates of this new attack (New) against UOV. Here the parameter sets shown in boldface denotes the proposed parameter sets of UOV scheme [8]. We propose several new parameter sets for the UOV scheme and analyze their concrete hardness using Algorithm 1.

(n, o, m)	(p, e, q)	(D, o', n')	New
(112, 44, 44)	**(2, 8, 256)**	(18, 18, 86)	140
	(3, 5, 243)	(30, 15, 83)	195
	(5, 3, 125)	(52, 13, 81)	265
	(7, 2, 49)	(72, 12, 80)	311
(160, 64, 64)	**(2, 4, 16)**	(22, 22, 118)	175
	(3, 2, 9)	(38, 19, 115)	252
	(5, 1, 5)	(67, 17, 113)	349
(184, 72, 72)	**(2, 8, 256)**	(26, 26, 138)	206
	(3, 5, 243)	(46, 23, 135)	301
	(5, 3, 125)	(79, 20, 132)	411
	(7, 2, 49)	(111, 19, 131)	490
(244, 96, 96)	**(2, 8, 256)**	(32, 32, 180)	257
	(3, 5, 243)	(57, 29, 177)	379
	(5, 3, 125)	(99, 25, 173)	523
	(7, 2, 49)	(138, 23, 171)	622

†Bit-cost estimates from [24].

To empirically demonstrate the p-sensitivity of our attack, we present cost estimates for UOV instances listed in Table 2. For each parameter set (n, o, m), we vary the field characteristic p as well as the field size $q = p^e$. Our results clearly demonstrate that the bit-cost of this attack increases with p, even in cases where the field size q decreases relatively.[2]

5.2 Attack on QR-UOV

Recall that for those four UOV-like schemes that advanced to the Round 2 of NIST's PQC additional signature algorithm competition, only QR-UOV [14] recommends parameter sets with *odd* characteristics. In this subsection, we shall apply our key-recovery attack presented in Algorithm 1 to analyze the concrete hardness of 12 recommended instances of QR-UOV [14].

It is well-established that the reconciliation attack achieves optimal performance against UOV-like schemes when parameters satisfy $n - o \leq m$. Since all QR-UOV recommended parameters meet this condition, the reconciliation

[2] Furthermore, as predicted by the cost estimation Formula (3), the influence of the extension degree e is negligible. In particular, when (n, m, p) are fixed, increasing q via a larger e leads to only a marginal increase in overall cost.

attack represents the most efficient known approach for these schemes. Therefore, we benchmark our algorithm's effectiveness by comparing its computational cost against the reconciliation attack.

Table 3. Bit-cost estimates of our attack and reconciliation attack on corresponding UOV(n, o, m, q) instances against the proposed parameter sets in QR-UOV [14]. Here the parameter sets shown in boldface denotes the main proposed parameter sets. And the complexity of our attack and the reconciliation attack shown in boldface indicates the two complexity value collides..

S.L.	(n, o, m)	(p, e, q)	(D, o', n')	Our	Rec.
I	**(70, 18, 54)**	**(127, 3, 2048383)**	(28, 1, 53)	**164**	**164**
	(84, 10, 100)	(7, 10, 282475249)	(20, 4, 78)	159	148
	(75, 20, 60)	(31, 3, 29791)	(23, 1, 56)	**151**	**151**
	(67, 7, 70)	(31, 10, 819628286980801)	(21, 1, 61)	**152**	**152**
III	**(102, 26, 78)**	**(127, 3, 2048383)**	(40, 1, 77)	**231**	**231**
	(124, 14, 140)	(7, 10, 282475249)	(30, 5, 115)	230	219
	(111, 29, 87)	(31, 3, 29791)	(37, 2, 84)	229	221
	(99, 10, 100)	(31, 10, 819628286980801)	(32, 2, 91)	221	216
V	**(137, 35, 105)**	**(127, 3, 2048383)**	(49, 1, 103)	**291**	**291**
	(168, 19, 190)	(7, 10, 282475249)	(39, 7, 156)	299	277
	(146, 38, 114)	(31, 3, 29791)	(47, 2, 110)	291	283
	(124, 12, 120)	(31, 10, 819628286980801)	(45, 2, 114)	291	283

QR-UOV remains secure against our attack because its characteristic is sufficiently large to render our approach inefficient. We observe that our algorithm achieves the same computational complexity as the reconciliation attack when $o' = 1$ illustrated in the table above. This equivalence occurs because, when $o' = 1$, the Macaulay matrix $\mathbf{M}_d$ in our XL algorithm (operating in the p-reduced symmetric algebra) coincides with the Macaulay matrix used in the reconciliation attack for dimensions $d < p$.

As shown in Table 3, our attack does not outperform the reconciliation attack for standard QR-UOV parameters due to the large characteristic of QR-UOV. However, when we modify only the characteristic of QR-UOV's recommended parameters—setting it to 3 or 5—our attack demonstrates superior efficiency compared to the reconciliation attack, as illustrated in the table below (Table 4)

Table 4. Bit-cost estimates of our XL attack (Our) and reconciliation attack (Rec.) against QR-UOV [14]. Here, we choose several new parameter sets for the QR-UOV scheme and analyze their concrete hardness.

(n, o, m)	(p, e, q)	(D, o', n')	Our	Rec.
(70, 18, 54)	(3, 3, 27)	(16, 8, 60)	122	145
	(5, 3, 125)	(23, 6, 58)	150	153
(102, 26, 78)	(3, 3, 27)	(21, 11, 87)	163	201
	(5, 3, 125)	(30, 8, 84)	201	215
(137, 35, 105)	(3, 3, 27)	(26, 13, 115)	204	255
	(5, 3, 125)	(38, 10, 112)	257	274

5.3 Parameter Suggestions

In this subsection, we demonstrate the connection between the characteristic p and the concrete hardness of UOV instance with the MAYO scheme [7]. To be precise, we choose several parameter sets for MAYO, and analyze their concrete hardness using our key-recovery attack, as well as those attacks considered in [7] (*e.g.*, the direct attack, the Kipnis-Shamir attack, the reconciliation attack, the intersection attack and the collision attack).

Some remarks are in order. First, it can be seen from Table 5 that for certain MAYO instances (or more generally, for certain UOV instances), our key-recovery attack presented in Algorithm 1 outperforms all other key-recovery attacks under consideration, or even those forgery attacks; this demonstrates the strength of our new attack concretely. Moreover, our argument that a larger p usually results in a more secure instance can be confirmed in Table 5; for instance, the MAYO instance with $\mathbb{k} = \mathbb{F}_{79}$ turns out to be more secure than the MAYO instance with $\mathbb{k} = \mathbb{F}_{81}$, provided that the other parameters remain the same.

Notice that our XL attack's performance depends heavily on the field characteristic p. This implies that when our key-recovery attack dominates the concrete hardness result, the simplest way for achieving security upgrade is to increase p while keeping all other parameters unchanged. For example, switching MAYO_2 [7] from $\mathbb{F}_{16}$ to $\mathbb{F}_{17}$ (or from $\mathbb{F}_{81}$ to $\mathbb{F}_{79}$) would boost the concrete hardness for obvious reasons.

Table 5. Bit-cost estimates of attacks including our new attack (New), direct attack (Direct), Kipnis-Shamir attack (KS), reconciliation attack (Rec.), intersection attack (Int.) as well as collision attack (Col.) against several MAYO instances. It should be noted those instances are not the recommended instances proposed in the MAYO submission [7].

(n, o, m)	(p, e, q)	(D, o', n')	New	Direct	KS	Rec.	Int.	Col.
(81, 64, 17)	(2, 4, 16)	(13, 13, 77)	**112**	155	211	167	228	141
	(17, 1, 17)	(46, 3, 67)	230	155	216	169	231	**145**
	(3, 4, 81)	(19, 10, 74)	**147**	177	323	190	302	217
	(79, 1, 79)	(110, 2, 66)	345	**176**	321	190	301	216
	(5, 4, 625)	(28, 7, 71)	**183**	192	462	205	394	312
	(7, 4, 2401)	(33, 6, 70)	199	**198**	554	211	455	374
	(31, 4, 923521)	(59, 2, 66)	263	**217**	959	232	723	649

†Bit-cost estimates from [24]
‡In these columns, we use the cryptographic estimator introduced in [13] when $p \neq 2$.

6 Conclusion

In summary, this work presents a novel cryptanalytic approach against UOV-based multivariate cryptographic schemes using polar forms and p-reduced symmetric algebras. We develop a generalized framework that extends beyond the characteristic 2 case studied by Ran, enabling attacks on odd characteristic scenarios through p-reduced algebraic structures. Our symmetric method leverages the symmetric properties of polar forms to construct an algebra isomorphic to symmetric algebras in characteristic 0 and to exterior algebras in characteristic 2. We propose an enhanced XL algorithm operating over p-reduced symmetric algebras that efficiently computes permanent minors of oil variable matrices, leading to oil space recovery.

Furthermore, we establish that our XL-based approach constitutes a reconciliation attack under certain conditions. When applied to QR-UOV parameters, we show that the attack scenario falls within the reconciliation framework, thereby confirming the security of QR-UOV against polar form attacks. Our results provide new insights into the algebraic structure of multivariate schemes and contribute to the security analysis of NIST PQC candidates.

Our work not only advances the theoretical understanding of multivariate cryptography but also delivers concrete tools for evaluating and improving the security of post-quantum signature schemes. Future research directions include extending this framework to other multivariate schemes, optimizing the proposed algorithms, and exploring further applications of symmetric algebra in cryptography.

Acknowledgments. The authors would like to thank Lars Ran for his valuable insights and helpful comments in writing this paper. Jintai Ding would like to thank the support of grant KJL2025101. Jintai Ding would like to thank the support of the Suzhou City Top Talent program and the Jiangsu Provincial Top Talent Program A.

References

1. Bardet, M., Bros, M., Cabarcas, D., Gaborit, P., Perlner, R., Smith-Tone, D., Tillich, J.-P., Verbel, J.: Improvements of Algebraic Attacks for Solving the Rank Decoding and MinRank Problems. In: Moriai, S., Wang, H. (eds.) ASIACRYPT 2020. LNCS, vol. 12491, pp. 507–536. Springer, Cham (2020). https://doi.org/10.1007/978-3-030-64837-4_17
2. Bellini, E., Makarim, R.H., Sanna, C., Verbel, J.: An Estimator for the Hardness of the MQ Problem. In: Batina, L., Daemen, J. (eds.) Progress in Cryptology - AFRICACRYPT 2022, pp. 323–347. Springer Nature Switzerland, Cham (2022)
3. Bettale, L., Faugere, J.C., Perret, L.: Hybrid Approach for Solving Multivariate Systems over Finite Fields. Journal of Mathematical Cryptology **3**(3), 177–197 (2009)
4. Beullens, W.: Improved Cryptanalysis of UOV and Rainbow. In: Canteaut, A., Standaert, F.-X. (eds.) EUROCRYPT 2021. LNCS, vol. 12696, pp. 348–373. Springer, Cham (2021). https://doi.org/10.1007/978-3-030-77870-5_13
5. Beullens, W.: Breaking rainbow takes a weekend on a laptop. In: Dodis, Y., Shrimpton, T. (eds.) Advances in Cryptology - CRYPTO 2022 - 42nd Annual International Cryptology Conference, CRYPTO 2022, Santa Barbara, CA, USA, August 15-18, 2022, Proceedings, Part II. Lecture Notes in Computer Science, vol. 13508, pp. 464–479. Springer (2022)
6. Beullens, W.: Improved Cryptanalysis of SNOVA. In: Annual International Conference on the Theory and Applications of Cryptographic Techniques. pp. 277–293. Springer (2025)
7. Beullens, W., Campos, F., Celi, S., Hess, B., Kannwischer, M.J.: MAYO. Round 2 Additional Signatures, Post-Quantum Cryptography: Digital Signature Schemes (2025), https://csrc.nist.gov/csrc/media/Projects/pqc-dig-sig/documents/round-2/spec-files/mayo-spec-round2-web.pdf
8. Beullens, W., Chen, M.S., Ding, J., Gong, B., Kannwischer, M.J., Patarin, J., Peng, B.Y., Schmidt, D., Shih, C.J., Tao, C., Yang, B.Y.: UOV: Unbalanced Oil and Vinegar - Algorithm Specifications and Supporting Documentation Version 2.0. Round 2 Additional Signatures, Post-Quantum Cryptography: Digital Signature Schemes (2025), https://csrc.nist.gov/csrc/media/Projects/pqc-dig-sig/documents/round-2/spec-files/uov-spec-round2-web.pdf
9. Bhatia, R.: Matrix Analysis. Springer, New York, NY (1997)
10. Courtois, N., Klimov, A., Patarin, J., Shamir, A.: Efficient Algorithms for Solving Overdefined Systems of Multivariate Polynomial Equations. In: Preneel, B. (ed.) EUROCRYPT 2000. LNCS, vol. 1807, pp. 392–407. Springer, Heidelberg (2000). https://doi.org/10.1007/3-540-45539-6_27
11. Ding, J., Gower, J.E., Schmidt, D.S.: Multivariate public key cryptosystems, vol. 25. Springer Science & Business Media (2006)
12. Ding, J., Yang, B.-Y., Chen, C.-H.O., Chen, M.-S., Cheng, C.-M.: New Differential-Algebraic Attacks and Reparametrization of Rainbow. In: Bellovin, S.M., Gennaro, R., Keromytis, A., Yung, M. (eds.) ACNS 2008. LNCS, vol. 5037, pp. 242–257. Springer, Heidelberg (2008). https://doi.org/10.1007/978-3-540-68914-0_15
13. Esser, A., Verbel, J.A., Zweydinger, F., Bellini, E.: SoK: CryptographicEstimators - a Software Library for Cryptographic Hardness Estimation. In: AsiaCCS. ACM (2024)

14. Furue, H., Ikematsu, Y., Hoshino, F., Takagi, T., Kosuge, H., Yamakoshi, K., Akiyama, R., Nakamura, S., Orihara, S., Kinjo, K.: QR-UOV. Round 2 Additional Signatures, Post-Quantum Cryptography: Digital Signature Schemes (2025), https://csrc.nist.gov/csrc/media/Projects/pqc-dig-sig/documents/qruov-spec-round2-web.pdf
15. Guo, H., Jin, Y., Pan, Y., He, X., Gong, B., Ding, J.: Practical and theoretical cryptanalysis of VOX. In: Saarinen, M.O., Smith-Tone, D. (eds.) Post-Quantum Cryptography - 15th International Workshop, PQCrypto 2024, Oxford, UK, June 12-14, 2024, Proceedings, Part II. Lecture Notes in Computer Science, vol. 14772, pp. 186–208. Springer (2024)
16. Kaltofen, E.: Analysis of Coppersmith's Block Wiedemann Algorithm for the Parallel Solution of Sparse Linear Systems. In: Cohen, G., Mora, T., Moreno, O. (eds.) Applied Algebra, Algebraic Algorithms and Error-Correcting Codes, pp. 195–212. Springer, Berlin Heidelberg, Berlin, Heidelberg (1993)
17. Kipnis, A., Shamir, A.: Cryptanalysis of the Oil and Vinegar Signature Scheme. In: Krawczyk, H. (ed.) Advances in Cryptology – CRYPTO '98, pp. 257–266. Springer, Berlin Heidelberg, Berlin, Heidelberg (1998)
18. Le, H., Bros, M., Lichtinger, J., Smith-Tone, D., Minaud, B., Perlner, R., Valenzuela, C.: Exploiting SNOVA's Structure in the Wedge Product Attack. Sixth PQC Standardization Conference (2025)
19. Matsumoto, T., Imai, H.: Public Quadratic Polynomial-Tuples for Efficient Signature-Verification and Message-Encryption. In: Barstow, D., Brauer, W., Brinch Hansen, P., Gries, D., Luckham, D., Moler, C., Pnueli, A., Seegmüller, G., Stoer, J., Wirth, N., Günther, C.G. (eds.) EUROCRYPT 1988. LNCS, vol. 330, pp. 419–453. Springer, Heidelberg (1988). https://doi.org/10.1007/3-540-45961-8_39
20. Call for Additional Digital Signature Schemes for the Post-Quantum Cryptography Standardization Process (September 2022), available at https://csrc.nist.gov/csrc/media/Projects/pqc-dig-sig/documents/call-for-proposals-dig-sig-sept-2022.pdf
21. Patarin, J.: Cryptanalysis of the Matsumoto and Imai Public Key Scheme of Eurocrypt'88. In: Coppersmith, D. (ed.) Advances in Cryptology – CRYPTO '95, pp. 248–261. Springer, Berlin Heidelberg, Berlin, Heidelberg (1995)
22. Patarin, J.: The Oil and Vinegar Signature Scheme. In: Dagstuhl Workshop on Cryptography (September 1997)
23. Pébereau, P.: Singular Points of UOV and VOX. In: Annual International Conference on the Theory and Applications of Cryptographic Techniques. pp. 294–323. Springer (2025)
24. Ran, L.: Wedges, Oil, and Vinegar – An analysis of UOV in Characteristic 2. Cryptology ePrint Archive, Paper 2025/1143 (2025), https://eprint.iacr.org/2025/1143
25. Scharlau, W.: Quadratic and hermitian forms. Springer-Verlag (1985)
26. Shor, P.W.: Polynomial-Time Algorithms for Prime Factorization and Discrete Logarithms on a Quantum Computer. SIAM J. Comput. **26**(5), 1484–1509 (1997)
27. Team, T.R.: Modified Parameters of Rainbow in Response to a Refined Analysis of the Rainbow Band Separation attack by the NIST Team and the Recent New Min-Rank Attacks (2020), http://precision.moscito.org/by-publ/recent/rainbow-pars.pdf
28. Wang, L.C., Chou, C.Y., Ding, J., Kuan, Y.L., Leegwater, J.A., Li, M.S., Tseng, B.S., Tseng, P.E., Wang, C.C.: SNOVA - Proposal for NISTPQC: Digital Signature Schemes Project. Round 2 Additional Signatures, Post-Quantum Cryptography: Digital Signature Schemes (2025), https://csrc.nist.gov/csrc/media/Projects/pqc-dig-sig/documents/round-2/spec-files/snova-spec-round2-web.pdf

29. Wang, L.C., Chou, C.Y., Ding, J., Kuan, Y.L., Li, M.S., Tseng, B.S., Tseng, P.E., Wang, C.C.: SNOVA - Proposal for NISTPQC: Digital Signature Schemes Project. Round 1 Additional Signatures, Post-Quantum Cryptography: Digital Signature Schemes (2023), https://csrc.nist.gov/csrc/media/Projects/pqc-dig-sig/documents/round-1/spec-files/SNOVA-spec-web.pdf
30. Yang, B.-Y., Chen, J.-M., Courtois, N.T.: On Asymptotic Security Estimates in XL and Gröbner Bases-Related Algebraic Cryptanalysis. In: Lopez, J., Qing, S., Okamoto, E. (eds.) ICICS 2004. LNCS, vol. 3269, pp. 401–413. Springer, Heidelberg (2004). https://doi.org/10.1007/978-3-540-30191-2_31
31. Yang, B.Y., Chen, O.C.H., Bernstein, D.J., Chen, J.M.: Analysis of QUAD. In: International Workshop on Fast Software Encryption. pp. 290–308. Springer (2007)

On the Dangers of RSA Exponent Transforms

Eugene Lau, Laura Shea(✉), and Nadia Heninger

Department of Computer Science and Engineering, University of California San Diego, San Diego, USA
{eylau,lmshea}@ucsd.edu, nadiah@cs.ucsd.edu

Abstract. We analyze the security of RSA keys where the public exponent e is larger than $\varphi(N)$. While nearly all real-world applications of RSA use a small set of pre-determined constant values for e, the literature contains a number of constructions involving large special-form exponents. Examples include proposed countermeasures against Wiener's attack on small RSA private exponents, exponent masking against side channels, a 2018 proposal by Joye and Michalevsky to extend the usefulness of hardware security modules, and a 2023 RSA blind signature construction by Amjad, Yeo, and Yung.

We give an efficient algorithm to factor an RSA modulus N given an integer a that is "close" to a multiple of $\varphi(N)$. That is, we can factor N in polynomial time given $\varphi(N) < a \leq N^{3/2}$ if there is an integer y with $|y| \leq aN^{-3/4}$ such that $a - y \equiv 0 \bmod \varphi(N)$. Our attack is a special case of Blömer and May's 2004 algorithm using Coppersmith's method that enables us to give stronger bounds for our application range of interest. We instantiate our attack against several constructions and exhibit families of weak public exponents that do not appear to have been analyzed in the literature. In particular, the Joye and Michalevsky exponent transform permits full key recovery if used for small public exponents. While it is well known that RSA is vulnerable for small private exponent d, our work suggests that care must also be taken when generating large public exponents, or when publishing transformed exponents.

1 Introduction

RSA is the most widely used digital signature scheme in practice for many use cases. While NIST has recently announced plans to deprecate RSA along with other quantum-vulnerable public-key cryptographic algorithms by 2035 [26], it is expected that many deployments will continue to use hybrid classical/post-quantum constructions for many years in the future.

RSA has been subjected to decades of cryptanalysis, and RSA public keys are typically generated following some common conventions. In practice, implementations almost always use small constant values for the public exponent e; $e = 65537$ is overwhelmingly the most popular choice in practice. In fact, the US federal government's FIPS 186-5 digital signature guidelines [14] require that

S. Bai and E. Persichetti (Eds.): PKC 2026, LNCS 16551, pp. 455–479, 2026.
https://doi.org/10.1007/978-3-032-26731-3_15

$2^{16} < e < 2^{256}$. Small values of e allow for more efficient signature verification, but implementers are nervous about *very* small RSA public exponents such as $e = 3$ because of Coppersmith's attacks against small RSA public exponents with fixed-pattern encryption padding [11]; $e = 65537$ seems to strike a balance somewhere in the middle of these concerns.

For the private exponent d, a classic 1989 attack due to Wiener [35] shows how to factor an RSA modulus N using continued fractions given a public exponent e whose corresponding private exponent $d < N^{1/4}$. Boneh and Durfee improved this attack in 1999 [6] to $d < N^{0.292}$ by applying a bivariate version of Coppersmith's method for finding small roots of polynomials modulo integers using lattice basis reduction. Requiring implementations to use a small public exponent e prevents the use of such small exponents d.

In this paper, we highlight a family of weak choices for the *public exponent* e when e is large. While not common in practice, there are a number of proposals in the academic literature that use customized or special-form values of e for special applications, including cases where $e > \varphi(N)$ or $e > N$.

We give a few examples:

- Wiener [35] suggests as a countermeasure to his small d attack to generate $e > N^{3/2}$ by adding multiples of $\varphi(N)$.
- Joye and Michalevsky [18] give an RSA exponent transform that allows users to convert RSA signatures generated using one exponent to a different exponent. The motivating application is to use a Hardware Security Module (HSM) that restricts the allowed class of public exponents to sign with an arbitrary choice of public exponent. Their construction maintains a secret HSM-only signature verification exponent e_s, and publishes the arbitrary public exponent e_p and a randomly chosen multiplier t that are related via $e_p t \equiv e_s \bmod \varphi(N)$. Here, $e_p t > \varphi(N)$.
- Amjad, Yeo, and Yung give several constructions for RSA blind signature schemes, some of which have motivated a recent IRTF draft [2]. One of their constructions [1, Appendix C] has potential exponent values of $\varphi(N) < e < N^{3/2}$.
- Lysanskaya, Micali, Reyzin, and Shacham [21, Section 5] give a construction for sequential aggregate RSA signatures that uses $e > N$.
- Kocher [19] suggests masking exponents by adding a multiple of $\varphi(N)$ as a potential countermeasure against modular exponentiation-based side-channel attacks. This applies to the private exponent d but our work highlights that it *must only* apply to the private exponent.

1.1 Contributions

In this paper, we show that several of the above constructions may allow efficient private key recovery for a range of parameters. Our attack is independent of the size of d. In particular, we give the following (simplified) theorem.

Theorem 1 (Simplified). *Let $N = pq$ where p,q are primes of the same size. Given an integer a such that $\varphi(N) < a \leq N^{3/2}$ and $a - y \equiv 0 \bmod \varphi(N)$ for secret $|y| \leq aN^{-3/4}$, then N can be factored in polynomial time.*

Our theorem is a specialization and strengthening of a 2004 theorem of Blömer and May [5], and uses Coppersmith's method for factoring from partial information via lattice basis reduction [11]. Interestingly, despite the numerous variants of Coppersmith-type theorems analyzing RSA constructions, parameter families, and partial key recovery problems [3,4,7,9–11,13,15,20,24,32,36], we have not seen this particular version articulated as such.

In Sect. 7 we experimentally validate the range of a and y for which the above theorem holds. The experiments match, and slightly outperform, our proven theoretical results. The above simplified theorem is more explicitly stated as Theorem 5 of Sect. 3.

As a corollary to the above theorem, we obtain the following impacts on some of the above schemes:

- The Joye and Michalevsky RSA exponent transform scheme reveals the private key if $e_p \leq N^{1/2}$ and $e_s < e_p N^{1/4}$—that is, it is insecure precisely for the case of the small RSA exponent sizes allowed by HSMs that motivate their construction.
- An RSA user who generates a public exponent $e = e' + t\varphi(N)$ for $e' < N^{3/4}$ and $t \leq N^{1/2}$ reveals the factors of N, *even when d is large* and e' is unknown to the attacker. Implementations that attempt to apply exponent masking to RSA public exponents out of an abundance of caution to protect against Wiener's attack or side-channel attacks may inadvertently reveal their private key if applied to the conventional practical construction of small public exponents.
- For the large, randomly generated public exponents as in [21, Section 5] and [1], our attacks give a previously undiscussed family of weak keys. These weak exponents are unlikely to arise for randomly generated instances, but a key generation algorithm may wish to verify that a particular key is not weak before publishing the public key.

We discuss these applications in detail in Sects. 5 and 6.

Our results suggest that designers of alternative RSA constructions with large public exponents should apply these security analyses to avoid insecure parameters and exponent choices. None of the constructions we mention above contains an analysis of weak choices for their published public exponents.

2 Preliminaries

Notation and Syntax. For an integer $z \in \mathbb{Z}$ we let $\lceil \log_2(z) \rceil$ be the number of bits in its representation as a binary string. For a set $\mathcal{X}$ we denote selection of a uniformly random element by $x \leftarrow_{\$} \mathcal{X}$. To denote a range of integers we write

$[a, b]$ to mean the set of integers between a and b, inclusive, or (a, b) to mean exclusive. We use $\perp$ to denote a special failure symbol.

For a modulus $M \in \mathbb{N}$ we let $\mathbb{Z}_M$ be the group consisting of $\{0, 1, \ldots, (M-1)\}$ under addition modulo M. We let $\mathbb{Z}_M^*$ denote the group consisting of $\{z \in \mathbb{Z}_M \mid \gcd(z, M) = 1\}$ under multiplication modulo M.

The prime-counting function $\pi : \mathbb{N} \rightarrow \mathbb{N}$ returns the number of primes up to a given bound. On input $x \in \mathbb{N}$, $\pi(x)$ is the number of prime integers less than or equal to x. Our algorithm will not run the function π, and we use it only to bound probabilities.

RSA. For primes p, q and $N = pq$ recall that $\varphi(N) = (p-1)(q-1)$ and this is the order of the group $\mathbb{Z}_N^*$. In classic RSA [29], the public key includes the modulus N and an exponent $e \in \mathbb{Z}_{\varphi(N)}^*$ while the secret key includes an exponent $d \in \mathbb{Z}_{\varphi(N)}^*$ such that $ed = 1 \bmod \varphi(N)$. We will define all variables as needed but may informally refer to an RSA scheme's "public e" or "secret d."

2.1 Related Work on RSA Cryptanalysis

RSA and related assumptions have undergone extensive cryptanalysis since its invention in [29]. A number of attacks use Coppersmith's method for finding small roots of polynomials modulo integers via lattice reduction [10,11].

Factoring with High Bits Known. Coppersmith gave an algorithm to factor an RSA modulus N when the most significant half of bits of one factor p are known [10]. In particular, we can phrase this as factoring when an approximaton to p is known, with additive error at most $N^{1/4}$. Coppersmith's original algorithm used lattice basis reduction to find small solutions to bivariate polynomials over the integers; Howgrave-Graham gave a reformulated algorithm as finding approximate integer common divisors [16]. We use this algorithm as a subroutine in our algorithm.

Theorem 2 (Bivariate Coppersmith). *Let $p(x, y) = \sum_{i,j} p_{ij} x^i y^j$ be a polynomial of degree at most δ in each separate variable x and y. Let X and Y be upper bounds on x and y respectively. Let $D = \max_{i,j}\{|p_{ij}| X^i Y^j\}$. If*

$$(XY)^{3\delta/2} < D$$

then there exists a polynomial time algorithm to find (x_0, y_0) such that $p(x_0, y_0) = 0$, $x_0, y_0 \in \mathbb{Z}$, $x_0 < X$, $y_0 < Y$.

To find a small root modulo p, we will use May's formulation [23] of the above Coppersmith and Howgrave-Graham results.

Theorem 3 (Coppersmith/Howgrave-Graham/May). *Let N be an integer of unknown factorization, which has a divisor $b \geq N^{\beta}, 0 < \beta \leq 1$. Let $0 < \varepsilon \leq (1/7)\beta$. Furthermore, let $f(x)$ be a univariate monic polynomial of* *degree δ with at least one root modulo b, i.e. there exists at least one value of x_0 such that*

$$f(x_0) = 0 \bmod b \text{ with } |x_0| \leq \frac{1}{2}N^{\beta^2/\delta - \varepsilon} .$$

Then, we can find all solutions for x_0 in polynomial time.

Attacks on Small Private Exponent d. In 1990 Wiener [34] proposed an attack on the RSA cryptosystem for small d. He used continued fractions to give an algorithm to factor the RSA modulus N given an RSA public key (N,e) with corresponding secret exponent $d < N^{1/4}$. Boneh and Durfee [6] improved this bound to $d < N^{0.292}$ in 1999 using an algorithm based on Coppersmith's method. Both methods consider the RSA equation $ed = 1 + k(N - (p+q) + 1)$ where d, k, and $p+q$ are unknown but bounded.

Attacks on Partially Known Private Exponent, with Exponent Masking. Some RSA-based schemes use a countermeasure known as exponent blinding or exponent masking, in which random multiples of $\varphi(N)$ are added to the private exponent d, typically to mitigate side channel attacks. Kocher [19] mentions this countermeasure in his work introducing timing attacks. In 2015, Cimato, Mella and Susella gave an algorithm in [9] to factor an RSA modulus N in this exponent masking setting, given partial information about an exponent-masked private exponent $d^* = d + j\varphi(N)$. They improved upon 2012 algorithms described by Joye and Lepoint [17], which had covered the general case of a private exponent $d > \varphi(N)$. In 2022, Zhou, van de Pol, Yu, and Standaert [36] gave an algorithm targeting key recovery in this setting for masked private RSA-CRT coefficients. We consider the somewhat unusual question of what happens if an implementation masks a *public* exponent in Sect. 6.

Extensions of Wiener's Attack. In 2004 Blömer and May [5] gave a generalization of Wiener's attack on short exponents d. For completeness, we give their full theorem.

Theorem 4 (Blomer-May). *Let $N \in \mathbb{N}$ be a product of two uniformly random primes p, q with $\lceil \log_2(p) \rceil = \lceil \log_2(q) \rceil$. Then with high probability N can be factored in polynomial time given N and an $e \in \mathbb{Z}^*_{\varphi(N)}$ satisfying*

$$ex + y = 0 \bmod \varphi(N)$$

for some unknown $x, y \in \mathbb{Z}$ when x, y satisfy

$$0 < x \leq \frac{1}{3}N^{1/4} \tag{1}$$

$$y \leq cex \cdot N^{-3/4} \tag{2}$$

where the probability is over the primes p and q, and c is a constant.

Wiener's attack is a special case of this attack where $y = -1$. This N attack proceeds in three steps: first, they use continued fractions to recover the value of x, and then they use x to recover an approximation to p, and finally apply Coppersmith's method to factor N given this partial information on p.

This is the most similar prior work to our attack; we observe that for our desired applications x is known, and thus we can obtain stronger bounds on y by re-analyzing their algorithm. We provide a detailed comparison in Sect. 4.

Further works have provided more exotic generalizations to even more special forms of e. In 2008 Nitaj [28] proposed another generalization of Wiener's 2004 attack where the public key satisfies $ex - (p-u)(q-v)y = 1$ where $1 \leq y < x < 2^{-1/4}N^{1/4}, |u| < N^{1/4}, v = \lceil -qu/(p-u) \rfloor$, and$(p-u)(q-v)$ is 10^{50}-smooth.

Deterministic Equivalence between Factoring and RSA Private Key Recovery. Coppersmith's method has also been used by May [22] to give a deterministic polynomial-time algorithm to factor N given both public and private exponents (e, d).

3 Factoring N from $\varphi(N)$ with Noise

In our setting, the attacker learns an integer $a = y + k\varphi(N)$ where y and k are relatively small unknown integers. As usual, $\varphi(N)$ and the prime factors of N are also unknown. From the integer a (which can be seen as $\varphi(N)$ with noise) and the public modulus N, our attacker wishes to factor N. In the following, we assume that N is an RSA modulus with balanced primes, that is, that $N = pq$ with $\lceil \log_2(p) \rceil = \lceil \log_2(q) \rceil$.

Notice that if more information than (a, N) is available to the attacker, then factoring may become easy:

- If the attacker learns $\varphi(N)$, they can write $p + q = \varphi(N) - N - 1$, learn $(p-q)^2 = (p+q)^2 - 4N$, and then solve for a factor p.
- If the attacker learns an exact multiple $a = k\varphi(N)$, they can solve for $k = \lceil a/N \rceil$, and then factor N as above.
- If the attacker learns both both a and y such that $a = y + k\varphi(N)$, they can apply the above to $a - y$.

The above cases have long been noted [25]. This section concerns the case where the multiplier k and the noise y are unknown to the attacker, resisting the trivial attacks above. The following theorem shows how to factor N given $a = y + k\varphi(N)$ where both k and y are unknown but small.

Theorem 5. *Let $N \in \mathbb{N}$ be a product of two uniformly random primes p, q with $\lceil \log_2(p) \rceil = \lceil \log_2(q) \rceil$. Then with high probability N can be factored in polynomial time given N and an $a \in \mathbb{Z}$ satisfying*

$$a \equiv y \bmod \varphi(N)$$

for some unknown $y \in \mathbb{Z}$ *when* a, y *satisfy*

$$\varphi(N) \leq a \leq N^{3/2} \tag{3}$$

$$y < a \cdot N^{-3/4} \tag{4}$$

where the probability is over the primes p *and* q.

The algorithm follows the second half of Blömer and May's algorithm [5], but since our setting and bounds are different, we re-analyze some steps. We prove Theorem 5 in the following sequence of lemmas, aligned with the steps of the algorithm. The proof concludes with Lemma 12.

Step 0: Take as input integers N and a. The algorithm begins by taking in the public information. Let $p > q$ be the larger factor of N. Lemma 6 below is a useful fact for the balanced-prime setting.

Lemma 6. *When* $\lceil \log_2(p) \rceil = \lceil \log_2(q) \rceil$, $(3/2)\sqrt{N} \leq p + q \leq 3\sqrt{N}$.

Proof. In the balanced prime case, $p < 2q$ and $q \leq \sqrt{N} \leq p$. Therefore $\sqrt{N} \leq p \leq 2q \leq 2\sqrt{N}$ and $(1/2)\sqrt{N} \leq p/2 \leq q \leq \sqrt{N}$. Therefore $p + q \geq \sqrt{N} + (1/2)\sqrt{N} = (3/2)\sqrt{N}$ and $p + q \leq 2\sqrt{N} + \sqrt{N} = 3\sqrt{N}$.

Step 1: Learn k. Let k be the integer multiplier such that $a = y + k\varphi(N)$. Approximate k as $\lfloor a/N \rfloor$. We show (in Lemma 7) that k is at most an additive error of 6 from this approximation, so we can try all possible values.

Lemma 7. $0 \leq k - a/N < 6$.

Proof. For the first inequality, we have

$$k - \frac{a}{N} = \frac{a - y}{\varphi(N)} - \frac{a}{N} = \frac{a(p + q - 1) - yN}{\varphi(N)N}.$$

Since we have $p+q > \sqrt{N}$, the numerator will be positive when $y < aN^{-1/2}$. For the second inequality, we can bound $p + q \leq 3\sqrt{N}$ and $\varphi(N) > N/2$ to obtain

$$(p + q - 1)a - Ny < 3\sqrt{N}a < 3\,N^2 < 6\,N\varphi(N)\,.$$

Dividing by $N\varphi(N)$ we have that $k - a/N < 6$.

Step 2: Approximate $\mathbf{p + q}$. Let $s = p + q$. We can approximate $\tilde{s} = N + 1 - \lfloor a/k \rfloor$. The error will be $|s - \tilde{s}| \leq y/k$, as stated in Lemma 8.

Lemma 8. $(p + q) - \tilde{s} \leq y/k$.

Proof. This follows from the definition of $\tilde{s}$.

Step 3: Approximate p − q. We approximate $p-q$ as $\bar{s} = \lfloor\sqrt{\tilde{s}^2 - 4N}\rfloor$. The following three lemmas (9, 10 and 11) are used to bound the error on this approximation; the final bound is stated in Lemma 11.

Lemma 9. *For uniformly random prime integers p,q of the same size* $\lceil\log_2(p)\rceil = \lceil\log_2(q)\rceil = b$*, and for a constant* $0 \leq c \leq 1/4$*, we have* $|p-q| \geq c \cdot N^{1/2}$ *with probability at least* $1 - 4/b - 6c$*. We assume* $b > 16$*.*

The proof of Lemma 9 is more than a few lines, and is postponed to the Appendix. (While $b > 16$ is a necessary assumption for our proof, we consider factoring to already be practically easy for 32-bit moduli.)

Lemma 10. $y/k \leq N^{1/4}$

Proof. $y \leq aN^{-3/4} - 1 \leq aN^{-3/4} - yN^{-3/4} \leq (a-y)N^{1/4}/\varphi(N) = kN^{1/4}$.

Lemma 11. $(p-q) - \bar{s} \leq (7/c)\cdot(y/k)$ *with probability at least* $1 - 4/b - 6c$*, where* $\lceil\log_2(p)\rceil = \lceil\log_2(q)\rceil = b$*.*

Proof. We have

$$p - q - \sqrt{\tilde{s}^2 - 4N} = \frac{(p-q-\sqrt{\tilde{s}^2-4N})(p-q+\sqrt{\tilde{s}^2-4N})}{p-q+\sqrt{\tilde{s}^2-4N}} = \frac{((p+q)-\tilde{s})((p+q)+\tilde{s})}{p-q+\sqrt{\tilde{s}^2-4N}}\,.$$

We have $(p+q) - \tilde{s} = y/k$ from Lemma 8, $y/k \leq N^{1/4}$ from Lemma 10, and $|p-q| \geq cN^{1/2}$ from Lemma 9 (with probability at least $1-4/b-6c$). Therefore we have

$$\frac{(p+q)+\tilde{s}}{\sqrt{\tilde{s}^2-4N}+(p-q)} \leq \frac{\tilde{s}+p+q}{(p-q)} \leq \frac{N^{1/4}+6N^{1/2}}{cN^{1/2}} \leq 7/c\,.$$

So the error on $(p-q)$ is at most $(7/c)\cdot(y/k)$, with probability at least $1-4/b-6c$.

Step 4: Approximate $\tilde{p} = (\tilde{s}+\bar{s})/2$ and apply Coppersmith/ Howgrave-Graham to recover p from $\tilde{p}$ and N. When $|p-\tilde{p}| < N^{1/4}$ this method is guaranteed to recover p in polynomial time. Lemma 12 below proves that our approximation is within this $N^{1/4}$ bound, plus a constant factor.

Lemma 12. *The error on the approximation of p is* $|p-\tilde{p}| \leq N^{1/4}\cdot(c+7)/(2c)$ *with probability at least* $1-4/b-6c$*.*

Proof. We apply Lemmas 8 and 11 to obtain

$$|p-\tilde{p}| \leq \frac{1}{2}\left(\frac{7}{c}\cdot\frac{y}{k}+\frac{y}{k}\right) = \frac{c+7}{2c}\frac{y}{k} \leq \frac{c+7}{2c}N^{1/4}\,.$$

To reach the full Coppersmith bound without the constant factors, we brute force $\lceil \log_2((c+7)/(2c)) \rceil$ bits of p. The success of Step 4 is then achieved by Coppersmith/Howgrave-Graham. The outcome is a recovery of p, meaning we have factored N.

This all occurs with probability at least $1-4/b-6c$. We have $b = \lceil \log_2(p) \rceil = \lceil \log_2(q) \rceil$, and can set $0 \leq c \leq 1/4$ to approach 0 so that the probability approaches 1 while the required number of bits to brute force is polynomial in $\log(1/c)$. Thus the algorithm succeeds with high probability, as claimed in Theorem 5.

To obtain a concrete bound, consider $b > 16$. Then our success probability is at least $0.75 - 6c$, and is at least $0.99 - 6c$ for practical (at least 1024-bit) moduli. The dependence on this $4/b$ term only reflects how primes are distributed at different bit sizes. □

We implemented and ran the above algorithm on 2048-bit moduli and a range of a, y values, and report the results in Sect. 7. For the best Coppersmith lattice parameters, our attack factored N in over 98% of cases, where the probability is over the uniformly random primes p, q. Even with brute-forcing a constant number of bits as in the remarks above, the largest cost was running LLL, which took at most seconds. The full details are in Sect. 7.

4 Comparison to Alternate Approaches

In this section, we explore related approaches to see whether other algorithmic tools can improve the bounds we obtain in Theorem 5.

4.1 Applying Blomer-May as a Black Box

An alternative approach to using Theorem 5 in the previous section is to apply Blomer-May's Theorem 4 as a black box. Note that since in our setting $a > \varphi(N)$ we cannot simply set their $e = a$ and $x = 1$, as this violates the requirement in Blomer-May that $e \in \mathbb{Z}^*_{\varphi(N)}$ and $e < \varphi(N)$. (The Blomer-May attack does not work when $e > \varphi(N)$.) If we are able to find two factors of a as $a = a_1 \cdot a_2$ such that $a_1 \in \mathbb{Z}^*_{\varphi(N)}$ and $a_2 \leq (1/3)N^{1/4}$ then the Blomer-May attack indeed applies as formulated in Theorem 4; we set $e = a_1$ and (known) $x = a_2$.

Unfortunately, even if we land in this case, the bound is worse than that of our attack in Sect. 3. Their bound results in $a = a_1 a_2 \leq (1/3)N^{5/4}$, while our theorem applies up to $a \leq N^{3/2}$. The bound on y relative to a is unchanged, but our re-analysis shows that it is possible to recover $y < N^{3/4}$ for maximal a, while simply applying their theorem results in a maximum value of $y < N^{1/2}$.

4.2 Bivariate Coppersmith

It is also tempting to try to improve Theorem 5 by applying bivariate Coppersmith's method.

After recovering k via elementary methods (Step 1 in the prior section), we can reformulate Steps 2–4 in our algorithm. We are solving for y in the equation $a - y = k\varphi(N)$ and can recast the problem as finding small roots of an integer bivariate polynomial, which is then solved via bivariate Coppersmith (Theorem 2). However this approach has strictly worse bounds than Theorem 5.

Let us rewrite $a - y = k\varphi(N)$ as a bivariate integer equation. Let $x = p + q$ be an unknown. Then we can rewrite the equation as

$$\begin{aligned} a - y &= k(N - x + 1) \\ kx - y + (a - kN - k) &= 0. \end{aligned}$$

We can apply Coppersmith's Theorem 2 to this integer equation. Let $f(x, y) = kx - y + (a - kN - k)$, and let X and Y be upper bounds on x and y respectively. Then $\delta = 1$. Since $p + q \leq 3N^{1/2}$, it follows that $X = 3N^{1/2}$. Now it remains to calculate D:

$$D = \max_{i,j}\{|p_{ij}|X^i Y^j\} = \max\{kX, Y, |a - kN - k|\}\ .$$

By Lemma 7, $k \approx a/N$, so kX is roughly equal to $3aN^{-1/2}$. $a - kN - k = k(p-1)(q-1) + y - kN - k = y - k(p+q)$, so $|a - kN - k| \approx a/\sqrt{N}$. Therefore, it follows that $D \approx \max\{Y, 3aN^{-1/2}\}$.

If $Y \geq 3aN^{-1/2}$, then $D = Y$, and $(XY)^{3/2} \geq Y$ meaning bivariate Coppersmith will fail. If $Y < 3aN^{-1/2}$, then $D = 3aN^{-1/2}$, and bivariate Coppersmith will succeed under the conditions

$$\begin{aligned} (XY)^{3\delta/2} &< D \\ (3N^{1/2}Y)^{3/2} &< 3aN^{-1/2} \\ Y &< a^{2/3}N^{-5/6}\ . \end{aligned}$$

This latter bound on Y (the upper bound on y) is strictly inferior to the bound $y < a \cdot N^{-3/4}$ of Theorem 5.

4.3 Primal and Multivariate Coppersmith

We also explored approaches via heuristic multivariate Coppersmith methods to improve upon the bounds. In [30], Ryan surveys the literature on optimizing customized lattice constructions for multivariate Coppersmith-type problems, and creates an umbrella technique that is implemented in an automatic tool. We applied this tool, `cuso` (Coppersmith Solver), to solve the same integer bivariate Coppersmith problem discussed in the subsection above.

Our problem falls into the case of a linear bivariate equation. For this, `cuso` automatically attempts three methods to find a solution. These include a specialized linear solver which uses a primal Coppersmith construction, a Gröbner basis method, and a generalized multivariate Coppersmith method. In the following we discuss "recovering y" but recall that for our setup, knowledge of y enables factoring N.

Empirically, we found that when used as a black box, `cuso` outperforms classic bivariate Coppersmith, but remains weaker than our approach. Table 1 gives `cuso`'s success rate for various sizes of a and y, compared to our algorithm, which performs strictly better. Let us explain here in more detail.

For concrete parameters of $\lceil \log_2(N) \rceil = 2048$ and $\lceil \log_2(a) \rceil = 3071$, the maximum size of y that `cuso` was able to recover is $\lceil \log_2(y) \rceil = 1023$. This outperforms classic bivariate Coppersmith, which, as shown in the previous subsection, can recover up to

$$\lceil \log_2(y) \rceil = (2/3) \cdot 3071 - (5/6) \cdot 2048 \approx 341 .$$

However `cuso` is weaker than our approach; by Theorem 5 our theoretical maximum bound is

$$\lceil \log_2(y) \rceil = 3071 - (3/4) \cdot 2048 = 1535 .$$

And as in Table 1, our approach works empirically up to $\lceil \log_2(y) \rceil = 1516$.

For concrete parameters of $\lceil \log_2(N) \rceil = 2048$ and $\lceil \log_2(a) \rceil = 2049$, we did not find a size of y that `cuso` could recover. However our approach was empirically able to recover y up to $\lceil \log_2(y) \rceil = 494$.

We conjecture that this is due to steps in our algorithm that fall outside of generalizable Coppersmith techniques, such as Steps 2 and 3 in Theorem 5, but do not have a proven answer. We give a more extensive discussion of experimental results for our attack in Sect. 7.

Table 1. We ran the `cuso` solver on a variety of parameters using $\lceil \log_2(N) \rceil = 2048$. For each experiment, we chose the size of a and the size of y. Note that we time-out any attack that takes longer than 20 min and count it as a failure. (Our attack always took at most 13 seconds.) The "Succ. %" columns give the experimental success rate for recovering y and factoring N out of 50 trials.

$\lceil \log_2(a) \rceil$	$\lceil \log_2(y) \rceil$	`cuso` Succ. %	Our Attack Succ. %
3071	512	1.00	1.00
3071	1023	0.94	1.00
3071	1323	0	0.98
3071	1516	0	0.98
2049	335	0	1.00
2049	494	0	1.00

5 Application to the Joye-Michalevsky Transform

In 2018 Joye and Michalevsky (JM) presented a variant of RSA signatures intended to overcome hardware restrictions [18]. Their motivation is the following. Hardware Security Modules (HSMs) are a popular mechanism to securely store signing keys and efficiently handle high volumes of signature requests. Many HSMs only allow certain RSA public exponents, or disallow other values. For example, the Thales Luna 7 HSM only allows RSA public exponents 3, 17, and 65537[1], and only 65537 is allowed in FIPS mode. FIPS 186-5 [14] disallows most choices of public exponent: it specifies that "the exponent e shall be an odd positive integer such that $2^{16} < e < 2^{256}$".

If the hardware disallows $e = 3$, but you would like to use it as your public exponent, is there a workaround? Joye and Michalevsky answered with a transform-signature scheme, which aims to do precisely this.

5.1 The JM Transform-Signature Scheme

$\mathsf{JM.Kg}(e_p)$:

1 $p, q \leftarrow_\$ \mathsf{PrimesGen}$; $N \leftarrow p \cdot q$; $\varphi(N) \leftarrow (p-1)(q-1)$
2 If $\gcd(e_p, \varphi(N)) \neq 1$ then restart
3 $t \leftarrow_\$ \{z \in \mathbb{Z} \,|\, 0 < z < N \text{ and } \gcd(z, \varphi(N)) = 1\}$
4 $e_s \leftarrow e_p \cdot t \bmod \varphi(N)$ s.t. e_s is supported on the HSM
5 $d_s \leftarrow e_s^{-1} \bmod \varphi(N)$
6 $sk \leftarrow (N, d_s)$ // Secret signing key
7 $tk \leftarrow (N, t)$ // Public transform key
8 $vk \leftarrow (N, e_p)$ // Public verification key
9 Return (sk, tk, vk)

$\mathsf{JM.Sign}(sk, m)$:

10 $(N, d_s) \leftarrow sk$
11 $\sigma' \leftarrow_\$ \mathsf{H}(m)^{d_s} \bmod N$
12 Return σ'

$\mathsf{JM.Transform}(tk, \sigma')$:

13 $(N, t) \leftarrow tk$
14 $\sigma \leftarrow (\sigma')^t \bmod N$
15 Return σ

$\mathsf{JM.Verify}(vk, m, \sigma)$:

16 $(N, e_p) \leftarrow vk$
17 Return true iff $\sigma^{e_p} = \mathsf{H}(m) \bmod N$

Fig. 1. The transform-signature scheme JM. Line 4, where e_s is generated but must be supported on the HSM, could be implemented in different ways depending on the particular restrictions; we discuss this in the body.

We begin by recalling the scheme in [18]. Scheme JM is not a standard signature scheme; we call it a *transform-signature scheme*. It consists of four algorithms

[1] https://thalesdocs.com/gphsm/luna/7/docs/network/Content/PDF_Network/Utilities%20Reference.pdf.

which, in practice, are run by three different parties. The parties are the signer (the HSM), the transformer (the operator of the HSM) and a verifier. Now scheme JM consists of algorithms:

- $\mathsf{JM.Kg}$: This takes as input a desired public exponent $e_p \in \mathbb{N}$ and returns keys sk, tk, vk for the signer, transformer and verifier, respectively. Only the signing key sk is secret; both tk and vk are public. In brief, the signing key is a secret exponent $d_s \in \mathbb{Z}^*_{\varphi(N)}$ with an associated but unused secret $e_s = d_s^{-1} \bmod \varphi(N)$. The verification key is e_p as desired from the input. The transform key is $t \in \mathbb{Z}^*_{\varphi(N)}$ such that $e_s = e_p \cdot t \bmod \varphi(N)$.
- $\mathsf{JM.Sign}$: This operates as a usual RSA signing algorithm. It takes as input $sk = (N, d_s)$ and a message $m \in \{0,1\}^*$ to return a signature $\sigma' \in \mathbb{Z}^*_N$. The signature is $\mathsf{H}(m)^{d_s} \bmod N$ for a full-domain hash function $\mathsf{H} : \{0,1\}^* \to \mathbb{Z}^*_N$.
- $\mathsf{JM.Transform}$: This takes as input the transform key $tk = (N, t)$ and a signature $\sigma' \in \mathbb{Z}^*_N$ to return a transformed signature $\sigma \in \mathbb{Z}^*_N$. The transformation specifies that $\sigma = (\sigma')^t \bmod N$.
- $\mathsf{JM.Verify}$: This is usual RSA verification, taking as input $vk = (N, e_p)$ and verifying whether the input σ and m satisfy $\sigma^{e_p} = \mathsf{H}(m) \bmod N$.

We provide the scheme JM in more detail in Fig. 1. We do so for completeness but in fact, the following attack only considers the key-generation method $\mathsf{JM.Kg}$. Note that one subtlety arises with the selection of t and e_s. Key generation must output values such that $e_s = e_p \cdot t$ and e_s is "supported on the HSM." If a large enough fraction of exponents are allowed, then (re-)sampling t until e_s is an allowed exponent is efficient. If the HSM has a very restrictive set of allowed exponents, then e_s can be sampled and t determined from e_s and e_p. However any implementation choices here would modify the distribution of possible exponents; in particular security of the scheme relies on high-entropy e_s.

5.2 Attacking Small Parameter Regimes

The transform-signature scheme JM produces public information (N, e_p, t) and secret information e_s. There is additional secret information including the factors p, q and $\varphi(N), d_s$. Our problem statement is the following:

Given (N, e_p, t), under what conditions can you efficiently factor N?

Recovering p, q is the strongest attack one can hope for, as it immediately yields the secret keys and all associated values.

Joye and Michalevsky observed that e_s must remain secret, else one can recover the secret key from the relationship between e_p and e_s. Our attack strengthens this observation: even if e_s is secret and drawn from a cryptographically large set, we can recover the secret key from the public key and transform key if the exponents e_p and e_s are small relative to N. In particular, the attack of Sect. 3 applies when $e_p \leq N^{1/2}$ and $e_s < e_p N^{1/4} < N^{3/4}$. This is detailed in the below corollary, which is a result of Theorem 5, as well as experimental results we conducted in Sect. 7.

Unfortunately, this means that the Joye-Michalevsky scheme is insecure in precisely the case for which it was designed, to, for example, generate signatures for $e_p = 3$ using an HSM that only supports RSA exponents allowed by FIPS 186-5, so that $2^{16} < e_s < 2^{256}$. For a 2048-bit modulus N, and $e_p = 3$, our attack would apply up to a 512-bit e_s.

Our attack suggests that care must be taken with parameter choices, and moreover that the usual RSA recommendations are necessary but not sufficient for this transform setting.

Corollary 13. *Let public* (N, e_p, t) *and secret* e_s *be generated by the Joye-Michalevsky transform, as described above. If* $t \geq N^{1-\varepsilon}$ *for* $0 < \varepsilon \leq 1$ *and if*

$$N^{\varepsilon} \leq e_p \leq N^{1/2} \tag{5}$$

$$e_s < e_p N^{1/4-\varepsilon} \tag{6}$$

then with high probability N *can be factored in polynomial time.*

Before presenting the proof, let us remark on the variable ε. In the transform, t is selected as $t \leftarrow_{\$} [1, (N-1)]$ subject to $\gcd(t, \varphi(N)) = 1$. With high probability $\lceil \log_2(t) \rceil \approx \lceil \log_2(N) \rceil$ and ε is very small.

Proof. To prove the corollary we need only translate e_p, e_s, t into a, y of Theorem 5. We set $a = e_p \cdot t$ and $y = e_s$. First, if $e_p \leq N^{1/2}$ then $e_p t < N^{3/2}$ since $t < N$. Moreover we have $e_p \geq N^{\varepsilon} \geq N/N^{1-\varepsilon} \geq \varphi(N)/t$ so $e_p t \geq \varphi(N)$. Together these are exactly the first condition of Theorem 5; that is, that $\varphi(N) \leq a \leq N^{3/2}$ for $a = e_p t$.

Moving to the second condition, if $e_s < e_p N^{1/4-\varepsilon}$ then $e_s < e_p N^{1-\varepsilon-3/4} < e_p t N^{-3/4}$. This is precisely the second condition of Theorem 5, which asks that $y < aN^{-3/4}$. Thus we can apply that theorem with $a = e_p \cdot t$ and $y = e_s$, which now says that with high probability N can be factored in polynomial time. □

5.3 Discussion

We have shown that the JM scheme can be attacked in polynomial time when e_p and e_s are small. We conclude our discussion of this application with three remarks. Joye and Michalevsky proved that their scheme satisfies existential unforgeability under a chosen-message attack (UF-CMA). First, to our knowledge, the security proof of [18] is not necessarily violated. The proof argues that if there is an efficient adversary violating UF-CMA (for a transform signature scheme) of JM then one can construct an efficient adversary violating the one-wayness of RSA. These hardness assumptions should depend on the distribution of keys output by an RSA key generator. When weak keys are generated, the proof argument still holds but is vacuous: there is already an efficient adversary violating the one-wayness of RSA. This is a reminder of the importance of considering, or at least parameterizing by, distributions of RSA keys in proofs.

Second, a simple countermeasure to the attack is to select e_p, e_s which are not vulnerable to Corollary 13. One or both must then be large. Unfortunately, from a practical perspective this means that either signature verification will be much slower (if e_p is large) or e_s may be unsupported by HSMs or other signing implementations that limit the size of allowed public exponents.

Third, one could modify the JM scheme in potentially useful ways. For example, given the use case, it seems that t could remain secret to the HSM operator. If t is secret, our attack doesn't apply, but Blomer-May will, where t translates to the unknown x, e_s to the unknown y, and e_p to the public e in Theorem 4. The Blomer-May attack succeeds if $t \leq (1/3)N^{1/4}$ and $e_s \leq cN^{-3/4}e_p t$. In any case, we reiterate that care should be taken when transforming RSA exponents.

6 Application to e Larger Than $\varphi(N)$

Recall that the attack of Sect. 3 applies when some $a \geq \varphi(N)$ is known to the attacker. A natural setting where this could arise is schemes that select the RSA public exponent e to be larger than $\varphi(N)$. This does not immediately lead to an attack. However it shows that there is a class of weak choices of e, in particular those such that $e \bmod \varphi(N)$ is small. We discuss applications where this may occur.

RSA with Public Metadata. One example of such a scheme is the RSA-with-public-metadata scheme of [1], published at PETS 2025 and motivating a recent IRTF draft [2]. The main scheme guarantees that $e < \varphi(N)$, but a variant with better concrete security [1, Appendix C] leads to potentially larger e. There, a public key is set to be $e \leftarrow e' \cdot \mathsf{H}(\text{data})$ for some specified metadata. The hash function maps to elements of size at most $\varphi(N)^{1/2}$. This is not immediately obvious so we explain. The authors prove, in their Lemma 1, that an output h of the hash function satisfies $h < p'$ and $h < q'$, where $\varphi(N) = 4p'q'$. It follows that $4h^2 < 4p'q'$ so $h < 1/2 \cdot \varphi(N)^{1/2}$.

If e' is full-size, or at least larger than $N^{1/2}$, it is thus possible to have $\varphi(N) < e < N^{3/2}$. Our attack applies in these parameter regimes if $e \bmod \varphi(N)$ is small, meaning $e \bmod \varphi(N) < N^{3/4}$. Note that one would need to be very unlucky to select such a weak key: for the most extreme parameters this happens with probability about $N^{-1/4}$. Nonetheless, it is a previously undescribed class of weak keys. There is no randomness in the selection of $e \leftarrow e' \cdot \mathsf{H}(\text{data})$, but the scheme could check and re-sample e if it is weak (for example, with a salt). Or, the exponent e' could also be specified to be small, with $e' < \varphi(N)^{1/2}$, so the product remains $e < \varphi(N)$.

Other Schemes with Large e. The aggregate signature scheme of Lysanskaya, Micali, Reyzin, and Shacham [21, Section 5] is another example of large RSA exponents appearing in the literature. The scheme "require[s] e to be a prime larger than N". Thus as above, we exhibit a class of previously un-analyzed weak keys for this construction.

Interestingly, there are schemes [8] which use large e but specifically require $e = N$. This avoids our attack because $N \bmod \varphi(N)$ is always about the size of $N^{1/2}$ so Eq. (4) of Theorem 5 does not hold. Intuitively, setting $e = N$ leaks no information about $\varphi(N)$.

Wiener's Attack and Countermeasure. In 1989, Wiener proposed an attack against RSA with a small private exponent d [34]. As a countermeasure, he suggested adding multiples of $\mathrm{lcm}(p-1, q-1)$: "In order to make k larger, one must make the public exponent e larger... This can be done by adding a multiple of $\mathrm{lcm}(p-1, q-1)$ to e." He goes on to argue that $e > N^{3/2}$ mitigates the continued fraction attack. Our work shows that generating an exponent e of this form may be vulnerable *even if d is full sized.* Consider an unwitting implementer who generates a relatively small e and a corresponding full-sized d as a starting point, but decides to apply Wiener's countermeasure and generate a large e out of an overabundance of caution.

In that case, the public exponent is $e' = e + j \cdot \mathrm{lcm}(p-1, q-1)$ for some integer j and some e that is unknown to the attacker. Then we can let $a = \gcd(p-1, q-1)e' = \gcd(p-1, q-1)e + j(p-1)(q-1)$ and $y = \gcd(p-1, q-1)e$. If $\gcd(p-1, q-1)e' < N^{3/2}$ and $e < e' \cdot N^{-3/4}$, then our attack will successfully factor N. Note that our attack requires $e' < N^{3/2}$, and thus does not apply for Wiener's recommended exponents of size $e > N^{3/2}$.

Exponent Masking. Kocher's paper introducing cryptographic timing attacks [19] suggests exponent masking as a potential countermasure: "If anonymity is important or if further masking is required, a random multiple of $\varphi(N)$ can be added to the exponent before each modular exponentiation." While this is intended to be applied to the private exponent d, and typically operations on e wouldn't need to be protected (and an implementation operating on e likely doesn't have access to the private key to mask anyway) an excessively cautious implementation that attempts to protect e by ensuring an attacker only has access to a blinded version may inadvertently introduce a vulnerability. Interestingly, this would also allow for key recovery even if the unmasked value of e is unknown, the recovered masked e' contains arbitrary noise in the least significant bits, or the attacker only obtains most significant bits of the recovered masked e'.

Let $e' = e + j\varphi(N)$ for some unknown j and unknown small e, and suppose that the attacker has observed the value of e' either openly in a blinded/masked public key, or via a side-channel attack on a blinded/masked implementation. Then we can set $a = e'$ and $y = e$. If $\varphi(N) < e' < N^{3/2}$ and $e < e'N^{-3/4}$, then our attack will succeed and we will be able to factor N successfully.

7 Experimental Results and Optimizations

We implemented our attack in Sage [33] to experimentally validate our bounds and gather timing data. We used the `flatter` algorithm of Ryan and Heninger [31] for lattice reduction. We ran our experiments on a computer with a 2.40GHz Intel Xeon E5-2673 processor and 32GB RAM, but for the parameters we report the experiments also run in seconds on a laptop.

7.1 Details on Applying Coppersmith/Howgrave-Graham

In Step 4 of our algorithm, we apply the Coppersmith/Howgrave-Graham approach [23] to recover a factor p of N from an approximation $\tilde{p}$. In theory, this algorithm runs in polynomial time to recover $N^{1/4}$ bits of p. However, actually implementing this algorithm requires choosing concrete parameters.

In Coppersmith's algorithm, given an upper bound $X > x$, our goal is to construct a polynomial h such that $h \equiv 0 \bmod p$, and $|h(xX)| < N^{\beta} = p \approx N^{1/2}$.

In May's algorithm, the lattice L that is constructed depends on two parameters: the multiplicity m and the maximum degree shift l. The algorithm's success can be predicted by verifying that LLL can recover a lattice vector shorter than the bound required by the algorithm. We heuristically assumed we could achieve LLL approximation factor $1.02^{\dim L}$, where $\dim L$ is the dimension of L, following Nguyen and Stehlé's experiments [27]. For given values of m and l it is straightforward to compute the determinant and dimension of L.

Given this heuristic assumption, the LLL algorithm guarantees that

$$|h(xX)| \leq 1.02^{\dim(L)} \det(L)^{1/\dim(L)}$$

where $\dim L$ is the dimension of L and $\det(L)$ is the determinant of L. Therefore, if we choose parameters m and l such that

$$1.02^{\dim(L)} \det(L)^{1/\dim(L)} \leq N^{1/2}$$

then we will have

$$|h(xX)| \leq N^{1/2}$$

meeting the sufficient condition for Coppersmith algorithm's to succeed. We computed optimal X bounds for various lattice sizes by ranging over possible values for m and for l and choosing the maximal X for each multiplicity m. This $\lceil \log_2(X) \rceil$ is included as a column in the coming Table 2.

7.2 Experimental Results

We summarize our results in Table 2. At a high level, they validate the parameters for which Theorem 5 implies we can factor N with high probability. To see this, consider the columns in Table 1 which report the size of a ($\lceil \log_2(a) \rceil$), the theoretical maximum y we can solve for ($\lceil \log_2(y) \rceil$) and the success rate (the fraction of experiments where we did recover y and factor N). This maximum

y is coming from our statement of Theorem 5; as long as $a \leq N^{3/2}$ we expect $y < a \cdot N^{-3/4}$. The theorem is proved "with high probability, where the probability is over the primes p and q." This is what we aim to experimentally validate. Our success rates for different parameter choices range from 0.88 to 1, justifying this claim of high probability.

In the remainder of this section we explain the experiments, and other intermediate data, in more detail.

Table 2. We implemented and ran our attack on a variety of parameters using $\lceil \log_2(N) \rceil = 2048$. For each experiment, we chose the size of a and the multiplicity and shift parameters (m and l) for Coppersmith. From these, we computed the dimension of the lattice constructed in Coppersmith ($\dim L = m + l$). The next two columns are perhaps the most important: $\lceil \log_2(y) \rceil$ gives the theoretical size of y for which Theorem 5 implies a 90% chance of successfully factoring N. The "Succ. %" column gives the experimental success rate for this value out of 50 trials. The remaining columns include intermediate calculations in the attack, which are explained in the body of this section, as well as the lattice reduction time.

$\lceil \log_2(a) \rceil$	m	l	dim L	$\lceil \log_2(y) \rceil$	Succ. %	$\lceil \log_2(X) \rceil$	$k - \lfloor \frac{a}{N} \rfloor$	$\frac{\lvert p-\tilde{p}\rvert}{(y/k)}$	LLL time
3071	1	4	5	1323	0.98	307	1.82	8.04	0.035s
3071	2	5	7	1406	0.96	389	1.90	7.01	0.055s
3071	3	6	9	1443	1.00	426	1.86	6.07	0.079s
3071	5	8	13	1476	0.96	459	1.94	6.20	0.192s
3071	10	13	23	1402	0.92	485	1.90	6.13	0.955s
3071	22	25	47	1516	0.98	500	1.74	6.80	12.068s
2049	1	4	5	335	1.00	341	1.00	6.12	0.032s
2049	2	5	7	384	0.88	389	1.00	8.34	0.056s
2049	3	6	9	421	0.98	426	1.00	5.73	0.079s
2049	5	8	13	454	1.00	459	1.00	6.02	0.190s
2049	10	13	23	480	0.96	485	1.00	7.72	0.956s
2049	22	25	47	494	0.98	500	1.00	7.41	12.059s

7.3 Experimental Details

We ran our experiments on 2048-bit N; the bounds are relative so they scale arbitrarily. We chose representative values of a at each end of our theoretical bounds. For each value of a, we chose a range of values of m, ranging from tiny to medium-sized lattices, and computed the maximal bound X on $p - \tilde{p}$ that the algorithm could tolerate in theory with those parameters.

We used Lemma 9 to choose a c that should result in $|p - q| \geq cN^{1/2}$ with probability ≥ 0.9. We set this value to $c = 1/40$.

Once we had $\log_2(X)$ and a chosen value of c, we applied Lemma 11 to obtain $|p-\tilde{p}| \le (c+7)/(2c)\cdot y/k \approx 140\cdot yN/a$. This gives the theoretical maximum size of y that could be recovered with success rate ≥ 0.9. This is included in Table 2 as the column "$\lceil\log_2(y)\rceil$".

We then experimentally verified these theoretical results by running the attack for our chosen parameters. For each parameter set in the table, we ran the experiment 50 times and compared our empirical success rate to the theoretical success rate (0.9).

We also computed the ratio $|p-\tilde{p}|/(y/k)$ empirically, to measure the distance between our theoretical bound of $|p-\tilde{p}| \approx 140\cdot y/k$ above to the observed size of $|p-\tilde{p}|$ in our experiments. We calculated the ratio by taking the median over 50 experiments for each choice of parameters and included it in the second-to-last column of Table 2.

In addition to experiments simulating the whole attack, we also ran experiments on approximating k. For each choice of N, a and y sizes that were in the table, we generated 50 sets of values for N, a, y, k, and then calculated $k - \lfloor a/N \rfloor$ for each set, and took the mean of these differences. We included this mean error on the approximation of k in the table, as the column "$k - \lfloor a/N \rfloor$".

Outperforming Theoretical Guarantees. Notice that our experiments outperformed our theoretically guaranteed success rate of 0.9. With the data in the table, we see two reasons for this. First, the ratio $|p-\tilde{p}|/(y/k)$ was lower than expected. Initially, we had an upper bound $|p-\tilde{p}| \lessapprox 140\cdot y/k$, assuming $|p-q| \ge (1/40)\sqrt{N}$. However, as the table suggests, it appears to be the case that $|p-\tilde{p}| \lessapprox 10(y/k)$. The theoretical bounds are thus a bit conservative on the size of y that can be recovered.

Second, we also found that, for our choices of the sizes of N, a, y, the value $k - \lfloor a/N \rfloor$ was smaller on average than the theoretical upper bound, which we calculated to be 7. In fact, in all the experiments on k we performed, the value $k - \lfloor a/N \rfloor$ never exceeded 3. This verifies that our theoretical result $k - a/N \le 6$ is conservative as an upper bound.

8 Conclusion

In this paper, we observe an apparently previously un-analyzed source of weak keys for RSA: large public exponents that are close to a small multiple of $\varphi(N)$. While such exponents are unlikely to arise through random chance, they do arise through exponent transforms and masking schemes.

The methods we apply in our attack are all quite elementary (except for the use of univariate Coppersmith's theorem); we ourselves were surprised that they apparently could not be outperformed by custom multivariate Coppersmith-type algorithms. We leave it to future work to improve further upon these bounds.

Acknowledgments. We thank Marc Joye and Yan Michalevsky for their feedback and suggestions, and Keegan Ryan for conversations about Coppersmiths method. Shea was sup ported by NSF grants CNS-2048563, CNS-1513671, and CNS-2154272, and an FMA fellowship award from Qualcomm. Heninger was supported by a gift from Google and NSF grant DMS-2411704.

Appendix

This appendix gives the proof of Lemma 9 which was introduced in Sect. 3.

Lemma 14. *For uniformly random prime integers* p,q *of the same size* $\lceil \log_2(p) \rceil = \lceil \log_2(q) \rceil = b$, *and for a constant* $0 \leq c \leq 1/4$, *we have* $|p-q| \geq c \cdot N^{1/2}$ *with probability at least* $1 - 4/b - 6c$. *We assume* $b > 16$.

Before proceeding to the proof, we remark that $b > 16$ is needed to apply Dusart's non-asymptotic statements of the prime number theorem [12]. The precise bound used by Dusart is $N \geq 60,184$, which is achieved if each prime factor of N is over 16 bits. If $b \leq 16$ we consider factoring to be (practically) easy.

Proof. We use the fact that the prime-counting function π can be bounded as

$$\frac{x}{\ln(x) - 1} \leq \pi(x) \leq \frac{x}{\ln(x) - 1.1}$$

for $x \geq 60184$ (or $\lceil \log_2(x) \rceil > 16$) as proved by Dusart [12]. From this fact, we give a lower bound on the total number of primes in the interval $(2^{b-1}, 2^b)$; we call this quantity D. For any prime p in the interval, we also give an upper bound on the number of primes q such that $|p-q| < c \cdot N^{1/2}$; we call this quantity Q. In particular we will prove that:

$$D = \pi(2^b) - \pi(2^{b-1}) \geq \log_2(e) 2^{b-1} \left(\frac{b - 3.8}{(b-1.4)(b-2.6)} \right) \quad (7)$$

$$Q = \pi(p + c \cdot N^{1/2}) - \pi(p - c \cdot N^{1/2}) \leq \log_2(e) 2^{b-1} \left(\frac{4bc + 2.4}{(b-1.4)(b-2.6)} \right) \quad (8)$$

From these two equations, we bound the probability that q is selected to be close to p. That is, for random and independent primes p, q the above two equations imply

$$\Pr[|p-q| < c \cdot N^{1/2}] \leq \frac{Q}{D} \leq \frac{4bc + 2.4}{b - 3.8} < \frac{4bc + 2.4}{0.75 \cdot b} < 6c + 4/b$$

and thus that

$$\Pr[|p-q| \geq c \cdot N^{1/2}] \geq 1 - 4/b - 6c \,.$$

Claim 1. First we prove Eq. (7), the lower bound on the whole interval D. This is the set of primes from which p, q are sampled. The following sequence of equations (1) applies Dusart's bounds from above, (2) simplifies logarithms (where e is the base of ln), (3) rearranges terms, and (4) uses simple hardcoded constants to replace some expressions involving e. We have:

$$\begin{aligned}
D &= \pi(2^b) - \pi(2^{b-1}) \\
&\geq \frac{2^b}{\ln(2^b) - 1} - \frac{2^{b-1}}{\ln(2^{b-1}) - 1.1} \\
&= \frac{2^b}{b/\log_2(e) - 1} - \frac{2^{b-1}}{(b-1)/\log_2(e) - 1.1} \\
&= \frac{\log_2(e)2^b}{b - \log_2(e)} - \frac{\log_2(e)2^{b-1}}{(b-1) - 1.1\log_2(e)} \\
&\geq \frac{\log_2(e)2^b}{b - 1.4} - \frac{\log_2(e)2^{b-1}}{b - 2.6} \\
&= \log_2(e)2^{b-1}\left(\frac{2}{b-1.4} - \frac{1}{b-2.6}\right) \\
&= \log_2(e)2^{b-1}\left(\frac{2(b-2.6) - 1(b-1.4)}{(b-1.4)(b-2.6)}\right) \\
&= \log_2(e)2^{b-1}\left(\frac{b-3.8}{(b-1.4)(b-2.6)}\right)
\end{aligned}$$

where this final line is the desired bound.

Claim 2. Next we prove Eq. (8), the upper bound on the number of primes q that are close to p. (This is also an upper bound on such primes q that are in the interval of interest.) We apply a similar sequence of simplifications as in the prior claim. We additionally use the facts that $N^{1/2} < 2^b$ (since each of $p, q < 2^b$), that $2^{b-1} < p < 2^b$, and that $\ln(1-c)$ for $0 < c \leq 1/4$ is *negative*. We have:

$$
\begin{aligned}
Q &= \pi(p + c \cdot N^{1/2}) - \pi(p - c \cdot N^{1/2}) \\
&\le \pi(p + c2^b) - \pi(p - c2^b) \\
&\le \frac{p + c2^b}{\ln(p + c2^b) - 1.1} - \frac{p - c2^b}{\ln(p - c2^b) - 1} \\
&\le \frac{p + c2^b}{\ln(2^{b-1} + c2^b) - 1.1} - \frac{p - c2^b}{\ln(2^b - c2^b) - 1} \\
&= \frac{p + c2^b}{\ln(2^{b-1}(1 + 2c)) - 1.1} - \frac{p - c2^b}{\ln(2^b(1 - c)) - 1} \\
&= \frac{p + c2^b}{\ln(2^{b-1}) + \ln(1 + 2c) - 1.1} - \frac{p - c2^b}{\ln(2^b) + \ln(1 - c) - 1} \\
&\le \frac{p + c2^b}{\ln(2^{b-1}) - 1.1} - \frac{p - c2^b}{\ln(2^b) - 1} \\
&= \frac{p + c2^b}{(b-1)/\log_2(e) - 1.1} - \frac{p - c2^b}{b/\log_2(e) - 1} \\
&= \frac{\log_2(e)p + \log_2(e)c2^b}{(b-1) - 1.1\log_2(e)} - \frac{\log_2(e)p - \log_2(e)c2^b}{b - \log_2(e)} \\
&\le \frac{\log_2(e)p + \log_2(e)c2^b}{b - 2.6} - \frac{\log_2(e)p - \log_2(e)c2^b}{b - 1.4} \\
&= \log_2(e)\left(\frac{p + c2^b}{b - 2.6} - \frac{p - c2^b}{b - 1.4}\right) \\
&= \log_2(e)\left(\frac{(p + c2^b)(b - 1.4) - (p - c2^b)(b - 2.6)}{(b - 2.6)(b - 1.4)}\right) \\
&= \log_2(e)\left(\frac{pb - 1.4p + bc2^b - 1.4c2^b - (pb - 2.6p - bc2^b + 2.6c2^b)}{(b - 2.6)(b - 1.4)}\right) \\
&= \log_2(e)\left(\frac{1.2p + 2bc2^b - 4c2^b}{(b - 2.6)(b - 1.4)}\right) \\
&\le \log_2(e)\left(\frac{1.2 \cdot 2^b + 2bc2^b - 4c2^b}{(b - 2.6)(b - 1.4)}\right) \\
&\le \log_2(e)2^{b-1}\left(\frac{2.4 + 4bc}{(b - 2.6)(b - 1.4)}\right)
\end{aligned}
$$

where the last line is the desired bound. Thus equations (7) and (8) both hold, completing the proof of Lemma 9. □

References

1. Amjad, G., Yeo, K., Yung, M.: RSA blind signatures with public metadata. In: PETS 2025 (2025). https://eprint.iacr.org/2023/1199
2. Amjad, G.A., Hendrickson, S., Wood, C.A., Yeo, K.W.L.: Partially blind RSA signatures (2025). https://datatracker.ietf.org/doc/draft-irtf-cfrg-partially-blind-rsa
3. Aono, Y.: A new lattice construction for partial key exposure attack for RSA. In: Jarecki, S., Tsudik, G. (eds.) PKC 2009. LNCS, vol. 5443, pp. 34–53. Springer, Berlin, Heidelberg (2009). https://doi.org/10.1007/978-3-642-00468-1_3
4. Blömer, J., May, A.: New partial key exposure attacks on RSA. In: Boneh, D. (ed.) CRYPTO 2003. LNCS, vol. 2729, pp. 27–43. Springer, Heidelberg (2003). https://doi.org/10.1007/978-3-540-45146-4_2
5. Blömer, J., May, A.: A generalized wiener attack on RSA. In: Bao, F., Deng, R., Zhou, J. (eds.) PKC 2004. LNCS, vol. 2947, pp. 1–13. Springer, Heidelberg (2004). https://doi.org/10.1007/978-3-540-24632-9_1
6. Boneh, D., Durfee, G.: Cryptanalysis of RSA with private key d less than $N^{0.292}$. In: Stern, J. (ed.) EUROCRYPT'99. LNCS, vol. 1592, pp. 1–11. Springer, Berlin, Heidelberg (1999). https://doi.org/10.1007/3-540-48910-X_1
7. Boneh, D., Durfee, G., Frankel, Y.: An attack on RSA given a small fraction of the private key bits. In: Ohta, K., Pei, D. (eds.) ASIACRYPT 1998. LNCS, vol. 1514, pp. 25–34. Springer, Heidelberg (1998). https://doi.org/10.1007/3-540-49649-1_3
8. Catalano, D., Gennaro, R., Howgrave-Graham, N., Nguyen, P.Q.: Paillier's cryptosystem revisited. In: Proceedings of the 8th ACM Conference on Computer and Communications Security, pp. 206–214. CCS '01, Association for Computing Machinery, New York, NY, USA (2001). https://doi.org/10.1145/501983.502012. https://doi.org/10.1145/501983.502012
9. Cimato, S., Mella, S., Susella, R.: New results for partial key exposure on RSA with exponent blinding. In: 2015 12th International Joint Conference on e-Business and Telecommunications (ICETE). vol. 04, pp. 136–147 (2015)
10. Coppersmith, D.: Finding a small root of a bivariate integer equation; factoring with high bits known. In: Maurer, U.M. (ed.) EUROCRYPT'96. LNCS, vol. 1070, pp. 178–189. Springer, Berlin, Heidelberg (1996). https://doi.org/10.1007/3-540-68339-9_16
11. Coppersmith, D.: Finding a small root of a univariate modular equation. In: Maurer, U.M. (ed.) EUROCRYPT'96. LNCS, vol. 1070, pp. 155–165. Springer, Berlin, Heidelberg (1996). https://doi.org/10.1007/3-540-68339-9_14
12. Dusart, P.: Estimates of some functions over primes without R.H. (2010). https://arxiv.org/abs/1002.0442
13. Ernst, M., Jochemsz, E., May, A., de Weger, B.: Partial key exposure attacks on RSA up to full size exponents. In: Cramer, R. (ed.) EUROCRYPT 2005. LNCS, vol. 3494, pp. 371–386. Springer, Heidelberg (2005). https://doi.org/10.1007/11426639_22
14. FIPS 186-5: digital signature standard (2023). https://csrc.nist.gov/pubs/fips/186-5/final
15. Howgrave-Graham, N.: Finding small roots of univariate modular equations revisited. In: Darnell, M. (ed.) 6th IMA International Conference on Cryptography and Coding. LNCS, vol. 1355, pp. 131–142. Springer, Berlin, Heidelberg (1997). https://doi.org/10.1007/bfb0024458

16. Howgrave-Graham, N.: Approximate integer common divisors. In: International cryptography and lattices conference, pp. 51–66. Springer (2001)
17. Joye, M., Lepoint, T.: Partial key exposure on RSA with private exponents larger than N. In: Ryan, M.D., Smyth, B., Wang, G. (eds.) Information Security Practice and Experience, pp. 369–380. Springer, Berlin Heidelberg, Berlin, Heidelberg (2012)
18. Joye, M., Michalevsky, Y.: RSA signatures under hardware restrictions. In: Proceedings of the 2018 Workshop on Attacks and Solutions in Hardware Security, pp. 51–54. ASHES '18, Association for Computing Machinery, New York, NY, USA (2018). https://doi.org/10.1145/3266444.3266451. https://doi.org/10.1145/3266444.3266451
19. Kocher, P.C.: Timing attacks on implementations of Diffie-Hellman, RSA, DSS, and other systems. In: Koblitz, N. (ed.) CRYPTO'96. LNCS, vol. 1109, pp. 104–113. Springer, Berlin, Heidelberg (1996). https://doi.org/10.1007/3-540-68697-5_9
20. Lu, Y., Zhang, R., Lin, D.: New partial key exposure attacks on CRT-RSA with large public exponents. In: Boureanu, I., Owesarski, P., Vaudenay, S. (eds.) ACNS 2014. LNCS, vol. 8479, pp. 151–162. Springer, Cham (2014). https://doi.org/10.1007/978-3-319-07536-5_10
21. Lysyanskaya, A., Micali, S., Reyzin, L., Shacham, H.: Sequential aggregate signatures from trapdoor permutations. In: Cachin, C., Camenisch, J.L. (eds.) EUROCRYPT 2004. LNCS, vol. 3027, pp. 74–90. Springer, Heidelberg (2004). https://doi.org/10.1007/978-3-540-24676-3_5
22. May, A.: Computing the RSA secret key is deterministic polynomial time equivalent to factoring. In: Franklin, M. (ed.) CRYPTO 2004. LNCS, vol. 3152, pp. 213–219. Springer, Heidelberg (2004). https://doi.org/10.1007/978-3-540-28628-8_13
23. May, A.: Using LLL-reduction for solving RSA and factorization problems. In: Nguyen, P.Q., Vallée, B. (eds.) The LLL Algorithm: Survey and Applications, pp. 315–348. Springer Berlin Heidelberg, Berlin, Heidelberg (2010). https://doi.org/10.1007/978-3-642-02295-1_10. https://doi.org/10.1007/978-3-642-02295-1_10
24. May, A., Nowakowski, J., Sarkar, S.: Partial key exposure attack on short secret exponent CRT-RSA. In: Tibouchi, M., Wang, H. (eds.) ASIACRYPT 2021, Part I. LNCS, vol. 13090, pp. 99–129. Springer, Cham (2021). https://doi.org/10.1007/978-3-030-92062-3_4
25. Miller, G.L.: Riemann's hypothesis and tests for primality. J. Comput. Syst. Sci. **13**(3), 300–317 (1976). https://doi.org/10.1016/S0022-0000(76)80043-8. https://www.sciencedirect.com/science/article/pii/S0022000076800438
26. Moody, D., Perlner, R., Regenscheid, A., Robinson, A., Cooper, D.: NIST transition to post-quantum cryptography standards (2024). https://nvlpubs.nist.gov/nistpubs/ir/2024/NIST.IR.8547.ipd.pdf
27. Nguyen, P.Q., Stehlé, D.: LLL on the average. In: Hess, F., Pauli, S., Pohst, M. (eds.) Algorithmic Number Theory, pp. 238–256. Springer, Berlin Heidelberg, Berlin, Heidelberg (2006)
28. Nitaj, A.: Another generalization of Wiener's attack on RSA. In: Vaudenay, S. (ed.) Progress in Cryptology - AFRICACRYPT 2008, pp. 174–190. Springer, Berlin Heidelberg, Berlin, Heidelberg (2008)
29. Rivest, R.L., Shamir, A., Adleman, L.M.: A method for obtaining digital signatures and public-key cryptosystems. Commun. Ass. Comput. Mach. **21**(2), 120–126 (1978). https://doi.org/10.1145/359340.359342
30. Ryan, K.: Solving multivariate coppersmith problems with known moduli. In: EUROCRYPT 2025 (2025)

31. Ryan, K., Heninger, N.: Fast practical lattice reduction through iterated compression. In: Handschuh, H., Lysyanskaya, A. (eds.) CRYPTO 2023, Part III. LNCS, vol. 14083, pp. 3–36. Springer, Cham (2023). https://doi.org/10.1007/978-3-031-38548-3_1
32. Sarkar, S., Maitra, S.: Partial key exposure attack on CRT-RSA. In: Abdalla, M., Pointcheval, D., Fouque, P.-A., Vergnaud, D. (eds.) ACNS 2009. LNCS, vol. 5536, pp. 473–484. Springer, Heidelberg (2009). https://doi.org/10.1007/978-3-642-01957-9_29
33. The sage developers: sagemath, the sage mathematics software system (Version 9.5)(2022). https://www.sagemath.org
34. Wiener, M.J.: Cryptanalysis of short RSA secret exponents. In: Quisquater, J.-J., Vandewalle, J. (eds.) EUROCRYPT 1989. LNCS, vol. 434, pp. 372–372. Springer, Heidelberg (1990). https://doi.org/10.1007/3-540-46885-4_36
35. Wiener, M.: Cryptanalysis of short RSA secret exponents. IEEE Trans. Inf. Theory **36**(3), 553–558 (1990). https://doi.org/10.1109/18.54902
36. Zhou, Y., van de Pol, J., Yu, Y., Standaert, F.X.: A third is all you need: extended partial key exposure attack on CRT-RSA with additive exponent blinding. In: Agrawal, S., Lin, D. (eds.) ASIACRYPT 2022, Part IV. LNCS, vol. 13794, pp. 508–536. Springer, Cham (2022). https://doi.org/10.1007/978-3-031-22972-5_18

Attacks on PRISM-id via Torsion over Small Extension Fields

Kohei Nakagawa[1] and Hiroshi Onuki[2(✉)]

[1] NTT Social Informatics Laboratories, Tokyo, Japan
kohei.nakagawa@ntt.com
[2] The University of Tokyo, Bunkyo, Japan
onuki@mist.i.u-tokyo.ac.jp

Abstract. PRISM is an isogeny-based cryptographic framework that relies on the hardness of computing a large prime-degree isogeny from a supersingular elliptic curve with an unknown endomorphism ring. It includes both an identification scheme PRISM-id and a signature scheme PRISM-sig. In this work, we present two attacks on PRISM-id. First, we analyze the probability that a randomly sampled prime q in PRISM-id results in a q-torsion subgroup defined over a small extension field, and we show that this probability is higher than claimed in the original proposal. Exploiting this observation, we construct classical forgery attacks on PRISM-id. The first attack addresses the scenario in which the attacker cannot reject a challenge. It succeeds with probability $\tilde{\Theta}(2^{-(\lambda+\log\lambda)(1-\varepsilon)})$ and runs in expected time $\tilde{O}(\max\{2^{3\lambda\varepsilon}, 2^{\lambda(\varepsilon+1/2)}\})$ for any positive real number $\varepsilon < 1/3$. Setting $\varepsilon = 1/4$ yields success probability $\tilde{\Theta}(2^{-3(\lambda+\log\lambda)/4})$ and expected time complexity $\tilde{O}(2^{3\lambda/4})$. The second forgery attack covers the scenario in which the attacker is allowed to reject challenges. It always succeeds and runs in expected time $\tilde{O}(2^{6\lambda/7})$. Finally, we describe an attack against the underlying hardness assumption of PRISM-id that runs in expected time $\tilde{O}(2^{\lambda/2})$. Note that our results do not affect the security of PRISM-sig.

Keywords: Isogenies · Post-Quantum · Identification Schemes · PRISM

1 Introduction

Isogeny-based cryptography is a promising candidate for post-quantum cryptography. A representative scheme within isogeny-based cryptography is SQIsign [1], which is one of the candidates for the NIST post-quantum additional digital signature standard. One advantage of isogeny-based cryptography is its small key size compared to other post-quantum schemes.

Many isogeny-based cryptographic protocols use supersingular elliptic curves and rely on the hardness of the *supersingular isogeny problem*, which requires computing an isogeny between two given supersingular elliptic curves. This problem is believed to be hard even in the quantum setting. Furthermore,

S. Bai and E. Persichetti (Eds.): PKC 2026, LNCS 16551, pp. 480–509, 2026.
https://doi.org/10.1007/978-3-032-26731-3_16

the supersingular isogeny problem is equivalent to the problem of computing the endomorphism ring of a supersingular elliptic curve [30,36].

Recently, a new problem has been proposed and has attracted attention: computing an isogeny of a given degree d from a given supersingular elliptic curve E over $\mathbb{F}_{p^2}$. We call this the *given-degree isogeny problem*. It can be solved in polynomial time if d is smooth or if the endomorphism ring of E is known. However, when d is a large prime and the endomorphism ring of E is unknown, no efficient algorithm is known.

The given-degree isogeny problem first appeared in the context of the security of SQIsignHD [13]. SQIsignHD and several variants [4,18,32,33,37] of SQIsign including the NIST SQIsign rely on the hardness of the supersingular isogeny problem with oracle access to the given-degree isogeny problem. On the other hand, a new cryptographic framework PRISM [3] has been proposed, assuming the hardness of the given-degree isogeny problem with d being a large prime. PRISM consists of an identification scheme PRISM-id and a signature scheme PRISM-sig. Due to its simple structure, PRISM-sig could serve as a building block for more advanced cryptographic protocols.

Consequently, analyzing the hardness of the given-degree isogeny problem is important for isogeny-based cryptography. If it turns out to be easy, the security of several SQIsign variants becomes clearer because the oracle access to the given-degree isogeny problem can be removed from their security analyses. If it remains hard, the security rationale for PRISM is reinforced. However, a detailed complexity analysis of the given-degree isogeny problem is still lacking. In the case of PRISM, only rough lower-bound estimates have been provided so far.

Contributions. We analyze the hardness of the given-degree isogeny problem in the classical setting. For this, we provide algorithms required to solve the problem and give a detailed complexity analysis of each algorithm. Based on these algorithms, we construct forgery attacks on PRISM-id showing that the proposed parameters of PRISM-id do not achieve the claimed security level.

The security of PRISM-id relies on the hardness of computing an isogeny of a given large prime degree $q \approx 2^\lambda$ from a given supersingular elliptic curve E over $\mathbb{F}_{p^2}$, where λ is the security parameter. The analysis of the original proposal of PRISM claims that q-torsion points of the elliptic curve E are defined over an extension field of $\mathbb{F}_{p^2}$ of degree approximately q, and thus the attack using q-torsion points costs more than 2^λ bit operations. We analyze the probability that a randomly sampled prime q in PRISM-id results in a q-torsion subgroup defined over a relatively small extension field, and we show that an attack whose cost is less than 2^λ bit operations succeeds with probability exponentially small but greater than $2^{-\lambda}$.

Based on this observation, we construct two forgery attacks on PRISM-id. In the first attack, we assume that the attacker cannot reject a challenge prime q. This attack succeeds with probability $\tilde{\Theta}(2^{-3\lambda/4})$ and has expected time complexity $\tilde{O}(2^{3\lambda/4})$ for a security parameter λ. In the second attack, we allow the attacker to reject a challenge prime q. This attack always succeeds and has expected time complexity $\tilde{O}(2^{6\lambda/7})$.

In addition, we analyze the hardness of the underlying problem of PRISM, which is a variant of the given-degree isogeny problem. We show that, for the parameters of PRISM-id that target λ-bit security, there exists an algorithm with expected time complexity $\tilde{O}(2^{\lambda/2})$ that solves this problem.

Note that our attacks do not affect the security of PRISM-sig.

1.1 Organization

In Sect. 2, we provide background knowledge used in this paper. In Sect. 3, we recall the construction and security claims of the PRISM framework. In Sect. 4, we present the foundational algorithms and heuristics used in our attacks. In Sect. 5, we present two forgery attacks on PRISM-id. In Sect. 6, we analyze an attack on the underlying problem of PRISM-id. Finally, in Sect. 7, we conclude the paper.

2 Preliminaries

In this section, we provide background knowledge used in this paper.

Throughout this paper, we use the following notation. We let p be a prime number greater than 3. The symbol log denotes the natural logarithm.

2.1 Supersingular Elliptic Curves and Isogenies

An elliptic curve E defined over $\overline{\mathbb{F}}_p$ is *supersingular* if the torsion subgroup $E[p]$ is trivial. A supersingular elliptic curve is isomorphic to a curve defined over $\mathbb{F}_{p^2}$. In addition, we can choose a curve E over $\mathbb{F}_{p^2}$ such that the p^2-th power Frobenius endomorphism on E is equal to the multiplication by $-p$. Then, for positive integers k and n such that $p \nmid n$, the group $E(\mathbb{F}_{p^{2k}})$ of rational points on E contains the n-torsion subgroup $E[n]$ if and only if $(-p)^k \equiv 1 \pmod{n}$. In particular, if n is prime, then $E[n] \subseteq E(\mathbb{F}_{p^{2(n-1)}})$ from the Fermat little theorem. We assume that all the supersingular elliptic curves considered in this paper are defined over $\mathbb{F}_{p^2}$ and have the above property. In addition, we can assume that E is a (twisted) Montgomery curve, which is defined by the equation $By^2 = x^3 + Ax^2 + x$ for some $A, B \in \mathbb{F}_{p^2}$. Thus, we assume that a supersingular elliptic curve E is represented by its coefficients A, B.

An *isogeny* between elliptic curves is a non-constant morphism of algebraic varieties that is also a group homomorphism. The *degree* of an isogeny φ is the degree of the corresponding morphism and is denoted by $\deg \varphi$. We say φ is a *d-isogeny* if $\deg \varphi = d$. Let $\varphi : E \to E'$ be a d-isogeny. Then, there exists a unique isogeny $\varphi' : E' \to E$ such that $\varphi' \circ \varphi$ is the multiplication by d on E. We call this isogeny the *dual isogeny* of φ and denote it by $\hat{\varphi}$. Assume that the degree d of φ decomposes as $d = d_1 \cdots d_k$. Then, there exist isogenies φ_i of degree d_i such that $\varphi = \varphi_k \circ \cdots \circ \varphi_1$. The order of the kernel of an isogeny φ is less than or equal to $\deg \varphi$, where the equality holds if and only if φ is separable. Conversely, for an elliptic curve E over $\overline{\mathbb{F}}_p$ and a finite subgroup G of

$E(\overline{\mathbb{F}}_p)$, there exists a separable isogeny φ with kernel G, which is unique up to post-composition by an isomorphism.

An *endomorphism* of an elliptic curve E is an isogeny from E to itself or the zero morphism. The set of endomorphisms of an elliptic curve E forms a ring $\mathrm{End}(E)$ by the addition on the images of endomorphisms and the composition of endomorphisms. We call this ring the *endomorphism ring* of E and denote it by $\mathrm{End}(E)$.

2.2 Quaternion Algebras

In this paper, we only consider quaternion algebras over $\mathbb{Q}$ ramified exactly at p and the infinite place. If p is fixed, such an algebra is unique up to isomorphism, so we denote it by $B_{p,\infty}$. There exist $\mathrm{i}, \mathrm{j} \in B_{p,\infty}$ such that $(1, \mathrm{i}, \mathrm{j}, \mathrm{ij})$ is a basis of $B_{p,\infty}$ as a $\mathbb{Q}$-vector space, i.e.,

$$B_{p,\infty} = \mathbb{Q} + \mathbb{Q}\mathrm{i} + \mathbb{Q}\mathrm{j} + \mathbb{Q}\mathrm{ij},$$

and that $\mathrm{i}^2 = -q$, $\mathrm{j}^2 = -p$, and $\mathrm{ij} = -\mathrm{ji}$, where $q = 1$ if $p \equiv 3 \pmod 4$, $q = 2$ if $p \equiv 5 \pmod 8$, and q is a prime such that $q \equiv 3 \pmod 4$ and $\left(\frac{q}{p}\right) = -1$ otherwise.

The *canonical involution* on $B_{p,\infty}$ is defined by

$$\overline{a + b\mathrm{i} + c\mathrm{j} + d\mathrm{ij}} = a - b\mathrm{i} - c\mathrm{j} + d\mathrm{ij},$$

for all $a, b, c, d \in \mathbb{Q}$. For $\alpha \in B_{p,\infty}$, the *reduced norm* of α is defined by $\mathrm{nrd}(\alpha) = \alpha\overline{\alpha}$. A *lattice* in $B_{p,\infty}$ is a $\mathbb{Z}$-submodule of $B_{p,\infty}$ of rank 4. An *order* in $B_{p,\infty}$ is a lattice that is a subring of $B_{p,\infty}$. Let $\mathcal{O}$ be an order in $B_{p,\infty}$. A left $\mathcal{O}$-ideal is a lattice I in $B_{p,\infty}$ such that $\mathcal{O}I \subseteq I$. Let I be a left $\mathcal{O}$-ideal. Then the set $\{\mathrm{nrd}(\alpha) \mid \alpha \in I\} \subset \mathbb{Q}$ is a $\mathbb{Z}$-module of rank 1, so this set has a unique positive generator. We define the *reduced norm* of I as the unique positive generator of this set and denote it by $\mathrm{nrd}(I)$. A left $\mathcal{O}$-ideal I is said to be *integral* if $I \subseteq \mathcal{O}$. In this paper, we only consider integral left $\mathcal{O}$-ideals, and therefore we omit the word "integral" in the following sections. For $\alpha \in \mathcal{O}$, the reduced norm of α is a positive integer. Thus, the reduced norm of an integral left $\mathcal{O}$-ideal I is also a positive integer.

An order in $B_{p,\infty}$ is called *maximal* if it is not properly contained in any other order in $B_{p,\infty}$. There exists a maximal order containing i and j. Examples of such maximal orders are given by Proposition 1 in [19]. These orders are called *special p-extremal* (see [25] for the definition). In the case $p \equiv 3 \pmod 4$, the following order is a special p-extremal order:

$$\mathcal{O}_0 = \mathbb{Z} + \mathbb{Z}\mathrm{i} + \mathbb{Z}\frac{\mathrm{i}+\mathrm{j}}{2} + \mathbb{Z}\frac{1+\mathrm{ij}}{2}.$$

The Deuring Correspondence. If E is a supersingular elliptic curve over $\mathbb{F}_{p^2}$, then $\mathrm{End}(E)$ is isomorphic to a maximal order in the quaternion algebra $B_{p,\infty}$.

Let $\mathcal{E}_p$ be the set of the isomorphism classes of supersingular elliptic curves over $\mathbb{F}_{p^2}$, and let $\mathscr{O}_p$ be the set of the isomorphism (as rings) classes of maximal orders in $B_{p,\infty}$. Then, we have the following map

$$\mathcal{E}_p \to \mathscr{O}_p, \quad E \mapsto \mathcal{O} \text{ such that } \mathcal{O} \cong \mathrm{End}(E).$$

This map is surjective and the images of two distinct elliptic curves are the same if and only if the two elliptic curves are p-th power Frobenius conjugate to each other. We call this map the *Deuring correspondence.*

Let E be a supersingular elliptic curve over $\mathbb{F}_{p^2}$, and let $\mathcal{O}$ be a maximal order in $B_{p,\infty}$ isomorphic to $\mathrm{End}(E)$. We fix an isomorphism $\iota : \mathcal{O} \to \mathrm{End}(E)$. For a left $\mathcal{O}$-ideal I, we define a set

$$E[I] := \bigcap_{\alpha \in I} \ker(\iota(\alpha)).$$

Then, $E[I]$ is a finite subgroup of $E(\mathbb{F}_{p^2})$. An isogeny with kernel $E[I]$ is called the *isogeny corresponding to the ideal* I.

In the case $p \equiv 3 \pmod 4$, the elliptic curve E_0 defined by $y^2 = x^3 + x$ over $\mathbb{F}_{p^2}$ is supersingular. The endomorphism ring $\mathrm{End}(E_0)$ is isomorphic to $\mathcal{O}_0$ defined above. An isomorphism is given by

$$((x, y) \mapsto (-x, \sqrt{-1}y)) \mapsto \mathrm{i} \text{ and } ((x, y) \mapsto (x^p, y^p)) \mapsto \mathrm{j},$$

where $\sqrt{-1}$ is a square root of -1 in $\mathbb{F}_{p^2}$.

2.3 Kani's Lemma

Since the attack on SIKE using 2-dimensional isogenies [9,29,34] appeared, there have been widespread efforts to incorporate 2-dimensional isogenies into the design of isogeny-based cryptography. The following lemma, which is called *Kani's lemma* because it comes from Kani's work [24], is a key tool in this context.

Lemma 1 (Theorem 1 in [29]). *Let d_1 and d_2 be coprime integers and let $D = d_1 + d_2$. Let E, E_1, E_2, and F be elliptic curves connected by the following commutative diagram of isogenies:*

$$\begin{array}{ccc} E & \xrightarrow{\varphi_1} & E_1 \\ \varphi_2 \downarrow & & \downarrow \varphi_2' \\ E_2 & \xrightarrow[\varphi_1']{} & F, \end{array}$$

where $\deg \varphi_i = \deg \varphi_i' = d_i$ *for* $i \in \{1, 2\}$. *Then, the map*

$$\Phi = \begin{pmatrix} \varphi_1 & -\widehat{\varphi}_2' \\ \varphi_2 & \widehat{\varphi}_1' \end{pmatrix} : E \times F \to E_1 \times E_2$$

is an isogeny with respect to the natural product polarizations on $E_1 \times E_2$ *and* $E \times F$*, and has kernel* $\{([d_2]P, \varphi_2' \circ \varphi_1(P)) \mid P \in E[D]\}$*, which is isomorphic to* $\mathbb{Z}/D\mathbb{Z} \oplus \mathbb{Z}/D\mathbb{Z}$*.*

This lemma tells us how to compute all the 1-dimensional isogenies in the component of the 2-dimensional isogeny Φ from the restriction of $\varphi_2' \circ \varphi_1$ to $E[D]$ and the degrees d_1 and d_2. Note that Φ can be computed from its kernel (for example by using the algorithms in [11] or [28]). In particular, when $D = 2^e$ for a positive integer e, we can use the efficient formulas proposed by Dartois, Maino, Pope, and Robert [14].

Remark 1. A higher-dimensional version of Kani's lemma is known [34, Lemma 3.6]. It can be used to represent a 1-dimensional isogeny as we will explain in Sect. 2.4.

2.4 Representation of Isogenies

An isogeny of degree d is a rational map consisting of polynomials of degree approximately d. If the degree d is exponential in $\log p$, which is the size of the coefficients of the elliptic curve, then we need to represent the isogeny by a more compact form. To describe such a representation, we introduce the notion of an *efficient representation* of an isogeny.

Definition 1. *Let* d *be a positive integer and* $\varphi : E \to E'$ *be an isogeny of degree* d *between elliptic curves over* $\mathbb{F}_q$*. An* efficient representation *of* φ *with respect to an algorithm* $\mathcal{A}$ *is some data* $D_\varphi \in \{0,1\}^*$ *of polynomial size in* $\log q$ *and* $\log d$ *such that for all* $P \in E(\mathbb{F}_{q^k})$*,* $\mathcal{A}$ *with input* (D_φ, P) *returns* E' *and* $\varphi(P)$ *in polynomial time in* $\log d$ *and* $k \log q$*.*

If the degree d is smooth, then we can decompose the isogeny φ into a composition of isogenies of small degree. The sequence of the representations of these small-degree isogenies as rational maps is an efficient representation of φ.

In the case where the degree d is not smooth, we can represent the isogeny φ using Kani's lemma (Lemma 1). Assume that there exists a smooth integer n such that $n^2 > d$ and $E[n]$ is rational over $\mathbb{F}_{q^k}$, where k is a positive integer in polynomial size in $\log q$. Then, a tuple $(E, P, Q, \varphi(P), \varphi(Q), d)$, where (P, Q) is a basis of $E[n]$, is an efficient representation of φ (see Theorem 1 and Remark 1 in [34]). The computation of the isogeny by this representation requires computing an 8-dimensional isogeny in general, and is not efficient in practice.

In some special cases, we can improve the efficiency of the computation of the isogeny. Assume that there exist integers d' and a with d' odd and $a > 0$ such that $d = d'(2^a - d')$ and $E[2^a]$ is rational over $\mathbb{F}_{q^k}$ for some positive integer k in polynomial size in $\log q$. Then, a tuple $(E, E', P, Q, \varphi(P), \varphi(Q), d')$, where (P, Q) is a basis of $E[2^a]$, is an efficient representation of φ. In this case, we can decompose φ into the composition of a d'-isogeny and a $(2^a - d')$-isogeny, and apply Kani's lemma (Lemma 1) to obtain efficient representations of these isogenies. Here, we can use the efficient method of [14] to compute a 2-dimensional isogeny. This representation is used in POKÉ [5] and PRISM [3]. We also use this representation in our attacks.

2.5 Ideal to Isogeny Translation

Translating ideals into the corresponding isogenies under the Deuring correspondence is a fundamental operation in isogeny-based cryptography.

Let E be a supersingular elliptic curve over $\mathbb{F}_{p^2}$, and $\mathcal{O}$ be a maximal order in $B_{p,\infty}$ such that $\mathcal{O} \cong \mathrm{End}(E)$. Assume that we are given E, a basis of $\mathcal{O}$, and efficient representations of the endomorphisms of E corresponding to the basis elements. In this setting, an algorithm to compute an efficient representation of the isogeny corresponding to a given left $\mathcal{O}$-ideal I is called an *ideal-to-isogeny algorithm.*

In this paper, we restrict our attention to the case where $\mathrm{End}(E)$ is isomorphic to a special p-extremal order. Several polynomial-time ideal-to-isogeny algorithms are known in this case (e.g., [15,16,19,20] for using 1-dimensional isogenies, and [4,27,31] for using 2-dimensional isogenies). Note that the general case can be reduced to the special case by using the above-mentioned algorithms twice.

In PRISM, the ideal-to-isogeny algorithm in [4] is used. This algorithm is efficient when the characteristic p of the base field is of the form $p = f2^e - 1$ for integers f and e such that f is odd and $p \approx 2^e$. For details of this algorithm, we refer the reader to [4, §3.2]. We denote this algorithm by `IdealToIsogeny`. More precisely, given a left $\mathcal{O}$-ideal I, the algorithm computes an efficient representation of the isogeny corresponding to I. We omit the elliptic curve and the special p-extremal order from the input of `IdealToIsogeny` since we regard these as system parameters.

2.6 Computational Problems

Isogeny-based protocols using supersingular elliptic curves are based on the hardness of the following computational problem.

Problem 1 (Supersingular isogeny problem). Given two supersingular elliptic curves E and E' over $\mathbb{F}_{p^2}$, find an isogeny $\varphi : E \to E'$.

One of the best algorithms for solving the supersingular isogeny problem is the Delfs-Galbraith algorithm [17], which has expected time complexity $\tilde{O}(p^{1/2})$ in classical computation and $\tilde{O}(p^{1/4})$ in quantum computation with Grover's algorithm [21].

The following related problem is also important in isogeny-based cryptography.

Problem 2 (Maximal order problem). Given a supersingular elliptic curve E over $\mathbb{F}_{p^2}$, find a maximal order $\mathcal{O}$ in $B_{p,\infty}$ such that $\mathcal{O} \cong \mathrm{End}(E)$.

Here, finding a maximal order in $B_{p,\infty}$ means finding a basis of $\mathcal{O}$ as a tuple of $\mathbb{Q}$-vectors with respect to the basis $(1, \mathrm{i}, \mathrm{j}, \mathrm{ij})$.

It is known that Problem 1 and Problem 2 are equivalent, i.e., there exist polynomial-time reductions between them. It was shown by assuming the generalized Riemann hypothesis in [36], and later unconditionally in [30].

Another problem relevant to isogenies between supersingular elliptic curves is computing an isogeny from a given elliptic curve E and degree d.

Problem 3 (Computing isogeny given degree problem). Given a supersingular elliptic curve E over $\mathbb{F}_{p^2}$ and a positive integer d, find an isogeny φ from E of degree d.

If d is smooth, then this problem can be solved efficiently by applying Vélu's formula [35] to each prime factor of d. Even if d is not smooth, if we are given a maximal order $\mathcal{O}$ in $B_{p,\infty}$ such that $\mathcal{O} \cong \mathrm{End}(E)$, then we can still compute an isogeny of degree d from E by using an ideal-to-isogeny algorithm. This is a core component of PRISM and will be explained in Sect. 3.1. On the other hand, if d is not smooth and we are not given a maximal order $\mathcal{O}$, then there is no known efficient algorithm to solve this problem. We will give a more detailed analysis of this problem when d is a prime (see Lemma 3).

3 PRISM

In this section, we recall PRISM, which consists of an identification scheme PRISM-id and a signature scheme PRISM-sig derived from PRISM-id. The security of PRISM is based on the hardness of a variant of Problem 3.

3.1 PRISM-id

We give an overview of the identification scheme PRISM-id. We refer to the original paper [3] for further details.

First, we define the notation used in the scheme. Let p be a prime of the form $p = f2^e - 1$ for some integers f and e. We require $p \approx 2^e$ so that we can use `IdealToIsogeny` efficiently. Let a be an integer less than e, and let Primes_a be the set of all primes in $[2^{a-1}, 2^a]$.

PRISM-id is a two-round identification scheme, which is based on the following diagram.

$$\begin{array}{ccc} E_0 & & \\ \downarrow{\scriptstyle \varphi_{\mathrm{sk}}} & & \\ E_{\mathrm{vk}} & \xrightarrow{\varphi_{\mathrm{rsp}}} & E_{\mathrm{rsp}} \end{array}$$

Here, E_0 is a supersingular elliptic curve whose endomorphism ring is isomorphic to a special p-extremal order $\mathcal{O}_0$.

The system parameter of PRISM-id is the tuple $(e, f, a, E_0, \mathcal{O}_0)$. The secret key for PRISM-id is a left $\mathcal{O}_0$-ideal I_{sk} of norm ℓ^n for some prime $\ell > 2^a$ and integer n. The public key is the codomain E_{vk} of the isogeny φ_{sk} corresponding to I_{sk}. The challenge for the identification scheme is a prime q sampled uniformly at random from Primes_a. The response to the challenge is an isogeny φ_{rsp} from E_{vk} of degree $q(2^a - q)$. The verifier checks whether the response φ_{rsp} is an isogeny from E_{vk} of degree $q(2^a - q)$. The procedure of the identification scheme is depicted in Table 1, where the algorithms `GenIsogeny` and `VerIsogeny` are defined as follows.

Table 1. PRISM-id identification scheme.

Prover($\mathrm{sk} = I_{\mathrm{sk}}$)		Verifier($\mathrm{vk} = E_{\mathrm{vk}}$)
		Sample a prime $q \xleftarrow{\$} \mathsf{Primes}_a$
	$\xleftarrow{q}$	
$\varphi_{\mathrm{rsp}} \leftarrow \mathtt{GenIsogeny}(E_{\mathrm{vk}}, I_{\mathrm{sk}}, q)$		
	$\xrightarrow{\varphi_{\mathrm{rsp}}}$	
		Return $\mathtt{VerIsogeny}(E_{\mathrm{vk}}, \varphi_{\mathrm{rsp}}, q)$

- $\mathtt{GenIsogeny}(E, I, q) \to \varphi$: On input a supersingular elliptic curve E over $\mathbb{F}_{p^2}$, a left $\mathcal{O}_0$-ideal I such that the codomain of the isogeny corresponding to I is E, and a prime $q \in \mathsf{Primes}_a$, outputs a $q(2^a - q)$-isogeny φ from E.
- $\mathtt{VerIsogeny}(E, \varphi, q) \to \mathtt{accept}/\mathtt{reject}$: On input a supersingular elliptic curve E over $\mathbb{F}_{p^2}$, an isogeny φ, and a prime $q \in \mathsf{Primes}_a$, outputs $\mathtt{accept}$ if the domain of φ is E and $\deg \varphi = q(2^a - q)$, and $\mathtt{reject}$ otherwise.

The algorithm $\mathtt{VerIsogeny}$ uses the decomposition of the response isogeny φ_{rsp} as $\varphi_{\mathrm{rsp}} = \varphi_{2^a-q} \circ \varphi_q = \psi_q \circ \psi_{2^a-q}$, where $\deg \varphi_q = \deg \psi_q = q$ and $\deg \varphi_{2^a-q} = \deg \psi_{2^a-q} = 2^a - q$. Thus, we have the following commutative diagram.

$$\begin{array}{ccc} E_{\mathrm{vk}} & \xrightarrow{\varphi_q} & E_1 \\ {\scriptstyle \psi_{2^a-q}} \downarrow & \searrow^{\varphi_{\mathrm{rsp}}} & \downarrow {\scriptstyle \varphi_{2^a-q}} \\ E_2 & \xrightarrow[\psi_q]{} & E_{\mathrm{rsp}} \end{array}$$

By applying Kani's lemma (Lemma 1), we can obtain efficient representations of the isogenies in the diagram. The degrees of these isogenies can be checked by computing the 2^a-Weil pairings of the images of 2^a-torsion points under the isogenies.

3.2 PRISM-sig

PRISM-sig is a signature scheme based on PRISM-id. For constructing PRISM-sig, we prepare a collision-resistant hash function $\mathtt{H}_{\mathrm{prime}}$ whose output is a prime number in Primes_a (see [3, §3.3] for construction details).

The key generation of PRISM-sig is the same as that of PRISM-id except that we take $a \approx 2\lambda$. Let E_{vk} be the public key and I_{sk} be the secret key. For a message $m \in \{0,1\}^*$, we let $q = \mathtt{H}_{\mathrm{prime}}(E_{\mathrm{vk}} || m)$. Then the signature is $\mathtt{GenIsogeny}(E_{\mathrm{vk}}, I_{\mathrm{sk}}, q)$, and the verification is done by $\mathtt{VerIsogeny}(E_{\mathrm{vk}}, \varphi_{\mathrm{rsp}}, q)$.

3.3 Security

In this subsection, we briefly recall the security analysis of PRISM from [3].

First, to define the underlying problem of PRISM-id, we recall the definition of the oracle SPEDIO defined in [3].

Definition 2 (Definition 5 in [3]). *A special degree isogeny oracle (SPEDIO) is an oracle which takes as input a supersingular elliptic curve E and a prime $q \in \mathsf{Primes}_a$, and returns a uniformly random isogeny of degree $q(2^a - q)$ from E.*

Using this oracle, we define the underlying problem of PRISM-id.

Problem 4 (Problem 2 in [3]). Given a supersingular elliptic curve E and SPEDIO, compute an isogeny of degree $q(2^a - q)$ from E with a prime $q \in \mathsf{Primes}_a$ different from all degrees previously queried to the oracle.

The security of PRISM-id and PRISM-sig is established based on this problem in [3] as follows.

Proposition 1 (Proposition 1 in [3]). *Under the assumption that Problem 4 is hard, the security against active attacks of PRISM-id performing N interactions has a winning probability bounded by $N/\#\mathsf{Primes}_a$.*

Proposition 2 (Proposition 2 in [3]). *If the hash function $\mathtt{H}_{\text{prime}}$ in Sect. 3.2 is a collision-resistant cryptographic hash function and Problem 4 is hard, then PRISM-sig is EUF-CMA secure.*

Next, we recall how to choose the parameters p and a to ensure a λ-bit security for classical attacks and a $\lambda/2$-bit security for quantum attacks, which is discussed in [3, §4.4].

One of the best methods for a key recovery attack on PRISM-id and PRISM-sig is to find an isogeny from E_0 to E_{vk} of smooth degree. We can use the Delfs-Galbraith algorithm [17] for this purpose. As we explained in Sect. 2.6, the expected time complexity of this algorithm is $\tilde{O}(\sqrt{p})$ in the classical setting, and $\tilde{O}(p^{1/4})$ in the quantum setting. Therefore, we require that p is at least approximately $2^{2\lambda}$.

The authors of [3] estimate the cost to compute a $q(2^a - q)$-isogeny from E_{vk} for $q \in \mathsf{Primes}_a$. They claim that its expected time complexity is at least $\tilde{O}(q^2)$ in the classical setting. Therefore, we require that a is at least approximately $\lambda/2$.

For PRISM-id, we require that the probability in Problem 4 is less than $2^{-\lambda}$. This leads to the requirement that $\#\mathsf{Primes}_a > 2^{\lambda}$. From the prime number theorem, we have

$$\#\mathsf{Primes}_a \approx \frac{2^a}{a \log 2} - \frac{2^{a-1}}{(a-1)\log 2} \approx \frac{2^a}{2a \log 2}.$$

Therefore, we require that $a > \lambda + \log_2 \lambda$.

For PRISM-sig, we require that the cost to find a collision in the hash function $\mathtt{H}_{\text{prime}}$ is greater than 2^{λ}. This can be achieved by ensuring that $\#\mathsf{Primes}_a > 2^{2\lambda}$, thus $a > 2\lambda + \log_2 \lambda$. However, they claim that $a > 2\lambda$ is enough to ensure security because one computation of $\mathtt{H}_{\text{prime}}$ requires another cryptographic hash function several times. For more details, see [3, §4.4].

4 Foundations of Our Attacks

In this section, we give algorithms and heuristics used in our attacks. From now on, the notation $\tilde{O}$ hides logarithmic factors in p as well as in its input. Our algorithms are classical algorithms and some of these are probabilistic. We consider the expected time complexity of these algorithms, not the worst-case time complexity.

4.1 Algorithms

We introduce the following algorithms used in our attacks.

- `ConstructField`$(p, k) \to \mathbb{F}_{p^{2k}}$: On input a prime p and a positive integer k, outputs the extension field $\mathbb{F}_{p^{2k}}$, whose representation will be explained later.
- `Isogeny`$(E, q, \mathbb{F}_{p^{2k}}) \to \varphi$: On input a supersingular elliptic curve E, a prime q, and the extension field $\mathbb{F}_{p^{2k}}$ such that $E[q] \subset E(\mathbb{F}_{p^{2k}})$, outputs an isogeny φ of degree q from E.
- `IsGoodPrime`$(p, q, B) \to$ True/False: On input distinct primes p and q and a bound B, outputs a boolean indicating whether there exists a positive integer $k \leq B$ such that $(-p)^k \equiv 1 \pmod{q}$.

Constructing Extension Fields (`ConstructField`(p, k)). Since our algorithms require operations in an extension field $\mathbb{F}_{p^{2k}}$ for some exponentially large k, we need an algorithm to construct a computable representation of $\mathbb{F}_{p^{2k}}$. We also need to analyze the cost of the construction and of the operations in $\mathbb{F}_{p^{2k}}$.

Let k be a positive integer, and consider the field extension $\mathbb{F}_{p^{2k}}/\mathbb{F}_{p^2}$. We assume that $\mathbb{F}_{p^{2k}}$ is expressed as $\mathbb{F}_{p^{2k}} = \mathbb{F}_{p^2}[X]/(F(X))$, where $F(X)$ is an irreducible polynomial of degree k over $\mathbb{F}_{p^2}$. Then, the cost of addition and multiplication in $\mathbb{F}_{p^{2k}}$ is in $\tilde{O}(k)$ times the cost of addition and multiplication in $\mathbb{F}_{p^2}$. This cost is achieved by using the polynomial multiplication algorithm [12, Algorithm 9.6.1] and polynomial modulo algorithm [12, Algorithm 9.6.4] with FFT integer multiplication (see [12, §9.5.8]).

Suppose that k is the product of $d_1, \ldots, d_n$, where d_i are positive integers. Consider the tower of field extensions

$$\mathcal{F}_0 = \mathbb{F}_{p^2} \subset \mathcal{F}_1 \subset \mathcal{F}_2 \subset \cdots \subset \mathcal{F}_n = \mathbb{F}_{p^{2k}},$$

where the extension degree of $\mathcal{F}_i$ over $\mathcal{F}_{i-1}$ is d_i. Similarly to the above, we assume that $\mathcal{F}_i = \mathcal{F}_{i-1}[X]/(F_i(X))$, where $F_i(X)$ is an irreducible polynomial of degree d_i over $\mathcal{F}_{i-1}$. Then, by the same discussion, we can show that the cost of addition and multiplication in $\mathbb{F}_{p^{2k}}$ is in $\tilde{O}(k)$.

The cost of inversion in $\mathbb{F}_{p^{2k}}$ is in $\tilde{O}(k^2)$ since the inversion can be done by the power of $p^{2k} - 2$ in $\mathbb{F}_{p^{2k}}$. The expected cost of square root in $\mathbb{F}_{p^{2k}}$ is in $\tilde{O}(k^2)$ by using a variant of the Tonelli-Shanks algorithm [2, Algorithm 5].

The remaining problem is how to construct $\mathbb{F}_{p^{2k}}$. To deal with this problem, we use the following lemma.

Lemma 2. *Let ℓ be a prime number, and i be a positive integer. Suppose that we are given a representation of $\mathbb{F}_{p^{2i}}$ by a tower of field extensions with the base field $\mathbb{F}_{p^2}$. Then there exists an algorithm with input ℓ and $\mathbb{F}_{p^{2i}}$ returning an irreducible polynomial of degree ℓ over $\mathbb{F}_{p^{2i}}$ having expected time complexity $\tilde{O}(\ell^3 \cdot i^2)$.*

Proof. We consider the following algorithm:

1. Choose a random monic polynomial $F(X) \in \mathbb{F}_{p^{2i}}[X]$ of degree ℓ.
2. Check whether $F(X)$ is irreducible over $\mathbb{F}_{p^{2i}}$.
3. If $F(X)$ is irreducible, return $F(X)$.
4. Otherwise, go to step 1.

The expected time complexity of step 1 is in $\tilde{O}(\ell \cdot i)$ since it can be done by generating $\ell \cdot i$ random elements in $\mathbb{F}_{p^2}$.

From Proposition 3.4.4 in [10], $F(X)$ is irreducible over $\mathbb{F}_{p^{2i}}$ if and only if $X^{p^{2\ell \cdot i}} \equiv X \pmod{F(X)}$ and $\gcd(X^{p^{2i}} - X, F(X)) = 1$. Let $r_1(X), r_\ell(X)$ be the representatives of the classes $X^{p^{2i}} \bmod F(X)$ and $X^{p^{2\ell \cdot i}} \bmod F(X)$ of degree less than ℓ, respectively. The expected time complexity of computing $r_\ell(X)$ is in $\tilde{O}(\ell^2 \cdot i^2)$. Thus, the expected time complexity of checking $X^{p^{2\ell \cdot i}} \equiv X \pmod{F(X)}$ is in $\tilde{O}(\ell^2 \cdot i^2)$. The expected time complexity of computing $r_1(X)$ is in $\tilde{O}(\ell \cdot i^2)$. The expected time complexity of computing $\gcd(r_1(X), F(X))$ is in $\tilde{O}(\ell^2 \cdot i)$. Therefore, the expected time complexity of step 2 is in $\tilde{O}(\ell^2 \cdot i^2)$.

A well-known result by Gauss (see [26, Exercise V.22]) tells us that the number of irreducible polynomials of degree ℓ over $\mathbb{F}_{p^{2i}}$ is $(p^{2\ell \cdot i} - p^{2i})/\ell$. Therefore, the probability that a random monic polynomial of degree ℓ over $\mathbb{F}_{p^{2i}}$ is irreducible is approximately $1/\ell$. Thus, the expected number of iterations of the above algorithm is approximately ℓ. Therefore, the expected time complexity of the algorithm is in $\tilde{O}(\ell^3 \cdot i^2)$. □

Now, we deal with the construction of $\mathbb{F}_{p^{2k}}$. Decompose k into prime factors $k = \ell_1 \cdots \ell_n$, where ℓ_i are (not necessarily distinct) prime numbers. We assume that ℓ_n is the largest prime factor of k. For $i = 1, \dots, n$, we define $q_i = p^{2\ell_1 \cdots \ell_i}$ and $q_0 = p^2$. Then, we construct $\mathbb{F}_{p^{2k}}$ by the tower of field extensions

$$\mathbb{F}_{p^2} = \mathbb{F}_{q_0} \subset \mathbb{F}_{q_1} \subset \cdots \subset \mathbb{F}_{q_n} = \mathbb{F}_{p^{2k}}.$$

For each $i = 1, \dots, n$, we construct $\mathbb{F}_{q_i}$ from $\mathbb{F}_{q_{i-1}}$ by finding an irreducible polynomial $f_i(X)$ of degree ℓ_i over $\mathbb{F}_{q_{i-1}}$. From Lemma 2, the expected time complexity of this procedure is $\tilde{O}(\ell_i^3(\ell_1 \cdots \ell_{i-1})^2)$. Therefore, the total expected time complexity is

$$\tilde{O}\left(\sum_{i=1}^{n} \ell_i^3 (\ell_1 \cdots \ell_{i-1})^2\right) \leq \tilde{O}\left(n \cdot \max_{i=1,\dots,n} \{\ell_i^3 (\ell_1 \cdots \ell_{i-1})^2\}\right)$$

Since $n \leq \log_2 k$ and $\ell_i^3(\ell_1 \cdots \ell_{i-1})^2 \leq k^3$, the total expected time complexity is $\tilde{O}(k^3)$. We denote the algorithm to construct a computable representation of $\mathbb{F}_{p^{2k}}$ by `ConstructField`(p, k).

Computing q-isogenies (Isogeny(E, q, $\mathbb{F}_{p^{2k}}$)). Next, we give an algorithm to compute a q-isogeny from a supersingular elliptic curve E for a prime q different from p.

Lemma 3. *Let E be a supersingular elliptic curve, q be a prime different from p, and k be a positive integer such that $(-p)^k \equiv 1 \pmod{q}$. Then there exists an algorithm with input E, q, and a computable representation of $\mathbb{F}_{p^{2k}}$ to compute (an efficient representation of) a q-isogeny with expected time complexity $\tilde{O}(\max\{k^2, k\sqrt{q}\})$.*

Proof (Special case). For simplicity, we prove the case where p and q satisfy the condition in PRISM. This case is sufficient for our attacks. In particular, we assume that $p = f2^e - 1$ for some odd integer f and $e \geq 2$, and that $q \in \mathsf{Primes}_a$ for some $a < e$. We give a proof for the general case in Appendix A.

We can assume that E is a Montgomery curve since a transformation to a Montgomery curve can be done in polynomial time. We consider the following algorithm to compute a q-isogeny φ from E.

1. Take a random point $P \in E(\mathbb{F}_{p^{2k}})$.
2. Compute the scalar multiplication $[((-p)^k - 1)/q]P$. Let Q be the result.
3. If $Q = 0$ then return to step 1.
4. Let φ be the isogeny of degree q with kernel $\langle Q \rangle$ and (P_a, Q_a) be a basis of $E[2^a]$. Compute the codomain E' and images $\varphi(P_a)$ and $\varphi(Q_a)$ by using the $\sqrt{\text{é}}$lu's formula by [6].
5. Output $(E', q, P_a, Q_a, \varphi(P_a), \varphi(Q_a))$ as an efficient representation of φ.

The point Q in step 2 has order q or 1 since $E(\mathbb{F}_{p^{2k}}) = E[(-p)^k - 1]$ and q is a prime. The output is an efficient representation of φ since $q < 2^a$. Therefore, the algorithm is correct.

In the following, we analyze the time complexity of each step. Note that these steps are done in the x-coordinates-only arithmetic on the Montgomery curve.

Step 1 consists of sampling a random element in $\mathbb{F}_{p^{2k}}$ as the x-coordinate of P and checking whether the corresponding y-coordinate is in $\mathbb{F}_{p^{2k}}$. The former requires k times random samplings in $\mathbb{F}_{p^2}$. The latter requires a constant number of additions and multiplications in $\mathbb{F}_{p^{2k}}$ and a square detection in $\mathbb{F}_{p^{2k}}$, which can be done by powering to $(p^{2k} - 1)/2$. These procedures are repeated until a $\mathbb{F}_{p^{2k}}$-rational point P is found. The expected number of iterations is 2. Therefore, the expected time complexity of step 1 is in $\tilde{O}(k^2)$.

Step 2 consists of $O(k)$ times differential additions and doublings on $E(\mathbb{F}_{p^{2k}})$. The differential addition and multiplication require a constant number of additions and multiplications in $\mathbb{F}_{p^{2k}}$. Therefore, the expected time complexity of step 2 is in $\tilde{O}(k^2)$.

The failure probability of step 3 is $1/q$. Therefore, we can expect that several iterations of steps 1–3 are sufficient to obtain a non-trivial point Q.

The $\sqrt{\text{é}}$lu's formula in step 4 requires $\tilde{O}(\sqrt{q})$ additions and multiplications in $\mathbb{F}_{p^{2k}}$. Therefore, the expected time complexity of step 4 is in $\tilde{O}(k\sqrt{q})$. This completes the proof. □

We denote the algorithm in Lemma 3 by $\texttt{Isogeny}(E, q, \mathbb{F}_{p^{2k}})$.

Checking the rationality of the q-torsion subgroup ($\texttt{IsGoodPrime}$ (p, q, B)). Finally, we give an algorithm to determine whether the q-torsion subgroup of a supersingular elliptic curve is rational over some extension field $\mathbb{F}_{p^{2k}}$ for $k \leq B$ for a given prime q and a positive integer B. As we explained in Sect. 2.1, the q-torsion subgroup of a supersingular elliptic curve is rational over $\mathbb{F}_{p^{2k}}$ if and only if $(-p)^k \equiv 1 \pmod{q}$ in our setting.

Lemma 4. *Let q be a prime different from p and B be a positive integer. Then there exists an algorithm with input q and B to determine whether q divides $\prod_{k=1}^{B}((-p)^k - 1)$ whose expected time complexity is in $\tilde{O}(\sqrt{B})$, where $\tilde{O}$ hides also polynomial factors in $\log q$.*

Proof. We use the algorithm given in [6, §3.2].

Let $b = \lfloor \sqrt{B} \rfloor$. Define two sets $I = \{1, \ldots, b\}$ and $J = \{0, b, \ldots, b(b-1)\}$. Then, the resultant of two polynomials $\prod_{i \in I}(X - (-p)^i)$ and $\prod_{j \in J}((-p)^j X - 1)$ in $\mathbb{F}_q[X]$ is equal to $\prod_{k=1}^{b^2}(1 - (-p)^k) \in \mathbb{F}_q$. This resultant can be computed in $\tilde{O}(b)$ operations in $\mathbb{F}_q$. Since q divides $\prod_{k=1}^{B}((-p)^k - 1)$ if and only if the resultant is equal to 0 or $\prod_{k=b^2+1}^{B}((-p)^k - 1) \equiv 0 \pmod{q}$, we can check whether q divides $\prod_{k=1}^{B}((-p)^k - 1)$ with expected time complexity in $\tilde{O}(\sqrt{B})$. □

We denote the algorithm in Lemma 4 by $\texttt{IsGoodPrime}(p, q, B)$.

4.2 Heuristic Assumptions

For positive integers a and B such that $B < 2^a$, we define a subset of Primes_a as

$$\mathsf{GoodPrimes}_{a,p,B} = \{q \in \mathsf{Primes}_a \mid \texttt{IsGoodPrime}(p, q, B) = \mathsf{True}\}.$$

We assume the following two heuristics related to this set.

Heuristic 1. *Let B be a positive integer less than 2^a. Then we assume that*

$$\#\mathsf{GoodPrimes}_{a,p,B} \approx \frac{B}{2a \log 2}.$$

Explanation. As we explained in Sect. 3.3, $\#\mathsf{Primes}_a \approx \frac{2^a}{2a \log 2}$. Let $\Phi_k(X)$ be the k-th cyclotomic polynomial. We assume that $\Phi_1(-p), \ldots, \Phi_B(-p)$ are independently and uniformly distributed over $\mathbb{Z}/q\mathbb{Z}$ for all $q \in \mathsf{Primes}_a$. For each k and q, the probability that q divides $\Phi_k(-p)$ is approximately $1/2^a$. Therefore, the expected number of primes $q \in \mathsf{Primes}_a$ such that q divides $\Phi_k(-p)$ for some $k \in [1, B]$ is approximately

$$\frac{B}{2^a} \cdot \#\mathsf{Primes}_a \approx \frac{B}{2a \log 2}.$$

Heuristic 2. *Let u be a positive real number in $[1, a]$ and B be a positive integer less than 2^a. Then we assume that for a prime q sampled uniformly at random from $\mathsf{GoodPrimes}_{a,p,B}$, the probability that $2^a - q$ is $2^{a/u}$-smooth depends only on u.*

Explanation. Let x be a positive real number. From the Dickman theorem [12, Theorem 1.4.9], the number of $x^{1/u}$-smooth positive integers less than x is asymptotically $x\rho(u)$, where $\rho(u)$ is the Dickman function. Assuming that 2^a is sufficiently large and that $2^a - q$ behaves as a uniform random integer in $[1, 2^a)$, we can expect that the probability that $2^a - q$ is $2^{a/u}$-smooth is approximately $\rho(u)$.

We conducted experiments to verify these heuristics. The results support our assumptions. The details of the experiments are given in Appendix B.

5 Attacks on PRISM-id

In this section, we give two classical forgery attacks on PRISM-id [3] whose expected time complexities are exponential in the security parameter, but slightly smaller than the claimed security level.

In the rest of the paper, we use the same notation as in Sect. 3. Let λ be the security parameter of PRISM-id. Hence the claimed expected time complexity of PRISM-id is at least proportional to 2^λ, up to polynomial factors in λ. Since PRISM-id uses $a \approx \lambda + \log \lambda$, our purpose is to show that the expected time complexity of our attacks is $\tilde{O}(2^{a\varepsilon})$ for some $\varepsilon < 1$.

We define a *forgery attack on PRISM-id* as a direct attack (Attack Game 18.1 in [8]). In this attack, the challenger and the attacker interact as follows.

1. The challenger generates a key pair $(E_{\mathrm{vk}}, I_{\mathrm{sk}})$ by the key generation algorithm of PRISM-id and sends E_{vk} to the attacker.
2. The challenger sends a challenge prime $q \in \mathsf{Primes}_a$ to the attacker.
3. The attacker outputs a response φ_{rsp}.

The attacker wins if $\texttt{VerIsogeny}(E_{\mathrm{vk}}, \varphi_{\mathrm{rsp}}, q) = \mathsf{True}$.

We also define a *forgery attack on PRISM-id with refusing challenge primes* as a forgery attack on PRISM-id in which the attacker can refuse a challenge prime q in step 2 and ask the challenger to send another challenge prime $q' \in \mathsf{Primes}_a$.

5.1 Forgery Attack on PRISM-idwithout refusing challenge primes

We first consider an attack in which the attacker cannot refuse a challenge prime q. This attack only succeeds when the challenge prime q is a good prime. Such a good prime appears with exponentially small probability, but the probability is greater than $2^{-a} \approx 2^{-(\lambda+\log \lambda)}$.

This attack is described in Algorithm 1. First, the attacker checks whether the challenge prime q is a good prime by using $\texttt{IsGoodPrime}(p, q, B_1)$ for some bound B_1 and $2^a - q$ is B_2-smooth for some bound B_2. If q does not satisfy these

Algorithm 1: Attack on PRISM-id

Input: A supersingular elliptic curve E, a prime q in Primes_a, and a positive real number $\varepsilon < 1/3$.
Output: An isogeny from E of degree $q(2^a - q)$.

1 $B_1 \leftarrow \lceil 2^{a\varepsilon} \rceil$;
2 $B_2 \leftarrow \max\{2^{a\varepsilon}, 2^{a(\varepsilon/3+1/6)}\}$;
3 **if** $\texttt{IsGoodPrime}(p, q, B_1) = \mathsf{False}$ *or* $2^a - q$ *is not* B_2*-smooth* **then**
4   **return** Failure;
5 $k \leftarrow 1$;
6 **while** $(-p)^k \not\equiv 1 \pmod{q}$ **do**
7     $k \leftarrow k + 1$;
8 $\mathbb{F}_{p^{2k}} \leftarrow \texttt{ConstructField}(p, k)$;
9 $\varphi \leftarrow \texttt{Isogeny}(E, q, \mathbb{F}_{p^{2k}})$;
10 $F \leftarrow$ the codomain of φ;
11 Let $\ell_1^{e_1} \cdots \ell_n^{e_n}$ be the prime factorization of $2^a - q$;
12 **for** $i \leftarrow 1$ **to** n **do**
13     $\mathbb{F}_{p^{2(\ell_i - 1)}} \leftarrow \texttt{ConstructField}(p, \ell_i - 1)$;
14   **for** $j \leftarrow 1$ **to** e_i **do**
15         $\psi \leftarrow \texttt{Isogeny}(F, \ell_i, \mathbb{F}_{p^{2(\ell_i - 1)}})$;
16         $F \leftarrow$ the codomain of ψ;
17         $\varphi \leftarrow \psi \circ \varphi$;
18 **return** φ;

conditions, the attacker fails. Otherwise, the attacker finds the smallest k such that $E[q] \subset E(\mathbb{F}_{p^{2k}})$. Then, the attacker computes a q-isogeny and ℓ-isogenies for all prime factors ℓ of $2^a - q$. Finally, the attacker outputs the composition of these isogenies as a response. The success probability and expected time complexity of this attack are given in the following theorem.

Theorem 1. *Assume Heuristic 1 and Heuristic 2. For any positive real number $\varepsilon < 1/3$, there exists a positive constant C_ε depending only on ε and a forgery attack on PRISM-id with success probability $C_\varepsilon \cdot 2^{-a(1-\varepsilon)}$ and expected time complexity $\tilde{O}(\max\{2^{3a\varepsilon}, 2^{a(\varepsilon+1/2)}\})$.*

Proof. We show the forgery attack on PRISM-id in Algorithm 1. From Heuristic 1 and Heuristic 2, we can expect that the number of primes $q \in \mathsf{Primes}_a$ which pass the check in line 3 is approximately $C_\varepsilon \cdot 2^{a\varepsilon}/(2a \log 2)$, where C_ε is a constant depending only on ε. Therefore, the success probability of this algorithm is approximately

$$\frac{C_\varepsilon \cdot 2^{a\varepsilon}}{2a \log 2} \cdot \frac{1}{\#\mathsf{Primes}_a} = C_\varepsilon \cdot 2^{-a(1-\varepsilon)}.$$

The expected time complexity is the sum of those of the following procedures:

1. $\texttt{ConstructField}(p, k)$,

2. `IsGoodPrime`(p, q, B_1),
3. the factorization of $2^a - q$,
4. finding k such that $(-p)^k \equiv 1 \pmod{q}$ (**while** loop in line 6),
5. `Isogeny`$(E, q, \mathbb{F}_{p^{2k}})$,
6. `ConstructField`$(p, \ell_i - 1)$ for $i = 1, \ldots, n$,
7. `Isogeny`$(F, \ell_i, \ell_i - 1)$ (e_i times) for $i = 1, \ldots, n$.

As in Algorithm 1, we let $B_2 = \max\{2^{a\varepsilon}, 2^{a(\varepsilon/3+1/6)}\}$. It suffices to show that each step has the expected time complexity in $\tilde{O}(B_2^3)$.

The expected time complexity of step 1 is $\tilde{O}(2^{3a\varepsilon})$ as explained in Sect. 4.1. The expected time complexity of step 2 is $\tilde{O}(2^{a\varepsilon/2})$ by Lemma 4. In the factorization in step 3, we can find all prime factors of $2^a - q$ less than B_2 with expected time complexity in $\tilde{O}(\sqrt{B_2})$ by the Pollard rho algorithm [12, Algorithm 5.2.1].[1] The expected time complexity of step 4 is $\tilde{O}(B_1) = \tilde{O}(2^{a\varepsilon})$ since $k \leq B_1$ and the exponentiation $(-p)^k \bmod q$ can be computed in $O(\log k)$ multiplications in $\mathbb{F}_q$. The expected time complexity of step 5 is $\tilde{O}(2^{a(\varepsilon+\frac{1}{2})})$ by Lemma 3. For each prime ℓ_i in the factorization of $2^a - q$, the expected time complexity of step 6 is $\tilde{O}(B_2^3)$ and the expected time complexity of step 7 is $\tilde{O}(B_2^2)$. The number $\sum_{i=1}^{n} e_i$ of iterations of the two **for** loops in Algorithm 1 is at most a. Therefore, the expected time complexity of Algorithm 1 is $\tilde{O}(B_2^3) = \tilde{O}(\max\{2^{3a\varepsilon}, 2^{a(\varepsilon+1/2)}\})$.
□

In particular, we have the following forgery attack on PRISM-id.

Corollary 1. *Assuming Heuristic 1 and Heuristic 2, there exists a forgery attack on PRISM-id with success probability $\tilde{\Theta}(2^{-3(\lambda+\log\lambda)/4})$ and expected time complexity $\tilde{O}(2^{3\lambda/4})$.*

Proof. Since $a \approx \lambda + \log \lambda$, it follows from Theorem 1 by taking $\varepsilon = 1/4$. □

Remark 2. The coefficient C_ε in the success probability in Theorem 1 is approximately $\rho(a/\log_2(B_2)) = \rho((\max\{\varepsilon, \varepsilon/3 + 1/6\})^{-1})$, where ρ is the Dickman function. This coefficient is not so small when ε is close to 1/3. For example, when $\varepsilon = 1/4$, we have $C_\varepsilon \approx 0.0049$.

Using a Proving Oracle. We consider an active attack (Attack Game 18.3 in [8]), where the attacker can interact with a proving oracle $\texttt{ProvingOracle}_{E_{\mathrm{vk}}}(q)$ that takes a prime $q \in \mathsf{Primes}_a$ as input and returns an efficient representation of an isogeny of degree $q(2^a - q)$ from E_{vk}.

By using a proving oracle, we can mitigate the second condition that $2^a - q$ is B_2-smooth in the attack in Algorithm 1. Instead, we only require that $2^a - q$ is the product of a B_2-smooth number and an integer t such that there exists

[1] ECM (elliptic curve method) [12, Algorithm 7.4.2] has subexponential expected time complexity in $\log B_2$, and is faster than the Pollard rho algorithm in most cases. However, it is enough to use the Pollard rho algorithm to prove the expected time complexity of our attack.

Algorithm 2: IsogenyFromOracle(q, t, ProvingOracle$_E$)

Input: A prime q in Primes$_a$, a positive integer t, and a proving oracle ProvingOracle$_E$.
Output: An isogeny from E of degree t.

$s \leftarrow 1$;
while $st < 2^{a-1}$ *and* $2^a - st$ *is not a prime in* Primes$_a \setminus \{q\}$ **do**
  $s \leftarrow s + 2$;
if $st \geq 2^{a-1}$ **then**
  return Failure;
$\varphi \leftarrow$ ProvingOracle$_E(2^a - st)$;
$\psi \leftarrow$ the st-isogeny from E obtained from φ; // Using Kani's lemma.
$k \leftarrow$ the smallest positive integer such that $(-p)^k \equiv 1 \pmod{s}$; // $k < s$.
$\mathbb{F}_{p^{2k}} \leftarrow$ ConstructField(p, k);
$(P, Q) \leftarrow$ a basis of $E[s]$; // P and Q are in $E(\mathbb{F}_{p^{2k}})$.
$\psi_s \leftarrow$ an isogeny of degree s with kernel $\langle \psi(P), \psi(Q) \rangle$; // $\psi = \hat{\psi}_s \circ \psi_t$ for a t-isogeny ψ_t.
$(P_a, Q_a) \leftarrow$ a basis of $E[2^a]$;
$\psi_t(P_a) \leftarrow [1/s]\psi_s \circ \psi(P_a)$, $\psi_t(Q_a) \leftarrow [1/s]\psi_s \circ \psi(Q_a)$;
return ψ_t; // expressed by $(P_a, Q_a, \psi_t(P_a), \psi_t(Q_a))$.

a small integer s such that $2^a - st$ is a prime in Primes$_a$ different from q. This mitigation does not improve the asymptotic success probability of the attack since the probability that $2^a - q$ is B_2-smooth is a constant depending only on ε by Heuristic 2. However, it can improve the constant factor in the success probability. In the following, we explain the reason why we can mitigate the condition by using a proving oracle.

Let d be the largest B_2-smooth number dividing $2^a - q$, and let $t = (2^a - q)/d$. Suppose that there exists a small integer s such that $2^a - st$ is a prime in Primes$_a$ different from q. We can expect that such an s exists when $2^{a-1}/t > 2a \log 2$ since the probability that $2^a - st$ is a prime is approximately $1/(2a \log 2)$ for a random $s \in [1, 2^a/t]$. Then the attacker can obtain an isogeny of degree t by calling a proving oracle with the input $2^a - st$. This is done as follows: First, the attacker obtains an isogeny of degree $(2^a - st)st$ from E by calling the oracle with the input $2^a - st$. Then, the attacker computes an isogeny φ of degree st from E by using Kani's lemma. By evaluating a basis of $E[s]$ under φ, the attacker obtains generators of the kernel of degree s part of $\hat{\varphi}$. This allows the attacker to compute an isogeny of degree t from E. We describe this algorithm in Algorithm 2. In the algorithm, we can expect that s is $O(a)$ as explained above. Therefore, the expected time complexity of the algorithm is a polynomial in $\log p$.

We describe the attack on PRISM-id using a proving oracle in Algorithm 3.

Algorithm 3: Attack on PRISM-id with a proving oracle

Input: A supersingular elliptic curve E, a prime q in Primes_a, a positive real number $\varepsilon < 1/3$, and a proving oracle $\mathtt{ProvingOracle}_E$.

Output: An isogeny from E of degree $q(2^a - q)$.

1 $B_1 \leftarrow \lceil 2^{a\varepsilon/3} \rceil$;
2 $B_2 \leftarrow \max\{2^{a\varepsilon}, 2^{a(\varepsilon/3+1/6)}\}$;
3 **if** $\mathtt{IsGoodPrime}(p, q, B_1) =$ False **then**
4   **return** Failure;
5 Let s be the largest B_2-smooth number dividing $2^a - q$;
6 $t \leftarrow (2^a - q)/s$;
7 **if** $t = 1$ **then**
8   Do the same as after line 5 in Algorithm 1;
9 **else**
10     $\varphi \leftarrow \mathtt{IsogenyFromOracle}(q, t, \mathtt{ProvingOracle}_E)$;
11   **if** $\varphi =$ Failure **then**
12   **return** Failure;
13     $F \leftarrow$ the codomain of φ;
14     $k \leftarrow 1$;
15   **while** $(-p)^k \not\equiv 1 \pmod{q}$ **do**
16         $k \leftarrow k + 1$;
17     $\mathbb{F}_{p^{2k}} \leftarrow \mathtt{ConstructField}(p, k)$;
18     $\psi \leftarrow \mathtt{Isogeny}(F, q, \mathbb{F}_{p^{2k}})$;
19     $\varphi \leftarrow \psi \circ \varphi$;
20     $F \leftarrow$ the codomain of φ;
21   Let $\ell_1^{e_1} \cdots \ell_n^{e_n}$ be the prime factorization of s;
22   **for** $i \leftarrow 1$ **to** n **do**
23         $\mathbb{F}_{p^{2(\ell_i-1)}} \leftarrow \mathtt{ConstructField}(p, \ell_i - 1)$;
24   **for** $j \leftarrow 1$ **to** e_i **do**
25             $\psi \leftarrow \mathtt{Isogeny}(F, \ell_i, \mathbb{F}_{p^{2(\ell_i-1)}})$;
26             $F \leftarrow$ the codomain of ψ;
27             $\varphi \leftarrow \psi \circ \varphi$;
28   **return** φ;

5.2 Forgery Attack on PRISM-idwith refusing challenge primes

If we allow the attacker to refuse a challenge prime q, then we can construct a forgery attack with expected time complexity in $\tilde{O}(2^{6a/7})$. This attack is obtained by refusing challenge primes until the condition in line 3 in Algorithm 3 is satisfied. At first glance, the expected time complexity of this attack seems to be greater than $2^{a(1-\varepsilon)} \cdot 2^{3a\varepsilon} = 2^{a(1+2\varepsilon)}$. However, the latter part of Algorithm 3 is executed only when the condition in line 3 is satisfied. Therefore, the expected time complexity of this attack is the sum of the expected computational complexities of obtaining a prime q passing the check in line 3 and the remaining part of the algorithm. We explicitly state this in the following theorem.

Theorem 2. *Assume Heuristic 1 and Heuristic 2. There exists a forgery attack on PRISM-id that allows the attacker to refuse a challenge prime q with expected time complexity in* $\tilde{O}(2^{6a/7})$.

Proof. Consider Algorithm 1 with $\varepsilon = 2/7$ and modify it as follows:

- q is not given as input, but sampled uniformly at random from Primes_a.
- If the condition in line 3 is not satisfied, then the algorithm resamples q uniformly at random from Primes_a and checks the condition again.

Since $B_1 = \lceil 2^{2a/7} \rceil$ in this case, the expected number of checks of the condition in line 3 is approximately $C(2a \log 2/B_1) \cdot \#\mathsf{Primes}_a \approx C \cdot 2^{5a/7}$, where C is a constant derived from Heuristic 2. The expected time complexity of checking the condition in line 3 is in $\tilde{O}(2^{a/7})$ by Lemma 4. Therefore, the expected time complexity of finding a prime q passing the check in line 3 is in $\tilde{O}(2^{6a/7})$.

The remaining part of the algorithm is in $\tilde{O}(2^{6a/7})$ as shown in the proof of Theorem 1. This completes the proof. □

5.3 Countermeasure

For PRISM-id to be secure against the forgery attacks in the previous subsections, the protocol should use a large enough a. Since the proposed p for PRISM-id in [3] is of the form $p = f2^e - 1$, where f is a small odd integer and $e \approx 2\lambda$, we can increase a as far as $a < 2\lambda$ while keeping $E[2^a]$ rational.

We propose two sizes of a for PRISM-id.

- **Conservative size:** $a = \frac{4}{3}\lambda$. This size ensures the following: In Algorithm 1 with any ε, the success probability is less than $2^{-\lambda}$ or the expected time complexity is greater than approximately 2^λ.
- **Aggressive size:** $a = \frac{7}{6}\lambda$. This size ensures that the expected time complexity of the forgery attack in §5.2 is greater than approximately 2^λ.

Note that for the aggressive size, there exists a forgery attack whose success probability is greater than $2^{-\lambda}$ and whose expected time complexity is less than 2^λ. For example, by taking $\varepsilon = 3/14$ in Algorithm 1, the success probability is proportional to $2^{-11\lambda/12}$ and the expected time complexity is $\tilde{O}(2^{5\lambda/6})$.

5.4 Quantum Setting

In the quantum setting, we can slightly improve the expected time complexities of our forgery attacks by using Grover's search algorithm [22]. However, the improvement does not affect the quantum security of PRISM-id.

In our attacks, we can apply Grover's search to irreducible polynomial search in the algorithm $\mathtt{ConstructField}(p, k)$. As a result, the expected time complexity of $\mathtt{ConstructField}(p, k)$ is improved from $\tilde{O}(k^3)$ to $\tilde{O}(k^{5/2})$. This improvement reduces the expected time complexities of the attack in Theorem 1 from

$\tilde{O}(\max\{2^{3a\varepsilon}, 2^{a(\varepsilon+1/2)}\})$ to $\tilde{O}(\max\{2^{5a\varepsilon/2}, 2^{a(\varepsilon+1/2)}\})$ and that of the attack in Theorem 2 from $\tilde{O}(2^{6a/7})$ to $\tilde{O}(2^{5a/6})$.

On the other hand, there are more efficient quantum algorithms to break PRISM-id. For example, the Delfs-Galbraith algorithm [17] combined with Grover's search can find an isogeny from E_0 to E_{vk} with expected time complexity in $\tilde{O}(p^{1/4})$ (see [7] for more details on the quantum algorithms for finding isogenies). Since $p \approx 2^{2\lambda}$ and $a \approx \lambda + \log_2 \lambda$ in PRISM-id, this expected time complexity is smaller than those of our forgery attacks in the quantum setting.

6 Attack on the Underlying Problem

In this section, we consider an attack on the underlying problem of PRISM-id (Problem 4), which is to find an isogeny of degree $q(2^a - q)$ for a prime $q \in \mathsf{Primes}_a$. The difference from the forgery attacks in Sect. 5 is that the attacker can choose the prime q as they like. This allows the attacker to take $\varepsilon = 0$ in Algorithm 1, thus there exists an attack with expected time complexity in $\tilde{O}(2^{a/2})$.

Note that an attack on the underlying problem does not immediately lead to a forgery attack on PRISM-id. Therefore, the results in this section should be regarded as a warning for constructing a cryptosystem based on the hardness of Problem 4.

To describe the attack, we define the following problem.

Problem 5. Given a supersingular elliptic curve E, compute an isogeny of degree $q(2^a - q)$ from E with a prime $q \in \mathsf{Primes}_a$.

Obviously, Problem 4 reduces to Problem 5. Our attack on Problem 5 is described in Algorithm 4. The difference from Algorithm 1 is that the attacker can choose the prime q as they like. To find a prime q such that $E[q] \subset E(\mathbb{F}_{p^{2k}})$ for some small k, the attacker uses the cyclotomic polynomials. Once the attacker finds a prime q such that $E[q] \subset E(\mathbb{F}_{p^{2k}})$ for some small k and that $2^a - q$ is smooth, the following steps are the same as those in Algorithm 1. The expected time complexity of this attack is given in the following theorem.

Theorem 3. *Assuming Heuristic 1 and Heuristic 2, there exists an algorithm to solve Problem 5 with expected time complexity* $\tilde{O}(2^{a/2})$.

Proof. We show the algorithm in Algorithm 4.

From Heuristic 1 and Heuristic 2, we can expect that the expected iteration number of the while loop in Algorithm 4 is proportional to a. Thus, k is also proportional to a. As explained in the proof of Theorem 1, finding a factor in Primes_a of $\Phi_k(-p)$ can be done in $\tilde{O}(2^{a/2})$ and finding all prime factors less than $2^{a/6}$ of $2^a - q$ can be done in $\tilde{O}(2^{a/12})$. Therefore, the expected time complexity of the while loop is in $\tilde{O}(2^{a/2})$.

The expected time complexity of `ConstructField`(p, k) in line 13 is bounded by some polynomial in $\log p$ since k is proportional to $a < \log p$.

Algorithm 4: Attack on Problem 5

Input: A supersingular elliptic curve E.
Output: An isogeny from E of degree $q(2^a - q)$ with a prime $q \in \mathsf{Primes}_a$.

$k \leftarrow 1$;
$q \leftarrow 0$;
while $q = 0$ **do**
  $\Phi \leftarrow$ the k-th cyclotomic polynomial;
  if *The prime factors of* $\Phi(-p)$ *contain a prime in* Primes_a **then**
    $q \leftarrow$ a prime factor of $\Phi(-p)$ in Primes_a;
    if $2^a - q$ *is not* $2^{a/6}$*-smooth* **then**
      $q \leftarrow 0$;
      $k \leftarrow k + 1$;
  else
    $k \leftarrow k + 1$;
Let $\ell_1^{e_1} \cdots \ell_n^{e_n}$ be the prime factorization of $2^a - q$;
$\mathbb{F}_{p^{2k}} \leftarrow \mathtt{ConstructField}(p, k)$;
$\varphi \leftarrow \mathtt{Isogeny}(E, q, \mathbb{F}_{p^{2k}})$;
$F \leftarrow$ the codomain of φ;
for $i \leftarrow 1$ **to** n **do**
  $\mathbb{F}_{p^{2(\ell_i - 1)}} \leftarrow \mathtt{ConstructField}(p, \ell_i - 1)$;
  for $j \leftarrow 1$ **to** e_i **do**
    $\psi \leftarrow \mathtt{Isogeny}(F, \ell_i, \mathbb{F}_{p^{2(\ell_i - 1)}})$;
    $F \leftarrow$ the codomain of ψ;
    $\varphi \leftarrow \psi \circ \varphi$;
return φ;

The isogeny φ in the algorithm is computed by the algorithm $\mathtt{Isogeny}(E, q, \mathbb{F}_{p^{2k}})$ in Lemma 3. The expected time complexity of this algorithm is in $\tilde{O}(2^{a/2})$.

The number $\sum_{i=1}^{t} e_i$ of iterations of the two **for** loops in Algorithm 4 is at most a. In each iteration, the expected time complexities of $\mathtt{ConstructField}(p, \ell_i - 1)$ and $\mathtt{Isogeny}(F, \ell_i, \ell_i - 1)$ are in $\tilde{O}(2^{a/2})$ and $\tilde{O}(2^{a/3})$, respectively.

Therefore, the total expected time complexity of the algorithm is in $\tilde{O}(2^{a/2})$. □

As in the attack on PRISM-id, we can mitigate the condition that $2^a - q$ is $2^{a/6}$-smooth by using SPEDIO. Unlike $\mathtt{ProvingOracle}_E$, we can call SPEDIO with input a supersingular elliptic curve different from E. In other words, we have $\mathtt{ProvingOracle}_{E'}$ for all supersingular elliptic curves E'. By using SPEDIO, the attacker could obtain a t-isogeny from E even in the case that Algorithm 2 fails.

This is done as follows: Let t be a non-smooth factor of $2^a - q$. Suppose that t decomposes into a product $t_1 \cdots t_n$ such that there exist small integers $s_1, \ldots, s_n$ satisfying $2^a - s_i t_i \in \mathsf{Primes}_a \setminus \{q\}$ for all $i = 1, \ldots, n$. Then the attacker can obtain a t-isogeny from E as follows:

1. Let E_1 be E.
2. For $i = 1, \ldots, n$,
   (a) $\varphi_i \leftarrow \texttt{IsogenyFromOracle}(E_i, t_i, \texttt{ProvingOracle}_{E_i})$
   (b) Let E_{i+1} be the codomain of φ_i.
3. Output $\varphi_n \circ \cdots \circ \varphi_2 \circ \varphi_1$.

7 Conclusion

We proposed classical forgery attacks on PRISM-id in scenarios where refusing a challenge is allowed and where it is not. In both cases, we showed that the original parameters in PRISM-id do not achieve the claimed security level. We also proposed a countermeasure against our attacks. Additionally, we analyzed the underlying problem of PRISM-id and gave an explicit expected time complexity for solving it. We believe that our work provides valuable insights into the security of PRISM-id and is useful for constructing new protocols based on the hardness of the given-degree isogeny problem.

Acknowledgments. The authors thank Shingo Sato for valuable discussions on attacks against identification schemes. This work was supported by JST K Program Grant Number JPMJKP24U2, Japan.

A Proof of Lemma 3 for the General Case

We give a proof of Lemma 3 for the general case. In particular, we allow p and q to be arbitrary primes distinct from each other.

Let ψ be the second Chebyshev function, i.e.,

$$\psi(x) = \sum_{k \in \mathbb{N}} \sum_{\ell^k \leq x} \log \ell = \sum_{\ell \leq x} \lfloor \log_\ell x \rfloor \log \ell,$$

where ℓ runs over all primes. From Theorem 414 in [23], there exists a constant C such that $\psi(x) > Cx$ for all $x > 0$. This means that there exists a $(\log q)/C$-powersmooth number greater than q. Let $\ell_1^{e_1} \ldots \ell_n^{e_n}$ be the prime factorization of this number.

For $i = 1, \ldots, n$, let (R_i, S_i) be a basis of $E[\ell_i^{e_i}]$. Note that $E[\ell_i^{e_i}]$ is rational over the extension field of $\mathbb{F}_{p^2}$ of degree $(\ell_i - 1)\ell_i^{e_i - 1}$. Since $\ell_i^{e_i} \leq (\log q)/C$ and $n < \log_2 q$, we can compute (R_i, S_i) for all $i = 1, \ldots, n$ with expected time complexity in polynomial in $\log p$ and $\log q$.

We use these bases $\{(R_i, S_i)\}_i$ instead of (P_a, Q_a) in the proof of Lemma 3 for the special case. The images $\varphi(R_i)$ and $\varphi(S_i)$ under the q-isogeny in step 4 can also be computed in $\tilde{O}(k\sqrt{q})$. Therefore, the expected time complexity of the algorithm for the general case is also in $\tilde{O}(\max\{k^2, k\sqrt{q}\})$.

As in the proof of the special case, we let E' be the codomain of φ. Then, $(E', q, \{R_i, S_i, \varphi(R_i), \varphi(S_i)\}_i)$ is an efficient representation of φ with respect to the 8-dimensional isogeny computation in [34] since $(\sum_i R_i, \sum_i S_i)$ is a basis of $E[\prod_i \ell_i^{e_i}]$. Note that we do not compute this basis explicitly and the computation can be done in polynomial time by using a similar approach as in [20, Algorithm 2].

B Experiments to Confirm Heuristics

We show experimental results to confirm Heuristic 1 and Heuristic 2.

B.1 Experiments for Heuristic 1

We show experimental results to confirm Heuristic 1. The setting in our experiment is as follows: For a given a, we chose a prime p of the form $2^{2a-1}f - 1$, where f is the smallest positive integer such that p is a prime number.

Then, we conducted two experiments:

1. We computed the cardinality of $\mathsf{GoodPrimes}_{a,p,B}$ in Heuristic 1 for $B = 1, \ldots, 2^a - 1$.
2. We searched for the prime factors of $\Phi_k(-p)$ in Primes_a for $k = 1, \ldots, 4a$.

The first experiment is conducted for $a = 10, 20$. The results are shown in Fig. 1. In the figure, the horizontal axis is B and the vertical axis is the cardinality of $\mathsf{GoodPrimes}_{a,p,B}$. The blue line is the exact cardinality of $\mathsf{GoodPrimes}_{a,p,B}$, and the orange line is the number predicted by Heuristic 1. The results show that there are slightly more good primes than predicted by Heuristic 1.

In the second experiment, we chose $a = 30, 40, 50$. For searching for the prime factors of $\Phi_k(-p)$ in Primes_a, we use the Pollard rho algorithm. The results are shown in Table 2. The number of the prime factors of $\Phi_k(-p)$ in Primes_a for $k = 1, \ldots, 4a$ is equal to the cardinality of $\mathsf{GoodPrimes}_{a,p,4a}$. Therefore, Heuristic 1 predicts that the number is $2/\log 2 \approx 2.8854$. The results almost match the expected number.

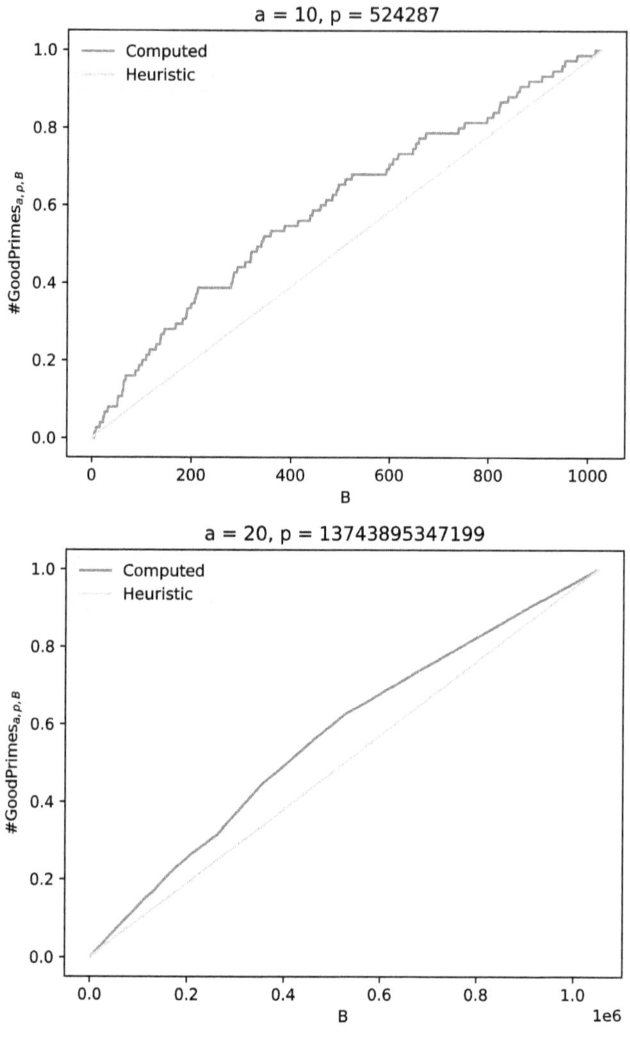

Fig. 1. The cardinality of $\mathsf{GoodPrimes}_{a,p,B}$ for $a = 10, 20$ and $B \in [1, 2^a - 1]$. The horizontal axis is B, and the vertical axis is the cardinality of $\mathsf{GoodPrimes}_{a,p,B}$. The blue line is the computed cardinality of $\mathsf{GoodPrimes}_{a,p,B}$, and the orange line is the cardinality predicted by Heuristic 1.

We also confirm that a proving oracle can help the attacker to obtain an isogeny of degree t, which is a non-smooth factor of $2^a - q$. The results are shown in Table 3. There are four cases where the search for another $q' \in \mathsf{Primes}_a$ fails. In these cases, the attack on PRISM-id with a proving oracle should search for a different prime q. On the other hand, the attack on Problem 4 can succeed in some of these cases by using SPEDIO as explained in Sect. 6. Indeed, except for the case of $q = 876847801$, we can find q' by decomposing a non-smooth factor t of $2^a - q$.

Table 2. Integers k such that $\Phi_k(-p)$ has a prime factor q in Primes_a and the factorization of $2^a - q$. The factors in red are prime factors greater than $2^{a/6}$.

a	p	k	q s.t. $q \mid \Phi_k(-p)$	$2^a - q$
30	$2^{61} - 1$	5	625343471	$13 \cdot 31 \cdot 1112651$
		62	715827883	$3 \cdot 7 \cdot 11 \cdot 31 \cdot 151 \cdot 331$
		100	876847801	$3 \cdot 65631341$
		110	627381701	$11 \cdot 109 \cdot 372277$
40	$2^{80} \cdot 15 - 1$	81	851187842929	$3 \cdot 577 \cdot 143456837$
		95	599173923731	$5 \cdot 479 \cdot 14033 \cdot 14887$
		160	710949960001	$3 \cdot 5^2 \cdot 5180822237$
50	$2^{99} \cdot 9 - 1$	75	815037005161201	$3^2 \cdot 7 \cdot 13 \cdot 263 \cdot 1443209059$
		170	710540400578051	$13 \cdot 461 \cdot 2039 \cdot 33990899$
		183	756997340934253	$3^2 \cdot 11 \cdot 3726288544529$

Table 3. Given $q \in \mathsf{Primes}_a$ and t a non-smooth factor of $2^a - q$, the table shows the result of searching s such that $q' := 2^a - st$ is a prime in Primes_a.

a	q	t	s	q'
30	625343471	1112651	$3 \cdot 5^2$	990292999
	715827883	$151 \cdot 331$	3	1073591881
	876847801	65631341	Failure	–
	627381701	$109 \cdot 372277$	Failure	–
		109	$3 \cdot 5$	1073740189
		372277	$5 \cdot 13$	1049543819
40	851187842929	$577 \cdot 143456837$	Failure	–
		577	$3 \cdot 5$	1099511619121
		143456837	3^2	1098220516243
	599173923731	$479 \cdot 14033 \cdot 14887$	3	799309005349
	710949960001	5180822237	19	1001076005273
50	815037005161201	1443209059	3	1125895577215447
	710540400578051	$461 \cdot 2039 \cdot 33990899$	Failure	–
		$461 \cdot 2039$	$3 \cdot 19$	1125899853263821
		33990899	3	1125899804869927
	756997340934253	3726288544529	49	943311768160703

B.2 Experiments for Heuristic 2

To confirm Heuristic 2, we computed the ratio

$$\frac{\#\{q \in \mathsf{GoodPrimes}_{a,p,B} \mid 2^a - q \text{ is } (2^{a/u})\text{-smooth}\}}{\#\mathsf{GoodPrimes}_{a,p,B}}$$

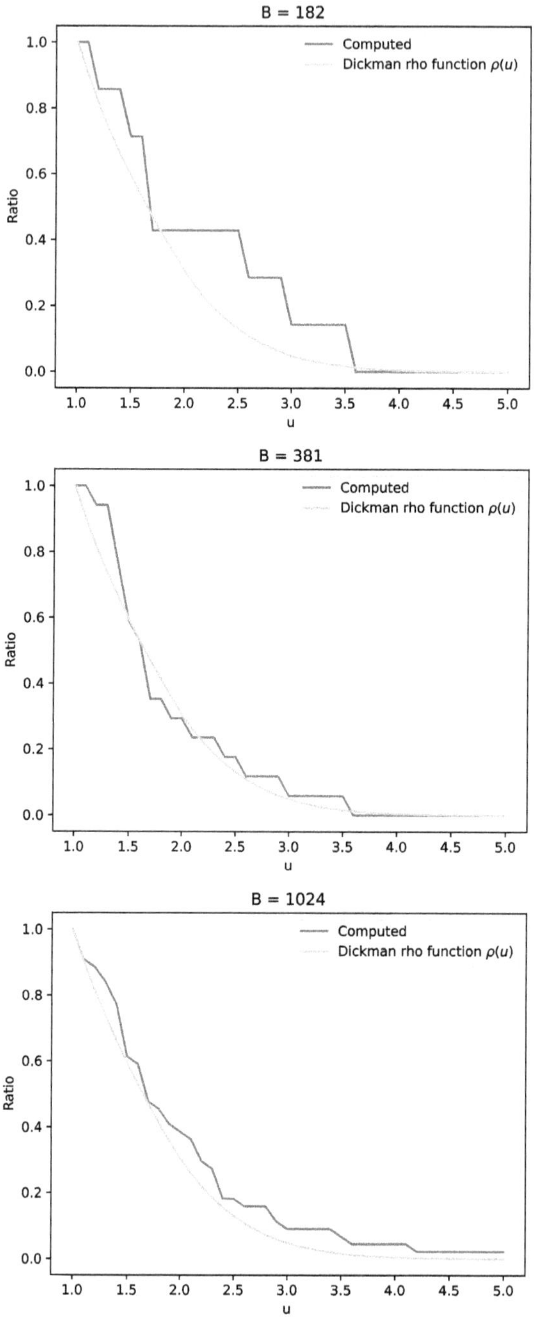

Fig. 2. The ratio of the number of $q \in \mathsf{GoodPrimes}_{a,p,B}$ such that $2^a - q$ is $(2^{a/u})$-smooth to the cardinality of $\mathsf{GoodPrimes}_{a,p,B}$ for $a = 30$ and $B = B_1 = \lceil 2^{a\varepsilon} \rceil$ with $\varepsilon = 1/4$ (top), $\varepsilon = 2/7$ (middle), and $\varepsilon = 1/3$ (bottom). The horizontal axis is u, and the vertical axis is the ratio. The blue line is the computed ratio, and the orange line is the Dickman function $\rho(u)$.

by listing all the primes $q \in \mathsf{GoodPrimes}_{a,p,B}$ and checking if $2^a - q$ is $(2^{a/u})$-smooth. As explained in Sect. 4.2, we expect this ratio to be close to the Dickman function $\rho(u)$.

We chose $a = 30$ and $p = 2^{61} - 1$, as in the previous experiments. The bound B was set to $B_1 = \lceil 2^{a\varepsilon} \rceil$ as in Algorithm 1 for $\varepsilon \in \left\{\frac{1}{4}, \frac{2}{7}, \frac{1}{3}\right\}$. Note that the first two values of ε are used in Corollary 1 and Theorem 2, respectively, and that the last value is the upper bound in Theorem 1. Then, we computed the above ratio for u in steps 0.1 over the interval $[1, 5]$. The results are shown in Fig. 2. As predicted by Heuristic 2, the ratio is close to the Dickman function $\rho(u)$.

References

1. Aardal, M.A., et al.: SQIsign. Technical report, National Institute of Standards and Technology (2024). https://csrc.nist.gov/Projects/pqc-dig-sig/round-2-additional-signatures
2. Adj, G., Rodríguez-Henríquez, F.: Square root computation over even extension fields. IEEE Trans. Comput. **63**(11), 2829–2841 (2014). https://doi.org/10.1109/TC.2013.145
3. Basso, A., et al.: PRISM: simple and compact identification and signatures from large prime degree isogenies. In: Jager, T., Pan, J. (eds.) Public-Key Cryptography - PKC 2025, pp. 300–332. Springer Nature Switzerland, Cham (2025)
4. Basso, A., et al.: SQIsign2D-West - the fast, the small, and the safer. In: Chung, K.M., Sasaki, Y. (eds.) ASIACRYPT 2024, Part III. LNCS, vol. 15486, pp. 339–370. Springer, Singapore (2024). https://doi.org/10.1007/978-981-96-0891-1_11
5. Basso, A., Maino, L.: POKÉ: A compact and efficient PKE from higher-dimensional isogenies. In: Fehr, S., Fouque, P.A. (eds.) EUROCRYPT 2025, Part II. LNCS, vol. 15602, pp. 94–123. Springer, Cham (2025). https://doi.org/10.1007/978-3-031-91124-8_4
6. Bernstein, D.J., De Feo, L., Leroux, A., Smith, B.: Faster computation of isogenies of large prime degree. In: Galbraith, S. (ed.) ANTS-XIV - 14th Algorithmic Number Theory Symposium. Proceedings of the Fourteenth Algorithmic Number Theory Symposium (ANTS-XIV), vol. 4, pp. 39–55. Mathematical Sciences Publishers, Auckland, New Zealand (2020). https://doi.org/10.2140/obs.2020.4.39, https://hal.inria.fr/hal-02514201
7. Biasse, J.F., Jao, D., Sankar, A.: A quantum algorithm for computing isogenies between supersingular elliptic curves. In: Meier, W., Mukhopadhyay, D. (eds.) INDOCRYPT 2014. LNCS, vol. 8885, pp. 428–442. Springer, Cham (2014). https://doi.org/10.1007/978-3-319-13039-2_25
8. Boneh, D., Shoup, V.: A graduate course in applied cryptography. Draft 0.5 (2020)
9. Castryck, W., Decru, T.: An efficient key recovery attack on SIDH. In: Hazay, C., Stam, M. (eds.) EUROCRYPT 2023, Part V. LNCS, vol. 14008, pp. 423–447. Springer, Cham (2023). https://doi.org/10.1007/978-3-031-30589-4_15
10. Cohen, H.: A course in computational algebraic number theory, vol. 138. Springer, Berlin, Heidelberg (2010)
11. Cosset, R., Robert, D.: Computing (l, l)-isogenies in polynomial time on Jacobians of genus 2 curves. Math. Comput. **84**(294), 1953–1975 (2015)
12. Crandall, R., Pomerance, C.B.: Prime numbers: a computational perspective. 2nd Edn. Springer New York (2005). https://doi.org/10.1007/0-387-28979-8

13. Dartois, P., Leroux, A., Robert, D., Wesolowski, B.: SQIsignHD: new dimensions in cryptography. In: Joye, M., Leander, G. (eds.) EUROCRYPT 2024, Part I. LNCS, vol. 14651, pp. 3–32. Springer, Cham (2024). https://doi.org/10.1007/978-3-031-58716-0_1
14. Dartois, P., Maino, L., Pope, G., Robert, D.: An algorithmic approach to (2, 2)-isogenies in the theta model and applications to isogeny-based cryptography. In: Chung, K.M., Sasaki, Y. (eds.) ASIACRYPT 2024, Part III. LNCS, vol. 15486, pp. 304–338. Springer, Singapore (2024). https://doi.org/10.1007/978-981-96-0891-1_10
15. De Feo, L., Kohel, D., Leroux, A., Petit, C., Wesolowski, B.: SQISign: compact post-quantum signatures from quaternions and isogenies. In: Moriai, S., Wang, H. (eds.) ASIACRYPT 2020, Part I. LNCS, vol. 12491, pp. 64–93. Springer, Cham (2020). https://doi.org/10.1007/978-3-030-64837-4_3
16. De Feo, L., Leroux, A., Longa, P., Wesolowski, B.: New algorithms for the Deuring correspondence - towards practical and secure SQISign signatures. In: Hazay, C., Stam, M. (eds.) EUROCRYPT 2023, Part V. LNCS, vol. 14008, pp. 659–690. Springer, Cham (2023). https://doi.org/10.1007/978-3-031-30589-4_23
17. Delfs, C., Galbraith, S.D.: Computing isogenies between supersingular elliptic curves over $\mathbb{F}_p$. Des. Codes Crypt. **78**(2), 425–440 (2014). https://doi.org/10.1007/s10623-014-0010-1
18. Duparc, M., Fouotsa, T.B.: SQIPrime: a dimension 2 variant of SQISignHD with non-smooth challenge isogenies. In: Chung, K.M., Sasaki, Y. (eds.) ASIACRYPT 2024, Part III. LNCS, vol. 15486, pp. 396–429. Springer, Singapore (2024). https://doi.org/10.1007/978-981-96-0891-1_13
19. Eisenträger, K., Hallgren, S., Lauter, K.E., Morrison, T., Petit, C.: Supersingular isogeny graphs and endomorphism rings: reductions and solutions. In: Nielsen, J.B., Rijmen, V. (eds.) EUROCRYPT 2018, Part III. LNCS, vol. 10822, pp. 329–368. Springer, Cham (2018). https://doi.org/10.1007/978-3-319-78372-7_11
20. Galbraith, S.D., Petit, C., Silva, J.: Identification protocols and signature schemes based on supersingular isogeny problems. In: Takagi, T., Peyrin, T. (eds.) ASIACRYPT 2017, Part I. LNCS, vol. 10624, pp. 3–33. Springer, Cham (2017). https://doi.org/10.1007/978-3-319-70694-8_1
21. Grover, L.K.: A fast quantum mechanical algorithm for database search. In: 28th ACM STOC, pp. 212–219. ACM Press (1996). https://doi.org/10.1145/237814.237866
22. Grover, L.K.: A fast quantum mechanical algorithm for database search. In: Proceedings of the Twenty-Eighth Annual ACM Symposium on Theory of Computing, pp. 212–219. STOC '96, Association for Computing Machinery, New York, NY, USA (1996). https://doi.org/10.1145/237814.237866
23. Hardy, G.H., Wright, E..M.: An introduction to the theory of numbers. Oxford University Press (2008). https://doi.org/10.1093/oso/9780199219858.001.0001
24. Kani, E.: The number of curves of genus two with elliptic differentials. Journal für die reine und angewandte Mathematik **485**, 93–122 (1997). https://doi.org/10.1515/crll.1997.485.93
25. Kohel, D., Lauter, K., Petit, C., Tignol, J.P.: On the quaternion ℓ-isogeny path problem. LMS J. Comput. Math. **17**(A), 418–432 (2014). https://doi.org/10.1112/S1461157014000151, https://hal.archives-ouvertes.fr/hal-01257092
26. Lang, S.: Algebra, Graduate Texts in Mathematics, vol. 211. Springer, New York, NY, revised 3rd edn. (2002). https://doi.org/10.1007/978-1-4613-0041-0

27. Leroux, A.: Verifiable random function from the deuring correspondence and higher dimensional isogenies. In: Fehr, S., Fouque, P.A. (eds.) EUROCRYPT 2025, Part VII. LNCS, vol. 15607, pp. 167–194. Springer, Cham (2025). https://doi.org/10.1007/978-3-031-91098-2_7
28. Lubicz, D., Robert, D.: Fast change of level and applications to isogenies. Res. Number Theory **9**(1), 7 (2023). https://doi.org/10.1007/s40993-022-00407-9
29. Maino, L., Martindale, C., Panny, L., Pope, G., Wesolowski, B.: A direct key recovery attack on SIDH. In: Hazay, C., Stam, M. (eds.) EUROCRYPT 2023, Part V. LNCS, vol. 14008, pp. 448–471. Springer, Cham (2023). https://doi.org/10.1007/978-3-031-30589-4_16
30. Merdy, A.H.L., Wesolowski, B.: Unconditional foundations for supersingular isogeny-based cryptography (2025). https://arxiv.org/abs/2502.17010
31. Nakagawa, K., Onuki, H.: QFESTA: Efficient algorithms and parameters for FESTA using quaternion algebras. In: Reyzin, L., Stebila, D. (eds.) CRYPTO 2024, Part V. LNCS, vol. 14924, pp. 75–106. Springer, Cham (2024). https://doi.org/10.1007/978-3-031-68388-6_4
32. Nakagawa, K., Onuki, H.: SQIsign2DPush: faster signature scheme using 2-dimensional isogenies. Cryptology ePrint Archive, Paper 2025/897 (2025). https://eprint.iacr.org/2025/897
33. Nakagawa, K., et al.: SQIsign2D-East: a new signature scheme using 2-dimensional isogenies. In: Chung, K.M., Sasaki, Y. (eds.) ASIACRYPT 2024, Part III. LNCS, vol. 15486, pp. 272–303. Springer, Singapore (2024). https://doi.org/10.1007/978-981-96-0891-1_9
34. Robert, D.: Breaking SIDH in polynomial time. In: Hazay, C., Stam, M. (eds.) EUROCRYPT 2023, Part V. LNCS, vol. 14008, pp. 472–503. Springer, Cham (2023). https://doi.org/10.1007/978-3-031-30589-4_17
35. Vélu, J.: Isogénies entre courbes elliptiques. Comptes-Rendues de l'Académie des Sciences **273**, 238–241 (1971)
36. Wesolowski, B.: The supersingular isogeny path and endomorphism ring problems are equivalent. In: 62nd FOCS, pp. 1100–1111. IEEE Computer Society Press (2022). https://doi.org/10.1109/FOCS52979.2021.00109
37. Xu, Z., Lin, K., Zhao, C.A., Ouyang, Y.: SQIsign2D^2: new SQIsign2D variant by leveraging power smooth isogenies in dimension one. Cryptology ePrint Archive, Paper 2025/920 (2025). https://eprint.iacr.org/2025/920

Simple Attacks Against (Extended) Fiat-Shamir

Chris Brzuska[1(✉)], Pavel Hubáček[2,3], and Aleksi Kalsta[1,4]

[1] Aalto University, Espoo, Finland
chris.brzuska@aalto.fi
[2] Institute of Mathematics, Czech Academy of Sciences, Prague, Czech Republic
hubacek@math.cas.cz
[3] Charles University, Faculty of Mathematics and Physics, Prague, Czech Republic
[4] VTT Technical Research Centre of Finland, Espoo, Finland
aleksi.kalsta@vtt.fi

Abstract. The Fiat-Shamir (FS) transform turns interactive public-coin arguments into non-interactive arguments while preserving soundness in the Random Oracle Model (ROM), whereas soundness in the standard model does not hold in general. One of the counterexamples is the work by Bartusek et al. (BBHMR, TCC 2019) which shows that FS fails for a (contrived) version of the Kilian-Micali protocol. Concretely, BBHMR design a collision-resistant hash-function and a sound PCP such that Kilian-Micali is sound, but its FS transform is not, regardless of which hash-function instantiates the random oracle. In a recent breakthrough, Khovratovich, Rothblum, and Soukhanov (KRS, CRYPTO 2025) show that FS-based attacks do not only apply to contrived argument systems, but actually apply to *deployed* versions of GKR-based succinct arguments. KRS, thus, clarifies that the gap between real-life hash functions and the ROM is of larger practical relevance than previously thought. In this work, we improve our understanding of FS counterexamples by simplifying (and modernizing) the BBHMR attack. Concretely, we determine simple (as well as more complex) equations relating the polynomial commitment scheme (PC) and the hash function whose solutions lead to attacks on soundness for GKR-style protocols, including more complex protocols such as PlonK. Notably, we show that such attacks can even apply to *secure* PCs.

Finally, we show a counterexample against the *extended Fiat-Shamir* transform (XFS), which was recently proposed by Arnon and Yogev (AY, CRYPTO 2025) to prevent KRS-style attacks. The existence of contrived counterexamples was conjectured by AY in relation to BBHMR and Barak (FOCS 2001). Our XFS counterexample is indeed contrived and uses universal argument systems similar to Barak. In turn, it is simpler than Barak and does not rely on the involved techniques developed by BBHMR.

Keywords: Fiat-Shamir · Argument Systems · Random Oracles · Polynomial Commitment Schemes · PIOP

S. Bai and E. Persichetti (Eds.): PKC 2026, LNCS 16551, pp. 510–543, 2026.
https://doi.org/10.1007/978-3-032-26731-3_17

1 Introduction

The Fiat–Shamir transform (FS [20]) converts a public-coin interactive protocol into a non-interactive one by replacing random challenges of the verifier with the output of a cryptographic hash function applied to the intermediate transcript. FS is an essential building block in a broad class of practical digital signatures, succinct proofs, and zero-knowledge systems because it dispenses with online interaction, reduces latency and enables deployment in asynchronous or broadcast environments such as the Internet and blockchains. Its appeal lies in its conceptual simplicity and low overhead: the prover and verifier evaluate the hash-function and, otherwise, proceed as in the interactive protocol. Therefore, FS is part of standards ranging from ISO/IEC 9798-4 authentication [1] to lattice-based signatures submitted to the recent NIST post-quantum competition [2]. Despite its ubiquity and decades of study, the security of FS ultimately rests on idealised assumptions about the hash function, leaving open avenues for both cryptanalytic advances and structural attacks on real-world deployments.

Positive Results. Pointcheval and Stern [33] prove that the FS transform results in a sound non-interactive protocol in the random-oracle model (ROM) when applied to 3-round public-message identification schemes. Similar results hold even for multi-round interactive *proofs* in the ROM [4] and its quantum variant [18]. In addition to the random oracle, these positive results rely on strong soundness guarantees of the original interactive scheme. Pursuing this point of view further, Mittelbach and Venturi [32] show a positive result in the *standard model* for a class of protocols with extremely strong soundness guarantees, trading the ROM for complexity leveraging. Motivated by FS-based constructions of modern SNARKs, Ganesh et al. [23] present a framework to prove in the (programmable) ROM that FS-transformed multi-round public-coin proofs achieve simulation-extractability. Note that the dependency on the ROM is somewhat justified by the impossibility result of Bitansky et al. [10] who gave a black-box separation ruling out reductions to "standard" security assumptions, and a similar result holds even with respect to quantum adversaries [19].

Uninstantiability and Attacks. Unfortunately, the above positive results shed little light on the application of the FS transform to interactive *arguments*, i.e., protocols with computational soundness. A line of *uninstantiability* results, beginning with examples by Canetti, Goldreich, and Halevi [11], shows that for certain identification schemes with computational security, no deterministic or efficiently sampleable hash family preserves security after the FS transformation: Barak [5] observes that there is a constant-round public-coin protocol for which the FS heuristic cannot be instantiated. Goldwasser and Kalai [25] leverage Barak's non-black-box techniques for uninstantiability results for three-round identification schemes. These impossibility results highlight a structural tension: the very properties that make a protocol efficient in the interactive world can undermine its robustness in hash-transformed transcripts, leading to potential signature forgeries or knowledge-extraction failures.

On the more practical side, Bernhard, Pereira, and Warinschi [9] give evidence that the security of FS is fragile, as even a minor error in its implementation can lead to major security breaches in deployed protocols. However, neither sensitivity to implementation mistakes nor general uninstantiability results provide strong arguments against the use of the FS transform in practice. Towards better understanding of the latter, Bartusek et al. [6] study the FS transform when applied to the classical Kilian-Micali construction of SNARKs for NP [29,31], showing insecurity of a popular and natural protocol, when replacing one of its building blocks by a tweaked variant.

The most damaging attack on practical deployments of FS is recent work by Khovratovich, Rothblum, and Soukhanov (KRS, [28]), which shows unsoundness of protocols following the work by Goldwasser, Kalai and Rothblum (GKR [26]). KRS showed that it suffices to choose a counterexample *statement* without tweaking the *protocol*. Moreover, KRS extend their basic idea so that any (false) statement can be transformed into an equivalent (false) statement such that a malicious prover can make the verifier believe that the latter is true.

As a response to KRS, Arnon and Yogev (AY, [3]) proposed an *extended* variant of the Fiat-Shamir (XFS) transform intended to prevent the possibility of embedding a hash-function into a statement as in the KRS attack. As evidence, AY suggested proving the security of the XFS in a *relativized* ROM, where not only the FS transform but also the protocol can make RO calls. When adding padding to the transform (to prevent the verifier from making the same query as the transform), AY were then able to prove security of the XFS transform in the relativized ROM for 3-round protocols. A proof of the XFS-collapsed GKR protocol (which has more than 3 rounds) in the relativized ROM (or another model capturing diagonalization attacks) remains an important open question left for future work.

1.1 Our Contribution

Inspired by KRS, we develop new (contrived) counterexamples against FS in the spirit of Barak and BBHMR, but with a much simpler design and analysis. In particular, we identify adversarially exploitable relations between the polynomial commitment scheme (PC) and the FS hash-function h. In the simplest case, it suffices for a malicious prover to find a digest value d such that:

$$d = h(\mathsf{Com}(x, d)), \tag{1}$$

where x is the description of the (false) statement that there is an input w on which the circuit $C(w_1, \ldots, w_k) := (w_1, w_1 - 1)$ returns $(0, 0)$. If so, then we show that a malicious prover can break the soundness of the GKR protocol by proving the aforementioned (false) statement.

While the relation in Eq. 1 suggests a natural target for cryptanalysis, one might suspect that the binding property of the PC or simple properties of the hash function, such as collision-resistance, prevent such an attack already. We observe that this is not so. Concretely, given an input-output value (a, d) of the hash-function h, we (1) modify Com to Com' which outputs a on input (x, d)

and (2) ensure via domain separation that Com' returns a on no other input. Now, Com' maintains the functionality and security (cf. Sect. 4.1 for details) of a polynomial commitment scheme and, in particular, is still binding, since a points to a *single* pre-image only. If we hardcode (a, d) into the public description of Com', a malicious prover easily finds d which satisfies Eq. 1 when replacing Com by Com'.

We generalize the above conceptual idea to a large class of polynomial interactive oracle proofs (PIOP, cf. Definition 11 and Definition 12), including PlonK and GKR. The abstractions we develop to capture large classes of PIOPs might be of independent interest. We then show that the argument system resulting from combining such a PIOP with our modified PC results in a sound interactive argument whose FS transform is unsound. Similar to KRS, we can take an *arbitrary* circuit C and output z, transform C into a circuit C' with *equal* input-output behaviour as C and prove that there exists an input w such that $C'(w) = y$, even when no such w exists.

Our techniques are inspired by Bartusek et al. (BBHMR [6]) who create a *fixed point* in the collision-resistant hash-function used in the Kilian-Micali protocol. Similarly, we program the polynomial commitment on a single point. Thus, our technique can be viewed as both a simplification and a modernization of BBHMR, targeting a different class of protocols—namely, those based on PIOPs. Loosely speaking, our approach can also be seen as generalizing BBHMR, since PIOPs are conceptually related to PCPs, which underlie the Kilian–Micali construction. In particular, PIOPs can be transformed into Interactive Oracle Proofs (IOP, [8]) via Interactive Oracle Proofs of Proximity (IOPP, [7]), and IOPs themselves can be viewed as interactive PCPs. In contrast, the BBHMR work does not directly extend to general IOPs, which represent a broader class of proof systems.

Dependency Between the Hash-Function and the PC. There are two ways to encode the dependency between the hash-function and the PC. One option is to either encode an input-output pair of the hash-function into the PC. In Sect. 4.1, we show that, alternatively, the PC can also *evaluate* the hash-function. Both approaches of casting the counterexample have their strengths: Hardcoding values means that neither the statement, nor the complexity of the proof system depend on the complexity of the hash-function, a property which none of the previous counterexamples achieved. In turn, *using* the same hash-function within the same polynomial commitment scheme is, perhaps, a more realistic setting where a weakness might arise unintentionally. We thus opt for the latter in the remainder of the paper.

Extended Fiat-Shamir. The observant reader might have noticed that our counter- example also works in the ROM—we can either hardcode an input-output pair from the ROM into the public parameters of the PC or have the PC make queries to the same RO as the FS transform. This issue is reminiscent of a pattern which the XFS transform by AY seeks to prevent.

Indeed, we were not able to adapt the above attack to protocols covered by the soundness results of the XFS in the relativized ROM. In turn, we found a simple alternative counterexample. Namely, given any sound 3-message proof system, we let the prover additionally send a hash-function h in his 1st message as well as a value y and a SNARG for the correct evaluation of h on a suitable input defined by the XFS transform. The verifier accepts if y is equal to its own randomness r. Soundness of this protocol follows from the soundness of the SNARG and the original 3-message proof system as well as a low collision probability of y and r for a uniformly random value r. In turn, the XFS transform of this protocol is insecure, because the verifier's randomness will always be equal to y and thus, the verifier always accepts.

AY indeed conjecture that contrived counterexamples exist which rely on SNARGs for evaluation proofs about the Fiat-Shamir hash-function similar to Barak [5] as well as counterexamples based on BBHMR-style techniques. Our simple example is similar to Barak since it relies on a universal argument system. Besides, no advanced techniques beyond a hash-function evaluation proof are necessary. It remains open to find more natural counterexamples against AY.

2 Preliminaries

We use $\mathbb{F}$ to denote an arbitrary prime field and $\mathbb{F}_{\mu}^{\leq d}$ to denote the ring of μ-variate polynomials over a field $\mathbb{F}$ with degree bound $d \in \mathbb{N}$ in each variable.

Lemma 1. (Schwartz-Zippel Lemma). *Let $f \in \mathbb{F}_{\mu}^{\leq d}$ be a non-zero polynomial over a field $\mathbb{F}$. Let $S \subseteq \mathbb{F}$ be a finite subset, and let $r_1, r_2, \ldots, r_\mu$ be chosen independently and uniformly at random from S. Then,* $\Pr[f(r_1, r_2, \ldots, r_\mu) = 0] \leq \mu d |S|^{-1}$.

Interactive Proofs. A relation $\mathscr{R}$ is a set of pairs (x, w), where x is called a *statement* and w a *witness*. The *language* $\mathcal{L}(\mathscr{R})$ consists of all statements x for which there exists a witness w such that $(x, w) \in \mathscr{R}$.

Definition 1 (Interactive Proof System). *An interactive proof system for relation $\mathscr{R}$ is a tuple $\Pi = (\mathscr{P}, \mathscr{V})$ of interactive PPT Turing machines, together with the* $\mathsf{Setup}(1^\lambda)$ *algorithm, which generates the public parameters* pp. *At the end of the interaction, the verifier outputs a single bit. The verifier's output is a random variable, denoted by $\langle \mathscr{P}(\mathsf{pp}, x, w), \mathscr{V}(\mathsf{pp}, x)\rangle$ and the system must satisfy the following properties:*

Completeness: *For every $(x, w) \in \mathscr{R}$,* $\Pr[\langle \mathscr{P}(\mathsf{pp}, x, w), \mathscr{V}(\mathsf{pp}, x)\rangle = 1] = 1$.
ϵ-Soundness: *For a function $\epsilon : \mathbb{N} \to [0, 1]$ and for any adversarial prover $\mathscr{P}^*$:*

$$x \notin \mathcal{L}(\mathscr{R}) \implies \Pr[\langle \mathscr{P}^*(\mathsf{pp}, x), \mathscr{V}(\mathsf{pp}, x)\rangle = 1] \leq \epsilon(|x|).$$

If the soundness error of Π is negligible against computationally unbounded adversaries, then Π is called an interactive *proof.* If the soundness error is negligible only against PPT adversaries, then Π is called an interactive *argument.*

Knowledge-Soundness is an alternative, stronger definition of soundness which formalizes the idea that a prover who convinces the verifier must *know* a valid witness for the proven statement.

Definition 2 (Knowledge-soundness). *An argument system $\Pi = (\mathsf{Setup}, \mathcal{P}, \mathcal{V})$ is κ-knowledge-sound for $\mathscr{R}$, if there exists a PPT extractor E such that for any pair of PPT adversaries $(\mathcal{A}_1, \mathcal{A}_2)$, it holds that*

$$\Pr\left[\begin{array}{l} \langle \mathcal{A}_2(\mathsf{pp}, x, \mathsf{st}), \mathcal{V}(\mathsf{pp}, x)\rangle = 1 \\ \wedge\ (x, w) \notin \mathscr{R} \end{array} \middle| \begin{array}{l} \mathsf{pp} \leftarrow \mathsf{Setup}(1^\lambda), \\ (x, \mathsf{st}) \leftarrow \mathcal{A}_1(\mathsf{pp}), \\ w \leftarrow \mathsf{E}^{\mathcal{A}_1, \mathcal{A}_2}(\mathsf{pp}, x) \end{array}\right] \leq \kappa(\lambda).$$

We say that Π is knowledge-sound, or an argument of knowledge, if Π is κ-knowledge-sound for some negligible κ. Note that we usually omit the Setup algorithm if it is not relevant for the analysis.

Polynomial Oracle Relations and Polynomial IOPs. A common approach to designing succinct arguments is to first construct an information-theoretically secure proof in an idealized model of so-called Polynomial Interactive Oracle Proofs (PIOPs, Definition 4), and then compile it into an interactive argument using a polynomial commitment scheme (PC, Definition 5). In this model, the prover can send oracles to polynomials, and the verifier is allowed to query these oracles to obtain evaluations at arbitrary points. Soundness in this setting is achieved by choosing a sufficiently large underlying field $\mathbb{F}$ and leveraging guarantees provided by the Schwartz–Zippel lemma (Lemma 1). Similarly to previous work (see, e.g., [12]), we use the following notion of polynomial oracle relations to formalize this approach.

Definition 3 (Polynomial Oracle Relation). *A polynomial oracle relation $\mathscr{R}$ is a relation in which the statement x may contain oracles to (instance-specific) polynomials over a field $\mathbb{F}$, and witness for x consists of polynomials corresponding to these oracles. The oracle to $\phi \in \mathbb{F}_\mu^{\leq d}$ is denoted by $[\phi]$ and oracles specify the degree d and the number of variables μ. These oracles can be queried at arbitrary points in $\mathbb{F}^\mu$ to obtain evaluations of the polynomial at these points.*

Definition 4 (Polynomial IOP). *Let $\mathbb{F}$ be a finite field selected from a family of finite fields $\{\mathbb{F}_\lambda\}_{\lambda \in \mathbb{N}}$ by the $\mathsf{Setup}(1^\lambda)$ algorithm. A tuple $\Pi = (\mathscr{P}, \mathscr{V})$ is said to be an ϵ-sound Polynomial Interactive Oracle Proof (PIOP) for a polynomial oracle relation $\mathscr{R}$ if the following conditions are satisfied:*

- *$(\mathscr{P}, \mathscr{V})$ is a public coin interactive proof system for $\mathscr{R}$ with soundness error $\epsilon : \mathbb{N} \to [0, 1]$.*
- *Each prover message is an oracle to a polynomial over $\mathbb{F}$.*
- *When the oracle $[\phi]$, associated with a polynomial $\phi \in \mathbb{F}_\mu^{\leq d}$, is queried at a point $u \in \mathbb{F}^\mu$, it returns the value $\phi(u)$.*

Polynomial Commitment Schemes. Polynomial commitment schemes were introduced by Kate, Zaverucha, and Goldberg [27] and generalize bit commitments to polynomials, allowing the committer to later prove that an evaluation of the committed polynomial is computed correctly.

Definition 5 (Polynomial Commitment (PC)). *A tuple of PPT algorithms* $\mathsf{PC} = (\mathsf{KGen}, \mathsf{Com}, \mathsf{Eval}, \mathsf{Verify})$ *is a μ-variate* polynomial commitment scheme *over a family of finite fields $\{\mathbb{F}_\lambda\}_{\lambda\in\mathbb{N}}$ with degree bounds $\mathbf{d} \in \mathbb{N}^\mu$ if it has the following syntax:*

- $\mathsf{KGen}(1^\lambda, \mathbf{d}, \mathsf{aux}) \xrightarrow{\$} \mathsf{ck}$ *takes the security parameter, degree bounds $\mathbf{d}$ and some auxiliary information as an input and returns a commitment key* ck.
- $\mathsf{Com}(\mathsf{ck}, \phi) \to C$ *takes as input a commitment key* ck *and a polynomial $\phi \in \mathbb{F}_\mu^{\leq d}$, and outputs a commitment C.*
- $\mathsf{Eval}(\mathsf{ck}, C, \phi, u) \to \pi$ *outputs a proof π that the committed polynomial $\phi \in \mathbb{F}_\mu^{\leq d}$ evaluates to $\phi(u)$ at the point u, given a commitment key* ck, *a commitment C and the evaluation point $u \in \mathbb{F}^\mu$.*
- $\mathsf{Verify}(\mathsf{ck}, C, u, z, \pi) \to b$ *takes as input a commitment key* ck, *a commitment C, an evaluation point $u \in \mathbb{F}^\mu$, a claimed image $z \in \mathbb{F}$, and an evaluation proof π, and outputs a bit b indicating whether π is a valid proof that the polynomial committed in C evaluates to z at the point u.*

Typically, the Verify and Eval algorithms are defined as interactive protocols. However, in this work, we focus on protocols that have been made non-interactive via the Fiat-Shamir transform, and accordingly directly consider non-interactive polynomial commitment schemes. We say that a polynomial commitment scheme is secure, if it satisfies binding, evaluation completeness and knowledge-soundness, which we define next.

Definition 6 (Binding). *A μ-variate polynomial commitment scheme* PC *satisfies binding if for all PPT adversaries $\mathcal{A}$:*

$$\Pr\left[\begin{array}{c}\mathsf{Com}(\mathsf{ck}, \phi_1) = \mathsf{Com}(\mathsf{ck}, \phi_2)\\ \wedge\\ \phi_1 \neq \phi_2\end{array}\middle|\begin{array}{l}\mathsf{ck} \leftarrow\!\$\ \mathsf{KGen}(1^\lambda, \mathbf{d}, \mathsf{aux})\\ (\phi_1, \phi_2) \leftarrow\!\$\ \mathcal{A}(\mathsf{ck})\end{array}\right] \leq \mathsf{negl}(\lambda) \qquad (2)$$

Definition 7 (Evaluation Completeness). *A μ-variate polynomial commitment scheme* PC *satisfies evaluation completeness, if for all $\phi \in \mathbb{F}_\mu^{\leq d}$ and $u \in \mathbb{F}^\mu$:*

$$\Pr\left[\mathsf{Verify}(\mathsf{ck}, C, u, \phi(u), \pi) = 1 \middle| \begin{array}{l}\mathsf{ck} \leftarrow\!\$\ \mathsf{KGen}(1^\lambda, \mathbf{d}, \mathsf{aux})\\ C \leftarrow \mathsf{Com}(\mathsf{ck}, \phi)\\ \pi \leftarrow \mathsf{Eval}(\mathsf{ck}, C, \phi, u)\end{array}\right] = 1 \qquad (3)$$

Definition 8 (Knowledge Soundness). *A μ-variate polynomial commitment scheme* PC *is knowledge-sound if for all PPT adversaries $\mathcal{A}$, there exists a PPT extractor $\mathcal{E}$ such that*

$$\Pr\left[\begin{array}{c|c} b=1 & \mathsf{ck} \leftarrow_{\$} \mathsf{KGen}(1^\lambda, \mathbf{d}, \mathsf{aux}) \\ \wedge & (C, u, z, \pi) \leftarrow_{\$} \mathcal{A}(\mathsf{ck}) \\ (\mathsf{Com}(\mathsf{ck}, \phi) \neq C \vee \phi(u) \neq z) & b \leftarrow \mathsf{Verify}(\mathsf{ck}, C, u, z, \pi) \\ & \phi \leftarrow \mathcal{E}^{\mathcal{A}}(\mathsf{ck}, C, u, z, \pi) \end{array}\right] \leq \mathsf{negl}(\lambda) \quad (4)$$

From PIOPs to Succinct Arguments via Polynomial Commitments. Let $\Pi = (\mathscr{P}, \mathscr{V})$ be a PIOP. Then Π can be compiled into an interactive (non-oracle) argument using a polynomial commitment scheme PC as follows:

- Each oracle $[f]$ is replaced by a commitment $C_f = \mathsf{PC.Com}(\mathsf{ck}, f)$ to the polynomial $f \in \mathbb{F}_{\mu}^{\leq d}$.
- Every query to polynomial oracle $[f]$ at a point $r \in \mathbb{F}^\mu$ is redirected to the prover, who computes $\pi_f^r \leftarrow \mathsf{PC.Eval}(\mathsf{ck}, C_f, f, r)$ and sends the claimed evaluation $z = f(r)$ along with the proof π_f^r to the verifier.
- The compiled verifier accepts if $\mathscr{V}$ accepts using the provided evaluations, and if $\mathsf{PC.Verify}(\mathsf{ck}, C_f, r, z, \pi_f^r)$ returns 1 for every query.

For any PIOP $\Pi = (\mathscr{P}, \mathscr{V})$ and polynomial commitment scheme PC, we denote the protocol obtained through the above compilation process by $\Pi^{\mathsf{PC}} = (\mathscr{P}^{\mathsf{PC}}, \mathscr{V}^{\mathsf{PC}})$. If both Π and PC are secure (in the appropriate sense), then Π^{PC} is an interactive argument (of knowledge) (see, e.g., Theorem 8.1 in Chiesa et al. [14] for a formal statement and proof).

Since PIOP Π is for a polynomial oracle relation (cf. Definition 3), the statements can contain oracles to polynomials, while the statements in the compiled protocol Π^{PC} do not. For instance, consider the relation

$$\mathscr{R}_\Omega = \{([f]; f) \mid f \in \mathbb{F}^{\leq d} \wedge \forall x \in \Omega \subseteq \mathbb{F} : f(x) = 0\},$$

which arises in the Zero-Test (Definition 16). After compilation, this relation is mapped to a new relation, defined as

$$\mathscr{R}_\Omega^{\mathsf{PC}} = \{(C_f; f) \mid f \in \mathbb{F}^{\leq d} \wedge C_f = \mathsf{PC.Com}(\mathsf{ck}, f) \ \wedge \ \forall x \in \Omega \subseteq \mathbb{F} : f(x) = 0\}.$$

Henceforth, $\mathscr{R}^{\mathsf{PC}}$ denotes the compiled relation obtained from $\mathscr{R}$ by replacing each oracle in the statement by the commitment to the corresponding polynomial under PC and requiring that the corresponding polynomial in the witness is an opening to this commitment.

Removing Interaction via the Fiat-Shamir Transform. Any interactive public-coin protocol can be converted into a non-interactive one in the random oracle model using the Fiat-Shamir transform [20].

Definition 9 (Fiat-Shamir Transformation). *Let $\Pi = (\mathscr{P}, \mathscr{V})$ be a $(2\rho + 1)$-round public-coin interactive proof system and denote the random oracle by* RO. *We define the non-interactive protocol $\mathsf{FS}(\Pi) = (\mathscr{P}_{\mathsf{FS}}, \mathscr{V}_{\mathsf{FS}})$ as follows:*

$\mathscr{P}_{\mathsf{FS}}(x, w)$: *runs* $\mathscr{P}(x, w)$ *but instead of asking the verifier for the challenge* c_i *on message* a_i, *the challenges are computed as* $c_i = \mathsf{RO}(x, a_1, \ldots, a_i)$ *for all* $1 \leq i \leq \rho$. *The output is the proof* $\pi = (a_1, \ldots, a_{\rho+1})$.
$\mathscr{V}_{\mathsf{FS}}(x, \pi)$: *accepts iff* $\mathscr{V}$ *accepts the transcript* $(x, a_1, c_1, \ldots, a_\rho, c_\rho, a_{\rho+1})$, *where* $c_i = \mathsf{RO}(x, a_1, \ldots, a_i)$ *for all* $1 \leq i \leq \rho$.

By combining the notation from the compilation step and the Fiat-Shamir transform, we obtain that $\Pi = (\mathscr{P}, \mathscr{V})$ is mapped to $\mathsf{FS}(\Pi^{\mathsf{PC}}) = (\mathscr{P}_{\mathsf{FS}}^{\mathsf{PC}}, \mathscr{V}_{\mathsf{FS}}^{\mathsf{PC}})$.

3 Simple PIOPs

In this section, we present a restricted class of PIOPs, which we call *simple PIOPs*. We then use simple PIOPs to demonstrate the core ideas underlying our main result in Sect. 4.

3.1 Polynomial Equality Test

The Schwartz-Zippel lemma (Lemma 1) implies that one can check whether polynomials $f_1, \ldots, f_k \in \mathbb{F}_{\mu}^{\leq d}$ satisfy an algebraic identity consisting of additions and multiplications by evaluating them at a uniformly random point $r \in \mathbb{F}^{\mu}$, as long as the field $\mathbb{F}$ is sufficiently large. With overwhelming probability, if the claimed polynomial identity does not hold, the evaluations $f_1(r), \ldots, f_k(r)$ will also fail to satisfy the algebraic expression. This kind of equality check is commonly used in proof systems to verify the claims of the prover. We formalize it in Definition 10. Throughout this section, we treat λ as the security parameter of the underlying argument system, and parametrize the other building blocks with respect to λ.

Definition 10 (Polynomial Equality Test). *Let* $\mathbb{F}$ *be a field whose cardinality is superpolynomial in* λ *and let* $d, \mu, \eta, d_i, k_i = \mathsf{poly}(\lambda)$. *Then, a* polynomial equality test $E = (\mathsf{pp}, p)$ *consists of a multivariate polynomial* $p \in \mathbb{F}_{\mu}^{\leq d}$ *and a tuple of public polynomials* $\mathsf{pp} = (f_1, \ldots, f_\nu) \in \mathbb{F}_{\eta}^{\leq d_1} \times \cdots \times \mathbb{F}_{\eta}^{\leq d_\nu}$, *where* $\nu \leq \mu$. *The public polynomials are composed with the first* ν *variables of* p, *while the prover selects* $\mu - \nu$ *additional polynomials, denoted by* $g_1, \ldots, g_{\mu-\nu} \in \mathbb{F}_{\eta}^{\leq k_i}$. *These polynomials are composed with the remaining variables of* p *and on input* $r \in \mathbb{F}^{\eta}$, *the test outputs* 1 *if* $p\big(f_1(r), \ldots, f_\nu(r), g_1(r), \ldots, g_{\mu-\nu}(r)\big) = 0$, *and* 0 *otherwise. We use* $E(\mathsf{pp}, g_1(r), \ldots, g_{\mu-\nu}(r); r)$ *to denote the outcome of the polynomial equality test evaluated with the specific input* $r \in \mathbb{F}^{\eta}$.

Additionally, we say that E is non-trivial with respect to the ith variable, *if, for any assignment* $v_1, \ldots, v_{i-1}, v_{i+1} v_{\mu-\nu} \in \mathbb{F}$, *there exists* $r \in \mathbb{F}^{\eta}$ *such that the polynomial* $h(x) = p(f_1(r), ..., f_\nu(r), v_1, \ldots, v_{i-1}, x, v_{i+1}, \ldots v_{\mu-\nu})$ *is not a constant polynomial.*

We also say that a polynomial equality test $E = (\mathsf{pp}, p)$ *is* linear with respect to the ith variable (or g_i) *if* $\deg_{\nu+i}(p) \leq 1$; *that is,* p *has degree at most one in its* $(\nu + i)$*th variable.*

We emphasize that the above definition of non-triviality is mainly technical, and that polynomial equality tests encountered in practice typically satisfy it. To make this formalism concrete, we prove in Lemma 2 that the final check in the Zero Test (Definition 16) can be viewed as a polynomial equality test which is linear and non-trivial with respect to the quotient polynomial q. The proof is presented in the full version of our work.

Lemma 2. *The final check of the verifier in the Zero Test (Definition 16) is a polynomial equality test as defined in Definition 10. Moreover, this polynomial equality test is linear and non-trivial with respect to the quotient polynomial q.*

We will later use that a polynomial equality test which is linear with respect to a variable makes it easy to find a (unique) solution. We thus state and prove the following lemma.

Lemma 3. *Let $E = (\mathsf{pp} = (f_1, \dots, f_\nu) \in \mathbb{F}_\eta^{\leq d_1} \times \dots \times \mathbb{F}_\eta^{d_\nu}, p \in \mathbb{F}_\mu^{\leq D})$ be a polynomial equality test, which is linear and non-trivial with respect to the i-th variable, and let $v_1, \dots, v_{i-1}, v_{i+1}, \dots, v_{\mu-\nu} \in \mathbb{F}$ be an arbitrary assignment to the remaining variables. If $n = \max\{d_i : i \in [\nu]\}$, then, with probability at least $1 - \frac{\mu\eta n D}{|\mathbb{F}|}$ over a uniformly random choice of $r \in \mathbb{F}^\eta$, the equation*

$$p(f_1(r), \dots, f_\nu(r), v_1, \dots, v_{i-1}, x, v_{i+1}, \dots, v_{\mu-\nu}) = 0$$

admits a unique solution in x over $\mathbb{F}$, which can be efficiently computed.

Proof. First, we note that the equation

$$p(f_1(r), ..., f_\nu(r), v_1, \dots, v_{i-1}, x, v_{i+1}, \dots v_{\mu-\nu}) = 0$$

can be simplified to $ax + b = 0$ for some $a, b \in \mathbb{F}$. If $a \neq 0$, then the solution is $x = -a^{-1}b$, where a^{-1} can be efficiently computed, for example, using the Euclidean algorithm. Observe that $a = g(r)$ and $b = h(r)$ for some $g, h \in \mathbb{F}_\eta^{\leq \mu n D}$. Since E is non-trivial, g cannot be identically zero. Therefore, by the Schwartz–Zippel lemma, the probability that $g(r) = 0$ is at most $\frac{\mu\eta n D}{|\mathbb{F}|} = \mathsf{negl}(\lambda)$. □

Given $v_1, \dots, v_k \in \mathbb{F}$, we write $v \leftarrow E(\mathsf{pp}, \cdot, v_1, \dots, v_k; r)$ to denote solving the polynomial equality test E for the variable in the placeholder position $\cdot$, using randomness r, and assigning the resulting value to v. If no solution exists for the given assignment and randomness, we set $v := 0$ by convention.

3.2 Simple PIOPs

Using the notation of polynomial equality tests (Definition 10), we formally define simple PIOPs below.

Definition 11 (Simple PIOP). *We say that PIOP $\Pi = (\mathscr{P}, \mathscr{V})$ for a polynomial oracle relation $\mathscr{R}$ is a simple PIOP if it satisfies the following properties:*

- *The relation* $\mathscr{R}$ *consists of pairs* $(x; w) = ([f]; f)$, *where* $f \in \mathbb{F}_{\eta}^{\leq d}$.
- *The prover sends the first message* $[\phi]$, *where* $\phi \in \mathbb{F}_{\eta}^{\leq k}$.
- *The verifier queries* $[\phi]$ *at exactly one uniformly random point* $r \in \mathbb{F}^{\eta}$ *and* r *is the only message the verifier sends to the prover.*
- *Let* $E = (\mathsf{pp}_E \in \mathbb{F}_{\eta}^{\leq d_1} \times ... \times \mathbb{F}_{\eta}^{\leq d_\nu}, p \in \mathbb{F}_{\mu}^{\leq D})$ *be a polynomial equality test. The verifier decides if a statement* $[f]$ *is in the language* $\mathcal{L}(\mathscr{R})$ *based on polynomial equality test* $E(\mathsf{pp}, \phi(r), f(r); r)$, *which is linear and non-trivial in* $\phi(r)$.

We note that certain proof gadgets, such as the zero test (Definition 16) used as a subroutine in SNARKs, have the above structure of a simple PIOP. Note that if $\mathscr{R}$ is the relation underlying a simple PIOP, then the statements in the compiled relation are simply commitments to the witnesses in $\mathscr{R}$.

4 Attacking Simple PIOPs

To illustrate our idea, we first present an attack against compiled and Fiat–Shamir-transformed *simple* PIOPs. In Sect. 4.1, we transform any secure polynomial commitment scheme PC into another secure polynomial commitment scheme PC′. Then, in Sect. 4.2, we take a simple PIOP Π for the relation $\mathscr{R}$ and show that, in $\mathsf{FS}(\Pi^{\mathsf{PC}'})$, a malicious prover can convince the verifier that the commitment C_g to g is in $\mathcal{L}(\mathscr{R}^{\mathsf{PC}'})$, even when $[g] \notin \mathcal{L}(\mathscr{R})$.

Note that polynomial commitment schemes are typically compressing, and thus there is no guarantee that $C_g \notin \mathcal{L}(\mathscr{R}^{\mathsf{PC}'})$, even if $[g] \notin \mathcal{L}(\mathscr{R})$. In particular, if $C_g \in \mathcal{L}(\mathscr{R}^{\mathsf{PC}'})$, then exhibiting a prover that convinces the verifier of this fact does not violate the (standard) soundness of the protocol. In the extreme case, every commitment may lie in the compiled language, making soundness vacuous. Therefore, in Sect. 4.3, we extend our analysis by showing that $\mathsf{FS}(\Pi^{\mathsf{PC}'})$ is not *knowledge-sound* (Definition 2).

4.1 Transforming the Polynomial Commitment Scheme

We now turn an arbitrary secure polynomial commitment scheme PC into its modified version PC′. By definition of a simple PIOP, the protocol Π employs a polynomial equality test E to decide the relation $\mathscr{R}$, consisting of pairs $(x; w) = ([f]; f)$ with $f \in \mathbb{F}_{\eta}^{\leq d}$. Moreover, let $g \in \mathbb{F}_{\eta}^{\leq d}$ be such that $[g] \notin \mathcal{L}(\mathscr{R})$. We now construct PC′ such that, in $\mathsf{FS}(\Pi^{\mathsf{PC}'})$, the verifier accepts the commitment C_g to g with overwhelming probability, regardless of whether C_g is in $\mathcal{L}(\mathscr{R}^{\mathsf{PC}'})$ or not.

Lemma 4. *For a polynomial commitment scheme* $\mathsf{PC} = (\mathsf{KGen}, \mathsf{Com}, \mathsf{Eval}, \mathsf{Verify})$, *let* PC′ *be the polynomial commitment scheme defined in Algorithms 1 to 3. If* PC *is secure, then* PC′ *is secure.*

Algorithm 1. $\mathsf{PC}'.\mathsf{Com}^{\mathsf{RO}}(\mathsf{ck}, \phi)$

$r \leftarrow \mathsf{RO}(\mathsf{pp}, (1, \mathsf{PC.Com}(\mathsf{ck}, g)), (0, 0))$ // challenge from the FS verifier
$v \leftarrow E(\mathsf{pp}_E, \cdot, g(r); r)$. // solve the equality test
if $\phi(x) = v$: // constant polynomial, equal to v
  return $(0, 0)$
else
  return $(1, \mathsf{PC.Com}(\mathsf{ck}, \phi))$

Algorithm 2. $\mathsf{PC}'.\mathsf{Eval}(\mathsf{ck}, C, \phi, u)$

$(b, c) \leftarrow C$ // parse the commitment
if $(b, c) = (0, 0)$:
  return $\perp$ // no need for an evaluation proof, there is only one option for ϕ and $\phi(u)$
else
  return $\mathsf{PC.Eval}(\mathsf{ck}, c, \phi, u)$

Algorithm 3. $\mathsf{PC}'.\mathsf{Verify}^{\mathsf{RO}}(\mathsf{ck}, C, u, z, \pi)$

$(b, c) \leftarrow C$ // parse the commitment
if $(b, c) = (0, 0)$:
  $r \leftarrow \mathsf{RO}(\mathsf{pp}, (1, \mathsf{PC.Com}(\mathsf{ck}, g)), (0, 0))$ // challenge from the FS verifier
  $v \leftarrow E(\mathsf{pp}_E, \cdot, g(r); r)$. // solve the equality test
  if $z = v$: **return** 1
  else : **return** 0
if $b = 1$:
  return $\mathsf{PC.Verify}(\mathsf{ck}, c, u, z, \pi)$
else return 0

Proof. We show that the new scheme PC' satisfies evaluation completeness, binding, and knowledge-soundness as per Definition 6 to 8.

Evaluation Completeness: Let $\phi \in \mathbb{F}_{\mu}^{\leq d}$ and suppose $C = \mathsf{PC}'.\mathsf{Com}^{\mathsf{RO}}(\mathsf{ck}, \phi) = (0, 0)$. Then $\phi(x) = v$ for all $x \in \mathbb{F}^{\mu}$, where v is either solution to the polynomial equality test in Algorithm 1, or $v = 0$, if the solution did not exist. Either way, we obtain that $\mathsf{PC}'.\mathsf{Verify}^{\mathsf{RO}}(\mathsf{ck}, C, u, v) = 1$ for all $u \in \mathbb{F}^{\mu}$. If $C = \mathsf{PC}'.\mathsf{Com}^{\mathsf{RO}}(\mathsf{ck}, \phi) = (1, \mathsf{PC.Com}(\mathsf{ck}, \phi))$, then the evaluation completeness follows from the evaluation completeness of PC.

Binding: Only one polynomial maps to the commitment $(0, 0)$. Therefore, if an adversary finds two distinct polynomials $\phi_1, \phi_2 \in \mathbb{F}_{\mu}^{\leq d}$ that produce the same commitment under $\mathsf{PC}'.\mathsf{Com}^{\mathsf{RO}}$, it must be that $(1, \mathsf{PC.Com}(\mathsf{ck}, \phi_1)) = (1, \mathsf{PC.Com}(\mathsf{ck}, \phi_2))$. This implies that $\mathsf{PC.Com}(\mathsf{ck}, \phi_1) = \mathsf{PC.Com}(\mathsf{ck}, \phi_2)$, which can occur only with negligible probability, since PC is binding.

Algorithm 4. $\mathcal{R}^{\mathcal{A}}(\mathsf{ck})$

$(C, u, z, \pi') \leftarrow\$ \mathcal{A}(\mathsf{ck})$
$(b, c) \leftarrow C$
return (c, u, z, π)

Algorithm 5. $\mathcal{E}'^{\mathcal{A},\mathsf{RO}}(\mathsf{ck}, C, u, z, \pi)$

$(b, c) \leftarrow C$ // parse the commitment
$r \leftarrow \mathsf{RO}(\mathsf{pp}, (1, \mathsf{Com}(\mathsf{ck}, g)), (0, 0))$
$v \leftarrow E(\mathsf{pp}_E, \cdot, g(r); r)$
if $C = (0, 0)$:
    return v // constant polynomial equal to v
else :
    $\mathcal{B} \leftarrow \mathcal{R}^{\mathcal{A}}$
    $\phi \leftarrow\$ \mathcal{E}^{\mathcal{B}}(\mathsf{ck}, c, u, z, \pi)$
    return ϕ

Knowledge-Soundness: Let $\mathcal{A}$ be a PPT adversary against the knowledge-soundness of PC'. Then, the reduction $\mathcal{R}^{\mathcal{A}}$, described in Algorithm 4, parses the tuple produced by $\mathcal{A}$ to conform to the syntax expected by PC. Note that if $\mathcal{A}$ produces an accepting tuple for $\mathsf{PC}'.\mathsf{Verify}^{\mathsf{RO}}$ and $C \neq (0, 0)$, then $\mathcal{R}^{\mathcal{A}}$ produces an accepting tuple for $\mathsf{PC}.\mathsf{Verify}$.

Since PC is secure, there exists a successful extractor $\mathcal{E}$ for PC. In Algorithm 5, we define an extractor $\mathcal{E}'$ for PC', constructed from $\mathcal{E}$ and $\mathcal{R}$. Observe that if $\mathcal{A}$ produces an accepting tuple for $\mathsf{PC}'.\mathsf{Verify}^{\mathsf{RO}}$ with $C = (0, 0)$, then by the definition of $\mathsf{PC}'.\mathsf{Verify}^{\mathsf{RO}}$, the only valid polynomial is the constant polynomial, which $\mathcal{E}'$ correctly extracts. Therefore, we can assume without loss of generality that the adversary returns a tuple (C, u, z, π) with $C = (1, c)$. Note that $((1, c), u, z, \pi)$ is accepted by $\mathsf{PC}'.\mathsf{Verify}^{\mathsf{RO}}$, if and only if (c, u, z, π) is accepted by $\mathsf{PC}.\mathsf{Verify}$. Thus, the adversary $\mathcal{A}$ succeeds if and only if $\mathcal{E}^{\mathcal{B}}$ fails to extract a satisfying polynomial for the commitment c and evaluation z at point u. Since $\mathcal{E}'$ correctly simulates the input to $\mathcal{E}$, the knowledge soundness of PC implies that the extractor fails with at most negligible probability. This concludes the proof. □

4.2 Proving a Potentially False Claim

In Lemma 5, we show that when the simple PIOP Π is compiled using the polynomial commitment scheme PC', then there exists a prover $\mathscr{P}^*$ that convinces the verifier in $\mathsf{FS}(\Pi^{\mathsf{PC}'})$ that $C_g \in \mathcal{L}(\mathscr{R}^{\mathsf{PC}'})$, regardless of whether the statement actually belongs to the language. Note that if the compiled statement C_g does not belong to the compiled language, then Lemma 5 immediately yields a soundness failure for $\mathsf{FS}(\Pi^{\mathsf{PC}'})$.

Algorithm 6. $\mathscr{P}^*(\mathsf{pp}, C_g)$

1: $r \leftarrow \mathsf{RO}(\mathsf{pp}, C_g, (0,0))$
2: $z \leftarrow g(r)$
3: $v \leftarrow E(\mathsf{pp}_E, \cdot, z; r)$ // solve the equality test
4: $C_v \leftarrow \mathsf{PC}'.\mathsf{Com}^{\mathsf{RO}}(\mathsf{ck}, v)$ // commit to the constant polynomial, equal to v
5: $\pi_g \leftarrow \mathsf{PC}'.\mathsf{Eval}(\mathsf{ck}, C_g, g(r), r)$
6: $\pi_v \leftarrow \mathsf{PC}'.\mathsf{Eval}(\mathsf{ck}, C_v, v, r)$
7: **return** $(C_g, C_v, z, \pi_g, v, \pi_v)$

Lemma 5. *Let Π be a simple PIOP, and let $\mathsf{FS}(\Pi^{\mathsf{PC}'}) = (\mathcal{P}_{\mathsf{FS}}^{\mathsf{PC}'}, \mathcal{V}_{\mathsf{FS}}^{\mathsf{PC}'})$ be the Fiat–Shamir-transformed argument for $\mathscr{R}^{\mathsf{PC}'}$, where PC' is the polynomial commitment scheme defined in Algorithms 1 to 3. Furthermore, let $C_g = \mathsf{PC}'.\mathsf{Com}^{\mathsf{RO}}(\mathsf{ck}, g)$, where g is the polynomial used to define PC'. Then there exists a negligible function ϵ such that*

$$\Pr[\langle \mathscr{P}^*(\mathsf{pp}, C_g), \mathcal{V}_{\mathsf{FS}}^{\mathsf{PC}'}(\mathsf{pp}, C_g)\rangle = 1] \geq 1 - \epsilon,$$

where $\mathscr{P}^*$ is defined in Algorithm 6 and the probability is taken over the choice of the random oracle.

Proof. Let $C_g = \mathsf{PC}'.\mathsf{Com}^{\mathsf{RO}}(\mathsf{ck}, g)$ be the commitment to the polynomial g, corresponding to the (potentially) false claim that the prover attempts to prove in the compiled protocol $\mathsf{FS}(\Pi^{\mathsf{PC}'})$. The adversarial prover $\mathscr{P}^*$ then generates the proof string as described in Algorithm 6 and sends it to $\mathscr{V}_{\mathsf{FS}}^{\mathsf{PC}'}$.

Upon receiving the proof string $(C_g, C_v, z, \pi_g, v, \pi_v)$, $\mathscr{V}_{\mathsf{FS}}^{\mathsf{PC}'}$ computes the challenge $r' \leftarrow \mathsf{RO}(\mathsf{pp}, C_g, C_v)$, and accepts if the following checks are satisfied:

(1) $\mathsf{PC}'.\mathsf{Verify}^{\mathsf{RO}}(\mathsf{ck}, C_g, r', z, \pi_g) = 1$ and $\mathsf{PC}'.\mathsf{Verify}^{\mathsf{RO}}(\mathsf{ck}, C_v, r', v, \pi_v) = 1$
(2) $E(\mathsf{pp}_E, v, z; r') = 1$

Since the prover $\mathscr{P}^*$ honestly generates the evaluation proofs π_g and π_v, we know that the verifications in the first condition are satisfied if the randomness r derived by the prover is equal to the randomness r' derived by the verifier. This occurs if and only if $\mathsf{RO}(\mathsf{pp}, C_g, C_v) = \mathsf{RO}(\mathsf{pp}, C_g, (0,0))$, which holds in particular when $C_v = (0,0)$. From the definition of $\mathsf{PC}'.\mathsf{Com}^{\mathsf{RO}}$ (Algorithm 1), we observe that this occurs if $C_g = (1, \mathsf{PC}.\mathsf{Com}(\mathsf{ck}, g))$, i.e. if g is not equal to the special constant polynomial v computed in Algorithm 1. If E additionally has a unique solution, then the second condition is satisfied by construction. Therefore, the verifier accepts the proof if E has a unique solution and $g \neq v$.

Let $\mathsf{E}_{\mathsf{unq}}$ denote the event that $E(\mathsf{pp}_E, x, g(r); r)$ has a unique solution for x, and let $\mathsf{E}_{g \neq v}$ denote the event that $g \neq v$. Since any non-constant polynomial isn't equal to v, we can lower bound the probability that the verifier accepts, by assuming that g is a constant polynomial equal to some $K \in \mathbb{F}$.

By Lemma 6 (see below), we may assume that the output of $E(\mathsf{pp}_E, \cdot, K; r)$ is non-constant (w.r.t $r \in \mathbb{F}_{\overline{\eta}}^{\leq d}$), even in the case where $g(x) = K$ is a constant polynomial. Therefore, the conditional probability $\Pr[\mathsf{E}_{g \neq v} \mid \mathsf{E}_{\mathsf{unq}}]$ can be lower bounded by the probability that $E(\mathsf{pp}, \cdot, K; r)$ does not return K. Taking the multivariate polynomial interpretation of $E = (\mathsf{pp}_E, p \in \mathbb{F}_{\bar{\mu}}^{\leq D})$ from Definition 10, we see that $E(\mathsf{pp}, \cdot, K; r)$ returns K if and only if the polynomial $h(r) = p(f_1(r), ..., f_\nu(r), K, K) = 0$ for a uniformly random $r \in \mathbb{F}^\eta$. Thus, by the Schwartz-Zippel Lemma, we have that $\Pr[\mathsf{E}_{g \neq v} \mid \mathsf{E}_{\mathsf{unq}}] \geq 1 - \frac{\eta\mu n D}{|\mathbb{F}|}$, where $n = \max\{d_1, ..., d_\nu\}$. Direct application of Lemma 3 yields the same lower bound for $\Pr[\mathsf{E}_{\mathsf{unq}}]$. Hence, we obtain that

$$\Pr[\langle \mathscr{P}^*(\mathsf{pp}, C_g), \mathscr{V}_{\mathsf{FS}}^{\mathsf{PC}'}(\mathsf{pp}, C_g)\rangle = 1] \geq \Pr[\mathsf{E}_{\mathsf{unq}} \cap \mathsf{E}_{g \neq v}] = \Pr[\mathsf{E}_{\mathsf{unq}}] \cdot \Pr\left[\mathsf{E}_{g \neq v} \mid \mathsf{E}_{\mathsf{unq}}\right]$$
$$\geq \left(1 - \frac{\eta\mu n D}{|\mathbb{F}|}\right)^2 \geq 1 - \mathsf{negl}(\lambda).$$

The last inequality follows from the fact that $\eta, \mu, n, D = \mathsf{poly}(\lambda)$, whereas $|\mathbb{F}|$ is assumed to be super-polynomial in λ. □

4.3 $\mathsf{FS}(\Pi^{\mathsf{PC}'})$ Is Not Knowledge-Sound

We now address the technical complication arising from the fact that polynomial commitment schemes are typically highly compressing. As a result, collisions in the domain of PC' may cause false statements in the oracle language $\mathcal{L}(\mathscr{R})$ to become true statements in the compiled language $\mathcal{L}(\mathscr{R}^{\mathsf{PC}'})$.

Theorem 1. *Let $\Pi = (\mathscr{P}, \mathscr{V})$ be a simple PIOP. Then, any secure polynomial commitment scheme* PC *can be modified into a secure* RO*-based commitment scheme* PC'*, such that the protocol* $\mathsf{FS}(\Pi^{\mathsf{PC}'}) = (\mathscr{P}_{\mathsf{FS}}^{\mathsf{PC}'}, \mathscr{V}_{\mathsf{FS}}^{\mathsf{PC}'})$ *is not knowledge-sound, with overwhelming probability, if* FS *uses the* same RO.

Remark 1. The theorem also holds for any concrete hash-function that is shared between PC' and FS, assuming that the outputs of the hash-function are sufficiently uniform. We omit the details.

Proof. Let g be the public polynomial that we used when we defined PC' and let $C_g = \mathsf{PC}'.\mathsf{Com}^{\mathsf{RO}}(\mathsf{ck}, g)$. By assumption, $[g] \notin \mathcal{L}(\mathscr{R})$, which implies that $(C_g, g) \notin \mathscr{R}^{\mathsf{PC}'}$. We will show that the knowledge-soundness of $\mathsf{FS}(\Pi^{\mathsf{PC}'})$ contradicts the binding of PC'.

In the definition of knowledge-soundness, let $\mathcal{A}_1$ be such that it always returns the commitment C_g to g. Assume towards contradiction that $\mathsf{FS}(\Pi^{\mathsf{PC}'})$ is knowledge sound, which implies that there exists a PPT extractor E with negligible knowledge-error κ. Then, consider an adversary $\mathcal{B}$ against the binding of PC', which on input ck works as follows:

- Sample public parameters $\mathsf{pp} \leftarrow\$ \mathsf{Setup}(1^\lambda)$ and let pp' be pp with its commitment key replaced by ck.
- Run $w \leftarrow\$ \mathsf{E}^{\mathcal{A}_1, \mathscr{P}^*}(\mathsf{pp}', C_g)$ to obtain a witness (candidate) w for the statement C_g.
- Output (g, w).

Let B denote the event that $\mathcal{B}$ breaks the binding of PC' and let W be the event that $\mathsf{E}^{\mathcal{A}_1,\mathscr{P}^*}$ outputs a valid witness during the knowledge-soundness game against $(\mathcal{A}_1, \mathscr{P}^*)$. Since g is not a valid witness for the statement C_g in $\mathscr{R}^{\mathsf{PC}'}$, any valid witness w for C_g must satisfy $w \neq g$ and $\mathsf{PC}'.\mathsf{Com}^{\mathsf{RO}}(\mathsf{ck}, w) = C_g$. Moreover, $\mathcal{B}$ perfectly simulates the knowledge-soundness game for $(\mathcal{A}_1, \mathscr{P}^*)$, so whenever W occurs, the adversary $\mathcal{B}$ outputs two distinct openings $g \neq w$ to the same commitment C_g, and thus breaks the binding of PC'. It follows that $\Pr[\mathsf{W}] \leq \Pr[\mathsf{B}]$.

Let A denote the event that $\mathcal{V}_{\mathsf{FS}}^{\mathsf{PC}'}$ accepts the proof during the knowledge-soundness game against $(\mathcal{A}_1, \mathscr{P}^*)$. Lemma 5 implies that $\Pr[A] \geq 1-\epsilon$ for some negligible function ϵ. Then, we observe that

$$\kappa \geq \Pr\left[\begin{array}{l|l} \langle \mathscr{P}^*(\mathsf{pp}, C_g, \mathsf{st}), \mathcal{V}_{\mathsf{FS}}^{\mathsf{PC}'}(\mathsf{pp}, C_g)\rangle = 1 & \mathsf{pp} \leftarrow \mathsf{Setup}(1^\lambda), \\ \wedge\ (C_g, w) \notin \mathscr{R}^{\mathsf{PC}'} & (C_g, \mathsf{st}) \leftarrow \mathcal{A}_1(\mathsf{pp}), \\ & w \leftarrow \mathsf{E}^{\mathcal{A}_1,\mathscr{P}^*}(\mathsf{pp}, C_g) \end{array}\right] = \Pr[\mathsf{A} \cap \neg\mathsf{W}]$$
$$= \Pr[\mathsf{A}] - \Pr[\mathsf{A} \cap \mathsf{W}] \geq \Pr[\mathsf{A}] - \Pr[\mathsf{W}] \geq 1 - \epsilon - \Pr[\mathsf{B}] \tag{5}$$

In particular, $\Pr[\mathsf{B}] \geq 1-\epsilon-\kappa$, where $\epsilon, \kappa \in \mathsf{negl}(\lambda)$. Thus, $\mathcal{B}$ finds two openings for C_g with overwhelming probability, contradicting the binding of PC'. Therefore, our original assumption must be false, which implies that $\mathsf{FS}(\Pi^{\mathsf{PC}'})$ is not knowledge-sound. □

5 Generalization to Multi-round PIOPs

In this section, we present our general result. For technical reasons, we have to restrict to PIOPs that have the structure presented in Definition 12 below.

Definition 12. (Structured PIOP). *Let $\Pi = (\mathscr{P}, \mathscr{V})$ be a public coin PIOP for an oracle relation $\mathscr{R}$ over a field $\mathbb{F}$. Suppose $|\mathbb{F}|$ is super-polynomial in λ. We say that Π is a* structured PIOP *if it satisfies the following:*

- *The verifier decides whether the statement x is in $\mathcal{L}(\mathscr{R})$ based on some set of polynomial equality tests, which includes $E = (\mathsf{pp}_E \in \mathbb{F}_{\overline{\eta}}^{\leq d_1} \times \ldots \times \mathbb{F}_{\overline{\eta}}^{\leq d_\nu}, p \in \mathbb{F}_{\overline{\mu}}^{\leq D})$.*
- *There exists a false statement $x \notin \mathcal{L}(\mathscr{R})$ and a prover strategy $\widetilde{\mathscr{P}}$ (in Π), such that $\widetilde{\mathscr{P}}(\mathsf{pp}, x)$ always passes all the other polynomial equality tests except E.*
- *In round t of Π^{PC}, the prover's message is a commitment to a polynomial $\phi \in \mathbb{F}_{\overline{\eta}}^{\leq d}$, which the verifier queries exactly once at a uniformly random point $r \in \mathbb{F}^{\eta}$ and uses the result only in E, which is linear and non-trivial in $\phi(r)$.*
- *All other inputs to E are determined at the latest in the same round as the evaluation of ϕ (in Π^{PC}).*
- *The compiled version of the false statement $x \notin \mathcal{L}(\mathscr{R})$ remains false in $\mathcal{L}(\mathscr{R}^{\mathsf{PC}})$.*

Intuitively, the second and third conditions of Definition 12 ensure that there exists a false claim and that it suffices to tweak a single polynomial evaluation to make the verifier accept. The fourth condition guarantees that the polynomial commitment scheme PC can be transformed to PC′, such that it can predict all other values involved in E by simulating the protocol before fixing the evaluation of ϕ. Moreover, the last condition is a technical requirement ensuring that if one can convince the verifier that the compiled instance of a false claim $x \notin \mathcal{L}(\mathscr{R})$ is in $\mathcal{L}(\mathscr{R}^{\mathsf{PC}})$, then this immediately yields a soundness failure of the (Fiat-Shamir transformed) argument system. This assumption is natural for many universal succinct argument systems, because if an arithmetic circuit $\mathcal{C} : \mathbb{F}^n \times \mathbb{F}^m \to \mathbb{F}$ does not output the claimed value for any witness $w \in \mathbb{F}^m$, then no polynomial witness exists for the corresponding claim. We can now state our main result.

Theorem 2. *Let $|\mathbb{F}|$ be super-polynomial in λ and let $\Pi = (\mathscr{P}, \mathscr{V})$ be a* structured PIOP *(cf. Definition 12). Then, any secure polynomial commitment scheme* PC *can be transformed into another secure polynomial commitment scheme* PC′*, which uses the Fiat-Shamir random oracle, such that* $\mathsf{FS}(\Pi^{\mathsf{PC}'}) = (\mathscr{P}_{\mathsf{FS}}^{\mathsf{PC}'}, \mathscr{V}_{\mathsf{FS}}^{\mathsf{PC}'})$ *is not sound in the random oracle model, with overwhelming probability.*

To prove Theorem 2, we again construct the polynomial commitment scheme PC′ in such a way that the prover can convince the verifier that the compiled statement in $\mathsf{FS}(\Pi^{\mathsf{PC}'})$ corresponding to $x \notin \mathcal{L}(\mathscr{R})$, is in the language.

To rule out a special case involving polynomial equality tests in structured PIOPs (and simple PIOPs), we state the following lemma.

Lemma 6. *Let Π be a structured PIOP. Using the notation from Definition 12, let z denote the variable corresponding to $\phi(r)$ in $E(\mathsf{pp}_E, z, g_1(r), \ldots, g_k(r); r)$, and let $g_1, \ldots, g_k$ denote the polynomials chosen by $\widetilde{\mathscr{P}}$ on input (pp, x). If $E(\mathsf{pp}_E, \cdot, g_1(r), \ldots, g_k(r); r)$ is constant with respect to r, then Π is not sound.*

Proof. Assume that the solution to $E(\mathsf{pp}, \cdot, g_1(r), ..., g_k(r); r)$ is constant for all $r \in \mathbb{F}^\eta$ and denote this constant by $c \in \mathbb{F}$. We define a new prover $\mathscr{P}^*$ such that it follows the same strategy as $\widetilde{\mathscr{P}}$, except that it sends $[\phi] = [c]$ instead of what $\widetilde{\mathscr{P}}$ would send in the corresponding round.

By assumption, $\widetilde{\mathscr{P}}(\mathsf{pp}, x)$ passes all polynomial equality tests except E, and the oracle $[c]$ is used exclusively for E. Since c is a valid solution to E and $\mathscr{P}^*(\mathsf{pp}, x)$ does everything else as $\widetilde{\mathscr{P}}(\mathsf{pp}, x)$ does, we conclude that $\mathscr{P}^*$ passes all tests. Therefore, the verifier accepts $x \notin \mathcal{L}(\mathscr{R})$, which implies that Π is not sound. □

5.1 Transforming the Polynomial Commitment Scheme

We adopt the notation used in Theorem 2 and Definition 12. In particular, PC denotes an arbitrary secure polynomial commitment scheme, Π is a structured PIOP, and E and $\widetilde{\mathscr{P}}$ refer to the associated polynomial equality test and prover strategy from Definition 12.

Algorithm 7. $\mathsf{Sim}^{\mathsf{RO}}(\mathscr{P}, \Pi, \mathsf{PC}, E, x, t)$

Simulate the prover $\mathscr{P}_{\mathsf{FS}}^{\mathsf{PC}}(\mathsf{pp}, x)$ in $\mathsf{FS}(\Pi^{\mathsf{PC}})$ for the first $t-1$ rounds.
In round t, use $(0, 0)$ as the commitment (to ϕ).
Continue simulating $\mathscr{P}_{\mathsf{FS}}^{\mathsf{PC}}(\mathsf{pp}, x)$ for the remaining rounds, until all assignments $v_1, \ldots, v_k$ to E, except the evaluation of ϕ are obtained.
Let r be the randomness used for E when computing the assignments.
return $(v_1, \ldots, v_k, r)$

Let $\mathcal{PC}$ denote a modified polynomial commitment scheme with identical KGen, defined as follows:

- $\mathcal{PC}.\mathsf{Com}(\mathsf{ck}, \phi) := (1, \mathsf{PC.Com}(\mathsf{ck}, \phi))$
- $\mathcal{PC}.\mathsf{Eval}(\mathsf{ck}, (1, C), \phi, u) := \mathsf{PC.Eval}(\mathsf{ck}, C, \phi, u)$
- $\mathcal{PC}.\mathsf{Verify}(\mathsf{ck}, (1, C), u, z, \pi) := \mathsf{PC.Verify}(\mathsf{ck}, C, u, z, \pi)$

Clearly, $\mathcal{PC}$ preserves all the security properties of PC. The purpose of this transformation is to facilitate the simulation of our final construction PC' on all inputs except one.

Before presenting PC', we define a simulation algorithm Sim (Algorithm 7), which will serve as a subroutine within PC'. This algorithm aims to simulate the prover compiled under the (as yet undefined) PC' and to compute all assignments to E except the evaluation of ϕ. As we will show in Lemma 7, it succeeds with overwhelming probability.

Note that when Π is a structured PIOP and E is a polynomial equality test satisfying the conditions of Definition 12, all values $v_1, \ldots, v_k$ computed by Sim are determined before the evaluation of ϕ. Next we define $\mathsf{PC}'.\mathsf{Com}$, such that the constant polynomial $\phi(x) = v$, which satisfies $E(\mathsf{pp}_E, v, v_1, \ldots, v_k)$, has the special commitment $(0, 0) = \mathsf{PC}'.\mathsf{Com}^{\mathsf{RO}}(\mathsf{ck}, \phi)$.

We present the formal construction of the polynomial commitment scheme PC' in Algorithms 8 to 10. Note that this polynomial commitment scheme is very similar to the modified polynomial commitment scheme we used to establish Theorem 1 for simple PIOPs. The only difference is that the scheme described in Algorithms 8 to 10 derives the solution to the polynomial equality test E in a more complicated way. Nevertheless, the proofs (cf. Lemma 4) for evaluation completeness, binding, and knowledge soundness remain valid in this setting as well (with only a minor adjustment to the extractor).

5.2 Proving the False Statement

To complete the proof of Theorem 2, it remains to show that an adversarial prover can successfully convince the verifier of a false statement in $\mathsf{FS}(\Pi^{\mathsf{PC}'})$. We first establish two supporting lemmas.

Algorithm 8. $\mathsf{PC}'.\mathsf{Com}(\mathsf{ck}, \phi)$

$(v_1, \ldots, v_k) \leftarrow \mathsf{Sim}(\mathscr{P}^{\mathcal{PC}}, x, t)$
$v \leftarrow E(\mathsf{pp}, \cdot, v_1, \ldots, v_k)$ // solve the polynomial equality test
if $\phi(x) = v$: // constant polynomial, equal to v
  return $(0, 0)$
else
  ïz£**return** $(1, \mathsf{PC}.\mathsf{Com}(\mathsf{ck}, \phi))$

Algorithm 9. $\mathsf{PC}'.\mathsf{Eval}(\mathsf{ck}, C, \phi, u)$

$(b, c) \leftarrow C$ // parse the commitment
if $(b, c) = (0, 0)$:
  return $\perp$ // no need for an evaluation proof, there is only one option for ϕ and $\phi(u)$
else
  return $\mathsf{PC}.\mathsf{Eval}(\mathsf{ck}, c, \phi, u)$ // returns $\perp$ if c is not a valid commitment for ϕ

Algorithm 10. $\mathsf{PC}'.\mathsf{Verify}^{\mathsf{RO}}(\mathsf{ck}, C, u, z, \pi)$

$(b, c) \leftarrow C$ // parse the commitment
if $(b, c) = (0, 0)$:
  $(v_1, \ldots, v_k, r) \leftarrow \mathsf{Sim}^{\mathsf{RO}}(\widetilde{\mathscr{P}}, \Pi, \mathcal{PC}, E, x, t)$
  $v \leftarrow E(\mathsf{pp}_E, \cdot, v_1, \ldots, v_k, r)$ // solve the polynomial equality test
  if $z = v$: **return** 1
  else : **return** 0
if $b = 1$:
  return $\mathsf{PC}.\mathsf{Verify}(\mathsf{ck}, c, u, z, \pi)$
else return 0

Lemma 7. *Let Π be a structured PIOP and recall the definitions of PC' and $\mathcal{PC}$. Fix the random oracle RO and let $f_1, \ldots, f_\ell$ be the polynomials to which the prover commits during the execution of simulator $\mathsf{Sim}^{\mathsf{RO}}(\widetilde{\mathscr{P}}, \Pi, \mathcal{PC}, E, x, t)$, and let $v_1, \ldots, v_k, r$ be the values that the simulator returns. Let ϕ denote the constant polynomial $\phi(x) := v$, where $v \leftarrow E(\mathsf{pp}, \cdot, v_1, \ldots, v_k, r)$. If $f_1, \ldots, f_\ell \neq \phi$, then the transcripts of $\mathsf{Sim}^{\mathsf{RO}}(\widetilde{\mathscr{P}}, \Pi, \mathcal{PC}, E, x, t)$ and $\mathsf{Sim}^{\mathsf{RO}}(\widetilde{\mathscr{P}}, \Pi, \mathsf{PC}', E, x, t)$ are identical, and both return the same values.*

Proof. Assume that none of the polynomials $f_1, \ldots, f_\ell$ is equal to ϕ. Then, by definition, we have

$$\mathcal{PC}.\mathsf{Com}(\mathsf{ck}, f_i) = \mathsf{PC}'.\mathsf{Com}(\mathsf{ck}, f_i) = (1, C_i)$$
$$\mathcal{PC}.\mathsf{Eval}(\mathsf{ck}, (1, C_i), f_i, u) = \mathsf{PC}'.\mathsf{Eval}(\mathsf{ck}, (1, C_i) f_i, u) = \pi_i,$$

for all $u \in \mathbb{F}^\mu$ and $i \in [\ell]$. For a fixed prover strategy and a fixed random oracle, the transcript in $\mathsf{FS}(\Pi^{\mathsf{PC}})$ is entirely determined by the commitments, evaluations, and evaluation proofs. Therefore, by induction, the transcripts must be identical. □

Algorithm 11. $\mathscr{P}^*(\mathsf{pp}, x)$

```
(v_1, ..., v_ν, r) ← Sim^RO(P̃, Π, PC′, E, x, t)
v ← E(pp_E, ·, v_1, ..., v_k; r)                      // Solve the polynomial equality test
Let φ(x) := v be the constant polynomial
Generate the proof π as follows:
    Follow the same strategy as P̃_FS^PC′(pp, x) for the first t − 1 rounds
    Set C_φ = PC′.Com^RO(ck, φ) as the prover's message for round t
    Follow the same strategy as P̃_FS^PC′(pp, x) for the remaining rounds
return π
```

Lemma 8. *If both* $\mathsf{Sim}^{\mathsf{RO}}(\widetilde{\mathscr{P}}, \Pi, \mathcal{PC}, E, x, t)$ *and* $\mathsf{Sim}^{\mathsf{RO}}(\widetilde{\mathscr{P}}, \Pi, \mathsf{PC}', E, x, t)$ *return the same values* $v_1, \ldots, v_k, r$*, and* $E(\mathsf{pp}, \cdot, v_1, \ldots, v_k; r)$ *has a unique solution, then the verifier* $\mathscr{V}_{\mathsf{FS}}^{\mathsf{PC}'}$ *accepts the proof string generated by* $\mathscr{P}^*$ *in Algorithm 11.*

Proof. The prover $\mathscr{P}^*$ generates all the evaluation proofs honestly, so it suffices to argue that all the polynomial equality tests are satisfied. Since $\widetilde{\mathscr{P}}$ passes all tests other than E by assumption, and since ϕ is not involved in any test other than E, it follows that $\mathscr{P}^*$ also passes (at least) all other tests except E. Thus, it suffices to show that E is also satisfied.

Since $\mathsf{Sim}^{\mathsf{RO}}(\Pi, \mathcal{PC}, E, x, t)$ and $\mathsf{Sim}^{\mathsf{RO}}(\Pi, \mathsf{PC}', E, x, t)$ return the same values $v_1, \ldots, v_k, r$, the value v computed in Algorithms 8 and 11 is identical. It follows that the commitment to ϕ in Algorithm 11 is $C_\phi = (0, 0)$, which matches the commitment used in both simulations in round t. Thus, the honest evaluation of ϕ (equal to v) is exactly the unique solution to $E(\mathsf{pp}, \cdot, v_1, ..., v_k; r)$, which implies that $\mathscr{V}_{\mathsf{FS}}^{\mathsf{PC}'}$ accepts the proof. □

Proof (Theorem 2). By Lemmas 7 and 8, it suffices to show that $E(\mathsf{pp}, \cdot, v_1, \ldots, v_k; r)$ has a unique solution and that $f_i \neq v \leftarrow E(\mathsf{pp}, \cdot, v_1, \ldots, v_k; r)$ holds for all $i \in [\ell]$ with overwhelming probability, where each f_i is a polynomial to which the prover commits during the execution of $\mathsf{Sim}^{\mathsf{RO}}(\widetilde{\mathscr{P}}, \Pi, \mathcal{PC}, E, x, t)$.

Let $\mathsf{E}_{\mathsf{unq}}$ denote the event that $E(\mathsf{pp}_E, \cdot, v_1, \ldots, v_k; r)$ has a unique solution, $\mathsf{E}_{\mathsf{f_i} \neq \mathsf{v}}$ to denote the event that $f_i \neq v$, and $\mathsf{E}_{\mathsf{F} \neq \mathsf{v}}$ to denote the event that $f_i \neq v$ for all $i \in [\ell]$. The probabilities of these events are taken over the choice of the random oracle. Thus, by Lemma 3, we obtain that $\Pr[\mathsf{E}_{\mathsf{unq}}] \geq 1 - \frac{\mu \eta n D}{|\mathbb{F}|}$, where $n = \max\{d_i : i \in [\nu]\}$. To lower bound $\Pr[\mathsf{E}_{\mathsf{F} \neq \mathsf{v}} \mid \mathsf{E}_{\mathsf{unq}}]$, we first note that according to Lemma 6, we can assume that the solution to $E(\mathsf{pp}_E, \cdot, v_1, ..., v_k; r)$ is non-constant over r. Since v is a constant polynomial, the lowest probability for $\mathsf{E}_{\mathsf{F} \neq \mathsf{v}}$ is obtained by assuming that each f_i is a distinct constant polynomial. Then, the union bound yields that

$$\Pr\left[\mathsf{E}_{\mathsf{F}\neq\mathsf{v}} \mid \mathsf{E}_{\mathsf{unq}}\right] = \Pr\left[\bigcap_{i\in[\ell]} \mathsf{E}_{\mathsf{f}_i\neq\mathsf{v}} \,\middle|\, \mathsf{E}_{\mathsf{unq}}\right] = 1 - \Pr\left[\bigcup_{i\in[\ell]} \mathsf{E}_{\mathsf{f}_i=\mathsf{v}} \,\middle|\, \mathsf{E}_{\mathsf{unq}}\right]$$
$$\geq 1 - \sum_{i\in[\ell]} \Pr\left[\mathsf{E}_{\mathsf{f}_i=\mathsf{v}} \mid \mathsf{E}_{\mathsf{unq}}\right] \geq 1 - \ell\frac{\eta\mu n D}{|\mathbb{F}|},$$

where the last inequality follows from the Schwartz–Zippel lemma applied to the multivariate polynomial interpretation of E (cf. proof of Lemma 5). Therefore,

$$\Pr[\langle \mathscr{P}^*(\mathsf{pp}, x), \mathscr{V}_{\mathsf{FS}}^{\mathsf{PC}'}(\mathsf{pp}, x)\rangle = 1] \geq \Pr[\mathsf{E}_{\mathsf{unq}} \cap \mathsf{E}_{\mathsf{F}\neq\mathsf{v}}] = \Pr[\mathsf{E}_{\mathsf{unq}}] \cdot \Pr\left[\mathsf{E}_{\mathsf{F}\neq\mathsf{v}} \mid \mathsf{E}_{\mathsf{unq}}\right]$$
$$\geq \left(1 - \frac{\eta\mu n D}{|\mathbb{F}|}\right) \cdot \left(1 - \ell \cdot \frac{\eta\mu n D}{|\mathbb{F}|}\right)$$
$$\geq 1 - \mathsf{negl}(\lambda),$$

The last inequality follows from the fact that $\ell, \eta, \mu, n, D = \mathsf{poly}(\lambda)$, whereas $|\mathbb{F}|$ is assumed to be super-polynomial in λ. □

6 Attacks Against Natural Protocols

6.1 GKR

The GKR protocol [26] is a doubly-efficient interactive proof system for verifying bounded-depth computations on arithmetic circuits. We begin with a high-level overview of the protocol and, inspired from the attacks described in [28], we demonstrate how our transformation of polynomial commitment schemes enables attacks on constant-depth circuits.

Suppose we are given a layered arithmetic circuit $\mathcal{C}$ over a field $\mathbb{F}$ with fan-in two. For a given input x, the vanilla GKR protocol is used to verify that $\mathcal{C}(x) = y$. The goal is for the prover to incur minimal overhead beyond evaluating the circuit, while the verifier gains a strong correctness guarantee using only logarithmic resources relative to the cost of evaluating the circuit.

We say that a polynomial p is *multilinear* if $p \in \mathbb{F}_{\overline{\mu}}^{\leq 1}$, that is, if it has degree at most one in each variable. In the GKR protocol, each gate in a given circuit layer is identified using a binary label, and then each layer is represented as a function $f : \{0,1\}^k \to \mathbb{F}$, mapping each gate label to the value of the gate. This representation is convenient because any such function admits a unique extension to a multilinear polynomial $\widetilde{f} : \mathbb{F}^k \to \mathbb{F}$ that agrees with f on all points in $\{0,1\}^k$. We refer to this extension as the MultiLinear Extension (MLE) of f. Equivalently, one can view each layer of the circuit as a vector of evaluations and apply Definition 13.

Definition 13 (MLE of a vector). *Let* $\mathbf{x} \in \mathbb{F}^n$ *be a vector, where* $n = 2^k$ *for some* $k \in \mathbb{N}$ *and denote the ith element of* $\mathbf{x}$ *by* $\mathbf{x}_i$. *Define a function* $f_{\mathbf{x}}$: $\{0,1\}^{\log n} \to \mathbb{F}$ *by* $f_{\mathbf{x}}(\langle i \rangle) := \mathbf{x}_i$, *where* $\langle i \rangle$ *denotes a binary encoding of* $i \in [n]$. *Then, the MLE of* $\mathbf{x}$ *is defined as* $\widetilde{\mathbf{x}} := \widetilde{f_{\mathbf{x}}}$.

Without loss of generality, we assume that all vectors have length equal to a power of two, since any vector can be padded with zeros. Next, in Definition 14, we present the SumCheck protocol [30] formalized as a PIOP, which serves as a key subroutine within the GKR protocol.

Definition 14 (SumCheck PIOP). *The SumCheck PIOP, for the relation* $\mathscr{R}^{\mathsf{SUM}} = \{((c, [f]); f) \mid \sum_{b \in B_\mu} f(b) = c\}$ *over the set* $\mathbb{F}_{\mu}^{\leq d}$*, where* $B_\mu = \{0,1\}^\mu$*, is defined as follows:*

1. *The prover computes a univariate polynomial* $g_1(x) = \sum_{\mathbf{b} \in B_{\mu-1}} f(x, \mathbf{b})$ *of degree* d *and sends an oracle* $[g_1]$ *to the verifier.*
2. *The verifier checks that* $c = g_1(0) + g_1(1)$*, and rejects if not.*
3. *The verifier samples a uniformly random value* $r_1 \in \mathbb{F}$*, sets* $c_1 \leftarrow g_1(r_1)$ *and sends* r_1 *to the prover.*
4. *For each round* $i = 2, \ldots, \mu$*:*
   - *The prover computes a univariate polynomial* $g_i(x) = \sum_{\mathbf{b} \in B_{\mu-i}} f(r_1, \ldots, r_{i-1}, x, \mathbf{b})$ *and sends an oracle* $[g_i]$ *to the verifier.*
   - *The verifier checks that* $c_{i-1} = g_i(0) + g_i(1)$*, and rejects if not.*
   - *The verifier samples a uniformly random value* $r_i \in \mathbb{F}$*, sets* $c_i \leftarrow g_i(r_i)$ *and sends* r_i *to the prover.*
5. *The verifier evaluates* f *at* $r = (r_1, \ldots, r_\mu)$ *by querying the oracle* $[f]$ *and accepts if* $c_\mu = g_\mu(r_\mu) = f(r)$*.*

Vanilla GKR. On the high level, the vanilla GKR works as follows:

- The prover claims that $\mathcal{C}(x) = y$ for some $x \in \mathbb{F}^n$ and $y \in \mathbb{F}^m$ and the verifier knows both of these values.
- The verifier evaluates the multilinear extension $\widetilde{y}$ at a randomly chosen point $r \in \mathbb{F}^{\lceil \log m \rceil}$ and sends r to the prover.
- Starting from the output layer, the verifier and the prover repeatedly run the SumCheck PIOP (Definition 14), which reduces a claim about the multilinear extension of layer i to the multilinear extension of layer $i+1$ until a claim about input layer is obtained.
- Finally, since the verifier knows the input x, it can compute its multilinear extension $\widetilde{x}$ and verify the claim directly.

Remark 2. In the GKR protocol, if a false claim about the multilinear extension at some layer agrees with the extension of the correct claim at that layer, then the prover can cause the verifier to accept by proceeding honestly with respect to the true claim for the remainder of the protocol.

GKR as a Succinct Argument. In practice, the GKR protocol is typically combined with a polynomial commitment scheme to construct an argument system for verifying the existence of a satisfying assignment for a given arithmetic circuit.

Given an arithmetic circuit $C : \mathbb{F}^n \times \mathbb{F}^m \rightarrow \mathbb{F}^\ell$, an input $x \in \{0,1\}^n$, and a claimed output $y \in \mathbb{F}^\ell$, the goal is to verify that there exists $w \in \mathbb{F}^m$ such that $C(x, w) = y$. The protocol works roughly as follows:

1. **Setup:** The verifier initializes the parameters for polynomial commitment scheme PC. The prover selects a circuit $C : \mathbb{F}^n \times \mathbb{F}^m \to \mathbb{F}^\ell$ and sends it to the verifier, who stores a constant length digest $\langle C \rangle$ of the circuit description.
2. **Commitment Phase:** The prover provides the input $x \in \{0,1\}^n$, the claimed output $y \in \mathbb{F}^\ell$, and a witness $w \in \mathbb{F}^m$. The input x and output y are sent directly to the verifier, while only the commitment $\alpha = \mathsf{PC}(\mathsf{ck}, \widetilde{w})$ to the witness is sent.
3. **Output Claim:** The verifier samples a random point $r \in \mathbb{F}^{\lceil \log l \rceil}$ and forms a claim regarding the value $\widetilde{y}(r)$, where $\widetilde{y}$ is the multilinear extension of the output y. Recall that y is viewed as a function from $\{0,1\}^k$ to $\mathbb{F}$ as explained in Definition 13.
4. **GKR Invocation:** The prover and verifier execute the GKR protocol to reduce the claim about $\widetilde{y}(r)$ to corresponding claims about the multilinear extensions $\widetilde{x}$ and $\widetilde{w}$ of the input and witness, respectively.
5. **Evaluation Checks:** The verifier evaluates the claim about $\widetilde{x}$ directly, and asks the prover to provide evaluation of $\widetilde{w}$ with the corresponding evaluation proofs. The verifier accepts the proof if the evaluation of $\widetilde{w}$ matches the (reduced) claim and the evaluation proofs are successfully verified.

The soundness of this interactive argument is ensured by the statistical soundness of the GKR protocol and the computational binding property of the commitment scheme PC.

Remark 3. If one views the succinct GKR protocol as a pure PIOP, then it clearly satisfies the definition of a structured PIOP (Definition 12), since it is sufficient to cheat only in the evaluation of $\widetilde{w}$. However, the polynomials used during the SumCheck protocol are sometimes sent in the clear, so that Theorem 2 cannot be applied directly. We nevertheless show how similar techniques can be used to mount attacks against GKR.

Simple Attack Against GKR. For the simple attack, we consider a constant depth circuit $\mathcal{C}^*$ that takes only the witness $w \in \mathbb{F}^k$ as input. More precisely, the circuit is defined as

$$\begin{aligned} \mathcal{C}^* : \mathbb{F}^k &\to \mathbb{F}^2 \\ (w_1, \ldots, w_k) &\mapsto (w_1, w_1 - 1). \end{aligned} \tag{6}$$

By construction, the circuit outputs two distinct values for any input, so that the claim that there exists a witness w such that $\mathcal{C}^*(w) = (0,0) =: y^*$ is false. Note that in the FS-transformed protocol, the first challenge point will be derived as $r \leftarrow \mathsf{RO}(\mathsf{pp}, \langle \mathcal{C}^* \rangle, y^*, \mathsf{PC.Com}(\mathsf{ck}, \widetilde{w}))$. In Algorithm 12 we show how PC is transformed to a new polynomial commitment scheme PC', which allows an attack for circuit $\mathcal{C}^*$. We omit the details of the remaining algorithms in PC', as they are analogous to ones we used in Theorems 1 and 2.

The prover can now simply compute $\gamma \leftarrow \mathsf{RO}(\mathsf{pp}, \langle \mathcal{C}^* \rangle, y^*, (0,0))$ and set the witness to $w = (\gamma, 0, \ldots, 0) \in \mathbb{F}^k$. It then follows that the first (random) challenge in the Fiat-Shamir transformed protocol is

$$r = \mathsf{RO}(\mathsf{pp}, \langle \mathcal{C}^* \rangle, y^*, \mathsf{PC}'.\mathsf{Com}(\mathsf{ck}, \widetilde{w})) = \mathsf{RO}(\mathsf{pp}, \langle \mathcal{C}^* \rangle, y^*, (0,0)) = \gamma.$$

Algorithm 12. $\mathsf{PC}'.\mathsf{Com}(\mathsf{ck}, \phi)$

1: $\gamma \leftarrow \mathsf{RO}(\mathsf{pp}, \langle \mathcal{C}^* \rangle, y^*, (0,0))$
2: $p \leftarrow (\gamma, 0, ..., 0) \in \mathbb{F}^k$
3: **if** $\phi = \widetilde{p}$
4: **return** $(0,0)$
5: **else**
6: **return** $(1, \mathsf{PC}.\mathsf{Com}(\mathsf{ck}, \phi))$

The MLE of the real output $\mathcal{C}^*(w) = y = (\gamma, \gamma - 1)$ is $\widetilde{y}(x) = \gamma - x$, while the MLE of the claimed output $y^* = (0,0)$ is $\widetilde{y}^*(x) = 0$. Since the multilinear extensions agree at the challenge point $r = \gamma$, Remark 2 implies that the prover can proceed honestly through the remainder of the protocol, causing the verifier to accept with probability 1.

6.2 PlonK

The PlonK protocol [22] is a popular universal succinct argument system for verifying computations on arithmetic circuits with a public input x and a private witness w. We begin with a high-level overview of the relevant parts of the protocol, followed by an explanation of how Theorem 2 applies in this setting.

Let $\mathcal{C} : \mathbb{F}^n \times \mathbb{F}^m \to \mathbb{F}$ be an arithmetic circuit in which each gate has fan-in two. The high level idea is that for any input-witness pair $(x, w) \in \mathbb{F}^n \times \mathbb{F}^m$, the prover encodes the complete computation trace of the circuit into a univariate polynomial. The prover then commits to this polynomial and convinces the verifier that it accurately represents the circuit's computation by performing few carefully designed polynomial equality tests.

We begin by defining a public constant $d = 3\,s + n + m$, where $s = |\mathcal{C}|$ denotes the number of gates in the circuit. We assume that the field $\mathbb{F}$ contains a primitive d-th root of unity ω, and define a cyclic subgroup $\Omega = \{1, \omega, \omega^2, \ldots, \omega^{d-1}\} \subseteq \mathbb{F}$, which has order d.

In PlonK, the computation $y = \mathcal{C}(x, w)$ is first expressed using vectors $L, R, O \in \mathbb{F}^s$, where for all $i \in [s]$, L_i, R_i, and O_i denote the left input, right input, and output of the ith gate, respectively. The prover then encodes the entire computation trace as a univariate polynomial $T \in \mathbb{F}^{\leq d}$, which interpolates these values such that

$$T(\omega^{3i}) = L_i,\ T(\omega^{3i+1}) = R_i,\ T(\omega^{3i+2}) = O_i, \tag{7}$$

for all $i \in [s]$. Additionally, the prover encodes the input $x \in \mathbb{F}^n$ by setting $T(\omega^{-i}) = x_i$ for all $i \in [n]$.

Informally, after constructing the polynomial T, which allegedly encodes the computation trace of the circuit with input $(x, w) \in \mathbb{F}^n \times \mathbb{F}^m$, the prover must convince the verifier of the following:

1. Every gate is correctly evaluated with respect to the input values and type of the gate.

2. The input x used in the computation matches the claimed input of the prover.
3. The wiring between each gate is consistent with the description of the circuit.
4. The value of the last gate matches the claimed output.

Intuitively, if all of the above conditions hold, the claimed output must result from a correctly executed computation. In PlonK, each of these conditions is verified through a carefully designed polynomial equality test. However, for our attack, it suffices to consider the first one, which is verified using a so-called *zero test* presented below (Definition 16).

Definition 15 (Vanishing Polynomial). *The* vanishing polynomial *of the set $\Omega \subseteq \mathbb{F}$ of cardinality d is the unique polynomial $Z_\Omega \in \mathbb{F}^{\leq d}$ that evaluates to zero everywhere on Ω, i.e.,*

$$Z_\Omega(x) := \prod_{\omega \in \Omega} (x - \omega).$$

Definition 16 (Zero Test). *The zero test is a PIOP for the relation $\mathscr{R}_\Omega^{\mathsf{ZERO}} = \{([f]; f) \mid f \in \mathbb{F}^{\leq d} \wedge \forall x \in \Omega \subseteq \mathbb{F} : f(x) = 0\}$ for some $d \in \mathbb{N}$. Let $Z_\Omega \in \mathbb{F}^{\leq d}$ denote the vanishing polynomial on Ω. Then, on input $(x; w) = ([g]; g)$ the protocol works as follows:*

- *The prover $\mathscr{P}$ computes the quotient polynomial $q \leftarrow g/Z_\Omega$ and sends $[q]$ to the verifier.*
- *The verifier samples a uniformly random point $r \in \mathbb{F}$, queries $[q]$ and $[g]$ at r, and accepts if $Z_\Omega(r) \cdot q(r) = g(r)$; rejects otherwise.*

Before describing how the zero test verifies the first condition, we note that the protocol includes a preprocessing phase in which a public selector polynomial $S \in \mathbb{F}[X]$ and its commitment are generated. The selector polynomial S is defined such that

$$S(\omega^{3l}) = \begin{cases} 1, & \text{if the } l\text{-th gate is an addition gate,} \\ 0, & \text{if the } l\text{-th gate is a multiplication gate} \end{cases}$$

for all $l \in [s]$.

Now, to verify that every gate is correctly evaluated, it suffices to verify that

$$f(x) := S(x)[T(x) + T(\omega x)] + [1 - S(x)]T(x)T(\omega x) - T(\omega^2 x) = 0, \qquad (8)$$

for all $x \in \Omega_{\mathsf{gates}} = \{\omega^{3k} \mid k \in [s]\}$. In PlonK, this is verified using the zero test for f on Ω_{gates}.

Attack Against PlonK. Let $\mathcal{C} : \mathbb{F}^n \times \mathbb{F}^m \to \mathbb{F}$ be an arithmetic circuit, for which we wish to prove a (potentially false) claim that for $x \in \mathbb{F}^n$, there exists a witness $w \in \mathbb{F}^m$ such that $\mathcal{C}(x, w) = y^*$.

Consider a prover strategy where $\widetilde{\mathscr{P}}$ selects an arbitrary witness $w \in \mathbb{F}^m$ and honestly interpolates the computation trace of $\mathcal{C}(x, w)$ using a polynomial

$T \in \mathbb{F}^{\leq d}$, except that it sets $T(\omega^{3s-1}) = y^*$, instead of $T(\omega^{3s-1}) = y = \mathcal{C}(x, w)$. Here the input ω^{3s-1} corresponds to the evaluation point of the last gate, which is the output gate. Then, T correctly interpolates all the input values, satisfies the wiring constraints, and its evaluation aligns with the claimed output. Thus, by construction, the polynomial T satisfies conditions (2) – (4), with respect to the false claim that $\mathcal{C}(x, w) = y^*$.

Now, the first condition is verified by the Zero Test applied to the polynomial f in Eq. 8, which requires oracle access to the quotient polynomial q (see Definition 16). The oracle for q is queried exactly once, and the evaluation $q(r)$ is used solely within this Zero Test, which can be viewed as a linear and non-trivial polynomial equality test with respect to q (Lemma 2). Moreover, $\widetilde{\mathscr{P}}$ passes all other polynomial equality tests, and all additional inputs required by the Zero Test are obtained in the same round as the evaluation of q. Consequently, PlonK satisfies the definition of a structured PIOP (Definition 12), allowing us to apply Theorem 2 directly to carry out our attack.

7 Counterexample Against XFS

The Extended Fiat-Shamir Transform. Arnon and Yogev [3] (AY) develop a new theory where the security of sigma protocols (SP) is proven in the *relativized* random oracle model (ROM). We give a counterexample against the XFS transformation using a CRS-based SNARG for some specific RAM computation. Next, we recall some preliminaries on the AY extended Fiat-Shamir (XFS) transform and CRS-based SNARGS for RAM programs. Note that, compared to AY, we consider sigma protocols with computational security.

Definition 17 (Relativized SP in the ROM [3]). *A triple of algorithms* $(I_{\mathsf{SP}}, P_{\mathsf{SP}}, V_{\mathsf{SP}})$ *is a relativized Sigma Protocol (SP) in the ROM for a family of Boolean circuits* $\mathcal{C}$ *if it is complete and the following hold:*

Adaptive (straightline) round-by-round knowledge: *There exists a polynomial-time extractor* E_{SP} *such that:*

1. *For every malicious t-query PPT prover* $\mathcal{P}$,

$$\Pr\left[\begin{array}{c} C \in \mathcal{C} \ \wedge \ C^f(x, w) = 0 \ \wedge \\ V^f_{\mathsf{SP}}(\psi, x, m_1, \rho, m_2) = 1 \end{array} \middle| \begin{array}{l} f \leftarrow U(\lambda), \\ (C, x, m_1, \mathrm{aux}) \xleftarrow{\mathrm{tr}_1} \mathcal{P}^f, \\ \rho \leftarrow \{0,1\}^\lambda, \\ m_2 \leftarrow \mathcal{P}^f(\mathrm{aux}, \rho), \\ w \leftarrow E_{\mathsf{SP}}(C, x, m_1, \mathrm{tr}_1), \\ \psi \leftarrow I^f_{\mathsf{SP}}(C) \end{array}\right] \leq \kappa_{\mathsf{SP}}(\lambda, t).$$

2. *For every malicious t-query PPT prover $\mathcal{P}$ and every t-query algorithm $\mathcal{A}$,*

$$\Pr\left[C \in \mathcal{C} \ \wedge \ w \neq w' \ \middle|\ \begin{array}{l} f \leftarrow U(\lambda), \\ (C, x, m_1, \mathrm{aux}) \xleftarrow{\mathrm{tr}_1} \mathcal{P}^f, \\ \bot \xleftarrow{\mathrm{tr}_2} \mathcal{A}^f(\mathrm{aux}), \\ w \leftarrow E_{\mathsf{SP}}(C, x, m_1, \mathrm{tr}_1), \\ w' \leftarrow E_{\mathsf{SP}}(C, x, m_1, \mathrm{tr}_1 \| \mathrm{tr}_2) \end{array} \right] \leq \kappa_{\mathsf{SP}}(\lambda, t).$$

Adaptive (straightline) indexer-knowledge: *There exists a polynomial-time extractor E_I such that:*

1. *For every malicious t-query adversary $\mathcal{A}$,*

$$\Pr\left[C \neq C' \ \wedge \ I^f_{\mathsf{SP}}(C) = \psi \ \middle|\ \begin{array}{l} f \leftarrow U(\lambda), \\ (\psi, \mathrm{aux}) \xleftarrow{\mathrm{tr}} \mathcal{A}^f, \\ C' \leftarrow E_I(\psi, \mathrm{tr}), \\ C \leftarrow \mathcal{A}^f(\mathrm{aux}) \end{array} \right] \leq \kappa_I(\lambda, t).$$

2. *For every malicious t-query adversaries $\mathcal{A}_1, \mathcal{A}_2$,*

$$\Pr\left[C \neq C' \ \middle|\ \begin{array}{l} f \leftarrow U(\lambda), \\ (\psi, \mathrm{aux}) \xleftarrow{\mathrm{tr}_1} \mathcal{A}^f_1, \\ C \leftarrow E_I(\psi, \mathrm{tr}_1), \\ \bot \xleftarrow{\mathrm{tr}_2} \mathcal{A}^f_2(\mathrm{aux}), \\ C' \leftarrow E_I(\psi, \mathrm{tr}_1 \| \mathrm{tr}_2) \end{array} \right] \leq \kappa_I(\lambda, t).$$

Given an SP in the relativized ROM, they suggested using the following extended Fiat-Shamir transform (XFS) based on a padding algorithm Padder and a strong proof of work (Setup, Sample, Solve, Check), whose definition we omit, since we do not prove security properties of XFS. We specify Padder after describing the transform.

Definition 18 (XFS transformation). *Given a sigma protocol $(\mathscr{I}, \mathscr{P}, \mathscr{V})$, a strong proof-of-work* (Setup, Sample, Solve, Check), *a padding algorithm* Padder *and a hash function h, let the transformed non-interactive protocol $(\mathscr{I}_{\mathsf{XFS}}, \mathscr{P}_{\mathsf{XFS}}, \mathscr{V}_{\mathsf{XFS}})$ be as follows:*

- $\mathcal{G}(1^\lambda, l)$: *Output* $\mathsf{pp} \leftarrow \mathsf{Setup}(1^\lambda, l)$.
- $\mathscr{I}_{\mathsf{XFS}}(i)$: *Output* $\psi \leftarrow \mathscr{I}(i)$.
- $\mathscr{P}_{\mathsf{XFS}}(i, x, w)$:
  1. *Compute the digest:* $\psi \leftarrow \mathscr{I}(i)$.
  2. *Compute the prover's first message:* $m_1 \leftarrow \mathscr{P}(i, x, w)$.
  3. *Derive the randomness of the puzzle:* $r \leftarrow h(\psi, x, m_1)$.

4. *Compute the puzzle:* $z \leftarrow \mathsf{Sample}(\mathsf{pp}, r)$.
5. *Solve the puzzle:* $s \leftarrow \mathsf{Solve}(\mathsf{pp}, z)$.
6. *Set the pad:* $\tau \leftarrow \mathsf{Padder}(\psi, x, m_1, s)$.
7. *Derive the verifier message:* $\rho \leftarrow h(\tau, \psi, x, m_1, s)$.
8. *Get the second prover message:* $m_2 \leftarrow \mathscr{P}(i, x, w, \rho)$.
9. *Output:* (m_1, s, m_2).

- $\mathscr{V}_{\mathsf{XFS}}(\psi, x, \pi = (m_1, s, m_2))$:
  1. *Derive puzzle randomness:* $r \leftarrow h(\psi, x, m_1)$.
  2. *Compute the puzzle:* $z \leftarrow \mathsf{Sample}(\mathsf{pp}, r)$.
  3. *Set the pad:* $\tau \leftarrow \mathsf{Padder}(\psi, x, m_1, s)$.
  4. *Derive the verifier message:* $\rho \leftarrow h(\tau, \psi, x, m_1, s)$.
  5. *Accept if* $\mathscr{V}(\psi, x, m_1, \rho, m_2) = 1$ *and* $\mathsf{Check}(\mathsf{pp}, z, s) = 1$.

AY require the padder to be *prefix-avoiding*, i.e., such that the hash-evaluation $h(\tau, \psi, x, m_1, s)$ in Step (4) of $\mathscr{V}_{\mathsf{XFS}}$ is "fresh" in the sense that the verifier $\mathscr{V}$ of the underlying SP has not made the same query before. Let $T_{\mathscr{V}}(|\psi|, |x|)$ be the size of the verifier circuit for the underlying SP. Then, AY prove the following statement. We defer the formal definition of prefix-avoidance to the full version.

Lemma 9 ([3] Lemma 5.2). *Let ℓ be such that $\ell(\lambda, |x|) > T_{\mathscr{V}}(|\psi|, |x|)$. Then,* $\mathsf{Padder}(\psi, x, m_1, s) := 0^{\ell(\lambda, |x|)}$ *is prefix-avoiding.*

CRS-Based SNARGs for RAM Computations. The universal language $\mathcal{L}_U$ is the set of instances (M, x, y, L, T) where M is a deterministic RAM machine such that $M(x)$ outputs y within T steps, and additionally $|y| \leq L$. A *CRS-based succinct non-interactive argument* for a language $\mathcal{L} \subseteq \mathcal{L}_U$ consists of algorithms (G, P, V) such that $G(1^\lambda)$ outputs a common reference string crs, the prover $P(\mathsf{crs}, (M, x, L, T))$ outputs a candidate output y together with a proof π, and the deterministic verifier $V(\mathsf{crs}, (M, x, y, L, T), \pi)$ outputs an accept/reject bit. Soundness requires that for every non-uniform polynomial-time adversarial prover P^* and every time bound $T(\lambda) \leq 2^\lambda$, the probability that P^* produces (M, x, y, L, π) such that V accepts while $(M, x, y, L, T(\lambda)) \notin \mathcal{L}$ is negligible in λ. Succinctness further requires formal bounds on verifier efficiency and communication complexity: for suitable polynomials q_1, q_2, whenever $(M, x, y, L, T) \in \mathcal{L}$ with $n, T \leq 2^\lambda$, the verifier work satisfies $\mathsf{work}_V(\mathsf{crs}, (M, x, y, L, T), \pi) \leq q_1(\lambda, |(M, x)|, L, \log T)$, the output length obeys $|y| \leq L$, and the proof length satisfies $|\pi| \leq q_2(\lambda, L, \log T)$. Additionally, we require the distribution output by $G(1^\lambda)$ to be pseudorandom.

A Simple Counterexample Against XFS**.** Our counterexample relies on a CRS-based SNARG for RAM computations specialized to the following language, which uses the program $\mathsf{Prog}[\psi, x, m_1, h]$ (cf. Algorithm 13) with hard-coded parameters ψ, x, m_1 and h as a building block.

Algorithm 13. $\mathsf{Prog}[\psi, x, m_1, h](l, s)$

1: $r \leftarrow h(\psi, x, m_1, h)$
2: $z \leftarrow \mathsf{Samp}(\mathsf{pp}, r)$
3: **if** $\mathsf{Check}(z, s) = 1$:
4: **return** $h(0^l, \psi, x, m_1, h, s)$
5: **else** :
6: **return** $\perp$

Definition 19 (Hash-Evaluation Language). *For constant $c \in \mathbb{N}$, the language $\mathcal{L}_{\mathsf{hash},c} \subseteq \mathcal{L}_U$ consists of all tuples*

$$(\mathsf{Prog}[\psi, x, m_1, h], (l, s), y, \lambda, T)$$

such that $\mathsf{Prog}[\psi, x, m_1, h](l, s)$ outputs y within $T = T(\lambda, |x|) := (\lambda|x|)^{\log(\lambda|x||y|)}$ steps and the input-length satisfies $|s|, |\psi|, |m_1|, |h| \leq I(\lambda, |x|) := (\lambda|x|)^c$.

1. $\mathscr{P}$ computes the message $m_1 \leftarrow \mathcal{P}_{\mathsf{SP}}(i, x, w)$ and selects a hash function h from the hash family $\mathcal{H}$. It then sends the pair (m_1, h) to $\mathscr{V}$.
2. $\mathscr{V}$ samples $\rho \leftarrow \{0,1\}^\lambda$ uniformly at random and sends ρ to $\mathscr{P}$.
3. $\mathscr{P}$ sends (m_2, d, s, π) to $\mathscr{V}$, where:
   m_2: the second prover message, i.e., $m_2 \leftarrow \mathcal{P}_{\mathsf{SP}}(i, x, w, \rho)$ for an honest prover.
   d: the claimed output of $\mathsf{Prog}[\psi, x, m_1, h](l, s)$, where $l \leftarrow \ell(\lambda, |x|)$ is computed as in Eq. 9.
   s: a solution to the puzzle $z \leftarrow \mathsf{Samp}(\mathsf{pp}; h(\psi, x, m_1, h))$.
   π: a succinct proof that $\mathsf{Prog}[\psi, x, m_1, h](l, s) = d$, computed as $(\pi, d) = \mathcal{P}_{\mathsf{Prog}}(\mathsf{crs}, (\mathsf{Prog}[\psi, x, m_1, h], (l, s), y, \lambda, T))$, where $\mathsf{crs} \leftarrow \tilde{f}(\rho)$ and $T \leftarrow (\lambda|x|)^{\log \lambda^2 |x|}$.
4. $\mathscr{V}$ computes $T \leftarrow (\lambda|x|)^{\log \lambda^2 |x|}$ and $l \leftarrow \ell(\lambda, |x|)$, where ℓ is defined in Eq. 9, and checks the following conditions:
   1. $\mathcal{V}_{\mathsf{SP}}(\psi, x, m_1, \rho, m_2) = 1$
   2. $\mathcal{V}_{\mathsf{Prog}}(\mathsf{crs}, (\mathsf{Prog}[\psi, x, m_1, h], (l, s), y, \lambda, T), \pi) = 1 \wedge d = \rho$, where $\mathsf{crs} \leftarrow \tilde{f}(\rho)$.

   $\mathscr{V}$ accepts if either condition holds, and rejects otherwise.

Fig. 1. Transformed relativized SP in the ROM for proving that $C^f(x, w) = 1$, for some Boolean circuit $C \in \mathcal{C}$.

Note that, due to the slightly super-polynomial time bound $T(\lambda, |x|)$, the hash evaluation language $\mathcal{L}_{\mathsf{hash},c}$ is not necessarily in P (or even NP). This ensures that we can capture all polynomial-time computable hash-functions h. The input-length bound allows (asymptotically) for all *uniform* polynomial-time computable hash-functions h, since their description is a constant. If they are salted, the input length requires a bounded salt-length. Jumping ahead, the constant c will be determined by a general SP which we transform, since $|\psi|$, $|m_1|$, $|h|$, and $|y|$ (the latter is the randomness length of the verifier) are all of polynomial-size in the product of the security parameter and the input length, i.e., there exists some constant c such that $(\lambda|x|)^c$ upper bounds them.

Towards our counterexample, we describe a generic transform to turn any SP $(\mathcal{I}, \mathcal{P}_{\mathsf{SP}}, \mathcal{V}_{\mathsf{SP}})$ in the relativized ROM into a new SP $(\mathcal{I}, \mathscr{P}, \mathscr{V})$ in the relativized ROM with the same indexer $\mathcal{I}$. We denote by $(\mathcal{G}_{\mathsf{Prog}}, \mathcal{P}_{\mathsf{Prog}}, \mathcal{V}_{\mathsf{Prog}})$ a CRS-based SNARG for $\mathcal{L}_{\mathsf{hash},c}$. The new SP $(\mathcal{I}, \mathscr{P}, \mathscr{V})$ resulting from the transformation is presented in Fig. 1. In the protocol, the CRS of the SNARG for $\mathcal{L}_{\mathsf{hash},c}$ is derived using the random oracle f from the verifier's message ρ (with domain separation), which we denote $\mathsf{crs} \leftarrow \tilde{f}(\rho)$. Next, we state the main theorem of this section.

Theorem 3. *Let $(\mathcal{I}, \mathcal{P}_{\mathsf{SP}}, \mathcal{V}_{\mathsf{SP}})$ be a relativized SP in the ROM for a family of Boolean circuits $\mathcal{C}$. Assume that, for any constant c, there exists a CRS-based SNARG $(\mathcal{G}_{\mathsf{Prog}}, \mathcal{P}_{\mathsf{Prog}}, \mathcal{V}_{\mathsf{Prog}})$ for $\mathcal{L}_{\mathsf{hash},c}$. Let $(\mathscr{I}, \mathscr{P}, \mathscr{V})$ be the transformed version of $(\mathcal{I}, \mathcal{P}_{\mathsf{SP}}, \mathcal{V}_{\mathsf{SP}})$ as in Fig. 1, where $\mathcal{I} = \mathscr{I}$. Then $(\mathscr{I}, \mathscr{P}, \mathscr{V})$ is also a relativized SP in the ROM, but for any uniform hash-function h, its* XFS *transform $(\mathscr{I}_{\mathsf{XFS}}, \mathscr{P}_{\mathsf{XFS}}, \mathscr{V}_{\mathsf{XFS}})$ is not sound whenever the strong PoW for the* XFS *has solution size $|s| \leq \frac{\lambda}{2}$.*

Before proving the theorem, we define a prefix-avoiding padding algorithm Padder for the transformed SP $(\mathscr{I}, \mathscr{P}, \mathscr{V})$, which will be used in the XFS transformation. We ultimately want to apply Lemma 9 to conclude that Padder is prefix-avoiding, so we first derive some helpful bounds. Note that if $l \leq (\lambda|x|)^N$ for some $N \in \mathbb{N}$ and it is encoded in binary, then $|l|$ is sublinear in $\lambda|x|$. Furthermore, since $|s|, |\psi|, |m_1|, |h| \leq (\lambda|x|)^c$, there exists some constant $S \in \mathbb{N}$ (which depends on c) such that $|\langle \mathsf{Prog}[\psi, x, m_1, h], (l, s)\rangle| = \mathcal{O}((\lambda|x|)^S)$. In particular, S can be fixed before knowing N as long as we know that l is polynomial in $(\lambda|x|)$. Then, let q_1 denote the polynomial upper bound of the verifier work, and let $K := \deg q_1 + 1$. We define the padder algorithm as

$$\mathsf{Padder}(\psi, x, m_1, s) := 0^{\ell(\lambda, |x|)}, \tag{9}$$

for $\ell(\lambda, |x|) = 3(\lambda|x|)^{dK(S+3)+3}$, where d is an integer s.t. $(\lambda|x|)^d$ upper bounds $T_{\mathcal{V}_{\mathsf{SP}}}(\lambda, |x|)$. Note that since the circuit of $\mathcal{V}_{\mathsf{SP}}$ is polynomial-size, the exponent d is a constant. Using Lemma 9, to show that Padder is prefix-avoiding, it suffices to show that $\ell(\lambda, |x|) > T_{\mathscr{V}}(|\psi|, |x|)$, which holds roughly because the runtime of the verifier $\mathcal{V}_{\mathsf{Prog}}$ of the CRS-based SNARG system only grows polylogarithmically in the running time of Prog. Next, we establish that the output-length of Padder is strictly larger than the run time of $\mathscr{V}$. See the full version for a formal proof.

Lemma 10 (Verifier Runtime vs. Padding Size). $\ell(\lambda, |x|) > T_{\mathscr{V}}(|\psi|, |x|)$

Fixing the padder Padder described above, the proof of Theorem 3 follows from Lemma 11 and 12 that we prove in the full version.

Lemma 11. *Let $(\mathcal{I}, \mathcal{P}_{\mathsf{SP}}, \mathcal{V}_{\mathsf{SP}})$ be a relativized SP in the ROM for a family of Boolean circuits $\mathcal{C}$ and let $(\mathscr{I}, \mathscr{P}, \mathscr{V})$ be its transformed version (cf. Fig. 1), where $\mathcal{I} = \mathscr{I}$. If $(\mathcal{G}_{\mathsf{Prog}}, \mathcal{P}_{\mathsf{Prog}}, \mathcal{V}_{\mathsf{Prog}})$ is sound for $\mathcal{L}_{\mathsf{hash},c}$, then $(\mathscr{I}, \mathscr{P}, \mathscr{V})$ is also* *a relativized SP in the ROM for $\mathcal{C}$ whenever the strong PoW for the* XFS *has solution size* $|s| \leq \frac{\lambda}{2}$.

Lemma 12. *The* XFS *transformation (Definition 18) of the protocol defined in Fig. 1 is not sound.*

Strong PoW with Short Solutions. To establish Lemma 11, we must show that the transformed SP from Fig. 1 remains secure. For this, it is convenient to work with a strong PoW whose solution length is short, say at most $\lambda/2$. In that case, a simple counting argument rules out that, after seeing the randomness ρ, the prover can still find a solution s that enables it to produce an accepting SNARG proof when the original SP statement is not in the language. For the simple strong PoW construction of AY (AY, Sect. 6.1), this can be achieved by introducing a separate PoW security parameter k, replacing the construction's internal parameter by k, and choosing $k \in \omega(\log \lambda)$ while keeping $k = O(\sqrt{\lambda / \log \lambda})$ when $\ell \in \mathsf{poly}(\lambda)$. Under this reparameterization, the solution length for their construction is at most $\lambda/2$ while the soundness error remains negligible in λ. We provide additional discussion in the full version.

Instantiating the CRS-Based SNARG for $\mathcal{L}_{\mathsf{hash},c}$. A CRS-based SNARK for RAM computation that we assume for our Theorem 3 can be constructed based on the line of work initiated by Choudhuri, Jain, and Jin [16] and extended in [13,15,17,21,24,34]. This line of work, in particular, established CRS-based publicly-verifiable SNARGS for RAM programs under LWE. Importantly, the CRS generation in those schemes is based on sampling LWE instances with trapdoors, which is computationally indistinguishable from sampling random CRS, allowing us to derive the CRS in our transformed SP from the verifier's challenge ρ using the random oracle.

Acknowledgments. Chris Brzuska was supported by Research Council of Finland grant 358950. Pavel Hubáček was partially supported by the Academy of Sciences of the Czech Republic (RVO 67985840), Czech Science Foundation GAČR grant No. 25-16311S, and by Zircuit. Aleksi Kalsta was supported by Business Finland through the BlimPQC project under decision number 422/31/2024. We thank Russell Lai for helpful discussions.

Disclosure of Interests. The authors have no competing interests to declare that are relevant to the content of this article.

References

1. Information technology — Security techniques — Entity authentication — Part 4: Mechanisms using a cryptographic check function. https://www.iso.org/standard/31488.html, International Standard (second edition, confirmed with Corr. 1:2009 and Corr. 2:2012)
2. Module-Lattice-Based Digital Signature Standard. https://doi.org/10.6028/NIST.FIPS.204, Federal Information Processing Standards Publication, effective 13 Aug 2024

3. Arnon, G., Yogev, E.: Towards a white-box secure Fiat-Shamir transformation. In: Kalai, Y.T., Kamara, S.F. (eds.) CRYPTO 2025, Part VI. LNCS, vol. 16005, pp. 27–56. Springer, Cham (2025). https://doi.org/10.1007/978-3-032-01887-8_2
4. Attema, T., Fehr, S., Klooß, M.: Fiat-Shamir transformation of multi-round interactive proofs (extended version). J. Cryptol. **36**(4), 36 (2023). https://doi.org/10.1007/s00145-023-09478-y
5. Barak, B.: How to go beyond the black-box simulation barrier. In: 42nd FOCS, pp. 106–115. IEEE Computer Society Press (2001). https://doi.org/10.1109/SFCS.2001.959885
6. Bartusek, J., Bronfman, L., Holmgren, J., Ma, F., Rothblum, R.D.: On the (in)security of kilian-based SNARGs. In: Hofheinz, D., Rosen, A. (eds.) TCC 2019, Part II. LNCS, vol. 11892, pp. 522–551. Springer, Cham (2019). https://doi.org/10.1007/978-3-030-36033-7_20
7. Ben-Sasson, E., Chiesa, A., Gabizon, A., Riabzev, M., Spooner, N.: Interactive oracle proofs with constant rate and query complexity. In: Chatzigiannakis, I., Indyk, P., Kuhn, F., Muscholl, A. (eds.) ICALP 2017. LIPIcs, vol. 80, pp. 40:1–40:15. Schloss Dagstuhl (2017). https://doi.org/10.4230/LIPIcs.ICALP.2017.40
8. Ben-Sasson, E., Chiesa, A., Spooner, N.: Interactive oracle proofs. In: Hirt, M., Smith, A.D. (eds.) TCC 2016-B, Part II. LNCS, vol. 9986, pp. 31–60. Springer, Berlin, Heidelberg (2016). https://doi.org/10.1007/978-3-662-53644-5_2
9. Bernhard, D., Pereira, O., Warinschi, B.: How not to prove yourself: pitfalls of the Fiat-Shamir heuristic and applications to Helios. In: Wang, X., Sako, K. (eds.) ASIACRYPT 2012. LNCS, vol. 7658, pp. 626–643. Springer, Berlin, Heidelberg (2012). https://doi.org/10.1007/978-3-642-34961-4_38
10. Bitansky, N., et al.: Why "Fiat-Shamir for proofs" lacks a proof. In: Sahai, A. (ed.) TCC 2013. LNCS, vol. 7785, pp. 182–201. Springer, Berlin, Heidelberg (2013). https://doi.org/10.1007/978-3-642-36594-2_11
11. Canetti, R., Goldreich, O., Halevi, S.: The random oracle methodology, revisited. J. ACM **51**(4), 557–594 (2004). https://doi.org/10.1145/1008731.1008734
12. Chen, B., Bünz, B., Boneh, D., Zhang, Z.: HyperPlonk: Plonk with linear-time prover and high-degree custom gates. In: Hazay, C., Stam, M. (eds.) EUROCRYPT 2023, Part II. LNCS, vol. 14005, pp. 499–530. Springer, Cham (2023). https://doi.org/10.1007/978-3-031-30617-4_17
13. Chen, L., Freitag, C., Jin, Z., Wichs, D.: Unambiguous SNARGs for P from LWE with applications to PPAD hardness. In: Koucký, M., Bansal, N. (eds.) 57th ACM STOC, pp. 944–954. ACM Press (2025). https://doi.org/10.1145/3717823.3718159
14. Chiesa, A., et al.: Marlin: preprocessing zkSNARKs with universal and updatable SRS. In: Canteaut, A., Ishai, Y. (eds.) EUROCRYPT 2020, Part I. LNCS, vol. 12105, pp. 738–768. Springer, Cham (2020). https://doi.org/10.1007/978-3-030-45721-1_26
15. Choudhuri, A.R., Garg, S., Jain, A., Jin, Z., Zhang, J.: Correlation intractability and SNARGs from sub-exponential DDH. In: Handschuh, H., Lysyanskaya, A. (eds.) CRYPTO 2023, Part IV. LNCS, vol. 14084, pp. 635–668. Springer, Cham (2023). https://doi.org/10.1007/978-3-031-38551-3_20
16. Choudhuri, A.R., Jain, A., Jin, Z.: SNARGs for $\mathcal{P}$ from LWE. In: 62nd FOCS, pp. 68–79. IEEE Computer Society Press (2022). https://doi.org/10.1109/FOCS52979.2021.00016
17. Devadas, L., Goyal, R., Kalai, Y., Vaikuntanathan, V.: Rate-1 non-interactive arguments for batch-NP and applications. In: 63rd FOCS, pp. 1057–1068. IEEE Computer Society Press (2022). https://doi.org/10.1109/FOCS54457.2022.00103

18. Don, J., Fehr, S., Majenz, C., Schaffner, C.: Security of the Fiat-Shamir transformation in the quantum random-oracle model. In: Boldyreva, A., Micciancio, D. (eds.) CRYPTO 2019, Part II. LNCS, vol. 11693, pp. 356–383. Springer, Cham (2019). https://doi.org/10.1007/978-3-030-26951-7_13
19. Dupuis, F., Lamontagne, P., Salvail, L.: Fiat-Shamir for proofs lacks a proof even in the presence of shared entanglement. Quantum **8**, 1568 (2024). https://doi.org/10.22331/Q-2024-12-17-1568
20. Fiat, A., Shamir, A.: How to prove yourself: practical solutions to identification and signature problems. In: Odlyzko, A.M. (ed.) CRYPTO'86. LNCS, vol. 263, pp. 186–194. Springer, Berlin, Heidelberg (1987). https://doi.org/10.1007/3-540-47721-7_12
21. Freitag, C., Pass, R., Sirkin, N.: Parallelizable delegation from LWE. In: Kiltz, E., Vaikuntanathan, V. (eds.) TCC 2022, Part II. LNCS, vol. 13748, pp. 623–652. Springer, Cham (2022). https://doi.org/10.1007/978-3-031-22365-5_22
22. Gabizon, A., Williamson, Z.J., Ciobotaru, O.: PLONK: permutations over Lagrange-bases for oecumenical noninteractive arguments of knowledge. Cryptology ePrint Archive, Report 2019/953 (2019). https://eprint.iacr.org/2019/953
23. Ganesh, C., Orlandi, C., Pancholi, M., Takahashi, A., Tschudi, D.: Fiat-Shamir bulletproofs are non-malleable (in the random oracle model). J. Cryptol. **38**(1), 11 (2025). https://doi.org/10.1007/s00145-024-09525-2
24. Garg, R., Sheridan, K., Waters, B., Wu, D.J.: Fully succinct batch arguments for np from indistinguishability obfuscation. In: Kiltz, E., Vaikuntanathan, V. (eds.) TCC 2022, Part I. LNCS, vol. 13747, pp. 526–555. Springer, Cham (2022). https://doi.org/10.1007/978-3-031-22318-1_19
25. Goldwasser, S., Kalai, Y.T.: On the (in)security of the Fiat-Shamir paradigm. In: 44th FOCS, pp. 102–115. IEEE Computer Society Press (2003). https://doi.org/10.1109/SFCS.2003.1238185
26. Goldwasser, S., Kalai, Y.T., Rothblum, G.N.: Delegating computation: interactive proofs for muggles. J. ACM **62**(4), 27:1–27:64 (2015). https://doi.org/10.1145/2699436
27. Kate, A., Zaverucha, G.M., Goldberg, I.: Constant-size commitments to polynomials and their applications. In: Abe, M. (ed.) ASIACRYPT 2010. LNCS, vol. 6477, pp. 177–194. Springer, Berlin, Heidelberg (2010). https://doi.org/10.1007/978-3-642-17373-8_11
28. Khovratovich, D., Rothblum, R.D., Soukhanov, L.: How to prove false statements: Practical attacks on Fiat-Shamir. In: Kalai, Y.T., Kamara, S.F. (eds.) CRYPTO 2025, Part VI. LNCS, vol. 16005, pp. 3–26. Springer, Cham (2025). https://doi.org/10.1007/978-3-032-01887-8_1
29. Kilian, J.: A note on efficient zero-knowledge proofs and arguments (extended abstract). In: 24th ACM STOC, pp. 723–732. ACM Press (1992). https://doi.org/10.1145/129712.129782
30. Lund, C., Fortnow, L., Karloff, H.J., Nisan, N.: Algebraic methods for interactive proof systems. J. ACM **39**(4), 859–868 (1992). https://doi.org/10.1145/146585.146605
31. Micali, S.: Computationally sound proofs. SIAM J. Comput. **30**(4), 1253–1298 (2000). https://doi.org/10.1137/S0097539795284959
32. Mittelbach, A., Venturi, D.: Fiat-Shamir for highly sound protocols is instantiable. Theor. Comput. Sci. **740**, 28–62 (2018). https://doi.org/10.1016/J.TCS.2018.05.001

33. Pointcheval, D., Stern, J.: Security proofs for signature schemes. In: Maurer, U.M. (ed.) EUROCRYPT'96. LNCS, vol. 1070, pp. 387–398. Springer, Berlin, Heidelberg (1996). https://doi.org/10.1007/3-540-68339-9_33
34. Waters, B., Wu, D.J.: Batch arguments for NP and more from standard bilinear group assumptions. In: Dodis, Y., Shrimpton, T. (eds.) CRYPTO 2022, Part II. LNCS, vol. 13508, pp. 433–463. Springer, Cham (2022). https://doi.org/10.1007/978-3-031-15979-4_15

Author Index

S. Bai and E. Persichetti (Eds.): PKC 2026, LNCS 16551, pp. 545–546, 2026.
https://doi.org/10.1007/978-3-032-26731-3

GPSR Compliance
The European Union's (EU) General Product Safety Regulation (GPSR) is a set of rules that requires consumer products to be safe and our obligations to ensure this.

If you have any concerns about our products, you can contact us on

ProductSafety@springernature.com

In case Publisher is established outside the EU, the EU authorized representative is:

Springer Nature Customer Service Center GmbH
Europaplatz 3
69115 Heidelberg, Germany

www.ingramcontent.com/pod-product-compliance
Ingram Content Group UK Ltd.
Pitfield, Milton Keynes, MK11 3LW, UK
UKHW022111180926
475695UK00002B/100
9783032267306